THE GREAT SPEECHES AND ORATIONS OF DANIEL WEBSTER

With an Essay on Daniel Webster as a Master of English Style

By Edwin P. Whipple

Originally published in 1923.

PREFACE.

The object of the present volume is not to supersede the standard edition of Daniel Webster's Works, in six octavo volumes, edited by Edward Everett, and originally issued in the year 1851, by the publishers of this volume of Selections. It is rather the purpose of the present publication to call attention anew to the genius and character of Daniel Webster, as a lawyer, statesman, diplomatist, patriot, and, citizen, and, by republishing some of his prominent orations and speeches of universally acknowledged excellence, to revive public interest in the great body of his works. In the task of selection, it has been impossible to do full justice to his powers; for among the speeches omitted in this collection are to be found passages of superlative eloquence, maxims of political and moral wisdom which might be taken as mottoes for elaborate treatises on the philosophy of law and legislation, and important facts and principles which no student of history of the United States can overlook without betraying an ignorance of the great forces which influenced the legislation of the two Houses of Congress, from the time Mr. Webster first entered public life to the day of his death.

It is to be supposed that, when Mr. Everett consented to edit the six volumes of his works, Mr. Webster indicated to him the orations, speeches, and diplomatic despatches which he really thought might be of service to the public, and that he intended them as a kind of legacy,--a bequest to his countrymen.

The publishers of this volume believe that a study of Mr. Webster's mind, heart, and character, as exhibited in the selections contained in the present volume, will inevitably direct all sympathetic readers to the great body of Mr. Webster's works. Among the eminent men who have influenced legislative assemblies in Great Britain and the United States, during the past hundred and twenty years, it is curious that only two have established themselves as men of the first class in English and American literature. These two men are Edmund Burke and Daniel Webster; and it is only by the complete study of every thing which they authorized to be published under their names, that we can adequately comprehend either their position among the political forces of their time, or their rank among the great masters of English eloquence and style.

CONTENTS.

DANIEL WEBSTER AS A MASTER OF ENGLISH STYLE.

From my own experience and observation I should say that every boy, who is ready enough in spelling, grammar, geography, and arithmetic, is appalled when he is commanded to write what is termed "a composition." When he enters college the same fear follows him and the Professor of Rhetoric is a more terrible personage to his imagination than the Professors of Greek, Latin, Mathematics, and Moral and Intellectual Philosophy. Both boys at school and young men in college show no lack of power in speaking their native language with a vehemence and fluency which almost stuns the ears of their seniors. Why, then, should they find such difficulty in writing it? When you listen to the animated talk of a bright school-boy or college student, full of a subject which really interests him, you say at once that such command of racy and idiomatic English words must of course be exhibited in his "compositions" or his "themes"; but when the latter are examined, they are commonly found to be feeble and lifeless, with hardly a thought or a word which bears any stamp of freshness or originality, and which are so inferior to his ordinary conversation, that we can hardly believe they came from the same mind.

The first quality which strikes an examiner of these exercises in English composition is their *falseness*. No boy or youth writes what he personally thinks and feels, but writes what a good boy or youth is expected to think or feel. This hypocrisy vitiates his writing from first to last, and is not absent in his "Class Oration," or in his "Speech at Commencement." I have a vivid memory of the first time the boys of my class, in a public school, were called upon to write "composition." The themes selected were the prominent moral virtues or vices. How we poor innocent urchins were tormented by the task imposed upon us! How we put more ink on our hands and faces than we shed upon the white paper on our desks! Our conclusions generally agreed with those announced by the greatest moralists of the world. Socrates and Plato, Cicero and Seneca, Cudworth and Butler, could not have been more austerely moral than were we little rogues, as we relieved the immense exertion involved in completing a single short baby-like sentence, by shying at one companion a rule, or hurling at another a paper pellet intended to light plump on his forehead or nose. Our custom was to begin every composition with the proposition that such or such a virtue "was one of the greatest blessings we enjoy"; and this triumph of accurate statement was not discovered by our teacher to be purely mechanical, until one juvenile thinker, having avarice to deal with, declared it to be "one of the greatest evils we enjoy." The whole thing was such a piece of monstrous hypocrisy, that I once timidly suggested to the schoolmaster that it would be well to allow me to select my own subject. The request was granted; and, as narrative is the natural form of composition which a boy adopts when he has his own way, I filled, in less than half the time heretofore consumed in writing a quarter of a page, four pages of letter-paper with an account of my being in a ship taken by a pirate; of the heroic defiance I launched at the pirate captain; and the sagacity I evinced in escaping the fate of my fellow-passengers, in not being ordered to "walk the plank." The story, though trashy enough, was so much better than any of the moral essays of the other pupils, that the teacher commanded me to read it before the whole school, as an evidence of the rapid strides I had made in the art of "composition."

This falseness of thought and feeling is but too apt to characterize the writing of the student, after he has passed from the common school to the academy or the college. The term "Sophomorical" is used to describe speeches which are full of emotion which the speaker does not feel, full of words in four or five syllables that mean nothing, and, in respect to imagery and illustrations, blazing with the cheap jewelry of rhetoric,--with those rubies and diamonds that can be purchased for a few pennies an ounce. The danger is that this "Sophomorical" style may continue to afflict the student after he has become a clergyman, a lawyer, or a legislator.

Practical men who may not be "college educated" still have the great virtue of using the few words they employ as identical with facts. When they meet a man who has half the dictionary at his disposal, and yet gives no evidence of apprehending the real import and meaning of one word among the many thousands he glibly pours forth, they naturally distrust him, as a person who does not know the vital connection of all good words with the real things they represent. Indeed, the best rule that a Professor of Rhetoric could adopt would be to insist that no student under his care should use an unusual word until he had *earned the right to use it* by making it the verbal sign of some new advance in his thinking, in his acquirements, or in his feelings. Shakspeare, the greatest of English writers, and perhaps the greatest of all writers, required fifteen thousand words to embody all that his vast exceptional intelligence acquired, thought, imagined, and discovered; and he had earned the right to use every one of them. Milton found that eight thousand words could fairly and fully represent all the power, grandeur, and creativeness of his almost seraphic soul, when he attempted to express his whole nature in a literary form. All the words used by Shakspeare and Milton are _alive_; "cut them and they will *bleed*." But it is ridiculous for a college student to claim that he has the mighty resources of the English language at his supreme disposal, when he has not verified, by his own thought, knowledge, and experience, one in a hundred of the words he presumptuously employs. Now Daniel Webster passed safely through all the stages of the "Sophomoric" disease of the mind, as he passed safely through the measles, the chicken-pox, and other eruptive maladies incident to childhood and youth. The process, however, by which he purified his style from this taint, and made his diction at last as robust and as manly, as simple and as majestic, as the nature it expressed, will reward a little study.

The mature style of Webster is perfect of its kind, being in words the express image of his mind and character,--plain, terse, clear, forcible; and rising from the level of lucid statement and argument into passages of superlative eloquence only when his whole nature is stirred by some grand sentiment of freedom, patriotism, justice, humanity, or religion, which absolutely lifts him, by its own inherent force and inspiration, to a region above that in which his mind habitually lives and moves. At the same time it will be observed that these thrilling passages, which the boys of two generations have ever been delighted to declaim in their shrillest tones, are strictly illustrative of the main purpose of the speech in which they appear. They are not mere purple patches of rhetoric, loosely stitched on the homespun gray of the reasoning, but they seem to be inwoven with it and to be a vital part of it. Indeed we can hardly decide, in reading these magnificent bursts of eloquence in connection with what precedes and follows them, whether the effect is due to the logic of the orator becoming suddenly morally impassioned, or to his moral passion becoming suddenly logical. What gave Webster his immense influence over the opinions of the people of New England was, first, his power of so "putting things" that everybody could understand his statements; secondly, his power of so framing his arguments that all the steps, from one point to another, in a logical series, could be clearly apprehended by every intelligent farmer or mechanic who had a thoughtful interest in the affairs of the country; and thirdly, his power of inflaming the sentiment of patriotism in all honest and well-intentioned men by overwhelming appeals to that sentiment, so that, after convincing their understandings, he clinched the matter by sweeping away their wills.

Perhaps to these sources of influence may be added another which many eminent statesmen have lacked. With all his great superiority to average men in force and breadth of mind, he had a genuine respect for the intellect, as well as for the manhood, of average men. He disdained the ignoble office of misleading the voters he aimed to instruct; and the farmers and mechanics who read his speeches felt ennobled when they found that the greatest statesman of the country frankly addressed them, as man to man, without pluming himself on his exceptional talents and accomplishments. Up to the crisis of 1850, he succeeded in domesticating himself at most of the pious, moral, and intelligent firesides of New England. Through his speeches he seemed to be almost bodily present wherever the family, gathered in the evening around the blazing hearth, discussed the questions of the day. It was not the great Mr. Webster, "the godlike Daniel," who had a seat by the fire. It was a person who talked *to* them, and argued *with* them, as though he was "one of the folks,"--a neighbor dropping in to make an evening call; there was not the slightest trace of assumption in his manner; but suddenly, after the discussion had become a little tiresome, certain fiery words would leap from his lips and make the whole household spring to their feet, ready to sacrifice life and property for "the Constitution and the Union." That Webster was thus a kind of invisible presence in thousands of homes where his face was never seen, shows that his rhetoric had caught an element of power from his early recollections of the independent, hard-headed farmers whom he met when a boy in his father's house. The bodies of these men had become tough and strong in their constant struggle to force scanty harvests from an unfruitful soil, which only persistent toil could compel to yield any thing; and their brains, though forcible and clear, were still not stored with the important facts and principles which it was his delight to state and expound. In truth, he ran a race with the demagogues of his time in an attempt to capture such men as these, thinking them the very backbone of the country. Whether he succeeded or failed, it would be vain to hunt through his works to find a single epithet in which he mentioned them with contempt. He was as incapable of insulting one member of this landed democracy,--sterile as most of their acres were,--as of insulting the memory of his father, who belonged to this class.

The late Mr. Peter Harvey used to tell with much zest a story illustrating the hold which these early associations retained on Webster's mind throughout his life. Some months after his removal from Portsmouth to Boston, a servant knocked at his chamber door late in an April afternoon in the year 1817, with the announcement that three men were in the drawing-room who insisted on seeing him. Webster was overwhelmed with fatigue, the result of his Congressional labors and his attendance on courts of law; and he had determined, after a night's sleep, to steal a vacation in order to recruit his energies by a fortnight's fishing and hunting. He suspected that the persons below were expectant clients; and he resolved, in descending the stairs, not to accept their offer. He found in the parlor three plain, country-bred, honest-looking men, who were believers in the innocence of Levi and Laban Kenniston, accused of robbing a certain Major Goodridge on the highway, and whose trial would take place at Ipswich the next day. They could find, they said, no member of the Essex bar who would undertake the defence of the Kennistons, and they had come to Boston to engage the services of Mr. Webster. Would he go down to Ipswich and defend the accused? Mr. Webster stated that he could not and would not go. He had made arrangements for an excursion to the sea-side; the state of his health absolutely demanded a short withdrawal from all business cares; and that no fee could tempt him to abandon his purpose. "Well," was the reply of one of the delegation, "it isn't the fee that we think of at all, though we are willing to pay what you may charge; but it's justice. Here are two New Hampshire men who are believed in Exeter, and Newbury, and Newburyport, and Salem to be rascals; but we in Newmarket believe, in spite of all evidence against them, that they are the victims of some conspiracy. We think you are the man to unravel it, though it seems a good deal tangled even to us. Still we suppose that men whom we know to have been honest all their lives can't have become such desperate rogues all of a sudden." "But I cannot take the case," persisted Mr. Webster; "I am worn to death with over-work. I have not had any real sleep for forty-eight hours. Besides, I know nothing of the case." "It's hard, I can see," continued the leader of the delegation; "but you're a New Hampshire man, and the *neighbors* thought that you would not allow two innocent New Hampshire men, however humble they may be in their circumstances, to suffer for lack of your skill in exposing the wiles of this scoundrel Goodridge. The *neighbors* all desire you to take the case." That phrase "the neighbors" settled the question. No resident of a city knows what the phrase means. But Webster knew it in all the intense significance of its meaning. His imagination flew back to the scattered homesteads of a New England village, where mutual sympathy and assistance are the necessities, as they are the commonplaces, of village life. The phrase remotely meant to him the combination of neighbors to resist an assault of Indian savages, or to send volunteers to the war which wrought the independence of the nation. It specially meant to him the help of neighbor to neighbor, in times of sickness, distress, sorrow, and calamity. In his childhood and boyhood the Christian question, "Who is my neighbor?" was instantly solved the moment a matron in good health heard that the wife of Farmer A, or Farmer B, was stricken down by fever, and needed a friendly nurse to sit by her bedside all night, though she had herself been toiling hard all day. Every thing philanthropists mean when they talk of brotherhood and sisterhood among men and women was condensed in that homely phrase, "the neighbors." "Oh!" said Webster, ruefully, "if the neighbors think I may be of service, of course I must go";--and, with his three companions, he was soon seated in the stage for Ipswich, where he arrived at about midnight. The court met the next morning; and his management of the case is still considered one of his masterpieces of legal acumen and eloquence. His cross-examination of Goodridge rivalled, in mental torture, every thing martyrologists tell us of the physical agony endured by the victim of the inquisitor, when roasted before slow fires or stretched upon the rack. Still it seemed impossible to assign any motive for the self-robbery and the self-maiming of Goodridge, which any judge or jury would accept as reasonable. The real motive has never been discovered. Webster argued that the motive might have originated in a desire to escape from the payment of his debts, or in a whimsical ambition to have his name sounded all over Maine and Massachusetts as the heroic tradesman who had parted with his money only when overpowered by superior force. It is impossible to say what motives may impel men who are half-crazed by vanity, or half-demonized by malice. Coleridge describes Iago's hatred of Othello as the hatred which a base nature instinctively feels for a noble one, and his assignment of motives for his acts as the mere "motive-hunting of a motiveless malignity."

Whatever may have been Goodridge's motive in his attempt to ruin the innocent men he falsely accused, it is certain that Webster saved these men from the unjust punishment of an imputed crime. Only the skeleton of his argument before the jury has been preserved; but what we have of it evidently passed under his revision. He knew that the plot of Goodridge had been so cunningly contrived, that every man of the twelve before him, whose verdict was to determine the fate of his clients, was inwardly persuaded of their guilt. Some small marked portions of the money which Goodridge swore he had on his person on the night of the pretended robbery were found in their house. Circumstantial evidence brought their guilt with a seemingly irresistible force literally "home" to them. It was the conviction of the leaders of the Essex bar that no respectable lawyer could appear in their defence without becoming, in some degree, their accomplice. But Webster, after damaging the character of the prosecutor by his stern cross-examination, addressed the jury, not as an advocate bearing down upon them with his arguments and appeals, but rather as a thirteenth juryman, who had cosily introduced himself into their company, and was arguing the case with them after they had retired for consultation among themselves. The simplicity of the language employed is not more notable than the power evinced in seizing the main points on which the question of guilt or innocence turned. At every quiet but deadly stab aimed at the theory of the prosecution, he is careful to remark, that "it is for the jury to say under their oaths" whether such inconsistencies or improbabilities should have any effect on their minds. Every strong argument closes with the ever-recurring phrase, "It is for the jury to say"; and, at the end, the jury, thoroughly convinced, said, "Not guilty." The Kennistons were vindicated; and the public, which had been almost unanimous in declaring them fit tenants for the State prison, soon blamed the infatuation which had made them the accomplices of a villain in hunting down two unoffending citizens, and of denouncing every lawyer who should undertake their defence as a legal rogue.

The detected scoundrel fled from the place where his rascality had been exposed, to seek some other locality, where the mingled jeers and curses of his dupes would be unheard. Some twenty years after the trial, Mr. Webster, while travelling in Western New York, stopped at an obscure village tavern to get a glass of water. The hand of the man behind the bar, who gave it to him, trembled violently; and Webster, wondering at the cause, looked the fellow steadily in the eye. He recognized Goodridge, and understood at once that Goodridge had just before recognized *him*. Not a word passed between the felon and the intrepid advocate who had stripped his villany of all its plausible disguises; but what immense meaning must there have been in the swift interchange of feeling as their eyes met! Mr. Webster entered his carriage and proceeded on his journey; but Goodridge,--who has since ever heard of him?

This story is a slight digression, but it illustrates that hold on reality, that truth to fact, which was one of the sources of the force and simplicity of Mr. Webster's mature style. He, however, only obtained these good qualities of rhetoric by long struggles with constant temptations, in his early life, to use resounding expressions and flaring images which he had not earned the right to use. His Fourth of July oration at Hanover, when he was only eighteen, and his college addresses, must have been very bad in their diction if we can judge of them by the style of his private correspondence at the time. The verses he incorporates in his letters are deformed by all the faults of false thinking and borrowed expression which characterized contemporary American imitators of English imitators of Pope and Gray. Think of the future orator, lawyer, and senator writing, even at the age of twenty, such balderdash as this!

"And Heaven grant me, whatever luck betide, Be fame or fortune given or denied, Some cordial friend to meet my warm desire, Honest as John and good as Nehemiah."

In reading such couplets we are reminded of the noted local poet of New Hampshire (or was it Maine?) who wrote "The Shepherd's Songs," and some of whose rustic lines still linger in the memory to be laughed at, such, for instance, as these:--

"This child who perished in the fire,-- His father's name was Nehemiah."

Or these:--

"Napoleon, that great ex_ile_, Who scoured all Europe like a file."

And Webster's prose was then almost as bad as his verse, though it was modelled on what was considered fine writing at the opening of the present century. He writes to his dearest student friends in a style which is profoundly insincere, though the thoughts are often good, and the fact of his love for his friends cannot be doubted. He had committed to memory Fisher Ames's noble speech on the British Treaty, and had probably read some of Burke's great pamphlets on the French Revolution. The stripling statesman aimed to talk in their high tone and in their richly ornamented language, before he had earned the right even to mimic their style of expression. There is a certain swell in some of his long sentences, and a kind of good sense in some of his short ones, which suggest that the writer is a youth endowed with elevation as well as strength of nature, and is only making a fool of himself because he thinks he must make a fool of himself in order that he may impress his correspondents with the idea that he is a master of the horrible jargon which all bright young fellows at that time innocently supposed to constitute eloquence. Thus, in February, 1800, he writes thus to his friend Bingham: "In my melancholy moments I presage the most dire calamities. I already see in my imagination the time when the banner of civil war shall be unfurled; when Discord's hydra form shall set up her hideous yell, and from her hundred mouths shall howl destruction through our empire; and when American blood shall be made to flow in rivers by American swords! But propitious Heaven prevent such dreadful calamities! Internally secure, we have nothing to fear. Let Europe pour her embattled millions around us, let her thronged cohorts cover our shores, from St. Lawrence to St. Marie's, yet United Columbia shall stand unmoved; the manes of her deceased Washington shall guard the liberties of his country, and direct the sword of freedom in the day of battle." And think of this, not in a Fourth of July oration, but in a private letter to an intimate acquaintance! The bones of Daniel Webster might be supposed to have moved in their coffin at the thought that this miserable trash--so regretted and so amply atoned for--should have ever seen the light; but it is from such youthful follies that we measure the vigor of the man who outgrows them.

It was fortunate that Webster, after he was admitted to the bar, came into constant collision, in the courts of New Hampshire, with one of the greatest masters of the common law that the country has ever produced, Jeremiah Mason. It has been said that Mr. Mason educated Webster into a lawyer by opposing him. He did more than this; he cured Webster of all the florid foolery of his early rhetorical style. Of all men that ever appeared before a jury, Mason was the most pitiless realist, the most terrible enemy of what is--in a slang term as vile almost as itself--called "Hifalutin"; and woe to the opposing lawyer who indulged in it! He relentlessly pricked all rhetorical bubbles, reducing them at once to the small amount of ignominious suds, which the orator's breath had converted into colored globes, having some appearance of stability as well as splendor. Six feet and seven inches high, and corpulent in proportion, this inexorable representative of good sense and sound law stood, while he was arguing a case, "quite near to the jury," says Webster,--"so near that he might have laid his finger on the foreman's nose; and then he talked to them in a plain conversational way, in short sentences, and using no word that was not level to the comprehension of the least educated man on the panel. This led me," he adds, "to examine my own style, and I set about reforming it altogether."

Mr. Mason was what the lawyers call a "cause-getting man," like Sir James Scarlett, Brougham's great opponent at the English bar. It was said of Scarlett, that he gained his verdicts because there were twelve Scarletts in the jury-box; and Mason so contrived to blend his stronger mind with the minds of the jurymen, that his thoughts appeared to be theirs, expressed in the same simple words and quaint illustrations which they would have used if asked to give their opinions on the case. It is to be added, that Mason's almost cynical disregard of ornament in his addresses to the jury gave to an opponent like Webster the advantage of availing himself of those real ornaments of speech which spring directly from a great heart and imagination. Webster, without ever becoming so supremely plain and simple in style as Mason, still strove to emulate, in his legal statements and arguments, the homely, robust common-sense of his antagonist; but, wherever the case allowed of it, he brought into the discussion an element of _un_-common sense, the gift of his own genius and individuality, which Mason could hardly comprehend sufficiently to controvert, but which was surely not without its effect in deciding the verdicts of juries.

It is probable that Webster was one of the few lawyers and statesmen that Mason respected. Mason's curt, sharp, "vitriolic" sarcasms on many men who enjoyed a national reputation, and who were popularly considered the lights of their time, still remain in the memories of his surviving associates, as things which may be quoted in conversation, but which it would be cruel to put into print. Of Webster, however, he never seems to have spoken a contemptuous word. Indeed, Mason, though fourteen years older than Webster, and fighting him at the Portsmouth bar with all the formidable force of his logic and learning, was from the first his cordial friend. That friendship, early established between strong natures so opposite in character, was never disturbed by any collision in the courts. In a letter written, I think, a few weeks after he had made that "Reply to Hayne" which is conceded to be one of the great masterpieces of eloquence in the recorded oratory of the world, Webster wrote jocularly to Mason: "I have been written to, to go to New Hampshire, to try a cause against you next August.... If it were an easy and plain case on our side, I might be willing to go; but I have some of your _pounding in my bones yet_, and I don't care about any more till that wears out."

It may be said that Webster's argument in the celebrated "Dartmouth College Case," before the Supreme Court of the United States, placed him, at the age of thirty-six, in the foremost rank of the constitutional lawyers of the country. For the main points of the reasoning, and for the exhaustive citation of authorities by which the reasoning was sustained, he was probably indebted to Mason, who had previously argued the case before the Superior Court of New Hampshire; but his superiority to Mason was shown in the eloquence, the moral power, he infused into his reasoning, so as to make the dullest citation of legal authority *tell* on the minds he addressed.

There is one incident connected with this speech which proves what immense force is given to simple words when a great man--great in his emotional nature as well as great in logical power--is behind the words. "It is, sir, as I have said, a small college. And yet there are those who love it." At this point the orator's lips quivered, his voice choked, his eyes filled with tears,--all the memories of sacrifices endured by his father and mother, his brothers and sisters, in order that he might enjoy its rather scanty advantages of a liberal education, and by means of which he was there to plead its cause before the supreme tribunal of the nation, rushed suddenly upon his mind in an overwhelming flood. The justices of the Supreme Court-- great lawyers, tried and toughened by experience into a certain obdurate sense of justice, and insensible to any common appeal to their hearts--melted into unwonted tenderness, as, in broken words, the advocate proceeded to state his own indebtedness to the "small college," whose rights and privileges he was there to defend. Chief Justice Marshall's eyes were filled with tears; and the eyes of the other justices were suffused with a moisture similar to that which afflicted the eyes of the Chief. As the orator gradually recovered his accustomed stern composure of manner, he turned to the counsel on the other side,--one of whom, at least, was a graduate of Dartmouth,--and in his deepest and most thrilling tones, thus concluded his argument: "Sir, I know not how others may feel; but for myself, when I see my Alma Mater surrounded, like Caesar in the senate-house, by those who are reiterating stab after stab, I would not, for this right hand, have her turn to me and say, _Et tu quoque, mi fili!_--And thou too, my son." The effect was overwhelming; yet by what simple means was it produced, and with what small expenditure of words! The eloquence was plainly "in the man, in the subject, and in the occasion," but most emphatically was it in the MAN.

Webster's extreme solicitude to make his style thoroughly _Websterian_--a style unimitated because it is in itself inimitable--is observable in the care he took in revising all his speeches and addresses which were published under his own authority. His great Plymouth oration of 1820 did not appear in a pamphlet form until a year after its delivery. The chief reason of this delay was probably due to his desire of stating the main political idea of the oration, that government is founded on property, so clearly that it could not be misconceived by any honest mind, and could only be perverted from its plain democratic meaning by the ingenious malignity of such minds as are deliberately dishonest, and consider lying as justifiable when lying will serve a party purpose. It is probable that Webster would have been President of the United States had it not been for one short sentence in this oration,--"Government is founded on property." It was of no use for his political friends to prove that he founded on this general proposition the most democratic views as to the distribution of property, and advised the enactment of laws calculated to frustrate the accumulation of large fortunes in a few hands. There were the words, words horrible to the democratic imagination, and Webster was proclaimed an aristocrat, and an enemy to the common people. But the delay in the publication of the oration may also be supposed to have been due to his desire to prune all its grand passages of eloquence of every epithet and image which should not be rigorously exact as expressions of his genuine sentiments and principles. It is probable that the Plymouth oration, as we possess it in print, is a better oration, in respect to composition, than that which was heard by the applauding crowd before which it was originally delivered. It is certain that the largeness, the grandeur, the weight of Webster's whole nature, were first made manifest to the intelligent portion of his countrymen by this noble commemorative address.

Yet it is also certain that he was not himself altogether satisfied with this oration; and his dissatisfaction with some succeeding popular speeches, memorable in the annals of American eloquence, was expressed privately to his friends in the most emphatic terms. On the day he completed his magnificent Bunker Hill oration, delivered on the 17th of June, 1825, he wrote to Mr. George Ticknor: "I did the deed this morning, i.e. I finished my speech; and I am pretty well persuaded that it will *finish* me as far as reputation is concerned. There is no more tone in it than in the weather in which it has been written; it is perpetual dissolution and thaw." Every critic will understand the force of that word "tone." He seemed to feel that it had not enough robust manliness,--that the ribs and backbone, the facts, thoughts, and real substance of the address, were not sufficiently prominent, owing to the frequency of those outbursts of magnetic eloquence, which made the immense audience that listened to it half crazy with the vehemence of their applause. On the morning after he had delivered his eulogy on Adams and Jefferson, he entered his office with his manuscript in his hand, and threw it down on the desk of a young student at law whom he specially esteemed, with the request, "There, Tom, please to take that discourse, and weed out all the Latin words."

Webster's liking for the Saxon element of our composite language was, however, subordinate to his main purpose of self-expression. Every word was good, whether of Saxon or Latin derivation, which aided him to embody the mood of mind dominant at the time he was speaking or writing. No man had less of what has been called "the ceremonial cleanliness of academical pharisees;" and the purity of expression he aimed at was to put into a form, at once intelligible and tasteful, his exact thoughts and emotions. He tormented reporters, proof-readers, and the printers who had the misfortune to be engaged in putting one of his performances into type, not because this or that word was or was not Saxon or Latin, but because it was inadequate to convey perfectly his meaning. Mr. Kemble, a great Anglo-Saxon scholar, once, in a company of educated gentlemen, defied anybody present to mention a single Latin phrase in our language for which he could not furnish a more forcible Saxon equivalent. "The impenetrability of matter" was suggested; and Kemble, after half a minute's reflection, answered, "The un-thorough-fareableness of stuff." Still, no English writer would think of discarding such an abstract, but convenient and accurate, term as "impenetrability," for the coarsely concrete and terribly ponderous word which declares that there is no possible thoroughfare, no road, by which we can penetrate that substance which we call "matter," and which our Saxon forefathers called "stuff." Wherever the Latin element in our language comes in to express ideas and sentiments which were absent from the Anglo-Saxon mind, Webster uses it without stint; and some of the most resounding passages of his eloquence owe to it their strange power to suggest a certain vastness in his intellect and sensibility, which the quaint, idiomatic, homely prose of his friend, Mason, would have been utterly incompetent to convey. Still, he preferred a plain, plump, simple verb or noun to any learned phrase, whenever he could employ it without limiting his opulent nature to a meagre vocabulary, incompetent fully to express it.

Yet he never departed from simplicity; that is, he rigidly confined himself to the use of such words as he had earned the right to use. Whenever the report of one of his extemporaneous speeches came before him for revision, he had an instinctive sagacity in detecting every word that had slipped unguardedly from his tongue, which he felt, on reflection, did not belong to *him*. Among the reporters of his speeches, he had a particular esteem for Henry J. Raymond, afterwards so well known as the editor of the New York Times. Mr. Raymond told me that, after he had made a report of one of Webster's speeches, and had presented it to him for revision, his conversation with him was always a lesson in rhetoric. "Did I use that phrase? I hope not. At any rate, substitute for it this more accurate definition." And then again: "That word does not express my meaning. Wait a moment, and I will give you a better one. That sentence is slovenly,--that image is imperfect and confused. I believe, my young friend, that you have a remarkable power of reporting what I say; but, if I said that, and that, and that, it must have been owing to the fact that I caught, in the hurry of the moment, such expressions as I could command at the moment; and you see they do not accurately represent the idea that was in my mind." And thus, Mr. Raymond said, the orator's criticism upon his own speech would go on,--correction following correction,--until the reporter feared he would not have it ready for the morning edition of his journal.

Webster had so much confidence in Raymond's power of reporting him accurately, that, when he intended to make an important speech in the Senate, he would send a note to him, asking him to come to Washington as a personal favor; for he knew that the accomplished editor had a rare power of apprehending a long train of reasoning, and of so reporting it that the separate thoughts would not only be exactly stated, but the relations of the thoughts to each other--a much more difficult task--would be preserved throughout, and that the argument would be presented in the symmetrical form in which it existed in the speaker's mind. Then would follow, as of old, the severe scrutiny of the phraseology of the speech; and Webster would give, as of old, a new lesson in rhetoric to the accomplished reporter who was so capable of following the processes of his mind.

The great difficulty with speakers who may be sufficiently clear in statement and cogent in argument is that turn in their discourse when their language labors to become figurative. Imagery makes palpable to the bodily eye the abstract thought seen only by the eye of the mind; and all orators aim at giving vividness to their thinking by thus making their thoughts *visible*. The investigation of the process of imagination by which this end is reached is an interesting study. Woe to the speaker who is ambitious to rise into the region of imagination without possessing the faculty! Everybody remembers the remark of Sheridan, when Tierney, the prosaic Whig leader of the English House of Commons, ventured to bring in, as an illustration of his argument, the fabulous but favorite bird of untrained orators, the phoenix, which is supposed always to spring up alive out of its own ashes. "It was," said Sheridan, "a poulterer's description of a phoenix."

That is, Tierney, from defect of imagination, could not lift his poetic bird above the rank of a common hen or chicken.

The test that may be most easily applied to all efforts of the imagination is sincerity; for, like other qualities of the mind, it acts strictly within the limits of a man's character and experience. The meaning of the word "experience," however, must not be confined to what he has personally seen and felt, but is also to be extended to every thing he has seen and felt through vital sympathy with facts, scenes, events, and characters, which he has learned by conversation with other men and through books. Webster laid great emphasis on conversation as one of the most important sources of imagery as well as of positive knowledge. "In my education," he once remarked to Charles Sumner, "I have found that conversation with the intelligent men I have had the good fortune to meet has done more for me than books ever did; for I learn more from them in a talk of half an hour than I could possibly learn from their books. Their minds, in conversation, come into intimate contact with my own mind; and I absorb certain secrets of their power, whatever may be its quality, which I could not have detected in their works. Converse, _converse_, CONVERSE with living men, face to face, and mind to mind,--that is one of the best sources of knowledge."

But my present object is simply to give what may be called the natural history of metaphor, comparison, image, trope, and the like, whether imagery be employed by an uneducated husbandman, or by a great orator and writer. Many readers may recollect the anecdote of the New Hampshire farmer, who was once complimented on the extremely handsome appearance of a horse which he was somewhat sullenly urging on to perform its work. "Yaas," was the churlish reply, "the critter looks well enough, but then he is as slow as--as--as--well, as slow as cold molasses." This perfectly answers to Bacon's definition of imagination, as "thought immersed in matter." The comparison is exactly on a level with the experience of the person who used it. He had seen his good wife, on so many bitter winter mornings, when he was eager for his breakfast, turn the molasses-jug upside down, and had noted so often the reluctance of the congealed sweetness to assume its liquid nature, that the thing had become to him the visible image of the abstract notion of slowness of movement. An imaginative dramatist or novelist, priding himself on the exactness with which he represented character, could not have invented a more appropriate comparison to be put into the mouth of an imagined New England farmer.

The only objection to such rustic poets is, that a comparatively few images serve them for a lifetime; and one tires of such "originals" after a few days' conversation has shown the extremely limited number of apt illustrations they have added to the homely poetry of agricultural life. The only person, belonging to this class, that I ever met, who possessed an imagination which was continually creative in quaint images, was a farmer by the name of Knowlton, who had spent fifty years in forcing some few acres of the rocky soil of Cape Ann to produce grass, oats, potatoes, and, it may be added, those ugly stone walls which carefully distinguish, at the cape, one patch of miserable sterile land from another. He was equal, in quickness of imaginative illustration, to the whole crowd of clergymen, lawyers, poets, and artists, who filled the boarding-houses of "Pigeon Cove"; and he was absolutely inexhaustible in fresh and original imagery. On one hot summer day, the continuation of fourteen hot summer days, when there was fear all over Cape Ann that the usual scanty crops would be withered up by the intense heat, and the prayer for rain was in almost every farmer's heart, I met Mr. Knowlton, as he was looking philosophically over one of his own sun-smitten fields of grass. Thinking that I was in full sympathy with his own feeling at the dolorous prospect before his eyes, I said, in accosting him, that it was bad weather for the farmers. He paused for half a minute; and then his mind flashed back on an incident of his weekly experience,--that of his wife "ironing" the somewhat damp clothes of the Monday's "washing,"--and he replied: "I see you've been talking with our farmers, who are too stupid to know what's for their good. Ye see the spring here was uncommonly rainy, and the ground became wet and cold; but now, for the last fortnight, _God has been putting his flat-iron over it_, and 'twill all come out right in the end."

Thus Mr. Knowlton went on, year after year, speaking poetry without knowing it, as Molière's Monsieur Jourdain found he had been speaking prose all his life without knowing it. But the conception of the sun as God's flat-iron, smoothing out and warming the moist earth, as a housewife smooths and warms the yet damp shirts, stockings, and bed-linen brought into the house from the clothes-lines in the yard, is an astounding illustration of that "familiar grasp of things divine," which obtains in so many of our rustic households. Dante or Chaucer, two of the greatest poets of the world, would, had they happened to be "uneducated" men, have seized on just such an image to express their idea of the Divine beneficence.

This natural, this instinctive operation of the imaginative faculty, is often observed in children. Numberless are the stories told by fond mothers of the wonderful things uttered by their babies, shortly after they have left their cradles. The most striking peculiarity running through them all is the astonishing audacity with which the child treats the most sacred things. He or she seems to have no sense of awe. All children are taught to believe that God resides above them in the sky; and I shall never forget the shock of surprise I felt at the answer of a boy of five years--whom I found glorying over the treasures of his first paint-box--to my question: "Which color do you like best?" "Oh," he carelessly replied, "I like best sky-blue,--God's color." And the little rogue went on, daubing the paper before him with a mixture of all colors, utterly unconscious that he had said any thing remarkable; and yet what Mrs. Browning specially distinguishes as the characteristic of the first and one of the greatest of English poets, Chaucer, namely, his "familiar grasp of things Divine," could not have found a more appropriate illustration than in this chance remark of a mere child, expressing the fearlessness of his faith in the Almighty Father above him.

Now in all these instinctive operations of the imagination, whether in the mind of a child or in that of a grown man, it is easy to discern the mark of sincerity. If the child is petted, and urged by his mother to display his brightness before a company of other mothers and other babies, he is in danger of learning early that trick of falsehood, which clings to him when he goes to school, when he leaves the school for the college, and when he leaves the college for the pursuits of professional life. The farmer or mechanic, not endowed with "college larnin'," is sure to become a bad declaimer, perhaps a demagogue, when he abandons those natural illustrations and ornaments of his speech which spring from his individual experience, and strives to emulate the grandiloquence of those graduates of colleges who have the heathen mythology at the ends of their fingers and tongues, and can refer to Jove, Juno, Minerva, Diana, Venus, Vulcan, and Neptune, as though they were resident deities and deesses of the college halls. The trouble with most "uneducated" orators is, that they become enamored of these shining gods and goddesses, after they have lost, through repetition, all of their old power to give point or force to any good sentence of modern oratory. During the times when, to be a speaker at Abolitionist meetings, the speaker ran the risk of being pelted with rotten eggs, I happened to be present, as one of a small antislavery audience, gathered in an equally small hall. Among the speakers was an honest, strong-minded, warm-hearted young mechanic, who, as long as he was true to his theme, spoke earnestly, manfully, and well; but alas! he thought he could not close without calling in some god or goddess to give emphasis--after the method of college students--to his previous statements. He selected, of course, that unfortunate phantom whom he called the Goddess of Liberty. "Here, in Boston," he thundered, "where she was cradled in Faneuil Hall, can it be that Liberty should be trampled under foot, when, after two generations have passed,--yes, sir, have elapsed,--she has grown--yes, sir, I repeat it, has grown--grown up, sir, into a great man?" The change in sex was, in this case, more violent than usual; but how many instances occur to everybody's recollection, where that poor Goddess has been almost equally outraged, through a puerile ambition on the part of the orator to endow her with an exceptional distinction by senseless rhodomontade, manufactured by the word-machine which he presumes to call his imagination! All imitative imagery is the grave of common-sense.

Now let us pass to an imagination which is, perhaps, the grandest in American oratory, but which was as perfectly natural as that of the "cold molasses," or "God's flat-iron," of the New England farmer,--as natural, indeed, as the "sky-blue, God's color," of the New England boy. Daniel Webster, standing on the heights of Quebec at an early hour of a summer morning, heard the ordinary morning drum-beat which called the garrison to their duty. Knowing that the British possessions belted the globe, the thought occurred to him that the morning drum would go on beating in some English post to the time when it would sound again in Quebec. Afterwards, in a speech on President Jackson's Protest, he dwelt on the fact that our Revolutionary forefathers engaged in a war with Great Britain on a strict question of principle, "while actual suffering was still afar off." How could he give most effect to this statement? It would have been easy for him to have presented statistical tables, showing the wealth, population, and resources of England, followed by an enumeration of her colonies and military stations, all going to prove the enormous strength of the nation against which the United American colonies raised their improvised flag. But the thought which had heretofore occurred to him at Quebec happily recurred to his mind the moment it was needed; and he flashed on the imagination an image of British power which no statistics could have conveyed to the understanding,--"a Power," he said, "which has dotted over the surface of the whole globe with her possessions and military posts, whose morning drum-beat, following the sun, and keeping company with the hours, circles the earth with one continuous and unbroken strain of the martial airs of

England." Perhaps a mere rhetorician might consider superfluous the word "whole," as applied to "globe," and "unbroken," as following "continuous"; yet they really add to the force and majesty of the expression. It is curious that, in Great Britain, this magnificent impersonation of the power of England is so little known. It is certain that it is unrivalled in British patriotic oratory. Not Chatham, not even Burke, ever approached it in the noblest passages in which they celebrated the greatness and glory of their country. Webster, it is to be noted, introduced it in his speech, not for the purpose of exalting England, but of exalting our Revolutionary forefathers, whose victory, after a seven years' war of terrible severity, waged in vindication of a principle, was made all the more glorious from having been won over an adversary so formidable and so vast.

It is reported that, at the conclusion of this speech on the President's Protest, John Sergeant, of Philadelphia, came up to the orator, and, after cordially shaking hands with him, eagerly asked, "Where, Webster, did you get that idea of the morning drum-beat?" Like other public men, accustomed to address legislative assemblies, he was naturally desirous of knowing the place, if place there was, where such images and illustrations were to be found. The truth was that, if Webster had ever read Goethe's Faust,-- which he of course never had done,--he might have referred his old friend to that passage where Faust, gazing at the setting sun, aches to follow it in its course for ever. "See," he exclaims, "how the green-girt cottages shimmer in the setting sun. He bends and sinks,--the day is outlived. Yonder he hurries off, and quickens other life. Oh, that I have no wing to lift me from the ground, to struggle after--for ever after-- him! I should see, in everlasting evening beams, the stilly world at my feet, every height on fire, every vale in repose, the silver brook flowing into golden streams. The rugged mountain, with all its dark defiles, would not then break my godlike course. Already the sea, with its heated bays, opens on my enraptured sight. Yet the god seems at last to sink away. But the new impulse wakes. I hurry on to drink his everlasting light,--_the day before me and the night behind_,--and under me the waves." In Faust, the wings of the mind follow the setting sun; in Webster, they follow the rising sun; but the thought of each circumnavigates the globe, in joyous companionship with the same centre of life, light, and heat,--though the suggestion which prompts the sublime idea is widely different. The sentiment of Webster, calmly meditating on the heights of Quebec, contrasts strangely with the fiery feeling of Faust, raging against the limitations of his mortal existence. A humorist, Charles Dickens, who never read either Goethe or Webster, has oddly seized on the same general idea: "The British empire," as he says, in one of his novels,--"on which the sun never sets, and where the tax-gatherer never goes to bed."

This celebrated image of the British "drum-beat" is here cited simply to indicate the natural way in which all the faculties of Webster are brought into harmonious co-operation, whenever he seriously discusses any great question. His understanding and imagination, when both are roused into action, always cordially join hands. His statement of facts is so combined with the argument founded on them, that they are interchangeable; his statement having the force of argument, and his argument having the "substantiality" which properly belongs to statement; and to these he commonly adds an imaginative illustration, which gives increased reality to both statement and argument. In rapidly turning over the leaves of the six volumes of his Works, one can easily find numerous instances of this instinctive operation of his mind. In his first Bunker Hill oration, he announces that "the *principle* of free governments adheres to the American soil. It is bedded in it, immovable as its mountains." Again he says: "A call for the representative system, wherever it is not enjoyed, and where there is already intelligence enough to estimate its value, is perseveringly made. Where men may speak out, they demand it where the bayonet is at their throats, they pray for it." And yet again: "If the true spark of religious and civil liberty be kindled, it will burn. Human agency cannot extinguish it. Like the earth's central fire, it may be smothered for a time; the ocean may overwhelm it; mountains may press it down; but its inherent and unconquerable force will heave both the ocean and the land, and at some time or other, in some place or other, the volcano will break out, and flame up to heaven." It would be difficult to find in any European literature a similar embodiment of an elemental sentiment of humanity, in an image which is as elemental as the sentiment to which it gives vivid expression.

And then with what majesty, with what energy, and with what simplicity, can he denounce a political transaction which, had it not attracted his ire, would hardly have survived in the memory of his countrymen! Thus, in his Protest against Mr. Benton's Expunging Resolution, speaking for himself and his Senatorial colleague, he says: "We rescue our own names, character, and honor from all participation in this matter; and, whatever the wayward character of the times, the headlong and plunging spirit of party devotion, or the fear or the love of power, may have been able to bring about elsewhere, we desire to thank God that they have not, as yet, overcome the love of liberty, fidelity to true republican principles, and a sacred regard for the Constitution in that State whose soil was drenched to a mire by the first and best blood of the Revolution." Perhaps the peculiar power of Webster in condemning a measure by a felicitous epithet, such as that he employs in describing "the *plunging* spirit of party devotion," was never more happily exercised. In that word "plunging," he intended to condense all his horror and hatred of a transaction which he supposed calculated to throw the true principles of constitutional government into a bottomless abyss of personal government, where right constitutional principles would cease to have existence, as well as cease to have authority.

There is one passage in his oration at the completion of the Bunker Hill Monument, which may be quoted as an illustration of his power of compact statement, and which, at the same time, may save readers from the trouble of reading many excellent histories of the origin and progress of the Spanish dominion in America, condensing, as it does, all which such histories can tell us in a few smiting sentences. "Spain," he says, "stooped on South America, like a vulture on its prey. Every thing was force. Territories were acquired by fire and sword. Cities were destroyed by fire and sword. Hundreds of thousands of human beings fell by fire and sword. Even conversion to Christianity was attempted by fire and sword." One is reminded, in this passage, of Macaulay's method of giving vividness to his confident generalization of facts by emphatic repetitions of the same form of words. The repetition of "fire and sword," in this series of short, sharp sentences, ends in forcing the reality of what the words mean on the dullest imagination; and the climax is capped by affirming that "fire and sword" were the means by which the religion of peace was recommended to idolaters, whose heathenism was more benignant, and more intrinsically Christian, than the military Christianity which was forced upon them.

And then, again, how easily Webster's imagination slips in, at the end of a comparatively bald enumeration of the benefits of a good government, to vitalize the statements of his understanding! "Everywhere," he says, "there is order, everywhere there is security. Everywhere the law reaches to the highest, and reaches to the lowest, to protect all in their rights, and to restrain all from wrong; and over all hovers liberty,--that liberty for which our fathers fought and fell on this very spot, with her eye ever watchful, and her eagle wing ever wide outspread." There is something astonishing in the dignity given in the last clause of this sentence to the American eagle,--a bird so degraded by the rhodomontade of fifth-rate declaimers, that it seemed impossible that the highest genius and patriotism could restore it to its primacy among the inhabitants of the air, and its just eminence as a symbol of American liberty. It is also to be noted, that Webster here alludes to "the bird of freedom" only as it appears on the American silver dollar that passes daily from hand to hand, where the watchful eye and the outspread wing are so inartistically represented that the critic is puzzled to account for the grandeur of the image which the orator contrived to evolve from the barbaric picture on the ugliest and clumsiest of civilized coins.

The compactness of Webster's statements occasionally reminds us of the epigrammatic point which characterizes so many of the statements of Burke. Thus, in presenting a memorial to Congress, signed by many prominent men of business, against President Jackson's system of finance, he saw at once that the Democrats would denounce it as another manifesto of the "moneyed aristocracy." Accordingly Webster introduced the paper to the attention of the Senate, with the preliminary remark: "The memorialists are not unaware, that, if rights are attacked, attempts will be made to render odious those whose rights are violated. Power always seeks such subjects on which to try its experiments." It is difficult to resist the impression that Webster must have been indebted to Burke for this maxim. Again, we are deluded into the belief that we must be reading Burke, when Webster refers to the *minimum* principle as the right one to be followed in imposing duties on certain manufactures. "It lays the impost," he says, "exactly where it will do good, and leaves the rest free. It is an intelligent, discerning, discriminating principle; not a blind, headlong, generalizing, uncalculating operation. Simplicity undoubtedly, is a great beauty in acts of legislation, as well as in the works of art; but in both it must be a simplicity resulting from congruity of parts and adaptation to the end designed; not a rude generalization, which either leaves the particular object unaccomplished, or, in accomplishing it, accomplishes a dozen others also, which were not desired. It is a simplicity wrought out by knowledge and skill; not the rough product of an undistinguishing, sweeping general principle."

An ingenuous reader, who has not learned from his historical studies that men generally act, not from arguments addressed to their understandings, but from vehement appeals which rouse their passions to defend their seeming interests, cannot comprehend why Webster's arguments against Nullification and Secession, which were apparently unanswerable, and which were certainly unanswered either by Hayne or Calhoun, should not have settled the question in debate between the North and the South. Such a reader, after patiently following all the turns and twists of the logic, all the processes of the reasoning employed on both sides of the intellectual contest, would naturally conclude that the party defeated in the conflict would gracefully acknowledge the fact of its defeat; and, as human beings, gifted with the faculty of reason, would cheerfully admit the demonstrated results of its exercise. He would find it difficult to comprehend why the men who were overcome in a fair gladiatorial strife in the open arena of debate, with brain pitted against brain, and manhood against manhood, should resort to the rough logic of "blood and iron," when the nobler kind of logic, that which is developed in the struggle of mind with mind, had failed to accomplish the purposes which their hearts and wills, independent of their understandings, were bent on accomplishing.

It may be considered certain that so wise a statesman as Webster--a statesman whose foresight was so palpably the consequence of his insight, and whose piercing intellect was so admirably adapted to read events in their principles--never indulged in such illusions as those which cheered so many of his own adherents, when they supposed his triumph in argumentation was to settle a matter which was really based on organic differences in the institutions of the two sections of the Union. He knew perfectly well that, while the Webster men were glorying in his victory over Calhoun, the Calhoun men were equally jubilant in celebrating Calhoun's victory over him. Which of them had the better in the argument was of little importance in comparison with the terrible fact that the people of the Southern States were widening, year by year, the distance which separated them from the people of the Northern States. We have no means of judging whether Webster clearly foresaw the frightful civil war between the two sections, which followed so soon after his own death. We only know that, to him, it was a conflict constantly impending, and which could be averted for the time only by compromises, concessions, and other temporary expedients. If he allowed his mind to pass from the pressing questions of the hour, and to consider the radical division between the two sections of the country which were only formally united, it would seem that he must have felt, as long as the institution of negro slavery existed, that he was only laboring to postpone a conflict which it was impossible for him to prevent.

But my present purpose is simply to indicate the felicity of Webster's intrepid assault on the principles which the Southern disunionists put forward in justification of their acts. Mr. Calhoun's favorite idea was this,--that Nullification was a conservative principle, to be exercised within the Union, and in accordance with a just interpretation of the Constitution. "To begin with nullification," Webster retorted, "with the avowed intent, nevertheless, not to proceed to secession, dismemberment, and general revolution, is as if one were to take the plunge of Niagara, and cry out that he would stop half-way down. In the one case, as in the other, the rash adventurer must go to the bottom of the dark abyss below, were it not that the abyss has no discovered bottom."

How admirable also is his exposure of the distinction attempted to be drawn between secession, as a State right to be exercised under the provisions of what was called "the Constitutional Compact," and revolution. "Secession," he says, "as a revolutionary right, is intelligible; as a right to be proclaimed in the midst of civil commotions, and asserted at the head of armies, I can understand it. But as a practical right, existing under the Constitution, and in conformity with its provisions, it seems to me nothing but a plain absurdity; for it supposes resistance to government, under the authority of government itself; it supposes dismemberment, without violating the principles of union; it supposes opposition to law, without crime, it supposes the total overthrow of government, without revolution."

After putting some pertinent interrogatories--which are arguments in themselves--relating to the inevitable results of secession, he adds, that "every man must see that these are all questions which can arise only after a revolution. They presuppose the breaking up of the government. While the Constitution lasts, they are repressed";--and then, with that felicitous use of the imagination as a handmaid of the understanding, which is the peculiar characteristic of his eloquence, he closes the sentence by saying, that "they spring up to annoy and startle us only from its grave." A mere reasoner would have stopped at the word "repressed"; the instantaneous conversion of "questions" into spectres, affrighting and annoying us as they spring up from the grave of the Constitution,--which is also by implication impersonated,--is the work of Webster's ready imagination; and it thoroughly vitalizes the statements which precede it.

A great test of the sincerity of a statesman's style is his moderation. Now, if we take the whole body of Mr.

Webster's speeches, whether delivered in the Senate or before popular assemblies, during the period of his opposition to President Jackson's administration, we may well be surprised at their moderation of tone and statement. Everybody old enough to recollect the singular virulence of political speech at that period must remember it as disgraceful equally to the national conscience and the national understanding. The spirit of party, always sufficiently fierce and unreasonable, was then stimulated into a fury resembling madness. Almost every speaker, Democrat or Whig, was in that state of passion which is represented by the physical sign of "foaming at the mouth." Few mouths then opened that did not immediately begin to "foam." So many fortunes were suddenly wrecked by President Jackson's financial policy, and the business of the country was so disastrously disturbed, that, whether the policy was right or wrong, those who assailed and those who defended it seemed to be equally devoid of common intellectual honesty. "I do well to be angry," appears to have been the maxim which inspired Democratic and Whig orators alike; and what reason there was on either side was submerged in the lies and libels, in the calumnies and caricatures, in the defamations and execrations, which accompanied the citation of facts and the affirmation of principles. Webster, during all this time, was selected as a shining mark, at which every puny writer or speaker who opposed him hurled his small or large contribution of verbal rotten eggs; and yet Webster was almost the only Whig statesman who preserved sanity of understanding during the whole progress of that political riot, in which the passions of men became the masters of their understandings. Pious Whig fathers, who worshipped the "godlike Daniel," went almost to the extent of teaching their children to curse Jackson in their prayers; equally pious Democratic fathers brought up their sons and daughters to anathematize the fiend-like Daniel as the enemy of human rights; and yet, in reading Webster's speeches, covering the whole space between 1832 and 1836, we can hardly find a statement which an historian of our day would not admit as a candid generalization of facts, or an argument which would not stand the test of logical examination. Such an historian might entirely disagree with the opinions of Webster; but he would certainly award to him the praise of being an honest reasoner and an honest rhetorician, in a time when reason was used merely as a tool of party passion, and when rhetoric rushed madly into the worst excesses of rhodomontade.

It is also to be said that Webster rarely indulged in personalities. When we consider how great were his powers of sarcasm and invective, how constant were the provocations to exercise them furnished by his political enemies, and how atrociously and meanly allusions to his private affairs were brought into discussions which should have been confined to refuting his reasoning, his moderation in this matter is to be ranked as a great virtue. He could not take a glass of wine without the trivial fact being announced all over the country as indisputable proof that he was an habitual drunkard, though the most remarkable characteristic of his speeches is their temperance,--their "total abstinence" from all the intoxicating moral and mental "drinks" which confuse the understanding and mislead the conscience. He could not borrow money on his note of hand, like any other citizen, without the circumstance being trumpeted abroad as incontrovertible evidence that Nick Biddle had paid him that sum to defend his diabolical Bank in the Senate of the United States. The plain fact that his speeches were confined strictly to the exposition and defence of sound opinions on trade and finance, and that it was difficult to answer them, only confirmed his opponents in the conviction that old Nick was at the bottom of it all. His great intellect was admitted; but on the high, broad brow, which was its manifestation to the eye, his enemies pasted the words, "To be let," or, "For sale." The more impersonal he became in his statements and arguments, the more truculently was he assailed by the personalities of the political gossip and scandal-monger. Indeed, from the time he first came to the front as a great lawyer, statesman, and patriot, he was fixed upon by the whole crew of party libellers as a man whose arguments could be answered most efficiently by staining his character. He passed through life with his head enveloped "in a cloud of poisonous flies"; and the head was the grandest-looking head that had ever been seen on the American continent. It was so pre-eminently noble and impressive, and promised so much more than it could possibly perform, that only one felicitous sarcasm of party malice, among many thousands of bad jokes, has escaped oblivion; and that was stolen from Charles Fox's remark on Lord Chancellor Thurlow, as Fox once viewed him sitting on the wool-sack, frowning on the English House of Lords, which he dominated by the terror of his countenance, and by the fear that he might, at any moment, burst forth in one of his short bullying, thundering retorts, should any comparatively weak baron, earl, marquis, or duke dare to oppose him. "Thurlow," said Fox, "must be an impostor, for nobody can be as wise as he looks." The American version of this was, "Webster must be a charlatan, for no one can be as great as he looks."

But during all the time that his antagonists attempted to elude the force of his arguments by hunting up the evidences of his debts, and by trying to show that the most considerate, the most accurate, and the most temperate of his lucid statements were the products of physical stimulants, Webster steadily kept in haughty reserve his power of retaliation. In his speech in reply to Hayne he hinted that, if he were imperatively called upon to meet blows with blows, he might be found fully equal to his antagonists in that ignoble province of intellectual pugilism; but that he preferred the more civilized struggle of brain with brain, in a contest which was to decide questions of principle. In the Senate, where he could meet his political opponents face to face, few dared to venture to degrade the subject in debate from the discussion of principles to the miserable subterfuge of imputing bad motives as a sufficient answer to good arguments; but still many of these dignified gentlemen smiled approval on the efforts of the low-minded, small-minded caucus-speakers of their party, when they declared that Webster's logic was unworthy of consideration, because he was bought by the Bank, or bought by the manufacturers of Massachusetts, or bought by some other combination of persons who were supposed to be the deadly enemies of the laboring men of the country. On some rare occasions Webster's wrath broke out in such smiting words that his adversaries were cowed into silence, and cursed the infatuation which had led them to overlook the fact that the "logic-machine" had in it invectives more terrible than its reasonings. But generally he refrained from using the giant's power "like a giant"; and it is almost pathetic to remember that, when Mr. Everett undertook to edit, in 1851, the standard edition of his works, Webster gave directions to expunge all personalities from his speeches, even when those personalities were the just punishment of unprovoked attacks on his integrity as a man. Readers will look in vain, in this edition of his works, for some of the most pungent passages which originally attracted their attention in the first report of the Defence of the Treaty of Washington. At the time these directions were given, Webster was himself the object of innumerable personalities, which were the natural, the inevitable results of his speech of the 7th of March, 1850.

It seems to be a law, that the fame of all public men shall be "half disfame." We are specially warned to beware of the man of whom all men speak well. Burke, complimenting his friend Fox for risking every thing, even his "darling popularity," on the success of the East India Bill, nobly says: "He is traduced and abused for his supposed motives. He will remember, that obloquy is a necessary ingredient in all true glory; he will remember, that it was not only in the Roman customs, but it is in the nature of human things, that calumny and abuse are essential parts of triumph."

It may be said, however, that Webster's virtue in this general abstinence from personalities is to be offset by the fact that he could throw into a glance of his eye, a contortion of his face, a tone of his voice, or a simple gesture of his hand, more scorn, contempt, and hatred than ordinary debaters could express by the profuse use of all the scurrilous terms in the English language. Probably many a sentence, which we now read with an even pulse, was, as originally delivered, accompanied by such pointing of the finger, or such flashing of the eye, or such raising of the voice, that the seemingly innocent words were poisoned arrows that festered in the souls of those against whom they were directed, and made deadly enemies of a number of persons whom he seems, in his printed speeches, never to have mentioned without the respect due from one Senator to another. In his speech in defence of the Treaty of Washington, he had to repel Mr. Ingersoll's indecent attack on his integrity, and his dreadful retort is described by those who heard it as coming within the rules which condemn cruelty to animals. But the "noble rage" which prompted him to indulge in such unwonted invective subsided with the occasion that called it forth, and he was careful to have it expunged when the speech was reprinted. An eminent judge of the Supreme Court of Massachusetts, in commending the general dignity and courtesy which characterized Webster's conduct of a case in a court of law, noted one exception. "When," he said, "the opposite counsel had got him into a corner, the way he 'trampled out' was something frightful to behold. The court itself could hardly restrain him in his gigantic efforts to extricate himself from the consequences of a blunder or an oversight."

Great writers and orators are commonly economists in the use of words. They compel common words to bear a burden of thought and emotion, which mere rhetoricians, with all the resources of the language at their disposal, would never dream of imposing upon them. But it is also to be observed, that some writers have the power of giving a new and special significance to a common word, by impressing on it a wealth of meaning which it cannot claim for itself. Three obvious examples of this peculiar power may be cited. Among poets, Chaucer infused into the simple word "green" a poetic ecstasy which no succeeding English poet, not even Wordsworth, has ever rivalled, in describing an English landscape in the month of May.

Jonathan Edwards fixed upon the term "sweetness" as best conveying his loftiest conception of the bliss which the soul of the saint can attain to on earth, or expect to be blessed with in heaven; but not one of his theological successors has ever caught the secret of using "sweetness" in the sense attached to it by him. Dr. Barrow gave to the word "rest," as embodying his idea of the spiritual repose of the soul fit for heaven, a significance which it bears in the works of no other great English divine. To descend a little, Webster was fond of certain words, commonplace enough in themselves, to which he insisted on imparting a more than ordinary import. Two of these, which meet us continually in reading his speeches, are "interesting" and "respectable." The first of these appears to him competent to express that rapture of attention called forth by a thing, an event, or a person, which other writers convey by such a term as "absorbing," or its numerous equivalents. If we should select one passage from his works which, more than any other, indicates his power of seeing and feeling, through a process of purely imaginative vision and sympathy, it is that portion of his Plymouth oration, where he places himself and his audience as spectators on the barren shore, when the *Mayflower* came into view. He speaks of "the *interesting* group upon the deck" of the little vessel. The very word suggests that we are to have a very commonplace account of the landing, and the circumstances which followed it. In an instant, however, we are made to "feel the cold which benumbed, and listen to the winds which pierced" this "interesting" group; and immediately after, the picture is flashed upon the imagination of "chilled and shivering childhood, houseless, but for a mother's arms, couchless, but for a mother's breast,"--an image which shows that the orator had not only transported himself into a spectator of the scene, but had felt his own blood "almost freeze" in intense sympathy with the physical sufferings of the shelterless mothers and children.

There is no word which the novelists, satirists, philanthropic reformers, and Bohemians of our day have done so much to discredit, and make dis-respectable to the heart and the imagination, as the word "respectable." Webster always uses it as a term of eulogy. A respectable man is, to his mind, a person who performs all his duties to his family, his country, and his God; a person who is not only virtuous, but who has a clear perception of the relation which connects one virtue with another by "the golden thread" of moderation, and who, whether he be a man of genius, or a business man of average talent, or an intelligent mechanic, or a farmer of sound moral and mental character, is to be considered "respectable" because he is one of those citizens whose intelligence and integrity constitute the foundation on which the Republic rests. As late as 1843, in his noble oration on the completion of the Bunker Hill Monument, he declared that if our American institutions had done nothing more than to produce the character of Washington, that alone would entitle them to the respect of mankind. "Washington is all our own!... I would cheerfully put the question to-day to the intelligence of Europe and the world, what character of the century, upon the whole, stands out in the relief of history, most pure, most _respectable_, most sublime; and I doubt not, that, by a suffrage approaching to unanimity, the answer would be Washington!" It is needless to quote other instances of the peculiar meaning he put into the word "respectable," when we thus find him challenging the Europe of the eighteenth century to name a match for Washington, and placing "most respectable" after "most pure," and immediately preceding "most sublime," in his enumeration of the three qualities in which Washington surpassed all men of his century.

It has been often remarked that Webster adapted his style, even his habits of mind and modes of reasoning, to the particular auditors he desired to influence; but that, whether he addressed an unorganized crowd of people, or a jury, or a bench of judges, or the Senate of the United States, he ever proved himself an orator of the first class.

His admirers commonly confine themselves to the admirable sagacity with which he discriminated between the kind of reasoning proper to be employed when he addressed courts and juries, and the kind of reasoning which is most effective in a legislative assembly. The lawyer and the statesman were, in Webster, kept distinct, except so far as he was a lawyer who had argued before the Supreme Court questions of constitutional law. An amusing instance of this abnegation of the lawyer, while incidentally bringing in a lawyer's knowledge of judicial decisions, occurs in a little episode in his debate with Mr. Calhoun, in 1849, as to the relation of Congress to the Territories. Mr. Calhoun said that he had been told that the Supreme Court of the United States had decided, in *one* case, that the Constitution did not extend to the Territories, but that he was "incredulous of the fact." "Oh!" replied Mr. Webster, "I can remove the gentleman's incredulity very easily, for I can assure him that the same thing has been decided by the United States courts over and over again for the last thirty years." It will be observed, however, that Mr. Webster, after communicating this important item of information, proceeded to discuss the question as if the

Supreme Court had no existence, and bases his argument on the plain terms of the Constitution, and the plain facts recorded in the history of the government established by it.

Macaulay, in his lively way, has shown the difficulty of manufacturing English statesmen out of English lawyers, though, as lawyers, their rank in the profession may be very high. "Their arguments," he says, "are intellectual prodigies, abounding with the happiest analogies and the most refined distinctions. The principles of their arbitrary science being once admitted, the statute-books and the reports being once assumed as the foundations of reasoning, these men must be allowed to be perfect masters of logic. But if a question arises as to the postulates on which their whole system rests, if they are called upon to vindicate the fundamental maxims of that system which they have passed their lives in studying, these very men often talk the language of savages or of children. Those who have listened to a man of this class in his own court, and who have witnessed the skill with which he analyzes and digests a vast mass of evidence, or reconciles a crowd of precedents which at first sight seem contradictory, scarcely know him again when, a few hours later, they hear him speaking on the other side of Westminster Hall in his capacity of legislator. They can scarcely believe that the paltry quirks which are faintly heard through a storm of coughing, and which do not impose on the plainest country gentleman, can proceed from the same sharp and vigorous intellect which had excited their admiration under the same roof, and on the same day." And to this keen distinction between an English lawyer, and an English lawyer as a member of the House of Commons, may be added the peculiar kind of sturdy manliness which is demanded in any person who aims to take a leading part in Parliamentary debates. Erskine, probably the greatest advocate who ever appeared in the English courts of law, made but a comparatively poor figure in the House of Commons, as a member of the Whig opposition. "The truth is, Erskine," Sheridan once said to him, "you are afraid of Pitt, and that is the flabby part of your character."

But Macaulay, in another article, makes a point against the leaders of party themselves. His definition of Parliamentary government is "government by speaking"; and he declares that the most effective speakers are commonly ill-informed, shallow in thought, devoid of large ideas of legislation, hazarding the loosest speculations with the utmost intellectual impudence, and depending for success on volubility of speech, rather than on accuracy of knowledge or penetration of intelligence. "The tendency of institutions like those of England," he adds, "is to encourage readiness in public men, at the expense both of fulness and of exactness. The keenest and most vigorous minds of every generation, minds often admirably fitted for the investigation of truth, are habitually employed in producing arguments such as no man of sense would ever put into a treatise intended for publication, arguments which are just good enough to be used once, when aided by fluent delivery and pointed language." And he despairingly closes with the remark, that he "would sooner expect a great original work on political science, such a work, for example, as the Wealth of Nations, from an apothecary in a country town, or from a minister in the Hebrides, than from a statesman who, ever since he was one-and-twenty, had been a distinguished debater in the House of Commons."

Now it is plain that neither of these contemptuous judgments applies to Webster. He was a great lawyer; but as a legislator the precedents of the lawyer did not control the action or supersede the principles of the statesman. He was one of the most formidable debaters that ever appeared in a legislative assembly; and yet those who most resolutely grappled with him in the duel of debate would be the last to impute to him inaccuracy of knowledge or shallowness of thought. He carried into the Senate of the United States a trained mind, disciplined by the sternest culture of his faculties, disdaining any plaudits which were not the honest reward of robust reasoning on generalized facts, and "gravitating" in the direction of truth, whether he hit or missed it. In his case, at least, there was nothing in his legal experience, or in his legislative experience, which would have unfitted him for producing a work on the science of politics. The best speeches in the House of Commons of Lord Palmerston and Lord John Russell appear very weak indeed, as compared with the Reply to Hayne, or the speech on "The Constitution not a Compact between Sovereign States," or the speech on the President's Protest.

In this connection it may be said, when we remember the hot contests between the two men, that there is something plaintive in Calhoun's dying testimony to Webster's austere intellectual conscientiousness. Mr. Venables, who attended the South Carolina statesman in his dying hours, wrote to Webster: "When your name was mentioned he remarked that 'Mr. Webster has as high a standard of truth as any statesman I have met in debate. Convince him, and he cannot reply; he is silenced; he cannot look truth in the face and oppose it by argument. I think that it can be readily perceived by his manner when he felt the unanswerable force of a reply.' He often spoke of you in my presence, and always kindly and most respectfully." Now it must be considered that, in debate, the minds of Webster and Calhoun had come into actual contact and collision. Each really felt the force of the other. An ordinary duel might be ranked among idle pastimes when compared with the stress and strain and pain of their encounters in the duel of debate. A sword-cut or pistol-bullet, maiming the body, was as nothing in comparison with the wounds they mutually inflicted on that substance which was immortal in both. It was a duel, or series of duels, in which mind was opposed to mind, and will to will, and where the object appeared to be to inflict moral and mental annihilation on one of the combatants. There never passed a word between them on which the most ingenious Southern jurists, in their interpretations of the "code" of honor, could have found matter for a personal quarrel; and yet these two proud and strong personalities knew that they were engaged in a mortal contest, in which neither gave quarter nor expected quarter. Mr. Calhoun's intellectual egotism was as great as his intellectual ability. He always supposed that he was the victor in every close logical wrestle with any mind to which his own was opposed. He never wrestled with a mind, until he met Webster's, which in tenacity, grasp, and power was a match for his own. He, of course, thought his antagonist was beaten by his superior strength and amplitude of argumentation; but it is still to be noted that he, the most redoubtable opponent that Webster ever encountered, testified, though in equivocal terms, to Webster's intellectual honesty. When he crept, half dead, into the Senate-Chamber to hear Webster's speech of the 7th of March, 1850, he objected emphatically at the end to Webster's declaration that the Union could not be dissolved. After declaring that Calhoun's supposed case of justifiable resistance came within the definition of the ultimate right of revolution, which is lodged in all oppressed communities, Webster added that he did not at that time wish to go into a discussion of the nature of the United States government. "The honorable gentleman and myself," he said, "have broken lances sufficiently often before on that subject." "I have no desire to do it now," replied Calhoun; and Webster blandly retorted, "I presume the gentleman has not, and I have quite as little." One is reminded here of Dr. Johnson's remark, when he was stretched on a sick-bed, with his gladiatorial powers of argument suspended by physical exhaustion. "If that fellow Burke were now present," the Doctor humorously murmured, "he would certainly kill me."

But to Webster's eminence as a lawyer and a statesman, it is proper to add, that he has never been excelled as a writer of state papers among the public men of the United States. Mr. Emerson has a phrase which is exactly applicable to these efforts of Webster's mind. That phrase is, "superb propriety." Throughout his despatches, he always seems to feel that he impersonates his country; and the gravity and weight of his style are as admirable as its simplicity and majestic ease. "Daniel Webster, his mark," is indelibly stamped on them all. When the Treaty of Washington was criticised by the Whigs in the English Parliament, Macaulay specially noticed the difference in the style of the two negotiators. Lord Ashburton, he said, had compromised the honor of his country by "the humble, caressing, wheedling tone" of his letters, a tone which contrasted strangely with "the firm, resolute, vigilant, and unyielding manner" of the American Secretary of State. It is to be noticed that no other opponent of Sir Robert Peel's administration, not even Lord Palmerston and Lord John Russell, struck at the essential weakness of Lord Ashburton's despatches with the force and sagacity which characterized Macaulay's assault on the treaty. Indeed, a rhetorician and critic less skilful than Macaulay can easily detect that "America" is represented fully in Webster's despatches, while "Britannia" has a very amiable, but not very forcible, representative in Lord Ashburton. Had Palmerston been the British plenipotentiary, we can easily imagine how different would have been the task imposed on Webster. As the American Secretary was generally in the right in every position he assumed, he would probably have triumphed even over Palmerston; but the letters of the "pluckiest" of English statesmen would, we may be sure, have never been criticised in the House of Commons as "humble, wheedling, and caressing."

In addition, however, to his legal arguments, his senatorial speeches, and his state papers, Webster is to be considered as the greatest orator our country has produced in his addresses before miscellaneous assemblages of the people. In saying this we do not confine the remark to such noble orations as those on the "First Settlement of New England," "The Bunker Hill Monument," and "Adams and Jefferson," but extend it so as to include speeches before great masses of people who could be hardly distinguished from a mob, and who were under no restraint but that imposed by their own self-respect and their respect for the orator. On these occasions he was uniformly successful. It is impossible to detect, in any reports of these popular addresses, that he ever stooped to employ a style of speech or mode of argument commonly supposed appropriate to a speaker on the "stump"; and yet he was the greatest "stump" orator that our country has ever seen. He seemed to delight in addressing five, or ten, or even twenty thousand people, in the open air, trusting that the penetrating tones of his voice would reach even the ears of those who were on the ragged edges of the swaying crowd before him; and he would thus speak to the sovereign people, in their unorganized state as a collection of uneasy and somewhat belligerent individuals, with a dignity and majesty similar to the dignity and majesty which characterized his arguments before the Senate of the United States, or before a bench of judges. A large portion of his published works consist of such speeches, and they rank only second among the remarkable productions of his mind.

The question arises, How could he hold the attention of such audiences without condescending to flatter their prejudices, or without occasionally acting the part of the sophist and the buffoon? Much may be said, in accounting for this phenomenon, about his widely extended reputation, his imposing presence, the vulgar curiosity to see a man whom even the smallest country newspaper thought of sufficient importance to defame, his power of giving vitality to simple words which the most ignorant of his auditors could easily understand, and the instinctive respect which the rudest kind of men feel for a grand specimen of robust manhood. But the real, the substantial source of his power over such audiences proceeded from his respect for _them_; and their respect for him was more or less consciously founded on the perception of this fact. Indeed, a close scrutiny of his speeches will show how conscientiously he regards the rights of other minds, however inferior they may be to his own; and this virtue, for it is a virtue, is never more apparent than in his arguments and appeals addressed to popular assemblies. No working-man, whether farmer, mechanic, factory "hand," or day-laborer, ever deemed himself insulted by a word from the lips of Daniel Webster; he felt himself rather exalted in his own esteem, for the time, by coming in contact with that beneficent and comprehensive intelligence, which cherished among its favorite ideas a scheme for lifting up the American laborer to a height of comfort and respectability which the European laborer could hardly hope to attain. Prominent politicians, men of wealth and influence, statesmen of high social and political rank, may, at times, have considered Webster as arrogant and bad-tempered, and may, at times, have felt disposed to fasten a quarrel upon him; even in Massachusetts this disposition broke out in conventions of the party to which he belonged; but it would be in vain to find a single laboring-man, whether he met Webster in private, or half pushed and half fought his way into a mass meeting, in order to get his ears into communication with the orator's voice, who ever heard a word from him which did not exalt the dignity of labor, or which was not full of sympathy for the laborer's occasional sorrows and privations. Webster seemed to have ever present to his mind the poverty of the humble home of his youth. His father, his brothers, he himself, had all been brought up to consider manual toil a dignified occupation, and as consistent with the exercise of all the virtues which flourish under the domestic roof. More than this, it may be said that, with the exception of a few intimate friends, his sympathies to the last were most warmly with common laborers. Indeed, if we closely study the private correspondence of this statesman, who was necessarily brought into relations, more or less friendly, with the conventionally great men of the world, European as well as American, we shall find that, after all, he took more real interest in Seth Peterson, and John Taylor, and Porter Wright, men connected with him in fishing and farming, than he did in the ambassadors of foreign states whom he met as Senator or as Secretary of State, or in all the members of the polite society of Washington, New York, and Boston. He was very near to Nature himself; and the nearer a man was to Nature, the more he esteemed him. Thus persons who superintended his farms and cattle, or who pulled an oar in his boat when he ventured out in search of cod and halibut, thought "Squire Webster" a man who realized their ideal and perfection of good-fellowship while it may confidently be said that many of his closest friends among men of culture, including lawyers, men of letters, and statesmen of the first rank, must have occasionally resented the "anfractuosities" of his mood and temper. But Seth Peterson, and Porter Wright, and John Taylor, never complained of these "anfractuosities." Webster, in fact, is one of the few public men of the country in whose championship of the rights and sympathy with the wrongs of labor there is not the slightest trace of the arts of the demagogue; and in this fact we may find the reason why even the "roughs," who are present in every mass meeting, always treated him with respect. Perhaps it would not be out of place to remark here, that, in his Speech of the 7th of March, he missed a grand opportunity to vindicate Northern labor, in the reference he made to a foolish tirade of a Senator from Louisiana, who "took pains to run a contrast between the slaves of the South and the laboring people of the North, giving the preference, in all points of condition, of comfort, and happiness, to the slaves of the South." Webster made a complete reply to this aspersion on Northern labor; but, as his purpose was to conciliate, he did not blast the libeller by quoting the most eminent example that could be named demonstrating the falsehood of the slave-holding Senator's assertion. Without deviating from the conciliatory attitude he had assumed, one could easily imagine him as lifting his large frame to its full height, flashing from his rebuking eyes a glance of scorn at the "amiable Senator," and simply saying, "*I* belong to the class which the Senator from Louisiana stigmatizes as more degraded than the slaves of the South." There was not at the time any Senator from the South, except Mr. Calhoun, that the most prejudiced Southern man would have thought of comparing with Webster in respect to intellectual eminence; and, if Webster had then and there placed himself squarely on his position as the son of a Northern laborer, we should have been spared all the rhetoric about Northern "mud-sills," with which the Senate was afterwards afflicted. Webster was our man of men; and it would seem that he should have crushed such talk at the outset, by proudly assuming that Northern labor was embodied and impersonated in him,--that HE had sprung from its ranks, and was proud of his ancestry.

An ingenious and powerful, but paradoxical thinker, once told me that I was mistaken in calling Jonathan Edwards and Daniel Webster great reasoners. "They were bad reasoners," he added, "but great poets." Without questioning the right of the author of "An Enquiry into the Modern Prevailing Notion of that Freedom of the Will, which is supposed to be Essential to Moral Agency," to be ranked among the most eminent of modern logicians, I could still understand why he was classed among poets; for whether Edwards paints the torments of hell or the bliss of heaven, his imagination almost rivals that of Dante in intensity of realization. But it was at first puzzling to comprehend why Webster should be depressed as a reasoner in order to be exalted as a poet. The images and metaphors scattered over his speeches are so evidently brought in to illustrate and enforce his statements and arguments, that, grand as they often are, the imagination displayed in them is still a faculty strictly subsidiary to the reasoning power. It was only after reflecting patiently for some time on the seeming paradox that I caught a glimpse of my friend's meaning; and it led me at once to consider an entirely novel question, not heretofore mooted by any of Webster's critics, whether friendly or unfriendly, in their endeavors to explain the reason of his influence over the best minds of the generation to which he belonged. In declaring that, as a poet, he far exceeded any capacity he evinced as a reasoner, my paradoxical friend must have meant that Webster had the poet's power of so *organizing* a speech, that it stood out to the eye of the mind as a palpable intellectual product and fact, possessing, not merely that vague reality which comes from erecting a plausible mental structure of deductive argumentation, based on strictly limited premises, but a positive reality, akin to the products of Nature herself, when she tries her hand in constructing a ledge of rocks or rearing a chain of hills.

In illustration, it may be well to cite the example of poets with whom Webster, of course, cannot be compared. Among the great mental facts, palpable to the eyes of all men interested in literature, are such creations as the Iliad, the Divine Comedy, the great Shakspearian dramas, the Paradise Lost, and Faust. The commentaries and criticisms on these are numerous enough to occupy the shelves of a large library; some of them attempt to show that Homer, Dante, Shakspeare, Milton, and Goethe were all wrong in their methods of creation; but they still cannot obscure, to ordinary vision, the lustre of these luminaries as they placidly shine in the intellectual firmament, which is literally *over* our heads. They are as palpable, to the eye of the mind, as Sirius, Arcturus, the Southern Cross, and the planets Venus, Mars, Jupiter, and Saturn, are to the bodily sense. M. Taine has recently assailed the Paradise Lost with the happiest of French epigrams; he tries to prove that, in construction, it is the most ridiculously inartistic monstrosity that the imagination of a great mind ever framed out of chaos; but, after we have thoroughly enjoyed the play of his wit, there the Paradise Lost remains, an undisturbed object in the intellectual heavens, disdaining to justify its right to exist on any other grounds than the mere fact of its existence; and, certainly, not more ridiculous than Saturn himself, as we look at him through a great equatorial telescope, swinging through space encumbered with his clumsy ring, and his wrangling family of satellites, but still, in spite of peculiarities on which M. Taine might exercise his wit until doomsday, one of the most beautiful and sublime objects which the astronomer can behold in the whole phenomena of the heavens.

Indeed, in reading criticisms on such durable poetic creations and organizations as we have named, one is reminded of Sydney Smith's delicious chaffing of his friend Jeffrey, on account of Jeffrey's sensitiveness of literary taste, and his inward rage that events, men, and books, outside of him, do not correspond to the exacting rules which are the products of his own subjective and somewhat peevish intelligence. "I like," says Sydney, "to tell you these things, because you never do so well as when you are humbled and frightened, and, if _you could be alarmed into the semblance of modesty_, you would charm everybody; but remember my joke against you about the moon: 'D--n the solar system! bad light--planets too distant-- pestered with comets--feeble contrivance; could make a better with great ease.'"

Now when a man, in whatever department or direction of thought his activity is engaged, succeeds in organizing, or even welding together, the materials on which he works, so that the product, as a whole, is *visible* to the mental eye, as a new creation or construction, he has an immense advantage over all critics of his performance. Refined reasonings are impotent to overthrow it; epigrams glance off from it, as rifle-bullets rebound when aimed at a granite wall; and it stands erect long after the reasonings and the epigrams are forgotten. Even when its symmetry is destroyed by a long and destructive siege, a pile of stones still remains, as at Fort Sumter, to attest what power of resistance it opposed to all the resources of modern artillery.

If we look at Webster's greatest speeches, as, for instance, "The Reply to Hayne," "The Constitution not a Compact between Sovereign States," "The President's Protest," and others that might be mentioned, we shall find that they partake of the character of organic formations, or at least of skilful engineering or architectural constructions. Even Mr. Calhoun never approached him in this art of giving objective reality to a speech, which, after all, is found, on analysis, to consist only of a happy collocation and combination of words, but in Webster the words are either all alive with the creative spirit of the poet, or, at the worst, resemble the blocks of granite or marble which the artisan piles, one on the other, and the result of which, though it may represent a poor style of architecture, is still a rude specimen of a Gothic edifice. The artist and artificer are both observable in Webster's work; but the reality and solidity of the construction cannot be questioned. At the present time, an educated reader would be specially interested in the mental processes by which Webster thus succeeded in giving objective existence and validity to the operations of his mind, and, whether sympathizing with his opinions or not, would as little think of refusing to read them because of their Whiggism, as he would think of refusing to read Homer because of his heathenism, or Dante because of his Catholicism, or Milton because of his compound of Arianism and Calvinism, or Goethe because of his Pantheism. The fact which would most interest such a reader would be, that Webster had, in some mysterious way, translated and transformed his abstract propositions into concrete substance and form. The form might offend his reason, his taste, or his conscience; but he could not avoid admitting that it *had* a form, while most speeches, even those made by able men, are comparatively formless, however lucid they may be in the array of facts, and plausible in the order and connection of arguments.

In trying to explain this power, the most obvious comparison which would arise in the mind of an intelligent reader would be, that Webster, as a rhetorician, resembled Vauban and Cohorn as military engineers. In the war of debate, he so *fortified* the propositions he maintained, that they could not be carried by direct assault, but must be patiently besieged. The words he employed were simple enough, and fell short of including the vocabulary of even fifth-rate declaimers; but he had the art of so disposing them that, to an honest reasoner, the position he took appeared to be impregnable. To assail it by the ordinary method of passionate protest and illogical reasoning, was as futile as a dash of light cavalry would have been against the defences of such cities as Namur and Lille. Indeed, in his speech, "The Constitution not a Compact between Sovereign States," he erected a whole Torres Vedras line of fortifications, on which legislative Massenas dashed themselves in vain, and, however strong in numbers in respect to the power of voting him down, recoiled defeated in every attempt to reason him down.

In further illustration of this peculiar power of Webster, the Speech of the 7th of March, 1850, may be cited, for its delivery is to be ranked with the most important historical events. For some years it was the object of the extremes of panegyric and the extremes of execration. But this effort is really the most loosely constructed of all the great productions of Webster's mind. In force, compactness, and completeness, in closeness of thought to things, in closeness of imagery to the reasoning it illustrates, and in general intellectual fibre, muscle, and bone, it cannot be compared to such an oration as that on the "First Settlement of New England," or such a speech as that which had for its theme, "The Constitution not a Compact between Sovereign States"; but, after all deductions have been made, it was still a speech which frowned upon its opponents as a kind of verbal fortress constructed both for the purpose of defence and aggression. Its fame is due, in a great degree, to its resistance to a storm of assaults, such as had rarely before been concentrated on any speech delivered in either branch of the Congress of the United States. Indeed, a very large portion of the intellect, the moral sentiment, and the moral passion of the free States was directed against it. There was not a weapon in the armory of the dialectician or the rhetorician which was not employed with the intent of demolishing it. Contempt of Webster was vehemently taught as the beginning of political wisdom. That a speech, thus assailed, should survive the attacks made upon it, appeared to be impossible. And yet it did survive, and is alive now, while better speeches, or what the present writer thought, at the time, to be more convincing speeches, have not retained individual existence, however deeply they may have influenced that public opinion which, in the end, determines political events. "I still live," was Webster's declaration on his death-bed, when the friends gathered around it imagined he had breathed his last; and the same words might be uttered by the Speech of the 7th of March, could it possess the vocal organ which announces personal existence. Between the time it was originally delivered and the present year there runs a great and broad stream of blood, shed from the veins of Northern and Southern men alike; the whole political and moral constitution of the country has practically suffered an abrupt change; new problems engage the attention of thoughtful statesmen; much is forgotten which was once considered of the first importance; but the 7th of March Speech, battered as it is by innumerable attacks, is still remembered at least as one which called forth more power than it embodied in itself. This persistence of life is due to the fact that it was "organized."

Is this power of organization common among orators? It seems to me that, on the contrary, it is very rare. In some of Burke's speeches, in which his sensibility and imagination were thoroughly under the control of his judgment, as, for instance, his speech on Conciliation with America, that on Economical Reform, and that to the Electors of Bristol, we find the orator to be a consummate master of the art of so constructing a speech that it serves the immediate object which prompted its delivery, while at the same time it has in it a principle of vitality which makes it survive the occasion that called it forth. But the greatest of Burke's speeches, if we look merely at the richness and variety of mental power and the force and depth of moral passion displayed in it, is his speech on the Nabob of Arcot's Debts. No speech ever delivered before any assembly, legislative, judicial, or popular, can rank with this in respect to the abundance of its facts, reasonings, and imagery, and the ferocity of its moral wrath. It resembles the El Dorado that Voltaire's Candide visited, where the boys played with precious stones of inestimable value, as our boys play with ordinary marbles; for to the inhabitants of El Dorado diamonds and pearls were as common as pebbles are with us.

But the defect of this speech, which must still be considered, on the whole, the most inspired product of Burke's great nature, was this,-- that it did not strike its hearers or readers as having *reality* for its basis or the superstructure raised upon it. Englishmen could not believe then, and most of them probably do not believe now, that it had any solid foundation in incontrovertible facts. It did not "fit in" to their ordinary modes of thought; and it has never been ranked with Burke's "organized" orations; it has never come home to what Bacon called the "business and bosoms" of his countrymen. They have generally dismissed it from their imaginations as "a phantasmagoria and a hideous dream" created by Burke under the impulse of the intense hatred he felt for the administration which succeeded the overthrow of the government, which was founded on the coalition of Fox and North.

Now, in simple truth, the speech is the most masterly statement of facts, relating to the oppression of millions of the people of India, which was ever forced on the attention of the House of Commons,--a legislative assembly which, it may be incidentally remarked, was practically responsible for the just government of the immense Indian empire of Great Britain. It is curious that the main facts on which the argument of Burke rests have been confirmed by James Mill, the coldest-blooded historian that ever narrated the enormous crimes which attended the rise and progress of the British power in Hindostan, and a man who also had a strong intellectual antipathy to the mind of Burke. In making the speech, Burke had documentary evidence of a large portion of the transactions he denounced, and had *divined* the rest. Mill supports him both as regards the facts of which Burke had positive knowledge, and the facts which he deductively inferred from the facts he knew. Having thus a strong foundation for his argument, he exerted every faculty of his mind, and every impulse of his moral sentiment and moral passion, to overwhelm the leading members of the administration of Pitt, by attempting to make them accomplices in crimes which would disgrace even slave-traders on the Guinea coast. The merely intellectual force of his reasoning is crushing; his analysis seems to be sharpened by his hatred; and there is no device of contempt, scorn, derision, and direct personal attack, which he does not unsparingly use. In the midst of all this mental tumult, inestimable maxims of moral and political wisdom are shot forth in short sentences, which have so much of the sting and brilliancy of epigram, that at first we do not appreciate their depth of thought; and through all there burns such a pitiless fierceness of moral reprobation of cruelty, injustice, and wrong, that all the accredited courtesies of debate are violated, once, at least, in every five minutes. In any American legislative assembly he would have been called to order at least once in five minutes. The images which the orator brings in to give vividness to his argument are sometimes coarse; but, coarse as they are, they admirably reflect the moral turpitude of the men against whom he inveighs. Among these is the image with which he covers Dundas, the special friend of Pitt, with a ridicule which promises to be immortal. Dundas, on the occasion when Fox and Burke called for papers by the aid of which they proposed to demonstrate the iniquity of the scheme by which the ministry proposed to settle the debts of the Nabob of Arcot, pretended that the production of such papers would be indelicate,--"that this inquiry is of a delicate nature, and that the state will suffer detriment by the exposure of this transaction." As Dundas had previously brought out six volumes of Reports, generally confirming Burke's own views of the corruption and oppression which marked the administration of affairs in India, he laid himself open to Burke's celebrated assault. Dundas and delicacy, he said, were "a rare and singular coalition." And then follows an image of colossal coarseness, such as might be supposed capable of rousing thunder-peals of laughter from a company of festive giants,--an image which Lord Brougham declared offended *his* sensitive taste,--the sensitive taste of one of the most formidable legal and legislative bullies that ever appeared before the juries or Parliament of Great Britain, and who never hesitated to use any illustration, however vulgar, which he thought would be effective to degrade his opponents.

But whatever may be thought of the indelicacy of Burke's image, it was one eminently adapted to penetrate through the thick hide of the minister of state at whom it was aimed, and it shamed him as far as a profligate politician like Dundas was capable of feeling the sensation of shame. But there are also flashes, or rather flames, of impassioned imagination, in the same speech, which rush up from the main body of its statements and arguments, and remind us of nothing so much as of those jets of incandescent gas which, we are told by astronomers, occasionally leap, from the extreme outer covering of the sun, to the height of a hundred or a hundred and sixty thousand miles, and testify to the terrible forces raging within it. After reading this speech for the fiftieth time, the critic cannot free himself from the rapture of admiration and amazement which he experienced in his first fresh acquaintance with it. Yet its delivery in the House of Commons (February 28, 1785) produced an effect so slight, that Pitt, after a few minutes' consultation with Grenville, concluded that it was not worth the trouble of being answered; and the House of Commons, obedient to the Prime Minister's direction, negatived, by a large majority, the motion in advocating which Burke poured out the wonderful treasures of his intellect and imagination. To be sure, the House was tired to death with the discussion, was probably very sleepy, and the orator spoke five hours after the members had already shouted, "Question! Question!"

The truth is, that this speech, unmatched though it is in the literature of eloquence, had not, as has been previously stated, the air of reality. It struck the House as a magnificent Oriental dream, as an Arabian Nights' Entertainment, as a tale told by an inspired madman, "full of sound and fury, signifying nothing"; and the evident partisan intention of the orator to blast Pitt's administration by exhibiting its complicity in one of the most enormous frauds recorded in history, confirmed the dandies, the cockneys, the bankers, and the country gentlemen, who, as members of the House of Commons, stood by Pitt with all the combined force of their levity, their venality, and their stupidity, in the propriety of voting Burke down. And even now, when the substantial truth of all the facts he alleged is established on evidence which convinces historians, the admiring reader can understand why it failed to convince Burke's contemporaries, and why it still appears to lack the characteristics of a speech thoroughly organized. Indeed, the mind of Burke, when it was delivered, can only be compared to a volcanic mountain in eruption;--not merely a volcano like that of Vesuvius, visited by scientists and amateurs in crowds, when it deigns to pour forth its flames and lava for the entertainment of the multitude; but a lonely volcano, like that of Etna, rising far above Vesuvius in height, far removed from all the vulgar curiosity of a body of tourists, but rending the earth on which it stands with the mighty earthquake throes of its fiery centre and heart. The moral passion,--perhaps it would be more just to say the moral fury,--displayed in the speech, is elemental, and can be compared to nothing less intense than the earth's interior fire and heat.

Now in Webster's great legislative efforts, his mind is never exhibited in a state of eruption. In the most excited debates in which he bore a prominent part, nothing strikes us more than the admirable self-possession, than the majestic inward calm, which presides over all the operations of his mind and the impulses of his sensibility, so that, in building up the fabric of his speech, he has his reason, imagination, and passion under full control,--using each faculty and feeling as the occasion may demand, but never allowing himself to be used *by* it,--and always therefore conveying the impression of power in reserve, while he may, in fact, be exercising all the power he has to the utmost. In laboriously erecting his edifice of reasoning he also studiously regards the intellects and the passions of ordinary men; strives to bring his mind into cordial relations with theirs; employs every faculty he possesses to give reality, to give even visibility, to his thoughts; and though he never made a speech which rivals that of Burke on the Nabob of Arcot's Debts, in respect to grasp of understanding, astounding wealth of imagination and depth of moral passion, he always so contrived to organize his materials into a complete whole, that the result stood out clearly to the sight of the mind, as a structure resting on strong foundations, and reared to due height by the mingled skill of the artisan and the artist. When he does little more than weld his materials together, he is still an artificer of the old school of giant workmen, the school that dates its pedigree from Tubal Cain. After all this wearisome detail and dilution of the idea attempted to be expressed, it may be that I have failed to convey an adequate impression of what constitutes Webster's distinction among orators, as far as orators have left speeches which are considered an invaluable addition to the literature of the language in which they were originally delivered. Everybody understands why any one of the great sermons of Jeremy Taylor, or the sermon of Dr. South on "Man created in the Image of God," or the sermon of Dr. Barrow on "Heavenly Rest," differs from the millions on millions of doubtless edifying sermons that have been preached and printed during the last two centuries and a half; but everybody does not understand the distinction between one brilliant oration and another, when both made a great sensation at the time, while only one survived in literature. Probably Charles James Fox was a more effective speaker in the House of Commons than Edmund Burke, probably Henry Clay was a more effective speaker in Congress than Daniel Webster; but when the occasions on which their speeches were made are found gradually to fade from the memory of men, why is it that the speeches of Fox and Clay have no recognized position in literature, while those of Burke and Webster are ranked with literary productions of the first class? The reason is as really obvious as that which explains the exceptional value of some of the efforts of the great orators of the pulpit. Jeremy Taylor, Dr. South, and Dr. Barrow, different as they were in temper and disposition, succeeded in "organizing" some masterpieces in their special department of intellectual and moral activity; and the same is true of Burke and Webster in the departments of legislation and political science. The "occasion" was merely an opportunity for the consolidation into a speech of the rare powers and attainments, the large personality and affluent thought, which were the spiritual possessions of the man who made it,--a speech which represented the whole intellectual manhood of the speaker,--a manhood in which knowledge, reason, imagination, and sensibility were all consolidated under the directing power of will.

A pertinent example of the difference we have attempted to indicate may be easily found in contrasting Fox's closing speech on the East India Bill with Burke's on the same subject. For immediate effect on the House of Commons, it ranks with the most masterly of Fox's Parliamentary efforts. The hits on his opponents were all "telling." The _argumentum ad hominem_, embodied in short, sharp statements, or startling interrogatories, was never employed with more brilliant success. The reasoning was rapid, compact, encumbered by no long enumeration of facts, and, though somewhat unscrupulous here and there, was driven home upon his adversaries with a skill that equalled its audacity. It may be said that there is not a sentence in the whole speech which was not calculated to sting a sleepy audience into attention, or to give delight to a fatigued audience which still managed to keep its eyes and minds wide open. Even in respect to the principles of liberty and justice, which were the animating life of the bill, Fox's terse sentences contrast strangely with the somewhat more lumbering and elaborate paragraphs of Burke. "What," he exclaims, putting his argument in his favorite interrogative form,--"what is the most odious species of tyranny? Precisely that which this bill is meant to annihilate. That a handful of men, free themselves, should exercise the most base and abominable despotism over millions of their fellow-creatures; that innocence should be the victim of oppression; that industry should toil for rapine; that the harmless laborer should sweat, not for his own benefit, but for the luxury and rapacity of tyrannic depredation;--in a word, that thirty millions of men, gifted by Providence with the ordinary endowments of humanity, should groan under a system of despotism unmatched in all the histories of the world? What is the end of all government? Certainly, the happiness of the governed. Others may hold different opinions; but this is mine, and I proclaim it. What, then, are we to think of a government whose good fortune is supposed to spring from the calamities of its subjects, whose aggrandizement grows out of the miseries of mankind? This is the kind of government exercised under the East Indian Company upon the natives of Hindostan; and the subversion of that infamous government is the main object of the bill in question." And afterwards he says, with admirable point and pungency of statement: "Every line in both the bills which I have had the honor to introduce, presumes the possibility of bad administration; for every word breathes suspicion. This bill supposes that men are but men. It confides in no integrity; it trusts no character; it inculcates the wisdom of a jealousy of power, and annexes responsibility, not only to every _action_, but even to the *inaction* of those who are to dispense it. The necessity of these provisions must be evident, when it is known that the different misfortunes of the company have resulted not more from what their servants _did_, than from what the *masters did not*."

There is a directness in such sentences as these which we do not find in Burke's speech on the East India Bill; but Burke's remains as a part of English literature, and in form and substance, especially in substance, is so immensely superior to that of Fox, that, in quoting sentences from the latter, one may almost be supposed to rescue them from that neglect which attends all speeches which do not reach beyond the occasion which calls them forth. In Bacon's phrase, the speech of Fox shows "small matter, and infinite agitation of wit"; in Burke's, we discern large matter with an abundance of "wit" proper to the discussion of the matter, but nothing which suggests the idea of mere "agitation." Fox, in his speeches, subordinated every thing to the immediate impression he might make on the House of Commons. He deliberately gave it as his opinion, that a speech that read well must be a bad speech; and, in a literary sense, the House of Commons, which he entered before he was twenty, may be called both the cradle and the grave of his fame. It has been said that he was a debater whose speeches should be studied by every man who wishes "to learn the science of logical defence"; that he alone, among English orators, resembles Demosthenes, inasmuch as his reasoning is "penetrated and made red-hot by passion"; and that nothing could excel the effect of his delivery when "he was in the full paroxysm of inspiration, foaming, screaming, choked by the rushing multitude of his words." But not one of his speeches, not even that on the East India Bill, or on the Westminster Scrutiny, or on the Russian Armament, or on Parliamentary Reform, or on Mr. Pitt's Rejection of Bonaparte's Overtures for Peace, has obtained an abiding place in the literature of Great Britain. It would be no disparagement to an educated man, if it were said that he had never read these speeches; but it would be a serious bar to his claim to be considered an English scholar, if he confessed to be ignorant of the great speeches of Burke; for such a confession would be like admitting that he had never read the first book of Hooker's Ecclesiastical Polity, Bacon's Essays and Advancement of Learning, Milton's Areopagitica, Butler's Analogy, and Adam Smith's Wealth of Nations.

When we reflect on the enormous number of American speeches which, when they were first delivered, were confidently predicted, by appreciating friends, to insure to the orators a fame which would be immortal, one wonders a little at the quiet persistence of the speeches of Webster in refusing to die with the abrupt suddenness of other orations, which, at the time of their delivery, seemed to have an equal chance of renown. The lifeless remains of such unfortunate failures are now entombed in that dreariest of all mausoleums, the dingy quarto volumes, hateful to all human eyes, which are lettered on the back with the title of "Congressional Debates,"--a collection of printed matter which members of Congress are wont to send to a favored few among their constituents, and which are immediately consigned to the dust-barrel or sold to pedlers in waste paper, according as the rage of the recipients takes a scornful or an economical direction. It would seem that the speeches of Webster are saved from this fate, by the fact that, in them, the mental and moral life of a great man, and of a great master of the English language, are organized in a palpable intellectual form. The reader feels that they have some of the substantial qualities which he recognizes in looking at the gigantic constructions of the master workmen among the crowd of the world's engineers and architects, in looking at the organic products of Nature herself, and in surveying, through the eye of his imagination, those novel reproductions of Nature which great poets have embodied in works which are indelibly stamped with the character of deathlessness.

But Webster is even more obviously a poet--subordinating "the shows of things to the desires of the mind"--in his magnificent idealization, or idolization, of the Constitution and the Union. By the magic of his imagination and sensibility he contrived to impress on the minds of a majority of the people of the free States a vague, grand idea that the Constitution was a sacred instrument of government,--a holy shrine of fundamental law, which no unhallowed hands could touch without profanation,--a digested system of rights and duties, resembling those institutes which were, in early times, devised by the immortal gods for the guidance of infirm mortal man; and the mysterious creatures, half divine and half human, who framed this remarkable document, were always reverently referred to as "the Fathers,"--as persons who excelled all succeeding generations in sagacity and wisdom; as inspired prophets, who were specially selected by Divine Providence to frame the political scriptures on which our political faith was to be based, and by which our political reason was to be limited. The splendor of the glamour thus cast over the imaginations and sentiments of the people was all the more effective because it was an effluence from the mind of a statesman who, of all other statesmen of the country, was deemed the most practical, and the least deluded by any misguiding lights of fancy and abstract speculation.

There can be little doubt that Webster's impressive idealization of the Constitution gave a certain narrowness to American thinking on constitutional government and the science of politics and legislation. Foreigners, of the most liberal views, could not sometimes restrain an expression of wonder, when they found that our most intelligent men, even our jurists and publicists, hardly condescended to notice the eminent European thinkers on the philosophy of government, so absorbed were they in the contemplation of the perfection of their own. When the great civil war broke out, hundreds of thousands of American citizens marched to the battle-field with the grand passages of Webster glowing in their hearts. They met death cheerfully in the cause of the "Constitution and Union," as by him expounded and idealized; and if they were so unfortunate as not to be killed, but to be taken captive, they still rotted to death in Southern prisons, sustained by sentences of Webster's speeches which they had declaimed as boys in their country schools. Of all the triumphs of Webster as a leader of public opinion, the most remarkable was his infusing into the minds of the people of the free States the belief that the Constitution as it existed in his time was an organic fact, springing from the intelligence, hearts, and wills of the people of the United States, and not, as it really was, an ingenious mechanical contrivance of wise men, to which the people, at the time, gave their assent.

The constitutions of the separate States of the Union were doubtless rooted in the habits, sentiments, and ideas of their inhabitants. But the Constitution of the United States could not possess this advantage, however felicitously it may have been framed for the purpose of keeping, for a considerable period, peace between the different sections of the country. As long, therefore, as the institution of negro slavery lasted, it could not be called a Constitution of States organically "United"; for it lacked the principle of _growth_, which characterizes all constitutions of government which are really adapted to the progressive needs of a people, if the people have in them any impulse which stimulates them to advance. The unwritten constitution of Great Britain has this advantage, that a decree of Parliament can alter the whole representative system, annihilating by a vote of the two houses all laws which the Parliament had enacted in former years. In Great Britain, therefore, a measure which any Imperial Parliament passes becomes at once the supreme law of the land, though it may nullify a great number of laws which previous Parliaments had passed under different conditions of the sentiment of the nation. Our Constitution, on the other hand, provides for the contingencies of growth in the public sentiment only by amendments to the Constitution. These amendments require more than a majority of all the political forces represented in Congress; and Mr. Calhoun, foreseeing that a collision must eventually occur between the two sections, carried with him, not only the South, but a considerable minority of the North, in resisting any attempt to limit the *extension* of slavery. On this point the passions and principles of the people of the slave-holding and the majority of the people of the non-slave-holding States came into violent opposition; and there was no possibility that any amendment to the Constitution could be ratified, which would represent either the growth of the Southern people in their ever-increasing belief that negro slavery was not only a good in itself, but a good which ought to be extended, or the growth of the Northern people in their ever-increasing hostility both to slavery and its extension. Thus two principles, each organic in its nature, and demanding indefinite development, came into deadly conflict under the mechanical forms of a Constitution which was not organic.

A considerable portion of the speeches in this volume is devoted to denunciations of violations of the Constitution perpetrated by Webster's political opponents. These violations, again, would seem to prove that written constitutions follow practically the same law of development which marks the progress of the unwritten. By a strained system of Congressional interpretation, the Constitution has been repeatedly compelled to yield to the necessities of the party dominant, for the time, in the government; and has, if we may believe Webster, been repeatedly changed without being constitutionally "amended." The causes which led to the most terrible civil war recorded in history were silently working beneath the forms of the Constitution,--both parties, by the way, appealing to its provisions,--while Webster was idealizing it as the utmost which humanity could come to in the way of civil government. In 1848, when nearly all Europe was in insurrection against its rulers, he proudly said that our Constitution promised to be the _oldest_, as well as the best, in civilized states. Meanwhile the institution of negro slavery was undermining the whole fabric of the Union. The moral division between the South and North was widening into a division between the religion of the two sections. The Southern statesmen, economists, jurists, publicists, and ethical writers had adapted their opinions to the demands which the defenders of the institution of slavery imposed on the action of the human intellect and conscience; but it was rather startling to discover that the Christian religion, as taught in the Southern States, was a religion which had no vital connection with the Christianity taught in the Northern States. There is nothing more astounding, to a patient explorer of the causes which led to the final explosion, than this opposition of religions. The mere form of the dogmas common to the religion of both sections might be verbally identical; but a volume of sermons by a Southern doctor of divinity, as far as he touched on the matter of slavery, was as different from one published by his Northern brother, in the essential moral and humane elements of Christianity, as though they were divided from each other by a gulf as wide as that which yawns between a Druid priest and a Christian clergyman.

The politicians of the South, whether they were the mouthpieces of the ideas and passions of their constituents, or were, as Webster probably thought, more or less responsible for their foolishness and bitterness, were ever eager to precipitate a conflict, which Webster was as eager to prevent, or at least to postpone. It was fortunate for the North, that the inevitable conflict did not come in 1850, when the free States were unprepared for it. Ten years of discussion and preparation were allowed; when the war broke out, it found the North in a position to meet and eventually to overcome the enemies of the Union; and the Constitution, not as it _was_, but as it _is_, now represents a form of government which promises to be permanent; for after passing through its baptism of fire and blood, the Constitution contains nothing which is not in harmony with any State government founded on the principle of equal rights which it guarantees, and is proof against all attacks but those which may proceed from the extremes of human folly and wickedness. But that, before the civil war, it was preserved so long under conditions which constantly threatened it with destruction, is due in a considerable degree to the circumstance that it found in Daniel Webster its poet as well as its "expounder."

In conclusion it may be said that the style of Webster is pre-eminently distinguished by manliness. Nothing little, weak, whining, or sentimental can be detected in any page of the six volumes of his works. A certain strength and grandeur of personality is prominent in all his speeches. When he says "I," or "my," he never appears to indulge in the bravado of self-assertion, because the words are felt to express a positive, stalwart, almost colossal manhood, which had already been implied in the close-knit sentences in which he embodied his statements and arguments. He is an eminent instance of the power which character communicates to style. Though evidently proud, self-respecting, and high-spirited, he is ever above mere vanity and egotism. Whenever he gives emphasis to the personal pronoun the reader feels that he had as much earned the right to make his opinion an authority, as he had earned the right to use the words he employs to express his ideas and sentiments. Thus, in the celebrated *Smith Will* trial, his antagonist, Mr. Choate, quoted a decision of Lord Chancellor Camden. In his reply, Webster argued against its validity as though it were merely a proposition laid down by Mr. Choate. "But it is not mine, it is Lord Camden's" was the instant retort. Webster paused for half a minute, and then, with his eye fixed on the presiding judge, he replied: "Lord Camden was a great judge; he is respected by every American, for he was on our side in the Revolution; but, may it please your honor, *I* differ from my Lord Camden." There was hardly a lawyer in the United States who could have made such a statement without exposing himself to ridicule; but it did not seem at all ridiculous, when the "I" stood for Daniel Webster. In his early career as a lawyer, his mode of reasoning was such as to make him practically a thirteenth juror in the panel; when his fame was fully established, he contrived, in some mysterious way, to seat himself by the side of the judges on the bench, and appear to be consulting with them as a jurist, rather than addressing them as an advocate. The personality of the man was always suppressed until there seemed to be need of asserting it; and then it was proudly pushed into prominence, though rarely passing beyond the limits which his acknowledged eminence as a statesman and lawyer did not justify him in asserting it. Among the selections in the present volume where his individuality becomes somewhat aggressive, and breaks loose from the restraints ordinarily self-imposed on it, may be mentioned his speech on his Reception at Boston (1842), his Marshfield Speech (1848), and his speech at his Reception at Buffalo (1851). Whatever may be thought of the course of argument pursued in these, they are at least thoroughly penetrated with a manly spirit,--a manliness somewhat haughty and defiant, but still consciously strong in its power to return blow for blow, from whatever quarter the assault may come.

But the real intellectual and moral manliness of Webster underlies all his great orations and speeches, even those where the animating life which gives them the power to persuade, convince, and uplift the reader's mind, seems to be altogether impersonal; and this plain force of manhood, this sturdy grapple with every question that comes before his understanding for settlement, leads him contemptuously to reject all the meretricious aids and ornaments of mere rhetoric, and is prominent, among the many exceptional qualities of his large nature, which have given him a high position among the prose-writers of his country as a consummate master of English style.

THE DARTMOUTH COLLEGE CASE.
ARGUMENT BEFORE THE SUPREME COURT OF THE UNITED STATES, AT WASHINGTON, ON THE 10TH OF MARCH, 1818.

[The action, The Trustees of Dartmouth College v. William H. Woodward, was commenced in the Court of Common Pleas, Grafton County, State of New Hampshire, February term, 1817. The declaration was trover for the books of record, original charter, common seal, and other corporate property of the College. The conversion was alleged to have been made on the 7th day of October, 1816. The proper pleas were filed, and by consent the cause was carried directly to the Superior Court of New Hampshire, by appeal, and entered at the May term, 1817. The general issue was pleaded by the defendant, and joined by the plaintiffs. The facts in the case were then agreed upon by the parties, and drawn up in the form of a special verdict, reciting the charter of the College and the acts of the legislature of the State, passed June and December, 1816, by which the said corporation of Dartmouth College was *enlarged* and _improved_, and the said charter *amended*.

The question made in the case was, whether those acts of the legislature were valid and binding upon the corporation, without their acceptance or assent, and not repugnant to the Constitution of the United States. If so, the verdict found for the defendants; otherwise, it found for the plaintiffs.

The cause was continued to the September term of the court in Rockingham County, where it was argued; and at the November term of the same year, in Grafton County, the opinion of the court was delivered by Chief Justice Richardson, in favor of the validity and constitutionality of the acts of the legislature; and judgment was accordingly entered for the defendant on the special verdict.

Thereupon a writ of error was sued out by the original plaintiffs, to remove the cause to the Supreme Court of the United States; where it was entered at the term of the court holden at Washington on the first Monday of February, 1818.

The cause came on for argument on the 10th day of March, 1818, before all the judges. It was argued by Mr. Webster and Mr. Hopkinson for the plaintiffs in error, and by Mr. Holmes and the Attorney-General (Wirt) for the defendant in error.

At the term of the court holden in February, 1819, the opinion of the judges was delivered by Chief Justice Marshall, declaring the acts of the legislature unconstitutional and invalid, and reversing the judgment of the State Court. The court, with the exception of Mr. Justice Duvall, were unanimous.

The following was the argument of Mr. Webster for the plaintiffs in error.]

The general question is, whether the acts of the legislature of New Hampshire of the 27th of June, and of the 18th and 26th of December, 1816, are valid and binding on the plaintiffs, *without their acceptance or assent*.

The charter of 1769 created and established a corporation, to consist of twelve persons, and no more; to be called the "Trustees of Dartmouth College." The preamble to the charter recites, that it is granted on the application and request of the Rev. Eleazer Wheelock: That Dr. Wheelock, about the year 1754, established a charity school, at his own expense, and on his own estate and plantation: That for several years, through the assistance of well-disposed persons in America, granted at his solicitation, he had clothed, maintained, and educated a number of native Indians, and employed them afterwards as missionaries and schoolmasters among the savage tribes: That, his design promising to be useful, he had constituted the Rev. Mr. Whitaker to be his attorney, with power to solicit contributions, in England, for the further extension and carrying on of his undertaking; and that he had requested the Earl of Dartmouth, Baron Smith, Mr. Thornton, and other gentlemen, to receive such sums as might be contributed, in England, towards supporting his school, and to be trustees thereof, for his charity; which these persons had agreed to do: That thereupon Dr. Wheelock had executed to them a deed of trust, in pursuance of such agreement between him and them, and, for divers good reasons, had referred it to these persons to determine the place in which the school should be finally established: And, to enable them to form a proper decision on this subject, had laid before them the several offers which had been made to him by the several governments in America, in order to induce him to settle and establish his school within the limits of such governments for their own emolument, and the increase of learning in their respective places, as well as for the furtherance of his general original design: And inasmuch as a number of the proprietors of lands in New Hampshire, animated by the example of the Governor himself and others, and in consideration that, without any impediment to its original design, the school might be enlarged and improved, to promote learning among the English, and to supply ministers to the people of that Province, had promised large tracts of land, provided the school should be established in that Province, the persons before mentioned, having weighed the reasons in favor of the several places proposed, had given the preference to this Province, and these offers: That Dr. Wheelock therefore represented the necessity of a legal incorporation, and proposed that certain gentlemen in America, whom he had already named and appointed in his will to be trustees of his charity after his decease, should compose the corporation. Upon this recital, and in consideration of the laudable original design of Dr. Wheelock, and willing that the best means of education be established in New Hampshire, for the benefit of the Province, the king granted the charter, by the advice of his Provincial Council.

The substance of the facts thus recited is, that Dr. Wheelock had founded a charity, on funds owned and procured by himself; that he was at that time the sole dispenser and sole administrator, as well as the legal owner, of these funds; that he had made his will, devising this property in trust, to continue the existence and uses of the school, and appointed trustees; that, in this state of things, he had been invited to fix his school permanently in New Hampshire, and to extend the design of it to the education of the youth of that Province; that before he removed his school, or accepted this invitation, which his friends in England had advised him to accept, he applied for a charter, to be granted, not to whomsoever the king or government of the Province should please, but to such persons as he named and appointed, namely, the persons whom he had already appointed to be the future trustees of his charity by his will.

The charter, or letters patent, then proceed to create such a corporation, and to appoint twelve persons to constitute it, by the name of the "Trustees of Dartmouth College"; to have perpetual existence as such corporation, and with power to hold and dispose of lands and goods, for the use of the college, with all the ordinary powers of corporations. They are in their discretion to apply the funds and property of the college to the support of the president, tutors, ministers, and other officers of the college, and such missionaries and schoolmasters as they may see fit to employ among the Indians. There are to be twelve trustees for ever, _and no more_; and they are to have the right of filling vacancies occurring in their own body. The Rev. Mr. Wheelock is declared to be the founder of the college, and is, by the charter, appointed first president, with power to appoint a successor by his last will. All proper powers of government, superintendence, and visitation are vested in the trustees. They are to appoint and remove all officers at their discretion; to fix their salaries, and assign their duties; and to make all ordinances, orders, and laws for the government of the students. To the end that the persons who had acted as depositaries of the contributions in England, and who had also been contributors themselves, might be satisfied of the good use of their contributions, the president was annually, or when required, to transmit to them an account of the progress of the institution and the disbursements of its funds, so long as they should continue to act in that trust. These letters patent are to be good and effectual, in law, _against the king, his heirs and successors for ever_, without further grant or confirmation; and the trustees are to hold all and singular these privileges, advantages, liberties, and immunities to them and to their successors for ever.

No funds are given to the college by this charter. A corporate existence and capacity are given to the trustees, with the privileges and immunities which have been mentioned, to enable the founder and his associates the better to manage the funds which they themselves had contributed, and such others as they might afterwards obtain.

After the institution thus created and constituted had existed, uninterruptedly and usefully, nearly fifty years, the legislature of New Hampshire passed the acts in question.

The first act makes the twelve trustees under the charter, and nine other individuals, to be appointed by the Governor and Council, a corporation, by a new name; and to this new corporation transfers all the _property, rights, powers, liberties, and privileges_ of the old corporation; with further power to establish new colleges and an institute, and to apply all or any part of the funds to these purposes; subject to the power and control of a board of twenty-five overseers, to be appointed by the Governor and Council.

The second act makes further provisions for executing the objects of the first, and the last act authorizes the defendant, the treasurer of the plaintiffs, to retain and hold their property, against their will.

If these acts are valid, the old corporation is abolished, and a new one created. The first act does, in fact, if it can have any effect, create a new corporation, and transfer to it all the property and franchises of the old. The two corporations are not the same in anything which essentially belongs to the existence of a corporation. They have different names, and different powers, rights, and duties. Their organization is wholly different. The powers of the corporation are not vested in the same, or similar hands. In one, the trustees are twelve, and no more. In the other, they are twenty-one. In one, the power is in a single board. In the other, it is divided between two boards. Although the act professes to include the old trustees in the new corporation, yet that was without their assent, and against their remonstrance; and no person can be compelled to be a member of such a corporation against his will. It was neither expected nor intended that they should be members of the new corporation. The act itself treats the old corporation as at an end, and, going on the ground that all its functions have ceased, it provides for the first meeting and organization of the new corporation. It expressly provides, also, that the new corporation shall have and hold all the property of the old; a provision which would be quite unnecessary upon any other ground, than that the old corporation was dissolved. But if it could be contended that the effect of these acts was not entirely to abolish the old corporation, yet it is manifest that they impair and invade the rights, property, and powers of the trustees under the charter, as a corporation, and the legal rights, privileges, and immunities which belong to them, as individual members of the corporation.

The twelve trustees were the *sole* legal owners of all the property acquired under the charter. By the acts, others are admitted, against *their* will, to be joint owners. The twelve individuals who are trustees were possessed of all the franchises and immunities conferred by the charter. By the acts, *nine* other trustees and _twenty-five_ overseers are admitted, against their will, to divide these franchises and immunities with them.

If, either as a corporation or as individuals, they have any legal rights, this forcible intrusion of others violates those rights, as manifestly as an entire and complete ouster and dispossession. These acts alter the whole constitution of the corporation. They affect the rights of the whole body as a corporation, and the rights of the individuals who compose it. They revoke corporate powers and franchises. They alienate and transfer the property of the college to others. By the charter, the trustees had a right to fill vacancies in their own number. This is now taken away. They were to consist of twelve, and, by express provision, of no more. This is altered. They and their successors, appointed by themselves, were for ever to hold the property. The legislature has found successors for them, before their seats are vacant. The powers and privileges which the twelve were to exercise exclusively, are now to be exercised by others. By one of the acts, they are subjected to heavy penalties if they exercise their offices, or any of those powers and privileges granted them by charter, and which they had exercised for fifty years. They are to be punished for not accepting the new grant and taking its benefits. This, it must be confessed, is rather a summary mode of settling a question of constitutional right. Not only are new trustees forced into the corporation, but new trusts and uses are created. The college is turned into a university. Power is given to create new colleges, and, to authorize any diversion of the funds which may be agreeable to the new boards, sufficient latitude is given by the undefined power of establishing an institute. To these new colleges, and this institute, the funds contributed by the founder, Dr. Wheelock, and by the original donors, the Earl of Dartmouth and others, are to be applied, in plain and manifest disregard of the uses to which they were given.

The president, one of the old trustees, had a right to his office, salary, and emoluments, subject to the twelve trustees alone. His title to these is now changed, and he is made accountable to new masters. So also all the professors and tutors. If the legislature can at pleasure make these alterations and changes in the rights and privileges of the plaintiffs, it may, with equal propriety, abolish these rights and privileges altogether. The same power which can do any part of this work can accomplish the whole. And, indeed, the argument on which these acts have been hitherto defended goes altogether on the ground, that this is such a corporation as the legislature may abolish at pleasure; and that its members have no _rights, liberties, franchises, property, or privileges_, which the legislature may not revoke, annul, alienate, or transfer to others, whenever it sees fit.

It will be contended by the plaintiffs, that these acts are not valid and binding on them without their assent,--

1. Because they are against common right, and the Constitution of New Hampshire.

2. Because they are repugnant to the Constitution of the United States.

I am aware of the limits which bound the jurisdiction of the court in this case, and that on this record nothing can be decided but the single question, whether these acts are repugnant to the Constitution of the United States. Yet it may assist in forming an opinion of their true nature and character to compare them with those fundamental principles introduced into the State governments for the purpose of limiting the exercise of the legislative power, and which the Constitution of New Hampshire expresses with great fulness and accuracy.

It is not too much to assert, that the legislature of New Hampshire would not have been competent to pass the acts in question, and to make them binding on the plaintiffs without their assent, even if there had been, in the Constitution of New Hampshire, or of the United States, no special restriction on their power, because these acts are not the exercise of a power properly legislative.[1] Their effect and object are to take away, from one, rights, property, and franchises, and to grant them to another. This is not the exercise of a legislative power. To justify the taking away of vested rights there must be a forfeiture, to adjudge upon and declare which is the proper province of the judiciary. Attainder and confiscation are acts of sovereign power, not acts of legislation. The British Parliament, among other unlimited powers, claims that of altering and vacating charters; not as an act of ordinary legislation, but of uncontrolled authority. It is theoretically omnipotent. Yet, in modern times, it has very rarely attempted the exercise of this power. In a celebrated instance, those who asserted this power in Parliament vindicated its exercise only in a case in which it could be shown, 1st. That the charter in question was a charter of political power; 2d. That there was a great and overruling state necessity, justifying the violation of the charter; 3d. That the charter had been abused and justly forfeited.[2] The bill affecting this charter did not pass. Its history is well known. The act which afterwards did pass, passed *with the assent of the corporation*. Even in the worst times, this power of Parliament to repeal and rescind charters has not often been exercised. The illegal proceedings in the reign of Charles the Second were under color of law. Judgments of forfeiture were obtained in the courts. Such was the case of the *quo warranto* against the city of London, and the proceedings by which the charter of Massachusetts was vacated.

The legislature of New Hampshire has no more power over the rights of the plaintiffs than existed somewhere, in some department of government, before the Revolution. The British Parliament could not have annulled or revoked this grant as an act of ordinary legislation. If it had done it at all, it could only have been in virtue of that sovereign power, called omnipotent, which does not belong to any legislature in the United States. The legislature of New Hampshire has the same power over this charter which belonged to the king who granted it, and no more. By the law of England, the power to create corporations is a part of the royal prerogative.[3] By the Revolution, this power may be considered as having devolved on the legislature of the State, and it has accordingly been exercised by the legislature. But the king cannot abolish a corporation, or new-model it, or alter its powers, without its assent. This is the acknowledged and well-known doctrine of the common law. "Whatever might have been the notion in former times," says Lord Mansfield, "it is most certain now that the corporations of the universities are lay corporations; and that the crown cannot take away from them any rights that have been formerly subsisting in them under old charters or prescriptive usage."[4] After forfeiture duly found, the king may re-grant the franchises; but a grant of franchises already granted, and of which no forfeiture has been found, is void.

Corporate franchises can only be forfeited by trial and judgment.[5] In case of a new charter or grant to an existing corporation, it may accept or reject it as it pleases.[6] It may accept such part of the grant as it chooses, and reject the rest.[7] In the very nature of things, a charter cannot be forced upon any body. No one can be compelled to accept a grant; and without acceptance the grant is necessarily void.[8] It cannot be pretended that the legislature, as successor to the king in this part of his prerogative, has any power to revoke, vacate, or alter this charter. If, therefore, the legislature has not this power by any specific grant contained in the Constitution; nor as included in its ordinary legislative powers; nor by reason of its succession to the prerogatives of the crown in this particular, on what ground would the authority to pass these acts rest, even if there were no prohibitory clauses in the Constitution and the Bill of Rights?

But there *are* prohibitions in the Constitution and Bill of Rights of New Hampshire, introduced for the purpose of limiting the legislative power and protecting the rights and property of the citizens. One prohibition is, "that no person shall be deprived of his property, immunities, or privileges, put out of the protection of the law, or deprived of his life, liberty, or estate, but by judgment of his peers or the law of the land."

In the opinion, however, which was given in the court below, it is denied that the trustees under the charter had any property, immunity, liberty, or privilege in this corporation, within the meaning of this prohibition in the Bill of Rights. It is said that it is a public corporation and public property; that the trustees have no greater interest in it than any other individuals; that it is not private property, which they can sell or transmit to their heirs, and that therefore they have no interest in it; that their office is a public trust, like that of the Governor or a judge, and that they have no more concern in the property of the college than the Governor in the property of the State, or than the judges in the fines which they impose on the culprits at their bar; that it is nothing to them whether their powers shall be extended or lessened, any more than it is to their honors whether their jurisdiction shall be enlarged or diminished. It is necessary, therefore, to inquire into the true nature and character of the corporation which was created by the charter of 1769.

There are divers sorts of corporations; and it may be safely admitted that the legislature has more power over some than others.[9] Some corporations are for government and political arrangement; such, for example, as cities, counties, and towns in New England. These may be changed and modified as public convenience may require, due regard being always had to the rights of property. Of such corporations, all who live within the limits are of course obliged to be members, and to submit to the duties which the law imposes on them as such. Other civil corporations are for the advancement of trade and business, such as banks, insurance companies, and the like. These are created, not by general law, but usually by grant. Their constitution is special. It is such as the legislature sees fit to give, and the grantees to accept.

The corporation in question is not a civil, although it is a lay corporation. It is an eleemosynary corporation. It is a private charity, originally founded and endowed by an individual, with a charter obtained for it at his request, for the better administration of his charity. "The eleemosynary sort of corporations are such as are constituted for the perpetual distributions of the free alms or bounty of the founder of them, to such persons as he has directed. Of this are all hospitals for the maintenance of the poor, sick, and impotent; and all colleges both in our universities and out of them."[10] Eleemosynary corporations are for the management of private property, according to the will of the donors. They are private corporations. A college is as much a private corporation as a hospital; especially a college founded, as this was, by private bounty. A college is a charity. "The establishment of learning," says Lord Hardwicke, "is a charity, and so considered in the statute of Elizabeth. A devise to a college, for their benefit, is a laudable charity, and deserves encouragement."[11]

The legal signification of *a charity* is derived chiefly from the statute 43 Eliz. ch. 4. "Those purposes," says Sir William Grant, "are considered *charitable* which that statute enumerates."[12] Colleges are enumerated as charities in that statute. The government, in these cases, lends its aid to perpetuate the beneficent intention of the donor, by granting a charter under which his private charity shall continue to be dispensed after his death. This is done either by incorporating the objects of the charity, as, for instance, the scholars in a college or the poor in a hospital, or by incorporating those who are to be governors or trustees of the charity.[13] In cases of the first sort, the founder is, by the common law, visitor. In early times it became a maxim, that he who gave the property might regulate it in future. "Cujus est dare, ejus est disponere." This right of visitation descended from the founder to his heir as a right of property, and precisely as his other property went to his heir; and in default of heirs it went to the king, as all other property goes to the king for the want of heirs. The right of visitation arises from the property. It grows out of the endowment. The founder may, if he please, part with it at the time when he establishes the charity, and may vest it in others. Therefore, if he chooses that governors, trustees, or overseers should be appointed in the charter, he may cause it to be done, and his power of visitation may be transferred to them, instead of descending to his heirs. The persons thus assigned or appointed by the founder will be visitors, with all the powers of the founder, in exclusion of his heir.[14] The right of visitation, then, accrues to them, as a matter of property, by the gift, transfer, or appointment of the founder. This is a private right, which they can assert in all legal modes, and in which they have the same protection of the law as in all other rights. As visitors they may make rules, ordinances, and statutes, and alter and repeal them, as far as permitted so to do by the charter.[15] Although the charter proceeds from the crown or the government, it is considered as the will of the donor. It is obtained at his request. He imposes it as the rule which is to prevail in the dispensation of his bounty in all future times. The king or government which grants the charter is not thereby the founder, but he who furnishes the funds. The gift of the revenues is the foundation.[16]

The leading case on this subject is _Phillips v. Bury_.[17] This was an ejectment brought to recover the rectory-house, &c. of Exeter College in Oxford. The question was whether the plaintiff or defendant was legal rector. Exeter College was founded by an individual, and incorporated by a charter granted by Queen Elizabeth. The controversy turned upon the power of the visitor, and, in the discussion of the cause, the nature of college charters and corporations was very fully considered. Lord Holt's judgment, copied from his own manuscript, is found in 2 Term Reports. 346. The following is an extract:--

"That we may the better apprehend the nature of a visitor, we are to consider that there are in law two sorts of corporations aggregate; such as are for public government, and such as are for private charity. Those that are for the public government of a town, city, mystery, or the like, being for public advantage, are to be governed according to the laws of the land. If they make any particular private laws and constitutions, the validity and justice of them is examinable in the king's courts. Of these there are no particular private founders, and consequently no particular visitor; there are no patrons of these; therefore, if no provision be in the charter how the succession shall continue, the law supplieth the defect of that constitution, and saith it shall be by election; as mayor, aldermen, common council, and the like. But *private* and particular corporations for charity, founded and endowed by private persons, are subject to the private government of those who erect them; and therefore, if there be no visitor appointed by the founder, the law appoints the founder and his heirs to be visitors, who are to act and proceed according to the particular laws and constitutions assigned them by the founder. It is now admitted on all hands that the founder is patron, and, as founder, is visitor, if no particular visitor be assigned; so that patronage and visitation are necessary consequents one upon another. For this visitatorial power was not introduced by any canons or constitutions ecclesiastical (as was said by a learned gentleman whom I have in my eye, in his argument of this case); it is an appointment of law. It ariseth from the property which the founder had in the lands assigned to support the charity; and as he is the author of the charity, the law gives him and his heirs a visitatorial power, that is, an authority to inspect the actions and regulate the behavior of the members that partake of the charity. For it is fit the members that are endowed, and that have the charity bestowed upon them, should not be left to themselves, but pursue the intent and design of him that bestowed it upon them. _Now, indeed, where the poor, or those that receive the charity, are not incorporated, but there are certain trustees who dispose of the charity, there is no visitor, because the interest of the revenue is not vested in the poor that have the benefit of the charity, but they are subject to the orders and directions of the trustees._ But where they who are to enjoy the benefit of the charity are incorporated, there to prevent all perverting of the charity, or to compose differences that may happen among them, there is by law a visitatorial power; and it being a creature of the founder's own, it is reason that he and his heirs should have that power, unless by the founder it is vested in some other. Now there is no manner of difference between a college and a hospital, except only in degree. A hospital is for those that are poor, and mean, and low, and sickly; a college is for another sort of indigent persons; but it hath another intent, to study in and breed up persons in the world that have no otherwise to live; but still it is as much within the reasons as hospitals. And if in a hospital the master and poor are incorporated, it is a college having a common seal to act by, although it hath not the name of a college (which always supposeth a corporation), because it is of an inferior degree; and in the one case and in the other there must be a visitor, either the founder and his heirs or one appointed by him; and both are eleemosynary."

Lord Holt concludes his whole argument by again repeating, that that college was a _private corporation_, and that the founder had a right to appoint a visitor, and to give him such power as he saw fit.[18]

The learned Bishop Stillingfleet's argument in the same cause, as a member of the House of Lords, when it was there heard, exhibits very clearly the nature of colleges and similar corporations. It is to the following effect: "That this absolute and conclusive power of visitors is no more than the law hath appointed in other cases, upon commissions of charitable uses: that the common law, and not any ecclesiastical canons, do place the power of visitation in the founder and his heirs, _unless he settle it upon others_: that although corporations for public government be subject to the courts of Westminster Hall, which have no particular or special visitors, yet corporations for charity, founded and endowed by private persons, are subject to the rule and government of those that erect them; but where the persons to whom the charity is given are not incorporated, there is no such visitatorial power, because the interest of the revenue is not invested in them; but where they are, the right of visitation ariseth from the foundation, and the founder may convey _it to whom and in what manner he pleases; and the visitor acts as founder, and by the same authority which he had, and consequently is no more accountable than he had been_: that the king by his charter can make a society to be incorporated so as to have the rights belonging to persons, as to legal capacities: that colleges, although founded by private persons, are yet incorporated by the king's charter; but although the kings by their charter made the colleges to be such in law, that is, to be legal corporations, yet they left to the particular founders authority to appoint what statutes they thought fit for the regulation of them. And not only the statutes, but the appointment of visitors, was left to them, and the manner of government, and the several conditions on which any persons were to be made or continue partakers of their bounty."[19] These opinions received the sanction of the House of Lords, and they seem to be settled and undoubted law. Where there is a charter, vesting proper powers in trustees, or governors, they are visitors; and there is no control in any body else; except only that the courts of equity or of law will interfere so far as to preserve the revenues and prevent the perversion of the funds, and to keep the visitors within their prescribed bounds. "If there be a charter with proper powers, the charity must be regulated in the manner prescribed by the charter. There is no ground for the controlling interposition of the courts of chancery. The interposition of the courts, therefore, in those instances in which the charities were founded on charters or by act of Parliament, and a visitor or governor and trustees appointed, must be referred to the general jurisdiction of the courts in all cases in which a trust conferred appears to have been abused, and not to an original right to direct the management of the charity, or the conduct of the governors or trustees."[20] "The original of all _visitatorial_ power is the property of the donor, and the power every one has to dispose, direct, and regulate his own property; like the case of patronage; _cujus est dare_, &c. Therefore, if either the crown or the subject creates an eleemosynary foundation, and vests the charity in the persons who are to receive the benefit of it, since a contest might arise about the government of it, the law allows the founder or his heirs, or the person specially appointed by him to be visitor, to determine concerning his own creature. If the charity is not vested in the persons who are to partake, but in trustees for their benefit, no visitor can arise by implication, but the trustees have that power."[21]

"There is nothing better established," says Lord Commissioner Eyre, "than that this court does not entertain a general jurisdiction, or regulate and control charities _established by charter_. There the establishment is fixed and determined; and the court has no power to vary it. If the governors established for the regulation of it are not those who have the management of the revenue, this court has no jurisdiction, and if it is ever so much abused, as far as it respects the jurisdiction of this court it is without remedy; but if those established as governors have also the management of the revenues, this court does assume a jurisdiction of necessity, so far as they are to be considered as trustees of the revenue."[22]

"The foundations of colleges," says Lord Mansfield, "are to be considered in two views; namely, as they are _corporations_ and as they are _eleemosynary_. As eleemosynary, they are the creatures of the founder; he may delegate his power, either generally or specially; he may prescribe particular modes and manners, as to the exercise of part of it. If he makes a general visitor (as by the general words _visitator sit_), the person so constituted has all incidental power; but he may be restrained as to particular instances. The founder may appoint a special visitor for a particular purpose, and no further. The founder may make a general visitor; and yet appoint an inferior particular power, to be executed without going to the visitor in the first instance."[23] And even if the king be founder, if he grant a charter, incorporating trustees and governors, _they are visitors_, and the king cannot visit.[24] A subsequent donation, or ingrafted fellowship, falls under the same general visitatorial power, if not otherwise specially provided.[25]

In New England, and perhaps throughout the United States, eleemosynary corporations have been generally established in the latter mode; that is, by incorporating governors, or trustees, and vesting in them the right of visitation. Small variations may have been in some instances adopted; as in the case of Harvard College, where some power of inspection is given to the overseers, but not, strictly speaking, a visitatorial power, which still belongs, it is apprehended, to the fellows or members of the corporation. In general, there are many donors. A charter is obtained, comprising them all, or some of them, and such others as they choose to include, with the right of appointing successors. They are thus the visitors of their own charity, and appoint others, such as they may see fit, to exercise the same office in time to come. All such corporations are private. The case before the court is clearly that of an eleemosynary corporation. It is, in the strictest legal sense, a private charity. In King v. St. Catherine's Hall,[26] that college is called a private eleemosynary lay corporation. It was endowed by a private founder, and incorporated by letters patent. And in the same manner was Dartmouth College founded and incorporated. Dr. Wheelock is declared by the charter to be its founder. It was established by him, on funds contributed and collected by himself.

As such founder, he had a right of visitation, which he assigned to the trustees, and they received it by his consent and appointment, and held it under the charter.[27] He appointed these trustees visitors, and in that respect to take place of his heir; as he might have appointed devisees, to take his estate instead of his heir. Little, probably, did he think, at that time, that the legislature would ever take away this property and these privileges, and give them to others. Little did he suppose that this charter secured to him and his successors no legal rights. Little did the other donors think so. If they had, the college would have been, what the university is now, a thing upon paper, existing only in name.

The numerous academies in New England have been established substantially in the same manner. They hold their property by the same tenure, and no other. Nor has Harvard College any surer title than Dartmouth College. It may to-day have more friends; but to-morrow it may have more enemies. Its legal rights are the same. So also of Yale College; and, indeed, of all the others. When the legislature gives to these institutions, it may and does accompany its grants with such conditions as it pleases. The grant of lands by the legislature of New Hampshire to Dartmouth College, in 1789, was accompanied with various conditions. When donations are made, by the legislature or others, to a charity already existing, without any condition, or the specification of any new use, the donation follows the nature of the charity. Hence the doctrine, that all eleemosynary corporations are private bodies. They are founded by private persons, and on private property. The public cannot be charitable in these institutions. It is not the money of the public, but of private persons, which is dispensed. It may be public, that is general, in its uses and advantages; and the State may very laudably add contributions of its own to the funds; but it is still private in the tenure of the property, and in the right of administering the funds.

If the doctrine laid down by Lord Holt, and the House of Lords, in _Phillips v. Bury_, and recognized and established in all the other cases, be correct, the property of this college was private property; it was vested in the trustees by the charter, and to be administered by them, according to the will of the founder and donors, as expressed in the charter. They were also visitors of the charity, in the most ample sense. They had, therefore, as they contend, privileges, property, and immunities, within the true meaning of the Bill of Rights. They had rights, and still have them, which they can assert against the legislature, as well as against other wrong-doers. It makes no difference, that the estate is holden for certain trusts. The legal estate is still theirs. They have a right in the property, and they have a right of visiting and superintending the trust; and this is an object of legal protection, as much as any other right. The charter declares that the powers conferred on the trustees are "privileges, advantages, liberties, and immunities"; and that they shall be for ever holden by them and their successors. The New Hampshire Bill of Rights declares that no one shall be deprived of his "property, privileges, or immunities," but by judgment of his peers, or the law of the land. The argument on the other side is, that, although these terms may mean something in the Bill of Rights, they mean nothing in this charter. But they are terms of legal signification, and very properly used in the charter. They are equivalent with *franchises*. Blackstone says that *franchise* and *liberty* are used as synonymous terms. And after enumerating other liberties and franchises, he says: "It is likewise a franchise for a number of persons to be incorporated and subsist as a body politic, with a power to maintain perpetual succession and do other corporate acts; and each individual member of such a corporation is also said to have a franchise or freedom."[28]

Liberties is the term used in Magna Charta as including franchises, privileges, immunities, and all the rights which belong to that class. Professor Sullivan says, the term signifies the "*privileges* that some of the subjects, whether single persons or bodies corporate, have above others by the lawful grant of the king; as the chattels of felons or outlaws, and the lands *and privileges of corporations*."[29]

The privilege, then, of being a member of a corporation, under a lawful grant, and of exercising the rights and powers of such member, is such a privilege, _liberty_, or _franchise_, as has been the object of legal protection, and the subject of a legal interest, from the time of Magna Charta to the present moment. The plaintiffs have such an interest in this corporation, individually, as they could assert and maintain in a court of law, not as agents of the public, but in their own right. Each trustee has a _franchise_, and if he be disturbed in the enjoyment of it, he would have redress, on appealing to the law, as promptly as for any other injury. If the other trustees should conspire against any one of them to prevent his equal right and voice in the appointment of a president or professor, or in the passing of any statute or ordinance of the college, he would be entitled to his action, for depriving him of his franchise. It makes no difference, that this property is to be holden and administered, and these franchises exercised, for the purpose of diffusing learning. No principle and no case establishes any such distinction. The public may be benefited by the use of this property. But this does not change the nature of the property, or the rights of the owners. The object of the charter may be public good; so it is in all other corporations; and this would as well justify the resumption or violation of the grant in any other case as in this. In the case of an advowson, the use is public, and the right cannot be turned to any private benefit or emolument. It is nevertheless a legal private right, and the *property* of the owner, as emphatically as his freehold. The rights and privileges of trustees, visitors, or governors of incorporated colleges, stand on the same foundation. They are so considered, both by Lord Holt and Lord Hardwicke.[30]

To contend that the rights of the plaintiffs may be taken away, because they derive from them no pecuniary benefit or private emolument, or because they cannot be transmitted to their heirs, or would not be assets to pay their debts, is taking an extremely narrow view of the subject. According to this notion, the case would be different, if, in the charter, they had stipulated for a commission on the disbursement of the funds; and they have ceased to have any interest in the property, because they have undertaken to administer it gratuitously.

It cannot be necessary to say much in refutation of the idea, that there cannot be a legal interest, or ownership, in any thing which does not yield a pecuniary profit; as if the law regarded no rights but the rights of money, and of visible, tangible property. Of what nature are all rights of suffrage? No elector has a particular personal interest; but each has a legal right, to be exercised at his own discretion, and it cannot be taken away from him. The exercise of this right directly and very materially affects the public; much more so than the exercise of the privileges of a trustee of this college. Consequences of the utmost magnitude may sometimes depend on the exercise of the right of suffrage by one or a few electors. Nobody was ever yet heard to contend, however, that on that account the public might take away the right, or impair it. This notion appears to be borrowed from no better source than the repudiated doctrine of the three judges in the Aylesbury case.[31] That was an action against a returning officer for refusing the plaintiff's vote, in the election of a member of Parliament. Three of the judges of the King's Bench held, that the action could not be maintained, because, among other objections, "it was not any matter of profit, either _in presenti_, or *in futuro*." It would not enrich the plaintiff _in presenti_, nor would it *in futuro* go to his heirs, or answer to pay his debts. But Lord Holt and the House of Lords were of another opinion. The judgment of the three judges was reversed, and the doctrine they held, having been exploded for a century, seems now for the first time to be revived.

Individuals have a right to use their own property for purposes of benevolence, either towards the public, or towards other individuals. They have a right to exercise this benevolence in such lawful manner as they may choose; and when the government has induced and excited it, by contracting to give perpetuity to the stipulated manner of exercising it, it is not law, but violence, to rescind this contract, and seize on the property. Whether the State will grant these franchises, and under what conditions it will grant them, it decides for itself. But when once granted, the constitution holds them to be sacred, till forfeited for just cause.

That all property, of which the use may be beneficial to the public, belongs therefore to the public, is quite a new doctrine. It has no precedent, and is supported by no known principle. Dr. Wheelock might have answered his purposes, in this case, by executing a private deed of trust. He might have conveyed his property to trustees, for precisely such uses as are described in this charter. Indeed, it appears that he had contemplated the establishing of his school in that manner, and had made his will, and devised the property to the same persons who were afterwards appointed trustees in the charter. Many literary and other charitable institutions are founded in that manner, and the trust is renewed, and conferred on other persons, from time to time, as occasion may require. In such a case, no lawyer would or could say, that the legislature might divest the trustees, constituted by deed or will, seize upon the property, and give it to other persons, for other purposes. And does the granting of a charter, which is only done to perpetuate the trust in a more convenient manner, make any difference? Does or can this change the nature of the charity, and turn it into a public political corporation? Happily, we are not without authority on this point. It has been considered and adjudged. Lord Hardwicke says, in so many words, "The charter of the crown cannot make a charity more or less public, but only more permanent than it would otherwise be."[32]

The granting of the corporation is but making the trust perpetual, and does not alter the nature of the charity. The very object sought in obtaining such charter, and in giving property to such a corporation, is to make and keep it private property, and to clothe it with all the security and inviolability of private property. The intent is, that there shall be a legal private ownership, and that the legal owners shall maintain and protect the property, for the benefit of those for whose use it was designed. Who ever endowed the public? Who ever appointed a legislature to administer his charity? Or who ever heard, before, that a gift to a college, or a hospital, or an asylum, was, in reality, nothing but a gift to the State?

The State of Vermont is a principal donor to Dartmouth College. The lands given lie in that State. This appears in the special verdict. Is Vermont to be considered as having intended a gift to the State of New Hampshire in this case, as, it has been said, is to be the reasonable construction of all donations to the college? The legislature of New Hampshire affects to represent the public, and therefore claims a right to control all property destined to public use. What hinders Vermont from considering herself equally the representative of the public, and from resuming her grants, at her own pleasure? Her right to do so is less doubtful than the power of New Hampshire to pass the laws in question.

In _University v. Foy_,[33] the Supreme Court of North Carolina pronounced unconstitutional and void a law repealing a grant to the University of North Carolina, although that university was originally erected and endowed by a statute of the State. That case was a grant of lands, and the court decided that it could not be resumed. This is the grant of a power and capacity to hold lands. Where is the difference of the cases, upon principle?

In _Terrett v. Taylor_,[34] this court decided that a legislative grant or confirmation of lands, for the purposes of moral and religious instruction, could no more be rescinded than other grants. The nature of the use was not holden to make any difference. A grant to a parish or church, for the purposes which have been mentioned, cannot be distinguished, in respect to the title it confers, from a grant to a college for the promotion of piety and learning. To the same purpose may be cited the case of _Pawlett v. Clark_. The State of Vermont, by statute, in 1794, granted to the respective towns in that State certain glebe lands lying within those towns for the sole use and support of religious worship. In 1799, an act was passed to repeal the act of 1794; but this court declared, that the act of 1794, "so far as it granted the glebes to the towns, could not afterwards be repealed by the legislature, so as to divest the rights of the towns under the grant."[35]

It will be for the other side to show that the nature of the use decides the question whether the legislature has power to resume its grants. It will be for those who maintain such a doctrine to show the principles and cases upon which it rests. It will be for them also to fix the limits and boundaries of their doctrine, and to show what are and what are not such uses as to give the legislature this power of resumption and revocation. And to furnish an answer to the cases cited, it will be for them further to show that a grant for the use and support of religious worship stands on other ground than a grant for the promotion of piety and learning.

I hope enough has been said to show that the trustees possessed vested liberties, privileges, and immunities, under this charter; and that such liberties, privileges, and immunities, being once lawfully obtained and vested, are as inviolable as any vested rights of property whatever. Rights to do certain acts, such, for instance, as the visitation and superintendence of a college and the appointment of its officers, may surely be vested rights, to all legal intents, as completely as the right to possess property. A late learned judge of this court has said, "When I say that a *right* is vested in a citizen, I mean that he has the power to do _certain actions_, or to possess _certain things_, according to the law of the land."[36]

If such be the true nature of the plaintiffs' interests under this charter, what are the articles in the New Hampshire Bill of Rights which these acts infringe?

They infringe the second article; which says, that the citizens of the State have a right to hold and possess property. The plaintiffs had a legal property in this charter; and they had acquired property under it. The acts deprive them of both. They impair and take away the charter; and they appropriate the property to new uses, against their consent. The plaintiffs cannot now hold the property acquired by themselves, and which this article says they have a right to hold.

They infringe the twentieth article. By that article it is declared that, in questions of property, there is a right to trial. The plaintiffs are divested, without trial or judgment.

They infringe the twenty-third article. It is therein declared that no retrospective laws shall be passed. This article bears directly on the case. These acts must be deemed to be retrospective, within the settled construction of that term. What a retrospective law is, has been decided, on the construction of this very article, in the Circuit Court for the First Circuit. The learned judge of that circuit says: "Every statute which takes away or impairs vested rights, acquired under existing laws, must be deemed retrospective."[37] That all such laws are retrospective was decided also in the case of _Dash v. Van Kleek_,[38] where a most learned judge quotes this article from the constitution of New Hampshire, with manifest approbation, as a plain and clear expression of those fundamental and unalterable principles of justice, which must lie at the foundation of every free and just system of laws. Can any man deny that the plaintiffs had rights, under the charter, which were legally vested, and that by these acts those rights are impaired?

"It is a principle in the English law," says Chief Justice Kent, in the case last cited, "as ancient as the law itself, that a statute, even of its omnipotent Parliament, is not to have a retrospective effect. 'Nova constitutio futuris formam imponere debet, et non praeteritis.'[39] The maxim in Bracton was taken from the civil law, for we find in that system the same principle, expressed substantially in the same words, that the lawgiver cannot alter his mind to the prejudice of a vested right. 'Nemo potest mutare concilium suum in alterius injuriam.'[40] This maxim of Papinian is general in its terms, but Dr. Taylor[41] applies it directly as a restriction upon the lawgiver, and a declaration in the Code leaves no doubt as to the sense of the civil law. 'Leges et constitutiones futuris certum est dare formam negotiis, non ad facta praeterita revocari, nisi nominatim, et de praeterito tempore, et adhuc pendentibus negotiis cautum sit.'[42] This passage, according to the best interpretation of the civilians, relates not merely to future suits, but to future, as contradistinguished from past, contracts and vested rights.[43] It is indeed admitted that the prince may enact a retrospective law, provided it be done _expressly_; for the will of the prince under the despotism of the Roman emperors was paramount to every obligation. Great latitude was anciently allowed to legislative expositions of statutes; for the separation of the judicial from the legislative power was not then distinctly known or prescribed. The prince was in the habit of interpreting his own laws for particular occasions. This was called the 'Interlocutio Principis'; and this, according to Huber's definition, was, 'quando principes inter partes loquuntur et jus dicunt.'[44] No correct civilian, and especially no proud admirer of the ancient republic (if any such then existed), could have reflected on this interference with private rights and pending suits without disgust and indignation; and we are rather surprised to find that, under the violent and arbitrary genius of the Roman government, the principle before us should have been acknowledged and obeyed to the extent in which we find it. The fact shows that it must be founded in the clearest justice. Our case is happily very different from that of the subjects of Justinian. With us the power of the lawgiver is limited and defined; the judicial is regarded as a distinct, independent power; private rights are better understood and more exalted in public estimation, as well as secured by provisions dictated by the spirit of freedom, and unknown to the civil law. Our constitutions do not admit the power assumed by the Roman prince, and the principle we are considering is now to be regarded as sacred."

These acts infringe also the thirty-seventh article of the constitution of New Hampshire; which says, that the powers of government shall be kept separate. By these acts, the legislature assumes to exercise a judicial power. It declares a forfeiture, and resumes franchises, once granted, without trial or hearing.

If the constitution be not altogether waste-paper, it has restrained the power of the legislature in these particulars. If it has any meaning, it is that the legislature shall pass no act directly and manifestly impairing private property and private privileges. It shall not judge by act. It shall not decide by act. It shall not deprive by act. But it shall leave all these things to be tried and adjudged by the law of the land.

The fifteenth article has been referred to before. It declares that no one shall be "deprived of his property, immunities, or privileges, but by the judgment of his peers or the law of the land." Notwithstanding the light in which the learned judges in New Hampshire viewed the rights of the plaintiffs under the charter, and which has been before adverted to, it is found to be admitted in their opinion, that those rights are privileges within the meaning of this fifteenth article of the Bill of Rights. Having quoted that article, they say: "That the right to manage the affairs of this college is a privilege, within the meaning of this clause of the Bill of Rights, is not to be doubted." In my humble opinion, this surrenders the point. To resist the effect of this admission, however, the learned judges add: "But how a privilege can be protected from the operation of the law of the land by a clause in the constitution, declaring that it shall not be taken away but by the law of the land, is not very easily understood." This answer goes on the ground, that the acts in question are laws of the land, within the meaning of the constitution. If they be so, the argument drawn from this article is fully answered. If they be not so, it being admitted that the plaintiffs' rights are "privileges," within the meaning of the article, the argument is not answered, and the article is infringed by the acts.

Are, then, these acts of the legislature, which affect only particular persons and their particular privileges, laws of the land? Let this question be answered by the text of Blackstone. "And first it (i.e. law) is a _rule_: not a transient, sudden order from a superior to or concerning a particular person; but something permanent, uniform, and universal. Therefore a particular act of the legislature to confiscate the goods of Titius, or to attaint him of high treason, does not enter into the idea of a municipal law; for the operation of this act is spent upon Titius only, and has no relation to the community in general; it is rather a sentence than a law."[45] Lord Coke is equally decisive and emphatic. Citing and commenting on the celebrated twenty-ninth chapter of Magna Charta, he says: "No man shall be disseized, &c., unless it be by the lawful judgment, that is, verdict of equals, or by the law of the land, that is (to speak it once for all), by the due course and process of law."[46] Have the plaintiffs lost their franchises by "due course and process of law"? On the contrary, are not these acts "particular acts of the legislature, which have no relation to the community in general, and which are rather sentences than laws"?

By the law of the land is most clearly intended the general law; a law which hears before it condemns; which proceeds upon inquiry, and renders judgment only after trial. The meaning is, that every citizen shall hold his life, liberty, property, and immunities under the protection of the general rules which govern society. Every thing which may pass under the form of an enactment is not therefore to be considered the law of the land. If this were so, acts of attainder, bills of pains and penalties, acts of confiscation, acts reversing judgments, and acts directly transferring one man's estate to another, legislative judgments, decrees, and forfeitures in all possible forms, would be the law of the land.

Such a strange construction would render constitutional provisions of the highest importance completely inoperative and void. It would tend directly to establish the union of all powers in the legislature. There would be no general, permanent law for courts to administer or men to live under. The administration of justice would be an empty form, an idle ceremony. Judges would sit to execute legislative judgments and decrees; not to declare the law or to administer the justice of the country. "Is that the law of the land," said Mr. Burke, "upon which, if a man go to Westminster Hall, and ask counsel by what title or tenure he holds his privilege or estate _according to the law of the land_, he should be told, that the law of the land is not yet known; that no decision or decree has been made in his case; that when a decree shall be passed, he will then know _what the law of the land is_? Will this be said to be the law of the land, by any lawyer who has a rag of a gown left upon his back, or a wig with one tie upon his head?"

That the power of electing and appointing the officers of this college is not only a right of the trustees as a corporation, generally, and in the aggregate, but that each individual trustee has also his own individual franchise in such right of election and appointment, is according to the language of all the authorities. Lord Holt says: "It is agreeable to reason and the rules of law, that a franchise should be vested in the corporation aggregate, and yet the benefit of it to redound to the particular members, and to be enjoyed by them in their private capacity. Where the privilege of election is used by particular persons, _it is a particular right, vested in every particular man_."[47]

It is also to be considered, that the president and professors of this college have rights to be affected by these acts. Their interest is similar to that of fellows in the English colleges; because they derive their living, wholly or in part, from the founders' bounty. The president is one of the trustees or corporators. The professors are not necessarily members of the corporation; but they are appointed by the trustees, are removable only by them, and have fixed salaries payable out of the general funds of the college. Both president and professors have freeholds in their offices; subject only to be removed by the trustees, as their legal visitors, for good cause. All the authorities speak of fellowships in colleges as freeholds, notwithstanding the fellows may be liable to be suspended or removed, for misbehavior, by their constituted visitors.

Nothing could have been less expected, in this age, than that there should have been an attempt, by acts of the legislature, to take away these college livings, the inadequate but the only support of literary men who have devoted their lives to the instruction of youth. The president and professors were appointed by the twelve trustees. They were accountable to nobody else, and could be removed by nobody else. They accepted their offices on this tenure. Yet the legislature has appointed other persons, with power to remove these officers and to deprive them of their livings; and those other persons have exercised that power. No description of private property has been regarded as more sacred than college livings. They are the estates and freeholds of a most deserving class of men; of scholars who have consented to forego the advantages of professional and public employments, and to devote themselves to science and literature and the instruction of youth in the quiet retreats of academic life. Whether to dispossess and oust them; to deprive them of their office, and to turn them out of their livings; to do this, not by the power of their legal visitors or governors, but by acts of the legislature, and to do it without forfeiture and without fault; whether all this be not in the highest degree an indefensible and arbitrary proceeding, is a question of which there would seem to be but one side fit for a lawyer or a scholar to espouse.

Of all the attempts of James the Second to overturn the law, and the rights of his subjects, none was esteemed more arbitrary or tyrannical than his attack on Magdalen College, Oxford; and yet that attempt was nothing but to put out one president and put in another. The president of that college, according to the charter and statutes, is to be chosen by the fellows, who are the corporators. There being a vacancy, the king chose to take the appointment out of the hands of the fellows, the legal electors of a president, into his own hands. He therefore sent down his mandate, commanding the fellows to admit for president a person of his nomination; and, inasmuch as this was directly against the charter and constitution of the college, he was pleased to add a *non obstante* clause of sufficiently comprehensive import. The fellows were commanded to admit the person mentioned in the mandate, "any statute, custom, or constitution to the contrary notwithstanding, wherewith we are graciously pleased to dispense, in this behalf." The fellows refused obedience to this mandate, and Dr. Hough, a man of independence and character, was chosen president by the fellows, according to the charter and statutes. The king then assumed the power, in virtue of his prerogative, to send down certain commissioners to turn him out; which was done accordingly; and Parker, a creature suited to the times, put in his place. Because the president, who was rightfully and legally elected, _would not deliver the keys, the doors were broken open_. "The nation as well as the university," says Bishop Burnet,[48] "looked on all these proceedings with just indignation. It was thought an open piece of robbery and burglary when men, authorized by no legal commission, came and forcibly turned men out of their possession and freehold." Mr. Hume, although a man of different temper, and of other sentiments, in some respects, than Dr. Burnet, speaks of this arbitrary attempt of prerogative in terms not less decisive. "The president, and all the fellows," says he, "except two, who complied, were expelled the college, and Parker was put in possession of the office. This act of violence, of all those which were committed during the reign of James, is perhaps the most illegal and arbitrary. When the dispensing power was the most strenuously insisted on by court lawyers, it had still been allowed that the statutes which regard private property could not legally be infringed by that prerogative. Yet, in this instance, it appeared that even these were not now secure from invasion. The privileges of a college are attacked; men are illegally dispossessed of their property for adhering to their duty, to their oaths, and to their religion."

This measure King James lived to repent, after repentance was too late. When the charter of London was restored, and other measures of violence were retracted, to avert the impending revolution, the expelled president and fellows of Magdalen College were permitted to resume their rights. It is evident that this was regarded as an arbitrary interference with private property. Yet private property was no otherwise attacked than as a person was appointed to administer and enjoy the revenues of a college in a manner and by persons not authorized by the constitution of the college. A majority of the members of the corporation would not comply with the king's wishes. A minority would. The object was therefore to make this minority a majority. To this end the king's commissioners were directed to interfere in the case, and they united with the two complying fellows, and expelled the rest; and thus effected a change in the government of the college. The language in which Mr. Hume and all other writers speak of this abortive attempt of oppression, shows that colleges were esteemed to be, as they truly are, private corporations, and the property and privileges which belong to them *private* property and *private* privileges. Court lawyers were found to justify the king in dispensing with the laws; that is, in assuming and exercising a legislative authority. But no lawyer, not even a court lawyer, in the reign of King James the Second, as far as appears, was found to say that, even by this high authority, he could infringe the franchises of the fellows of a college, and take away their livings. Mr. Hume gives the reason; it is, that such franchises were regarded, in a most emphatic sense, as *private property*.[49]

If it could be made to appear that the trustees and the president and professors held their offices and franchises during the pleasure of the legislature, and that the property holden belonged to the State, then indeed the legislature have done no more than they had a right to do. But this is not so. The charter is a charter of privileges and immunities; and these are holden by the trustees expressly against the State for ever.

It is admitted that the State, by its courts of law, can enforce the will of the donor, and compel a faithful execution of the trust. The plaintiffs claim no exemption from legal responsibility. They hold themselves at all times answerable to the law of the land, for their conduct in the trust committed to them. They ask only to hold the property of which they are owners, and the franchises which belong to them, until they shall be found, by due course and process of law, to have forfeited them.

It can make no difference whether the legislature exercise the power it has assumed by removing the trustees and the president and professors, directly and by name, or by appointing others to expel them. The principle is the same, and in point of fact the result has been the same. If the entire franchise cannot be taken away, neither can it be essentially impaired. If the trustees are legal owners of the property, they are sole owners. If they are visitors, they are sole visitors. No one will be found to say, that, if the legislature may do what it has done, it may not do any thing and every thing which it may choose to do, relative to the property of the corporation, and the privileges of its members and officers.

If the view which has been taken of this question be at all correct, this was an eleemosynary corporation, a private charity. The property was private property. The trustees were visitors, and the right to hold the charter, administer the funds, and visit and govern the college, was a franchise and privilege, solemnly granted to them. The use being public in no way diminishes their legal estate in the property, or their title to the franchise. There is no principle, nor any case, which declares that a gift to such a corporation is a gift to the public. The acts in question violate property. They take away privileges, immunities, and franchises. They deny to the trustees the protection of the law; and they are retrospective in their operation. In all which respects they are against the constitution of New Hampshire.

The plaintiffs contend, in the second place, that the acts in question are repugnant to the tenth section of the first article of the Constitution of the United States. The material words of that section are: "No State shall pass any bill of attainder, *ex post facto* law, or law impairing the obligation of contacts."

The object of these most important provisions in the national constitution has often been discussed, both here and elsewhere. It is exhibited with great clearness and force by one of the distinguished persons who framed that instrument. "Bills of attainder, *ex post facto* laws, and laws impairing the obligation of contracts, are contrary to the first principles of the social compact, and to every principle of sound legislation. The two former are expressly prohibited by the declarations prefixed to some of the State constitutions, and all of them are prohibited by the spirit and scope of these fundamental charters. Our own experience has taught us, nevertheless, that additional fences against these dangers ought not to be omitted. Very properly, therefore, have the convention added this constitutional bulwark, in favor of personal security and private rights; and I am much deceived, if they have not, in so doing, as faithfully consulted the genuine sentiments as the undoubted interests of their constituents. The sober people of America are weary of the fluctuating policy which has directed the public councils. They have seen with regret, and with indignation, that sudden changes, and legislative interferences in cases affecting personal rights, become jobs in the hands of enterprising and influential speculators, and snares to the more industrious and less informed part of the community. They have seen, too, that one legislative interference is but the link of a long chain of repetitions; every subsequent interference being naturally produced by the effects of the preceding."[50]

It has already been decided in this court, that a *grant* is a contract, within the meaning of this provision; and that a grant by a State is also a contract, as much as the grant of an individual. In the case of _Fletcher v. Peck_[51] this court says: "A contract is a compact between two or more parties, and is either executory or executed. An executory contract is one in which a party binds himself to do, or not to do, a particular thing; such was the law under which the conveyance was made by the government. A contract executed is one in which the object of contract is performed; and this, says Blackstone, differs in nothing from a grant. The contract between Georgia and the purchasers was executed by the grant. A contract executed, as well as one which is executory, contains obligations binding on the parties. A grant, in its own nature, amounts to an extinguishment of the right of the grantor, and implies a contract not to reassert that right. If, under a fair construction of the Constitution, grants are comprehended under the term contracts, is a grant from the State excluded from the operation of the provision? Is the clause to be considered as inhibiting the State from impairing the obligation of contracts between two individuals, but as excluding from that inhibition contracts made with itself? The words themselves contain no such distinction. They are general, and are applicable to contracts of every description. If contracts made with the State are to be exempted from their operation, the exception must arise from the character of the contracting party, not from the words which are employed. Whatever respect might have been felt for the State sovereignties, it is not to be disguised that the framers of the Constitution viewed with some apprehension the violent acts which might grow out of the feelings of the moment; and that the people of the United States, in adopting that instrument, have manifested a determination to shield themselves and their property from the effects of those sudden and strong passions to which men are exposed. The restrictions on the legislative power of the States are obviously founded in this sentiment; and the Constitution of the United States contains what may be deemed a bill of rights for the people of each State."

It has also been decided, that a grant by a State before the Revolution is as much to be protected as a grant since.[52] But the case of _Terrett v. Taylor_, before cited, is of all others most pertinent to the present argument. Indeed, the judgment of the court in that case seems to leave little to be argued or decided in this. "A private corporation," say the court, "created by the legislature, may lose its franchises by a *misuser* or a *nonuser* of them; and they may be resumed by the government under a judicial judgment upon a *quo warranto* to ascertain and enforce the forfeiture. This is the common law of the land, and is a tacit condition annexed to the creation of every such corporation. Upon a change of government, too, it may be admitted, that such exclusive privileges attached to a private corporation as are inconsistent with the new government may be abolished. In respect, also, to *public* corporations which exist only for public purposes, such as counties, towns, cities, and so forth, the legislature may, under proper limitations, have a right to change, modify, enlarge, or restrain them, securing, however, the property for the uses of those for whom and at whose expense it was originally purchased. But that the legislature can repeal statutes creating private corporations, or confirming to them property already acquired under the faith of previous laws, and by such repeal can vest the property of such corporations exclusively in the State, or dispose of the same to such purposes as they please, without the consent or default of the corporators, we are not prepared to admit; and we think ourselves standing upon the principles of natural justice, upon the fundamental laws of every free government, upon the spirit and letter of the Constitution of the United States, and upon the decisions of most respectable judicial tribunals, in resisting such a doctrine."

This court, then, does not admit the doctrine, that a legislature can repeal statutes creating private corporations. If it cannot repeal them altogether, of course it cannot repeal any part of them, or impair them, or essentially alter them, without the consent of the corporators. If, therefore, it has been shown that this college is to be regarded as a private charity, this case is embraced within the very terms of that decision. A grant of corporate powers and privileges is as much a contract as a grant of land. What proves all charters of this sort to be contracts is, that they must be accepted to give them force and effect. If they are not accepted, they are void. And in the case of an existing corporation, if a new charter is given it, it may even accept part and reject the rest. In _Rex v. Vice-Chancellor of Cambridge_,[53] Lord Mansfield says: "There is a vast deal of difference between a new charter granted to a new corporation, (who must take it as it is given,) and a new charter given to a corporation already in being, and acting either under a former charter or under prescriptive usage. The latter, a corporation already existing, are not obliged to accept the new charter _in toto_, and to receive either all or none of it; they may act partly under it, and partly under their old charter or prescription. The validity of these new charters must turn upon the acceptance of them." In the same case Mr. Justice Wilmot says: "It is the concurrence and acceptance of the university that gives the force to the charter of the crown." In the _King v. Pasmore_,[54] Lord Kenyon observes: "Some things are clear: when a corporation exists capable of discharging its functions, the crown cannot obtrude another charter upon them; they may either accept or reject it."[55]

In all cases relative to charters, the acceptance of them is uniformly alleged in the pleadings. This shows the general understanding of the law, that they are grants or contracts; and that parties are necessary to give them force and validity. In _King v. Dr. Askew_,[56] it is said: "The crown cannot oblige a man to be a corporator, without his consent; he shall not be subject to the inconveniences of it, without accepting it and assenting to it." These terms, "acceptance" and "assent," are the very language of contract. In _Ellis v. Marshall_,[57] it was expressly adjudged that the naming of the defendant among others, in an act of incorporation, did not of itself make him a corporator; and that his assent was necessary to that end. The court speak of the act of incorporation as a grant, and observe: "That a man may refuse a grant, whether from the government or an individual, seems to be a principle too clear to require the support of authorities." But Justice Buller, in _King v. Pasmore_, furnishes, if possible, a still more direct and explicit authority. Speaking of a corporation for government, he says: "I do not know how to reason on this point better than in the manner urged by one of the relator's counsel; who considered the grant of incorporation to be a compact between the crown and a certain number of the subjects, the latter of whom undertake, in consideration of the privileges which are bestowed, to exert themselves for the good government of the place." This language applies with peculiar propriety and force to the case before the court. It was in consequence of the "privileges bestowed," that Dr. Wheelock and his associates undertook to exert themselves for the instruction and education of youth in this college; and it was on the same consideration that the founder endowed it with his property.

And because charters of incorporation are of the nature of contracts, they cannot be altered or varied but by consent of the original parties. If a charter be granted by the king, it may be altered by a new charter granted by the king, and accepted by the corporators. But if the first charter be granted by Parliament, the consent of Parliament must be obtained to any alteration. In _King v. Miller_,[58] Lord Kenyon says: "Where a corporation takes its rise from the king's charter, the king by granting, and the corporation by accepting another charter, may alter it, because it is done with the consent of all the parties who are competent to consent to the alteration."[59]

There are, in this case, all the essential constituent parts of a contract. There is something to be contracted about, there are parties, and there are plain terms in which the agreement of the parties on the subject of the contract is expressed. There are mutual considerations and inducements. The charter recites, that the founder, on his part, has agreed to establish his seminary in New Hampshire, and to enlarge it beyond its original design, among other things, for the benefit of that Province; and thereupon a charter is given to him and his associates, designated by himself, promising and assuring to them, under the plighted faith of the State, the right of governing the college and administering its concerns in the manner provided in the charter. There is a complete and perfect grant to them of all the power of superintendence, visitation, and government. Is not this a contract? If lands or money had been granted to him and his associates, for the same purposes, such grant could not be rescinded. And is there any difference, in legal contemplation, between a grant of corporate franchises and a grant of tangible property? No such difference is recognized in any decided case, nor does it exist in the common apprehension of mankind.

It is therefore contended, that this case falls within the true meaning of this provision of the Constitution, as expounded in the decisions of this court; that the charter of 1769 is a contract, a stipulation or agreement, mutual in its considerations, express and formal in its terms, and of a most binding and solemn nature. That the acts in question impair this contract, has already been sufficiently shown. They repeal and abrogate its most essential parts.

A single observation may not be improper on the opinion of the court of New Hampshire, which has been published. The learned judges who delivered that opinion have viewed this question in a very different light from that in which the plaintiffs have endeavored to exhibit it. After some general remarks, they assume that this college is a public corporation; and on this basis their judgment rests. Whether all colleges are not regarded as private and eleemosynary corporations, by all law writers and all judicial decisions; whether this college was not founded by Dr. Wheelock; whether the charter was not granted at his request, the better to execute a trust, which he had already created; whether he and his associates did not become visitors, by the charter; and whether Dartmouth College be not, therefore, in the strictest sense, a private charity, are questions which the learned judges do not appear to have discussed.

It is admitted in that opinion, that, if it be a private corporation, its rights stand on the same ground as those of an individual. The great question, therefore, to be decided is, To which class of corporations do colleges thus founded belong? And the plaintiffs have endeavored to satisfy the court, that, according to the well-settled principles and uniform decisions of law, they are private, eleemosynary corporations.

Much has heretofore been said on the necessity of admitting such a power in the legislature as has been assumed in this case. Many cases of possible evil have been imagined, which might otherwise be without remedy. Abuses, it is contended, might arise in the management of such institutions, which the ordinary courts of law would be unable to correct. But this is only another instance of that habit of supposing extreme cases, and then of reasoning from them, which is the constant refuge of those who are obliged to defend a cause, which, upon its merits, is indefensible. It would be sufficient to say in answer, that it is not pretended that there was here any such case of necessity. But a still more satisfactory answer is, that the apprehension of danger is groundless, and therefore the whole argument fails. Experience has not taught us that there is danger of great evils or of great inconvenience from this source. Hitherto, neither in our own country nor elsewhere have such cases of necessity occurred. The judicial establishments of the State are presumed to be competent to prevent abuses and violations of trust, in cases of this kind, as well as in all others. If they be not, they are imperfect, and their amendment would be a most proper subject for legislative wisdom. Under the government and protection of the general laws of the land, these institutions have always been found safe, as well as useful. They go on, with the progress of society, accommodating themselves easily, without sudden change or violence, to the alterations which take place in its condition, and in the knowledge, the habits, and pursuits of men. The English colleges were founded in Catholic ages. Their religion was reformed with the general reformation of the nation; and they are suited perfectly well to the purpose of educating the Protestant youth of modern times. Dartmouth College was established under a charter granted by the Provincial government; but a better constitution for a college, or one more adapted to the condition of things under the present government, in all material respects, could not now be framed. Nothing in it was found to need alteration at the Revolution. The wise men of that day saw in it one of the best hopes of future times, and commended it as it was, with parental care, to the protection and guardianship of the government of the State. A charter of more liberal sentiments, of wiser provisions, drawn with more care, or in a better spirit, could not be expected at any time or from any source. The college needed no change in its organization or government. That which it did need was the kindness, the patronage, the bounty of the legislature; not a mock elevation to the character of a university, without the solid benefit of a shilling's donation to sustain the character; not the swelling and empty authority of establishing institutes and other colleges. This unsubstantial pageantry would seem to have been in derision of the scanty endowment and limited means of an unobtrusive, but useful and growing seminary. Least of all was there a necessity, or pretence of necessity, to infringe its legal rights, violate its franchises and privileges, and pour upon it these overwhelming streams of litigation.

But this argument from necessity would equally apply in all other cases. If it be well founded, it would prove, that, whenever any inconvenience or evil is experienced from the restrictions imposed on the legislature by the Constitution, these restrictions ought to be disregarded. It is enough to say, that the people have thought otherwise. They have, most wisely, chosen to take the risk of occasional inconvenience from the want of power, in order that there might be a settled limit to its exercise, and a permanent security against its abuse. They have imposed prohibitions and restraints; and they have not rendered these altogether vain and nugatory by conferring the power of dispensation. If inconvenience should arise which the legislature cannot remedy under the power conferred upon it, it is not answerable for such inconvenience. That which it cannot do within the limits prescribed to it, it cannot do at all. No legislature in this country is able, and may the time never come when it shall be able, to apply to itself the memorable expression of a Roman pontiff: "Licet hoc *de jure* non possumus, volumus tamen *de plenitudine potestatis*."

The case before the court is not of ordinary importance, nor of every-day occurrence. It affects not this college only, but every college, and all the literary institutions of the country. They have nourished hitherto, and have become in a high degree respectable and useful to the community. They have all a common principle of existence, the inviolability of their charters. It will be a dangerous, a most dangerous experiment, to hold these institutions subject to the rise and fall of popular parties, and the fluctuations of political opinions. If the franchise may be at any time taken away, or impaired, the property also may be taken away, or its use perverted. Benefactors will have no certainty of effecting the object of their bounty; and learned men will be deterred from devoting themselves to the service of such institutions, from the precarious title of their offices. Colleges and halls will be deserted by all better spirits, and become a theatre for the contentions of politics. Party and faction will be cherished in the places consecrated to piety and learning. These consequences are neither remote nor possible only. They are certain and immediate.

When the court in North Carolina declared the law of the State, which repealed a grant to its university, unconstitutional and void, the legislature had the candor and the wisdom to repeal the law. This example, so honorable to the State which exhibited it, is most fit to be followed on this occasion. And there is good reason to hope that a State, which has hitherto been so much distinguished for temperate counsels, cautious legislation, and regard to law, will not fail to adopt a course which will accord with her highest and best interests, and in no small degree elevate her reputation.

It was for many and obvious reasons most anxiously desired that the question of the power of the legislature over this charter should have been finally decided in the State court. An earnest hope was entertained that the judges of the court might have viewed the case in a light favorable to the rights of the trustees. That hope has failed. It is here that those rights are now to be maintained, or they are prostrated for ever. "Omnia alia perfugia bonorum, subsidia, consilia, auxilia, jura ceciderunt. Quem enim alium appellem? quem obtester? quem implorem? Nisi hoc loco, nisi apud vos, nisi per vos, judices, salutem nostram, quae spe exigua extremaque pendet, tenuerimus; nihil est praeterea quo confugere possimus."

[Footnote 1: Calder et ux. v. Bull, 3 Dallas, 386.][Footnote 2: Annual Register, 1784, p. 160; Parl. Reg. 1783; Mr. Burke's Speech on Mr. Fox's East India Bill, Burke's Works, Vol. II. pp. 414, 417, 467, 468, 486.][Footnote 3: 1 Black. 472, 473.][Footnote 4: 3 Burr. 1656.][Footnote 5: King v. Pasmore, 3 Term Rep. 244.][Footnote 6: King v. Vice-Chancellor of Cambridge, 3 Burr. 1656; 3 Term Rep. 240,--Lord Kenyon.][Footnote 7: 3 Burr. 1661, and King v. Pasmore, *ubi supra*.][Footnote 8: Ellis v. Marshall, 2 Mass. Rep. 277; 1 Kyd on Corporations, 65, 66.] [Footnote 9: 1 Wooddeson, 474; 1 Black. 467.][Footnote 10: 1 Black. 471.][Footnote 11: Ves. 537.][Footnote 12: 9 Ves. Jun. 405.][Footnote 13: 1 Wood. 474.][Footnote 14: 1 Black. 471.][Footnote 15: 2 Term Rep. 350, 351.][Footnote 16: 1 Black. 480.][Footnote 17: 1 Lord Raymond, 5; Comb. 265; Holt, 715; 1 Shower. 360; 4 Mod. 106; Skinn. 447.][Footnote 18: 1 Lord Raymond, 9.][Footnote 19: 1 Burn's Eccles. Law, 443, Appendix No. 3][Footnote 20: 2 Forb. 205, 206.][Footnote 21: Green v. Rutherforth, 1 Ves. 472, per Lord Hardwicke.][Footnote 22: Attorney-General v. Foundling Hospital, 2 Ves. Jun. 47. See also 2 Kyd on Corporations, 195; Cooper's Equity Pleading, 292.][Footnote 23: St. John's College, Cambridge, v. Todington, 1 Burr. 200.][Footnote 24: Attorney-General v. Middleton, 2 Ves. 328.][Footnote 25: Green v. Rutherforth, _ubi supra_; St. John's College v. Todington, *ubi supra*.][Footnote 26: 4 Term Rep. 233.][Footnote 27: Black., *ubi supra*.][Footnote 28: 2 Black. Com. 37.][Footnote 29: Sull. 41st Lect.][Footnote 30: Phillips v. Bury, and Green v. Rutherforth, *ubi supra*. See also 2 Black. 21.][Footnote 31: Ashby v. White, 2 Lord Raymond, 938.][Footnote 32: Attorney-General v. Pearce, 2 Atk. 87.][Footnote 33: 2 Haywood's Rep.][Footnote 34: 9 Cranch, 43.][Footnote 35: 9 Cranch. 292.][Footnote 36: 3 Dallas, 394.][Footnote 37: Society v. Wheeler, 2 Gal. 103.][Footnote 38: 7 Johnson's Rep. 477.][Footnote 39: Bracton, Lib. 4, fol. 228. 2 Inst. 292.][Footnote 40: Dig. 50. 17. 75.][Footnote 41: Elements of the Civil Law, p. 168.][Footnote 42: Cod. 1. 14. 7.][Footnote 43: Perezii Praelect. h. t.][Footnote 44: Praelect. Juris. Civ., Vol. II. p. 545.][Footnote 45: 1 Black. Com. 44.][Footnote 46: Coke, 2 Inst. 46.][Footnote 47: Lord Raymond, 952.][Footnote 48: History of his own Times, Vol. III. p. 119.][Footnote 49: See a full account of this case in State Trials, 4th ed., Vol. IV. p. 262.][Footnote 50: The Federalist, No. 44, by Mr. Madison.][Footnote 51: 6 Cranch, 87.][Footnote 52: New Jersey v. Wilson, 7 Cranch, 164.][Footnote 53: 3 Burr. 1656.][Footnote 54: 3 Term Rep. 240.][Footnote 55: See also 1 Kyd on Corp. 65.][Footnote 56: 4 Burr. 2200.][Footnote 57: 2 Mass. Rep. 269.][Footnote 58: 6 Term Rep. 277.][Footnote 59: See also Ex parte Bolton School, 2 Brown's Ch. Rep. 662.]

FIRST SETTLEMENT OF NEW ENGLAND.
A DISCOURSE DELIVERED AT PLYMOUTH, ON THE 22D OF DECEMBER, 1820.

[The first public anniversary celebration of the landing of the Pilgrims at Plymouth took place under the auspices of the "Old Colony Club," of whose formation an account may be found in the interesting little work of William S. Russell, Esq., entitled "Guide to Plymouth and Recollections of the Pilgrims."
This club was formed for general purposes of social intercourse, in 1769; but its members determined, by a vote passed on Monday, the 18th of December, of that year, "to keep" Friday, the 22d, in commemoration of the landing of the fathers. A particular account of the simple festivities of this first public celebration of the landing of the Pilgrims will be found at page 220 of Mr. Russell's work.
The following year, the anniversary was celebrated much in the same manner as in 1769, with the addition of a short address, pronounced "with modest and decent firmness, by a member of the club, Edward Winslow, Jr., Esq.," being the first address ever delivered on this occasion.
In 1771, it was suggested by Rev. Chandler Robbins, pastor of the First Church at Plymouth, in a letter addressed to the club, "whether it would not be agreeable, for the entertainment and instruction of the

rising generation on these anniversaries, to have a sermon in public, some part of the day, peculiarly adapted to the occasion." This recommendation prevailed, and an appropriate discourse was delivered the following year by the Rev. Dr. Robbins.

In 1773 the Old Colony Club was dissolved, in consequence of the conflicting opinions of its members on the great political questions then agitated. Notwithstanding this event, the anniversary celebrations of the 22d of December continued without interruption till 1780, when they were suspended. After an interval of fourteen years, a public discourse was again delivered by the Rev. Dr. Robbins. Private celebrations took place the four following years, and from that time till the year 1819, with one or two exceptions, the day was annually commemorated, and public addresses were delivered by distinguished clergymen and laymen of Massachusetts.

In 1820 the "Pilgrim Society" was formed by the citizens of Plymouth and the descendants of the Pilgrims in other places, desirous of uniting "to commemorate the landing, and to honor the memory of the intrepid men who first set foot on Plymouth rock." The foundation of this society gave a new impulse to the anniversary celebrations of this great event. The Hon. Daniel Webster was requested to deliver the public address on the 22d of December of that year, and the following discourse was pronounced by him on the ever-memorable occasion. Great public expectation was awakened by the fame of the orator; an immense concourse assembled at Plymouth to unite in the celebration; and it may be safely anticipated, that some portion of the powerful effect of the following address on the minds of those who were so fortunate as to hear it, will be perpetuated by the press to the latest posterity.

From 1820 to the present day, with occasional interruptions, the 22d of December has been celebrated by the Pilgrim Society. A list of all those by whom anniversary discourses have been delivered since the first organization of the Old Colony Club, in 1769, may be found in Mr. Russell's work.

Nor has the notice of the day been confined to New England. Public celebrations of the landing of the Pilgrims have been frequent in other parts of the country, particularly in New York. The New England Society of that city has rarely permitted the day to pass without appropriate honors. Similar societies have been formed at Philadelphia, Charleston, S.C., and Cincinnati, and the day has been publicly commemorated in several other parts of the country.]

Let us rejoice that we behold this day. Let us be thankful that we have lived to see the bright and happy breaking of the auspicious morn, which commences the third century of the history of New England. Auspicious, indeed,--bringing a happiness beyond the common allotment of Providence to men,--full of present joy, and gilding with bright beams the prospect of futurity, is the dawn that awakens us to the commemoration of the landing of the Pilgrims.

Living at an epoch which naturally marks the progress of the history of our native land, we have come hither to celebrate the great event with which that history commenced. For ever honored be this, the place of our fathers' refuge! For ever remembered the day which saw them, weary and distressed, broken in every thing but spirit, poor in all but faith and courage, at last secure from the dangers of wintry seas, and impressing this shore with the first footsteps of civilized man!

It is a noble faculty of our nature which enables us to connect our thoughts, our sympathies, and our happiness with what is distant in place or time; and, looking before and after, to hold communion at once with our ancestors and our posterity. Human and mortal although we are, we are nevertheless not mere insulated beings, without relation to the past or the future. Neither the point of time, nor the spot of earth, in which we physically live, bounds our rational and intellectual enjoyments. We live in the past by a knowledge of its history; and in the future, by hope and anticipation. By ascending to an association with our ancestors; by contemplating their example and studying their character; by partaking their sentiments, and imbibing their spirit; by accompanying them in their toils, by sympathizing in their sufferings, and rejoicing in their successes and their triumphs; we seem to belong to their age, and to mingle our own existence with theirs. We become their contemporaries, live the lives which they lived, endure what they endured, and partake in the rewards which they enjoyed. And in like manner, by running along the line of future time, by contemplating the probable fortunes of those who are coming after us, by attempting something which may promote their happiness, and leave some not dishonorable memorial of ourselves for their regard, when we shall sleep with the fathers, we protract our own earthly being, and seem to crowd whatever is future, as well as all that is past, into the narrow compass of our earthly existence. As it is not a vain and false, but an exalted and religious imagination, which leads us to raise our thoughts from the orb, which, amidst this universe of worlds, the Creator has given us to inhabit, and to send them with something of the feeling which nature prompts, and teaches to be proper among children of the same Eternal Parent, to the contemplation of the myriads of fellow-beings with which his goodness has peopled the infinite of space; so neither is it false or vain to consider ourselves as interested and connected with our whole race, through all time; allied to our ancestors; allied to our posterity; closely compacted on all sides with others; ourselves being but links in the great chain of being, which begins with the origin of our race, runs onward through its successive generations, binding together the past, the present, and the future, and terminating at last, with the consummation of all things earthly, at the throne of God.

There may be, and there often is, indeed, a regard for ancestry, which nourishes only a weak pride; as there is also a care for posterity, which only disguises an habitual avarice, or hides the workings of a low and grovelling vanity. But there is also a moral and philosophical respect for our ancestors, which elevates the character and improves the heart. Next to the sense of religious duty and moral feeling, I hardly know what should bear with stronger obligation on a liberal and enlightened mind, than a consciousness of alliance with excellence which is departed; and a consciousness, too, that in its acts and conduct, and even in its sentiments and thoughts, it may be actively operating on the happiness of those who come after it. Poetry is found to have few stronger conceptions, by which it would affect or overwhelm the mind, than those in which it presents the moving and speaking image of the departed dead to the senses of the living. This belongs to poetry, only because it is congenial to our nature. Poetry is, in this respect, but the handmaid of true philosophy and morality; it deals with us as human beings, naturally reverencing those whose visible connection with this state of existence is severed, and who may yet exercise we know not what sympathy with ourselves; and when it carries us forward, also, and shows us the long continued result of all the good we do, in the prosperity of those who follow us, till it bears us from ourselves, and absorbs us in an intense interest for what shall happen to the generations after us, it speaks only in the language of our nature, and affects us with sentiments which belong to us as human beings.

Standing in this relation to our ancestors and our posterity, we are assembled on this memorable spot, to perform the duties which that relation and the present occasion impose upon us. We have come to this Rock, to record here our homage for our Pilgrim Fathers; our sympathy in their sufferings; our gratitude for their labors; our admiration of their virtues; our veneration for their piety; and our attachment to those principles of civil and religious liberty, which they encountered the dangers of the ocean, the storms of heaven, the violence of savages, disease, exile, and famine, to enjoy and to establish. And we would leave here, also, for the generations which are rising up rapidly to fill our places, some proof that we have endeavored to transmit the great inheritance unimpaired; that in our estimate of public principles and private virtue, in our veneration of religion and piety, in our devotion to civil and religious liberty, in our regard for whatever advances human knowledge or improves human happiness, we are not altogether unworthy of our origin.

There is a local feeling connected with this occasion, too strong to be resisted; a sort of _genius of the place_, which inspires and awes us. We feel that we are on the spot where the first scene of our history was laid; where the hearths and altars of New England were first placed; where Christianity, and civilization, and letters made their first lodgement, in a vast extent of country, covered with a wilderness, and peopled by roving barbarians. We are here, at the season of the year at which the event took place. The imagination irresistibly and rapidly draws around us the principal features and the leading characters in the original scene. We cast our eyes abroad on the ocean, and we see where the little bark, with the interesting group upon its deck, made its slow progress to the shore. We look around us, and behold the hills and promontories where the anxious eyes of our fathers first saw the places of habitation and of rest. We feel the cold which benumbed, and listen to the winds which pierced them. Beneath us is the Rock,[1] on which New England received the feet of the Pilgrims. We seem even to behold them, as they struggle with the elements, and, with toilsome efforts, gain the shore. We listen to the chiefs in council; we see the unexampled exhibition of female fortitude and resignation; we hear the whisperings of youthful impatience, and we see, what a painter of our own has also represented by his pencil,[2] chilled and shivering childhood, houseless, but for a mother's arms, couchless, but for a mother's breast, till our own blood almost freezes. The mild dignity of Carver and of Bradford; the decisive and soldier-like air and manner of Standish; the devout Brewster; the enterprising Allerton;[3] the general firmness and thoughtfulness of the whole band; their conscious joy for dangers escaped; their deep solicitude about dangers to come; their trust in Heaven; their high religious faith, full of confidence and anticipation; all of these seem to belong to this place, and to be present upon this occasion, to fill us with reverence and admiration.

The settlement of New England by the colony which landed here[4] on the twenty-second[5] of December, sixteen hundred and twenty, although not the first European establishment in what now constitutes the United States, was yet so peculiar in its causes and character, and has been followed and must still be followed by such consequences, as to give it a high claim to lasting commemoration. On these causes and consequences, more than on its immediately attendant circumstances, its importance, as an historical event, depends. Great actions and striking occurrences, having excited a temporary admiration, often pass away and are forgotten, because they leave no lasting results, affecting the prosperity and happiness of communities. Such is frequently the fortune of the most brilliant military achievements. Of the ten thousand battles which have been fought, of all the fields fertilized with carnage, of the banners which have been bathed in blood, of the warriors who have hoped that they had risen from the field of conquest to a glory as bright and as durable as the stars, how few that continue long to interest mankind! The victory of yesterday is reversed by the defeat of to-day; the star of military glory, rising like a meteor, like a meteor has fallen; disgrace and disaster hang on the heels of conquest and renown; victor and vanquished presently pass away to oblivion, and the world goes on in its course, with the loss only of so many lives and so much treasure.

But if this be frequently, or generally, the fortune of military achievements, it is not always so. There are enterprises, military as well as civil, which sometimes check the current of events, give a new turn to human affairs, and transmit their consequences through ages. We see their importance in their results, and call them great, because great things follow. There have been battles which have fixed the fate of nations. These come down to us in history with a solid and permanent interest, not created by a display of glittering armor, the rush of adverse battalions, the sinking and rising of pennons, the flight, the pursuit, and the victory; but by their effect in advancing or retarding human knowledge, in overthrowing or establishing despotism, in extending or destroying human happiness. When the traveller pauses on the plain of Marathon, what are the emotions which most strongly agitate his breast? What is that glorious recollection, which thrills through his frame, and suffuses his eyes? Not, I imagine, that Grecian skill and Grecian valor were here most signally displayed; but that Greece herself was saved. It is because to this spot, and to the event which has rendered it immortal, he refers all the succeeding glories of the republic. It is because, if that day had gone otherwise, Greece had perished. It is because he perceives that her philosophers and orators, her poets and painters, her sculptors and architects, her governments and free institutions, point backward to Marathon, and that their future existence seems to have been suspended on the contingency, whether the Persian or the Grecian banner should wave victorious in the beams of that day's setting sun. And, as his imagination kindles at the retrospect, he is transported back to the interesting moment; he counts the fearful odds of the contending hosts; his interest for the result overwhelms him; he trembles, as if it were still uncertain, and seems to doubt whether he may consider Socrates and Plato, Demosthenes, Sophocles, and Phidias, as secure, yet, to himself and to the world.

"If we conquer," said the Athenian commander on the approach of that decisive day, "if we conquer, we shall make Athens the greatest city of Greece."[6] A prophecy how well fulfilled! "If God prosper us," might have been the more appropriate language of our fathers, when they landed upon this Rock, "if God prosper us, we shall here begin a work which shall last for ages; we shall plant here a new society, in the principles of the fullest liberty and the purest religion; we shall subdue this wilderness which is before us; we shall fill this region of the great continent, which stretches almost from pole to pole, with civilization and Christianity; the temples of the true God shall rise, where now ascends the smoke of idolatrous sacrifice; fields and gardens, the flowers of summer, and the waving and golden harvest of autumn, shall spread over a thousand hills, and stretch along a thousand valleys, never yet, since the creation, reclaimed to the use of civilized man. We shall whiten this coast with the canvas of a prosperous commerce; we shall stud the long and winding shore with a hundred cities. That which we sow in weakness shall be raised in strength. From our sincere, but houseless worship, there shall spring splendid temples to record God's goodness; from the simplicity of our social union, there shall arise wise and politic constitutions of government, full of the liberty which we ourselves bring and breathe; from our zeal for learning, institutions shall spring which shall scatter the light of knowledge throughout the land, and, in time, paying back where they have borrowed, shall contribute their part to the great aggregate of human knowledge; and our descendants, through all generations, shall look back to this spot, and to this hour, with unabated affection and regard."

A brief remembrance of the causes which led to the settlement of this place; some account of the peculiarities and characteristic qualities of that settlement, as distinguished from other instances of colonization; a short notice of the progress of New England in the great interests of society, during the century which is now elapsed; with a few observations on the principles upon which society and government are established in this country; comprise all that can be attempted, and much more than can be satisfactorily performed, on the present occasion.

Of the motives which influenced the first settlers to a voluntary exile, induced them to relinquish their native country, and to seek an asylum in this then unexplored wilderness, the first and principal, no doubt, were connected with religion. They sought to enjoy a higher degree of religious freedom, and what they esteemed a purer form of religious worship, than was allowed to their choice, or presented to their imitation, in the Old World. The love of religious liberty is a stronger sentiment, when fully excited, than an attachment to civil or political freedom. That freedom which the conscience demands, and which men feel bound by their hope of salvation to contend for, can hardly fail to be attained. Conscience, in the cause of religion and the worship of the Deity, prepares the mind to act and to suffer beyond almost all other causes. It sometimes gives an impulse so irresistible, that no fetters of power or of opinion can withstand it. History instructs us that this love of religious liberty, a compound sentiment in the breast of man, made up of the clearest sense of right and the highest conviction of duty, is able to look the sternest despotism in the face, and, with means apparently most inadequate, to shake principalities and powers. There is a boldness, a spirit of daring, in religious reformers, not to be measured by the general rules which control men's purposes and actions. If the hand of power be laid upon it, this only seems to augment its force and its elasticity, and to cause its action to be more formidable and violent. Human invention has devised nothing, human power has compassed nothing, that can forcibly restrain it, when it breaks forth. Nothing can stop it, but to give way to it; nothing can check it, but indulgence. It loses its power only when it has gained its object. The principle of toleration, to which the world has come so slowly, is at once the most just and the most wise of all principles. Even when religious feeling takes a character of extravagance and enthusiasm, and seems to threaten the order of society and shake the columns of the social edifice, its principal danger is in its restraint. If it be allowed indulgence and expansion, like the elemental fires, it only agitates, and perhaps purifies, the atmosphere; while its efforts to throw off restraint would burst the world asunder.

It is certain, that, although many of them were republicans in principle, we have no evidence that our New England ancestors would have emigrated, as they did, from their own native country, would have become wanderers in Europe, and finally would have undertaken the establishment of a colony here, merely from their dislike of the political systems of Europe. They fled not so much from the civil government, as from the hierarchy, and the laws which enforced conformity to the church establishment. Mr. Robinson had left England as early as 1608, on account of the persecutions for non-conformity, and had retired to Holland. He left England from no disappointed ambition in affairs of state, from no regrets at the want of preferment in the church, nor from any motive of distinction or of gain. Uniformity in matters of religion was pressed with such extreme rigor, that a voluntary exile seemed the most eligible mode of escaping from the penalties of non-compliance. The accession of Elizabeth had, it is true, quenched the fires of Smithfield, and put an end to the easy acquisition of the crown of martyrdom. Her long reign had established the Reformation, but toleration was a virtue beyond her conception, and beyond the age. She left no example of it to her successor; and he was not of a character which rendered a sentiment either so wise or so liberal would originate with him. At the present period it seems incredible that the learned, accomplished, unassuming, and inoffensive Robinson should neither be tolerated in his peaceable mode of worship in his own country, nor suffered quietly to depart from it. Yet such was the fact. He left his country by stealth, that he might elsewhere enjoy those rights which ought to belong to men in all countries. The departure of the Pilgrims for Holland is deeply interesting, from its circumstances, and also as it marks the character of the times, independently of its connection with names now incorporated with the history of empire. The embarkation was intended to be made in such a manner that it might escape the notice of the officers of government. Great pains had been taken to secure boats, which should come undiscovered to the shore, and receive the fugitives; and frequent disappointments had been experienced in this respect.

At length the appointed time came, bringing with it unusual severity of cold and rain. An unfrequented and barren heath, on the shores of Lincolnshire, was the selected spot, where the feet of the Pilgrims were to tread, for the last time, the land of their fathers. The vessel which was to receive them did not come until the next day, and in the mean time the little band was collected, and men and women and children and baggage were crowded together, in melancholy and distressed confusion. The sea was rough, and the women and children were already sick, from their passage down the river to the place of embarkation on the sea. At length the wished-for boat silently and fearfully approaches the shore, and men and women and children, shaking with fear and with cold, as many as the small vessel could bear, venture off on a dangerous sea. Immediately the advance of horses is heard from behind, armed men appear, and those not yet embarked are seized and taken into custody. In the hurry of the moment, the first parties had been sent on board without any attempt to keep members of the same family together, and on account of the appearance of the horsemen, the boat never returned for the residue. Those who had got away, and those who had not, were in equal distress. A storm, of great violence and long duration, arose at sea, which not only protracted the voyage, rendered distressing by the want of all those accommodations which the interruption of the embarkation had occasioned, but also forced the vessel out of her course, and menaced immediate shipwreck; while those on shore, when they were dismissed from the custody of the officers of justice, having no longer homes or houses to retire to, and their friends and protectors being already gone, became objects of necessary charity, as well as of deep commiseration.

As this scene passes before us, we can hardly forbear asking whether this be a band of malefactors and felons flying from justice. What are their crimes, that they hide themselves in darkness? To what punishment are they exposed, that, to avoid it, men, and women, and children, thus encounter the surf of the North Sea and the terrors of a night storm? What induces this armed pursuit, and this arrest of fugitives, of all ages and both sexes? Truth does not allow us to answer these inquiries in a manner that does credit to the wisdom or the justice of the times. This was not the flight of guilt, but of virtue. It was an humble and peaceable religion, flying from causeless oppression. It was conscience, attempting to escape from the arbitrary rule of the Stuarts. It was Robinson and Brewster, leading off their little band from their native soil, at first to find shelter on the shore of the neighboring continent, but ultimately to come hither; and having surmounted all difficulties and braved a thousand dangers, to find here a place of refuge and of rest. Thanks be to God, that this spot was honored as the asylum of religious liberty! May its standard, reared here, remain for ever! May it rise up as high as heaven, till its banner shall fan the air of both continents, and wave as a glorious ensign of peace and security to the nations!

The peculiar character, condition, and circumstances of the colonies which introduced civilization and an English race into New England, afford a most interesting and extensive topic of discussion. On these, much of our subsequent character and fortune has depended. Their influence has essentially affected our whole history, through the two centuries which have elapsed; and as they have become intimately connected with government, laws, and property, as well as with our opinions on the subjects of religion and civil liberty, that influence is likely to continue to be felt through the centuries which shall succeed. Emigration from one region to another, and the emission of colonies to people countries more or less distant from the residence of the parent stock, are common incidents in the history of mankind; but it has not often, perhaps never, happened, that the establishment of colonies should be attempted under circumstances, however beset with present difficulties and dangers, yet so favorable to ultimate success, and so conducive to magnificent results, as those which attended the first settlements on this part of the American continent. In other instances, emigration has proceeded from a less exalted purpose, in periods of less general intelligence, or more without plan and by accident; or under circumstances, physical and moral, less favorable to the expectation of laying a foundation for great public prosperity and future empire.

A great resemblance exists, obviously, between all the English colonies established within the present limits of the United States; but the occasion attracts our attention more immediately to those which took possession of New England, and the peculiarities of these furnish a strong contrast with most other instances of colonization.

Among the ancient nations, the Greeks, no doubt, sent forth from their territories the greatest number of colonies. So numerous, indeed, were they, and so great the extent of space over which they were spread, that the parent country fondly and naturally persuaded herself, that by means of them she had laid a sure foundation for the universal civilization of the world. These establishments, from obvious causes, were most numerous in places most contiguous; yet they were found on the coasts of France, on the shores of the Euxine Sea, in Africa, and even, as is alleged, on the borders of India. These emigrations appear to have been sometimes voluntary and sometimes compulsory; arising from the spontaneous enterprise of individuals, or the order and regulation of government. It was a common opinion with ancient writers, that they were undertaken in religious obedience to the commands of oracles, and it is probable that impressions of this sort might have had more or less influence; but it is probable, also, that on these occasions the oracles did not speak a language dissonant from the views and purposes of the state. Political science among the Greeks seems never to have extended to the comprehension of a system, which should be adequate to the government of a great nation upon principles of liberty. They were accustomed only to the contemplation of small republics, and were led to consider an augmented population as incompatible with free institutions. The desire of a remedy for this supposed evil, and the wish to establish marts for trade, led the governments often to undertake the establishment of colonies as an affair of state expediency. Colonization and commerce, indeed, would naturally become objects of interest to an ingenious and enterprising people, inhabiting a territory closely circumscribed in its limits, and in no small part mountainous and sterile; while the islands of the adjacent seas, and the promontories and coasts of the neighboring continents, by their mere proximity, strongly solicited the excited spirit of emigration. Such was this proximity, in many instances, that the new settlements appeared rather to be the mere extension of population over contiguous territory, than the establishment of distant colonies. In proportion as they were near to the parent state, they would be under its authority, and partake of its fortunes. The colony at Marseilles might perceive lightly, or not at all, the sway of Phocis; while the islands in the Aegean Sea could hardly attain to independence of their Athenian origin. Many of these establishments took place at an early age; and if there were defects in the governments of the parent states, the colonists did not possess philosophy or experience sufficient to correct such evils in their own institutions, even if they had not been, by other causes, deprived of the power. An immediate necessity, connected with the support of life, was the main and direct inducement to these undertakings, and there could hardly exist more than the hope of a successful imitation of institutions with which they were already acquainted, and of holding an equality with their neighbors in the course of improvement. The laws and customs, both political and municipal, as well as the religious worship of the parent city, were transferred to the colony; and the parent city herself, with all such of her colonies as were not too far remote for frequent intercourse and common sentiments, would appear like a family of cities, more or less dependent, and more or less connected. We know how imperfect this system was, as a system of general politics, and what scope it gave to those mutual dissensions and conflicts which proved so fatal to Greece.

But it is more pertinent to our present purpose to observe, that nothing existed in the character of Grecian emigrations, or in the spirit and intelligence of the emigrants, likely to give a new and important direction to human affairs, or a new impulse to the human mind. Their motives were not high enough, their views were not sufficiently large and prospective. They went not forth, like our ancestors, to erect systems of more perfect civil liberty, or to enjoy a higher degree of religious freedom. Above all, there was nothing in the religion and learning of the age, that could either inspire high purposes, or give the ability to execute them. Whatever restraints on civil liberty, or whatever abuses in religious worship, existed at the time of our fathers' emigration, yet even then all was light in the moral and mental world, in comparison with its condition in most periods of the ancient states. The settlement of a new continent, in an age of progressive knowledge and improvement, could not but do more than merely enlarge the natural boundaries of the habitable world. It could not but do much more even than extend commerce and increase wealth among the human race. We see how this event has acted, how it must have acted, and wonder only why it did not act sooner, in the production of moral effects, on the state of human knowledge, the general tone of human sentiments, and the prospects of human happiness. It gave to civilized man not only a new continent to be inhabited and cultivated, and new seas to be explored; but it gave him also a new range for his thoughts, new objects for curiosity, and new excitements to knowledge and improvement.

Roman colonization resembled, far less than that of the Greeks, the original settlements of this country. Power and dominion were the objects of Rome, even in her colonial establishments. Her whole exterior aspect was for centuries hostile and terrific. She grasped at dominion, from India to Britain, and her measures of colonization partook of the character of her general system. Her policy was military, because her objects were power, ascendency, and subjugation. Detachments of emigrants from Rome incorporated themselves with, and governed, the original inhabitants of conquered countries. She sent citizens where she had first sent soldiers; her law followed her sword. Her colonies were a sort of military establishment; so many advanced posts in the career of her dominion. A governor from Rome ruled the new colony with absolute sway, and often with unbounded rapacity. In Sicily, in Gaul, in Spain, and in Asia, the power of

Rome prevailed, not nominally only, but really and effectually. Those who immediately exercised it were Roman; the tone and tendency of its administration, Roman. Rome herself continued to be the heart and centre of the great system which she had established. Extortion and rapacity, finding a wide and often rich field of action in the provinces, looked nevertheless to the banks of the Tiber, as the scene in which their ill-gotten treasures should be displayed; or, if a spirit of more honest acquisition prevailed, the object, nevertheless, was ultimate enjoyment in Rome itself. If our own history and our own times did not sufficiently expose the inherent and incurable evils of provincial government, we might see them portrayed, to our amazement, in the desolated and ruined provinces of the Roman empire. We might hear them, in a voice that terrifies us, in those strains of complaint and accusation, which the advocates of the provinces poured forth in the Roman Forum:--"Quas res luxuries in flagitiis, crudelitas in suppliciis, avaritia in rapinis, superbia in contumeliis, efficere potuisset, eas omnes sese pertulisse."

As was to be expected, the Roman Provinces partook of the fortunes, as well as of the sentiments and general character, of the seat of empire. They lived together with her, they flourished with her, and fell with her. The branches were lopped away even before the vast and venerable trunk itself fell prostrate to the earth. Nothing had proceeded from her which could support itself, and bear up the name of its origin, when her own sustaining arm should be enfeebled or withdrawn. It was not given to Rome to see, either at her zenith or in her decline, a child of her own, distant, indeed, and independent of her control, yet speaking her language and inheriting her blood, springing forward to a competition with her own power, and a comparison with her own great renown. She saw not a vast region of the earth peopled from her stock, full of states and political communities, improving upon the models of her institutions, and breathing in fuller measure the spirit which she had breathed in the best periods of her existence; enjoying and extending her arts and her literature; rising rapidly from political childhood to manly strength and independence; her offspring, yet now her equal; unconnected with the causes which might affect the duration of her own power and greatness; of common origin, but not linked to a common fate; giving ample pledge, that her name should not be forgotten, that her language should not cease to be used among men; that whatsoever she had done for human knowledge and human happiness should be treasured up and preserved; that the record of her existence and her achievements should not be obscured, although, in the inscrutable purposes of Providence, it might be her destiny to fall from opulence and splendor; although the time might come, when darkness should settle on all her hills; when foreign or domestic violence should overturn her altars and her temples; when ignorance and despotism should fill the places where Laws, and Arts, and Liberty had flourished; when the feet of barbarism should trample on the tombs of her consuls, and the walls of her senate-house and forum echo only to the voice of savage triumph. She saw not this glorious vision, to inspire and fortify her against the possible decay or downfall of her power. Happy are they who in our day may behold it, if they shall contemplate it with the sentiments which it ought to inspire!

The New England Colonies differ quite as widely from the Asiatic establishments of the modern European nations, as from the models of the ancient states. The sole object of those establishments was originally trade; although we have seen, in one of them, the anomaly of a mere trading company attaining a political character, disbursing revenues, and maintaining armies and fortresses, until it has extended its control over seventy millions of people. Differing from these, and still more from the New England and North American Colonies, are the European settlements in the West India Islands. It is not strange, that, when men's minds were turned to the settlement of America, different objects should be proposed by those who emigrated to the different regions of so vast a country. Climate, soil, and condition were not all equally favorable to all pursuits. In the West Indies, the purpose of those who went thither was to engage in that species of agriculture, suited to the soil and climate, which seems to bear more resemblance to commerce than to the hard and plain tillage of New England. The great staples of these countries, being partly an agricultural and partly a manufactured product, and not being of the necessaries of life, become the object of calculation, with respect to a profitable investment of capital, like any other enterprise of trade or manufacture. The more especially, as, requiring, by necessity or habit, slave labor for their production, the capital necessary to carry on the work of this production is very considerable. The West Indies are resorted to, therefore, rather for the investment of capital than for the purpose of sustaining life by personal labor. Such as possess a considerable amount of capital, or such as choose to adventure in commercial speculations without capital, can alone be fitted to be emigrants to the islands. The agriculture of these regions, as before observed, is a sort of commerce; and it is a species of employment in which labor seems to form an inconsiderable ingredient in the productive causes, since the portion of white labor is exceedingly small, and slave labor is rather more like profit on stock or capital than *labor* properly so called. The individual who undertakes an establishment of this kind takes into the account the cost of the necessary number of slaves, in the same manner as he calculates the cost of the land. The uncertainty, too, of this species of employment, affords another ground of resemblance to commerce. Although gainful on the whole, and in a series of years, it is often very disastrous for a single year, and, as the capital is not readily invested in other pursuits, bad crops or bad markets not only affect the profits, but the capital itself. Hence the sudden depressions which take place in the value of such estates.

But the great and leading observation, relative to these establishments, remains to be made. It is, that the owners of the soil and of the capital seldom consider themselves *at home* in the colony. A very great portion of the soil itself is usually owned in the mother country; a still greater is mortgaged for capital obtained there; and, in general, those who are to derive an interest from the products look to the parent country as the place for enjoyment of their wealth. The population is therefore constantly fluctuating. Nobody comes but to return. A constant succession of owners, agents, and factors takes place. Whatsoever the soil, forced by the unmitigated toil of slavery, can yield, is sent home to defray rents, and interest, and agencies, or to give the means of living in a better society. In such a state, it is evident that no spirit of permanent improvement is likely to spring up. Profits will not be invested with a distant view of benefiting posterity. Roads and canals will hardly be built; schools will not be founded; colleges will not be endowed. There will be few fixtures in society; no principles of utility or of elegance, planted now, with the hope of being developed and expanded hereafter. Profit, immediate profit, must be the principal active spring in the social system. There may be many particular exceptions to these general remarks, but the outline of the whole is such as is here drawn.

Another most important consequence of such a state of things is, that no idea of independence of the parent country is likely to arise; unless, indeed, it should spring up in a form that would threaten universal desolation. The inhabitants have no strong attachment to the place which they inhabit. The hope of a great portion of them is to leave it; and their great desire, to leave it soon. However useful they may be to the parent state, how much soever they may add to the conveniences and luxuries of life, these colonies are not favored spots for the expansion of the human mind, for the progress of permanent improvement, or for sowing the seeds of future independent empire.

Different, indeed, most widely different, from all these instances of emigration and plantation, were the condition, the purposes, and the prospects of our fathers, when they established their infant colony upon this spot. They came hither to a land from which they were never to return. Hither they had brought, and here they were to fix, their hopes, their attachments, and their objects in life. Some natural tears they shed, as they left the pleasant abodes of their fathers, and some emotions they suppressed, when the white cliffs of their native country, now seen for the last time, grew dim to their sight. They were acting, however, upon a resolution not to be daunted. With whatever stifled regrets, with whatever occasional hesitation, with whatever appalling apprehensions, which might sometimes arise with force to shake the firmest purpose, they had yet committed themselves to Heaven and the elements; and a thousand leagues of water soon interposed to separate them for ever from the region which gave them birth. A new existence awaited them here; and when they saw these shores, rough, cold, barbarous, and barren, as then they were, they beheld their country. That mixed and strong feeling, which we call love of country, and which is, in general, never extinguished in the heart of man, grasped and embraced its proper object here. Whatever constitutes _country_, except the earth and the sun, all the moral causes of affection and attachment which operate upon the heart, they had brought with them to their new abode. Here were now their families and friends, their homes, and their property. Before they reached the shore, they had established the elements of a social system,[7] and at a much earlier period had settled their forms of religious worship. At the moment of their landing, therefore, they possessed institutions of government, and institutions of religion: and friends and families, and social and religious institutions, framed by consent, founded on choice and preference, how nearly do these fill up our whole idea of country! The morning that beamed on the first night of their repose saw the Pilgrims already *at home* in their country. There were political institutions, and civil liberty, and religious worship. Poetry has fancied nothing, in the wanderings of heroes, so distinct and characteristic. Here was man, indeed, unprotected, and unprovided for, on the shore of a rude and fearful wilderness; but it was politic, intelligent, and educated man. Every thing was civilized but the physical world. Institutions, containing in substance all that ages had done for human government, were organized in a forest. Cultivated mind was to act on uncultivated nature; and, more than all, a government and a country were to commence, with the very first foundations laid under the divine light of the Christian religion. Happy auspices of a happy futurity! Who would wish that his country's existence had otherwise begun? Who would desire the power of going back to the ages of fable? Who would wish for an origin obscured in the darkness of antiquity? Who would wish for other emblazoning of his country's heraldry, or other ornaments of her genealogy, than to be able to say, that her first existence was with intelligence, her first breath the inspiration of liberty, her first principle the truth of divine religion?

Local attachments and sympathies would ere long spring up in the breasts of our ancestors, endearing to them the place of their refuge. Whatever natural objects are associated with interesting scenes and high efforts obtain a hold on human feeling, and demand from the heart a sort of recognition and regard. This Rock soon became hallowed in the esteem of the Pilgrims,[8] and these hills grateful to their sight. Neither they nor their children were again to till the soil of England, nor again to traverse the seas which surround her.[9] But here was a new sea, now open to their enterprise, and a new soil, which had not failed to respond gratefully to their laborious industry, and which was already assuming a robe of verdure. Hardly had they provided shelter for the living, ere they were summoned to erect sepulchres for the dead. The ground had become sacred, by enclosing the remains of some of their companions and connections. A parent, a child, a husband, or a wife, had gone the way of all flesh, and mingled with the dust of New England. We naturally look with strong emotions to the spot, though it be a wilderness, where the ashes of those we have loved repose. Where the heart has laid down what it loved most, there it is desirous of laying itself down. No sculptured marble, no enduring monument, no honorable inscription, no ever-burning taper that would drive away the darkness of the tomb, can soften our sense of the reality of death, and hallow to our feelings the ground which is to cover us, like the consciousness that we shall sleep, dust to dust, with the objects of our affections.

In a short time other causes sprung up to bind the Pilgrims with new cords to their chosen land. Children were born, and the hopes of future generations arose, in the spot of their new habitation. The second generation found this the land of their nativity, and saw that they were bound to its fortunes. They beheld their fathers' graves around them, and while they read the memorials of their toils and labors, they rejoiced in the inheritance which they found bequeathed to them.

Under the influence of these causes, it was to be expected that an interest and a feeling should arise here, entirely different from the interest and feeling of mere Englishmen; and all the subsequent history of the Colonies proves this to have actually and gradually taken place. With a general acknowledgment of the supremacy of the British crown, there was, from the first, a repugnance to an entire submission to the control of British legislation. The Colonies stood upon their charters, which, as they contended, exempted them from the ordinary power of the British Parliament, and authorized them to conduct their own concerns by their own counsels. They utterly resisted the notion that they were to be ruled by the mere authority of the government at home, and would not endure even that their own charter governments should be established on the other side of the Atlantic. It was not a controlling or protecting board in England, but a government of their own, and existing immediately within their limits, which could satisfy their wishes. It was easy to foresee, what we know also to have happened, that the first great cause of collision and jealousy would be, under the notion of political economy then and still prevalent in Europe, an attempt on the part of the mother country to monopolize the trade of the Colonies. Whoever has looked deeply into the causes which produced our Revolution has found, if I mistake not, the original principle far back in this claim, on the part of England, to monopolize our trade, and a continued effort on the part of the Colonies to resist or evade that monopoly; if, indeed, it be not still more just and philosophical to go farther back, and to consider it decided, that an independent government must arise here, the moment it was ascertained that an English colony, such as landed in this place, could sustain itself against the dangers which surrounded it, and, with other similar establishments, overspread the land with an English population. Accidental causes retarded at times, and at times accelerated, the progress of the controversy. The Colonies wanted strength, and time gave it to them. They required measures of strong and palpable injustice, on the part of the mother country, to justify resistance; the early part of the late king's reign furnished them. They needed spirits of high order, of great daring, of long foresight, and of commanding power, to seize the favoring occasion to strike a blow, which should sever, for all time, the tie of colonial dependence; and these spirits were found, in all the extent which that or any crisis could demand, in Otis, Adams, Hancock, and the other immediate authors of our independence.

Still, it is true that, for a century, causes had been in operation tending to prepare things for this great result. In the year 1660 the English Act of Navigation was passed; the first and grand object of which seems to have been, to secure to England the whole trade with her plantations.[10] It was provided by that act, that none but English ships should transport American produce over the ocean, and that the principal articles of that produce should be allowed to be sold only in the markets of the mother country. Three years afterwards another law was passed, which enacted, that such commodities as the Colonies might wish to purchase should be bought only in the markets of the mother country. Severe rules were prescribed to enforce the provisions of these laws, and heavy penalties imposed on all who should violate them. In the subsequent years of the same reign, other statutes were enacted to re-enforce these statutes, and other rules prescribed to secure a compliance with these rules. In this manner was the trade to and from the Colonies restricted, almost to the exclusive advantage of the parent country. But laws, which rendered the interest of a whole people subordinate to that of another people, were not likely to execute themselves, nor was it easy to find many on the spot, who could be depended upon for carrying them into execution. In fact, these laws were more or less evaded or resisted, in all the Colonies. To enforce them was the constant endeavor of the government at home; to prevent or elude their operation, the perpetual object here. "The laws of navigation," says a living British writer, "were nowhere so openly disobeyed and contemned as in New England." "The people of Massachusetts Bay," he adds, "were from the first disposed to act as if independent of the mother country, and having a governor and magistrates of their own choice, it was difficult to enforce any regulation which came from the English Parliament, adverse to their interests." To provide more effectually for the execution of these laws, we know that courts of admiralty were afterwards established by the crown, with power to try revenue causes, as questions of admiralty, upon the construction given by the crown lawyers to an act of Parliament; a great departure from the ordinary principles of English jurisprudence, but which has been maintained, nevertheless, by the force of habit and precedent, and is adopted in our own existing systems of government.

"There lie," says another English writer, whose connection with the Board of Trade has enabled him to ascertain many facts connected with Colonial history, "There lie among the documents in the board of trade and state-paper office, the most satisfactory proofs, from the epoch of the English Revolution in 1688, throughout every reign, and during every administration, of the settled purpose of the Colonies to acquire direct independence and positive sovereignty." Perhaps this may be stated somewhat too strongly; but it cannot be denied, that, from the very nature of the establishments here, and from the general character of the measures respecting their concerns early adopted and steadily pursued by the English government, a division of the empire was the natural and necessary result to which every thing tended.[11] I have dwelt on this topic, because it seems to me, that the peculiar original character of the New England Colonies, and certain causes coeval with their existence, have had a strong and decided influence on all their subsequent history, and especially on the great event of the Revolution. Whoever would write our history, and would understand and explain early transactions, should comprehend the nature and force of the feeling which I have endeavored to describe. As a son, leaving the house of his father for his own, finds, by the order of nature, and the very law of his being, nearer and dearer objects around which his affections circle, while his attachment to the parental roof becomes moderated, by degrees, to a composed regard and an affectionate remembrance; so our ancestors, leaving their native land, not without some violence to the feelings of nature and affection, yet, in time, found here a new circle of engagements, interests, and affections; a feeling, which more and more encroached upon the old, till an undivided sentiment, _that this was their country_, occupied the heart; and patriotism, shutting out from its embraces the parent realm, became *local* to America.

Some retrospect of the century which has now elapsed is among the duties of the occasion. It must, however, necessarily be imperfect, to be compressed within the limits of a single discourse. I shall content myself, therefore, with taking notice of a few of the leading and most important occurrences which have distinguished the period.

When the first century closed, the progress of the country appeared to have been considerable; notwithstanding that, in comparison with its subsequent advancement, it now seems otherwise. A broad and lasting foundation had been laid; excellent institutions had been established; many of the prejudices of former times had been removed; a more liberal and catholic spirit on subjects of religious concern had begun to extend itself, and many things conspired to give promise of increasing future prosperity. Great men had arisen in public life, and the liberal professions. The Mathers, father and son, were then sinking low in the western horizon; Leverett, the learned, the accomplished, the excellent Leverett, was about to withdraw his brilliant and useful light. In Pemberton great hopes had been suddenly extinguished, but Prince and Colman were in our sky; and along the east had begun to flash the crepuscular light of a great luminary which was about to appear, and which was to stamp the age with his own name, as the age of Franklin.

The bloody Indian wars, which harassed the people for a part of the first century; the restrictions on the trade of the Colonies, added to the discouragements inherently belonging to all forms of colonial government; the distance from Europe, and the small hope of immediate profit to adventurers, are among the causes which had contributed to retard the progress of population. Perhaps it may be added, also, that during the period of the civil wars in England, and the reign of Cromwell, many persons, whose religious opinions and religious temper might, under other circumstances, have induced them to join the New England colonists, found reasons to remain in England; either on account of active occupation in the scenes which were passing, or of an anticipation of the enjoyment, in their own country, of a form of government, civil and religious, accommodated to their views and principles. The violent measures, too, pursued against the Colonies in the reign of Charles the Second, the mockery of a trial, and the forfeiture of the charters, were serious evils. And during the open violences of the short reign of James the Second, and the tyranny of Andros, as the venerable historian of Connecticut observes, "All the motives to great actions, to industry, economy, enterprise, wealth, and population, were in a manner annihilated. A general inactivity and languishment pervaded the public body. Liberty, property, and every thing which ought to be dear to men, every day grew more and more insecure."

With the Revolution in England, a better prospect had opened on this country, as well as on that. The joy had been as great at that event, and far more universal, in New than in Old England. A new charter had been granted to Massachusetts, which, although it did not confirm to her inhabitants all their former privileges, yet relieved them from great evils and embarrassments, and promised future security. More than all, perhaps, the Revolution in England had done good to the general cause of liberty and justice. A blow had been struck in favor of the rights and liberties, not of England alone, but of descendants and kinsmen of England all over the world. Great political truths had been established. The champions of liberty had been successful in a fearful and perilous conflict. Somers, and Cavendish, and Jekyl, and Howard, had triumphed in one of the most noble causes ever undertaken by men. A revolution had been made upon principle. A monarch had been dethroned for violating the original compact between king and people. The rights of the people to partake in the government, and to limit the monarch by fundamental rules of government, had been maintained; and however unjust the government of England might afterwards be towards other governments or towards her colonies, she had ceased to be governed herself by the arbitrary maxims of the Stuarts.

New England had submitted to the violence of James the Second not longer than Old England. Not only was it reserved to Massachusetts, that on her soil should be acted the first scene of that great revolutionary drama, which was to take place near a century afterwards, but the English Revolution itself, as far as the Colonies were concerned, commenced in Boston. The seizure and imprisonment of Andros, in April, 1689, were acts of direct and forcible resistance to the authority of James the Second. The pulse of liberty beat as high in the extremities as at the heart. The vigorous feeling of the Colony burst out before it was known how the parent country would finally conduct herself. The king's representative, Sir Edmund Andros, was a prisoner in the castle at Boston, before it was or could be known that the king himself had ceased to exercise his full dominion on the English throne.

Before it was known here whether the invasion of the Prince of Orange would or could prove successful, as soon as it was known that it had been undertaken, the people of Massachusetts, at the imminent hazard of their lives and fortunes, had accomplished the Revolution as far as respected themselves. It is probable that, reasoning on general principles and the known attachment of the English people to their constitution and liberties, and their deep and fixed dislike of the king's religion and politics, the people of New England expected a catastrophe fatal to the power of the reigning prince. Yet it was neither certain enough, nor near enough, to come to their aid against the authority of the crown, in that crisis which had arrived, and in which they trusted to put themselves, relying on God and their own courage. There were spirits in Massachusetts congenial with the spirits of the distinguished friends of the Revolution in England. There were those who were fit to associate with the boldest asserters of civil liberty; and Mather himself, then in England, was not unworthy to be ranked with those sons of the Church, whose firmness and spirit in resisting kingly encroachments in matters of religion, entitled them to the gratitude of their own and succeeding ages.

The second century opened upon New England under circumstances which evinced that much had already been accomplished, and that still better prospects and brighter hopes were before her. She had laid, deep and strong, the foundations of her society. Her religious principles were firm, and her moral habits exemplary. Her public schools had begun to diffuse widely the elements of knowledge; and the College, under the excellent and acceptable administration of Leverett, had been raised to a high degree of credit and usefulness.

The commercial character of the country, notwithstanding all discouragements, had begun to display itself, and _five hundred vessels_, then belonging to Massachusetts, placed her, in relation to commerce, thus early at the head of the Colonies. An author who wrote very near the close of the first century says:--"New England is almost deserving that _noble name_, so mightily hath it increased; and from a small settlement at first, is now become a *very populous* and *flourishing* government. The _capital city_, Boston, is a place of _great wealth and trade_; and by much the largest of any in the English empire of America; and not exceeded but by few cities, perhaps two or three, in all the American world."

But if our ancestors at the close of the first century could look back with joy and even admiration, at the progress of the country, what emotions must we not feel, when, from the point on which we stand, we also look back and run along the events of the century which has now closed! The country which then, as we have seen, was thought deserving of a "noble name,"--which then had "mightily increased," and become "very populous,"--what was it, in comparison with what our eyes behold it? At that period, a very great proportion of its inhabitants lived in the eastern section of Massachusetts proper, and in Plymouth Colony. In Connecticut, there were towns along the coast, some of them respectable, but in the interior all was a wilderness beyond Hartford. On Connecticut River, settlements had proceeded as far up as Deerfield, and Fort Dummer had been built near where is now the south line of New Hampshire. In New Hampshire no settlement was then begun thirty miles from the mouth of Piscataqua River, and in what is now Maine the inhabitants were confined to the coast. The aggregate of the whole population of New England did not exceed one hundred and sixty thousand. Its present amount (1820) is probably one million seven hundred thousand. Instead of being confined to its former limits, her population has rolled backward, and filled up the spaces included within her actual local boundaries. Not this only, but it has overflowed those boundaries, and the waves of emigration have pressed farther and farther toward the West. The Alleghany has not checked it; the banks of the Ohio have been covered with it. New England farms, houses, villages, and churches spread over and adorn the immense extent from the Ohio to Lake Erie, and stretch along from the Alleghany onwards, beyond the Miamis, and toward the Falls of St. Anthony. Two thousand miles westward from the rock where their fathers landed, may now be found the sons of the Pilgrims, cultivating smiling fields, rearing towns and villages, and cherishing, we trust, the patrimonial blessings of wise institutions, of liberty, and religion. The world has seen nothing like this. Regions large enough to be empires, and which, half a century ago, were known only as remote and unexplored wildernesses, are now teeming with population, and prosperous in all the great concerns of life; in good governments, the means of subsistence, and social happiness. It may be safely asserted, that there are now more than a million of people, descendants of New England ancestry, living, free and happy, in regions which scarce sixty years ago were tracts of unpenetrated forest. Nor do rivers, or mountains, or seas resist the progress of industry and enterprise. Erelong, the sons of the Pilgrims will be on the shores of the Pacific.[12] The imagination hardly keeps pace with the progress of population, improvement, and civilization.

It is now five-and-forty years since the growth and rising glory of America were portrayed in the English Parliament, with inimitable beauty, by the most consummate orator of modern times. Going back somewhat more than half a century, and describing our progress as foreseen from that point by his amiable friend Lord Bathurst, then living, he spoke of the wonderful progress which America had made during the period of a single human life. There is no American heart, I imagine, that does not glow, both with conscious, patriotic pride, and admiration for one of the happiest efforts of eloquence, so often as the vision of "that little speck, scarce visible in the mass of national interest, a small seminal principle, rather than a formed body," and the progress of its astonishing development and growth, are recalled to the recollection. But a stronger feeling might be produced, if we were able to take up this prophetic description where he left it, and, placing ourselves at the point of time in which he was speaking, to set forth with equal felicity the subsequent progress of the country. There is yet among the living a most distinguished and venerable name, a descendant of the Pilgrims; one who has been attended through life by a great and fortunate genius; a man illustrious by his own great merits, and favored of Heaven in the long continuation of his years.[13] The time when the English orator was thus speaking of America preceded but by a few days the actual opening of the revolutionary drama at Lexington. He to whom I have alluded, then at the age of forty, was among the most zealous and able defenders of the violated rights of his country. He seemed already to have filled a full measure of public service, and attained an honorable fame. The moment was full of difficulty and danger, and big with events of immeasurable importance. The country was on the very brink of a civil war, of which no man could foretell the duration or the result. Something more than a courageous hope, or characteristic ardor, would have been necessary to impress the glorious prospect on his belief, if, at that moment, before the sound of the first shock of actual war had reached his ears, some attendant spirit had opened to him the vision of the future;--if it had said to him, "The blow is struck, and America is severed from England for ever!"--if it had informed him, that he himself, during the next annual revolution of the sun, should put his own hand to the great instrument of independence, and write his name where all nations should behold it and all time should not efface it; that erelong he himself should maintain the interests and represent the sovereignty of his newborn country in the proudest courts of Europe; that he should one day exercise her supreme magistracy; that he should yet live to behold ten millions of fellow-citizens paying him the homage of their deepest gratitude and kindest affections; that he should see distinguished talent and high public trust resting where his name rested; that he should even see with his own unclouded eyes the close of the second century of New England, who had begun life almost with its commencement, and lived through nearly half the whole history of his country; and that on the morning of this auspicious day he should be found in the political councils of his native State, revising, by the light of experience, that system of government which forty years before he had assisted to frame and establish; and, great and happy as he should then behold his country, there should be nothing in prospect to cloud the scene, nothing to check the ardor of that confident and patriotic hope which should glow in his bosom to the end of his long protracted and happy life.

It would far exceed the limits of this discourse even to mention the principal events in the civil and political history of New England during the century; the more so, as for the last half of the period that history has, most happily, been closely interwoven with the general history of the United States. New England bore an honorable part in the wars which took place between England and France. The capture of Louisburg gave her a character for military achievement; and in the war which terminated with the peace of 1763, her exertions on the frontiers wore of most essential service, as well to the mother country as to all the Colonies.

In New England the war of the Revolution commenced. I address those who remember the memorable 19th of April, 1775; who shortly after saw the burning spires of Charlestown; who beheld the deeds of Prescott, and heard the voice of Putnam amidst the storm of war, and saw the generous Warren fall, the first distinguished victim in the cause of liberty. It would be superfluous to say, that no portion of the country did more than the States of New England to bring the Revolutionary struggle to a successful issue. It is scarcely less to her credit, that she saw early the necessity of a closer union of the States, and gave an efficient and indispensable aid to the establishment and organization of the Federal government.

Perhaps we might safely say, that a new spirit and a new excitement began to exist here about the middle of the last century. To whatever causes it may be imputed, there seems then to have commenced a more rapid improvement. The Colonies had attracted more of the attention of the mother country, and some renown in arms had been acquired. Lord Chatham was the first English minister who attached high importance to these possessions of the crown, and who foresaw any thing of their future growth and extension. His opinion was, that the great rival of England was chiefly to be feared as a maritime and commercial power, and to drive her out of North America and deprive her of her West Indian possessions was a leading object in his policy. He dwelt often on the fisheries, as nurseries for British seamen, and the colonial trade, as furnishing them employment. The war, conducted by him with so much vigor, terminated in a peace, by which Canada was ceded to England. The effect of this was immediately visible in the New England Colonies; for, the fear of Indian hostilities on the frontiers being now happily removed, settlements went on with an activity before that time altogether unprecedented, and public affairs wore a new and encouraging aspect. Shortly after this fortunate termination of the French war, the interesting topics connected with the taxation of America by the British Parliament began to be discussed, and the attention and all the faculties of the people drawn towards them. There is perhaps no portion of our history more full of interest than the period from 1760 to the actual commencement of the war. The progress of opinion in this period, though less known, is not less important than the progress of arms afterwards. Nothing deserves more consideration than those events and discussions which affected the public sentiment and settled the Revolution in men's minds, before hostilities openly broke out.

Internal improvement followed the establishment and prosperous commencement of the present government. More has been done for roads, canals, and other public works, within the last thirty years, than in all our former history. In the first of these particulars, few countries excel the New England States. The astonishing increase of their navigation and trade is known to every one, and now belongs to the history of our national wealth.

We may flatter ourselves, too, that literature and taste have not been stationary, and that some advancement has been made in the elegant, as well as in the useful arts.

The nature and constitution of society and government in this country are interesting topics, to which I would devote what remains of the time allowed to this occasion. Of our system of government the first thing to be said is, that it is really and practically a free system. It originates entirely with the people, and rests on no other foundation than their assent. To judge of its actual operation, it is not enough to look merely at the form of its construction. The practical character of government depends often on a variety of considerations, besides the abstract frame of its constitutional organization. Among these are the condition and tenure of property; the laws regulating its alienation and descent; the presence or absence of a military power; an armed or unarmed yeomanry; the spirit of the age, and the degree of general intelligence. In these respects it cannot be denied that the circumstances of this country are most favorable to the hope of maintaining the government of a great nation on principles entirely popular. In the absence of military power, the nature of government must essentially depend on the manner in which property is holden and distributed. There is a natural influence belonging to property, whether it exists in many hands or few; and it is on the rights of property that both despotism and unrestrained popular violence ordinarily commence their attacks. Our ancestors began their system of government here under a condition of comparative equality in regard to wealth, and their early laws were of a nature to favor and continue this equality.

A republican form of government rests not more on political constitutions, than on those laws which regulate the descent and transmission of property. Governments like ours could not have been maintained, where property was holden according to the principles of the feudal system; nor, on the other hand, could the feudal constitution possibly exist with us. Our New England ancestors brought hither no great capitals from Europe; and if they had, there was nothing productive in which they could have been invested. They left behind them the whole feudal policy of the other continent. They broke away at once from the system of military service established in the Dark Ages, and which continues, down even to the present time, more or less to affect the condition of property all over Europe. They came to a new country. There were, as yet, no lands yielding rent, and no tenants rendering service. The whole soil was unreclaimed from barbarism. They were themselves, either from their original condition, or from the necessity of their common interest, nearly on a general level in respect to property. Their situation demanded a parcelling out and division of the lands, and it may be fairly said, that this necessary act *fixed the future frame and form of their government*. The character of their political institutions was determined by the fundamental laws respecting property. The laws rendered estates divisible among sons and daughters. The right of primogeniture, at first limited and curtailed, was afterwards abolished. The property was all freehold. The entailment of estates, long trusts, and the other processes for fettering and tying up inheritances, were not applicable to the condition of society, and seldom made use of. On the contrary, alienation of the land was every way facilitated, even to the subjecting of it to every species of debt. The establishment of public registries, and the simplicity of our forms of conveyance, have greatly facilitated the change of real estate from one proprietor to another. The consequence of all these causes has been a great subdivision of the soil, and a great equality of condition; the true basis, most certainly, of a popular government. "If the people," says Harrington, "hold three parts in four of the territory, it is plain there can neither be any single person nor nobility able to dispute the government with them; in this case, therefore, _except force be interposed_, they govern themselves."

The history of other nations may teach us how favorable to public liberty are the division of the soil into small freeholds, and a system of laws, of which the tendency is, without violence or injustice, to produce and to preserve a degree of equality of property. It has been estimated, if I mistake not, that about the time of Henry the Seventh four fifths of the land in England was holden by the great barons and ecclesiastics.

The effects of a growing commerce soon afterwards began to break in on this state of things, and before the Revolution, in 1688, a vast change had been wrought. It may be thought probable, that, for the last half-century, the process of subdivision in England has been retarded, if not reversed; that the great weight of taxation has compelled many of the lesser freeholders to dispose of their estates, and to seek employment in the army and navy, in the professions of civil life, in commerce, or in the colonies. The effect of this on the British constitution cannot but be most unfavorable. A few large estates grow larger; but the number of those who have no estates also increases; and there may be danger, lest the inequality of property become so great, that those who possess it may be dispossessed by force; in other words, that the government may be overturned.

A most interesting experiment of the effect of a subdivision of property on government is now making in France. It is understood, that the law regulating the transmission of property in that country, now divides it, real and personal, among all the children equally, both sons and daughters; and that there is, also, a very great restraint on the power of making dispositions of property by will. It has been supposed, that the effects of this might probably be, in time, to break up the soil into such small subdivisions, that the proprietors would be too poor to resist the encroachments of executive power. I think far otherwise. What is lost in individual wealth will be more than gained in numbers, in intelligence, and in a sympathy of sentiment. If, indeed, only one or a few landholders were to resist the crown, like the barons of England, they must, of course, be great and powerful landholders, with multitudes of retainers, to promise success. But if the proprietors of a given extent of territory are summoned to resistance, there is no reason to believe that such resistance would be less forcible, or less successful, because the number of such proprietors happened to be great. Each would perceive his own importance, and his own interest, and would feel that natural elevation of character which the consciousness of property inspires. A common sentiment would unite all, and numbers would not only add strength, but excite enthusiasm. It is true, that France possesses a vast military force, under the direction of an hereditary executive government; and military power, it is possible, may overthrow any government. It is in vain, however, in this period of the world, to look for security against military power to the arm of the great landholders. That notion is derived from a state of things long since past; a state in which a feudal baron, with his retainers, might stand against the sovereign and his retainers, himself but the greatest baron. But at present, what could the richest landholder do, against one regiment of disciplined troops? Other securities, therefore, against the prevalence of military power must be provided. Happily for us, we are not so situated as that any purpose of national defence requires, ordinarily and constantly, such a military force as might seriously endanger our liberties.

In respect, however, to the recent law of succession in France, to which I have alluded, I would, presumptuously perhaps, hazard a conjecture, that, if the government do not change the law, the law in half a century will change the government; and that this change will be, not in favor of the power of the crown, as some European writers have supposed, but against it. Those writers only reason upon what they think correct general principles, in relation to this subject. They acknowledge a want of experience. Here we have had that experience; and we know that a multitude of small proprietors, acting with intelligence, and that enthusiasm which a common cause inspires, constitute not only a formidable, but an invincible power.[14]

The true principle of a free and popular government would seem to be, so to construct it as to give to all, or at least to a very great majority, an interest in its preservation; to found it, as other things are founded, on men's interest. The stability of government demands that those who desire its continuance should be more powerful than those who desire its dissolution. This power, of course, is not always to be measured by mere numbers. Education, wealth, talents, are all parts and elements of the general aggregate of power; but numbers, nevertheless, constitute ordinarily the most important consideration, unless, indeed, there be *a military force* in the hands of the few, by which they can control the many. In this country we have actually existing systems of government, in the maintenance of which, it should seem, a great majority, both in numbers and in other means of power and influence, must see their interest. But this state of things is not brought about solely by written political constitutions, or the mere manner of organizing the government; but also by the laws which regulate the descent and transmission of property. The freest government, if it could exist, would not be long acceptable, if the tendency of the laws were to create a rapid accumulation of property in few hands, and to render the great mass of the population dependent and penniless. In such a case, the popular power would be likely to break in upon the rights of property, or else the influence of property to limit and control the exercise of popular power. Universal suffrage, for example, could not long exist in a community where there was great inequality of property. The holders of estates would be obliged, in such case, in some way to restrain the right of suffrage, or else such right of suffrage would, before long, divide the property. In the nature of things, those who have not property, and see their neighbors possess much more than they think them to need, cannot be favorable to laws made for the protection of property. When this class becomes numerous, it grows clamorous. It looks on property as its prey and plunder, and is naturally ready, at all times, for violence and revolution.

It would seem, then, to be the part of political wisdom to found government on property; and to establish such distribution of property, by the laws which regulate its transmission and alienation, as to interest the great majority of society in the support of the government. This is, I imagine, the true theory and the actual practice of our republican institutions. With property divided as we have it, no other government than that of a republic could be maintained, even were we foolish enough to desire it. There is reason, therefore, to expect a long continuance of our system. Party and passion, doubtless, may prevail at times, and much temporary mischief be done. Even modes and forms may be changed, and perhaps for the worse. But a great revolution in regard to property must take place, before our governments can be moved from their republican basis, unless they be violently struck off by military power. The people possess the property, more emphatically than it could ever be said of the people of any other country, and they can have no interest to overturn a government which protects that property by equal laws.

Let it not be supposed, that this state of things possesses too strong tendencies towards the production of a dead and uninteresting level in society. Such tendencies are sufficiently counteracted by the infinite diversities in the characters and fortunes of individuals. Talent, activity, industry, and enterprise tend at all times to produce inequality and distinction; and there is room still for the accumulation of wealth, with its great advantages, to all reasonable and useful extent. It has been often urged against the state of society in America, that it furnishes no class of men of fortune and leisure. This may be partly true, but it is not entirely so, and the evil, if it be one, would affect rather the progress of taste and literature, than the general prosperity of the people. But the promotion of taste and literature cannot be primary objects of political institutions; and if they could, it might be doubted whether, in the long course of things, as much is not gained by a wide diffusion of general knowledge, as is lost by diminishing the number of those who are enabled by fortune and leisure to devote themselves exclusively to scientific and literary pursuits. However this may be, it is to be considered that it is the spirit of our system to be equal and general, and if there be particular disadvantages incident to this, they are far more than counterbalanced by the benefits which weigh against them. The important concerns of society are generally conducted, in all countries, by the men of business and practical ability; and even in matters of taste and literature, the advantages of mere leisure are liable to be overrated. If there exist adequate means of education and a love of letters be excited, that love will find its way to the object of its desire, through the crowd and pressure of the most busy society.

Connected with this division of property, and the consequent participation of the great mass of people in its possession and enjoyments, is the system of representation, which is admirably accommodated to our condition, better understood among us, and more familiarly and extensively practised, in the higher and in the lower departments of government, than it has been by any other people. Great facility has been given to this in New England by the early division of the country into townships or small districts, in which all concerns of local police are regulated, and in which representatives to the legislature are elected. Nothing can exceed the utility of these little bodies. They are so many councils or parliaments, in which common interests are discussed, and useful knowledge acquired and communicated.

The division of governments into departments, and the division, again, of the legislative department into two chambers, are essential provisions in our system. This last, although not new in itself, yet seems to be new in its application to governments wholly popular. The Grecian republics, it is plain, knew nothing of it; and in Rome, the check and balance of legislative power, such as it was, lay between the people and the senate. Indeed, few things are more difficult than to ascertain accurately the true nature and construction of the Roman commonwealth. The relative power of the senate and the people, of the consuls and the tribunes, appears not to have been at all times the same, nor at any time accurately defined or strictly observed. Cicero, indeed, describes to us an admirable arrangement of political power, and a balance of the constitution, in that beautiful passage, in which he compares the democracies of Greece with the Roman commonwealth. "O morem preclarum, disciplinamque, quam a majoribus accepimus, si quidem teneremus!

sed nescio quo pacto jam de manibus elabitur. Nullam enim illi nostri sapientissimi et sanctissimi viri vim concionis esse voluerunt, quae scisseret plebs, aut quae populus juberet; summota concione, distributis partibus, tributim et centuriatim descriptis ordinibus, classibus, aetatibus, auditis auctoribus, re multos dies promulgata et cognita, juberi vetarique voluerunt. Graecorum autem totae respublicae sedentis concionis temeritate administrantur."[15]

But at what time this wise system existed in this perfection at Rome, no proofs remain to show. Her constitution, originally framed for a monarchy, never seemed to be adjusted in its several parts after the expulsion of the kings. Liberty there was, but it was a disputatious, an uncertain, an ill-secured liberty. The patrician and plebeian orders, instead of being matched and joined, each in its just place and proportion, to sustain the fabric of the state, were rather like hostile powers, in perpetual conflict. With us, an attempt has been made, and so far not without success, to divide representation into chambers, and, by difference of age, character, qualification, or mode of election, to establish salutary checks, in governments altogether elective.

Having detained you so long with these observations, I must yet advert to another most interesting topic,-- the Free Schools. In this particular, New England may be allowed to claim, I think, a merit of a peculiar character. She early adopted, and has constantly maintained the principle, that it is the undoubted right and the bounden duty of government to provide for the instruction of all youth. That which is elsewhere left to chance or to charity, we secure by law.[16] For the purpose of public instruction, we hold every man subject to taxation in proportion to his property, and we look not to the question, whether he himself have, or have not, children to be benefited by the education for which he pays. We regard it as a wise and liberal system of police, by which property, and life, and the peace of society are secured. We seek to prevent in some measure the extension of the penal code, by inspiring a salutary and conservative principle of virtue and of knowledge in an early age. We strive to excite a feeling of respectability, and a sense of character, by enlarging the capacity and increasing the sphere of intellectual enjoyment. By general instruction, we seek, as far as possible, to purify the whole moral atmosphere; to keep good sentiments uppermost, and to turn the strong current of feeling and opinion, as well as the censures of the law and the denunciations of religion, against immorality and crime. We hope for a security beyond the law, and above the law, in the prevalence of an enlightened and well-principled moral sentiment. We hope to continue and prolong the time, when, in the villages and farm-houses of New England, there may be undisturbed sleep within unbarred doors. And knowing that our government rests directly on the public will, in order that we may preserve it we endeavor to give a safe and proper direction to that public will. We do not, indeed, expect all men to be philosophers or statesmen; but we confidently trust, and our expectation of the duration of our system of government rests on that trust, that, by the diffusion of general knowledge and good and virtuous sentiments, the political fabric may be secure, as well against open violence and overthrow, as against the slow, but sure, undermining of licentiousness.

We know that, at the present time, an attempt is making in the English Parliament to provide by law for the education of the poor, and that a gentleman of distinguished character (Mr. Brougham) has taken the lead in presenting a plan to government for carrying that purpose into effect. And yet, although the representatives of the three kingdoms listened to him with astonishment as well as delight, we hear no principles with which we ourselves have not been familiar from youth; we see nothing in the plan but an approach towards that system which has been established in New England for more than a century and a half. It is said that in England not more than *one child in fifteen* possesses the means of being taught to read and write; in Wales, _one in twenty_; in France, until lately, when some improvement was made, not more than _one in thirty-five_. Now, it is hardly too strong to say, that in New England *every child possesses* such means. It would be difficult to find an instance to the contrary, unless where it should be owing to the negligence of the parent; and, in truth, the means are actually used and enjoyed by nearly every one. A youth of fifteen, of either sex, who cannot both read and write, is very seldom to be found. Who can make this comparison, or contemplate this spectacle, without delight and a feeling of just pride? Does any history show property more beneficently applied? Did any government ever subject the property of those who have estates to a burden, for a purpose more favorable to the poor, or more useful to the whole community?

A conviction of the importance of public instruction was one of the earliest sentiments of our ancestors. No lawgiver of ancient or modern times has expressed more just opinions, or adopted wiser measures, than the early records of the Colony of Plymouth show to have prevailed here. Assembled on this very spot, a hundred and fifty-three years ago, the legislature of this Colony declared, "Forasmuch as the maintenance of good literature doth much tend to the advancement of the weal and flourishing state of societies and republics, this Court doth therefore order, that in whatever township in this government, consisting of fifty families or upwards, any meet man shall be obtained to teach a grammar school, such township shall allow at least twelve pounds, to be raised by rate on all the inhabitants."

Having provided that all youth should be instructed in the elements of learning by the institution of free schools, our ancestors had yet another duty to perform. Men were to be educated for the professions and the public. For this purpose they founded the University, and with incredible zeal and perseverance they cherished and supported it, through all trials and discouragements.[17] On the subject of the University, it is not possible for a son of New England to think without pleasure, or to speak without emotion. Nothing confers more honor on the State where it is established, or more utility on the country at large. A respectable university is an establishment which must be the work of time. If pecuniary means were not wanting, no new institution could possess character and respectability at once. We owe deep obligation to our ancestors, who began, almost on the moment of their arrival, the work of building up this institution. Although established in a different government, the Colony of Plymouth manifested warm friendship for Harvard College. At an early period, its government took measures to promote a general subscription throughout all the towns in this Colony, in aid of its small funds. Other colleges were subsequently founded and endowed, in other places, as the ability of the people allowed; and we may flatter ourselves, that the means of education at present enjoyed in New England are not only adequate to the diffusion of the elements of knowledge among all classes, but sufficient also for respectable attainments in literature and the sciences.

Lastly, our ancestors established their system of government on morality and religious sentiment. Moral habits, they believed, cannot safely be trusted on any other foundation than religious principle, nor any government be secure which is not supported by moral habits. Living under the heavenly light of revelation, they hoped to find all the social dispositions, all the duties which men owe to each other and to society, enforced and performed. Whatever makes men good Christians, makes them good citizens. Our fathers came here to enjoy their religion free and unmolested; and, at the end of two centuries, there is nothing upon which we can pronounce more confidently, nothing of which we can express a more deep and earnest conviction, than of the inestimable importance of that religion to man, both in regard to this life and that which is to come.

If the blessings of our political and social condition have not been too highly estimated, we cannot well overrate the responsibility and duty which they impose upon us. We hold these institutions of government, religion, and learning, to be transmitted, as well as enjoyed. We are in the line of conveyance, through which whatever has been obtained by the spirit and efforts of our ancestors is to be communicated to our children.

We are bound to maintain public liberty, and, by the example of our own systems, to convince the world that order and law, religion and morality, the rights of conscience, the rights of persons, and the rights of property, may all be preserved and secured, in the most perfect manner, by a government entirely and purely elective. If we fail in this, our disaster will be signal, and will furnish an argument, stronger than has yet been found, in support of those opinions which maintain that government can rest safely on nothing but power and coercion. As far as experience may show errors in our establishments, we are bound to correct them; and if any practices exist contrary to the principles of justice and humanity within the reach of our laws or our influence, we are inexcusable if we do not exert ourselves to restrain and abolish them. I deem it my duty on this occasion to suggest, that the land is not yet wholly free from the contamination of a traffic, at which every feeling of humanity must for ever revolt,--I mean the African slave-trade.[18] Neither public sentiment, nor the law, has hitherto been able entirely to put an end to this odious and abominable trade. At the moment when God in his mercy has blessed the Christian world with a universal peace, there is reason to fear, that, to the disgrace of the Christian name and character, new efforts are making for the extension of this trade by subjects and citizens of Christian states, in whose hearts there dwell no sentiments of humanity or of justice, and over whom neither the fear of God nor the fear of man exercises a control. In the sight of our law, the African slave-trader is a pirate and a felon; and in the sight of Heaven, an offender far beyond the ordinary depth of human guilt. There is no brighter page of our history, than that which records the measures which have been adopted by the government at an early day, and at different times since, for the suppression of this traffic; and I would call on all the true sons of New

England to co-operate with the laws of man, and the justice of Heaven. If there be, within the extent of our knowledge or influence, any participation in this traffic, let us pledge ourselves here, upon the rock of Plymouth, to extirpate and destroy it. It is not fit that the land of the Pilgrims should bear the shame longer. I hear the sound of the hammer, I see the smoke of the furnaces where manacles and fetters are still forged for human limbs. I see the visages of those who by stealth and at midnight labor in this work of hell, foul and dark, as may become the artificers of such instruments of misery and torture. Let that spot be purified, or let it cease to be of New England. Let it be purified, or let it be set aside from the Christian world; let it be put out of the circle of human sympathies and human regards, and let civilized man henceforth have no communion with it.

I would invoke those who fill the seats of justice, and all who minister at her altar, that they execute the wholesome and necessary severity of the law. I invoke the ministers of our religion, that they proclaim its denunciation of these crimes, and add its solemn sanctions to the authority of human laws. If the pulpit be silent whenever or wherever there may be a sinner bloody with this guilt within the hearing of its voice, the pulpit is false to its trust. I call on the fair merchant, who has reaped his harvest upon the seas, that he assist in scourging from those seas the worst pirates that ever infested them. That ocean, which seems to wave with a gentle magnificence to waft the burden of an honest commerce, and to roll along its treasures with a conscious pride,--that ocean, which hardy industry regards, even when the winds have ruffled its surface, as a field of grateful toil,--what is it to the victim of this oppression, when he is brought to its shores, and looks forth upon it, for the first time, loaded with chains, and bleeding with stripes? What is it to him but a wide-spread prospect of suffering, anguish, and death? Nor do the skies smile longer, nor is the air longer fragrant to him. The sun is cast down from heaven. An inhuman and accursed traffic has cut him off in his manhood, or in his youth, from every enjoyment belonging to his being, and every blessing which his Creator intended for him.

The Christian communities send forth their emissaries of religion and letters, who stop, here and there, along the coast of the vast continent of Africa, and with painful and tedious efforts make some almost imperceptible progress in the communication of knowledge, and in the general improvement of the natives who are immediately about them. Not thus slow and imperceptible is the transmission of the vices and bad passions which the subjects of Christian states carry to the land. The slave-trade having touched the coast, its influence and its evils spread, like a pestilence, over the whole continent, making savage wars more savage and more frequent, and adding new and fierce passions to the contests of barbarians.

I pursue this topic no further, except again to say, that all Christendom, being now blessed with peace, is bound by every thing which belongs to its character, and to the character of the present age, to put a stop to this inhuman and disgraceful traffic.

We are bound, not only to maintain the general principles of public liberty, but to support also those existing forms of government which have so well secured its enjoyment, and so highly promoted the public prosperity. It is now more than thirty years that these States have been united under the Federal Constitution, and whatever fortune may await them hereafter, it is impossible that this period of their history should not be regarded as distinguished by signal prosperity and success. They must be sanguine indeed, who can hope for benefit from change. Whatever division of the public judgment may have existed in relation to particular measures of the government, all must agree, one should think, in the opinion, that in its general course it has been eminently productive of public happiness. Its most ardent friends could not well have hoped from it more than it has accomplished; and those who disbelieved or doubted ought to feel less concern about predictions which the event has not verified, than pleasure in the good which has been obtained. Whoever shall hereafter write this part of our history, although he may see occasional errors or defects, will be able to record no great failure in the ends and objects of government. Still less will he be able to record any series of lawless and despotic acts, or any successful usurpation. His page will contain no exhibition of provinces depopulated, of civil authority habitually trampled down by military power, or of a community crushed by the burden of taxation. He will speak, rather, of public liberty protected, and public happiness advanced; of increased revenue, and population augmented beyond all example; of the growth of commerce, manufactures, and the arts; and of that happy condition, in which the restraint and coercion of government are almost invisible and imperceptible, and its influence felt only in the benefits which it confers. We can entertain no better wish for our country, than that this government may be preserved; nor have a clearer duty than to maintain and support it in the full exercise of all its just constitutional powers.

The cause of science and literature also imposes upon us an important and delicate trust. The wealth and population of the country are now so far advanced, as to authorize the expectation of a correct literature and a well formed taste, as well as respectable progress in the abstruse sciences. The country has risen from a state of colonial subjection; it has established an independent government, and is now in the undisturbed enjoyment of peace and political security. The elements of knowledge are universally diffused, and the reading portion of the community is large. Let us hope that the present may be an auspicious era of literature. If, almost on the day of their landing, our ancestors founded schools and endowed colleges, what obligations do not rest upon us, living under circumstances so much more favorable both for providing and for using the means of education? Literature becomes free institutions. It is the graceful ornament of civil liberty, and a happy restraint on the asperities which political controversies sometimes occasion. Just taste is not only an embellishment of society, but it rises almost to the rank of the virtues, and diffuses positive good throughout the whole extent of its influence. There is a connection between right feeling and right principles, and truth in taste is allied with truth in morality. With nothing in our past history to discourage us, and with something in our present condition and prospects to animate us, let us hope, that, as it is our fortune to live in an age when we may behold a wonderful advancement of the country in all its other great interests, we may see also equal progress and success attend the cause of letters.

Finally, let us not forget the religious character of our origin. Our fathers were brought hither by their high veneration for the Christian religion. They journeyed by its light, and labored in its hope. They sought to incorporate its principles with the elements of their society, and to diffuse its influence through all their institutions, civil, political, or literary. Let us cherish these sentiments, and extend this influence still more widely; in the full conviction, that that is the happiest society which partakes in the highest degree of the mild and peaceful spirit of Christianity.

The hours of this day are rapidly flying, and this occasion will soon be passed. Neither we nor our children can expect to behold its return. They are in the distant regions of futurity, they exist only in the all-creating power of God, who shall stand here a hundred years hence, to trace, through us, their descent from the Pilgrims, and to survey, as we have now surveyed, the progress of their country, during the lapse of a century. We would anticipate their concurrence with us in our sentiments of deep regard for our common ancestors. We would anticipate and partake the pleasure with which they will then recount the steps of New England's advancement. On the morning of that day, although it will not disturb us in our repose, the voice of acclamation and gratitude, commencing on the Rock of Plymouth, shall be transmitted through millions of the sons of the Pilgrims, till it lose itself in the murmurs of the Pacific seas.

We would leave for the consideration of those who shall then occupy our places, some proof that we hold the blessings transmitted from our fathers in just estimation; some proof of our attachment to the cause of good government, and of civil and religious liberty; some proof of a sincere and ardent desire to promote every thing which may enlarge the understandings and improve the hearts of men. And when, from the long distance of a hundred years, they shall look back upon us, they shall know, at least, that we possessed affections, which, running backward and warming with gratitude for what our ancestors have done for our happiness, run forward also to our posterity, and meet them with cordial salutation, ere yet they have arrived on the shore of being.

Advance, then, ye future generations! We would hail you, as you rise in your long succession, to fill the places which we now fill, and to taste the blessings of existence where we are passing, and soon shall have passed, our own human duration. We bid you welcome to this pleasant land of the fathers. We bid you welcome to the healthful skies and the verdant fields of New England. We greet your accession to the great inheritance which we have enjoyed. We welcome you to the blessings of good government and religious liberty. We welcome you to the treasures of science and the delights of learning. We welcome you to the transcendent sweets of domestic life, to the happiness of kindred, and parents, and children. We welcome you to the immeasurable blessings of rational existence, the immortal hope of Christianity, and the light of everlasting truth!

* * * * *

NOTES.

NOTE A.--PAGE 27.

The allusion in the Discourse is to the large historical painting of the Landing of the Pilgrims at Plymouth, executed by Henry Sargent, Esq., of Boston, and, with great liberality, presented by him to the Pilgrim Society. It appeared in their hall (of which it forms the chief ornament) for the first time at the celebration of 1824. It represents the principal personages of the company at the moment of landing, with the Indian Samoset, who approaches them with a friendly welcome. A very competent judge, himself a distinguished artist, the late venerable Colonel Trumbull, has pronounced that this painting has great merit. An interesting account of it will be found in Dr. Thacher's History of Plymouth, pp. 249 and 257.

An historical painting, by Robert N. Weir, Esq., of the largest size, representing the embarkation of the Pilgrims from Delft-Haven, in Holland, and executed by order of Congress, fills one of the panels of the Rotunda of the Capitol at Washington. The moment chosen by the artist for the action of the picture is that in which the venerable pastor Robinson, with tears, and benedictions, and prayers to Heaven, dismisses the beloved members of his little flock to the perils and the hopes of their great enterprise. The characters of the personages introduced are indicated with discrimination and power, and the accessories of the work marked with much taste and skill. It is a painting of distinguished historical interest and of great artistic merit.

The "Landing of the Pilgrims" has also been made the subject of a very interesting painting by Mr. Flagg, intended to represent the deep religious feeling which so strikingly characterized the first settlers of New England. With this object in view, the central figure is that of Elder Brewster. It is a picture of cabinet size, and is in possession of a gentleman of New Haven, descended from Elder Brewster, and of that name.

NOTE B.--PAGE 45.

As the opinion of contemporaneous thinkers on this important subject cannot fail to interest the general reader, it is deemed proper to insert here the following extract from a letter, written in 1849, to show how powerfully the truths uttered in 1820, in the spirit of prophecy, as it were, impressed themselves upon certain minds, and how closely the verification of the prediction has been watched.

"I do not remember any political prophecy, founded on the spirit of a wide and far-reaching statesmanship, that has been so remarkably fulfilled as the one made by Mr. Webster, in his Discourse delivered at Plymouth in 1820, on the effect which the laws of succession to property in France, then in operation, would be likely to produce on the forms and working of the French government. But to understand what he said, and what he foresaw, I must explain a little what had been the course of legislation in France on which his predictions were founded.

"Before the Revolution of 1789, there had been a great accumulation of the landed property of the country, and, indeed, of all its property,--by means of laws of entail, _majorats_, and other legal contrivances,--in the hands of the privileged classes; chiefly in those of the nobility and the clergy. The injury and injustice done by long continued legislation in this direction were obviously great; and it was not, perhaps, unnatural, that the opposite course to that which had brought on the mischief should be deemed the best one to cure it. At any rate, such was the course taken.

"In 1791 a law was passed, preventing any man from having any interest beyond the period of his own life in any of his property, real, personal, or mixed, and distributing all his possessions for him, immediately after his death, among his children, in equal shares, or if he left no children, then among his next of kin, on the same principle. This law, with a slight modification, made under the influence of Robespierre, was in force till 1800. But the period was entirely revolutionary, and probably quite as much property changed hands from violence and the consequences of violence, during the nine years it continued, as was transmitted by the laws that directly controlled its succession.

"With the coming in of Bonaparte, however, there was established a new order of things, which has continued, with little modification, ever since, and has had its full share in working out the great changes in French society which we now witness. A few experiments were first made, and then the great Civil Code, often called the _Code Napoleon_, was adopted. This was in 1804. By this remarkable code, which is still in force, a man, if he has but one child, can give away by his last will, as he pleases, half of his property,--the law insuring the other half to the child; if he has two children, then he can so give away only one third,--the law requiring the other two thirds to be given equally to the two children; if three, then only one fourth under similar conditions; but if he has a greater number, it restricts the rights of the parent more and more, and makes it more and more difficult for him to distribute his property according to his own judgment; the restrictions embarrassing him even in his lifetime.

"The consequences of such laws are, from their nature, very slowly developed. When Mr. Webster spoke in 1820, the French code had been in operation sixteen years, and similar principles had prevailed for nearly a generation. But still its wide results were not even suspected. Those who had treated the subject at all supposed that the tendency was to break up the great estates in France, and make the larger number of the holders of small estates more accessible to the influence of the government, then a limited monarchy, and so render it stronger and more despotic.

"Mr. Webster held a different opinion. He said, 'In respect, however, to the recent law of succession in France, to which I have alluded, _I would, presumptuously perhaps, hazard a conjecture, that, if the government do not change the law, the law in half a century will change the government; and that this change will be, not in favor of the power of the crown, as some European writers have supposed, but against it_. Those writers only reason upon what they think correct general principles, in relation to this subject. They acknowledge a want of experience. Here we have had that experience; and we know that a multitude of small proprietors, acting with intelligence, and that enthusiasm which a common cause inspires, constitute not only a formidable, but an invincible power.'

"In less than six years after Mr. Webster uttered this remarkable prediction, the king of France himself, at the opening of the Legislative Chambers, thus strangely echoed it:--'Legislation ought to provide, by successive improvements, for all the wants of society. The progressive partitioning of landed estates, essentially contrary to the spirit of a monarchical government, would enfeeble the guaranties which the charter has given to my throne and to my subjects. Measures will be proposed to you, gentlemen, to establish the consistency which ought to exist between the political law and the civil law, and to preserve the patrimony of families, without restricting the liberty of disposing of one's property. The preservation of families is connected with, and affords a guaranty to, political stability, which is the first want of states, and which is especially that of France, after so many vicissitudes.'

"Still, the results to which such subdivision and comminution of property tended were not foreseen even in France. The Revolution of 1830 came, and revealed a part of them; for that revolution was made by the influence of men possessing very moderate estates, who believed that the guaranties of a government like that of the elder branch of the Bourbons were not sufficient for their safety. But when the revolution was made, and the younger branch of the Bourbons reigned instead of the elder, the laws for the descent of property continued to be the same, and the subdivision went on as if it were an admitted benefit to society.

"In consequence of this, in 1844 it was found that there were in France at least five millions and a half of families, or about twenty-seven millions of souls, who were proprietary families, and that of these about four millions of families had each less than nine English acres to the family on the average. Of course, a vast majority of these twenty-seven millions of persons, though they might be interested in some small portion of the soil, were really poor, and multitudes of them were dependent.

"Now, therefore, the results began to appear in a practical form. One third of all the rental of France was discovered to be absolutely mortgaged, and another third was swallowed up by other encumbrances, leaving but one third free for the use and benefit of its owners. In other words, a great proportion of the people of France were embarrassed and poor, and a great proportion of the remainder were fast becoming so.

"Such a state of things produced, of course, a wide-spread social uneasiness. Part of this uneasiness was directed against the existing government; another and more formidable portion was directed against *all* government, and against the very institution of property. The convulsion of 1848 followed; France is still unsettled; and Mr. Webster's prophecy seems still to be in the course of a portentous fulfilment."

In the London Quarterly Review for 1846 there is an interesting discussion on so much of the matter as relates to the subdivision of real estate for agricultural purposes in France, as far as it had then advanced, and from which many of the facts here alluded to are taken.

[Footnote 1: An interesting account of the Rock may be found in Dr. Thacher's History of the Town of Plymouth, pp. 29, 198, 199.][Footnote 2: See Note A, at the end of the Discourse.]
[Footnote 3: For notices of Carver, Bradford, Standish, Brewster, and Allerton, see Young's Chronicles of Plymouth and Massachusetts; Morton's Memorial, p. 126; Belknap's American Biography, Vol. II.; Hutchinson's History, Vol. II., App., pp. 456 _et seq._; Collections of the Massachusetts Historical Society; Winthrop's Journal; and Thacher's History.][Footnote 4: For the original name of what is now Plymouth, see Lives of American Governors, p. 38, note, a work prepared with great care by J.B. Moore, Esq.][Footnote 5: The twenty-first is now acknowledged to be the true anniversary. See the Report of the Pilgrim Society on the subject.][Footnote 6: Herodot. VI. § 109.][Footnote 7: For the compact to which reference is made in the text, signed on board the Mayflower, see Hutchinson's History, Vol. II., Appendix, No. I. For an eloquent description of the manner in which the first Christian Sabbath was passed on board

the Mayflower, at Plymouth, see Barne's Discourse at Worcester.][Footnote 8: The names of the passengers in the Mayflower, with some account of them, may be found in the New England Genealogical Register, Vol. I. p. 47, and a narration of some of the incidents of the voyage, Vol. II. p. 186. For an account of Mrs. White, the mother of the first child born in New England, see Baylies's History of Plymouth, Vol. II. p. 18, and for a notice of her son Peregrine, see Moore's Lives of American Governors, Vol. I. p. 31, note.][Footnote 9: See the admirable letter written on board the Arbella, in Hutchinson's History, Vol. I. Appendix, No. I.][Footnote 10: In reference to the British policy respecting Colonial manufactures, see Representations of the Board of Trade to the House of Lords, 23d Jan., 1734; also, 8th June, 1749. For an able vindication of the British Colonial policy, see "Political Essays concerning the Present State of the British Empire." London. 1772.][Footnote 11: Many interesting papers, illustrating the early history of the Colony, may be found in Hutchinson's "Collection of Original Papers relating to the History of the Colony of Massachusetts Bay."][Footnote 12: In reference to the fulfilment of this prediction, see Mr. Webster's Address at the Celebration of the New England Society of New York, on the 23d of December, 1850.][Footnote 13: John Adams, second President of the United States.][Footnote 14: See note B, at the end of the Discourse.][Footnote 15: Oratio pro Flacco, § 7.][Footnote 16: The first free school established by law in the Plymouth Colony was in 1670-72. One of the early teachers in Boston taught school more than *seventy* years. See Cotton Mather's "Funeral Sermon upon Mr. Ezekiel Cheever, the ancient and honorable Master of the Free School in Boston."

For the impression made upon the mind of an intelligent foreigner by the general attention to popular education, as characteristic of the American polity, see Mackay's Western World, Vol. III. p. 225 _et seq._ Also, Edinburgh Review, No. 186.][Footnote 17: By a law of the Colony of Massachusetts Bay, passed as early as 1647, it was ordered, that, "when any town shall increase to the number of one hundred families or householders, they shall set up a grammar school, the master thereof being able to instruct youth so far as they may be fitted for the University."]

[Footnote 18: In reference to the opposition of the Colonies to the slave-trade, see a representation of the Board of Trade to the House of Lords, 23d January, 1733-4.]

DEFENCE OF JUDGE JAMES PRESCOTT.
THE CLOSING APPEAL TO THE SENATE OF MASSACHUSETTS, IN MR. WEBSTER'S "ARGUMENT ON THE IMPEACHMENT OF JAMES PRESCOTT," APRIL 24TH, 1821.

Mr. President, the case is closed! The fate of the respondent is in your hands. It is for you now to say, whether, from the law and the facts as they have appeared before you, you will proceed to disgrace and disfranchise him. If your duty calls on you to convict him, let justice be done, and convict him; but, I adjure you, let it be a clear, undoubted case. Let it be so for his sake, for you are robbing him of that for which, with all your high powers, you can yield him no compensation; let it be so for your own sakes, for the responsibility of this day's judgment is one which you must carry with you through life. For myself, I am willing here to relinquish the character of an advocate, and to express opinions by which I am prepared to be bound as a citizen and a man. And I say upon my honor and conscience, that I see not how, with the law and constitution for your guides, you can pronounce the respondent guilty. I declare that I have seen no case of wilful and corrupt official misconduct, set forth according to the requisitions of the constitution, and proved according to the common rules of evidence. I see many things imprudent and ill-judged; many things that I could wish had been otherwise; but corruption and crime I do not see.

Sir, the prejudices of the day will soon be forgotten; the passions, if any there be, which have excited or favored this prosecution will subside; but the consequence of the judgment you are about to render will outlive both them and you. The respondent is now brought, a single, unprotected individual, to this formidable bar of judgment, to stand against the power and authority of the State. I know you can crush him, as he stands before you, and clothed as you are with the sovereignty of the State. You have the power "to change his countenance and to send him away." Nor do I remind you, that your judgment is to be rejudged by the community; and, as you have summoned him for trial to this high tribunal, that you are soon to descend yourselves from these seats of justice, and stand before the higher tribunal of the world. I would not fail so much in respect to this honorable court as to hint that it could pronounce a sentence which the community will reverse. No, Sir, it is not the world's revision which I would call on you to regard; but that of your own consciences, when years have gone by and you shall look back on the sentence you are about to render. If you send away the respondent, condemned and sentenced, from your bar, you are yet to meet him in the world on which you cast him out. You will be called to behold him a disgrace to his family, a sorrow and a shame to his children, a living fountain of grief and agony to himself.

If you shall then be able to behold him only as an unjust judge, whom vengeance has overtaken and justice has blasted, you will be able to look upon him, not without pity, but yet without remorse. But if, on the other hand, you shall see, whenever and wherever you meet him, a victim of prejudice or of passion, a sacrifice to a transient excitement; if you shall see in him a man for whose condemnation any provision of the constitution has been violated or any principle of law broken down, then will he be able, humble and low as may be his condition, then will he be able to turn the current of compassion backward, and to look with pity on those who have been his judges. If you are about to visit this respondent with a judgment which shall blast his house; if the bosoms of the innocent and the amiable are to be made to bleed under your infliction, I beseech you to be able to state clear and strong grounds for your proceeding. Prejudice and excitement are transitory, and will pass away. Political expediency, in matters of judicature, is a false and hollow principle, and will never satisfy the conscience of him who is fearful that he may have given a hasty judgment. I earnestly entreat you, for your own sakes, to possess yourselves of solid reasons, founded in truth and justice, for the judgment you pronounce, which you can carry with you till you go down into your graves; reasons which it will require no argument to revive, no sophistry, no excitement, no regard to popular favor, to render satisfactory to your consciences; reasons which you can appeal to in every crisis of your lives, and which shall be able to assure you, in your own great extremity, that you have not judged a fellow-creature without mercy.

Sir, I have done with the case of this individual, and now leave it in your hands. But I would yet once more appeal to you as public men; as statesmen; as men of enlightened minds, capable of a large view of things, and of foreseeing the remote consequences of important transactions; and, as such, I would most earnestly implore you to consider fully of the judgment you may pronounce. You are about to give a construction to constitutional provisions which may adhere to that instrument for ages, either for good or evil. I may perhaps overrate the importance of this occasion to the public welfare; but I confess it does appear to me that, if this body give its sanction to some of the principles which have been advanced on this occasion, then there is a power in the State above the constitution and the law; a power essentially arbitrary and despotic, the exercise of which may be most dangerous. If impeachment be not under the rule of the constitution and the laws, then may we tremble, not only for those who may be impeached, but for all others. If the full benefit of every constitutional provision be not extended to the respondent, his case becomes the case of all the people of the Commonwealth. The constitution is their constitution. They have made it for their own protection, and for his among the rest. They are not eager for his conviction. They desire not his ruin. If he be condemned, without having his offences set forth in the manner which they, by their constitution, have prescribed, and in the manner which they, by their laws, have ordained, then not only is he condemned unjustly, but the rights of the whole people are disregarded. For the sake of the people themselves, therefore, I would resist all attempts to convict by straining the laws or getting over their prohibitions. I hold up before him the broad shield of the constitution; if through that he be pierced and fall, he will be but one sufferer in a common catastrophe.

THE REVOLUTION IN GREECE.
A SPEECH DELIVERED IN THE HOUSE OF REPRESENTATIVES OF THE UNITED STATES, ON THE 19TH OF JANUARY, 1824.

[The rise and progress of the revolution in Greece attracted great attention in the United States. Many obvious causes contributed to this effect, and their influence was seconded by the direct appeal made to the people of America, by the first political body organized in Greece after the breaking out of the revolution, viz. "The Messenian Senate of Calamata." A formal address was made by that body to the people of the United States, and forwarded by their committee (of which the celebrated Koray was chairman), to a friend and correspondent in this country. This address was translated and widely circulated; but it was not to be expected that any great degree of confidence should be at once generally felt in a movement undertaken against such formidable odds.

The progress of events, however, in 1822 and 1823, was such as to create an impression that the revolution in Greece had a substantial foundation in the state of affairs, in the awakened spirit of that country, and in the condition of public opinion throughout Christendom. The interest felt in the struggle rapidly increased in the United States. Local committees were formed, animated appeals were made, and funds collected, with a view to the relief of the victims of the war.

On the assembling of Congress, in December, 1823, President Monroe made the revolution in Greece the subject of a paragraph in his annual message, and on the 8th of December Mr. Webster moved the following resolution in the House of Representatives:--

"_Resolved_, That provision ought to be made, by law, for defraying the expense incident to the appointment of an Agent or Commissioner to Greece, whenever the President shall deem it expedient to make such appointment."

These, it is believed, are the first official expressions favorable to the independence of Greece uttered by any of the governments of Christendom, and no doubt contributed powerfully towards the creation of that feeling throughout the civilized world which eventually led to the battle of Navarino, and the liberation of a portion of Greece from the Turkish yoke.

The House of Representatives having, on the 19th of January, resolved itself into a committee of the whole, and this resolution being taken into consideration, Mr. Webster spoke to the following effect.]

I am afraid, Mr. Chairman, that, so far as my part in this discussion is concerned, those expectations which the public excitement existing on the subject, and certain associations easily suggested by it, have conspired to raise, may be disappointed. An occasion which calls the attention to a spot so distinguished, so connected with interesting recollections, as Greece, may naturally create something of warmth and enthusiasm. In a grave, political discussion, however, it is necessary that those feelings should be chastised. I shall endeavor properly to repress them, although it is impossible that they should be altogether extinguished. We must, indeed, fly beyond the civilized world; we must pass the dominion of law and the boundaries of knowledge; we must, more especially, withdraw ourselves from this place, and the scenes and objects which here surround us,--if we would separate ourselves entirely from the influence of all those memorials of herself which ancient Greece has transmitted for the admiration and the benefit of mankind. This free form of government, this popular assembly, the common council held for the common good,--where have we contemplated its earliest models? This practice of free debate and public discussion, the contest of mind with mind, and that popular eloquence, which, if it were now here, on a subject like this, would move the stones of the Capitol,--whose was the language in which all these were first exhibited? Even the edifice in which we assemble, these proportioned columns, this ornamented architecture, all remind us that Greece has existed, and that we, like the rest of mankind, are greatly her debtors.[1]

But I have not introduced this motion in the vain hope of discharging any thing of this accumulated debt of centuries. I have not acted upon the expectation, that we who have inherited this obligation from our ancestors should now attempt to pay it to those who may seem to have inherited from _their_ ancestors a right to receive payment. My object is nearer and more immediate. I wish to take occasion of the struggle of an interesting and gallant people, in the cause of liberty and Christianity, to draw the attention of the House to the circumstances which have accompanied that struggle, and to the principles which appear to have governed the conduct of the great states of Europe in regard to it; and to the effects and consequences of these principles upon the independence of nations, and especially upon the institutions of free governments. What I have to say of Greece, therefore, concerns the modern, not the ancient; the living, and not the dead. It regards her, not as she exists in history, triumphant over time, and tyranny, and ignorance; but as she now is, contending, against fearful odds, for being, and for the common privileges of human nature.

As it is never difficult to recite commonplace remarks and trite aphorisms, so it may be easy, I am aware, on this occasion, to remind me of the wisdom which dictates to men a care of their own affairs, and admonishes them, instead of searching for adventures abroad, to leave other men's concerns in their own hands. It may be easy to call this resolution _Quixotic_, the emanation of a crusading or propagandist spirit. All this, and more, may be readily said; but all this, and more, will not be allowed to fix a character upon this proceeding, until that is proved which it takes for granted. Let it first be shown, that in this question there is nothing which can affect the interest, the character, or the duty of this country. Let it be proved, that we are not called upon, by either of these considerations, to express an opinion on the subject to which the resolution relates. Let this be proved, and then it will indeed be made out, that neither ought this resolution to pass, nor ought the subject of it to have been mentioned in the communication of the President to us. But, in my opinion, this cannot be shown. In my judgment, the subject is interesting to the people and the government of this country, and we are called upon, by considerations of great weight and moment, to express our opinions upon it. These considerations, I think, spring from a sense of our own duty, our character, and our own interest. I wish to treat the subject on such grounds, exclusively, as are truly _American_; but then, in considering it as an American question, I cannot forget the age in which we live, the prevailing spirit of the age, the interesting questions which agitate it, and our own peculiar relation in regard to these interesting questions. Let this be, then, and as far as I am concerned I hope it will be, purely an American discussion; but let it embrace, nevertheless, every thing that fairly concerns America. Let it comprehend, not merely her present advantage, but her permanent interest, her elevated character as one of the free states of the world, and her duty towards those great principles which have hitherto maintained the relative independence of nations, and which have, more especially, made her what she is.

At the commencement of the session, the President, in the discharge of the high duties of his office, called our attention to the subject to which this resolution refers. "A strong hope," says that communication, "has been long entertained, founded on the heroic struggle of the Greeks, that they would succeed in their contest, and resume their equal station among the nations of the earth. It is believed that the whole civilized world takes a deep interest in their welfare. Although no power has declared in their favor, yet none, according to our information, has taken part against them. Their cause and their name have protected them from dangers which might ere this have overwhelmed any other people. The ordinary calculations of interest, and of acquisition with a view to aggrandizement, which mingle so much in the transactions of nations, seem to have had no effect in regard to them. From the facts which have come to our knowledge, there is good cause to believe that their enemy has lost for ever all dominion over them; that Greece will become again an independent nation."

It has appeared to me that the House should adopt some resolution reciprocating these sentiments, so far as it shall approve them. More than twenty years have elapsed since Congress first ceased to receive such a communication from the President as could properly be made the subject of a general answer. I do not mean to find fault with this relinquishment of a former and an ancient practice. It may have been attended with inconveniences which justified its abolition. But, certainly, there was one advantage belonging to it; and that is, that it furnished a fit opportunity for the expression of the opinion of the Houses of Congress upon those topics in the executive communication which were not expected to be made the immediate subjects of direct legislation. Since, therefore, the President's message does not now receive a general answer, it has seemed to me to be proper that, in some mode, agreeable to our own usual form of proceeding, we should express our sentiments upon the important and interesting topics on which it treats. If the sentiments of the message in respect to Greece be proper, it is equally proper that this House should reciprocate those sentiments. The present resolution is designed to have that extent, and no more. If it pass, it will leave any future proceeding where it now is, in the discretion of the executive government. It is but an expression, under those forms in which the House is accustomed to act, of the satisfaction of the House with the general sentiments expressed in regard to this subject in the message, and of its readiness to defray the expense incident to any inquiry for the purpose of further information, or any other agency which the President, in his discretion, shall see fit, in whatever manner and at whatever time, to institute. The whole matter is still left in his judgment, and this resolution can in no way restrain its unlimited exercise.

I might well, Mr. Chairman, avoid the responsibility of this measure, if it had, in my judgment, any tendency to change the policy of the country. With the general course of that policy I am quite satisfied. The nation is prosperous, peaceful, and happy; and I should very reluctantly put its peace, prosperity, or happiness at risk. It appears to me, however, that this resolution is strictly conformable to our general policy, and not only consistent with our interests, but even demanded by a large and liberal view of those interests.

It is certainly true that the just policy of this country is, in the first place, a peaceful policy. No nation ever had less to expect from forcible aggrandizement. The mighty agents which are working out our greatness are time, industry, and the arts. Our augmentation is by growth, not by acquisition; by internal development, not by external accession. No schemes can be suggested to us so magnificent as the prospects which a sober contemplation of our own condition, unaided by projects, uninfluenced by ambition, fairly spreads before us. A country of such vast extent, with such varieties of soil and climate, with so much public spirit and private enterprise, with a population increasing so much beyond former example, with capacities of improvement not only unapplied or unexhausted, but even, in a great measure, as yet unexplored,--so free in its institutions, so mild in its laws, so secure in the title it confers on every man to his own acquisitions,--needs nothing but time and peace to carry it forward to almost any point of advancement.

In the next place, I take it for granted that the policy of this country, springing from the nature of our government and the spirit of all our institutions, is, so far as it respects the interesting questions which agitate the present age, on the side of liberal and enlightened sentiments. The age is extraordinary; the spirit that actuates it is peculiar and marked; and our own relation to the times we live in, and to the questions which interest them, is equally marked and peculiar. We are placed, by our good fortune and the wisdom and valor of our ancestors, in a condition in which we *can* act no obscure part. Be it for honor, or be it for dishonor, whatever we do is sure to attract the observation of the world. As one of the free states among the nations, as a great and rapidly rising republic, it would be impossible for us, if we were so disposed, to prevent our principles, our sentiments, and our example from producing some effect upon the opinions and hopes of society throughout the civilized world. It rests probably with ourselves to determine whether the influence of these shall be salutary or pernicious.

It cannot be denied that the great political question of this age is that between absolute and regulated governments. The substance of the controversy is whether society shall have any part in its own government. Whether the form of government shall be that of limited monarchy, with more or less mixture of hereditary power, or wholly elective or representative, may perhaps be considered as subordinate. The main controversy is between that absolute rule, which, while it promises to govern well, means, nevertheless, to govern without control, and that constitutional system which restrains sovereign discretion, and asserts that society may claim as matter of right some effective power in the establishment of the laws which are to regulate it. The spirit of the times sets with a most powerful current in favor of these last-mentioned opinions. It is opposed, however, whenever and wherever it shows itself, by certain of the great potentates of Europe; and it is opposed on grounds as applicable in one civilized nation as in another, and which would justify such opposition in relation to the United States, as well as in relation to any other state or nation, if time and circumstances should render such opposition expedient.

What part it becomes this country to take on a question of this sort, so far as it is called upon to take any part, cannot be doubtful. Our side of this question is settled for us, even without our own volition. Our history, our situation, our character, necessarily decide our position and our course, before we have even time to ask whether we have an option. Our place is on the side of free institutions. From the earliest settlement of these States, their inhabitants were accustomed, in a greater or less degree, to the enjoyment of the powers of self-government; and for the last half-century they have sustained systems of government entirely representative, yielding to themselves the greatest possible prosperity, and not leaving them without distinction and respect among the nations of the earth. This system we are not likely to abandon; and while we shall no farther recommend its adoption to other nations, in whole or in part, than it may recommend itself by its visible influence on our own growth and prosperity, we are, nevertheless, interested to resist the establishment of doctrines which deny the legality of its foundations. We stand as an equal among nations, claiming the full benefit of the established international law; and it is our duty to oppose, from the earliest to the latest moment, any innovations upon that code which shall bring into doubt or question our own equal and independent rights.

I will now, Mr. Chairman, advert to those pretensions put forth by the allied sovereigns of Continental Europe, which seem to me calculated, if unresisted, to bring into disrepute the principles of our government, and, indeed, to be wholly incompatible with any degree of national independence. I do not introduce these considerations for the sake of topics. I am not about to declaim against crowned heads, nor to quarrel with any country for preferring a form of government different from our own. The right of choice that we exercise for ourselves, I am quite willing to leave also to others. But it appears to me that the pretensions to which I have alluded are wholly inconsistent with the independence of nations generally, without regard to the question whether their governments be absolute, monarchical and limited, or purely popular and representative. I have a most deep and thorough conviction, that a new era has arisen in the world, that new and dangerous combinations are taking place, promulgating doctrines and fraught with consequences wholly subversive in their tendency of the public law of nations and of the general liberties of mankind. Whether this be so, or not, is the question which I now propose to examine, upon such grounds of information as are afforded by the common and public means of knowledge.

Everybody knows that, since the final restoration of the Bourbons to the throne of France, the Continental powers have entered into sundry alliances, which have been made public, and have held several meetings or congresses, at which the principles of their political conduct have been declared. These things must necessarily have an effect upon the international law of the states of the world. If that effect be good, and according to the principles of that law, they deserve to be applauded. If, on the contrary, their effect and tendency be most dangerous, their principles wholly inadmissible, their pretensions such as would abolish every degree of national independence, then they are to be resisted.

I begin, Mr. Chairman, by drawing your attention to the treaty concluded at Paris in September, 1815, between Russia, Prussia, and Austria, commonly called the Holy Alliance. This singular alliance appears to have originated with the Emperor of Russia; for we are informed that a draft of it was exhibited by him, personally, to a plenipotentiary of one of the great powers of Europe, before it was presented to the other sovereigns who ultimately signed it.[2] This instrument professes nothing, certainly, which is not extremely commendable and praiseworthy. It promises only that the contracting parties, both in relation to other states, and in regard to their own subjects, will observe the rules of justice and Christianity. In confirmation of these promises, it makes the most solemn and devout religious invocations. Now, although such an alliance is a novelty in European history, the world seems to have received this treaty, upon its first promulgation, with general charity. It was commonly understood as little or nothing more than an expression of thanks for the successful termination of the momentous contest in which those sovereigns had been engaged. It still seems somewhat unaccountable, however, that these good resolutions should require to be confirmed by treaty. Who doubted that these august sovereigns would treat each other with justice, and rule their own subjects in mercy? And what necessity was there for a solemn stipulation by treaty, to insure the performance of that which is no more than the ordinary duty of every government? It would hardly be admitted by these sovereigns, that by this compact they consider themselves bound to introduce an entire change, or any change in the course of their own conduct. Nothing substantially new, certainly, can be supposed to have been intended. What principle, or what practice, therefore, called for this solemn declaration of the intention of the parties to observe the rules of religion and justice?

It is not a little remarkable, that a writer of reputation upon the Public Law, described, many years ago, not inaccurately, the character of this alliance. I allude to Puffendorf. "It seems useless," says he, "to frame any pacts or leagues, barely for the defence and support of universal peace; for by such a league nothing is superadded to the obligation of natural law, and no agreement is made for the performance of any thing which the parties were not previously bound to perform; nor is the original obligation rendered firmer or stronger by such an addition. Men of any tolerable culture and civilization might well be ashamed of entering into any such compact, the conditions of which imply only that the parties concerned shall not offend in any clear point of duty. Besides, we should be guilty of great irreverence towards God, should we suppose that his injunctions had not already laid a sufficient obligation upon us to act justly, unless we ourselves voluntarily consented to the same engagement; as if our obligation to obey his will depended upon our own pleasure.

"If one engage to serve another, he does not set it down expressly and particularly among the terms and conditions of the bargain, that he will not betray nor murder him, nor pillage nor burn his house. For the same reason, that would be a dishonorable engagement in which men should bind themselves to act properly and decently, and not break the peace."[3]

Such were the sentiments of that eminent writer. How nearly he had anticipated the case of the Holy Alliance will appear from the preamble to that alliance. After stating that the allied sovereigns had become persuaded, by the events of the last three years, that "their relations with each other ought to be regulated exclusively by the sublime truths taught by the eternal religion of God the Saviour," they solemnly declare their fixed resolution "to adopt as the sole rule of their conduct, both in the administration of their respective states, and in their political relations with every other government, the precepts of that holy religion, namely, the precepts of justice, charity, and peace, which, far from being applicable to private life alone, ought, on the contrary, to have a direct influence upon the counsels of princes, and guide all their steps, as being the only means of consolidating human institutions, and remedying their imperfections."[4]

This measure, however, appears principally important, as it was the first of a series, and was followed afterwards by others of a more marked and practical nature. These measures, taken together, profess to establish two principles, which the Allied Powers would introduce as a part of the law of the civilized world; and the establishment of which is to be enforced by a million and a half of bayonets.

The first of these principles is, that all popular or constitutional rights are held no otherwise than as grants from the crown. Society, upon this principle, has no rights of its own; it takes good government, when it gets it, as a boon and a concession, but can demand nothing. It is to live by that favor which emanates from royal authority, and if it have the misfortune to lose that favor, there is nothing to protect it against any degree of injustice and oppression. It can rightfully make no endeavor for a change, by itself; its whole privilege is to receive the favors that may be dispensed by the sovereign power, and all its duty is described in the single word *submission*. This is the plain result of the principal Continental state papers; indeed, it is nearly the identical text of some of them.

The circular despatch addressed by the sovereigns assembled at Laybach, in the spring of 1821, to their ministers at foreign courts, alleges, "that useful and necessary changes in legislation and in the administration of states ought only to emanate from the free will and intelligent and well-weighed conviction of those whom God has rendered responsible for power. All that deviates from this line necessarily leads to disorder, commotions, and evils far more insufferable than those which they pretend to remedy."[5] Now, Sir, this principle would carry Europe back again, at once, into the middle of the Dark Ages. It is the old doctrine of the Divine right of kings, advanced now by new advocates, and sustained by a formidable array of power. That the people hold their fundamental privileges as matter of concession or indulgence from the sovereign power, is a sentiment not easy to be diffused in this age, any farther than it is enforced by the direct operation of military means. It is true, certainly, that some six centuries ago the early founders of English liberty called the instrument which secured their rights a *charter*. It was, indeed, a concession; they had obtained it sword in hand from the king; and in many other cases, whatever was obtained, favorable to human rights, from the tyranny and despotism of the feudal sovereigns, was called by the names of *privileges* and _liberties_, as being matter of special favor. Though we retain this language at the present time, the principle itself belongs to ages that have long passed by us. The civilized world has done with "the enormous faith, of many made for one." Society asserts its own rights, and alleges them to be original, sacred, and unalienable. It is not satisfied with having kind masters; it demands a participation in its own government; and in states much advanced in civilization, it urges this demand with a constancy and an energy that cannot well nor long be resisted. There are, happily, enough of regulated governments in the world, and those among the most distinguished, to operate as constant examples, and to keep alive an unceasing panting in the bosoms of men for the enjoyment of similar free institutions.

When the English Revolution of 1688 took place, the English people did not content themselves with the example of Runnymede; they did not build their hopes upon royal charters; they did not, like the authors of the Laybach circular, suppose that all useful changes in constitutions and laws must proceed from those only whom God has rendered responsible for power. They were somewhat better instructed in the principles of civil liberty, or at least they were better lovers of those principles than the sovereigns of Laybach. Instead of petitioning for charters, they declared their rights, and while they offered to the Prince of Orange the crown with one hand, they held in the other an enumeration of those privileges which they did not profess to hold as favors, but which they demanded and insisted upon as their undoubted rights.

I need not stop to observe, Mr. Chairman, how totally hostile are these doctrines of Laybach to the fundamental principles of our government. They are in direct contradiction; the principles of good and evil are hardly more opposite. If these principles of the sovereigns be true, we are but in a state of rebellion or of anarchy, and are only tolerated among civilized states because it has not yet been convenient to reduce us to the true standard.

But the second, and, if possible, the still more objectionable principle, avowed in these papers, is the right of forcible interference in the affairs of other states. A right to control nations in their desire to change their own government, wherever it maybe conjectured, or pretended, that such change might furnish an example to the subjects of other states, is plainly and distinctly asserted. The same Congress that made the declaration at Laybach had declared, before its removal from Troppau, "that the powers have an undoubted right to take a hostile attitude in regard to those states in which the overthrow of the government may operate as an example."

There cannot, as I think, be conceived a more flagrant violation of public law, or national independence, than is contained in this short declaration.

No matter what be the character of the government resisted; no matter with what weight the foot of the oppressor bears on the neck of the oppressed; if he struggle, or if he complain, he sets a dangerous example of resistance,--and from that moment he becomes an object of hostility to the most powerful potentates of the earth. I want words to express my abhorrence of this abominable principle. I trust every enlightened man throughout the world will oppose it, and that, especially, those who, like ourselves, are fortunately out of the reach of the bayonets that enforce it, will proclaim their detestation of it, in a tone both loud and decisive. The avowed object of such declarations is to preserve the peace of the world. But by what means is it proposed to preserve this peace? Simply, by bringing the power of all governments to bear against all subjects. Here is to be established a sort of double, or treble, or quadruple, or, for aught I know, quintuple allegiance. An offence against one king is to be an offence against all kings, and the power of all is to be put forth for the punishment of the offender. A right to interfere in extreme cases, in the case of contiguous states, and where imminent danger is threatened to one by what is occurring in another, is not without precedent in modern times, upon what has been called the law of vicinage; and when confined to extreme cases, and limited to a certain extent, it may perhaps be defended upon principles of necessity and self-defence. But to maintain that sovereigns may go to war upon the subjects of another state to repress an example, is monstrous indeed. What is to be the limit to such a principle, or to the practice growing out of it? What, in any case, but sovereign pleasure, is to decide whether the example be good or bad? And what, under the operation of such a rule, may be thought of our example? Why are we not as fair objects for the operation of the new principle, as any of those who may attempt a reform of government on the other side of the Atlantic?

The ultimate effect of this alliance of sovereigns, for objects personal to themselves, or respecting only the permanence of their own power, must be the destruction of all just feeling, and all natural sympathy, between those who exercise the power of government and those who are subject to it. The old channels of mutual regard and confidence are to be dried up, or cut off. Obedience can now be expected no longer than it is enforced. Instead of relying on the affections of the governed, sovereigns are to rely on the affections and friendship of other sovereigns. There are, in short, no longer to be nations. Princes and people are no longer to unite for interests common to them both. There is to be an end of all patriotism, as a distinct national feeling. Society is to be divided horizontally; all sovereigns above, and all subjects below; the former coalescing for their own security, and for the more certain subjection of the undistinguished multitude beneath. This, Sir, is no picture drawn by imagination. I have hardly used language stronger than that in which the authors of this new system have commented on their own work. M. de Chateaubriand, in his speech in the French Chamber of Deputies, in February last, declared, that he had a conference with the Emperor of Russia at Verona, in which that august sovereign uttered sentiments which appeared to him so precious, that he immediately hastened home, and wrote them down while yet fresh in his recollection. "The Emperor declared," said he, "that there can no longer be such a thing as an English, French, Russian, Prussian, or Austrian policy; there is henceforth but one policy, which, for the safety of all, should be adopted both by people and kings. It was for me first to show myself convinced of the principles upon which I founded the alliance; an occasion offered itself,--the rising in Greece. Nothing certainly could occur more for my interests, for the interests of my people, nothing more acceptable to my country, than a religious war in Turkey. But I have thought I perceived in the troubles of the Morea the sign of revolution, and I have held back. Providence has not put under my command eight hundred thousand soldiers to satisfy my ambition, but to protect religion, morality, and justice, and to secure the prevalence of those principles of order on which human society rests. It may well be permitted, that kings may have public alliances to defend themselves against secret enemies."

These, Sir, are the words which the French minister thought so important that they deserved to be recorded; and I, too, Sir, am of the same opinion. But if it be true that there is hereafter to be neither a Russian policy, nor a Prussian policy, nor an Austrian policy, nor a French policy, nor even, which yet I will not believe, an English policy, there will be, I trust in God, an American policy. If the authority of all these governments be hereafter to be mixed and blended, and to flow in one augmented current of prerogative over the face of Europe, sweeping away all resistance in its course, it will yet remain for us to secure our own happiness by the preservation of our own principles; which I hope we shall have the manliness to express on all proper occasions, and the spirit to defend in every extremity. The end and scope of this amalgamated policy are neither more nor less than this: to interfere, by force, for any government against any people who may resist it. Be the state of the people what it may, they shall not rise; be the government what it will, it shall not be opposed.

The practical commentary has corresponded with the plain language of the text. Look at Spain, and at

Greece. If men may not resist the Spanish Inquisition, and the Turkish cimeter, what is there to which humanity must not submit? Stronger cases can never arise. Is it not proper for us, at all times, is it not our duty, at this time, to come forth, and deny, and condemn, these monstrous principles? Where, but here, and in one other place, are they likely to be resisted? They are advanced with equal coolness and boldness; and they are supported by immense power. The timid will shrink and give way, and many of the brave may be compelled to yield to force. Human liberty may yet, perhaps, be obliged to repose its principal hopes on the intelligence and the vigor of the Saxon race. As far as depends on us, at least, I trust those hopes will not be disappointed; and that, to the extent which may consist with our own settled, pacific policy, our opinions and sentiments may be brought to act on the right side, and to the right end, on an occasion which is, in truth, nothing less than a momentous question between an intelligent age, full of knowledge, thirsting for improvement, and quickened by a thousand impulses, on one side, and the most arbitrary pretensions, sustained by unprecedented power, on the other.

This asserted right of forcible intervention in the affairs of other nations is in open violation of the public law of the world. Who has authorized these learned doctors of Troppau to establish new articles in this code? Whence are their diplomas? Is the whole world expected to acquiesce in principles which entirely subvert the independence of nations? On the basis of this independence has been reared the beautiful fabric of international law. On the principle of this independence, Europe has seen a family of nations flourishing within its limits, the small among the large, protected not always by power, but by a principle above power, by a sense of propriety and justice. On this principle, the great commonwealth of civilized states has been hitherto upheld. There have been occasional departures or violations, and always disastrous, as in the case of Poland; but, in general, the harmony of the system has been wonderfully preserved. In the production and preservation of this sense of justice, this predominating principle, the Christian religion has acted a main part. Christianity and civilization have labored together; it seems, indeed, to be a law of our human condition, that they can live and flourish only together. From their blended influence has arisen that delightful spectacle of the prevalence of reason and principle over power and interest, so well described by one who was an honor to the age;--

"And sovereign Law, the state's collected will, O'er thrones and globes elate, Sits empress,--crowning good, repressing ill: Smit by her sacred frown, The fiend, Discretion, like a vapor, sinks, And e'en the all-dazzling crown Hides his faint rays, and at her bidding shrinks."

But this vision is past. While the teachers of Laybach give the rule, there will be no law but the law of the strongest.

It may now be required of me to show what interest *we* have in resisting this new system. What is it to _us_, it may be asked, upon what principles, or what pretences, the European governments assert a right of interfering in the affairs of their neighbors? The thunder, it may be said, rolls at a distance. The wide Atlantic is between us and danger; and, however others may suffer, *we* shall remain safe.

I think it is a sufficient answer to this to say, that we are one of the nations of the earth; that we have an interest, therefore, in the preservation of that system of national law and national intercourse which has heretofore subsisted, so beneficially for all. Our system of government, it should also be remembered, is, throughout, founded on principles utterly hostile to the new code; and if we remain undisturbed by its operation, we shall owe our security either to our situation or our spirit. The enterprising character of the age, our own active, commercial spirit, the great increase which has taken place in the intercourse among civilized and commercial states, have necessarily connected us with other nations, and given us a high concern in the preservation of those salutary principles upon which that intercourse is founded. We have as clear an interest in international law, as individuals have in the laws of society.

But apart from the soundness of the policy, on the ground of direct interest, we have, Sir, a duty connected with this subject, which I trust we are willing to perform. What do *we* not owe to the cause of civil and religious liberty? to the principle of lawful resistance? to the principle that society has a right to partake in its own government? As the leading republic of the world, living and breathing in these principles, and advanced, by their operation, with unequalled rapidity in our career, shall we give *our* consent to bring them into disrepute and disgrace? It is neither ostentation nor boasting to say, that there lies before this country, in immediate prospect, a great extent and height of power. We are borne along towards this without effort, and not always even with a full knowledge of the rapidity of our own motion.

Circumstances which never combined before have co-operated in our favor, and a mighty current is setting us forward which we could not resist even if we would, and which, while we would stop to make an observation, and take the sun, has set us, at the end of the operation, far in advance of the place where we commenced it. Does it not become us, then, is it not a duty imposed on us, to give our weight to the side of liberty and justice, to let mankind know that we are not tired of our own institutions, and to protest against the asserted power of altering at pleasure the law of the civilized world?

But whatever we do in this respect, it becomes us to do upon clear and consistent principles. There is an important topic in the message to which I have yet hardly alluded. I mean the rumored combination of the European Continental sovereigns against the newly established free states of South America. Whatever position this government may take on that subject, I trust it will be one which can be defended on known and acknowledged grounds of right. The near approach or the remote distance of danger may affect policy, but cannot change principle. The same reason that would authorize us to protest against unwarrantable combinations to interfere between Spain and her former colonies, would authorize us equally to protest if the same combination were directed against the smallest state in Europe, although our duty to ourselves, our policy, and wisdom, might indicate very different courses as fit to be pursued by us in the two cases. We shall not, I trust, act upon the notion of dividing the world with the Holy Alliance, and complain of nothing done by them in their hemisphere if they will not interfere with ours. At least this would not be such a course of policy as I could recommend or support. We have not offended, and I hope we do not intend to offend, in regard to South America, against any principle of national independence or of public law. We have done nothing, we shall do nothing, that we need to hush up or to compromise by forbearing to express our sympathy for the cause of the Greeks, or our opinion of the course which other governments have adopted in regard to them.

It may, in the next place, be asked, perhaps, Supposing all this to be true, what can *we* do? Are we to go to war? Are we to interfere in the Greek cause, or any other European cause? Are we to endanger our pacific relations? No, certainly not. What, then, the question recurs, remains for us? If we will not endanger our own peace, if we will neither furnish armies nor navies to the cause which we think the just one, what is there within our power?

Sir, this reasoning mistakes the age. The time has been, indeed, when fleets, and armies, and subsidies, were the principal reliances even in the best cause. But, happily for mankind, a great change has taken place in this respect. Moral causes come into consideration, in proportion as the progress of knowledge is advanced; and the public opinion of the civilized world is rapidly gaining an ascendency over mere brutal force. It is already able to oppose the most formidable obstruction to the progress of injustice and oppression; and as it grows more intelligent and more intense, it will be more and more formidable. It may be silenced by military power, but it cannot be conquered. It is elastic, irrepressible, and invulnerable to the weapons of ordinary warfare. It is that impassible, inextinguishable enemy of mere violence and arbitrary rule, which, like Milton's angels,

"Vital in every part, ... Cannot, but by annihilating, die."

Until this be propitiated or satisfied, it is vain for power to talk either of triumphs or of repose. No matter what fields are desolated, what fortresses surrendered, what armies subdued, or what provinces overrun. In the history of the year that has passed by us, and in the instance of unhappy Spain, we have seen the vanity of all triumphs in a cause which violates the general sense of justice of the civilized world. It is nothing that the troops of France have passed from the Pyrenees to Cadiz; it is nothing that an unhappy and prostrate nation has fallen before them; it is nothing that arrests, and confiscation, and execution, sweep away the little remnant of national resistance. There is an enemy that still exists to check the glory of these triumphs. It follows the conqueror back to the very scene of his ovations; it calls upon him to take notice that Europe, though silent, is yet indignant; it shows him that the sceptre of his victory is a barren sceptre; that it shall confer neither joy nor honor, but shall moulder to dry ashes in his grasp. In the midst of his exultation, it pierces his ear with the cry of injured justice; it denounces against him the indignation of an enlightened and civilized age; it turns to bitterness the cup of his rejoicing, and wounds him with the sting which belongs to the consciousness of having outraged the opinion of mankind.

In my opinion, Sir, the Spanish nation is now nearer, not only in point of time, but in point of circumstance, to the acquisition of a regulated government, than at the moment of the French invasion. Nations must, no doubt, undergo these trials in their progress to the establishment of free institutions. The very trials benefit them, and render them more capable both of obtaining and of enjoying the object which they seek.

I shall not detain the committee, Sir, by laying before it any statistical, geographical, or commercial account of Greece. I have no knowledge on these subjects which is not common to all. It is universally admitted, that, within the last thirty or forty years, the condition of Greece has been greatly improved. Her marine is at present respectable, containing the best sailors in the Mediterranean, better even, in that sea, than our own, as more accustomed to the long quarantines and other regulations which prevail in its ports. The number of her seamen has been estimated as high as 50,000, but I suppose that estimate must be much too large. She has, probably, 150,000 tons of shipping. It is not easy to ascertain the amount of the Greek population. The Turkish government does not trouble itself with any of the calculations of political economy, and there has never been such a thing as an accurate census, probably, in any part of the Turkish empire. In the absence of all official information, private opinions widely differ. By the tables which have been communicated, it would seem that there are 2,400,000 Greeks in Greece proper and the islands; an amount, as I am inclined to think, somewhat overrated. There are, probably, in the whole of European Turkey, 5,000,000 Greeks, and 2,000,000 more in the Asiatic dominions of that power.

The moral and intellectual progress of this numerous population, under the horrible oppression which crushes it, has been such as may well excite regard. Slaves, under barbarous masters, the Greeks have still aspired after the blessings of knowledge and civilization. Before the breaking out of the present revolution, they had established schools, and colleges, and libraries, and the press. Wherever, as in Scio, owing to particular circumstances, the weight of oppression was mitigated, the natural vivacity of the Greeks, and their aptitude for the arts, were evinced. Though certainly not on an equality with the civilized and Christian states of Europe,--and how is it possible, under such oppression as they endured, that they should be?--they yet furnished a striking contrast with their Tartar masters. It has been well said, that it is not easy to form a just conception of the nature of the despotism exercised over them. Conquest and subjugation, as known among European states, are inadequate modes of expression by which to denote the dominion of the Turks. A conquest in the civilized world is generally no more than an acquisition of a new dominion to the conquering country. It does not imply a never-ending bondage imposed upon the conquered, a perpetual mark,--an opprobrious distinction between them and their masters; a bitter and unending persecution of their religion; an habitual violation of their rights of person and property, and the unrestrained indulgence towards them of every passion which belongs to the character of a barbarous soldiery. Yet such is the state of Greece. The Ottoman power over them, obtained originally by the sword, is constantly preserved by the same means. Wherever it exists, it is a mere military power. The religious and civil code of the state being both fixed in the Koran, and equally the object of an ignorant and furious faith, have been found equally incapable of change. "The Turk," it has been said, "has been *encamped* in Europe for four centuries." He has hardly any more participation in European manners, knowledge, and arts, than when he crossed the Bosphorus. But this is not the worst. The power of the empire is fallen into anarchy, and as the principle which belongs to the head belongs also to the parts, there are as many despots as there are pachas, beys, and viziers. Wars are almost perpetual between the Sultan and some rebellious governor of a province; and in the conflict of these despotisms, the people are necessarily ground between the upper and the nether millstone. In short, the Christian subjects of the Sublime Porte feel daily all the miseries which flow from despotism, from anarchy, from slavery, and from religious persecution. If any thing yet remains to heighten such a picture, let it be added, that every office in the government is not only actually, but professedly, venal,--the pachalics, the vizierates, the cadiships, and whatsoever other denomination may denote the depositary of power. In the whole world, Sir, there is no such oppression felt as by the Christian Greeks. In various parts of India, to be sure, the government is bad enough; but then it is the government of barbarians over barbarians, and the feeling of oppression is, of course, not so keen. There the oppressed are perhaps not better than their oppressors; but in the case of Greece, there are millions of Christian men, not without knowledge, not without refinement, not without a strong thirst for all the pleasures of civilized life, trampled into the very earth, century after century, by a pillaging, savage, relentless soldiery. Sir, the case is unique. There exists, and has existed, nothing like it. The world has no such misery to show; there is no case in which Christian communities can be called upon with such emphasis of appeal.

But I have said enough, Mr. Chairman, indeed I need have said nothing to satisfy the House, that it must be some new combination of circumstances, or new views of policy in the cabinets of Europe, which have caused this interesting struggle not merely to be regarded with indifference, but to be marked with opprobrium. The very statement of the case, as a contest between the Turks and Greeks, sufficiently indicates what must be the feeling of every individual, and every government, that is not biassed by a particular interest, or a particular feeling, to disregard the dictates of justice and humanity.

And now, Sir, what has been the conduct pursued by the Allied Powers in regard to this contest? When the revolution broke out, the sovereigns were assembled in congress at Laybach; and the papers of that assembly sufficiently manifest their sentiments. They proclaim their abhorrence of those "criminal combinations which had been formed in the eastern parts of Europe"; and, although it is possible that this denunciation was aimed, more particularly, at the disturbances in the provinces of Wallachia and Moldavia, yet no exception is made, from its general terms, in favor of those events in Greece which were properly the commencement of her revolution, and which could not but be well known at Laybach, before the date of these declarations. Now it must be remembered, that Russia was a leading party in this denunciation of the efforts of the Greeks to achieve their liberation; and it cannot but be expected by Russia, that the world should also remember what part she herself has heretofore acted in the same concern. It is notorious, that within the last half-century she has again and again excited the Greeks to rebellion against the Porte, and that she has constantly kept alive in them the hope that she would, one day, by her own great power, break the yoke of their oppressor. Indeed, the earnest attention with which Russia has regarded Greece goes much farther back than to the time I have mentioned. Ivan the Third, in 1482, having espoused a Grecian princess, heiress of the last Greek Emperor, discarded St. George from the Russian arms, and adopted the Greek two-headed black eagle, which has continued in the Russian arms to the present day. In virtue of the same marriage, the Russian princes claim the Greek throne as their inheritance.

Under Peter the Great, the policy of Russia developed itself more fully. In 1696, he rendered himself master of Azof, and, in 1698, obtained the right to pass the Dardanelles, and to maintain, by that route, commercial intercourse with the Mediterranean. He had emissaries throughout Greece, and particularly applied himself to gain the clergy. He adopted the *Labarum* of Constantine, "In hoc signo vinces"; and medals were struck, with the inscription, "Petrus I. Russo-Graecorum Imperator." In whatever new direction the principles of the Holy Alliance may now lead the politics of Russia, or whatever course she may suppose Christianity now prescribes to her, in regard to the Greek cause, the time has been when she professed to be contending for that cause, as identified with Christianity. The white banner under which the soldiers of Peter the First usually fought, bore, as its inscription, "In the name of the Prince, and for our country." Relying on the aid of the Greeks, in his war with the Porte, he changed the white flag to red, and displayed on it the words, "In the name of God, and for Christianity." The unfortunate issue of this war is well known. Though Anne and Elizabeth, the successors of Peter, did not possess his active character, they kept up a constant communication with Greece, and held out hopes of restoring the Greek empire.

Catharine the Second, as is well known, excited a general revolt in 1769. A Russian fleet appeared in the Mediterranean, and a Russian army was landed in the Morea. The Greeks in the end were disgusted at being expected to take an oath of allegiance to Russia, and the Empress was disgusted because they refused to take it. In 1774, peace was signed between Russia and the Porte, and the Greeks of the Morea were left to their fate. By this treaty the Porte acknowledged the independence of the Khan of the Crimea; a preliminary step to the acquisition of that country by Russia. It is not unworthy of remark, as a circumstance which distinguished this from most other diplomatic transactions, that it conceded to the cabinet of St. Petersburg the right of intervention in the interior affairs of Turkey, in regard to whatever concerned the religion of the Greeks. The cruelties and massacres that happened to the Greeks after the peace between Russia and the Porte, notwithstanding the general pardon which had been stipulated for them, need not now be recited. Instead of retracing the deplorable picture, it is enough to say, that in this respect the past is justly reflected in the present. The Empress soon after invaded and conquered the Crimea, and on one of the gates of Kerson, its capital, caused to be inscribed, "The road to Byzantium." The present Emperor, on his accession to the throne, manifested an intention to adopt the policy of Catharine the Second as his own, and the world has not been right in all its suspicions, if a project for the partition of Turkey did not form a part of the negotiations of Napoleon and Alexander at Tilsit.

All this course of policy seems suddenly to be changed. Turkey is no longer regarded, it would appear, as an object of partition or acquisition, and Greek revolts have all at once become, according to the declaration of Laybach, "criminal combinations." The recent congress at Verona exceeded its predecessor at Laybach in its denunciations of the Greek struggle. In the circular of the 14th of December, 1822, it declared the Grecian resistance to the Turkish power to be rash and culpable, and lamented that "the firebrand of rebellion had been thrown into the Ottoman empire." This rebuke and crimination we know to have proceeded on those settled principles of conduct which the Continental powers had prescribed for themselves. The sovereigns saw, as well as others, the real condition of the Greeks; they knew as well as others that it was most natural and most justifiable, that they should endeavor, at whatever hazard, to change that condition. They knew that they themselves, or at least one of them, had more than once urged the Greeks to similar efforts; that they themselves had thrown the same firebrand into the midst of the Ottoman empire. And yet, so much does it seem to be their fixed object to discountenance whatsoever threatens to disturb the actual government of any country, that, Christians as they were, and allied, as they professed to be, for purposes most important to human happiness and religion, they have not hesitated to declare to the world that they have wholly forborne to exercise any compassion to the Greeks, simply because they thought that they saw, in the struggles of the Morea, the sign of revolution. This, then, is coming to a plain, practical result. The Grecian revolution has been discouraged, discountenanced, and denounced, solely because it *is* a revolution. Independent of all inquiry into the reasonableness of its causes or the enormity of the oppression which produced it; regardless of the peculiar claims which Greece possesses upon the civilized world; and regardless of what has been their own conduct towards her for a century; regardless of the interest of the Christian religion,--the sovereigns at Verona seized upon the case of the Greek revolution as one above all others calculated to illustrate the fixed principles of their policy. The abominable rule of the Porte on one side, the value and the sufferings of the Christian Greeks on the other, furnished a case likely to convince even an incredulous world of the sincerity of the professions of the Allied Powers. They embraced the occasion with apparent ardor: and the world, I trust, is satisfied. We see here, Mr. Chairman, the direct and actual application of that system which I have attempted to describe. We see it in the very case of Greece. We learn, authentically and indisputably, that the Allied Powers, holding that all changes in legislation and administration ought to proceed from kings alone, were wholly inexorable to the sufferings of the Greeks, and entirely hostile to their success. Now it is upon this practical result of the principle of the Continental powers that I wish this House to intimate its opinion. The great question is a question of principle. Greece is only the signal instance of the application of that principle. If the principle be right, if we esteem it conformable to the law of nations, if we have nothing to say against it, or if we deem ourselves unfit to express an opinion on the subject, then, of course, no resolution ought to pass. If, on the other hand, we see in the declarations of the Allied Powers principles, not only utterly hostile to our own free institutions, but hostile also to the independence of all nations, and altogether opposed to the improvement of the condition of human nature; if, in the instance before us, we see a most striking exposition and application of those principles, and if we deem our opinions to be entitled to any weight in the estimation of mankind,--then I think it is our duty to adopt some such measure as the proposed resolution.

It is worthy of observation, Sir, that as early as July, 1821, Baron Strogonoff, the Russian minister at Constantinople, represented to the Porte, that, if the undistinguished massacres of the Greeks, both of such as were in open resistance and of those who remained patient in their submission were continued, and should become a settled habit, they would give just cause of war against the Porte to all Christian states. This was in 1821.[6] It was followed, early in the next year, by that indescribable enormity, that appalling monument of barbarian cruelty, the destruction of Scio; a scene I shall not attempt to describe; a scene from which human nature shrinks shuddering away; a scene having hardly a parallel in the history of fallen man. This scene, too, was quickly followed by the massacres in Cyprus; and all these things were perfectly known to the Christian powers assembled at Verona. Yet these powers, instead of acting upon the case supposed by Baron Strogonoff, and which one would think had been then fully made out,--instead of being moved by any compassion for the sufferings of the Greeks,--these powers, these Christian powers, rebuke their gallantry and insult their sufferings by accusing them of "throwing a firebrand into the Ottoman empire." Such, Sir, appear to me to be the principles on which the Continental powers of Europe have agreed hereafter to act; and this, an eminent instance of the application of those principles.

I shall not detain the committee, Mr. Chairman, by any attempt to recite the events of the Greek struggle up to the present time. Its origin may be found, doubtless, in that improved state of knowledge which, for some years, has been gradually taking place in that country. The emancipation of the Greeks has been a subject frequently discussed in modern times. They themselves are represented as having a vivid remembrance of the distinction of their ancestors, not unmixed with an indignant feeling that civilized and Christian Europe should not ere now have aided them in breaking their intolerable fetters.

In 1816 a society was founded in Vienna for the encouragement of Grecian literature. It was connected with a similar institution at Athens, and another in Thessaly, called the "Gymnasium of Mount Pelion." The treasury and general office of the institution were established at Munich. No political object was avowed by these institutions, probably none contemplated. Still, however, they had their effect, no doubt, in hastening that condition of things in which the Greeks felt competent to the establishment of their independence. Many young men have been for years annually sent to the universities in the western states of Europe for their education; and, after the general pacification of Europe, many military men, discharged from other employment, were ready to enter even into so unpromising a service as that of the revolutionary Greeks.

In 1820, war commenced between the Porte and Ali, the well-known Pacha of Albania. Differences existed also with Persia and with Russia. In this state of things, at the beginning of 1821, an insurrection broke out in Moldavia, under the direction of Alexander Ypsilanti, a well-educated soldier, who had been major-general in the Russian service. From his character, and the number of those who seemed inclined to join him, he was supposed to be countenanced by the court of St. Petersburg. This, however, was a great mistake, which the Emperor, then at Laybach, took an early opportunity to rectify. The Turkish government was alarmed at these occurrences in the northern provinces of European Turkey, and caused search to be made of all vessels entering the Black Sea, lest arms or other military means should be sent in that manner to the insurgents. This proved inconvenient to the commerce of Russia, and caused some unsatisfactory correspondence between the two powers. It may be worthy of remark, as an exhibition of national character, that, agitated by these appearances of intestine commotion, the Sultan issued a proclamation, calling on all true Mussulmans to renounce the pleasures of social life, to prepare arms and horses, and to return to the manner of their ancestors, the life of the plains. The Turk seems to have thought that he had, at last, caught something of the dangerous contagion of European civilization, and that it was necessary to reform his habits, by recurring to the original manners of military roving barbarians.

It was about this time, that is to say, at the commencement of 1821, that the revolution burst out in various parts of Greece and the isles. Circumstances, certainly, were not unfavorable to the movement, as one portion of the Turkish army was employed in the war against Ali Pacha in Albania, and another part in the provinces north of the Danube. The Greeks soon possessed themselves of the open country of the Morea, and drove their enemy into the fortresses. Of these, that of Tripolitza, with the city, fell into their hands, in the course of the summer. Having after these first movements obtained time to breathe, it became, of course, an early object to establish a government. For this purpose delegates of the people assembled, under that name which describes the assembly in which we ourselves sit, that name which "freed the Atlantic," a *Congress*. A writer, who undertakes to render to the civilized world that service which was once performed by Edmund Burke, I mean the compiler of the English Annual Register, asks, by what authority this assembly could call itself a Congress. Simply, Sir, by the same authority by which the people of the United States have given the same name to their own legislature. We, at least, should be naturally inclined to think, not only as far as names, but things also, are concerned, that the Greeks could hardly have begun their revolution under better auspices; since they have endeavored to render applicable to themselves the general principles of our form of government, as well as its name. This constitution went into operation at the commencement of the next year. In the mean time, the war with Ali Pacha was ended, he having surrendered, and being afterwards assassinated, by an instance of treachery and perfidy, which, if it had happened elsewhere than under the government of the Turks, would have deserved notice. The negotiation with Russia, too, took a turn unfavorable to the Greeks. The great point upon which Russia insisted, beside the abandonment of the measure of searching vessels bound to the Black Sea, was, that the Porte should withdraw its armies from the neighborhood of the Russian frontiers; and the immediate consequence of this, when effected, was to add so much more to the disposable force ready to be employed against the Greeks. These events seemed to have left the whole force of the Ottoman empire, at the commencement of 1822, in a condition to be employed against the Greek rebellion; and, accordingly, very many anticipated the immediate destruction of the cause. The event, however, was ordered otherwise. Where the greatest effort was made, it was met and defeated. Entering the Morea with an army which seemed capable of bearing down all resistance, the Turks were nevertheless defeated and driven back, and pursued beyond the isthmus, within which, as far as it appears, from that time to the present, they have not been able to set their foot.

It was in April of this year that the destruction of Scio took place. That island, a sort of appanage of the Sultana mother, enjoyed many privileges peculiar to itself. In a population of 130,000 or 140,000, it had no more than 2,000 or 3,000 Turks; indeed, by some accounts, not near as many. The absence of these ruffian masters had in some degree allowed opportunity for the promotion of knowledge, the accumulation of wealth, and the general cultivation of society. Here was the seat of modern Greek literature; here were libraries, printing-presses, and other establishments, which indicate some advancement in refinement and knowledge. Certain of the inhabitants of Samos, it would seem, envious of this comparative happiness of Scio, landed upon the island in an irregular multitude, for the purpose of compelling its inhabitants to make common cause with their countrymen against their oppressors. These, being joined by the peasantry, marched to the city and drove the Turks into the castle. The Turkish fleet, lately reinforced from Egypt, happened to be in the neighboring seas, and, learning these events, landed a force on the island of fifteen thousand men. There was nothing to resist such an army. These troops immediately entered the city and began an indiscriminate massacre. The city was fired; and in four days the fire and sword of the Turk rendered the beautiful Scio a clotted mass of blood and ashes. The details are too shocking to be recited. Forty thousand women and children, unhappily saved from the general destruction, were afterwards sold in the market of Smyrna, and sent off into distant and hopeless servitude. Even on the wharves of our own cities, it has been said, have been sold the utensils of those hearths which now exist no longer. Of the whole population which I have mentioned, not above nine hundred persons were left living upon the island. I will only repeat, Sir, that these tragical scenes were as fully known at the Congress of Verona, as they are now known to us; and it is not too much to call on the powers that constituted that congress, in the name of conscience and in the name of humanity, to tell us if there be nothing even in these unparalleled excesses of Turkish barbarity to excite a sentiment of compassion; nothing which they regard as so objectionable as even the very idea of popular resistance to power.

The events of the year which has just passed by, as far as they have become known to us, have been even more favorable to the Greeks than those of the year preceding. I omit all details, as being as well known to others as to myself. Suffice it to say, that with no other enemy to contend with, and no diversion of his force to other objects, the Porte has not been able to carry the war into the Morea; and that, by the last accounts, its armies were acting defensively in Thessaly. I pass over, also, the naval engagements of the Greeks, although that is a mode of warfare in which they are calculated to excel, and in which they have already performed actions of such distinguished skill and bravery, as would draw applause upon the best mariners in the world. The present state of the war would seem to be, that the Greeks possess the whole of the Morea with the exception of the three fortresses of Patras, Coron, and Modon; all Candia, but one fortress; and most of the other islands. They possess the citadel of Athens, Missolonghi, and several other places in Livadia. They have been able to act on the offensive, and to carry the war beyond the isthmus. There is no reason to believe their marine is weakened; more probably, it is strengthened. But, what is most important of all, they have obtained time and experience. They have awakened a sympathy throughout Europe and throughout America; and they have formed a government which seems suited to the emergency of their condition.

Sir, they have done much. It would be great injustice to compare their achievements with our own. We began our Revolution, already possessed of government, and, comparatively, of civil liberty. Our ancestors had from the first been accustomed in a great measure to govern themselves. They were familiar with popular elections and legislative assemblies, and well acquainted with the general principles and practice of free governments. They had little else to do than to throw off the paramount authority of the parent state. Enough was still left, both of law and of organization, to conduct society in its accustomed course, and to unite men together for a common object. The Greeks, of course, could act with little concert at the beginning; they were unaccustomed to the exercise of power, without experience, with limited knowledge, without aid, and surrounded by nations which, whatever claims the Greeks might seem to have upon them, have afforded them nothing but discouragement and reproach. They have held out, however, for three campaigns; and that, at least, is something. Constantinople and the northern provinces have sent forth thousands of troops;--they have been defeated. Tripoli, and Algiers, and Egypt, have contributed their marine contingents;--they have not kept the ocean. Hordes of Tartars have crossed the Bosphorus;--they have died where the Persians died. The powerful monarchies in the neighborhood have denounced their cause, and admonished them to abandon it and submit to their fate. They have answered them, that, although two hundred thousand of their countrymen have offered up their lives, there yet remain lives to offer; and that it is the determination of _all_, "yes, of ALL," to persevere until they shall have established their liberty, or until the power of their oppressors shall have relieved them from the burden of existence.

It may now be asked, perhaps, whether the expression of our own sympathy, and that of the country, may do them good? I hope it may. It may give them courage and spirit, it may assure them of public regard, teach them that they are not wholly forgotten by the civilized world, and inspire them with constancy in the pursuit of their great end. At any rate, Sir, it appears to me that the measure which I have proposed is due to our own character, and called for by our own duty. When we shall have discharged that duty, we may leave the rest to the disposition of Providence.

I do not see how it can be doubted that this measure is entirely *pacific*. I profess my inability to perceive that it has any possible tendency to involve our neutral relations. If the resolution pass, it is not of necessity to be immediately acted on. It will not be acted on at all, unless, in the opinion of the President, a proper and safe occasion for acting upon it shall arise. If we adopt the resolution to-day, our relations with every foreign state will be to-morrow precisely what they now are. The resolution will be sufficient to express our sentiments on the subjects to which I have adverted. Useful for that purpose, it can be mischievous for no purpose. If the topic were properly introduced into the message, it cannot be improperly introduced into discussion in this House. If it were proper, which no one doubts, for the President to express his opinions upon it, it cannot, I think, be improper for us to express ours. The only certain effect of this resolution is to signify, in a form usual in bodies constituted like this, our approbation of the general sentiment of the message. Do we wish to withhold that approbation? The resolution confers on the President no new power, nor does it enjoin on him the exercise of any new duty; nor does it hasten him in the discharge of any existing duty.

I cannot imagine that this resolution can add any thing to those excitements which it has been supposed, I think very causelessly, might possibly provoke the Turkish government to acts of hostility. There is already the message, expressing the hope of success to the Greeks and disaster to the Turks, in a much stronger manner than is to be implied from the terms of this resolution. There is the correspondence between the Secretary of State and the Greek Agent in London, already made public, in which similar wishes are expressed, and a continuance of the correspondence apparently invited. I might add to this, the unexampled burst of feeling which this cause has called forth from all classes of society, and the notorious fact of pecuniary contributions made throughout the country for its aid and advancement. After all this, whoever can see cause of danger to our pacific relations from the adoption of this resolution has a keener vision than I can pretend to. Sir, there is no augmented danger; there is no danger. The question comes at last to this, whether, on a subject of this sort, this House holds an opinion which is worthy to be expressed.

Even suppose, Sir, an agent or commissioner were to be immediately sent,--a measure which I myself believe to be the proper one,--there is no breach of neutrality, nor any just cause of offence. Such an agent, of course, would not be accredited; he would not be a public minister. The object would be inquiry and information; inquiry which we have a right to make, information which we are interested to possess. If a dismemberment of the Turkish empire be taking place, or has already taken place; if a new state be rising, or be already risen, in the Mediterranean,--who can doubt, that, without any breach of neutrality, we may inform ourselves of these events for the government of our own concerns? The Greeks have declared the Turkish coasts in a state of blockade; may we not inform ourselves whether this blockade be *nominal* or _real_? and, of course, whether it shall be regarded or disregarded? The greater our trade may happen to be with Smyrna, a consideration which seems to have alarmed some gentlemen, the greater is the reason, in my opinion, why we should seek to be accurately informed of those events which may affect its safety. It seems to me impossible, therefore, for any reasonable man to imagine that this resolution can expose us to the resentment of the Sublime Porte.

As little reason is there for fearing its consequences upon the conduct of the Allied Powers. They may, very naturally, dislike our sentiments upon the subject of the Greek revolution; but what those sentiments are they will much more explicitly learn in the President's message than in this resolution. They might, indeed, prefer that we should express no dissent from the doctrines which they have avowed, and the application which they have made of those doctrines to the case of Greece. But I trust we are not disposed to leave them in any doubt as to our sentiments upon these important subjects. They have expressed their opinions, and do not call that expression of opinion an interference; in which respect they are right, as the expression of opinion in such cases is not such an interference as would justify the Greeks in considering the powers at war with them. For the same reason, any expression which we may make of different principles and different sympathies is no interference. No one would call the President's message an interference; and yet it is much stronger in that respect than this resolution. If either of them could be construed to be an interference, no doubt it would be improper, at least it would be so according to my view of the subject; for the very thing which I have attempted to resist in the course of these observations is the right of foreign interference. But neither the message nor the resolution has that character. There is not a power in Europe which can suppose, that, in expressing our opinions on this occasion, we are governed by any desire of aggrandizing ourselves or of injuring others. We do no more than to maintain those established principles in which we have an interest in common with other nations, and to resist the introduction of new principles and new rules, calculated to destroy the relative independence of states, and particularly hostile to the whole fabric of our government.

I close, then, Sir, with repeating, that the object of this resolution is to avail ourselves of the interesting occasion of the Greek revolution to make our protest against the doctrines of the Allied Powers, both as they are laid down in principle and as they are applied in practice. I think it right, too, Sir, not to be unseasonable in the expression of our regard, and, as far as that goes, in a manifestation of our sympathy with a long oppressed and now struggling people. I am not of those who would, in the hour of utmost peril, withhold such encouragement as might be properly and lawfully given, and, when the crisis should be past, overwhelm the rescued sufferer with kindness and caresses. The Greeks address the civilized world with a pathos not easy to be resisted. They invoke our favor by more moving considerations than can well belong to the condition of any other people. They stretch out their arms to the Christian communities of the earth, beseeching them, by a generous recollection of their ancestors, by the consideration of their desolated and ruined cities and villages, by their wives and children sold into an accursed slavery, by their blood, which they seem willing to pour out like water, by the common faith, and in the name, which unites all Christians, that they would extend to them at least some token of compassionate regard.

[Footnote 1: The interior of the hall of the House of Representatives is surrounded by a magnificent colonnade of the composite order. [1824.]][Footnote 2: See Lord Castlereagh's speech in the House of Commons, February 3, 1816. Debates in Parliament, Vol. XXXVI. p. 355; where also the treaty may be found at length.][Footnote 3: Law of Nature and Nations, Book II. cap. 2, § 11.][Footnote 4: Martens, Recueil des Traités, Tome XIII. p. 656.][Footnote 5: Annual Register for 1821, p. 601.][Footnote 6: Annual Register for 1821, p. 251.]

THE TARIFF.

A SPEECH DELIVERED IN THE HOUSE OF REPRESENTATIVES OF THE UNITED STATES, ON THE 1ST AND 2D OF APRIL, 1824.

[At an early period of the session of Congress of 1823-24 a bill was introduced into the House of Representatives to amend the several acts laying duties on imports. The object of the bill was a comprehensive revision of the existing laws, with a view to the extension of the protective system. The bill became the subject of a protracted debate, in which much of the talent of the House on both sides was engaged. Mr. Webster took an active part in the discussion, and spoke upon many of the details of the bill, while it remained in the committee of the whole House on the state of the Union. Several objectionable provisions were removed, and various amendments were introduced upon his motion; and it was a matter of regret to him, as seen in the following speech, that the friends of the bill were not able or willing to bring it into a form in which, as a whole, he could give it his support. On the 30th and 31st of March, Mr. Clay, Speaker of the House, addressed the committee of the whole, at length and with great ability, on the general principles of the bill; and he was succeeded by Mr. Webster, on the 1st and 2d of April, in the following speech.]

MR. CHAIRMAN,--I will avail myself of the present occasion to make some remarks on certain principles and opinions which have been recently advanced, and on those considerations which, in my judgment, ought to govern us in deciding upon the several and respective parts of this very important and complex measure. I can truly say that this is a painful duty. I deeply regret the necessity which is likely to be imposed upon me of giving a general affirmative or negative vote on the whole of the bill. I cannot but think this mode of proceeding liable to great objections. It exposes both those who support and those who oppose the measure to very unjust and injurious misapprehensions. There may be good reasons for favoring some of the provisions of the bill, and equally strong reasons for opposing others; and these provisions do not stand to each other in the relation of principal and incident. If that were the case, those who are in favor of the principal might forego their opinions upon incidental and subordinate provisions. But the bill proposes enactments entirely distinct and different from one another in character and tendency. Some of its clauses are intended merely for revenue; and of those which regard the protection of home manufactures, one part stands upon very different grounds from those of other parts. So that probably every gentleman who may ultimately support the bill will vote for much which his judgment does not approve; and those who oppose it will oppose something which they would very gladly support.

Being intrusted with the interests of a district highly commercial, and deeply interested in manufactures also, I wish to state my opinions on the present measure, not as on a whole, for it has no entire and homogeneous character, but as on a collection of different enactments, some of which meet my approbation and some of which do not.

And allow me, Sir, in the first place, to state my regret, if indeed I ought not to express a warmer sentiment, at the names or designations which Mr. Speaker[1] has seen fit to adopt for the purpose of describing the advocates and the opposers of the present bill. It is a question, he says, between the friends of an "American policy" and those of a "foreign policy." This, Sir, is an assumption which I take the liberty most directly to deny. Mr. Speaker certainly intended nothing invidious or derogatory to any part of the House by this mode of denominating friends and enemies. But there is power in names, and this manner of distinguishing those who favor and those who oppose particular measures may lead to inferences to which no member of the House can submit. It may imply that there is a more exclusive and peculiar regard to American interests in one class of opinions than in another. Such an implication is to be resisted and repelled. Every member has a right to the presumption, that he pursues what he believes to be the interest of his country with as sincere a zeal as any other member. I claim this in my own case; and while I shall not, for any purpose of description or convenient arrangement use terms which may imply any disrespect to other men's opinions, much less any imputation upon other men's motives, it is my duty to take care that the use of such terms by others be not, against the will of those who adopt them, made to produce a false impression.

Indeed, Sir, it is a little astonishing, if it seemed convenient to Mr. Speaker, for the purposes of distinction, to make use of the terms "American policy" and "foreign policy," that he should not have applied them in a manner precisely the reverse of that in which he has in fact used them. If names are thought necessary, it would be well enough, one would think, that the name should be in some measure descriptive of the thing; and since Mr. Speaker denominates the policy which he recommends "a new policy in this country"; since he speaks of the present measure as a new era in our legislation; since he professes to invite us to depart from our accustomed course, to instruct ourselves by the wisdom of others, and to adopt the policy of the most distinguished foreign states,--one is a little curious to know with what propriety of speech this imitation of other nations is denominated an "American policy," while, on the contrary, a preference for our own established system, as it now actually exists and always has existed, is called a "foreign policy." This favorite American policy is what America has never tried; and this odious foreign policy is what, as we are told, foreign states have never pursued. Sir, that is the truest American policy which shall most usefully employ American capital and American labor, and best sustain the whole population. With me it is a fundamental axiom, it is interwoven with all my opinions, that the great interests of the country are united and inseparable; that agriculture, commerce, and manufactures will prosper together or languish together; and that all legislation is dangerous which proposes to benefit one of these without looking to consequences which may fall on the others.

Passing from this, Sir, I am bound to say that Mr. Speaker began his able and impressive speech at the proper point of inquiry,--I mean the present state and condition of the country,--although I am so unfortunate, or rather although I am so happy, as to differ from him very widely in regard to that condition. I dissent entirely from the justice of that picture of distress which he has drawn. I have not seen the reality, and know not where it exists. Within my observation, there is no cause for so gloomy and terrifying a representation. In respect to the New England States, with the condition of which I am of course best acquainted, the present appears to me a period of very general prosperity. Not, indeed, a time for sudden acquisition and great profits, not a day of extraordinary activity and successful speculation. There is no doubt a considerable depression of prices, and, in some degree, a stagnation of business. But the case presented by Mr. Speaker was not one of _depression_, but of _distress_; of universal, pervading, intense distress, limited to no class and to no place. We are represented as on the very verge and brink of national ruin. So far from acquiescing in these opinions, I believe there has been no period in which the general prosperity was better secured, or rested on a more solid foundation. As applicable to the Eastern States, I put this remark to their representatives, and ask them if it is not true. When has there been a time in which the means of living have been more accessible and more abundant? When has labor been rewarded, I do not say with a larger, but with a more certain success? Profits, indeed, are low; in some pursuits of life, which it is not proposed to benefit, but to _burden_, by this bill, very low. But still I am unacquainted with any proofs of extraordinary distress. What, indeed, are the general indications of the state of the country? There is no famine nor pestilence in the land, nor war, nor desolation. There is no writhing under the burden of taxation. The means of subsistence are abundant; and at the very moment when the miserable condition of the country is asserted, it is admitted that the wages of labor are high in comparison with those of any other country. A country, then, enjoying a profound peace, perfect civil liberty, with the means of subsistence cheap and abundant, with the reward of labor sure, and its wages higher than anywhere else, cannot be represented as in gloom, melancholy, and distress, but by the effort of extraordinary powers of tragedy.

Even if, in judging of this question, we were to regard only those proofs to which we have been referred, we shall probably come to a conclusion somewhat different from that which has been drawn. Our exports, for example, although certainly less than in some years, were not, last year, so much below an average formed upon the exports of a series of years, and putting those exports at a fixed value, as might be supposed. The value of the exports of agricultural products, of animals, of the products of the forest and of the sea, together with gunpowder, spirits, and sundry unenumerated articles, amounted in the several years to the following sums, viz.:--

In 1790, $27,716,152 1804, 33,842,316 1807, 38,465,854

Coming up now to our own times, and taking the exports of the years 1821, 1822, and 1823, of the same articles and products, at the same prices, they stand thus:--

In 1821, $45,643,175 1822, 48,782,295 1823, 55,863,491

Mr. Speaker has taken the very extraordinary year of 1803, and, adding to the exportation of that year what he thinks ought to have been a just augmentation, in proportion to the increase of our population, he swells the result to a magnitude, which, when compared with our actual exports, would exhibit a great deficiency. But is there any justice in this mode of calculation? In the first place, as before observed, the year 1803 was a year of extraordinary exportation. By reference to the accounts, that of the article of flour, for example, there was an export that year of thirteen hundred thousand barrels; but the very next year it fell to eight hundred thousand, and the next year to seven hundred thousand. In the next place, there never was any reason to expect that the increase of our exports of agricultural products would keep pace with the increase of our population. That would be against all experience. It is, indeed, most desirable, that there should be an augmented demand for the products of agriculture; but, nevertheless, the official returns of our exports do not show that absolute want of all foreign market which has been so strongly stated.

But there are other means by which to judge of the general condition of the people. The quantity of the means of subsistence consumed, or, to make use of a phraseology better suited to the condition of our own people, the quantity of the comforts of life enjoyed, is one of those means. It so happens, indeed, that it is not so easy in this country as elsewhere to ascertain facts of this sort with accuracy. Where most of the articles of subsistence and most of the comforts of life are taxed, there is, of course, great facility in ascertaining, from official statements, the amount of consumption. But in this country, most fortunately, the government neither knows, nor is concerned to know, the annual consumption; and estimates can only be formed in another mode, and in reference only to a few articles. Of these articles, tea is one. It is not quite a luxury, and yet is something above the absolute necessaries of life. Its consumption, therefore, will be diminished in times of adversity, and augmented in times of prosperity. By deducting the annual export from the annual import, and taking a number of years together, we may arrive at a probable estimate of consumption. The average of eleven years, from 1790 to 1800, inclusive, will be found to be two millions and a half of pounds. From 1801 to 1812, inclusive, the average was three millions seven hundred thousand; and the average of the last three years, to wit, 1821, 1822, and 1823, was five millions and a half. Having made a just allowance for the increase of our numbers, we shall still find, I think, from these statements, that there is no distress which has limited our means of subsistence and enjoyment.

In forming an opinion of the degree of general prosperity, we may regard, likewise, the progress of internal improvements, the investment of capital in roads, bridges, and canals. All these prove a balance of income over expenditure; they afford evidence that there is a surplus of profits, which the present generation is usefully vesting for the benefit of the next. It cannot be denied, that, in this particular, the progress of the country is steady and rapid.

We may look, too, to the sums expended for education. Are our colleges deserted? Do fathers find themselves less able than usual to educate their children? It will be found, I imagine, that the amount paid for the purpose of education is constantly increasing, and that the schools and colleges were never more full than at the present moment. I may add, that the endowment of public charities, the contributions to objects of general benevolence, whether foreign or domestic, the munificence of individuals towards whatever promises to benefit the community, are all so many proofs of national prosperity. And, finally, there is no defalcation of revenue, no pressure of taxation.

The general result, therefore, of a fair examination of the present condition of things, seems to me to be, that there is a considerable depression of prices, and curtailment of profit; and in some parts of the country, it must be admitted, there is a great degree of pecuniary embarrassment, arising from the difficulty of paying debts which were contracted when prices were high. With these qualifications, the general state of the country may be said to be prosperous; and these are not sufficient to give to the whole face of affairs any appearance of general distress.

Supposing the evil, then, to be a depression of prices, and a partial pecuniary pressure, the next inquiry is into the causes of that evil; and it appears to me that there are several; and in this respect, I think, too much has been imputed by Mr. Speaker to the single cause of the diminution of exports. Connected, as we are, with all the commercial nations of the world, and having observed great changes to take place elsewhere, we should consider whether the causes of those changes have not reached us, and whether we are not suffering by the operation of them, in common with others. Undoubtedly, there has been a great fall in the price of all commodities throughout the commercial world, in consequence of the restoration of a state of peace. When the Allies entered France in 1814, prices rose astonishingly fast, and very high. Colonial produce, for instance, in the ports of this country, as well as elsewhere, sprung up suddenly from the lowest to the highest extreme. A new and vast demand was created for the commodities of trade. These were the natural consequences of the great political changes which then took place in Europe.

We are to consider, too, that our own war created new demand, and that a government expenditure of twenty-five or thirty million dollars a year had the usual effect of enhancing prices. We are obliged to add, that the paper issues of our banks carried the same effect still further. A depreciated currency existed in a great part of the country; depreciated to such an extent, that, at one time, exchange between the centre and the North was as high as twenty per cent. The Bank of the United States was instituted to correct this evil; but, for causes which it is not necessary now to enumerate, it did not for some years bring back the currency of the country to a sound state. This depreciation of the circulating currency was so much, of course, added to the nominal prices of commodities, and these prices, thus unnaturally high, seemed, to those who looked only at the appearance, to indicate great prosperity. But such prosperity is more specious than real. It would have been better, probably, as the shock would have been less, if prices had fallen sooner. At length, however, they fell; and as there is little doubt that certain events in Europe had an influence in determining the time at which this fall took place, I will advert shortly to some of the principal of those events.

In May, 1819, the British House of Commons decided, by a unanimous vote, that the resumption of cash payments by the Bank of England should not be deferred beyond the ensuing February. The restriction had been continued from time to time, and from year to year, Parliament always professing to look to the restoration of a specie currency whenever it should be found practicable. Having been, in July, 1818, continued to July, 1819, it was understood that, in the interim, the important question of the time at which cash payments should be resumed should be finally settled. In the latter part of the year 1818, the circulation of the bank had been greatly reduced, and a severe scarcity of money was felt in the London market. Such was the state of things in England. On the Continent, other important events took place. The French Indemnity Loan had been negotiated in the summer of 1818, and the proportion of it belonging to Austria, Russia, and Prussia had been sold. This created an unusual demand for gold and silver in those countries. It has been stated, that the amount of the precious metals transmitted to Austria and Russia in that year was at least twenty millions sterling. Other large sums were sent to Prussia and to Denmark. The effect of this sudden drain of specie, felt first at Paris, was communicated to Amsterdam and Hamburg, and all other commercial places in the North of Europe.

The paper system of England had certainly communicated an artificial value to property. It had encouraged speculation, and excited over-trading. When the shock therefore came, and this violent pressure for money acted at the same moment on the Continent and in England, inflated and unnatural prices could be kept up no longer. A reduction took place, which has been estimated to have been at least equal to a fall of thirty, if not forty per cent. The depression was universal; and the change was felt in the United States severely, though not equally so in every part. There are those, I am aware, who maintain that the events to which I have alluded did not cause the great fall of prices, but that that fall was natural and inevitable, from the previously existing state of things, the abundance of commodities, and the want of demand. But that would only prove that the effect was produced in another way, rather than by another cause. If these great and sudden calls for money did not reduce prices, but prices fell, as of themselves, to their natural state, still the result is the same; for we perceive that, after these new calls for money, prices could not be kept longer at their unnatural height.

About the time of these foreign events, our own bank system underwent a change; and all these causes, in my view of the subject, concurred to produce the great shock which took place in our commercial cities, and in many parts of the country. The year 1819 was a year of numerous failures, and very considerable distress, and would have furnished far better grounds than exist at present for that gloomy representation of our condition which has been presented. Mr. Speaker has alluded to the strong inclination which exists, or has existed, in various parts of the country, to issue paper money, as a proof of great existing difficulties. I regard it rather as a very productive cause of those difficulties; and the committee will not fail to observe, that there is, at this moment, much the loudest complaint of distress precisely where there has been the greatest attempt to relieve it by systems of paper credit. And, on the other hand, content, prosperity, and happiness are most observable in those parts of the country where there has been the least endeavor to administer relief by law. In truth, nothing is so baneful, so utterly ruinous to all true industry, as interfering with the legal value of money, or attempting to raise artificial standards to supply its place. Such remedies suit well the spirit of extravagant speculation, but they sap the very foundation of all honest acquisition. By weakening the security of property, they take away all motive for exertion. Their effect is to transfer property. Whenever a debt is allowed to be paid by any thing less valuable than the legal currency in respect to which it was contracted, the difference between the value of the paper given in payment and the legal currency is precisely so much property taken from one man and given to another, by legislative enactment.

When we talk, therefore, of protecting industry, let us remember that the first measure for that end is to secure it in its earnings; to assure it that it shall receive its own. Before we invent new modes of raising prices, let us take care that existing prices are not rendered wholly unavailable, by making them capable of being paid in depreciated paper. I regard, Sir, this issue of irredeemable paper as the most prominent and deplorable cause of whatever pressure still exists in the country; and, further, I would put the question to the members of this committee, whether it is not from that part of the people who have tried this paper system, and tried it to their cost, that this bill receives the most earnest support? And I cannot forbear to ask, further, whether this support does not proceed rather from a general feeling of uneasiness under the present condition of things, than from the clear perception of any benefit which the measure itself can confer? Is not all expectation of advantage centred in a sort of vague hope, that change may produce relief? Debt certainly presses hardest where prices have been longest kept up by artificial means. They find the shock lightest who take it soonest; and I fully believe that, if those parts of the country which now suffer most had not augmented the force of the blow by deferring it, they would have now been in a much better condition than they are. We may assure ourselves, once for all, Sir, that there can be no such thing as payment of debts by legislation. We may abolish debts indeed; we may transfer property by visionary and violent laws. But we deceive both ourselves and our constituents, if we flatter either ourselves or them with the hope that there is any relief against whatever pressure exists, but in economy and industry. The depression of prices and the stagnation of business have been in truth the necessary result of circumstances. No government could prevent them, and no government can altogether relieve the people from their effect. We have enjoyed a day of extraordinary prosperity; we had been neutral while the world was at war, and had found a great demand for our products, our navigation, and our labor. We had no right to expect that that state of things would continue always. With the return of peace, foreign nations would struggle for themselves, and enter into competition with us in the great objects of pursuit.

Now, Sir, what is the remedy for existing evils? What is the course of policy suited to our actual condition? Certainly it is not our wisdom to adopt any system that may be offered to us, without examination, and in the blind hope that whatever changes our condition may improve it. It is better that we should

"bear those ills we have, Than fly to others that we know not of."

We are bound to see that there is a fitness and an aptitude in whatever measures may be recommended to relieve the evils that afflict us; and before we adopt a system that professes to make great alterations, it is our duty to look carefully to each leading interest of the community, and see how it may probably be affected by our proposed legislation.

And, in the first place, what is the condition of our commerce? Here we must clearly perceive, that it is not enjoying that rich harvest which fell to its fortune during the continuance of the European wars. It has been greatly depressed, and limited to small profits. Still, it is elastic and active, and seems capable of recovering itself in some measure from its depression. The shipping interest, also, has suffered severely, still more severely, probably, than commerce. If any thing should strike us with astonishment, it is that the navigation of the United States should be able to sustain itself. Without any government protection whatever, it goes abroad to challenge competition with the whole world; and, in spite of all obstacles, it has yet been able to maintain eight hundred thousand tons in the employment of foreign trade. How, Sir, do the ship-owners and navigators accomplish this? How is it that they are able to meet, and in some measure overcome, universal competition? It is not, Sir, by protection and bounties: but by unwearied exertion, by extreme economy, by unshaken perseverance, by that manly and resolute spirit which relies on itself to protect itself. These causes alone enable American ships still to keep their element, and show the flag of their country in distant seas. The rates of insurance may teach us how thoroughly our ships are built, and how skilfully and safely they are navigated. Risks are taken, as I learn, from the United States to Liverpool, at one per cent; and from the United States to Canton and back, as low as three per cent. But when we look to the low rate of freight, and when we consider, also, that the articles entering into the composition of a ship, with the exception of wood, are dearer here than in other countries, we cannot but be utterly surprised that the shipping interest has been able to sustain itself at all. I need not say that the navigation of the country is essential to its honor and its defence. Yet, instead of proposing benefits for it in this hour of its depression, we threaten by this measure to lay upon it new and heavy burdens. In the discussion, the other day, of that provision of the bill which proposes to tax tallow for the benefit of the oil-merchants and whalemen, we had the pleasure of hearing eloquent eulogiums upon that portion of our shipping employed in the whale-fishery, and strong statements of its importance to the public interest. But the same bill proposes a severe tax upon that interest, for the benefit of the iron-manufacturer and the hemp-grower. So that the tallow-chandlers and soapboilers are sacrificed to the oil-merchants, in order that these again may contribute to the manufacturers of iron and the growers of hemp.

If such be the state of our commerce and navigation, what is the condition of our home manufactures? How are they amidst the general depression? Do they need further protection? and if any, how much? On all these points, we have had much general statement, but little precise information. In the very elaborate speech of Mr. Speaker, we are not supplied with satisfactory grounds of judging with respect to these various particulars. Who can tell, from any thing yet before the committee, whether the proposed duty be too high or too low on any one article? Gentlemen tell us, that they are in favor of domestic industry; so am I. They would give it protection; so would I. But then all domestic industry is not confined to manufactures. The employments of agriculture, commerce, and navigation are all branches of the same domestic industry; they all furnish employment for American capital and American labor. And when the question is, whether new duties shall be laid, for the purpose of giving further encouragement to particular manufactures, every reasonable man must ask himself, both whether the proposed new encouragement be necessary, and whether it can be given without injustice to other branches of industry.

It is desirable to know, also, somewhat more distinctly, how the proposed means will produce the intended effect. One great object proposed, for example, is the increase of the home market for the consumption of agricultural products. This certainly is much to be desired; but what provisions of the bill are expected wholly or principally to produce this, is not stated. I would not deny that some increase of the home market may follow, from the adoption of this bill, but all its provisions have not an equal tendency to produce this effect. Those manufactures which employ most labor, create, of course, most demand for articles of consumption; and those create least in the production of which capital and skill enter as the chief ingredients of cost. I cannot, Sir, take this bill merely because a committee has recommended it. I cannot espouse a side, and fight under a flag. I wholly repel the idea that we must take this law, or pass no law on the subject. What should hinder us from exercising our own judgments upon these provisions, singly and severally? Who has the power to place us, or why should we place ourselves, in a condition where we cannot give to every measure, that is distinct and separate in itself, a separate and distinct consideration? Sir, I presume no member of the committee will withhold his assent from what he thinks right, until others will yield their assent to what they think wrong. There are many things in this bill acceptable, probably, to the general sense of the House. Why should not these provisions be passed into a law, and others left to be decided upon their own merits, as a majority of the House shall see fit? To some of these provisions I am myself decidedly favorable; to others I have great objections; and I should have been very glad of an opportunity of giving my own vote distinctly on propositions which are, in their own nature, essentially and substantially distinct from one another.

But, Sir, before expressing my own opinion upon the several provisions of this bill, I will advert for a moment to some other general topics. We have heard much of the policy of England, and her example has been repeatedly urged upon us, as proving, not only the expediency of encouragement and protection, but of exclusion and direct prohibition also. I took occasion the other day to remark, that more liberal notions were becoming prevalent on this subject; that the policy of restraints and prohibitions was getting out of repute, as the true nature of commerce became better understood; and that, among public men, those most distinguished were most decided in their reprobation of the broad principle of exclusion and prohibition. Upon the truth of this representation, as matter of fact, I supposed there could not be two opinions among those who had observed the progress of political sentiment in other countries, and were acquainted with its present state. In this respect, however, it would seem that I was greatly mistaken. We have heard it again and again declared, that the English government still adheres, with immovable firmness, to its old doctrines of prohibition; that although journalists, theorists, and scientific writers advance other doctrines, yet the practical men, the legislators, the government of the country, are too wise to follow them. It has even been most sagaciously hinted, that the promulgation of liberal opinions on these subjects is intended only to delude other governments, to cajole them into the folly of liberal ideas, while England retains to herself all the benefits of the admirable old system of prohibition. We have heard from Mr. Speaker a warm commendation of the complex mechanism of this system. The British empire, it is said, is, in the first place, to be protected against the rest of the world; then the British Isles against the colonies; next, the isles respectively against each other, England herself, as the heart of the empire, being protected most of all, and against all.

Truly, Sir, it appears to me that Mr. Speaker's imagination has seen system, and order, and beauty, in that which is much more justly considered as the result of ignorance, partiality, or violence. This part of English legislation has resulted, partly from considering Ireland as a conquered country, partly from the want of a complete union, even with Scotland, and partly from the narrow views of colonial regulation, which in early and uninformed periods influenced the European states.

Nothing, I imagine, would strike the public men of England more singularly, than to find gentlemen of real information and much weight in the councils of this country expressing sentiments like these, in regard to the existing state of these English laws. I have never said, indeed, that prohibitory laws do not exist in England; we all know they do; but the question is, Does she owe her prosperity and greatness to these laws? I venture to say, that such is not the opinion of public men now in England, and the continuance of the laws, even without any alteration, would not be evidence that their opinion is different from what I have represented it; because the laws having existed long, and great interests having been built up on the faith of them, they cannot now be repealed without great and overwhelming inconvenience. Because a thing has been wrongly done, it does not therefore follow that it can now be undone; and this is the reason, as I understand it, for which exclusion, prohibition, and monopoly are suffered to remain in any degree in the English system; and for the same reason, it will be wise in us to take our measures, on all subjects of this kind, with great caution. We may not be able, but at the hazard of much injury to individuals, hereafter to retrace our steps. And yet, whatever is extravagant or unreasonable is not likely to endure. There may come a moment of strong reaction; and if no moderation be shown in laying on duties, there may be as little scruple in taking them off.

It may be here observed, that there is a broad and marked distinction between entire prohibition and reasonable encouragement. It is one thing, by duties or taxes on foreign articles, to awaken a home competition in the production of the same articles; it is another thing to remove all competition by a total exclusion of the foreign article; and it is quite another thing still, by total prohibition, to raise up at home manufactures not suited to the climate, the nature of the country, or the state of the population. These are substantial distinctions, and although it may not be easy in every case to determine which of them applies to a given article, yet the distinctions themselves exist, and in most cases will be sufficiently clear to indicate the true course of policy; and, unless I have greatly mistaken the prevailing sentiment in the councils of England, it grows every day more and more favorable to the diminution of restrictions, and to the wisdom of leaving much (I do not say every thing, for that would not be true) to the enterprise and the discretion of individuals. I should certainly not have taken up the time of the committee to state at any length the opinions of other governments, or of the public men of other countries, upon a subject like this; but an occasional remark made by me the other day, having been so directly controverted, especially by Mr. Speaker, in his observations yesterday, I must take occasion to refer to some proofs of what I have stated.

What, then, is the state of English opinion? Everybody knows that, after the termination of the late European war, there came a time of great pressure in England. Since her example has been quoted, let it be asked in what mode her government sought relief. Did it aim to maintain artificial and unnatural prices? Did it maintain a swollen and extravagant paper circulation? Did it carry further the laws of prohibition and exclusion? Did it draw closer the cords of colonial restraint? No, Sir, but precisely the reverse. Instead of relying on legislative contrivances and artificial devices, it trusted to the enterprise and industry of the people, which it sedulously sought to excite, not by imposing restraint, but by removing it, wherever its removal was practicable. In May, 1820, the attention of the government having been much turned to the state of foreign trade, a distinguished member[2] of the House of Peers brought forward a Parliamentary motion upon that subject, followed by an ample discussion and a full statement of his own opinions. In the course of his remarks, he observed, "that there ought to be no prohibitory duties as such; for that it was evident, that, where a manufacture could not be carried on, or a production raised, but under the protection of a prohibitory duty, that manufacture, or that produce, could not be brought to market but at a loss. In his opinion, the name of strict prohibition might, therefore, in commerce, be got rid of altogether; but he did not see the same objection to protecting duties, which, while they admitted of the introduction of commodities from abroad similar to those which we ourselves manufactured, placed them so much on a level as to allow a competition between them." "No axiom," he added, "was more true than this: that it was by growing what the territory of a country could grow most cheaply, and by receiving from other countries what it could not produce except at too great an expense, that the greatest degree of happiness was to be communicated to the greatest extent of population."

In assenting to the motion, the first minister[3] of the crown expressed his own opinion of the great advantage resulting from unrestricted freedom of trade. "Of the soundness of that general principle," he observed, "I can entertain no doubt. I can entertain no doubt of what would have been the great advantages to the civilized world, if the system of unrestricted trade had been acted upon by every nation from the earliest period of its commercial intercourse with its neighbors. If to those advantages there could have been any exceptions, I am persuaded that they would have been but few; and I am also persuaded that the cases to which they would have referred would not have been, in themselves, connected with the trade and commerce of England. But we are now in a situation in which, I will not say that a reference to the principle of unrestricted trade can be of no use, because such a reference may correct erroneous reasoning, but in which it is impossible for us, or for any country in the world but the United States of America, to act unreservedly on that principle. The commercial regulations of the European world have been long established, and cannot suddenly be departed from." Having supposed a proposition to be made to England by a foreign state for free commerce and intercourse, and an unrestricted exchange of agricultural products and of manufactures, he proceeds to observe: "It would be impossible to accede to such a proposition. We have risen to our present greatness under a different system. Some suppose that we have risen in consequence of that system; _others, of whom I am one, believe that we have risen in spite of that system_. But, whichever of these hypotheses be true, certain it is that we have risen under a very different system than that of free and unrestricted trade. It is utterly impossible, with our debt and taxation, even if they were but half their existing amount, that we can suddenly adopt the system of free trade."

Lord Ellenborough, in the same debate, said, "that he attributed the general distress then existing in Europe to the regulations that had taken place since the destruction of the French power. Most of the states on the Continent had surrounded themselves as with walls of brass, to inhibit intercourse with other states. Intercourse was prohibited, even in districts of the same state, as was the case in Austria and Sardinia.

Thus, though the taxes on the people had been lightened, the severity of their condition had been increased. He believed that the discontent which pervaded most parts of Europe, and especially Germany, was more owing to commercial restrictions than to any theoretical doctrines on government; and that a free communication among them would do more to restore tranquillity, than any other step that could be adopted. He objected to all attempts to frustrate the benevolent intentions of Providence, which had given to various countries various wants, in order to bring them together. He objected to it as anti-social; he objected to it as making commerce the means of barbarizing instead of enlightening nations. The state of the trade with France was most disgraceful to both countries; the two greatest civilized nations of the world, placed at a distance of scarcely twenty miles from each other, had contrived, by their artificial regulations, to reduce their commerce with each other to a mere nullity." Every member speaking on this occasion agreed in the general sentiments favorable to unrestricted intercourse, which had thus been advanced; one of them remarking, at the conclusion of the debate, that "the principles of free trade, which he was happy to see so fully recognized, were of the utmost consequence; for, though, in the present circumstances of the country, a free trade was unattainable, yet their task hereafter was to approximate to it. Considering the prejudices and interests which were opposed to the recognition of that principle, it was no small indication of the firmness and liberality of government to have so fully conceded it."

Sir, we have seen, in the course of this discussion, that several gentlemen have expressed their high admiration of the *silk manufacture* of England. Its commendation was begun, I think, by the honorable member from Vermont, who sits near me, who thinks that that alone gives conclusive evidence of the benefits produced by attention to manufactures, inasmuch as it is a great source of wealth to the nation, and has amply repaid all the cost of its protection. Mr. Speaker's approbation of this part of the English example was still warmer. Now, Sir, it does so happen, that both these gentlemen differ very widely on this point from the opinions entertained in England, by persons of the first rank, both as to knowledge and power. In the debate to which I have already referred, the proposer of the motion urged the expediency of providing for the admission of the silks of France into England. "He was aware," he said, "that there was a poor and industrious body of manufacturers, whose interests must suffer by such an arrangement; and therefore he felt that it would be the duty of Parliament to provide for the present generation by a large Parliamentary grant. It was conformable to every principle of sound justice to do so, when the interests of a particular class were sacrificed to the good of the whole." In answer to these observations, Lord Liverpool said that, with reference to several branches of manufactures, time, and the change of circumstances, had rendered the system of protecting duties merely nominal; and that, in his opinion, if all the protecting laws which regarded both the woollen and cotton manufactures were to be repealed, no injurious effects would thereby be occasioned. "But," he observes, "with respect to silk, that manufacture in this kingdom is so completely artificial, that any attempt to introduce the principles of free trade with reference to it might put an end to it altogether. I allow that the silk manufacture is not natural to this country. _I wish we had never had a silk manufactory._ I allow that it is natural to France; I allow that it might have been better, had each country adhered exclusively to that manufacture in which each is superior; and had the silks of France been exchanged for British cottons. But I must look at things as they are; and when I consider the extent of capital, and the immense population, consisting, I believe, of about fifty thousand persons, engaged in our silk manufacture, I can only say, that one of the few points in which I totally disagree with the proposer of the motion is the expediency, under existing circumstances, of holding out any idea that it would be possible to relinquish the silk manufacture, and to provide for those who live by it, by Parliamentary enactment. Whatever objections there may be to the continuance of the protecting system, I repeat, that it is impossible altogether to relinquish it. I may regret that the system was ever commenced; but as I cannot recall that act, I must submit to the inconvenience by which it is attended, rather than expose the country to evils of greater magnitude." Let it be remembered, Sir, that these are not the sentiments of a theorist, nor the fancies of speculation; but the operative opinions of the first minister of England, acknowledged to be one of the ablest and most practical statesmen of his country.

Gentlemen could have hardly been more unfortunate than in the selection of the silk manufacture in England as an example of the beneficial effects of that system which they would recommend. It is, in the language which I have quoted, completely artificial. It has been sustained by I know not how many laws, breaking in upon the plainest principles of general expediency. At the last session of Parliament, the manufacturers petitioned for the repeal of three or four of these statutes, complaining of the vexatious restrictions which they impose on the wages of labor; setting forth, that a great variety of orders has from time to time been issued by magistrates under the authority of these laws, interfering in an oppressive manner with the minutest details of the manufacture,--such as limiting the number of threads to an inch, restricting the widths of many sorts of work, and determining the quantity of labor not to be exceeded without extra wages; that by the operation of these laws, the rate of wages, instead of being left to the recognized principles of regulation, has been arbitrarily fixed by persons whose ignorance renders them incompetent to a just decision; that masters are compelled by law to pay an equal price for all work, whether well or ill performed; and that they are wholly prevented from using improved machinery, it being ordered, that work, in the weaving of which machinery is employed, shall be paid precisely at the same rate as if done by hand; that these acts have frequently given rise to the most vexatious regulations, the unintentional breach of which has subjected manufacturers to ruinous penalties; and that the introduction of all machinery being prevented, by which labor might be cheapened, and the manufacturers being compelled to pay at a fixed price, under all circumstances, they are unable to afford employment to their workmen, in times of stagnation of trade, and are compelled to stop their looms. And finally, they complain that, notwithstanding these grievances under which they labor, while carrying on their manufacture in London, the law still prohibits them, while they continue to reside there, from employing any portion of their capital in the same business in any other part of the kingdom, where it might be more beneficially conducted. Now, Sir, absurd as these laws must appear to be to every man, the attempt to repeal them did not, as far as I recollect, altogether succeed. The weavers were too numerous, their interests too great, or their prejudices too strong; and this notable instance of protection and monopoly still exists, to be lamented in England with as much sincerity as it seems to be admired here.

In order further to show the prevailing sentiment of the English government, I would refer to a report of a select committee of the House of Commons, at the head of which was the Vice-President of the Board of Trade (Mr. Wallace), in July, 1820. "The time," say that committee, "when monopolies could be successfully supported, or would be patiently endured, either in respect to subjects against subjects, or particular countries against the rest of the world, seems to have passed away. Commerce, to continue undisturbed and secure, must be, as it was intended to be, a source of reciprocal amity between nations, and an interchange of productions to promote the industry, the wealth, and the happiness of mankind." In moving for the re-appointment of the committee in February, 1823, the same gentleman said: "We must also get rid of that feeling of appropriation which exhibited itself in a disposition to produce every thing necessary for our own consumption, and to render ourselves independent of the world. No notion could be more absurd or mischievous; it led, even in peace, to an animosity and rancor greater than existed in time of war. Undoubtedly there would be great prejudices to combat, both in this country and elsewhere, in the attempt to remove the difficulties which are most obnoxious. It would be impossible to forget the attention which was in some respects due to the present system of protections, although that attention ought certainly not to be carried beyond the absolute necessity of the case." And in a second report of the committee, drawn by the same gentleman, in that part of it which proposes a diminution of duties on timber from the North of Europe, and the policy of giving a legislative preference to the importation of such timber in the log, and a discouragement of the importation of deals, it is stated that the committee reject this policy, because, among other reasons, "it is founded on a principle of exclusion, which they are most averse to see brought into operation, in any _new instance_, without the warrant of some evident and great political expediency." And on many subsequent occasions the same gentleman has taken occasion to observe, that he differed from those who thought that manufactures could not nourish without restrictions on trade; that old prejudices of that sort were dying away, and that more liberal and just sentiments were taking their place.

These sentiments appear to have been followed by important legal provisions, calculated to remove restrictions and prohibitions where they were most severely felt; that is to say, in several branches of navigation and trade. They have relaxed their colonial system, they have opened the ports of their islands, and have done away the restriction which limited the trade of the colony to the mother country. Colonial products can now be carried directly from the islands to any part of Europe; and it may not be improbable, considering our own high duties on spirits, that that article may be exchanged hereafter by the English West India colonies directly for the timber and deals of the Baltic. It may be added, that Mr. Lowe, whom the gentleman has cited, says, that nobody supposes that the three great staples of English manufactures, cotton, woollen, and hardware, are benefited by any existing protecting duties; and that one object of all these protecting laws is usually overlooked, and that is, that they have been intended to reconcile the various interests to taxation; the corn law, for example, being designed as some equivalent to the agricultural interest for the burden of tithes and of poor-rates.

In fine, Sir, I think it is clear, that, if we now embrace the system of prohibitions and restrictions, we shall show an affection for what others have discarded, and be attempting to ornament ourselves with cast-off apparel.

Sir, I should not have gone into this prolix detail of opinions from any consideration of their special importance on the present occasion; but having happened to state that such was the actual opinion of the government of England at the present time, and the accuracy of this representation having been so confidently denied, I have chosen to put the matter beyond doubt or cavil, although at the expense of these tedious citations. I shall have occasion hereafter to refer more particularly to sundry recent British enactments, by way of showing the diligence and spirit with which that government strives to sustain its navigating interest, by opening the widest possible range to the enterprise of individual adventurers. I repeat, that I have not alluded to these examples of a foreign state as being fit to control our own policy. In the general principle, I acquiesce. Protection, when carried to the point which is now recommended, that is, to entire prohibition, seems to me destructive of all commercial intercourse between nations. We are urged to adopt the system upon general principles; and what would be the consequence of the universal application of such a general principle, but that nations would abstain entirely from all intercourse with one another? I do not admit the general principle; on the contrary, I think freedom of trade to be the general principle, and restriction the exception. And it is for every state, taking into view its own condition, to judge of the propriety, in any case, of making an exception, constantly preferring, as I think all wise governments will, not to depart without urgent reason from the general rule.

There is another point in the existing policy of England to which I would most earnestly invite the attention of the committee; I mean the warehouse system, or what we usually call the system of drawback. Very great prejudices appear to me to exist with us on that subject. We seem averse to the extension of the principle. The English government, on the contrary, appear to have carried it to the extreme of liberality. They have arrived, however, at their present opinions and present practice by slow degrees. The transit system was commenced about the year 1803, but the first law was partial and limited. It admitted the importation of raw materials for exportation, but it excluded almost every sort of manufactured goods. This was done for the same reason that we propose to prevent the transit of Canadian wheat through the United States, the fear of aiding the competition of the foreign article with our own in foreign markets. Better reflection or more experience has induced them to abandon that mode of reasoning, and to consider all such means of influencing foreign markets as nugatory; since, in the present active and enlightened state of the world, nations will supply themselves from the best sources, and the true policy of all producers, whether of raw materials or of manufactured articles, is, not vainly to endeavor to keep other vendors out of the market, but to conquer them in it by the quality and the cheapness of their articles. The present policy of England, therefore, is to allure the importation of commodities into England, there to be deposited in English warehouses, thence to be exported in assorted cargoes, and thus enabling her to carry on a general export trade to all quarters of the globe. Articles of all kinds, with the single exception of tea, may be brought into England, from any part of the world, in foreign as well as British ships, there warehoused, and again exported, at the pleasure of the owner, without the payment of any duty or government charge whatever.

While I am upon this subject, I would take notice also of the recent proposition in the English Parliament to abolish the tax on imported wool; and it is observable that those who support this proposition give the same reasons that have been offered here, within the last week, against the duty which we propose on the same article. They say that their manufacturers require a cheap and coarse wool, for the supply of the Mediterranean and Levant trade, and that, without a more free admission of the wool of the Continent, that trade will all fall into the hands of the Germans and Italians, who will carry it on through Leghorn and Trieste. While there is this duty on foreign wool to protect the wool-growers of England, there is, on the other hand, a prohibition on the exportation of the native article in aid of the manufacturers. The opinion seems to be gaining strength, that the true policy is to abolish both.

Laws have long existed in England preventing the emigration of artisans and the exportation of machinery; but the policy of these, also, has become doubted, and an inquiry has been instituted in Parliament into the expediency of repealing them. As to the emigration of artisans, say those who disapprove the laws, if that were desirable, no law could effect it; and as to the exportation of machinery, let us make it and export it as we would any other commodity. If France is determined to spin and weave her own cotton, let us, if we may, still have the benefit of furnishing the machinery.

I have stated these things, Sir, to show what seems to be the general tone of thinking and reasoning on these subjects in that country, the example of which has been so much pressed upon us. Whether the present policy of England be right or wrong, wise or unwise, it cannot, as it seems clearly to me, be quoted as an authority for carrying further the restrictive and exclusive system, either in regard to manufactures or trade. To re-establish a sound currency, to meet at once the shock, tremendous as it was, of the fall of prices, to enlarge her capacity for foreign trade, to open wide the field of individual enterprise and competition, and to say plainly and distinctly that the country must relieve itself from the embarrassments which it felt, by economy, frugality, and renewed efforts of enterprise,--these appear to be the general outline of the policy which England has pursued.

Mr. Chairman, I will now proceed to say a few words upon a topic, but for the introduction of which into this debate I should not have given the committee on this occasion the trouble of hearing me. Some days ago, I believe it was when we were settling the controversy between the oil-merchants and the tallow-chandlers, the *balance of trade* made its appearance in debate, and I must confess, Sir, that I spoke of it, or rather spoke to it, somewhat freely and irreverently. I believe I used the hard names which have been imputed to me, and I did it simply for the purpose of laying the spectre, and driving it back to its tomb. Certainly, Sir, when I called the old notion on this subject nonsense, I did not suppose that I should offend any one, unless the dead should happen to hear me. All the living generation, I took it for granted, would think the term very properly applied. In this, however, I was mistaken. The dead and the living rise up together to call me to account, and I must defend myself as well as I am able.

Let us inquire, then, Sir, what is meant by an unfavorable balance of trade, and what the argument is, drawn from that source. By an unfavorable balance of trade, I understand, is meant that state of things in which importation exceeds exportation. To apply it to our own case, if the value of goods imported exceed the value of those exported, then the balance of trade is said to be against us, inasmuch as we have run in debt to the amount of this difference. Therefore it is said, that, if a nation continue long in a commerce like this, it must be rendered absolutely bankrupt. It is in the condition of a man that buys more than he sells; and how can such a traffic be maintained without ruin? Now, Sir, the whole fallacy of this argument consists in supposing, that, whenever the value of imports exceeds that of exports, a debt is necessarily created to the extent of the difference, whereas, ordinarily, the import is no more than the result of the export, augmented in value by the labor of transportation. The excess of imports over exports, in truth, usually shows the gains, not the losses, of trade; or, in a country that not only buys and sells goods, but employs ships in carrying goods also, it shows the profits of commerce, and the earnings of navigation. Nothing is more certain than that, in the usual course of things, and taking a series of years together, the value of our imports is the aggregate of our exports and our freights. If the value of commodities imported in a given instance did not exceed the value of the outward cargo, with which they were purchased, then it would be clear to every man's common sense, that the voyage had not been profitable. If such commodities fell far short in value of the cost of the outward cargo, then the voyage would be a very losing one; and yet it would present exactly that state of things, which, according to the notion of a balance of trade, can alone indicate a prosperous commerce. On the other hand, if the return cargo were found to be worth much more than the outward cargo, while the merchant, having paid for the goods exported, and all the expenses of the voyage, finds a handsome sum yet in his hands, which he calls profits, the balance of trade is still against him, and, whatever he may think of it, he is in a very bad way. Although one individual or all individuals gain, the nation loses; while all its citizens grow rich, the country grows poor. This is the doctrine of the balance of trade.

Allow me, Sir, to give an instance tending to show how unaccountably individuals deceive themselves, and imagine themselves to be somewhat rapidly mending their condition, while they ought to be persuaded that, by that infallible standard, the balance of trade, they are on the high road to ruin. Some years ago, in better times than the present, a ship left one of the towns of New England with 70,000 specie dollars. She proceeded to Mocha, on the Red Sea, and there laid out these dollars in coffee, drugs, spices, and other articles procured in that market. With this new cargo she proceeded to Europe; two thirds of it were sold in Holland for $130,000, which the ship brought back, and placed in the same bank from the vaults of which she had taken her original outfit. The other third was sent to the ports of the Mediterranean, and produced a return of $25,000 in specie, and $15,000 in Italian merchandise. These sums together make $170,000 imported, which is $100,000 more than was exported, and is therefore proof of an unfavorable balance of trade, to that amount, in this adventure. We should find no great difficulty, Sir, in paying off our balances, if this were the nature of them all.

The truth is, Mr. Chairman, that all these obsolete and exploded notions had their origin in very mistaken ideas of the true nature of commerce. Commerce is not a gambling among nations for a stake, to be won by some and lost by others. It has not the tendency necessarily to impoverish one of the parties to it, while it enriches the other; all parties gain, all parties make profits, all parties grow rich, by the operations of just and liberal commerce. If the world had but one clime and but one soil; if all men had the same wants and the same means, on the spot of their existence, to gratify those wants,--then, indeed, what one obtained from the other by exchange would injure one party in the same degree that it benefited the other; then, indeed, there would be some foundation for the balance of trade. But Providence has disposed our lot much more kindly. We inhabit a various earth. We have reciprocal wants, and reciprocal means for gratifying one another's wants. This is the true origin of commerce, which is nothing more than an exchange of equivalents, and, from the rude barter of its primitive state, to the refined and complex condition in which we see it, its principle is uniformly the same, its only object being, in every stage, to produce that exchange of commodities between individuals and between nations which shall conduce to the advantage and to the happiness of both. Commerce between nations has the same essential character as commerce between individuals, or between parts of the same nation. Cannot two individuals make an interchange of commodities which shall prove beneficial to both, or in which the balance of trade shall be in favor of both? If not, the tailor and the shoemaker, the farmer and the smith, have hitherto very much misunderstood their own interests. And with regard to the internal trade of a country, in which the same rule would apply as between nations, do we ever speak of such an intercourse as prejudicial to one side because it is useful to the other? Do we ever hear that, because the intercourse between New York and Albany is advantageous to one of those places, it must therefore be ruinous to the other?

May I be allowed, Sir, to read a passage on this subject from the observations of a gentleman, in my opinion one of the most clear and sensible writers and speakers of the age upon subjects of this sort?[4] "There is no political question on which the prevalence of false principles is so general, as in what relates to the nature of commerce and to the pretended balance of trade; and there are few which have led to a greater number of practical mistakes, attended with consequences extensively prejudicial to the happiness of mankind. In this country, our Parliamentary proceedings, our public documents, and the works of several able and popular writers, have combined to propagate the impression, that we are indebted for much of our riches to what is called the balance of trade." "Our true policy would surely be to profess, as the object and guide of our commercial system, that which every man who has studied the subject must know to be the true principle of commerce, the interchange of reciprocal and equivalent benefit. We may rest assured that it is not in the nature of commerce to enrich one party at the expense of the other. This is a purpose at which, if it were practicable, we ought not to aim; and which, if we aimed at, we could not accomplish." These remarks, I believe, Sir, were written some ten or twelve years ago. They are in perfect accordance with the opinions, advanced in more elaborate treatises, and now that the world has returned to a state of peace, and commerce has resumed its natural channels, and different nations are enjoying, or seeking to enjoy, their respective portions of it, all see the justness of these ideas,--all see, that, in this day of knowledge and of peace, there can be no commerce between nations but that which shall benefit all who are parties to it.

If it were necessary, Mr. Chairman, I might ask the attention of the committee to refer to a document before us, on this subject of the balance of trade. It will be seen by reference to the accounts, that, in the course of the last year, our total export to Holland exceeded two millions and a half; our total import from the same country was but seven hundred thousand dollars. Now, can any man be wild enough to make any inference from this as to the gain or loss of our trade with Holland for that year? Our trade with Russia for the same year produced a balance the other way, our import being two millions, and our export but half a million. But this has no more tendency to show the Russian trade a losing trade, than the other statement has to show that the Dutch trade has been a gainful one. Neither of them, by itself, proves any thing.

Springing out of this notion of a balance of trade, there is another idea, which has been much dwelt upon in the course of this debate; that is, that we ought not to buy of nations who do not buy of us; for example, that the Russian trade is a trade disadvantageous to the country, and ought to be discouraged, because, in the ports of Russia, we buy more than we sell. Now allow me to observe, in the first place, Sir, that we have no account showing how much we do sell in the ports of Russia. Our official returns show us only what is the amount of our direct trade with her ports. But then we all know that the proceeds of another portion of our exports go to the same market, though indirectly. We send our own products, for example, to Cuba, or to Brazil; we there exchange them for the sugar and the coffee of those countries, and these articles we carry to St. Petersburg, and there sell them. Again; our exports to Holland and Hamburg are connected directly or indirectly with our imports from Russia. What difference does it make, in sense or reason, whether a cargo of iron be bought at St. Petersburg, by the exchange of a cargo of tobacco, or whether the tobacco has been sold on the way, in a better market, in a port of Holland, the money remitted to England, and the iron paid for by a bill on London? There might indeed have been an augmented freight, there might have been some saving of commissions, if tobacco had been in brisk demand in the Russian market. But still there is nothing to show that the whole voyage may not have been highly profitable. That depends upon the original cost of the article here, the amount of freight and insurance to Holland, the price obtained there, the rate of exchange between Holland and England, the expense, then, of proceeding to St. Petersburg, the price of iron there, the rate of exchange between that place and England, the amount of freight and insurance at home, and, finally, the value of the iron when brought to our own market. These are the calculations which determine the fortune of the adventure; and nothing can be judged of it, one way or the other, by the relative state of our imports or exports with Holland, England, or Russia.

I would not be understood to deny, that it may often be our interest to cultivate a trade with countries that require most of such commodities as we can furnish, and which are capable also of directly supplying our own wants. This is the original and the simplest form of all commerce, and is no doubt highly beneficial. Some countries are so situated, that commerce, in this original form, or something near it, may be all that they can, without considerable inconvenience, carry on. Our trade, for example, with Madeira and the Western Islands has been useful to the country, as furnishing a demand for some portion of our agricultural products, which probably could not have been bought had we not received their products in return. Countries situated still farther from the great marts and highways of the commercial world may afford still stronger instances of the necessity and utility of conducting commerce on the original principle of barter, without much assistance from the operations of credit and exchange. All I would be understood to say is, that it by no means follows that we can carry on nothing but a losing trade with a country from which we receive more of her products than she receives of ours. Since I was supposed, the other day, in speaking upon this subject, to advance opinions which not only this country ought to reject, but which also other countries, and those the most distinguished for skill and success in commercial intercourse, do reject, I will ask leave to refer again to the discussion which I first mentioned in the English Parliament, relative to the foreign trade of that country. "With regard," says the mover[5] of the proposition, "to the argument employed against renewing our intercourse with the North of Europe, namely, that those who supplied us with timber from that quarter would not receive British manufactures in return, it appeared to him futile and ungrounded. If they did not send direct for our manufactures at home, they would send for them to Leipsic and other fairs of Germany. Were not the Russian and Polish merchants purchasers there to a great amount? But he would never admit the principle, that a trade was not profitable because we were obliged to carry it on with the precious metals, or that we ought to renounce it, because our manufactures were not received by the foreign nation in return for its produce. Whatever we received must be paid for in the produce of our land and labor, directly or circuitously, and he was glad to have the noble Earl's[6] marked concurrence in this principle."

Referring ourselves again, Sir, to the analogies of common life, no one would say that a farmer or a mechanic should buy *only* where he can do so by the exchange of his own produce, or of his own manufacture. Such exchange may be often convenient; and, on the other hand, the cash purchase may be often more convenient. It is the same in the intercourse of nations. Indeed, Mr. Speaker has placed this argument on very clear grounds. It was said, in the early part of the debate, that, if we cease to import English cotton fabrics, England will no longer continue to purchase our cotton. To this Mr. Speaker replied, with great force and justice, that, as she must have cotton in large quantities, she will buy the article where she can find it best and cheapest; and that it would be quite ridiculous in her, manufacturing as she still would be, for her own vast consumption and the consumption of millions in other countries, to reject our uplands because we had learned to manufacture a part of them for ourselves. Would it not be equally ridiculous in us, if the commodities of Russia were both cheaper and better suited to our wants than could be found elsewhere, to abstain from commerce with her, because she will not receive in return other commodities which we have to sell, but which she has no occasion to buy?

Intimately connected, Sir, with this topic, is another which has been brought into the debate; I mean the evil so much complained of, the exportation of specie. We hear gentlemen imputing the loss of market at home to a want of money, and this want of money to the exportation of the precious metals. We hear the India and China trade denounced, as a commerce conducted on our side, in a great measure, with gold and silver. These opinions, Sir, are clearly void of all just foundation, and we cannot too soon get rid of them. There are no shallower reasoners than those political and commercial writers who would represent it to be the only true and gainful end of commerce, to accumulate the precious metals. These are articles of use, and articles of merchandise, with this additional circumstance belonging to them, that they are made, by the general consent of nations, the standard by which the value of all other merchandise is to be estimated. In regard to weights and measures, something drawn from external nature is made a common standard, for the purposes of general convenience: and this is precisely the office performed by the precious metals, in addition to those uses to which, as metals, they are capable of being applied. There may be of these too much or too little in a country at a particular time, as there may be of any other articles. When the market is overstocked with them, as it often is, their exportation becomes as proper and as useful as that of other commodities, under similar circumstances. We need no more repine, when the dollars which have been brought here from South America are despatched to other countries, than when coffee and sugar take the same direction. We often deceive ourselves, by attributing to a scarcity of money that which is the result of other causes. In the course of this debate, the honorable member from Pennsylvania[7] has represented the country as full of every thing but money. But this I take to be a mistake. The agricultural products, so abundant in Pennsylvania, will not, he says, sell for money; but they will sell for money as quick as for any other article which happens to be in demand. They will sell for money, for example, as easily as for coffee or for tea, at the prices which properly belong to those articles. The mistake lies in imputing that to want of money which arises from want of demand. Men do not buy wheat because they have money, but because they want wheat. To decide whether money be plenty or not, that is, whether there be a large portion of capital unemployed or not, when the currency of a country is metallic, we must look, not only to the prices of commodities, but also to the rate of interest. A low rate of interest, a facility of obtaining money on loans, a disposition to invest in permanent stocks, all of which are proofs that money is plenty, may nevertheless often denote a state not of the highest prosperity. They may, and often do, show a want of employment for capital; and the accumulation of specie shows the same thing. We have no occasion for the precious metals as money, except for the purposes of circulation, or rather of sustaining a safe paper circulation. And whenever there is a prospect of a profitable investment abroad, all the gold and silver, except what these purposes require, will be exported. For the same reason, if a demand exist abroad for sugar and coffee, whatever amount of those articles might exist in the country, beyond the wants of its own consumption, would be sent abroad to meet that demand.

Besides, Sir, how should it ever occur to anybody, that we should continue to export gold and silver, if we did not continue to import them also? If a vessel take our own products to the Havana, or elsewhere, exchange them for dollars, proceed to China, exchange them for silks and teas, bring these last to the ports of the Mediterranean, sell them there for dollars, and return to the United States,--this would be a voyage resulting in the importation of the precious metals. But if she had returned from Cuba, and the dollars obtained there had been shipped direct from the United States to China, the China goods sold in Holland, and the proceeds brought home in the hemp and iron of Russia, this would be a voyage in which they were exported. Yet everybody sees that both might be equally beneficial to the individual and to the public. I believe, Sir, that, in point of fact, we have enjoyed great benefit in our trade with India and China, from the liberty of going from place to place all over the world, without being obliged in the mean time to return home, a liberty not heretofore enjoyed by the private traders of England, in regard to India and China. Suppose the American ship to be at Brazil, for example; she could proceed with her dollars direct to India, and, in return, could distribute her cargo in all the various ports of Europe or America; while an English ship, if a private trader, being at Brazil, must first return to England, and then could only proceed in the direct line from England to India. This advantage our countrymen have not been backward to improve; and in the debate to which I have already so often referred, it was stated, not without some complaint of the inconvenience of exclusion, and the natural sluggishness of monopoly, that American ships were at that moment fitting out in the Thames, to supply France, Holland, and other countries on the Continent, with tea; while the East India Company would not do this of themselves, nor allow any of their fellow-countrymen to do it for them.

There is yet another subject, Mr. Chairman, upon which I would wish to say something, if I might presume upon the continued patience of the committee. We hear sometimes in the House, and continually out of it, of the rate of exchange, as being one proof that we are on the downward road to ruin. Mr. Speaker himself has adverted to that topic, and I am afraid that his authority may give credit to opinions clearly unfounded, and which lead to very false and erroneous conclusions. Sir, let us see what the facts are. Exchange on England has recently risen one or one and a half per cent, partly owing, perhaps, to the introduction of this bill into Congress. Before this recent rise, and for the last six months, I understand its average may have been about seven and a half per cent advance. Now, supposing this to be the _real_, and not merely, as it is, the nominal, par of exchange between us and England, what would it prove? Nothing, except that funds were wanted by American citizens in England for commercial operations, to be carried on either in England or elsewhere. It would not necessarily show that we were indebted to England; for, if we had occasion to pay debts in Russia or Holland, funds in England would naturally enough be required for such a purpose. Even if it did prove that a balance was due England at the moment, it would have no tendency to explain to us whether our commerce with England had been profitable or unprofitable.

But it is not true, in point of fact, that the *real* price of exchange is seven and a half per cent advance, nor, indeed, that there is at the present moment any advance at all. That is to say, it is not true that merchants will give such an advance, or any advance, for *money* in England, beyond what they would give for the same amount, in the same currency, here. It will strike every one who reflects upon it, that, if there were a real difference of seven and a half per cent, money would be immediately shipped to England; because the expense of transportation would be far less than that difference. Or commodities of trade would be shipped to Europe, and the proceeds remitted to England. If it could so happen, that American merchants should be willing to pay ten per cent premium for money in England, or, in other words, that a real difference to that amount in the exchange should exist, its effects would be immediately seen in new shipments of our own commodities to Europe, because this state of things would create new motives. A cargo of tobacco, for example, might sell at Amsterdam for the same price as before; but if its proceeds, when remitted to London, were advanced, as they would be in such case, ten per cent by the state of exchange, this would be so much added to the price, and would operate therefore as a motive for the exportation; and in this way national balances are, and always will be, adjusted.

To form any accurate idea of the true state of exchange between two countries, we must look at their currencies, and compare the quantities of gold and silver which they may respectively represent. This usually explains the state of the exchanges; and this will satisfactorily account for the apparent advance now existing on bills drawn on England. The English standard of value is gold; with us that office is performed by gold, and by silver also, at a fixed relation to each other. But our estimate of silver is rather higher, in proportion to gold, than most nations give it; it is higher, especially, than in England, at the present moment. The consequence is, that silver, which remains a legal currency with us, stays here, while the gold has gone abroad; verifying the universal truth, that, if *two* currencies be allowed to exist, of different values, that which is cheapest will fill up the whole circulation. For as much gold as will suffice to pay here a debt of a given amount, we can buy in England more silver than would be necessary to pay the same debt here; and from this difference in the value of silver arises wholly or in a great measure the present apparent difference in exchange. Spanish dollars sell now in England for four shillings and nine pence sterling per ounce, equal to one dollar and six cents. By our standard the same ounce is worth one dollar and sixteen cents, being a difference of about nine per cent. The true par of exchange, therefore, is nine per cent. If a merchant here pay one hundred Spanish dollars for a bill on England, at nominal par, in sterling money, that is for a bill of £22 10s., the proceeds of this bill, when paid in England in the legal currency, will there purchase, at the present price of silver, one hundred and nine Spanish dollars. Therefore, if the nominal advance on English bills do not exceed nine per cent, the real exchange is not against this country; in other words, it does not show that there is any pressing or particular occasion for the remittance of funds to England.

As little can be inferred from the occasional transfer of United States stock to England. Considering the interest paid on our stocks, the entire stability of our credit, and the accumulation of capital in England, it is not at all wonderful that investments should occasionally be made in our funds. As a sort of countervailing fact, it may be stated that English stocks are now actually held in this country, though probably not to any considerable amount.

I will now proceed, Sir, to state some objections of a more general nature to the course of Mr. Speaker's observations.

He seems to me to argue the question as if all domestic industry were confined to the production of manufactured articles; as if the employment of our own capital and our own labor, in the occupations of commerce and navigation, were not as emphatically domestic industry as any other occupation. Some other gentlemen, in the course of the debate, have spoken of the price paid for every foreign manufactured article as so much given for the encouragement of foreign labor, to the prejudice of our own. But is not every such article the product of our own labor as truly as if we had manufactured it ourselves? Our labor has earned it, and paid the price for it. It is so much added to the stock of national wealth. If the commodity were dollars, nobody would doubt the truth of this remark; and it is precisely as correct in its application to any other commodity as to silver. One man makes a yard of cloth at home; another raises agricultural products and buys a yard of imported cloth. Both these are equally the earnings of domestic industry, and the only questions that arise in the case are two: the first is, which is the best mode, under all the circumstances, of obtaining the article; the second is, how far this first question is proper to be decided by government, and how far it is proper to be left to individual discretion. There is no foundation for the distinction which attributes to certain employments the peculiar appellation of American industry; and it is, in my judgment, extremely unwise to attempt such discriminations.

We are asked, What nations have ever attained eminent prosperity without encouraging manufactures? I may ask, What nation ever reached the like prosperity without promoting foreign trade? I regard these interests as closely connected, and am of opinion that it should be our aim to cause them to flourish together. I know it would be very easy to promote manufactures, at least for a time, but probably for a short time only, if we might act in disregard of other interests. We could cause a sudden transfer of capital, and a violent change in the pursuits of men. We could exceedingly benefit some classes by these means. But what, then, becomes of the interests of others? The power of collecting revenue by duties on imports, and the habit of the government of collecting almost its whole revenue in that mode, will enable us, without exceeding the bounds of moderation, to give great advantages to those classes of manufactures which we may think most useful to promote at home. What I object to is the immoderate use of the power,-- exclusions and prohibitions; all of which, as I think, not only interrupt the pursuits of individuals, with great injury to themselves and little or no benefit to the country, but also often divert our own labor, or, as it may very properly be called, our own domestic industry, from those occupations in which it is well employed and well paid, to others in which it will be worse employed and worse paid. For my part, I see very little relief to those who are likely to be deprived of their employments, or who find the prices of the commodities which they need raised, in any of the alternatives which Mr. Speaker has presented. It is nothing to say that they may, if they choose, continue to buy the foreign article; the answer is, the price is augmented: nor that they may use the domestic article; the price of that also is increased. Nor can they supply themselves by the substitution of their own fabric. How can the agriculturist make his own iron? How can the ship-owner grow his own hemp?

But I have a yet stronger objection to the course of Mr. Speaker's reasoning; which is, that he leaves out of the case all that has been already done for the protection of manufactures, and argues the question as if those interests were now for the first time to receive aid from duties on imports. I can hardly express the surprise I feel that Mr. Speaker should fall into the common mode of expression used elsewhere, and ask if we will give our manufacturers no protection. Sir, look to the history of our laws; look to the present state of our laws. Consider that our whole revenue, with a trifling exception, is collected at the custom-house, and always has been; and then say what propriety there is in calling on the government for protection, as if no protection had heretofore been afforded. The real question before us, in regard to all the important clauses of the bill, is not whether we will *lay* duties, but whether we will *augment* duties. The demand is for something more than exists, and yet it is pressed as if nothing existed. It is wholly forgotten that iron and hemp, for example, already pay a very heavy and burdensome duty; and, in short, from the general tenor of Mr. Speaker's observations, one would infer that, hitherto, we had rather taxed our own manufactures than fostered them by taxes on those of other countries. We hear of the fatal policy of the tariff of 1816; and yet the law of 1816 was passed avowedly for the benefit of manufacturers, and, with very few exceptions, imposed on imported articles very great additions of tax; in some important instances, indeed, amounting to a prohibition.

Sir, on this subject, it becomes us at least to understand the real posture of the question. Let us not suppose that we are *beginning* the protection of manufactures, by duties on imports. What we are asked to do is, to render those duties much higher, and therefore, instead of dealing in general commendations of the benefits of protection, the friends of the bill, I think, are bound to make out a fair case for each of the manufactures which they propose to benefit. The government has already done much for their protection, and it ought to be presumed to have done enough, unless it be shown, by the facts and considerations applicable to each, that there is a necessity for doing more.

On the general question, Sir, allow me to ask if the doctrine of prohibition, as a general doctrine, be not preposterous. Suppose all nations to act upon it; they would be prosperous, then, according to the argument, precisely in the proportion in which they abolished intercourse with one another. The less of mutual commerce the better, upon this hypothesis. Protection and encouragement may be, and doubtless are, sometimes, wise and beneficial, if kept within proper limits; but when carried to an extravagant height, or the point of prohibition, the absurd character of the system manifests itself. Mr. Speaker has referred to the late Emperor Napoleon, as having attempted to naturalize the manufacture of cotton in France. He did not cite a more extravagant part of the projects of that ruler, that is, his attempt to naturalize the growth of that plant itself, in France; whereas, we have understood that considerable districts in the South of France, and in Italy, of rich and productive lands, were at one time withdrawn from profitable uses, and devoted to raising, at great expense, a little bad cotton. Nor have we been referred to the attempts, under the same system, to make sugar and coffee from common culinary vegetables; attempts which served to fill the print-shops of Europe, and to show us how easy is the transition from what some think sublime to that which all admit to be ridiculous. The folly of some of these projects has not been surpassed, nor hardly equalled, unless it be by the philosopher in one of the satires of Swift, who so long labored to extract sunbeams from cucumbers.

The poverty and unhappiness of Spain have been attributed to the want of protection to her own industry. If by this it be meant that the poverty of Spain is owing to bad government and bad laws, the remark is, in a great measure, just. But these very laws are bad because they are restrictive, partial, and prohibitory. If prohibition were protection, Spain would seem to have had enough of it. Nothing can exceed the barbarous rigidity of her colonial system, or the folly of her early commercial regulations. Unenlightened and bigoted legislation, the multitude of holidays, miserable roads, monopolies on the part of government, restrictive laws, that ought long since to have been abrogated, are generally, and I believe truly, reckoned the principal causes of the bad state of the productive industry of Spain. Any partial improvement in her condition, or increase of her prosperity, has been, in all cases, the result of relaxation, and the abolition of what was intended for favor and protection.

In short, Sir, the general sense of this age sets, with a strong current, in favor of freedom of commercial intercourse, and unrestrained individual action. Men yield up their notions of monopoly and restriction, as they yield up other prejudices, slowly and reluctantly; but they cannot withstand the general tide of opinion.

Let me now ask, Sir, what relief this bill proposes to some of those great and essential interests of the country, the condition of which has been referred to as proof of national distress; and which condition, although I do not think it makes out a case of _distress_, yet does indicate depression.

And first, Sir, as to our foreign trade. Mr. Speaker has stated that there has been a considerable falling off in the tonnage employed in that trade. This is true, lamentably true. In my opinion, it is one of those occurrences which ought to arrest our immediate, our deep, our most earnest attention. What does this bill propose for its relief? It proposes nothing but new burdens. It proposes to diminish its employment, and it proposes, at the same time, to augment its expense, by subjecting it to heavier taxation. Sir, there is no interest, in regard to which a stronger case for protection can be made out, than the navigating interest. Whether we look at its present condition, which is admitted to be depressed, the number of persons connected with it, and dependent upon it for their daily bread, or its importance to the country in a political point of view, it has claims upon our attention which cannot be surpassed. But what do we propose to do for it? I repeat, Sir, simply to burden and to tax it. By a statement which I have already submitted to the committee, it appears that the shipping interest pays, annually, more than half a million of dollars in duties on articles used in the construction of ships. We propose to add nearly, or quite, fifty per cent to this amount, at the very moment that we appeal to the languishing state of this interest as a proof of national distress. Let it be remembered that our shipping employed in foreign commerce has, at this moment, not the shadow of government protection. It goes abroad upon the wide sea to make its own way, and earn its own bread, in a professed competition with the whole world. Its resources are its own frugality, its own skill, its own enterprise. It hopes to succeed, if it shall succeed at all, not by extraordinary aid of government, but by patience, vigilance, and toil. This right arm of the nation's safety strengthens its own muscle by its own efforts, and by unwearied exertion in its own defence becomes strong for the defence of the country.

No one acquainted with this interest can deny that its situation, at this moment, is extremely critical. We have left it hitherto to maintain itself or perish; to swim if it can, and to sink if it must. But at this moment of its apparent struggle, can we as men, can we as patriots, add another stone to the weight that threatens to carry it down? Sir, there is a limit to human power, and to human effort. I know the commercial marine of this country can do almost every thing, and bear almost every thing. Yet some things are impossible to be done, and some burdens may be impossible to be borne; and as it was the last ounce that broke the back of the camel, so the last tax, although it were even a small one, may be decisive as to the power of our marine to sustain the conflict in which it is now engaged with all the commercial nations on the globe.

Again, Mr. Chairman, the failures and the bankruptcies which have taken place in our large cities have been mentioned as proving the little success attending _commerce_, and its general decline. But this bill has no balm for those wounds. It is very remarkable, that when the losses and disasters of certain manufacturers, those of iron, for instance, are mentioned, it is done for the purpose of invoking aid for the distressed. Not so with the losses and disasters of commerce; these last are narrated, and not unfrequently much exaggerated, to prove the ruinous nature of the employment, and to show that it ought to be abandoned, and the capital engaged in it turned to other objects.

It has been often said, Sir, that our manufacturers have to contend, not only against the natural advantages of those who produce similar articles in foreign countries, but also against the action of foreign governments, who have great political interest in aiding their own manufactures to suppress ours. But have not these governments as great an interest to cripple our marine, by preventing the growth of our commerce and navigation? What is it that makes us the object of the highest respect, or the most suspicious jealousy, to foreign states? What is it that most enables us to take high relative rank among the nations? I need not say that this results, more than from any thing else, from that quantity of military power which we can cause to be water-borne, and from that extent of commerce which we are able to maintain throughout the world.

Mr. Chairman, I am conscious of having detained the committee much too long with these observations. My apology for now proceeding to some remarks upon the particular clauses of the bill is, that, representing a district at once commercial and highly manufacturing, and being called upon to vote upon a bill containing provisions so numerous and so various, I am naturally desirous to state as well what I approve, as what I would reject.

The first section proposes an augmented duty upon woollen manufactures. This, if it were unqualified, would no doubt be desirable to those who are engaged in that business. I have myself presented a petition from the woollen manufacturers of Massachusetts, praying an augmented *ad valorem* duty upon imported woollen cloths; and I am prepared to accede to that proposition, to a reasonable extent. But then this bill proposes, also, a very high duty upon imported wool; and, as far as I can learn, a majority of the manufacturers are at least extremely doubtful whether, taking these two provisions together, the state of the law is not better for them now than it would be if this bill should pass. It is said, this tax on raw wool will benefit the agriculturist; but I know it to be the opinion of some of the best informed of that class, that it will do them more hurt than good. They fear it will check the manufacturer, and consequently check his demand for their article. The argument is, that a certain quantity of coarse wool, cheaper than we can possibly furnish, is necessary to enable the manufacturer to carry on the general business, and that if this cannot be had, the consequence will be, not a greater, but a less, manufacture of our own wool. I am aware that very intelligent persons differ upon this point; but if we may safely infer from that difference of opinion, that the proposed benefit is at least doubtful, it would be prudent perhaps to abstain from the experiment. Certain it is, that the same reasoning has been employed, as I have before stated, on the same subject, when a renewed application was made to the English Parliament to repeal the duty on imported wool, I believe scarcely two months ago; those who supported the application pressing urgently the necessity of an unrestricted use of the cheap, imported raw material, with a view to supply with coarse cloths the markets of warm climates, such as those of Egypt and Turkey, and especially a vast newly created demand in the South American states.

As to the manufactures of cotton, it is agreed, I believe, that they are generally successful. It is understood that the present existing duty operates pretty much as a prohibition over those descriptions of fabrics to which it applies. The proposed alteration would probably enable the American manufacturer to commence competition with higher-priced fabrics; and so, perhaps, would an augmentation less than is here proposed. I consider the cotton manufactures not only to have reached, but to have passed, the point of competition. I regard their success as certain, and their growth as rapid as the most impatient could well expect. If, however, a provision of the nature of that recommended here were thought necessary, to commence new operations in the same line of manufacture, I should cheerfully agree to it, if it were not at the cost of sacrificing other great interests of the country. I need hardly say, that whatever promotes the cotton and woollen manufactures promotes most important interests of my constituents. They have a great stake in the success of those establishments, and, as far as those manufactures are concerned, would be as much benefited by the provisions of this bill as any part of the community. It is obvious, too, I should think, that, for some considerable time, manufactures of this sort, to whatever magnitude they may rise, will be principally established in those parts of the country where population is most dense, capital most abundant, and where the most successful beginnings have already been made.

But if these be thought to be advantages, they are greatly counterbalanced by other advantages enjoyed by other portions of the country. I cannot but regard the situation of the West as highly favorable to human happiness. It offers, in the abundance of its new and fertile lands, such assurances of permanent property and respectability to the industrious, it enables them to lay such sure foundations for a competent provision for their families, it makes such a nation of freeholders, that it need not envy the happiest and most prosperous of the manufacturing communities. We may talk as we will of well-fed and well-clothed day-laborers or journeymen; they are not, after all, to be compared, either for happiness or respectability, with him who sleeps under his own roof and cultivates his own fee-simple inheritance.

With respect to the proposed duty on glass, I would observe, that, upon the best means of judging which I possess, I am of opinion that the chairman of the committee is right in stating that there is in effect a bounty upon the exportation of the British article. I think it entirely proper, therefore, to raise our own duty by such an amount as shall be equivalent to that bounty.

And here, Mr. Chairman, before proceeding to those parts of the bill to which I most strenuously object, I will be so presumptuous as to take up a challenge which Mr. Speaker has thrown down. He has asked us, in a tone of interrogatory indicative of the feeling of anticipated triumph, to mention any country in which manufactures have flourished without the aid of prohibitory laws. He has demanded if it be not policy, protection, ay, and prohibition, that have carried other states to the height of their prosperity, and whether any one has succeeded with such tame and inert legislation as ours. Sir, I am ready to answer this inquiry. There is a country, not undistinguished among the nations, in which the progress of manufactures has been far more rapid than in any other, and yet unaided by prohibitions or unnatural restrictions. That country, the happiest which the sun shines on, is our own.

The woollen manufactures of England have existed from the early ages of the monarchy. Provisions designed to aid and foster them are in the black-letter statutes of the Edwards and the Henrys. Ours, on the contrary, are but of yesterday; and yet, with no more than the protection of existing laws, they are already at the point of close and promising competition. Sir, nothing is more unphilosophical than to refer us, on these subjects, to the policy adopted by other nations in a very different state of society, or to infer that what was judged expedient by them, in their early history, must also be expedient for us, in this early part of our own. This would be reckoning our age chronologically, and estimating our advance by our number of years; when, in truth, we should regard only the state of society, the knowledge, the skill, the capital, and the enterprise which belong to our times. We have been transferred from the stock of Europe, in a comparatively enlightened age, and our civilization and improvement date as far back as her own. Her original history is also our original history; and if, since the moment of separation, she has gone ahead of us in some respects, it may be said, without violating truth, that we have kept up in others, and, in others again, are ahead ourselves. We are to legislate, then, with regard to the present actual state of society; and our own experience shows us, that, commencing manufactures at the present highly enlightened and emulous moment, we need not resort to the clumsy helps with which, in less auspicious times, governments have sought to enable the ingenuity and industry of their people to hobble along.

The English cotton manufactures began about the commencement of the last reign. Ours can hardly be said to have commenced with any earnestness, until the application of the power-loom, in 1814, not more than ten years ago. Now, Sir, I hardly need again speak of its progress, its present extent, or its assurance of future enlargement. In some sorts of fabrics we are already exporters, and the products of our factories are, at this moment, in the South American markets. We see, then, what *can* be done without prohibition or extraordinary protection, because we see what *has* been done; and I venture to predict, that, in a few years, it will be thought wonderful that these branches of manufactures, at least, should have been thought to require additional aid from government.

Mr. Chairman, the best apology for laws of prohibition and laws of monopoly will be found in that state of society, not only unenlightened but sluggish, in which they are most generally established. Private industry, in those days, required strong provocatives, which governments were seeking to administer by these means. Something was wanted to actuate and stimulate men, and the prospects of such profits as would, in our times, excite unbounded competition, would hardly move the sloth of former ages. In some instances, no doubt, these laws produced an effect, which, in that period, would not have taken place without them. But our age is of a wholly different character, and its legislation takes another turn. Society is full of excitement; competition comes in place of monopoly; and intelligence and industry ask only for fair play and an open field. Profits, indeed, in such a state of things, will be small, but they will be extensively diffused; prices will be low, and the great body of the people prosperous and happy. It is worthy of remark, that, from the operation of these causes, commercial wealth, while it is increased beyond calculation in its general aggregate, is, at the same time, broken and diminished in its subdivisions. Commercial prosperity should be judged of, therefore, rather from the extent of trade, than from the magnitude of its apparent profits. It has been remarked, that Spain, certainly one of the poorest nations, made very great profits on the amount of her trade; but with little other benefit than the enriching of a few individuals and companies. Profits to the English merchants engaged in the Levant and Turkey trade were formerly very great, and there were richer merchants in England some centuries ago, considering the comparative value of money, than at the present highly commercial period. When the diminution of profits arises from the extent of competition, it indicates rather a salutary than an injurious change.[8]

The true course then, Sir, for us to pursue, is, in my opinion, to consider what our situation is; what our means are; and how they can be best applied. What amount of population have we in comparison with our extent of soil, what amount of capital, and labor at what price? As to skill, knowledge, and enterprise, we may safely take it for granted that in these particulars we are on an equality with others. Keeping these considerations in view, allow me to examine two or three of those provisions of the bill to which I feel the strongest objections.

To begin with the article of iron. Our whole annual consumption of this article is supposed by the chairman of the committee to be forty-eight or fifty thousand tons. Let us suppose the latter. The amount of our own manufacture he estimates, I think, at seventeen thousand tons. The present duty on the imported article is $15 per ton, and as this duty causes, of course, an equivalent augmentation of the price of the home manufacture, the whole increase of price is equal to $750,000 annually. This sum we pay on a raw material, and on an absolute necessary of life. The bill proposes to raise the duty from $15 to $22.50 per ton, which would be equal to $1,125,000 on the whole annual consumption. So that, suppose the point of prohibition which is aimed at by some gentlemen to be attained, the consumers of the article would pay this last-mentioned sum every year to the producers of it, over and above the price at which they could supply themselves with the same article from other sources. There would be no mitigation of this burden, except from the prospect, whatever that might be, that iron would fall in value, by domestic competition, after the importation should be prohibited. It will be easy, I think, to show that it cannot fall; and supposing for the present that it shall not, the result will be, that we shall pay annually the sum of $1,125,000, constantly augmented, too, by increased consumption of the article, *to support a business that cannot support itself.*

It is of no consequence to the argument, that this sum is expended at home; so it would be if we taxed the people to support any other useless and expensive establishment, to build another Capitol, for example, or incur an unnecessary expense of any sort. The question still is, Are the money, time, and labor well laid out in these cases? The present price of iron at Stockholm, I am assured by importers, is $53 per ton on board, $48 in the yard before loading, and probably not far from $40 at the mines. Freight, insurance, &c. may be fairly estimated at $15, to which add our present duty of $15 more, and these two last sums, together with the cost on board at Stockholm, give $83 as the cost of Swedes iron in our market. In fact, it is said to have been sold last year at $81.50 to $82 per ton. We perceive, by this statement, that the cost of the iron is doubled in reaching us from the mine in which it is produced. In other words, our present duty, with the expense of transportation, gives an advantage to the American over the foreign manufacturer of one hundred per cent. Why, then, cannot the iron be manufactured at home? Our ore is said to be as good, and some of it better. It is under our feet, and the chairman of the committee tells us that it might be wrought by persons who otherwise will not be employed. Why, then, is it not wrought? Nothing could be more sure of constant sale. It is not an article of changeable fashion, but of absolute, permanent necessity, and such, therefore, as would always meet a steady demand. Sir, I think it would be well for the chairman of the committee to revise his premises, for I am persuaded that there is an ingredient properly belonging to the calculation which he has misstated or omitted. Swedes iron in England pays a duty, I think, of about $27 per ton; yet it is imported in considerable quantities, notwithstanding the vast capital, the excellent coal, and, more important than all perhaps, the highly improved state of inland navigation in England; although I am aware that the English use of Swedes iron may be thought to be owing in some degree to its superior quality.

Sir, the true explanation of this appears to me to lie in the different prices _of labor_; and here I apprehend is the grand mistake in the argument of the chairman of the committee. He says it would cost the nation, as a nation, nothing, to make our ore into iron. Now, I think it would cost us precisely that which we can worst afford; that is, great *labor*. Although bar-iron is very properly considered a raw material in respect to its various future uses, yet, as bar-iron, the principal ingredient in its cost is labor. Of manual labor, no nation has more than a certain quantity, nor can it be increased at will. As to some operations, indeed, its place may be supplied by machinery; but there are other services which machinery cannot perform for it, and which it must perform for itself. A most important question for every nation, as well as for every individual, to propose to itself, is, how it can best apply that quantity of labor which it is able to perform. Labor is the great producer of wealth; it moves all other causes. If it call machinery to its aid, it is still employed, not only in using the machinery, but in making it. Now, with respect to the quantity of labor, as we all know, different nations are differently circumstanced. Some need, more than any thing, work for hands, others require hands for work; and if we ourselves are not absolutely in the latter class, we are still most fortunately very near it. I cannot find that we have those idle hands, of which the chairman of the committee speaks. The price of labor is a conclusive and unanswerable refutation of that idea; it is known to be higher with us than in any other civilized state, and this is the greatest of all proofs of general happiness. Labor in this country is independent and proud. It has not to ask the patronage of capital, but capital solicits the aid of labor. This is the general truth in regard to the condition of our whole population, although in the large cities there are doubtless many exceptions. The mere capacity to labor in common agricultural employments, gives to our young men the assurance of independence. We have been asked, Sir, by the chairman of the committee, in a tone of some pathos, whether we will allow to the serfs of Russia and Sweden the benefit of making iron for us. Let me inform the gentleman, Sir, that those same serfs do not earn more than seven cents a day, and that they work in these mines for that compensation because they are serfs. And let me ask the gentleman further, whether we have any labor in this country that cannot be better employed than in a business which does not yield the laborer more than seven cents a day? This, it appears to me, is the true question for our consideration. There is no reason for saying that we will work iron because we have mountains that contain the ore. We might for the same reason dig among our rocks for the scattered grains of gold and silver which might be found there. The true inquiry is, Can we produce the article in a useful state at the same cost, or nearly at the same cost, or at any reasonable approximation towards the same cost, at which we can import it?

Some general estimates of the price and profits of labor, in those countries from which we import our iron, might be formed by comparing the reputed products of different mines, and their prices, with the number of hands employed. The mines of Danemora are said to yield about 4,000 tons, and to employ in the mines twelve hundred workmen. Suppose this to be worth $50 per ton; any one will find by computation, that the whole product would not pay, in this country, for one quarter part of the necessary labor. The whole export of Sweden was estimated, a few years ago, at 400,000 ship pounds, or about 54,000 tons. Comparing this product with the number of workmen usually supposed to be employed in the mines which produce iron for exportation, the result will not greatly differ from the foregoing. These estimates are general, and might not conduct us to a precise result; but we know, from intelligent travellers, and eye-witnesses, that the price of labor in the Swedish mines does not exceed seven cents a day.[9]

The true reason, Sir, why it is not our policy to compel our citizens to manufacture our own iron, is that they are far better employed. It is an unproductive business, and they are not poor enough to be obliged to follow it. If we had more of poverty, more of misery, and something of servitude, if we had an ignorant, idle, starving population, we might set up for iron makers against the world.

The committee will take notice, Mr. Chairman, that, under our present duty, together with the expense of transportation, our manufacturers are able to supply their own immediate neighborhood; and this proves the magnitude of that substantial encouragement which these two causes concur to give. There is little or no foreign iron, I presume, used in the county of Lancaster. This is owing to the heavy expense of land carriage; and as we recede farther from the coast, the manufacturers are still more completely secured, as to their own immediate market, against the competition of the imported article. But what they ask is to be allowed to supply the sea-coast, at such a price as shall be formed by adding to the cost at the mines the expense of land carriage to the sea; and this appears to me most unreasonable. The effect of it would be to compel the consumer to pay the cost of two land transportations; for, in the first place, the price of iron at the inland furnaces will always be found to be at, or not much below, the price of the imported article in the seaport, and the cost of transportation to the neighborhood of the furnace; and to enable the home product to hold a competition with the imported in the seaport, the cost of another transportation downward, from the furnace to the coast, must be added. Until our means of inland commerce be improved, and the charges of transportation by that means lessened, it appears to me wholly impracticable, with such duties as any one would think of proposing, to meet the wishes of the manufacturers of this article. Suppose we were to add the duty proposed by this bill, although it would benefit the capital invested in works near the sea and the navigable rivers, yet the benefit would not extend far in the interior. Where, then, are we to stop, or what limit is proposed to us?

The freight of iron has been afforded from Sweden to the United States as low as eight dollars per ton. This is not more than the price of fifty miles of land carriage. Stockholm, therefore, for the purpose of this argument, may be considered as within fifty miles of Philadelphia. Now, it is at once a just and a strong view of this case, to consider, that there are, within fifty miles of our market, vast multitudes of persons who are willing to labor in the production of this article for us, at the rate of seven cents per day, while we have no labor which will not command, upon the average, at least five or six times that amount. The question is, then, shall we buy this article of these manufacturers, and suffer our own labor to earn its greater reward, or shall we employ our own labor in a similar manufacture, and make up to it, by a tax on consumers, the loss which it must necessarily sustain.

I proceed, Sir, to the article of hemp. Of this we imported last year, in round numbers, 6,000 tons, paying a duty of $30 a ton, or $180,000 on the whole amount; and this article, it is to be remembered, is consumed almost entirely in the uses of navigation. The whole burden may be said to fall on one interest. It is said we can produce this article if we will raise the duties. But why is it not produced now? or why, at least, have we not seen some specimens? for the present is a very high duty, when expenses of importation are added. Hemp was purchased at St. Petersburg, last year, at $101.67 per ton. Charges attending shipment, &c., $14.25. Freight may be stated at $30 per ton, and our existing duty $30 more. These three last sums, being the charges of transportation, amount to a protection of near seventy-five per cent in favor of the home manufacturer, if there be any such. And we ought to consider, also, that the price of hemp at St. Petersburg is increased by all the expense of transportation from the place of growth to that port; so that probably the whole cost of transportation, from the place of growth to our market, including our duty, is equal to the first cost of the article; or, in other words, is a protection in favor of our own product of one hundred per cent.

And since it is stated that we have great quantities of fine land for the production of hemp, of which I have no doubt, the question recurs, Why is it not produced? I speak of the water-rotted hemp, for it is admitted that that which is dew-rotted is not sufficiently good for the requisite purposes. I cannot say whether the cause be in climate, in the process of rotting, or what else, but the fact is certain, that there is no American water-rotted hemp in the market. We are acting, therefore, upon an hypothesis. Is it not reasonable that those who say that they *can* produce the article shall at least prove the truth of that allegation, before new taxes are laid on those who use the foreign commodity? Suppose this bill passes; the price of hemp is immediately raised $14.80 per ton, and this burden falls immediately on the ship-builder; and no part of it, for the present, will go for the benefit of the American grower, because he has none of the article than can be used, nor is it expected that much of it will be produced for a considerable time. Still the tax takes effect upon the imported article; and the ship-owners, to enable the Kentucky farmer to receive an additional $14 on his ton of hemp, whenever he may be able to raise and manufacture it, pay, in the mean time, an equal sum per ton into the treasury on all the imported hemp which they are still obliged to use; and this is called "protection"! Is this just or fair? A particular interest is here burdened, not only for the benefit of another particular interest, but burdened also beyond that, for the benefit of the treasury. It is said to be important for the country that this article should be raised in it; then let the country bear the expense, and pay the bounty. If it be for the good of the whole, let the sacrifice be made by the whole, and not by a part. If it be thought useful and necessary, from political considerations, to encourage the growth and manufacture of hemp, government has abundant means of doing it. It might give a direct bounty, and such a measure would, at least, distribute the burden equally; or, as government itself is a great consumer of this article, it might stipulate to confine its own purchases to the home product, so soon as it should be shown to be of the proper quality. I see no objection to this proceeding, if it be thought to be an object to encourage the production. It might easily, and perhaps properly, be provided by law, that the navy should be supplied with American hemp, the quality being good, at any price not exceeding, by more than a given amount, the current price of foreign hemp in our market. Every thing conspires to render some such course preferable to the one now proposed. The encouragement in that way would be ample, and, if the experiment should succeed, the whole object would be gained; and, if it should fail, no considerable loss or evil would be felt by any one.

I stated, some days ago, and I wish to renew the statement, what was the amount of the proposed augmentation of the duties on iron and hemp, in the cost of a vessel. Take the case of a common ship of three hundred tons, not coppered, nor copper-fastened. It would stand thus, by the present duties:--

14-1/2 tons of iron, for hull, rigging, and and anchors, at $15 per ton, $217.50 10 tons of hemp, at $30, 300.00 40 bolts Russia duck, at $2, 80.00 20 bolts Ravens duck, at $1.25, 25.00 On articles of ship-chandlery, cabin furniture, hard-ware, &c., 40.00 _____ $662.50 -------

The bill proposes to add,--

$7.40 per ton on iron, which will be $107.30 $14.80 per ton on hemp, equal to 148.00 And on duck, by the late amendment of the bill, say 25 per cent, 25.00 _____ $280.30 _____

But to the duties on iron and hemp should be added those paid on copper, whenever that article is used. By the statement which I furnished the other day, it appeared that the duties received by government on articles used in the construction of a vessel of three hundred and fifty-nine tons, with copper fastenings, amounted to $1,056. With the augmentations of this bill, they would be equal to $1,400.

Now I cannot but flatter myself, Mr. Chairman, that, before the committee will consent to this new burden upon the shipping interest, it will very deliberately weigh the probable consequences. I would again urgently solicit its attention to the condition of that interest. We are told that government has protected it, by discriminating duties, and by an exclusive right to the coasting trade. But it would retain the coasting trade by its own natural efforts, in like manner, and with more certainty, than it now retains any portion of foreign trade. The discriminating duties are now abolished, and while they existed, they were nothing more than countervailing measures; not so much designed to give our navigation an advantage over that of other nations, as to put it upon an equality; and we have, accordingly, abolished ours, when they have been willing to abolish theirs. Look to the rate of freights. Were they ever lower, or even so low? I ask gentlemen who know, whether the harbor of Charleston, and the river of Savannah, be not crowded with ships seeking employment, and finding none? I would ask the gentlemen from New Orleans, if their magnificent Mississippi does not exhibit, for furlongs, a forest of masts? The condition, Sir, of the shipping interest is not that of those who are insisting on high profits, or struggling for monopoly; but it is the condition of men content with the smallest earnings, and anxious for their bread. The freight of cotton has formerly been three pence sterling, from Charleston to Liverpool, in time of peace. It is now I know not what, or how many fractions of a penny; I think, however, it is stated at five eighths. The producers, then, of this great staple, are able, by means of this navigation, to send it, for a cent a pound, from their own doors to the best market in the world.

Mr. Chairman, I will now only remind the committee that, while we are proposing to add new burdens to the shipping interest, a very different line of policy is followed by our great commercial and maritime rival. It seems to be announced as the sentiment of the government of England, and undoubtedly it is its real sentiment, that the first of all manufactures is the manufacture of ships. A constant and wakeful attention is paid to this interest, and very important regulations, favorable to it, have been adopted within the last year, some of which I will beg leave to refer to, with the hope of exciting the notice, not only of the committee, but of all others who may feel, as I do, a deep interest in this subject. In the first place, a general amendment has taken place in the register acts, introducing many new provisions, and, among others, the following:--

A direct mortgage of the interest of a ship is allowed, without subjecting the mortgagee to the responsibility of an owner.

The proportion of interest held by each owner is exhibited in the register, thereby facilitating both sales and mortgages, and giving a new value to shipping among the moneyed classes.

Shares, in the ships of copartnerships, may be registered as joint property, and subject to the same rules as other partnership effects.

Ships may be registered in the name of trustees, for the benefit of joint-stock companies.

And many other regulations are adopted, with the same general view of rendering the mode of holding the property as convenient and as favorable as possible.

By another act, British registered vessels, of every description, are allowed to enter into the general and the coasting trade in the India seas, and may now trade to and from India, with any part of the world except China.

By a third, all limitations and restrictions, as to latitude and longitude, are removed from ships engaged in the Southern whale-fishery. These regulations, I presume, have not been made without first obtaining the consent of the East India Company; so true is it found, that real encouragement of enterprise oftener consists, in our days, in restraining or buying off monopolies and prohibitions, than in imposing or extending them.

The trade with Ireland is turned into a free coasting trade; light duties have been reduced, and various other beneficial arrangements made, and still others proposed. I might add, that, in favor of general commerce, and as showing their confidence in the principles of liberal intercourse, the British government has perfected the warehouse system, and authorized a reciprocity of duties with foreign states, at the discretion of the Privy Council.

This, Sir, is the attention which our great rival is paying to these important subjects, and we may assure ourselves that, if we do not cherish a proper sense of our own interests, she will not only beat us, but will deserve to beat us.

Sir, I will detain you no longer. There are some parts of this bill which I highly approve; there are others in which I should acquiesce; but those to which I have now stated my objections appear to me so destitute of all justice, so burdensome and so dangerous to that interest which has steadily enriched, gallantly defended, and proudly distinguished us, that nothing can prevail upon me to give it my support.[10]

NOTE.

This is commonly called Mr. Webster's "Free Trade" speech. It has been found difficult to select one among his many speeches in support of the policy of Protection which would fully represent his views on the subject; but the reasons for his change of opinion, and for his advocacy of Protection, are fully stated in many of the speeches printed in this volume, delivered after the year 1830. Perhaps as good a statement as can be selected from his many speeches on the Tariff, in explanation of his change of position as to the need, policy, and duty of protection to American manufactures, may be found in his speech delivered in the Senate of the United States, on the 25th and 26th of July, 1846, on the Bill "To reduce the Duties on Imports, and for other Purposes." In this speech, he made the following frank avowal of the reasons which induced him to reconsider and reverse his original opinions on the subject:--

"But, Sir, before I proceed further with this part of the case, I will take notice of what appears, latterly, to be an attempt, by the republication of opinions and expressions, arguments and speeches of mine, at an earlier and later period of life, to found against me a charge of inconsistency, on this subject of the protective policy of the country. Mr. President, if it be an inconsistency to hold an opinion upon a subject at one time and in one state of circumstances, and to hold a different opinion upon the same subject at another time and in a different state of circumstances, I admit the charge. Nay, Sir, I will go further; and in regard to questions which, from their nature, do not depend upon circumstances for their true and just solution, I mean constitutional questions, if it be an inconsistency to hold an opinion to-day, even upon such a question, and on that same question to hold a different opinion a quarter of a century afterwards, upon a more comprehensive view of the whole subject, with a more thorough investigation into the original purposes and objects of that Constitution, and especially after a more thorough exposition of those objects and purposes by those who framed it, and have been trusted to administer it, I should not shrink even from that imputation. I hope I know more of the Constitution of my country than I did when I was twenty years old. I hope I have contemplated its great objects more broadly. I hope I have read with deeper interest the sentiments of the great men who framed it. I hope I have studied with more care the condition of the country when the convention assembled to form it. And yet I do not know that I have much to retract or to change on these points.

"But, Sir, I am of the opinion of a very eminent person, who had occasion, not long since, to speak of this topic in another place. Inconsistencies of opinion, arising from changes of circumstances, are often justifiable. But there is one sort of inconsistency which is culpable. It is the inconsistency between a man's conviction and his vote; between his conscience and his conduct. No man shall ever charge me with an inconsistency like that. And now, Sir, allow me to say, that I am quite indifferent, or rather thankful, to those conductors of the public press who think they cannot do better than now and then to spread my poor opinions before the public.

"I have said many times, and it is true, that, up to the year 1824, the people of that part of the country to which I belong, being addicted to commerce, having been successful in commerce, their capital being very much engaged in commerce, were averse to entering upon a system of manufacturing operations. Every member in Congress from the State of Massachusetts, with the exception, I think, of one, voted against the act of 1824. But what were we to do? Were we not bound, after 1817 and 1824, to consider that the policy of the country was settled, had become settled, as a policy, to protect the domestic industry of the country by solemn laws? The leading speech[11] which ushered in the act of 1824 was called a speech for the 'American System.' The bill was carried principally by the Middle States. Pennsylvania and New York would have it so; and what were we to do? Were we to stand aloof from the occupations which others were pursuing around us? Were we to pick clean teeth on a constitutional doubt which a majority in the councils of the nation had overruled? No, Sir; we had no option. All that was left us was to fall in with the settled policy of the country; because, if any thing can ever settle the policy of the country, or if any thing can ever settle the practical construction of the Constitution of the country, it must be these repeated decisions of Congress, and enactments of successive laws conformable to these decisions. New England, then, did fall in. She went into manufacturing operations, not from original choice, but from the necessity of the circumstances in which the legislation of the country had placed her. And, for one, I resolved then, and have acted upon the resolution ever since, that, having compelled the Eastern States to go into these pursuits for a livelihood, the country was bound to fulfil the just expectations which it had inspired."

[Footnote 1: Mr. Clay.] [Footnote 2: Lord Lansdowne.] [Footnote 3: Lord Liverpool.]
[Footnote 4: Mr. Huskisson, President of the English Board of Trade.] [Footnote 5: The Marquess of Lansdowne.] [Footnote 6: Lord Liverpool.] [Footnote 7: Mr. Tod.][Footnote 8: "The present equable diffusion of moderate wealth cannot be better illustrated, than by remarking that in this age many palaces and superb mansions have been pulled down, or converted to other purposes, while none have been erected on a like scale. The numberless baronial castles and mansions, in all parts of England, now in ruins, may all be adduced as examples of the decrease of inordinate wealth. On the other hand, the multiplication of commodious dwellings for the upper and middle classes of society, and the increased comforts of all ranks, exhibit a picture of individual happiness, unknown in any other age."--_Sir G. Blane's Letter to Lord Spencer, in_ 1800.]
[Footnote 9: The price of labor in Russia may be pretty well collected from Tooke's "View of the Russian Empire." "The workmen in the mines and the founderies are, indeed, all called master-people; but they distinguish themselves into masters, under-masters, apprentices, delvers, servants, carriers, washers, and separators. In proportion to their ability their wages are regulated, which proceed from fifteen to upwards of thirty roubles per annum. The provisions which they receive from the magazines are deducted from this pay." The value of the rouble at that time (1799) was about twenty-four pence sterling, or forty-five cents of our money.
"By the edict of 1799," it is added, "a laborer with a horse shall receive, daily, in summer, twenty, and in winter, twelve copecks; a laborer without a horse, in summer, ten, in winter, eight copecks."
A copeck is the hundredth part of a rouble, or about half a cent of our money. The price of labor may have risen, in some degree, since that period, but probably not much.]

[Footnote 10: Since the delivery of this speech, an arrival has brought London papers containing the speech of the English Chancellor of the Exchequer (Mr. Robinson), on the 23d of February last, in submitting to Parliament the annual financial statement. Abundant confirmation will be found in that statement of the remarks made in the preceding speech, as to the prevailing sentiment, in the English government, on the general subject of prohibitory laws, and on the silk manufacture and the wool tax particularly.][Footnote 11: That of Mr. Clay.]

THE CASE OF GIBBONS AND OGDEN.
AN ARGUMENT MADE IN THE CASE OF GIBBONS AND OGDEN IN THE SUPREME COURT OF THE UNITED STATES, FEBRUARY TERM, 1824.

[This was an appeal from the Court for the Trial of Impeachments and Correction of Errors of the State of New York. Aaron Ogden filed his bill in the Court of Chancery of that State, against Thomas Gibbons, setting forth the several acts of the legislature thereof, enacted for the purpose of securing to Robert R. Livingston and Robert Fulton the exclusive navigation of all the waters within the jurisdiction of that State, with boats moved by fire or steam, for a term of years which had not then expired; and authorizing the Chancellor to award an injunction, restraining any person whatever from navigating those waters with boats of that description. The bill stated an assignment from Livingston and Fulton to one John R. Livingston, and from him to the complainant, Ogden, of the right to navigate the waters between Elizabethtown, and other places in New Jersey, and the city of New York; and that Gibbons, the defendant below, was in possession of two steamboats, called the Stoudinger and the Bellona, which were actually employed in running between New York and Elizabethtown, in violation of the exclusive privilege conferred on the complainant, and praying an injunction to restrain the said Gibbons from using the said boats, or any other propelled by fire or steam, in navigating the waters within the territory of New York. The injunction having been awarded, the answer of Gibbons was filed, in which he stated, that the boats employed by him were duly enrolled and licensed to be employed in carrying on the coasting trade, under the act of Congress, passed the 18th of February, 1793, ch. 8, entitled, "An Act for enrolling and licensing ships and vessels to be employed in the coasting trade and fisheries, and for regulating the same." And the defendant insisted on his right, in virtue of such licenses, to navigate the waters between Elizabethtown and the city of New York, the said acts of the legislature of the State of New York to the contrary notwithstanding. At the hearing, the Chancellor perpetuated the injunction, being of the opinion that the said acts were not repugnant to the Constitution and laws of the United States, and were valid. This decree was affirmed in the Court for the Trial of Impeachments and Correction of Errors, which is the highest court of law and equity in the State of New York before which the cause could be carried, and it was thereupon carried up to the Supreme Court of the United States by appeal.
The following argument was made by Mr. Webster, for the plaintiff in error.]
It is admitted, that there is a very respectable weight of authority in favor of the decision which is sought to be reversed. The laws in question, I am aware, have been deliberately re-enacted by the legislature of New York; and they have also received the sanction, at different times, of all her judicial tribunals, than which there are few, if any, in the country, more justly entitled to respect and deference. The disposition of the court will be, undoubtedly, to support, if it can, laws so passed and so sanctioned. I admit, therefore, that it is justly expected of us that we should make out a clear case; and unless we do so, we cannot hope for a reversal. It should be remembered, however, that the whole of this branch of power, as exercised by this court, is a power of revision. The question must be decided by the State courts, and decided in a particular manner, before it can be brought here at all. Such decisions alone give this court jurisdiction; and therefore, while they are to be respected as the judgments of learned judges, they are yet in the condition of all decisions from which the law allows an appeal.
It will not be a waste of time to advert to the existing state of the facts connected with the subject of this litigation. The use of steamboats on the coasts and in the bays and rivers of the country, has become very general. The intercourse of its different parts essentially depends upon this mode of conveyance and transportation. Rivers and bays, in many cases, form the divisions between States; and thence it is obvious, that, if the States should make regulations for the navigation of these waters, and such regulations should be repugnant and hostile, embarrassment would necessarily be caused to the general intercourse of the

community. Such events have actually occurred, and have created the existing state of things.

By the law of New York, no one can navigate the bay of New York, the North River, the Sound, the lakes, or any of the waters of that State, by steam-vessels, without a license from the grantees of New York, under penalty of forfeiture of the vessel.

By the law of the neighboring State of Connecticut, no one can enter her waters with a steam-vessel having such license.

By the law of New Jersey, if any citizen of that State shall be restrained, under the New York law, from using steamboats between the ancient shores of New Jersey and New York, he shall be entitled to an action for damages, in New Jersey, with treble costs against the party who thus restrains or impedes him under the law of New York! This act of New Jersey is called an act of retortion against the illegal and oppressive legislation of New York; and seems to be defended on those grounds of public law which justify reprisals between independent States.

It will hardly be contended, that all these acts are consistent with the laws and Constitution of the United States. If there is no power in the general government to control this extreme belligerent legislation of the States, the powers of the government are essentially deficient in a most important and interesting particular. The present controversy respects the earliest of these State laws, those of New York. On these, this court is now to pronounce; and if they should be declared to be valid and operative, I hope somebody will point out where the State right stops, and on what grounds the acts of other States are to be held inoperative and void.

It will be necessary to advert more particularly to the laws of New York, as they are stated in the record. The first was passed March 19th, 1787. By this act, a sole and exclusive right was granted to John Fitch, of making and using every kind of boat or vessel impelled by steam, in all creeks, rivers, bays, and waters within the territory and jurisdiction of New York for fourteen years.

On the 27th of March, 1798, an act was passed, on the suggestion that Fitch was dead, or had withdrawn from the State without having made any attempt to use his privilege, repealing the grant to him, and conferring similar privileges on Robert R. Livingston, for the term of twenty years, on a suggestion, made by him, that he was possessor of a mode of applying the steam-engine to propel a boat, on new and advantageous principles. On the 5th of April, 1803, another act was passed, by which it was declared, that the rights and privileges granted to Robert R. Livingston by the last act should be extended to him and Robert Fulton, for twenty years from the passing of the act. Then there is the act of April 11, 1808, purporting to extend the monopoly, in point of time, five years for every additional boat, the whole duration, however, not to exceed thirty years; and forbidding any and all persons to navigate the waters of the State with any steam boat or vessel, without the license of Livingston and Fulton, under penalty of forfeiture of the boat or vessel. And lastly comes the act of April 9, 1811, for enforcing the provisions of the last-mentioned act, and declaring, that the forfeiture of the boat or vessel found navigating against the provisions of the previous acts shall be deemed to accrue on the day on which such boat or vessel should navigate the waters of the State; and that Livingston and Fulton might immediately have an action for such boat or vessel, in like manner as if they themselves had been dispossessed thereof by force; and that, on bringing any such suit, the defendant therein should be prohibited, by injunction, from removing the boat or vessel out of the State, or using it within the State. There are one or two other acts mentioned in the pleadings, which principally respect the time allowed for complying with the condition of the grant, and are not material to the discussion of the case.

By these acts, then, an exclusive right is given to Livingston and Fulton to use steam navigation on all the waters of New York, for thirty years from 1808.

It is not necessary to recite the several conveyances and agreements, stated in the record, by which Ogden, the plaintiff below, derives title under Livingston and Fulton to the exclusive use of part of these waters for steam navigation.

The appellant being owner of a steamboat, and being found navigating the waters between New Jersey and the city of New York, over which waters Ogden, the plaintiff below, claims an exclusive right, under Livingston and Fulton, this bill was filed against him by Ogden, in October, 1818, and an injunction granted, restraining him from such use of his boat. This injunction was made perpetual, on the final hearing of the cause, in the Court of Chancery; and the decree of the Chancellor has been duly affirmed in the Court of Errors. The right, therefore, which the plaintiff below asserts, to have and maintain his injunction, depends obviously on the general validity of the New York laws, and especially on their force and operation as against the right set up by the defendant. This right he states in his answer to be, that he is a citizen of New Jersey, and owner of the steamboat in question; that the boat is a vessel of more than twenty tons burden, duly enrolled and licensed for carrying on the coasting trade, and intended to be employed by him in that trade, between Elizabethtown, in New Jersey, and the city of New York; and that it was actually employed in navigating between those places at the time of, and until notice of, the injunction from the Court of Chancery was served on him.

On these pleadings the substantial question is raised, Are these laws such as the legislature of New York has a right to pass? If so, do they, secondly, in their operation, interfere with any right enjoyed under the Constitution and laws of the United States, and are they therefore void, as far as such interference extends? It may be well to state again their general purport and effect, and the purport and effect of the other State laws which have been enacted by way of retaliation.

A steam-vessel, of any description, going to New York, is forfeited to the representatives of Livingston and Fulton, unless she have their license. Going from New York or elsewhere to Connecticut, she is prohibited from entering the waters of that State if she have such license.

If the representatives of Livingston and Fulton in New York carry into effect, by judicial process, the provision of the New York laws, against any citizen of New Jersey, they expose themselves to a statute action in New Jersey for all damages, and treble costs.

The New York laws extend to all steam-vessels; to steam frigates, steam ferry-boats, and all intermediate classes. They extend to public as well as private ships; and to vessels employed in foreign commerce, as well as to those employed in the coasting trade.

The remedy is as summary as the grant itself is ample; for immediate confiscation, without seizure, trial, or judgment, is the penalty of infringement.

In regard to these acts, I shall contend, in the first place, that they exceed the power of the legislature; and, secondly, that, if they could be considered valid for any purpose, they are void still, as against any right enjoyed under the laws of the United States with which they come in collision; and that in this case they are found interfering with such rights.

I shall contend that the power of Congress to regulate commerce is complete and entire, and, to a certain extent, necessarily exclusive; that the acts in question are regulations of commerce, in a most important particular, affecting it in those respects in which it is under the exclusive authority of Congress. I state this first proposition guardedly. I do not mean to say, that all regulations which may, in their operation, affect commerce, are exclusively in the power of Congress; but that such power as has been exercised in this case does not remain with the States. Nothing is more complex than commerce; and in such an age as this, no words embrace a wider field than *commercial regulation*. Almost all the business and intercourse of life may be connected incidentally, more or less, with commercial regulations. But it is only necessary to apply to this part of the Constitution the well-settled rules of construction. Some powers are held to be exclusive in Congress, from the use of exclusive words in the grant; others, from the prohibitions on the States to exercise similar powers; and others, again, from the nature of the powers themselves. It has been by this mode of reasoning that the court has adjudicated many important questions; and the same mode is proper here. And, as some powers have been held to be exclusive, and others not so, under the same form of expression, from the nature of the different powers respectively; so where the power, on any one subject, is given in general words, like the power to regulate commerce, the true method of construction will be to consider of what parts the grant is composed, and which of those, from the nature of the thing, ought to be considered exclusive. The right set up in this case, under the laws of New York, is a monopoly. Now I think it very reasonable to say, that the Constitution never intended to leave with the States the power of granting monopolies either of trade or of navigation; and therefore, that, as to this, the commercial power is exclusive in Congress.

It is in vain to look for a precise and exact *definition* of the powers of Congress on several subjects. The Constitution does not undertake the task of making such exact definitions. In conferring powers, it proceeds by the way of _enumeration_, stating the powers conferred, one after another, in few words and where the power is general or complex in its nature, the extent of the grant must necessarily be judged of, and limited, by its object, and by the nature of the power.

Few things are better known than the immediate causes which led to the adoption of the present Constitution; and there is nothing, as I think, clearer, than that the prevailing motive was _to regulate commerce_; to rescue it from the embarrassing and destructive consequences resulting from the legislation of so many different States, and to place it under the protection of a uniform law. The great objects were commerce and revenue; and they were objects indissolubly connected. By the Confederation, divers restrictions had been imposed on the States; but these had not been found sufficient. No State, it is true, could send or receive an embassy; nor make any treaty; nor enter into any compact with another State, or with a foreign power; nor lay duties interfering with treaties which had been entered into by Congress. But all these were found to be far short of what the actual condition of the country required. The States could still, each for itself, regulate commerce, and the consequence was a perpetual jarring and hostility of commercial regulation.

In the history of the times, it is accordingly found, that the great topic, urged on all occasions, as showing the necessity of a new and different government, was the state of trade and commerce. To benefit and improve these was a great object in itself; and it became greater when it was regarded as the only means of enabling the country to pay the public debt, and to do justice to those who had most effectually labored for its independence. The leading state papers of the time are full of this topic. The New Jersey resolutions[1] complain that the regulation of trade was in the power of the several States, within their separate jurisdiction, to such a degree as to involve many difficulties and embarrassments; and they express an earnest opinion, that the sole and exclusive power of regulating trade with foreign states ought to be in Congress. Mr. Witherspoon's motion in Congress, in 1781, is of the same general character; and the report of a committee of that body, in 1785, is still more emphatic. It declares that Congress ought to possess the sole and exclusive power of regulating trade, as well with foreign nations as between the States.[2] The resolutions of Virginia, in January, 1786, which were the immediate cause of the Convention, put forth this same great object. Indeed, it is the only object stated in those resolutions. There is not another idea in the whole document. The sole purpose for which the delegates assembled at Annapolis was to devise means for the uniform regulation of trade. They found no means but in a general government; and they recommended a convention to accomplish that purpose. Over whatever other interests of the country this government may diffuse its benefits and its blessings, it will always be true, as matter of historical fact, that it had its immediate origin in the necessities of commerce; and for its immediate object, the relief of those necessities, by removing their causes, and by establishing a uniform and steady system. It will be easy to show, by reference to the discussions in the several State conventions, the prevalence of the same general topics; and if any one would look to the proceedings of several of the States, especially to those of Massachusetts and New York, he would see very plainly, by the recorded lists of votes, that wherever this commercial necessity was most strongly felt, there the proposed new Constitution had most friends. In the New York convention, the argument arising from this consideration was strongly pressed, by the distinguished person[3] whose name is connected with the present question.

We do not find, in the history of the formation and adoption of the Constitution, that any man speaks of a general concurrent power, in the regulation of foreign and domestic trade, as still residing in the States. The very object intended, more than any other, was to take away such power. If it had not so provided, the Constitution would not have been worth accepting.

I contend, therefore, that the people intended, in establishing the Constitution, to transfer from the several States to a general government those high and important powers over commerce, which, in their exercise, were to maintain a uniform and general system. From the very nature of the case, these powers must be exclusive; that is, the higher branches of commercial regulation must be exclusively committed to a single hand. What is it that is to be regulated? Not the commerce of the several States, respectively, but the commerce of the United States. Henceforth, the commerce of the States was to be a _unit_, and the system by which it was to exist and be governed must necessarily be complete, entire, and uniform. Its character was to be described in the flag which waved over it, E PLURIBUS UNUM. Now, how could individual States assert a right of concurrent legislation, in a case of this sort, without manifest encroachment and confusion? It should be repeated, that the words used in the Constitution, "to regulate commerce," are so very general and extensive, that they may be construed to cover a vast field of legislation, part of which has always been occupied by State laws; and therefore the words must have a reasonable construction, and the power should be considered as exclusively vested in Congress so far, and so far only, as the nature of the power requires. And I insist, that the nature of the case, and of the power, did imperiously require, that such important authority as that of granting monopolies of trade and navigation should not be considered as still retained by the States.

It is apparent from the prohibitions on the power of the States, that the general concurrent power was not supposed to be left with them. And the exception out of these prohibitions of the inspection laws proves this still more clearly. Which most concerns the commerce of this country, that New York and Virginia should have an uncontrolled power to establish their inspection of flour and tobacco, or that they should have an uncontrolled power of granting either a monopoly of trade in their own ports, or a monopoly of navigation over all the waters leading to those ports? Yet the argument on the other side must be, that, although the Constitution has sedulously guarded and limited the first of these powers, it has left the last wholly unlimited and uncontrolled.

But although much has been said, in the discussion on former occasions, about this supposed concurrent power in the States, I find great difficulty in understanding what is meant by it. It is generally qualified by saying, that it is a power by which the States could pass laws on subjects of commercial regulation, which would be valid until Congress should pass other laws controlling them, or inconsistent with them, and that then the State laws must yield. What sort of concurrent powers are these, which cannot exist together? Indeed, the very reading of the clause in the Constitution must put to flight this notion of a general concurrent power. The Constitution was formed for all the States; and Congress was to have power to regulate commerce. Now, what is the import of this, but that Congress is to give the rule, to establish the system, to exercise the control over the subject? And can more than one power, in cases of this sort, give the rule, establish the system, or exercise the control? As it is not contended that the power of Congress is to be exercised by a supervision of State legislation, and as it is clear that Congress is to give the general rule, I contend that this power of giving the general rule is transferred, by the Constitution, from the States to Congress, to be exercised as that body may see fit; and consequently, that all those high exercises of power, which might be considered as giving the rule, or establishing the system, in regard to great commercial interests, are necessarily left with Congress alone. Of this character I consider monopolies of trade or navigation; embargoes; the system of navigation laws; the countervailing laws, as against foreign states; and other important enactments respecting our connection with such states. It appears to me a most reasonable construction to say, that in these respects the power of Congress is exclusive, from the nature of the power. If it be not so, where is the limit, or who shall fix a boundary for the exercise of the power of the States? Can a State grant a monopoly of trade? Can New York shut her ports to all but her own citizens? Can she refuse admission to ships of particular nations? The argument on the other side is, and must be, that she might do all these things, until Congress should revoke her enactments. And this is called *concurrent* legislation! What confusion such notions lead to is obvious enough. A power in the States to do any thing, and every thing, in regard to commerce, till Congress shall undo it, would suppose a state of things at least as bad as that which existed before the present Constitution. It is the true wisdom of these governments to keep their action as distinct as possible. The general government should not seek to operate where the States can operate with more advantage to the community; nor should the States encroach on ground which the public good, as well as the Constitution, refers to the exclusive control of Congress.

If the present state of things, these laws of New York, the laws of Connecticut, and the laws of New Jersey, had been all presented, in the convention of New York, to the eminent person whose name is on this record, and who acted on that occasion so important a part; if he had been told, that, after all he had said in favor of the new government, and of its salutary effects on commercial regulations, the time would yet come when the North River would be shut up by a monopoly from New York, the Sound interdicted by a penal law of Connecticut, reprisals authorized by New Jersey against citizens of New York, and when one could not cross a ferry without transshipment, does any one suppose he would have admitted all this as compatible with the government which he was recommending?

This doctrine of a general concurrent power in the States is insidious and dangerous. If it be admitted, no one can say where it will stop. The States may legislate, it is said, wherever Congress has not made a plenary exercise of its power. But who is to judge whether Congress has made this plenary exercise of power? Congress has acted on this power; it has done all that it deemed wise; and are the States now to do whatever Congress has left undone? Congress makes such rules as, in its judgment, the case requires; and those rules, whatever they are, constitute the system.

All useful regulation does not consist in restraint; and that which Congress sees fit to leave free is a part of its regulation, as much as the rest.

The practice under the Constitution sufficiently evinces, that this portion of the commercial power is exclusive in Congress. When, before this instance, have the States granted monopolies? When, until now, have they interfered with the navigation of the country? The pilot laws, the health laws, or quarantine laws, and various regulations of that class, which have been recognized by Congress, are no arguments to prove, even if they are to be called commercial regulations (which they are not), that other regulations, more directly and strictly commercial, are not solely within the power of Congress. There is a singular fallacy, as I venture to think, in the argument of very learned and most respectable persons on this subject. That argument alleges, that the States have a concurrent power with Congress of regulating commerce; and the proof of this position is, that the States have, without any question of their right, passed acts respecting turnpike roads, toll-bridges, and ferries. These are declared to be acts of commercial regulation, affecting not only the interior commerce of the State itself, but also commerce between different States. Therefore, as all these are commercial regulations, and are yet acknowledged to be rightfully established by the States, it follows, as is supposed, that the States must have a concurrent power to regulate commerce.

Now, what is the inevitable consequence of this mode of reasoning? Does it not admit the power of Congress, at once, upon all these minor objects of legislation? If all these be regulations of commerce, within the meaning of the Constitution, then certainly Congress, having a concurrent power to regulate commerce, may establish ferries, turnpike-roads, and bridges, and provide for all this detail of interior legislation. To sustain the interference of the State in a high concern of maritime commerce, the argument adopts a principle which acknowledges the right of Congress over a vast scope of internal legislation, which no one has heretofore supposed to be within its powers. But this is not all; for it is admitted that, when Congress and the States have power to legislate over the same subject, the power of Congress, when exercised, controls or extinguishes the State power; and therefore the consequence would seem to follow, from the argument, that all State legislation over such subjects as have been mentioned is, at all times, liable to the superior power of Congress; a consequence which no one would admit for a moment. The truth is, in my judgment, that all these things are, in their general character, rather regulations of police than of commerce, in the constitutional understanding of that term. A road, indeed, may be a matter of great commercial concern. In many cases it is so; and when it is so, there is no doubt of the power of Congress to make it. But, generally speaking, roads, and bridges, and ferries, though of course they affect commerce and intercourse, do not possess such importance and elevation as to be deemed commercial regulations. A reasonable construction must be given to the Constitution; and such construction is as necessary to the just power of the States, as to the authority of Congress. Quarantine laws, for example, may be considered as affecting commerce; yet they are, in their nature, health laws. In England, we speak of the power of regulating commerce as in Parliament, or the king, as arbiter of commerce; yet the city of London enacts health laws. Would any one infer from that circumstance, that the city of London had concurrent power with Parliament or the crown to regulate commerce? or that it might grant a monopoly of the navigation of the Thames? While a health law is reasonable, it is a health law; but if, under color of it, enactments should be made for other purposes, such enactments might be void.

In the discussion in the New York courts, no small reliance was placed on the law of that State prohibiting the importation of slaves, as an example of a commercial regulation enacted by State authority. That law may or may not be constitutional and valid. It has been referred to generally, but its particular provisions have not been stated. When they are more clearly seen, its character may be better determined.

It might further be argued, that the power of Congress over these high branches of commerce is exclusive, from the consideration that Congress possesses an exclusive admiralty jurisdiction. That it does possess such exclusive jurisdiction will hardly be contested. No State pretends to exercise any jurisdiction of that kind. The States abolished their courts of admiralty, when the Constitution went into operation. Over these waters, therefore, or at least some of them, which are the subject of this monopoly, New York has no jurisdiction whatever. They are a part of the high seas, and not within the body of any county. The authorities of that State could not punish for a murder, committed on board one of these boats, in some places within the range of this exclusive grant. This restraining of the States from all jurisdiction out of the body of their own counties, shows plainly enough that navigation on the high seas was understood to be a matter to be regulated only by Congress. It is not unreasonable to say, that what are called the waters of New York are, for purposes of navigation and commercial regulation, the waters of the United States. There is no cession, indeed, of the waters themselves, but their use for those purposes seems to be intrusted to the exclusive power of Congress. Several States have enacted laws which would appear to imply their conviction of the power of Congress over navigable waters to a greater extent.

If there be a concurrent power of regulating commerce on the high seas, there must be a concurrent admiralty jurisdiction, and a concurrent control of the waters. It is a common principle, that arms of the sea, including navigable rivers, belong to the sovereign, so far as navigation is concerned. Their use is navigation. The United States possess the general power over navigation, and, of course, ought to control, in general, the use of navigable waters. If it be admitted that, for purposes of trade and navigation, the North River and its bay are the river and bay of New York and the Chesapeake the bay of Virginia, very great inconveniences and much confusion might be the result.

It may now be well to take a nearer view of these laws, to see more exactly what their provisions are, what consequences have followed from them, and what would and might follow from other similar laws.

The first grant to John Fitch gave him the sole and exclusive right of making, employing, and navigating all boats impelled by fire or steam, "in all creeks, rivers, bays, and waters within the territory and jurisdiction of the State." Any other person navigating such boat, was to forfeit it, and to pay a penalty of a hundred pounds. The subsequent acts repeal this, and grant similar privileges to Livingston and Fulton; and the act of 1811 provides the extraordinary and summary remedy which has been already stated. The river, the bay, and the marine league along the shore, are all within the scope of this grant. Any vessel, therefore, of this description, coming into any of those waters, without a license, whether from another State or from abroad, whether it be a public or private vessel, is instantly forfeited to the grantees of the monopoly.

Now it must be remembered that this grant is made as an exercise of sovereign political power. It is not an inspection law, nor a health law, nor passed by any derivative authority; it is professedly an act of sovereign power. Of course, there is no limit to the power, to be derived from the purpose for which it is exercised. If exercised for one purpose, it may be also for another. No one can inquire into the motives which influence sovereign authority. It is enough that such power manifests its will. The motive alleged in this case is, to remunerate the grantees for a benefit conferred by them on the public. But there is no necessary connection between that benefit and this mode of rewarding it; and if the State could grant this monopoly for that purpose, it could also grant it for any other purpose. It could make the grant for money; and so make the monopoly of navigation over those waters a direct source of revenue. When this monopoly shall expire, in 1838, the State may continue it, for any pecuniary consideration which the holders may see fit to offer, and the State to receive.

If the State may grant this monopoly, it may also grant another, for other descriptions of vessels; for instance, for all sloops.

If it can grant these exclusive privileges to a few, it may grant them to many; that is, it may grant them to all its own citizens, to the exclusion of everybody else.

But the waters of New York are no more the subject of exclusive grants by that State, than the waters of other States are subjects of such grants by those other States. Virginia may well exercise, over the entrance of the Chesapeake, all the power that New York can exercise over the bay of New York, and the waters on her shores. The Chesapeake, therefore, upon the principle of these laws, may be the subject of State monopoly; and so may the bay of Massachusetts. But this is not all. It requires no greater power to grant a monopoly of trade, than a monopoly of navigation. Of course, New York, if these acts can be maintained, may give an exclusive right of entry of vessels into her ports; and the other States may do the same. These are not extreme cases. We have only to suppose that other States should do what New York has already done, and that the power should be carried to its full extent.

To all this, no answer is to be given but one, that the concurrent power of the States, concurrent though it be, is yet subordinate to the legislation of Congress; and that therefore Congress may, whenever it pleases, annul the State legislation; but until it does so annul it, the State legislation is valid and effectual. What is there to recommend a construction which leads to a result like this? Here would be a perpetual hostility; one legislature enacting laws, till another legislature should repeal them; one sovereign power giving the rule, till another sovereign power should abrogate it; and all this under the idea of concurrent legislation! But, further, under this concurrent power, the State does that which Congress cannot do; that is, it gives preferences to the citizens of some States over those of others. I do not mean here the advantages conferred by the grant on the grantees; but the disadvantages to which it subjects all the other citizens of New York. To impose an extraordinary tax on steam navigation visiting the ports of New York, and leaving it free everywhere else, is giving a preference to the citizens of other States over those of New York. This Congress could not do; and yet the State does it; so that this power, at first subordinate, then concurrent, now becomes paramount.

The people of New York have a right to be protected against this monopoly. It is one of the objects for which they agreed to this Constitution, that they should stand on an equality in commercial regulations; and if the government should not insure them that, the promises made to them in its behalf would not be performed.

I contend, therefore, in conclusion on this point, that the power of Congress over these high branches of commercial regulation is shown to be exclusive, by considering what was wished and intended to be done, when the convention for forming the Constitution was called; by what was understood, in the State conventions, to have been accomplished by the instrument; by the prohibitions on the States, and the express exception relative to inspection laws; by the nature of the power itself; by the terms used, as connected with the nature of the power; by the subsequent understanding and practice, both of Congress and the States; by the grant of exclusive admiralty jurisdiction to the federal government; by the manifest danger of the opposite doctrine, and the ruinous consequences to which it directly leads.

Little is now required to be said, to prove that this exclusive grant is a law regulating commerce; although, in some of the discussions elsewhere, it has been called a law of police. If it be not a regulation of commerce, then it follows, against the constant admission on the other side, that Congress, even by an express act, cannot annul or control it. For if it be not a regulation of commerce, Congress has no concern with it. But the granting of monopolies of this kind is always referred to the power over commerce. It was as arbiter of commerce that the king formerly granted such monopolies.[4] This is a law regulating commerce, inasmuch as it imposes new conditions and terms on the coasting trade, on foreign trade generally, and on foreign trade as regulated by treaties; and inasmuch as it interferes with the free navigation of navigable waters.

If, then, the power of commercial regulation possessed by Congress be, in regard to the great branches of it, exclusive; and if this grant of New York be a commercial regulation, affecting commerce in respect to these great branches, then the grant is void, whether any case of actual collision has happened or not.

But I contend, in the second place, that whether the grant were to be regarded as wholly void or not, it must, at least, be inoperative, when the rights claimed under it come in collision with other rights, enjoyed and secured under the laws of the United States; and such collision, I maintain, clearly exists in this case. It will not be denied that the law of Congress is paramount. The Constitution has expressly provided for that. So that the only question in this part of the case is, whether the two rights be inconsistent with each other. The appellant has a right to go from New Jersey to New York, in a vessel owned by himself, of the proper legal description, and enrolled and licensed according to law. This right belongs to him as a citizen of the United States. It is derived under the laws of the United States, and no act of the legislature of New York can deprive him of it, any more than such act could deprive him of the right of holding lands in that State, or of suing in its courts. It appears from the record, that the boat in question was regularly enrolled at Perth Amboy, and properly licensed for carrying on the coasting trade. Under this enrolment, and with this license, she was proceeding to New York, when she was stopped by the injunction of the Chancellor, on the application of the New York grantees. There can be no doubt that here is a collision, in fact; that which the appellant claimed as a right, the respondent resisted; and there remains nothing now but to determine whether the appellant had, as he contends, a right to navigate these waters; because, if he had such right, it must prevail.

Now, this right is expressly conferred by the laws of the United States. The first section of the act of February, 1793, ch. 8, regulating the coasting trade and fisheries, declares, that all ships and vessels, enrolled and licensed as that act provides, "and no others, shall be deemed ships or vessels of the United States, entitled to the privileges of ships or vessels employed in the coasting trade or fisheries." The fourth section of the same act declares, "that, in order to the licensing of any ship or vessel, for carrying on the coasting trade or fisheries," bond shall be given, according to the provisions of the act. And the same section declares, that, the owner having complied with the requisites of the law, "it shall be the duty of the collector to grant a license for carrying on the coasting trade"; and the act proceeds to give the form and words of the license, which is, therefore, of course, to be received as a part of the act; and the words of the license, after the necessary recitals, are, "License is hereby granted for the said vessel to be employed in carrying on the coasting trade." Words could not make this authority more express.

The court below seems to me, with great deference, to have mistaken the object and nature of the license. It seems to have been of opinion, that the license has no other intent or effect than to ascertain the ownership and character of the vessel. But this is the peculiar office and object of the enrolment. That document ascertains that the regular proof of ownership and character has been given; and the license is given to confer the right to which the party has shown himself entitled. It is the authority which the master carries with him, to prove his right to navigate freely the waters of the United States, and to carry on the coasting trade.

In some of the discussions which have been had on this question, it has been said, that Congress has only provided for ascertaining the ownership and property of vessels, but has not prescribed to what use they may be applied. But this is an obvious error. The whole object of the act regulating the coasting trade is to declare what vessels shall enjoy the benefit of being employed in that trade. To secure this use to certain vessels, and to deny it to others, is precisely the purpose for which the act was passed. The error, or what I humbly suppose to be the error, in the judgment of the court below, consists in that court's having thought, that, although Congress might act, it had not yet acted, in such a way as to confer a right on the appellant; whereas, if a right was not given by this law, it never could be given. No law can be more express. It has been admitted, that, supposing there is a provision in the act of Congress, that all vessels duly licensed shall be at liberty to navigate, for the purpose of trade and commerce, all the navigable harbors, bays, rivers, and lakes within the several States, any law of the States creating particular privileges as to any particular class of vessels to the contrary notwithstanding, the only question that could arise, in such a case, would be, whether the law was constitutional; and that, if that was to be granted or decided, it would certainly, in all courts and places, overrule and set aside the State grant.

Now, I do not see that such supposed case could be distinguished from the present. We show a provision in an act of Congress, that all vessels, duly licensed, may carry on the coasting trade; nobody doubts the constitutional validity of that law; and we show that this vessel was duly licensed according to its provisions. This is all that is essential in the case supposed. The presence or absence of a *non obstante* clause cannot affect the extent or operation of the act of Congress. Congress has no power of revoking State laws, as a distinct power. It legislates over subjects; and over those subjects which are within its power, its legislation is supreme, and necessarily overrules all inconsistent or repugnant State legislation. If Congress were to pass an act expressly revoking or annulling, in whole or in part, this New York grant, such an act would be wholly useless and inoperative. If the New York grant be opposed to, or inconsistent with, any constitutional power which Congress has exercised, then, so far as the incompatibility exists, the grant is nugatory and void, necessarily, and by reason of the supremacy of the law of Congress. But if the grant be not inconsistent with any exercise of the powers of Congress, then, certainly, Congress has no authority to revoke or annul it. Such an act of Congress, therefore, would be either unconstitutional or supererogatory. The laws of Congress need no *non obstante* clause. The Constitution makes them supreme, when State laws come into opposition to them. So that in these cases there is no question except this; whether there be, or be not, a repugnancy or hostility between the law of Congress and the law of the State. Nor is it at all material, in this view, whether the law of the State be a law regulating commerce, or a law of police, nor by what other name or character it may be designated. If its provisions be inconsistent with an act of Congress, they are void, so far as that inconsistency extends. The whole argument, therefore, is substantially and effectually given up, when it is admitted that Congress might, by express terms, abrogate the State grant, or declare that it should not stand in the way of its own legislation; because such express terms would add nothing to the effect and operation of an act of Congress.

I contend, therefore, upon the whole of this point, that a case of actual collision has been made out between the State grant and the act of Congress; and as the act of Congress is entirely unexceptionable, and clearly in pursuance of its constitutional powers, the State grant must yield.

There are other provisions of the Constitution of the United States, which have more or less bearing on this question. "No State shall, without the consent of Congress, lay any duty of tonnage." Under color of grants like this, that prohibition might be wholly evaded. This grant authorizes Messrs. Livingston and Fulton to license navigation in the waters of New York. They, of course, license it on their own terms. They may require a pecuniary consideration, ascertained by the tonnage of the vessel, or in any other manner. Probably, in fact, they govern themselves, in this respect, by the size or tonnage of the vessels to which they grant licenses. Now, what is this but substantially a tonnage duty, under the law of the State? Or does it make any difference, whether the receipts go directly into her own treasury, or into the hands of those to whom she has made the grant?

There is, lastly, that provision of the Constitution which gives Congress power to promote the progress of science and the useful arts, by securing to authors and inventors, for a limited time, an exclusive right to their own writings and discoveries. Congress has exercised this power, and made all the provisions which it deemed useful or necessary. The States may, indeed, like munificent individuals, exercise their own bounty towards authors and inventors, at their own discretion. But to confer reward by exclusive grants, even if it were but a part of the use of the writing or invention, is not supposed to be a power properly to be exercised by the States. Much less can they, under the notion of conferring rewards in such cases, grant monopolies, the enjoyment of which is essentially incompatible with the exercise of rights possessed under the laws of the United States. I shall insist, however, the less on these points, as they are open to counsel who will come after me on the same side, and as I have said so much upon what appears to me the more important and interesting part of the argument.

[Footnote 1: 1 Laws U.S., p. 28, Bioren and Duane's ed.][Footnote 2: 1 Laws U.S., p. 50.]
[Footnote 3: Chancellor Livingston.][Footnote 4: 1 Black. Com. 273; 4 Black. Com. 160.]

THE BUNKER HILL MONUMENT.
AN ADDRESS DELIVERED AT THE LAYING OF THE CORNER-STONE OF THE BUNKER HILL MONUMENT AT CHARLESTOWN, MASSACHUSETTS, ON THE 17TH OF JUNE, 1825.

[As early as 1776, some steps were taken toward the commemoration of the battle of Bunker Hill and the fall of General Warren, who was buried upon the hill the day after the action. The Massachusetts Lodge of Masons, over which he presided, applied to the provisional government of Massachusetts, for permission to take up his remains and to bury them with the usual solemnities. The Council granted this request, on condition that it should be carried into effect in such a manner that the government of *the Colony* might have an opportunity to erect a monument to his memory. A funeral procession was had, and a Eulogy on General Warren was delivered by Perez Morton, but no measures were taken toward building a monument. A resolution was adopted by the Congress of the United States on the 8th of April, 1777, directing that monuments should be erected to the memory of General Warren, in Boston, and of General Mercer, at Fredericksburg; but this resolution has remained to the present time unexecuted.

On the 11th of November, 1794, a committee was appointed by King Solomon's Lodge, at Charlestown,[1] to take measures for the erection of a monument to the memory of General Joseph Warren at the expense of the Lodge. This resolution was promptly carried into effect. The land for this purpose was presented to the Lodge by the Hon. James Russell, of Charlestown, and it was dedicated with appropriate ceremonies on the 2d of December, 1794. It was a wooden pillar of the Tuscan order, eighteen feet in height, raised on a pedestal eight feet square, and of an elevation of ten feet from the ground. The pillar was surmounted by a gilt urn. An appropriate inscription was placed on the south side of the pedestal.

In February, 1818, a committee of the legislature of Massachusetts was appointed to consider the expediency of building a monument of American marble of the memory of General Warren, but this proposal was not carried into effect.

As the half-century from the date of the battle drew toward a close, a stronger feeling of the duty of commemorating it began to be awakened in the community. Among those who from the first manifested the greatest interest in the subject, was the late William Tudor, Esq. He expressed the wish, in a letter still preserved, to see upon the battle-ground "the noblest monument in the world," and he was so ardent and persevering in urging the project, that it has been stated that he first conceived the idea of it. The steps taken in execution of the project, from the earliest private conferences among the gentlemen first engaged in it to its final completion, are accurately sketched by Mr. Richard Frothingham, Jr., in his valuable History of the Siege of Boston. All the material facts contained in this note are derived from his chapter on the Bunker Hill Monument. After giving an account of the organization of the society, the measures adopted for the collection of funds, and the deliberations on the form of the monument, Mr. Frothingham proceeds as follows:--

"It was at this stage of the enterprise that the directors proposed to lay the corner-stone of the monument, and ground was broken (June 7th) for this purpose. As a mark of respect to the liberality and patriotism of

King Solomon's Lodge, they invited the Grand Master of the Grand Lodge of Massachusetts to perform the ceremony. They also invited General Lafayette to accompany the President of the Association, Hon. Daniel Webster, and assist in it.

"This celebration was unequalled in magnificence by any thing of the kind that had been seen in New England. The morning proved propitious. The air was cool, the sky was clear, and timely showers the previous day had brightened the vesture of nature into its loveliest hue. Delighted thousands flocked into Boston to bear a part in the proceedings, or to witness the spectacle. At about ten o'clock a procession moved from the State House towards Bunker Hill. The military, in their fine uniforms, formed the van. About two hundred veterans of the Revolution, of whom forty were survivors of the battle, rode in barouches next to the escort. These venerable men, the relics of a past generation, with emaciated frames, tottering limbs, and trembling voices, constituted a touching spectacle. Some wore, as honorable decorations, their old fighting equipments, and some bore the scars of still more honorable wounds. Glistening eyes constituted their answer to the enthusiastic cheers of the grateful multitudes who lined their pathway and cheered their progress. To this patriot band succeeded the Bunker Hill Monument Association. Then the Masonic fraternity, in their splendid regalia, thousands in number. Then Lafayette, continually welcomed by tokens of love and gratitude, and the invited guests. Then a long array of societies, with their various badges and banners. It was a splendid procession, and of such length that the front nearly reached Charlestown Bridge ere the rear had left Boston Common. It proceeded to Breed's Hill, where the Grand Master of the Freemasons, the President of the Monument Association, and General Lafayette, performed the ceremony of laying the corner-stone, in the presence of a vast concourse of people."

The procession then moved to a spacious amphitheatre on the northern declivity of the hill, when the following address was delivered by Mr. Webster, in the presence of as great a multitude as was ever perhaps assembled within the sound of a human voice.]

This uncounted multitude before me and around me proves the feeling which the occasion has excited. These thousands of human faces, glowing with sympathy and joy, and from the impulses of a common gratitude turned reverently to heaven in this spacious temple of the firmament, proclaim that the day, the place, and the purpose of our assembling have made a deep impression on our hearts.

If, indeed, there be any thing in local association fit to affect the mind of man, we need not strive to repress the emotions which agitate us here. We are among the sepulchres of our fathers. We are on ground, distinguished by their valor, their constancy, and the shedding of their blood. We are here, not to fix an uncertain date in our annals, nor to draw into notice an obscure and unknown spot. If our humble purpose had never been conceived, if we ourselves had never been born, the 17th of June, 1775, would have been a day on which all subsequent history would have poured its light, and the eminence where we stand a point of attraction to the eyes of successive generations. But we are Americans. We live in what may be called the early age of this great continent; and we know that our posterity, through all time, are here to enjoy and suffer the allotments of humanity. We see before us a probable train of great events; we know that our own fortunes have been happily cast; and it is natural, therefore, that we should be moved by the contemplation of occurrences which have guided our destiny before many of us were born, and settled the condition in which we should pass that portion of our existence which God allows to men on earth.

We do not read even of the discovery of this continent, without feeling something of a personal interest in the event; without being reminded how much it has affected our own fortunes and our own existence. It would be still more unnatural for us, therefore, than for others, to contemplate with unaffected minds that interesting, I may say that most touching and pathetic scene, when the great discoverer of America stood on the deck of his shattered bark, the shades of night falling on the sea, yet no man sleeping; tossed on the billows of an unknown ocean, yet the stronger billows of alternate hope and despair tossing his own troubled thoughts; extending forward his harassed frame, straining westward his anxious and eager eyes, till Heaven at last granted him a moment of rapture and ecstasy, in blessing his vision with the sight of the unknown world.

Nearer to our times, more closely connected with our fates, and therefore still more interesting to our feelings and affections, is the settlement of our own country by colonists from England. We cherish every memorial of these worthy ancestors; we celebrate their patience and fortitude; we admire their daring enterprise; we teach our children to venerate their piety; and we are justly proud of being descended from men who have set the world an example of founding civil institutions on the great and united principles of human freedom and human knowledge. To us, their children, the story of their labors and sufferings can never be without its interest. We shall not stand unmoved on the shore of Plymouth, while the sea continues to wash it; nor will our brethren in another early and ancient Colony forget the place of its first establishment, till their river shall cease to flow by it.[2] No vigor of youth, no maturity of manhood, will lead the nation to forget the spots where its infancy was cradled and defended.

But the great event in the history of the continent, which we are now met here to commemorate, that prodigy of modern times, at once the wonder and the blessing of the world, is the American Revolution. In a day of extraordinary prosperity and happiness, of high national honor, distinction, and power, we are brought together, in this place, by our love of country, by our admiration of exalted character, by our gratitude for signal services and patriotic devotion.

The Society whose organ I am[3] was formed for the purpose of rearing some honorable and durable monument to the memory of the early friends of American Independence. They have thought, that for this object no time could be more propitious than the present prosperous and peaceful period; that no place could claim preference over this memorable spot; and that no day could be more auspicious to the undertaking, than the anniversary of the battle which was here fought. The foundation of that monument we have now laid. With solemnities suited to the occasion, with prayers to Almighty God for his blessing, and in the midst of this cloud of witnesses, we have begun the work. We trust it will be prosecuted, and that, springing from a broad foundation, rising high in massive solidity and unadorned grandeur, it may remain as long as Heaven permits the works of man to last, a fit emblem, both of the events in memory of which it is raised, and of the gratitude of those who have reared it.

We know, indeed, that the record of illustrious actions is most safely deposited in the universal remembrance of mankind. We know, that if we could cause this structure to ascend, not only till it reached the skies, but till it pierced them, its broad surfaces could still contain but part of that which, in an age of knowledge, hath already been spread over the earth, and which history charges itself with making known to all future times. We know that no inscription on entablatures less broad than the earth itself can carry information of the events we commemorate where it has not already gone; and that no structure, which shall not outlive the duration of letters and knowledge among men, can prolong the memorial. But our object is, by this edifice, to show our own deep sense of the value and importance of the achievements of our ancestors; and, by presenting this work of gratitude to the eye, to keep alive similar sentiments, and to foster a constant regard for the principles of the Revolution. Human beings are composed, not of reason only, but of imagination also, and sentiment; and that is neither wasted nor misapplied which is appropriated to the purpose of giving right direction to sentiments, and opening proper springs of feeling in the heart. Let it not be supposed that our object is to perpetuate national hostility, or even to cherish a mere military spirit. It is higher, purer, nobler. We consecrate our work to the spirit of national independence, and we wish that the light of peace may rest upon it for ever. We rear a memorial of our conviction of that unmeasured benefit which has been conferred on our own land, and of the happy influences which have been produced, by the same events, on the general interests of mankind. We come, as Americans, to mark a spot which must for ever be dear to us and our posterity. We wish that whosoever, in all coming time, shall turn his eye hither, may behold that the place is not undistinguished where the first great battle of the Revolution was fought. We wish that this structure may proclaim the magnitude and importance of that event to every class and every age. We wish that infancy may learn the purpose of its erection from maternal lips, and that weary and withered age may behold it, and be solaced by the recollections which it suggests. We wish that labor may look up here, and be proud, in the midst of its toil. We wish that, in those days of disaster, which, as they come upon all nations, must be expected to come upon us also, desponding patriotism may turn its eyes hitherward, and be assured that the foundations of our national power are still strong. We wish that this column, rising towards heaven among the pointed spires of so many temples dedicated to God, may contribute also to produce, in all minds, a pious feeling of dependence and gratitude. We wish, finally, that the last object to the sight of him who leaves his native shore, and the first to gladden his who revisits it, may be something which shall remind him of the liberty and the glory of his country. Let it rise! let it rise, till it meet the sun in his coming; let the earliest light of the morning gild it, and parting day linger and play on its summit.

We live in a most extraordinary age. Events so various and so important that they might crowd and distinguish centuries are, in our times, compressed within the compass of a single life. When has it happened that history has had so much to record, in the same term of years, as since the 17th of June,

1775? Our own Revolution, which, under other circumstances, might itself have been expected to occasion a war of half a century, has been achieved; twenty-four sovereign and independent States erected; and a general government established over them, so safe, so wise, so free, so practical, that we might well wonder its establishment should have been accomplished so soon, were it not for the greater wonder that it should have been established at all. Two or three millions of people have been augmented to twelve, the great forests of the West prostrated beneath the arm of successful industry, and the dwellers on the banks of the Ohio and the Mississippi become the fellow-citizens and neighbors of those who cultivate the hills of New England.[4] We have a commerce, that leaves no sea unexplored; navies, which take no law from superior force; revenues, adequate to all the exigencies of government, almost without taxation; and peace with all nations, founded on equal rights and mutual respect.

Europe, within the same period, has been agitated by a mighty revolution, which, while it has been felt in the individual condition and happiness of almost every man, has shaken to the centre her political fabric, and dashed against one another thrones which had stood tranquil for ages. On this, our continent, our own example has been followed, and colonies have sprung up to be nations.[5] Unaccustomed sounds of liberty and free government have reached us from beyond the track of the sun; and at this moment the dominion of European power in this continent, from the place where we stand to the south pole, is annihilated for ever. In the mean time, both in Europe and America, such has been the general progress of knowledge, such the improvement in legislation, in commerce, in the arts, in letters, and, above all, in liberal ideas and the general spirit of the age, that the whole world seems changed.

Yet, notwithstanding that this is but a faint abstract of the things which have happened since the day of the battle of Bunker Hill, we are but fifty years removed from it; and we now stand here to enjoy all the blessings of our own condition, and to look abroad on the brightened prospects of the world, while we still have among us some of those who were active agents in the scenes of 1775, and who are now here, from every quarter of New England, to visit once more, and under circumstances so affecting, I had almost said so overwhelming, this renowned theatre of their courage and patriotism.

VENERABLE MEN! you have come down to us from a former generation. Heaven has bounteously lengthened out your lives, that you might behold this joyous day. You are now where you stood fifty years ago, this very hour, with your brothers and your neighbors, shoulder to shoulder, in the strife for your country. Behold, how altered! The same heavens are indeed over your heads; the same ocean rolls at your feet; but all else how changed! You hear now no roar of hostile cannon, you see no mixed volumes of smoke and flame rising from burning Charlestown. The ground strewed with the dead and the dying; the impetuous charge; the steady and successful repulse; the loud call to repeated assault; the summoning of all that is manly to repeated resistance; a thousand bosoms freely and fearlessly bared in an instant to whatever of terror there may be in war and death;--all these you have witnessed, but you witness them no more. All is peace. The heights of yonder metropolis, its towers and roofs, which you then saw filled with wives and children and countrymen in distress and terror, and looking with unutterable emotions for the issue of the combat, have presented you to-day with the sight of its whole happy population, come out to welcome and greet you with a universal jubilee. Yonder proud ships, by a felicity of position appropriately lying at the foot of this mount, and seeming fondly to cling around it, are not means of annoyance to you, but your country's own means of distinction and defence.[6] All is peace; and God has granted you this sight of your country's happiness, ere you slumber in the grave. He has allowed you to behold and to partake the reward of your patriotic toils; and he has allowed us, your sons and countrymen, to meet you here, and in the name of the present generation, in the name of your country, in the name of liberty, to thank you!

But, alas! you are not all here! Time and the sword have thinned your ranks. Prescott, Putnam, Stark, Brooks, Read, Pomeroy, Bridge! our eyes seek for you in vain amid this broken band. You are gathered to your fathers, and live only to your country in her grateful remembrance and your own bright example. But let us not too much grieve, that you have met the common fate of men. You lived at least long enough to know that your work had been nobly and successfully accomplished. You lived to see your country's independence established, and to sheathe your swords from war. On the light of Liberty you saw arise the light of Peace, like

"another morn, Risen on mid-noon";

and the sky on which you closed your eyes was cloudless.

But ah! Him! the first great martyr in this great cause! Him! the premature victim of his own self-devoting heart! Him! the head of our civil councils, and the destined leader of our military bands, whom nothing brought hither but the unquenchable fire of his own spirit! Him! cut off by Providence in the hour of overwhelming anxiety and thick gloom; falling ere he saw the star of his country rise; pouring out his generous blood like water, before he knew whether it would fertilize a land of freedom or of bondage!-- how shall I struggle with the emotions that stifle the utterance of thy name![7] Our poor work may perish; but thine shall endure! This monument may moulder away; the solid ground it rests upon may sink down to a level with the sea; but thy memory shall not fail! Wheresoever among men a heart shall be found that beats to the transports of patriotism and liberty, its aspirations shall be to claim kindred with thy spirit!

But the scene amidst which we stand does not permit us to confine our thoughts or our sympathies to those fearless spirits who hazarded or lost their lives on this consecrated spot. We have the happiness to rejoice here in the presence of a most worthy representation of the survivors of the whole Revolutionary army. VETERANS! you are the remnant of many a well-fought field. You bring with you marks of honor from Trenton and Monmouth, from Yorktown, Camden, Bennington, and Saratoga. VETERANS OF HALF A CENTURY! when in your youthful days you put every thing at hazard in your country's cause, good as that cause was, and sanguine as youth is, still your fondest hopes did not stretch onward to an hour like this! At a period to which you could not reasonably have expected to arrive, at a moment of national prosperity such as you could never have foreseen, you are now met here to enjoy the fellowship of old soldiers, and to receive the overflowings of a universal gratitude.

But your agitated countenances and your heaving breasts inform me that even this is not an unmixed joy. I perceive that a tumult of contending feelings rushes upon you. The images of the dead, as well as the persons of the living, present themselves before you. The scene overwhelms you, and I turn from it. May the Father of all mercies smile upon your declining years, and bless them! And when you shall here have exchanged your embraces, when you shall once more have pressed the hands which have been so often extended to give succor in adversity, or grasped in the exultation of victory, then look abroad upon this lovely land which your young valor defended, and mark the happiness with which it is filled; yea, look abroad upon the whole earth, and see what a name you have contributed to give to your country, and what a praise you have added to freedom, and then rejoice in the sympathy and gratitude which beam upon your last days from the improved condition of mankind!

The occasion does not require of me any particular account of the battle of the 17th of June, 1775, nor any detailed narrative of the events which immediately preceded it. These are familiarly known to all. In the progress of the great and interesting controversy, Massachusetts and the town of Boston had become early and marked objects of the displeasure of the British Parliament. This had been manifested in the act for altering the government of the Province, and in that for shutting up the port of Boston. Nothing sheds more honor on our early history, and nothing better shows how little the feelings and sentiments of the Colonies were known or regarded in England, than the impression which these measures everywhere produced in America. It had been anticipated, that, while the Colonies in general would be terrified by the severity of the punishment inflicted on Massachusetts, the other sea-ports would be governed by a mere spirit of gain; and that, as Boston was now cut off from all commerce, the unexpected advantage which this blow on her was calculated to confer on other towns would be greedily enjoyed. How miserably such reasoners deceived themselves! How little they knew of the depth, and the strength, and the intenseness of that feeling of resistance to illegal acts of power, which possessed the whole American people! Everywhere the unworthy boon was rejected with scorn. The fortunate occasion was seized, everywhere, to show to the whole world that the Colonies were swayed by no local interest, no partial interest, no selfish interest. The temptation to profit by the punishment of Boston was strongest to our neighbors of Salem. Yet Salem was precisely the place where this miserable proffer was spurned, in a tone of the most lofty self-respect and the most indignant patriotism. "We are deeply affected," said its inhabitants, "with the sense of our public calamities; but the miseries that are now rapidly hastening on our brethren in the capital of the Province greatly excite our commiseration. By shutting up the port of Boston, some imagine that the course of trade might be turned hither and to our benefit; but we must be dead to every idea of justice, lost to all feelings of humanity, could we indulge a thought to seize on wealth and raise our fortunes on the ruin of our suffering neighbors." These noble sentiments were not confined to our immediate vicinity. In that day of general affection and brotherhood, the blow given to Boston smote on every patriotic heart from one end of the country to the other. Virginia and the Carolinas, as well as Connecticut and New Hampshire, felt and proclaimed the cause to be their own. The Continental Congress, then holding its first session in

Philadelphia, expressed its sympathy for the suffering inhabitants of Boston, and addresses were received from all quarters, assuring them that the cause was a common one, and should be met by common efforts and common sacrifices. The Congress of Massachusetts responded to these assurances; and in an address to the Congress at Philadelphia, bearing the official signature, perhaps among the last, of the immortal Warren, notwithstanding the severity of its suffering and the magnitude of the dangers which threatened it, it was declared, that this Colony "is ready, at all times, to spend and to be spent in the cause of America." But the hour drew nigh which was to put professions to the proof, and to determine whether the authors of these mutual pledges were ready to seal them in blood. The tidings of Lexington and Concord had no sooner spread, than it was universally felt that the time was at last come for action. A spirit pervaded all ranks, not transient, not boisterous, but deep, solemn, determined,

"totamque infusa per artus Mens agitat molem, et magno se corpore miscet."

War, on their own soil and at their own doors, was, indeed, a strange work to the yeomanry of New England; but their consciences were convinced of its necessity, their country called them to it, and they did not withhold themselves from the perilous trial. The ordinary occupations of life were abandoned; the plough was staid in the unfinished furrow; wives gave up their husbands, and mothers gave up their sons, to the battles of a civil war. Death might come, in honor, on the field; it might come, in disgrace, on the scaffold. For either and for both they were prepared. The sentiment of Quincy was full in their hearts. "Blandishments," said that distinguished son of genius and patriotism, "will not fascinate us, nor will threats of a halter intimidate; for, under God, we are determined that, wheresoever, whensoever, or howsoever we shall be called to make our exit, we will die free men."

The 17th of June saw the four New England Colonies standing here, side by side, to triumph or to fall together; and there was with them from that moment to the end of the war, what I hope will remain with them for ever, one cause, one country, one heart.

The battle of Bunker Hill was attended with the most important effects beyond its immediate results as a military engagement. It created at once a state of open, public war. There could now be no longer a question of proceeding against individuals, as guilty of treason or rebellion. That fearful crisis was past. The appeal lay to the sword, and the only question was, whether the spirit and the resources of the people would hold out, till the object should be accomplished. Nor were its general consequences confined to our own country. The previous proceedings of the Colonies, their appeals, resolutions, and addresses, had made their cause known to Europe. Without boasting, we may say, that in no age or country has the public cause been maintained with more force of argument, more power of illustration, or more of that persuasion which excited feeling and elevated principle can alone bestow, than the Revolutionary state papers exhibit. These papers will for ever deserve to be studied, not only for the spirit which they breathe, but for the ability with which they were written.

To this able vindication of their cause, the Colonies had now added a practical and severe proof of their own true devotion to it, and given evidence also of the power which they could bring to its support. All now saw, that, if America fell, she would not fall without a struggle. Men felt sympathy and regard, as well as surprise, when they beheld these infant states, remote, unknown, unaided, encounter the power of England, and, in the first considerable battle, leave more of their enemies dead on the field, in proportion to the number of combatants, than had been recently known to fall in the wars of Europe.

Information of these events, circulating throughout the world, at length reached the ears of one who now hears me.[8] He has not forgotten the emotion which the fame of Bunker Hill, and the name of Warren, excited in his youthful breast.

SIR, we are assembled to commemorate the establishment of great public principles of liberty, and to do honor to the distinguished dead. The occasion is too severe for eulogy of the living. But, Sir, your interesting relation to this country, the peculiar circumstances which surround you and surround us, call on me to express the happiness which we derive from your presence and aid in this solemn commemoration. Fortunate, fortunate man! with what measure of devotion will you not thank God for the circumstances of your extraordinary life! You are connected with both hemispheres and with two generations. Heaven saw fit to ordain, that the electric spark of liberty should be conducted, through you, from the New World to the Old; and we, who are now here to perform this duty of patriotism, have all of us long ago received it in charge from our fathers to cherish your name and your virtues. You will account it an instance of your good fortune, Sir, that you crossed the seas to visit us at a time which enables you to be present at this solemnity. You now behold the field, the renown of which reached you in the heart of France, and caused a thrill in your ardent bosom. You see the lines of the little redoubt thrown up by the incredible diligence of Prescott; defended, to the last extremity, by his lion-hearted valor; and within which the corner-stone of our monument has now taken its position. You see where Warren fell, and where Parker, Gardner, McCleary, Moore, and other early patriots, fell with him. Those who survived that day, and whose lives have been prolonged to the present hour, are now around you. Some of them you have known in the trying scenes of the war. Behold! they now stretch forth their feeble arms to embrace you. Behold! they raise their trembling voices to invoke the blessing of God on you and yours for ever.

Sir, you have assisted us in laying the foundation of this structure. You have heard us rehearse, with our feeble commendation, the names of departed patriots. Monuments and eulogy belong to the dead. We give them this day to Warren and his associates. On other occasions they have been given to your more immediate companions in arms, to Washington, to Greene, to Gates, to Sullivan, and to Lincoln. We have become reluctant to grant these, our highest and last honors, further. We would gladly hold them yet back from the little remnant of that immortal band. _Serus in coelum redeas._ Illustrious as are your merits, yet far, O very far distant be the day, when any inscription shall bear your name, or any tongue pronounce its eulogy!

The leading reflection to which this occasion seems to invite us, respects the great changes which have happened in the fifty years since the battle of Bunker Hill was fought. And it peculiarly marks the character of the present age, that, in looking at these changes, and in estimating their effect on our condition, we are obliged to consider, not what has been done in our own country only, but in others also. In these interesting times, while nations are making separate and individual advances in improvement, they make, too, a common progress; like vessels on a common tide, propelled by the gales at different rates, according to their several structure and management, but all moved forward by one mighty current, strong enough to bear onward whatever does not sink beneath it.

A chief distinction of the present day is a community of opinions and knowledge amongst men in different nations, existing in a degree heretofore unknown. Knowledge has, in our time, triumphed, and is triumphing, over distance, over difference of languages, over diversity of habits, over prejudice, and over bigotry. The civilized and Christian world is fast learning the great lesson, that difference of nation does not imply necessary hostility, and that all contact need not be war. The whole world is becoming a common field for intellect to act in. Energy of mind, genius, power, wheresoever it exists, may speak out in any tongue, and the *world* will hear it. A great chord of sentiment and feeling runs through two continents, and vibrates over both. Every breeze wafts intelligence from country to country; every wave rolls it; all give it forth, and all in turn receive it. There is a vast commerce of ideas; there are marts and exchanges for intellectual discoveries, and a wonderful fellowship of those individual intelligences which make up the mind and opinion of the age. Mind is the great lever of all things; human thought is the process by which human ends are ultimately answered; and the diffusion of knowledge, so astonishing in the last half-century, has rendered innumerable minds, variously gifted by nature, competent to be competitors or fellow-workers on the theatre of intellectual operation.

From these causes important improvements have taken place in the personal condition of individuals. Generally speaking, mankind are not only better fed and better clothed, but they are able also to enjoy more leisure; they possess more refinement and more self-respect. A superior tone of education, manners, and habits prevails. This remark, most true in its application to our own country, is also partly true when applied elsewhere. It is proved by the vastly augmented consumption of those articles of manufacture and of commerce which contribute to the comforts and the decencies of life; an augmentation which has far outrun the progress of population. And while the unexampled and almost incredible use of machinery would seem to supply the place of labor, labor still finds its occupation and its reward; so wisely has Providence adjusted men's wants and desires to their condition and their capacity.

Any adequate survey, however, of the progress made during the last half-century in the polite and the mechanic arts, in machinery and manufactures, in commerce and agriculture, in letters and in science, would require volumes. I must abstain wholly from these subjects, and turn for a moment to the contemplation of what has been done on the great question of politics and government. This is the master topic of the age; and during the whole fifty years it has intensely occupied the thoughts of men. The nature of civil government, its ends and uses, have been canvassed and investigated; ancient opinions attacked and defended; new ideas recommended and resisted, by whatever power the mind of man could bring to the controversy. From the closet and the public halls the debate has been transferred to the field; and the world has been shaken by wars of unexampled magnitude, and the greatest variety of fortune. A day of peace has at length succeeded; and now that the strife has subsided, and the smoke cleared away, we may begin to see what has actually been done, permanently changing the state and condition of human society. And, without dwelling on particular circumstances, it is most apparent, that, from the before-mentioned causes of augmented knowledge and improved individual condition, a real, substantial, and important change has taken place, and is taking place, highly favorable, on the whole, to human liberty and human happiness.

The great wheel of political revolution began to move in America. Here its rotation was guarded, regular, and safe. Transferred to the other continent, from unfortunate but natural causes, it received an irregular and violent impulse; it whirled along with a fearful celerity; till at length, like the chariot-wheels in the races of antiquity, it took fire from the rapidity of its own motion, and blazed onward, spreading conflagration and terror around.

We learn from the result of this experiment, how fortunate was our own condition, and how admirably the character of our people was calculated for setting the great example of popular governments. The possession of power did not turn the heads of the American people, for they had long been in the habit of exercising a great degree of self-control. Although the paramount authority of the parent state existed over them, yet a large field of legislation had always been open to our Colonial assemblies. They were accustomed to representative bodies and the forms of free government; they understood the doctrine of the division of power among different branches, and the necessity of checks on each. The character of our countrymen, moreover, was sober, moral, and religious; and there was little in the change to shock their feelings of justice and humanity, or even to disturb an honest prejudice. We had no domestic throne to overturn, no privileged orders to cast down, no violent changes of property to encounter. In the American Revolution, no man sought or wished for more than to defend and enjoy his own. None hoped for plunder or for spoil. Rapacity was unknown to it; the axe was not among the instruments of its accomplishment; and we all know that it could not have lived a single day under any well-founded imputation of possessing a tendency adverse to the Christian religion.

It need not surprise us, that, under circumstances less auspicious, political revolutions elsewhere, even when well intended, have terminated differently. It is, indeed, a great achievement, it is the master-work of the world, to establish governments entirely popular on lasting foundations; nor is it easy, indeed, to introduce the popular principle at all into governments to which it has been altogether a stranger. It cannot be doubted, however, that Europe has come out of the contest, in which she has been so long engaged, with greatly superior knowledge, and, in many respects, in a highly improved condition. Whatever benefit has been acquired is likely to be retained, for it consists mainly in the acquisition of more enlightened ideas. And although kingdoms and provinces may be wrested from the hands that hold them, in the same manner they were obtained; although ordinary and vulgar power may, in human affairs, be lost as it has been won; yet it is the glorious prerogative of the empire of knowledge, that what it gains it never loses. On the contrary, it increases by the multiple of its own power; all its ends become means; all its attainments, helps to new conquests. Its whole abundant harvest is but so much seed wheat, and nothing has limited, and nothing can limit, the amount of ultimate product.

Under the influence of this rapidly increasing knowledge, the people have begun, in all forms of government, to think and to reason, on affairs of state. Regarding government as an institution for the public good, they demand a knowledge of its operations, and a participation in its exercise. A call for the representative system, wherever it is not enjoyed, and where there is already intelligence enough to estimate its value, is perseveringly made. Where men may speak out, they demand it; where the bayonet is at their throats, they pray for it.

When Louis the Fourteenth said, "I am the state," he expressed the essence of the doctrine of unlimited power. By the rules of that system, the people are disconnected from the state; they are its subjects; it is their lord. These ideas, founded in the love of power, and long supported by the excess and the abuse of it, are yielding, in our age, to other opinions; and the civilized world seems at last to be proceeding to the conviction of that fundamental and manifest truth, that the powers of government are but a trust, and that they cannot be lawfully exercised but for the good of the community. As knowledge is more and more extended, this conviction becomes more and more general. Knowledge, in truth, is the great sun in the firmament. Life and power are scattered with all its beams. The prayer of the Grecian champion, when enveloped in unnatural clouds and darkness, is the appropriate political supplication for the people of every country not yet blessed with free institutions:--

"Dispel this cloud, the light of heaven restore, Give me TO SEE,--and Ajax asks no more."

We may hope that the growing influence of enlightened sentiment will promote the permanent peace of the world. Wars to mantain family alliances, to uphold or to cast down dynasties, and to regulate successions to thrones, which have occupied so much room in the history of modern times, if not less likely to happen at all, will be less likely to become general and involve many nations, as the great principle shall be more and more established, that the interest of the world is peace, and its first great statute, that every nation possesses the power of establishing a government for itself. But public opinion has attained also an influence over governments which do not admit the popular principle into their organization. A necessary respect for the judgment of the world operates, in some measure, as a control over the most unlimited forms of authority. It is owing, perhaps, to this truth, that the interesting struggle of the Greeks has been suffered to go on so long, without a direct interference, either to wrest that country from its present masters, or to execute the system of pacification by force, and, with united strength, lay the neck of Christian and civilized Greek at the foot of the barbarian Turk. Let us thank God that we live in an age when something has influence besides the bayonet, and when the sternest authority does not venture to encounter the scorching power of public reproach. Any attempt of the kind I have mentioned should be met by one universal burst of indignation; the air of the civilized world ought to be made too warm to be comfortably breathed by any one who would hazard it.

It is, indeed, a touching reflection, that, while, in the fulness of our country's happiness, we rear this monument to her honor, we look for instruction in our undertaking to a country which is now in fearful contest, not for works of art or memorials of glory, but for her own existence. Let her be assured, that she is not forgotten in the world; that her efforts are applauded, and that constant prayers ascend for her success. And let us cherish a confident hope for her final triumph. If the true spark of religious and civil liberty be kindled, it will burn. Human agency cannot extinguish it. Like the earth's central fire, it may be smothered for a time; the ocean may overwhelm it; mountains may press it down; but its inherent and unconquerable force will heave both the ocean and the land, and at some time or other, in some place or other, the volcano will break out and flame up to heaven.

Among the great events of the half-century, we must reckon, certainly, the revolution of South America; and we are not likely to overrate the importance of that revolution, either to the people of the country itself or to the rest of the world. The late Spanish colonies, now independent states, under circumstances less favorable, doubtless, than attended our own revolution, have yet successfully commenced their national existence. They have accomplished the great object of establishing their independence; they are known and acknowledged in the world; and although in regard to their systems of government, their sentiments on religious toleration, and their provisions for public instruction, they may have yet much to learn, it must be admitted that they have risen to the condition of settled and established states more rapidly than could have been reasonably anticipated. They already furnish an exhilarating example of the difference between free governments and despotic misrule. Their commerce, at this moment, creates a new activity in all the great marts of the world. They show themselves able, by an exchange of commodities, to bear a useful part in the intercourse of nations.

A new spirit of enterprise and industry begins to prevail; all the great interests of society receive a salutary impulse; and the progress of information not only testifies to an improved condition, but itself constitutes the highest and most essential improvement.

When the battle of Bunker Hill was fought, the existence of South America was scarcely felt in the civilized world. The thirteen little Colonies of North America habitually called themselves the "Continent." Borne down by colonial subjugation, monopoly, and bigotry, these vast regions of the South were hardly visible above the horizon. But in our day there has been, as it were, a new creation. The southern hemisphere emerges from the sea. Its lofty mountains begin to lift themselves into the light of heaven; its broad and fertile plains stretch out, in beauty, to the eye of civilized man, and at the mighty bidding of the voice of political liberty the waters of darkness retire.

And, now, let us indulge an honest exultation in the conviction of the benefit which the example of our country has produced, and is likely to produce, on human freedom and human happiness. Let us endeavor to comprehend in all its magnitude, and to feel in all its importance, the part assigned to us in the great drama of human affairs. We are placed at the head of the system of representative and popular governments. Thus far our example shows that such governments are compatible, not only with respectability and power, but with repose, with peace, with security of personal rights, with good laws, and a just administration.

We are not propagandists. Wherever other systems are preferred, either as being thought better in themselves, or as better suited to existing condition, we leave the preference to be enjoyed. Our history hitherto proves, however, that the popular form is practicable, and that with wisdom and knowledge men may govern themselves; and the duty incumbent on us is, to preserve the consistency of this cheering example, and take care that nothing may weaken its authority with the world. If, in our case, the representative system ultimately fail, popular governments must be pronounced impossible. No combination of circumstances more favorable to the experiment can ever be expected to occur. The last hopes of mankind, therefore, rest with us; and if it should be proclaimed, that our example had become an argument against the experiment, the knell of popular liberty would be sounded throughout the earth.

These are excitements to duty; but they are not suggestions of doubt. Our history and our condition, all that is gone before us, and all that surrounds us, authorize the belief, that popular governments, though subject to occasional variations, in form perhaps not always for the better, may yet, in their general character, be as durable and permanent as other systems. We know, indeed, that in our country any other is impossible. The *principle* of free governments adheres to the American soil. It is bedded in it, immovable as its mountains. And let the sacred obligations which have devolved on this generation, and on us, sink deep into our hearts. Those who established our liberty and our government are daily dropping from among us. The great trust now descends to new hands. Let us apply ourselves to that which is presented to us, as our appropriate object. We can win no laurels in a war for independence. Earlier and worthier hands have gathered them all. Nor are there places for us by the side of Solon, and Alfred, and other founders of states. Our fathers have filled them. But there remains to us a great duty of defence and preservation; and there is opened to us, also, a noble pursuit, to which the spirit of the times strongly invites us. Our proper business is improvement. Let our age be the age of improvement. In a day of peace, let us advance the arts of peace and the works of peace. Let us develop the resources of our land, call forth its powers, build up its institutions, promote all its great interests, and see whether we also, in our day and generation, may not perform something worthy to be remembered. Let us cultivate a true spirit of union and harmony. In pursuing the great objects which our condition points out to us, let us act under a settled conviction, and an habitual feeling, that these twenty-four States are one country. Let our conceptions be enlarged to the circle of our duties. Let us extend our ideas over the whole of the vast field in which we are called to act. Let our object be, OUR COUNTRY, OUR WHOLE COUNTRY, AND NOTHING BUT OUR COUNTRY. And, by the blessing of God, may that country itself become a vast and splendid monument, not of oppression and terror, but of Wisdom, of Peace, and of Liberty, upon which the world may gaze with admiration for ever!

[Footnote 1: General Warren, at the time of his decease, was Grand Master of the Masonic Lodges in America.][Footnote 2: An interesting account of the voyage of the early emigrants to the Maryland Colony, and of its settlement, is given in the official report of Father White, written probably within the first month after the landing at St. Mary's. The original Latin manuscript is still preserved among the archives of the Jesuits at Rome. The "Ark" and the "Dove" are remembered with scarcely less interest by the descendants of the sister colony, than is the "Mayflower" in New England, which thirteen years earlier, at the same season of the year, bore thither the Pilgrim Fathers.][Footnote 3: Mr. Webster was at this time President of the Bunker Hill Monument Association, chosen on the decease of Governor John Brooks, the first President.]

[Footnote 4: That which was spoken of figuratively in 1825 has, in the lapse of a quarter of a century, by the introduction of railroads and telegraphic lines, become a reality. It is an interesting circumstance, that the first railroad on the Western Continent was constructed for the purpose of accelerating the erection of this monument.][Footnote 5: See President Monroe's Message to Congress in 1823, and Mr. Webster's speech on the Panama Mission, in 1826.]

[Footnote 6: It is necessary to inform those only who are unacquainted with the localities, that the United States Navy Yard at Charlestown is situated at the base of Bunker Hill.][Footnote 7: See the North American Review, Vol. XIII. p. 242.][Footnote 8: Among the earliest of the arrangements for the celebration of the 17th of June, 1825, was the invitation to General Lafayette to be present; and he had so timed his progress through the other States as to return to Massachusetts in season for the great occasion.]

THE COMPLETION OF THE BUNKER HILL MONUMENT.
AN ADDRESS DELIVERED ON BUNKER HILL, ON THE 17th OF JUNE, 1843, ON OCCASION OF THE COMPLETION OF THE MONUMENT.

[In the introductory note to the preceding Address, a brief account is given of the origin and progress of the measures adopted for the erection of the Bunker Hill Monument, down to the time of laying the corner-stone, compiled from Mr. Frothingham's History of the Siege of Boston. The same valuable work (pp. 345-352) relates the obstacles which presented themselves to the rapid execution of the design, and the means by which they were overcome. In this narrative, Mr. Frothingham has done justice to the efforts and exertions of the successive boards of direction and officers of the Association, to the skill and disinterestedness of the architect, to the liberality of distinguished individuals, to the public spirit of the Massachusetts Charitable Mechanic Association, in promoting a renewed subscription, and to the patriotic zeal of the ladies of Boston and the vicinity, in holding a most successful fair. As it would be difficult farther to condense the information contained in this interesting summary, we must refer the reader to Mr. Frothingham's work for an adequate account of the causes which delayed the completion of the monument for nearly seventeen years, and of the resources and exertions by which the desired end was finally attained. The last stone was raised to its place on the morning of the 23d of July, 1842.

It was determined by the directors of the Association, that the completion of the work should be celebrated in a manner not less imposing than that in which the laying of the corner-stone had been celebrated, seventeen years before. The co-operation of Mr. Webster was again invited, and, notwithstanding the pressure of his engagements as Secretary of State at Washington, was again patriotically yielded. Many circumstances conspired to increase the interest of the occasion. The completion of the monument had been long delayed, but in the interval the subject had been kept much before the public mind. Mr. Webster's address on the 17th of June, 1825, had obtained the widest circulation throughout the country; passages from it had passed into household words throughout the Union. Wherever they were repeated, they made the Bunker Hill Monument a familiar thought with the people. Meantime, Boston and Charlestown had doubled their population, and the multiplication of rail roads in every direction enabled a person, in almost any part of New England, to reach the metropolis in a day. The President of the United States and his Cabinet had accepted invitations to be present; delegations of the descendants of New England were present from the remotest parts of the Union; one hundred and eight surviving veterans of the Revolution, among whom were some who were in the battle of Bunker Hill, imparted a touching interest to the scene.

Every thing conspired to promote the success of the ceremonial. The day was uncommonly fine; cool for the season, and clear. A large volunteer force from various parts of the country had assembled for the occasion, and formed a brilliant escort to an immense procession, as it moved from Boston to the battle-ground on the hill. The bank which slopes down from the obelisk on the eastern side of Monument Square was covered with seats, rising in the form of an amphitheatre, under the open sky. These had been prepared for ladies, who had assembled in great numbers, awaiting the arrival of the procession. When it arrived, it was received into a large open area in front of these seats. Mr. Webster was stationed upon an elevated platform, in front of the audience and of the monument towering in the background. According to Mr. Frothingham's estimate, a hundred thousand persons were gathered about the spot, and nearly half that number are supposed to have been within the reach of the orator's voice. The ground rises slightly between the platform and the Monument Square, so that the whole of this immense concourse, compactly crowded together, breathless with attention, swayed by one sentiment of admiration and delight, was within the full view of the speaker. The position and the occasion were the height of the moral sublime. "When, after saying, 'It is not from my lips, it could not be from any human lips, that that strain of eloquence is this day to flow most competent to move and excite the vast multitude around me,--the powerful speaker stands motionless before us,'--he paused, and pointed in silent admiration to the sublime structure, the audience burst into long and loud applause. It was some moments before the speaker could go on with the address."]

A duty has been performed. A work of gratitude and patriotism is completed. This structure, having its foundations in soil which drank deep of early Revolutionary blood, has at length reached its destined height, and now lifts its summit to the skies.

We have assembled to celebrate the accomplishment of this undertaking, and to indulge afresh in the recollection of the great event which it is designed to commemorate. Eighteen years, more than half the ordinary duration of a generation of mankind, have elapsed since the corner-stone of this monument was laid. The hopes of its projectors rested on voluntary contributions, private munificence, and the general favor of the public. These hopes have not been disappointed. Donations have been made by individuals, in some cases of large amount, and smaller sums have been contributed by thousands. All who regard the object itself as important, and its accomplishment, therefore, as a good attained, will entertain sincere respect and gratitude for the unwearied efforts of the successive presidents, boards of directors, and committees of the Association which has had the general control of the work. The architect, equally entitled to our thanks and commendation, will find other reward, also, for his labor and skill, in the beauty and elegance of the obelisk itself, and the distinction which, as a work of art, it confers upon him.

At a period when the prospects of further progress in the undertaking were gloomy and discouraging, the Mechanic Association, by a most praiseworthy and vigorous effort, raised new funds for carrying it forward, and saw them applied with fidelity, economy, and skill. It is a grateful duty to make public acknowledgments of such timely and efficient aid.

The last effort and the last contribution were from a different source. Garlands of grace and elegance were destined to crown a work which had its commencement in manly patriotism. The winning power of the sex addressed itself to the public, and all that was needed to carry the monument to its proposed height, and to give to it its finish, was promptly supplied. The mothers and the daughters of the land contributed thus, most successfully, to whatever there is of beauty in the monument itself, or whatever of utility and public benefit and gratification there is in its completion.

Of those with whom the plan originated of erecting on this spot a monument worthy of the event to be commemorated, many are now present; but others, alas! have themselves become subjects of monumental inscription. William Tudor, an accomplished scholar, a distinguished writer, a most amiable man, allied both by birth and sentiment to the patriots of the Revolution, died while on public service abroad, and now lies buried in a foreign land.[1] William Sullivan, a name fragrant of Revolutionary merit, and of public service and public virtue, who himself partook in a high degree of the respect and confidence of the community, and yet was always most loved where best known, has also been gathered to his fathers. And last, George Blake, a lawyer of learning and eloquence, a man of wit and of talent, of social qualities the most agreeable and fascinating, and of gifts which enabled him to exercise large sway over public assemblies, has closed his human career.[2] I know that in the crowds before me there are those from whose eyes tears will flow at the mention of these names. But such mention is due to their general character, their public and private virtues, and especially, on this occasion, to the spirit and zeal with which they entered into the undertaking which is now completed.

I have spoken only of those who are no longer numbered with the living. But a long life, now drawing towards its close, always distinguished by acts of public spirit, humanity, and charity, forming a character which has already become historical, and sanctified by public regard and the affection of friends, may confer even on the living the proper immunity of the dead, and be the fit subject of honorable mention and warm commendation. Of the early projectors of the design of this monument, one of the most prominent, the most zealous, and the most efficient, is Thomas H. Perkins. It was beneath his ever-hospitable roof that those whom I have mentioned, and others yet living and now present, having assembled for the purpose, adopted the first step towards erecting a monument on Bunker Hill. Long may he remain, with unimpaired faculties, in the wide field of his usefulness! His charities have distilled, like the dews of heaven; he has fed the hungry, and clothed the naked; he has given sight to the blind; and for such virtues there is a reward on high, of which all human memorials, all language of brass and stone, are but humble types and attempted imitations.

Time and nature have had their course, in diminishing the number of those whom we met here on the 17th of June, 1825. Most of the Revolutionary characters then present have since deceased; and Lafayette sleeps in his native land. Yet the name and blood of Warren are with us; the kindred of Putnam are also here; and near me, universally beloved for his character and his virtues, and now venerable for his years, sits the son of the noble-hearted and daring Prescott.[3] Gideon Foster of Danvers, Enos Reynolds of Boxford, Phineas Johnson, Robert Andrews, Elijah Dresser, Josiah Cleaveland, Jesse Smith, Philip Bagley, Needham Maynard, Roger Plaisted, Joseph Stephens, Nehemiah Porter, and James Harvey, who bore arms for their country either at Concord and Lexington, on the 19th of April, or on Bunker Hill, all now far advanced in age, have come here to-day, to look once more on the field where their valor was proved, and to receive a hearty outpouring of our respect.

They have long outlived the troubles and dangers of the Revolution; they have outlived the evils arising from the want of a united and efficient government; they have outlived the menace of imminent dangers to the public liberty; they have outlived nearly all their contemporaries;--but they have not outlived, they cannot outlive, the affectionate gratitude of their country. Heaven has not allotted to this generation an opportunity of rendering high services, and manifesting strong personal devotion, such as they rendered and manifested, and in such a cause as that which roused the patriotic fires of their youthful breasts, and nerved the strength of their arms. But we may praise what we cannot equal, and celebrate actions which we were not born to perform. _Pulchrum est benefacere reipublica, etiam bene dicere haud absurdum est._

The Bunker Hill Monument is finished. Here it stands. Fortunate in the high natural eminence on which it is placed, higher, infinitely higher in its objects and purpose, it rises over the land and over the sea; and, visible, at their homes, to three hundred thousand of the people of Massachusetts, it stands a memorial of the last, and a monitor to the present, and to all succeeding generations. I have spoken of the loftiness of its purpose. If it had been without any other design than the creation of a work of art, the granite of which it is composed would have slept in its native bed. It has a purpose, and that purpose gives it its character. That purpose enrobes it with dignity and moral grandeur. That well-known purpose it is which causes us to look up to it with a feeling of awe. It is itself the orator of this occasion. It is not from my lips, it could not be from any human lips, that that strain of eloquence is this day to flow most competent to move and excite the vast multitudes around me. The powerful speaker stands motionless before us. It is a plain shaft. It bears no inscriptions, fronting to the rising sun, from which the future antiquary shall wipe the dust. Nor does the rising sun cause tones of music to issue from its summit. But at the rising of the sun, and at the setting of the sun; in the blaze of noonday, and beneath the milder effulgence of lunar light; it looks, it speaks, it acts, to the full comprehension of every American mind, and the awakening of glowing enthusiasm in every American heart. Its silent, but awful utterance; its deep pathos, as it brings to our contemplation the 17th of June, 1775, and the consequences which have resulted to us, to our country, and to the world, from the events of that day, and which we know must continue to rain influence on the destinies of mankind to the end of time; the elevation with which it raises us high above the ordinary feelings of life,--surpass all that the study of the closet, or even the inspiration of genius, can produce. To-day it speaks to us. Its future auditories will be the successive generations of men, as they rise up before it and gather around it. Its speech will be of patriotism and courage; of civil and religious liberty; of free government; of the moral improvement and elevation of mankind; and of the immortal memory of those who, with heroic devotion, have sacrificed their lives for their country.[4]

In the older world, numerous fabrics still exist, reared by human hands, but whose object has been lost in the darkness of ages. They are now monuments of nothing but the labor and skill which constructed them. The mighty pyramid itself, half buried in the sands of Africa, has nothing to bring down and report to us, but the power of kings and the servitude of the people. If it had any purpose beyond that of a mausoleum, such purpose has perished from history and from tradition. If asked for its moral object, its admonition, its sentiment, its instruction to mankind, or any high end in its erection, it is silent; silent as the millions which lie in the dust at its base, and in the catacombs which surround it. Without a just moral object, therefore, made known to man, though raised against the skies, it excites only conviction of power, mixed with strange wonder. But if the civilization of the present race of men, founded, as it is, in solid science, the true knowledge of nature, and vast discoveries in art, and which is elevated and purified by moral sentiment and by the truths of Christianity, be not destined to destruction before the final termination of human existence on earth, the object and purpose of this edifice will be known till that hour shall come. And even if civilization should be subverted, and the truths of the Christian religion obscured by a new deluge of barbarism, the memory of Bunker Hill and the American Revolution will still be elements and parts of the knowledge which shall be possessed by the last man to whom the light of civilization and Christianity shall be extended.

This celebration is honored by the presence of the chief executive magistrate of the Union. An occasion so national in its object and character, and so much connected with that Revolution from which the government sprang at the head of which he is placed, may well receive from him this mark of attention and respect. Well acquainted with Yorktown, the scene of the last great military struggle of the Revolution, his eye now surveys the field of Bunker Hill, the theatre of the first of those important conflicts. He sees where Warren fell, where Putnam, and Prescott, and Stark, and Knowlton, and Brooks fought. He beholds the spot where a thousand trained soldiers of England were smitten to the earth, in the first effort of revolutionary war, by the arm of a bold and determined yeomanry, contending for liberty and their country. And while all assembled here entertain towards him sincere personal good wishes and the high respect due to his elevated office and station, it is not to be doubted that he enters, with true American feeling, into the patriotic enthusiasm kindled by the occasion which animates the multitudes that surround him.

His Excellency, the Governor of the Commonwealth, the Governor of Rhode Island, and the other distinguished public men whom we have the honor to receive as visitors and guests to-day, will cordially unite in a celebration connected with the great event of the Revolutionary war.

No name in the history of 1775 and 1776 is more distinguished than that borne by an ex-President of the United States, whom we expected to see here, but whose ill health prevents his attendance. Whenever popular rights were to be asserted, an Adams was present; and when the time came for the formal Declaration of Independence, it was the voice of an Adams that shook the halls of Congress. We wish we could have welcomed to us this day the inheritor of Revolutionary blood, and the just and worthy representative of high Revolutionary names, merit, and services.

Banners and badges, processions and flags, announce to us, that amidst this uncounted throng are thousands of natives of New England now residents in other States. Welcome, ye kindred names, with kindred blood! From the broad savannas of the South, from the newer regions of the West, from amidst the hundreds of thousands of men of Eastern origin who cultivate the rich valley of the Genesee or live along the chain of the Lakes, from the mountains of Pennsylvania, and from the thronged cities of the coast, welcome, welcome! Wherever else you may be strangers, here you are all at home. You assemble at this shrine of liberty, near the family altars at which your earliest devotions were paid to Heaven, near to the temples of worship first entered by you, and near to the schools and colleges in which your education was received. You come hither with a glorious ancestry of liberty. You bring names which are on the rolls of Lexington, Concord, and Bunker Hill. You come, some of you, once more to be embraced by an aged Revolutionary father, or to receive another, perhaps a last, blessing, bestowed in love and tears, by a mother, yet surviving to witness and to enjoy your prosperity and happiness.

But if family associations and the recollections of the past bring you hither with greater alacrity, and mingle with your greeting much of local attachment and private affection, greeting also be given, free and hearty greeting, to every American citizen who treads this sacred soil with patriotic feeling, and respires with pleasure in an atmosphere perfumed with the recollections of 1775! This occasion is respectable, nay, it is grand, it is sublime, by the nationality of its sentiment. Among the seventeen millions of happy people who form the American community, there is not one who has not an interest in this monument, as there is not one that has not a deep and abiding interest in that which it commemorates.

Woe betide the man who brings to this day's worship feeling less than wholly American! Woe betide the man who can stand here with the fires of local resentments burning, or the purpose of fomenting local jealousies and the strifes of local interests festering and rankling in his heart! Union, established in justice, in patriotism, and the most plain and obvious common interest,--union, founded on the same love of liberty, cemented by blood shed in the same common cause,--union has been the source of all our glory and greatness thus far, and is the ground of all our highest hopes. This column stands on Union. I know not that it might not keep its position, if the American Union, in the mad conflict of human passions, and in the strife of parties and factions, should be broken up and destroyed. I know not that it would totter and fall to the earth, and mingle its fragments with the fragments of Liberty and the Constitution, when State should be separated from State, and faction and dismemberment obliterate for ever all the hopes of the founders of our republic, and the great inheritance of their children. It might stand. But who, from beneath the weight of mortification and shame that would oppress him, could look up to behold it? Whose eyeballs would not be seared by such a spectacle? For my part, should I live to such a time, I shall avert my eyes from it for ever.

It is not as a mere military encounter of hostile armies that the battle of Bunker Hill presents its principal claim to attention. Yet, even as a mere battle, there were circumstances attending it extraordinary in character, and entitling it to peculiar distinction. It was fought on this eminence; in the neighborhood of yonder city; in the presence of many more spectators than there were combatants in the conflict. Men, women, and children, from every commanding position, were gazing at the battle, and looking for its results with all the eagerness natural to those who knew that the issue was fraught with the deepest consequences to themselves, personally, as well as to their country. Yet, on the 16th of June, 1775, there was nothing around this hill but verdure and culture. There was, indeed, the note of awful preparation in

Boston. There was the Provincial army at Cambridge, with its right flank resting on Dorchester, and its left on Chelsea. But here all was peace. Tranquillity reigned around. On the 17th, every thing was changed. On this eminence had arisen, in the night, a redoubt, built by Prescott, and in which he held command. Perceived by the enemy at dawn, it was immediately cannonaded from the floating batteries in the river, and from the opposite shore. And then ensued the hurried movement in Boston, and soon the troops of Britain embarked in the attempt to dislodge the Colonists. In an hour every thing indicated an immediate and bloody conflict. Love of liberty on one side, proud defiance of rebellion on the other, hopes and fears, and courage and daring, on both sides, animated the hearts of the combatants as they hung on the edge of battle.

I suppose it would be difficult, in a military point of view, to ascribe to the leaders on either side any just motive for the engagement which followed. On the one hand, it could not have been very important to the Americans to attempt to hem the British within the town, by advancing one single post a quarter of a mile; while, on the other hand, if the British found it essential to dislodge the American troops, they had it in their power at no expense of life. By moving up their ships and batteries, they could have completely cut off all communication with the mainland over the Neck, and the forces in the redoubt would have been reduced to a state of famine in forty-eight hours.

But that was not the day for any such consideration on either side! Both parties were anxious to try the strength of their arms. The pride of England would not permit the rebels, as she termed them, to defy her to the teeth; and, without for a moment calculating the cost, the British general determined to destroy the fort immediately. On the other side, Prescott and his gallant followers longed and thirsted for a decisive trial of strength and of courage. They wished a battle, and wished it at once. And this is the true secret of the movements on this hill.

I will not attempt to describe that battle. The cannonading; the landing of the British; their advance; the coolness with which the charge was met; the repulse; the second attack; the second repulse; the burning of Charlestown; and, finally, the closing assault, and the slow retreat of the Americans,--the history of all these is familiar.

But the consequences of the battle of Bunker Hill were greater than those of any ordinary conflict, although between armies of far greater force, and terminating with more immediate advantage on the one side or the other. It was the first great battle of the Revolution; and not only the first blow, but the blow which determined the contest. It did not, indeed, put an end to the war, but in the then existing hostile state of feeling, the difficulties could only be referred to the arbitration of the sword. And one thing is certain: that after the New England troops had shown themselves able to face and repulse the regulars, it was decided that peace never could be established, but upon the basis of the independence of the Colonies. When the sun of that day went down, the event of Independence was no longer doubtful. In a few days Washington heard of the battle, and he inquired if the militia had stood the fire of the regulars. When told that they had not only stood that fire, but reserved their own till the enemy was within eight rods, and then poured it in with tremendous effect, "Then," exclaimed he, "the liberties of the country are safe!"

The consequences of this battle were just of the same importance as the Revolution itself.

If there was nothing of value in the principles of the American Revolution, then there is nothing valuable in the battle of Bunker Hill and its consequences. But if the Revolution was an era in the history of man favorable to human happiness, if it was an event which marked the progress of man all over the world from despotism to liberty, then this monument is not raised without cause. Then the battle of Bunker Hill is not an event undeserving; celebrations, commemorations, and rejoicings, now and in all coming times.

What, then, is the true and peculiar principle of the American Revolution, and of the systems of government which it has confirmed and established? The truth is, that the American Revolution was not caused by the instantaneous discovery of principles of government before unheard of, or the practical adoption of political ideas such as had never before entered into the minds of men. It was but the full development of principles of government, forms of society, and political sentiments, the origin of all which lay back two centuries in English and American history.

The discovery of America, its colonization by the nations of Europe, the history and progress of the colonies, from their establishment to the time when the principal of them threw off their allegiance to the respective states by which they had been planted, and founded governments of their own, constitute one of the most interesting portions of the annals of man. These events occupied three hundred years; during which period civilization and knowledge made steady progress in the Old World; so that Europe, at the commencement of the nineteenth century, had become greatly changed from that Europe which began the colonization of America at the close of the fifteenth, or the commencement of the sixteenth. And what is most material to my present purpose is, that in the progress of the first of these centuries, that is to say, from the discovery of America to the settlements of Virginia and Massachusetts, political and religious events took place, which most materially affected the state of society and the sentiments of mankind, especially in England and in parts of Continental Europe. After a few feeble and unsuccessful efforts by England, under Henry the Seventh, to plant colonies in America, no designs of that kind were prosecuted for a long period, either by the English government or any of its subjects. Without inquiring into the causes of this delay, its consequences are sufficiently clear and striking. England, in this lapse of a century, unknown to herself, but under the providence of God and the influence of events, was fitting herself for the work of colonizing North America, on such principles, and by such men, as should spread the English name and English blood, in time, over a great portion of the Western hemisphere. The commercial spirit was greatly fostered by several laws passed in the reign of Henry the Seventh; and in the same reign encouragement was given to arts and manufactures in the eastern counties, and some not unimportant modifications of the feudal system took place, by allowing the breaking of entails. These and other measures, and other occurrences, were making way for a new class of society to emerge, and show itself, in a military and feudal age; a middle class, between the barons or great landholders and the retainers of the crown, on the one side, and the tenants of the crown and barons, and agricultural and other laborers, on the other side. With the rise and growth of this new class of society, not only did commerce and the arts increase, but better education, a greater degree of knowledge, juster notions of the true ends of government, and sentiments favorable to civil liberty, began to spread abroad, and become more and more common. But the plants springing from these seeds were of slow growth. The character of English society had indeed begun to undergo a change; but changes of national character are ordinarily the work of time. Operative causes were, however, evidently in existence, and sure to produce, ultimately, their proper effect. From the accession of Henry the Seventh to the breaking out of the civil wars, England enjoyed much greater exemption from war, foreign and domestic, than for a long period before, and during the controversy between the houses of York and Lancaster. These years of peace were favorable to commerce and the arts. Commerce and the arts augmented general and individual knowledge; and knowledge is the only fountain, both of the love and the principles of human liberty.

Other powerful causes soon came into active play. The Reformation of Luther broke out, kindling up the minds of men afresh, leading to new habits of thought, and awakening in individuals energies before unknown even to themselves. The religious controversies of this period changed society, as well as religion; indeed, it would be easy to prove, if this occasion were proper for it, that they changed society to a considerable extent, where they did not change the religion of the state. They changed man himself, in his modes of thought, his consciousness of his own powers, and his desire of intellectual attainment. The spirit of commercial and foreign adventure, therefore, on the one hand, which had gained so much strength and influence since the time of the discovery of America, and, on the other, the assertion and maintenance of religious liberty, having their source indeed in the Reformation, but continued, diversified, and constantly strengthened by the subsequent divisions of sentiment and opinion among the Reformers themselves, and this love of religious liberty drawing after it, or bringing along with it, as it always does, an ardent devotion to the principle of civil liberty also, were the powerful influences under which character was formed, and men trained, for the great work of introducing English civilization, English law, and, what is more than all, Anglo-Saxon blood, into the wilderness of North America. Raleigh and his companions may be considered as the creatures, principally, of the first of these causes. High-spirited, full of the love of personal adventure, excited, too, in some degree, by the hopes of sudden riches from the discovery of mines of the precious metals, and not unwilling to diversify the labors of settling a colony with occasional cruising against the Spaniards in the West Indian seas, they crossed and recrossed the ocean, with a frequency which surprises us, when we consider the state of navigation, and which evinces a most daring spirit.

The other cause peopled New England. The Mayflower sought our shores under no high-wrought spirit of commercial adventure, no love of gold, no mixture of purpose warlike or hostile to any human being. Like the dove from the ark, she had put forth only to find rest. Solemn supplications on the shore of the sea, in Holland, had invoked for her, at her departure, the blessings of Providence. The stars which guided her were the unobscured constellations of civil and religious liberty. Her deck was the altar of the living God.

Fervent prayers on bended knees mingled, morning and evening, with the voices of ocean, and the sighing of the wind in her shrouds. Every prosperous breeze, which, gently swelling her sails, helped the Pilgrims onward in their course, awoke new anthems of praise; and when the elements were wrought into fury, neither the tempest, tossing their fragile bark like a feather, nor the darkness and howling of the midnight storm, ever disturbed, in man or woman, the firm and settled purpose of their souls, to undergo all, and to do all, that the meekest patience, the boldest resolution, and the highest trust in God, could enable human beings to suffer or to perform.

Some differences may, doubtless, be traced at this day between the descendants of the early colonists of Virginia and those of New England, owing to the different influences and different circumstances under which the respective settlements were made; but only enough to create a pleasing variety in the midst of a general family resemblance.

"Facies, non omnibus una, Nec diversa tamen, qualem decet esse sororum."

But the habits, sentiments, and objects of both soon became modified by local causes, growing out of their condition in the New World; and as this condition was essentially alike in both, and as both at once adopted the same general rules and principles of English jurisprudence, and became accustomed to the authority of representative bodies, these differences gradually diminished. They disappeared by the progress of time, and the influence of intercourse. The necessity of some degree of union and co-operation to defend themselves against the savage tribes, tended to excite in them mutual respect and regard. They fought together in the wars against France. The great and common cause of the Revolution bound them to one another by new links of brotherhood; and at length the present constitution of government united them happily and gloriously, to form the great republic of the world, and bound up their interests and fortunes, till the whole earth sees that there is now for them, in present possession as well as in future hope, but "One Country, One Constitution, and One Destiny."

The colonization of the tropical region, and the whole of the southern parts of the continent, by Spain and Portugal, was conducted on other principles, under the influence of other motives, and followed by far different consequences. From the time of its discovery, the Spanish government pushed forward its settlements in America, not only with vigor, but with eagerness; so that long before the first permanent English settlement had been accomplished in what is now the United States, Spain had conquered Mexico, Peru, and Chili, and stretched her power over nearly all the territory she ever acquired on this continent. The rapidity of these conquests is to be ascribed in a great degree to the eagerness, not to say the rapacity, of those numerous bands of adventurers, who were stimulated by individual interests and private hopes to subdue immense regions, and take possession of them in the name of the crown of Spain. The mines of gold and silver were the incitements to these efforts, and accordingly settlements were generally made, and Spanish authority established immediately on the subjugation of territory, that the native population might be set to work by their new Spanish masters in the mines. From these facts, the love of gold--gold, not produced by industry, nor accumulated by commerce, but gold dug from its native bed in the bowels of the earth, and that earth ravished from its rightful possessors by every possible degree of enormity, cruelty, and crime--was long the governing passion in Spanish wars and Spanish settlements in America. Even Columbus himself did not wholly escape the influence of this base motive. In his early voyages we find him passing from island to island, inquiring everywhere for gold; as if God had opened the New World to the knowledge of the Old, only to gratify a passion equally senseless and sordid, and to offer up millions of an unoffending race of men to the destruction of the sword, sharpened both by cruelty and rapacity. And yet Columbus was far above his age and country. Enthusiastic, indeed, but sober, religious, and magnanimous; born to great things and capable of high sentiments, as his noble discourse before Ferdinand and Isabella, as well as the whole history of his life, shows. Probably he sacrificed much to the known sentiments of others, and addressed to his followers motives likely to influence them. At the same time, it is evident that he himself looked upon the world which he discovered as a world of wealth, all ready to be seized and enjoyed.

The conquerors and the European settlers of Spanish America were mainly military commanders and common soldiers. The monarchy of Spain was not transferred to this hemisphere, but it acted in it, as it acted at home, through its ordinary means, and its true representative, military force. The robbery and destruction of the native race was the achievement of standing armies, in the right of the king, and by his authority, fighting in his name, for the aggrandizement of his power and the extension of his prerogatives, with military ideas under arbitrary maxims,--a portion of that dreadful instrumentality by which a perfect despotism governs a people. As there was no liberty in Spain, how could liberty be transmitted to Spanish colonies?

The colonists of English America were of the people, and a people already free. They were of the middle, industrious, and already prosperous class, the inhabitants of commercial and manufacturing cities, among whom liberty first revived and respired, after a sleep of a thousand years in the bosom of the Dark Ages. Spain descended on the New World in the armed and terrible image of her monarchy and her soldiery; England approached it in the winning and popular garb of personal rights, public protection, and civil freedom. England transplanted liberty to America; Spain transplanted power. England, through the agency of private companies and the efforts of individuals, colonized this part of North America by industrious individuals, making their own way in the wilderness, defending themselves against the savages, recognizing their right to the soil, and with a general honest purpose of introducing knowledge as well as Christianity among them. Spain stooped on South America, like a vulture on its prey. Every thing was force. Territories were acquired by fire and sword. Cities were destroyed by fire and sword. Hundreds of thousands of human beings fell by fire and sword. Even conversion to Christianity was attempted by fire and sword.

Behold, then, fellow-citizens, the difference resulting from the operation of the two principles! Here, to-day, on the summit of Bunker Hill, and at the foot of this monument, behold the difference! I would that the fifty thousand voices present could proclaim it with a shout which should be heard over the globe. Our inheritance was of liberty, secured and regulated by law, and enlightened by religion and knowledge; that of South America was of power, stern, unrelenting, tyrannical, military power. And now look to the consequences of the two principles on the general and aggregate happiness of the human race. Behold the results, in all the regions conquered by Cortéz and Pizarro, and the contrasted results here. I suppose the territory of the United States may amount to one eighth, or one tenth, of that colonized by Spain on this continent; and yet in all that vast region there are but between one and two millions of people of European color and European blood, while in the United States there are fourteen millions who rejoice in their descent from the people of the more northern part of Europe.

But we may follow the difference in the original principle of colonization, and in its character and objects, still further. We must look to moral and intellectual results; we must consider consequences, not only as they show themselves in hastening or retarding the increase of population and the supply of physical wants, but in their civilization, improvement, and happiness. We must inquire what progress has been made in the true science of liberty, in the knowledge of the great principles of self-government, and in the progress of man, as a social, moral, and religious being.

I would not willingly say any thing on this occasion discourteous to the new governments founded on the demolition of the power of the Spanish monarchy. They are yet on their trial, and I hope for a favorable result. But truth, sacred truth, and fidelity to the cause of civil liberty, compel me to say, that hitherto they have discovered quite too much of the spirit of that monarchy from which they separated themselves. Quite too frequent resort is made to military force; and quite too much of the substance of the people is consumed in maintaining armies, not for defence against foreign aggression, but for enforcing obedience to domestic authority. Standing armies are the oppressive instruments for governing the people, in the hands of hereditary and arbitrary monarchs. A military republic, a government founded on mock elections and supported only by the sword, is a movement indeed, but a retrograde and disastrous movement, from the regular and old-fashioned monarchical systems. If men would enjoy the blessings of republican government, they must govern themselves by reason, by mutual counsel and consultation, by a sense and feeling of general interest, and by the acquiescence of the minority in the will of the majority, properly expressed; and, above all, the military must be kept, according to the language of our Bill of Rights, in strict subordination to the civil authority. Wherever this lesson is not both learned and practised, there can be no political freedom. Absurd, preposterous is it, a scoff and a satire on free forms of constitutional liberty, for frames of government to be prescribed by military leaders, and the right of suffrage to be exercised at the point of the sword.

Making all allowance for situation and climate, it cannot be doubted by intelligent minds, that the difference now existing between North and South America is justly attributable, in a great degree, to political institutions in the Old World and in the New. And how broad that difference is! Suppose an assembly, in one of the valleys or on the side of one of the mountains of the southern half of the hemisphere, to be held, this day, in the neighborhood of a large city;--what would be the scene presented?

Yonder is a volcano, flaming and smoking, but shedding no light, moral or intellectual. At its foot is the mine, sometimes yielding, perhaps, large gains to capital, but in which labor is destined to eternal and unrequited toil, and followed only by penury and beggary. The city is filled with armed men; not a free people, armed and coming forth voluntarily to rejoice in a public festivity, but hireling troops, supported by forced loans, excessive impositions on commerce, or taxes wrung from a half-fed and a half-clothed population. For the great there are palaces covered with gold; for the poor there are hovels of the meanest sort. There is an ecclesiastical hierarchy, enjoying the wealth of princes; but there are no means of education for the people. Do public improvements favor intercourse between place and place? So far from this, the traveller cannot pass from town to town, without danger, every mile, of robbery and assassination. I would not overcharge or exaggerate this picture; but its principal features are all too truly sketched.

And how does it contrast with the scene now actually before us? Look round upon these fields; they are verdant and beautiful, well cultivated, and at this moment loaded with the riches of the early harvest. The hands which till them are those of the free owners of the soil, enjoying equal rights, and protected by law from oppression and tyranny. Look to the thousand vessels in our sight, filling the harbor, or covering the neighboring sea. They are the vehicles of a profitable commerce, carried on by men who know that the profits of their hardy enterprise, when they make them, are their own; and this commerce is encouraged and regulated by wise laws, and defended, when need be, by the valor and patriotism of the country. Look to that fair city, the abode of so much diffused wealth, so much general happiness and comfort, so much personal independence, and so much general knowledge, and not undistinguished, I may be permitted to add, for hospitality and social refinement. She fears no forced contributions, no siege or sacking from military leaders of rival factions. The hundred temples in which her citizens worship God are in no danger of sacrilege. The regular administration of the laws encounters no obstacle. The long processions of children and youth, which you see this day, issuing by thousands from her free schools, prove the care and anxiety with which a popular government provides for the education and morals of the people. Everywhere there is order; everywhere there is security. Everywhere the law reaches to the highest and reaches to the lowest, to protect all in their rights, and to restrain all from wrong; and over all hovers liberty,--that liberty for which our fathers fought and fell on this very spot, with her eye ever watchful, and her eagle wing ever wide outspread.

The colonies of Spain, from their origin to their end, were subject to the sovereign authority of the mother country. Their government, as well as their commerce, was a strict home monopoly. If we add to this the established usage of filling important posts in the administration of the colonies exclusively by natives of Old Spain, thus cutting off for ever all hopes of honorable preferment from every man born in the Western hemisphere, causes enough rise up before us at once to account fully for the subsequent history and character of these provinces. The viceroys and provincial governors of Spain were never at home in their governments in America. They did not feel that they were of the people whom they governed. Their official character and employment have a good deal of resemblance to those of the proconsuls of Rome, in Asia, Sicily, and Gaul; but obviously no resemblance to those of Carver and Winthrop, and very little to those of the governors of Virginia after that Colony had established a popular House of Burgesses.

The English colonists in America, generally speaking, were men who were seeking new homes in a new world. They brought with them their families and all that was most dear to them. This was especially the case with the colonists of Plymouth and Massachusetts. Many of them were educated men, and all possessed their full share, according to their social condition, of the knowledge and attainments of that age. The distinctive characteristic of their settlement is the introduction of the civilization of Europe into a wilderness, without bringing with it the political institutions of Europe. The arts, sciences, and literature of England came over with the settlers. That great portion of the common law which regulates the social and personal relations and conduct of men, came also. The jury came; the *habeas corpus* came; the testamentary power came; and the law of inheritance and descent came also, except that part of it which recognizes the rights of primogeniture, which either did not come at all, or soon gave way to the rule of equal partition of estates among children. But the monarchy did not come, nor the aristocracy, nor the church, as an estate of the realm. Political institutions were to be framed anew, such as should be adapted to the state of things. But it could not be doubtful what should be the nature and character of these institutions. A general social equality prevailed among the settlers, and an equality of political rights seemed the natural, if not the necessary consequence. After forty years of revolution, violence, and war, the people of France have placed at the head of the fundamental instrument of their government, as the great boon obtained by all their sufferings and sacrifices, the declaration that all Frenchmen are equal before the law. What France has reached only by the expenditure of so much blood and treasure, and the perpetration of so much crime, the English colonists obtained by simply changing their place, carrying with them the intellectual and moral culture of Europe, and the personal and social relations to which they were accustomed, but leaving behind their political institutions. It has been said with much vivacity, that the felicity of the American colonists consisted in their escape from the past. This is true so far as respects political establishments, but no further. They brought with them a full portion of all the riches of the past, in science, in art, in morals, religion, and literature. The Bible came with them. And it is not to be doubted, that to the free and universal reading of the Bible, in that age, men were much indebted for right views of civil liberty. The Bible is a book of faith, and a book of doctrine, and a book of morals, and a book of religion, of especial revelation from God; but it is also a book which teaches man his own individual responsibility, his own dignity, and his equality with his fellow-man.

Bacon and Locke, and Shakspeare and Milton, also came with the colonists. It was the object of the first settlers to form new political systems, but all that belonged to cultivated man, to family, to neighborhood, to social relations, accompanied them. In the Doric phrase of one of our own historians, "they came to settle on bare creation"; but their settlement in the wilderness, nevertheless, was not a lodgement of nomadic tribes, a mere resting-place of roaming savages. It was the beginning of a permanent community, the fixed residence of cultivated men. Not only was English literature read, but English, good English, was spoken and written, before the axe had made way to let in the sun upon the habitations and fields of Plymouth and Massachusetts. And whatever may be said to the contrary, a correct use of the English language is, at this day, more general throughout the United States, than it is throughout England herself. But another grand characteristic is, that, in the English colonies, political affairs were left to be managed by the colonists themselves. This is another fact wholly distinguishing them in character, as it has distinguished them in fortune, from the colonists of Spain. Here lies the foundation of that experience in self-government, which has preserved order, and security, and regularity, amidst the play of popular institutions. Home government was the secret of the prosperity of the North American settlements. The more distinguished of the New England colonists, with a most remarkable sagacity and a long-sighted reach into futurity, refused to come to America unless they could bring with them charters providing for the administration of their affairs in this country.[5] They saw from the first the evils of being governed in the New World by a power fixed in the Old. Acknowledging the general superiority of the crown, they still insisted on the right of passing local laws, and of local administration. And history teaches us the justice and the value of this determination in the example of Virginia. The early attempts to settle that Colony failed, sometimes with the most melancholy and fatal consequences, from want of knowledge, care, and attention on the part of those who had the charge of their affairs in England; and it was only after the issuing of the third charter, that its prosperity fairly commenced. The cause was, that by that third charter the people of Virginia, for by this time they deserved to be so called, were allowed to constitute and establish the first popular representative assembly which ever convened on this continent, the Virginia House of Burgesses.

The great elements, then, of the American system of government, originally introduced by the colonists, and which were early in operation, and ready to be developed, more and more, as the progress of events should justify or demand, were,--

Escape from the existing political systems of Europe, including its religious hierarchies, but the continued possession and enjoyment of its science and arts, its literature, and its manners;

Home government, or the power of making in the colony the municipal laws which were to govern it;

Equality of rights;

Representative assemblies, or forms of government founded on popular elections.

Few topics are more inviting, or more fit for philosophical discussion, than the effect on the happiness of mankind of institutions founded upon these principles; or, in other words, the influence of the New World upon the Old.

Her obligations to Europe for science and art, laws, literature, and manners, America acknowledges as she ought, with respect and gratitude. The people of the United States, descendants of the English stock, grateful for the treasures of knowledge derived from their English ancestors, admit also, with thanks and filial regard, that among those ancestors, under the culture of Hampden and Sydney and other assiduous friends, that seed of popular liberty first germinated, which on our soil has shot up to its full height, until its branches overshadow all the land.

But America has not failed to make returns. If she has not wholly cancelled the obligation, or equalled it by others of like weight, she has, at least, made respectable advances towards repaying the debt. And she admits, that, standing in the midst of civilized nations, and in a civilized age, a nation among nations, there is a high part which she is expected to act, for the general advancement of human interests and human welfare.

American mines have filled the mints of Europe with the precious metals. The productions of the American soil and climate have poured out their abundance of luxuries for the tables of the rich, and of necessaries for the sustenance of the poor. Birds and animals of beauty and value have been added to the European stocks; and transplantations from the unequalled riches of our forests have mingled themselves profusely with the elms, and ashes, and Druidical oaks of England.

America has made contributions to Europe far more important. Who can estimate the amount, or the value, of the augmentation of the commerce of the world that has resulted from America? Who can imagine to himself what would now be the shock to the Eastern Continent, if the Atlantic were no longer traversable, or if there were no longer American productions, or American markets?

But America exercises influences, or holds out examples, for the consideration of the Old World, of a much higher, because they are of a moral and political character.

America has furnished to Europe proof of the fact, that popular institutions, founded on equality and the principle of representation, are capable of maintaining governments, able to secure the rights of person, property, and reputation.

America has proved that it is practicable to elevate the mass of mankind,--that portion which in Europe is called the laboring, or lower class,--to raise them to self-respect, to make them competent to act a part in the great right and great duty of self-government; and she has proved that this may be done by education and the diffusion of knowledge. She holds out an example, a thousand times more encouraging than ever was presented before, to those nine tenths of the human race who are born without hereditary fortune or hereditary rank.

America has furnished to the world the character of Washington! And if our American institutions had done nothing else, that alone would have entitled them to the respect of mankind.

Washington! "First in war, first in peace, and first in the hearts of his countrymen!" Washington is all our own! The enthusiastic veneration and regard in which the people of the United States hold him, prove them to be worthy of such a countryman; while his reputation abroad reflects the highest honor on his country. I would cheerfully put the question to-day to the intelligence of Europe and the world, what character of the century, upon the whole, stands out in the relief of history, most pure, most respectable, most sublime; and I doubt not, that, by a suffrage approaching to unanimity, the answer would be Washington!

The structure now standing before us, by its uprightness, its solidity, its durability, is no unfit emblem of his character. His public virtues and public principles were as firm as the earth on which it stands; his personal motives, as pure as the serene heaven in which its summit is lost. But, indeed, though a fit, it is an inadequate emblem. Towering high above the column which our hands have builded, beheld, not by the inhabitants of a single city or a single State, but by all the families of man, ascends the colossal grandeur of the character and life of Washington. In all the constituents of the one, in all the acts of the other, in all its titles to immortal love, admiration, and renown, it is an American production. It is the embodiment and vindication of our Transatlantic liberty. Born upon our soil, of parents also born upon it; never for a moment having had sight of the Old World; instructed, according to the modes of his time, only in the spare, plain, but wholesome elementary knowledge which our institutions provide for the children of the people; growing up beneath and penetrated by the genuine influences of American society; living from infancy to manhood and age amidst our expanding, but not luxurious civilization; partaking in our great destiny of labor, our long contest with unreclaimed nature and uncivilized man, our agony of glory, the war of Independence, our great victory of peace, the formation of the Union, and the establishment of the Constitution,--he is all, all our own! Washington is ours. That crowded and glorious life,

"Where multitudes of virtues passed along, Each pressing foremost, in the mighty throng Ambitious to be seen, then making room For greater multitudes that were to come,"--

that life was the life of an American citizen.

I claim him for America. In all the perils, in every darkened moment of the state, in the midst of the reproaches of enemies and the misgiving of friends, I turn to that transcendent name for courage and for consolation. To him who denies or doubts whether our fervid liberty can be combined with law, with order, with the security of property, with the pursuits and advancement of happiness; to him who denies that our forms of government are capable of producing exaltation of soul, and the passion of true glory; to him who denies that we have contributed any thing to the stock of great lessons and great examples;--to all these I reply by pointing to Washington!

And now, friends and fellow-citizens, it is time to bring this discourse to a close.

We have indulged in gratifying recollections of the past, in the prosperity and pleasures of the present, and in high hopes for the future. But let us remember that we have duties and obligations to perform, corresponding to the blessings which we enjoy. Let us remember the trust, the sacred trust, attaching to the rich inheritance which we have received from our fathers. Let us feel our personal responsibility, to the full extent of our power and influence, for the preservation of the principles of civil and religious liberty. And let us remember that it is only religion, and morals, and knowledge, that can make men respectable and happy, under any form of government. Let us hold fast the great truth, that communities are responsible, as well as individuals; that no government is respectable, which is not just; that without unspotted purity of public faith, without sacred public principle, fidelity, and honor, no mere forms of government, no machinery of laws, can give dignity to political society. In our day and generation let us seek to raise and improve the moral sentiment, so that we may look, not for a degraded, but for an elevated and improved future. And when both we and our children shall have been consigned to the house appointed for all living, may love of country and pride of country glow with equal fervor among those to whom our names and our blood shall have descended! And then, when honored and decrepit age shall lean against the base of this monument, and troops of ingenuous youth shall be gathered round it, and when the one shall speak to the other of its objects, the purposes of its construction, and the great and glorious events with which it is connected, there shall rise from every youthful breast the ejaculation, "Thank God, I--I also--AM AN AMERICAN!"

NOTE. Page 139. The following description of the Bunker Hill Monument and Square is from Mr. Frothingham's History of the Siege of Boston, pp. 355, 356. "Monument Square is four hundred and seventeen feet from north to south, and four hundred feet from east to west, and contains nearly six acres. It embraces the whole site of the redoubt, and a part of the site of the breastwork. According to the most accurate plan of the town and the battle (Page's), the monument stands where the southwest angle of the redoubt was, and the whole of the redoubt was between the monument and the street that bounds it on the west. The small mound in the northeast corner of the square is supposed to be the remains of the breastwork. Warren fell about two hundred feet west of the monument. An iron fence encloses the square, and another surrounds the monument. The square has entrances on each of its sides, and at each of its corners, and is surrounded by a walk and rows of trees.

"The obelisk is thirty feet in diameter at the base, about fifteen feet at the top of the truncated part, and was designed to be two hundred and twenty feet high; but the mortar and the seams between the stones make the precise height two hundred and twenty-one feet. Within the shaft is a hollow cone, with a spiral stairway winding round it to its summit, which enters a circular chamber at the top. There are ninety courses of stone in the shaft,--six of them below the ground, and eighty-four above the ground. The capstone, or apex, is a single stone four feet square at the base, and three feet six inches in height, weighing two and half tons."

[Footnote 1: William Tudor died at Rio de Janeiro, as Chargé d'Affaires of the United States, in 1830.][Footnote 2: William Sullivan died in Boston in 1839, George Blake in 1841, both gentlemen of great political and legal eminence.][Footnote 3: William Prescott (since deceased, in 1844), son of Colonel William Prescott, who commanded on the 17th of June, 1775, and father of William H. Prescott, the historian.][Footnote 4: See the Note at the end of the Address.]

[Footnote 5: See the "Records of the Company of the Massachusetts Bay in New England," as published in the third volume of the Transactions of the American Antiquarian Society, pp. 47-50.]

OUR RELATIONS TO THE SOUTH AMERICAN REPUBLICS.
EXTRACTS FROM THE SPEECH ON "THE PANAMA MISSION," DELIVERED IN THE HOUSE OF REPRESENTATIVES OF THE UNITED STATES, ON THE 14TH OF APRIL, 1826.

It has been affirmed, that this measure, and the sentiments expressed by the Executive relative to its objects, are an acknowledged departure from the neutral policy of the United States. Sir, I deny that there is an acknowledged departure, or any departure at all, from the neutral policy of the country. What do we mean by our neutral policy? Not, I suppose, a blind and stupid indifference to whatever is passing around us; not a total disregard to approaching events, or approaching evils, till they meet us full in the face. Nor do we mean, by our neutral policy, that we intend never to assert our rights by force. No, Sir. We mean by our policy of neutrality, that the great objects of national pursuit with us are connected with peace. We covet no provinces; we desire no conquests; we entertain no ambitious projects of aggrandizement by war. This is our policy. But it does not follow from this, that we rely less than other nations on our own power to vindicate our own rights. We know that the last logic of kings is also our last logic; that our own interests must be defended and maintained by our own arm; and that peace or war may not always be of our own choosing. Our neutral policy, therefore, not only justifies, but requires, our anxious attention to the political events which take place in the world, a skilful perception of their relation to our own concerns, and an early anticipation of their consequences, and firm and timely assertion of what we hold to be our own rights and our own interests. Our neutrality is not a predetermined abstinence, either from remonstrances, or from force. Our neutral policy is a policy that protects neutrality, that defends neutrality, that takes up arms, if need be, for neutrality. When it is said, therefore, that this measure departs from our neutral policy, either that policy, or the measure itself, is misunderstood. It implies either that the object or the tendency of the measure is to involve us in the war of other states, which I think cannot be shown, or that the assertion of our own sentiments, on points affecting deeply our own interests, may place us in a hostile attitude toward other states, and that therefore we depart from neutrality; whereas the truth is, that the decisive assertion and the firm support of these sentiments may be most essential to the maintenance of neutrality.

An honorable member from Pennsylvania thinks this congress will bring a dark day over the United States. Doubtless, Sir, it is an interesting moment in our history; but I see no great proofs of thick-coming darkness. But the object of the remark seemed to be to show that the President himself saw difficulties on all sides, and, making a choice of evils, preferred rather to send ministers to this congress, than to run the risk of exciting the hostility of the states by refusing to send. In other words, the gentleman wished to prove that the President intended an alliance; although such intention is expressly disclaimed.

Much commentary has been bestowed on the letters of invitation from the ministers. I shall not go through with verbal criticisms on these letters. Their general import is plain enough. I shall not gather together small and minute quotations, taking a sentence here, a word there, and a syllable in a third place, dovetailing them into the course of remark, till the printed discourse bristles in every line with inverted commas. I look to the general tenor of the invitations, and I find that we are asked to take part only in such things as concern ourselves. I look still more carefully to the answers, and I see every proper caution and proper guard. I look to the message, and I see that nothing is there contemplated likely to involve us in other men's quarrels, or that may justly give offence to any foreign state. With this I am satisfied.

I must now ask the indulgence of the committee to an important point in the discussion, I mean the declaration of the President in 1823.[1] Not only as a member of the House, but as a citizen of the country, I have an anxious desire that this part of our public history should stand in its proper light. The country has, in my judgment, a very high honor connected with that occurrence, which we may maintain, or which we may sacrifice. I look upon it as a part of its treasures of reputation; and, for one, I intend to guard it. Sir, let us recur to the important political events which led to that declaration, or accompanied it. In the fall of 1822, the allied sovereigns held their congress at Verona. The great subject of consideration was the condition of Spain, that country then being under the government of the Cortes. The question was, whether Ferdinand should be reinstated in all his authority, by the intervention of foreign force. Russia, Prussia, France, and Austria were inclined to that measure; England dissented and protested; but the course was agreed on, and France, with the consent of these other Continental powers, took the conduct of the operation into her own hands. In the spring of 1823, a French army was sent into Spain. Its success was complete. The popular government was overthrown, and Ferdinand re-established in all his power. This invasion, Sir, was determined on, and undertaken, precisely on the doctrines which the allied monarchs had proclaimed the year before, at Laybach; that is, that they had a right to interfere in the concerns of another state, and reform its government, in order to prevent the effects of its bad example; this bad example, be it remembered, always being the example of free government. Now, Sir, acting on this principle of supposed dangerous example, and having put down the example of the Cortes in Spain, it was natural to inquire with what eyes they would look on the colonies of Spain, that were following still worse examples. Would King Ferdinand and his allies be content with what had been done in Spain itself, or would he solicit their aid, and was it likely they would grant it, to subdue his rebellious American provinces?

Sir, it was in this posture of affairs, on an occasion which has already been alluded to, that I ventured to say, early in the session of December, 1823, that these allied monarchs might possibly turn their attention to America; that America came within their avowed doctrine, and that her examples might very possibly attract their notice. The doctrines of Laybach were not limited to any continent. Spain had colonies in America, and having reformed Spain herself to the true standard, it was not impossible that they might see fit to complete the work by reconciling, in their way, the colonies to the mother country. Now, Sir, it did so happen, that, as soon as the Spanish king was completely re-established, he invited the co-operation of his allies in regard to South America. In the same month of December, of 1823, a formal invitation was addressed by Spain to the courts of St. Petersburg, Vienna, Berlin, and Paris, proposing to establish a conference at Paris, in order that the plenipotentiaries there assembled might aid Spain in adjusting the affairs of her revolted provinces. These affairs were proposed to be adjusted in such manner as should retain the sovereignty of Spain over them; and though the co-operation of the allies by force of arms was not directly solicited, such was evidently the object aimed at. The king of Spain, in making this request to the members of the Holy Alliance, argued as it has been seen he might argue. He quoted their own doctrines of Laybach; he pointed out the pernicious example of America; and he reminded them that their success in Spain itself had paved the way for successful operations against the spirit of liberty on this side of the Atlantic.

The proposed meeting, however, did not take place. England had already taken a decided course; for as early as October, Mr. Canning, in a conference with the French minister in London, informed him distinctly and expressly, that England would consider any foreign interference, by force or by menace, in the dispute between Spain and the colonies, as a motive for recognizing the latter without delay. It is probable this determination of the English government was known here at the commencement of the session of Congress; and it was under these circumstances, it was in this crisis, that Mr. Monroe's declaration was made. It was not then ascertained whether a meeting of the Allies would or would not take place, to concert with Spain the means of re-establishing her power; but it was plain enough they would be pressed by Spain to aid her operations; and it was plain enough, also, that they had no particular liking to what was taking place on this side of the Atlantic, nor any great disinclination to interfere. This was the posture of affairs; and, Sir, I concur entirely in the sentiment expressed in the resolution of a gentleman from Pennsylvania,[2] that this declaration of Mr. Monroe was wise, seasonable, and patriotic.

It has been said, in the course of this debate, to have been a loose and vague declaration. It was, I believe, sufficiently studied. I have understood, from good authority, that it was considered, weighed, and distinctly and decidedly approved, by every one of the President's advisers at that time. Our government could not adopt on that occasion precisely the course which England had taken. England threatened the immediate recognition of the provinces, if the Allies should take part with Spain against them. We had already recognized them. It remained, therefore, only for our government to say how we should consider a combination of the Allied Powers, to effect objects in America, as affecting ourselves; and the message was intended to say, what it does say, that we should regard such combination as dangerous to us. Sir, I agree with those who maintain the proposition, and I contend against those who deny it, that the message did mean something; that it meant much; and I maintain, against both, that the declaration effected much good, answered the end designed by it, did great honor to the foresight and the spirit of the government, and that it cannot now be taken back, retracted, or annulled, without disgrace. It met, Sir, with the entire concurrence and the hearty approbation of the country. The tone which it uttered found a corresponding response in the breasts of the free people of the United States. That people saw, and they rejoiced to see, that, on a fit occasion, our weight had been thrown into the right scale, and that, without departing from our duty, we had done something useful, and something effectual, for the cause of civil liberty. One general glow of exultation, one universal feeling of the gratified love of liberty, one conscious and proud perception of the consideration which the country possessed, and of the respect and honor which belonged to it, pervaded all bosoms. Possibly the public enthusiasm went too far; it certainly did go far. But, Sir, the sentiment which this declaration inspired was not confined to ourselves. Its force was felt everywhere, by all those who could understand its object and foresee its effect. In that very House of Commons of which the gentleman from South Carolina has spoken with such commendation, how was it received? Not only, Sir, with approbation, but, I may say, with no little enthusiasm. While the leading minister[3] expressed his entire concurrence in the sentiments and opinions of the American President, his distinguished competitor[4] in that popular body, less restrained by official decorum, and more at liberty to give utterance to all the feeling of the occasion, declared that no event had ever created greater joy, exultation, and gratitude among all the free men in Europe; that he felt pride in being connected by blood and language with the people of the United States; that the policy disclosed by the message became a great, a free, and an independent nation; and that he hoped his own country would be prevented by no mean pride, or paltry jealousy, from following so noble and glorious an example.

It is doubtless true, as I took occasion to observe the other day, that this declaration must be considered as founded on our rights, and to spring mainly from a regard to their preservation. It did not commit us, at all events, to take up arms on any indication of hostile feeling by the powers of Europe towards South America. If, for example, all the states of Europe had refused to trade with South America until her states should return to their former allegiance, that would have furnished no cause of interference to us. Or if an armament had been furnished by the Allies to act against provinces the most remote from us, as Chili or Buenos Ayres, the distance of the scene of action diminishing our apprehension of danger, and diminishing also our means of effectual interposition, might still have left us to content ourselves with remonstrance. But a very different case would have arisen, if an army, equipped and maintained by these powers, had been landed on the shores of the Gulf of Mexico, and commenced the war in our own immediate neighborhood. Such an event might justly be regarded as dangerous to ourselves, and, on that ground, call for decided and immediate interference by us. The sentiments and the policy announced by the declaration, thus understood, were, therefore, in strict conformity to our duties and our interest.

Sir, I look on the message of December, 1823, as forming a bright page in our history. I will help neither to erase it nor tear it out; nor shall it be, by any act of mine, blurred or blotted. It did honor to the sagacity of the government, and I will not diminish that honor. It elevated the hopes, and gratified the patriotism, of the people. Over those hopes I will not bring a mildew; nor will I put that gratified patriotism to shame.

[Footnote 1: In the message of President Monroe to Congress at the commencement of the session of 1823-24, the following passage occurs:--"In the wars of the European powers, in matters relating to themselves, we have never taken any part, nor does it comport with our policy so to do. It is only when our rights are invaded, or seriously menaced, that we resent injuries or make preparations for defence. With the movements in this hemisphere we are of necessity more immediately connected, and by causes which must be obvious to all enlightened and impartial observers. The political system of the Allied Powers is essentially different, in this respect, from that of America. This difference proceeds from that which exists in their respective governments. And to the defence of our own, which has been achieved by the loss of so much blood and treasure, and matured by the wisdom of their most enlightened citizens, and under which we have enjoyed such unexampled felicity, this whole nation is devoted. We owe it, therefore, to candor, and to the amicable relations existing between the United States and those powers, to declare that we should consider any attempt on their part to extend their system to any portion of this hemisphere as dangerous to our peace and safety. With the existing colonies or dependencies of any European power, we have not interfered, and shall not interfere. But with the governments who have declared their independence and maintained it, and whose independence we have on great consideration and on just principles acknowledged, we could not view any interposition for the purpose of oppressing them, or controlling in any other manner their destiny, in any other light than as the manifestation of an unfriendly disposition toward the United States."]

[Footnote 2: Mr. Markley.][Footnote 3: Mr. Canning.][Footnote 4: Mr. Brougham.]

ADAMS AND JEFFERSON.

DISCOURSE IN COMMEMORATION OF THE LIVES AND SERVICES OF JOHN ADAMS AND THOMAS JEFFERSON, DELIVERED IN FANEUIL HALL, BOSTON, ON THE 2D OF AUGUST, 1826.

[Since the decease of General Washington, on the 14th of December, 1799, the public mind has never been so powerfully affected in this part of the country by any similar event, as by the death of John Adams, on the 4th of July, 1826. The news reached Boston in the evening of that day. The decease of this venerable fellow-citizen must at all times have appealed with much force to the patriotic sympathies of the people of Massachusetts. It acquired a singular interest from the year and the day on which it took place;--the 4th of July of the year completing the half-century from that ever memorable era in the history of this country and the world, the Declaration of Independence; a measure in which Mr. Adams himself had taken so distinguished a part. The emotions of the public were greatly increased by the indications given by Mr. Adams in his last hours, that he was fully aware that the day was the anniversary of Independence, and by his dying allusion to the supposed fact that his colleague, Jefferson, survived him. When, in the course of a few days, the news arrived from Virginia, that he also had departed this life, on the same day and a few hours before Mr. Adams, the sensibility of the community, as of the country at large, was touched beyond all example. The occurrence was justly deemed without a parallel in history. The various circumstances of association and coincidence which marked the characters and careers of these great men, and especially those of their simultaneous decease on the 4th of July, were dwelt upon with melancholy but untiring interest. The circles of private life, the press, public bodies, and the pulpit, were for some time almost engrossed with the topic; and solemn rites of commemoration were performed throughout the country. An early day was appointed for this purpose by the City Council of Boston. The whole community manifested its sympathy in the extraordinary event; and on the 2d of August, 1826, at the request of the municipal authorities, and in the presence of an immense audience, the following Discourse was delivered in Faneuil Hall.]

This is an unaccustomed spectacle. For the first time, fellow-citizens, badges of mourning shroud the columns and overhang the arches of this hall. These walls, which were consecrated, so long ago, to the cause of American liberty, which witnessed her infant struggles, and rung with the shouts of her earliest victories, proclaim, now, that distinguished friends and champions of that great cause have fallen. It is right that it should be thus. The tears which flow, and the honors that are paid, when the founders of the republic die, give hope that the republic itself may be immortal. It is fit that, by public assembly and solemn observance, by anthem and by eulogy, we commemorate the services of national benefactors, extol their virtues, and render thanks to God for eminent blessings, early given and long continued, through their agency, to our favored country.

ADAMS and JEFFERSON are no more; and we are assembled, fellow-citizens, the aged, the middle-aged, and the young, by the spontaneous impulse of all, under the authority of the municipal government, with the presence of the chief magistrate of the Commonwealth, and others its official representatives, the University, and the learned societies, to bear our part in those manifestations of respect and gratitude which pervade the whole land. ADAMS and JEFFERSON are no more. On our fiftieth anniversary, the great day of national jubilee, in the very hour of public rejoicing, in the midst of echoing and re-echoing voices of thanksgiving, while their own names were on all tongues, they took their flight together to the world of spirits.

If it be true that no one can safely be pronounced happy while he lives, if that event which terminates life can alone crown its honors and its glory, what felicity is here! The great epic of their lives, how happily concluded! Poetry itself has hardly terminated illustrious lives, and finished the career of earthly renown, by such a consummation. If we had the power, we could not wish to reverse this dispensation of the Divine Providence. The great objects of life were accomplished, the drama was ready to be closed. It has closed; our patriots have fallen; but so fallen, at such age, with such coincidence, on such a day, that we cannot rationally lament that that end has come, which we knew could not be long deferred.

Neither of these great men, fellow-citizens, could have died, at any time, without leaving an immense void in our American society. They have been so intimately, and for so long a time, blended with the history of the country, and especially so united, in our thoughts and recollections, with the events of the Revolution, that the death of either would have touched the chords of public sympathy. We should have felt that one great link, connecting us with former times, was broken; that we had lost something more, as it were, of the presence of the Revolution itself, and of the act of independence, and were driven on, by another great remove from the days of our country's early distinction, to meet posterity, and to mix with the future. Like the mariner, whom the currents of the ocean and the winds carry along, till he sees the stars which have directed his course and lighted his pathless way descend, one by one, beneath the rising horizon, we should have felt that the stream of time had borne us onward till another great luminary, whose light had cheered us and whose guidance we had followed, had sunk away from our sight.

But the concurrence of their death on the anniversary of Independence has naturally awakened stronger emotions. Both had been Presidents, both had lived to great age, both were early patriots, and both were distinguished and ever honored by their immediate agency in the act of independence. It cannot but seem striking and extraordinary, that these two should live to see the fiftieth year from the date of that act; that they should complete that year; and that then, on the day which had fast linked for ever their own fame with their country's glory, the heavens should open to receive them both at once. As their lives themselves were the gifts of Providence, who is not willing to recognize in their happy termination, as well as in their long continuance, proofs that our country and its benefactors are objects of His care?

ADAMS and JEFFERSON, I have said, are no more. As human beings, indeed, they are no more. They are no more, as in 1776, bold and fearless advocates of independence; no more, as at subsequent periods, the head of the government; no more, as we have recently seen them, aged and venerable objects of admiration and regard. They are no more. They are dead. But how little is there of the great and good which can die! To their country they yet live, and live for ever. They live in all that perpetuates the remembrance of men on earth; in the recorded proofs of their own great actions, in the offspring of their intellect, in the deep-engraved lines of public gratitude, and in the respect and homage of mankind. They live in their example; and they live, emphatically, and will live, in the influence which their lives and efforts, their principles and opinions, now exercise, and will continue to exercise, on the affairs of men, not only in their own country, but throughout the civilized world. A superior and commanding human intellect, a truly great man, when Heaven vouchsafes so rare a gift, is not a temporary flame, burning brightly for a while, and then giving place to returning darkness. It is rather a spark of fervent heat, as well as radiant light, with power to enkindle the common mass of human mind; so that when it glimmers in its own decay, and finally goes out in death, no night follows, but it leaves the world all light, all on fire, from the potent contact of its own spirit. Bacon died; but the human understanding, roused by the touch of his miraculous wand to a perception of the true philosophy and the just mode of inquiring after truth, has kept on its course successfully and gloriously. Newton died; yet the courses of the spheres are still known, and they yet move on by the laws which he discovered, and in the orbits which he saw, and described for them, in the infinity of space.

No two men now live, fellow-citizens, perhaps it may be doubted whether any two men have ever lived in one age, who, more than those we now commemorate, have impressed on mankind their own sentiments in regard to politics and government, infused their own opinions more deeply into the opinions of others, or given a more lasting direction to the current of human thought. Their work doth not perish with them. The tree which they assisted to plant will flourish, although they water it and protect it no longer; for it has struck its roots deep, it has sent them to the very centre; no storm, not of force to burst the orb, can overturn it; its branches spread wide; they stretch their protecting arms broader and broader, and its top is destined to reach the heavens. We are not deceived. There is no delusion here. No age will come in which the American Revolution will appear less than it is, one of the greatest events in human history. No age will come in which it shall cease to be seen and felt, on either continent, that a mighty step, a great advance, not only in American affairs, but in human affairs, was made on the 4th of July, 1776. And no age will come, we trust, so ignorant or so unjust as not to see and acknowledge the efficient agency of those we now honor in producing that momentous event.

We are not assembled, therefore, fellow-citizens, as men overwhelmed with calamity by the sudden disruption of the ties of friendship or affection, or as in despair for the republic by the untimely blighting of its hopes. Death has not surprised us by an unseasonable blow. We have, indeed, seen the tomb close, but it has closed only over mature years, over long-protracted public service, over the weakness of age, and over life itself only when the ends of living had been fulfilled. These suns, as they rose slowly and steadily, amidst clouds and storms, in their ascendant, so they have not rushed from their meridian to sink suddenly in the west. Like the mildness, the serenity, the continuing benignity of a summer's day, they have gone down with slow-descending, grateful, long-lingering light; and now that they are beyond the visible margin of the world, good omens cheer us from "the bright track of their fiery car"!

There were many points of similarity in the lives and fortunes of these great men. They belonged to the same profession, and had pursued its studies and its practice, for unequal lengths of time indeed, but with diligence and effect. Both were learned and able lawyers. They were natives and inhabitants, respectively, of those two of the Colonies which at the Revolution were the largest and most powerful, and which naturally had a lead in the political affairs of the times. When the Colonies became in some degree united, by the assembling of a general Congress, they were brought to act together in its deliberations, not indeed at the same time, but both at early periods. Each had already manifested his attachment to the cause of the country, as well as his ability to maintain it, by printed addresses, public speeches, extensive correspondence, and whatever other mode could be adopted for the purpose of exposing the encroachments of the British Parliament and animating the people to a manly resistance. Both were not only decided, but early, friends of Independence. While others yet doubted, they were resolved; where others hesitated, they pressed forward. They were both members of the committee for preparing the Declaration of Independence, and they constituted the sub-committee appointed by the other members to make the draft. They left their seats in Congress, being called to other public employments, at periods not remote from each other, although one of them returned to it afterwards for a short time. Neither of them was of the assembly of great men which formed the present Constitution, and neither was at any time a member of Congress under its provisions. Both have been public ministers abroad, both Vice-Presidents and both Presidents of the United States. These coincidences are now singularly crowned and completed. They have died together; and they died on the anniversary of liberty.

When many of us were last in this place, fellow-citizens, it was on the day of that anniversary. We were met to enjoy the festivities belonging to the occasion, and to manifest our grateful homage to our political fathers. We did not, we could not here, forget our venerable neighbor of Quincy. We knew that we were standing, at a time of high and palmy prosperity, where he had stood in the hour of utmost peril; that we saw nothing but liberty and security, where he had met the frown of power; that we were enjoying every thing, where he had hazarded every thing; and just and sincere plaudits rose to his name, from the crowds which filled this area, and hung over these galleries. He whose grateful duty it was to speak to us,[1] on that day, of the virtues of our fathers, had, indeed, admonished us that time and years were about to level his venerable frame with the dust. But he bade us hope that "the sound of a nation's joy, rushing from our cities, ringing from our valleys, echoing from our hills, might yet break the silence of his aged ear; that the rising blessings of grateful millions might yet visit with glad light his decaying vision." Alas! that vision was then closing for ever. Alas! the silence which was then settling on that aged ear was an everlasting silence! For, lo! in the very moment of our festivities, his freed spirit ascended to God who gave it! Human aid and human solace terminate at the grave; or we would gladly have borne him upward, on a nation's outspread hands; we would have accompanied him, and with the blessings of millions and the prayers of millions, commended him to the Divine favor.

While still indulging our thoughts, on the coincidence of the death of this venerable man with the anniversary of Independence, we learn that Jefferson, too, has fallen; and that these aged patriots, these illustrious fellow-laborers, have left our world together. May not such events raise the suggestion that they are not undesigned, and that Heaven does so order things, as sometimes to attract strongly the attention and excite the thoughts of men? The occurrence has added new interest to our anniversary, and will be remembered in all time to come.

The occasion, fellow-citizens, requires some account of the lives and services of JOHN ADAMS and THOMAS JEFFERSON. This duty must necessarily be performed with great brevity, and in the discharge of it I shall be obliged to confine myself, principally, to those parts of their history and character which belonged to them as public men.

JOHN ADAMS was born at Quincy, then part of the ancient town of Braintree, on the 19th day of October (old style), 1735. He was a descendant of the Puritans, his ancestors having early emigrated from England, and settled in Massachusetts. Discovering in childhood a strong love of reading and of knowledge, together with marks of great strength and activity of mind, proper care was taken by his worthy father to provide for his education. He pursued his youthful studies in Braintree, under Mr. Marsh, a teacher whose fortune it was that Josiah Quincy, Jr., as well as the subject of these remarks, should receive from him his instruction in the rudiments of classical literature. Having been admitted, in 1751, a member of Harvard

College, Mr. Adams was graduated, in course, in 1755; and on the catalogue of that institution, his name, at the time of his death, was second among the living Alumni, being preceded only by that of the venerable Holyoke. With what degree of reputation he left the University is not now precisely known. We know only that he was distinguished in a class which numbered Locke and Hemmenway among its members.

Choosing the law for his profession, he commenced and prosecuted its studies at Worcester, under the direction of Samuel Putnam, a gentleman whom he has himself described as an acute man, an able and learned lawyer, and as being in large professional practice at that time. In 1758 he was admitted to the bar, and entered upon the practice of the law in Braintree. He is understood to have made his first considerable effort, or to have attained his first signal success, at Plymouth, on one of those occasions which furnish the earliest opportunity for distinction to many young men of the profession, a jury trial, and a criminal cause. His business naturally grew with his reputation, and his residence in the vicinity afforded the opportunity, as his growing eminence gave the power, of entering on a larger field of practice in the capital. In 1766 he removed his residence to Boston, still continuing his attendance on the neighboring circuits, and not unfrequently called to remote parts of the Province. In 1770 his professional firmness was brought to a test of some severity, on the application of the British officers and soldiers to undertake their defence, on the trial of the indictments found against them on account of the transactions of the memorable 5th of March. He seems to have thought, on this occasion, that a man can no more abandon the proper duties of his profession, than he can abandon other duties. The event proved, that, as he judged well for his own reputation, so, too, he judged well for the interest and permanent fame of his country. The result of that trial proved, that, notwithstanding the high degree of excitement then existing in consequence of the measures of the British government, a jury of Massachusetts would not deprive the most reckless enemies, even the officers of that standing army quartered among them, which they so perfectly abhorred, of any part of that protection which the law, in its mildest and most indulgent interpretation, affords to persons accused of crimes.

Without following Mr. Adams's professional course further, suffice it to say, that on the first establishment of the judicial tribunals under the authority of the State, in 1776, he received an offer of the high and responsible station of Chief Justice of the Supreme Court of Massachusetts. But he was destined for another and a different career. From early life the bent of his mind was toward politics; a propensity which the state of the times, if it did not create, doubtless very much strengthened. Public subjects must have occupied the thoughts and filled up the conversation in the circles in which he then moved; and the interesting questions at that time just arising could not but seize on a mind like his, ardent, sanguine, and patriotic. A letter, fortunately preserved, written by him at Worcester, so early as the 12th of October, 1755, is a proof of very comprehensive views, and uncommon depth of reflection, in a young man not yet quite twenty. In this letter he predicted the transfer of power, and the establishment of a new seat of empire in America; he predicted, also, the increase of population in the Colonies; and anticipated their naval distinction, and foretold that all Europe combined could not subdue them. All this is said, not on a public occasion or for effect, but in the style of sober and friendly correspondence, as the result of his own thoughts. "I sometimes retire," said he, at the close of the letter, "and, laying things together, form some reflections pleasing to myself. The produce of one of these reveries you have read above." This prognostication so early in his own life, so early in the history of the country, of independence, of vast increase of numbers, of naval force, of such augmented power as might defy all Europe, is remarkable. It is more remarkable that its author should live to see fulfilled to the letter what could have seemed to others, at the time, but the extravagance of youthful fancy. His earliest political feelings were thus strongly American, and from this ardent attachment to his native soil he never departed.

While still living at Quincy, and at the age of twenty-four, Mr. Adams was present, in this town, at the argument before the Supreme Court respecting _Writs of Assistance_, and heard the celebrated and patriotic speech of JAMES OTIS. Unquestionably, that was a masterly performance. No flighty declamation about liberty, no superficial discussion of popular topics, it was a learned, penetrating, convincing, constitutional argument, expressed in a strain of high and resolute patriotism. He grasped the question then pending between England and her Colonies with the strength of a lion; and if he sometimes sported, it was only because the lion himself is sometimes playful. Its success appears to have been as great as its merits, and its impression was widely felt. Mr. Adams himself seems never to have lost the feeling it produced, and to have entertained constantly the fullest conviction of its important effects. "I do say," he observes, "in the most solemn manner, that Mr. Otis's Oration against Writs of Assistance breathed into this nation the breath of life."[2]

In 1765 Mr. Adams laid before the public, anonymously, a series of essays, afterwards collected in a volume in London, under the title of "A Dissertation on the Canon and Feudal Law."[3] The object of this work was to show that our New England ancestors, in consenting to exile themselves from their native land, were actuated mainly by the desire of delivering themselves from the power of the hierarchy, and from the monarchical and aristocratical systems of the other continent; and to make this truth bear with effect on the politics of the times. Its tone is uncommonly bold and animated for that period. He calls on the people, not only to defend, but to study and understand, their rights and privileges; urges earnestly the necessity of diffusing general knowledge; invokes the clergy and the bar, the colleges and academies, and all others who have the ability and the means to expose the insidious designs of arbitrary power, to resist its approaches, and to be persuaded that there is a settled design on foot to enslave all America. "Be it remembered," says the author, "that liberty must, at all hazards, be supported. We have a right to it, derived from our Maker. But if we had not, our fathers have earned and bought it for us, at the expense of their ease, their estates, their pleasure, and their blood. And liberty cannot be preserved without a general knowledge among the people, who have a right, from the frame of their nature, to knowledge, as their great Creator, who does nothing in vain, has given them understandings and a desire to know. But, besides this, they have a right, an indisputable unalienable, indefeasible, divine right, to that most dreaded and envied kind of knowledge, I mean of the characters and conduct of their rulers. Rulers are no more than attorneys, agents, and trustees for the people; and if the cause, the interest and trust, is insidiously betrayed, or wantonly trifled away, the people have a right to revoke the authority that they themselves have deputed, and to constitute abler and better agents, attorneys, and trustees."

The citizens of this town conferred on Mr. Adams his first political distinction, and clothed him with his first political trust, by electing him one of their representatives, in 1770. Before this time he had become extensively known throughout the Province, as well by the part he had acted in relation to public affairs, as by the exercise of his professional ability. He was among those who took the deepest interest in the controversy with England, and, whether in or out of the legislature, his time and talents were alike devoted to the cause. In the years 1773 and 1774 he was chosen a Councillor by the members of the General Court, but rejected by Governor Hutchinson in the former of those years, and by Governor Gage in the latter.

The time was now at hand, however, when the affairs of the Colonies urgently demanded united counsels throughout the country. An open rupture with the parent state appeared inevitable, and it was but the dictate of prudence that those who were united by a common interest and a common danger should protect that interest and guard against that danger by united efforts. A general Congress of Delegates from all the Colonies having been proposed and agreed to, the House of Representatives, on the 17th of June, 1774, elected James Bowdoin, Thomas Cushing, Samuel Adams, John Adams, and Robert Treat Paine, delegates from Massachusetts. This appointment was made at Salem, where the General Court had been convened by Governor Gage, in the last hour of the existence of a House of Representatives under the Provincial Charter. While engaged in this important business, the Governor, having been informed of what was passing, sent his secretary with a message dissolving the General Court. The secretary, finding the door locked, directed the messenger to go in and inform the Speaker that the secretary was at the door with a message from the Governor. The messenger returned, and informed the secretary that the orders of the House were that the doors should be kept fast; whereupon the secretary soon after read upon the stairs a proclamation dissolving the General Court. Thus terminated, for ever, the actual exercise of the political power of England in or over Massachusetts. The four last-named delegates accepted their appointments, and took their seats in Congress the first day of its meeting, the 5th of September, 1774, in Philadelphia. The proceedings of the first Congress are well known, and have been universally admired. It is in vain that we would look for superior proofs of wisdom, talent, and patriotism. Lord Chatham said, that, for himself, he must declare that he had studied and admired the free states of antiquity, the master states of the world, but that for solidity of reasoning, force of sagacity, and wisdom of conclusion, no body of men could stand in preference to this Congress. It is hardly inferior praise to say, that no production of that great man himself can be pronounced superior to several of the papers published as the proceedings of this most able, most firm, most patriotic assembly. There is, indeed, nothing superior to them in the range of political disquisition. They not only embrace, illustrate, and enforce every thing which political philosophy, the love of liberty, and the spirit of free inquiry had antecedently produced, but they add new and striking views of their own, and apply the whole, with irresistible force, in support of the cause which had drawn them together.

Mr. Adams was a constant attendant on the deliberations of this body, and bore an active part in its important measures. He was of the committee to state the rights of the Colonies, and of that also which reported the Address to the King.

As it was in the Continental Congress, fellow-citizens, that those whose deaths have given rise to this occasion were first brought together, and called upon to unite their industry and their ability in the service of the country, let us now turn to the other of these distinguished men, and take a brief notice of his life up to the period when he appeared within the walls of Congress.

THOMAS JEFFERSON, descended from ancestors who had been settled in Virginia for some generations, was born near the spot on which he died, in the county of Albemarle, on the 2d of April (old style), 1743. His youthful studies were pursued in the neighborhood of his father's residence until he was removed to the College of William and Mary, the highest honors of which he in due time received. Having left the College with reputation, he applied himself to the study of the law under the tuition of George Wythe, one of the highest judicial names of which that State can boast. At an early age he was elected a member of the legislature, in which he had no sooner appeared than he distinguished himself by knowledge, capacity, and promptitude.

Mr. Jefferson appears to have been imbued with an early love of letters and science, and to have cherished a strong disposition to pursue these objects. To the physical sciences, especially, and to ancient classic literature, he is understood to have had a warm attachment, and never entirely to have lost sight of them in the midst of the busiest occupations. But the times were times for action, rather than for contemplation. The country was to be defended, and to be saved, before it could be enjoyed. Philosophic leisure and literary pursuits, and even the objects of professional attention, were all necessarily postponed to the urgent calls of the public service. The exigency of the country made the same demand on Mr. Jefferson that it made on others who had the ability and the disposition to serve it; and he obeyed the call; thinking and feeling in this respect with the great Roman orator: "Quis enim est tam cupidus in perspicienda cognoscendaque rerum natura, ut, si ei tractanti contemplantique res cognitione dignissimas subito sit allatum periculum discrimenque patriae, cui subvenire opitularique possit, non illa omnia relinquat atque abjiciat, etiam si dinumerare se stellas, aut metiri mundi magnitudinem posse arbitretur?"[4]

Entering with all his heart into the cause of liberty, his ability, patriotism, and power with the pen naturally drew upon him a large participation in the most important concerns. Wherever he was, there was found a soul devoted to the cause, power to defend and maintain it, and willingness to incur all its hazards. In 1774 he published a "Summary View of the Rights of British America," a valuable production among those intended to show the dangers which threatened the liberties of the country, and to encourage the people in their defence. In June, 1775, he was elected a member of the Continental Congress, as successor to Peyton Randolph, who had resigned his place on account of ill health, and took his seat in that body on the 21st of the same month.

And now, fellow-citizens, without pursuing the biography of these illustrious men further, for the present, let us turn our attention to the most prominent act of their lives, their participation in the DECLARATION OF INDEPENDENCE.

Preparatory to the introduction of that important measure, a committee, at the head of which was Mr. Adams, had reported a resolution, which Congress adopted on the 10th of May, recommending, in substance, to all the Colonies which had not already established governments suited to the exigencies of their affairs, _to adopt such government as would, in the opinion of the representatives of the people, best conduce to the happiness and safety of their constituents in particular, and America in general_.

This significant vote was soon followed by the direct proposition which Richard Henry Lee had the honor to submit to Congress, by resolution, on the 7th day of June. The published journal does not expressly state it, but there is no doubt, I suppose, that this resolution was in the same words, when originally submitted by Mr. Lee, as when finally passed. Having been discussed on Saturday, the 8th, and Monday, the 10th of June, this resolution was on the last-mentioned day postponed for further consideration to the first day of July; and at the same time it was voted, that a committee be appointed to prepare a Declaration to the effect of the resolution. This committee was elected by ballot, on the following day, and consisted of Thomas Jefferson, John Adams, Benjamin Franklin, Roger Sherman, and Robert R. Livingston.

It is usual, when committees are elected by ballot, that their members should be arranged in order, according to the number of votes which each has received. Mr. Jefferson, therefore, had received the highest, and Mr. Adams the next highest number of votes. The difference is said to have been but of a single vote. Mr. Jefferson and Mr. Adams, standing thus at the head of the committee, were requested by the other members to act as a subcommittee to prepare the draft; and Mr. Jefferson drew up the paper. The original draft, as brought by him from his study, and submitted to the other members of the committee, with interlineations in the handwriting of Dr. Franklin, and others in that of Mr. Adams, was in Mr. Jefferson's possession at the time of his death.[5] The merit of this paper is Mr. Jefferson's. Some changes were made in it at the suggestion of other members of the committee, and others by Congress while it was under discussion. But none of them altered the tone, the frame, the arrangement, or the general character of the instrument. As a composition, the Declaration is Mr. Jefferson's. It is the production of his mind, and the high honor of it belongs to him, clearly and absolutely.

It has sometimes been said, as if it were a derogation from the merits of this paper, that it contains nothing new; that it only states grounds of proceeding, and presses topics of argument, which had often been stated and pressed before. But it was not the object of the Declaration to produce any thing new. It was not to invent reasons for independence, but to state those which governed the Congress. For great and sufficient causes, it was proposed to declare independence; and the proper business of the paper to be drawn was to set forth those causes, and justify the authors of the measure, in any event of fortune, to the country and to posterity. The cause of American independence, moreover, was now to be presented to the world in such manner, if it might so be, as to engage its sympathy, to command its respect, to attract its admiration; and in an assembly of most able and distinguished men, THOMAS JEFFERSON had the high honor of being the selected advocate of this cause. To say that he performed his great work well, would be doing him injustice. To say that he did excellently well, admirably well, would be inadequate and halting praise. Let us rather say, that he so discharged the duty assigned him, that all Americans may well rejoice that the work of drawing the title-deed of their liberties devolved upon him.

With all its merits, there are those who have thought that there was one thing in the Declaration to be regretted; and that is, the asperity and apparent anger with which it speaks of the person of the king; the industrious ability with which it accumulates and charges upon him all the injuries which the Colonies had suffered from the mother country. Possibly some degree of injustice, now or hereafter, at home or abroad, may be done to the character of Mr. Jefferson, if this part of the Declaration be not placed in its proper light. Anger or resentment, certainly much less personal reproach and invective, could not properly find place in a composition of such high dignity, and of such lofty and permanent character.

A single reflection on the original ground of dispute between England and the Colonies is sufficient to remove any unfavorable impression in this respect.

The inhabitants of all the Colonies, while Colonies, admitted themselves bound by their allegiance to the king; but they disclaimed altogether the authority of Parliament; holding themselves, in this respect, to resemble the condition of Scotland and Ireland before the respective unions of those kingdoms with England, when they acknowledged allegiance to the same king, but had each its separate legislature. The tie, therefore, which our Revolution was to break did not subsist between us and the British Parliament, or between us and the British government in the aggregate, but directly between us and the king himself. The Colonies had never admitted themselves subject to Parliament. That was precisely the point of the original controversy. They had uniformly denied that Parliament had authority to make laws for them. There was, therefore, no subjection to Parliament to be thrown off.[6] But allegiance to the king did exist, and had been uniformly acknowledged; and down to 1775 the most solemn assurances had been given that it was not intended to break that allegiance, or to throw it off. Therefore, as the direct object and only effect of the Declaration, according to the principles on which the controversy had been maintained on our part, were to sever the tie of allegiance which bound us to the king, it was properly and necessarily founded on acts of the crown itself, as its justifying causes. Parliament is not so much as mentioned in the whole instrument. When odious and oppressive acts are referred to, it is done by charging the king with confederating with others "in pretended acts of legislation"; the object being constantly to hold the king himself directly responsible for those measures which were the grounds of separation. Even the precedent of the English Revolution was not overlooked, and in this case, as well as in that, occasion was found to say that the king had *abdicated* the government. Consistency with the principles upon which resistance began, and with all the previous state papers issued by Congress, required that the Declaration should be bottomed on the misgovernment of the king; and therefore it was properly framed with that aim and to that end. The king was known, indeed, to have acted, as in other cases, by his ministers, and with his Parliament; but as our ancestors had never admitted themselves subject either to ministers or to Parliament, there were no reasons to be given for now refusing obedience to their authority. This clear and obvious necessity of founding the Declaration on the misconduct of the king himself, gives to that instrument its personal application, and its character of direct and pointed accusation.

The Declaration having been reported to Congress by the committee, the resolution itself was taken up and debated on the first day of July, and again on the second, on which last day it was agreed to and adopted, in these words:--

"_Resolved_, That these united Colonies are, and of right ought to be, free and independent States; that they are absolved from all allegiance to the British crown, and that all political connection between them and the state of Great Britain is, and ought to be, totally dissolved."

Having thus passed the main resolution, Congress proceeded to consider the reported draught of the Declaration. It was discussed on the second, and third, and FOURTH days of the month, in committee of the whole; and on the last of those days, being reported from that committee, it received the final approbation and sanction of Congress. It was ordered, at the same time, that copies be sent to the several States, and that it be proclaimed at the head of the army. The Declaration thus published did not bear the names of the members, for as yet it had not been signed by them. It was authenticated, like other papers of the Congress, by the signatures of the President and Secretary. On the 19th of July, as appears by the secret journal, Congress "_Resolved_, That the Declaration, passed on the fourth, be fairly engrossed on parchment, with the title and style of 'THE UNANIMOUS DECLARATION OF THE THIRTEEN UNITED STATES OF AMERICA'; and that the same, when engrossed, be signed by every member of Congress." And on the SECOND DAY OF AUGUST following, "the Declaration, being engrossed and compared at the table, was signed by the members." So that it happens, fellow-citizens, that we pay these honors to their memory on the anniversary of that day (2d of August) on which these great men actually signed their names to the Declaration. The Declaration was thus made, that is, it passed and was adopted as an act of Congress, on the fourth of July; it was then signed, and certified by the President and Secretary, like other acts. The FOURTH OF JULY, therefore, is the ANNIVERSARY OF THE DECLARATION. But the signatures of the members present were made to it, being then engrossed on parchment, on the second day of August. Absent members afterwards signed, as they came in; and indeed it bears the names of some who were not chosen members of Congress until after the fourth of July. The interest belonging to the subject will be sufficient, I hope, to justify these details.[7]

The Congress of the Revolution, fellow-citizens, sat with closed doors, and no report of its debates was ever made. The discussion, therefore, which accompanied this great measure, has never been preserved, except in memory and by tradition. But it is, I believe, doing no injustice to others to say, that the general opinion was, and uniformly has been, that in debate, on the side of independence, JOHN ADAMS had no equal. The great author of the Declaration himself has expressed that opinion uniformly and strongly. "JOHN ADAMS," said he, in the hearing of him who has now the honor to address you, "JOHN ADAMS was our colossus on the floor. Not graceful, not elegant, not always fluent, in his public addresses, he yet came out with a power, both of thought and of expression, which moved us from our seats."

For the part which he was here to perform, Mr. Adams doubtless was eminently fitted. He possessed a bold spirit, which disregarded danger, and a sanguine reliance on the goodness of the cause, and the virtues of the people, which led him to overlook all obstacles. His character, too, had been formed in troubled times. He had been rocked in the early storms of the controversy, and had acquired a decision and a hardihood proportioned to the severity of the discipline which he had undergone.

He not only loved the American cause devoutly, but had studied and understood it. It was all familiar to him. He had tried his powers on the questions which it involved, often and in various ways; and had brought to their consideration whatever of argument or illustration the history of his own country, the history of England, or the stores of ancient or of legal learning, could furnish. Every grievance enumerated in the long catalogue of the Declaration had been the subject of his discussion, and the object of his remonstrance and reprobation. From 1760, the Colonies, the rights of the Colonies, the liberties of the Colonies, and the wrongs inflicted on the Colonies, had engaged his constant attention; and it has surprised those who have had the opportunity of witnessing it, with what full remembrance and with what prompt recollection he could refer, in his extreme old age, to every act of Parliament affecting the Colonies, distinguishing and stating their respective titles, sections, and provisions; and to all the Colonial memorials, remonstrances, and petitions, with whatever else belonged to the intimate and exact history of the times from that year to 1775. It was, in his own judgment, between these years that the American people came to a full understanding and thorough knowledge of their rights, and to a fixed resolution of maintaining them; and bearing himself an active part in all important transactions, the controversy with England being then in effect the business of his life, facts, dates, and particulars made an impression which was never effaced. He was prepared, therefore, by education and discipline, as well as by natural talent and natural temperament, for the part which he was now to act.

The eloquence of Mr. Adams resembled his general character, and formed, indeed, a part of it. It was bold, manly, and energetic; and such the crisis required. When public bodies are to be addressed on momentous occasions, when great interests are at stake, and strong passions excited, nothing is valuable in speech farther than as it is connected with high intellectual and moral endowments. Clearness, force, and earnestness are the qualities which produce conviction. True eloquence, indeed, does not consist in speech. It cannot be brought from far. Labor and learning may toil for it, but they will toil in vain. Words and phrases may be marshalled in every way, but they cannot compass it. It must exist in the man, in the subject, and in the occasion. Affected passion, intense expression, the pomp of declamation, all may aspire to it; they cannot reach it. It comes, if it come at all, like the outbreaking of a fountain from the earth, or the bursting forth of volcanic fires, with spontaneous, original, native force. The graces taught in the schools, the costly ornaments and studied contrivances of speech, shock and disgust men, when their own lives, and the fate of their wives, their children, and their country, hang on the decision of the hour. Then words have lost their power, rhetoric is vain, and all elaborate oratory contemptible. Even genius itself then feels rebuked and subdued, as in the presence of higher qualities. Then patriotism is eloquent; then self-devotion is eloquent. The clear conception, outrunning the deductions of logic, the high purpose, the firm resolve, the dauntless spirit, speaking on the tongue, beaming from the eye, informing every feature, and urging the whole man onward, right onward to his object,--this, this is eloquence; or rather, it is something greater and higher than all eloquence,--it is action, noble, sublime, godlike action.

In July, 1776, the controversy had passed the stage of argument. An appeal had been made to force, and opposing armies were in the field. Congress, then, was to decide whether the tie which had so long bound us to the parent state was to be severed at once, and severed for ever. All the Colonies had signified their resolution to abide by this decision, and the people looked for it with the most intense anxiety. And surely, fellow-citizens, never, never were men called to a more important political deliberation. If we contemplate it from the point where they then stood, no question could be more full of interest; if we look at it now, and judge of its importance by its effects, it appears of still greater magnitude.

Let us, then, bring before us the assembly, which was about to decide a question thus big with the fate of empire. Let us open their doors and look in upon their deliberations. Let us survey the anxious and careworn countenances, let us hear the firm-toned voices, of this band of patriots.

HANCOCK presides over the solemn sitting; and one of those not yet prepared to pronounce for absolute independence is on the floor, and is urging his reasons for dissenting from the Declaration.

"Let us pause! This step, once taken, cannot be retraced. This resolution, once passed, will cut off all hope of reconciliation. If success attend the arms of England, we shall then be no longer Colonies, with charters and with privileges; these will all be forfeited by this act; and we shall be in the condition of other conquered people, at the mercy of the conquerors. For ourselves, we may be ready to run the hazard; but are we ready to carry the country to that length? Is success so probable as to justify it? Where is the military, where the naval power, by which we are to resist the whole strength of the arm of England,--for she will exert that strength to the utmost? Can we rely on the constancy and perseverance of the people? or will they not act as the people of other countries have acted, and, wearied with a long war, submit, in the end, to a worse oppression? While we stand on our old ground, and insist on redress of grievances, we know we are right, and are not answerable for consequences. Nothing, then, can be imputed to us. But if we now change our object, carry our pretensions farther, and set up for absolute independence, we shall lose the sympathy of mankind. We shall no longer be defending what we possess, but struggling for something which we never did possess, and which we have solemnly and uniformly disclaimed all intention of pursuing, from the very outset of the troubles. Abandoning thus our old ground, of resistance only to arbitrary acts of oppression, the nations will believe the whole to have been mere pretence, and they will look on us, not as injured, but as ambitious subjects. I shudder before this responsibility. It will be on us, if, relinquishing the ground on which we have stood so long, and stood so safely, we now proclaim independence, and carry on the war for that object, while these cities burn, these pleasant fields whiten and bleach with the bones of their owners, and these streams run blood. It will be upon us, it will be upon us, if, failing to maintain this unseasonable and ill-judged declaration, a sterner despotism, maintained by military power, shall be established over our posterity, when we ourselves, given up by an exhausted, a harassed, a misled people, shall have expiated our rashness and atoned for our presumption on the scaffold."

It was for Mr. Adams to reply to arguments like these. We know his opinions, and we know his character. He would commence with his accustomed directness and earnestness.

"Sink or swim, live or die, survive or perish, I give my hand and my heart to this vote. It is true, indeed, that in the beginning we aimed not at independence. But there's a Divinity which shapes our ends. The injustice of England has driven us to arms; and, blinded to her own interest for our good, she has obstinately persisted, till independence is now within our grasp. We have but to reach forth to it, and it is ours. Why, then, should we defer the Declaration? Is any man so weak as now to hope for a reconciliation with England, which shall leave either safety to the country and its liberties, or safety to his own life and his own honor? Are not you, Sir, who sit in that chair,--is not he, our venerable colleague near you,--are you not both already the proscribed and predestined objects of punishment and of vengeance? Cut off from all hope of royal clemency, what are you, what can you be, while the power of England remains, but outlaws? If we postpone independence, do we mean to carry on, or to give up, the war? Do we mean to submit to the measures of Parliament, Boston Port Bill and all? Do we mean to submit, and consent that we ourselves shall be ground to powder, and our country and its rights trodden down in the dust? I know we do not mean to submit. We never shall submit. Do we intend to violate that most solemn obligation ever entered into by men, that plighting, before God, of our sacred honor to Washington, when, putting him forth to incur the dangers of war, as well as the political hazards of the times, we promised to adhere to him, in every extremity, with our fortunes and our lives? I know there is not a man here, who would not rather see a general conflagration sweep over the land, or an earthquake sink it, than one jot or tittle of that plighted faith fall to the ground. For myself, having, twelve months ago, in this place, moved you, that George Washington be appointed commander of the forces raised, or to be raised, for defence of American liberty,[8] may my right hand forget her cunning, and my tongue cleave to the roof of my mouth, if I hesitate or waver in the support I give him.

"The war, then, must go on. We must fight it through. And if the war must go on, why put off longer the Declaration of Independence? That measure will strengthen us. It will give us character abroad. The nations will then treat with us, which they never can do while we acknowledge ourselves subjects, in arms against our sovereign. Nay, I maintain that England herself will sooner treat for peace with us on the footing of independence, than consent, by repealing her acts, to acknowledge that her whole conduct towards us has been a course of injustice and oppression. Her pride will be less wounded by submitting to that course of things which now predestinates our independence, than by yielding the points in controversy to her rebellious subjects. The former she would regard as the result of fortune; the latter she would feel as her own deep disgrace. Why, then, why then, Sir, do we not as soon as possible change this from a civil to a national war? And since we must fight it through, why not put ourselves in a state to enjoy all the benefits of victory, if we gain the victory?

"If we fail, it can be no worse for us. But we shall not fail. The cause will raise up armies; the cause will create navies. The people, the people, if we are true to them, will carry us, and will carry themselves, gloriously, through this struggle. I care not how fickle other people have been found. I know the people of these Colonies, and I know that resistance to British aggression is deep and settled in their hearts and cannot be eradicated. Every Colony, indeed, has expressed its willingness to follow, if we but take the lead. Sir, the Declaration will inspire the people with increased courage. Instead of a long and bloody war for the restoration of privileges, for redress of grievances, for chartered immunities, held under a British king, set before them the glorious object of entire independeuce, and it will breathe into them anew the breath of life. Read this Declaration at the head of the army; every sword will be drawn from its scabbard, and the solemn vow uttered, to maintain it, or to perish on the bed of honor. Publish it from the pulpit; religion will approve it, and the love of religious liberty will cling round it, resolved to stand with it, or fall with it. Send it to the public halls; proclaim it there; let them hear it who heard the first roar of the enemy's cannon; let them see it who saw their brothers and their sons fall on the field of Bunker Hill, and in the streets of Lexington and Concord, and the very walls will cry out in its support.

"Sir, I know the uncertainty of human affairs, but I see, I see clearly, through this day's business. You and

I, indeed, may rue it. We may not live to the time when this Declaration shall be made good. We may die; die colonists; die slaves; die, it may be, ignominiously and on the scaffold. Be it so. Be it so. If it be the pleasure of Heaven that my country shall require the poor offering of my life, the victim shall be ready, at the appointed hour of sacrifice, come when that hour may. But while I do live, let me have a country, or at least the hope of a country, and that a free country.

"But whatever may be our fate, be assured, be assured that this Declaration will stand. It may cost treasure, and it may cost blood; but it will stand, and it will richly compensate for both. Through the thick gloom of the present, I see the brightness of the future, as the sun in heaven. We shall make this a glorious, an immortal day. When we are in our graves, our children will honor it. They will celebrate it with thanksgiving, with festivity, with bonfires, and illuminations. On its annual return they will shed tears, copious, gushing tears, not of subjection and slavery, not of agony and distress, but of exultation, of gratitude, and of joy. Sir, before God, I believe the hour is come. My judgment approves this measure, and my whole heart is in it. All that I have, and all that I am, and all that I hope, in this life, I am now ready here to stake upon it; and I leave off as I begun, that live or die, survive or perish, I am for the Declaration. It is my living sentiment, and by the blessing of God it shall be my dying sentiment, Independence _now_, and INDEPENDENCE FOR EVER."[9]

And so that day shall be honored, illustrious prophet and patriot! so that day shall be honored, and as often as it returns, thy renown shall come along with it, and the glory of thy life, like the day of thy death, shall not fail from the remembrance of men.

It would be unjust, fellow-citizens, on this occasion, while we express our veneration for him who is the immediate subject of these remarks, were we to omit a most respectful, affectionate, and grateful mention of those other great men, his colleagues, who stood with him, and with the same spirit, the same devotion, took part in the interesting transaction. HANCOCK, the proscribed HANCOCK, exiled from his home by a military governor, cut off by proclamation from the mercy of the crown,--Heaven reserved for him the distinguished honor of putting this great question to the vote, and of writing his own name first, and most conspicuously, on that parchment which spoke defiance to the power of the crown of England. There, too, is the name of that other proscribed patriot, SAMUEL ADAMS, a man who hungered and thirsted for the independence of his country, who thought the Declaration halted and lingered, being himself not only ready, but eager, for it, long before it was proposed; a man of the deepest sagacity, the clearest foresight, and the profoundest judgment in men. And there is GERRY, himself among the earliest and the foremost of the patriots, found, when the battle of Lexington summoned them to common counsels, by the side of WARREN; a man who lived to serve his country at home and abroad, and to die in the second place in the government. There, too, is the inflexible, the upright, the Spartan character, ROBERT TREAT PAINE. He also lived to serve his country through the struggle, and then withdrew from her councils, only that he might give his labors and his life to his native State, in another relation. These names, fellow-citizens, are the treasures of the Commonwealth; and they are treasures which grow brighter by time.

It is now necessary to resume the narrative, and to finish with great brevity the notice of the lives of those whose virtues and services we have met to commemorate.

Mr. Adams remained in Congress from its first meeting till November, 1777, when he was appointed Minister to France. He proceeded on that service in the February following, embarking in the frigate Boston, from the shore of his native town, at the foot of Mount Wollaston. The year following, he was appointed commissioner to treat of peace with England. Returning to the United States, he was a delegate from Braintree in the Convention for framing the Constitution of this Commonwealth, in 1780.[10] At the latter end of the same year, he again went abroad in the diplomatic service of the country, and was employed at various courts, and occupied with various negotiations, until 1788. The particulars of these interesting and important services this occasion does not allow time to relate. In 1782 he concluded our first treaty with Holland. His negotiations with that republic, his efforts to persuade the States-General to recognize our independence, his incessant and indefatigable exertions to represent the American cause favorably on the Continent, and to counteract the designs of its enemies, open and secret, and his successful undertaking to obtain loans on the credit of a nation yet new and unknown, are among his most arduous, most useful, most honorable services. It was his fortune to bear a part in the negotiation for peace with England, and in something more than six years from the Declaration which he had so strenuously supported, he had the satisfaction of seeing the minister plenipotentiary of the crown subscribe his name to the instrument which declared that his "Britannic Majesty acknowledged the United States to be free, sovereign, and independent." In these important transactions, Mr. Adams's conduct received the marked approbation of Congress and of the country.

While abroad, in 1787, he published his "Defence of the American Constitutions"; a work of merit and ability, though composed with haste, on the spur of a particular occasion, in the midst of other occupations, and under circumstances not admitting of careful revision. The immediate object of the work was to counteract the weight of opinions advanced by several popular European writers of that day, M. Turgot, the Abbé de Mably, and Dr. Price, at a time when the people of the United States were employed in forming and revising their systems of government.

Returning to the United States in 1788, he found the new government about going into operation, and was himself elected the first Vice-President, a situation which he filled with reputation for eight years, at the expiration of which he was raised to the Presidential chair, as immediate successor to the immortal Washington. In this high station he was succeeded by Mr. Jefferson, after a memorable controversy between their respective friends, in 1801; and from that period his manner of life has been known to all who hear me. He has lived, for five-and-twenty years, with every enjoyment that could render old age happy. Not inattentive to the occurrences of the times, political cares have yet not materially, or for any long time, disturbed his repose. In 1820 he acted as Elector of President and Vice-President, and in the same year we saw him, then at the age of eighty-five, a member of the Convention of this Commonwealth called to revise the Constitution. Forty years before, he had been one of those who formed that Constitution; and he had now the pleasure of witnessing that there was little which the people desired to change.[11] Possessing all his faculties to the end of his long life, with an unabated love of reading and contemplation, in the centre of interesting circles of friendship and affection, he was blessed in his retirement with whatever of repose and felicity the condition of man allows. He had, also, other enjoyments. He saw around him that prosperity and general happiness which had been the object of his public cares and labors. No man ever beheld more clearly, and for a longer time, the great and beneficial effects of the services rendered by himself to his country. That liberty which he so early defended, that independence of which he was so able an advocate and supporter, he saw, we trust, firmly and securely established. The population of the country thickened around him faster, and extended wider, than his own sanguine predictions had anticipated; and the wealth, respectability, and power of the nation sprang up to a magnitude which it is quite impossible he could have expected to witness in his day. He lived also to behold those principles of civil freedom which had been developed, established, and practically applied in America, attract attention, command respect, and awaken imitation, in other regions of the globe; and well might, and well did, he exclaim, "Where will the consequences of the American Revolution end?"

If any thing yet remain to fill this cup of happiness, let it be added, that he lived to see a great and intelligent people bestow the highest honor in their gift where he had bestowed his own kindest parental affections and lodged his fondest hopes. Thus honored in life, thus happy at death, he saw the JUBILEE, and he died; and with the last prayers which trembled on his lips was the fervent supplication for his country, "Independence for ever!"[12]

Mr. Jefferson, having been occupied in the years 1778 and 1779 in the important service of revising the laws of Virginia, was elected Governor of that State, as successor to Patrick Henry, and held the situation when the State was invaded by the British arms. In 1781 he published his Notes on Virginia, a work which attracted attention in Europe as well as America, dispelled many misconceptions respecting this continent, and gave its author a place among men distinguished for science. In November, 1783, he again took his seat in the Continental Congress, but in the May following was appointed Minister Plenipotentiary, to act abroad, in the negotiation of commercial treaties, with Dr. Franklin and Mr. Adams. He proceeded to France, in execution of this mission, embarking at Boston; and that was the only occasion on which he ever visited this place. In 1785 he was appointed Minister to France, the duties of which situation he continued to perform until October, 1789, when he obtained leave to retire, just on the eve of that tremendous revolution which has so much agitated the world in our times. Mr. Jefferson's discharge of his diplomatic duties was marked by great ability, diligence, and patriotism; and while he resided at Paris, in one of the most interesting periods, his character for intelligence, his love of knowledge and of the society of learned men, distinguished him in the highest circles of the French capital. No court in Europe had at that time in Paris a representative commanding or enjoying higher regard, for political knowledge or for general attainments, than the minister of this then infant republic. Immediately on his return to his native country, at the organization of the government under the present Constitution, his talents and experience recommended him to President Washington for the first office in his gift. He was placed at the head of the Department of State. In this situation, also, he manifested conspicuous ability. His correspondence with the ministers of other powers residing here, and his instructions to our own diplomatic agents abroad, are among our ablest state papers. A thorough knowledge of the laws and usages of nations, perfect acquaintance with the immediate subject before him, great felicity, and still greater facility, in writing, show themselves in whatever effort his official situation called on him to make. It is believed by competent judges, that the diplomatic intercourse of the government of the United States, from the first meeting of the Continental Congress in 1774 to the present time, taken together, would not suffer, in respect to the talent with which it has been conducted, by comparison with any thing which other and older governments can produce; and to the attainment of this respectability and distinction Mr. Jefferson has contributed his full part.

On the retirement of General Washington from the Presidency, and the election of Mr. Adams to that office in 1797, he was chosen Vice-President. While presiding in this capacity over the deliberations of the Senate, he compiled and published a Manual of Parliamentary Practice, a work of more labor and more merit than is indicated by its size. It is now received as the general standard by which proceedings are regulated, not only in both Houses of Congress, but in most of the other legislative bodies in the country. In 1801 he was elected President, in opposition to Mr. Adams, and re-elected in 1805, by a vote approaching towards unanimity.

From the time of his final retirement from public life, in 1809, Mr. Jefferson lived as became a wise man. Surrounded by affectionate friends, his ardor in the pursuit of knowledge undiminished, with uncommon health and unbroken spirits, he was able to enjoy largely the rational pleasures of life, and to partake in that public prosperity which he had so much contributed to produce. His kindness and hospitality, the charm of his conversation, the ease of his manners, the extent of his acquirements, and, especially, the full store of Revolutionary incidents which he had treasured in his memory, and which he knew when and how to dispense, rendered his abode in a high degree attractive to his admiring countrymen, while his high public and scientific character drew towards him every intelligent and educated traveller from abroad. Both Mr. Adams and Mr. Jefferson had the pleasure of knowing that the respect which they so largely received was not paid to their official stations. They were not men made great by office; but great men, on whom the country for its own benefit had conferred office. There was that in them which office did not give, and which the relinquishment of office did not, and could not, take away. In their retirement, in the midst of their fellow-citizens, themselves private citizens, they enjoyed as high regard and esteem as when filling the most important places of public trust.

There remained to Mr. Jefferson yet one other work of patriotism and beneficence, the establishment of a university in his native State. To this object he devoted years of incessant and anxious attention, and by the enlightened liberality of the Legislature of Virginia, and the co-operation of other able and zealous friends, he lived to see it accomplished. May all success attend this infant seminary; and may those who enjoy its advantages, as often as their eyes shall rest on the neighboring height, recollect what they owe to their disinterested and indefatigable benefactor; and may letters honor him who thus labored in the cause of letters![13]

Thus useful, and thus respected, passed the old age of Thomas Jefferson. But time was on its ever-ceaseless wing, and was now bringing the last hour of this illustrious man. He saw its approach with undisturbed serenity. He counted the moments as they passed, and beheld that his last sands were falling. That day, too, was at hand which he had helped to make immortal. One wish, one hope, if it were not presumptuous, beat in his fainting breast. Could it be so, might it please God, he would desire once more to see the sun, once more to look abroad on the scene around him, on the great day of liberty. Heaven, in its mercy, fulfilled that prayer. He saw that sun, he enjoyed its sacred light, he thanked God for this mercy, and bowed his aged head to the grave. "Felix, non vitae tantum claritate, sed etiam opportunitate mortis." The last public labor of Mr. Jefferson naturally suggests the expression of the high praise which is due, both to him and to Mr. Adams, for their uniform and zealous attachment to learning, and to the cause of general knowledge. Of the advantages of learning, indeed, and of literary accomplishments, their own characters were striking recommendations and illustrations. They were scholars, ripe and good scholars; widely acquainted with ancient, as well as modern literature, and not altogether uninstructed in the deeper sciences. Their acquirements, doubtless, were different, and so were the particular objects of their literary pursuits; as their tastes and characters, in these respects, differed like those of other men. Being, also, men of busy lives, with great objects requiring action constantly before them, their attainments in letters did not become showy or obtrusive. Yet I would hazard the opinion, that, if we could now ascertain all the causes which gave them eminence and distinction in the midst of the great men with whom they acted, we should find not among the least their early acquisitions in literature, the resources which it furnished, the promptitude and facility which it communicated, and the wide field it opened for analogy and illustration; giving them thus, on every subject, a larger view and a broader range, as well for discussion as for the government of their own conduct.

Literature sometimes disgusts, and pretension to it much oftener disgusts, by appearing to hang loosely on the character, like something foreign or extraneous, not a part, but an ill-adjusted appendage; or by seeming to overload and weigh it down by its unsightly bulk, like the productions of bad taste in architecture, where there is massy and cumbrous ornament without strength or solidity of column. This has exposed learning, and especially classical learning, to reproach. Men have seen that it might exist without mental superiority, without vigor, without good taste, and without utility. But in such cases classical learning has only not inspired natural talent; or, at most, it has but made original feebleness of intellect, and natural bluntness of perception, something more conspicuous. The question, after all, if it be a question, is, whether literature, ancient as well as modern, does not assist a good understanding, improve natural good taste, add polished armor to native strength, and render its possessor, not only more capable of deriving private happiness from contemplation and reflection, but more accomplished also for action in the affairs of life, and especially for public action. Those whose memories we now honor were learned men; but their learning was kept in its proper place, and made subservient to the uses and objects of life. They were scholars, not common nor superficial; but their scholarship was so in keeping with their character, so blended and inwrought, that careless observers, or bad judges, not seeing an ostentatious display of it, might infer that it did not exist; forgetting, or not knowing, that classical learning in men who act in conspicuous public stations, perform duties which exercise the faculty of writing, or address popular, deliberative, or judicial bodies, is often felt where it is little seen, and sometimes felt more effectually because it is not seen at all.

But the cause of knowledge, in a more enlarged sense, the cause of general knowledge and of popular education, had no warmer friends, nor more powerful advocates, than Mr. Adams and Mr. Jefferson. On this foundation they knew the whole republican system rested; and this great and all-important truth they strove to impress, by all the means in their power. In the early publication already referred to, Mr. Adams expresses the strong and just sentiment, that the education of the poor is more important, even to the rich themselves, than all their own riches. On this great truth, indeed, is founded that unrivalled, that invaluable political and moral institution, our own blessing and the glory of our fathers, the New England system of free schools.

As the promotion of knowledge had been the object of their regard through life, so these great men made it the subject of their testamentary bounty. Mr. Jefferson is understood to have bequeathed his library to the University of Virginia, and that of Mr. Adams is bestowed on the inhabitants of Quincy.

Mr. Adams and Mr. Jefferson, fellow-citizens, were successively Presidents of the United States. The comparative merits of their respective administrations for a long time agitated and divided public opinion. They were rivals, each supported by numerous and powerful portions of the people, for the highest office. This contest, partly the cause and partly the consequence of the long existence of two great political parties in the country, is now part of the history of our government. We may naturally regret that any thing should have occurred to create difference and discord between those who had acted harmoniously and efficiently in the great concerns of the Revolution. But this is not the time, nor this the occasion, for entering into the grounds of that difference, or for attempting to discuss the merits of the questions which it involves. As practical questions, they were canvassed when the measures which they regarded were acted on and adopted; and as belonging to history, the time has not come for their consideration.

It is, perhaps, not wonderful, that, when the Constitution of the United States first went into operation, different opinions should be entertained as to the extent of the powers conferred by it. Here was a natural source of diversity of sentiment. It is still less wonderful, that that event, nearly contemporary with our government under the present Constitution, which so entirely shocked all Europe, and disturbed our relations with her leading powers, should be thought, by different men, to have different bearings on our own prosperity; and that the early measures adopted by the government of the United States, in consequence of this new state of things, should be seen in opposite lights. It is for the future historian, when what now remains of prejudice and misconception shall have passed away, to state these different opinions, and pronounce impartial judgment. In the mean time, all good men rejoice, and well may rejoice, that the sharpest differences sprung out of measures which, whether right or wrong, have ceased with the exigencies that gave them birth, and have left no permanent effect, either on the Constitution or on the general prosperity of the country. This remark, I am aware, may be supposed to have its exception in one measure, the alteration of the Constitution as to the mode of choosing President; but it is true in its general application. Thus the course of policy pursued towards France in 1798, on the one hand, and the measures of commercial restriction commenced in 1807, on the other, both subjects of warm and severe opposition, have passed away and left nothing behind them. They were temporary, and, whether wise or unwise, their consequences were limited to their respective occasions. It is equally clear, at the same time, and it is equally gratifying, that those measures of both administrations which were of durable importance, and which drew after them momentous and long remaining consequences, have received general approbation. Such was the organization, or rather the creation, of the navy, in the administration of Mr. Adams; such the acquisition of Louisiana in that of Mr. Jefferson. The country, it may safely be added, is not likely to be willing either to approve, or to reprobate, indiscriminately, and in the aggregate, all the measures of either, or of any, administration. The dictate of reason and of justice is, that, holding each one his own sentiments on the points of difference, we imitate the great men themselves in the forbearance and moderation which they have cherished, and in the mutual respect and kindness which they have been so much inclined to feel and to reciprocate.

No men, fellow-citizens, ever served their country with more entire exemption from every imputation of selfish and mercenary motives, than those to whose memory we are paying these proofs of respect. A suspicion of any disposition to enrich themselves or to profit by their public employments, never rested on either. No sordid motive approached them. The inheritance which they have left to their children is of their character and their fame.

Fellow-citizens, I will detain you no longer by this faint and feeble tribute to the memory of the illustrious dead. Even in other hands, adequate justice could not be done to them, within the limits of this occasion. Their highest, their best praise, is your deep conviction of their merits, your affectionate gratitude for their labors and their services. It is not my voice, it is this cessation of ordinary pursuits, this arresting of all attention, these solemn ceremonies, and this crowded house, which speak their eulogy. Their fame, indeed, is safe. That is now treasured up beyond the reach of accident. Although no sculptured marble should rise to their memory, nor engraved stone bear record of their deeds, yet will their remembrance be as lasting as the land they honored. Marble columns may, indeed, moulder into dust, time may erase all impress from the crumbling stone, but their fame remains; for with AMERICAN LIBERTY it rose, and with AMERICAN LIBERTY ONLY can it perish. It was the last swelling peal of yonder choir, "THEIR BODIES ARE BURIED IN PEACE, BUT THEIR NAME LIVETH EVERMORE." I catch that solemn song, I echo that lofty strain of funeral triumph, "THEIR NAME LIVETH EVERMORE."

Of the illustrious signers of the Declaration of Independence there now remains only CHARLES CARROLL. He seems an aged oak, standing alone on the plain, which time has spared a little longer after all its contemporaries have been levelled with the dust. Venerable object! we delight to gather round its trunk, while yet it stands, and to dwell beneath its shadow. Sole survivor of an assembly of as great men as the world has witnessed, in a transaction one of the most important that history records, what thoughts, what interesting reflections, must fill his elevated and devout soul! If he dwell on the past, how touching its recollections; if he survey the present, how happy, how joyous, how full of the fruition of that hope which his ardent patriotism indulged; if he glance at the future, how does the prospect of his country's advancement almost bewilder his weakened conception! Fortunate, distinguished patriot! Interesting relic of the past! Let him know that, while we honor the dead, we do not forget the living; and that there is not a heart here which does not fervently pray that Heaven may keep him yet back from the society of his companions.

And now, fellow-citizens, let us not retire from this occasion without a deep and solemn conviction of the duties which have devolved upon us. This lovely land, this glorious liberty, these benign institutions, the dear purchase of our fathers, are ours; ours to enjoy, ours to preserve, ours to transmit. Generations past and generations to come hold us responsible for this sacred trust. Our fathers, from behind, admonish us, with their anxious paternal voices; posterity calls out to us, from the bosom of the future; the world turns hither its solicitous eyes; all, all conjure us to act wisely, and faithfully, in the relation which we sustain.

We can never, indeed, pay the debt which is upon us; but by virtue, by morality, by religion, by the cultivation of every good principle and every good habit, we may hope to enjoy the blessing, through our day, and to leave it unimpaired to our children. Let us feel deeply how much of what we are and of what we possess we owe to this liberty, and to these institutions of government. Nature has, indeed, given us a soil which yields bounteously to the hand of industry, the mighty and fruitful ocean is before us, and the skies over our heads shed health and vigor. But what are lands, and seas, and skies, to civilized man, without society, without knowledge, without morals, without religious culture; and how can these be enjoyed, in all their extent and all their excellence, but under the protection of wise institutions and a free government? Fellow-citizens, there is not one of us, there is not one of us here present, who does not, at this moment, and at every moment, experience, in his own condition, and in the condition of those most near and dear to him, the influence and the benefits of this liberty and these institutions. Let us then acknowledge the blessing, let us feel it deeply and powerfully, let us cherish a strong affection for it, and resolve to maintain and perpetuate it. The blood of our fathers, let it not have been shed in vain; the great hope of posterity, let it not be blasted.

The striking attitude, too, in which we stand to the world around us, a topic to which, I fear, I advert too often, and dwell on too long, cannot be altogether omitted here. Neither individuals nor nations can perform their part well, until they understand and feel its importance, and comprehend and justly appreciate all the duties belonging to it. It is not to inflate national vanity, nor to swell a light and empty feeling of self-importance, but it is that we may judge justly of our situation, and of our own duties, that I earnestly urge upon you this consideration of our position and our character among the nations of the earth. It cannot be denied, but by those who would dispute against the sun, that with America, and in America, a new era commences in human affairs. This era is distinguished by free representative governments, by entire religious liberty, by improved systems of national intercourse, by a newly awakened and an unconquerable spirit of free inquiry, and by a diffusion of knowledge through the community, such as has been before altogether unknown and unheard of. America, America, our country, fellow-citizens, our own dear and native land, is inseparably connected, fast bound up, in fortune and by fate, with these great interests. If they fall, we fall with them; if they stand, it will be because we have maintained them. Let us contemplate, then, this connection, which binds the prosperity of others to our own; and let us manfully discharge all the duties which it imposes. If we cherish the virtues and the principles of our fathers, Heaven will assist us to carry on the work of human liberty and human happiness. Auspicious omens cheer us. Great examples are before us. Our own firmament now shines brightly upon our path. WASHINGTON is in the clear, upper sky. These other stars have now joined the American constellation; they circle round their centre, and the heavens beam with new light. Beneath this illumination let us walk the course of life, and at its close devoutly commend our beloved country, the common parent of us all, to the Divine Benignity.

NOTE. Page 170. The question has often been asked, whether the anonymous speech against the Declaration of Independence, and the speech in support of it ascribed to John Adams in the preceding Discourse, are a portion of the debates which actually took place in 1776 in the Continental Congress. Not only has this inquiry been propounded in the public papers, but several letters on the subject have been addressed to Mr. Webster and his friends. For this reason, it may be proper to state, that those speeches were composed by Mr. Webster, after the manner of the ancient historians, as embodying in an impressive form the arguments relied upon by the friends and opponents of the measure, respectively. They of course represent the speeches that were actually made on both sides, but no report of the debates of this period has been preserved, and the orator on the present occasion had no aid in framing these addresses, but what was furnished by general tradition and the known line of argument pursued by the speakers and writers of that day for and against the measure of Independence. The first sentence of the speech ascribed to Mr. Adams was of course suggested by the parting scene with Jonathan Sewall, as described by Mr. Adams himself, in the Preface to the Letters of Novanglus and Massachusettensis.

So much interest has been taken in this subject, that it has been thought proper, by way of settling the question in the most authentic manner, to give publicity to the following answer, written by Mr. Webster to one of the letters of inquiry above alluded to.

"Washington, 22 January, 1846

"Dear Sir:--

"I have the honor to acknowledge the receipt of your letter of the 18th instant. Its contents hardly surprise me, as I have received very many similar communications.

"Your inquiry is easily answered. The Congress of the Revolution sat with closed doors. Its proceedings were made known to the public from time to time, by printing its journal; but the debates were not published. So far as I know, there is not existing, in print or manuscript, the speech, or any part or fragment of the speech, delivered by Mr. Adams on the question of the Declaration of Independence. We only know, from the testimony of his auditors, that he spoke with remarkable ability and characteristic earnestness.

"The day after the Declaration was made, Mr. Adams, in writing to a friend,[14] declared the event to be one that 'ought to be commemorated, as the day of deliverance, by solemn acts of devotion to God Almighty. It ought to be solemnized with pomp and parade, with shows, games, sports, guns, bells, bonfires, and illuminations, from one end of this continent to the other, from this time forward, for evermore.'

"And on the day of his death, hearing the noise of bells and cannon, he asked the occasion. On being reminded that it was 'Independent day,' he replied, 'Independence for ever!' These expressions were introduced into the speech *supposed* to have been made by him. For the rest I must be answerable. The speech was written by me, in my house in Boston, the day before the delivery of the Discourse in Faneuil Hall; a poor substitute, I am sure it would appear to be, if we could now see the speech actually made by Mr. Adams on that transcendently important occasion.

"I am, respectfully,

"Your obedient servant,

"DANIEL WEBSTER."

[Footnote 1: Hon. Josiah Quincy.][Footnote 2: Nearly all that was known of this celebrated argument, at the time the present Discourse was delivered, was derived from the recollections of John Adams, as preserved in Minot's History of Massachusetts, Vol. II. p. 91. See Life and Works of John Adams, Vol. II. p. 124, published in the course of the past year (1850), in the Appendix to which, p. 521, will be found a paper hitherto unpublished, containing notes of the argument of Otis, "which seem to be the foundation of the sketch published by Minot." Tudor's Life of James Otis, p. 61.][Footnote 3: See Life and Works of John Adams, Vol. II. p. 150, Vol. III. p. 447, and North American Review, Vol. LXXI. p. 430.][Footnote 4: Cicero de Officiis, Lib. I. § 43.]

[Footnote 5: A fac-simile of this ever-memorable state paper, as drafted by Mr. Jefferson, with the interlineations alluded to in the text, is contained in Mr. Jefferson's Writings, Vol. I. p. 146. See, also, in reference to the history of the Declaration, the Life and Works of John Adams, Vol. II. p. 512 _et seq._][Footnote 6: This question, of the power of Parliament over the Colonies, was discussed, with singular ability, by Governor Hutchinson on the one side, and the House of Representatives of Massachusetts on the other, in 1773. The argument of the House is in the form of an answer to the Governor's Message, and was reported by Mr. Samuel Adams, Mr. Hancock, Mr. Hawley, Mr. Bowers, Mr. Hobson, Mr. Foster, Mr. Phillips, and Mr. Thayer. As the power of the Parliament had been acknowledged, so far at least as to affect us by laws of trade, it was not easy to settle the line of distinction. It was thought, however, to be very clear, that the charters of the Colonies had exempted them from the general legislation of the British Parliament. See Massachusetts State Papers, p. 351. The important assistance rendered by John Adams in the preparation of the answer of the House to the Message of the Governor may be learned from the Life and Works of John Adams, Vol. II. p. 311 _et seq._][Footnote 7: The official copy of the Declaration, as engrossed and signed by the members of Congress, is framed and preserved in the Hall over the Patent-Office at Washington.][Footnote 8: See Life and Works of John Adams, Vol. II. p. 417 _et seq._][Footnote 9: On the authorship of this speech, see Note at the end of the Discourse.][Footnote 10: In this Convention he served as chairman of the committee for preparing the draft of a Constitution.][Footnote 11: Upon the organization of this body, 15th November, 1820, John Adams was elected its President; an office which the infirmities of age compelled him to decline. For the interesting proceedings of the Convention on this occasion, the address of Chief Justice Parker, and the reply of Mr. Adams, see Journal of Debates and Proceedings in the Convention of Delegates chosen to revise the Constitution of Massachusetts, p. 8 _et seq._][Footnote 12: For an account of Mr. Webster's last interview with Mr. Adams, see March's Reminiscences of Congress, p. 62.][Footnote 13: Mr. Jefferson himself considered his services in establishing the University of Virginia as among the most important rendered by him to the country. In Mr. Wirt's Eulogy, it is stated that a private memorandum was found among his papers, containing the following inscription to be placed on his monument.--"Here was buried Thomas Jefferson, Author of the Declaration of Independence, of the Statutes of Virginia for Religious Freedom, and Father of the University of Virginia." Eulogies on Adams and Jefferson, p. 426.][Footnote 14: See Letters of John Adams to his Wife, Vol. I. p. 128, note.]

THE CASE OF OGDEN AND SAUNDERS.
AN ARGUMENT MADE IN THE CASE OF OGDEN AND SAUNDERS, IN THE SUPREME COURT OF THE UNITED STATES, JANUARY TERM, 1827.

[This was an action of _assumpsit_, brought originally in the Circuit Court of Louisiana, by Saunders, a citizen of Kentucky, against Ogden, a citizen of Louisiana. The plaintiff below declared upon certain bills of exchange, drawn on the 30th of September, 1806, by one Jordan, at Lexington, in the State of Kentucky, upon the defendant below, Ogden, in the city of New York, (the defendant then being a citizen and resident of the State of New York,) accepted by him at the city of New York, and protested for non-payment. The defendant below pleaded several pleas, among which was a certificate of discharge under the act of the legislature of the State of New York, of April 3d, 1801, for the relief of insolvent debtors, commonly called the Three-Fourths Act. The jury found the facts in the form of a special verdict, on which the court rendered a judgment for the plaintiff below, and the cause was brought by writ of error before this court. The question which arose under this plea, as to the validity of the law of New York as being repugnant to the Constitution of the United States, was argued at February term, 1824, by Mr. Clay, Mr. D.B. Ogden, and Mr. Haines, for the plaintiff in error, and by Mr. Webster and Mr. Wheaton, for the defendant in error, and the cause was continued for advisement until the present term. It was again argued at the present term, by Mr. Webster and Mr. Wheaton, against the validity, and by the Attorney-General, Mr. E. Livingston, Mr. D.B. Ogden, Mr. Jones, and Mr. Sampson, for the validity. Mr. Wheaton opened the argument for the defendant in error; he was followed by the counsel for the plaintiff in error; and Mr. Webster replied as follows.]

The question arising in this case is not more important, nor so important even, in its bearing on individual cases of private right, as in its character of a public political question. The Constitution was intended to accomplish a great political object. Its design was not so much to prevent injustice or injury in one case, or in successive single cases, as it was to make general salutary provisions, which, in their operation, should give security to all contracts, stability to credit, uniformity among all the States in those things which materially concern the foreign commerce of the country, and their own credit, trade, and intercourse with each other. The real question, is, therefore, a much broader one than has been argued. It is this: Whether the Constitution has not, for general political purposes, ordained that bankrupt laws should be established only by national authority? We contend that such was the intention of the Constitution; an intention, as we think, plainly manifested in several of its provisions.

The act of New York, under which this question arises, provides that a debtor may be discharged from all his debts, upon assigning his property to trustees for the use of his creditors. When applied to the discharge of debts contracted before the date of the law, this court has decided that the act is invalid.[1] The act itself makes no distinction between past and future debts, but provides for the discharge of both in the same manner. In the case, then, of a debt already existing, it is admitted that the act does impair the obligation of contracts. We wish the full extent of this decision to be well considered. It is not merely that the legislature of the State cannot interfere by law, in the particular case of A or B, to injure or impair rights which have become vested under contracts; but it is, that they have no power by general law to regulate the manner in which all debtors may be discharged from subsisting contracts; in other wrords, they cannot pass general bankrupt laws to be applied *in presenti*. Now, it is not contended that such laws are unjust, and ought not to be passed by any legislature. It is not said that they are unwise or impolitic. On the contrary, we know the general practice to be, that, when bankrupt laws are established, they make no distinction between present and future debts. While all agree that special acts, made for individual cases, are unjust, all admit that a general law, made for all cases, may be both just and politic. The question, then, which meets us on the threshold is this: If the Constitution meant to leave the States the power of establishing systems of bankruptcy to act upon future debts, what great or important object of a political nature is answered by denying the power of making such systems applicable to existing debts?

The argument used in _Sturges v. Crowninshield_ was, at least, a plausible and consistent argument. It maintained that the prohibition of the Constitution was levelled only against interferences in individual cases, and did not apply to general laws, whether those laws were retrospective or prospective in their operation. But the court rejected that conclusion. It decided that the Constitution was intended to apply to general laws or systems of bankruptcy; that an act providing that all debtors might be discharged from all creditors, upon certain conditions, was of no more validity than an act providing that a particular debtor, A, should be discharged on the same conditions from his particular creditor, B.

It being thus decided that general laws are within the prohibition of the Constitution, it is for the plaintiff in error now to show on what ground, consistent with the general objects of the Constitution, he can establish a distinction which can give effect to those general laws in their application to future debts, while it denies them effect in their application to subsisting debts. The words are, that "no State shall pass any law impairing the obligation of contracts." The general operation of all such laws is to impair that obligation; that is, to discharge the obligation without fulfilling it. This is admitted; and the only ground taken for the distinction to stand on is, that, when the law was in existence at the time of the making of the contract, the parties must be supposed to have reference to it, or, as it is usually expressed, the law is made a part of the contract. Before considering what foundation there is for this argument, it may be well to inquire what is that obligation of contracts of which the Constitution speaks, and whence is it derived.

The definition given by the court in _Sturges v. Crowninshield_ is sufficient for our present purpose. "A contract," say the court, "is an agreement to do some particular thing; the law binds the party to perform this agreement, and this is the obligation of the contract."

It is indeed probable that the Constitution used the words in a somewhat more popular sense. We speak, for example, familiarly of a usurious contract, and yet we say, speaking technically, that a usurious agreement is no contract.

By the obligation of a contract, we should understand the Constitution to mean, the duty of performing a legal agreement. If the contract be lawful, the party is bound to perform it. But bound by what? What is it that binds him? And this leads us to what we regard as a principal fallacy in the argument on the other side. That argument supposes, and insists, that the whole obligation of a contract has its origin in the municipal law. This position we controvert. We do not say that it is that obligation which springs from conscience merely; but we deny that it is only such as springs from the particular law of the place where the contract is made. It must be a lawful contract, doubtless; that is, permitted and allowed; because society has a right to prohibit all such contracts, as well as all such actions, as it deems to be mischievous or injurious. But if the contract be such as the law of society tolerates, in other words, if it be lawful, then we say, the duty of performing it springs from universal law. And this is the concurrent sense of all the writers of authority. The duty of performing promises is thus shown to rest on universal law; and if, departing from this well-established principle, we now follow the teachers who instruct us that the obligation of a contract has its origin in the law of a particular State, and is in all cases what that law makes it, and no more, and no less, we shall probably find ourselves involved in inextricable difficulties. A man promises, for a valuable consideration, to pay money in New York. Is the obligation of that contract created by the laws of that State, or does it subsist independent of those laws? We contend that the obligation of a contract, that is, the duty of performing it, is not created by the law of the particular place where it is made, and dependent on that law for its existence; but that it may subsist, and does subsist, without that law, and independent of it. The obligation is in the contract itself, in the assent of the parties, and in the sanction of universal law. This is the doctrine of Grotius, Vattel, Burlamaqui, Pothier, and Rutherforth. The contract, doubtless, is necessarily to be enforced by the municipal law of the place where performance is demanded. The municipal law acts on the contract after it is made, to compel its execution, or give damages for its violation. But this is a very different thing from the same law being the origin or fountain of the contract. Let us illustrate this matter by an example. Two persons contract together in New York for the delivery, by one to the other, of a domestic animal, a utensil of husbandry, or a weapon of war. This is a lawful contract, and, while the parties remain in New York, it is to be enforced by the laws of that State. But if they remove with the article to Pennsylvania or Maryland, there a new law comes to act upon the contract, and to apply other remedies if it be broken. Thus far the remedies are furnished by the laws of society. But suppose the same parties to go together to a savage wilderness, or a desert island, beyond the reach of the laws of any society. The obligation of the contract still subsists, and is as perfect as ever, and is now to be enforced by another law, that is, the law of nature; and the party to whom the promise was made has a right to take by force the animal, the utensil, or the weapon that was promised him. The right is as perfect here as it was in Pennsylvania, or even in New York; but this could not be so if the obligation were created by the law of New York, or were dependent on that law for its existence, because the laws of that State can have no operation beyond its territory. Let us reverse this example. Suppose a contract to be made between two persons cast ashore on an uninhabited territory, or in a place over which no law of society extends. There are such places, and contracts have been made by individuals casually there, and these contracts have been enforced in courts of law in civilized communities. Whence do such contracts derive their obligation, if not from universal law?

If these considerations show us that the obligation of a lawful contract does not derive its force from the particular law of the place where made, but may exist where that law does not exist, and be enforced where that law has no validity, then it follows, we contend, that any statute which diminishes or lessens its obligation does impair it, whether it precedes or succeeds the contract in date. The contract having an independent origin, whenever the law comes to exist together with it, and interferes with it, it lessens, we say, and impairs, its own original and independent obligation. In the case before the court, the contract did not owe its existence to the particular law of New York; it did not depend on that law, but could be enforced without the territory of that State, as well as within it. Nevertheless, though legal, though thus independently existing, though thus binding the party everywhere, and capable of being enforced everywhere, yet the statute of New York says that it shall be discharged without payment. This, we say, impairs the obligation of that contract. It is admitted to have been legal in its inception, legal in its full extent, and capable of being enforced by other tribunals according to its terms. An act, then, purporting to discharge it without payment, is, as we contend, an act impairing its obligation.

Here, however, we meet the opposite argument, stated on different occasions in different terms, but usually summed up in this, that the law itself is a part of the contract, and therefore cannot impair it. What does this mean? Let us seek for clear ideas. It does not mean that the law gives any particular construction to the terms of the contract, or that it makes the promise, or the consideration, or the time of performance, other than is expressed in the instrument itself. It can only mean, that it is to be taken as a part of the contract, or understanding of the parties, that the contract itself shall be enforced by such laws and regulations, respecting remedy and for the enforcement of contracts, as are in being in the State where it is made at the time of entering into it. This is meant, or nothing very clearly intelligible is meant, by saying the law is part of the contract.

There is no authority in adjudged cases for the plaintiff in error but the State decisions which have been cited, and, as has already been stated, they all rest on this reason, that the law is part of the contract. Against this we contend,--

1st. That, if the proposition were true, the consequence would not follow.

2d. That the proposition itself cannot be maintained.

1. If it were true that the law is to be considered as part of the contract, the consequence contended for would not follow; because, if this statute be part of the contract, so is every other legal or constitutional provision existing at the time which affects the contract, or which is capable of affecting it; and especially this very article of the Constitution of the United States is part of the contract. The plaintiff in error argues in a complete circle. He supposes the parties to have had reference to it because it was a binding law, and yet he proves it to be a binding law only upon the ground that such reference was made to it. We come before the court alleging the law to be void, as unconstitutional; they stop the inquiry by opposing to us the law itself. Is this logical? Is it not precisely _objectio ejus, cujus dissolutio petitur_? If one bring a bill to set aside a judgment, is that judgment itself a good plea in bar to the bill? We propose to inquire if this law is of force to control our contract, or whether, by the Constitution of the United States, such force be not denied to it. The plaintiff in error stops us by saying that it does control the contract, and so arrives shortly at the end of the debate. Is it not obvious, that, supposing the act of New York to be a part of the contract, the question still remains as undecided as ever. What is that act? Is it a law, or is it a nullity? a thing of force, or a thing of no force? Suppose the parties to have contemplated this act, what did they contemplate? its words only, or its legal effect? its words, or the force which the Constitution of the United States allows to it? If the parties contemplated any law, they contemplated all the law that bore on their contract, the aggregate of all the statute and constitutional provisions. To suppose that they had in view one statute

without regarding others, or that they contemplated a statute without considering that paramount constitutional provisions might control or qualify that statute, or abrogate it altogether, is unreasonable and inadmissible. "This contract," says one of the authorities relied on, "is to be construed as if the law were specially recited in it." Let it be so for the sake of argument. But it is also to be construed as if the prohibitory clause of the Constitution were recited in it, and this brings us back again to the precise point from which we departed.

The Constitution always accompanies the law, and the latter can have no force which the former does not allow to it. If the reasoning were thrown into the form of special pleading, it would stand thus: the plaintiff declares on his debt; the defendant pleads his discharge under the law; the plaintiff alleges the law unconstitutional; but the defendant says, You knew of its existence; to which the answer is obvious and irresistible, I knew its existence on the statute-book of New York, but I knew, at the same time, it was null and void under the Constitution of the United States.

The language of another leading decision is, "A law in force at the time of making the contract does not violate that contract"; but the very question is, whether there be any such law "in force"; for if the States have no authority to pass such laws, then no such law can be in force. The Constitution is a part of the contract as much as the law, and was as much in the contemplation of the parties. So that the proposition, if it be admitted that the law is part of the contract, leaves us just where it found us: that is to say, under the necessity of comparing the law with the Constitution, and of deciding by such comparison whether it be valid or invalid. If the law be unconstitutional, it is void, and no party can be supposed to have had reference to a void law. If it be constitutional, no reference to it need be supposed.

2. But the proposition itself cannot be maintained. The law is no part of the contract. What part is it? the promise? the consideration? the condition? Clearly, it is neither of these. It is no term of the contract. It acts upon the contract only when it is broken, or to discharge the party from its obligation after it is broken. The municipal law is the force of society employed to compel the performance of contracts. In every judgment in a suit on contract, the damages are given, and the imprisonment of the person or sale of goods awarded, not in performance of the contract, or as part of the contract, but as an indemnity for the breach of the contract. Even interest, which is a strong case, where it is not expressed in the contract itself, can only be given as damages. It is all but absurd to say that a man's goods are sold on a _fieri facias_, or that he himself goes to jail, in pursuance of his contract. These are the penalties which the law inflicts for the breach of his contract. Doubtless, parties, when they enter into contracts, may well consider both what their rights and what their liabilities will be by the law, if such contracts be broken; but this contemplation of consequences which can ensue only when the contract is broken, is no part of the contract itself. The law has nothing to do with the contract till it be broken; how, then, can it be said to form a part of the contract itself?

But there are other cogent and more specific reasons against considering the law as part of the contract. (1.) If the law be part of the contract, it cannot be repealed or altered; because, in such case, the repealing or modifying law itself would impair the obligation of the contract. The insolvent law of New York, for example, authorizes the discharge of a debtor on the consent of two thirds of his creditors. A subsequent act requires the consent of three fourths; but if the existing law be part of the contract, this latter law would be void. In short, nothing which is part of the contract can be varied but by consent of the parties; therefore the argument runs _in absurdum_; for it proves that no laws for enforcing the contract, or giving remedies upon it, or any way affecting it, can be changed or modified between its creation and its end. If the law in question binds one party on the ground of assent to it, it binds both, and binds them until they agree to terminate its operation. (2.) If the party be bound by an implied assent to the law, as thereby making the law a part of the contract, how would it be if the parties had expressly dissented, and agreed that the law should make no part of the contract? Suppose the promise to have been, that the promisor would pay at all events, and not take advantage of the statute; still, would not the statute operate on the whole,--on this particular agreement and all? and does not this show that the law is no part of the contract, but something above it? (3.) If the law of the place be part of the contract, one of its terms and conditions, how could it be enforced, as we all know it might be, in another jurisdiction, which should have no regard to the law of the place? Suppose the parties, after the contract, to remove to another State, do they carry the law with them as part of their contract? We all know they do not. Or take a common case. Some States have laws abolishing imprisonment for debt; these laws, according to the argument, are all parts of the contract; how, then, can the party, when sued in another State, be imprisoned contrary to the terms of his contract? (4.)

The argument proves too much, inasmuch as it applies as strongly to prior as to subsequent contracts. It is founded on a supposed assent to the exercise of legislative authority, without considering whether that exercise be legal or illegal. But it is equally fair to found the argument on an implied assent to the potential exercise of that authority. The implied reference to the control of legislative power is as reasonable and as strong when that power is dormant, as while it is in exercise. In one case, the argument is, "The law existed, you knew it, and acquiesced." In the other it is, "The power to pass the law existed, you knew it, and took your chance." There is as clear an assent in one instance as in the other. Indeed, it is more reasonable and more sensible to imply a general assent to all the laws of society, present and to come, from the fact of living in it, than it is to imply a particular assent to a particular existing enactment. The true view of the matter is, that every man is presumed to submit to all power which may be lawfully exercised over him or his right, and no one should be presumed to submit to illegal acts of power, whether actual or contingent. (5.) But a main objection to this argument is, that it would render the whole constitutional provision idle and inoperative; and no explanatory words, if such words had been added in the Constitution, could have prevented this consequence. The law, it is said, is part of the contract; it cannot, therefore, impair the contract, because a contract cannot impair itself. Now, if this argument be sound, the case would have been the same, whatever words the Constitution had used. If, for example, it had declared that no State should pass any law impairing contracts *prospectively* or _retrospectively_; or any law impairing contracts, whether existing or future; or, whatever terms it had used to prohibit precisely such a law as is now before the court,--the prohibition would be totally nugatory if the law is to be taken as part of the contract; and the result would be, that, whatever may be the laws which the States by this clause of the Constitution are prohibited from passing, yet, if they in fact do pass such laws, those laws are valid, and bind parties by a supposed assent.

But further, this idea, if well founded, would enable the States to defeat the whole constitutional provision by a general enactment. Suppose a State should declare, by law, that all contracts entered into therein should be subject to such laws as the legislature, at any time, or from time to time, might see fit to pass. This law, according to the argument, would enter into the contract, become a part of it, and authorize the interference of the legislative power with it, for any and all purposes, wholly uncontrolled by the Constitution of the United States.

So much for the argument that the law is a part of the contract. We think it is shown to be not so; and if it were, the expected consequence would not follow.

The inquiry, then, recurs, whether the law in question be such a law as the legislature of New York had authority to pass. The question is general. We differ from our learned adversaries on general principles. We differ as to the main scope and end of this constitutional provision. They think it entirely remedial; we regard it as preventive. They think it adopted to secure redress for violated private rights; to us, it seems intended to guard against great public mischiefs. They argue it as if it were designed as an indemnity or protection for injured private rights, in individual cases of *meum* and _tuum_; we look upon it as a great political provision, favorable to the commerce and credit of the whole country. Certainly we do not deny its application to cases of violated private right. Such cases are clearly and unquestionably within its operation. Still, we think its main scope to be general and political. And this, we think, is proved by reference to the history of the country, and to the great objects which were sought to be attained by the establishment of the present government. Commerce, credit, and confidence were the principal things which did not exist under the old Confederation, and which it was a main object of the present Constitution to create and establish. A vicious system of legislation, a system of paper money and tender laws, had completely paralyzed industry, threatened to beggar every man of property, and ultimately to ruin the country. The relation between debtor and creditor, always delicate, and always dangerous whenever it divides society, and draws out the respective parties into different ranks and classes, was in such a condition in the years 1787, 1788, and 1789, as to threaten the overthrow of all government; and a revolution was menaced, much more critical and alarming than that through which the country had recently passed. The object of the new Constitution was to arrest these evils; to awaken industry by giving security to property; to establish confidence, credit, and commerce, by salutary laws, to be enforced by the power of the whole community. The Revolutionary War was over, the country had peace, but little domestic tranquillity; it had liberty, but few of its enjoyments, and none of its security. The States had struggled together, but their union was imperfect. They had freedom, but not an established course of justice. The Constitution was therefore framed, as it professes, "to form a more perfect union, to establish justice, to secure the blessings of liberty, and to insure domestic tranquillity."

It is not pertinent to this occasion to advert to all the means by which these desirable ends were to be obtained. Some of them, closely connected with the subject now under consideration, are obvious and prominent. The objects were commerce, credit, and mutual confidence in matters of property; and these required, among other things, a uniform standard of value or medium of payments. One of the first powers given to Congress, therefore, is that of coining money and fixing the value of foreign coins; and one of the first restraints imposed on the States is the total prohibition to coin money. These two provisions are industriously followed up and completed by denying to the States all power to emit bills of credit, or to make any thing but gold and silver a tender in the payment of debts. The whole control, therefore, over the standard of value and medium of payments is vested in the general government. And here the question instantly suggests itself. Why should such pains be taken to confide to Congress alone this exclusive power of fixing on a standard of value, and of prescribing the medium in which debts shall be paid, if it is, after all, to be left to every State to declare that debts may be discharged, and to prescribe how they may be discharged, without any payment at all? Why say that no man shall be obliged to take, in discharge of a debt, paper money issued by the authority of a State, and yet say that by the same authority the debt may be discharged without any payment whatever?

We contend, that the Constitution has not left its work thus unfinished. We contend, that, taking its provisions together, it is apparent it was intended to provide for two things, intimately connected with each other. These are,--

1. A medium for the payment of debts; and,

2. A uniform manner of discharging debts, when they are to be discharged without payment.

The arrangement of the grants and prohibitions contained in the Constitution is fit to be regarded on this occasion. The grant to Congress and the prohibition on the States, though they are certainly to be construed together, are not contained in the same clauses. The powers granted to Congress are enumerated one after another in the eighth section; the principal limitations on those powers, in the ninth section; and the prohibitions to the States, in the tenth section. Now, in order to understand whether any particular power be exclusively vested in Congress, it is necessary to read the terms of the grant, together with the terms of the prohibition. Take an example from that power of which we have been speaking, the coinage power. Here the grant to Congress is, "To coin money, regulate the value thereof, and of foreign coins." Now, the correlative prohibition on the States, though found in another section, is undoubtedly to be taken in immediate connection with the foregoing, as much as if it had been found in the same clause. The only just reading of these provisions, therefore, is this: "Congress shall have power to coin money, regulate the value thereof, and of foreign coin; but no State shall coin money, emit bills of credit, or make any thing but gold and silver coin a tender in payment of debts."

These provisions respect the medium of payment, or standard of value, and, thus collated, their joint result is clear and decisive. We think the result clear, also, of those provisions which respect the discharge of debts without payment. Collated in like manner, they stand thus: "Congress shall have power to establish uniform laws on the subject of bankruptcies throughout the United States, but no State shall pass any law impairing the obligation of contracts." This collocation cannot be objected to, if they refer to the same subject-matter; and that they do refer to the same subject-matter we have the authority of this court for saying, because this court solemnly determined, in _Sturges v. Crowninshield_, that this prohibition on the States did apply to systems of bankruptcy. It must be now taken, therefore, that State bankrupt laws were in the mind of the Convention when the prohibition was adopted, and therefore the grant to Congress on the subject of bankrupt laws, and the prohibition to the States on the same subject, are properly to be taken and read together; and being thus read together, is not the intention clear to take away from the States the power of passing bankrupt laws, since, while enacted by them, such laws would not be uniform, and to confer the power exclusively on Congress, by whom uniform laws could be established?

Suppose the order of arrangement in the Constitution had been otherwise than it is, and that the prohibitions to the States had preceded the grants of power to Congress, the two powers, when collated, would then have read thus: "No State shall pass any law impairing the obligation of contracts; but Congress may establish uniform laws on the subject of bankruptcies." Could any man have doubted, in that case, that the meaning was, that the States should not pass laws discharging debts without payment, but that Congress might establish uniform bankrupt acts? And yet this inversion of the order of the clauses does not alter their sense. We contend, that Congress alone possesses the power of establishing bankrupt laws; and although we are aware that, in _Sturges v. Crowninshield_, the court decided that such an exclusive power could not be inferred from the words of the grant in the seventh section, we yet would respectfully request the bench to reconsider this point. We think it could not have been intended that both the States and general government should exercise this power; and therefore, that a grant to one implies a prohibition on the other. But not to press a topic which the court has already had under its consideration, we contend, that, even without reading the clauses of the Constitution in the connection which we have suggested, and which is believed to be the true one, the prohibition in the tenth section, taken by itself, does forbid the enactment of State bankrupt laws, as applied to future as well as present debts. We argue this from the words of the prohibition, from the association they are found in, and from the objects intended.

1. The words are general. The States can pass no law impairing contracts; that is, any contract. In the nature of things a law may impair a future contract, and therefore such contract is within the protection of the Constitution. The words being general, it is for the other side to show a limitation; and this, it is submitted, they have wholly failed to do, unless they shall have established the doctrine that the law itself is part of the contract. It may be added, that the particular expression of the Constitution is worth regarding. The thing prohibited is called a _law_, not an *act*. A law, in its general acceptation, is a rule prescribed for future conduct, not a legislative interference with existing rights. The framers of the Constitution would hardly have given the appellation of *law* to violent invasions of individual right, or individual property, by acts of legislative power. Although, doubtless, such acts fall within this prohibition, yet they are prohibited also by general principles, and by the constitutions of the States, and therefore further provision against such acts was not so necessary as against other mischiefs.

2. The most conclusive argument, perhaps, arises from the connection in which the clause stands. The words of the prohibition, so far as it applies to civil rights, or rights of property, are, that "no State shall coin money, emit bills of credit, make any thing but gold and silver coin a tender in the payment of debts, or pass any law impairing the obligation of contracts." The prohibition of attainders, and *ex post facto* laws, refers entirely to criminal proceedings, and therefore should be considered as standing by itself; but the other parts of the prohibition are connected by the subject-matter, and ought, therefore, to be construed together. Taking the words thus together, according to their natural connection, how is it possible to give a more limited construction to the term "contracts," in the last branch of the sentence, than to the word "debts," in that immediately preceding? Can a State make any thing but gold and silver a tender in payment of future debts? This nobody pretends. But what ground is there for a distinction? No State shall make any thing but gold and silver a tender in the payment of debts, nor pass any law impairing the obligation of contracts. Now, by what reasoning is it made out that the debts here spoken of are any debts, either existing or future, but that the contracts spoken of are subsisting contracts only? Such a distinction seems to us wholly arbitrary. We see no ground for it. Suppose the article, where it uses the word _debts_, had used the word *contracts*. The sense would have been the same then that it now is; but the identity of terms would have made the nature of the distinction now contended for somewhat more obvious. Thus altered, the clause would read, that no State should make any thing but gold and silver a tender in discharge of _contracts_, nor pass any law impairing the obligation of _contracts_; yet the first of these expressions would have been held to apply to all contracts, and the last to subsisting contracts only. This shows the consequence of what is now contended for in a strong light. It is certain that the substitution of the word *contracts* for *debts* would not alter the sense; and an argument that could not be sustained, if such substitution were made, cannot be sustained now. We maintain, therefore, that, if tender laws may not be made for future debts, neither can bankrupt laws be made for future contracts. All the arguments used here may be applied with equal force to tender laws for future debts. It may be said, for instance, that, when it speaks of _debts_, the Constitution means existing debts, and not mere possibilities of future debt; that the object was to preserve vested rights; and that if a man, after a tender law had passed, had contracted a debt, the manner in which that tender law authorized that debt to be discharged became part of the contract, and that the whole debt, or whole obligation, was thus qualified by the pre-existing law, and was no more than a contract to deliver so much paper money, or whatever other article might be made a tender, as the original bargain expressed. Arguments of this sort will not be found wanting in favor of tender laws, if the court yield to similar arguments in favor of bankrupt laws.

These several prohibitions of the Constitution stand in the same paragraph; they have the same purpose, and were introduced for the same object; they are expressed in words of similar import, in grammar, and in sense; they are subject to the same construction, and we think no reason has yet been given for imposing an important restriction on one part of them, which does not equally show that the same restriction might be imposed also on the other part.

We have already endeavored to maintain, that one great political object intended by the Constitution would be defeated, if this construction were allowed to prevail. As an object of political regulation, it was not important to prevent the States from passing bankrupt laws applicable to present debts, while the power was left to them in regard to future debts; nor was it at all important, in a political point of view, to prohibit tender laws as to future debts, while it was yet left to the States to pass laws for the discharge of such debts, which, after all, are little different in principle from tender laws. Look at the law before the court in this view. It provides, that, if the debtor will surrender, offer, or tender to trustees, for the benefit of his creditors, all his estate and effects, he shall be discharged from all his debts. If it had authorized a tender of any thing but money to any one creditor, though it were of a value equal to the debt, and thereupon provided for a discharge, it would have been clearly invalid. Yet it is maintained to be good, merely because it is made for all creditors, and seeks a discharge from all debts; although the thing tendered may not be equivalent to a shilling in the pound of those debts. This shows, again, very clearly, how the Constitution has failed of its purpose, if, having in terms prohibited all tender laws, and taken so much pains to establish a uniform medium of payment, it has yet left the States the power of discharging debts, as they may see fit, without any payment at all.

To recapitulate what has been said, we maintain, first, that the Constitution, by its grants to Congress and its prohibitions on the States, has sought to establish one uniform standard of value, or medium of payment. Second, that, by like means, it has endeavored to provide for one uniform mode of discharging debts, when they are to be discharged without payment. Third, that these objects are connected, and that the first loses much of its importance, if the last, also, be not accomplished. Fourth, that, reading the grant to Congress and the prohibition on the States together, the inference is strong that the Constitution intended to confer an exclusive power to pass bankrupt laws on Congress. Fifth, that the prohibition in the tenth section reaches to all contracts, existing or future, in the same way that the other prohibition in the same section extends to all debts existing or future. Sixthly, that, upon any other construction, one great political object of the Constitution will fail of its accomplishment.
[Footnote 1: Sturges v. Crowninshield, 4 Wheat. Rep. 122.]

THE MURDER OF CAPTAIN JOSEPH WHITE.
AN ARGUMENT ON THE TRIAL OF JOHN FRANCIS KNAPP, FOR THE MURDER OF JOSEPH WHITE, OF SALEM, IN ESSEX COUNTY, MASSACHUSETTS, ON THE NIGHT OF THE 6TH OF APRIL, 1830.

[The following argument was addressed to the jury at a trial for a remarkable murder. A more extraordinary case never occurred in this country, nor is it equalled in strange interest by any trial in the French _Causes Célèbres_ or the English *State Trials*. Deep sensation and intense curiosity were excited through the whole country, at the time of the occurrence of the event, not only by the atrocity of the crime, but by the position of the victim, and the romantic incidents in the detection and fate of the assassin and his accomplices.

The following outline of the facts will assist the reader to understand the bearings of the argument. Joseph White, Esq. was found murdered in his bed, in his mansion-house, on the morning of the 7th of April, 1830. He was a wealthy merchant of Salem, eighty-two years of age, and had for many years given up active business. His servant-man rose that morning at six o'clock, and on going down into the kitchen, and opening the shutters of the window, saw that the back window of the east parlor was open, and that a plank was raised to the window from the back yard; he then went into the parlor, but saw no trace of any person having been there. He went to the apartment of the maid-servant, and told her, and then into Mr. White's chamber by its back door, and saw that the door of his chamber, leading into the front entry, was open. On approaching the bed, he found the bed-clothes turned down, and Mr. White dead, his countenance pallid, and his night-clothes and bed drenched in blood. He hastened to the neighboring houses to make known the event. He and the maid-servant were the only persons who slept in the house that night, except Mr. White himself, whose niece, Mrs. Beckford, his house-keeper, was then absent on a visit to her daughter, at Wenham.

The physicians and the coroner's jury, who were called to examine the body, found on it thirteen deep stabs, made as if by a sharp dirk or poniard, and the appearance of a heavy blow on the left temple, which had fractured the skull, but not broken the skin. The body was cold, and appeared to have been lifeless many hours.

On examining the apartments of the house, it did not appear that any valuable articles had been taken, or the house ransacked for them; there was a *rouleau* of doubloons in an iron chest in his chamber, and costly plate in other apartments, none of which was missing.

The perpetration of such an atrocious crime, in the most populous and central part of the town and in the most compactly built street, and under circumstances indicating the utmost coolness, deliberation, and audacity, deeply agitated and aroused the whole community; ingenuity was baffled in attempting even to conjecture a *motive* for the deed; and all the citizens were led to fear that the same fate might await them in the defenceless and helpless hours of slumber. For several days, persons passing through the streets might hear the continual sound of the hammer, while carpenters and smiths were fixing bolts to doors and fastenings to windows. Many, for defence, furnished themselves with cutlasses, fire-arms, and watch-dogs. Large rewards for the detection of the author or authors of the murder were offered by the heirs of the deceased, by the selectmen of the town, and by the Governor of the State. The citizens held a public meeting, and appointed a Committee of Vigilance, of twenty-seven members, to make all possible exertions to ferret out the offenders.

While the public mind was thus excited and anxious, it was announced that a bold attempt at highway robbery was made in Wenham, by three footpads, on Joseph J. Knapp, Jr. and John Francis Knapp, on the evening of the 27th of April, while they were returning in a chaise from Salem to their residence in Wenham. They appeared before the investigating committee, and testified that, after nine o'clock, near the Wenham Pond, they discovered three men approaching. One came near, seized the bridle, and stopped the horse, while the other two came, one on each side, and seized a trunk in the bottom of the chaise. Frank Knapp drew a sword from his cane and made a thrust at one, and Joseph with the but-end of his whip gave the other a heavy blow across the face. This bold resistance made them fall back. Joseph sprung from the chaise to assail the robbers. One of them then gave a shrill whistle, when they fled, and, leaping over the wall, were soon lost in the darkness. One had a weapon like an ivory dirk-handle, was clad in a sailor's short jacket, cap, and had whiskers; another wore a long coat, with bright buttons; all three were good-sized men. Frank, too, sprung from the chaise, and pursued with vigor, but all in vain.

The account of this unusual and bold attempt at robbery, thus given by the Knapps was immediately published in the Salem newspapers, with the editorial remark, that "these gentlemen are well known in this town, and their respectability and veracity are not questioned by any of our citizens."

Not the slightest clew to the murder could be found for several weeks, and the mystery seemed to be impenetrable. At length a rumor reached the ear of the committee that a prisoner in the jail at New Bedford, seventy miles from Salem, confined there on a charge of shoplifting, had intimated that he could make important disclosures. A confidential messenger was immediately sent, to ascertain what he knew on the subject. The prisoner's name was Hatch; he had been committed before the murder. He stated that, some months before the murder, while he was at large, he had associated in Salem with Richard Crowninshield, Jr., of Danvers, and had often heard Crowninshield express his intention to destroy the life of Mr. White. Crowninshield was a young man, of bad reputation; though he had never been convicted of any offence, he was strongly suspected of several heinous robberies. He was of dark and reserved deportment, temperate and wicked, daring and wary, subtle and obdurate, of great adroitness, boldness, and self-command. He had for several years frequented the haunts of vice in Salem; and though he was often spoken of as a dangerous man, his person was known to few, for he never walked the streets by daylight. Among his few associates he was a leader and a despot.

The disclosures of Hatch received credit. When the Supreme Court met at Ipswich, the Attorney-General, Morton, moved for a writ of _habeas corpus ad testif._, and Hatch was carried in chains from New Bedford before the grand jury, and on his testimony an indictment was found against Crowninshield. Other witnesses testified that, on the night of the murder, his brother, George Crowninshield, Colonel Benjamin Selman, of Marblehead, and Daniel Chase, of Lynn, were together in Salem, at a gambling-house usually frequented by Richard; these were indicted as accomplices in the crime. They were all arrested on the 2d of May, arraigned on the indictment, and committed to prison to await the sitting of a court that should have jurisdiction of the offence.

The Committee of Vigilance, however, continued to hold frequent meetings in order to discover further proof, for it was doubted by many whether the evidence already obtained would be sufficient to convict the accused.

A fortnight afterwards, on the 15th of May, Captain Joseph J. Knapp, a shipmaster and merchant, a man of good character, received by mail the following letter:--

CHARLES GRANT, JR., TO JOSEPH J. KNAPP.

"_Belfast, May 12, 1830._

"Dear Sir,--I have taken the pen at this time to address an utter stranger, and, strange as it may seem to you, it is for the purpose of requesting the loan of three hundred and fifty-dollars, for which I can give you no security but my word, and in this case consider this to be sufficient. My call for money at this time is pressing, or I would not trouble you; but with that sum, I have the prospect of turning it to so much advantage, as to be able to refund it with interest in the course of six months. At all events, I think it will be for your interest to comply with my request, and that immediately,--that is, not to put off any longer than you receive this. Then set down and enclose me the money with as much despatch as possible, for your own interest. This, Sir, is my advice; and if you do not comply with it, the short period between now and November will convince you that you have denied a request, the granting of which will never injure you, the refusal of which will ruin you. Are you surprised at this assertion--rest assured that I make it, reserving to myself the reasons and a series of facts, which are founded on such a bottom as will bid defiance to property or quality. It is useless for me to enter into a discussion of facts which must inevitably harrow up your soul. No, I will merely tell you that I am acquainted with your brother Franklin, and also the business that he was transacting for you on the 2d of April last; and that I think that you was very extravagant in giving one thousand dollars to the person that would execute the business for you. But you know best about that; you see that such things will leak out. To conclude, Sir, I will inform you that there is a gentleman of my acquaintance in Salem, that will observe that you do not leave town before the first of June, giving you sufficient time between now and then to comply with my request: and if I do not receive a line from you, together with the above sum, before the 22d of this month, I shall wait upon you with an assistant. I have said enough to convince you of my knowledge, and merely inform you that you can, when you answer, be as brief as possible.

"Direct yours to

"CHARLES GRANT, Jr., of Prospect, Maine."

This letter was an unintelligible enigma to Captain Knapp; he knew no man of the name of Charles Grant, Jr., and had no acquaintance at Belfast, a town in Maine, two hundred miles distant from Salem. After poring over it in vain, he handed it to his son, Nathaniel Phippen Knapp, a young lawyer; to him also the letter was an inexplicable riddle. The receiving of such a *threatening* letter, at a time when so many felt insecure, and were apprehensive of danger, demanded their attention. Captain Knapp and his son Phippen, therefore, concluded to ride to Wenham, seven miles distant, and show the letter to Captain Knapp's other two sons, Joseph J. Knapp, Jr. and John Francis Knapp, who were then residing at Wenham with Mrs. Beckford, the niece and late house-keeper of Mr. White, and the mother of the wife of J.J. Knapp, Jr. The latter perused the letter, told his father it "contained a devilish lot of trash," and requested him to hand it to the Committee of Vigilance. Captain Knapp, on his return to Salem that evening, accordingly delivered the letter to the chairman of the Committee.

The next day J.J. Knapp, Jr. went to Salem, and requested one of his friends to drop into the Salem post-office the two following pseudonymous letters.

"_May 13, 1830._

"GENTLEMEN OF THE COMMITTEE OF VIGILANCE,--Hearing that you have taken up four young men on suspicion of being concerned in the murder of Mr. White, I think it time to inform you that Steven White came to me one night and told me, if I would *remove* the old gentleman, he would give me five thousand dollars; he said he was afraid he would alter his will if he lived any longer. I told him I would do it, but I was afeared to go into the house, so he said he would go with me, that he would try to get into the house in the evening and open the window, would then go home and go to bed and meet me again about eleven. I found him, and we both went into his chamber. I struck him on the head with a heavy piece of lead, and then stabbed him with a dirk; he made the finishing strokes with another. He promised to send me the money next evening, and has not sent it yet which is the reason that I mention this.

"Yours, &c.,

"GRANT."

This letter was directed on the outside to the "Hon. Gideon Barstow, Salem," and put into the post-office on Sunday evening, May 16, 1830.

"_Lynn, May 12, 1830._

"Mr. White will send the $5,000, or a part of it, before to-morrow night, or suffer the painful consequences.

"N. CLAXTON, 4TH."

This letter was addressed to the "Hon. Stephen White, Salem, Mass.," and was also put into the post-office in Salem on Sunday evening.

When Knapp delivered these letters to his friend, he said his father had received an anonymous letter, and "What I want you for is to put these in the post-office in order to nip this silly affair in the bud."

The Hon. Stephen White, mentioned in these letters, was a nephew of Joseph White, and the legatee of the principal part of his large property.

When the Committee of Vigilance read and considered the letter, purporting to be signed by Charles Grant, Jr., which had been delivered to them by Captain Knapp, they were impressed with the belief that it contained a clew which might lead to important disclosures. As they had spared no pains or expense in their investigations, they immediately despatched a discreet messenger to Prospect, in Maine; he explained his business confidentially to the postmaster there, deposited a letter addressed to Charles Grant, Jr., and awaited the call of Grant to receive it. He soon called for it, when an officer, stationed in the house, stepped forward and arrested Grant. On examining him, it appeared that his true name was Palmer, a young man of genteel appearance, resident in the adjoining town of Belfast. He had been a convict in Maine, and had served a term in the State's prison in that State. Conscious that the circumstances justified the belief that he had had a hand in the murder, he readily made known, while he protested his own innocence, that he could unfold the whole mystery. He then disclosed that he had been an associate of R. Crowninshield, Jr. and George Crowninshield; had spent part of the winter at Danvers and Salem, under the name of Carr; part of the time he had been their inmate, concealed in their father's house in Danvers; that on the 2d of April he saw from the windows of the house Frank Knapp and a young man named Allen ride up to the house; that George walked away with Frank, and Richard with Allen; that on their return, George told Richard that Frank wished them to undertake to kill Mr. White, and that J.J. Knapp, Jr. would pay one thousand dollars for the job. They proposed various modes of executing it, and asked Palmer to be concerned, which he declined. George said the house-keeper would be away at the time; that the object of Joseph J. Knapp, Jr. was to destroy the will, because it gave most of the property to Stephen White; that Joseph J. Knapp, Jr. was first to destroy the will; that he could get from the house-keeper the keys of the iron chest in which it was kept; that Frank called again the same day, in a chaise, and rode away with Richard; and that on the night of the murder Palmer stayed at the Half-way House, in Lynn.

The messenger, on obtaining this disclosure from Palmer, without delay communicated it by mail to the Committee, and on the 26th of May, a warrant was issued against Joseph J. Knapp, Jr. and John Francis Knapp, and they were taken into custody at Wenham, where they were residing in the family of Mrs. Beckford, mother of the wife of Joseph J. Knapp, Jr. They were then imprisoned to await the arrival of Palmer, for their examination.

The two Knapps were young shipmasters, of a respectable family.

Joseph J. Knapp, Jr., on the third day of his imprisonment, made a full confession that he projected the murder. He knew that Mr. White had made his will, and given to Mrs. Beckford a legacy of fifteen thousand dollars; but if he died without leaving a will, he expected she would inherit nearly two hundred thousand dollars. In February he made known to his brother his desire to make way with Mr. White, intending first to abstract and destroy the will. Frank agreed to employ an assassin, and negotiated with R. Crowninshield, Jr., who agreed to do the deed for a reward of one thousand dollars; Joseph agreed to pay that sum, and, as he had access to the house at his pleasure, he was to unbar and unfasten the back window, so that Crowninshield might gain easy entrance. Four days before the murder, while they were deliberating on the mode of compassing it, he went into Mr. White's chamber, and, finding the key in the iron chest, unlocked it, took the will, put it in his chaise-box, covered it with hay, carried it to Wenham, kept it till after the murder, and then burned it. After securing the will, he gave notice to Crowninshield that all was ready. In the evening of that day he had a meeting with Crowninshield at the centre of the common, who showed him a bludgeon and dagger, with which the murder was to be committed. Knapp asked him if he meant to do it that night; Crowninshield said he thought not, he did not feel like it; Knapp then went to Wenham. Knapp ascertained on Sunday, the 4th of April, that Mr. White had gone to take tea with a relative in Chestnut Street. Crowninshield intended to dirk him on his way home in the evening, but Mr. White returned before dark. It was next arranged for the night of the 6th, and Knapp was on some pretext to prevail on Mrs. Beckford to visit her daughters at Wenham, and to spend the night there. He said that, all preparations being thus complete, Crowninshield and Frank met about ten o'clock in the evening of the 6th, in Brown Street, which passes the rear of the garden of Mr. White, and stood some time in a spot from which they could observe the movements in the house, and perceive when Mr. White and his two servants retired to bed. Crowninshield requested Frank to go home; he did so, but soon returned to the same spot. Crowninshield, in the mean time, had started and passed round through Newbury Street and Essex Street to the front of the house, entered the postern gate, passed to the rear of the house, placed a plank against the house, climbed to the window, opened it, entered the house alone, passed up the staircase, opened the door of the sleeping-chamber, approached the bedside, gave Mr. White a heavy and mortal blow on the head with a bludgeon, and then with a dirk gave him many stabs in his body. Crowninshield said, that, after he had "done for the old man," he put his fingers on his pulse to make certain he was dead. He then retired from the house, hurried back through Brown Street, where he met Frank, waiting to learn the event. Crowninshield ran down Howard Street, a solitary place, and hid the club under the steps of a meeting-house. He then went home to Danvers.

Joseph confessed further that the account of the Wenham robbery, on the 27th of April, was a sheer fabrication. After the murder Crowninshield went to Wenham in company with Frank to call for the one thousand dollars. He was not able to pay the whole, but gave him one hundred five-franc pieces. Crowninshield related to him the particulars of the murder, told him where the club was hid, and said he was sorry Joseph had not got the right will, for if he had known there was another, he would have got it. Joseph sent Frank afterwards to find and destroy the club, but he said he could not find it. When Joseph made the confession, he told the place where the club was concealed, and it was there found; it was heavy, made of hickory, twenty-two and a half inches long, of a smooth surface and large oval head, loaded with lead, and of a form adapted to give a mortal blow on the skull without breaking the skin; the handle was suited for a firm grasp. Crowninshield said he turned it in a lathe. Joseph admitted he wrote the two anonymous letters.

Crowninshield had hitherto maintained a stoical composure of feeling; but when he was informed of Knapp's arrest, his knees smote beneath him, the sweat started out on his stern and pallid face, and he subsided upon his bunk.

Palmer was brought to Salem in irons on the 3d of June, and committed to prison. Crowninshield saw him taken from the carriage. He was put in the cell directly under that in which Crowninshield was kept. Several members of the Committee entered Palmer's cell to talk with him; while they were talking, they heard a loud whistle, and, on looking up, saw that Crowninshield had picked away the mortar from the crevice between the blocks of the granite floor of his cell. After the loud whistle, he cried out, "Palmer! Palmer!" and soon let down a string, to which were tied a pencil and a slip of paper. Two lines of poetry were written on the paper, in order that, if Palmer was really there, he should make it known by capping the verses. Palmer shrunk away into a corner, and was soon transferred to another cell. He seemed to stand in awe of Crowninshield.

On the 12th of June a quantity of stolen goods was found concealed in the barn of Crowninshield, in consequence of information from Palmer.

Crowninshield, thus finding the proofs of his guilt and depravity thicken, on the 15th of June committed suicide by hanging himself to the bars of his cell with a handkerchief. He left letters to his father and brother, expressing in general terms the viciousness of his life, and his hopelessness of escape from punishment. When his associates in guilt heard his fate, they said it was not unexpected by them, for they had often heard him say he would never live to submit to an ignominious punishment.

A special term of the Supreme Court was held at Salem on the 20th of July, for the trial of the prisoners charged with the murder; it continued in session till the 20th of August, with a few days' intermission. An indictment for the murder was found against John Francis Knapp, as principal, and Joseph J. Knapp, Jr. and George Crowninshield, as accessories. Selman and Chase were discharged by the Attorney-General. The principal, John Francis Knapp, was first put on trial. As the law then stood, an accessory in a murder could not be tried until a principal had been convicted. He was defended by Messrs. Franklin Dexter and William H. Gardiner, advocates of high reputation for ability and eloquence; the trial was long and arduous, and the witnesses numerous. His brother Joseph, who had made a full confession, on the government's promise of impunity if he would in good faith testify the truth, was brought into court, called to the stand as a witness, but declined to testify. To convict the prisoner, it was necessary for the government to prove that he was _present_, actually or constructively, as an aider or abettor in the murder. The evidence was strong that there was a conspiracy to commit the murder, that the prisoner was one of the conspirators, that at the time of the murder he was in Brown Street at the rear of Mr. White's garden, and the jury were satisfied that he was in that place to aid and abet in the murder, ready to afford assistance, if necessary. He was convicted.

Joseph J. Knapp, Jr. was afterwards tried as an accessory before the fact, and convicted.

George Crowninshield proved an _alibi_, and was discharged.

The execution of John Francis Knapp and Joseph J. Knapp, Jr. closed the tragedy.

If Joseph, after turning State's evidence, had not changed his mind, neither he nor his brother, nor any of the conspirators, could have been convicted; if he had testified, and disclosed the whole truth, it would have appeared that John Francis Knapp was in Brown Street, not to render assistance to the assassin; but that Crowninshield, when he started to commit the murder, requested Frank to go home and go to bed; that Frank did go home, retire to bed, soon after arose, secretly left his father's house, and hastened to Brown Street, to await the coming out of the assassin, in order to learn whether the deed was accomplished, and all the particulars. If Frank had not been convicted as principal, none of the accessories could by law have been convicted. Joseph would not have been even tried, for the government stipulated, that, if he would be a witness for the State, he should go clear.

The whole history of this occurrence is of romantic interest. The murder itself, the _corpus delicti_, was strange; planned with deliberation and sagacity, and executed with firmness and vigor. While conjecture was baffled in ascertaining either the motive or the perpetrator, it was certain that the assassin had acted upon design, and not at random. He must have had knowledge of the house, for the window had been unfastened from within. He had entered stealthily, threaded his way in silence through the apartments, corridors, and staircases, and coolly given the mortal blow. To make assurance doubly sure, he inflicted many fatal stabs, "the least a death to nature," and stayed not his hand till he had deliberately felt the pulse of his victim, to make certain that life was extinct.

It was strange that Crowninshield, the real assassin, should have been indicted and arrested on the testimony of Hatch, who was himself in prison, in a distant part of the State, at the time of the murder, and had no actual knowledge on the subject.

It was very strange that J.J. Knapp, Jr. should have been the instrument of bringing to light the mystery of the whole murderous conspiracy; for when he received from the hand of his father the threatening letter of Palmer, consciousness of guilt so confounded his faculties, that, instead of destroying it, he stupidly handed it back and requested his father to deliver it to the Committee of Vigilance.

It was strange that the murder should have been committed on a mistake in law. Joseph, some time previous to the murder, had made inquiry how Mr. White's estate would be distributed in case he died without a will, and had been erroneously told that Mrs. Beckford, his mother-in-law, the sole issue and representative of a deceased sister of Mr. White, would inherit half of the estate, and that the four children and representatives of a deceased brother of Mr. White, of whom the Hon. Stephen White was one, would inherit the other half. Joseph had privately read the will, and knew that Mr. White had bequeathed to Mrs. Beckford much less than half.

It was strange that the murder should have been committed on a mistake in fact also. Joseph furtively abstracted *a* will, and expected Mr. White would die intestate; but, after the decease, *the* will, the *last* will, was found by his heirs in its proper place; and it could never have been known, or conjectured, without the aid of Joseph's confession, that he had made either of those blunders.

Finally, it was a strange fact that Knapp should, on the night following the murder, have watched with the mangled corpse, and at the funeral followed the hearse as one of the chief mourners, without betraying on either occasion the slightest emotion which could awaken a suspicion of his guilt.

The following note was prefixed to this argument in the former edition:--

Mr. White, a highly respectable and wealthy citizen of Salem, about eighty years of age, was found, on the morning of the 7th of April, 1830, in his bed, murdered, under such circumstances as to create a strong sensation in that town and throughout the community.

Richard Crowninshield, George Crowninshield, Joseph J. Knapp, and John F. Knapp were, a few weeks after, arrested on a charge of having perpetrated the murder, and committed for trial. Joseph J. Knapp, soon after, under the promise of favor from government, made a full confession of the crime and the circumstances attending it. In a few days after this disclosure was made, Richard Crowninshield, who was supposed to have been the principal assassin, committed suicide.

A special session of the Supreme Court was ordered by the legislature, for the trial of the prisoners, at Salem, in July. At that time, John F. Knapp was indicted as principal in the murder, and George Crowninshield and Joseph J. Knapp as accessories.

On account of the death of Chief Justice Parker, which occurred on the 26th of July, the court adjourned to Tuesday, the third day of August, when it proceeded in the trial of John F. Knapp. Joseph J. Knapp, being called upon, refused to testify, and the pledge of the government was withdrawn.

At the request of the prosecuting officers of the government, Mr. Webster appeared as counsel, and assisted in the trial.

Mr. Franklin Dexter addressed the jury on behalf of the prisoner, and was succeeded by Mr. Webster in the following speech.]

I am little accustomed, Gentlemen, to the part which I am now attempting to perform. Hardly more than once or twice has it happened to me to be concerned on the side of the government in any criminal prosecution whatever; and never, until the present occasion, in any case affecting life.

But I very much regret that it should have been thought necessary to suggest to you that I am brought here to "hurry you against the law and beyond the evidence." I hope I have too much regard for justice, and too much respect for my own character, to attempt either; and were I to make such attempt, I am sure that in this court nothing can be carried against the law, and that gentlemen, intelligent and just as you are, are not, by any power, to be hurried beyond the evidence. Though I could well have wished to shun this occasion, I have not felt at liberty to withhold my professional assistance, when it is supposed that I may be in some degree useful in investigating and discovering the truth respecting this most extraordinary murder. It has seemed to be a duty incumbent on me, as on every other citizen, to do my best and my utmost to bring to light the perpetrators of this crime. Against the prisoner at the bar, as an individual, I cannot have the slightest prejudice. I would not do him the smallest injury or injustice. But I do not affect to be indifferent to the discovery and the punishment of this deep guilt. I cheerfully share in the opprobrium, how great soever it may be, which is cast on those who feel and manifest an anxious concern that all who had a part in planning, or a hand in executing, this deed of midnight assassination, may be brought to answer for their enormous crime at the bar of public justice.

Gentlemen, it is a most extraordinary case. In some respects, it has hardly a precedent anywhere; certainly none in our New England history. This bloody drama exhibited no suddenly excited, ungovernable rage. The actors in it were not surprised by any lion-like temptation springing upon their virtue, and overcoming it, before resistance could begin. Nor did they do the deed to glut savage vengeance, or satiate long-settled and deadly hate. It was a cool, calculating, money-making murder. It was all "hire and salary, not revenge." It was the weighing of money against life; the counting out of so many pieces of silver against so many ounces of blood.

An aged man, without an enemy in the world, in his own house, and in his own bed, is made the victim of a butcherly murder, for mere pay. Truly, here is a new lesson for painters and poets. Whoever shall hereafter draw the portrait of murder, if he will show it as it has been exhibited, where such example was last to have been looked for, in the very bosom of our New England society, let him not give it the grim visage of Moloch, the brow knitted by revenge, the face black with settled hate, and the bloodshot eye emitting livid fires of malice. Let him draw, rather, a decorous, smooth-faced, bloodless demon; a picture in repose, rather than in action; not so much an example of human nature in its depravity, and in its paroxysms of crime, as an infernal being, a fiend, in the ordinary display and development of his character. The deed was executed with a degree of self-possession and steadiness equal to the wickedness with which it was planned. The circumstances now clearly in evidence spread out the whole scene before us. Deep sleep had fallen on the destined victim, and on all beneath his roof. A healthful old man, to whom sleep was sweet, the first sound slumbers of the night held him in their soft but strong embrace. The assassin enters, through the window already prepared, into an unoccupied apartment. With noiseless foot he paces the lonely hall, half lighted by the moon; he winds up the ascent of the stairs, and reaches the door of the chamber. Of this, he moves the lock, by soft and continued pressure, till it turns on its hinges without noise; and he enters, and beholds his victim before him. The room is uncommonly open to the admission of light. The face of the innocent sleeper is turned from the murderer, and the beams of the moon, resting on the gray locks of his aged temple, show him where to strike. The fatal blow is given! and the victim passes, without a struggle or a motion, from the repose of sleep to the repose of death! It is the assassin's purpose to make sure work; and he plies the dagger, though it is obvious that life has been destroyed by the blow of the bludgeon. He even raises the aged arm, that he may not fail in his aim at the heart, and replaces it again over the wounds of the poniard! To finish the picture, he explores the wrist for the pulse! He feels for it, and ascertains that it beats no longer! It is accomplished. The deed is done. He retreats, retraces his steps to the window, passes out through it as he came in, and escapes. He has done the murder. No eye has seen him, no ear has heard him. The secret is his own, and it is safe!

Ah! Gentlemen, that was a dreadful mistake. Such a secret can be safe nowhere. The whole creation of God has neither nook nor corner where the guilty can bestow it, and say it is safe. Not to speak of that eye which pierces through all disguises, and beholds every thing as in the splendor of noon, such secrets of guilt are never safe from detection, even by men. True it is, generally speaking, that "murder will out." True it is, that Providence hath so ordained, and doth so govern things, that those who break the great law of Heaven by shedding man's blood seldom succeed in avoiding discovery. Especially, in a case exciting so much attention as this, discovery must come, and will come, sooner or later. A thousand eyes turn at once to explore every man, every thing, every circumstance, connected with the time and place; a thousand ears catch every whisper; a thousand excited minds intensely dwell on the scene, shedding all their light, and ready to kindle the slightest circumstance into a blaze of discovery. Meantime the guilty soul cannot keep its own secret. It is false to itself; or rather it feels an irresistible impulse of conscience to be true to itself. It labors under its guilty possession, and knows not what to do with it. The human heart was not made for the residence of such an inhabitant. It finds itself preyed on by a torment, which it dares not acknowledge to God or man. A vulture is devouring it, and it can ask no sympathy or assistance, either from heaven or earth. The secret which the murderer possesses soon comes to possess him; and, like the evil spirits of which we read, it overcomes him, and leads him whithersoever it will. He feels it beating at his heart, rising to his throat, and demanding disclosure. He thinks the whole world sees it in his face, reads it in his eyes, and almost hears its workings in the very silence of his thoughts. It has become his master. It betrays his discretion, it breaks down his courage, it conquers his prudence. When suspicions from without begin to embarrass him, and the net of circumstance to entangle him, the fatal secret struggles with still greater violence to burst forth. It must be confessed, it will be confessed; there is no refuge from confession but suicide, and suicide is confession.

Much has been said, on this occasion, of the excitement which has existed, and still exists, and of the extraordinary measures taken to discover and punish the guilty. No doubt there has been, and is, much excitement, and strange indeed it would be had it been otherwise. Should not all the peaceable and well-disposed naturally feel concerned, and naturally exert themselves to bring to punishment the authors of this secret assassination? Was it a thing to be slept upon or forgotten? Did you, Gentlemen, sleep quite as quietly in your beds after this murder as before? Was it not a case for rewards, for meetings, for committees, for the united efforts of all the good, to find out a band of murderous conspirators, of midnight ruffians, and to bring them to the bar of justice and law? If this be excitement, is it an unnatural or an improper excitement?

It seems to me, Gentlemen, that there are appearances of another feeling, of a very different nature and character; not very extensive, I would hope, but still there is too much evidence of its existence. Such is human nature, that some persons lose their abhorrence of crime in their admiration of its magnificent exhibitions. Ordinary vice is reprobated by them, but extraordinary guilt, exquisite wickedness, the high flights and poetry of crime, seize on the imagination, and lead them to forget the depths of the guilt, in admiration of the excellence of the performance, or the unequalled atrocity of the purpose. There are those in our day who have made great use of this infirmity of our nature, and by means of it done infinite injury to the cause of good morals. They have affected not only the taste, but I fear also the principles, of the young, the heedless, and the imaginative, by the exhibition of interesting and beautiful monsters. They render depravity attractive, sometimes by the polish of its manners, and sometimes by its very extravagance; and study to show off crime under all the advantages of cleverness and dexterity.

Gentlemen, this is an extraordinary murder, but it is still a murder. We are not to lose ourselves in wonder at its origin, or in gazing on its cool and skilful execution. We are to detect and to punish it; and while we proceed with caution against the prisoner, and are to be sure that we do not visit on his head the offences of others, we are yet to consider that we are dealing with a case of most atrocious crime, which has not the slightest circumstance about it to soften its enormity. It is murder; deliberate, concerted, malicious murder. Although the interest of this case may have diminished by the repeated investigation of the facts; still, the additional labor which it imposes upon all concerned is not to be regretted, if it should result in removing all doubts of the guilt of the prisoner.

The learned counsel for the prisoner has said truly, that it is your individual duty to judge the prisoner; that it is your individual duty to determine his guilt or innocence; and that you are to weigh the testimony with candor and fairness. But much at the same time has been said, which, although it would seem to have no distinct bearing on the trial, cannot be passed over without some notice.

A tone of complaint so peculiar has been indulged, as would almost lead us to doubt whether the prisoner at the bar, or the managers of this prosecution, are now on trial. Great pains have been taken to complain of the manner of the prosecution. We hear of getting up a case; of setting in motion trains of machinery; of foul testimony; of combinations to overwhelm the prisoner; of private prosecutors; that the prisoner is hunted, persecuted, driven to his trial; that everybody is against him; and various other complaints, as if those who would bring to punishment the authors of this murder were almost as bad as they who committed it.

In the course of my whole life, I have never heard before so much said about the particular counsel who happen to be employed; as if it were extraordinary that other counsel than the usual officers of the government should assist in the management of a case on the part of the government. In one of the last criminal trials in this county, that of Jackman for the "Goodridge robbery" (so called), I remember that the learned head of the Suffolk Bar, Mr. Prescott, came down in aid of the officers of the government. This was regarded as neither strange nor improper. The counsel for the prisoner, in that case, contented themselves with answering his arguments, as far as they were able, instead of carping at his presence. Complaint is made that rewards were offered, in this case, and temptations held out to obtain testimony. Are not rewards always offered, when great and secret offences are committed? Rewards were offered in the case to which I have alluded; and every other means taken to discover the offenders, that ingenuity or the most persevering vigilance could suggest. The learned counsel have suffered their zeal to lead them into a strain of complaint at the manner in which the perpetrators of this crime were detected, almost indicating that they regard it as a positive injury to them to have found out their guilt. Since no man witnessed it, since they do not now confess it, attempts to discover it are half esteemed as officious intermeddling and impertinent inquiry.

It is said, that here even a Committee of Vigilance was appointed. This is a subject of reiterated remark. This committee are pointed at, as though they had been officiously intermeddling with the administration of justice. They are said to have been "laboring for months" against the prisoner. Gentlemen, what must we do in such a case? Are people to be dumb and still, through fear of overdoing? Is it come to this, that an effort cannot be made, a hand cannot be lifted, to discover the guilty, without its being said there is a combination to overwhelm innocence? Has the community lost all moral sense? Certainly, a community that would not be roused to action upon an occasion such as this was, a community which should not deny sleep to their eyes, and slumber to their eyelids, till they had exhausted all the means of discovery and detection, must indeed be lost to all moral sense, and would scarcely deserve protection from the laws. The learned counsel have endeavored to persuade you, that there exists a prejudice against the persons accused of this murder. They would have you understand that it is not confined to this vicinity alone; but that even the legislature have caught this spirit. That through the procurement of the gentleman here styled private prosecutor, who is a member of the Senate, a special session of this court was appointed for the trial of these offenders. That the ordinary movements of the wheels of justice were too slow for the purposes devised. But does not everybody see and know, that it was matter of absolute necessity to have a special session of the court? When or how could the prisoners have been tried without a special session? In the ordinary arrangement of the courts, but one week in a year is allotted for the whole court to sit in this county. In the trial of all capital offences a majority of the court, at least, is required to be present. In the trial of the present case alone, three weeks have already been taken up. Without such special session, then, three years would not have been sufficient for the purpose. It is answer sufficient to all complaints on this subject to say, that the law was drawn by the late Chief Justice himself,[1] to enable the court to accomplish its duties, and to afford the persons accused an opportunity for trial without delay.

Again, it is said that it was not thought of making Francis Knapp, the prisoner at the bar, a PRINCIPAL till after the death of Richard Crowninshield, Jr.; that the present indictment is an after-thought; that "testimony was got up" for the occasion. It is not so. There is no authority for this suggestion. The case of the Knapps had not then been before the grand jury. The officers of the government did not know what the testimony would be against them. They could not, therefore, have determined what course they should pursue. They intended to arraign all as principals who should appear to have been principals, and all as accessories who should appear to have been accessories. All this could be known only when the evidence should be produced.

But the learned counsel for the defendant take a somewhat loftier flight still. They are more concerned, they assure us, for the law itself, than even for their client. Your decision in this case, they say, will stand as a precedent. Gentlemen, we hope it will. We hope it will be a precedent both of candor and intelligence, of fairness and of firmness; a precedent of good sense and honest purpose pursuing their investigation discreetly, rejecting loose generalities, exploring all the circumstances, weighing each, in search of truth, and embracing and declaring the truth when found.

It is said, that "laws are made, not for the punishment of the guilty, but for the protection of the innocent." This is not quite accurate, perhaps, but if so, we hope they will be so administered as to give that protection. But who are the innocent whom the law would protect? Gentlemen, Joseph White was innocent. They are innocent who, having lived in the fear of God through the day, wish to sleep in his peace through the night, in their own beds. The law is established that those who live quietly may sleep quietly; that they who do no harm may feel none. The gentleman can think of none that are innocent except the prisoner at the bar, not yet convicted. Is a proved conspirator to murder innocent? Are the Crowninshields and the Knapps innocent? What is innocence? How deep stained with blood, how reckless in crime, how deep in depravity may it be, and yet retain innocence? The law is made, if we would speak with entire accuracy, to protect the innocent by punishing the guilty. But there are those innocent out of a court, as well as in; innocent citizens not suspected of crime, as well as innocent prisoners at the bar. The criminal law is not founded in a principle of vengeance. It does not punish that it may inflict suffering. The humanity of the law feels and regrets every pain it causes, every hour of restraint it imposes, and more deeply still every life it forfeits. But it uses evil as the means of preventing greater evil. It seeks to deter from crime by the example of punishment. This is its true, and only true main object. It restrains the liberty of the few offenders, that the many who do not offend may enjoy their liberty. It takes the life of the murderer, that other murders may not be committed. The law might open the jails, and at once set free all persons accused of offences, and it ought to do so if it could be made certain that no other offences would hereafter be committed, because it punishes, not to satisfy any desire to inflict pain, but simply to prevent the repetition of crimes. When the guilty, therefore, are not punished, the law has so far failed of its purpose; the safety of the innocent is so far endangered. Every unpunished murder takes away something from the security of every man's life. Whenever a jury, through whimsical and ill-founded scruples, suffer the guilty to escape, they make themselves answerable for the augmented danger of the innocent.

We wish nothing to be strained against this defendant. Why, then, all this alarm? Why all this complaint against the manner in which the crime is discovered? The prisoner's counsel catch at supposed flaws of evidence, or bad character of witnesses, without meeting the case. Do they mean to deny the conspiracy? Do they mean to deny that the two Crowninshields and the two Knapps were conspirators? Why do they rail against Palmer, while they do not disprove, and hardly dispute, the truth of any one fact sworn to by him? Instead of this, it is made matter of sentimentality that Palmer has been prevailed upon to betray his bosom companions and to violate the sanctity of friendship. Again I ask, Why do they not meet the case? If the fact is out, why not meet it? Do they mean to deny that Captain White is dead? One would have almost supposed even that, from some remarks that have been made. Do they mean to deny the conspiracy? Or, admitting a conspiracy, do they mean to deny only that Frank Knapp, the prisoner at the bar, was abetting in the murder, being present, and so deny that he was a principal? If a conspiracy is proved, it bears closely upon every subsequent subject of inquiry. Why do they not come to the fact? Here the defence is wholly indistinct. The counsel neither take the ground, nor abandon it. They neither fly, nor light. They hover. But they must come to a closer mode of contest. They must meet the facts, and either deny or admit them. Had the prisoner at the bar, then, a knowledge of this conspiracy or not? This is the question. Instead of laying out their strength in complaining of the *manner* in which the deed is discovered, of the extraordinary pains taken to bring the prisoner's guilt to light, would it not be better to show there was no guilt? Would it not be better to show his innocence? They say, and they complain, that the community feel a great desire that he should be punished for his crimes. Would it not be better to convince you that he has committed no crime?

Gentlemen, let us now come to the case. Your first inquiry, on the evidence, will be, Was Captain White murdered in pursuance of a conspiracy, and was the defendant one of this conspiracy? If so, the second inquiry is, Was he so connected with the murder itself as that he is liable to be convicted as a _principal_? The defendant is indicted as a *principal*. If not guilty _as such_, you cannot convict him. The indictment contains three distinct classes of counts. In the first, he is charged as having done the deed with his own hand; in the second, as an aider and abettor to Richard Crowninshield, Jr., who did the deed; in the third, as an aider and abettor to some person unknown. If you believe him guilty on either of these counts, or in either of these ways, you must convict him.

It may be proper to say, as a preliminary remark, that there are two extraordinary circumstances attending this trial. One is, that Richard Crowninshield, Jr., the supposed immediate perpetrator of the murder, since his arrest, has committed suicide. He has gone to answer before a tribunal of perfect infallibility. The other is, that Joseph Knapp, the supposed originator and planner of the murder, having once made a full disclosure of the facts, under a promise of indemnity, is, nevertheless, not now a witness. Notwithstanding his disclosure and his promise of indemnity, he now refuses to testify. He chooses to return to his original state, and now stands answerable himself, when the time shall come for his trial. These circumstances it is fit you should remember, in your investigation of the case.

Your decision may affect more than the life of this defendant. If he be not convicted as principal, no one can be. Nor can any one be convicted of a participation in the crime as accessory. The Knapps and George Crowninshield will be again on the community. This shows the importance of the duty you have to perform, and serves to remind you of the care and wisdom necessary to be exercised in its performance. But certainly these considerations do not render the prisoner's guilt any clearer, nor enhance the weight of the evidence against him. No one desires you to regard consequences in that light. No one wishes any thing to be strained, or too far pressed against the prisoner. Still, it is fit you should see the full importance of the duty which devolves upon you.

And now, Gentlemen, in examining this evidence, let us begin at the beginning, and see first what we know independent of the disputed testimony. This is a case of circumstantial evidence. And these circumstances, we think, are full and satisfactory. The case mainly depends upon them, and it is common that offences of this kind must be proved in this way. Midnight assassins take no witnesses. The evidence of the facts relied on has been somewhat sneeringly denominated, by the learned counsel, "circumstantial stuff," but it is not such stuff as dreams are made of. Why does he not rend this stuff? Why does he not scatter it to the winds? He dismisses it a little too summarily. It shall be my business to examine this stuff, and try its cohesion.

The letter from Palmer at Belfast, is that no more than flimsy stuff?

The fabricated letters from Knapp to the committee and to Mr. White, are they nothing but stuff?

The circumstance, that the house-keeper was away at the time the murder was committed, as it was agreed she would be, is that, too, a useless piece of the same stuff?

The facts, that the key of the chamber door was taken out and secreted; that the window was unbarred and unbolted; are these to be so slightly and so easily disposed of?

It is necessary, Gentlemen, to settle now, at the commencement, the great question of a conspiracy. If there was none, or the defendant was not a party, then there is no evidence here to convict him. If there was a conspiracy, and he is proved to have been a party, then these two facts have a strong bearing on others, and all the great points of inquiry. The defendant's counsel take no distinct ground, as I have already said, on this point, either to admit or to deny. They choose to confine themselves to a hypothetical mode of speech. They say, supposing there was a conspiracy, *non sequitur* that the prisoner is guilty as principal. Be it so. But still, if there was a conspiracy, and if he was a conspirator, and helped to plan the murder, this may shed much light on the evidence which goes to charge him with the execution of that plan.

We mean to make out the conspiracy; and that the defendant was a party to it; and then to draw all just inferences from these facts.

Let me ask your attention, then, in the first place, to those appearances, on the morning after the murder, which have a tendency to show that it was done in pursuance of a preconcerted plan of operation. What are they? A man was found murdered in his bed. No stranger had done the deed, no one unacquainted with the house had done it. It was apparent that somebody within had opened, and that somebody without had entered. There had obviously and certainly been concert and co-operation. The inmates of the house were not alarmed when the murder was perpetrated. The assassin had entered without any riot or any violence. He had found the way prepared before him. The house had been previously opened. The window was unbarred from within, and its fastening unscrewed. There was a lock on the door of the chamber in which Mr. White slept, but the key was gone. It had been taken away and secreted. The footsteps of the murderer were visible, out-doors, tending toward the window. The plank by which he entered the window still remained. The road he pursued had been thus prepared for him. The victim was slain, and the murderer had escaped. Every thing indicated that somebody within had co-operated with somebody without. Every thing proclaimed that some of the inmates, or somebody having access to the house, had had a hand in the murder. On the face of the circumstances, it was apparent, therefore, that this was a premeditated, concerted murder; that there had been a conspiracy to commit it. Who, then, were the conspirators? If not now found out, we are still groping in the dark, and the whole tragedy is still a mystery.

If the Knapps and the Crowninshields were not the conspirators in this murder, then there is a whole set of conspirators not yet discovered. Because, independent of the testimony of Palmer and Leighton, independent of all disputed evidence, we know, from uncontroverted facts, that this murder was, and must have been, the result of concert and co-operation between two or more. We know it was not done without plan and deliberation; we see, that whoever entered the house, to strike the blow, was favored and aided by some one who had been previously in the house, without suspicion, and who had prepared the way. This is concert, this is co-operation, this is conspiracy. If the Knapps and the Crowninshields, then, were not the conspirators, who were? Joseph Knapp had a motive to desire the death of Mr. White, and that motive has been shown.

He was connected by marriage with the family of Mr. White. His wife was the daughter of Mrs. Beckford, who was the only child of a sister of the deceased. The deceased was more than eighty years old, and had no children. His only heirs were nephews and nieces. He was supposed to be possessed of a very large fortune, which would have descended, by law, to his several nephews and nieces in equal shares; or, if there was a will, then according to the will. But as he had but two branches of heirs, the children of his brother, Henry White, and of Mrs. Beckford, each of these branches, according to the common idea, would have shared one half of his property.

This popular idea is not legally correct. But it is common, and very probably was entertained by the parties. According to this idea, Mrs. Beckford, on Mr. White's death without a will, would have been entitled to one half of his ample fortune; and Joseph Knapp had married one of her three children. There was a will, and this will gave the bulk of the property to others; and we learn from Palmer that one part of the design was to destroy the will before the murder was committed. There had been a previous will, and that previous will was known or believed to have been more favorable than the other to the Beckford family. So that, by destroying the last will, and destroying the life of the testator at the same time, either the first and more favorable will would be set up, or the deceased would have no will, which would be, as was supposed, still more favorable. But the conspirators not having succeeded in obtaining and destroying the last will, though they accomplished the murder, that will being found in existence and safe, and that will bequeathing the mass of the property to others, it seemed at the time impossible for Joseph Knapp, as for any one else, indeed, but the principal devisee, to have any motive which should lead to the murder. The key which unlocks the whole mystery is the knowledge of the intention of the conspirators to steal the will. This is derived from Palmer, and it explains all. It solves the whole marvel. It shows the motive which actuated those, against whom there is much evidence, but who, without the knowledge of this intention, were not seen to have had a motive. This intention is proved, as I have said, by Palmer; and it is so congruous with all the rest of the case, it agrees so well with all facts and circumstances, that no man could well withhold his belief, though the facts were stated by a still less credible witness. If one desirous of opening a lock turns over and tries a bunch of keys till he finds one that will open it, he naturally supposes he has found *the* key of *that* lock. So, in explaining circumstances of evidence which are apparently irreconcilable or unaccountable, if a fact be suggested which at once accounts for all, and reconciles all, by whomsoever it may be stated, it is still difficult not to believe that such fact is the true fact belonging to the case. In this respect, Palmer's testimony is singularly confirmed. If it were false, his ingenuity could not furnish us such clear exposition of strange appearing circumstances. Some truth not before known can alone do that.

When we look back, then, to the state of things immediately on the discovery of the murder, we see that suspicion would naturally turn at once, not to the heirs at law, but to those principally benefited by the will. They, and they alone, would be supposed or seem to have a direct object for wishing Mr. White's life to be terminated. And, strange as it may seem, we find counsel now insisting, that, if no apology, it is yet mitigation of the atrocity of the Knapps' conduct in attempting to charge this foul murder on Mr. White, the nephew and principal devisee, that public suspicion was already so directed! As if assassination of character were excusable in proportion as circumstances may render it easy. Their endeavors, when they knew they were suspected themselves, to fix the charge on others, by foul means and by falsehood, are fair and strong proof of their own guilt. But more of that hereafter.

The counsel say that they might safely admit that Richard Crowninshield, Jr. was the perpetrator of this murder.

But how could they safely admit that? If that were admitted, every thing else would follow. For why should Richard Crowninshield, Jr. kill Mr. White? He was not his heir, nor his devisee; nor was he his enemy. What could be his motive? If Richard Crowninshield, Jr. killed Mr. White, he did it at some one's procurement who himself had a motive. And who, having any motive, is shown to have had any intercourse with Richard Crowninshield, Jr., but Joseph Knapp, and this principally through the agency of the prisoner at the bar? It is the infirmity, the distressing difficulty of the prisoner's case, that his counsel cannot and dare not admit what they yet cannot disprove, and what all must believe. He who believes, on this evidence, that Richard Crowninshield, Jr. was the immediate murderer, cannot doubt that both the Knapps were conspirators in that murder. The counsel, therefore, are wrong, I think, in saying they might safely admit this. The admission of so important and so connected a fact would render it impossible to contend further against the proof of the entire conspiracy, as we state it.

What, then, was this conspiracy? J.J. Knapp, Jr., desirous of destroying the will, and of taking the life of the deceased, hired a ruffian, who, with the aid of other ruffians, was to enter the house, and murder him in his bed.

As far back as January this conspiracy began. Endicott testifies to a conversation with J.J. Knapp at that time, in which Knapp told him that Captain White had made a will, and given the principal part of his property to Stephen White. When asked how he knew, he said, "Black and white don't lie." When asked if the will was not locked up, he said, "There is such a thing as two keys to the same lock." And speaking of the then late illness of Captain White, he said, that Stephen White would not have been sent for if *he* had been there.

Hence it appears, that as early as January Knapp had a knowledge of the will, and that he had access to it by means of false keys. This knowledge of the will, and an intent to destroy it, appear also from Palmer's testimony, a fact disclosed to him by the other conspirators. He says that he was informed of this by the Crowninshields on the 2d of April. But then it is said, that Palmer is not to be credited; that by his own confession he is a felon; that he has been in the State prison in Maine; and, above all, that he was intimately associated with these conspirators themselves. Let us admit these facts. Let us admit him to be as bad as they would represent him to be; still, in law, he is a competent witness. How else are the secret designs of the wicked to be proved, but by their wicked companions, to whom they have disclosed them? The government does not select its witnesses. The conspirators themselves have chosen Palmer. He was the confidant of the prisoners. The fact, however, does not depend on his testimony alone. It is corroborated by other proof; and, taken in connection with the other circumstances, it has strong probability. In regard to the testimony of Palmer, generally, it may be said that it is less contradicted, in all parts of it, either by himself or others, than that of any other material witness, and that every thing he has told is corroborated by other evidence, so far as it is susceptible of confirmation. An attempt has been made to impair his testimony, as to his being at the Half-way House on the night of the murder; you have seen with what success. Mr. Babb is called to contradict him. You have seen how little he knows, and even that not certainly; for he himself is proved to have been in an error by supposing Palmer to have been at the Half-way House on the evening of the 9th of April. At that time he is proved to have been at Dustin's, in Danvers. If, then, Palmer, bad as he is, has disclosed the secrets of the conspiracy, and has told the truth, there is no reason why it should not be believed. Truth is truth, come whence it may.

The facts show that this murder had been long in agitation; that it was not a new proposition on the 2d of

April; that it had been contemplated for five or six weeks. Richard Crowninshield was at Wenham in the latter part of March, as testified by Starrett. Frank Knapp was at Danvers in the latter part of February, as testified by Allen. Richard Crowninshield inquired whether Captain Knapp was about home, when at Wenham. The probability is, that they would open the case to Palmer as a new project. There are other circumstances that show it to have been some weeks in agitation. Palmer's testimony as to the transaction on the 2d of April is corroborated by Allen, and by Osborn's books. He says that Frank Knapp came there in the afternoon, and again in the evening. So the book shows. He says that Captain White had gone out to his farm on that day. So others prove. How could this fact, or these facts, have been known to Palmer, unless Frank Knapp had brought the knowledge? And was it not the special object of this visit to give information of this fact, that they might meet him and execute their purpose on his return from his farm? The letter of Palmer, written at Belfast, bears intrinsic marks of genuineness. It was mailed at Belfast, May 13th. It states facts that he could not have known, unless his testimony be true. This letter was not an afterthought; it is a genuine narrative. In fact, it says, "I know the business your brother Frank was transacting on the 2d of April." How could he have possibly known this, unless he had been there? The "one thousand dollars that was to be paid,"--where could he have obtained this knowledge? The testimony of Endicott, of Palmer, and these facts, are to be taken together; and they most clearly show that the death of Captain White was caused by somebody interested in putting an end to his life.

As to the testimony of Leighton, as far as manner of testifying goes, he is a bad witness; but it does not follow from this that he is not to be believed. There are some strange things about him. It is strange, that he should make up a story against Captain Knapp, the person with whom he lived; that he never voluntarily told any thing: all that he has said was screwed out of him. But the story could not have been invented by him; his character for truth is unimpeached; and he intimated to another witness, soon after the murder happened, that he knew something he should not tell. There is not the least contradiction in his testimony, though he gives a poor account of withholding it. He says that he was extremely *bothered* by those who questioned him. In the main story that he relates, he is entirely consistent with himself. Some things are for him, and some against him. Examine the intrinsic probability of what he says. See if some allowance is not to be made for him, on account of his ignorance of things of this kind. It is said to be extraordinary, that he should have heard just so much of the conversation, and no more; that he should have heard just what was necessary to be proved, and nothing else. Admit that this is extraordinary; still, this does not prove it untrue. It is extraordinary that you twelve gentlemen should be called upon, out of all the men in the county, to decide this case; no one could have foretold this three weeks since. It is extraordinary that the first clew to this conspiracy should have been derived from information given by the father of the prisoner at the bar. And in every case that comes to trial there are many things extraordinary. The murder itself is a most extraordinary one; but still we do not doubt its reality.

It is argued, that this conversation between Joseph and Frank could not have been as Leighton has testified, because they had been together for several hours before; this subject must have been uppermost in their minds, whereas this appears to have been the commencement of their conversation upon it. Now this depends altogether upon the tone and manner of the expression; upon the particular word in the sentence which was emphatically spoken. If he had said, "When did you *see* Dick, Frank?" this would not seem to be the beginning of the conversation. With what emphasis it was uttered, it is not possible to learn; and therefore nothing can be made of this argument. If this boy's testimony stood alone, it should be received with caution. And the same may be said of the testimony of Palmer. But they do not stand alone. They furnish a clew to numerous other circumstances, which, when known, mutually confirm what would have been received with caution without such corroboration. How could Leighton have made up this conversation? "When did you see Dick?" "I saw him this morning." "When is he going to kill the old man?" "I don't know." "Tell him, if he don't do it soon, I won't pay him." Here is a vast amount in few words. Had he wit enough to invent this? There is nothing so powerful as truth; and often nothing so strange. It is not ever suggested that the story was made for him. There is nothing so extraordinary in the whole matter, as it would have been for this ignorant country boy to invent this story.

The acts of the parties themselves furnish strong presumption of their guilt. What was done on the receipt of the letter from Maine? This letter was signed by Charles Grant, Jr., a person not known to either of the Knapps, nor was it known to them that any other person beside the Crowninshields knew of the conspiracy. This letter, by the accidental omission of the word Jr., fell into the hands of the father, when intended for the son. The father carried it to Wenham, where both the sons were. They both read it. Fix your eye steadily on this part of the *circumstantial stuff* which is in the case, and see what can be made of it. This was shown to the two brothers on Saturday, the 15th of May. Neither of them knew Palmer. And if they had known him, they could not have known him to have been the writer of this letter. It was mysterious to them how any one at Belfast could have had knowledge of this affair. Their conscious guilt prevented due circumspection. They did not see the bearing of its publication. They advised their father to carry it to the Committee of Vigilance, and it was so carried. On the Sunday following, Joseph began to think there might be something in it. Perhaps, in the mean time, he had seen one of the Crowninshields. He was apprehensive that they might be suspected; he was anxious to turn attention from their family. What course did he adopt to effect this? He addressed one letter, with a false name, to Mr. White, and another to the Committee; and to complete the climax of his folly, he signed the letter addressed to the Committee, "Grant," the same name as that which was signed to the letter received from Belfast. It was in the knowledge of the Committee, that no person but the Knapps had seen this letter from Belfast; and that no other person knew its signature. It therefore must have been irresistibly plain to them that one of the Knapps was the writer of the letter received by the Committee, charging the murder on Mr. White. Add to this the fact of its having been dated at Lynn, and mailed at Salem four days after it was dated, and who could doubt respecting it? Have you ever read or known of folly equal to this? Can you conceive of crime more odious and abominable? Merely to explain the apparent mysteries of the letter from Palmer, they excite the basest suspicions against a man, whom, if they were innocent, they had no reason to believe guilty; and whom, if they were guilty, they most certainly knew to be innocent. Could they have adopted a more direct method of exposing their own infamy? The letter to the Committee has intrinsic marks of a knowledge of this transaction. It tells the *time* and the *manner* in which the murder was committed. Every line speaks the writer's condemnation. In attempting to divert attention from his family, and to charge the guilt upon another, he indelibly fixes it upon himself.

Joseph Knapp requested Allen to put these letters into the post-office, because, said he, "I wish to nip this silly affair in the bud." If this were not the order of an overruling Providence, I should say that it was the silliest piece of folly that was ever practised. Mark the destiny of crime. It is ever obliged to resort to such subterfuges; it trembles in the broad light; it betrays itself in seeking concealment. He alone walks safely who walks uprightly. Who for a moment can read these letters and doubt of Joseph Knapp's guilt? The constitution of nature is made to inform against him. There is no corner dark enough to conceal him. There is no turnpike-road broad enough or smooth enough for a man so guilty to walk in without stumbling. Every step proclaims his secret to every passenger. His own acts come out to fix his guilt. In attempting to charge another with his own crime, he writes his own confession. To do away the effect of Palmer's letter, signed Grant, he writes a letter himself and affixes to it the name of Grant. He writes in a disguised hand; but could it happen that the same Grant should be in Salem that was at Belfast? This has brought the whole thing out. Evidently he did it, because he has adopted the same style. Evidently he did it, because he speaks of the price of blood, and of other circumstances connected with the murder, that no one but a conspirator could have known.

Palmer says he made a visit to the Crowninshields, on the 9th of April. George then asked him whether he had heard of the murder. Richard inquired whether he had heard the music at Salem. They said that they were suspected, that a committee had been appointed to search houses; and that they had melted up the dagger, the day after the murder, because it would be a suspicious circumstance to have it found in their possession. Now this committee was not appointed, in fact, until Friday evening. But this proves nothing against Palmer; it does not prove that George did not tell him so; it only proves that he gave a false reason for a fact. They had heard that they were suspected; how could they have heard this, unless it were from the whisperings of their own consciences? Surely this rumor was not then public.

About the 27th of April, another attempt was made by the Knapps to give a direction to public suspicion. They reported themselves to have been robbed, in passing from Salem to Wenham, near Wenham Pond. They came to Salem and stated the particulars of the adventure. They described persons, their dress, size, and appearance, who had been suspected of the murder. They would have it understood that the community was infested by a band of ruffians, and that they themselves were the particular objects of their vengeance. Now this turns out to be all fictitious, all false. Can you conceive of any thing more enormous, any wickedness greater, than the circulation of such reports? than the allegation of crimes, if committed, capital? If no such crime had been committed, then it reacts with double force upon themselves, and goes very far to show their guilt. How did they conduct themselves on this occasion? Did they make hue and cry? Did they give information that they had been assaulted that night at Wenham? No such thing. They rested quietly that night; they waited to be called on for the particulars of their adventure; they made no attempt to arrest the offenders; this was not their object. They were content to fill the thousand mouths of rumor, to spread abroad false reports, to divert the attention of the public from themselves; for they thought every man suspected them, because they knew they ought to be suspected.

The manner in which the compensation for this murder was paid is a circumstance worthy of consideration. By examining the facts and dates, it will satisfactorily appear that Joseph Knapp paid a sum of money to Richard Crowninshield, in five-franc pieces, on the 24th of April. On the 21st of April, Joseph Knapp received five hundred five-franc pieces, as the proceeds of an adventure at sea. The remainder of this species of currency that came home in the vessel was deposited in a bank at Salem. On Saturday, the 24th of April, Frank and Richard rode to Wenham. They were there with Joseph an hour or more, and appeared to be negotiating private business. Richard continued in the chaise; Joseph came to the chaise and conversed with him. These facts are proved by Hart and Leighton, and by Osborn's books. On Saturday evening, about this time, Richard Crowninshield is proved, by Lummus, to have been at Wenham, with another person whose appearance corresponds with Frank's. Can any one doubt this being the same evening? What had Richard Crowninshield to do at Wenham, with Joseph, unless it were this business? He was there before the murder; he was there after the murder; he was there clandestinely, unwilling to be seen. If it were not upon this business, let it be told what it was for. Joseph Knapp could explain it; Frank Knapp might explain it. But they do not explain it; and the inference is against them.

Immediately after this, Richard passes five-franc pieces; on the same evening, one to Lummus, five to Palmer; and near this time George passes three or four in Salem. Here are nine of these pieces passed by them in four days; this is extraordinary. It is an unusual currency; in ordinary business, few men would pass nine such pieces in the course of a year. If they were not received in this way, why not explain how they came by them? Money was not so flush in their pockets that they could not tell whence it came, if it honestly came there. It is extremely important to them to explain whence this money came, and they would do it if they could. If, then, the price of blood was paid at this time, in the presence and with the knowledge of this defendant, does not this prove him to have been connected with this conspiracy?

Observe, also, the effect on the mind of Richard of Palmer's being arrested and committed to prison; the various efforts he makes to discover the fact; the lowering, through the crevices of the rock, the pencil and paper for him to write upon; the sending two lines of poetry, with the request that he would return the corresponding lines; the shrill and peculiar whistle; the inimitable exclamations of "Palmer! Palmer! Palmer!" All these things prove how great was his alarm; they corroborate Palmer's story, and tend to establish the conspiracy.

Joseph Knapp had a part to act in this matter. He must have opened the window, and secreted the key; he had free access to every part of the house; he was accustomed to visit there; he went in and out at his pleasure; he could do this without being suspected. He is proved to have been there the Saturday preceding.

If all these things, taken in connection, do not prove that Captain White was murdered in pursuance of a conspiracy, then the case is at an end.

Savary's testimony is wholly unexpected. He was called for a different purpose. When asked who the person was that he saw come out of Captain White's yard between three and four o'clock in the morning, he answered, Frank Knapp. It is not clear that this is not true. There may be many circumstances of importance connected with this, though we believe the murder to have been committed between ten and eleven o'clock. The letter to Dr. Barstow states it to have been done about eleven o'clock; it states it to have been done with a blow on the head, from a weapon loaded with lead. Here is too great a correspondence with the reality not to have some meaning in it. Dr. Peirson was always of the opinion, that the two classes of wounds were made with different instruments, and by different hands. It is possible that one class was inflicted at one time, and the other at another. It is possible that on the last visit the pulse might not have entirely ceased to beat, and then the finishing stroke was given. It is said, that, when the body was discovered, some of the wounds wept, while the others did not. They may have been inflicted from mere wantonness. It was known that Captain White was accustomed to keep specie by him in his chamber; this perhaps may explain the last visit. It is proved, that this defendant was in the habit of retiring to bed, and leaving it afterwards, without the knowledge of his family; perhaps he did so on this occasion. We see no reason to doubt the fact; and it does not shake our belief that the murder was committed early in the night.

What are the probabilities as to the time of the murder? Mr. White was an aged man; he usually retired to bed at about half-past nine. He slept soundest in the early part of the night; usually awoke in the middle and latter part; and his habits were perfectly well known. When would persons, with a knowledge of these facts, be most likely to approach him? Most certainly, in the first hour of his sleep. This would be the safest time. If seen then going to or from the house, the appearance would be least suspicious. The earlier hour would then have been most probably selected.

Gentlemen, I shall dwell no longer on the evidence which tends to prove that there was a conspiracy, and that the prisoner was a conspirator. All the circumstances concur to make out this point. Not only Palmer swears to it, in effect, and Leighton, but Allen mainly supports Palmer, and Osborn's books lend confirmation, so far as possible, from such a source. Palmer is contradicted in nothing, either by any other witness, or any proved circumstance or occurrence. Whatever could be expected to support him does support him. All the evidence clearly manifests, I think, that there was a conspiracy; that it originated with Joseph Knapp; that defendant became a party to it, and was one of its conductors, from first to last. One of the most powerful circumstances is Palmer's letter from Belfast. The amount of this is a direct charge on the Knapps of the authorship of this murder. How did they treat this charge; like honest men, or like guilty men? We have seen how it was treated. Joseph Knapp fabricated letters, charging another person, and caused them to be put into the post-office.

I shall now proceed on the supposition, that it is proved that there was a conspiracy to murder Mr. White, and that the prisoner was party to it.

The second and the material inquiry is, Was the prisoner present at the murder, aiding and abetting therein? This leads to the legal question in the case. What does the law mean, when it says, that, in order to charge him as a principal, "he must be present aiding and abetting in the murder"?

In the language of the late Chief Justice, "It is not required that the abettor shall be actually upon the spot when the murder is committed, or even in sight of the more immediate perpetrator of the victim, to make him a principal. If he be at a distance, co-operating in the act, by watching to prevent relief, or to give an alarm, or to assist his confederate in escape, having knowledge of the purpose and object of the assassin, this in the eye of the law is being present, aiding and abetting, so as to make him a principal in the murder."

"If he be at a distance co-operating." This is not a distance to be measured by feet or rods; if the intent to lend aid combine with a knowledge that the murder is to be committed, and the person so intending be so situate that he can by any possibility lend this aid in any manner, then he is present in legal contemplation. He need not lend any actual aid; to be ready to assist is assisting.

There are two sorts of murder; the distinction between them it is of essential importance to bear in mind: 1. Murder in an affray, or upon sudden and unexpected provocation. 2. Murder secretly, with a deliberate, predetermined intention to commit the crime. Under the first class, the question usually is, whether the offence be murder or manslaughter, in the person who commits the deed. Under the second class, it is often a question whether others than he who actually did the deed were present, aiding and assisting therein. Offences of this kind ordinarily happen when there is nobody present except those who go on the same design. If a riot should happen in the court-house, and one should kill another, this may be murder, or it may not, according to the intention with which it was done; which is always matter of fact, to be collected from the circumstances at the time. But in secret murders, premeditated and determined on, there can be no doubt of the murderous intention; there can be no doubt, if a person be present, knowing a murder is to be done, of his concurring in the act. His being there is a proof of his intent to aid and abet; else, why is he there?

It has been contended, that proof must be given that the person accused did actually afford aid, did lend a hand in the murder itself; and without this proof, although he may be near by, he may be presumed to be there for an innocent purpose; he may have crept silently there to hear the news, or from mere curiosity to see what was going on.[2] Preposterous, absurd! Such an idea shocks all common sense. A man is found to be a conspirator to commit a murder; he has planned it; he has assisted in arranging the time, the place and the means; and he is found in the place, and at the time, and yet it is suggested that he might have been there, not for co-operation and concurrence, but from curiosity! Such an argument deserves no answer. It would be difficult to give it one, in decorous terms. Is it not to be taken for granted, that a man seeks to accomplish his own purposes? When he has planned a murder, and is present at its execution, is he there to forward or to thwart his own design? is he there to assist, or there to prevent? But "Curiosity"! He may be there from mere "curiosity"! Curiosity to witness the success of the execution of his own plan of murder! The very walls of a court-house ought not to stand, the ploughshare should run through the ground it stands on, where such an argument could find toleration.[3]

It is not necessary that the abettor should actually lend a hand, that he should take a part in the act itself; if he be present ready to assist, that is assisting. Some of the doctrines advanced would acquit the defendant, though he had gone to the bedchamber of the deceased, though he had been standing by when the assassin gave the blow. This is the argument we have heard to-day.

The court here said, they did not so understand the argument of the counsel for defendant. Mr. Dexter said, "The intent and power alone must co-operate."

No doubt the law is, that being ready to assist is assisting, if the party has the power to assist, in case of need. It is so stated by Foster, who is a high authority. "If A happeneth to be present at a murder, for instance, and taketh no part in it, nor endeavoreth to prevent it, nor apprehendeth the murderer, nor levyeth hue and cry after him, this strange behavior of his, though highly criminal, will not of itself render him either principal or accessory." "But if a fact amounting to murder should be committed in prosecution of some unlawful purpose, though it were but a bare trespass, to which A in the case last stated had consented, and he had gone in order to give assistance, if need were, for carrying it into execution, this would have amounted to murder in him, and in every person present and joining with him." "If the fact was committed in prosecution of the original purpose which was unlawful, the whole party will be involved in the guilt of him who gave the blow. For in combinations of this kind, the mortal stroke, though given by one of the party, is considered in the eye of the law, and of sound reason too, as given by every individual present and abetting. The person actually giving the stroke is no more than the hand or instrument by which the others strike." The author, in speaking of being present, means actual presence; not actual in opposition to constructive, for the law knows no such distinction. There is but one presence, and this is the situation from which aid, or supposed aid, may be rendered. The law does not say where the person is to go, or how near he is to go, but that he must be where he may give assistance, or where the perpetrator may believe that he may be assisted by him. Suppose that he is acquainted with the design of the murderer, and has a knowledge of the time when it is to be carried into effect, and goes out with a view to render assistance, if need be; why, then, even though the murderer does not know of this, the person so going out will be an abettor in the murder.

It is contended that the prisoner at the bar could not be a principal, he being in Brown Street, because he could not there render assistance; and you are called upon to determine this case, according as you may be of opinion whether Brown Street was, or was not, a suitable, convenient, well-chosen place to aid in this murder. This is not the true question. The inquiry is not whether you would have selected this place in preference to all others, or whether you would have selected it at all. If the parties chose it, why should we doubt about it? How do we know the use they intended to make of it, or the kind of aid that he was to afford by being there? The question for you to consider is, Did the defendant go into Brown Street in aid of this murder? Did he go there by agreement, by appointment with the perpetrator?[4] If so, every thing else follows. The main thing, indeed the only thing, is to inquire whether he was in Brown Street by appointment with Richard Crowninshield. It might be to keep general watch; to observe the lights, and advise as to time of access; to meet the murderer on his return, to advise him as to his escape; to examine his clothes, to see if any marks of blood were upon them; to furnish exchange of clothes, or new disguise, if necessary; to tell him through what streets he could safely retreat, or whether he could deposit the club in the place designed; or it might be without any distinct object, but merely to afford that encouragement which would proceed from Richard Crowninshield's consciousness that he was near. It is of no consequence whether, in your opinion, the place was well chosen or not, to afford aid; if it was so chosen, if it was by appointment that he was there, it is enough. Suppose Richard Crowninshield, when applied to to commit the murder, had said, "I won't do it unless there can be some one near by to favor my escape; I won't go unless you will stay in Brown Street." Upon the gentleman's argument, he would not be an aider and abettor in the murder, because the place was not well chosen; though it is apparent that the being in the place chosen was a condition, without which the murder would never have happened.

You are to consider the defendant as one in the league, in the combination to commit the murder. If he was there by appointment with the perpetrator, he is an abettor. The concurrence of the perpetrator in his being there is proved by the previous evidence of the conspiracy. If Richard Crowninshield, for any purpose whatsoever, made it a condition of the agreement, that Frank Knapp should stand as backer, then Frank Knapp was an aider and abettor; no matter what the aid was, or what sort it was, or degree, be it ever so little; even if it were to judge of the hour when it was best to go, or to see when the lights were extinguished, or to give an alarm if any one approached. Who better calculated to judge of these things than the murderer himself? and if he so determined them, that is sufficient.

Now as to the facts. Frank Knapp knew that the murder was that night to be committed; he was one of the conspirators, he knew the object, he knew the time. He had that day been to Wenham to see Joseph, and probably to Danvers to see Richard Crowninshield, for he kept his motions secret. He had that day hired a horse and chaise of Osborn, and attempted to conceal the purpose for which it was used; he had intentionally left the *place* and the *price* blank on Osborn's books. He went to Wenham by the way of Danvers; he had been told the week before to hasten Dick; he had seen the Crowninshields several times within a few days; he had a saddle-horse the Saturday night before; he had seen Mrs. Beckford at Wenham, and knew she would not return that night. She had not been away before for six weeks, and probably would not soon be again. He had just come from Wenham. Every day, for the week previous, he had visited one or another of these conspirators, save Sunday, and then probably he saw them in town. When he saw Joseph on the 6th, Joseph had prepared the house, and would naturally tell him of it; there were constant communications between them; daily and nightly visitation; too much knowledge of these parties and this transaction, to leave a particle of doubt on the mind of any one, that Frank Knapp knew the murder was to be committed this night. The hour was come, and he knew it; if so, and he was in Brown Street, without explaining why he was there, can the jury for a moment doubt whether he was there to countenance, aid, or support; or for curiosity alone; or to learn how the wages of sin and death were earned by the perpetrator?

Here Mr. Webster read the law from Hawkins. 1 Hawk. 204, Lib. 1, ch. 32 sec. 7.

The perpetrator would derive courage, and strength, and confidence, from the knowledge that one of his associates was near by. If he was in Brown Street, he could have been there for no other purpose. If there for this purpose, then he was, in the language of the law, _present_, aiding and abetting in the murder. His interest lay in being somewhere else. If he had nothing to do with the murder, no part to act, why not stay at home? Why should he jeopard his own life, if it was not agreed that he should be there? He would not voluntarily go where the very place would cause him to swing if detected. He would not voluntarily assume the place of danger. His taking this place proves that he went to give aid. His staying away would have made an *alibi*. If he had nothing to do with the murder, he would be at home, where he could prove his *alibi*. He knew he was in danger, because he was guilty of the conspiracy, and, if he had nothing to do, would not expose himself to suspicion or detection.

Did the prisoner at the bar countenance this murder? Did he concur, or did he non-concur, in what the perpetrator was about to do? Would he have tried to shield him? Would he have furnished his cloak for protection? Would he have pointed out a safe way of retreat? As you would answer these questions, so you should answer the general question, whether he was there consenting to the murder, or whether he was there as a spectator only.

One word more on this presence, called constructive presence. What aid is to be rendered? Where is the line to be drawn, between acting, and omitting to act? Suppose he had been in the house, suppose he had followed the perpetrator to the chamber, what could he have done? This was to be a murder by stealth; it was to be a secret assassination. It was not their purpose to have an open combat; they were to approach their victim unawares, and silently give the fatal blow. But if he had been in the chamber, no one can doubt that he would have been an abettor; because of his presence, and ability to render services, if needed. What service could he have rendered, if there? Could he have helped him to fly? Could he have aided the silence of his movements? Could he have facilitated his retreat, on the first alarm? Surely, this was a case where there was more of safety in going alone than with another; where company would only embarrass. Richard Crowninshield would prefer to go alone. He knew his errand too well. His nerves needed no collateral support. He was not the man to take with him a trembling companion. He would prefer to have his aid at a distance. He would not wish to be encumbered by his presence. He would prefer to have him out of the house. He would prefer that he should be in Brown Street. But whether in the chamber, in the house, in the garden, or in the street, whatsoever is aiding in *actual presence* is aiding in _constructive presence_; any thing that is aid in one case is aid in the other.[5]

If, then, the aid be anywhere, so as to embolden the perpetrator, to afford him hope or confidence in his enterprise, it is the same as though the person stood at his elbow with his sword drawn. His being there ready to act, with the power to act, is what makes him an abettor.

Here Mr. Webster referred to the cases of Kelly, of Hyde, and others, cited by counsel for the defendant, and showed that they did not militate with the doctrine for which he contended. The difference is, in those cases there was open violence; this was a case of secret assassination. The aid must meet the occasion. Here no *acting* was necessary, but watching, concealment of escape, management.

What are the *facts* in relation to this presence? Frank Knapp is proved to have been a conspirator, proved to have known that the deed was now to be done. Is it not probable that he was in Brown Street to concur in the murder? There were four conspirators. It was natural that some one of them should go with the perpetrator. Richard Crowninshield was to be the perpetrator; he was to give the blow. There is no evidence of any casting of the parts for the others. The defendant would probably be the man to take the second part. He was fond of exploits, he was accustomed to the use of sword-canes and dirks. If any aid was required, he was the man to give it. At least, there is no evidence to the contrary of this.

Aid could not have been received from Joseph Knapp, or from George Crowninshield. Joseph Knapp was at Wenham, and took good care to prove that he was there. George Crowninshield has proved satisfactorily where he was; that he was in other company, such as it was, until eleven o'clock. This narrows the inquiry. This demands of the prisoner to show, if he was not in this place, where he was. It calls on him loudly to show this, and to show it truly. If he could show it, he would do it. If he does not tell, and that truly, it is against him. The defence of an *alibi* is a double-edged sword. He knew that he was in a situation where he might be called upon to account for himself. If he had had no particular appointment or business to attend to, he would have taken care to be able so to account. He would have been out of town, or in some good company. Has he accounted for himself on that night to your satisfaction?

The prisoner has attempted to prove an *alibi* in two ways. In the first place, by four young men with whom he says he was in company, on the evening of the murder, from seven o'clock till near ten o'clock. This depends upon the certainty of the night. In the second place, by his family, from ten o'clock afterwards. This depends upon the certainty of the time of the night. These two classes of proof have no connection with each other. One may be true, and the other false; or they may both be true, or both be false. I shall examine this testimony with some attention, because, on a former trial, it made more impression on the minds of the court than on my own mind. I think, when carefully sifted and compared, it will be found to have in it more of plausibility than reality.

Mr. Page testifies, that on the evening of the 6th of April he was in company with Burchmore, Balch, and Forrester, and that he met the defendant about seven o'clock, near the Salem Hotel; that he afterwards met him at Remond's, about nine o'clock, and that he was in company with him a considerable part of the evening. This young gentleman is a member of college, and says that he came to town the Saturday evening previous; that he is now able to say that it was the night of the murder when he walked with Frank Knapp, from the recollection of the fact, that he called himself to an account, on the morning after the murder, as it is natural for men to do when an extraordinary occurrence happens. Gentlemen, this kind of evidence is not satisfactory; general impressions as to time are not to be relied on. If I were called on to state the particular day on which any witness testified in this cause, I could not do it. Every man will notice the same thing in his own mind. There is no one of these young men that could give an account of himself for any *other* day in the month of April. They are made to remember the fact, and then they think they remember the time. The witness has no means of knowing it was Tuesday rather than any other time. He did not know it at first; he could not know it afterwards. He says he called himself to an account. This has no more to do with the murder than with the man in the moon. Such testimony is not worthy to be relied on in any forty-shilling cause. What occasion had he to call himself to an account? Did he suppose that he should be suspected? Had he any intimation of this conspiracy?

Suppose, Gentlemen, you were either of you asked where you were, or what you were doing, on the fifteenth day of June; you could not answer this question without calling to mind some events to make it certain. Just as well may you remember on what you dined each day of the year past. Time is identical. Its subdivisions are all alike. No man knows one day from another, or one hour from another, but by some fact connected with it. Days and hours are not visible to the senses, nor to be apprehended and distinguished by the understanding. The flow of time is known only by something which marks it; and he who speaks of the date of occurrences with nothing to guide his recollection speaks at random, and is not to be relied on. This young gentleman remembers the facts and occurrences; he knows nothing why they should not have happened on the evening of the 6th; but he knows no more. All the rest is evidently conjecture or impression.

Mr. White informs you, that he told him he could not tell what night it was. The first thoughts are all that are valuable in such case. They miss the mark by taking second aim.

Mr. Balch believes, but is not sure, that he was with Frank Knapp on the evening of the murder. He has given different accounts of the time. He has no means of making it certain. All he knows is, that it was some evening before Fast-day. But whether Monday, Tuesday, or Saturday, he cannot tell.

Mr. Burchmore says, to the best of his belief, it was the evening of the murder. Afterwards he attempts to speak positively, from recollecting that he mentioned the circumstance to William Peirce, as he went to the Mineral Spring on Fast-day. Last Monday morning he told Colonel Putnam he could not fix the time. This witness stands in a much worse plight than either of the others. It is difficult to reconcile all he has said with any belief in the accuracy of his recollections.

Mr. Forrester does not speak with any certainty as to the night; and it is very certain that he told Mr. Loring and others, that he did not know what night it was.

Now, what does the testimony of these four young men amount to? The only circumstance by which they approximate to an identifying of the night is, that three of them say it was cloudy; they think their walk was either on Monday or Tuesday evening, and it is admitted that Monday evening was clear, whence they draw the inference that it must have been Tuesday.

But, fortunately, there is one *fact* disclosed in their testimony that settles the question. Balch says, that on the evening, whenever it was, he saw the prisoner; the prisoner told him he was going out of town on horseback, for a distance of about twenty minutes' drive, and that he was going to get a horse at Osborn's. This was about seven o'clock. At about nine, Balch says he saw the prisoner again, and was then told by him that he had had his ride, and had returned. Now it appears by Osborn's books, that the prisoner had a saddle-horse from his stable, not on Tuesday evening, the night of the murder, but on the Saturday evening previous. This fixes the time about which these young men testify, and is a complete answer and refutation of the attempted *alibi* on Tuesday evening.

I come now to speak of the testimony adduced by the defendant to explain where he was after ten o'clock on the night of the murder. This comes chiefly from members of the family; from his father and brothers. It is agreed that the affidavit of the prisoner should be received as evidence of what his brother, Samuel H. Knapp, would testify if present. Samuel H. Knapp says, that, about ten minutes past ten o'clock, his brother, Frank Knapp, on his way to bed, opened his chamber door, made some remarks, closed the door, and went to his chamber; and that he did not hear him leave it afterwards. How is this witness able to fix the time at ten minutes past ten? There is no circumstance mentioned by which he fixes it. He had been in bed, probably asleep, and was aroused from his sleep by the opening of the door. Was he in a situation to speak of time with precision? Could he know, under such circumstances, whether it was ten minutes past ten, or ten minutes before eleven, when his brother spoke to him? What would be the natural result in such a case? But we are not left to conjecture this result. We have positive testimony on this point. Mr. Webb tells you that Samuel told him, on the 8th of June, "that he did not know what time his brother Frank came home, and that he was not at home when *he* went to bed." You will consider this testimony of Mr. Webb as indorsed upon this affidavit; and with this indorsement upon it, you will give it its due weight. This statement was made to him after Frank was arrested.

I come to the testimony of the father. I find myself incapable of speaking of him or his testimony with severity. Unfortunate old man! Another Lear, in the conduct of his children; another Lear, I apprehend, in the effect of his distress upon his mind and understanding. He is brought here to testify, under circumstances that disarm severity, and call loudly for sympathy. Though it is impossible not to see that his story cannot be credited, yet I am unable to speak of him otherwise than in sorrow and grief. Unhappy father! he strives to remember, perhaps persuades himself that he does remember, that on the evening of the murder he was himself at home at ten o'clock. He thinks, or seems to think, that his son came in at about five minutes past ten. He fancies that he remembers his conversation; he thinks he spoke of bolting the door; he thinks he asked the time of night; he seems to remember his then going to his bed. Alas! these are but the swimming fancies of an agitated and distressed mind. Alas! they are but the dreams of hope, its uncertain lights, flickering on the thick darkness of parental distress. Alas! the miserable father knows nothing, in reality, of all these things.

Mr. Shepard says that the first conversation he had with Mr. Knapp was soon after the murder, and *before* the arrest of his sons. Mr. Knapp says it was *after* the arrest of his sons. His own fears led him to say to Mr. Shepard, that his "son Frank was at home that night; and so Phippen told him," or "as Phippen told him." Mr. Shepard says that he was struck with the remark at the time; that it made an unfavorable impression on his mind; he does not tell you what that impression was, but when you connect it with the previous inquiry he had made, whether Frank had continued to associate with the Crowninshields, and recollect that the Crowninshields were then known to be suspected of this crime, can you doubt what this impression was? can you doubt as to the fears he then had?

This poor old man tells you, that he was greatly perplexed at the time; that he found himself in embarrassed circumstances; that on this very night he was engaged in making an assignment of his property to his friend, Mr. Shepard. If ever charity should furnish a mantle for error, it should be here. Imagination cannot picture a more deplorable, distressed condition.

The same general remarks may be applied to his conversation with Mr. Treadwell, as have been made upon that with Mr. Shepard. He told him, that he believed Frank was at home about the usual time. In his conversations with either of these persons, he did not pretend to know, of his own knowledge, the time that he came home. He now tells you positively that he recollects the time, and that he so told Mr. Shepard. He is directly contradicted by both these witnesses, as respectable men as Salem affords.

This idea of an *alibi* is of recent origin. Would Samuel Knapp have gone to sea if it were then thought of? His testimony, if true, was too important to be lost. If there be any truth in this part of the _alibi_, it is so near in point or time that it cannot be relied on. The mere variation of half an hour would avoid it. The mere variations of different timepieces would explain it.

Has the defendant proved where he was on that night? If you doubt about it, there is an end of it. The burden is upon him to satisfy you beyond all reasonable doubt. Osborn's books, in connection with what the young men state, are conclusive, I think, on this point. He has not, then, accounted for himself; he has attempted it, and has failed. I pray you to remember, Gentlemen, that this is a case in which the prisoner would, more than any other, be rationally able to account for himself on the night of the murder, if he could do so. He was in the conspiracy, he knew the murder was then to be committed, and if he himself was to have no hand in its actual execution, he would of course, as a matter of safety and precaution, be somewhere else, and be able to prove afterwards that he had been somewhere else. Having this motive to prove himself elsewhere, and the power to do it if he were elsewhere, his failing in such proof must necessarily leave a very strong inference against him.

But, Gentlemen, let us now consider what is the evidence produced on the part of the government to prove that John Francis Knapp, the prisoner at the bar, was in Brown Street on the night of the murder. This is a point of vital importance in this cause. Unless this be made out, beyond reasonable doubt, the law of *presence* does not apply to the case. The government undertake to prove that he was present aiding in the murder, by proving that he was in Brown Street for this purpose. Now, what are the undoubted facts? They are, that two persons were seen in that street, several times during that evening, under suspicious circumstances; under such circumstances as induced those who saw them to watch their movements. Of this there can be no doubt. Mirick saw a man standing at the post opposite his store from fifteen minutes before nine until twenty minutes after, dressed in a full frock-coat, glazed cap, and so forth, in size and general appearance answering to the prisoner at the bar. This person was waiting there; and whenever any one approached him, he moved to and from the corner, as though he would avoid being suspected or recognized. Afterwards, two persons were seen by Webster, walking in Howard Street, with a slow, deliberate movement that attracted his attention. This was about half-past nine. One of these he took to be the prisoner at the bar, the other he did not know.

About half-past ten a person is seen sitting on the rope-walk steps, wrapped in a cloak. He drops his head when passed, to avoid being known. Shortly after, two persons are seen to meet in this street, without ceremony or salutation, and in a hurried manner to converse for a short time; then to separate, and run off with great speed. Now, on this same night a gentleman is slain, murdered in his bed, his house being entered by stealth from without; and his house situated within three hundred feet of this street. The windows of his chamber were in plain sight from this street; a weapon of death is afterwards found in a place where these persons were seen to pass, in a retired place, around which they had been seen lingering. It is now known that this murder was committed by four persons, conspiring together for this purpose. No account is given who these suspected persons thus seen in Brown Street and its neighborhood were. Now, I ask, Gentlemen, whether you or any man can doubt that this murder was committed by the persons who were thus in and about Brown Street. Can any person doubt that they were there for purposes connected with this murder? If not for this purpose, what were they there for? When there is a cause so near at hand, why wander into conjecture for an explanation? Common-sense requires you to take the nearest adequate cause for a known effect. Who were these suspicious persons in Brown Street? There was something extraordinary about them; something noticeable, and noticed at the time; something in their appearance that aroused suspicion. And a man is found the next morning murdered in the near vicinity.

Now, so long as no other account shall be given of those suspicious persons, so long the inference must remain irresistible that they were the murderers. Let it be remembered, that it is already shown that this murder was the result of conspiracy and of concert; let it be remembered, that the house, having been opened from within, was entered by stealth from without. Let it be remembered that Brown Street, where these persons were repeatedly seen under such suspicious circumstances, was a place from which every occupied room in Mr. White's house is clearly seen; let it be remembered, that the place, though thus very near to Mr. White's house, is a retired and lonely place; and let it be remembered that the instrument of death was afterwards found concealed very near the same spot.

Must not every man come to the conclusion, that these persons thus seen in Brown Street were the murderers? Every man's own judgment, I think, must satisfy him that this must be so. It is a plain deduction of common sense. It is a point on which each one of you may reason like a Hale or a Mansfield. The two occurrences explain each other. The murder shows why these persons were thus lurking, at that hour, in Brown Street; and their lurking in Brown Street shows who committed the murder.

If, then, the persons in and about Brown Street were the plotters and executers of the murder of Captain White, we know who they were, and you know that *there* is one of them.

This fearful concatenation of circumstances puts him to an account. He was a conspirator. He had entered into this plan of murder. The murder is committed, and he is known to have been within three minutes' walk of the place. He must account for himself, He has attempted this, and failed. Then, with all these general reasons to show he was actually in Brown Street, and his failures in his _alibi_, let us see what is the direct proof of his being there. But first, let me ask, is it not very remarkable that there is no attempt to show where Richard Crowninshield, Jr. was on that night? We hear nothing of him. He was seen in none of his usual haunts about the town. Yet, if he was the actual perpetrator of the murder, which nobody doubts, he was in the town somewhere. Can you, therefore, entertain a doubt that he was one of the persons seen in Brown Street? And as to the prisoner, you will recollect, that, since the testimony of the young men has failed to show where he was on that evening, the last we hear or know of him, on the day preceding the murder, is, that at four o'clock, P.M., he was at his brother's in Wenham. He had left home, after dinner, in a manner doubtless designed to avoid observation, and had gone to Wenham, probably by way of Danvers. As we hear nothing of him after four o'clock, P.M., for the remainder of the day and evening; as he was one of the conspirators; as Richard Crowninshield, Jr. was another; as Richard Crowninshield, Jr. was in town in the evening, and yet seen in no usual place of resort,--the inference is very fair, that Richard Crowninshield, Jr. and the prisoner were together, acting in execution of their conspiracy. Of the four conspirators, J.J. Knapp, Jr. was at Wenham, and George Crowninshield has been accounted for; so that if the persons seen in Brown Street were the murderers, one of them must have been Richard Crowninshield, Jr., and the other must have been the prisoner at the bar.

Now, as to the proof of his identity with one of the persons seen in Brown Street, Mr. Mirick, a cautious witness, examined the person he saw, closely, in a light night, and says that he thinks the prisoner at the bar is the person; and that he should not hesitate at all, if he were seen in the same dress. His opinion is formed partly from his own observation, and partly from the description of others. But this description turns out to be only in regard to the dress. It is said, that he is now more confident than on the former trial. If he has varied in his testimony make such allowance as you may think proper. I do not perceive any material variance. He thought him the same person, when he was first brought to court, and as he saw him get out of the chaise. This is one of the cases in which a witness is permitted to give an opinion. This witness is as honest as yourselves, neither willing nor swift; but he says, he believes it was the man. His words are, "This is my opinion "; and this opinion it is proper for him to give. If partly founded on what he has _heard_, then this opinion is not to be taken; but if on what he _saw_, then you can have no better evidence. I lay no stress on similarity of dress. No man will ever lose his life by my voice on such evidence. But then it is proper to notice, that no inferences drawn from any *dissimilarity* of dress can be given in the prisoner's favor; because, in fact, the person seen by Mirick was dressed like the prisoner.

The description of the person seen by Mirick answers to that of the prisoner at the bar. In regard to the supposed discrepancy of statements, before and now, there would be no end to such minute inquiries. It would not be strange if witnesses should vary. I do not think much of slight shades of variation. If I believe the witness is honest, that is enough. If he has expressed himself more strongly now than then, this does not prove him false.

Peter E. Webster saw the prisoner at the bar, as he then thought, and still thinks, walking in Howard Street at half-past nine o'clock. He then thought it was Frank Knapp, and has not altered his opinion since. He knew him well; he had long known him. If he then thought it was he, this goes far to prove it. He observed him the more, as it was unusual to see gentlemen walk there at that hour. It was a retired, lonely street. Now, is there reasonable doubt that Mr. Webster did see him there that night? How can you have more proof than this? He judged by his walk, by his general appearance, by his deportment. We all judge in this manner. If you believe he is right, it goes a great way in this case. But then this person, it is said, had a cloak on, and that he could not, therefore, be the same person that Mirick saw. If we were treating of men that had no occasion to disguise themselves or their conduct, there might be something in this argument. But as it is, there is little in it. It may be presumed that they would change their dress. This would help their disguise. What is easier than to throw off a cloak, and again put it on? Perhaps he was less fearful of being known when alone, than when with the perpetrator.

Mr. Southwick swears all that a man can swear. He has the best means of judging that could be had at the time. He tells you that he left his father's house at half-past ten o'clock, and as he passed to his own house in Brown Street he saw a man sitting on the steps of the rope-walk; that he passed him three times, and each time he held down his head, so that he did not see his face. That the man had on a cloak, which was not wrapped around him, and a glazed cap. That he took the man to be Frank Knapp at the time; that, when he went into his house, he told his wife that he thought it was Frank Knapp; that he knew him well, having known him from a boy. And his wife swears that he did so tell her when he came home. What could mislead this witness at the time? He was not then suspecting Frank Knapp of any thing. He could not then be influenced by any prejudice. If you believe that the witness saw Frank Knapp in this position at this time, it proves the case. Whether you believe it or not depends upon the credit of the witness. He swears it. If true, it is solid evidence. Mrs. Southwick supports her husband. Are they true? Are they worthy of belief? If he deserves the epithets applied to him, then he ought not to be believed. In this fact they cannot be mistaken; they are right, or they are perjured. As to his not speaking to Frank Knapp, that depends upon their intimacy. But a very good reason is, Frank chose to disguise himself. This makes nothing against his credit. But it is said that he should not be believed. And why? Because, it is said, he himself now tells you, that, when he testified before the grand jury at Ipswich, he did not then say that he thought the person he saw in Brown Street was Frank Knapp, but that "the person was about the size of Selman." The means of attacking him, therefore, come from himself. If he is a false man, why should he tell truths against himself? They rely on his veracity to prove that he is a liar. Before you can come to this conclusion, you will consider whether all the circumstances are now known, that should have a bearing on this point. Suppose that, when he was before the grand jury, he was asked by the attorney this question, "Was the person you saw in Brown Street about the size of Selman?" and he answered Yes. This was all true. Suppose, also, that he expected to be inquired of further, and no further questions were put to him. Would it not be extremely hard to impute to him perjury for this? It is not uncommon for witnesses to think that they have done all their duty, when they have answered the questions put to them. But suppose that we admit that he did not then tell all he knew, this does not affect the *fact* at all; because he did tell, at the time, in the hearing of others, that the person he saw was Frank Knapp. There is not the slightest suggestion against the veracity or accuracy of Mrs. Southwick. Now she swears positively, that her husband came into the house and told her that he had seen a person on the rope-walk steps, and believed it was Frank Knapp.

It is said that Mr. Southwick is contradicted, also, by Mr. Shillaber. I do not so understand Mr. Shillaber's testimony. I think what they both testify is reconcilable, and consistent. My learned brother said, on a similar occasion, that there is more probability, in such cases, that the persons hearing should misunderstand, than that the person speaking should contradict himself. I think the same remark applicable here.

You have all witnessed the uncertainty of testimony, when witnesses are called to testify what other witnesses said. Several respectable counsellors have been summoned, on this occasion, to give testimony of that sort. They have, every one of them, given different versions. They all took minutes at the time, and without doubt intend to state the truth. But still they differ. Mr. Shillaber's version is different from every thing that Southwick has stated elsewhere. But little reliance is to be placed on slight variations in testimony, unless they are manifestly intentional. I think that Mr. Shillaber must be satisfied that he did not rightly understand Mr. Southwick. I confess I misunderstood Mr. Shillaber on the former trial, if I now rightly understand him. I, therefore, did not then recall Mr. Southwick to the stand. Mr. Southwick, as I read it, understood Mr. Shillaber as asking him about a person coming out of Newbury Street, and whether, for aught he knew, it might not be Richard Crowninshield, Jr. He answered, that he could not tell. He did not understand Mr. Shillaber as questioning him as to the person whom he saw sitting on the steps of the rope-walk. Southwick, on this trial, having heard Mr. Shillaber, has been recalled to the stand, and states that Mr. Shillaber entirely misunderstood him. This is certainly most probable, because the controlling fact in the case is not controverted; that is, that Southwick did tell his wife, at the very moment he entered his house, that he had seen a person on the rope-walk steps, whom he believed to be Frank Knapp. Nothing can prove with more certainty than this, that Southwick, at the time, *thought* the person whom he thus saw to be the prisoner at the bar.

Mr. Bray is an acknowledged accurate and intelligent witness. He was highly complimented by my brother on the former trial, although he now charges him with varying his testimony. What could be his motive? You will be slow in imputing to him any design of this kind. I deny altogether that there is any contradiction. There may be differences, but not contradiction. These arise from the difference in the questions put; the difference between believing and knowing. On the first trial, he said he did not know the person, and now says the same. Then, we did not do all we had a right to do. We did not ask him who he thought it was. Now, when so asked, he says he believes it was the prisoner at the bar. If he had then been asked this question, he would have given the same answer. That he has expressed himself more strongly, I admit; but he has not contradicted himself. He is more confident now; and that is all. A man may not assert a thing, and still may have no doubt upon it. Cannot every man see this distinction to be consistent? I leave him in that attitude; that only is the difference. On questions of identity, opinion is evidence. We may ask the witness, either if he knew who the person seen was, or who he thinks he was. And he may well answer, as Captain Bray has answered, that he does not know who it was, but that he thinks it was the prisoner.

We have offered to produce witnesses to prove, that, as soon as Bray saw the prisoner, he pronounced him the same person. We are not at liberty to call them to corroborate our own witness. How, then, could this fact of the prisoner's being in Brown Street be better proved? If ten witnesses had testified to it, it would be no better. Two men, who knew him well, took it to be Frank Knapp, and one of them so said, when there was nothing to mislead them. Two others, who examined him closely, now swear to their opinion that he is the man.

Miss Jaqueth saw three persons pass by the rope-walk, several evenings before the murder. She saw one of them pointing towards Mr. White's house. She noticed that another had something which appeared to be like an instrument of music; that he put it behind him and attempted to conceal it. Who were these persons? This was but a few steps from the place where this apparent instrument of music (of *music* such as Richard Crowninshield, Jr. spoke of to Palmer) was afterwards found. These facts prove this a point of rendezvous for these parties. They show Brown Street to have been the place for consultation and observation; and to this purpose it was well suited.

Mr. Burns's testimony is also important. What was the defendant's object in his private conversation with Burns? He knew that Burns was out that night; that he lived near Brown Street, and that he had probably seen him; and he wished him to say nothing. He said to Burns, "If you saw any of your friends out that night, say nothing about it; my brother Joe and I are your friends." This is plain proof that he wished to say to him, if you saw me in Brown Street that night, say nothing about it.

But it is said that Burns ought not to be believed, because he mistook the color of the dagger, and because he has varied in his description of it. These are slight circumstances, if his general character be good. To my mind they are of no importance. It is for you to make what deduction you may think proper, on this account, from the weight of his evidence. His conversation with Burns, if Burns is believed, shows two things; first, that he desired Burns not to mention it, if he had seen him on the night of the murder; second, that he wished to fix the charge of murder on Mr. Stephen White. Both of these prove his own guilt.

I think you will be of opinion, that Brown Street was a probable place for the conspirators to assemble, and for an aid to be stationed. If we knew their whole plan, and if we were skilled to judge in such a case, then we could perhaps determine on this point better. But it is a retired place, and still commands a full view of the house; a lonely place, but still a place of observation. Not so lonely that a person would excite suspicion to be seen walking there in an ordinary manner; not so public as to be noticed by many. It is near enough to the scene of action in point of law. It was their point of centrality. The club was found near the spot, in a place provided for it, in a place that had been previously hunted out, in a concerted place of concealment. _Here was their point of rendezvous._ Here might the lights be seen. Here might an aid be secreted. Here was he within call. Here might he be aroused by the sound of the whistle. Here might he carry the weapon. Here might he receive the murderer after the murder.

Then, Gentlemen, the general question occurs, Is it satisfactorily proved, by all these facts and circumstances, that the defendant was in and about Brown Street on the night of the murder? Considering that the murder was effected by a conspiracy; considering that he was one of the four conspirators; considering that two of the conspirators have accounted for themselves on the night of the murder, and were not in Brown Street; considering that the prisoner does not account for himself, nor show where he was; considering that Richard Crowninshield, the other conspirator and the perpetrator, is not accounted for, nor shown to be elsewhere; considering that it is now past all doubt that two persons were seen lurking in and about Brown Street at different times, avoiding observation, and exciting so much suspicion that the neighbors actually watched them; considering that, if these persons thus lurking in Brown Street at that hour were not the murderers, it remains to this day wholly unknown who they were or what their business was; considering the testimony of Miss Jaqueth, and that the club was afterwards found near this place; considering, finally, that Webster and Southwick saw these persons, and then took one of them for the defendant, and that Southwick then told his wife so, and that Bray and Mirick examined them closely, and now swear to their belief that the prisoner was one of them;--it is for you to say, putting these considerations together, whether you believe the prisoner was actually in Brown Street at the time of the murder.

By the counsel for the prisoner, much stress has been laid upon the question, whether Brown Street was a place in which aid could be given, a place in which actual assistance could be rendered in this transaction. This must be mainly decided by their own opinion who selected the place; by what they thought at the time, according to their plan of operation.

If it was agreed that the prisoner should be there to assist, it is enough. If they thought the place proper for their purpose, according to their plan, it is sufficient. Suppose we could prove expressly that they agreed that Frank should be there, and he was there, and you should think it not a well-chosen place for aiding and abetting, must he be acquitted? No! It is not what _I_ think or _you_ think of the appropriateness of the place; it is what _they_ thought _at the time_. If the prisoner was in Brown Street by appointment and agreement with the perpetrator, for the purpose of giving assistance if assistance should be needed, it may safely be presumed that the place was suited to such assistance as it was supposed by the parties might chance to become requisite.

If in Brown Street, was he there by appointment? was he there to aid, if aid were necessary? was he there for, or against, the murderer? to concur, or to oppose? to favor, or to thwart? Did the perpetrator know he was there, there waiting? If so, then it follows that he was there by appointment. He was at the post half an hour; he was waiting for somebody. This proves appointment, arrangement, previous agreement; then it follows that he was there to aid, to encourage, to embolden the perpetrator; and that is enough. If he were in such a situation as to afford aid, or that he was relied upon for aid, then he was aiding and abetting. It is enough that the conspirator desired to have him there. Besides, it may be well said, that he could afford just as much aid there as if he had been in Essex Street, as if he had been standing even at the gate, or at the window. It was not an act of power against power that was to be done; it was a secret act, to be done by stealth. The aid was to be placed in a position secure from observation. It was important to the security of both that he should be in a lonely place. Now it is obvious that there are many purposes for which he might be in Brown Street.

1. Richard Crowninshield might have been secreted in the garden, and waiting for a signal;
2. Or he might be in Brown Street to advise him as to the time of making his entry into the house;
3. Or to favor his escape;
4. Or to see if the street was clear when he came out;
5. Or to conceal the weapon or the clothes;
6. To be ready for any unforeseen contingency.

Richard Crowninshield lived in Danvers. He would retire by the most secret way. Brown Street is that way.

If you find him there, can you doubt why he was there?

If, Gentlemen, the prisoner went into Brown Street, by appointment with the perpetrator, to render aid or encouragement in any of these ways, he was _present_, in legal contemplation, aiding and abetting in this murder. It is not necessary that he should have done any thing; it is enough that he was ready to act, and in a place to act. If his being in Brown Street, by appointment, at the time of the murder, emboldened the purpose and encouraged the heart of the murderer, by the hope of instant aid, if aid should become necessary, then, without doubt, he was present, aiding and abetting, and was a principal in the murder.

I now proceed, Gentlemen, to the consideration of the testimony of Mr. Colman. Although this evidence bears on every material part of the cause, I have purposely avoided every comment on it till the present moment, when I have done with the other evidence in the case. As to the admission of this evidence, there has been a great struggle, and its importance demanded it. The general rule of law is, that confessions are to be received as evidence. They are entitled to great or to little consideration, according to the circumstances under which they are made. Voluntary, deliberate confessions are the most important and satisfactory evidence, but confessions hastily made, or improperly obtained, are entitled to little or no consideration. It is always to be inquired, whether they were purely voluntary, or were made under any undue influence of hope or fear; for, in general, if any influence were exerted on the mind of the person confessing, such confessions are not to be submitted to a jury.

Who is Mr. Colman? He is an intelligent, accurate, and cautious witness; a gentleman of high and well-known character, and of unquestionable veracity; as a clergyman, highly respectable; as a man, of fair name and fame.

Why was Mr. Colman with the prisoner? Joseph J. Knapp was his parishioner; he was the head of a family, and had been married by Mr. Colman. The interests of that family were dear to him. He felt for their afflictions, and was anxious to alleviate their sufferings. He went from the purest and best of motives to visit Joseph Knapp. He came to save, not to destroy; to rescue, not to take away life. In this family he thought there might be a chance to save one. It is a misconstruction of Mr. Colman's motives, at once the most strange and the most uncharitable, a perversion of all just views of his conduct and intentions the most unaccountable, to represent him as acting, on this occasion, in hostility to any one, or as desirous of injuring or endangering any one. He has stated his own motives, and his own conduct, in a manner to command universal belief and universal respect. For intelligence, for consistency, for accuracy, for caution, for candor, never did witness acquit himself better, or stand fairer. In all that he did as a man, and all he has said as a witness, he has shown himself worthy of entire regard.

Now, Gentlemen, very important confessions made by the prisoner are sworn to by Mr. Colman. They were made in the prisoner's cell, where Mr. Colman had gone with the prisoner's brother, N. Phippen Knapp. Whatever conversation took place was in the presence of N.P. Knapp. Now, on the part of the prisoner, two things are asserted; first, that such inducements were suggested to the prisoner, in this interview, that no confessions made by him ought to be received; second, that, in point of fact, he made no such confessions as Mr. Colman testifies to, nor, indeed, any confessions at all. These two propositions are attempted to be supported by the testimony of N.P. Knapp. These two witnesses, Mr. Colman and N.P. Knapp, differ entirely. There is no possibility of reconciling them. No charity can cover both. One or the other has sworn falsely. If N.P. Knapp be believed, Mr. Colman's testimony must be wholly disregarded. It is, then, a question of credit, a question of belief between the two witnesses. As you decide between these, so you will decide on all this part of the case.

Mr. Colman has given you a plain narrative, a consistent account, and has uniformly stated the same things. He is not contradicted, except by the testimony of Phippen Knapp. He is influenced, as far as we can see, by no bias, or prejudice, any more than other men, except so far as his character is now at stake. He has feelings on this point, doubtless, and ought to have. If what he has stated be not true, I cannot see any ground for his escape. If he be a true man, he must have heard what he testifies. No treachery of memory brings to memory things that never took place. There is no reconciling his evidence with good intention, if the facts in it are not as he states them. He is on trial as to his veracity.

The relation in which the other witness stands deserves your careful consideration. He is a member of the family. He has the lives of two brothers depending, as he may think, on the effect of his evidence; depending on every word he speaks. I hope he has not another responsibility resting upon him. By the advice of a friend, and that friend Mr. Colman, J. Knapp made a full and free confession, and obtained a promise of pardon. He has since, as you know, probably by the advice of other friends, retracted that confession, and rejected the offered pardon. Events will show who of these friends and advisers advised him best, and befriended him most. In the mean time, if this brother, the witness, be one of these advisers, and advised the retraction, he has, most emphatically, the lives of his brothers resting upon his evidence and upon his conduct. Compare the situation of these two witnesses. Do you not see mighty motive enough on the one side, and want of all motive on the other? I would gladly find an apology for that witness, in his agonized feelings, in his distressed situation; in the agitation of that hour, or of this. I would gladly impute it to error, or to want of recollection, to confusion of mind, or disturbance of feeling. I would gladly impute to any pardonable source that which cannot be reconciled to facts and to truth; but, even in a case calling for so much sympathy, justice must yet prevail, and we must come to the conclusion, however reluctantly, which that demands from us.

It is said, Phippen Knapp was probably correct, because he knew he should probably be called as a witness. Witness to what? When he says there was no confession, what could he expect to bear witness of? But I do not put it on the ground that he did not hear; I am compelled to put it on the other ground, that he did hear, and does not now truly tell what he heard.

If Mr. Colman were out of the case, there are other reasons why the story of Phippen Knapp should not be believed. It has in it inherent improbabilities. It is unnatural, and inconsistent with the accompanying circumstances. He tells you that they went "to the cell of Frank, to see if he had any objection to taking a trial, and suffering his brother to accept the offer of pardon"; in other words, to obtain Frank's consent to Joseph's making a confession; and in case this consent was not obtained, that the pardon would be offered to Frank. Did they bandy about the chance of life, between these two, in this way? Did Mr. Colman, after having given this pledge to Joseph, and after having received a disclosure from Joseph, go to the cell of Frank for such a purpose as this? It is impossible; it cannot be so.

Again, we know that Mr. Colman found the club the next day; that he went directly to the place of deposit, and found it at the first attempt, exactly where he says he had been informed it was. Now Phippen Knapp says, that Frank had stated nothing respecting the club; that it was not mentioned in that conversation. He says, also, that he was present in the cell of Joseph all the time that Mr. Colman was there; that he believes he heard all that was said in Joseph's cell; and that he did not himself know where the club was, and never had known where it was, until he heard it stated in court. Now it is certain that Mr. Colman says he did not learn the particular place of deposit of the club from Joseph; that he only learned from him that it was deposited under the steps of the Howard Street meeting-house, without defining the particular steps. It is certain, also, that he had more knowledge of the position of the club than this; else how could he have placed his hand on it so readily? and where else could he have obtained this knowledge, except from Frank?

Here Mr. Dexter said that Mr. Colman had had other interviews with Joseph, and might have derived the information from him at previous visits. Mr. Webster replied, that Mr. Colman had testified that he learned nothing in relation to the club until this visit. Mr. Dexter denied there being any such testimony. Mr. Colman's evidence was read, from the notes of the judges, and several other persons, and Mr. Webster then proceeded.

My point is to show that Phippen Knapp's story is not true, is not consistent with itself; that, taking it for granted, as he says, that he heard all that was said to Mr. Colman in both cells, by Joseph and by Frank; and that Joseph did not state particularly where the club was deposited; and that he knew as much about the place of deposit of the club as Mr. Colman knew; why, then Mr. Colman must either have been miraculously informed respecting the club, or Phippen Knapp has not told you the whole truth. There is no reconciling this, without supposing that Mr. Colman has misrepresented what took place in Joseph's cell, as well as what took place in Frank's cell.

Again, Phippen Knapp is directly contradicted by Mr. Wheatland. Mr. Wheatland tells the same story, as coming from Phippen Knapp, that Colman now tells. Here there are two against one. Phippen Knapp says that Frank made no confessions, and that he said he had none to make. In this he is contradicted by Wheatland. He, Phippen Knapp, told Wheatland, that Mr. Colman did ask Frank some questions, and that Frank answered them. He told him also what these answers were. Wheatland does not recollect the questions or answers, but recollects his reply; which was, "Is not this _premature_? I think this answer is sufficient to make Frank a principal." Here Phippen Knapp opposes himself to Wheatland, as well as to Mr. Colman. Do you believe Phippen Knapp against these two respectable witnesses, or them against him? Is not Mr. Colman's testimony credible, natural, and proper? To judge of this, you must go back to that scene.

The murder had been committed; the two Knapps were now arrested; four persons were already in jail supposed to be concerned in it, the Crowninshields, and Selman, and Chase. Another person at the Eastward was supposed to be in the plot; it was important to learn the facts. To do this, some one of those suspected must be admitted to turn state's witness. The contest was, Who should have this privilege? It was understood that it was about to be offered to Palmer, then in Maine; there was no good reason why he should have the preference. Mr. Colman felt interested for the family of the Knapps, and particularly for Joseph. He was a young man who had hitherto maintained a fair standing in society; he was a husband. Mr. Colman was particularly intimate with his family. With these views he went to the prison. He believed that he might safely converse with the prisoner, because he thought confessions made to a clergyman were sacred, and that he could not be called upon to disclose them. He went, the first time, in the morning, and was requested to come again. He went again at three o'clock; and was requested to call again at five o'clock. In the mean time he saw the father and Phippen, and they wished he would not go again, because it would be said the prisoners were making confession. He said he had engaged to go again at five o'clock; but would not, if Phippen would excuse him to Joseph. Phippen engaged to do this, and to meet him at his office at five o'clock. Mr. Colman went to the office at the time, and waited; but, as Phippen was not there, he walked down street, and saw him coming from the jail. He met him, and while in conversation near the church, he saw Mrs. Beckford and Mrs. Knapp going in a chaise towards the jail. He hastened to meet them, as he thought it not proper for them to go in at that time. While conversing with them near the jail, he received two distinct messages from Joseph, that he wished to see him. He thought it proper to go; and accordingly went to Joseph's cell, and it was while there that the disclosures were made. Before Joseph had finished his statement, Phippen came to the door; he was soon after admitted. A short interval ensued, and they went together to the cell of Frank. Mr. Colman went in by invitation of Phippen; he had come directly from the cell of Joseph, where he had for the first time learned the incidents of the tragedy. He was incredulous as to some of the facts which he had learned, they were so different from his previous impressions. He was desirous of knowing whether he could place confidence in what Joseph had told him. He, therefore, put the questions to Frank, as he has testified before you; in answer to which Frank Knapp informed him,--

1. "That the murder took place between ten and eleven o'clock."
2. "That Richard Crowninshield was alone in the house."
3. "That he, Frank Knapp, went home afterwards."
4. "That the club was deposited under the steps of the Howard Street meeting-house, and under the part nearest the burying-ground, in a rat hole."
5. "That the dagger or daggers had been worked up at the factory."

It is said that these five answers just fit the case; that they are just what was wanted, and neither more nor less. True, they are; but the reason is, because truth always fits. Truth is always congruous and agrees with itself: every truth in the universe agrees with every other truth in the universe, whereas falsehoods not only disagree with truths, but usually quarrel among themselves. Surely Mr. Colman is influenced by no bias, no prejudice; he has no feelings to warp him, except, now that he is contradicted, he may feel an interest to be believed.

If you believe Mr. Colman, then the evidence is fairly in the case.

I shall now proceed on the ground that you do believe Mr. Colman.

When told that Joseph had determined to confess, the defendant said, "It is hard, or unfair, that Joseph should have the benefit of confessing, since the thing was done for his benefit." What thing was done for his benefit? Does not this carry an implication of the guilt of the defendant? Does it not show that he had a knowledge of the object and history of the murder?

The defendant said, "I told Joseph, when he proposed it, that it was a silly business, and would get us into trouble." He knew, then, what this business was; he knew that Joseph proposed it, and that he agreed to it, else he could not get *us* into trouble; he understood its bearing and its consequences. Thus much was said, under circumstances that make it clearly evidence against him, before there is any pretence of an inducement held out. And does not this prove him to have had a knowledge of the conspiracy?

He knew the daggers had been destroyed, and he knew who committed the murder. How could he have innocently known these facts? Why, if by Richard's story, this shows him guilty of a knowledge of the murder, and of the conspiracy. More than all, he knew when the deed was done, and that he went home afterwards. This shows his participation in that deed. "Went home afterwards"! Home, from what scene? home, from what fact? home, from what transaction? home, from what place? This confirms the supposition that the prisoner was in Brown Street for the purposes ascribed to him. These questions were directly put, and directly answered. He does not intimate that he received the information from another. Now, if he knows the time, and went home afterwards, and does not excuse himself, is not this an admission that he had a hand in this murder? Already proved to be a conspirator in the murder, he now confesses that he knew who did it, at what time it was done, that he was himself out of his own house at the time, and went home afterwards. Is not this conclusive, if not explained? Then comes the club. He told where it was. This is like possession of stolen goods. He is charged with the guilty knowledge of this concealment. He must show, not say, how he came by this knowledge. If a man be found with stolen goods, he must prove how he came by them. The place of deposit of the club was premeditated and selected, and he knew where it was.

Joseph Knapp was an accessory, and an accessory only; he knew only what was told him. But the prisoner knew the particular spot in which the club might be found. This shows his knowledge something more than that of an accessory. This presumption must be rebutted by evidence, or it stands strong against him. He has too much knowledge of this transaction to have come innocently by it. It must stand against him until he explains it.

This testimony of Mr. Colman is represented as new matter, and therefore an attempt has been made to excite a prejudice against it. It is not so. How little is there in it, after all, that did not appear from other sources? It is mainly confirmatory. Compare what you learn from this confession with what you before knew.

As to its being proposed by Joseph, was not that known?

As to Richard's being alone in the house, was not that known?

As to the daggers, was not that known?

As to the time of the murder, was not that known?

As to his being out that night, was not that known?

As to his returning afterwards, was not that known?

As to the club, was not that known?

So this information confirms what was known before, and fully confirms it.

One word as to the interview between Mr. Colman and Phippen Knapp on the turnpike. It is said that Mr. Colman's conduct in this matter is inconsistent with his testimony. There does not appear to me to be any inconsistency. He tells you that his object was to save Joseph, and to hurt no one, and least of all the prisoner at the bar. He had probably told Mr. White the substance of what he heard at the prison. He had probably told him that Frank confirmed what Joseph had confessed. He was unwilling to be the instrument of harm to Frank. He therefore, at the request of Phippen Knapp, wrote a note to Mr. White, requesting him to consider Joseph as authority for the information he had received. He tells you that this is the only thing he has to regret, as it may seem to be an evasion, as he doubts whether it was entirely correct. If it was an evasion, if it was a deviation, if it was an error, it was an error of mercy, an error of kindness,--an error that proves he had no hostility to the prisoner at the bar. It does not in the least vary his testimony, or affect its correctness. Gentlemen, I look on the evidence of Mr. Colman as highly important; not as bringing into the cause new facts, but as confirming, in a very satisfactory manner, other evidence. It is incredible that he can be false, and that he is seeking the prisoner's life through false swearing. If he is true, it is incredible that the prisoner can be innocent.

Gentlemen, I have gone through with the evidence in this case, and have endeavored to state it plainly and fairly before you. I think there are conclusions to be drawn from it, the accuracy of which you cannot doubt. I think you cannot doubt that there was a conspiracy formed for the purpose of committing this murder, and who the conspirators were:

That you cannot doubt that the Crowninshields and the Knapps were the parties in this conspiracy:

That you cannot doubt that the prisoner at the bar knew that the murder was to be done on the night of the 6th of April:

That you cannot doubt that the murderers of Captain White were the suspicious persons seen in and about Brown Street on that night:

That you cannot doubt that Richard Crowninshield was the perpetrator of that crime:

That you cannot doubt that the prisoner at the bar was in Brown Street on that night.

If there, then it must be by agreement, to countenance, to aid the perpetrator. And if so, then he is guilty as PRINCIPAL.

Gentlemen, your whole concern should be to do your duty, and leave consequences to take care of themselves. You will receive the law from the court. Your verdict, it is true, may endanger the prisoner's life, but then it is to save other lives. If the prisoner's guilt has been shown and proved beyond all reasonable doubt, you will convict him. If such reasonable doubts of guilt still remain, you will acquit him. You are the judges of the whole case. You owe a duty to the public, as well as to the prisoner at the bar. You cannot presume to be wiser than the law. Your duty is a plain, straightforward one. Doubtless we would all judge him in mercy. Towards him, as an individual, the law inculcates no hostility; but towards him, if proved to be a murderer, the law, and the oaths you have taken, and public justice, demand that you do your duty.

With consciences satisfied with the discharge of duty, no consequences can harm you. There is no evil that we cannot either face or fly from, but the consciousness of duty disregarded. A sense of duty pursues us ever. It is omnipresent, like the Deity. If we take to ourselves the wings of the morning, and dwell in the uttermost parts of the sea, duty performed, or duty violated, is still with us, for our happiness or our misery. If we say the darkness shall cover us, in the darkness as in the light our obligations are yet with us. We cannot escape their power, nor fly from their presence. They are with us in this life, will be with us at its close; and in that scene of inconceivable solemnity, which lies yet farther onward, we shall still find ourselves surrounded by the consciousness of duty, to pain us wherever it has been violated, and to console us so far as God may have given us grace to perform it.

[Footnote 1: Chief Justice Parker.][Footnote 2: This seems to have been actually the case as regards J.F. Knapp.][Footnote 3: And yet this argument, so absurd in Mr. Webster's opinion, was based on the exact fact.][Footnote 4: He did not.][Footnote 5: 4 Hawk. 201, Lib. 4, ch. 29, sec. 8.]

THE REPLY TO HAYNE.
SECOND SPEECH ON "FOOT'S RESOLUTION," DELIVERED IN THE SENATE OF THE UNITED STATES, ON THE 26TH AND 27TH OF JANUARY, 1830.

[Mr. Webster having completed on January 20th his first speech on Foot's resolution, Mr. Benton spoke in reply, on the 20th and 21st of January, 1830. Mr. Hayne of South Carolina followed on the same side, but, after some time, gave way for a motion for adjournment. On Monday, the 25th, Mr. Hayne resumed, and concluded his argument. Mr. Webster immediately rose in reply, but yielded the floor for a motion for adjournment.

The next day (26th January, 1830) Mr. Webster took the floor and delivered the following speech, which has given such great celebrity to the debate. The circumstances connected with this remarkable effort of parliamentary eloquence are vividly set forth in Mr. Everett's Memoir, prefixed to the first volume of Mr. Webster's Works.]

Mr. President,--When the mariner has been tossed for many days in thick weather, and on an unknown sea, he naturally avails himself of the first pause in the storm, the earliest glance of the sun, to take his latitude, and ascertain how far the elements have driven him from his true course. Let us imitate this prudence, and, before we float farther on the waves of this debate, refer to the point from which we departed, that we may at least be able to conjecture where we now are. I ask for the reading of the resolution before the Senate.

The Secretary read the resolution, as follows:--

"_Resolved_, That the Committee on Public Lands be instructed to inquire and report the quantity of public lands remaining unsold within each State and Territory, and whether it be expedient to limit for a certain period the sales of the public lands to such lands only as have heretofore been offered for sale, and are now subject to entry at the minimum price. And, also, whether the office of Surveyor-General, and some of the land offices, may not be abolished without detriment to the public interest; or whether it be expedient to adopt measures to hasten the sales and extend more rapidly the surveys of the public lands."

We have thus heard, Sir, what the resolution is which is actually before us for consideration; and it will readily occur to every one, that it is almost the only subject about which something has not been said in the speech, running through two days, by which the Senate has been entertained by the gentleman from South Carolina. Every topic in the wide range of our public affairs, whether past or present,--every thing, general or local, whether belonging to national politics or party politics,--seems to have attracted more or less of the honorable member's attention, save only the resolution before the Senate. He has spoken of every thing but the public lands; they have escaped his notice. To that subject, in all his excursions, he has not paid even the cold respect of a passing glance.

When this debate, Sir, was to be resumed, on Thursday morning, it so happened that it would have been convenient for me to be elsewhere. The honorable member, however, did not incline to put off the discussion to another day. He had a shot, he said, to return, and he wished to discharge it. That shot, Sir, which he thus kindly informed us was coming, that we might stand out of the way, or prepare ourselves to fall by it and die with decency, has now been received. Under all advantages, and with expectation awakened by the tone which preceded it, it has been discharged, and has spent its force. It may become me to say no more of its effect, than that, if nobody is found, after all, either killed or wounded, it is not the first time, in the history of human affairs, that the vigor and success of the war have not quite come up to the lofty and sounding phrase of the manifesto.

The gentleman, Sir, in declining to postpone the debate, told the Senate, with the emphasis of his hand upon his heart, that there was something rankling _here_, which he wished to relieve. [Mr. Hayne rose, and disclaimed having used the word *rankling*.] It would not, Mr. President, be safe for the honorable member to appeal to those around him, upon the question whether he did in fact make use of that word. But he may have been unconscious of it. At any rate, it is enough that he disclaims it. But still, with or without the use of that particular word, he had yet something _here_, he said, of which he wished to rid himself by an immediate reply. In this respect, Sir, I have a great advantage over the honorable gentleman. There is nothing _here_, Sir, which gives me the slightest uneasiness; neither fear, nor anger, nor that which is sometimes more troublesome than either, the consciousness of having been in the wrong. There is nothing, either originating _here_, or now received *here* by the gentleman's shot. Nothing originating here, for I had not the slightest feeling of unkindness towards the honorable member. Some passages, it is true, had occurred since our acquaintance in this body, which I could have wished might have been otherwise; but I had used philosophy and forgotten them. I paid the honorable member the attention of listening with respect to his first speech; and when he sat down, though surprised, and I must even say astonished, at some of his opinions, nothing was farther from my intention than to commence any personal warfare. Through the whole of the few remarks I made in answer, I avoided, studiously and carefully, every thing which I thought possible to be construed into disrespect. And, Sir, while there is thus nothing originating *here* which I have wished at any time, or now wish, to discharge, I must repeat, also, that nothing has been received *here* which _rankles_, or in any way gives me annoyance. I will not accuse the honorable member of violating the rules of civilized war; I will not say, that he poisoned his arrows. But whether his shafts were, or were not, dipped in that which would have caused rankling if they had reached their destination, there was not, as it happened, quite strength enough in the bow to bring them to their mark. If he wishes now to gather up those shafts, he must look for them elsewhere; they will not be found fixed and quivering in the object at which they were aimed.

The honorable member complained that I had slept on his speech. I must have slept on it, or not slept at all. The moment the honorable member sat down, his friend from Missouri rose, and, with much honeyed commendation of the speech, suggested that the impressions which it had produced were too charming and delightful to be disturbed by other sentiments or other sounds, and proposed that the Senate should adjourn. Would it have been quite amiable in me, Sir, to interrupt this excellent good feeling? Must I not have been absolutely malicious, if I could have thrust myself forward, to destroy sensations thus pleasing? Was it not much better and kinder, both to sleep upon them myself, and to allow others also the pleasure of sleeping upon them? But if it be meant, by sleeping upon his speech, that I took time to prepare a reply to it, it is quite a mistake. Owing to other engagements, I could not employ even the interval between the adjournment of the Senate and its meeting the next morning, in attention to the subject of this debate. Nevertheless, Sir, the mere matter of fact is undoubtedly true. I did sleep on the gentleman's speech, and slept soundly. And I slept equally well on his speech of yesterday, to which I am now replying. It is quite possible that in this respect, also, I possess some advantage over the honorable member, attributable, doubtless, to a cooler temperament on my part; for, in truth, I slept upon his speeches remarkably well. But the gentleman inquires why *he* was made the object of such a reply. Why was *he* singled out? If an attack has been made on the East, he, he assures us, did not begin it; it was made by the gentleman from Missouri. Sir, I answered the gentleman's speech because I happened to hear it; and because, also, I chose to give an answer to that speech, which, if unanswered, I thought most likely to produce injurious impressions. I did not stop to inquire who was the original drawer of the bill. I found a responsible indorser before me, and it was my purpose to hold him liable, and to bring him to his just responsibility, without delay. But, Sir, this interrogatory of the honorable member was only introductory to another. He proceeded to ask me whether I had turned upon him, in this debate, from the consciousness that I should find an overmatch, if I ventured on a contest with his friend from Missouri. If, Sir, the honorable member, _modestiae gratia_, had chosen thus to defer to his friend, and to pay him a compliment, without intentional disparagement to others, it would have been quite according to the friendly courtesies of debate, and not at all ungrateful to my own feelings. I am not one of those, Sir, who esteem any tribute of regard, whether light and occasional, or more serious and deliberate, which may be bestowed on others, as so much unjustly withholden from themselves. But the tone and manner of the gentleman's question forbid me thus to interpret it. I am not at liberty to consider it as nothing more than a civility to his friend. It had an air of taunt and disparagement, something of the loftiness of asserted superiority, which does not allow me to pass it over without notice. It was put as a question for me to answer, and so put as if it were difficult for me to answer, whether I deemed the member from Missouri an overmatch for myself in debate here. It seems to me, Sir, that this is extraordinary language, and an extraordinary tone, for the discussions of this body.

Matches and overmatches! Those terms are more applicable elsewhere than here, and fitter for other assemblies than this. Sir, the gentleman seems to forget where and what we are. This is a Senate, a Senate of equals, of men of individual honor and personal character, and of absolute independence. We know no masters, we acknowledge no dictators. This is a hall for mutual consultation and discussion; not an arena for the exhibition of champions. I offer myself, Sir, as a match for no man; I throw the challenge of debate at no man's feet. But then, Sir, since the honorable member has put the question in a manner that calls for an answer, I will give him an answer; and I tell him, that, holding myself to be the humblest of the members here, I yet know nothing in the arm of his friend from Missouri, either alone or when aided by the arm of *his* friend from South Carolina, that need deter even me from espousing whatever opinions I may choose to espouse, from debating whenever I may choose to debate, or from speaking whatever I may see fit to say, on the floor of the Senate. Sir, when uttered as matter of commendation or compliment, I should dissent from nothing which the honorable member might say of his friend. Still less do I put forth any pretensions of my own. But when put to me as matter of taunt, I throw it back, and say to the gentleman, that he could possibly say nothing less likely than such a comparison to wound my pride of personal character. The anger of its tone rescued the remark from intentional irony, which otherwise, probably, would have been its general acceptation. But, Sir, if it be imagined that by this mutual quotation and commendation; if it be supposed that, by casting the characters of the drama assigning to each his part, to one the attack, to another the cry of onset; or if it be thought that, by a loud and empty vaunt of anticipated victory, any laurels are to be won here; if it be imagined, especially, that any or all these things will shake any purpose of mine,--I can tell the honorable member, once for all, that he is greatly mistaken, and that he is dealing with one of whose temper and character he has yet much to learn. Sir, I shall not allow myself, on this occasion, I hope on no occasion, to be betrayed into any loss of temper; but if provoked, as I trust I never shall be, into crimination and recrimination, the honorable member may perhaps find, that, in that contest, there will be blows to take as well as blows to give; that others can state comparisons as significant, at least, as his own, and that his impunity may possibly demand of him whatever powers of taunt and sarcasm he may possess. I commend him to a prudent husbandry of his resources.

But, Sir, the Coalition! The Coalition! Ay, "the murdered Coalition!" The gentleman asks, if I were led or frighted into this debate by the spectre of the Coalition. "Was it the ghost of the murdered Coalition," he exclaims, "which haunted the member from Massachusetts; and which, like the ghost of Banquo, would never down?" "The murdered Coalition!" Sir, this charge of a coalition, in reference to the late administration, is not original with the honorable member. It did not spring up in the Senate. Whether as a fact, as an argument, or as an embellishment, it is all borrowed. He adopts it, indeed, from a very low origin, and a still lower present condition. It is one of the thousand calumnies with which the press teemed, during an excited political canvass. It was a charge, of which there was not only no proof or probability, but which was in itself wholly impossible to be true. No man of common information ever believed a syllable of it. Yet it was of that class of falsehoods, which, by continued repetition, through all the organs of detraction and abuse, are capable of misleading those who are already far misled, and of further fanning passion already kindling into flame. Doubtless it served in its day, and in greater or less degree, the end designed by it. Having done that, it has sunk into the general mass of stale and loathed calumnies. It is the very cast-off slough of a polluted and shameless press. Incapable of further mischief, it lies in the sewer, lifeless and despised. It is not now, Sir, in the power of the honorable member to give it dignity or decency, by attempting to elevate it, and to introduce it into the Senate. He cannot change it from what it is, an object of general disgust and scorn. On the contrary, the contact, if he choose to touch it, is more likely to drag him down, down, to the place where it lies itself.

But, Sir, the honorable member was not, for other reasons, entirely happy in his allusion to the story of Banquo's murder and Banquo's ghost. It was not, I think, the friends, but the enemies of the murdered Banquo, at whose bidding his spirit would not *down*. The honorable gentleman is fresh in his reading of the English classics, and can put me right if I am wrong: but, according to my poor recollection, it was at those who had begun with caresses and ended with foul and treacherous murder that the gory locks were shaken. The ghost of Banquo, like that of Hamlet, was an honest ghost. It disturbed no innocent man. It knew where its appearance would strike terror, and who would cry out, A ghost! It made itself visible in the right quarter, and compelled the guilty and the conscience-smitten, and none others, to start, with, "Pr'ythee, see there! behold!--look! lo, If I stand here, I saw him!"

THEIR eyeballs were seared (was it not so, Sir?) who had thought to shield themselves by concealing their own hand, and laying the imputation of the crime on a low and hireling agency in wickedness; who had vainly attempted to stifle the workings of their own coward consciences by ejaculating through white lips and chattering teeth, "Thou canst not say I did it!" I have misread the great poet if those who had no way partaken in the deed of the death, either found that they were, or _feared that they should be_, pushed from their stools by the ghost of the slain, or exclaimed to a spectre created by their own fears and their own remorse, "Avaunt! and quit our sight!"

There is another particular, Sir, in which the honorable member's quick perception of resemblances might, I should think, have seen something in the story of Banquo, making it not altogether a subject of the most pleasant contemplation. Those who murdered Banquo, what did they win by it? Substantial good? Permanent power? Or disappointment, rather, and sore mortification,--dust and ashes, the common fate of vaulting ambition overleaping itself? Did not even-handed justice erelong commend the poisoned chalice to their own lips? Did they not soon find that for another they had "filed their mind"? that their ambition, though apparently for the moment successful, had but put a barren sceptre in their grasp? Ay, Sir, "a barren sceptre in their gripe, _Thence to be wrenched with an unlineal hand, No son of theirs succeeding_."

Sir, I need pursue the allusion no farther. I leave the honorable gentleman to run it out at his leisure, and to derive from it all the gratification it is calculated to administer. If he finds himself pleased with the associations, and prepared to be quite satisfied, though the parallel should be entirely completed, I had almost said, I am satisfied also; but that I shall think of. Yes, Sir, I will think of that.

In the course of my observations the other day, Mr. President, I paid a passing tribute of respect to a very worthy man, Mr. Dane of Massachusetts. It so happened that he drew the Ordinance of 1787, for the government of the Northwestern Territory. A man of so much ability, and so little pretence; of so great a capacity to do good, and so unmixed a disposition to do it for its own sake; a gentleman who had acted an important part, forty years ago, in a measure the influence of which is still deeply felt in the very matter which was the subject of debate,--might, I thought, receive from me a commendatory recognition. But the honorable member was inclined to be facetious on the subject. He was rather disposed to make it matter of ridicule, that I had introduced into the debate the name of one Nathan Dane, of whom he assures us he had never before heard. Sir, if the honorable member had never before heard of Mr. Dane, I am sorry for it. It shows him less acquainted with the public men of the country than I had supposed. Let me tell him, however, that a sneer from him at the mention of the name of Mr. Dane is in bad taste. It may well be a high mark of ambition, Sir, either with the honorable gentleman or myself, to accomplish as much to make our names known to advantage, and remembered with gratitude, as Mr. Dane has accomplished. But the truth is, Sir, I suspect, that Mr. Dane lives a little too far north. He is of Massachusetts, and too near the north star to be reached by the honorable gentleman's telescope. If his sphere had happened to range south of Mason and Dixon's line, he might, probably, have come within the scope of his vision.

I spoke, Sir, of the Ordinance of 1787, which prohibits slavery, in all future times, northwest of the Ohio, as a measure of great wisdom and foresight, and one which had been attended with highly beneficial and permanent consequences. I supposed that, on this point, no two gentlemen in the Senate could entertain different opinions. But the simple expression of this sentiment has led the gentleman, not only into a labored defence of slavery, in the abstract, and on principle, but also into a warm accusation against me, as having attacked the system of domestic slavery now existing in the Southern States. For all this, there was not the slightest foundation, in any thing said or intimated by me. I did not utter a single word which any ingenuity could torture into an attack on the slavery of the South. I said, only, that it was highly wise and useful, in legislating for the Northwestern country while it was yet a wilderness, to prohibit the introduction of slaves; and I added, that I presumed there was no reflecting and intelligent person, in the neighboring State of Kentucky, who would doubt that, if the same prohibition had been extended, at the same early period, over that commonwealth, her strength and population would, at this day, have been far greater than they are. If these opinions be thought doubtful, they are nevertheless, I trust, neither extraordinary nor disrespectful. They attack nobody and menace nobody. And yet, Sir, the gentleman's optics have discovered, even in the mere expression of this sentiment, what he calls the very spirit of the Missouri question! He represents me as making an onset on the whole South, and manifesting a spirit which would interfere with, and disturb, their domestic condition!

Sir, this injustice no otherwise surprises me, than as it is committed here, and committed without the slightest pretence of ground for it. I say it only surprises me as being done here; for I know full well, that it is, and has been, the settled policy of some persons in the South, for years, to represent the people of the North as disposed to interfere with them in their own exclusive and peculiar concerns. This is a delicate and sensitive point in Southern feeling; and of late years it has always been touched, and generally with effect, whenever the object has been to unite the whole South against Northern men or Northern measures. This feeling, always carefully kept alive, and maintained at too intense a heat to admit discrimination or reflection, is a lever of great power in our political machine. It moves vast bodies, and gives to them one and the same direction. But it is without adequate cause, and the suspicion which exists is wholly groundless. There is not, and never has been, a disposition in the North to interfere with these interests of the South. Such interference has never been supposed to be within the power of government; nor has it been in any way attempted. The slavery of the South has always been regarded as a matter of domestic policy, left with the States themselves, and with which the Federal government had nothing to do. Certainly, Sir, I am, and ever have been, of that opinion. The gentleman, indeed, argues that slavery, in the abstract, is no evil. Most assuredly I need not say I differ with him, altogether and most widely, on that point. I regard domestic slavery as one of the greatest evils, both moral and political. But whether it be a malady, and whether it be curable, and if so, by what means; or, on the other hand, whether it be the *vulnus immedicabile* of the social system, I leave it to those whose right and duty it is to inquire and to decide. And this I believe, Sir, is, and uniformly has been, the sentiment of the North. Let us look a little at the history of this matter.

When the present Constitution was submitted for the ratification of the people, there were those who imagined that the powers of the government which it proposed to establish might, in some possible mode, be exerted in measures tending to the abolition of slavery. This suggestion would of course attract much attention in the Southern conventions. In that of Virginia, Governor Randolph said:--

"I hope there is none here, who, considering the subject in the calm light of philosophy, will make an objection dishonorable to Virginia; that, at the moment they are securing the rights of their citizens, an objection is started, that there is a spark of hope that those unfortunate men now held in bondage may, by the operation of the general government, be made free."

At the very first Congress, petitions on the subject were presented, if I mistake not, from different States. The Pennsylvania society for promoting the abolition of slavery took a lead, and laid before Congress a memorial, praying Congress to promote the abolition by such powers as it possessed. This memorial was referred, in the House of Representatives, to a select committee, consisting of Mr. Foster of New Hampshire, Mr. Gerry of Massachusetts, Mr. Huntington of Connecticut, Mr. Lawrence of New York, Mr. Sinnickson of New Jersey, Mr. Hartley of Pennsylvania, and Mr. Parker of Virginia,--all of them, Sir, as you will observe, Northern men but the last. This committee made a report, which was referred to a committee of the whole House, and there considered and discussed for several days; and being amended, although without material alteration, it was made to express three distinct propositions, on the subject of slavery and the slave-trade. First, in the words of the Constitution, that Congress could not, prior to the year 1808, prohibit the migration or importation of such persons as any of the States then existing should think proper to admit; and, secondly, that Congress had authority to restrain the citizens of the United States from carrying on the African slave-trade, for the purpose of supplying foreign countries. On this proposition, our early laws against those who engage in that traffic are founded. The third proposition, and that which bears on the present question, was expressed in the following terms:--

"_Resolved_, That Congress have no authority to interfere in the emancipation of slaves, or in the treatment of them in any of the States; it remaining with the several States alone to provide rules and regulations therein which humanity and true policy may require."

This resolution received the sanction of the House of Representatives so early as March, 1790. And now, Sir, the honorable member will allow me to remind him, that not only were the select committee who reported the resolution, with a single exception, all Northern men, but also that, of the members then composing the House of Representatives, a large majority, I believe nearly two thirds, were Northern men also.

The House agreed to insert these resolutions in its journal; and from that day to this it has never been maintained or contended at the North, that Congress had any authority to regulate or interfere with the condition of slaves in the several States. No Northern gentleman, to my knowledge, has moved any such question in either House of Congress.

The fears of the South, whatever fears they might have entertained, were allayed and quieted by this early decision; and so remained till they were excited afresh, without cause, but for collateral and indirect purposes. When it became necessary, or was thought so, by some political persons, to find an unvarying ground for the exclusion of Northern men from confidence and from lead in the affairs of the republic, then, and not till then, the cry was raised, and the feeling industriously excited, that the influence of Northern men in the public counsels would endanger the relation of master and slave. For myself, I claim no other merit than that this gross and enormous injustice towards the whole North has not wrought upon me to change my opinions or my political conduct. I hope I am above violating my principles, even under the smart of injury and false imputations. Unjust suspicions and undeserved reproach, whatever pain I may experience from them, will not induce me, I trust, to overstep the limits of constitutional duty, or to encroach on the rights of others. The domestic slavery of the Southern States I leave where I find it,--in the hands of their own governments. It is their affair, not mine. Nor do I complain of the peculiar effect which the magnitude of that population has had in the distribution of power under this Federal government. We know, Sir, that the representation of the States in the other house is not equal. We know that great advantage in that respect is enjoyed by the slave-holding States; and we know, too, that the intended equivalent for that advantage, that is to say, the imposition of direct taxes in the same ratio, has become merely nominal, the habit of the government being almost invariably to collect its revenue from other sources and in other modes. Nevertheless, I do not complain; nor would I countenance any movement to alter this arrangement of representation. It is the original bargain, the compact; let it stand; let the advantage of it be fully enjoyed. The Union itself is too full of benefit to be hazarded in propositions for changing its original basis. I go for the Constitution as it is, and for the Union as it is. But I am resolved not to submit in silence to accusations, either against myself individually or against the North, wholly unfounded and unjust,--accusations which impute to us a disposition to evade the constitutional compact, and to extend the power of the government over the internal laws and domestic condition of the States. All such accusations, wherever and whenever made, all insinuations of the existence of any such purposes, I know and feel to be groundless and injurious. And we must confide in Southern gentlemen themselves; we must trust to those whose integrity of heart and magnanimity of feeling will lead them to a desire to maintain and disseminate truth, and who possess the means of its diffusion with the Southern public; we must leave it to them to disabuse that public of its prejudices. But in the mean time, for my own part, I shall continue to act justly, whether those towards whom justice is exercised receive it with candor or with contumely.

Having had occasion to recur to the Ordinance of 1787, in order to defend myself against the inferences which the honorable member has chosen to draw from my former observations on that subject, I am not willing now entirely to take leave of it without another remark. It need hardly be said, that that paper expresses just sentiments on the great subject of civil and religious liberty. Such sentiments were common, and abound in all our state papers of that day. But this Ordinance did that which was not so common, and which is not even now universal; that is, it set forth and declared it to be a high and binding duty of government itself to support schools and advance the means of education, on the plain reason that religion, morality, and knowledge are necessary to good government, and to the happiness of mankind. One observation further. The important provision incorporated into the Constitution of the United States, and into several of those of the States, and recently, as we have seen, adopted into the reformed constitution of Virginia, restraining legislative power in questions of private right, and from impairing the obligation of contracts, is first introduced and established, as far as I am informed, as matter of express written constitutional law, in this Ordinance of 1787. And I must add, also, in regard to the author of the Ordinance, who has not had the happiness to attract the gentleman's notice heretofore, nor to avoid his sarcasm now, that he was chairman of that select committee of the old Congress, whose report first expressed the strong sense of that body, that the old Confederation was not adequate to the exigencies of the country, and recommended to the States to send delegates to the convention which formed the present Constitution.

An attempt has been made to transfer from the North to the South the honor of this exclusion of slavery from the Northwestern Territory. The journal, without argument or comment, refutes such attempts. The cession by Virginia was made in March, 1784. On the 19th of April following, a committee, consisting of Messrs. Jefferson, Chase, and Howell, reported a plan for a temporary government of the territory, in which was this article: "That, after the year 1800, there shall be neither slavery nor involuntary servitude in any of the said States, otherwise than in punishment of crimes, whereof the party shall have been convicted." Mr. Spaight of North Carolina moved to strike out this paragraph. The question was put, according to the form then practised, "Shall these words stand as a part of the plan?" New Hampshire, Massachusetts, Rhode Island, Connecticut, New York, New Jersey, and Pennsylvania, seven States, voted in the affirmative; Maryland, Virginia, and South Carolina, in the negative. North Carolina was divided. As the consent of nine States was necessary, the words could not stand, and were struck out accordingly. Mr. Jefferson voted for the clause, but was overruled by his colleagues.

In March of the next year (1785), Mr. King of Massachusetts, seconded by Mr. Ellery of Rhode Island, proposed the formerly rejected article, with this addition: "And that this regulation shall be an article of compact, and remain a fundamental principle of the constitutions between the thirteen original States, and each of the States described in the resolve." On this clause, which provided the adequate and thorough security, the eight Northern States at that time voted affirmatively, and the four Southern States negatively. The votes of nine States were not yet obtained, and thus the provision was again rejected by the Southern States. The perseverance of the North held out, and two years afterwards the object was attained. It is no derogation from the credit, whatever that may be, of drawing the Ordinance, that its principles had before been prepared and discussed, in the form of resolutions. If one should reason in that way, what would become of the distinguished honor of the author of the Declaration of Independence? There is not a sentiment in that paper which had not been voted and resolved in the assemblies, and other popular bodies in the country, over and over again.

But the honorable member has now found out that this gentleman, Mr. Dane, was a member of the Hartford Convention. However uninformed the honorable member may be of characters and occurrences at the North, it would seem that he has at his elbow, on this occasion, some high-minded and lofty spirit, some magnanimous and true-hearted monitor, possessing the means of local knowledge, and ready to supply the honorable member with every thing, down even to forgotten and moth-eaten two-penny pamphlets, which may be used to the disadvantage of his own country. But as to the Hartford Convention, Sir, allow me to say, that the proceedings of that body seem now to be less read and studied in New England than farther South. They appear to be looked to, not in New England, but elsewhere, for the purpose of seeing how far they may serve as a precedent. But they will not answer the purpose, they are quite too tame. The latitude in which they originated was too cold. Other conventions, of more recent existence, have gone a whole bar's length beyond it. The learned doctors of Colleton and Abbeville have pushed their commentaries on the Hartford collect so far, that the original text-writers are thrown entirely into the shade. I have nothing to do, Sir, with the Hartford Convention. Its journal, which the gentleman has quoted, I never read. So far as the honorable member may discover in its proceedings a spirit in any degree resembling that which was avowed and justified in those other conventions to which I have alluded, or so far as those proceedings can be shown to be disloyal to the Constitution, or tending to disunion, so far I shall be as ready as any one to bestow on them reprehension and censure.

Having dwelt long on this convention, and other occurrences of that day, in the hope, probably, (which will not be gratified,) that I should leave the course of this debate to follow him at length in those excursions, the honorable member returned, and attempted another object. He referred to a speech of mine in the other house, the same which I had occasion to allude to myself, the other day; and has quoted a passage or two from it, with a bold, though uneasy and laboring, air of confidence, as if he had detected in me an inconsistency. Judging from the gentleman's manner, a stranger to the course of the debate and to the point in discussion would have imagined, from so triumphant a tone, that the honorable member was about to overwhelm me with a manifest contradiction. Any one who heard him, and who had not heard what I had, in fact, previously said, must have thought me routed and discomfited, as the gentleman had promised. Sir, a breath blows all this triumph away. There is not the slightest difference in the purport of my remarks on the two occasions. What I said here on Wednesday is in exact accordance with the opinion expressed by me in the other house in 1825. Though the gentleman had the metaphysics of Hudibras, though he were able

"to sever and divide A hair 'twixt north and northwest side,"

he yet could not insert his metaphysical scissors between the fair reading of my remarks in 1825, and what I said here last week. There is not only no contradiction, no difference, but, in truth, too exact a similarity, both in thought and language, to be entirely in just taste. I had myself quoted the same speech; had recurred to it, and spoke with it open before me; and much of what I said was little more than a repetition from it. In order to make finishing work with this alleged contradiction, permit me to recur to the origin of this debate, and review its course. This seems expedient, and may be done as well now as at any time. Well, then, its history is this. The honorable member from Connecticut moved a resolution, which constitutes the first branch of that which is now before us; that is to say, a resolution, instructing the committee on public lands to inquire into the expediency of limiting, for a certain period, the sales of the public lands, to such as have heretofore been offered for sale; and whether sundry offices connected with the sales of the lands might not be abolished without detriment to the public service. In the progress of the discussion which arose on this resolution, an honorable member from New Hampshire moved to amend the resolution, so as entirely to reverse its object; that is, to strike it all out, and insert a direction to the committee to inquire into the expediency of adopting measures to hasten the sales, and expend more rapidly the surveys, of the lands.

The honorable member from Maine[1] suggested that both those propositions might well enough go for consideration to the committee; and in this state of the question, the member from South Carolina addressed the Senate in his first speech. He rose, he said, to give us his own free thoughts on the public lands. I saw him rise with pleasure, and listened with expectation, though before he concluded I was filled with surprise. Certainly, I was never more surprised, than to find him following up, to the extent he did, the sentiments and opinions which the gentleman from Missouri had put forth, and which it is known he has long entertained.

I need not repeat at large the general topics of the honorable gentleman's speech. When he said yesterday that he did not attack the Eastern States, he certainly must have forgotten, not only particular remarks, but the whole drift and tenor of his speech; unless he means by not attacking, that he did not commence hostilities, but that another had preceded him in the attack. He, in the first place, disapproved of the whole course of the government, for forty years, in regard to its disposition of the public lands; and then, turning northward and eastward, and fancying he had found a cause for alleged narrowness and niggardliness in the "accursed policy of the tariff", to which he represented the people of New England as wedded, he went on for a full hour with remarks, the whole scope of which was to exhibit the results of this policy, in feelings and in measures unfavorable to the West. I thought his opinions unfounded and erroneous, as to the general course of the government, and ventured to reply to them.

The gentleman had remarked on the analogy of other cases, and quoted the conduct of European governments towards their own subjects settling on this continent, as in point, to show that we had been harsh and rigid in selling, when we should have given the public lands to settlers without price. I thought the honorable member had suffered his judgment to be betrayed by a false analogy; that he was struck with an appearance of resemblance where there was no real similitude. I think so still. The first settlers of North America were enterprising spirits, engaged in private adventure, or fleeing from tyranny at home. When arrived here, they were forgotten by the mother country, or remembered only to be oppressed. Carried away again by the appearance of analogy, or struck with the eloquence of the passage, the honorable member yesterday observed, that the conduct of government towards the Western emigrants, or my representation of it, brought to his mind a celebrated speech in the British Parliament. It was, Sir, the speech of Colonel Barre. On the question of the stamp act, or tea tax, I forget which, Colonel Barre had heard a member on the treasury bench argue, that the people of the United States, being British colonists, planted by the maternal care, nourished by the indulgence, and protected by the arms of England, would not grudge their mite to relieve the mother country from the heavy burden under which she groaned. The language of Colonel Barre, in reply to this, was: "They planted by your care? Your oppression planted them in America. They fled from your tyranny, and grew by your neglect of them. So soon as you began to care for them, you showed your care by sending persons to spy out their liberties, misrepresent their character, prey upon them, and eat out their substance."

And how does the honorable gentleman mean to maintain, that language like this is applicable to the conduct of the government of the United States towards the Western emigrants, or to any representation given by me of that conduct? Were the settlers in the West driven thither by our oppression? Have they flourished only by our neglect of them? Has the government done nothing but prey upon them, and eat out their substance? Sir, this fervid eloquence of the British speaker, just when and where it was uttered, and fit to remain an exercise for the schools, is not a little out of place, when it is brought thence to be applied here to the conduct of our own country towards her own citizens. From America to England, it may be true; from Americans to their own government, it would be strange language. Let us leave it, to be recited and declaimed by our boys against a foreign nation; not introduce it here, to recite and declaim ourselves against our own.

But I come to the point of the alleged contradiction. In my remarks on Wednesday, I contended that we could not give away gratuitously all the public lands; that we held them in trust; that the government had solemnly pledged itself to dispose of them as a common fund for the common benefit, and to sell and settle them as its discretion should dictate. Now, Sir, what contradiction does the gentleman find to this sentiment in the speech of 1825? He quotes me as having then said, that we ought not to hug these lands as a very great treasure. Very well, Sir, supposing me to be accurately reported in that expression, what is the contradiction? I have not now said, that we should hug these lands as a favorite source of pecuniary income. No such thing. It is not my view. What I have said, and what I do say, is, that they are a common fund, to be disposed of for the common benefit, to be sold at low prices for the accommodation of settlers, keeping the object of settling the lands as much in view as that of raising money from them. This I say now, and this I have always said. Is this hugging them as a favorite treasure? Is there no difference between hugging and hoarding this fund, on the one hand, as a great treasure, and, on the other, of disposing of it at low prices, placing the proceeds in the general treasury of the Union? My opinion is, that as much is to be made of the land as fairly and reasonably may be, selling it all the while at such rates as to give the fullest effect to settlement. This is not giving it all away to the States, as the gentleman would propose; nor is it hugging the fund closely and tenaciously, as a favorite treasure; but it is, in my judgment, a just and wise policy, perfectly according with all the various duties which rest on government. So much for my contradiction. And what is it? Where is the ground of the gentleman's triumph? What inconsistency in word or doctrine has he been able to detect? Sir, if this be a sample of that discomfiture with which the honorable gentleman threatened me, commend me to the word *discomfiture* for the rest of my life.

But, after all, this is not the point of the debate; and I must now bring the gentleman back to what is the point.

The real question between me and him is, Has the doctrine been advanced at the South or the East, that the population of the West should be retarded, or at least need not be hastened, on account of its effect to drain off the people from the Atlantic States? Is this doctrine, as has been alleged, of Eastern origin? That is the question. Has the gentleman found any thing by which he can make good his accusation? I submit to the Senate, that he has entirely failed; and, as far as this debate has shown, the only person who has advanced such sentiments is a gentleman from South Carolina, and a friend of the honorable member himself. The honorable gentleman has given no answer to this; there is none which can be given. The simple fact, while it requires no comment to enforce it, defies all argument to refute it. I could refer to the speeches of another Southern gentleman, in years before, of the same general character, and to the same effect, as that which has been quoted; but I will not consume the time of the Senate by the reading of them.

So then, Sir, New England is guiltless of the policy of retarding Western population, and of all envy and jealousy of the growth of the new States. Whatever there be of that policy in the country, no part of it is hers. If it has a local habitation, the honorable member has probably seen by this time where to look for it; and if it now has received a name, he has himself christened it.

We approach, at length, Sir, to a more important part of the honorable gentleman's observations. Since it does not accord with my views of justice and policy to give away the public lands altogether, as a mere matter of gratuity, I am asked by the honorable gentleman on what ground it is that I consent to vote them away in particular instances. How, he inquires, do I reconcile with these professed sentiments, my support of measures appropriating portions of the lands to particular roads, particular canals, particular rivers, and particular institutions of education in the West? This leads, Sir, to the real and wide difference in political opinion between the honorable gentleman and myself. On my part, I look upon all these objects as connected with the common good, fairly embraced in its object and its terms; he, on the contrary, deems them all, if good at all, only local good. This is our difference. The interrogatory which he proceeded to put at once explains this difference. "What interest," asks he, "has South Carolina in a canal in Ohio?" Sir, this very question is full of significance. It develops the gentleman's whole political system; and its answer expounds mine. Here we differ. I look upon a road over the Alleghanies, a canal round the falls of the Ohio, or a canal or railway from the Atlantic to the Western waters, as being an object large and extensive enough to be fairly said to be for the common benefit. The gentleman thinks otherwise, and this is the key to his construction of the powers of the government. He may well ask what interest has South Carolina in a canal in Ohio. On his system, it is true, she has no interest. On that system, Ohio and Carolina are different governments, and different countries; connected here, it is true, by some slight and ill-defined bond of union, but in all main respects separate and diverse. On that system, Carolina has no more interest in a canal in Ohio than in Mexico. The gentleman, therefore, only follows out his own principles; he does no more than arrive at the natural conclusions of his own doctrines; he only announces the true results of that creed which he has adopted himself, and would persuade others to adopt, when he thus declares that South Carolina has no interest in a public work in Ohio.

Sir, we narrow-minded people of New England do not reason thus. Our *notion* of things is entirely different. We look upon the States, not as separated, but as united. We love to dwell on that union, and on the mutual happiness which it has so much promoted, and the common renown which it has so greatly contributed to acquire. In our contemplation, Carolina and Ohio are parts of the same country; States, united under the same general government, having interests, common, associated, intermingled. In whatever is within the proper sphere of the constitutional power of this government, we look upon the States as one. We do not impose geographical limits to our patriotic feeling or regard; we do not follow rivers and mountains, and lines of latitude, to find boundaries, beyond which public improvements do not benefit us. We who come here, as agents and representatives of these narrow-minded and selfish men of New England, consider ourselves as bound to regard with an equal eye the good of the whole, in whatever is within our powers of legislation. Sir, if a railroad or canal, beginning in South Carolina and ending in South Carolina, appeared to me to be of national importance and national magnitude, believing, as I do, that the power of government extends to the encouragement of works of that description, if I were to stand up here and ask, What interest has Massachusetts in a railroad in South Carolina? I should not be willing to face my constituents. These same narrow-minded men would tell me, that they had sent me to act for the whole country, and that one who possessed too little comprehension, either of intellect or feeling, one who was not large enough, both in mind and in heart, to embrace the whole, was not fit to be intrusted with the interest of any part.

Sir, I do not desire to enlarge the powers of the government by unjustifiable construction, nor to exercise any not within a fair interpretation. But when it is believed that a power does exist, then it is, in my judgment, to be exercised for the general benefit of the whole. So far as respects the exercise of such a power, the States are one. It was the very object of the Constitution to create unity of interests to the extent of the powers of the general government. In war and peace we are one; in commerce, one; because the authority of the general government reaches to war and peace, and to the regulation of commerce. I have never seen any more difficulty in erecting light-houses on the lakes, than on the ocean; in improving the harbors of inland seas, than if they were within the ebb and flow of the tide; or in removing obstructions in the vast streams of the West, more than in any work to facilitate commerce on the Atlantic coast. If there be any power for one, there is power also for the other; and they are all and equally for the common good of the country.

There are other objects, apparently more local, or the benefit of which is less general, towards which, nevertheless, I have concurred with others, to give aid by donations of land. It is proposed to construct a road, in or through one of the new States, in which this government possesses large quantities of land.

Have the United States no right, or, as a great and untaxed proprietor, are they under no obligation to contribute to an object thus calculated to promote the common good of all the proprietors, themselves included? And even with respect to education, which is the extreme case, let the question be considered. In the first place, as we have seen, it was made matter of compact with these States, that they should do their part to promote education. In the next place, our whole system of land laws proceeds on the idea that education is for the common good; because, in every division, a certain portion is uniformly reserved and appropriated for the use of schools. And, finally, have not these new States singularly strong claims, founded on the ground already stated, that the government is a great untaxed proprietor, in the ownership of the soil? It is a consideration of great importance, that probably there is in no part of the country, or of the world, so great call for the means of education, as in these new States, owing to the vast numbers of persons within those ages in which education and instruction are usually received, if received at all. This is the natural consequence of recency of settlement and rapid increase. The census of these States shows how great a proportion of the whole population occupies the classes between infancy and manhood. These are the wide fields, and here is the deep and quick soil for the seeds of knowledge and virtue; and this is the favored season, the very spring-time for sowing them. Let them be disseminated without stint. Let them be scattered with a bountiful hand, broadcast. Whatever the government can fairly do towards these objects, in my opinion, ought to be done.

These, Sir, are the grounds, succinctly stated, on which my votes for grants of lands for particular objects rest; while I maintain, at the same time, that it is all a common fund, for the common benefit. And reasons like these, I presume, have influenced the votes of other gentlemen from New England. Those who have a different view of the powers of the government, of course, come to different conclusions, on these, as on other questions. I observed, when speaking on this subject before, that if we looked to any measure, whether for a road, a canal, or any thing else, intended for the improvement of the West, it would be found that, if the New England *ayes* were struck out of the lists of votes, the Southern *noes* would always have rejected the measure. The truth of this has not been denied, and cannot be denied. In stating this, I thought it just to ascribe it to the constitutional scruples of the South, rather than to any other less favorable or less charitable cause. But no sooner had I done this, than the honorable gentleman asks if I reproach him and his friends with their constitutional scruples. Sir, I reproach nobody. I stated a fact, and gave the most respectful reason for it that occurred to me. The gentleman cannot deny the fact; he may, if he choose, disclaim the reason. It is not long since I had occasion, in presenting a petition from his own State, to account for its being intrusted to my hands, by saying, that the constitutional opinions of the gentleman and his worthy colleague prevented them from supporting it. Sir, did I state this as matter of reproach? Far from it. Did I attempt to find any other cause than an honest one for these scruples? Sir, I did not. It did not become me to doubt or to insinuate that the gentleman had either changed his sentiments, or that he had made up a set of constitutional opinions accommodated to any particular combination of political occurrences. Had I done so, I should have felt, that, while I was entitled to little credit in thus questioning other people's motives, I justified the whole world in suspecting my own. But how has the gentleman returned this respect for others' opinions? His own candor and justice, how have they been exhibited towards the motives of others, while he has been at so much pains to maintain, what nobody has disputed, the purity of his own? Why, Sir, he has asked _when_, and _how_, and *why* New England votes were found going for measures favorable to the West. He has demanded to be informed whether all this did not begin in 1825, and while the election of President was still pending.

Sir, to these questions retort would be justified; and it is both cogent and at hand. Nevertheless, I will answer the inquiry, not by retort, but by facts. I will tell the gentleman _when_, and _how_, and *why* New England has supported measures favorable to the West. I have already referred to the early history of the government, to the first acquisition of the lands, to the original laws for disposing of them, and for governing the territories where they lie; and have shown the influence of New England men and New England principles in all these leading measures. I should not be pardoned were I to go over that ground again. Coming to more recent times, and to measures of a less general character, I have endeavored to prove that every thing of this kind, designed for Western improvement, has depended on the votes of New England; all this is true beyond the power of contradiction. And now, Sir, there are two measures to which I will refer, not so ancient as to belong to the early history of the public lands, and not so recent as to be on this side of the period when the gentleman charitably imagines a new direction may have been given to New England feeling and New England votes. These measures, and the New England votes in support of them, may be taken as samples and specimens of all the rest.

In 1820 (observe, Mr. President, in 1820) the people of the West besought Congress for a reduction in the price of lands. In favor of that reduction, New England, with a delegation of forty members in the other house, gave thirty-three votes, and one only against it. The four Southern States, with more than fifty members, gave thirty-two votes for it, and seven against it. Again, in 1821, (observe again, Sir, the time,) the law passed for the relief of the purchasers of the public lands. This was a measure of vital importance to the West, and more especially to the Southwest. It authorized the relinquishment of contracts for lands which had been entered into at high prices, and a reduction in other cases of not less than thirty-seven and a half per cent on the purchase-money. Many millions of dollars, six or seven, I believe, probably much more, were relinquished by this law. On this bill, New England, with her forty members, gave more affirmative votes than the four Southern States, with their fifty-two or fifty-three members. These two are far the most important general measures respecting the public lands which have been adopted within the last twenty years. They took place in 1820 and 1821. That is the time *when*.

As to the manner _how_, the gentleman already sees that it was by voting in solid column for the required relief; and, lastly, as to the cause _why_, I tell the gentleman it was because the members from New England thought the measures just and salutary; because they entertained towards the West neither envy, hatred, nor malice; because they deemed it becoming them, as just and enlightened public men, to meet the exigency which had arisen in the West with the appropriate measure of relief; because they felt it due to their own characters, and the characters of their New England predecessors in this government, to act towards the new States in the spirit of a liberal, patronizing, magnanimous policy. So much, Sir, for the cause _why_; and I hope that by this time, Sir, the honorable gentleman is satisfied; if not, I do not know _when_, or _how_, or *why* he ever will be.

Having recurred to these two important measures, in answer to the gentleman's inquiries, I must now beg permission to go back to a period somewhat earlier, for the purpose of still further showing how much, or rather how little, reason there is for the gentleman's insinuation that political hopes or fears, or party associations, were the grounds of these New England votes. And after what has been said, I hope it may be forgiven me if I allude to some political opinions and votes of my own, of very little public importance certainly, but which, from the time at which they were given and expressed, may pass for good witnesses on this occasion.

This government, Mr. President, from its origin to the peace of 1815, had been too much engrossed with various other important concerns to be able to turn its thoughts inward, and look to the development of its vast internal resources. In the early part of President Washington's administration, it was fully occupied with completing its own organization, providing for the public debt, defending the frontiers, and maintaining domestic peace. Before the termination of that administration, the fires of the French Revolution blazed forth, as from a new-opened volcano, and the whole breadth of the ocean did not secure us from its effects. The smoke and the cinders reached us, though not the burning lava. Difficult and agitating questions, embarrassing to government and dividing public opinion, sprung out of the new state of our foreign relations, and were succeeded by others, and yet again by others, equally embarrassing and equally exciting division and discord, through the long series of twenty years, till they finally issued in the war with England. Down to the close of that war, no distinct, marked, and deliberate attention had been given, or could have been given, to the internal condition of the country, its capacities of improvement, or the constitutional power of the government in regard to objects connected with such improvement.

The peace, Mr. President, brought about an entirely new and a most interesting state of things; it opened to us other prospects and suggested other duties. We ourselves were changed, and the whole world was changed. The pacification of Europe, after June, 1815, assumed a firm and permanent aspect. The nations evidently manifested that they were disposed for peace. Some agitation of the waves might be expected, even after the storm had subsided; but the tendency was, strongly and rapidly, towards settled repose.

It so happened, Sir, that I was at that time a member of Congress, and, like others, naturally turned my thoughts to the contemplation of the recently altered condition of the country and of the world. It appeared plainly enough to me, as well as to wiser and more experienced men, that the policy of the government would naturally take a start in a new direction; because new directions would necessarily be given to the pursuits and occupations of the people. We had pushed our commerce far and fast, under the advantage of a neutral flag. But there were now no longer flags, either neutral or belligerent. The harvest of neutrality had been great, but we had gathered it all. With the peace of Europe, it was obvious there would spring up in her circle of nations a revived and invigorated spirit of trade, and a new activity in all the business and objects of civilized life. Hereafter, our commercial gains were to be earned only by success in a close and intense competition. Other nations would produce for themselves, and carry for themselves, and manufacture for themselves, to the full extent of their abilities. The crops of our plains would no longer sustain European armies, nor our ships longer supply those whom war had rendered unable to supply themselves. It was obvious, that, under these circumstances, the country would begin to survey itself, and to estimate its own capacity of improvement.

And this improvement,--how was it to be accomplished, and who was to accomplish it? We were ten or twelve millions of people, spread over almost half a world. We were more than twenty States, some stretching along the same seaboard, some along the same line of inland frontier, and others on opposite banks of the same vast rivers. Two considerations at once presented themselves with great force, in looking at this state of things. One was, that that great branch of improvement which consisted in furnishing new facilities of intercourse necessarily ran into different States in every leading instance, and would benefit the citizens of all such States. No one State, therefore, in such cases, would assume the whole expense, nor was the co-operation of several States to be expected. Take the instance of the Delaware breakwater. It will cost several millions of money. Would Pennsylvania alone ever have constructed it? Certainly never, while this Union lasts, because it is not for her sole benefit. Would Pennsylvania, New Jersey, and Delaware have united to accomplish it at their joint expense? Certainly not, for the same reason. It could not be done, therefore, but by the general government. The same may be said of the large inland undertakings, except that, in them, government, instead of bearing the whole expense, co-operates with others who bear a part. The other consideration is, that the United States have the means. They enjoy the revenues derived from commerce, and the States have no abundant and easy sources of public income. The custom-houses fill the general treasury, while the States have scanty resources, except by resort to heavy direct taxes.

Under this view of things, I thought it necessary to settle, at least for myself, some definite notions with respect to the powers of the government in regard to internal affairs. It may not savor too much of self-commendation to remark, that, with this object, I considered the Constitution, its judicial construction, its contemporaneous exposition, and the whole history of the legislation of Congress under it; and I arrived at the conclusion, that government had power to accomplish sundry objects, or aid in their accomplishment, which are now commonly spoken of as INTERNAL IMPROVEMENTS. That conclusion, Sir, may have been right, or it may have been wrong. I am not about to argue the grounds of it at large. I say only, that it was adopted and acted on even so early as in 1816. Yes, Mr. President, I made up my opinion, and determined on my intended course of political conduct, on these subjects, in the Fourteenth Congress, in 1816. And now, Mr. President, I have further to say, that I made up these opinions, and entered on this course of political conduct, *Teucro duce*.[2] Yes, Sir, I pursued in all this a South Carolina track on the doctrines of internal improvement. South Carolina, as she was then represented in the other house, set forth in 1816 under a fresh and leading breeze, and I was among the followers. But if my leader sees new lights and turns a sharp corner, unless I see new lights also, I keep straight on in the same path. I repeat, that leading gentlemen from South Carolina were first and foremost in behalf of the doctrines of internal improvements, when those doctrines came first to be considered and acted upon in Congress. The debate on the bank question, on the tariff of 1816, and on the direct tax, will show who was who, and what was what, at that time.

The tariff of 1816, (one of the plain cases of oppression and usurpation, from which, if the government does not recede, individual States may justly secede from the government,) is, Sir, in truth, a South Carolina tariff, supported by South Carolina votes. But for those votes, it could not have passed in the form in which it did pass; whereas, if it had depended on Massachusetts votes, it would have been lost. Does not the honorable gentleman well know all this? There are certainly those who do, full well, know it all. I do not say this to reproach South Carolina. I only state the fact; and I think it will appear to be true, that among the earliest and boldest advocates of the tariff, as a measure of protection, and on the express ground of protection, were leading gentlemen of South Carolina in Congress. I did not then, and cannot now, understand their language in any other sense. While this tariff of 1816 was under discussion in the House of Representatives, an honorable gentleman from Georgia, now of this house,[3] moved to reduce the proposed duty on cotton. He failed, by four votes, South Carolina giving three votes (enough to have turned the scale) against his motion. The act, Sir, then passed, and received on its passage the support of a majority of the Representatives of South Carolina present and voting. This act is the first in the order of those now denounced as plain usurpations. We see it daily in the list, by the side of those of 1824 and 1828, as a case of manifest oppression, justifying disunion. I put it home to the honorable member from South Carolina, that his own State was not only "art and part" in this measure, but the *causa causans*. Without her aid, this seminal principle of mischief, this root of Upas, could not have been planted. I have already said, and it is true, that this act proceeded on the ground of protection. It interfered directly with existing interests of great value and amount. It cut up the Calcutta cotton trade by the roots; but it passed, nevertheless, and it passed on the principle of protecting manufactures, on the principle against free trade, on the principle opposed to that *which lets us alone.*

Such, Mr. President, were the opinions of important and leading gentlemen from South Carolina, on the subject of internal improvement, in 1816. I went out of Congress the next year, and, returning again in 1823, thought I found South Carolina where I had left her. I really supposed that all things remained as they were, and that the South Carolina doctrine of internal improvements would be defended by the same eloquent voices, and the same strong arms, as formerly. In the lapse of these six years, it is true, political associations had assumed a new aspect and new divisions. A strong party had arisen in the South hostile to the doctrine of internal improvements. Anti-consolidation was the flag under which this party fought; and its supporters inveighed against internal improvements, much after the manner in which the honorable gentleman has now inveighed against them, as part and parcel of the system of consolidation. Whether this party arose in South Carolina itself, or in the neighborhood, is more than I know. I think the latter. However that may have been, there were those found in South Carolina ready to make war upon it, and who did make intrepid war upon it. Names being regarded as things in such controversies, they bestowed on the anti-improvement gentlemen the appellation of Radicals. Yes, Sir, the appellation of Radicals, as a term of distinction applicable and applied to those who denied the liberal doctrines of internal improvement, originated, according to the best of my recollection, somewhere between North Carolina and Georgia. Well, Sir, these mischievous Radicals were to be put down, and the strong arm of South Carolina was stretched out to put them down. About this time I returned to Congress. The battle with the Radicals had been fought, and our South Carolina champions of the doctrines of internal improvement had nobly maintained their ground, and were understood to have achieved a victory. We looked upon them as conquerors. They had driven back the enemy with discomfiture, a thing, by the way, Sir, which is not always performed when it is promised. A gentleman to whom I have already referred in this debate had come into Congress, during my absence from it, from South Carolina, and had brought with him a high reputation for ability. He came from a school with which we had been acquainted, *et noscitur a sociis.* I hold in my hand, Sir, a printed speech of this distinguished gentleman,[4] "ON INTERNAL IMPROVEMENTS," delivered about the period to which I now refer, and printed with a few introductory remarks upon _consolidation_; in which, Sir, I think he quite consolidated the arguments of his opponents, the Radicals, if to *crush* be to consolidate. I give you a short but significant quotation from these remarks. He is speaking of a pamphlet, then recently published, entitled "Consolidation"; and, having alluded to the question of renewing the charter of the former Bank of the United States, he says:--

"Moreover, in the early history of parties, and when Mr. Crawford advocated a renewal of the old charter, it was considered a Federal measure; which internal improvement _never was_, as this author erroneously states. This latter measure originated in the administration of Mr. Jefferson, with the appropriation for the Cumberland Road; and was first proposed, _as a system_, by Mr. Calhoun, and carried through the House of Representatives by a large majority of the Republicans, including almost every one of the leading men who carried us through the late war."

So, then, internal improvement is not one of the Federal heresies. One paragraph more, Sir:--

"The author in question, not content with denouncing as Federalists, General Jackson, Mr. Adams, Mr. Calhoun, and the majority of the South Carolina delegation in Congress, modestly extends the denunciation to Mr. Monroe and the whole Republican party. Here are his words: 'During the administration of Mr. Monroe much has passed which the Republican party would be glad to approve if they could!! But the principal feature, and that which has chiefly elicited these observations, is the renewal of the SYSTEM OF INTERNAL IMPROVEMENTS.' Now this measure was adopted by a vote of 115 to 86 of a Republican Congress, and sanctioned by a Republican President. Who, then, is this author, who assumes the high prerogative of denouncing, in the name of the Republican party, the Republican administration of the country? A denunciation including within its sweep _Calhoun, Lowndes, and

Cheves_, men who will be regarded as the brightest ornaments of South Carolina, and the strongest pillars of the Republican party, as long as the late war shall be remembered, and talents and patriotism shall be regarded as the proper objects of the admiration and gratitude of a free people!!"

Such are the opinions, Sir, which were maintained by South Carolina gentlemen, in the House of Representatives, on the subject of internal improvements, when I took my seat there as a member from Massachusetts in 1823. But this is not all. We had a bill before us, and passed it in that house, entitled, "An Act to procure the necessary surveys, plans, and estimates upon the subject of roads and canals." It authorized the President to cause surveys and estimates to be made of the routes of such roads and canals as he might deem of national importance in a commercial or military point of view, or for the transportation of the mail, and appropriated thirty thousand dollars out of the treasury to defray the expense. This act, though preliminary in its nature, covered the whole ground. It took for granted the complete power of internal improvement, as far as any of its advocates had ever contended for it. Having passed the other house, the bill came up to the Senate, and was here considered and debated in April, 1824. The honorable member from South Carolina was a member of the Senate at that time. While the bill was under consideration here, a motion was made to add the following proviso: "_Provided_, That nothing herein contained shall be construed to affirm *or admit* a power in Congress, on their own authority, to make roads or canals within any of the States of the Union." The yeas and nays were taken on this proviso, and the honorable member voted _in the negative_! The proviso failed.

A motion was then made to add this proviso, viz.: "_Provided_, That the faith of the United States is hereby pledged, that no money shall ever be expended for roads or canals, except it shall be among the several States, and in the same proportion as direct taxes are laid and assessed by the provisions of the Constitution." The honorable member voted *against this proviso* also, and it failed. The bill was then put on its passage, and the honorable member voted _for it_, and it passed, and became a law.

Now, it strikes me, Sir, that there is no maintaining these votes, but upon the power of internal improvement, in its broadest sense. In truth, these bills for surveys and estimates have always been considered as test questions; they show who is for and who against internal improvement. This law itself went the whole length, and assumed the full and complete power. The gentleman's votes sustained that power, in every form in which the various propositions to amend presented it. He went for the entire and unrestrained authority, without consulting the States, and without agreeing to any proportionate distribution. And now suffer me to remind you, Mr. President, that it is this very same power, thus sanctioned, in every form, by the gentleman's own opinion, which is so plain and manifest a usurpation, that the State of South Carolina is supposed to be justified in refusing submission to any laws carrying the power into effect. Truly, Sir, is not this a little too hard? May we not crave some mercy, under favor and protection of the gentleman's own authority? Admitting that a road, or a canal, must be written down flat usurpation as was ever committed, may we find no mitigation in our respect for his place, and his vote, as one that knows the law?

The tariff, which South Carolina had an efficient hand in establishing, in 1816, and this asserted power of internal improvement, advanced by her in the same year, and, as we have seen, approved and sanctioned by her Representatives in 1824,--these two measures are the great grounds on which she is now thought to be justified in breaking up the Union, if she sees fit to break it up!

I may now safely say, I think, that we have had the authority of leading and distinguished gentlemen from South Carolina in support of the doctrine of internal improvement. I repeat, that, up to 1824, I for one followed South Carolina; but when that star, in its ascension, veered off in an unexpected direction, I relied on its light no longer.

Here the Vice-President said, "Does the chair understand the gentleman from Massachusetts to say that the person now occupying the chair of the Senate has changed his opinions on the subject of internal improvements?"

From nothing ever said to me, Sir, have I had reason to know of any change in the opinions of the person filling the chair of the Senate. If such change has taken place, I regret it. I speak generally of the State of South Carolina. Individuals we know there are who hold opinions favorable to the power. An application for its exercise, in behalf of a public work in South Carolina itself, is now pending, I believe, in the other house, presented by members from that State.

I have thus, Sir, perhaps not without some tediousness of detail, shown, if I am in error on the subject of internal improvement, how, and in what company, I fell into that error. If I am wrong, it is apparent who misled me.

I go to other remarks of the honorable member; and I have to complain of an entire misapprehension of what I said on the subject of the national debt, though I can hardly perceive how any one could misunderstand me. What I said was, not that I wished to put off the payment of the debt, but, on the contrary, that I had always voted for every measure for its reduction, as uniformly as the gentleman himself. He seems to claim the exclusive merit of a disposition to reduce the public charge. I do not allow it to him. As a debt, I was, I am for paying it, because it is a charge on our finances, and on the industry of the country. But I observed, that I thought I perceived a morbid fervor on that subject, an excessive anxiety to pay off the debt, not so much because it is a debt simply, as because, while it lasts, it furnishes one objection to disunion. It is, while it continues, a tie of common interest. I did not impute such motives to the honorable member himself, but that there is such a feeling in existence I have not a particle of doubt. The most I said was, that, if one effect of the debt was to strengthen our Union, that effect itself was not regretted by me, however much others might regret it. The gentleman has not seen how to reply to this, otherwise than by supposing me to have advanced the doctrine that a national debt is a national blessing. Others, I must hope, will find much less difficulty in understanding me. I distinctly and pointedly cautioned the honorable member not to understand me as expressing an opinion favorable to the continuance of the debt. I repeated this caution, and repeated it more than once; but it was thrown away. On yet another point, I was still more unaccountably misunderstood. The gentleman had harangued against "consolidation." I told him, in reply, that there was one kind of consolidation to which I was attached, and that was the consolidation of our Union; that this was precisely that consolidation to which I feared others were not attached, and that such consolidation was the very end of the Constitution, the leading object, as they had informed us themselves, which its framers had kept in view. I turned to their communication,[5] and read their very words, "the consolidation of the Union," and expressed my devotion to this sort of consolidation. I said, in terms, that I wished not in the slightest degree to augment the powers of this government; that my object was to preserve, not to enlarge; and that by consolidating the Union I understood no more than the strengthening of the Union, and perpetuating it. Having been thus explicit, having thus read from the printed book the precise words which I adopted, as expressing my own sentiments, it passes comprehension how any man could understand me as contending for an extension of the powers of the government, or for consolidation in that odious sense in which it means an accumulation, in the federal government, of the powers properly belonging to the States.

I repeat, Sir, that, in adopting the sentiment of the framers of the Constitution, I read their language audibly, and word for word; and I pointed out the distinction, just as fully as I have now done, between the consolidation of the Union and that other obnoxious consolidation which I disclaimed. And yet the honorable member misunderstood me. The gentleman had said that he wished for no fixed revenue,--not a shilling. If by a word he could convert the Capitol into gold, he would not do it. Why all this fear of revenue? Why, Sir, because, as the gentleman told us, it tends to consolidation. Now this can mean neither more nor less than that a common revenue is a common interest, and that all common interests tend to preserve the union of the States. I confess I like that tendency; if the gentleman dislikes it, he is right in deprecating a shilling of fixed revenue. So much, Sir, for consolidation.

As well as I recollect the course of his remarks, the honorable gentleman next recurred to the subject of the tariff. He did not doubt the word must be of unpleasant sound to me, and proceeded, with an effort neither new nor attended with new success, to involve me and my votes in inconsistency and contradiction. I am happy the honorable gentleman has furnished me an opportunity of a timely remark or two on that subject. I was glad he approached it, for it is a question I enter upon without fear from anybody. The strenuous toil of the gentleman has been to raise an inconsistency between my dissent to the tariff in 1824, and my vote in 1828. It is labor lost. He pays undeserved compliment to my speech in 1824; but this is to raise me high, that my fall, as he would have it, in 1828, may be more signal. Sir, there was no fall. Between the ground I stood on in 1824 and that I took in 1828, there was not only no precipice, but no declivity. It was a change of position to meet new circumstances, but on the same level. A plain tale explains the whole matter. In 1816 I had not acquiesced in the tariff, then supported by South Carolina. To some parts of it, especially, I felt and expressed great repugnance. I held the same opinions in 1820, at the meeting in Faneuil Hall, to which the gentleman has alluded. I said then, and say now, that, as an original question, the authority of Congress to exercise the revenue power, with direct reference to the protection of manufactures, is a questionable authority, far more questionable, in my judgment, than the power of internal improvements. I must confess, Sir, that in one respect some impression has been made on my opinions lately. Mr. Madison's publication has put the power in a very strong light. He has placed it, I must acknowledge, upon grounds of construction and argument which seem impregnable. But even if the power were doubtful, on the face of the Constitution itself, it had been assumed and asserted in the first revenue law ever passed under that same Constitution and on this ground, as a matter settled by contemporaneous practice, I had refrained from expressing the opinion that the tariff laws transcended constitutional limits, as the gentleman supposes. What I did say at Faneuil Hall, as far as I now remember, was, that this was originally matter of doubtful construction. The gentleman himself, I suppose, thinks there is no doubt about it, and that the laws are plainly against the Constitution. Mr. Madison's letters, already referred to, contain, in my judgment, by far the most able exposition extant of this part of the Constitution. He has satisfied me, so far as the practice of the government had left it an open question.

With a great majority of the Representatives of Massachusetts, I voted against the tariff of 1824. My reasons were then given, and I will not now repeat them. But, notwithstanding our dissent, the great States of New York, Pennsylvania, Ohio, and Kentucky went for the bill, in almost unbroken column, and it passed. Congress and the President sanctioned it, and it became the law of the land. What, then, were we to do? Our only option was, either to fall in with this settled course of public policy, and accommodate ourselves to it as well as we could, or to embrace the South Carolina doctrine, and talk of nullifying the statute by State interference.

This last alternative did not suit our principles, and of course we adopted the former. In 1827, the subject came again before Congress, on a proposition to afford some relief to the branch of wool and woollens. We looked upon the system of protection as being fixed and settled. The law of 1824 remained. It had gone into full operation, and, in regard to some objects intended by it, perhaps most of them, had produced all its expected effects. No man proposed to repeal it; no man attempted to renew the general contest on its principle. But, owing to subsequent and unforeseen occurrences, the benefit intended by it to wool and woollen fabrics had not been realized. Events not known here when the law passed had taken place, which defeated its object in that particular respect. A measure was accordingly brought forward to meet this precise deficiency, to remedy this particular defect. It was limited to wool and woollens. Was ever any thing more reasonable? If the policy of the tariff laws had become established in principle, as the permanent policy of the government, should they not be revised and amended, and made equal, like other laws, as exigencies should arise, or justice require? Because we had doubted about adopting the system, were we to refuse to cure its manifest defects, after it had been adopted, and when no one attempted its repeal? And this, Sir, is the inconsistency so much bruited. I had voted against the tariff of 1824, but it passed; and in 1827 and 1828 I voted to amend it, in a point essential to the interest of my constituents. Where is the inconsistency? Could I do otherwise? Sir, does political consistency consist in always giving negative votes? Does it require of a public man to refuse to concur in amending laws, because they passed against his consent? Having voted against the tariff originally, does consistency demand that I should do all in my power to maintain an unequal tariff, burdensome to my own constituents in many respects, favorable in none? To consistency of that sort, I lay no claim. And there is another sort to which I lay as little, and that is, a kind of consistency by which persons feel themselves as much bound to oppose a proposition after it has become a law of the land as before.

The bill of 1827, limited, as I have said, to the single object in which the tariff of 1824 had manifestly failed in its effect, passed the House of Representatives, but was lost here. We had then the act of 1828. I need not recur to the history of a measure so recent. Its enemies spiced it with whatsoever they thought would render it distasteful; its friends took it, drugged as it was. Vast amounts of property, many millions, had been invested in manufactures, under the inducements of the act of 1824. Events called loudly, as I thought, for further regulation to secure the degree of protection intended by that act. I was disposed to vote for such regulation, and desired nothing more; but certainly was not to be bantered out of my purpose by a threatened augmentation of duty on molasses, put into the bill for the avowed purpose of making it obnoxious. The vote may have been right or wrong, wise or unwise; but it is little less than absurd to allege against it an inconsistency with opposition to the former law.

Sir, as to the general subject of the tariff, I have little now to say. Another opportunity may be presented. I remarked the other day, that this policy did not begin with us in New England; and yet, Sir, New England is charged with vehemence as being favorable, or charged with equal vehemence as being unfavorable, to the tariff policy, just as best suits the time, place, and occasion for making some charge against her. The credulity of the public has been put to its extreme capacity of false impression relative to her conduct in this particular. Through all the South, during the late contest, it was New England policy and a New England administration that were afflicting the country with a tariff beyond all endurance; while on the other side of the Alleghanies even the act of 1828 itself, the very sublimated essence of oppression, according to Southern opinions, was pronounced to be one of those blessings for which the West was indebted to the "generous South."

With large investments in manufacturing establishments, and many and various interests connected with and dependent on them, it is not to be expected that New England, any more than other portions of the country, will now consent to any measure destructive or highly dangerous. The duty of the government, at the present moment, would seem to be to preserve, not to destroy; to maintain the position which it has assumed; and, for one, I shall feel it an indispensable obligation to hold it steady, as far as in my power, to that degree of protection which it has undertaken to bestow. No more of the tariff.

Professing to be provoked by what he chose to consider a charge made by me against South Carolina, the honorable member, Mr. President, has taken up a new crusade against New England. Leaving altogether the subject of the public lands, in which his success, perhaps, had been neither distinguished nor satisfactory, and letting go, also, of the topic of the tariff, he sallied forth in a general assault on the opinions, politics, and parties of New England, as they have been exhibited in the last thirty years. This is natural. The "narrow policy" of the public lands had proved a legal settlement in South Carolina, and was not to be removed. The "accursed policy" of the tariff, also, had established the fact of its birth and parentage in the same State. No wonder, therefore, the gentleman wished to carry the war, as he expressed it, into the enemy's country. Prudently willing to quit these subjects, he was, doubtless, desirous of fastening on others, which could not be transferred south of Mason and Dixon's line. The politics of New England became his theme; and it was in this part of his speech, I think, that he menaced me with such sore discomfiture. Discomfiture! Why, Sir, when he attacks any thing which I maintain, and overthrows it, when he turns the right or left of any position which I take up, when he drives me from any ground I choose to occupy, he may then talk of discomfiture, but not till that distant day. What has he done? Has he maintained his own charges? Has he proved what he alleged? Has he sustained himself in his attack on the government, and on the history of the North, in the matter of the public lands? Has he disproved a fact, refuted a proposition, weakened an argument, maintained by me? Has he come within beat of drum of any position of mine? O, no; but he has "carried the war into the enemy's country"! Carried the war into the enemy's country! Yes, Sir, and what sort of a war has he made of it? Why, Sir, he has stretched a drag-net over the whole surface of perished pamphlets, indiscreet sermons, frothy paragraphs, and fuming popular addresses,--over whatever the pulpit in its moments of alarm, the press in its heats, and parties in their extravagance, have severally thrown off in times of general excitement and violence. He has thus swept together a mass of such things as, but that they are now old and cold, the public health would have required him rather to leave in their state of dispersion. For a good long hour or two, we had the unbroken pleasure of listening to the honorable member, while he recited with his usual grace and spirit, and with evident high gusto, speeches, pamphlets, addresses, and all the *et caeteras* of the political press, such as warm heads produce in warm times; and such as it would be "discomfiture" indeed for any one, whose taste did not delight in that sort of reading, to be obliged to peruse. This is his war. This it is to carry war into the enemy's country. It is in an invasion of this sort, that he flatters himself with the expectation of gaining laurels fit to adorn a Senator's brow!

Mr. President, I shall not, it will not, I trust, be expected that I should, either now or at any time, separate this farrago into parts, and answer and examine its components. I shall barely bestow upon it all a general remark or two. In the run of forty years, Sir, under this Constitution, we have experienced sundry successive violent party contests. Party arose, indeed, with the Constitution itself, and, in some form or other, has attended it through the greater part of its history. Whether any other constitution than the old Articles of Confederation was desirable, was itself a question on which parties divided; if a new constitution were framed, what powers should be given to it was another question; and when it had been formed, what was, in fact, the just extent of the powers actually conferred was a third. Parties, as we know, existed under the first administration, as distinctly marked as those which have manifested themselves at any subsequent period. The contest immediately preceding the political change in 1801, and that, again, which existed at the commencement of the late war, are other instances of party excitement, of something more than usual strength and intensity. In all these conflicts there was, no doubt, much of violence on both and all sides. It would be impossible, if one had a fancy for such employment, to adjust the relative *quantum* of violence between these contending parties. There was enough in each, as must always be expected in popular governments. With a great deal of popular and decorous discussion, there was mingled a great deal, also, of declamation, virulence, crimination, and abuse. In regard to any party, probably, at one of the leading epochs in the history of parties, enough may be found to make out another inflamed exhibition, not unlike that with which the honorable member has edified us. For myself, Sir, I shall not rake among the rubbish of bygone times, to see what I can find, or whether I cannot find something by which I can fix a blot on the escutcheon of any State, any party, or any part of the country. General Washington's administration was steadily and zealously maintained, as we all know, by New England. It was violently opposed elsewhere. We know in what quarter he had the most earnest, constant, and persevering support, in all his great and leading measures. We know where his private and personal character was held in the highest degree of attachment and veneration; and we know, too, where his measures were opposed, his services slighted, and his character vilified. We know, or we might know, if we turned to the journals, who expressed respect, gratitude, and regret, when he retired from the chief magistracy, and who refused to express either respect, gratitude, or regret. I shall not open those journals. Publications more abusive or scurrilous never saw the light, than were sent forth against Washington, and all his leading measures, from presses south of New England. But I shall not look them up. I employ no scavengers, no one is in attendance on me, furnishing such means of retaliation; and if there were, with an ass's load of them, with a bulk as huge as that which the gentleman himself has produced, I would not touch one of them. I see enough of the violence of our own times, to be no way anxious to rescue from forgetfulness the extravagances of times past.

Besides, what is all this to the present purpose? It has nothing to do with the public lands, in regard to which the attack was begun; and it has nothing to do with those sentiments and opinions which, I have thought, tend to disunion and all of which the honorable member seems to have adopted himself, and undertaken to defend. New England has, at times, so argues the gentleman, held opinions as dangerous as those which he now holds. Suppose this were so; why should *he* therefore abuse New England? If he finds himself countenanced by acts of hers, how is it that, while he relies on these acts, he covers, or seeks to cover, their authors with reproach? But, Sir, if, in the course of forty years, there have been undue effervescences of party in New England, has the same thing happened nowhere else? Party animosity and party outrage, not in New England, but elsewhere, denounced President Washington, not only as a Federalist, but as a Tory, a British agent, a man who, in his high office, sanctioned corruption. But does the honorable member suppose, if I had a tender here who should put such an effusion of wickedness and folly into my hand, that I would stand up and read it against the South? Parties ran into great heats again in 1799 and 1800. What was said, Sir, or rather what was not said, in those years, against John Adams, one of the committee that drafted the Declaration of Independence, and its admitted ablest defender on the floor of Congress? If the gentleman wishes to increase his stores of party abuse and frothy violence, if he has a determined proclivity to such pursuits, there are treasures of that sort south of the Potomac, much to his taste, yet untouched. I shall not touch them.

The parties which divided the country at the commencement of the late war were violent. But then there was violence on both sides, and violence in every State. Minorities and majorities were equally violent. There was no more violence against the war in New England, than in other States; nor any more appearance of violence, except that, owing to a dense population, greater facility of assembling, and more presses, there may have been more in quantity spoken and printed there than in some other places. In the article of sermons, too, New England is somewhat more abundant than South Carolina; and for that reason the chance of finding here and there an exceptionable one may be greater. I hope, too, there are more good ones. Opposition may have been more formidable in New England, as it embraced a larger portion of the whole population; but it was no more unrestrained in principle, or violent in manner. The minorities dealt quite as harshly with their own State governments as the majorities dealt with the administration here. There were presses on both sides, popular meetings on both sides, ay, and pulpits on both sides also. The gentleman's purveyors have only catered for him among the productions of one side. I certainly shall not supply the deficiency by furnishing samples of the other. I leave to him, and to them, the whole concern. It is enough for me to say, that if, in any part of this their grateful occupation, if, in all their researches, they find any thing in the history of Massachusetts, or New England, or in the proceedings of any legislative or other public body, disloyal to the Union, speaking slightingly of its value, proposing to break it up, or recommending non-intercourse with neighboring States, on account of difference of political opinion, then, Sir, I give them all up to the honorable gentleman's unrestrained rebuke; expecting, however, that he will extend his buffetings in like manner _to all similar proceedings, wherever else found_.

The gentleman, Sir, has spoken at large of former parties, now no longer in being, by their received appellations, and has undertaken to instruct us, not only in the knowledge of their principles, but of their respective pedigrees also. He has ascended to their origin, and run out their genealogies. With most exemplary modesty, he speaks of the party to which he professes to have himself belonged, as the true Pure, the only honest, patriotic party, derived by regular descent, from father to son, from the time of the virtuous Romans! Spreading before us the *family tree* of political parties, he takes especial care to show himself snugly perched on a popular bough! He is wakeful to the expediency of adopting such rules of descent as shall bring him in, to the exclusion of others, as an heir to the inheritance of all public virtue, and all true political principle. His party and his opinions are sure to be orthodox; heterodoxy is confined to his opponents. He spoke, Sir, of the Federalists, and I thought I saw some eyes begin to open and stare a little, when he ventured on that ground. I expected he would draw his sketches rather lightly, when he looked on the circle round him, and especially if he should cast his thoughts to the high places out of the Senate. Nevertheless, he went back to Rome, _ad annum urbis conditae_, and found the fathers of the Federalists in the primeval aristocrats of that renowned city! He traced the flow of Federal blood down through successive ages and centuries, till he brought it into the veins of the American Tories, of whom, by the way, there were twenty in the Carolinas for one in Massachusetts. From the Tories he followed it to the Federalists; and, as the Federal party was broken up, and there was no possibility of transmitting it further on this side the Atlantic, he seems to have discovered that it has gone off collaterally, though against all the canons of descent, into the Ultras of France, and finally become extinguished, like exploded gas, among the adherents of Don Miguel! This, Sir, is an abstract of the gentleman's history of Federalism. I am not about to controvert it. It is not, at present, worth the pains of refutation; because, Sir, if at this day any one feels the sin of Federalism lying heavily on his conscience, he can easily procure remission. He may even obtain an indulgence, if he be desirous of repeating the same transgression. It is an affair of no difficulty to get into this same right line of patriotic descent. A man now-a-days is at liberty to choose his political parentage. He may elect his own father. Federalist or not, he may, if he choose, claim to belong to the favored stock, and his claim will be allowed. He may carry back his pretensions just as far as the honorable gentleman himself; nay, he may make himself out the honorable gentleman's cousin, and prove, satisfactorily, that he is descended from the same political great-grandfather. All this is allowable. We all know a process, Sir, by which the whole Essex Junto could, in one hour, be all washed white from their ancient Federalism, and come out, every one of them, original Democrats, dyed in the wool! Some of them have actually undergone the operation, and they say it is quite easy. The only inconvenience it occasions, as they tell us, is a slight tendency of the blood to the face, a soft suffusion, which, however, is very transient, since nothing is said by those whom they join calculated to deepen the red on the cheek, but a prudent silence is observed in regard to all the past. Indeed, Sir, some smiles of approbation have been bestowed, and some crumbs of comfort have fallen, not a thousand miles from the door of the Hartford Convention itself. And if the author of the Ordinance of 1787 possessed the other requisite qualifications, there is no knowing, notwithstanding his Federalism, to what heights of favor he might not yet attain.

Mr. President, in carrying his warfare, such as it is, into New England, the honorable gentleman all along professes to be acting on the defensive. He chooses to consider me as having assailed South Carolina, and insists that he comes forth only as her champion, and in her defence. Sir, I do not admit that I made any attack whatever on South Carolina. Nothing like it. The honorable member, in his first speech, expressed opinions, in regard to revenue and some other topics, which I heard both with pain and with surprise. I told the gentleman I was aware that such sentiments were entertained *out* of the government, but had not expected to find them advanced in it; that I knew there were persons in the South who speak of our Union with indifference or doubt, taking pains to magnify its evils, and to say nothing of its benefits; that the honorable member himself, I was sure, could never be one of these; and I regretted the expression of such opinions as he had avowed, because I thought their obvious tendency was to encourage feelings of disrespect to the Union, and to impair its strength. This, Sir, is the sum and substance of all I said on the subject. And this constitutes the attack which called on the chivalry of the gentleman, in his own opinion, to harry us with such a foray among the party pamphlets and party proceedings of Massachusetts! If he means that I spoke with dissatisfaction or disrespect of the ebullitions of individuals in South Carolina, it is true. But if he means that I assailed the character of the State, her honor, or patriotism, that I reflected on her history or her conduct, he has not the slightest ground for any such assumption. I did not even refer, I think, in my observations, to any collection of individuals. I said nothing of the recent conventions. I spoke in the most guarded and careful manner, and only expressed my regret for the publication of opinions, which I presumed the honorable member disapproved as much as myself. In this, it seems, I was mistaken. I do not remember that the gentleman has disclaimed any sentiment, or any opinion, of a supposed anti-union tendency, which on all or any of the recent occasions has been expressed. The whole drift of his speech has been rather to prove, that, in divers times and manners, sentiments equally liable to my objection have been avowed in New England. And one would suppose that his object, in this reference to Massachusetts, was to find a precedent to justify proceedings in the South, were it not for the reproach and contumely with which he labors, all along, to load these his own chosen precedents. By way of defending South Carolina from what he chooses to think an attack on her, he first quotes the example of Massachusetts, and then denounces that example in good set terms. This twofold purpose, not very consistent, one would think, with itself, was exhibited more than once in the course of his speech. He referred, for instance, to the Hartford Convention. Did he do this for authority, or for a topic of reproach? Apparently for both, for he told us that he should find no fault with the mere fact of holding such a convention, and considering and discussing such questions as he supposes were then and there discussed; but what rendered it obnoxious was its being held at the time, and under the circumstances of the country then existing. We were in a war, he said, and the country needed all our aid: the hand of government required to be strengthened, not weakened; and patriotism should have postponed such proceedings to another day. The thing itself, then, is a precedent; the time and manner of it only, a subject of censure. Now, Sir, I go much further, on this point, than the honorable member. Supposing, as the gentleman seems to do, that the Hartford Convention assembled for any such purpose as breaking up the Union, because they thought unconstitutional laws had been passed, or to consult on that subject, or _to calculate the value of the Union_; supposing this to be their purpose, or any part of it, then I say the meeting itself was disloyal, and was obnoxious to censure, whether held in time of peace or time of war, or under whatever circumstances. The material question is the *object*. Is dissolution the _object_? If it be, external circumstances may make it a more or less aggravated case, but cannot affect the principle. I do not hold, therefore, Sir, that the Hartford Convention was pardonable, even to the extent of the gentleman's admission, if its objects were really such as have been imputed to it. Sir, there never was a time, under any degree of excitement, in which the Hartford Convention, or any other convention, could have maintained itself one moment in New England, if assembled for any such purpose as the gentleman says would have been an allowable purpose. To hold conventions to decide constitutional law! To try the binding validity of statutes by votes in a convention! Sir, the Hartford Convention, I presume, would not desire that the honorable gentleman should be their defender or advocate, if he puts their case upon such untenable and extravagant grounds.

Then, Sir, the gentleman has no fault to find with these recently promulgated South Carolina opinions. And certainly he need have none; for his own sentiments, as now advanced, and advanced on reflection, as far as I have been able to comprehend them, go the full length of all these opinions. I propose, Sir, to say something on these, and to consider how far they are just and constitutional. Before doing that, however, let me observe that the eulogium pronounced by the honorable gentleman on the character of the State of South Carolina, for her Revolutionary and other merits, meets my hearty concurrence. I shall not acknowledge that the honorable member goes before me in regard for whatever of distinguished talent, or distinguished character, South Carolina has produced. I claim part of the honor, I partake in the pride, of her great names. I claim them for countrymen, one and all, the Laurenses, the Rutledges, the Pinckneys, the Sumpters, the Marions, Americans all, whose fame is no more to be hemmed in by State lines, than their talents and patriotism were capable of being circumscribed within the same narrow limits. In their day and generation, they served and honored the country, and the whole country; and their renown is of the treasures of the whole country. Him whose honored name the gentleman himself bears,--does he esteem me less capable of gratitude for his patriotism, or sympathy for his sufferings, than if his eyes had first opened upon the light of Massachusetts, instead of South Carolina? Sir, does he suppose it in his power to exhibit a Carolina name so bright as to produce envy in my bosom? No, Sir, increased gratification and delight, rather. I thank God, that, if I am gifted with little of the spirit which is able to raise mortals to the skies, I have yet none, as I trust, of that other spirit, which would drag angels down. When I shall be found, Sir, in my place here in the Senate, or elsewhere, to sneer at public merit, because it happens to spring up beyond the little limits of my own State or neighborhood; when I refuse, for any such cause or for any cause, the homage due to American talent, to elevated patriotism, to sincere devotion to liberty and the country; or, if I see an uncommon endowment of Heaven, if I see extraordinary capacity and virtue, in any son of the South, and if, moved by local prejudice or gangrened by State jealousy, I get up here to abate the tithe of a hair from his just character and just fame, may my tongue cleave to the roof of my mouth!

Sir, let me recur to pleasing recollections; let me indulge in refreshing remembrance of the past; let me remind you that, in early times, no States cherished greater harmony, both of principle and feeling, than Massachusetts and South Carolina. Would to God that harmony might again return. Shoulder to shoulder they went through the Revolution, hand in hand they stood round the administration of Washington, and felt his own great arm lean on them for support. Unkind feeling, if it exist, alienation, and distrust are the growth, unnatural to such soils, of false principles since sown. They are weeds, the seeds of which that same great arm never scattered.

Mr. President, I shall enter on no encomium upon Massachusetts; she needs none. There she is. Behold her, and judge for yourselves. There is her history; the world knows it by heart. The past, at least, is secure. There is Boston, and Concord, and Lexington, and Bunker Hill; and there they will remain for ever. The bones of her sons, falling in the great struggle for Independence, now lie mingled with the soil of every State from New England to Georgia; and there they will lie for ever. And, Sir, where American Liberty raised its first voice, and where its youth was nurtured and sustained, there it still lives, in the strength of its manhood and full of its original spirit. If discord and disunion shall wound it, if party strife and blind ambition shall hawk at and tear it, if folly and madness, if uneasiness under salutary and necessary restraint, shall succeed in separating it from that Union, by which alone its existence is made sure, it will stand, in the end, by the side of that cradle in which its infancy was rocked; it will stretch forth its arm with whatever of vigor it may still retain over the friends who gather round it; and it will fall at last, if fall it must, amidst the proudest monuments of its own glory, and on the very spot of its origin.

There yet remains to be performed, Mr. President, by far the most grave and important duty, which I feel to be devolved on me by this occasion. It is to state, and to defend, what I conceive to be the true principles of the Constitution under which we are here assembled. I might well have desired that so weighty a task should have fallen into other and abler hands. I could have wished that it should have been executed by those whose character and experience give weight and influence to their opinions, such as cannot possibly belong to mine. But, Sir, I have met the occasion, not sought it; and I shall proceed to state my own sentiments, without challenging for them any particular regard, with studied plainness, and as much precision as possible.

I understand the honorable gentleman from South Carolina to maintain, that it is a right of the State legislatures to interfere, whenever, in their judgment, this government transcends its constitutional limits, and to arrest the operation of its laws.

I understand him to maintain this right, as a right existing *under* the Constitution, not as a right to overthrow it on the ground of extreme necessity, such as would justify violent revolution.

I understand him to maintain an authority, on the part of the States, thus to interfere, for the purpose of correcting the exercise of power by the general government, of checking it, and of compelling it to conform to their opinion of the extent of its powers.

I understand him to maintain, that the ultimate power of judging of the constitutional extent of its own authority is not lodged exclusively in the general government, or any branch of it; but that, on the contrary, the States may lawfully decide for themselves, and each State for itself, whether, in a given case, the act of the general government transcends its power.

I understand him to insist, that, if the exigency of the case, in the opinion of any State government, require it, such State government may, by its own sovereign authority, annul an act of the general government which it deems plainly and palpably unconstitutional.

This is the sum of what I understand from him to be the South Carolina doctrine, and the doctrine which he maintains. I propose to consider it, and compare it with the Constitution. Allow me to say, as a preliminary remark, that I call this the South Carolina doctrine only because the gentleman himself has so denominated it. I do not feel at liberty to say that South Carolina, as a State, has ever advanced these sentiments. I hope she has not, and never may. That a great majority of her people are opposed to the tariff laws, is doubtless true. That a majority, somewhat less than that just mentioned, conscientiously believe these laws unconstitutional, may probably also be true. But that any majority holds to the right of direct State interference at State discretion, the right of nullifying acts of Congress by acts of State legislation, is more than I know, and what I shall be slow to believe.

That there are individuals besides the honorable gentleman who do maintain these opinions, is quite certain. I recollect the recent expression of a sentiment, which circumstances attending its utterance and publication justify us in supposing was not unpremeditated. "The sovereignty of the State,--never to be controlled, construed, or decided on, but by her own feelings of honorable justice."

Mr. Hayne here rose and said, that, for the purpose of being clearly understood he would state that his proposition was in the words of the Virginia resolution, as follows:--

"That this assembly doth explicitly and peremptorily declare, that it views the powers of the federal government as resulting from the compact to which the States are parties, as limited by the plain sense and intention of the instrument constituting that compact, as no farther valid than they are authorized by the grants enumerated in that compact; and that, in case of a deliberate, palpable, and dangerous exercise of other powers not granted by the said compact, the States who are parties thereto have the right, and are in duty bound, to interpose, for arresting the progress of the evil, and for maintaining within their respective limits the authorities, rights, and liberties appertaining to them."

Mr. Webster resumed:--#/

I am quite aware, Mr. President, of the existence of the resolution which the gentleman read, and has now repeated, and that he relies on it as his authority. I know the source, too, from which it is understood to have proceeded. I need not say that I have much respect for the constitutional opinions of Mr. Madison; they would weigh greatly with me always. But before the authority of his opinion be vouched for the gentleman's proposition, it will be proper to consider what is the fair interpretation of that resolution, to which Mr. Madison is understood to have given his sanction. As the gentleman construes it, it is an authority for him. Possibly he may not have adopted the right construction. That resolution declares, that, _in the case of the dangerous exercise of powers not granted by the general government, the States may interpose to arrest the progress of the evil_. But how interpose, and what does this declaration purport? Does it mean no more than that there may be extreme cases, in which the people, in any mode of assembling, may resist usurpation, and relieve themselves from a tyrannical government? No one will deny this. Such resistance is not only acknowledged to be just in America, but in England also Blackstone admits as much, in the theory, and practice, too, of the English constitution. We, Sir, who oppose the Carolina doctrine, do not deny that the people may, if they choose, throw off any government when it becomes oppressive and intolerable, and erect a better in its stead. We all know that civil institutions are established for the public benefit, and that when they cease to answer the ends of their existence they may be changed. But I do not understand the doctrine now contended for to be that, which, for the sake of distinction, we may call the right of revolution. I understand the gentleman to maintain, that, without revolution, without civil commotion, without rebellion, a remedy for supposed abuse and transgression of the powers of the general government lies in a direct appeal to the interference of the State governments.

Mr. Hayne here rose and said: He did not contend for the mere right of revolution, but for the right of constitutional resistance. What he maintained was, that in case of a plain, palpable violation of the Constitution by the general government, a State may interpose; and that this interposition is constitutional.

Mr. Webster resumed:--#/

So, Sir, I understood the gentleman, and am happy to find that I did not misunderstand him. What he contends for is, that it is constitutional to interrupt the administration of the Constitution itself, in the hands of those who are chosen and sworn to administer it, by the direct interference, in form of law, of the States, in virtue of their sovereign capacity. The inherent right in the people to reform their government I do not deny; and they have another right, and that is, to resist unconstitutional laws, without overturning the government. It is no doctrine of mine that unconstitutional laws bind the people. The great question is, Whose prerogative is it to decide on the constitutionality or unconstitutionality of the laws? On that, the main debate hinges. The proposition, that, in case of a supposed violation of the Constitution by Congress, the States have a constitutional right to interfere and annul the law of Congress, is the proposition of the gentleman. I do not admit it. If the gentleman had intended no more than to assert the right of revolution for justifiable cause, he would have said only what all agree to. But I cannot conceive that there can be a middle course, between submission to the laws, when regularly pronounced constitutional, on the one hand, and open resistance, which is revolution or rebellion, on the other. I say, the right of a State to annul a law of Congress cannot be maintained, but on the ground of the inalienable right of man to resist oppression; that is to say, upon the ground of revolution. I admit that there is an ultimate violent remedy, above the Constitution and in defiance of the Constitution, which may be resorted to when a revolution is to be justified. But I do not admit, that, under the Constitution and in conformity with it, there is any mode in which a State government, as a member of the Union, can interfere and stop the progress of the general government, by force of her own laws, under any circumstances whatever.

This leads us to inquire into the origin of this government and the source of its power. Whose agent is it? Is it the creature of the State legislatures, or the creature of the people? If the government of the United States be the agent of the State governments, then they may control it, provided they can agree in the manner of controlling it; if it be the agent of the people, then the people alone can control it, restrain it, modify, or reform it. It is observable enough, that the doctrine for which the honorable gentleman contends leads him to the necessity of maintaining, not only that this general government is the creature of the States, but that it is the creature of each of the States severally, so that each may assert the power for itself of determining whether it acts within the limits of its authority. It is the servant of four-and-twenty masters, of different wills and different purposes, and yet bound to obey all. This absurdity (for it seems no less) arises from a misconception as to the origin of this government and its true character. It is, Sir, the people's Constitution, the people's government, made for the people, made by the people, and answerable to the people. The people of the United States have declared that this Constitution shall be the supreme law. We must either admit the proposition, or dispute their authority. The States are, unquestionably, sovereign, so far as their sovereignty is not affected by this supreme law. But the State legislatures, as political bodies, however sovereign, are yet not sovereign over the people. So far as the people have given power to the general government, so far the grant is unquestionably good, and the government holds of the people, and not of the State governments. We are all agents of the same supreme power, the people. The general government and the State governments derive their authority from the same source. Neither can, in relation to the other, be called primary, though one is definite and restricted, and the other general and residuary. The national government possesses those powers which it can be shown the people have conferred on it, and no more. All the rest belongs to the State governments, or to the people themselves. So far as the people have restrained State sovereignty, by the expression of their will, in the Constitution of the United States, so far, it must be admitted, State sovereignty is effectually controlled. I do not contend that it is, or ought to be, controlled farther. The sentiment to which I have referred propounds that State sovereignty is only to be controlled by its own "feeling of justice"; that is to say, it is not to be controlled at all, for one who is to follow his own feelings is under no legal control. Now, however men may think this ought to be, the fact is, that the people of the United States have chosen to impose control on State sovereignties. There are those, doubtless, who wish they had been left without restraint; but the Constitution has ordered the matter differently. To make war, for instance, is an exercise of sovereignty; but the Constitution declares that no State shall make war. To coin money is another exercise of sovereign power; but no State is at liberty to coin money. Again, the Constitution says that no sovereign State shall be so sovereign as to make a treaty. These prohibitions, it must be confessed, are a control on the State sovereignty of South Carolina, as well as of the other States, which does not arise "from her own feelings of honorable justice." The opinion referred to, therefore, is in defiance of the plainest provisions of the Constitution.

There are other proceedings of public bodies which have already been alluded to, and to which I refer again for the purpose of ascertaining more fully what is the length and breadth of that doctrine, denominated the Carolina doctrine, which the honorable member has now stood up on this floor to maintain. In one of them I find it resolved, that "the tariff of 1828, and every other tariff designed to promote one branch of industry at the expense of others, is contrary to the meaning and intention of the federal compact; and such a dangerous, palpable, and deliberate usurpation of power, by a determined majority, wielding the general government beyond the limits of its delegated powers, as calls upon the States which compose the suffering minority, in their sovereign capacity, to exercise the powers which, as sovereigns, necessarily devolve upon them, when their compact is violated."

Observe, Sir, that this resolution holds the tariff of 1828, and every other tariff designed to promote one branch of industry at the expense of another, to be such a dangerous, palpable, and deliberate usurpation of power, as calls upon the States, in their sovereign capacity, to interfere by their own authority. This denunciation, Mr. President, you will please to observe, includes our old tariff of 1816, as well as all others; because that was established to promote the interest of the manufacturers of cotton, to the manifest and admitted injury of the Calcutta cotton trade. Observe, again, that all the qualifications are here rehearsed and charged upon the tariff, which are necessary to bring the case within the gentleman's proposition. The tariff is a usurpation; it is a dangerous usurpation; it is a palpable usurpation; it is a deliberate usurpation. It is such a usurpation, therefore, as calls upon the States to exercise their right of interference. Here is a case, then, within the gentleman's principles, and all his qualifications of his principles. It is a case for action. The Constitution is plainly, dangerously, palpably, and deliberately violated; and the States must interpose their own authority to arrest the law. Let us suppose the State of South Carolina to express this same opinion, by the voice of her legislature. That would be very imposing; but what then? Is the voice of one State conclusive? It so happens that, at the very moment when South Carolina resolves that the tariff laws are unconstitutional, Pennsylvania and Kentucky resolve exactly the reverse. *They* hold those laws to be both highly proper and strictly constitutional. And now, Sir, how does the honorable member propose to deal with this case? How does he relieve us from this difficulty, upon any principle of his? His construction gets us into it; how does he propose to get us out?

In Carolina, the tariff is a palpable, deliberate usurpation; Carolina, therefore, may nullify it, and refuse to pay the duties. In Pennsylvania, it is both clearly constitutional and highly expedient; and there the duties are to be paid. And yet we live under a government of uniform laws, and under a Constitution too, which contains an express provision, as it happens, that all duties shall be equal in all the States. Does not this approach absurdity?

If there be no power to settle such questions, independent of either of the States, is not the whole Union a rope of sand? Are we not thrown back again, precisely, upon the old Confederation?

It is too plain to be argued. Four-and-twenty interpreters of constitutional law, each with a power to decide for itself, and none with authority to bind anybody else, and this constitutional law the only bond of their union! What is such a state of things but a mere connection during pleasure, or, to use the phraseology of the times, _during feeling_? And that feeling, too, not the feeling of the people, who established the Constitution, but the feeling of the State governments.

In another of the South Carolina addresses, having premised that the crisis requires "all the concentrated energy of passion," an attitude of open resistance to the laws of the Union is advised. Open resistance to the laws, then, is the constitutional remedy, the conservative power of the State, which the South Carolina doctrines teach for the redress of political evils, real or imaginary. And its authors further say, that, appealing with confidence to the Constitution itself, to justify their opinions, they cannot consent to try their accuracy by the courts of justice. In one sense, indeed, Sir, this is assuming an attitude of open resistance in favor of liberty. But what sort of liberty? The liberty of establishing their own opinions, in defiance of the opinions of all others; the liberty of judging and of deciding exclusively themselves, in a matter in which others have as much right to judge and decide as they; the liberty of placing their own opinions above the judgment of all others, above the laws, and above the Constitution. This is their liberty, and this is the fair result of the proposition contended for by the honorable gentleman. Or, it may be more properly said, it is identical with it, rather than a result from it.

In the same publication we find the following: "Previously to our Revolution, when the arm of oppression was stretched over New England, where did our Northern brethren meet with a braver sympathy than that which sprung from the bosoms of Carolinians? We had no extortion, no oppression, no collision with the king's ministers, no navigation interests springing up, in envious rivalry of England."

This seems extraordinary language. South Carolina no collision with the king's ministers in 1775! No extortion! No oppression! But, Sir, it is also most significant language. Does any man doubt the purpose for which it was penned? Can anyone fail to see that it was designed to raise in the reader's mind the question, whether, _at this time_,--that is to say, in 1828,--South Carolina has any collision with the king's ministers, any oppression, or extortion, to fear from England? whether, in short, England is not as naturally the friend of South Carolina as New England, with her navigation interests springing up in envious rivalry of England?

Is it not strange, Sir, that an intelligent man in South Carolina, in 1828, should thus labor to prove that, in 1775, there was no hostility, no cause of war, between South Carolina and England? That she had no occasion, in reference to her own interest, or from a regard to her own welfare, to take up arms in the Revolutionary contest? Can any one account for the expression of such strange sentiments, and their circulation through the State, otherwise than by supposing the object to be what I have already intimated, to raise the question, if they had no "_collision_" (mark the expression) with the ministers of King George the Third, in 1775, what *collision* have they, in 1828, with the ministers of King George the Fourth? What is there now, in the existing state of things, to separate Carolina from _Old_, more, or rather, than from *New* England?

Resolutions, Sir, have been recently passed by the legislature of South Carolina. I need not refer to them; they go no farther than the honorable gentleman himself has gone, and I hope not so far. I content myself, therefore, with debating the matter with him.

And now, Sir, what I have first to say on this subject is, that at no time, and under no circumstances, has New England, or any State in New England, or any respectable body of persons in New England, or any public man of standing in New England, put forth such a doctrine as this Carolina doctrine.

The gentleman has found no case, he can find none, to support his own opinions by New England authority. New England has studied the Constitution in other schools, and under other teachers. She looks upon it with other regards, and deems more highly and reverently both of its just authority and its utility and excellence. The history of her legislative proceedings may be traced. The ephemeral effusions of temporary bodies, called together by the excitement of the occasion, may be hunted up; they have been hunted up. The opinions and votes of her public men, in and out of Congress, may be explored. It will all be in vain. The Carolina doctrine can derive from her neither countenance nor support. She rejects it now; she always did reject it; and till she loses her senses, she always will reject it. The honorable member has referred to expressions on the subject of the embargo law, made in this place, by an honorable and venerable gentleman,[6] now favoring us with his presence. He quotes that distinguished Senator as saying, that, in his judgment, the embargo law was unconstitutional, and that therefore, in his opinion, the people were not bound to obey it. That, Sir, is perfectly constitutional language. An unconstitutional law is not binding; *but then it does not rest with a resolution or a law of a State legislature to decide whether an act of Congress be or be not constitutional.* An unconstitutional act of Congress would not bind the people of this District, although they have no legislature to interfere in their behalf; and, on the other hand, a constitutional law of Congress does bind the citizens of every State, although all their legislatures should undertake to annul it by act or resolution. The venerable Connecticut Senator is a constitutional lawyer, of sound principles and enlarged knowledge; a statesman practised and experienced, bred in the company of Washington, and holding just views upon the nature of our governments. He believed the embargo unconstitutional, and so did others; but what then? Who did he suppose was to decide that question? The State legislatures? Certainly not. No such sentiment ever escaped his lips.

Let us follow up, Sir, this New England opposition to the embargo laws; let us trace it, till we discern the principle which controlled and governed New England throughout the whole course of that opposition. We shall then see what similarity there is between the New England school of constitutional opinions, and this modern Carolina school. The gentleman, I think, read a petition from some single individual addressed to the legislature of Massachusetts, asserting the Carolina doctrine; that is, the right of State interference to arrest the laws of the Union. The fate of that petition shows the sentiment of the legislature. It met no favor. The opinions of Massachusetts were very different. They had been expressed in 1798, in answer to the resolutions of Virginia, and she did not depart from them, nor bend them to the times. Misgoverned, wronged, oppressed, as she felt herself to be, she still held fast her integrity to the Union. The gentleman may find in her proceedings much evidence of dissatisfaction with the measures of government, and great and deep dislike to the embargo; all this makes the case so much the stronger for her; for, notwithstanding all this dissatisfaction and dislike, she still claimed no right to sever the bonds of the Union. There was heat, and there was anger in her political feeling. Be it so; but neither her heat nor her anger betrayed her into infidelity to the government. The gentleman labors to prove that she disliked the embargo as much as South Carolina dislikes the tariff, and expressed her dislike as strongly. Be it so; but did she propose the Carolina remedy? did she threaten to interfere, by State authority, to annul the laws of the Union? That is the question for the gentleman's consideration.

No doubt, Sir, a great majority of the people of New England conscientiously believed the embargo law of 1807 unconstitutional; as conscientiously, certainly, as the people of South Carolina hold that opinion of the tariff. They reasoned thus: Congress has power to regulate commerce; but here is a law, they said, stopping all commerce, and stopping it indefinitely. The law is perpetual; that is, it is not limited in point of time, and must of course continue until it shall be repealed by some other law. It is as perpetual, therefore, as the law against treason or murder. Now, is this regulating commerce, or destroying it? Is it guiding, controlling, giving the rule to commerce, as a subsisting thing or is it putting an end to it altogether? Nothing is more certain, than that a majority in New England deemed this law a violation of the Constitution. The very case required by the gentleman to justify State interference had then arisen. Massachusetts believed this law to be "a deliberate, palpable, and dangerous exercise of a power not granted by the Constitution." Deliberate it was, for it was long continued; palpable she thought it, as no words in the Constitution gave the power, and only a construction, in her opinion most violent, raised it; dangerous it was, since it threatened utter ruin to her most important interests. Here, then, was a Carolina case. How did Massachusetts deal with it? It was, as she thought, a plain, manifest, palpable violation of the Constitution, and it brought ruin to her doors. Thousands of families, and hundreds of thousands of individuals, were beggared by it. While she saw and felt all this, she saw and felt also, that, as a measure of national policy, it was perfectly futile; that the country was no way benefited by that which caused so much individual distress; that it was efficient only for the production of evil, and all that evil inflicted on ourselves. In such a case, under such circumstances, how did Massachusetts demean herself? Sir, she remonstrated, she memorialized, she addressed herself to the general government, not exactly "with the concentrated energy of passion," but with her own strong sense, and the energy of sober conviction. But she did not interpose the arm of her own power to arrest the law, and break the embargo. Far from it. Her principles bound her to two things; and she followed her principles, lead where they might. First, to submit to every constitutional law of Congress, and secondly, if the constitutional validity of the law be doubted, to refer that question to the decision of the proper tribunals. The first principle is vain and ineffectual without the second. A majority of us in New England believed the embargo law unconstitutional; but the great question was, and always will be in such cases, Who is to decide this? Who is to judge between the people and the government? And, Sir, it is quite plain, that the Constitution of the United States confers on the government itself, to be exercised by its appropriate department, and under its own responsibility to the people, this power of deciding ultimately and conclusively upon the just extent of its own authority. If this had not been done, we should not have advanced a single step beyond the old Confederation.

Being fully of opinion that the embargo law was unconstitutional, the people of New England were yet equally clear in the opinion, (it was a matter they did doubt upon,) that the question, after all, must be decided by the judicial tribunals of the United States. Before those tribunals, therefore, they brought the question. Under the provisions of the law, they had given bonds to millions in amount, and which were alleged to be forfeited. They suffered the bonds to be sued, and thus raised the question. In the old-fashioned way of settling disputes, they went to law. The case came to hearing and solemn argument; and he who espoused their cause, and stood up for them against the validity of the embargo act, was none other than that great man, of whom the gentleman has made honorable mention, Samuel Dexter. He was then, Sir, in the fulness of his knowledge, and the maturity of his strength. He had retired from long and distinguished public service here, to the renewed pursuit of professional duties, carrying with him all that enlargement and expansion, all the new strength and force, which an acquaintance with the more general subjects discussed in the national councils is capable of adding to professional attainment, in a mind of true greatness and comprehension. He was a lawyer, and he was also a statesman. He had studied the Constitution, when he filled public station, that he might defend it; he had examined its principles that he might maintain them. More than all men, or at least as much as any man, he was attached to the general government and to the union of the States. His feelings and opinions all ran in that direction. A question of constitutional law, too, was, of all subjects, that one which was best suited to his talents and learning. Aloof from technicality, and unfettered by artificial rule, such a question gave opportunity for that deep and clear analysis, that mighty grasp of principle, which so much distinguished his higher efforts. His very statement was argument; his inference seemed demonstration. The earnestness of his own conviction wrought conviction in others. One was convinced, and believed, and assented, because it was gratifying, delightful, to think, and feel, and believe, in unison with an intellect of such evident superiority.

Mr. Dexter, Sir, such as I have described him, argued the New England cause. He put into his effort his whole heart, as well as all the powers of his understanding; for he had avowed, in the most public manner, his entire concurrence with his neighbors on the point in dispute. He argued the cause; it was lost, and New England submitted. The established tribunals pronounced the law constitutional, and New England acquiesced. Now, Sir, is not this the exact opposite of the doctrine of the gentleman from South Carolina? According to him, instead of referring to the judicial tribunals, we should have broken up the embargo by laws of our own; we should have repealed it, *quoad* New England; for we had a strong, palpable, and oppressive case. Sir, we believed the embargo unconstitutional; but still that was matter of opinion, and who was to decide it? We thought it a clear case; but, nevertheless, we did not take the law into our own hands, because we did not wish to bring about a revolution, nor to break up the Union; for I maintain, that between submission to the decision of the constituted tribunals, and revolution, or disunion, there is no middle ground; there is no ambiguous condition, half allegiance and half rebellion. And, Sir, how futile, how very futile it is, to admit the right of State interference, and then attempt to save it from the character of unlawful resistance, by adding terms of qualification to the causes and occasions, leaving all these qualifications, like the case itself, in the discretion of the State governments. It must be a clear case, it is said, a deliberate case, a palpable case, a dangerous case. But then the State is still left at liberty to decide for herself what is clear, what is deliberate, what is palpable, what is dangerous. Do adjectives and epithets avail any thing?

Sir, the human mind is so constituted, that the merits of both sides of a controversy appear very clear, and very palpable, to those who respectively espouse them; and both sides usually grow clearer as the controversy advances. South Carolina sees unconstitutionality in the tariff; she sees oppression there also, and she sees danger. Pennsylvania, with a vision not less sharp, looks at the same tariff, and sees no such thing in it; she sees it all constitutional, all useful, all safe. The faith of South Carolina is strengthened by opposition, and she now not only sees, but _resolves_, that the tariff is palpably unconstitutional, oppressive, and dangerous; but Pennsylvania, not to be behind her neighbors, and equally willing to strengthen her own faith by a confident asseveration, _resolves_ also, and gives to every warm affirmative of South Carolina, a plain, downright, Pennsylvania negative. South Carolina, to show the strength and unity of her opinion, brings her assembly to a unanimity, within seven voices; Pennsylvania, not to be outdone in this respect any more than in others, reduces her dissentient fraction to a single vote. Now, Sir, again, I ask the gentleman, What is to be done? Are these States both right? Is he bound to consider them both right? If not, which is in the wrong? or rather, which has the best right to decide? And if he, and if I, are not to know what the Constitution means, and what it is, till those two State legislatures, and the twenty-two others, shall agree in its construction, what have we sworn to, when we have sworn to maintain it? I was forcibly struck, Sir, with one reflection, as the gentleman went on in his speech. He quoted Mr. Madison's resolutions, to prove that a State may interfere, in a case of deliberate, palpable, and dangerous exercise of a power not granted. The honorable member supposes the tariff law to be such an exercise of power; and that consequently a case has arisen in which the State may, if it see fit, interfere by its own law. Now it so happens, nevertheless, that Mr. Madison deems this same tariff law quite constitutional. Instead of a clear and palpable violation, it is, in his judgment, no violation at all. So that, while they use his authority for a hypothetical case, they reject it in the very case before them. All this, Sir, shows the inherent futility, I had almost used a stronger word, of conceding this power of interference to the State, and then attempting to secure it from abuse by imposing qualifications of which the States themselves are to judge. One of two things is true; either the laws of the Union are beyond the discretion and beyond the control of the States; or else we have no constitution of general government, and are thrust back again to the days of the Confederation.

Let me here say, Sir, that if the gentleman's doctrine had been received and acted upon in New England, in the times of the embargo and non-intercourse, we should probably not now have been here. The government would very likely have gone to pieces, and crumbled into dust. No stronger case can ever arise than existed under those laws; no States can ever entertain a clearer conviction than the New England States then entertained; and if they had been under the influence of that heresy of opinion, as I must call it, which the honorable member espouses, this Union would, in all probability, have been scattered to the four winds. I ask the gentleman, therefore, to apply his principles to that case; I ask him to come forth and declare, whether, in his opinion, the New England States would have been justified in interfering to break up the embargo system under the conscientious opinions which they held upon it? Had they a right to annul that law? Does he admit or deny? If what is thought palpably unconstitutional in South Carolina justifies that State in arresting the progress of the law, tell me whether that which was thought palpably unconstitutional also in Massachusetts would have justified her in doing the same thing. Sir, I deny the whole doctrine. It has not a foot of ground in the Constitution to stand on. No public man of reputation ever advanced it in Massachusetts in the warmest times, or could maintain himself upon it there at any time.

I wish now, Sir, to make a remark upon the Virginia resolutions of 1798. I cannot undertake to say how these resolutions were understood by those who passed them. Their language is not a little indefinite. In the case of the exercise by Congress of a dangerous power not granted to them, the resolutions assert the right, on the part of the State, to interfere and arrest the progress of the evil. This is susceptible of more than one interpretation. It may mean no more than that the States may interfere by complaint and remonstrance, or by proposing to the people an alteration of the Federal Constitution. This would all be quite unobjectionable. Or it may be that no more is meant than to assert the general right of revolution, as against all governments, in cases of intolerable oppression. This no one doubts, and this, in my opinion, is all that he who framed the resolutions could have meant by it; for I shall not readily believe that he was ever of opinion that a State, under the Constitution and in conformity with it, could, upon the ground of her own opinion of its unconstitutionality, however clear and palpable she might think the case, annul a law of Congress, so far as it should operate on herself by her own legislative power.

I must now beg to ask, Sir, Whence is this supposed right of the States derived? Where do they find the power to interfere with the laws of the Union? Sir, the opinion which the honorable gentleman maintains is a notion founded in a total misapprehension, in my judgment, of the origin of this government, and of the foundation on which it stands. I hold it to be a popular government, erected by the people; those who administer it, responsible to the people; and itself capable of being amended and modified, just as the people may choose it should be. It is as popular, just as truly emanating from the people, as the State governments. It is created for one purpose; the State governments for another. It has its own powers; they have theirs. There is no more authority with them to arrest the operation of a law of Congress, than with Congress to arrest the operation of their laws. We are here to administer a Constitution emanating immediately from the people, and trusted by them to our administration. It is not the creature of the State governments. It is of no moment to the argument, that certain acts of the State legislatures are necessary to fill our seats in this body. That is not one of their original State powers, a part of the sovereignty of the State. It is a duty which the people, by the Constitution itself, have imposed on the State legislatures; and which they might have left to be performed elsewhere, if they had seen fit. So they have left the choice of President with electors; but all this does not affect the proposition that this whole government, President, Senate, and House of Representatives, is a popular government. It leaves it still all its popular character. The governor of a State (in some of the States) is chosen, not directly by the people, but by those who are chosen by the people, for the purpose of performing, among other duties, that of electing a governor. Is the government of the State, on that account, not a popular government? This government, Sir, is the independent offspring of the popular will. It is not the creature of State legislatures; nay, more, if the whole truth must be told, the people brought it into existence, established it, and have hitherto supported it, for the very purpose, amongst others, of imposing certain salutary restraints on State sovereignties. The States cannot now make war; they cannot contract alliances; they cannot make, each for itself, separate regulations of commerce; they cannot lay imposts; they cannot coin money. If this Constitution, Sir, be the creature of State legislatures, it must be admitted that it has obtained a strange control over the volitions of its creators.

The people, then, Sir, erected this government. They gave it a Constitution, and in that Constitution they have enumerated the powers which they bestow on it. They have made it a limited government. They have defined its authority. They have restrained it to the exercise of such powers as are granted; and all others, they declare, are reserved to the States or the people. But, Sir, they have not stopped here. If they had, they would have accomplished but half their work. No definition can be so clear, as to avoid possibility of doubt; no limitation so precise as to exclude all uncertainty. Who, then, shall construe this grant of the people? Who shall interpret their will, where it may be supposed they have left it doubtful? With whom do they repose this ultimate right of deciding on the powers of the government? Sir, they have settled all this in the fullest manner. They have left it with the government itself, in its appropriate branches. Sir, the very chief end, the main design, for which the whole Constitution was framed and adopted, was to establish a government that should not be obliged to act through State agency, or depend on State opinion and State discretion. The people had had quite enough of that kind of government under the Confederation. Under that system, the legal action, the application of law to individuals, belonged exclusively to the States. Congress could only recommend; their acts were not of binding force, till the States had adopted and sanctioned them. Are we in that condition still? Are we yet at the mercy of State discretion and State construction? Sir, if we are, then vain will be our attempt to maintain the Constitution under which we sit. But, Sir, the people have wisely provided, in the Constitution itself, a proper, suitable mode and tribunal for settling questions of constitutional law. There are in the Constitution grants of powers to Congress, and restrictions on these powers. There are, also, prohibitions on the States. Some authority must, therefore, necessarily exist, having the ultimate jurisdiction to fix and ascertain the interpretation of these grants, restrictions, and prohibitions. The Constitution has itself pointed out, ordained, and established that authority. How has it accomplished this great and essential end? By declaring, Sir, that "_the Constitution, and the laws of the United States made in pursuance thereof, shall be the supreme law of the land, any thing in the constitution or laws of any State to the contrary notwithstanding_."

This, Sir, was the first great step. By this the supremacy of the Constitution and laws of the United States is declared. The people so will it. No State law is to be valid which comes in conflict with the Constitution, or any law of the United States passed in pursuance of it. But who shall decide this question of interference? To whom lies the last appeal? This, Sir, the Constitution itself decides also, by declaring, "*that the judicial power shall extend to all cases arising under the Constitution and laws of the United States.*" These two provisions cover the whole ground. They are, in truth, the keystone of the arch! With these it is a government; without them it is a confederation. In pursuance of these clear and express provisions, Congress established, at its very first session, in the judicial act, a mode for carrying them into full effect, and for bringing all questions of constitutional power to the final decision of the Supreme Court. It then, Sir, became a government. It then had the means of self-protection; and but for this, it would, in all probability, have been now among things which are past. Having constituted the government, and declared its powers, the people have further said, that, since somebody must decide on the extent of these powers, the government shall itself decide; subject, always, like other popular governments, to its responsibility to the people. And now, Sir, I repeat, how is it that a State legislature acquires any power to interfere? Who, or what, gives them the right to say to the people, "We, who are your agents and servants for one purpose, will undertake to decide, that your other agents and servants, appointed by you for another purpose, have transcended the authority you gave them!" The reply would be, I think, not impertinent, "Who made you a judge over another's servants? To their own masters they stand or fall."

Sir, I deny this power of State legislatures altogether. It cannot stand the test of examination. Gentlemen may say, that, in an extreme case, a State government might protect the people from intolerable oppression. Sir, in such a case, the people might protect themselves, without the aid of the State governments. Such a case warrants revolution. It must make, when it comes, a law for itself. A nullifying act of a State legislature cannot alter the case, nor make resistance any more lawful. In maintaining these sentiments, Sir, I am but asserting the rights of the people. I state what they have declared, and insist on their right to declare it. They have chosen to repose this power in the general government, and I think it my duty to support it, like other constitutional powers.

For myself, Sir, I do not admit the competency of South Carolina, or any other State, to prescribe my constitutional duty; or to settle, between me and the people, the validity of laws of Congress for which I have voted. I decline her umpirage. I have not sworn to support the Constitution according to her construction of its clauses. I have not stipulated, by my oath of office or otherwise, to come under any responsibility, except to the people, and those whom they have appointed to pass upon the question, whether laws, supported by my votes, conform to the Constitution of the country. And, Sir, if we look to the general nature of the case, could any thing have been more preposterous, than to make a government for the whole Union, and yet leave its powers subject, not to one interpretation, but to thirteen or twenty-four interpretations? Instead of one tribunal, established by all, responsible to all, with power to decide for all, shall constitutional questions be left to four-and-twenty popular bodies, each at liberty to decide for itself, and none bound to respect the decisions of others,--and each at liberty, too, to give a new construction on every new election of its own members? Would any thing, with such a principle in it, or rather with such a destitution of all principle, be fit to be called a government? No, Sir. It should not be denominated a Constitution. It should be called, rather, a collection of topics for everlasting controversy; heads of debate for a disputatious people. It would not be a government. It would not be adequate to any practical good, or fit for any country to live under.

To avoid all possibility of being misunderstood, allow me to repeat again, in the fullest manner, that I claim no powers for the government by forced or unfair construction. I admit that it is a government of strictly limited powers; of enumerated, specified, and particularized powers; and that whatsoever is not granted, is withheld. But notwithstanding all this, and however the grant of powers may be expressed, its limit and extent may yet, in some cases, admit of doubt; and the general government would be good for nothing, it would be incapable of long existing, if some mode had not been provided in which those doubts, as they should arise, might be peaceably, but authoritatively, solved.

And now, Mr. President, let me run the honorable gentleman's doctrine a little into its practical application. Let us look at his probable *modus operandi*. If a thing can be done, an ingenious man can tell *how* it is to be done, and I wish to be informed *how* this State interference is to be put in practice, without violence, bloodshed, and rebellion. We will take the existing case of the tariff law. South Carolina is said to have made up her opinion upon it. If we do not repeal it, (as we probably shall not,) she will then apply to the case the remedy of her doctrine. She will, we must suppose, pass a law of her legislature, declaring the several acts of Congress usually called the tariff laws null and void, so far as they respect South Carolina, or the citizens thereof. So far, all is a paper transaction, and easy enough. But the collector at Charleston is collecting the duties imposed by these tariff laws. He, therefore, must be stopped. The collector will seize the goods if the tariff duties are not paid. The State authorities will undertake their rescue, the marshal, with his posse, will come to the collector's aid, and here the contest begins. The militia of the State will be called out to sustain the nullifying act. They will march, Sir, under a very gallant leader; for I believe the honorable member himself commands the militia of that part of the State. He will raise the NULLIFYING ACT on his standard, and spread it out as his banner! It will have a preamble, setting forth that the tariff laws are palpable, deliberate, and dangerous violations of the Constitution! He will proceed, with this banner flying, to the custom-house in Charleston,

"All the while Sonorous metal blowing martial sounds."

Arrived at the custom-house, he will tell the collector that he must collect no more duties under any of the tariff laws. This he will be somewhat puzzled to say, by the way, with a grave countenance, considering what hand South Carolina herself had in that of 1816. But, Sir, the collector would not, probably, desist, at his bidding. He would show him the law of Congress, the treasury instruction, and his own oath of office. He would say, he should perform his duty, come what come might.

Here would ensue a pause; for they say that a certain stillness precedes the tempest. The trumpeter would hold his breath awhile, and before all this military array should fall on the custom-house, collector, clerks, and all, it is very probable some of those composing it would request of their gallant commander-in-chief to be informed a little upon the point of law; for they have, doubtless, a just respect for his opinions as a lawyer, as well as for his bravery as a soldier. They know he has read Blackstone and the Constitution, as well as Turenne and Vauban. They would ask him, therefore, something concerning their rights in this matter. They would inquire, whether it was not somewhat dangerous to resist a law of the United States. What would be the nature of their offence, they would wish to learn, if they, by military force and array, resisted the execution in Carolina of a law of the United States, and it should turn out, after all, that the law _was constitutional_? He would answer, of course, Treason. No lawyer could give any other answer. John Fries, he would tell them, had learned that, some years ago. How, then, they would ask, do you propose to defend us? We are not afraid of bullets, but treason has a way of taking people off that we do not much relish. How do you propose to defend us? "Look at my floating banner," he would reply; "see there the _nullifying law_!" Is it your opinion, gallant commander, they would then say, that, if we should be indicted for treason, that same floating banner of yours would make a good plea in bar? "South Carolina is a sovereign State," he would reply. That is true; but would the judge admit our plea? "These tariff laws," he would repeat, "are unconstitutional, palpably, deliberately, dangerously." That may all be so; but if the tribunal should not happen to be of that opinion, shall we swing for it? We are ready to die for our country, but it is rather an awkward business, this dying without touching the ground! After all, that is a sort of hemp tax worse than any part of the tariff.

Mr. President, the honorable gentleman would be in a dilemma, like that of another great general. He would have a knot before him which he could not untie. He must cut it with his sword. He must say to his followers, "Defend yourselves with your bayonets"; and this is war,--civil war.

Direct collision, therefore, between force and force, is the unavoidable result of that remedy for the revision of unconstitutional laws which the gentleman contends for. It must happen in the very first case to which it is applied. Is not this the plain result? To resist by force the execution of a law, generally, is treason. Can the courts of the United States take notice of the indulgence of a State to commit treason? The common saying, that a State cannot commit treason herself, is nothing to the purpose. Can she authorize others to do it? If John Fries had produced an act of Pennsylvania, annulling the law of Congress, would it have helped his case? Talk about it as we will, these doctrines go the length of revolution. They are incompatible with any peaceable administration of the government. They lead directly to disunion and civil commotion; and therefore it is, that at their commencement, when they are first found to be maintained by respectable men, and in a tangible form, I enter my public protest against them all.

The honorable gentleman argues, that, if this government be the sole judge of the extent of its own powers, whether that right of judging be in Congress or the Supreme Court, it equally subverts State sovereignty. This the gentleman sees, or thinks he sees, although he cannot perceive how the right of judging, in this matter, if left to the exercise of State legislatures, has any tendency to subvert the government of the Union. The gentleman's opinion may be, that the right *ought not* to have been lodged with the general government; he may like better such a constitution as we should have under the right of State interference; but I ask him to meet me on the plain matter of fact. I ask him to meet me on the Constitution itself. I ask him if the power is not found there, clearly and visibly found there?

But, Sir, what is this danger, and what are the grounds of it? Let it be remembered, that the Constitution of the United States is not unalterable. It is to continue in its present form no longer than the people who established it shall choose to continue it. If they shall become convinced that they have made an injudicious or inexpedient partition and distribution of power between the State governments and the general government, they can alter that distribution at will.

If any thing be found in the national Constitution, either by original provision or subsequent interpretation, which ought not to be in it, the people know how to get rid of it. If any construction, unacceptable to them, be established, so as to become practically a part of the Constitution, they will amend it, at their own sovereign pleasure. But while the people choose to maintain it as it is, while they are satisfied with it, and refuse to change it, who has given, or who can give, to the State legislatures a right to alter it, either by interference, construction, or otherwise? Gentlemen do not seem to recollect that the people have any power to do any thing for themselves. They imagine there is no safety for them, any longer than they are under the close guardianship of the State legislatures. Sir, the people have not trusted their safety, in regard to the general Constitution, to these hands. They have required other security, and taken other bonds. They have chosen to trust themselves, first, to the plain words of the instrument, and to such construction as the government themselves, in doubtful cases, should put on their own powers, under their oaths of office, and subject to their responsibility to them; just as the people of a State trust their own State governments with a similar power. Secondly, they have reposed their trust in the efficacy of frequent elections, and in their own power to remove their own servants and agents whenever they see cause. Thirdly, they have reposed trust in the judicial power, which, in order that it might be trustworthy, they have made as respectable, as disinterested, and as independent as was practicable. Fourthly, they have seen fit to rely, in case of necessity, or high expediency, on their known and admitted power to alter or amend the Constitution, peaceably and quietly, whenever experience shall point out defects or imperfections. And, finally, the people of the United States have at no time, in no way, directly or indirectly, authorized any State legislature to construe or interpret *their* high instrument of government; much less, to interfere, by their own power, to arrest its course and operation.

If, Sir, the people in these respects had done otherwise than they have done, their Constitution could neither have been preserved, nor would it have been worth preserving. And if its plain provisions shall now be disregarded, and these new doctrines interpolated in it, it will become as feeble and helpless a being as its enemies, whether early or more recent, could possibly desire. It will exist in every State but as a poor dependent on State permission. It must borrow leave to be; and will be, no longer than State pleasure, or State discretion, sees fit to grant the indulgence, and to prolong its poor existence.

But, Sir, although there are fears, there are hopes also. The people have preserved this, their own chosen Constitution, for forty years, and have seen their happiness, prosperity, and renown grow with its growth, and strengthen with its strength. They are now, generally, strongly attached to it. Overthrown by direct assault, it cannot be; evaded, undermined, NULLIFIED, it will not be, if we and those who shall succeed us here, as agents and representatives of the people, shall conscientiously and vigilantly discharge the two great branches of our public trust, faithfully to preserve, and wisely to administer it.

Mr. President, I have thus stated the reasons of my dissent to the doctrines which have been advanced and maintained. I am conscious of having detained you and the Senate much too long. I was drawn into the debate with no previous deliberation, such as is suited to the discussion of so grave and important a subject. But it is a subject of which my heart is full, and I have not been willing to suppress the utterance of its spontaneous sentiments. I cannot, even now, persuade myself to relinquish it, without expressing once more my deep conviction, that, since it respects nothing less than the Union of the States, it is of most vital and essential importance to the public happiness. I profess, Sir, in my career hitherto, to have kept steadily in view the prosperity and honor of the whole country, and the preservation of our Federal Union. It is to that Union we owe our safety at home, and our consideration and dignity abroad. It is to that Union that we are chiefly indebted for whatever makes us most proud of our country. That Union we reached only by the discipline of our virtues in the severe school of adversity. It had its origin in the necessities of disordered finance, prostrate commerce, and ruined credit. Under its benign influences, these great interests immediately awoke, as from the dead, and sprang forth with newness of life. Every year of its duration has teemed with fresh proofs of its utility and its blessings; and although our territory has stretched out wider and wider, and our population spread farther and farther, they have not outrun its protection or its benefits. It has been to us all a copious fountain of national, social, and personal happiness.

I have not allowed myself, Sir, to look beyond the Union, to see what might lie hidden in the dark recess behind. I have not coolly weighed the chances of preserving liberty when the bonds that unite us together shall be broken asunder. I have not accustomed myself to hang over the precipice of disunion, to see whether, with my short sight, I can fathom the depth of the abyss below; nor could I regard him as a safe counsellor in the affairs of this government, whose thoughts should be mainly bent on considering, not how the Union may be best preserved, but how tolerable might be the condition of the people when it should be broken up and destroyed. While the Union lasts, we have high, exciting, gratifying prospects spread out before us, for us and our children. Beyond that I seek not to penetrate the veil. God grant that, in my day, at least, that curtain may not rise! God grant that on my vision never may be opened what lies behind! When my eyes shall be turned to behold for the last time the sun in heaven, may I not see him shining on the broken and dishonored fragments of a once glorious Union; on States dissevered, discordant, belligerent; on a land rent with civil feuds, or drenched, it may be, in fraternal blood! Let their last feeble and lingering glance rather behold the gorgeous ensign of the republic, now known and honored throughout the earth, still full high advanced, its arms and trophies streaming in their original lustre, not a stripe erased or polluted, nor a single star obscured, bearing for its motto, no such miserable interrogatory as "What is all this worth?" nor those other words of delusion and folly, "Liberty first and Union afterwards"; but everywhere, spread all over in characters of living light, blazing on all its ample folds, as they float over the sea and over the land, and in every wind under the whole heavens, that other sentiment, dear to every true American heart,--Liberty *and* Union, now and for ever, one and inseparable!

Mr. Hayne having rejoined to Mr. Webster, especially on the constitutional question, Mr. Webster rose, and, in conclusion, said:--#/

A few words, Mr. President, on this constitutional argument, which the honorable gentleman has labored to reconstruct.

His argument consists of two propositions and an inference. His propositions are,--

1. That the Constitution is a compact between the States.

2. That a compact between two, with authority reserved to one to interpret its terms, would be a surrender to that one of all power whatever.

3. Therefore, (such is his inference,) the general government does not possess the authority to construe its own powers.

Now, Sir, who does not see, without the aid of exposition or detection, the utter confusion of ideas involved in this so elaborate and systematic argument.

The Constitution, it is said, is a compact _between States_; the States, then, and the States only, *are parties* to the compact. How comes the general government itself _a party_? Upon the honorable gentleman's hypothesis, the general government is the result of the compact, the creature of the compact, not one of the parties to it. Yet the argument, as the gentleman has now stated it, makes the government itself one of its own creators. It makes it a party to that compact to which it owes its own existence.

For the purpose of erecting the Constitution on the basis of a compact, the gentleman considers the States as parties to that compact; but as soon as his compact is made, then he chooses to consider the general government, which is the offspring of that compact, not its offspring, but one of its parties; and so, being a party, without the power of judging on the terms of compact. Pray, Sir, in what school is such reasoning as this taught?

If the whole of the gentleman's main proposition were conceded to him,--that is to say, if I admit, for the sake of the argument, that the Constitution is a compact between States,--the inferences which he draws from that proposition are warranted by no just reasoning. If the Constitution be a compact between States, still that Constitution, or that compact, has established a government, with certain powers; and whether it be one of those powers, that it shall construe and interpret for itself the terms of the compact, in doubtful cases, is a question which can only be decided by looking to the compact, and inquiring what provisions it contains on this point. Without any inconsistency with natural reason, the government even thus created might be trusted with this power of construction. The extent of its powers, therefore, must still be sought for in the instrument itself.

If the old Confederation had contained a clause, declaring that resolutions of the Congress should be the supreme law of the land, any State law or constitution to the contrary notwithstanding, and that a committee of Congress, or any other body created by it, should possess judicial powers, extending to all cases arising under resolutions of Congress, then the power of ultimate decision would have been vested in Congress under the Confederation, although that Confederation was a compact between States; and for this plain reason,--that it would have been competent to the States, who alone were parties to the compact, to agree who should decide in cases of dispute arising on the construction of the compact.

For the same reason, Sir, if I were now to concede to the gentleman his principal proposition, namely, that the Constitution is a compact between States, the question would still be, What provision is made, in this compact, to settle points of disputed construction, or contested power, that shall come into controversy? And this question would still be answered, and conclusively answered, by the Constitution itself.

While the gentleman is contending against construction, he himself is setting up the most loose and dangerous construction. The Constitution declares, that *the laws of Congress passed in pursuance of the Constitution shall be the supreme law of the land*. No construction is necessary here. It declares, also, with equal plainness and precision, *that the judicial power of the United States shall extend to every case arising under the laws of Congress*. This needs no construction. Here is a law, then, which is declared to be supreme; and here is a power established, which is to interpret that law. Now, Sir, how has the gentleman met this? Suppose the Constitution to be a compact, yet here are its terms; and how does the gentleman get rid of them? He cannot argue the _seal off the bond_, nor the words out of the instrument. Here they are; what answer does he give to them? None in the world, Sir, except, that the effect of this would be to place the States in a condition of inferiority; and that it results from the very nature of things, there being no superior, that the parties must be their own judges! Thus closely and cogently does the honorable gentleman reason on the words of the Constitution. The gentleman says, if there be such a power of final decision in the general government, he asks for the grant of that power. Well, Sir, I show him the grant. I turn him to the very words. I show him that the laws of Congress are made supreme; and that the judicial power extends, by express words, to the interpretation of these laws. Instead of answering this, he retreats into the general reflection, that it must result _from the nature of things_, that the States, being parties, must judge for themselves.

I have admitted, that, if the Constitution were to be considered as the creature of the State governments, it might be modified, interpreted, or construed according to their pleasure. But, even in that case, it would be necessary that they should *agree*. One alone could not interpret it conclusively; one alone could not construe it; one alone could not modify it. Yet the gentleman's doctrine is, that Carolina alone may construe and interpret that compact which equally binds all, and gives equal rights to all.

So, then, Sir, even supposing the Constitution to be a compact between the States, the gentleman's doctrine, nevertheless, is not maintainable; because, first, the general government is not a party to that compact, but a *government* established by it, and vested by it with the powers of trying and deciding doubtful questions; and secondly, because, if the Constitution be regarded as a compact, not one State only, but all the States, are parties to that compact, and one can have no right to fix upon it her own peculiar construction.

So much, Sir, for the argument, even if the premises of the gentleman were granted, or could be proved. But, Sir, the gentleman has failed to maintain his leading proposition. He has not shown, it cannot be shown, that the Constitution is a compact between State governments. The Constitution itself, in its very front, refutes that idea; it declares that it is ordained and established *by the people of the United States*. So far from saying that it is established by the governments of the several States, it does not even say that it is established by the people _of the several States_; but it pronounces that it is established by the people of the United States, in the aggregate. The gentleman says, it must mean no more than the people of the several States. Doubtless, the people of the several States, taken collectively, constitute the people of the United States; but it is in this, their collective capacity, it is as all the people of the United States, that they establish the Constitution. So they declare; and words cannot be plainer than the words used.

When the gentleman says the Constitution is a compact between the States, he uses language exactly applicable to the old Confederation. He speaks as if he were in Congress before 1789. He describes fully that old state of things then existing. The Confederation was, in strictness, a compact; the States, as States, were parties to it. We had no other general government. But that was found insufficient, and inadequate to the public exigencies. The people were not satisfied with it, and undertook to establish a better. They undertook to form a general government, which should stand on a new basis; not a confederacy, not a league, not a compact between States, but a _Constitution_; a popular government, founded in popular election, directly responsible to the people themselves, and divided into branches with prescribed limits of power, and prescribed duties. They ordained such a government, they gave it the name of a _Constitution_, and therein they established a distribution of powers between this, their general government, and their several State governments. When they shall become dissatisfied with this distribution, they can alter it. Their own power over their own instrument remains. But until they shall alter it, it must stand as their will, and is equally binding on the general government and on the States.

The gentleman, Sir, finds analogy where I see none. He likens it to the case of a treaty, in which, there being no common superior, each party must interpret for itself, under its own obligation of good faith. But this is not a treaty, but a constitution of government, with powers to execute itself, and fulfil its duties.

I admit, Sir, that this government is a government of checks and balances; that is, the House of Representatives is a check on the Senate, and the Senate is a check on the House, and the President a check on both. But I cannot comprehend him, or, if I do, I totally differ from him, when he applies the notion of checks and balances to the interference of different governments. He argues, that, if we transgress our constitutional limits, each State, as a State, has a right to check us. Does he admit the converse of the proposition, that we have a right to check the States? The gentleman's doctrines would give us a strange jumble of authorities and powers, instead of governments of separate and defined powers. It is the part of wisdom, I think, to avoid this; and to keep the general government and the State government each in its proper sphere, avoiding as carefully as possible every kind of interference.

Finally, Sir, the honorable gentleman says, that the States will only interfere, by their power, to preserve the Constitution. They will not destroy it, they will not impair it; they will only save, they will only preserve, they will only strengthen it! Ah! Sir, this is but the old story. All regulated governments, all free governments, have been broken by similar disinterested and well-disposed interference. It is the common pretence. But I take leave of the subject.

[Footnote 1: Mr. Sprague.][Footnote 2: Mr. Calhoun, when this speech was made, was President of the Senate, and Vice-President of the United States.][Footnote 3: Mr. Forsyth.]

[Footnote 4: Mr. McDuffie.][Footnote 5: The letter of the Federal Convention to the Congress of the Confederation transmitting the plan of the Constitution.][Footnote 6: Mr. Hillhouse, of Connecticut.]

THE CONSTITUTION NOT A COMPACT BETWEEN SOVEREIGN STATES.
A SPEECH DELIVERED IN THE SENATE OF THE UNITED STATES, ON THE 16TH OF FEBRUARY, 1833, IN REPLY TO MR. CALHOUN'S SPEECH ON THE BILL "FURTHER TO PROVIDE FOR THE COLLECTION OF DUTIES ON IMPORTS."

[On the 21st of January, 1833, Mr. Wilkins, chairman of the Judiciary Committee of the Senate, introduced the bill further to provide for the collection of duties. On the 22d day of the same month, Mr. Calhoun submitted the following resolutions:--

"_Resolved_, That the people of the several States composing these United States are united as parties to a constitutional compact, to which the people of each State acceded as a separate govereign community, each binding itself by its own particular ratification; and that the union, of which the said compact is the bond, is a union *between the States* ratifying the same.

"_Resolved_, That the people of the several States thus united by the constitutional compact, in forming that instrument, and in creating a general government to carry into effect the objects for which they were formed, delegated to that government, for that purpose, certain definite powers, to be exercised jointly, reserving, at the same time, each State to itself, the residuary mass of powers, to be exercised by its own separate government; and that whenever the general government assumes the exercise of powers not delegated by the compact, its acts are unauthorized, and are of no effect; and that the same government is not made the final judge of the powers delegated to it, since that would make its discretion, and not the Constitution, the measure of its powers; but that, as in all other cases of compact among sovereign parties, without any common judge, each has an equal right to judge for itself, as well of the infraction as of the mode and measure of redress.

"_Resolved_, That the assertions, that the people of these United States, taken collectively as individuals, are now, or ever have been, united on the principle of the social compact, and, as such, are now formed into one nation or people, or that they have ever been so united in any one stage of their political existence; that the people of the several States composing the Union have not, as members thereof, retained their sovereignty; that the allegiance of their citizens has been transferred to the general government; that they have parted with the right of punishing treason through their respective State governments; and that they have not the right of judging in the last resort as to the extent of the powers reserved, and of consequence of those delegated,--are not only without foundation in truth, but are contrary to the most certain and plain historical facts, and the clearest deductions of reason; and that all exercise of power on the part of the general government, or any of its departments, claiming authority from such erroneous assumptions, must of necessity be unconstitutional,--must tend, directly and inevitably, to subvert the sovereignty of the States, to destroy the federal character of the Union, and to rear on its ruins a consolidated government, without constitutional check or limitation, and which must necessarily terminate in the loss of liberty itself."

On Saturday, the 16th of February, Mr. Calhoun spoke in opposition to the bill, and in support of these resolutions. He was followed by Mr. Webster in this speech.]

Mr. President,--The gentleman from South Carolina has admonished us to be mindful of the opinions of those who shall come after us. We must take our chance, Sir, as to the light in which posterity will regard us. I do not decline its judgment, nor withhold myself from its scrutiny. Feeling that I am performing my public duty with singleness of heart and to the best of my ability, I fearlessly trust myself to the country, now and hereafter, and leave both my motives and my character to its decision.

The gentleman has terminated his speech in a tone of threat and defiance towards this bill, even should it become a law of the land, altogether unusual in the halls of Congress. But I shall not suffer myself to be excited into warmth by his denunciation of the measure which I support. Among the feelings which at this moment fill my breast, not the least is that of regret at the position in which the gentleman has placed himself. Sir, he does himself no justice. The cause which he has espoused finds no basis in the Constitution, no succor from public sympathy, no cheering from a patriotic community. He has no foothold on which to stand while he might display the powers of his acknowledged talents. Every thing beneath his feet is hollow and treacherous. He is like a strong man struggling in a morass: every effort to extricate himself only sinks him deeper and deeper. And I fear the resemblance may be carried still farther; I fear that no friend can safely come to his relief, that no one can approach near enough to hold out a helping hand, without danger of going down himself, also, into the bottomless depths of this Serbonian bog.

The honorable gentleman has declared, that on the decision of the question now in debate may depend the cause of liberty itself. I am of the same opinion; but then, Sir, the liberty which I think is staked on the contest is not political liberty, in any general and undefined character, but our own well-understood and long-enjoyed *American* liberty.

Sir, I love Liberty no less ardently than the gentleman himself, in whatever form she may have appeared in the progress of human history. As exhibited in the master states of antiquity, as breaking out again from amidst the darkness of the Middle Ages, and beaming on the formation of new communities in modern Europe, she has, always and everywhere, charms for me. Yet, Sir, it is our own liberty, guarded by constitutions and secured by union, it is that liberty which is our paternal inheritance, it is our established, dear-bought, peculiar American liberty, to which I am chiefly devoted, and the cause of which I now mean, to the utmost of my power, to maintain and defend.

Mr. President, if I considered the constitutional question now before us as doubtful as it is important, and if I supposed that its decision, either in the Senate or by the country, was likely to be in any degree influenced by the manner in which I might now discuss it, this would be to me a moment of deep solicitude. Such a moment has once existed. There has been a time, when, rising in this place, on the same question, I felt, I must confess, that something for good or evil to the Constitution of the country might depend on an effort of mine. But circumstances are changed. Since that day, Sir, the public opinion has become awakened to this great question; it has grasped it; it has reasoned upon it, as becomes an intelligent and patriotic community, and has settled it, or now seems in the progress of settling it, by an authority which none can disobey, the authority of the people themselves.

I shall not, Mr. President, follow the gentleman, step by step, through the course of his speech. Much of what he has said he has deemed necessary to the just explanation and defence of his own political character and conduct. On this I shall offer no comment. Much, too, has consisted of philosophical remark upon the general nature of political liberty, and the history of free institutions; and upon other topics, so general in their nature as to possess, in my opinion, only a remote bearing on the immediate subject of this debate. But the gentleman's speech made some days ago, upon introducing his resolutions, those resolutions themselves, and parts of the speech now just concluded, may, I presume, be justly regarded as containing the whole South Carolina doctrine. That doctrine it is my purpose now to examine, and to compare it with the Constitution of the United States. I shall not consent, Sir, to make any new constitution, or to establish another form of government. I will not undertake to say what a constitution for these United States ought to be. That question the people have decided for themselves; and I shall take the instrument as they have established it, and shall endeavor to maintain it, in its plain sense and meaning, against opinions and notions which, in my judgment, threaten its subversion.

The resolutions introduced by the gentleman were apparently drawn up with care, and brought forward upon deliberation. I shall not be in danger, therefore, of misunderstanding him, or those who agree with him, if I proceed at once to these resolutions, and consider them as an authentic statement of those opinions upon the great constitutional question by which the recent proceedings in South Carolina are attempted to be justified.

These resolutions are three in number.

The third seems intended to enumerate, and to deny, the several opinions expressed in the President's proclamation, respecting the nature and powers of this government. Of this third resolution, I purpose, at present, to take no particular notice.

The first two resolutions of the honorable member affirm these propositions, viz.:--

1. That the political system under which we live, and under which Congress is now assembled, is a _compact_, to which the people of the several States, as separate and sovereign communities, are *the parties*.

2. That these sovereign parties have a right to judge, each for itself, of any alleged violation of the Constitution by Congress; and, in case of such violation, to choose, each for itself, its own mode and measure of redress.

It is true, Sir, that the honorable member calls this a "constitutional" compact; but still he affirms it to be a compact between sovereign States. What precise meaning, then, does he attach to the term _constitutional_? When applied to compacts between sovereign States, the term *constitutional* affixes to the word *compact* no definite idea. Were we to hear of a constitutional league or treaty between England and France, or a constitutional convention between Austria and Russia, we should not understand what could be intended by such a league, such a treaty, or such a convention. In these connections, the word is void of all meaning; and yet, Sir, it is easy, quite easy, to see why the honorable gentleman has used it in these resolutions. He cannot open the book, and look upon our written frame of government, without seeing that it is called a *constitution*. This may well be appalling to him. It threatens his whole doctrine of compact, and its darling derivatives, nullification and secession, with instant confutation. Because, if he admits our instrument of government to be a _constitution_, then, for that very reason, it is not a compact between sovereigns; a constitution of government and a compact between sovereign powers being things essentially unlike in their very natures, and incapable of ever being the same. Yet the word *constitution* is on the very front of the instrument. He cannot overlook it. He seeks, therefore, to compromise the matter, and to sink all the substantial sense of the word, while he retains a resemblance of its sound. He introduces a new word of his own, viz. _compact_, as importing the principal idea, and designed to play the principal part, and degrades *constitution* into an insignificant, idle epithet, attached to *compact*. The whole then stands as a "_constitutional compact_"! And in this way he hopes to pass off a plausible gloss, as satisfying the words of the instrument. But he will find himself disappointed. Sir, I must say to the honorable gentleman, that, in our American political grammar, CONSTITUTION is a noun substantive; it imports a distinct and clear idea of itself; and it is not to lose its importance and dignity, it is not to be turned into a poor, ambiguous, senseless, unmeaning adjective, for the purpose of accommodating any new set of political notions. Sir, we reject his new rules of syntax altogether. We will not give up our forms of political speech to the grammarians of the school of nullification. By the Constitution, we mean, not a "constitutional compact," but, simply and directly, the Constitution, the fundamental law; and if there be one word in the language which the people of the United States understand, this is that word. We know no more of a constitutional compact between sovereign powers, than we know of a *constitutional* indenture of copartnership, a *constitutional* deed of conveyance, or a *constitutional* bill of exchange. But we know what the *Constitution* is; we know what the plainly written fundamental law is; we know what the bond of our Union and the security of our liberties is; and we mean to maintain and to defend it, in its plain sense and unsophisticated meaning.

The sense of the gentleman's proposition, therefore, is not at all affected, one way or the other, by the use of this word. That proposition still is, that our system of government is but a *compact* between the people of separate and sovereign States.

Was it Mirabeau, Mr. President, or some other master of the human passions, who has told us that words are things? They are indeed things, and things of mighty influence, not only in addresses to the passions and high-wrought feelings of mankind, but in the discussion of legal and political questions also; because a just conclusion is often avoided, or a false one reached, by the adroit substitution of one phrase, or one word, for another. Of this we have, I think, another example in the resolutions before us.

The first resolution declares that the people of the several States "_acceded_" to the Constitution, or to the constitutional compact, as it is called. This word "accede," not found either in the Constitution itself, or in the ratification of it by any one of the States, has been chosen for use here, doubtless, not without a well-considered purpose.

The natural converse of *accession* is _secession_; and, therefore, when it is stated that the people of the States acceded to the Union, it may be more plausibly argued that they may secede from it. If, in adopting the Constitution, nothing was done but acceding to a compact, nothing would seem necessary, in order to break it up, but to secede from the same compact. But the term is wholly out of place. _Accession_, as a word applied to political associations, implies coming into a league, treaty, or confederacy, by one hitherto a stranger to it; and *secession* implies departing from such league or confederacy. The people of the United States have used no such form of expression in establishing the present government. They do not say that they *accede* to a league, but they declare that they *ordain* and *establish* a Constitution, Such are the very words of the instrument itself; and in all the States, without an exception, the language used by their conventions was, that they "_ratified the Constitution_"; some of them employing the additional words "assented to" and "adopted," but all of them "ratifying."

There is more importance than may, at first sight, appear, in the introduction of this new word, by the honorable mover of these resolutions. Its adoption and use are indispensable to maintain those premises from which his main conclusion is to be afterwards drawn. But before showing that, allow me to remark, that this phraseology tends to keep out of sight the just view of a previous political history, as well as to suggest wrong ideas as to what was actually done when the present Constitution was agreed to. In 1789, and before this Constitution was adopted, the United States had already been in a union, more or less close, for fifteen years. At least as far back as the meeting of the first Congress, in 1774, they had been in some measure, and for some national purposes, united together. Before the Confederation of 1781, they had declared independence jointly, and had carried on the war jointly, both by sea and land; and this not as separate States, but as one people. When, therefore, they formed that Confederation, and adopted its articles as articles of perpetual union, they did not come together for the first time; and therefore they did not speak of the States as *acceding* to the Confederation, although it was a league, and nothing but a league, and rested on nothing but plighted faith for its performance. Yet, even then, the States were not strangers to each other; there was a bond of union already subsisting between them; they were associated, united States; and the object of the Confederation was to make a stronger and better bond of union. Their representatives deliberated together on these proposed Articles of Confederation, and, being authorized by their respective States, finally "_ratified and confirmed_" them. Inasmuch as they were already in union, they did not speak of *acceding* to the new Articles of Confederation, but of *ratifying and confirming* them;

and this language was not used inadvertently, because, in the same instrument, *accession* is used in its proper sense, when applied to Canada, which was altogether a stranger to the existing union. "Canada," says the eleventh article, "*acceding* to this Confederation, and joining in the measures of the United States, shall be admitted into the Union."

Having thus used the terms *ratify* and _confirm_, even in regard to the old Confederation, it would have been strange indeed, if the people of the United States, after its formation, and when they came to establish the present Constitution, had spoken of the States, or the people of the States, as *acceding* to this Constitution. Such language would have been ill-suited to the occasion. It would have implied an existing separation or disunion among the States, such as never has existed since 1774. No such language, therefore, was used. The language actually employed is, _adopt, ratify, ordain, establish_.

Therefore, Sir, since any State, before she can prove her right to dissolve the Union, must show her authority to undo what has been done, no State is at liberty to _secede_, on the ground that she and other States have done nothing but *accede*. She must show that she has a right to *reverse* what has been _ordained_, to *unsettle* and *overthrow* what has been _established_, to *reject* what the people have _adopted_, and to *break up* what they have _ratified_; because these are the terms which express the transactions which have actually taken place. In other words, she must show her right to make a revolution. If, Mr. President, in drawing these resolutions, the honorable member had confined himself to the use of constitutional language, there would have been a wide and awful *hiatus* between his premises and his conclusion. Leaving out the two words *compact* and _accession_, which are not constitutional modes of expression, and stating the matter precisely as the truth is, his first resolution would have affirmed that _the people of the several States ratified this Constitution, or form of government_. These are the very words of South Carolina herself, in her act of ratification. Let, then, his first resolution tell the exact truth; let it state the fact precisely as it exists; let it say that the people of the several States ratified a constitution, or form of government, and then, Sir, what will become of his inference in his second resolution, which is in these words, viz. "that, as in all other cases of compact among sovereign parties, each has an equal right to judge for itself, as well of the infraction as of the mode and measure of redress"? It is obvious, is it not, Sir? that this conclusion requires for its support quite other premises; it requires premises which speak of *accession* and of *compact* between sovereign powers; and, without such premises, it is altogether unmeaning.

Mr. President, if the honorable member will truly state what the people did in forming this Constitution, and then state what they must do if they would now undo what they then did, he will unavoidably state a case of revolution. Let us see if it be not so. He must state, in the first place, that the people of the several States adopted and ratified this Constitution, or form of government; and, in the next place, he must state that they have a right to undo this; that is to say, that they have a right to discard the form of government which they have adopted, and to break up the Constitution which they have ratified. Now, Sir, this is neither more nor less than saying that they have a right to make a revolution. To reject an established government, to break up a political constitution, is revolution.

I deny that any man can state accurately what was done by the people, in establishing the present Constitution, and then state accurately what the people, or any part of them, must now do to get rid of its obligations, without stating an undeniable case of the overthrow of government. I admit, of course, that the people may, if they choose, overthrow the government. But, then, that is revolution. The doctrine now contended for is, that, by _nullification_, or _secession_, the obligations and authority of the government may be set aside or rejected, without revolution. But that is what I deny; and what I say is, that no man can state the case with historical accuracy, and in constitutional language, without showing that the honorable gentleman's right, as asserted in his conclusion, is a revolutionary right merely; that it does not and cannot exist under the Constitution, or agreeably to the Constitution, but can come into existence only when the Constitution is overthrown. This is the reason, Sir, which makes it necessary to abandon the use of constitutional language for a new vocabulary, and to substitute, in the place of plain historical facts, a series of assumptions. This is the reason why it is necessary to give new names to things, to speak of the Constitution, not as a constitution, but as a compact, and of the ratifications by the people, not as ratifications, but as acts of accession.

Sir, I intend to hold the gentleman to the written record. In the discussion of a constitutional question, I intend to impose upon him the restraints of constitutional language. The people have ordained a Constitution; can they reject it without revolution? They have established a form of government; can they overthrow it without revolution? These are the true questions.

Allow me now, Mr. President, to inquire further into the extent of the propositions contained in the resolutions, and their necessary consequences.

Where sovereign communities are parties, there is no essential difference between a compact, a confederation, and a league. They all equally rest on the plighted faith of the sovereign party. A league, or confederacy, is but a subsisting or continuing treaty.

The gentleman's resolutions, then, affirm, in effect, that these twenty-four United States are held together only by a subsisting treaty, resting for its fulfilment and continuance on no inherent power of its own, but on the plighted faith of each State; or, in other words, that our Union is but a league; and, as a consequence from this proposition, they further affirm that, as sovereigns are subject to no superior power, the States must judge, each for itself, of any alleged violation of the league; and if such violation be supposed to have occurred, each may adopt any mode or measure of redress which it shall think proper.

Other consequences naturally follow, too, from the main proposition. If a league between sovereign powers have no limitation as to the time of its duration, and contain nothing making it perpetual, it subsists only during the good pleasure of the parties, although no violation be complained of. If, in the opinion of either party, it be violated, such party may say that he will no longer fulfil its obligations on his part, but will consider the whole league or compact at an end, although it might be one of its stipulations that it should be perpetual. Upon this principle, the Congress of the United States, in 1798, declared null and void the treaty of alliance between the United States and France, though it professed to be a perpetual alliance. If the violation of the league be accompanied with serious injuries, the suffering party, being sole judge of his own mode and measure of redress, has a right to indemnify himself by reprisals on the offending members of the league; and reprisals, if the circumstances of the case require it, may be followed by direct, avowed, and public war.

The necessary import of the resolution, therefore, is, that the United States are connected only by a league; that it is in the good pleasure of every State to decide how long she will choose to remain a member of this league; that any State may determine the extent of her own obligations under it, and accept or reject what shall be decided by the whole; that she may also determine whether her rights have been violated, what is the extent of the injury done her, and what mode and measure of redress her wrongs may make it fit and expedient for her to adopt. The result of the whole is, that any State may secede at pleasure; that any State may resist a law which she herself may choose to say exceeds the power of Congress; and that, as a sovereign power, she may redress her own grievances, by her own arm, at her own discretion. She may make reprisals; she may cruise against the property of other members of the league; she may authorize captures, and make open war.

If, Sir, this be our political condition, it is time the people of the United States understood it. Let us look for a moment to the practical consequences of these opinions. One State, holding an embargo law unconstitutional, may declare her opinion, and withdraw from the Union. *She* secedes. Another, forming and expressing the same judgment on a law laying duties on imports, may withdraw also. *She* secedes. And as, in her opinion, money has been taken out of the pockets of her citizens illegally, under pretence of this law, and as she has power to redress their wrongs, she may demand satisfaction: and, if refused, she may take it with a strong hand. The gentleman has himself pronounced the collection of duties, under existing laws, to be nothing but robbery. Robbers, of course, may be rightfully dispossessed of the fruits of their flagitious crimes; and therefore, reprisals, impositions on the commerce of other States, foreign alliances against them, or open war, are all modes of redress justly open to the discretion and choice of South Carolina; for she is to judge of her own rights, and to seek satisfaction for her own wrongs, in her own way.

But, Sir, a *third* State is of opinion, not only that these laws of imposts are constitutional, but that it is the absolute duty of Congress to pass and to maintain such laws; and that, by omitting to pass and maintain them, its constitutional obligations would be grossly disregarded. She herself relinquished the power of protection, she might allege, and allege truly, and gave it up to Congress, on the faith that Congress would exercise it. If Congress now refuse to exercise it, Congress does, as she may insist, break the condition of the grant, and thus manifestly violate the Constitution; and for this violation of the Constitution, *she* may threaten to secede also. Virginia may secede, and hold the fortresses in the Chesapeake. The Western States may secede, and take to their own use the public lands. Louisiana may secede, if she choose, form a foreign alliance, and hold the mouth of the Mississippi. If one State may secede, ten may do so, twenty may do so, twenty-three may do so. Sir, as these secessions go on, one after another, what is to constitute the United States? Whose will be the army? Whose the navy? Who will pay the debts? Who fulfil the public treaties? Who perform the constitutional guaranties? Who govern this District and the Territories? Who retain the public property?

Mr. President, every man must see that these are all questions which can arise only *after a revolution*. They presuppose the breaking up of the government. While the Constitution lasts, they are repressed; they spring up to annoy and startle us only from its grave.

The Constitution does not provide for events which must be preceded by its own destruction.

SECESSION, therefore, since it must bring these consequences with it, is REVOLUTIONARY, and NULLIFICATION is equally REVOLUTIONARY. What is revolution? Why, Sir, that is revolution which overturns, or controls, or successfully resists, the existing public authority; that which arrests the exercise of the supreme power; that which introduces a new paramount authority into the rule of the State. Now, Sir, this is the precise object of nullification. It attempts to supersede the supreme legislative authority. It arrests the arm of the executive magistrate. It interrupts the exercise of the accustomed judicial power. Under the name of an ordinance, it declares null and void, within the State, all the revenue laws of the United States. Is not this revolutionary? Sir, so soon as this ordinance shall be carried into effect, *a revolution* will have commenced in South Carolina. She will have thrown off the authority to which her citizens have heretofore been subject. She will have declared her own opinions and her own will to be above the laws and above the power of those who are intrusted with their administration. If she makes good these declarations, she is revolutionized. As to her, it is as distinctly a change of the supreme power as the American Revolution of 1776. That revolution did not subvert government in all its forms. It did not subvert local laws and municipal administrations. It only threw off the dominion of a power claiming to be superior, and to have a right, in many important respects, to exercise legislative authority. Thinking this authority to have been usurped or abused, the American Colonies, now the United States, bade it defiance, and freed themselves from it by means of a revolution. But that revolution left them with their own municipal laws still, and the forms of local government. If Carolina now shall effectually resist the laws of Congress; if she shall be her own judge, take her remedy into her own hands, obey the laws of the Union when she pleases and disobey them when she pleases, she will relieve herself from a paramount power as distinctly as the American Colonies did the same thing in 1776. In other words, she will achieve, as to herself, a revolution.

But, Sir, while practical nullification in South Carolina would be, as to herself, actual and distinct revolution, its necessary tendency must also be to spread revolution, and to break up the Constitution, as to all the other States. It strikes a deadly blow at the vital principle of the whole Union. To allow State resistance to the laws of Congress to be rightful and proper, to admit nullification in some States, and yet not expect to see a dismemberment of the entire government, appears to me the wildest illusion, and the most extravagant folly. The gentleman seems not conscious of the direction or the rapidity of his own course. The current of his opinions sweeps him along, he knows not whither. To begin with nullification, with the avowed intent, nevertheless, not to proceed to secession, dismemberment, and general revolution, is as if one were to take the plunge of Niagara, and cry out that he would stop half-way down. In the one case, as in the other, the rash adventurer must go to the bottom of the dark abyss below, were it not that that abyss has no discovered bottom.

Nullification, if successful, arrests the power of the law, absolves citizens from their duty, subverts the foundation both of protection and obedience, dispenses with oaths and obligations of allegiance, and elevates another authority to supreme command. Is not this revolution? And it raises to supreme command four-and-twenty distinct powers, each professing to be under a general government, and yet each setting its laws at defiance at pleasure. Is not this anarchy, as well as revolution? Sir, the Constitution of the United States was received as a whole, and for the whole country. If it cannot stand altogether, it cannot stand in parts; and if the laws cannot be executed everywhere, they cannot long be executed anywhere. The gentleman very well knows that all duties and imposts must be uniform throughout the country. He knows that we cannot have one rule or one law for South Carolina, and another for other States. He must see, therefore, and does see, and every man sees, that the only alternative is a repeal of the laws throughout the whole Union, or their execution in Carolina as well as elsewhere. And this repeal is demanded because a single State interposes her veto, and threatens resistance! The result of the gentleman's opinion, or rather the very text of his doctrine, is, that no act of Congress can bind all the States, the constitutionality of which is not admitted by all; or, in other words, that no single State is bound, against its own dissent, by a law of imposts. This is precisely the evil experienced under the old Confederation, and for remedy of which this Constitution was adopted. The leading object in establishing this government, an object forced on the country by the condition of the times and the absolute necessity of the law, was to give to Congress power to lay and collect imposts *without the consent of particular States*. The Revolutionary debt remained unpaid; the national treasury was bankrupt; the country was destitute of credit; Congress issued its requisitions on the States, and the States neglected them; there was no power of coercion but war, Congress could not lay imposts, or other taxes, by its own authority; the whole general government, therefore, was little more than a name. The Articles of Confederation, as to purposes of revenue and finance, were nearly a dead letter. The country sought to escape from this condition, at once feeble and disgraceful, by constituting a government which should have power, of itself, to lay duties and taxes, and to pay the public debt, and provide for the general welfare; and to lay these duties and taxes in all the States, without asking the consent of the State governments. This was the very power on which the new Constitution was to depend for all its ability to do good; and without it, it can be no government, now or at any time. Yet, Sir, it is precisely against this power, so absolutely indispensable to the very being of the government, that South Carolina directs her ordinance. She attacks the government in its authority to raise revenue, the very main-spring of the whole system; and if she succeed, every movement of that system must inevitably cease. It is of no avail that she declares that she does not resist the law as a revenue law, but as a law for protecting manufactures. It is a revenue law; it is the very law by force of which the revenue is collected; if it be arrested in any State, the revenue ceases in that State; it is, in a word, the sole reliance of the government for the means of maintaining itself and performing its duties.

Mr. President, the alleged right of a State to decide constitutional questions for herself necessarily leads to force, because other States must have the same right, and because different States will decide differently; and when these questions arise between States, if there be no superior power, they can be decided only by the law of force. On entering into the Union, the people of each State gave up a part of their own power to make laws for themselves, in consideration, that, as to common objects, they should have a part in making laws for other States. In other words, the people of all the States agreed to create a common government, to be conducted by common counsels. Pennsylvania, for example, yielded the right of laying imposts in her own ports, in consideration that the new government, in which she was to have a share, should possess the power of laying imposts on all the States. If South Carolina now refuses to submit to this power, she breaks the condition on which other States entered into the Union. She partakes of the common counsels, and therein assists to bind others, while she refuses to be bound herself. It makes no difference in the case, whether she does all this without reason or pretext, or whether she sets up as a reason, that, in her judgment, the acts complained of are unconstitutional. In the judgment of other States, they are not so. It is nothing to them that she offers some reason or some apology for her conduct, if it be one which they do not admit. It is not to be expected that any State will violate her duty without some plausible pretext. That would be too rash a defiance of the opinion of mankind. But if it be a pretext which lies in her own breast, if it be no more than an opinion which she says she has formed, how can other States be satisfied with this? How can they allow her to be judge of her own obligations? Or, if she may judge of her obligations, may they not judge of their rights also? May not the twenty-three entertain an opinion as well as the twenty-fourth? And if it be their right, in their own opinion, as expressed in the common council, to enforce the law against her, how is she to say that her right and her opinion are to be every thing, and their right and their opinion nothing?

Mr. President, if we are to receive the Constitution as the text, and then to lay down in its margin the contradictory commentaries which have been, and which maybe, made by different States, the whole page would be a polyglot indeed. It would speak with as many tongues as the builders of Babel, and in dialects as much confused, and mutually as unintelligible. The very instance now before us presents a practical illustration. The law of the last session is declared unconstitutional in South Carolina, and obedience to it is refused. In other States, it is admitted to be strictly constitutional. You walk over the limit of its authority, therefore, when you pass a State line. On one side it is law, on the other side a nullity; and yet it is passed by a common government, having the same authority in all the States.

Such, Sir, are the inevitable results of this doctrine. Beginning with the original error, that the Constitution of the United States is nothing but a compact between sovereign States; asserting, in the next step, that each State has a right to be its own sole judge of the extent of its own obligations, and consequently of the constitutionality of laws of Congress; and, in the next, that it may oppose whatever it sees fit to declare unconstitutional, and that it decides for itself on the mode and measure of redress,--the argument arrives at once at the conclusion, that what a State dissents from, it may nullify; what it opposes, it may oppose by force; what it decides for itself, it may execute by its own power; and that, in short, it is itself supreme over the legislation of Congress, and supreme over the decisions of the national judicature; supreme over the constitution of the country, supreme over the supreme law of the land. However it seeks to protect itself against these plain inferences, by saying that an unconstitutional law is no law, and that it only opposes such laws as are unconstitutional, yet this does not in the slightest degree vary the result; since it insists on deciding this question for itself; and, in opposition to reason and argument, in opposition to practice and experience, in opposition to the judgment of others, having an equal right to judge, it says, only, "Such is my opinion, and my opinion shall be my law, and I will support it by my own strong hand. I denounce the law; I declare it unconstitutional; that is enough; it shall not be executed. Men in arms are ready to resist its execution. An attempt to enforce it shall cover the land with blood. Elsewhere it may be binding; but here it is trampled underfoot."

This, Sir, is practical nullification.

And now, Sir, against all these theories and opinions, I maintain,--

1. That the Constitution of the United States is not a league, confederacy, or compact between the people of the several States in their sovereign capacities; but a government proper, founded on the adoption of the people, and creating direct relations between itself and individuals.

2. That no State authority has power to dissolve these relations; that nothing can dissolve them but revolution; and that, consequently, there can be no such thing as secession without revolution.

3. That there is a supreme law, consisting of the Constitution of the United States, and acts of Congress passed in pursuance of it, and treaties; and that, in cases not capable of assuming the character of a suit in law or equity, Congress must judge of, and finally interpret, this supreme law so often as it has occasion to pass acts of legislation; and in cases capable of assuming, and actually assuming, the character of a suit, the Supreme Court of the United States is the final interpreter.

4. That an attempt by a State to abrogate, annul, or nullify an act of Congress, or to arrest its operation within her limits, on the ground that, in her opinion, such law is unconstitutional, is a direct usurpation on the just powers of the general government, and on the equal rights of other States; a plain violation of the Constitution, and a proceeding essentially revolutionary in its character and tendency.

Whether the Constitution be a compact between States in their sovereign capacities, is a question which must be mainly argued from what is contained in the instrument itself. We all agree that it is an instrument which has been in some way clothed with power. We all admit that it speaks with authority. The first question then is, What does it say of itself? What does it purport to be? Does it style itself a league, confederacy, or compact between sovereign States? It is to be remembered, Sir, that the Constitution began to speak only after its adoption. Until it was ratified by nine States, it was but a proposal, the mere draught of an instrument. It was like a deed drawn, but not executed. The Convention had framed it; sent it to Congress, then sitting under the Confederation; Congress had transmitted it to the State legislatures; and by these last it was laid before conventions of the people in the several States. All this while it was inoperative paper. It had received no stamp of authority, no sanction; it spoke no language. But when ratified by the people in their respective conventions, then it had a voice, and spoke authentically. Every word in it had then received the sanction of the popular will, and was to be received as the expression of that will. What the Constitution says of itself, therefore, is as conclusive as what it says on any other point. Does it call itself a "compact"? Certainly not. It uses the word *compact* but once, and that is when it declares that the States shall enter into no compact. Does it call itself a "league," a "confederacy," a "subsisting treaty between the States"? Certainly not. There is not a particle of such language in all its pages. But it declares itself a CONSTITUTION. What is a _constitution_? Certainly not a league, compact, or confederacy, but *a fundamental law*. That fundamental regulation which determines the manner in which the public authority is to be executed, is what forms the *constitution* of a state. Those primary rules which concern the body itself, and the very being of the political society, the form of government, and the manner in which power is to be exercised,--all, in a word, which form together the _constitution of a state_,--these are the fundamental laws. This, Sir, is the language of the public writers. But do we need to be informed, in this country, what a *constitution* is? Is it not an idea perfectly familiar, definite, and well settled? We are at no loss to understand what is meant by the constitution of one of the States; and the

Constitution of the United States speaks of itself as being an instrument of the same nature. It says this *Constitution* shall be the law of the land, any thing in any State *constitution* to the contrary notwithstanding. And it speaks of itself, too, in plain contradistinction from a confederation; for it says that all debts contracted, and all engagements entered into, by the United States, shall be as valid under this *Constitution* as under the *Confederation*. It does not say, as valid under this _compact_, or this league, or this confederation, as under the former confederation, but as valid under this *Constitution*.

This, then, Sir, is declared to be a *constitution*. A constitution is the fundamental law of the state; and this is expressly declared to be the supreme law. It is as if the people had said, "We prescribe this fundamental law," or "this supreme law," for they do say that they establish this Constitution, and that it shall be the supreme law. They say that they *ordain and establish* it. Now, Sir, what is the common application of these words? We do not speak of *ordaining* leagues and compacts. If this was intended to be a compact or league, and the States to be parties to it, why was it not so said? Why is there found no one expression in the whole instrument indicating such intent? The old Confederation was expressly called a _league_, and into this league it was declared that the States, as States, severally entered. Why was not similar language used in the Constitution, if a similar intention had existed? Why was it not said, "the States enter into this new league," "the States form this new confederation," or "the States agree to this new compact"? Or why was it not said, in the language of the gentleman's resolution, that the people of the several States acceded to this compact in their sovereign capacities? What reason is there for supposing that the framers of the Constitution rejected expressions appropriate to their own meaning, and adopted others wholly at war with that meaning?

Again, Sir, the Constitution speaks of that political system which is established as "the government of the United States." Is it not doing strange violence to language to call a league or a compact between sovereign powers a _government_? The government of a state is that organization in which the political power resides. It is the political being created by the constitution or fundamental law. The broad and clear difference between a government and a league or compact is, that a government is a body politic; it has a will of its own; and it possesses powers and faculties to execute its own purposes. Every compact looks to some power to enforce its stipulations. Even in a compact between sovereign communities, there always exists this ultimate reference to a power to insure its execution; although, in such case, this power is but the force of one party against the force of another; that is to say, the power of war. But a *government* executes its decisions by its own supreme authority. Its use of force in compelling obedience to its own enactments is not war. It contemplates no opposing party having a right of resistance. It rests on its own power to enforce its own will; and when it ceases to possess this power, it is no longer a government.

Mr. President, I concur so generally in the very able speech of the gentleman from Virginia near me,[1] that it is not without diffidence and regret that I venture to differ with him on any point. His opinions, Sir, are redolent of the doctrines of a very distinguished school, for which I have the highest regard, of whose doctrines I can say, what I can also say of the gentleman's speech, that, while I concur in the results, I must be permitted to hesitate about some of the premises. I do not agree that the Constitution is a compact between States in their sovereign capacities. I do not agree, that, in strictness of language, it is a compact at all. But I do agree that it is founded on consent or agreement, or on compact, if the gentleman prefers that word, and means no more by it than voluntary consent or agreement. The Constitution, Sir, is not a contract, but the result of a contract; meaning by contract no more than assent. Founded on consent, it is a government proper. Adopted by the agreement of the people of the United States, when adopted, it has become a Constitution. The people have agreed to make a Constitution; but when made, that Constitution becomes what its name imports. It is no longer a mere agreement. Our laws, Sir, have their foundation in the agreement or consent of the two houses of Congress. We say, habitually, that one house proposes a bill, and the other agrees to it; but the result of this agreement is not a compact, but a law. The law, the statute, is not the agreement, but something created by the agreement; and something which, when created, has a new character, and acts by its own authority. So the Constitution of the United States, founded in or on the consent of the people, may be said to rest on compact or consent; but it is not itself the compact, but its result. When the people agree to erect a government, and actually erect it, the thing is done, and the agreement is at an end. The compact is executed, and the end designed by it attained. Henceforth, the fruit of the agreement exists, but the agreement itself is merged in its own accomplishment; since there can be no longer a subsisting agreement or compact *to form* a constitution or government, after that constitution or government has been actually formed and established.

It appears to me, Mr. President, that the plainest account of the establishment of this government presents the most just and philosophical view of its foundation. The people of the several States had their separate State governments; and between the States there also existed a Confederation. With this condition of things the people were not satisfied, as the Confederation had been found not to fulfil its intended objects. It was _proposed_, therefore, to erect a new, common government, which should possess certain definite powers, such as regarded the prosperity of the people of all the States, and to be formed upon the general model of American constitutions. This proposal was assented to, and an instrument was presented to the people of the several States for their consideration. They approved it, and agreed to adopt it, as a Constitution. They executed that agreement; they adopted the Constitution as a Constitution, and henceforth it must stand as a Constitution until it shall be altogether destroyed. Now, Sir, is not this the truth of the whole matter? And is not all that we have heard of compact between sovereign States the mere effect of a theoretical and artificial mode of reasoning upon the subject? a mode of reasoning which disregards plain facts for the sake of hypothesis?

Mr. President, the nature of sovereignty or sovereign power has been extensively discussed by gentlemen on this occasion, as it generally is when the origin of our government is debated. But I confess myself not entirely satisfied with arguments and illustrations drawn from that topic. The sovereignty of government is an idea belonging to the other side of the Atlantic. No such thing is known in North America. Our governments are all limited. In Europe, sovereignty is of feudal origin, and imports no more than the state of the sovereign. It comprises his rights, duties, exemptions, prerogatives, and powers. But with us, all power is with the people. They alone are sovereign; and they erect what governments they please, and confer on them such powers as they please. None of these governments is sovereign, in the European sense of the word, all being restrained by written constitutions. It seems to me, therefore, that we only perplex ourselves when we attempt to explain the relations existing between the general government and the several State governments, according to those ideas of sovereignty which prevail under systems essentially different from our own.

But, Sir, to return to the Constitution itself; let me inquire what it relies upon for its own continuance and support. I hear it often suggested, that the States, by refusing to appoint Senators and Electors, might bring this government to an end. Perhaps that is true; but the same may be said of the State governments themselves. Suppose the legislature of a State, having the power to appoint the governor and the judges, should omit that duty, would not the State government remain unorganized? No doubt, all elective governments may be broken up by a general abandonment, on the part of those intrusted with political powers, of their appropriate duties. But one popular government has, in this respect, as much security as another. The maintenance of this Constitution does not depend on the plighted faith of the States, as States, to support it; and this again shows that it is not a league. It relies on individual duty and obligation.

The Constitution of the United States creates direct relations between this government and individuals. This government may punish individuals for treason, and all other crimes in the code, when committed against the United States. It has power, also, to tax individuals, in any mode, and to any extent; and it possesses the further power of demanding from individuals military service. Nothing, certainly, can more clearly distinguish a government from a confederation of states than the possession of these powers. No closer relations can exist between individuals and any government.

On the other hand, the government owes high and solemn duties to every citizen of the country. It is bound to protect him in his most important rights and interests. It makes war for his protection, and no other government in the country can make war. It makes peace for his protection, and no other government can make peace. It maintains armies and navies for his defence and security, and no other government is allowed to maintain them. He goes abroad beneath its flag, and carries over all the earth a rational character imparted to him by this government, and which no other government can impart. In whatever relates to war, to peace, to commerce, he knows no other government. All these, Sir, are connections as dear and as sacred as can bind individuals to any government on earth. It is not, therefore, a compact between States, but a government proper, operating directly upon individuals, yielding to them protection on the one hand, and demanding from them obedience on the other.

There is no language in the whole Constitution applicable to a confederation of States. If the States be parties, as States, what are their rights, and what their respective covenants and stipulations? And where are their rights, covenants, and stipulations expressed? The States engage for nothing, they promise nothing. In the Articles of Confederation, they did make promises, and did enter into engagements, and did plight the faith of each State for their fulfilment; but in the Constitution there is nothing of that kind. The reason is, that, in the Constitution, it is the *people* who speak, and not the States. The people ordain the Constitution, and therein address themselves to the States, and to the legislatures of the States, in the language of injunction and prohibition. The Constitution utters its behests in the name and by authority of the people, and it does not exact from States any plighted public faith to maintain it. On the contrary, it makes its own preservation depend on individual duty and individual obligation. Sir, the States cannot omit to appoint Senators and Electors. It is not a matter resting in State discretion or State pleasure. The Constitution has taken better care of its own preservation. It lays its hand on individual conscience and individual duty. It incapacitates any man to sit in the legislature of a State, who shall not first have taken his solemn oath to support the Constitution of the United States. From the obligation of this oath, no State power can discharge him. All the members of all the State legislatures are as religiously bound to support the Constitution of the United States as they are to support their own State constitution. Nay, Sir, they are as solemnly sworn to support it as we ourselves are, who are members of Congress.

No member of a State legislature can refuse to proceed, at the proper time, to elect Senators to Congress, or to provide for the choice of Electors of President and Vice-President, any more than the members of this Senate can refuse, when the appointed day arrives, to meet the members of the other house, to count the votes for those officers, and ascertain who are chosen. In both cases, the duty binds, and with equal strength, the conscience of the individual member, and it is imposed on all by an oath in the same words. Let it then never be said, Sir, that it is a matter of discretion with the States whether they will continue the government, or break it up by refusing to appoint Senators and to elect Electors. They have no discretion in the matter. The members of their legislatures cannot avoid doing either, so often as the time arrives, without a direct violation of their duty and their oaths; such a violation as would break up any other government.

Looking still further to the provisions of the Constitution itself, in order to learn its true character, we find its great apparent purpose to be, to unite the people of all the States under one general government, for certain definite objects, and, to the extent of this union, to restrain the separate authority of the States. Congress only can declare war; therefore, when one State is at war with a foreign nation, all must be at war. The President and the Senate only can make peace; when peace is made for one State, therefore, it must be made for all.

Can any thing be conceived more preposterous, than that any State should have power to nullify the proceedings of the general government respecting peace and war? When war is declared by a law of Congress, can a single State nullify that law, and remain at peace? And yet she may nullify that law as well as any other. If the President and Senate make peace, may one State, nevertheless, continue the war? And yet, if she can nullify a law, she may quite as well nullify a treaty.

The truth is, Mr. President, and no ingenuity of argument, no subtilty of distinction can evade it, that, as to certain purposes, the people of the United States are one people. They are one in making war, and one in making peace; they are one in regulating commerce, and one in laying duties of imposts. The very end and purpose of the Constitution was, to make them one people in these particulars; and it has effectually accomplished its object. All this is apparent on the face of the Constitution itself. I have already said, Sir, that to obtain a power of direct legislation over the people, especially in regard to imposts, was always prominent as a reason for getting rid of the Confederation, and forming a new Constitution. Among innumerable proofs of this, before the assembling of the Convention, allow me to refer only to the report of the committee of the old Congress, July, 1785.

But, Sir, let us go to the actual formation of the Constitution; let us open the journal of the Convention itself, and we shall see that the very first resolution which the Convention adopted was, "THAT A NATIONAL GOVERNMENT OUGHT TO BE ESTABLISHED, CONSISTING OF A SUPREME LEGISLATURE, JUDICIARY, AND EXECUTIVE."

This itself completely negatives all idea of league, and compact, and confederation. Terms could not be chosen more fit to express an intention to establish a national government, and to banish for ever all notion of a compact between sovereign States.

This resolution was adopted on the 30th of May, 1787. Afterwards, the style was altered, and, instead of being called a national government, it was called the government of the United States; but the substance of this resolution was retained, and was at tha head of that list of resolutions which was afterwards sent to the committee who were to frame the instrument.

It is true, there were gentlemen in the Convention, who were for retaining the Confederation, and amending its Articles; but the majority was against this, and was for a national government. Mr. Patterson's propositions, which were for continuing the Articles of Confederation with additional powers, were submitted to the Convention on the 15th of June, and referred to the committee of the whole. The resolutions forming the basis of a national government, which had once been agreed to in the committee of the whole, and reported, were recommitted to the same committee, on the same day. The Convention, then, in committee of the whole, on the 19th of June, had both these plans before them; that is to say, the plan of a confederacy, or compact, between States, and the plan of a national government. Both these plans were considered and debated, and the committee reported, "That they do not agree to the propositions offered by the honorable Mr. Patterson, but that they again submit the resolutions formerly reported." If, Sir, any historical fact in the world be plain and undeniable, it is that the Convention deliberated on the expediency of continuing the Confederation, with some amendments, and rejected that scheme, and adopted the plan of a national government, with a legislature, an executive, and a judiciary of its own. They were asked to preserve the league; they rejected the proposition. They were asked to continue the existing compact between States; they rejected it. They rejected compact, league, and confederation, and set themselves about framing the constitution of a national government; and they accomplished what they undertook.

If men will open their eyes fairly to the lights of history, it is impossible to be deceived on this point. The great object was to supersede the Confederation by a regular government; because, under the Confederation, Congress had power only to make requisitions on States; and if States declined compliance, as they did, there was no remedy but war against such delinquent States. It would seem, from Mr. Jefferson's correspondence, in 1786 and 1787, that he was of opinion that even this remedy ought to be tried. "There will be no money in the treasury," said he, "till the confederacy shows its teeth"; and he suggests that a single frigate would soon levy, on the commerce of a delinquent State, the deficiency of its contribution. But this would be war; and it was evident that a confederacy could not long hold together, which should be at war with its members. The Constitution was adopted to avoid this necessity. It was adopted that there might be a government which should act directly on individuals, without borrowing aid from the State governments. This is clear as light itself on the very face of the provisions of the Constitution, and its whole history tends to the same conclusion. Its framers gave this very reason for their work in the most distinct terms. Allow me to quote but one or two proofs, out of hundreds. That State, so small in territory, but so distinguished for learning and talent, Connecticut, had sent to the general Convention, among other members, Samuel Johnston and Oliver Ellsworth. The Constitution having been framed, it was submitted to a convention of the people of Connecticut for ratification on the part of that State; and Mr. Johnston and Mr. Ellsworth were also members of this convention. On the first day of the debates, being called on to explain the reasons which led the Convention at Philadelphia to recommend such a Constitution, after showing the insufficiency of the existing confederacy, inasmuch as it applied to States, as States, Mr. Johnston proceeded to say:--

"The Convention saw this imperfection in attempting to legislate for States in their political capacity, that the coercion of law can he exercised by nothing but a military force. They have, therefore, gone upon entirely new ground. They have formed one new nation out of the individual States. The Constitution vests in the general legislature a power to make laws in matters of national concern; to appoint judges to decide upon these laws; and to appoint officers to carry them into execution. This excludes the idea of an armed force. The power which is to enforce these laws is to be a legal power, vested in proper magistrates. The force which is to be employed is the energy of law; and this force is to operate only upon individuals who fail in their duty to their country. This is the peculiar glory of the Constitution, that it depends upon the mild and equal energy of the magistracy for the execution of the laws."

In the further course of the debate, Mr. Ellsworth said:--

"In republics it is a fundamental principle, that the majority govern, and that the minority comply with the general voice. How contrary, then, to republican principles, how humiliating, is our present situation! A single State can rise up, and put a *veto* upon the most important public measures. We have seen this actually take place; a single State has controlled the general voice of the Union; a minority, a very small minority, has governed us. So far is this from being consistent with republican principles, that it is, in effect, the worst species of monarchy.

"Hence we see how necessary for the Union is a coercive principle. No man pretends the contrary. We all see and feel this necessity. The only question is, Shall it be a coercion of law, or a coercion of arms? There is no other possible alternative. Where will those who oppose a coercion of law come out? Where will they end? A necessary consequence of their principles is a war of the States one against another. I am for coercion by law; that coercion which acts only upon delinquent individuals. This Constitution does not attempt to coerce sovereign bodies, States, in their political capacity. No coercion is applicable to such bodies, but that of an armed force. If we should attempt to execute the laws of the Union by sending an armed force against a delinquent State, it would involve the good and bad, the innocent and guilty, in the same calamity. But this legal coercion singles out the guilty individual, and punishes him for breaking the laws of the Union."

Indeed, Sir, if we look to all contemporary history, to the numbers of the Federalist, to the debates in the conventions, to the publications of friends and foes, they all agree, that a change had been made from a confederacy of States to a different system; they all agree, that the Convention had formed a Constitution for a national government. With this result some were satisfied, and some were dissatisfied; but all admitted that the thing had been done. In none of these various productions and publications did any one intimate that the new Constitution was but another compact between States in their sovereign capacities. I do not find such an opinion advanced in a single instance. Everywhere, the people were told that the old Confederation was to be abandoned, and a new system to be tried; that a proper government was proposed, to be founded in the name of the people, and to have a regular organization of its own. Everywhere, the people were told that it was to be a government with direct powers to make laws over individuals, and to lay taxes and imposts without the consent of the States. Everywhere, it was understood to be a popular Constitution. It came to the people for their adoption, and was to rest on the same deep foundation as the State constitutions themselves. Its most distinguished advocates, who had been themselves members of the Convention, declared that the very object of submitting the Constitution to the people was, to preclude the possibility of its being regarded as a mere compact. "However gross a heresy," say the writers of the Federalist, "it may be to maintain that a party to a *compact* has a right to revoke that _compact_, the doctrine itself has had respectable advocates. The possibility of a question of this nature proves the necessity of laying the foundations of our national government deeper than in the mere sanction of delegated authority. The fabric of American empire ought to rest on the solid basis of THE CONSENT OF THE PEOPLE."

Such is the language, Sir, addressed to the people, while they yet had the Constitution under consideration. The powers conferred on the new government were perfectly well understood to be conferred, not by any State, or the people of any State, but by the people of the United States. Virginia is more explicit, perhaps, in this particular, than any other State. Her convention, assembled to ratify the Constitution, "in the name and behalf of the people of Virginia, declare and make known, that the powers granted under the Constitution, _being derived from the people of the United States_, may be resumed by them whenever the same shall be perverted to their injury or oppression."

Is this language which describes the formation of a compact between States? or language describing the grant of powers to a new government, by the whole people of the United States?

Among all the other ratifications, there is not one which speaks of the Constitution as a compact between States. Those of Massachusetts and New Hampshire express the transaction, in my opinion, with sufficient accuracy. They recognize the Divine goodness "in affording THE PEOPLE OF THE UNITED STATES an opportunity of entering into an explicit and solemn compact with each other, *by assenting to and ratifying a new Constitution*." You will observe, Sir, that it is the PEOPLE, and not the States, who have entered into this compact; and it is the PEOPLE of all the United States. These conventions, by this form of expression, meant merely to say, that the people of the United States had, by the blessing of Providence, enjoyed the opportunity of establishing a new Constitution, *founded in the consent of the people*. This consent of the people has been called, by European writers, the _social compact_; and, in conformity to this common mode of expression, these conventions speak of that assent, on which the new Constitution was to rest, as an explicit and solemn compact, not which the States had entered into with each other, but which the *people* of the United States had entered into.

Finally, Sir, how can any man get over the words of the Constitution itself?--"WE, THE PEOPLE OF THE UNITED STATES, DO ORDAIN AND ESTABLISH THIS CONSTITUTION." These words must cease to be a part of the Constitution, they must be obliterated from the parchment on which they are written, before any human ingenuity or human argument can remove the popular basis on which that Constitution rests, and turn the instrument into a mere compact between sovereign States.

The second proposition, Sir, which I propose to maintain, is, that no State authority can dissolve the relations subsisting between the government of the United States and individuals; that nothing can dissolve these relations but revolution; and that, therefore, there can be no such thing as *secession* without revolution. All this follows, as it seems to me, as a just consequence, if it be first proved that the Constitution of the United States is a government proper, owing protection to individuals, and entitled to their obedience.

The people, Sir, in every State, live under two governments. They owe obedience to both. These governments, though distinct, are not adverse. Each has its separate sphere, and its peculiar powers and duties. It is not a contest between two sovereigns for the same power, like the wars of the rival houses in England; nor is it a dispute between a government *de facto* and a government *de jure*. It is the case of a division of powers between two governments, made by the people, to whom both are responsible. Neither can dispense with the duty which individuals owe to the other; neither can call itself master of the other: the people are masters of both. This division of power, it is true, is in a great measure unknown in Europe. It is the peculiar system of America; and, though new and singular, it is not incomprehensible. The State constitutions are established by the people of the States. This Constitution is established by the people of all the States. How, then, can a State secede? How can a State undo what the whole people have done? How can she absolve her citizens from their obedience to the laws of the United States? How can she annul their obligations and oaths? How can the members of her legislature renounce their own oaths? Sir, secession, as a revolutionary right, is intelligible; as a right to be proclaimed in the midst of civil commotions, and asserted at the head of armies, I can understand it. But as a practical right, existing under the Constitution, and in conformity with its provisions, it seems to me to be nothing but a plain absurdity; for it supposes resistance to government, under the authority of government itself; it supposes dismemberment, without violating the principles of union; it supposes opposition to law, without crime; it supposes the violation of oaths, without responsibility; it supposes the total overthrow of government, without revolution.

The Constitution, Sir, regards itself as perpetual and immortal. It seeks to establish a union among the people of the States, which shall last through all time. Or, if the common fate of things human must be expected at some period to happen to it, yet that catastrophe is not anticipated.

The instrument contains ample provisions for its amendment, at all times; none for its abandonment, at any time. It declares that new States may come into the Union, but it does not declare that old States may go out. The Union is not a temporaly partnership of States. It is the association of the people, under a constitution of government, uniting their power, joining together their highest interests, cementing their present enjoyments, and blending, in one indivisible mass, all their hopes for the future. Whatsoever is steadfast in just political principles; whatsoever is permanent in the structure of human society; whatsoever there is which can derive an enduring character from being founded on deep-laid principles of constitutional liberty and on the broad foundations of the public will,--all these unite to entitle this instrument to be regarded as a permanent constitution of government.

In the next place, Mr. President, I contend that there is a supreme law of the land, consisting of the Constitution, acts of Congress passed in pursuance of it, and the public treaties. This will not be denied, because such are the very words of the Constitution. But I contend, further, that it rightfully belongs to Congress, and to the courts of the United States, to settle the construction of this supreme law, in doubtful cases. This is denied; and here arises the great practical question, _Who is to construe finally the Constitution of the United States_? We all agree that the Constitution is the supreme law; but who shall interpret that law? In our system of the division of powers between different governments, controversies will necessarily sometimes arise, respecting the extent of the powers of each. Who shall decide these controversies? Does it rest with the general government, in all or any of its departments, to exercise the office of final interpreter? Or may each of the States, as well as the general government, claim this right of ultimate decision? The practical result of this whole debate turns on this point. The gentleman contends that each State may judge for itself of any alleged violation of the Constitution, and may finally decide for itself, and may execute its own decisions by its own power. All the recent proceedings in South Carolina are founded on this claim of right. Her convention has pronounced the revenue laws of the United States unconstitutional; and this decision she does not allow any authority of the United States to overrule or reverse. Of course she rejects the authority of Congress, because the very object of the ordinance is to reverse the decision of Congress; and she rejects, too, the authority of the courts of the United States, because she expressly prohibits all appeal to those courts. It is in order to sustain this asserted right of being her own judge, that she pronounces the Constitution of the United States to be but a compact, to which she is a party, and a sovereign party. If this be established, then the inference is supposed to follow, that, being sovereign, there is no power to control her decision; and her own judgment on her own compact is, and must be, conclusive.

I have already endeavored, Sir, to point out the practical consequences of this doctrine, and to show how utterly inconsistent it is with all ideas of regular government, and how soon its adoption would involve the whole country in revolution and absolute anarchy. I hope it is easy now to show, Sir, that a doctrine bringing such consequences with it is not well founded; that it has nothing to stand on but theory and assumption; and that it is refuted by plain and express constitutional provisions. I think the government of the United States does possess, in its appropriate departments, the authority of final decision on questions of disputed power. I think it possesses this authority, both by necessary implication and by express grant. It will not be denied, Sir, that this authority naturally belongs to all governments. They all exercise it from necessity, and as a consequence of the exercise of other powers. The State governments themselves possess it, except in that class of questions which may arise between them and the general government, and in regard to which they have surrendered it, as well by the nature of the case as by clear constitutional provisions. In other and ordinary cases, whether a particular law be in conformity to the constitution of the State is a question which the State legislature or the State judiciary must determine. We all know that these questions arise daily in the State governments, and are decided by those governments; and I know no government which does not exercise a similar power.

Upon general principles, then, the government of the United States possesses this authority; and this would hardly be denied were it not that there are other governments. But since there are State governments, and since these, like other governments, ordinarily construe their own powers, if the government of the United States construes its own powers also, which construction is to prevail in the case of opposite constructions? And again, as in the case now actually before us, the State governments may undertake, not only to construe their own powers, but to decide directly on the extent of the powers of Congress. Congress has passed a law as being within its just powers; South Carolina denies that this law is within its just powers, and insists that she has the right so to decide this point, and that her decision is final. How are these questions to be settled?

In my opinion, Sir, even if the Constitution of the United States had made no express provision for such cases, it would yet be difficult to maintain, that, in a Constitution existing over four-and-twenty States, with equal authority over all, *one* could claim a right of construing it for the whole. This would seem a manifest impropriety; indeed, an absurdity. If the Constitution is a government existing over all the States, though with limited powers, it necessarily follows, that, to the extent of those powers, it must be supreme. If it be not superior to the authority of a particular State, it is not a national government. But as it is a government, as it has a legislative power of its own, and a judicial power coextensive with the legislative, the inference is irresistible that this government, thus created *by* the whole and *for* the whole, must have an authority superior to that of the particular government of any one part. Congress is the legislature of all the people of the United States; the judiciary of the general government is the judiciary of all the people of the United States. To hold, therefore, that this legislature and this judiciary are subordinate in authority to the legislature and judiciary of a single State, is doing violence to all common sense, and overturning all established principles. Congress must judge of the extent of its own powers so often as it is called on to exercise them, or it cannot act at all; and it must also act independent of State control, or it cannot act at all. The right of State interposition strikes at the very foundation of the legislative power of Congress. It possesses no effective legislative power, if such right of State interposition exists; because it can pass no law not subject to abrogation. It cannot make laws for the Union, if any part of the Union may pronounce its enactments void and of no effect. Its forms of legislation would be an idle ceremony, if, after all, any one of four-and-twenty States might bid defiance to its authority. Without express provision in the Constitution, therefore, Sir, this whole question is necessarily decided by those provisions which create a legislative power and a judicial power. If these exist in a government intended for the whole, the inevitable consequence is, that the laws of this legislative power and the decisions of this judicial power must be binding on and over the whole. No man can form the conception of a government existing over four-and-twenty States, with a regular legislative and judicial power, and of the existence at the same time of an authority, residing elsewhere, to resist, at pleasure or discretion, the enactments and the decisions of such a government. I maintain, therefore, Sir, that, from the nature of the case, and as an inference wholly unavoidable, the acts of Congress and the decisions of the national courts must be of higher authority than State laws and State decisions. If this be not so, there is, there can be, no general government.

But, Mr. President, the Constitution has not left this cardinal point without full and explicit provisions. First, as to the authority of Congress. Having enumerated the specific powers conferred on Congress, the Constitution adds, as a distinct and substantive clause, the following, viz.: "To make all laws which shall be necessary and proper for carrying into execution the foregoing powers, and all other powers vested by this Constitution in the government of the United States, or in any department or officer thereof." If this means any thing, it means that Congress may judge of the true extent and just interpretation of the specific powers granted to it, and may judge also of what is necessary and proper for executing those powers. If Congress is to judge of what is necessary for the execution of its powers, it must, of necessity, judge of the extent and interpretation of those powers.

And in regard, Sir, to the judiciary, the Constitution is still more express and emphatic. It declares that the judicial power shall extend to all *cases* in law or equity arising under the Constitution, laws of the United States, and treaties; that there shall be *one* Supreme Court, and that this Supreme Court shall have appellate jurisdiction of all these cases, subject to such exceptions as Congress may make. It is impossible to escape from the generality of these words. If a case arises under the Constitution, that is, if a case arises depending on the construction of the Constitution, the judicial power of the United States extends to it. It reaches _the case, the question_; it attaches the power of the national judicature to the *case* itself, in whatever court it may arise or exist; and in this *case* the Supreme Court has appellate jurisdiction over all courts whatever. No language could provide with more effect and precision than is here done, for subjecting constitutional questions to the ultimate decision of the Supreme Court. And, Sir, this is exactly what the Convention found it necessary to provide for, and intended to provide for. It is, too, exactly what the people were universally told was done when they adopted the Constitution. One of the first resolutions adopted by the Convention was in these words, viz.: "That the jurisdiction of the national judiciary shall extend to cases which respect _the collection of the national revenue_, and questions which involve the national peace and harmony." Now, Sir, this either had no sensible meaning at all, or else it meant that the jurisdiction of the national judiciary should extend to these questions, *with a paramount authority.* It is not to be supposed that the Convention intended that the power of the national judiciary should extend to these questions, and that the power of the judicatures of the States should also extend to them, *with equal power of final decision.* This would be to defeat the whole object of the provision. There were thirteen judicatures already in existence. The evil complained of, or the danger to be guarded against, was contradiction and repugnance in the decisions of these judicatures. If the framers of the Constitution meant to create a fourteenth, and yet not to give it power to revise and control the decisions of the existing thirteen, then they only intended to augment the existing evil and the apprehended danger by increasing still further the chances of discordant judgments. Why, Sir, has it become a settled axiom in politics that every government must have a judicial power coextensive with its legislative power? Certainly, there is only this reason, namely, that the laws may receive a uniform interpretation and a uniform execution. This object cannot be otherwise attained. A statute is what it is judicially interpreted to be; and if it be construed one way in New Hampshire, and another way in Georgia, there is no uniform law. One supreme court, with appellate and final jurisdiction, is the natural and only adequate means, in any government, to secure this uniformity. The Convention saw all this clearly; and the resolution which I have quoted, never afterwards rescinded, passed through various modifications, till it finally received the form which the article now bears in the Constitution.

It is undeniably true, then, that the framers of the Constitution intended to create a national judicial power, which should be paramount on national subjects. And after the Constitution was framed, and while the whole country was engaged in discussing its merits, one of its most distinguished advocates, Mr. Madison, told the people that it _was true, that, in controversies relating to the boundary between the two jurisdictions, the tribunal which is ultimately to decide is to be established under the general government_. Mr. Martin, who had been a member of the Convention, asserted the same thing to the legislature of Maryland, and urged it as a reason for rejecting the Constitution. Mr. Pinckney, himself also a leading member of the Convention, declared it to the people of South Carolina. Everywhere it was admitted, by friends and foes, that this power was in the Constitution. By some it was thought dangerous, by most it was thought necessary; but by all it was agreed to be a power actually contained in the instrument. The

Convention saw the absolute necessity of some control in the national government over State laws. Different modes of establishing this control were suggested and considered. At one time, it was proposed that the laws of the States should, from time to time, be laid before Congress, and that Congress should possess a negative over them. But this was thought inexpedient and inadmissible; and in its place, and expressly as a substitute for it, the existing provision was introduced; that is to say, a provision by which the federal courts should have authority to overrule such State laws as might be in manifest contravention of the Constitution. The writers of the Federalist, in explaining the Constitution, while it was yet pending before the people, and still unadopted, give this account of the matter in terms, and assign this reason for the article as it now stands. By this provision Congress escaped the necessity of any revision of State laws, left the whole sphere of State legislation quite untouched, and yet obtained a security against any infringement of the constitutional power of the general government. Indeed, Sir, allow me to ask again, if the national judiciary was not to exercise a power of revision on constitutional questions over the judicatures of the States, why was any national judicature erected at all? Can any man give a sensible reason for having a judicial power in this government, unless it be for the sake of maintaining a uniformity of decision on questions arising under the Constitution and laws of Congress, and insuring its execution? And does not this very idea of uniformity necessarily imply that the construction given by the national courts is to be the prevailing construction? How else, Sir, is it possible that uniformity can be preserved? Gentlemen appear to me, Sir, to look at but one side of the question. They regard only the supposed danger of trusting a government with the interpretation of its own powers. But will they view the question in its other aspect? Will they show us how it is possible for a government to get along with four-and-twenty interpreters of its laws and powers? Gentlemen argue, too, as if, in these cases, the State would be always right, and the general government always wrong. But suppose the reverse,--suppose the State wrong (and, since they differ, some of them must be wrong),--are the most important and essential operations of the government to be embarrassed and arrested, because one State holds the contrary opinion? Mr. President, every argument which refers the constitutionality of acts of Congress to State decision appeals from the majority to the minority; it appeals from the common interest to a particular interest; from the counsels of all to the counsel of one; and endeavors to supersede the judgment of the whole by the judgment of a part. I think it is clear. Sir, that the Constitution, by express provision, by definite and unequivocal words, as well as by necessary implication, has constituted the Supreme Court of the United States the appellate tribunal in all cases of a constitutional nature which assume the shape of a suit, in law or equity. And I think I cannot do better than to leave this part of the subject by reading the remarks made upon it in the convention of Connecticut, by Mr. Ellsworth; a gentleman, Sir, who has left behind him, on the records of the government of his country, proofs of the clearest intelligence and of the deepest sagacity, as well as of the utmost purity and integrity of character. "This Constitution," says he, "defines the extent of the powers of the general government. If the general legislature should, at any time, overleap their limits, the judicial department is a constitutional check. If the United States go beyond their powers, if they make a law which the Constitution does not authorize, it is void; and the judiciary power, the national judges, who, to secure their impartiality, are to be made independent, will declare it to be void. On the other hand, if the States go beyond their limits, if they make a law which is a usurpation upon the general government, the law is void; and upright, independent judges will declare it to be so." Nor did this remain merely matter of private opinion. In the very first session of the first Congress, with all these well-known objects, both of the Convention and the people, full and fresh in his mind, Mr. Ellsworth, as is generally understood, reported the bill for the organization of the judicial department, and in that bill made provision for the exercise of this appellate power of the Supreme Court, in all the proper cases, in whatsoever court arising; and this appellate power has now been exercised for more than forty years, without interruption, and without doubt. As to the cases, Sir, which do not come before the courts, those political questions which terminate with the enactments of Congress, it is of necessity that these should be ultimately decided by Congress itself. Like other legislatures, it must be trusted with this power. The members of Congress are chosen by the people, and they are answerable to the people; like other public agents, they are bound by oath to support the Constitution. These are the securities that they will not violate their duty, nor transcend their powers. They are the same securities that prevail in other popular governments; nor is it easy to see how grants of power can be more safely guarded, without rendering them nugatory. If the case cannot come before the courts, and if Congress be not trusted with its decision, who shall decide it? The gentleman says, each State is to decide it for herself. If so, then, as I have already urged, what is law in one State is not law in another. Or, if the resistance of one State compels an entire repeal of the law, then a minority, and that a small one, governs the whole country.

Sir, those who espouse the doctrines of nullification reject, as it seems to me, the first great principle of all republican liberty; that is, that the majority *must* govern. In matters of common concern, the judgment of a majority *must* stand as the judgment of the whole. This is a law imposed on us by the absolute necessity of the case; and if we do not act upon it, there is no possibility of maintaining any government but despotism. We hear loud and repeated denunciations against what is called *majority government*. It is declared, with much warmth, that a majority government cannot be maintained in the United States. What, then, do gentlemen wish? Do they wish to establish a *minority* government? Do they wish to subject the will of the many to the will of the few? The honorable gentleman from South Carolina has spoken of absolute majorities and majorities concurrent; language wholly unknown to our Constitution, and to which it is not easy to affix definite ideas. As far as I understand it, it would teach us that the absolute majority may be found in Congress, but the majority concurrent must be looked for in the States; that is to say, Sir, stripping the matter of this novelty of phrase, that the dissent of one or more States, as States, renders void the decision of a majority of Congress, so far as that State is concerned. And so this doctrine, running but a short career, like other dogmas of the day, terminates in nullification.

If this vehement invective against *majorities* meant no more than that, in the construction of government, it is wise to provide checks and balances, so that there should be various limitations on the power of the mere majority, it would only mean what the Constitution of the United States has already abundantly provided. It is full of such checks and balances. In its very organization, it adopts a broad and most effective principle in restraint of the power of mere majorities. A majority of the people elects the House of Representatives, but it does not elect the Senate. The Senate is elected by the States, each State having, in this respect, an equal power. No law, therefore, can pass, without the assent of the representatives of the people, and a majority of the representatives of the States also. A majority of the representatives of the people must concur, and a majority of the States must concur, in every act of Congress; and the President is elected on a plan compounded of both these principles. But having composed one house of representatives chosen by the people in each State, according to their numbers, and the other of an equal number of members from every State, whether larger or smaller, the Constitution gives to majorities in these houses thus constituted the full and entire power of passing laws, subject always to the constitutional restrictions and to the approval of the President. To subject them to any other power is clear usurpation. The majority of one house may be controlled by the majority of the other; and both may be restrained by the President's negative. These are checks and balances provided by the Constitution, existing in the government itself, and wisely intended to secure deliberation and caution in legislative proceedings. But to resist the will of the majority in both houses, thus constitutionally exercised, to insist on the lawfulness of interposition by an extraneous power; to claim the right of defeating the will of Congress, by setting up against it the will of a single State,--is neither more nor less, as it strikes me, than a plain attempt to overthrow the government. The constituted authorities of the United States are no longer a government, if they be not masters of their own will; they are no longer a government, if an external power may arrest their proceedings; they are no longer a government, if acts passed by both houses, and approved by the President, may be nullified by State vetoes or State ordinances. Does any one suppose it could make any difference, as to the binding authority of an act of Congress, and of the duty of a State to respect it, whether it passed by a mere majority of both houses, or by three fourths of each, or the unanimous vote of each? Within the limits and restrictions of the Constitution, the government of the United States, like all other populpr governments, acts by majorities. It can act no otherwise. Whoever, therefore, denounces the government of majorities, denounces the government of his own country, and denounces all free governments. And whoever would restrain these majorities, while acting within their constitutional limits, by an external power, whatever he may intend, asserts principles which, if adopted, can lead to nothing else than the destruction of the government itself.

Does not the gentleman perceive, Sir, how his argument against majorities might here be retorted upon him? Does he not see how cogently he might be asked, whether it be the character of nullification to practise what it preaches? Look to South Carolina, at the present moment. How far are the rights of minorities there respected? I confess, Sir, I have not known, in peaceable times, the power of the majority carried with a higher hand, or upheld with more relentless disregard of the rights, feelings and principles of the minority;--a minority embracing, as the gentleman himself will admit, a large portion of the worth and respectability of the State;--a minority comprehending in its numbers men who have been associated with him, and with us, in these halls of legislation; men who have served their country at home and honored it abroad; men who would cheerfully lay down their lives for their native State, in any cause which they could regard as the cause of honor and duty; men above fear, and above reproach, whose deepest grief and distress spring from the conviction, that the present proceedings of the State must ultimately reflect discredit upon her. How is this minority, how are these men, regarded? They are enthralled and disfranchised by ordinances and acts of legislation; subjected to tests and oaths, incompatible, as they conscientiously think, with oaths already taken, and obligations already assumed; they are proscribed and denounced as recreants to duty and patriotism, and slaves to a foreign power. Both the spirit which pursues them, and the positive measures which emanate from that spirit, are harsh and proscriptive beyond all precedent within my knowledge, except in periods of professed revolution.

It is not, Sir, one would think, for those who approve these proceedings to complain of the power of majorities.

Mr. President, all popular governments rest on two principles, or two assumptions:--

First, That there is so far a common interest among those over whom the government extends, as that it may provide for the defence, protection, and good government of the whole, without injustice or oppression to parts; and

Secondly, That the representatives of the people, and especially the people themselves, are secure against general corruption, and may be trusted, therefore, with the exercise of power.

Whoever argues against these principles argues against the practicability of all free governments. And whoever admits these, must admit, or cannot deny, that power is as safe in the hands of Congress as in those of other representative bodies. Congress is not irresponsible. Its members are agents of the people, elected by them, answerable to them, and liable to be displaced or superseded, at their pleasure; and they possess as fair a claim to the confidence of the people, while they continue to deserve it, as any other public political agents.

If, then, Sir, the manifest intention of the Convention, and the contemporary admission of both friends and foes, prove any thing; if the plain text of the instrument itself, as well as the necessary implication from other provisions, prove any thing; if the early legislation of Congress, the course of judicial decisions, acquiesced in by all the States for forty years, prove any thing,--then it is proved that there is a supreme law, and a final interpreter.

My fourth and last proposition, Mr. President, was, that any attempt by a State to abrogate or nullify acts of Congress is a usurpation on the powers of the general government and on the equal rights of other States, a violation of the Constitution, and a proceeding essentially revolutionary. This is undoubtedly true, if the preceding propositions be regarded as proved. If the government of the United States be trusted with the duty, in any department, of declaring the extent of its own powers, then a State ordinance, or act of legislation, authorizing resistance to an act of Congress, on the alleged ground of its unconstitutionally, is manifestly a usurpation upon its powers. If the States have equal rights in matters concerning the whole, then for one State to set up her judgment against the judgment of the rest, and to insist on executing that judgment by force, is also a manifest usurpation on the rights of other States. If the Constitution of the United States be a government proper, with authority to pass laws, and to give them a uniform interpretation and execution, then the interposition of a State, to enforce her own construction, and to resist, as to herself, that law which binds the other States, is a violation of the Constitution.

If that be revolutionary which arrests the legislative, executive, and judicial power of government, dispenses with existing oaths and obligations of obedience, and elevates another power to supreme dominion, then nullification is revolutionary. Or if that be revolutionary the natural tendency and practical effect of which are to break the Union into fragments, to sever all connection among the people of the respective States, and to prostrate this general government in the dust, then nullification is revolutionary. Nullification, Sir, is as distinctly revolutionary as secession; but I cannot say that the revolution which it seeks is one of so respectable a character. Secession would, it is true, abandon the Constitution altogether; but then it would profess to abandon it. Whatever other inconsistencies it might run into, one, at least, it would avoid. It would not belong to a government, while it rejected its authority. It would not repel the burden, and continue to enjoy the benefits. It would not aid in passing laws which others are to obey, and yet reject their authority as to itself. It would not undertake to reconcile obedience to public authority with an asserted right of command over that same authority. It would not be in the government, and above the government, at the same time. But though secession may be a more respectable mode of attaining the object than nullification, it is not more truly revolutionary. Each, and both, resist the constitutional authorities; each, and both, would sever the Union and subvert the government.

Mr. President, having detained the Senate so long already, I will not now examine at length the ordinance and laws of South Carolina. These papers are well drawn for their purpose. Their authors understood their own objects. They are called a peaceable remedy, and we have been told that South Carolina, after all, intends nothing but a lawsuit. A very few words, Sir, will show the nature of this peaceable remedy, and of the lawsuit which South Carolina contemplates.

In the first place, the ordinance declares the law of last July, and all other laws of the United States laying duties, to be absolutely null and void, and makes it unlawful for the constituted authorities of the United States to enforce the payment of such duties. It is therefore, Sir, an indictable offence, at this moment, in South Carolina, for any person to be concerned in collecting revenue under the laws of the United States. It being declared, by what is considered a fundamental law of the State, unlawful to collect these duties, an indictment lies, of course, against any one concerned in such collection; and he is, on general principles, liable to be punished by fine and imprisonment. The terms, it is true, are, that it is unlawful "to enforce the payment of duties"; but every custom-house officer enforces payment while he detains the goods in order to obtain such payment. The ordinance, therefore, reaches everybody concerned in the collection of the duties.

This is the first step in the prosecution of the peaceable remedy. The second is more decisive. By the act commonly called the _replevin_ law, any person whose goods are seized or detained by the collector for the payment of duties may sue out a writ of replevin, and, by virtue of that writ, the goods are to be restored to him. A writ of replevin is a writ which the sheriff is bound to execute, and for the execution of which he is bound to employ force, if necessary. He may call out the _posse_, and must do so, if resistance be made. This _posse_ may be armed or unarmed. It may come forth with military array, and under the lead of military men. Whatever number of troops may be assembled in Charleston, they may be summoned, with the governor, or commander-in-chief, at their head, to come in aid of the sheriff. It is evident, then, Sir, that the whole military power of the State is to be employed, if necessary, in dispossessing the custom-house officers, and in seizing and holding the goods, without paying the duties. This is the second step in the peaceable remedy.

Sir, whatever pretences may be set up to the contrary, this is the direct application of force, and of military force. It is unlawful, in itself, to replevy goods in the custody of the collectors. But this unlawful act is to be done, and it is to be done by power. Here is a plain interposition, by physical force, to resist the laws of the Union. The legal mode of collecting duties is to detain the goods till such duties are paid or secured. But force comes, and overpowers the collector and his assistants, and takes away the goods, leaving the duties unpaid. There cannot be a clearer case of forcible resistance to law. And it is provided that the goods thus seized shall be held against any attempt to retake them, by the same force which seized them.

Having thus dispossessed the officers of the government of the goods, without payment of duties, and seized and secured them by the strong arm of the State, only one thing more remains to be done, and that is, to cut off all possibility of legal redress; and that, too, is accomplished, or thought to be accomplished. The ordinance declares, _that all judicial proceedings, founded on the revenue laws_ (including, of course, proceedings in the courts of the United States), _shall be null and void_. This nullifies the judicial power of the United States. Then comes the test-oath act. This requires all State judges and jurors in the State courts to swear that they will execute the ordinance, and all acts of the legislature passed in pursuance thereof. The ordinance declares, that no appeal shall be allowed from the decision of the State courts to the Supreme Court of the United States; and the replevin act makes it an indictable offence for any clerk to furnish a copy of the record, for the purpose of such appeal.

The two principal provisions on which South Carolina relies, to resist the laws of the United States, and nullify the authority of this government, are, therefore, these:--

1. A forcible seizure of goods, before duties are paid or secured, by the power of the State, civil and military.

2. The taking away, by the most effectual means in her power, of all legal redress in the courts of the United States; the confining of judicial proceedings to her own State tribunals; and the compelling of her judges and jurors of these her own courts to take an oath, beforehand, that they will decide all cases according to the ordinance, and the acts passed under it; that is, that they will decide the cause one way.

They do not swear to *try* it, on its own merits; they only swear to *decide* it as nullification requires. The character, Sir, of these provisions defies comment. Their object is as plain as their means are extraordinary. They propose direct resistance, by the whole power of the State, to laws of Congress, and cut off, by methods deemed adequate, any redress by legal and judicial authority. They arrest legislation, defy the executive, and banish the judicial power of this government. They authorize and command acts to be done, and done by force, both of numbers and of arms, which, if done, and done by force, are clearly acts of rebellion and treason.

Such, Sir, are the laws of South Carolina; such, Sir, is the peaceable remedy of nullification. Has not nullification reached, Sir, even thus early, that point of direct and forcible resistance to law to which I intimated, three years ago, it plainly tended?

And now, Mr. President, what is the reason for passing laws like these? What are the oppressions experienced under the Union, calling for measures which thus threaten to sever and destroy it? What invasions of public liberty, what ruin to private happiness, what long list of rights violated, or wrongs unredressed, is to justify to the country, to posterity, and to the world, this assault upon the free Constitution of the United States, this great and glorious work of our fathers? At this very moment, Sir, the whole land smiles in peace, and rejoices in plenty. A general and a high prosperity pervades the country; and, judging by the common standard, by increase of population and wealth, or judging by the opinions of that portion of her people not embarked in these dangerous and desperate measures, this prosperity overspreads South Carolina herself.

Thus happy at home, our country, at the same time, holds high the character of her institutions, her power, her rapid growth, and her future destiny, in the eyes of all foreign states. One danger only creates hesitation; one doubt only exists, to darken the otherwise unclouded brightness of that aspect which she exhibits to the view and to the admiration of the world. Need I say, that that doubt respects the permanency of our Union? and need I say, that that doubt is now caused, more than any thing else, by these very proceedings of South Carolina? Sir, all Europe is, at this moment, beholding us, and looking for the issue of this controversy; those who hate free institutions, with malignant hope; those who love them, with deep anxiety and shivering fear.

The cause, then, Sir, the cause! Let the world know the cause which has thus induced one State of the Union to bid defiance to the power of the whole, and openly to talk of secession. Sir, the world will scarcely believe that this whole controversy, and all the desperate measures which its support requires, have no other foundation than a difference of opinion upon a provision of the Constitution, between a majority of the people of South Carolina, on one side, and a vast majority of the whole people of the United States, on the other. It will not credit the fact, it will not admit the possibility, that, in an enlightened age, in a free, popular republic, under a constitution where the people govern, as they must always govern under such systems, by majorities, at a time of unprecedented prosperity, without practical oppression, without evils such as may not only be pretended, but felt and experienced,--evils not slight or temporary, but deep, permanent, and intolerable,--a single State should rush into conflict with all the rest, attempt to put down the power of the Union by her own laws, and to support those laws by her military power, and thus break up and destroy the world's last hope. And well the world may be incredulous. We, who see and hear it, can ourselves hardly yet believe it. Even after all that had preceded it, this ordinance struck the country with amazement. It was incredible and inconceivable that South Carolina should plunge headlong into resistance to the laws on a matter of opinion, and on a question in which the preponderance of opinion, both of the present day and of all past time, was so overwhelmingly against her. The ordinance declares that Congress has exceeded its just power by laying duties on imports, intended for the protection of manufactures. This is the opinion of South Carolina; and on the strength of that opinion she nullifies the laws. Yet has the rest of the country no right to its opinion also? Is one State to sit sole arbitress? She maintains that those laws are plain, deliberate, and palpable violations of the Constitution; that she has a sovereign right to decide this matter; and that, having so decided, she is authorized to resist their execution by her own sovereign power; and she declares that she will resist it, though such resistance should shatter the Union into atoms.

Mr. President, I do not intend to discuss the propriety of these laws at large; but I will ask, How are they shown to be thus plainly and palpably unconstitutional? Have they no countenance at all in the Constitution itself? Are they quite new in the history of the government? Are they a sudden and violent usurpation on the rights of the States? Sir, what will the civilized world say, what will posterity say, when they learn that similar laws have existed from the very foundation of the government, that for thirty years the power was never questioned, and that no State in the Union has more freely and unequivocally admitted it than South Carolina herself?

To lay and collect duties and imposts is an *express power* granted by the Constitution to Congress. It is, also, an _exclusive power_; for the Constitution as expressly prohibits all the States from exercising it themselves. This express and exclusive power is unlimited in the terms of the grant, but is attended with two specific restrictions: first, that all duties and imposts shall be equal in all the States; second, that no duties shall be laid on exports. The power, then, being granted, and being attended with these two restrictions, and no more, who is to impose a third restriction on the general words of the grant? If the power to lay duties, as known among all other nations, and as known in all our history, and as it was perfectly understood when the Constitution was adopted, includes a right of discriminating while exercising the power, and of laying some duties heavier and some lighter, for the sake of encouraging our own domestic products, what authority is there for giving to the words used in the Constitution a new, narrow, and unusual meaning? All the limitations which the Constitution intended, it has expressed; and what it has left unrestricted is as much a part of its will as the restraints which it has imposed.

But these laws, it is said, are unconstitutional on account of the *motive*. How, Sir, can a law be examined on any such ground? How is the motive to be ascertained? One house, or one member, may have one motive; the other house, or another member, another. One motive may operate to-day, and another to-morrow. Upon any such mode of reasoning as this, one law might be unconstitutional now, and another law, in exactly the same words, perfectly constitutional next year. Besides, articles may not only be taxed for the purpose of protecting home products, but other articles may be left free, for the same purpose and with the same motive. A law, therefore, would become unconstitutional from what it omitted, as well as from what it contained. Mr. President, it is a settled principle, acknowledged in all legislative halls, recognized before all tribunals, sanctioned by the general sense and understanding of mankind, that there can be no inquiry into the motives of those who pass laws, for the purpose of determining on their validity. If the law be within the fair meaning of the words in the grant of the power, its authority must be admitted until it is repealed. This rule, everywhere acknowledged, everywhere admitted, is so universal and so completely without exception, that even an allegation of fraud, in the majority of a legislature, is not allowed as a ground to set aside a law.

But, Sir, is it true that the motive for these laws is such as is stated? I think not. The great object of all these laws is, unquestionably, revenue. If there were no occasion for revenue, the laws would not have been passed; and it is notorious that almost the entire revenue of the country is derived from them. And as yet we have collected none too much revenue. The treasury has not been more reduced for many years than it is at the present moment. All that South Carolina can say is, that, in passing the laws which she now undertakes to nullify, _particular imported articles were taxed, from a regard to the protection of certain articles of domestic manufacture, higher than they would have been had no such regard been entertained_. And she insists, that, according to the Constitution, no such discrimination can be allowed; that duties should be laid for revenue, and revenue only; and that it is unlawful to have reference, in any case, to protection. In other words, she denies the power of DISCRIMINATION. She does not, and cannot, complain of excessive taxation; on the contrary, she professes to be willing to pay any amount for revenue, merely as revenue; and up to the present moment there is no surplus of revenue. Her grievance, then, that plain and palpable violation of the Constitution which she insists has taken place, is simply the exercise of the power of DISCRIMINATION. Now, Sir, is the exercise of this power of discrimination plainly and palpably unconstitutional?

I have already said, the power to lay duties is given by the Constitution in broad and general terms. There is also conferred on Congress the whole power of regulating commerce, in another distinct provision. Is it clear and palpable, Sir, can any man say it is a case beyond doubt, that, under these two powers, Congress may not justly _discriminate_, in laying duties, _for the purpose of countervailing the policy of foreign nations, or of favoring our own home productions_? Sir, what ought to conclude this question for ever, as it would seem to me, is, that the regulation of commerce and the imposition of duties are, in all commercial nations, powers avowedly and constantly exercised for this very end. That undeniable truth ought to settle the question; because the Constitution ought to be considered, when it uses well-known language, as using it in its well-known sense. But it is equally undeniable, that it has been, from the very first, fully believed that this power of discrimination was conferred on Congress; and the Constitution was itself recommended, urged upon the people, and enthusiastically insisted on in some of the States, for that very reason. Not that, at that time, the country was extensively engaged in manufactures, especially of the kinds now existing. But the trades and crafts of the seaport towns, the business of the artisans and manual laborers,--those employments, the work in which supplies so great a portion of the daily wants of all classes,--all these looked to the new Constitution as a source of relief from the severe distress which followed the war. It would, Sir, be unpardonable, at so late an hour, to go into details on this point; but the truth is as I have stated. The papers of the day, the resolutions of public meetings, the debates in the contentions, all that we open our eyes upon in the history of the times, prove it.

Sir, the honorable gentleman from South Carolina has referred to two incidents connected with the proceedings of the Convention at Philadelphia, which he thinks are evidence to show that the power of protecting manufactures by laying duties, and by commercial regulations, was not intended to be given to Congress. The first is, as he says, that a power to protect manufactures was expressly proposed, but not granted. I think, Sir, the gentleman is quite mistaken in relation to this part of the proceedings of the Convention. The whole history of the occurrence to which he alludes is simply this. Towards the conclusion of the Convention, after the provisions of the Constitution had been mainly agreed upon, after the power to lay duties and the power to regulate commerce had both been granted, a long list of propositions was made and referred to the committee, containing various miscellaneous powers, some or all of which it was thought might be properly vested in Congress. Among these was a power to establish a university; to grant charters of incorporation; to regulate stage-coaches on the post-roads, and also the power to which the gentleman refers, and which is expressed in these words: "To establish public institutions, rewards, and immunities, for the promotion of agriculture, commerce, trades, and manufactures." The committee made no report on this or various other propositions in the same list. But the only inference from this omission is, that neither the committee nor the Convention thought it proper to authorize Congress "to establish public institutions, rewards, and immunities," for the promotion of manufactures, and other interests. The Convention supposed it had done enough,--at any rate, it had done all it intended,--when it had given to Congress, in general terms, the power to lay imposts and the power to regulate trade. It is not to be argued, from its omission to give more, that it meant to take back what it had already given. It had given the impost power; it had given the regulation of trade; and it did not deem it necessary to give the further and distinct power of establishing public institutions.

The other fact, Sir, on which the gentleman relies, is the declaration of Mr. Martin to the legislature of Maryland. The gentleman supposes Mr. Martin to have urged against the Constitution, that it did not contain the power of protection. But if the gentleman will look again at what Mr. Martin said, he will find, I think, that what Mr. Martin complained of was, that the Constitution, by its prohibitions on the States, had taken away from the States themselves the power of protecting their own manufactures by duties on imports. This is undoubtedly true; but I find no expression of Mr. Martin intimating that the Constitution had not conferred on Congress the same power which it had thus taken from the States.

But, Sir, let us go to the first Congress; let us look in upon this and the other house, at the first session of their organization.

We see, in both houses, men distinguished among the framers, friends, and advocates of the Constitution. We see in both, those who had drawn, discussed, and matured the instrument in the Convention, explained and defended it before the people, and were now elected members of Congress, to put the new government into motion, and to carry the powers of the Constitution into beneficial execution. At the head of the government was WASHINGTON himself, who had been President of the Convention; and in his cabinet were others most thoroughly acquainted with the history of the Constitution, and distinguished for the part taken in its discussion. If these persons were not acquainted with the meaning of the Constitution, if they did not understand the work of their own hands, who can understand it, or who shall now interpret it to us?

Sir, the volume which records the proceedings and debates of the first session of the House of Representatives lies before me. I open it, and I find that, having provided for the administration of the necessary oaths, the very first measure proposed for consideration is, the laying of imposts; and in the very first committee of the whole into which the House of Representatives ever resolved itself, on this its earliest subject, and in this its very first debate, the duty of so laying the imposts as to encourage manufactures was advanced and enlarged upon by almost every speaker, and doubted or denied by none. The first gentleman who suggests this as the clear duty of Congress, and as an object necessary to be attended to, is Mr. Fitzsimons, of Pennsylvania; the second, Mr. White, of VIRGINIA; the third, Mr.

Tucker, of SOUTH CAROLINA.

But the great leader, Sir, on this occasion, was Mr. Madison. Was *he* likely to know the intentions of the Convention and the people? Was *he* likely to understand the Constitution? At the second sitting of the committee, Mr. Madison explained his own opinions of the duty of Congress, fully and explicitly. I must not detain you, Sir, with more than a few short extracts from these opinions, but they are such as are clear, intelligible, and decisive. "The States," says he, "that are most advanced in population, and ripe for manufactures, ought to have their particular interest attended to, in some degree. While these States retained the power of making regulations of trade, they had the power to cherish such institutions. By adopting the present Constitution, they have thrown the exercise of this power into other hands; they must have done this with an expectation that those interests would not be neglected here." In another report of the same speech, Mr. Madison is represented as using still stronger language; as saying that, the Constitution having taken this power away from the States and conferred it on Congress, it would be a *fraud* on the States and on the people were Congress to refuse to exercise it.

Mr. Madison argues, Sir, on this early and interesting occasion, very justly and liberally, in favor of the general principles of unrestricted commerce. But he argues, also, with equal force and clearness, for certain important exceptions to these general principles. The first, Sir, respects those manufactures which had been brought forward under encouragement by the State governments. "It would be cruel," says Mr. Madison, "to neglect them, and to divert their industry into other channels; for it is not possible for the hand of man to shift from one employment to another without being injured by the change." Again: "There may be some manufactures which, being once formed, can advance towards perfection without any adventitious aid; while others, for want of the fostering hand of government, will be unable to go on at all. Legislative provision, therefore, will be necessary to collect the proper objects for this purpose; and this will form another exception to my general principle." And again: "The next exception that occurs is one on which great stress is laid by some well-informed men, and this with great plausibility; that each nation should have, within itself, the means of defence, independent of foreign supplies; that, in whatever relates to the operations of war, no State ought to depend upon a precarious supply from any part of the world. There may be some truth in this remark; and therefore it is proper for legislative attention."

In the same debate, Sir, Mr. Burk, from SOUTH CAROLINA, supported a duty on hemp, for the express purpose of encouraging its growth on the strong lands of South Carolina. "Cotton," he said, "was also in contemplation among them, and, if good seed could be procured, he hoped might succeed." Afterwards, Sir, the cotton was obtained, its culture was protected, and it did succeed. Mr. Smith, a very distinguished member from the SAME STATE, observed: "It has been said, and justly, that the States which adopted this Constitution expected its administration would be conducted with a favorable hand. The manufacturing States wished the encouragement of manufactures, the maritime States the encouragement of ship-building, and the agricultural States the encouragement of agriculture."

Sir, I will detain the Senate by reading no more extracts from these debates. I have already shown a majority of the members of SOUTH CAROLINA, in this very first session, acknowledging this power of protection, voting for its exercise, and proposing its extension to their own products. Similar propositions came from Virginia; and, indeed, Sir, in the whole debate, at whatever page you open the volume, you find the power admitted, and you find it applied to the protection of particular articles, or not applied, according to the discretion of Congress. No man denied the power, no man doubted it; the only questions were, in regard to the several articles proposed to be taxed, whether they were fit subjects for protection, and what the amount of that protection ought to be. Will gentlemen, Sir, now answer the argument drawn from these proceedings of the first Congress? Will they undertake to deny that that Congress did act on the avowed principle of protection? Or, if they admit it, will they tell us how those who framed the Constitution fell, thus early, into this great mistake about its meaning? Will they tell us how it should happen that they had so soon forgotten their own sentiments and their own purposes? I confess I have seen no answer to this argument, nor any respectable attempt to answer it. And, Sir, how did this debate terminate? What law was passed? There it stands, Sir, among the statutes, the second law in the book. It has a _preamble_, and that preamble expressly recites, that the duties which it imposes are laid "for the support of government, for the discharge of the debts of the United States, and *the encouragement and protection of manufactures*." Until, Sir, this early legislation, thus coeval with the Constitution itself, thus full and explicit, can be explained away, no man can doubt of the meaning of that instrument in this respect.

Mr. President, this power of _discrimination_, thus admitted, avowed, and practised upon in the first revenue act, has never been denied or doubted until within a few years past. It was not at all doubted in 1816, when it became necessary to adjust the revenue to a state of peace. On the contrary, the power was then exercised, not without opposition as to its expediency, but, as far as I remember or have understood, without the slightest opposition founded on any supposed want of constitutional authority. Certainly, SOUTH CAROLINA did not doubt it. The tariff of 1816 was introduced, carried through, and established, under the lead of South Carolina. Even the minimum policy is of South Carolina origin. The honorable gentleman himself supported, and ably supported, the tariff of 1816. He has informed us, Sir, that his speech on that occasion was sudden and off-hand, he being called up by the request of a friend. I am sure the gentleman so remembers it, and that it was so; but there is, nevertheless, much method, arrangement, and clear exposition in that extempore speech. It is very able, very, very much to the point, and very decisive. And in another speech, delivered two months earlier, on the proposition to repeal the internal taxes, the honorable gentleman had touched the same subject, and had declared "*that a certain encouragement ought to be extended at least to our woollen and cotton manufactures.*" I do not quote these speeches, Sir, for the purpose of showing that the honorable gentleman has changed his opinion: my object is other and higher. I do it for the sake of saying that that cannot be so plainly and palpably unconstitutional as to warrant resistance to law, nullification, and revolution, which the honorable gentleman and his friends have heretofore agreed to and acted upon without doubt and without hesitation. Sir, it is no answer to say that the tariff of 1816 was a revenue bill. So are they all revenue bills. The point is, and the truth is, that the tariff of 1816, like the rest, _did discriminate_; it did distinguish one article from another; it did lay duties for protection. Look to the case of coarse cottons under the minimum calculation: the duty on these was from sixty to eighty per cent. Something beside revenue, certainly, was intended in this; and, in fact, the law cut up our whole commerce with India in that article.

It is, Sir, only within a few years that Carolina has denied the constitutionality of these protective laws. The gentleman himself has narrated to us the true history of her proceedings on this point. He says, that, after the passing of the law of 1828, despairing then of being able to abolish the system of protection, political men went forth among the people, and set up the doctrine that the system was unconstitutional. "_And the people_," says the honorable gentleman, "*received the doctrine.*" This, I believe, is true, Sir. The people did then receive the doctrine; they had never entertained it before. Down to that period, the constitutionality of these laws had been no more doubted in South Carolina than elsewhere. And I suspect it is true, Sir, and I deem it a great misfortune, that, to the present moment, a great portion of the people of the State have never yet seen more than one side of the argument. I believe that thousands of honest men are involved in scenes now passing, led away by one-sided views of the question, and following their leaders by the impulses of an unlimited confidence. Depend upon it, Sir, if we can avoid the shock of arms, a day for reconsideration and reflection will come; truth and reason will act with their accustomed force, and the public opinion of South Carolina will be restored to its usual constitutional and patriotic tone.

But, Sir, I hold South Carolina to her ancient, her cool, her uninfluenced, her deliberate opinions. I hold her to her own admissions, nay, to her own claims and pretensions, in 1789, in the first Congress, and to her acknowledgments and avowed sentiments through a long series of succeeding years. I hold her to the principles on which she led Congress to act in 1816; or, if she have changed her own opinions, I claim some respect for those who still retain the same opinions. I say she is precluded from asserting that doctrines, which she has herself so long and so ably sustained, are plain, palpable, and dangerous violations of the Constitution.

Mr. President, if the friends of nullification should be able to propagate their opinions, and give them practical effect, they would, in my judgment, prove themselves the most skilful "architects of ruin," the most effectual extinguishers of high-raised expectation, the greatest blasters of human hopes, that any age has produced. They would stand up to proclaim, in tones which would pierce the ears of half the human race, that the last great experiment of representative government had failed. They would send forth sounds, at the hearing of which the doctrine of the divine right of kings would feel, even in its grave, a returning sensation of vitality and resuscitation. Millions of eyes, of those who now feed their inherent love of liberty on the success of the American example, would turn away from beholding our dismemberment, and find no place on earth whereon to rest their gratified sight. Amidst the incantations and orgies of nullification, secession, disunion, and revolution, would be celebrated the funeral rites of constitutional and republican liberty.

But, Sir, if the government do its duty, if it act with firmness and with moderation, these opinions cannot

prevail. Be assured, Sir, be assured, that, among the political sentiments of this people, the love of union is still uppermost. They will stand fast by the Constitution, and by those who defend it. I rely on no temporary expedients, on no political combination; but I rely on the true American feeling, the genuine patriotism of the people, and the imperative decision of the public voice. Disorder and confusion, indeed, may arise; scenes of commotion and contest are threatened, and perhaps may come. With my whole heart, I pray for the continuance of the domestic peace and quiet of the country. I desire, most ardently, the restoration of affection and harmony to all its parts. I desire that every citizen of the whole country may look to this government with no other sentiments than those of grateful respect and attachment. But I cannot yield even to kind feelings the cause of the Constitution, the true glory of the country, and the great trust which we hold in our hands for succeeding ages. If the Constitution cannot be maintained without meeting these scenes of commotion and contest, however unwelcome, they must come. We cannot, we must not, we dare not, omit to do that which, in our judgment, the safety of the Union requires. Not regardless of consequences, we must yet meet consequences; seeing the hazards which surround the discharge of public duty, it must yet be discharged. For myself, Sir, I shun no responsibility justly devolving on me, here or elsewhere, in attempting to maintain the cause. I am bound to it by indissoluble ties of affection and duty, and I shall cheerfully partake in its fortunes and its fate. I am ready to perform my own appropriate part, whenever and wherever the occasion may call on me, and to take my chance among those upon whom blows may fall first and fall thickest. I shall exert every faculty I possess in aiding to prevent the Constitution from being nullified, destroyed, or impaired; and even should I see it fall, I will still, with a voice feeble, perhaps, but earnest as ever issued from human lips, and with fidelity and zeal which nothing shall extinguish, call on the PEOPLE to come to its rescue.
[Footnote 1: Mr. Rives.]

PUBLIC DINNER AT NEW YORK.
A SPEECH DELIVERED AT A PUBLIC DINNER GIVEN BY A LARGE NUMBER OF CITIZENS OF NEW YORK, IN HONOR OF MR. WEBSTER, ON MARCH 10TH, 1831.

[In February, 1831, several distinguished gentlemen of the city of New York, in behalf of themselves and a large number of other citizens, invited Mr. Webster to a public dinner, as a mark of their respect for the value and success of his efforts, in the preceding session of Congress, in defence of the Constitution of the United States. His speech in reply to Mr. Hayne (contained in an earlier part of this volume), which, by that time, had been circulated and read through the country to a greater extent than any speech ever before delivered in Congress, was the particular effort which led to this invitation.
The dinner took place at the City Hotel, on the 10th of March, and was attended by a very large assembly. Chancellor Kent presided, and, in proposing to the company the health of their guest, made the following remarks:--
"New England has been long fruitful in great men, the necessary consequence of the admirable discipline of her institutions; and we are this day honored with the presence of one of those cherished objects of her attachment and pride, who has an undoubted and peculiar title to our regard. It is a plain truth, that he who defends the constitution of his country by his wisdom in council is entitled to share her gratitude with those who protect it by valor in the field. Peace has its victories as well as war. We all recollect a late memorable occasion, when the exalted talents and enlightened patriotism of the gentleman to whom I have alluded were exerted in the support of our national Union and the sound interpretation of its charter.
"If there be any one political precept pre-eminent above all others and acknowledged by all, it is that which dictates the absolute necessity of a union of the States under one government, and that government clothed with those attributes and powers with which the existing Constitution has invested it. We are indebted, under Providence, to the operation and influence of the powers of that Constitution for our national honor abroad and for unexampled prosperity at home. Its future stability depends upon the firm support and due exercise of its legitimate powers in all their branches. A tendency to disunion, to anarchy among the members rather than to tyranny in the head, has been heretofore the melancholy fate of all the federal governments of ancient and modern Europe. Our Union and national Constitution were formed, as we have hitherto been led to believe, under better auspices and with improved wisdom. But there was a deadly principle of disease inherent in the system. The assumption by any member of the Union of the right to

question and resist, or annul, as its own judgment should dictate, either the laws of Congress, or the treaties, or the decisions of the federal courts, or the mandates of the executive power, duly made and promulgated as the Constitution prescribes, was a most dangerous assumption of power, leading to collision and the destruction of the system. And if, contrary to all our expectations, we should hereafter fail in the grand experiment of a confederate government extending over some of the fairest portions of this continent, and destined to act, at the same time, with efficiency and harmony, we should most grievously disappoint the hopes of mankind, and blast for ever the fruits of the Revolution.

"But, happily for us, the refutation of such dangerous pretensions, on the occasion referred to, was signal and complete. The false images and delusive theories which had perplexed the thoughts and disturbed the judgments of men, were then dissipated in like manner as spectres disappear at the rising of the sun. The inestimable value of the Union, and the true principles of the Constitution, were explained by clear and accurate reasonings, and enforced by pathetic and eloquent illustrations. The result was the more auspicious, as the heretical doctrines which were then fairly reasoned down had been advanced by a very respectable portion of the Union, and urged on the floor of the Senate by the polished mind, manly zeal, and honored name of a distinguished member from the South.

"The consequences of that discussion have been extremely beneficial. It turned the attention of the public to the great doctrines of national rights and national union. Constitutional law ceased to remain wrapped up in the breasts, and taught only by the responses, of the living oracles of the law. Socrates was said to have drawn down philosophy from the skies, and scattered it among the schools. It may with equal truth be said, that constitutional law, by means of those senatorial discussions and the master genius that guided them, was rescued from the archives of our tribunals and the libraries of lawyers, and placed under the eye, and submitted to the judgment, of the American people. _Their verdict is with us, and from it, there lies no appeal._"

As soon as the immense cheering and acclamations with which this address and toast were received had subsided, Mr. Webster rose and addressed the company as follows.]

I owe the honor of this occasion, Gentlemen, to your patriotic and affectionate attachment to the Constitution of our country. For an effort, well intended, however otherwise of unpretending character, made in the discharge of public duty, and designed to maintain the Constitution and vindicate its just powers, you have been pleased to tender me this token of your respect. It would be idle affectation to deny that it gives me singular gratification. Every public man must naturally desire the approbation of his fellow-citizens; and though it may be supposed that I should be anxious, in the first place, not to disappoint the expectations of those whose immediate representative I am, it is not possible but that I should feel, nevertheless, the high value of such a mark of esteem as is here offered. But, Gentlemen, I am conscious that the main purpose of this occasion is higher than mere manifestation of personal regard. It is to evince your devotion to the Constitution, your sense of its transcendent value, and your just alarm at whatever threatens to weaken its proper authority, or endanger its existence.

Gentlemen, this could hardly be otherwise. It would be strange, indeed, if the members of this vast commercial community should not be first and foremost to rally for the Constitution, whenever opinions and doctrines are advanced hostile to its principles. Where sooner than here, where louder than here, may we expect a patriotic voice to be raised, when the union of the States is threatened? In this great emporium, at this central point of the united commerce of the United States, of all places, we may expect the warmest, the most determined and universal feeling of attachment to the national government. Gentlemen, no one can estimate more highly than I do the natural advantages of your city. No one entertains a higher opinion than myself, also, of that spirit of wise and liberal policy, which has actuated the government of your own great State in the accomplishment of high objects, important to the growth and prosperity both of the State and the city. But all these local advantages, and all this enlightened state policy, could never have made your city what it now is, without the aid and protection of a general government, extending over all the States, and establishing for all a common and uniform system of commercial regulation. Without national character, without public credit, without systematic finance, without uniformity of commercial laws, all other advantages possessed by this city would have decayed and perished, like unripe fruit. A general government was, for years before it was instituted, the great object of desire to the inhabitants of this city. New York, at a very early day, was conscious of her local advantages for commerce; she saw her destiny, and was eager to embrace it; but nothing else than a general government could make free her path before her, and set her forward on her brilliant career. She early saw all this, and to the accomplishment of this great and indispensable object she bent every faculty, and exerted every effort. She was not mistaken. She formed no false judgment. At the moment of the adoption of the Constitution, New York was the capital of one State, and contained thirty-two or three thousand people. It now contains more than two hundred thousand people, and is justly regarded as the commercial capital, not only of all the United States, but of the whole continent also, from the pole to the South Sea. Every page of her history, for the last forty years, bears high and irresistible testimony to the benefits and blessings of the general government. Her astonishing growth is referred to, and quoted, all the world over, as one of the most striking proofs of the effects of our Federal Union. To suppose her now to be easy and indifferent, when notions are advanced tending to its dissolution, would be to suppose her equally forgetful of the past and blind to the present, alike ignorant of her own history and her own interest, metamorphosed, from all that she has been, into a being tired of its prosperity, sick of its own growth and greatness, and infatuated for its own destruction. Every blow aimed at the union of the States strikes on the tenderest nerve of her interest and her happiness. To bring the Union into debate is to bring her own future prosperity into debate also. To speak of arresting the laws of the Union, of interposing State power in matters of commerce and revenue, of weakening the full and just authority of the general government, would be, in regard to this city, but another mode of speaking of commercial ruin, of abandoned wharfs, of vacated houses, of diminished and dispersing population, of bankrupt merchants, of mechanics without employment, and laborers without bread. The growth of this city and the Constitution of the United States are coevals and contemporaries. They began together, they have flourished together, and if rashness and folly destroy one, the other will follow it to the tomb.

Gentlemen, it is true, indeed, that the growth of this city is extraordinary, and almost unexampled. It is now, I believe, sixteen or seventeen years since I first saw it. Within that comparatively short period, it has added to its number three times the whole amount of its population when the Constitution was adopted. Of all things having power to check this prosperity, of all things potent to blight and blast it, of all things capable of compelling this city to recede as fast as she has advanced, a disturbed government, an enfeebled public authority, a broken or a weakened union of the States, would be most efficacious. This would be cause efficient enough. Every thing else, in the common fortune of communities, she may hope to resist or to prevent; but this would be fatal as the arrow of death.

Gentlemen, you have personal recollections and associations, connected with the establishment and adoption of the Constitution, which are necessarily called up on an occasion like this. It is impossible to forget the prominent agency exercised by eminent citizens of your own, in regard to that great measure. Those great men are now recorded among the illustrious dead; but they have left names never to be forgotten, and never to be remembered without respect and veneration. Least of all can they be forgotten by you, when assembled here for the purpose of signifying your attachment to the Constitution, and your sense of its inestimable importance to the happiness of the people.

I should do violence to my own feelings, Gentlemen, I think I should offend yours, if I omitted respectful mention of distinguished names yet fresh in your recollections. How can I stand here, to speak of the Constitution of the United States, of the wisdom of its provisions, of the difficulties attending its adoption, of the evils from which it rescued the country, and of the prosperity and power to which it has raised it, and yet pay no tribute to those who were highly instrumental in accomplishing the work? While we are here to rejoice that it yet stands firm and strong, while we congratulate one another that we live under its benign influence, and cherish hopes of its long duration, we cannot forget who they were that, in the day of our national infancy, in the times of despondency and despair, mainly assisted to work out our deliverance. I should feel that I was unfaithful to the strong recollections which the occasion presses upon us, that I was not true to gratitude, not true to patriotism, not true to the living or the dead, not true to your feelings or my own, if I should forbear to make mention of ALEXANDER HAMILTON.

Coming from the military service of the country yet a youth, but with knowledge and maturity, even in civil affairs far beyond his years, he made this city the place of his adoption; and he gave the whole powers of his mind to the contemplation of the weak and distracted condition of the country. Daily increasing in acquaintance and confidence with the people of New York, he saw, what they also saw, the absolute necessity of some closer bond of union for the States. This was the great object of desire. He never appears to have lost sight of it, but was found in the lead whenever any thing was to be attempted for its accomplishment. One experiment after another, as is well known, was tried, and all failed. The States were urgently called on to confer such further powers on the old Congress as would enable it to redeem the public faith, or to adopt, themselves, some general and common principle of commercial regulation. But the States had not agreed, and were not likely to agree. In this posture of affairs, so full of public difficulty and public distress, commissioners from five or six of the States met, on the request of Virginia, at Annapolis, in September, 1786. The precise object of their appointment was to take into consideration the trade of the United States; to examine the relative situations and trade of the several States; and to consider how far a uniform system of commercial regulations was necessary to their common interest and permanent harmony. Mr. Hamilton was one of these commissioners; and I have understood, though I cannot assert the fact, that their report was drawn by him. His associate from this State was the venerable Judge Benson, who has lived long, and still lives, to see the happy results of the counsels which originated in this meeting. Of its members, he and Mr. Madison are, I believe, now the only survivors. These commissioners recommended, what took place the next year, a general Convention of all the States, to take into serious deliberation the condition of the country, and devise such provisions as should render the constitution of the federal government adequate to the exigencies of the Union. I need not remind you, that of this Convention Mr. Hamilton was an active and efficient member. The Constitution was framed, and submitted to the country. And then another great work was to be undertaken. The Constitution would naturally find, and did find, enemies and opposers. Objections to it were numerous, and powerful, and spirited. They were to be answered; and they were effectually answered. The writers of the numbers of the Federalist, Mr. Hamilton, Mr. Madison, and Mr. Jay, so greatly distinguished themselves in their discussions of the Constitution, that those numbers are generally received as important commentaries on the text, and accurate expositions, in general, of its objects and purposes. Those papers were all written and published in this city. Mr. Hamilton was elected one of the distinguished delegation from the city to the State Convention at Poughkeepsie, called to ratify the new Constitution. Its debates are published. Mr. Hamilton appears to have exerted, on this occasion, to the utmost, every power and faculty of his mind. The whole question was likely to depend on the decision of New York. He felt the full importance of the crisis; and the reports of his speeches, imperfect as they probably are, are yet lasting monuments to his genius and patriotism. He saw at last his hopes fulfilled; he saw the Constitution adopted, and the government under it established and organized. The discerning eye of Washington immediately called him to that post, which was far the most important in the administration of the new system. He was made Secretary of the Treasury; and how he fulfilled the duties of such a place, at such a time, the whole country perceived with delight and the whole world saw with admiration. He smote the rock of the national resources, and abundant streams of revenue gushed forth. He touched the dead corpse of the Public Credit, and it sprung upon its feet. The fabled birth of Minerva, from the brain of Jove, was hardly more sudden or more perfect than the financial system of the United States, as it burst forth from the conceptions of ALEXANDER HAMILTON.

Your recollections, Gentlemen, your respect, and your affections, all conspire to bring before you, at such a time as this, another great man, now too numbered with the dead. I mean the pure, the disinterested, the patriotic JOHN JAY. His character is a brilliant jewel in the sacred treasures of national reputation. Leaving his profession at an early period, yet not before he had singularly distinguished himself in it, his whole life, from the commencement of the Revolution until his final retirement, was a life of public service. A member of the first Congress, he was the author of that political paper which is generally acknowledged to stand first among the incomparable productions of that body;[1] productions which called forth that decisive strain of commendation from the great Lord Chatham, in which he pronounced them not inferior to the finest productions of the master states of the world. Mr. Jay had been abroad, and he had also been long intrusted with the difficult duties of our foreign correspondence at home. He had seen and felt, in the fullest measure and to the greatest possible extent, the difficulty of conducting our foreign affairs honorably and usefully, without a stronger and more perfect domestic union. Though not a member of the Convention which framed the Constitution, he was yet present while it was in session, and looked anxiously for its result. By the choice of this city, he had a seat in the State Convention, and took an active and zealous part for the adoption of the Constitution. On the organization of the new government, he was selected by Washington to be the first Chief Justice of the Supreme Court of the United States; and surely the high and most responsible duties of that station could not have been trusted to abler or safer hands. It is the duty of that tribunal, one of equal importance and delicacy, to decide constitutional questions, occasionally arising on State laws. The general learning and ability, and especially the prudence, the mildness, and the firmness of his character, eminently fitted Mr. Jay to be the head of such a court.

When the spotless ermine of the judicial robe fell on John Jay, it touched nothing less spotless than itself. These eminent men, Gentlemen, the contemporaries of some of you, known to most, and revered by all, were so conspicuous in the framing and adopting of the Constitution, and called so early to important stations under it, that a tribute, better, indeed, than I have given, or am able to give, seemed due to them from us, on this occasion.

There was yet another, of whom mention is to be made. In the Revolutionary history of the country, the name of CHANCELLOR LIVINGSTON became early prominent. He was a member of that Congress which declared Independence; and a member, too, of the committee which drew and reported the immortal Declaration. At the period of the adoption of the Constitution, he was its firm friend and able advocate. He was a member of the State Convention, being one of that list of distinguished and gifted men who represented this city in that body; and he threw the whole weight of his talents and influence into the doubtful scale of the Constitution.

Gentlemen, as connected with the Constitution, you have also local recollections which must bind it still closer to your attachment and affection. It commenced its being and its blessings here. It was in this city, in the midst of friends, anxious, hopeful, and devoted, that the new government started in its course. To us, Gentlemen, who are younger, it has come down by tradition; but some around me are old enough to have witnessed, and did witness, the interesting scene of the first inauguration. They remember what voices of gratified patriotism, what shouts of enthusiastic hope, what acclamations rent the air, how many eyes were suffused with tears of joy, how cordially each man pressed the hand of him who was next to him, when, standing in the open air, in the centre of the city, in the view of assembled thousands, the first President of the United States was heard solemnly to pronounce the words of his official oath, repeating them from the lips of Chancellor Livingston. You then thought, Gentlemen, that the great work of the Revolution was accomplished. You then felt that you had a government; that the United States were then, indeed, united. Every benignant star seemed to shed its selectest influence on that auspicious hour. Here were heroes of the Revolution; here were sages of the Convention; here were minds, disciplined and schooled in all the various fortunes of the country, acting now in several relations, but all co-operating to the same great end, the successful administration of the new and untried Constitution. And he,--how shall I speak of him?--he was at the head, who was already first in war, who was already first in the hearts of his countrymen, and who was now shown also, by the unanimous suffrage of the country, to be first in peace.

Gentlemen, how gloriously have the hopes then indulged been fulfilled! Whose expectation was then so sanguine, I may almost ask, whose imagination then so extravagant, as to run forward, and contemplate as probable, the one half of what has been accomplished in forty years? Who among you can go back to 1789, and see what this city, and this country, too, then were; and, beholding what they now are, can be ready to consent that the Constitution of the United States shall be weakened,--dishonored,--_nullified_?

Gentlemen, before I leave these pleasant recollections, I feel it an irresistible impulse of duty to pay a tribute of respect to another distinguished person, not, indeed, a fellow-citizen of your own, but associated with those I have already mentioned in important labors, and an early and indefatigable friend and advocate in the great cause of the Constitution. I refer to MR. MADISON. I am aware, Gentlemen, that a tribute of regard from me to him is of little importance; but if it shall receive your approbation and sanction, it will become of value. Mr. Madison, thanks to a kind Providence, is yet among the living, and there is certainly no other individual living, to whom the country is so much indebted for the blessings of the Constitution. He was one of the commissioners who met at Annapolis, in 1786, to which meeting I have already referred, and which, to the great credit of Virginia, had its origin in a proceeding of that State. He was a member of the Convention of 1787, and of that of Virginia in the following year. He was thus intimately acquainted with the whole progress of the formation of the Constitution, from its very first step to its final adoption. If ever man had the means of understanding a written instrument, Mr. Madison has the means of understanding the Constitution. If it be possible to know what was designed by it, he can tell us. It was in this city, that, in conjunction with Mr. Hamilton and Mr. Jay, he wrote the numbers of the Federalist; and it was in this city that he commenced his brilliant career under the new Constitution, having been elected into the House of Representatives of the first Congress. The recorded votes and debates of those times show his active and efficient agency in every important measure of that Congress. The necessary organization of the government, the arrangement of the departments, and especially the paramount subject of revenue, engaged his attention, and divided his labors.

The legislative history of the first two or three years of the government is full of instruction. It presents, in striking light, the evils intended to be remedied by the Constitution, and the provisions which were deemed essential to the remedy of those evils. It exhibits the country, in the moment of its change from a weak and ill-defined confederacy of States, into a general, efficient, but still restrained and limited government. It shows the first working of our peculiar system, moved, as it then was, by master hands.

Gentlemen, for one, I confess I like to dwell on this part of our history. It is good for us to be here. It is good for us to study the situation of the country at this period, to survey its difficulties, to look at the conduct of its public men, to see how they struggled with obstacles, real and formidable, and how gloriously they brought the Union out of its state of depression and distress. Truly, Gentlemen, these founders and fathers of the Constitution were great men, and thoroughly furnished for every good work. All that reading and learning could do; all that talent and intelligence could do; and, what perhaps is still more, all that long experience in difficult and troubled times and a deep and intimate practical knowledge of the condition of the country could do,--conspired to fit them for the great business of forming a general, but limited government, embracing common objects, extending over all the States, and yet touching the power of the States no further than those common objects require. I confess I love to linger around these original fountains, and to drink deep of their waters. I love to imbibe, in as full measure as I may, the spirit of those who laid the foundations of the government, and so wisely and skilfully balanced and adjusted its bearings and proportions.

Having been afterwards, for eight years, Secretary of State, and as long President, Mr. Madison has had an experience in the affairs of the Constitution, certainly second to no man. More than any other man living, and perhaps more than any other who has lived, his whole public life has been incorporated, as it were, into the Constitution; in the original conception and project of attempting to form it, in its actual framing, in explaining and recommending it, by speaking and writing, in assisting at the first organization of the government under it, and in a long administration of its executive powers,--in these various ways he has lived near the Constitution, and with the power of imbibing its true spirit, and inhaling its very breath, from its first pulsation of life. Again, therefore, I ask, If he cannot tell us what the Constitution is, and what it means, who can? He had retired with the respect and regard of the community, and might naturally be supposed not willing to interfere again in matters of political concern. He has, nevertheless, not withholden his opinions on the vital question discussed on that occasion, which has caused this meeting. He has stated, with an accuracy almost peculiar to himself, and so stated as, in my opinion, to place almost beyond further controversy, the true doctrines of the Constitution. He has stated, not notions too loose and irregular to be called even a theory, not ideas struck out by the feeling of present inconvenience or supposed maladministration, not suggestions of expediency, or evasions of fair and straightforward construction, but elementary principles, clear and sound distinctions, and indisputable truths. I am sure, Gentlemen, that I speak your sentiments, as well as my own, when I say, that, for making public so clearly and distinctly as he has done his own opinions on these vital questions of constitutional law, Mr. Madison has founded a new and strong claim on the gratitude of a grateful country. You will think, with me, that, at his advanced age, and in the enjoyment of general respect and approbation for a long career of public services, it was an act of distinguished patriotism, when he saw notions promulgated and maintained which he deemed unsound and dangerous, not to hesitate to come forward and to place the weight of his own opinion in what he deemed the right scale, come what come might. I am sure, Gentlemen, it cannot be doubted,--the manifestation is clear,--that the country feels deeply the force of this new obligation.[2]

Gentlemen, what I have said of the benefits of the Constitution to your city might be said, with little change, in respect to every other part of the country. Its benefits are not exclusive. What has it left undone, which any government could do, for the whole country? In what condition has it placed us? Where do we now stand? Are we elevated, or degraded, by its operation? What is our condition under its influence, at the very moment when some talk of arresting its power and breaking its unity? Do we not feel ourselves on an eminence? Do we not challenge the respect of the whole world? What has placed us thus high? What has given us this just pride? What else is it, but the unrestrained and free operation of that same Federal Constitution, which it has been proposed now to hamper, and manacle, and nullify? Who is there among us, that, should he find himself on any spot of the earth where human beings exist, and where the existence of other nations is known, would not be proud to say, I am an American? I am a countryman of Washington? I am a citizen of that republic, which, although it has suddenly sprung up, yet there are none on the globe who have ears to hear, and have not heard of it; who have eyes to see, and have not read of it; who know any thing, and yet do not know of its existence and its glory? And, Gentlemen, let me now reverse the picture. Let me ask, who there is among us, if he were to be found to-morrow in one of the civilized countries of Europe, and were there to learn that this goodly form of government had been overthrown, that the United States were no longer united, that a death-blow had been struck upon their bond of union, that they themselves had destroyed their chief good and their chief honor,--who is there whose heart would not sink within him? Who is there who would not cover his face for very shame?

At this very moment, Gentlemen, our country is a general refuge for the distressed and the persecuted of other nations. Whoever is in affliction from political occurrences in his own country looks here for shelter. Whether he be republican, flying from the oppression of thrones, or whether he be monarch or monarchist, flying from thrones that crumble and fall under or around him, he feels equal assurance, that, if he get foothold on our soil, his person will be safe, and his rights will be respected.

And who will venture to say, that, in any government now existing in the world, there is greater security for persons or property than in that of the United States? We have tried these popular institutions in times of great excitement and commotion, and they have stood, substantially, firm and steady, while the fountains of the great political deep have been elsewhere broken up; while thrones, resting on ages of prescription, have tottered and fallen; and while, in other countries, the earthquake of unrestrained popular commotion has swallowed up all law, and all liberty, and all right together. Our government has been tried in peace, and it has been tried in war, and has proved itself fit for both. It has been assailed from without, and it has successfully resisted the shock; it has been disturbed within, and it has effectually quieted the disturbance. It can stand trial, it can stand assault, it can stand adversity, it can stand every thing, but the marring of its own beauty, and the weakening of its own strength. It can stand every thing but the effects of our own rashness and our own folly. It can stand every thing but disorganization, disunion, and nullification.

It is a striking fact, and as true as it is striking, that at this very moment, among all the principal civilized states of the world, *that* government is most secure against the danger of popular commotion which is itself entirely popular. It seems, indeed, that the submission of every thing to the public will, under constitutional restraints, imposed by the people themselves, furnishes itself security that they will desire nothing wrong. Certain it is, that popular, constitutional liberty, as we enjoy it, appears, in the present state of the world, as sure and stable a basis for government to rest upon, as any government of enlightened states can find, or does find. Certain it is, that, in these times of so much popular knowledge, and so much popular activity, those governments which do not admit the people to partake in their administration, but keep them under and beneath, sit on materials for an explosion, which may take place at any moment, and blow them into a thousand atoms.

Gentlemen, let any man who would degrade and enfeeble the national Constitution, let any man who would nullify its laws, stand forth and tell us what he would wish. What does he propose? Whatever he may be, and whatever substitute he may hold forth, I am sure the people of this country will decline his kind interference, and hold on by the Constitution which they possess. Any one who would willingly destroy it, I rejoice to know, would be looked upon with abhorrence. It is deeply intrenched in the regards of the people. Doubtless it may be undermined by artful and long-continued hostility; it may be imperceptibly weakened by secret attack; it may be insidiously shorn of its powers by slow degrees; the public vigilance may be lulled, and when it awakes, it may find the Constitution frittered away. In these modes, or some of them, it is possible that the union of the States may be dissolved.

But if the general attention of the people be kept alive, if they see the intended mischief before it is effected, they will prevent it by their own sovereign power. They will interpose themselves between the meditated blow and the object of their regard and attachment. Next to the controlling authority of the people themselves, the preservation of the government is mainly committed to those who administer it. If conducted in wisdom, it cannot but stand strong. Its genuine, original spirit is a patriotic, liberal, and generous spirit; a spirit of conciliation, of moderation, of candor, and charity; a spirit of friendship, and not a spirit of hostility toward the States; a spirit careful not to exceed, and equally careful not to relinquish, its just powers. While no interest can or ought to feel itself shut out from the benefits of the Constitution, none should consider those benefits as exclusively its own. The interests of all must be consulted, and reconciled, and provided for, as far as possible, that all may perceive the benefits of a united government. Among other things, we are to remember that new States have arisen, possessing already an immense population, spreading and thickening over vast regions which were a wilderness when the Constitution was adopted. Those States are not, like New York, directly connected with maritime commerce. They are entirely agricultural, and need markets for consumption; and they need, too, access to those markets. It is the duty of the government to bring the interests of these new States into the Union, and incorporate them closely in the family compact. Gentlemen, it is not impracticable to reconcile these various interests, and so to administer the government as to make it useful to all. It was never easier to administer the government than it is now. We are beset with none, or with few, of its original difficulties; and it is a time of great general prosperity and happiness. Shall we admit ourselves incompetent to carry on the government, so as to be satisfactory to the whole country? Shall we admit that there has so little descended to us of the wisdom and prudence of our fathers? If the government could be administered in Washington's time, when it was yet new, when the country was heavily in debt, when foreign relations were in a threatening condition, and when Indian wars pressed on the frontiers, can it not be administered now? Let us not acknowledge ourselves so unequal to our duties.

Gentlemen, on the occasion referred to by the chair, it became necessary to consider the judicial power, and its proper functions under the Constitution. In every free and balanced government, this is a most essential and important power. Indeed, I think it is a remark of Mr. Hume, that the administration of justice seems to be the leading object of institutions of government; that legislatures assemble, that armies are embodied, that both war and peace are made, with a sort of ultimate reference to the proper administration of laws, and the judicial protection of private rights. The judicial power comes home to every man. If the legislature passes incorrect or unjust general laws, its members bear the evil as well as others. But judicature acts on individuals. It touches every private right, every private interest, and almost every private feeling. What we possess is hardly fit to be called our own, unless we feel secure in its possession; and this security, this feeling of perfect safety, cannot exist under a wicked, or even under a weak and ignorant, administration of the laws. There is no happiness, there is no liberty, there is no enjoyment of life, unless a man can say when he rises in the morning, I shall be subject to the decision of no unjust judge to-day.

But, Gentlemen, the judicial department, under the Constitution of the United States, possesses still higher duties. It is true, that it may be called on, and is occasionally called on, to decide questions which are, in one sense, of a political nature. The general and State governments, both established by the people, are established for different purposes, and with different powers. Between those powers questions may arise; and who shall decide them? Some provision for this end is absolutely necessary. What shall it be? This was the question before the Convention; and various schemes were suggested. It was foreseen that the States might inadvertently pass laws inconsistent with the Constitution of the United States, or with acts of Congress. At least, laws might be passed which would be charged with such inconsistency. How should these questions be disposed of? Where shall the power of judging, in cases of alleged interference, be lodged? One suggestion in the Convention was, to make it an executive power, and to lodge it in the hands of the President, by requiring all State laws to be submitted to him, that he might negative such as he thought appeared repugnant to the general Constitution. This idea, perhaps, may have been borrowed from the power exercised by the crown over the laws of the Colonies. It would evidently have been, not only an inconvenient and troublesome proceeding, but dangerous also to the powers of the States. It was not pressed. It was thought wiser and safer, on the whole, to require State legislatures and State judges to take an oath to support the Constitution of the United States, and then leave the States at liberty to pass whatever laws they pleased, and if interference, in point of fact, should arise, to refer the question to judicial decision. To this end, the judicial power, under the Constitution of the United States, was made coextensive with the legislative power. It was extended to all cases arising under the Constitution and the laws of Congress. The judiciary became thus possessed of the authority of deciding, in the last resort, in all cases of alleged interference, between State laws and the Constitution and laws of Congress.

Gentlemen, this is the actual Constitution, this is the law of the land. There may be those who think it unnecessary, or who would prefer a different mode of deciding such questions. But this is the established mode, and, till it be altered, the courts can no more decline their duty on these occasions than on other occasions. But can any reasonable man doubt the expediency of this provision, or suggest a better? Is it not absolutely essential to the peace of the country that this power should exist somewhere? Where can it exist, better than where it now does exist? The national judiciary is the common tribunal of the whole country. It is organized by the common authority, and its places filled by the common agent. This is a plain and practical provision. It was framed by no bunglers, nor by any wild theorists. And who can say that it has failed? Who can find substantial fault with its operation or its results? The great question is, whether we shall provide for the peaceable decision of cases of collision. Shall they be decided by law, or by force? Shall the decisions be decisions of peace, or decisions of war?

On the occasion which has given rise to this meeting, the proposition contended for in opposition to the doctrine just stated was that every State, under certain supposed exigencies, and in certain supposed cases, might decide for itself, and act for itself, and oppose its own force to the execution of the laws. By what argument, do you imagine, Gentlemen, was such a proposition maintained? I should call it metaphysical and subtle; but these terms would imply at least ingenuity, and some degree of plausibility; whereas the argument appears to me plain assumption, mere perverse construction of plain language in the body of the Constitution itself. As I understand it, when put forth in its revised and most authentic shape, it is this: that the Constitution provides that any amendments may be made to it which shall be agreed to by three fourths of the States; there is, therefore, to be nothing in the Constitution to which three fourths of the States have not agreed. All this is true; but then comes this inference, namely, that, when one State denies the constitutionality of any law of Congress, she may arrest its execution as to herself, and keep it arrested, till the States can all be consulted by their conventions, and three fourths of them shall have decided that the law is constitutional. Indeed, the inference is still stranger than this; for State conventions have no authority to construe the Constitution, though they have authority to amend it; therefore the argument must prove, if it prove any thing, that, when any one State denies that any particular power is included in the Constitution, it is to be considered as not included, and cannot be found there till three fourths of the States agree to insert it. In short, the result of the whole is, that, though it requires three fourths of the States to insert any thing in the Constitution, yet any one State can strike any thing out of it. For the power to strike out, and the power of deciding, without appeal, upon the construction of what is already in, are substantially and practically the same.

And, Gentlemen, what a spectacle should we have exhibited under the actual operation of notions like these! At the very moment when our government was quoted, praised, and commended all over the world, when the friends of republican liberty everywhere were gazing at it with delight, and were in perfect admiration at the harmony of its movements, one State steps forth, and, by the power of nullification, breaks up the whole system, and scatters the bright chain of the Union into as many sundered links as there are separate States!

Seeing the true grounds of the Constitution thus attacked, I raised my voice in its favor, I must confess with no preparation or previous intention. I can hardly say that I embarked in the contest from a sense of duty. It was an instantaneous impulse of inclination, not acting against duty, I trust, but hardly waiting for its suggestions. I felt it to be a contest for the integrity of the Constitution, and I was ready to enter into it, not thinking, or caring, personally, how I might come out.

Gentlemen, I have true pleasure in saying that I trust the crisis has in some measure passed by. The doctrines of nullification have received a severe and stern rebuke from public opinion. The general reprobation of the country has been cast upon them. Recent expressions of the most numerous branch of the national legislature are decisive and imposing. Everywhere, the general tone of public feeling is for the Constitution. While much will be yielded--every thing, almost, but the integrity of the Constitution, and the essential interests of the country--to the cause of mutual harmony and mutual conciliation, no ground can be granted, not an inch, to menace and bluster. Indeed, menace and bluster, and the putting forth of daring, unconstitutional doctrines, are, at this very moment, the chief obstacles to mutual harmony and satisfactory accommodation. Men cannot well reason, and confer, and take counsel together, about the discreet exercise of a power, with those who deny that any such power rightfully exists, and who threaten to blow up the whole Constitution if they cannot otherwise get rid of its operation. It is matter of sincere gratification, Gentlemen, that the voice of this great State has been so clear and strong, and her vote all but unanimous, on the most interesting of these occasions, in the House of Representatives. Certainly, such respect to the Union becomes New York. It is consistent with her interests and her character. That singularly prosperous State, which now is, and is likely to continue to be, the greatest link in the chain of the Union, will ever be, I am sure, the strongest link also. The great States which lie in her neighborhood agreed with her fully in this matter. Pennsylvania, I believe, was loyal to the Union, to a man; and Ohio raises her voice, like that of a lion, against whatsoever threatens disunion and dismemberment. This harmony of sentiment is truly gratifying. It is not to be gainsaid, that the union of opinion in this great central mass of our population, on this momentous point of the Constitution, augurs well for our future prosperity and security.

I have said, Gentlemen, what I verily believe to be true, that there is no danger to the Union from open and avowed attacks on its essential principles. Nothing is to be feared from those who will march up boldly to their own propositions, and tell us that they mean to annihilate powers exercised by Congress. But, certainly, there are dangers to the Constitution, and we ought not to shut our eyes to them. We know the importance of a firm and intelligent judiciary; but how shall we secure the continuance of a firm and intelligent judiciary? Gentlemen, the judiciary is in the appointment of the executive power. It cannot continue or renew itself. Its vacancies are to be filled in the ordinary modes of executive appointment. If the time shall ever come (which Heaven avert), when men shall be placed in the supreme tribunal of the country, who entertain opinions hostile to the just powers of the Constitution, we shall then be visited by an evil defying all remedy. Our case will be past surgery. From that moment the Constitution is at an end. If they who are appointed to defend the castle shall betray it, woe betide those within! If I live to see that day come, I shall despair of the country. I shall be prepared to give it back to all its former afflictions in the days of the Confederation. I know no security against the possibility of this evil, but an awakened public vigilance. I know no safety, but in that state of public opinion which shall lead it to rebuke and put down every attempt, either to gratify party by judicial appointments, or to dilute the Constitution by creating a court which shall construe away its provisions. If members of Congress betray their trust, the people will find it out before they are ruined. If the President should at any time violate his duty, his term of office is short, and popular elections may supply a seasonable remedy. But the judges of the Supreme Court possess, for very good reasons, an independent tenure of office. No election reaches them. If, with this tenure, they betray their trusts, Heaven save us! Let us hope for better results. The past, certainly, may encourage us. Let us hope that we shall never see the time when there shall exist such an awkward posture of affairs, as that the government shall be found in opposition to the Constitution, and when the guardians of the Union shall become its betrayers.

Gentlemen, our country stands, at the present time, on commanding ground. Older nations, with different systems of government, may be somewhat slow to acknowledge all that justly belongs to us. But we may feel without vanity, that America is doing her part in the great work of improving human affairs. There are two principles, Gentlemen, strictly and purely American, which are now likely to prevail throughout the civilized world. Indeed, they seem the necessary result of the progress of civilization and knowledge. These are, first, popular governments, restrained by written constitutions; and, secondly, universal education. Popular governments and general education, acting and reacting, mutually producing and reproducing each other, are the mighty agencies which in our days appear to be exciting, stimulating, and changing civilized societies. Man, everywhere, is now found demanding a participation in government,-- and he will not be refused; and he demands knowledge as necessary to self-government. On the basis of these two principles, liberty and knowledge, our own American systems rest. Thus far we have not been disappointed in their results. Our existing institutions, raised on these foundations, have conferred on us almost unmixed happiness. Do we hope to better our condition by change? When we shall have nullified the present Constitution, what are we to receive in its place? As fathers, do we wish for our children better government, or better laws? As members of society, as lovers of our country, is there any thing we can desire for it better than that, as ages and centuries roll over it, it may possess the same invaluable institutions which it now enjoys? For my part, Gentlemen, I can only say, that I desire to thank the beneficent Author of all good for being born *where* I was born, and *when* I was born; that the portion of human existence allotted to me has been meted out to me in this goodly land, and at this interesting period. I rejoice that I have lived to see so much development of truth, so much progress of liberty, so much diffusion of virtue and happiness. And, through good report and evil report, it will be my consolation to be a citizen of a republic unequalled in the annals of the world for the freedom of its institutions, its high prosperity, and the prospects of good which yet lie before it. Our course, Gentlemen, is onward, straight onward, and forward. Let us not turn to the right hand, nor to the left. Our path is marked out for us, clear, plain, bright, distinctly defined, like the milky way across the heavens. If we are true to our country, in our day and generation, and those who come after us shall be true to it also, assuredly, assuredly, we shall elevate her to a pitch of prosperity and happiness, of honor and power, never yet reached by any nation beneath the sun.

Gentlemen, before I resume my seat, a highly gratifying duty remains to be performed. In signifying your sentiments of regard, you have kindly chosen to select as your organ for expressing them the eminent person[3] near whom I stand. I feel, I cannot well say how sensibly, the manner in which he has seen fit to speak on this occasion. Gentlemen, if I may be supposed to have made any attainment in the knowledge of constitutional law, he is among the masters in whose schools I have been taught. You see near him a distinguished magistrate,[4] long associated with him in judicial labors, which have conferred lasting benefits and lasting character, not only on the State, but on the whole country. Gentlemen, I acknowledge myself much their debtor. While yet a youth, unknown, and with little expectation of becoming known beyond a very limited circle, I have passed days and nights, not of tedious, but of happy and gratified labor, in the study of the judicature of the State of New York. I am most happy to have this public opportunity of acknowledging the obligation, and of repaying it, as far as it can be repaid, by the poor tribute of my profound regard, and the earnest expression of my sincere respect.

Gentlemen, I will no longer detain you than to propose a toast:--

The City of New York; herself the noblest eulogy on the Union of the States.

[Footnote 1: Address to the People of Great Britain.][Footnote 2: The reference is to Mr. Madison's letter on the subject of _Nullification_, in the North American Review, Vol. XXXI. p. 537.][Footnote 3: Chancellor Kent, the presiding officer.][Footnote 4: Judge Spencer.]

THE PRESIDENTIAL VETO OF THE UNITED STATES BANK BILL.
A SPEECH DELIVERED IN THE SENATE OF THE UNITED STATES, ON THE 11TH OF JULY, 1832, ON THE PRESIDENT'S VETO OF THE BANK BILL.

Mr. President,--No one will deny the high importance of the subject now before us. Congress, after full deliberation and discussion, has passed a bill, by decisive majorities, in both houses, for extending the duration of the Bank of the United States. It has not adopted this measure until its attention had been called to the subject, in three successive annual messages of the President. The bill having been thus passed by both houses, and having been duly presented to the President, instead of signing and approving it, he has returned it with objections. These objections go against the whole substance of the law originally creating the bank. They deny, in effect, that the bank is constitutional; they deny that it is expedient; they deny that it is necessary for the public service.

It is not to be doubted, that the Constitution gives the President the power which he has now exercised; but while the power is admitted, the grounds upon which it has been exerted become fit subjects of examination. The Constitution makes it the duty of Congress, in cases like this, to reconsider the measure which they have passed, to weigh the force of the President's objections to that measure, and to take a new vote upon the question.

Before the Senate proceeds to this second vote, I propose to make some remarks upon those objections. And, in the first place, it is to be observed, that they are such as to extinguish all hope that the present bank, or any bank at all resembling it, or resembling any known similar institution, can ever receive his approbation. He states no terms, no qualifications, no conditions, no modifications, which can reconcile him to the essential provisions of the existing charter. He is against the bank, and against any bank constituted in a manner known either to this or any other country. One advantage, therefore, is certainly obtained by presenting him the bill. It has caused the President's sentiments to be made known. There is no longer any mystery, no longer a contest between hope and fear, or between those prophets who predicted a *veto* and those who foretold an approval. The bill is negatived; the President has assumed the responsibility of putting an end to the bank; and the country must prepare itself to meet that change in its concerns which the expiration of the charter will produce. Mr. President, I will not conceal my opinion that the affairs of the country are approaching an important and dangerous crisis. At the very moment of almost unparalleled general prosperity, there appears an unaccountable disposition to destroy the most useful and most approved institutions of the government. Indeed, it seems to be in the midst of all this national happiness that some are found openly to question the advantages of the Constitution itself and many more ready to embarrass the exercise of its just power, weaken its authority, and undermine its foundations. How far these notions may be carried, it is impossible yet to say. We have before us the practical result of one of them. The bank has fallen, or is to fall.

It is now certain, that, without a change in our public counsels, this bank will not be continued, nor will any other be established, which, according to the general sense and language of mankind, can be entitled to the name. Within three years and nine months from the present moment, the charter of the bank expires; within that period, therefore, it must wind up its concerns. It must call in its debts, withdraw its bills from circulation, and cease from all its ordinary operations. All this is to be done in three years and nine months; because, although there is a provision in the charter rendering it lawful to use the corporate name for two years after the expiration of the charter, yet this is allowed only for the purpose of suits and for the sale of the estate belonging to the bank, and for no other purpose whatever. The whole active business of the bank, its custody of public deposits, its transfer of public moneys, its dealing in exchange, all its loans and discounts, and all its issues of bills for circulation, must cease and determine on or before the third day of March, 1836; and within the same period its debts must be collected, as no new contract can be made with it, as a corporation, for the renewal of loans, or discount of notes or bills, after that time.

The President is of opinion, that this time is long enough to close the concerns of the institution without inconvenience. His language is, "The time allowed the bank to close its concerns is ample, and if it has been well managed, its pressure will be light, and heavy only in case its management has been bad. If, therefore, it shall produce distress, the fault will be its own." Sir, this is all no more than general statement, without fact or argument to support it. We know what the management of the bank has been, and we know the present state of its affairs. We can judge, therefore, whether it be probable that its capital can be all called in, and the circulation of its bills withdrawn, in three years and nine months, by any discretion or prudence in management, without producing distress. The bank has discounted liberally, in compliance with the wants of the community. The amount due to it on loans and discounts, in certain large divisions of the country, is great; so great, that I do not perceive how any man can believe that it can be paid, within the time now limited, without distress. Let us look at known facts. Thirty millions of the capital of the bank are now out, on loans and discounts, in the States on the Mississippi and its waters; ten millions of which are loaned on the discount of bills of exchange, foreign and domestic, and twenty millions on promissory notes. Now, Sir, how is it possible that this vast amount can be collected in so short a period without suffering, by any management whatever? We are to remember, that, when the collection of this debt begins, at that same time the existing medium of payment, that is, the circulation of the bills of the bank, will begin also to be restrained and withdrawn; and thus the means of payment must be limited just when the necessity of making payment becomes pressing. The whole debt is to be paid, and within the same time the whole circulation withdrawn.

The local banks, where there are such, will be able to afford little assistance; because they themselves will feel a full share of the pressure. They will not be in a condition to extend their discounts, but, in all probability, obliged to curtail them. Whence, then, are the means to come for paying this debt? and in what medium is payment to be made? If all this may be done with but slight pressure on the community, what course of conduct is to accomplish it? How is it to be done? What other thirty millions are to supply the place of these thirty millions now to be called in? What other circulation or medium of payment is to be adopted in the place of the bills of the bank? The message, following a singular train of argument, which had been used in this house, has a loud lamentation upon the suffering of the Western States on account of their being obliged to pay even interest on this debt. This payment of interest is itself represented as exhausting their means and ruinous to their prosperity. But if the interest cannot be paid without pressure, can both interest and principal be paid in four years without pressure? The truth is, the interest has been paid, is paid, and may continue to be paid, without any pressure at all; because the money borrowed is profitably employed by those who borrow it, and the rate of interest which they pay is at least two per cent lower than the actual value of money in that part of the country. But to pay the whole principal in less than four years, losing, at the same time, the existing and accustomed means and facilities of payment created by the bank itself, and to do this without extreme embarrassment, without absolute distress, is, in my judgment, impossible. I hesitate not to say, that, as this *veto* travels to the West, it will depreciate the value of every man's property from the Atlantic States to the capital of Missouri. Its effects will be felt in the price of lands, the great and leading article of Western property, in the price of crops, in the products of labor, in the repression of enterprise, and in embarrassment to every kind of business and occupation. I state this opinion strongly, because I have no doubt of its truth, and am willing its correctness should be judged by the event. Without personal acquaintance with the Western States, I know enough of their condition to be satisfied that what I have predicted must happen. The people of the West are rich, but their riches consist in their immense quantities of excellent land, in the products of these lands, and in their spirit of enterprise. The actual value of money, or rate of interest, with them is high, because their pecuniary capital bears little proportion to their landed interest. At an average rate, money is not worth less than eight per cent per annum throughout the whole Western country, notwithstanding that it has now a loan or an advance from the bank of thirty millions, at six per cent. To call in this loan, at the rate of eight millions a year, in addition to the interest on the whole, and to take away, at the same time, that circulation which constitutes so great a portion of the medium of payment throughout that whole region, is an operation, which, however wisely conducted, cannot but inflict a blow on the community of tremendous force and frightful consequences. The thing cannot be done without distress, bankruptcy, and ruin, to many. If the President had seen any practical manner in which this change might be effected without producing these consequences, he would have rendered infinite service to the community by pointing it out. But he has pointed out nothing, he has suggested nothing; he contents himself with saying, without giving any reason, that, if the pressure be heavy, the fault will be the bank's. I hope this is not merely an attempt to forestall opinion, and to throw on the bank the responsibility of those evils which threaten the country, for the sake of removing it from himself.

The responsibility justly lies with him, and there it ought to remain. A great majority of the people are satisfied with the bank as it is, and desirous that it should be continued. They wished no change. The strength of this public sentiment has carried the bill through Congress, against all the influence of the administration, and all the power of organized party. But the President has undertaken, on his own responsibility, to arrest the measure, by refusing his assent to the bill. He is answerable for the consequences, therefore, which necessarily follow the change which the expiration of the bank charter may produce; and if these consequences shall prove disastrous, they can fairly be ascribed to his policy only, and the policy of his administration.

Although, Sir, I have spoken of the effects of this _veto_ in the Western country, it has not been because I considered that part of the United States exclusively affected by it. Some of the Atlantic States may feel its consequences, perhaps, as sensibly as those of the West, though not for the same reasons. The concern manifested by Pennsylvania for the renewal of the charter shows her sense of the importance of the bank to her own interest, and that of the nation. That great and enterprising State has entered into an extensive system of internal improvements, which necessarily makes heavy demands on her credit and her resources; and by the sound and acceptable currency which the bank affords, by the stability which it gives to private credit, and by occasional advances, made in anticipation of her revenues, and in aid of her great objects, she has found herself benefited, doubtless, in no inconsiderable degree. Her legislature has instructed her Senators here to advocate the renewal of the charter, at this session. They have obeyed her voice, and yet they have the misfortune to find that, in the judgment of the President, _the measure is unconstitutional, unnecessary, dangerous to liberty, and is, moreover, ill-timed_.

But, Mr. President, it is not the local interest of the West, nor the particular interest of Pennsylvania, or any other State, which has influenced Congress in passing this bill. It has been governed by a wise foresight, and by a desire to avoid embarrassment in the pecuniary concerns of the country, to secure the safe collection and convenient transmission of public moneys, to maintain the circulation of the country, sound and safe as it now happily is, against the possible effects of a wild spirit of speculation. Finding the bank highly useful, Congress has thought fit to provide for its continuance.

As to the _time_ of passing this bill, it would seem to be the last thing to be thought of, as a ground of objection, by the President; since, from the date of his first message to the present time, he has never failed to call our attention to the subject with all possible apparent earnestness. So early as December, 1829, in his message to the two houses, he declares, that he "cannot, in justice to the parties interested, too soon present the subject to the deliberate consideration of the legislature, in order to avoid the evils resulting from precipitancy, in a measure involving such important principles and such deep pecuniary interests." Aware of this early invitation given to Congress to take up the subject, by the President himself, the writer of the message seems to vary the ground of objection, and, instead of complaining that the time of bringing forward this measure was premature, to insist, rather, that, after the report of the committee of the other house, the bank should have withdrawn its application for the present! But that report offers no just ground, surely, for such withdrawal. The subject was before Congress; it was for Congress to decide upon it, with all the light shed by the report; and the question of postponement, having been made in both houses, was lost, by clear majorities, in each. Under such circumstances, it would have been somewhat singular, to say the least, if the bank itself had withdrawn its application. It is indeed known to everybody, that neither the report of the committee, nor any thing contained in that report, was relied on by the opposers of the renewal. If it has been discovered elsewhere, that that report contained matter important in itself, or which should have led to further inquiry, this may be proof of superior sagacity; for certainly no such thing was discerned by either house of Congress.

But, Sir, do we not now see that it was time, and high time, to press this bill, and to send it to the President? Does not the event teach us, that the measure was not brought forward one moment too early? The time had come when the people wished to know the decision of the administration on the question of the bank? Why conceal it, or postpone its declaration? Why, as in regard to the tariff, give out one set of opinions for the North, and another for the South?

An important election is at hand, and the renewal of the bank charter is a pending object of great interest, and some excitement. Should not the opinions of men high in office, and candidates for re-election, be known on this, as on other important public questions? Certainly, it is to be hoped that the people of the United States are not yet mere man-worshippers, that they do not choose their rulers without some regard to their political principles, or political opinions. Were they to do this, it would be to subject themselves voluntarily to the evils which the hereditary transmission of power, independent of all personal qualifications, inflicts on other nations. They will judge their public servants by their acts, and continue or withhold their confidence, as they shall think it merited, or as they shall think it forfeited. In every point of view, therefore, the moment had arrived, when it became the duty of Congress to come to a result, in regard to this highly important measure. The interests of the government, the interests of the people, the clear and indisputable voice of public opinion, all called upon Congress to act without further loss of time. It has acted, and its act has been negatived by the President; and this result of the proceedings here places the question, with all its connections and all its incidents, fully before the people.

Before proceeding to the constitutional question, there are some other topics, treated in the message, which ought to be noticed. It commences by an inflamed statement of what it calls the "favor" bestowed upon the original bank by the government, or, indeed, as it is phrased, the "monopoly of its favor and support"; and through the whole message all possible changes are rung on the "gratuity," the "exclusive privileges," and "monopoly," of the bank charter. Now, Sir, the truth is, that the powers conferred on the bank are such, and no others, as are usually conferred on similar institutions. They constitute no monopoly, although some of them are of necessity, and with propriety, exclusive privileges. "The original act," says the message, "operated as a gratuity of many millions to the stockholders." What fair foundation is there for this remark? The stockholders received their charter, not gratuitously, but for a valuable consideration in money, prescribed by Congress, and actually paid. At some times the stock has been above _par_, at other times below _par_, according to prudence in management, or according to commercial occurrences. But if, by a judicious administration of its affairs, it had kept its stock always above _par_, what pretence would there be, nevertheless, for saying that such augmentation of its value was a "gratuity" from government? The message proceeds to declare, that the present act proposes another donation, another gratuity, to the same men, of at least seven millions more. It seems to me that this is an extraordinary statement, and an extraordinary style of argument, for such a subject and on such an occasion. In the first place, the facts are all assumed; they are taken for true without evidence. There are no proofs that any benefit to that amount will accrue to the stockholders, nor any experience to justify the expectation of it. It rests on random estimates, or mere conjecture. But suppose the continuance of the charter should prove beneficial to the stockholders; do they not pay for it? They give twice as much for a charter of fifteen years, as was given before for one of twenty. And if the proposed _bonus_, or premium, be not, in the President's judgment, large enough, would he, nevertheless, on such a mere matter of opinion as that, negative the whole bill? May not Congress be trusted to decide even on such a subject as the amount of the money premium to be received by government for a charter of this kind?

But, Sir, there is a larger and a much more just view of this subject. The bill was not passed for the purpose of benefiting the present stockholders. Their benefit, if any, is incidental and collateral. Nor was it passed on any idea that they had a *right* to a renewed charter, although the message argues against such right, as if it had been somewhere set up and asserted. No such right has been asserted by anybody. Congress passed the bill, not as a bounty or a favor to the present stockholders, nor to comply with any demand of right on their part; but to promote great public interests, for great public objects. Every bank must have some stockholders, unless it be such a bank as the President has recommended, and in regard to which he seems not likely to find much concurrence of other men's opinions; and if the stockholders, whoever they may be, conduct the affairs of the bank prudently, the expectation is always, of course, that they will make it profitable to themselves, as well as useful to the public. If a bank charter is not to be granted, because, to some extent, it may be profitable to the stockholders, no charter can be granted. The objection lies against all banks.

Sir, the object aimed at by such institutions is to connect the public safety and convenience with private interests. It has been found by experience, that banks are safest under private management, and that government banks are among the most dangerous of all inventions. Now, Sir, the whole drift of the message is to reverse the settled judgment of all the civilized world, and to set up government banks, independent of private interest or private control. For this purpose the message labors, even beyond the measure of all its other labors, to create jealousies and prejudices, on the ground of the alleged benefit which individuals will derive from the renewal of this charter. Much less effort is made to show that government, or the public, will be injured by the bill, than that individuals will profit by it. Following up the impulses of the same spirit, the message goes on gravely to allege, that the act, as passed by Congress, proposes to make a *present* of some millions of dollars to foreigners, because a portion of the stock is held by foreigners. Sir, how would this sort of argument apply to other cases? The President has shown himself not only willing, but anxious, to pay off the three per cent stock of the United States at _par_, notwithstanding that it is notorious that foreigners are owners of the greater part of it. Why should he not call that a donation to foreigners of many millions?

I will not dwell particularly on this part of the message. Its tone and its arguments are all in the same strain. It speaks of the certain gain of the present stockholders, of the value of the monopoly; it says that all monopolies are granted at the expense of the public; that the many millions which this bill bestows on the stockholders come out of the earnings of the people; that, if government sells monopolies, it ought to sell them in open market; that it is an erroneous idea, that the present stockholders have a prescriptive right either to the favor or the bounty of government; that the stock is in the hands of a few, and that the whole American people are excluded from competition in the purchase of the monopoly. To all this I say, again, that much of it is assumption without proof; much of it is an argument against that which nobody has maintained or asserted; and the rest of it would be equally strong against any charter, at any time. These objections existed in their full strength, whatever that was, against the first bank. They existed, in like manner, against the present bank at its creation, and will always exist against all banks. Indeed, all the fault found with the bill now before us is, that it proposes to continue the bank substantially as it now exists. "All the objectionable principles of the existing corporation," says the message, "and most of its odious features, are retained without alleviation"; so that the message is aimed against the bank, as it has existed from the first, and against any and all others resembling it in its general features.

Allow me, now, Sir, to take notice of an argument founded on the practical operation of the bank. That argument is this. Little of the stock of the bank is held in the West, the capital being chiefly owned by citizens of the Southern and Eastern States, and by foreigners. But the Western and Southwestern States owe the bank a heavy debt, so heavy that the interest amounts to a million six hundred thousand a year. This interest is carried to the Eastern States, or to Europe, annually, and its payment is a burden on the people of the West, and a drain of their currency, which no country can bear without inconvenience and distress. The true character and the whole value of this argument are manifest by the mere statement of it. The people of the West are, from their situation, necessarily large borrowers. They need money, capital, and they borrow it, because they can derive a benefit from its use, much beyond the interest which they pay. They borrow at six per cent of the bank, although the value of money with them is at least as high as eight. Nevertheless, although they borrow at this low rate of interest, and although they use all they borrow thus profitably, yet they cannot pay the interest without "inconvenience and distress"; and then, Sir, follows the logical conclusion, that, although they cannot pay even the interest without inconvenience and distress, yet less than four years is ample time for the bank to call in the whole, both principal and interest, without causing more than a light pressure. This is the argument.

Then follows another, which may be thus stated. It is competent to the States to tax the property of their citizens vested in the stock of this bank; but the power is denied of taxing the stock of foreigners; therefore the stock will be worth ten or fifteen per cent more to foreigners than to residents, and will of course inevitably leave the country, and make the American people debtors to aliens in nearly the whole amount due the bank, and send across the Atlantic from two to five millions of specie every year, to pay the bank dividends.

Mr. President, arguments like these might be more readily disposed of, were it not that the high and official source from which they proceed imposes the necessity of treating them with respect. In the first place, it may safely be denied that the stock of the

uable to foreigners than to our own citizens, or an object of greater desire to them, except in so far as capital may be more abundant in the foreign country, and therefore its owners more in want of opportunity of investment. The foreign stockholder enjoys no exemption from taxation. He is, of course, taxed by his own government for his incomes, derived from this as well as other property; and this is a full answer to the whole statement. But it may be added, in the second place, that it is not the practice of civilized states to tax the property of foreigners under such circumstances. Do we tax, or did we ever tax, the foreign holders of our public debt? Does Pennsylvania, New York, or Ohio tax the foreign holders of stock in the loans contracted by either of these States? Certainly not. Sir, I must confess I had little expected to see, on such an occasion as the present, a labored and repeated attempt to produce an impression on the public opinion unfavorable to the bank, from the circumstance that foreigners are among its stockholders. I have no hesitation in saying, that I deem such a train of remark as the message contains on this point, coming from the President of the United States, to be injurious to the credit and character of the country abroad; because it manifests a jealousy, a lurking disposition not to respect the property, of foreigners invited hither by our own laws. And, Sir, what is its tendency but to excite this jealousy, and create groundless prejudices?

From the commencement of the government, it has been thought desirable to invite, rather than to repel, the introduction of foreign capital. Our stocks have all been open to foreign subscriptions; and the State banks, in like manner, are free to foreign ownership. Whatever State has created a debt has been willing that foreigners should become purchasers, and desirous of it. How long is it, Sir, since Congress itself passed a law vesting new powers in the President of the United States over the cities in this District, for the very purpose of increasing their credit abroad, the better to enable them to borrow money to pay their subscriptions to the Chesapeake and Ohio Canal? It is easy to say that there is danger to liberty, danger to independence, in a bank open to foreign stockholders, because it is easy to say any thing. But neither reason nor experience proves any such danger. The foreign stockholder cannot be a director. He has no voice even in the choice of directors. His money is placed entirely in the management of the directors appointed by the President and Senate and by the American stockholders. So far as there is dependence or influence either way, it is to the disadvantage of the foreign stockholder. He has parted with the control over his own property, instead of exercising control over the property or over the actions of others. And, Sir, let it now be added, in further answer to this class of objections, that experience has abundantly confuted them all. This government has existed forty-three years, and has maintained, in full being and operation, a bank, such as is now proposed to be renewed, for thirty-six years out of the forty-three. We have never for a moment had a bank not subject to every one of these objections. Always, foreigners might be stockholders; always, foreign stock has been exempt from State taxation, as much as at present; always, the same power and privileges; always, all that which is now called a "monopoly," a "gratuity," a "present," have been possessed by the bank. And yet there has been found no danger to liberty, no introduction of foreign influence, and no accumulation of irresponsible power in a few hands. I cannot but hope, therefore, that the people of the United States will not now yield up their judgment to those notions which would reverse all our best experience, and persuade us to discontinue a useful institution from the influence of vague and unfounded declamation against its danger to the public liberties. Our liberties, indeed, must stand upon very frail foundations, if the government cannot, without endangering them, avail itself of those common facilities, in the collection of its revenues and the management of its finances, which all other governments, in commercial countries, find useful and necessary.

In order to justify its alarm for the security of our independence, the message supposes a case. It supposes that the bank should pass principally into the hands of the subjects of a foreign country, and that we should be involved in war with that country, and then it exclaims, "What would be our condition?" Why, Sir, it is plain that all the advantages would be on our side. The bank would still be our institution, subject to our own laws, and all its directors elected by ourselves; and our means would be enhanced, not by the confiscation and plunder, but by the proper use, of the foreign capital in our hands. And, Sir, it is singular enough that this very state of war, from which this argument against a bank is drawn, is the very thing which, more than all others, convinced the country and the government of the necessity of a national bank. So much was the want of such an institution felt in the late war, that the subject engaged the attention of Congress, constantly, from the declaration of that war down to the time when the existing bank was actually established; so that in this respect, as well as in others, the argument of the message is directly opposed to the whole experience of the government, and to the general and long-settled convictions of the country.

I now proceed, Sir, to a few remarks upon the President's constitutional objections to the bank; and I cannot forbear to say, in regard to them, that he appears to me to have assumed very extraordinary grounds of reasoning. He denies that the constitutionality of the bank is a settled question. If it be not, will it ever become so, or what disputed question ever can be settled? I have already observed, that for thirty-six years out of the forty-three during which the government has been in being, a bank has existed, such as is now proposed to be continued.

As early as 1791, after great deliberation, the first bank charter was passed by Congress, and approved by President Washington. It established an institution, resembling, in all things now objected to, the present bank. That bank, like this, could take lands in payment of its debts; that charter, like the present, gave the States no power of taxation; it allowed foreigners to hold stock; it restrained Congress from creating other banks. It gave also exclusive privileges, and in all particulars it was, according to the doctrine of the message, as objectionable as that now existing. That bank continued twenty years. In 1816, the present institution was established, and has been ever since in full operation. Now, Sir, the question of the power of Congress to create such institutions has been contested in every manner known to our Constitution and laws. The forms of the government furnish no new mode in which to try this question. It has been discussed over and over again, in Congress; it has been argued and solemnly adjudged in the Supreme Court; every President, except the present, has considered it a settled question; many of the State legislatures have instructed their Senators to vote for the bank; the tribunals of the States, in every instance, have supported its constitutionality; and, beyond all doubt and dispute, the general public opinion of the country has at all times given, and does now give, its full sanction and approbation to the exercise of this power, as being a constitutional power. There has been no opinion questioning the power expressed or intimated, at any time, by either house of Congress, by any President, or by any respectable judicial tribunal. Now, Sir, if this practice of near forty years, if these repeated exercises of the power, if this solemn adjudication of the Supreme Court, with the concurrence and approbation of public opinion, do not settle the question, how is any question ever to be settled, about which any one may choose to raise a doubt?

The argument of the message upon the Congressional precedents is either a bold and gross fallacy, or else it is an assertion without proofs, and against known facts. The message admits, that, in 1791, Congress decided in favor of a bank; but it adds, that another Congress, in 1811, decided against it. Now, if it be meant that, in 1811, Congress decided against the bank on constitutional ground, then the assertion is wholly incorrect, and against notorious fact. It is perfectly well known, that many members, in both houses, voted against the bank in 1811, who had no doubt at all of the constitutional power of Congress. They were entirely governed by other reasons given at the time. I appeal, Sir, to the honorable member from Maryland, who was then a member of the Senate, and voted against the bank, whether he, and others who were on the same side, did not give those votes on other well-known grounds, and not at all on constitutional ground?

General Smith here rose, and said, that he voted against the bank in 1811, but not at all on constitutional grounds, and had no doubt such was the case with other members.

We all know, Sir, the fact to be as the gentleman from Maryland has stated it. Every man who recollects, or who has read, the political occurrences of that day, knows it. Therefore, if the message intends to say, that in 1811 Congress denied the existence of any such constitutional power, the declaration is unwarranted, and altogether at variance with the facts. If, on the other hand, it only intends to say, that Congress decided against the proposition then before it on some other grounds, then it alleges that which is nothing at all to the purpose. The argument, then, either assumes for truth that which is not true, or else the whole statement is immaterial and futile.

But whatever value others may attach to this argument, the message thinks so highly of it, that it proceeds to repeat it. "One Congress," it says, "in 1815, decided against a bank, another, in 1816, decided in its favor. There is nothing in precedent, therefore, which, if its authority were admitted, ought to weigh in favor of the act before me." Now, Sir, since it is known to the whole country, one cannot but wonder how it should remain unknown to the President, that Congress *did not* decide against a bank in 1815. On the contrary, that very Congress passed a bill for erecting a bank, by very large majorities. In one form, it is true, the bill failed in the House of Representatives; but the vote was reconsidered, the bill recommitted, and finally passed by a vote of one hundred and twenty to thirty-nine. There is, therefore, not only no solid ground, but not even any plausible pretence, for the assertion, that Congress in 1815 decided against the bank. That very Congress passed a bill to create a bank, and its decision, therefore, is precisely the other way, and is a direct practical precedent in favor of the constitutional power. What are we to think of a constitutional argument which deals in this way with historical facts? When the message declares, as it does declare, that there is nothing in precedent which ought to weigh in favor of the power, it sets at naught repeated acts of Congress affirming the power, and it also states other acts, which were in fact, and which are well known to have been, directly the reverse of what the message represents them. There is not, Sir, the slightest reason to think that any Senate or any House of Representatives, ever assembled under the Constitution, contained a majority that doubted the constitutional existence of the power of Congress to establish a bank. Whenever the question has arisen, and has been decided, it has always been decided one way. The legislative precedents all assert and maintain the power; and these legislative precedents have been the law of the land for almost forty years. They settle the construction of the Constitution, and sanction the exercise of the power in question, so far as these effects can ever be produced by any legislative precedents whatever.

But the President does not admit the authority of precedent. Sir, I have always found, that those who habitually deny most vehemently the general force of precedent, and assert most strongly the supremacy of private opinion, are yet, of all men, most tenacious of that very authority of precedent, whenever it happens to be in their favor. I beg leave to ask, Sir, upon what ground, except that of precedent, and precedent alone, the President's friends have placed his power of removal from office. No such power is given by the Constitution, in terms, nor anywhere intimated, throughout the whole of it; no paragraph or clause of that instrument recognizes such a power. To say the least, it is as questionable, and has been as often questioned, as the power of Congress to create a bank; and, enlightened by what has passed under our own observation, we now see that it is of all powers the most capable of flagrant abuse. Now, Sir, I ask again, What becomes of this power, if the authority of precedent be taken away? It has all along been denied to exist; it is nowhere found in the Constitution; and its recent exercise, or, to call things by their right names, its recent abuse, has, more than any other single cause, rendered good men either cool in their affections toward the government of their country, or doubtful of its long continuance. Yet there is *precedent* in favor of this power, and the President exercises it. We know, Sir, that, without the aid of that _precedent_, his acts could never have received the sanction of this body, even at a time when his voice was somewhat more potential here than it now is, or, as I trust, ever again will be. Does the President, then, reject the authority of all precedent except what it is suitable to his own purpose to use? And does he use, without stint or measure, all precedents which may augment his own power, or gratify his own wishes?

But if the President thinks lightly of the authority of Congress in construing the Constitution, he thinks still more lightly of the authority of the Supreme Court. He asserts a right of individual judgment on constitutional questions, which is totally inconsistent with any proper administration of the government, or any regular execution of the laws. Social disorder, entire uncertainty in regard to individual rights and individual duties, the cessation of legal anthority, confusion, the dissolution of free government,--all these are the inevitable consequences of the principles adopted by the message, whenever they shall be carried to their full extent. Hitherto it has been thought that the final decision of constitutional questions belonged to the supreme judicial tribunal. The very nature of free government, it has been supposed, enjoins this; and our Constitution, moreover, has been understood so to provide, clearly and expressly. It is true, that each branch of the legislature has an undoubted right, in the exercise of its functions, to consider the constitutionality of a law proposed to be passed. This is naturally a part of its duty; and neither branch can be compelled to pass any law, or do any other act, which it deems to be beyond the reach of its constitutional power. The President has the same right, when a bill is presented for his approval; for he is, doubtless, bound to consider, in all cases, whether such bill be compatible with the Constitution, and whether he can approve it consistently with his oath of office. But when a law has been passed by Congress, and approved by the President, it is now no longer in the power, either of the same President, or his successors, to say whether the law is constitutional or not. He is not at liberty to disregard it; he is not at liberty to feel or to affect "constitutional scruples," and to sit in judgment himself on the validity of a statute of the government, and to nullify it, if he so chooses. After a law has passed through all the requisite forms; after it has received the requisite legislative sanction and the executive approval, the question of its constitutionality then becomes a judicial question, and a judicial question alone. In the courts that question may be raised, argued, and adjudged; it can be adjudged nowhere else.

The President is as much bound by the law as any private citizen, and can no more contest its validity than any private citizen. He may refuse to obey the law, and so may a private citizen; but both do it at their own peril, and neither of them can settle the question of its validity. The President may *say* a law is unconstitutional, but he is not the judge. Who is to decide that question? The judiciary alone possesses this unquestionable and hitherto unquestioned right. The judiciary is the constitutional tribunal of appeal for the citizens, against both Congress and the executive, in regard to the constitutionality of laws. It has this jurisdiction expressly conferred upon it, and when it has decided the question, its judgment must, from the very nature of all judgments that are final, and from which there is no appeal, be conclusive. Hitherto, this opinion, and a correspondent practice, have prevailed, in America, with all wise and considerate men. If it were otherwise, there would be no government of laws; but we should all live under the government, the rule, the caprices, of individuals. If we depart from the observance of these salutary principles, the executive power becomes at once purely despotic; for the President, if the principle and the reasoning of the message be sound, may either execute or not execute the laws of the land, according to his sovereign pleasure. He may refuse to put into execution one law, pronounced valid by all branches of the government, and yet execute another, which may have been by constitutional authority pronounced void.

On the argument of the message, the President of the United States holds, under a new pretence and a new name, a *dispensing power* over the laws as absolute as was claimed by James the Second of England, a month before he was compelled to fly the kingdom. That which is now claimed by the President is in truth nothing less, and nothing else, than the old dispensing power asserted by the kings of England in the worst of times; the very climax, indeed, of all the preposterous pretensions of the Tudor and the Stuart races. According to the doctrines put forth by the President, although Congress may have passed a law, and although the Supreme Court may have pronounced it constitutional, yet it is, nevertheless, no law at all, if he, in his good pleasure, sees fit to deny it effect; in other words, to repeal and annul it. Sir, no President and no public man ever before advanced such doctrines in the face of the nation. There never before was a moment in which any President would have been tolerated in asserting such a claim to despotic power. After Congress has passed the law, and after the Supreme Court has pronounced its judgment on the very point in controversy, the President has set up his own private judgment against its constitutional interpretation. It is to be remembered, Sir, that it is the present law, it is the act of 1816, it is the present charter of the bank, which the President pronounces to be unconstitutional. It is no bank _to be created_, it is no law proposed to be passed, which he denounces; it is the _law now existing_, passed by Congress, approved by President Madison, and sanctioned by a solemn judgment of the Supreme Court, which he now declares unconstitutional, and which, of course, so far as it may depend on him, cannot be executed. If these opinions of the President be maintained, there is an end of all law and all judicial authority. Statutes are but recommendations, judgments no more than opinions. Both are equally destitute of binding force.

Such a universal power as is now claimed for him, a power of judging over the laws and over the decisions of the judiciary, is nothing else but pure despotism. If conceded to him, it makes him at once what Louis the Fourteenth proclaimed himself to be when he said, "I am the State."

The Supreme Court has unanimously declared and adjudged that the existing bank *is* created by a constitutional law of Congress. As has been before observed, this bank, so far as the present question is concerned, is like that which was established in 1791 by Washington, and sanctioned by the great men of that day. In every form, therefore, in which the question can be raised, it has been raised and has been settled. Every process and every mode of trial known to the Constitution and laws have been exhausted, and always and without exception the decision has been in favor of the validity of the law. But all this practice, all this precedent, all this public approbation, all this solemn adjudication directly on the point, is to be disregarded and rejected, and the constitutional power flatly denied. And, Sir, if we are startled at this conclusion, our surprise will not be lessened when we examine the argument by which it is maintained.

By the Constitution, Congress is authorized to pass all laws "necessary and proper" for carrying its own legislative powers into effect. Congress has deemed a bank to be "necessary and proper" for these purposes, and it has therefore established a bank. But although the law has been passed, and the bank established, and the constitutional validity of its charter solemnly adjudged, yet the President pronounces it unconstitutional, because some of the powers bestowed on the bank are, in his opinion, not necessary or proper. It would appear that powers which in 1791 and in 1816, in the time of Washington and in the time of Madison, were deemed "necessary and proper," are no longer to be so regarded, and therefore the bank is unconstitutional. It has really come to this, that the constitutionality of a bank is to depend upon the opinion which one particular man may form of the utility or necessity of some of the clauses in its charter! If that individual chooses to think that a particular power contained in the charter is not necessary to the proper constitution of the bank, then the act is unconstitutional!

Hitherto it has always been supposed that the question was of a very different nature. It has been thought that the policy of granting a particular charter may be materially dependent on the structure and organization and powers of the proposed institution. But its general constitutionality has never before been understood to turn on such points. This would be making its constitutionality depend on subordinate questions; on questions of expediency and questions of detail; upon that which one man may think necessary, and another may not. If the constitutional question were made to hinge on matters of this kind, how could it ever be decided? All would depend on conjecture; on the complexional feeling, on the prejudices, on the passions, of individuals; on more or less practical skill or correct judgment in regard to banking operations among those who should be the judges; on the impulse of momentary interests, party objects, or personal purposes. Put the question in this manner to a court of seven judges, to decide whether a particular bank was constitutional, and it might be doubtful whether they could come to any result, as they might well hold very various opinions on the practical utility of many clauses of the charter.

The question in that case would be, not whether the bank, in its general frame, character, and objects, was a proper instrument to carry into effect the powers of the government, but whether the particular powers, direct or incidental, conferred on a particular bank, were better calculated than all others to give success to its operations. For if not, then the charter, according to this sort of reasoning, would be unwarranted by the Constitution. This mode of construing the Constitution is certainly a novel discovery. Its merits belong entirely to the President and his advisers. According to this rule of interpretation, if the President should be of opinion, that the capital of the bank was larger, by a thousand dollars, than it ought to be; or that the time for the continuance of the charter was a year too long; or that it was unnecessary to require it, under penalty, to pay specie; or needless to provide for punishing, as forgery, the counterfeiting of its bills,-- either of these reasons would be sufficient to render the charter, in his opinion, unconstitutional, invalid, and nugatory. This is a legitimate conclusion from the argument. Such a view of the subject has certainly never before been taken. This train of reasoning has hitherto not been heard within the halls of Congress, nor has any one ventured upon it before the tribunals of justice. The first exhibition, its first appearance, as an argument, is in a message of the President of the United States.

According to that mode of construing the Constitution which was adopted by Congress in 1791, and approved by Washington, and which has been sanctioned by the judgment of the Supreme Court, and affirmed by the practice of nearly forty years, the question upon the constitutionality of the bank involves two inquiries. First, whether a bank, in its general character, and with regard to the general objects with which banks are usually connected, be, in itself, a fit means, a suitable instrument, to carry into effect the powers granted to the government. If it be so, then the second, and the only other question is, whether the powers given in a particular charter are appropriate for a bank. If they are powers which are appropriate for a bank, powers which Congress may fairly consider to be useful to the bank or the country, then Congress may confer these powers; because the discretion to be exercised in framing the constitution of the bank belongs to Congress. One man may think the granted powers not indispensable to the particular bank; another may suppose them injudicious, or injurious; a third may imagine that other powers, if granted in their stead, would be more beneficial; but all these are matters of expediency, about which men may differ; and the power of deciding upon them belongs to Congress.

I again repeat, Sir, that if, for reasons of this kind, the President sees fit to negative a bill, on the ground of its being inexpedient or impolitic, he has a right to do so. But remember, Sir, that we are now on the constitutional question; remember that the argument of the President is, that, because powers were given to the bank by the charter of 1816 which he thinks unnecessary, that charter is unconstitutional. Now, Sir, it will hardly be denied, or rather it was not denied or doubted before this message came to us, that, if there was to be a bank, the powers and duties of that bank must be prescribed in the law creating it. Nobody but Congress, it has been thought, could grant these powers and privileges, or prescribe their limitations. It is true, indeed, that the message pretty plainly intimates, that the President should have been *first* consulted, and that he should have had the framing of the bill; but we are not yet accustomed to that order of things in enacting laws, nor do I know a parallel to this claim, thus now brought forward, except that, in some peculiar cases in England, highly affecting the royal prerogative, the assent of the monarch is necessary before either the House of Peers, or his Majesty's faithful Commons, are permitted to act upon the subject, or to entertain its consideration. But supposing, Sir, that our accustomed forms and our republican principles are still to be followed, and that a law creating a bank is, like all other laws, to originate with Congress, and that the President has nothing to do with it till it is presented for his approval, then it is clear that the powers and duties of a proposed bank, and all the terms and conditions annexed to it, must, in the first place, be settled by Congress.

This power, if constitutional at all, is only constitutional in the hands of Congress. Anywhere else, its exercise would be plain usurpation. If, then, the authority to decide what powers ought to be granted to a bank belong to Congress, and Congress shall have exercised that power, it would seem little better than absurd to say, that its act, nevertheless would be unconstitutional and invalid, if, in the opinion of a third party, it had misjudged, on a question of expediency, in the arrangement of details. According to such a mode of reasoning, a mistake in the exercise of jurisdiction takes away the jurisdiction. If Congress decide right, its decision may stand; if it decide wrong, its decision is nugatory; and whether its decision be right or wrong, another is to judge, although the original power of making the decision must be allowed to be exclusively in Congress. This is the end to which the argument of the message will conduct its followers.

Sir, in considering the authority of Congress to invest the bank with the particular powers granted to it, the inquiry is not, and cannot be, how appropriate these powers are, but whether they be at all appropriate; whether they come within the range of a just and honest discretion; whether Congress may fairly esteem them to be necessary. The question is not, Are they the fittest means, the best means? or whether the bank might not be established without them; but the question is, Are they such as Congress, _bona fide_, may have regarded as appropriate to the end? If any other rule were to be adopted, nothing could ever be settled. A law would be constitutional to-day and unconstitutional to-morrow. Its constitutionality would altogether depend upon individual opinion on a matter of mere expediency. Indeed, such a case as that is now actually before us. Mr. Madison deemed the powers given to the bank, in its present charter, proper and necessary. He held the bank, therefore, to be constitutional. But the present President, not acknowledging that the power of deciding on these points rests with Congress, nor with Congress and the then President, but setting up his own opinion as the standard, declares the law now in being unconstitutional, because the powers granted by it are, in his estimation, not necessary and proper. I pray to be informed, Sir, whether, upon similar grounds of reasoning, the President's own scheme for a bank, if Congress should do so unlikely a thing as to adopt it, would not become unconstitutional also, if it should so happen that his successor should hold his bank in as light esteem as he holds those established under the auspices of Washington and Madison?

If the reasoning of the message be well founded, it is clear that the charter of the existing bank is not a law. The bank has no legal existence; it is not responsible to government; it has no authority to act; it is incapable of being an agent; the President may treat it as a nullity to-morrow, withdraw from it all the public deposits, and set afloat all the existing national arrangements of revenue and finance. It is enough to state these monstrous consequences, to show that the doctrine, principles, and pretensions of the message are entirely inconsistent with a government of laws. If that which Congress has enacted, and the Supreme Court has sanctioned, be not the law of the land, then the reign of law has ceased, and the reign of individual opinion has already begun.

The President, in his commentary on the details of the existing bank charter, undertakes to prove that one provision, and another provision, is not necessary and proper; because, as he thinks, the same objects proposed to be accomplished by them might have been better attained in another mode; and therefore such provisions are not necessary, and so not warranted by the Constitution. Does not this show, that, according to his own mode of reasoning, his *own* scheme would not be constitutional, since another scheme, which probably most people would think a better one, might be substituted for it? Perhaps, in any bank charter, there may be no provisions which may be justly regarded as absolutely indispensable; since it is probable that for any of them some others might be substituted. No bank, therefore, ever could be established; because there never has been, and never could be, any charter, of which every provision should appear to be indispensable, or necessary and proper, in the judgment of every individual. To admit, therefore, that there may be a constitutional bank, and yet to contend for such a mode of judging of its provisions and details as the message adopts, involves an absurdity. Any charter which may be framed may be taken up, and each power conferred by it successively denied, on the ground, that, in regard to each, either no such power is "necessary or proper" in a bank, or, which is the same thing in effect, some other power might be substituted for it, and supply its place. That can never be necessary, in the sense in which the message understands that term, which may be dispensed with; and it cannot be said that any power may not be dispensed with, if there be some other which might be substituted for it, and which would accomplish the same end. Therefore, no bank could ever be constitutional, because none could be established which should not contain some provisions which might have been omitted, and their place supplied by others.

Mr. President, I have understood the true and well-established doctrine to be, that, after it has been decided that it is competent for Congress to establish a bank, then it follows that it may create such a bank as it judges, in its discretion, to be best, and invest it with all such power as it may deem fit and suitable; with this limitation, always, that all is to be done in the *bona fide* execution of the power to create a bank. If the granted powers are appropriate to the professed end, so that the granting of them cannot be regarded as usurpation of authority by Congress, or an evasion of constitutional restrictions, under color of establishing a bank, then the charter is constitutional, whether these powers be thought indispensable by others or not, or whether even Congress itself deemed them absolutely indispensable, or only thought them fit and suitable, or whether they are more or less appropriate to their end. It is enough that they are appropriate; it is enough that they are suited to produce the effects designed; and no comparison is to be instituted, in order to try their constitutionality, between them and others which may be suggested. A case analogous to the present is found in the constitutional power of Congress over the mail. The Constitution says no more than that "Congress shall have power to establish post-offices and post-roads"; and, in the general clause, "all powers necessary and proper" to give effect to this. In the execution of this power, Congress has protected the mail, by providing that robbery of it shall be punished with death. Is this infliction of capital punishment constitutional? Certainly it is not, unless it be both "proper and necessary." The President may not think it necessary or proper; the law, then, according to the system of reasoning enforced by the message, is of no binding force, and the President may disobey it, and refuse to see it executed.

The truth is, Mr. President, that if the general object, the subject-matter, properly belong to Congress, all its incidents belong to Congress also. If Congress is to establish post-offices and post-roads, it may, for that end, adopt one set of regulations or another; and either would be constitutional. So the details of one bank are as constitutional as those of another, if they are confined fairly and honestly to the purpose of organizing the institution, and rendering it useful. One *bank* is as constitutional as another *bank*. If Congress possesses the power to make a bank, it possesses the power to make it efficient, and competent to produce the good expected from it. It may clothe it with all such power and privileges, not otherwise inconsistent with the Constitution, as may be necessary, in its own judgment, to make it what government deems it should be. It may confer on it such immunities as may induce individuals to become stockholders, and to furnish the capital; and since the extent of these immunities and privileges is matter of discretion, and matter of opinion, Congress only can decide it, because Congress alone can frame or grant the charter. A charter, thus granted to individuals, becomes a contract with them, upon their compliance with its terms. The bank becomes an agent, bound to perform certain duties, and entitled to certain stipulated rights and privileges, in compensation for the proper discharge of these duties; and all these stipulations, so long as they are appropriate to the object professed, and not repugnant to any other constitutional injunction, are entirely within the competency of Congress. And yet, Sir, the message of the President toils through all the commonplace topics of monopoly, the right of taxation, the suffering of the poor, and the arrogance of the rich, with as much painful effort, as if one, or another, or all of them, had something to do with the constitutional question.

What is called the "monopoly" is made the subject of repeated rehearsal, in terms of special complaint. By this "monopoly," I suppose, is understood the restriction contained in the charter, that Congress shall not, during the twenty years, create another bank. Now, Sir, let me ask, Who would think of creating a bank, inviting stockholders into it, with large investments, imposing upon it heavy duties, as connected with the government, receiving some millions of dollars as a *bonus* or premium, and yet retaining the power of granting, the next day, another charter, which would destroy the whole value of the first? If this be an unconstitutional restraint on Congress, the Constitution must be strangely at variance with the dictates both of good sense and sound morals. Did not the first Bank of the United States contain a similar restriction? And have not the States granted bank charters with a condition, that, if the charter should be accepted, they would not grant others? States have certainly done so; and, in some instances, where no *bonus* or premium was paid at all; but from the mere desire to give effect to the charter, by inducing individuals to accept it and organize the institution. The President declares that this restriction is not necessary to the efficiency of the bank; but that is the very thing which Congress and his predecessor in office were called on to decide, and which they did decide, when the one passed and the other approved the act. And he has now no more authority to pronounce his judgment on that act than any other individual in society. It is not his province to decide on the constitutionality of statutes which Congress has passed, and his predecessors approved.

There is another sentiment in this part of the message, which we should hardly have expected to find in a paper which is supposed, whoever may have drawn it up, to have passed under the review of professional characters. The message declares, that this limitation to create no other bank is unconstitutional, because, although Congress may use the discretion vested in them, "they may not limit the discretion of their successors." This reason is almost too superficial to require an answer. Every one at all accustomed to the consideration of such subjects knows that every Congress can bind its successors to the same extent that it can bind itself. The power of Congress is always the same; the authority of law always the same. It is true, we speak of the Twentieth Congress and the Twenty-first Congress, but this is only to denote the period of time, or to mark the successive organizations of the House of Representatives under the successive periodical election of its members. As a politic body, as the legislative power of the government, Congress is always continuous, always identical. A particular Congress, as we speak of it, for instance, the present Congress, can no farther restrain itself from doing what it may choose to do at the next session, than it can restrain any succeeding Congress from doing what it may choose. Any Congress may repeal the act or law of its predecessor, if in its nature it be repealable, just as it may repeal its own act; and if a law or an act be irrepealable in its nature, it can no more be repealed by a subsequent Congress than by that which passed it. All this is familiar to everybody. And Congress, like every other legislature, often passes acts which, being in the nature of grants or contracts, are irrepealable ever afterwards. The message, in a strain of argument which it is difficult to treat with ordinary respect, declares that this restriction on the power of Congress, as to the establishment of other banks, is a palpable attempt to amend the Constitution by an act of legislation. The reason on which this observation purports to be founded is, that Congress, by the Constitution, is to have exclusive legislation over the District of Columbia; and when the bank charter declares that Congress will create no new bank within the District, it annuls this power of exclusive legislation! I must say, that this reasoning hardly rises high enough to entitle it to a passing notice. It would be doing it too much credit to call it plausible. No one needs to be informed that exclusive power of legislation is not unlimited power of legislation; and if it were, how can that legislative power be unlimited that cannot restrain itself, that cannot bind itself by contract? Whether as a government or as an individual, that being is fettered and restrained which is not capable of binding itself by ordinary obligation. Every legislature binds itself, whenever it makes a grant, enters into a contract, bestows an office, or does any other act or thing which is in its nature irrepealable. And this, instead of detracting from its legislative power, is one of the modes of exercising that power. The legislative power of Congress over the District of Columbia would not be full and complete, if it might not make just such a stipulation as the bank charter contains.

As to the taxing power of the States, about which the message says so much, the proper answer to all it says is, that the States possess no power to tax any instrument of the government of the United States. It was no part of their power before the Constitution, and they derive no such power from any of its provisions. It is nowhere given to them. Could a State tax the *coin* of the United States at the mint? Could a State lay a stamp tax on the process of the courts of the United States, and on custom-house papers? Could it tax the transportation of the mail, or the ships of war, or the ordnance, or the muniments of war, of the United States? The reason that these cannot be taxed by a State is, that they are means and instruments of the government of the United States. The establishment of a bank exempt from State taxation takes away no existing right in a State. It leaves it all it ever possessed. But the complaint is, that the bank charter does not *confer* the power of taxation. This, certainly, though not a new, (for the same argument was urged here,) appears to me to be a strange, mode of asserting and maintaining State rights. The power of taxation is a sovereign power; and the President and those who think with him are of opinion, in a given case, that this sovereign power should be conferred on the States by an act of Congress. There is, if I mistake not, Sir, as little compliment to State sovereignty in this idea, as there is of sound constitutional doctrine. Sovereign rights held under the grant of an act of Congress present a proposition quite new in constitutional law.

The President himself even admits that an instrument of the government of the United States ought not, as such, to be taxed by the States; yet he contends for such a power of taxing property connected with this instrument, and essential to its very being, as places its whole existence in the pleasure of the States. It is not enough that the States may tax all the property of all their own citizens, wherever invested or however employed. The complaint is, that the power of State taxation does not reach so far as to take cognizance over persons out of the State, and to tax them for a franchise lawfully exercised under the authority of the United States. Sir, when did the power of the States, or indeed of any government, go to such an extent as that? Clearly never. The taxing power of all communities is necessarily and justly limited to the property of its own citizens, and to the property of others, having a distinct local existence as property, within its jurisdiction; it does not extend to rights and franchises, rightly exercised, under the authority of other governments, nor to persons beyond its jurisdiction. As the Constitution has left the taxing power of the States, so the bank charter leaves it. Congress has not undertaken either to take away, or to confer, a taxing power; nor to enlarge, or to restrain it; if it were to do either, I hardly know which of the two would be the least excusable.

I beg leave to repeat, Mr. President, that what I have now been considering are the President's objections, not to the policy or expediency, but to the constitutionality, of the bank; and not to the constitutionality of any new or proposed bank, but of the bank as it now is, and as it has long existed. If the President had declined to approve this bill because he thought the original charter unwisely granted, and the bank, in point of policy and expediency, objectionable or mischievous, and in that view only had suggested the reasons now urged by him, his argument, however inconclusive, would have been intelligible, and not, in its whole frame and scope, inconsistent with all well-established first principles. His rejection of the bill, in that case, would have been, no doubt, an extraordinary exercise of power; but it would have been, nevertheless, the exercise of a power belonging to his office, and trusted by the Constitution to his discretion. But when he puts forth an array of arguments such as the message employs, not against the expediency of the bank, but against its constitutional existence, he confounds all distinctions, mixes questions of policy and questions of right together, and turns all constitutional restraints into mere matters of opinion. As far as its power extends, either in its direct effects or as a precedent, the message not only unsettles every thing which has been settled under the Constitution, but would show, also, that the Constitution itself is utterly incapable of any fixed construction or definite interpretation, and that there is no possibility of establishing, by its authority, any practical limitations on the powers of the respective branches of the government.

When the message denies, as it does, the authority of the Supreme Court to decide on constitutional questions, it effects, so far as the opinion of the President and his authority can effect it, a complete change in our government. It does two things: first, it converts constitutional limitations of power into mere matters of opinion, and then it strikes the judicial department, as an efficient department, out of our system. But the message by no means stops even at this point. Having denied to Congress the authority of judging what powers may be constitutionally conferred on a bank, and having erected the judgment of the President himself into a standard by which to try the constitutional character of such powers, and having denounced the authority of the Supreme Court to decide finally on constitutional questions, the message proceeds to claim for the President, not the power of approval, but the primary power, the power of originating laws. The President informs Congress, that *he* would have sent them such a charter, if it had been properly asked for, as they ought to confer. He very plainly intimates, that, in his opinion, the establishment of all laws, of this nature at least, belongs to the functions of the executive government; and that Congress ought to have waited for the manifestation of the executive will, before it presumed to touch the subject. Such, Mr. President, stripped of their disguises, are the real pretences set up in behalf of the executive power in this most extraordinary paper.

Mr. President, we have arrived at a new epoch. We are entering on experiments, with the government and the Constitution of the country, hitherto untried, and of fearful and appalling aspect. This message calls us to the contemplation of a future which little resembles the past. Its principles are at war with all that public opinion has sustained, and all which the experience of the government has sanctioned. It denies first principles; it contradicts truths, heretofore received as indisputable. It denies to the judiciary the interpretation of law, and claims to divide with Congress the power of originating statutes. It extends the grasp of executive pretension over every power of the government. But this is not all. It presents the chief magistrate of the Union in the attitude of arguing away the powers of that government over which he has been chosen to preside; and adopting for this purpose modes of reasoning which, even under the influence of all proper feeling towards high official station, it is difficult to regard as respectable. It appeals to every prejudice which may betray men into a mistaken view of their own interests, and to every passion which may lead them to disobey the impulses of their understanding. It urges all the specious topics of State rights and national encroachment against that which a great majority of the States have affirmed to be rightful, and in which all of them have acquiesced. It sows, in an unsparing manner, the seeds of jealousy and ill-will against that government of which its author is the official head. It raises a cry, that liberty is in danger, at the very moment when it puts forth claims to powers heretofore unknown and unheard of. It affects alarm for the public freedom, when nothing endangers that freedom so much as its own unparalleled pretences. This, even, is not all. It manifestly seeks to inflame the poor against the rich; it wantonly attacks whole classes of the people, for the purpose of turning against them the prejudices and the resentments of other classes. It is a state paper which finds no topic too exciting for its use, no passion too inflammable for its address and its solicitation.

Such is this message. It remains now for the people of the United States to choose between the principles here avowed and their government. These cannot subsist together. The one or the other must be rejected. If the sentiments of the message shall receive general approbation, the Constitution will have perished even earlier than the moment which its enemies originally allowed for the termination of its existence. It will not have survived to its fiftieth year.

THE CHARACTER OF WASHINGTON
A SPEECH DELIVERED AT A PUBLIC DINNER IN THE CITY OF WASHINGTON ON THE 22D OF FEBRUARY, 1832, THE CENTENNIAL ANNIVERSARY OF WASHINGTON'S BIRTHDAY.

[On the 22d of February, 1832, being the centennial birthday of GEORGE WASHINGTON, a number of gentlemen, members of Congress and others, from different parts of the Union, united in commemorating the occasion by a public dinner in the city of Washington.
At the request of the Committee of Arrangements, Mr. Webster, then a Senator from Massachusetts, occupied the chair. After the cloth was removed, he addressed the company in the following manner.]
I rise, Gentlemen, to propose to you the name of that great man, in commemoration of whose birth, and in honor of whose character and services, we are here assembled.
I am sure that I express a sentiment common to every one present, when I say that there is something more than ordinarily solemn and affecting in this occasion.
We are met to testify our regard for him whose name is intimately blended with whatever belongs most essentially to the prosperity, the liberty, the free institutions, and the renown of our country. That name was of power to rally a nation, in the hour of thick-thronging public disasters and calamities; that name shone, amid the storm of war, a beacon light, to cheer and guide the country's friends; it flamed, too, like a meteor, to repel her foes. That name, in the days of peace, was a loadstone, attracting to itself a whole people's confidence, a whole people's love, and the whole world's respect. That name, descending with all time, spreading over the whole earth, and uttered in all the languages belonging to the tribes and races of men, will for ever be pronounced with affectionate gratitude by every one in whose breast there shall arise an aspiration for human rights and human liberty.
We perform this grateful duty, Gentlemen, at the expiration of a hundred years from his birth, near the place, so cherished and beloved by him, where his dust now reposes, and in the capital which bears his own immortal name.
All experience evinces that human sentiments are strongly influenced by associations. The recurrence of anniversaries, or of longer periods of time, naturally freshens the recollection, and deepens the impression, of events with which they are historically connected. Renowned places, also, have a power to awaken feeling, which all acknowledge. No American can pass by the fields of Bunker Hill, Monmouth, and Camden, as if they were ordinary spots on the earth's surface. Whoever visits them feels the sentiment of love of country kindling anew, as if the spirit that belonged to the transactions which have rendered these places distinguished still hovered round, with power to move and excite all who in future time may approach them.
But neither of these sources of emotion equals the power with which great moral examples affect the mind. When sublime virtues cease to be abstractions, when they become embodied in human character, and exemplified in human conduct, we should be false to our own nature, if we did not indulge in the spontaneous effusions of our gratitude and our admiration. A true lover of the virtue of patriotism delights to contemplate its purest models; and that love of country may be well suspected which affects to soar so high into the regions of sentiment as to be lost and absorbed in the abstract feeling, and becomes too elevated or too refined to glow with fervor in the commendation or the love of individual benefactors. All this is unnatural. It is as if one should be so enthusiastic a lover of poetry, as to care nothing for Homer or Milton; so passionately attached to eloquence as to be indifferent to Tully and Chatham; or such a devotee to the arts, in such an ecstasy with the elements of beauty, proportion, and expression, as to regard the masterpieces of Raphael and Michael Angelo with coldness or contempt. We may be assured, Gentlemen, that he who really loves the thing itself, loves its finest exhibitions. A true friend of his country loves her friends and benefactors, and thinks it no degradation to commend and commemorate them. The voluntary outpouring of the public feeling, made to-day, from the North to the South, and from the East to the West,

proves this sentiment to be both just and natural. In the cities and in the villages, in the public temples and in the family circles, among all ages and sexes, gladdened voices to-day bespeak grateful hearts and a freshened recollection of the virtues of the Father of his Country. And it will be so, in all time to come, so long as public virtue is itself an object of regard. The ingenuous youth of America will hold up to themselves the bright model of Washington's example, and study to be what they behold; they will contemplate his character till all its virtues spread out and display themselves to their delighted vision; as the earliest astronomers, the shepherds on the plains of Babylon, gazed at the stars till they saw them form into clusters and constellations, overpowering at length the eyes of the beholders with the united blaze of a thousand lights.

Gentlemen, we are at a point of a century from the birth of Washington; and what a century it has been! During its course, the human mind has seemed to proceed with a sort of geometric velocity, accomplishing for human intelligence and human freedom more than had been done in fives or tens of centuries preceding. Washington stands at the commencement of a new era, as well as at the head of the New World. A century from the birth of Washington has changed the world. The country of Washington has been the theatre on which a great part of that change has been wrought, and Washington himself a principal agent by which it has been accomplished. His age and his country are equally full of wonders; and of both he is the chief.

If the poetical prediction, uttered a few years before his birth, be true; if indeed it be designed by Providence that the grandest exhibition of human character and human affairs shall be made on this theatre of the Western world; if it be true that,

"The four first acts already past, A fifth shall close the drama with the day, Time's noblest offspring is the last";--

how could this imposing, swelling, final scene be appropriately opened, how could its intense interest be adequately sustained, but by the introduction of just such a character as our Washington?

Washington had attained his manhood when that spark of liberty was struck out in his own country, which has since kindled into a flame, and shot its beams over the earth. In the flow of a century from his birth, the world has changed in science, in arts, in the extent of commerce, in the improvement of navigation, and in all that relates to the civilization of man. But it is the spirit of human freedom, the new elevation of individual man, in his moral, social, and political character, leading the whole long train of other improvements, which has most remarkably distinguished the era. Society, in this century, has not made its progress, like Chinese skill, by a greater acuteness of ingenuity in trifles; it has not merely lashed itself to an increased speed round the old circles of thought and action; but it has assumed a new character; it has raised itself from *beneath* governments to a participation *in* governments; it has mixed moral and political objects with the daily pursuits of individual men; and, with a freedom and strength before altogether unknown, it has applied to these objects the whole power of the human understanding. It has been the era, in short, when the social principle has triumphed over the feudal principle; when society has maintained its rights against military power, and established, on foundations never hereafter to be shaken, its competency to govern itself.

It was the extraordinary fortune of Washington, that, having been intrusted, in revolutionary times, with the supreme military command, and having fulfilled that trust with equal renown for wisdom and for valor, he should be placed at the head of the first government in which an attempt was to be made on a large scale to rear the fabric of social order on the basis of a written constitution and of a pure representative principle. A government was to be established, without a throne, without an aristocracy, without castes, orders, or privileges; and this government, instead of being a democracy, existing and acting within the walls of a single city, was to be extended over a vast country, of different climates, interests, and habits, and of various communions of our common Christian faith. The experiment certainly was entirely new. A popular government of this extent, it was evident, could be framed only by carrying into full effect the principle of representation or of delegated power; and the world was to see whether society could, by the strength of this principle, maintain its own peace and good government, carry forward its own great interests, and conduct itself to political renown and glory.

By the benignity of Providence, this experiment, so full of interest to us and to our posterity for ever, so full of interest, indeed, to the world in its present generation and in all its generations to come, was suffered to commence under the guidance of Washington. Destined for this high career, he was fitted for it by wisdom, by virtue, by patriotism, by discretion, by whatever can inspire confidence in man toward man.

In entering on the untried scenes, early disappointment and the premature extinction of all hope of success would have been certain, had it not been that there did exist throughout the country, in a most extraordinary degree, an unwavering trust in him who stood at the helm.

I remarked, Gentlemen, that the whole world was and is interested in the result of this experiment. And is it not so? Do we deceive ourselves, or is it true that at this moment the career which this government is running is among the most attractive objects to the civilized world? Do we deceive ourselves, or is it true that at this moment that love of liberty and that understanding of its true principles which are flying over the whole earth, as on the wings of all the winds, are really and truly of American origin?

At the period of the birth of Washington, there existed in Europe no political liberty in large communities, except in the provinces of Holland, and except that England herself had set a great example, so far as it went, by her glorious Revolution of 1688. Everywhere else, despotic power was predominant, and the feudal or military principle held the mass of mankind in hopeless bondage. One half of Europe was crushed beneath the Bourbon sceptre, and no conception of political liberty, no hope even of religious toleration, existed among that nation which was America's first ally. The king was the state, the king was the country, the king was all. There was one king, with power not derived from his people, and too high to be questioned; and the rest were all subjects, with no political right but obedience. All above was intangible power, all below quiet subjection. A recent occurrence in the French Chambers shows us how public opinion on these subjects is changed. A minister had spoken of the "king's subjects." "There are no subjects," exclaimed hundreds of voices at once, "in a country where the people make the king!"

Gentlemen, the spirit of human liberty and of free government, nurtured and grown into strength and beauty in America, has stretched its course into the midst of the nations. Like an emanation from Heaven, it has gone forth, and it will not return void. It must change, it is fast changing, the face of the earth. Our great, our high duty is to show, in our own example, that this spirit is a spirit of health as well as a spirit of power; that its benignity is as great as its strength; that its efficiency to secure individual rights, social relations, and moral order, is equal to the irresistible force with which it prostrates principalities and powers. The world, at this moment, is regarding us with a willing, but something of a fearful admiration. Its deep and awful anxiety is to learn whether free states may be stable, as well as free; whether popular power may be trusted, as well as feared; in short, whether wise, regular, and virtuous self-government is a vision for the contemplation of theorists, or a truth established, illustrated, and brought into practice in the country of Washington.

Gentlemen, for the earth which we inhabit, and the whole circle of the sun, for all the unborn races of mankind, we seem to hold in our hands, for their weal or woe, the fate of this experiment. If we fail, who shall venture the repetition? If our example shall prove to be one, not of encouragement, but of terror, not fit to be imitated, but fit only to be shunned, where else shall the world look for free models? If this great *Western Sun* be struck out of the firmament, at what other fountain shall the lamp of liberty hereafter be lighted? What other orb shall emit a ray to glimmer, even, on the darkness of the world?

There is no danger of our overrating or overstating the important part which we are now acting in human affairs. It should not flatter our personal self-respect, but it should reanimate our patriotic virtues, and inspire us with a deeper and more solemn sense, both of our privileges and of our duties. We cannot wish better for our country, nor for the world, than that the same spirit which influenced Washington may influence all who succeed him; and that the same blessing from above, which attended his efforts, may also attend theirs.

The principles of Washington's administration are not left doubtful. They are to be found in the Constitution itself, in the great measures recommended and approved by him, in his speeches to Congress, and in that most interesting paper, his Farewell Address to the People of the United States. The success of the government under his administration is the highest proof of the soundness of these principles. And, after an experience of thirty-five years, what is there which an enemy could condemn? What is there which either his friends, or the friends of the country, could wish to have been otherwise? I speak, of course, of great measures and leading principles.

In the first place, all his measures were right in their intent. He stated the whole basis of his own great character, when he told the country, in the homely phrase of the proverb, that honesty is the best policy. One of the most striking things ever said of him is, that "_he changed mankind's ideas of political greatness_."[1] To commanding talents, and to success, the common elements of such greatness, he added a disregard of self, a spotlessness of motive, a steady submission to every public and private duty, which threw far into the shade the whole crowd of vulgar great. The object of his regard was the whole country. No part of it was enough to fill his enlarged patriotism. His love of glory, so far as that may be supposed to have influenced him at all, spurned every thing short of general approbation. It would have been nothing to him, that his partisans or his favorites outnumbered, or outvoted, or outmanaged, or outclamored, those of other leaders. He had no favorites; he rejected all partisanship; and, acting honestly for the universal good, he deserved, what he has so richly enjoyed, the universal love.

His principle it was to act right, and to trust the people for support; his principle it was not to follow the lead of sinister and selfish ends, nor to rely on the little arts of party delusion to obtain public sanction for such a course. Born for his country and for the world, he did not give up to party what was meant for mankind. The consequence is, that his fame is as durable as his principles, as lasting as truth and virtue themselves. While the hundreds whom party excitement, and temporary circumstances, and casual combinations, have raised into transient notoriety, sink again, like thin bubbles, bursting and dissolving into the great ocean, Washington's fame is like the rock which bounds that ocean, and at whose feet its billows are destined to break harmlessly for ever.

The maxims upon which Washington conducted our foreign relations were few and simple. The first was an entire and indisputable impartiality towards foreign states. He adhered to this rule of public conduct, against very strong inducements to depart from it, and when the popularity of the moment seemed to favor such a departure. In the next place, he maintained true dignity and unsullied honor in all communications with foreign states. It was among the high duties devolved upon him, to introduce our new government into the circle of civilized states and powerful nations. Not arrogant or assuming, with no unbecoming or supercilious bearing, he yet exacted for it from all others entire and punctilious respect. He demanded, and he obtained at once, a standing of perfect equality for his country in the society of nations; nor was there a prince or potentate of his day, whose personal character carried with it, into the intercourse of other states, a greater degree of respect and veneration.

He regarded other nations only as they stood in political relations to us. With their internal affairs, their political parties and dissensions, he scrupulously abstained from all interference; and, on the other hand, he repelled with spirit all such interference by others with us or our concerns. His sternest rebuke, the most indignant measure of his whole administration, was aimed against such an attempted interference. He felt it as an attempt to wound the national honor, and resented it accordingly.

The reiterated admonitions in his Farewell Address show his deep fears that foreign influence would insinuate itself into our counsels through the channels of domestic dissension, and obtain a sympathy with our own temporary parties. Against all such dangers, he most earnestly entreats the country to guard itself. He appeals to its patriotism, to its self-respect, to its own honor, to every consideration connected with its welfare and happiness, to resist, at the very beginning, all tendencies towards such connection of foreign interests with our own affairs. With a tone of earnestness nowhere else found, even in his last affectionate farewell advice to his countrymen, he says, "Against the insidious wiles of foreign influence, (I conjure you to believe me, fellow-citizens,) the jealousy of a free people ought to be *constantly* awake; since history and experience prove, that foreign influence is one of the most baneful foes of republican government."

Lastly, on the subject of foreign relations, Washington never forgot that we had interests peculiar to ourselves. The primary political concerns of Europe, he saw, did not affect us. We had nothing to do with her balance of power, her family compacts, or her successions to thrones. We were placed in a condition favorable to neutrality during European wars, and to the enjoyment of all the great advantages of that relation. "Why, then," he asks us, "why forego the advantages of so peculiar a situation? Why quit our own to stand upon foreign ground? Why, by interweaving our destiny with that of any part of Europe, entangle our peace and prosperity in the toils of European ambition, rivalship, interest, humor, or caprice?"

Indeed, Gentlemen, Washington's Farewell Address is full of truths important at all times, and particularly deserving consideration at the present. With a sagacity which brought the future before him, and made it like the present, he saw and pointed out the dangers that even at this moment most imminently threaten us. I hardly know how a greater service of that kind could now be done to the community, than by a renewed and wide diffusion of that admirable paper, and an earnest invitation to every man in the country to reperuse and consider it. Its political maxims are invaluable; its exhortations to love of country and to brotherly affection among citizens, touching; and the solemnity with which it urges the observance of moral duties, and impresses the power of religious obligation, gives to it the highest character of truly disinterested, sincere, parental advice.

The domestic policy of Washington found its pole-star in the avowed objects of the Constitution itself. He sought so to administer that Constitution, as to form a more perfect union, establish justice, insure domestic tranquillity, provide for the common defence, promote the general welfare, and secure the blessings of liberty. These were objects interesting, in the highest degree, to the whole country, and his policy embraced the whole country.

Among his earliest and most important duties was the organization of the government itself, the choice of his confidential advisers, and the various appointments to office. This duty, so important and delicate, when a whole government was to be organized, and all its offices for the first time filled, was yet not difficult to him; for he had no sinister ends to accomplish, no clamorous partisans to gratify, no pledges to redeem, no object to be regarded but simply the public good. It was a plain, straightforward matter, a mere honest choice of men for the public service.

His own singleness of purpose, his disinterested patriotism, were evinced by the selection of his first Cabinet, and by the manner in which he filled the seats of justice, and other places of high trust. He sought for men fit for offices; not for offices which might suit men. Above personal considerations, above local considerations, above party considerations, he felt that he could only discharge the sacred trust which the country had placed in his hands, by a diligent inquiry after real merit, and a conscientious preference of virtue and talent. The whole country was the field of his selection. He explored that whole field, looking only for whatever it contained most worthy and distinguished. He was, indeed, most successful, and he deserved success for the purity of his motives, the liberality of his sentiments, and his enlarged and manly policy.

Washington's administration established the national credit, made provision for the public debt, and for that patriotic army whose interests and welfare were always so dear to him; and, by laws wisely framed, and of admirable effect, raised the commerce and navigation of the country, almost at once, from depression and ruin to a state of prosperity. Nor were his eyes open to these interests alone. He viewed with equal concern its agriculture and manufactures, and, so far as they came within the regular exercise of the powers of this government, they experienced regard and favor.

It should not be omitted, even in this slight reference to the general measures and general principles of the first President, that he saw and felt the full value and importance of the judicial department of the government. An upright and able administration of the laws he held to be alike indispensable to private happiness and public liberty. The temple of justice, in his opinion, was a sacred place, and he would profane and pollute it who should call any to minister in it, not spotless in character, not incorruptible in integrity, not competent by talent and learning, not a fit object of unhesitating trust.

Among other admonitions, Washington has left us, in his last communication to his country, an exhortation against the excesses of party spirit. A fire not to be quenched, he yet conjures us not to fan and feed the flame. Undoubtedly, Gentlemen, it is the greatest danger of our system and of our time. Undoubtedly, if that system should be overthrown, it will be the work of excessive party spirit, acting on the government, which is dangerous enough, or acting in the government, which is a thousand times more dangerous; for government then becomes nothing but organized party, and, in the strange vicissitudes of human affairs, it may come at last, perhaps, to exhibit the singular paradox of government itself being in opposition to its own powers, at war with the very elements of its own existence. Such cases are hopeless. As men may be protected against murder, but cannot be guarded against suicide, so government may be shielded from the assaults of external foes, but nothing can save it when it chooses to lay violent hands on itself.

Finally, Gentlemen, there was in the breast of Washington one sentiment so deeply felt, so constantly uppermost, that no proper occasion escaped without its utterance. From the letter which he signed in behalf of the Convention when the Constitution was sent out to the people, to the moment when he put his hand to that last paper in which he addressed his countrymen, the Union,--the Union was the great object of his thoughts. In that first letter he tells them that, to him and his brethren of the Convention, union appears to be the greatest interest of every true American; and in that last paper he conjures them to regard that unity of government which constitutes them one people as the very palladium of their prosperity and safety, and the security of liberty itself. He regarded the union of these States less as one of our blessings, than as the great treasure-house which contained them all. Here, in his judgment, was the great magazine of all our means of prosperity; here, as he thought, and as every true American still thinks, are deposited all our animating prospects, all our solid hopes for future greatness. He has taught us to maintain this union, not by seeking to enlarge the powers of the government, on the one hand, nor by surrendering them, on the other; but by an administration of them at once firm and moderate, pursuing objects truly national, and carried on in a spirit of justice and equity.

The extreme solicitude for the preservation of the Union, at all times manifested by him, shows not only the opinion he entertained of its importance, but his clear perception of those causes which were likely to spring up to endanger it, and which, if once they should overthrow the present system, would leave little hope of any future beneficial reunion. Of all the presumptions indulged by presumptuous man, that is one of the rashest which looks for repeated and favorable opportunities for the deliberate establishment of a united government over distinct and widely extended communities. Such a thing has happened once in human affairs, and but once; the event stands out as a prominent exception to all ordinary history; and unless we suppose ourselves running into an age of miracles, we may not expect its repetition. Washington, therefore, could regard, and did regard, nothing as of paramount political interest, but the integrity of the Union itself. With a united government, well administered, he saw that we had nothing to fear; and without it, nothing to hope. The sentiment is just, and its momentous truth should solemnly impress the whole country. If we might regard our country as personated in the spirit of Washington, if we might consider him as representing her, in her past renown, her present prosperity, and her future career, and as in that character demanding of us all to account for our conduct, as political men or as private citizens, how should he answer him who has ventured to talk of disunion and dismemberment? Or how should he answer him who dwells perpetually on local interests, and fans every kindling flame of local prejudice? How should he answer him who would array State against State, interest against interest, and party against party, careless of the continuance of that _unity of government which constitutes us one people_?

The political prosperity which this country has attained, and which it now enjoys, has been acquired mainly through the instrumentality of the present government. While this agent continues, the capacity of attaining to still higher degrees of prosperity exists also. We have, while this lasts, a political life capable of beneficial exertion, with power to resist or overcome misfortunes, to sustain us against the ordinary accidents of human affairs, and to promote, by active efforts, every public interest. But dismemberment strikes at the very being which preserves these faculties. It would lay its rude and ruthless hand on this great agent itself. It would sweep away, not only what we possess, but all power of regaining lost, or acquiring new possessions. It would leave the country, not only bereft of its prosperity and happiness, but without limbs, or organs, or faculties, by which to exert itself hereafter in the pursuit of that prosperity and happiness.

Other misfortunes may be borne, or their effects overcome. If disastrous war should sweep our commerce from the ocean, another generation may renew it; if it exhaust our treasury, future industry may replenish it; if it desolate and lay waste our fields, still, under a new cultivation, they will grow green again, and ripen to future harvests. It were but a trifle even if the walls of yonder Capitol were to crumble, if its lofty pillars should fall, and its gorgeous decorations be all covered by the dust of the valley. All these might be rebuilt. But who shall reconstruct the fabric of demolished government? Who shall rear again the well-proportioned columns of constitutional liberty? Who shall frame together the skilful architecture which unites national sovereignty with State rights, individual security, and public prosperity? No, if these columns fall, they will be raised not again. Like the Coliseum and the Parthenon, they will be destined to a mournful, a melancholy immortality. Bitterer tears, however, will flow over them, than were ever shed over the monuments of Roman or Grecian art; for they will be the remnants of a more glorious edifice than Greece or Rome ever saw, the edifice of constitutional American liberty.

But let us hope for better things. Let us trust in that gracious Being who has hitherto held our country as in the hollow of his hand. Let us trust to the virtue and the intelligence of the people, and to the efficacy of religious obligation. Let us trust to the influence of Washington's example. Let us hope that that fear of Heaven which expels all other fear, and that regard to duty which transcends all other regard, may influence public men and private citizens, and lead our country still onward in her happy career. Full of these gratifying anticipations and hopes, let us look forward to the end of that century which is now commenced. A hundred years hence, other disciples of Washington will celebrate his birth, with no less of sincere admiration than we now commemorate it. When they shall meet, as we now meet, to do themselves and him that honor, so surely as they shall see the blue summits of his native mountains rise in the horizon, so surely as they shall behold the river on whose banks he lived, and on whose banks he rests, still flowing on toward the sea, so surely may they see, as we now see, the flag of the Union floating on the top of the Capitol; and then, as now, may the sun in his course visit no land more free, more happy, more lovely, than this our own country!

Gentlemen, I propose--"THE MEMORY OF GEORGE WASHINGTON."

[Footnote 1: See Works of Fisher Ames, pp. 122, 123.]

EXECUTIVE PATRONAGE AND REMOVALS FROM OFFICE.
FROM A SPEECH DELIVERED AT THE NATIONAL REPUBLICAN CONVENTION HELD AT WORCESTER (MASS.), ON THE 12th OF OCTOBER, 1832.

I begin, Sir, with the subject of removals from office for opinion's sake, one of the most signal instances, as I think, of the attempt to extend executive power. This has been a leading measure, a cardinal point, in the course of the administration. It has proceeded, from the first, on a settled proscription for political opinions; and this system it has carried into operation to the full extent of its ability. The President has not only filled all vacancies with his own friends, generally those most distinguished as personal partisans, but he has turned out political opponents, and thus created vacancies, in order that he might fill them with his own friends. I think the number of removals and appointments is said to be *two thousand*. While the administration and its friends have been attempting to circumscribe and to decry the powers belonging to other branches, it has thus seized into its own hands a patronage most pernicious and corrupting, an authority over men's means of living most tyrannical and odious, and a power to punish free men for political opinions altogether intolerable.

You will remember, Sir, that the Constitution says not one word about the President's power of removal from office. It is a power raised entirely by construction. It is a constructive power, introduced at first to meet cases of extreme public necessity. It has now become coextensive with the executive will, calling for no necessity, requiring no exigency for its exercise; to be employed at all times, without control, without question, without responsibility. When the question of the President's power of removal was debated in the first Congress, those who argued for it limited it to *extreme cases*. Cases, they said, might arise, in which it would be *absolutely necessary* to remove an officer before the Senate could be assembled. An officer might become insane; he might abscond; and from these and other supposable cases, it was said, the public service might materially suffer if the President could not remove the incumbent. And it was further said, that there was little or no danger of the abuse of the power for party or personal objects. No President, it was thought, would ever commit such an outrage on public opinion. Mr. Madison, who thought the power ought to exist, and to be exercised in cases of high necessity, declared, nevertheless, that if a President should resort to the power when not required by any public exigency, and merely for personal objects, *he would deserve to be impeached*. By a very small majority,--I think, in the Senate, by the casting vote of the Vice-President,--Congress decided in favor of the existence of the power of removal, upon the grounds which I have mentioned; granting the power in a case of clear and absolute necessity, and denying its existence everywhere else.

Mr. President, we should recollect that this question was discussed, and thus decided, when Washington was in the executive chair. Men knew that in his hands the power would not be abused; nor did they conceive it possible that any of his successors could so far depart from his great and bright example, as, by abuse of the power, and by carrying that abuse to its utmost extent, to change the essential character of the executive from that of an impartial guardian and executor of the laws into that of the chief dispenser of party rewards. Three or four instances of removal occurred in the first twelve years of the government. At the commencement of Mr. Jefferson's administration, he made several others, not without producing much dissatisfaction; so much so, that he thought it expedient to give reasons to the people, in a public paper, for even the limited extent to which he had exercised the power. He rested his justification on particular circumstances and peculiar grounds; which, whether substantial or not, showed, at least, that he did not regard the power of removal as an ordinary power, still less as a mere arbitrary one, to be used as he pleased, for whatever ends he pleased, and without responsibility. As far as I remember, Sir, after the early part of Mr. Jefferson's administration, hardly an instance occurred for near thirty years. If there were any instances, they were few. But at the commencement of the present administration, the precedent of these previous cases was seized on, and a _system_, a regular _plan of government_, a well-considered scheme for the maintenance of party power by the patronage of office, and this patronage to be created by general removal, was adopted, and has been carried into full operation. Indeed, before General Jackson's inauguration, the party put the system into practice. In the last session of Mr. Adams's administration, the friends of General Jackson constituted a majority in the Senate; and nominations, made by Mr. Adams to fill vacancies which had occurred in the ordinary way, were postponed, by this majority, beyond the 3d of March, _for the purpose, openly avowed, of giving the nominations to General Jackson_. A nomination for a judge of the Supreme Court, and many others of less magnitude, were thus disposed of.

And what did we witness, Sir, when the administration actually commenced, in the full exercise of its authority? One universal sweep, one undistinguishing blow, levelled against all who were not of the successful party. No worth, public or private, no service, civil or military, was of power to resist the relentless greediness of proscription. Soldiers of the late war, soldiers of the Revolutionary war, the very contemporaries of the independence of the country, all lost their situations. No office was too high, and none too low; for *office* was the spoil, and "_all the spoils_," it is said, "belong to the _victors_"! If a man holding an office necessary for his daily support had presented himself covered with the scars of wounds received in every battle, from Bunker Hill to Yorktown, these would not have protected him against this reckless rapacity. Nay, Sir, if Warren himself had been among the living, and had possessed any office under government, high or low, he would not have been suffered to hold it a single hour, unless he could show that he had strictly complied with the party statutes, and had put a well-marked party collar round his own neck. Look, Sir, to the case of the late venerable Major Melville. He was a personification of the spirit of 1776, one of the earliest to venture in the cause of liberty. He was of the Tea Party; one of the very first to expose himself to British power. And his whole life was consonant with this, its beginning. Always ardent in the cause of liberty, always a zealous friend to his country, always acting with the party which he supposed cherished the genuine republican spirit most fervently, always estimable and respectable in private life, he seemed armed against this miserable petty tyranny of party as far as man could be. But he felt its blow, and he fell. He held an office in the custom-house, and had held it for a long course of years; and he was deprived of it, as if unworthy to serve the country which he loved, and for whose liberties, in the vigor of his early manhood, he had thrust himself into the very jaws of its enemies. There was no mistake in the matter. His character, his standing, his Revolutionary services, were all well known; but they were known to no purpose; they weighed not one feather against party pretensions. It cost no pains to remove him; it cost no compunction to wring his aged heart with this retribution from his country for his services, his zeal, and his fidelity. Sir, you will bear witness,[1] that, when his successor was nominated to the Senate, and the Senate were informed who had been removed to make way for that nomination, its members were struck with horror. They had not conceived the administration to be capable of such a thing; and yet they said, What can *we* do? The man is removed; *we* cannot recall him; we can only act upon the nomination before us. Sir, you and I thought otherwise; and I rejoice that we did think otherwise. We thought it our duty to resist the nomination to fill a vacancy thus created. We thought it our duty to oppose this proscription, when, and where, and as, we constitutionally could. We besought the Senate to go with us, and to take a stand before the country on this great question. We invoked them to try the deliberate sense of the people; to trust themselves before the tribunal of public opinion; to resist at first, to resist at last, to resist always, the introduction of this unsocial, this mischievous, this dangerous, this belligerent principle into the practice of the government.

Mr. President, as far as I know, there is no civilized country on earth, in which, on a change of rulers, there is such an *inquisition for spoil* as we have witnessed in this free republic. The Inaugural Address of 1829 spoke of a *searching operation* of government. The most searching operation, Sir, of the present administration, has been its search for office and place. When, Sir, did any English minister, Whig or Tory, ever make such an inquest? When did he ever go down to low-water mark, to make an ousting of tide-waiters? When did he ever take away the daily bread of weighers, and gaugers, and measurers? When did he ever go into the villages, to disturb the little post-offices, the mail contracts, and every thing else in the remotest degree connected with government? Sir, a British minister who should do this, and should afterwards show his head in a British House of Commons, would be received by a universal hiss.

I have little to say of the selections made to fill vacancies thus created. It is true, however, and it is a natural consequence of the system which has been acted on, that, within the last three years, more nominations have been rejected on the ground of _unfitness_, than in all the preceding forty years of the government. And these nominations, you know, Sir, could not have been rejected but by votes of the

President's own friends. The cases were too strong to be resisted. Even party attachment could not stand them In some not a third of the Senate, in others not ten votes, and in others not a single vote, could be obtained; and this for no particular reason known only to the Senate, but on general grounds of the want of character and qualifications; on grounds known to everybody else, as well as to the Senate. All this, Sir, is perfectly natural and consistent. The same party selfishness which drives good men out of office will push bad men in. Political proscription leads necessarily to the filling of offices with incompetent persons, and to a consequent malexecution of official duties. And in my opinion, Sir, this principle of claiming a monopoly of office by the right of conquest, unless the public shall effectually rebuke and restrain it, will entirely change the character of our government. It elevates party above country; it forgets the common weal in the pursuit of personal emolument; it tends to form, it does form, we see that it has formed, a political combination, united by no common principles or opinions among its members, either upon the powers of the government, or the true policy of the country; but held together simply as an association, under the charm of a popular head, seeking to maintain possession of the government by a _vigorous exercise of its patronage_; and for this purpose agitating, and alarming, and distressing social life by the exercise of a tyrannical party proscription. Sir, if this course of things cannot be checked, good men will grow tired of the exercise of political privileges. They will have nothing to do with popular elections. They will see that such elections are but a mere selfish contest for office; and they will abandon the government to the scramble of the bold, the daring, and the desperate.

It seems, Mr. President, to be a peculiar and singular characteristic of the present administration, that it came into power on a cry against abuses, _which did not exist_, and then, as soon as it was in, as if in mockery of the perception and intelligence of the people, _it created those very abuses_, and carried them to a great length. Thus the chief magistrate himself, before he came into the chair, in a formal public paper, denounced the practice of appointing members of Congress to office. He said, that, if that practice continued, _corruption would become the order of the day_; and, as if to fasten and nail down his own consistency to that point, he declared that it was *due to himself to practise what he recommended to others.* Yet, Sir, as soon as he was in power, these fastenings gave way, the nails all flew, and the promised *consistency* remains a striking proof of the manner in which political assurances are sometimes fulfilled. He has already appointed more members of Congress to office than any of his predecessors, in the longest period of administration. Before his time, there was no reason to complain of these appointments. They had not been numerous under any administration. Under this, they have been numerous, and some of them such as may well justify complaint.

Another striking instance of the exhibition of the same characteristics may be found in the sentiments of the Inaugural Address, and in the subsequent practice, on the subject of *interfering with the freedom of elections.* The Inaugural Address declares, that it is necessary to reform abuses which have *brought the patronage of the government into conflict with the freedom of elections.* And what has been the subsequent practice? Look to the newspapers; look to the published letters of officers of the government, advising, exhorting, soliciting, friends and partisans to greater exertions in the cause of the party; see all done, everywhere, which patronage and power can do, to affect, not only elections in the general government, but also in every State government, and then say how well *this* promise of reforming abuses has been kept. At what former period, under what former administration, did public officers of the United States thus interfere in elections? Certainly, Sir, never. In this respect, then, as well as in others, that which was not true as a charge against previous administrations would have been true, if it had assumed the form of a prophecy respecting the acts of the present.

But there is another attempt to grasp and to wield a power over public opinion, of a still more daring character, and far more dangerous effects.

In all popular governments, a FREE PRESS is the most important of all agents and instruments. It not only expresses public opinion, but, to a very great degree, it contributes to form that opinion. It is an engine for good or for evil, as it may be directed; but an engine of which nothing can resist the force. The conductors of the press, in popular governments, occupy a place, in the social and political system, of the very highest consequence. They wear the character of public instructors. Their daily labors bear directly on the intelligence, the morals, the taste, and the public spirit of the country. Not only are they journalists, recording political occurrences, but they discuss principles, they comment on measures, they canvass characters; they hold a power over the reputation, the feelings, the happiness of individuals. The public ear is always open to their addresses, the public sympathy easily made responsive to their sentiments. It is indeed, Sir, a distinction of high honor, that theirs is the only profession expressly protected and guarded by constitutional enactments. Their employment soars so high, in its general consequences it is so intimately connected with the public happiness, that its security is provided for by the fundamental law. While it acts in a manner worthy of this distinction, the press is a fountain of light, and a source of gladdening warmth. It instructs the public mind, and animates the spirit of patriotism. Its loud voice suppresses every thing which would raise itself against the public liberty; and its blasting rebuke causes incipient despotism to perish in the bud.

But remember, Sir, that these are the attributes of a FREE press only. And is a press that is purchased or pensioned more free than a press that is fettered? Can the people look for truths to partial sources, whether rendered partial through fear or through favor? Why shall not a manacled press be trusted with the maintenance and defence of popular rights? Because it is supposed to be under the influence of a power which may prove greater than the love of truth. Such a press may screen abuses in government, or be silent. It may fear to speak. And may it not fear to speak, too, when its conductors, if they speak in any but one way, may lose their means of livelihood? Is dependence on government for bread no temptation to screen its abuses? Will the press always speak the truth, when the truth, if spoken, may be the means of silencing it for the future? Is the truth in no danger, is the watchman under no temptation, when he can neither proclaim the approach of national evils, nor seem to descry them, without the loss of his place? Mr. President, an open attempt to secure the aid and friendship of the public press, by bestowing the emoluments of office on its active conductors, seems to me, of every thing we have witnessed, to be the most reprehensible. It degrades both the government and the press. As far as its natural effect extends, it turns the palladium of liberty into an engine of party. It brings the agency, activity, energy, and patronage of government all to bear, with united force, on the means of general intelligence, and on the adoption or rejection of political opinions. It so completely perverts the true object of government, it so entirely revolutionizes our whole system, that the chief business of those in power is directed rather to the propagation of opinions favorable to themselves, than to the execution of the laws. This propagation of opinions, through the press, becomes the main administrative duty. Some fifty or sixty editors of leading journals have been appointed to office by the present executive. A stand has been made against this proceeding, in the Senate, with partial success; but, by means of appointments which do not come before the Senate, or other means, the number has been carried to the extent I have mentioned. Certainly, Sir, the editors of the public journals are not to be disfranchised. Certainly they are fair candidates, either for popular elections, or a just participation in office. Certainly they reckon in their number some of the first geniuses, the best scholars, and the most honest and well-principled men in the country. But the complaint is against the _system_, against the _practice_, against the undisguised attempt to secure the favor of the press by means addressed to its pecuniary interest, and these means, too, drawn from the public treasury, being no other than the appointed compensations for the performance of official duties. Sir, the press itself should resent this. Its own character for purity and independence is at stake. It should resist a connection rendering it obnoxious to so many imputations. It should point to its honorable denomination in our constitutions of government, and it should maintain the character, there ascribed to it, of a FREE PRESS. There can, Sir, be no objection to the appointment of an editor to office, if he is the fittest man. There can be no objection to considering the services which, in that or in any other capacity, he may have rendered his country. He may have done much to maintain her rights against foreign aggression, and her character against insult. He may have honored, as well as defended her; and may, therefore, be justly regarded and selected, in the choice of faithful public agents. But the ground of complaint is, that the aiding, by the press, of the election of an individual, is rewarded, by that same individual, with the gift of moneyed offices. Men are turned out of office, and others put in, and receive salaries from the public treasury, on the ground, either openly avowed or falsely denied, that they have rendered service in the election of the very individual who makes this removal and makes this appointment. Every man, Sir, must see that this is a vital stab at the purity of the press. It not only assails its independence, by addressing sinister motives to it, but it furnishes from the public treasury the means of exciting these motives. It extends the executive power over the press in a most daring manner. It operates to give a direction to opinion, not favorable to the government, in the aggregate; not favorable to the Constitution and laws; not favorable to the legislature; but favorable to the executive alone. The consequence often is, just what might be looked for, that the portion of the press thus made fast to the executive interest denounces Congress, denounces the judiciary, complains of the laws, and quarrels with the Constitution. This exercise of the right of appointment to this end is an augmentation, and a vast one, of the executive power, singly and alone. It uses that power strongly against all other branches of the government, and it uses it strongly, too, for any struggle which it may be called on to make with the public opinion of the country. Mr. President, I will quit this topic. There is much in it, in my judgment, affecting, not only the purity and independence of the press, but also the character and honor, the peace and security, of the government. I leave it, in all its bearings, to the consideration of the people.

[Footnote 1: Hon. Nathaniel Silsbee, President of the Convention, was Mr. Webster's colleague in the Senate at the time referred to.]

EXECUTIVE USURPATION.
FROM THE SAME SPEECH AT WORCESTER.

Mr. President, the executive has not only used these unaccustomed means to prevent the passage of laws, but it has also refused to enforce the execution of laws actually passed. An eminent instance of this is found in the course adopted relative to the Indian intercourse law of 1802. Upon being applied to, in behalf of the MISSIONARIES, to execute that law, for their relief and protection, the President replied, that _the State of Georgia having extended her laws over the Indian territory, the laws of Congress had thereby been superseded_. This is the substance of his answer, as communicated through the Secretary of War. He holds, then, that the law of the State is paramount to the law of Congress. The Supreme Court has adjudged this act of Georgia to be void, as being repugnant to a constitutional law of the United States. But the President pays no more regard to this decision than to the act of Congress itself. The missionaries remain in prison, held there by a condemnation under a law of a State which the supreme judicial tribunal has pronounced to be null and void. The Supreme Court have decided that the act of Congress is constitutional; that it is a binding statute; that it has the same force as other laws, and is as much entitled to be obeyed and executed as other laws. The President, on the contrary, declares that the law of Congress has been superseded by the law of the State, and therefore he will not carry its provisions into effect. Now we know, Sir, that the Constitution of the United States declares, that that Constitution, and all acts of Congress passed in pursuance of it, shall be the supreme law of the land, any thing in any State law to the contrary notwithstanding. This would seem to be a plain case, then, in which the law should be executed. It has been solemnly decided to be in actual force, by the highest judicial authority; its execution is demanded for the relief of free citizens, now suffering the pains of unjust and unlawful imprisonment; yet the President refuses to execute it.

In the case of the Chicago Road, some sessions ago, the President approved the bill, but accompanied his approval by a message, saying how far he deemed it a proper law, and how far, therefore, it ought to be carried into execution.

In the case of the harbor bill of the late session, being applied to by a member of Congress for directions for carrying parts of the law into effect, he declined giving them, and made a distinction between such parts of the law as he should cause to be executed, and such as he should not; and his right to make this distinction has been openly maintained, by those who habitually defend his measures. Indeed, Sir, these, and other instances of liberties taken with plain statute laws, flow naturally from the principles expressly avowed by the President, under his own hand. In that important document, Sir, upon which it seems to be his fate to stand or to fall before the American people, the veto message, he holds the following language: "Each public officer who takes an oath to support the Constitution, swears that he will support it as he understands it, and not as it is understood by others." Mr. President, the general adoption of the sentiments expressed in this sentence would dissolve our government. It would raise every man's private opinions into a standard for his own conduct; and there certainly is, there can be, no government, where every man is to judge for himself of his own rights and his own obligations. Where every one is his own arbiter, force, and not law, is the governing power. He who may judge for himself, and decide for himself, must execute his own decisions; and this is the law of force. I confess, Sir, it strikes me with astonishment, that so wild, so disorganizing, a sentiment should be uttered by a President of the United States. I should think it must have escaped from its author through want of reflection, or from the habit of little reflection on such subjects, if I could suppose it possible, that, on a question exciting so much public attention, and of so much national importance, any such extraordinary doctrine could find its way, through inadvertence, into a formal and solemn public act. Standing as it does, it affirms a proposition which would effectually repeal all constitutional and all legal obligations. The Constitution declares, that every public officer, in the State governments as well as in the general government, shall take an oath to support the Constitution of the United States. This is all. Would it not have cast an air of ridicule on the whole provision, if the Constitution had gone on to add the words, "as he understands it"? What could come nearer to a solemn farce, than to bind a man by oath, and still leave him to be his own interpreter of his own obligation? Sir, those who are to execute the laws have no more a license to construe them for themselves, than those whose only duty is to obey them. Public officers are bound to support the Constitution; private citizens are bound to obey it; and there is no more indulgence granted to the public officer to support the Constitution only _as he understands it_, than to a private citizen to obey it only _as he understands it_, and what is true of the Constitution, in this respect, is equally true of any law. Laws are to be executed, and to be obeyed, not as individuals may interpret them, but according to public, authoritative interpretation and adjudication. The sentiment of the message would abrogate the obligation of the whole criminal code. If every man is to judge of the Constitution and the laws for himself, if he is to obey and support them only as he may say he understands them, a revolution, I think, would take place in the administration of justice; and discussions about the law of treason, murder, and arson should be addressed, not to the judicial bench, but to those who might stand charged with such offences. The object of discussion should be, if we run out this notion to its natural extent, to enlighten the culprit himself how he ought to understand the law.

Mr. President, how is it possible that a sentiment so wild, and so dangerous, so encouraging to all who feel a desire to oppose the laws, and to impair the Constitution, should have been uttered by the President of the United States at this eventful and critical moment? Are we not threatened with dissolution of the Union? Are we not told that the laws of the government shall be openly and directly resisted? Is not the whole country looking, with the utmost anxiety, to what may be the result of these threatened courses? And at this very moment, so full of peril to the state, the chief magistrate puts forth opinions and sentiments as truly subversive of all government, as absolutely in conflict with the authority of the Constitution, as the wildest theories of nullification. Mr. President, I have very little regard for the law, or the logic, of nullification. But there is not an individual in its ranks, capable of putting two ideas together, who, if you will grant him the principles of the veto message, cannot defend all that nullification has ever threatened.

To make this assertion good, Sir, let us see how the case stands. The Legislature of South Carolina, it is said, will nullify the late revenue or tariff law, because, _they say_, it is not warranted by the Constitution of the United States, *as they understand the Constitution*. They, as well as the President of the United States, have sworn to support the Constitution. Both he and they have taken the same oath, in the same words. Now, Sir, since he claims the right to interpret the Constitution as he pleases, how can he deny the same right to them? Is his oath less stringent than theirs? Has he a prerogative of dispensation which they do not possess? How can he answer them, when they tell him, that the revenue laws are unconstitutional, _as they understand the Constitution_, and that therefore they will nullify them? Will he reply to them, according to the doctrines of his annual message in 1830, that *precedent* has settled the question, if it was ever doubtful? They will answer him in his own words in the veto message, that, in such a case, *precedent* is not binding. Will he say to them, that the revenue law is a law of Congress, which must be executed until it shall be declared void? They will answer him, that, in other cases, he has himself refused to execute laws of Congress which had not been declared void, but which had been, on the contrary, declared valid. Will he urge the force of judicial decisions? They will answer, that he himself does not admit the binding obligation of such decisions. Sir, the President of the United States is of opinion, that an individual, called on to execute a law, may himself judge of its constitutional validity. Does nullification teach any thing more revolutionary than that? The President is of opinion, that judicial interpretations of the Constitution and the laws do not bind the consciences, and ought not to bind the conduct, of men. Is nullification at all more disorganizing than that? The President is of opinion, that every officer is bound to support the Constitution only according to what ought to be, in his private opinion, its construction. Has nullification, in its wildest flight, ever reached to an extravagance like that? No, Sir, never. The doctrine of nullification, in my judgment a most false, dangerous, and revolutionary doctrine, is this: that _the State_, or _a State_, may declare the extent of the obligations which its citizens are under to the United States; in other words, that a State, by State laws and State judicatures, may conclusively construe the Constitution for its own citizens. But that every individual may construe it for himself is a refinement on the theory of resistance to constitutional power, a sublimation of the right of being disloyal to the Union, a free charter for the elevation of private opinion above the authority of the fundamental law of the state, such as was never presented to the public view, and the public astonishment, even by nullification itself. Its first appearance is in the veto message. Melancholy, lamentable, indeed, Sir, is our condition, when, at a moment of serious danger and wide-spread alarm, such sentiments are found to proceed from the chief magistrate of the government. Sir, I cannot feel that the Constitution is safe in such hands. I cannot feel that the present administration is its fit and proper guardian.

But let me ask, Sir, what evidence there is, that the President is himself opposed to the doctrines of nullification: I do not say to the political party which now pushes these doctrines, but to the doctrines themselves. Has he anywhere rebuked them? Has he anywhere discouraged them? Has his influence been exerted to inspire respect for the Constitution, and to produce obedience to the laws? Has he followed the bright example of his predecessors? Has he held fast by the institutions of the country? Has he summoned the good and the wise around him? Has he admonished the country that the Union is in danger, and called on all the patriotic to come out in its support? Alas! Sir, we have seen nothing, nothing, of all this.

Mr. President, I shall not discuss the doctrine of nullification. I am sure it can have no friends here. Gloss it and disguise it as we may, it is a pretence incompatible with the authority of the Constitution. If direct separation be not its only mode of operation, separation is, nevertheless, its direct consequence. That a State may nullify a law of the Union, and still remain *in* the Union; that she may have Senators and Representatives in the government, and yet be at liberty to disobey and resist that government; that she may partake in the common councils, and yet not be bound by their results; that she may control a law of Congress, so that it shall be one thing with her, while it is another thing with the rest of the States;--all these propositions seem to me so absolutely at war with common sense and reason, that I do not understand how any intelligent person can yield the slightest assent to them. Nullification, it is in vain to attempt to conceal it, is dissolution; it is dismemberment; it is the breaking up of the Union. If it shall practically succeed in any one State, from that moment there are twenty-four States in the Union no longer. Now, Sir, I think it exceedingly probable that the President may come to an open rupture with that portion of his original party which now constitutes what is called the Nullification party. I think it likely he will oppose the proceedings of that party, if they shall adopt measures coming directly in conflict with the laws of the United States. But how will he oppose? What will be his course of remedy? Sir, I wish to call the attention of the Convention, and of the people, earnestly to this question,--How will the President attempt to put down nullification, if he shall attempt it at all?

Sir, for one, I protest in advance against such remedies as I have heard hinted. The administration itself keeps a profound silence, but its friends have spoken for it. We are told, Sir, that the President will immediately employ the military force, and at once blockade Charleston! A military remedy, a remedy by direct belligerent operation, has been thus suggested, and nothing else has been suggested, as the intended means of preserving the Union. Sir, there is no little reason to think, that this suggestion is true. We cannot be altogether unmindful of the past, and therefore we cannot be altogether unapprehensive for the future. For one, Sir, I raise my voice beforehand against the unauthorized employment of military power, and against superseding the authority of the laws, by an armed force, under pretence of putting down nullification. The President has no authority to blockade Charleston; the President has no authority to employ military force, till he shall be duly required so to do, by law, and by the civil authorities. His duty is to cause the laws to be executed. His duty is to support the civil authority. His duty is, if the laws be resisted, to employ the military force of the country, if necessary, for their support and execution; but to do all this in compliance only with law, and with decisions of the tribunals. If, by any ingenious devices, those who resist the laws escape from the reach of judicial authority, as it is now provided to be exercised, it is entirely competent to Congress to make such new provisions as the exigency of the case may demand. These provisions undoubtedly would be made. With a constitutional and efficient head of the government, with an administration really and truly in favor of the Constitution, the country can grapple with nullification. By the force of reason, by the progress of enlightened opinion, by the natural, genuine patriotism of the country, and by the steady and well-sustained operations of law, the progress of disorganization may be successfully checked, and the Union maintained. Let it be remembered, that, where nullification is most powerful, it is not unopposed. Let it be remembered, that they who would break up the Union by force have to march toward that object through thick ranks of as brave and good men as the country can show,--men strong in character, strong in intelligence, strong in the purity of their own motives, and ready, always ready, to sacrifice their fortunes and their lives to the preservation of the constitutional union of the States. If we can relieve the country from an administration which denies to the Constitution those powers which are the breath of its life; if we can place the government in the hands of its friends; if we can secure it against the dangers of irregular and unlawful military force; if it can be under the lead of an administration whose moderation, firmness, and wisdom shall inspire confidence and command respect,--we may yet surmount the dangers, numerous and formidable as they are, which surround us.

Sir, I see little prospect of overcoming these dangers without a change of men. After all that has passed, the re-election of the present executive will give the national sanction to sentiments and to measures which will effectually change the government; which, in short, must destroy the government. If the President be re-elected, with concurrent and co-operating majorities in both houses of Congress, I do not see, that, in four years more, all the power which is suffered to remain in the government will not be held by the executive hand. Nullification will proceed, or will be put down by a power as unconstitutional as itself. The revenues will be managed by a treasury bank. The use of the veto will be considered as sanctioned by the public voice. The Senate, if not "cut down," will be bound down, and, the President commanding the army and the navy, and holding all places of trust to be party property, what will then be left, Sir, for constitutional reliance?

Sir, we have been accustomed to venerate the judiciary, and to repose hopes of safety on that branch of the government. But let us not deceive ourselves. The judicial power cannot stand for a long time against the executive power. The judges, it is true, hold their places by an independent tenure; but they are mortal. That which is the common lot of humanity must make it necessary to renew the benches of justice. And how will they be filled? Doubtless, Sir, they will be filled by judges agreeing with the President in his constitutional opinions. If the court is felt as an obstacle, the first opportunity and every opportunity will certainly be embraced to give it less and less the character of an obstacle. Sir, without pursuing these suggestions, I only say that the country must prepare itself for any change in the judicial department such as it shall deliberately sanction in other departments.

But, Sir, what is the prospect of change? Is there any hope that the national sentiment will recover its accustomed tone, and restore to the government a just and efficient administration?

Sir, if there be something of doubt on this point, there is also something, perhaps much, of hope. The popularity of the present chief magistrate, springing from causes not connected with his administration of the government, has been great. Public gratitude for military service has remained fast to him, in defiance of many things in his civil administration calculated to weaken its hold. At length there are indications, not to be mistaken, of new sentiments and new impressions. At length, a conviction of danger to important interests, and to the security of the government, has made its lodgement in the public mind. At length, public sentiment begins to have its free course and to produce its just effects. I fully believe, Sir, that a great majority of the nation desire a change in the administration; and that it will be difficult for party organization or party denunciation to suppress the effective utterance of that general wish. There are unhappy differences, it is true, about the fit person to be successor to the present incumbent in the chief magistracy; and it is possible that this disunion may, in the end, defeat the will of the majority. But so far as we agree together, let us act together. Wherever our sentiments concur, let our hands co-operate. If we cannot at present agree who should be President, we are at least agreed who ought not to be. I fully believe, Sir, that gratifying intelligence is already on the wing. While we are yet deliberating in Massachusetts, Pennsylvania is voting. This week, she elects her members to the next Congress. I doubt not the result of that election will show an important change in public sentiment in that State; nor can I doubt that the great States adjoining her, holding similar constitutional principles and having similar interests, will feel the impulse of the same causes which affect her. The people of the United States, by a countless majority, are attached to the Constitution. If they shall be convinced that it is in danger, they will come to its rescue, and will save it. It cannot be destroyed, even now, if THEY will undertake its guardianship and protection.

But suppose, Sir, there was less hope than there is, would that consideration weaken the force of our obligations? Are we at a post which we are at liberty to desert when it becomes difficult to hold it? May we fly at the approach of danger? Does our fidelity to the Constitution require no more of us than to enjoy its blessings, to bask in the prosperity which it has shed around us and our fathers? and are we at liberty to abandon it in the hour of its peril, or to make for it but a faint and heartless struggle, for the want of encouragement and the want of hope? Sir, if no State come to our succor, if everywhere else the contest should be given up, here let it be protracted to the last moment. Here, where the first blood of the Revolution was shed, let the last effort be made for that which is the greatest blessing obtained by the Revolution, a free and united government. Sir, in our endeavors to maintain our existing forms of government, we are acting not for ourselves alone, but for the great cause of constitutional liberty all over the globe. We are trustees holding a sacred treasure, in which all the lovers of freedom have a stake. Not only in revolutionized France, where there are no longer subjects, where the monarch can no longer say, I am the state; not only in reformed England, where our principles, our institutions, our practice of free government, are now daily quoted and commended; but in the depths of Germany, also, and among the desolated fields and the still smoking ashes of Poland, prayers are uttered for the preservation of our union and happiness. We are surrounded, Sir, by a cloud of witnesses. The gaze of the sons of liberty, everywhere, is upon us, anxiously, intently, upon us. They may see us fall in the struggle for our Constitution and government, but Heaven forbid that they should see us recreant.

At least, Sir, let the star of Massachusetts be the last which shall be seen to fall from heaven, and to plunge into the utter darkness of disunion. Let her shrink back, let her hold others back if she can, at any rate, let her keep herself back, from this gulf, full at once of fire and of blackness; yes, Sir, as far as human foresight can scan, or human imagination fathom, full of the fire and the blood of civil war, and of the thick darkness of general political disgrace, ignominy, and ruin. Though the worst may happen that can happen, and though she may not be able to prevent the catastrophe, yet let her maintain her own integrity, her own high honor, her own unwavering fidelity, so that with respect and decency, though with a broken and a bleeding heart, she may pay the last tribute to a glorious, departed, free Constitution.

THE NATURAL HATRED OF THE POOR TO THE RICH.
FROM A SPEECH IN THE SENATE OF THE UNITED STATES, JANUARY 31st 1834, ON "THE REMOVAL OF THE DEPOSITS."

Sir, there is one other subject on which I wish to raise my voice. There is a topic which I perceive is to become the general war-cry of party, on which I take the liberty to warn the country against delusion. Sir, the cry is to be raised that this is a question between the poor and the rich. I know, Sir, it has been proclaimed, that one thing was certain, that there was always a hatred on the part of the poor toward the rich; and that this hatred would support the late measures, and the putting down of the bank. Sir, I will not be silent at the threat of such a detestable fraud on public opinion. If but ten men, or one man, in the nation will hear my voice, I will still warn them against this attempted imposition.

Mr. President, this is an eventful moment. On the great questions which occupy us, we all look for some decisive movement of public opinion. As I wish that movement to be free, intelligent, and unbiassed, the true manifestation of the public will, I desire to prepare the country for another appeal, which I perceive is about to be made to popular prejudice, another attempt to obscure all distinct views of the public good, to overwhelm all patriotism and all enlightened self-interest, by loud cries against false danger, and by exciting the passions of one class against another. I am not mistaken in the omen; I see the magazine whence the weapons of this warfare are to be drawn. I hear already the din of the hammering of arms preparatory to the combat. They may be such arms, perhaps, as reason, and justice, and honest patriotism cannot resist. Every effort at resistance, it is possible, may be feeble and powerless; but, for one, I shall make an effort,--an effort to be begun now, and to be carried on and continued, with untiring zeal, till the end of the contest.

Sir, I see, in those vehicles which carry to the people sentiments from high places, plain declarations that the present controversy is but a strife between one part of the community and another. I hear it boasted as the unfailing security, the solid ground, never to be shaken, on which recent measures rest, *that the poor naturally hate the rich.* I know that, under the cover of the roofs of the Capitol, within the last twenty-four hours, among men sent here to devise means for the public safety and the public good, it has been vaunted forth, as matter of boast and triumph, that one cause existed powerful enough to support every thing and to defend every thing; and that was, *the natural hatred of the poor to the rich.*

Sir, I pronounce the author of such sentiments to be guilty of attempting a detestable fraud on the community; a double fraud; a fraud which is to cheat men out of their property, and out of the earnings of their labor, by first cheating them out of their understandings.

"The natural hatred of the poor to the rich!" Sir, it shall not be till the last moment of my existence,--it shall be only when I am drawn to the verge of oblivion, when I shall cease to have respect or affection for any thing on earth,--that I will believe the people of the United States capable of being effectually deluded, cajoled, and _driven about in herds_, by such abominable frauds as this. If they shall sink to that point, if they so far cease to be men, thinking men, intelligent men, as to yield to such pretences and such clamor, they will be slaves already; slaves to their own passions, slaves to the fraud and knavery of pretended friends. They will deserve to be blotted out of all the records of freedom; they ought not to dishonor the cause of self-government, by attempting any longer to exercise it; they ought to keep their unworthy hands entirely off from the cause of republican liberty, if they are capable of being the victims of artifices so shallow, of tricks so stale, so threadbare, so often practised, so much worn out, on serfs and slaves.

"The natural hatred of the poor against the rich!" "The danger of a moneyed aristocracy!" "A power as great and dangerous as that resisted by the Revolution!" "A call to a new declaration of independence!" Sir, I admonish the people against the object of outcries like these. I admonish every industrious laborer in the country to be on his guard against such delusion. I tell him the attempt is to play off his passions against his interests, and to prevail on him, in the name of liberty, to destroy all the fruits of liberty; in the name of patriotism, to injure and afflict his country; and in the name of his own independence, to destroy that very independence, and make him a beggar and a slave. Has he a dollar? He is advised to do that which will destroy half its value. Has he hands to labor? Let him rather fold them, and sit still, than be pushed on, by fraud and artifice, to support measures which will render his labor useless and hopeless. Sir, the very man, of all others, who has the deepest interest in a sound currency, and who suffers most by mischievous legislation in money matters, is the man who earns his daily bread by his daily toil. A depreciated currency, sudden changes of prices, paper money, falling between morning and noon, and falling still lower between noon and night,--these things constitute the very harvest-time of speculators, and of the whole race of those who are at once idle and crafty; and of that other race, too, the Catilines of all times, marked, so as to be known for ever by one stroke of the historian's pen, _those greedy of other men's property and prodigal of their own_. Capitalists, too, may outlive such times. They may either prey on the earnings of labor, by their _cent. per cent._, or they may hoard. But the laboring man, what can he hoard? Preying on nobody, he becomes the prey of all. His property is in his hands. His reliance, his fund, his productive freehold, his all, is his labor. Whether he work on his own small capital, or another's, his living is still earned by his industry; and when the money of the country becomes depreciated and debased, whether it be adulterated coin or paper without credit, that industry is robbed of its reward. He then labors for a country whose laws cheat him out of his bread. I would say to every owner of every quarter-section of land in the West, I would say to every man in the East who follows his own plough, and to every mechanic, artisan, and laborer in every city in the country,--I would say to every man, everywhere, who wishes by honest means to gain an honest living, "Beware of wolves in sheep's clothing. Whoever attempts, under whatever popular cry, to shake the stability of the public currency, bring on distress in money matters, and drive the country into the use of paper money, stabs your interest and your happiness to the heart."

The herd of hungry wolves who live on other men's earnings will rejoice in such a state of things. A system which absorbs into their pockets the fruits of other men's industry is the very system for them. A government that produces or countenances uncertainty, fluctuations, violent risings and fallings in prices, and, finally, paper money, is a government exactly after their own heart. Hence these men are always for change. They will never let well enough alone. A condition of public affairs in which property is safe, industry certain of its reward, and every man secure in his own hard-earned gains, is no paradise for them. Give them just the reverse of this state of things; bring on change, and change after change; let it not be known to-day what will be the value of property to-morrow; let no man be able to say whether the money in his pockets at night will be money or worthless rags in the morning; and depress labor till double work shall earn but half a living,--give them this state of things, and you give them the consummation of their earthly bliss.

Sir, the great interest of this great country, the producing cause of all its prosperity, is labor! labor! labor! We are a laboring community. A vast majority of us all live by industry and actual employment in some of their forms. The Constitution was made to protect this industry, to give it both encouragement and security; but, above all, security. To that very end, with that precise object in view, power was given to Congress over the currency, and over the money system of the country. In forty years' experience, we have found nothing at all adequate to the beneficial execution of this trust but a well-conducted national bank. That has been tried, returned to, tried again, and always found successful. If it be not the proper thing for us, let it be soberly argued against; let something better be proposed; let the country examine the matter coolly, and decide for itself. But whoever shall attempt to carry a question of this kind by clamor, and violence, and prejudice; whoever would rouse the people by appeals, false and fraudulent appeals, to their love of independence, to resist the establishment of a useful institution, because it is a bank, and deals in money, and who artfully urges these appeals wherever he thinks there is more of honest feeling than of enlightened judgment,--means nothing but deception. And whoever has the wickedness to conceive, and the hardihood to avow, a purpose to break down what has been found, in forty years' experience, essential to the protection of all interests, by arraying one class against another, and by acting on such a principle as _that the poor always hate the rich_, shows himself the reckless enemy of all. An enemy to his whole country, to all classes, and to every man in it, he deserves to be marked especially _as the poor man's curse_!

A REDEEMABLE PAPER CURRENCY.
FROM A SPEECH DELIVERED IN THE SENATE OF THE UNITED STATES, ON THE 22D OF FEBRUARY, 1834.

Mr. President,--The honorable member from Georgia stated yesterday, more distinctly than I have before learned it, what that experiment is which the government is now trying on the revenues and the currency, and, I may add, on the commerce, manufactures, and agriculture of this country. If I rightly apprehend him, this experiment is an attempt to return to an exclusive specie currency, first, by employing the State banks as a substitute for the Bank of the United States; and then by dispensing with the use of the State banks themselves.

This, Sir, is the experiment. I thank the gentleman for thus stating its character. He has done his duty, and dealt fairly with the people, by this exhibition of what the views of the executive government are, at this interesting moment. It is certainly most proper that the people should see distinctly to what end or for what object it is that so much suffering is already upon them, and so much more already in visible and near prospect.

And now, Sir, is it possible,--is it possible that twelve millions of intelligent people can be expected voluntarily to subject themselves to severe distress, of unknown duration, for the purpose of making trial of an experiment like this? Will a nation that is intelligent, well informed of its own interest, enlightened, and capable of self-government, submit to suffer embarrassment in all its pursuits, loss of capital, loss of employment, and a sudden and dead stop in its onward movement in the path of prosperity and wealth, until it shall be ascertained whether this new-hatched theory shall answer the hopes of those who have devised it? Is the country to be persuaded to bear every thing, and bear patiently, until the operation of such an experiment, adopted for such an avowed object, and adopted, too, without the co-operation or consent of Congress, and by the executive power alone, shall exhibit its results?

In the name of the hundreds of thousands of our suffering fellow-citizens, I ask, for what reasonable end is this experiment to be tried? What great and good object, worth so much cost, is it to accomplish? What enormous evil is to be remedied by all this inconvenience and all this suffering? What great calamity is to be averted? Have the people thronged our doors, and loaded our tables with petitions for relief against the pressure of some political mischief, some notorious misrule, which this experiment is to redress? Has it been resorted to in an hour of misfortune, calamity, or peril, to save the state? Is it a measure of remedy, yielded to the importunate cries of an agitated and distressed nation? Far, Sir, very far from all this. There was no calamity, there was no suffering, there was no peril, when these measures began. At the moment when this experiment was entered upon, these twelve millions of people were prosperous and happy, not only beyond the example of all others, but even beyond their own example in times past.

There was no pressure of public or private distress throughout the whole land. All business was prosperous, all industry was rewarded, and cheerfulness and content universally prevailed. Yet, in the midst of all this enjoyment, with so much to heighten and so little to mar it, this experiment comes upon us, to harass and oppress us at present, and to affright us for the future. Sir, it is incredible; the world abroad will not believe it; it is difficult even for us to credit, who see it with our own eyes, that the country, at such a moment, should put itself upon an experiment fraught with such immediate and overwhelming evils, and threatening the property and the employments of the people, and all their social and political blessings, with severe and long-enduring future inflictions.

And this experiment, with all its cost, is to be tried, for what? Why, simply, Sir, to enable us to try another "experiment"; and that other experiment is, to see whether an exclusive specie currency may not be better than a currency partly specie and partly bank paper! The object which it is hoped we may effect, by patiently treading this path of endurance, is to banish all bank paper, of all kinds, and to have coined money, and coined money only, as the actual currency of the country!

Now, Sir, I altogether deny that such an object is at all desirable, even if it could be attained. I know, indeed, that all paper ought to circulate on a specie basis; that all bank-notes, to be safe, must be convertible into gold and silver at the will of the holder; and I admit, too, that the issuing of very small notes by many of the State banks has too much reduced the amount of specie actually circulating. It may be remembered that I called the attention of Congress to this subject in 1832, and that the bill which then passed both houses for renewing the bank charter contained a provision designed to produce some restraint on the circulation of very small notes. I admit there are conveniences in making small payments in specie; and I have always, not only admitted, but contended, that, if all issues of bank-notes under five dollars were discontinued, much more specie would be retained in the country, and in the circulation; and that great security would result from this. But we are now debating about an *exclusive* specie currency; and I deny that an exclusive specie currency is the best currency for any highly commercial country; and I deny, especially, that such a currency would be best suited to the condition and circumstances of the United States. With the enlightened writers and practical statesmen of all commercial communities in modern times, I have supposed it to be admitted that a well regulated, properly restrained, safely limited paper currency, circulating on an adequate specie basis, was a thing to be desired, a political public advantage to be obtained, if it might be obtained; and, more especially, I have supposed that in a new country, with resources not yet half developed, with a rapidly increasing population and a constant demand for more and more capital,--that is to say, in just such a country as the United States are, I have supposed that it was admitted that there are particular and extraordinary advantages in a safe and well regulated paper currency; because in such a country well regulated bank paper not only supplies a convenient medium of payments and of exchange, but also, by the expansion of that medium in a reasonable and safe degree, the amount of circulation is kept more nearly commensurate with the constantly increasing amount of property; and an extended capital, in the shape of credit, comes to the aid of the enterprising and the industrious. It is precisely on this credit, created by reasonable expansion of the currency in a new country, that men of small capital carry on their business. It is exactly by means of this, that industry and enterprise are stimulated. If we were driven back to an exclusively metallic currency, the necessary and inevitable consequence would be, that all trade would fall into the hands of large capitalists. This is so plain, that no man of reflection can doubt it. I know not, therefore, in what words to express my astonishment, when I hear it said that the present measures of government are intended for the good of the many instead of the few, for the benefit of the poor, and against the rich; and when I hear it proposed, at the same moment, to do away with the whole system of credit, and place all trade and commerce, therefore, in the hands of those who have adequate capital to carry them on without the use of any credit at all. This, Sir, would be dividing society, by a precise, distinct, and well-defined line, into two classes; first, the small class, who have competent capital for trade, when credit is out of the question; and, secondly, the vastly numerous class of those whose living must become, in such a state of things, a mere manual occupation, without the use of capital or of any substitute for it.

Now, Sir, it is the effect of a well-regulated system of paper credit to break in upon this line thus dividing the many from the few, and to enable more or less of the more numerous class to pass over it, and to participate in the profits of capital by means of a safe and convenient substitute for capital; and thus to diffuse far more widely the general earnings, and therefore the general prosperity and happiness, of society. Every man of observation must have witnessed, in this country, that men of heavy capital have constantly complained of bank circulation, and a consequent credit system, as injurious to the rights of capital. They undoubtedly feel its effects. All that is gained by the use of credit is just so much subtracted from the amount of their own accumulations, and so much the more has gone to the benefit of those who bestow their own labor and industry on capital in small amounts. To the great majority, this has been of incalculable benefit in the United States; and therefore, Sir, whoever attempts the entire overthrow of the system of bank credit aims a deadly blow at the interest of that great and industrious class, who, having some capital, cannot, nevertheless, transact business without some credit. He can mean nothing else, if he have any intelligible meaning at all, than to turn all such persons over to the long list of mere manual laborers. What else can they do, with not enough of absolute capital, and with no credit? This, Sir, this is the true tendency and the unavoidable result of these measures, which have been undertaken with the patriotic object of assisting the poor against the rich!

I am well aware that bank credit may be abused. I know that there is another extreme, exactly the opposite of that of which I have now been speaking, and no less sedulously to be avoided. I know that the issue of bank paper may become excessive; that depreciation will then follow; and that the evils, the losses, and the frauds consequent on a disordered currency fall on the rich and the poor together, but with especial weight of ruin on the poor. I know that the system of bank credit must always rest on a specie basis, and that it constantly needs to be strictly guarded and properly restrained; and it may be so guarded and restrained. We need not give up the good which belongs to it, through fear of the evils which may follow from its abuse. We have the power to take security against these evils. It is our business, as statesmen, to adopt that security; it is our business not to prostrate, or attempt to prostrate, the system, but to use those means of precaution, restraint, and correction which experience has sanctioned, and which are ready at our hands. It would be to our everlasting reproach, it would be placing us below the general level of the intelligence of civilized states, to admit that we cannot contrive means to enjoy the benefits of bank circulation, and of avoiding, at the same time, its dangers. Indeed, Sir, no contrivance is necessary. It is _contrivance_, and the love of contrivance, that spoil all. We are destroying ourselves by a remedy which no evil called for. We are ruining perfect health by nostrums and quackery. We have lived hitherto under a well constructed, practical, and beneficial system; a system not surpassed by any in the world; and it seems to me to be presuming largely, largely indeed, on the credulity and self-denial of the people, to rush with such sudden and impetuous haste into new schemes and new theories, to overturn and annihilate all that we have so long found useful.

Our system has hitherto been one in which paper has been circulating on the strength of a specie basis; that is to say, when every bank-note was convertible into specie at the will of the holder. This has been our guard against excess. While banks are bound to redeem their bills by paying gold and silver on demand, and are at all times able to do this, the currency is safe and convenient. Such a currency is not paper money, in its odious sense. It is not like the Continental paper of Revolutionary times; it is not like the worthless bills of banks which have suspended specie payments. On the contrary, it is the representative of gold and silver, and convertible into gold and silver on demand, and therefore answers the purposes of gold and silver; and so long as its credit is in this way sustained, it is the cheapest, the best, and the most convenient circulating medium. I have already endeavored to warn the country against irredeemable paper; against the paper of banks which do not pay specie for their own notes; against that miserable, abominable, and fraudulent policy, which attempts to give value to any paper, of any bank, one single moment longer than such paper is redeemable on demand in gold and silver. I wish most solemnly and earnestly to repeat that warning. I see danger of that state of things ahead. I see imminent danger that a portion of the State banks will stop specie payments. The late measure of the Secretary, and the infatuation with which it seems to be supported, tend directly and strongly to that result. Under pretence, then, of a design to return to a currency which shall be all specie, we are likely to have a currency in which there shall be no specie at all. We are in danger of being overwhelmed with irredeemable paper, mere paper, representing not gold nor silver; no, Sir, representing nothing but broken promises, bad faith, bankrupt corporations, cheated creditors, and a ruined people. This, I fear, Sir, may be the consequence, already alarmingly near, of this attempt, unwise if it be real, and grossly fraudulent if it be only pretended, of establishing an exclusively hard-money currency.

But, Sir, if this shock could be avoided, and if we could reach the object of an exclusive metallic circulation, we should find in that very success serious and insurmountable inconveniences. We require neither irredeemable paper, nor yet exclusively hard money. We require a mixed system. We require specie, and we require, too, good bank paper, founded on specie, representing specie, and convertible into specie on demand. We require, in short, just such a currency as we have long enjoyed, and the advantages of which we seem now, with unaccountable rashness, about to throw away.

I avow myself, therefore, decidedly against the object of a return to an exclusive specie currency. I find great difficulty, I confess, in believing any man serious in avowing such an object. It seems to me rather a subject for ridicule, at this age of the world, than for sober argument. But if it be true that any are serious for the return of the gold and silver age, I am seriously against it.

Let us, Sir, anticipate, in imagination, the accomplishment of this grand experiment. Let us suppose that, at this moment, all bank paper were out of existence, and the country full of specie. Where, Sir, should we put it, and what should we do with it? Should we ship it, by cargoes, every day, from New York to New Orleans, and from New Orleans back to New York? Should we encumber the turnpikes, the railroads, and the steamboats with it, whenever purchases and sales were to be made in one place of articles to be transported to another? The carriage of the money would, in some cases, cost half as much as the carriage of the goods. Sir, the very first day, under such a state of things, we should set ourselves about the creation of banks. This would immediately become necessary and unavoidable. We may assure ourselves, therefore, without danger of mistake, that the idea of an exclusively metallic currency is totally incompatible, in the existing state of the world, with an active and extensive commerce. It is inconsistent, too, with the greatest good of the greatest number; and therefore I oppose it.

But, Sir, how are we to get through the first experiment, so as to be able to try that which is to be final and ultimate, that is to say, how are we to get rid of the State banks? How is this to be accomplished? Of the Bank of the United States, indeed, we may free ourselves readily; but how are we to annihilate the State banks? We did not speak them into being; we cannot speak them out of being. They did not originate in any exercise of our power; nor do they owe their continuance to our indulgence. They are responsible to the States; to us they are irresponsible. We cannot act upon them; we can only act with them; and the expectation, as it would appear, is, that, by zealously co-operating with the government in carrying into operation its new theory, they may disprove the necessity of their own existence, and fairly work themselves out of the world! Sir, I ask once more, Is a great and intelligent community to endure patiently all sorts of suffering for fantasies like these? How charmingly practicable, how delightfully probable, all this looks!

I find it impossible, Mr. President, to believe that the removal of the deposits arose in any such purpose as is now avowed. I believe all this to be an after-thought. The removal was resolved on as a strong measure against the bank; and now that it has been attended with consequences not at all apprehended from it, instead of being promptly retracted, as it should have been, it is to be justified on the ground of a grand experiment, above the reach of common sagacity, and dropped down, as it were, from the clouds, "to witch the world with noble policy." It is not credible, not possible, Sir, that, six months ago, the administration suddenly started off to astonish mankind with its new inventions in politics, and that it then began its magnificent project by removing the deposits as its first operation. No, Sir, no such thing. The removal of the deposits was a blow at the bank, and nothing more; and if it had succeeded, we should have heard nothing of any project for the final putting down of all State banks. No, Sir, not one word. We should have heard, on the contrary, only of their usefulness, their excellence, and their exact adaptation to the uses and necessities of this government. But the experiment of making successful use of State banks having failed, completely failed, in this the very first endeavor; the State banks having already proved themselves not able to fill the place and perform the duties of a national bank, although highly useful in their appropriate sphere; and the disastrous consequences of the measures of government coming thick and fast upon us, the professed object of the whole movement is at once changed, and the cry now is, Down with all the State banks! Down with all the State banks! and let us return to our embraces of solid gold and solid silver!

THE PRESIDENTIAL PROTEST.

A SPEECH DELIVERED IN THE SENATE OF THE UNITED STATES, ON THE 7th OF MAY, 1834, ON THE SUBJECT OF THE PRESIDENT'S PROTEST AGAINST THE RESOLUTION OF THE SENATE OF THE 28TH OF MARCH.

Mr. President,--I feel the magnitude of this question. We are coming to a vote which cannot fail to produce important effects on the character of the Senate, and the character of the government.

Unhappily, Sir, the Senate finds itself involved in a controversy with the President of the United States; a man who has rendered most distinguished services to his country, who has hitherto possessed a degree of popular favor perhaps never exceeded, and whose honesty of motive and integrity of purpose are still admitted by those who maintain that his administration has fallen into lamentable errors.

On some of the interesting questions in regard to which the President and Senate hold opposite opinions, the more popular branch of the legislature concurs with the executive. It is not to be concealed that the Senate is engaged against imposing odds. It can sustain itself only by its own prudence and the justice of its cause. It has no patronage by which to secure friends; it can raise up no advocates through the dispensation of favors, for it has no favors to dispense. Its very constitution, as a body whose members are elected for a long term, is capable of being rendered obnoxious, and is daily made the subject of opprobrious remark. It is already denounced as independent of the people, and aristocratic. Nor is it, like the other house, powerful in its numbers; not being, like that, so large as that its members come constantly in direct and extensive contact with the whole people. Under these disadvantages, Sir, which, we may be assured, will be pressed and urged to the utmost length, there is but one course for us. The Senate must stand on its rendered reasons. It must put forth the grounds of its proceedings, and it must then rely on the intelligence and patriotism of the people to carry it through the contest.

As an individual member of the Senate, it gives me great pain to be engaged in such a conflict with the executive government. The occurrences of the last session are fresh in the recollection of all of us; and having felt it to be my duty, at that time, to give my cordial support to highly important measures of the administration, I ardently hoped that nothing might occur to place me afterwards in an attitude of opposition. In all respects, and in every way, it would have been far more agreeable to me to find nothing in the measures of the executive government which I could not cheerfully support. The present occasion of difference has not been sought or made by me. It is thrust upon me, in opposition to strong opinions and wishes, on my part not concealed. The interference with the public deposits dispelled all hope of continued concurrence with the administration, and was a measure so uncalled for, so unnecessary, and, in my judgment, so illegal and indefensible, that, with whatever reluctance it might be opposed by me, opposition was unavoidable.

The paper before us has grown out of this interference. It is a paper which cannot be treated with indifference. The doctrines which it advances, the circumstances which have attended its transmission to the Senate, and the manner in which the Senate may now dispose of it, will form a memorable era in the history of the government. We are either to enter it on our journals, concur in its sentiments, and submit to its rebuke, or we must answer it, with the respect due to the chief magistrate, but with such animadversion on its doctrines as they deserve, and with the firmness imposed upon us by our public duties.

I shall proceed, then, Sir, to consider the circumstances which gave rise to this Protest; to examine the principles which it attempts to establish; and to compare those principles with the Constitution and the laws.

On the 28th day of March, the Senate adopted a resolution declaring that, "in the late executive proceedings in relation to the public revenue, the President had assumed a power not conferred by the Constitution and laws, but in derogation of both." In that resolution I concurred.

It is not a direct question, now again before us, whether the President really had assumed such illegal power; that point is decided, so far as the Senate ever can decide it. But the Protest denies that, supposing the President to have assumed such illegal power, the Senate could properly pass the resolution; or, what is the same thing, it denies that the Senate could, in this way, express any opinion about it. It denies that the Senate has any right, by resolution, in this or any other case, to express disapprobation of the President's conduct, let that conduct be what it may; and this, one of the leading doctrines of the Protest, I propose to consider. But as I concurred in the resolution of the 28th of March, and did not trouble the Senate, at that time, with any statement of my own reasons, I will avail myself of this opportunity to explain, shortly, what those reasons were.

In the first place, then, I have to say, that I did not vote for the resolution on the mere ground of the removal of Mr. Duane from the office of Secretary of the Treasury. Although I disapprove of the removal altogether, yet the power of removal does exist in the President, according to the established construction of the Constitution; and therefore, although in a particular case it may be abused, and, in my opinion, was abused in this case, yet its exercise cannot be justly said to be an assumption or usurpation. We must all agree that Mr. Duane is out of office. He has, therefore, been removed by a power constitutionally competent to remove him, whatever may be thought of the exercise of that power under the circumstances of the case.

If, then, the act of removing the Secretary be not the assumption of power which the resolution declares, in what is that assumption found? Before giving a precise answer to this inquiry, allow me to recur to some of the principal previous events.

At the end of the last session of Congress, the public moneys of the United States were still in their proper place. That place was fixed by the law of the land, and no power of change was conferred on any other human being than the Secretary of the Treasury. On him the power of change was conferred, to be exercised by himself, if emergency should arise, and to be exercised for reasons which he was bound to lay before Congress. No other officer of the government had the slightest pretence of authority to lay his hand on these moneys for the purpose of changing the place of their custody. All the other heads of departments together could not touch them. The President could not touch them. The power of change was a trust confided to the discretion of the Secretary, and to his discretion alone. The President had no more authority to take upon himself this duty, thus assigned expressly by law to the Secretary, than he had to make the annual report to Congress, or the annual commercial statements, or to perform any other service which the law specially requires of the Secretary. He might just as well sign the warrants for moneys, in the ordinary daily disbursements of government, instead of the Secretary. The statute had assigned the especial duty of removing the deposits, if removed at all, to the Secretary of the Treasury, and to him alone. The consideration of the propriety or necessity of removal must be the consideration of the Secretary; the decision to remove, his decision; and the act of removal, his act.

Now, Sir, on the 18th day of September last, a resolution was taken to remove these deposits from their legislative, that is to say, their legal custody. _Whose resolution was this?_ On the 1st of October, they were removed. _By whose power was this done?_ The papers necessary to accomplish the removal (that is, the orders and drafts) are, it is true, signed by the Secretary. The President's name is not subscribed to them; nor does the Secretary, in any of them, recite or declare that he does the act by direction of the President, or on the President's responsibility. In form, the whole proceeding is the proceeding of the Secretary, and, as such, had the legal effect. The deposits were removed. But whose act was it, in truth and reality? Whose will accomplished it? On whose responsibility was it adopted?

These questions are all explicitly answered by the President himself, in the paper, under his own hand, read to the Cabinet on the 18th of September, and published by his authority. In this paper the President declares, in so many words, that he begs his Cabinet to consider the proposed measure as his own; that its responsibility has been assumed by him; and that he names the first day of October as a period proper for its execution.

Now, Sir, it is precisely this which I deem an assumption of power not conferred by the Constitution and laws. I think the law did not give this authority to the President, nor impose on him the responsibility of its exercise. It is evident that, in this removal, the Secretary was in reality nothing but the scribe; he was the pen in the President's hand, and no more. Nothing depended on his discretion, his judgment, or his responsibility. The removal, indeed, has been admitted and defended in the Senate, as the direct act of the President himself. This, Sir, is what I call assumption of power. If the President had issued an order for the removal of the deposits in his own name, and under his own hand, it would have been an illegal order, and the bank would not have been at liberty to obey it. For the same reason, if the Secretary's order had recited that it was issued by the President's direction, and on the President's authority, it would have shown on its face that it was illegal and invalid. No one can doubt that. The act of removal, to be lawful, must be the _bonâ fide_ act of the Secretary; _his_ judgment, the result of _his_ deliberations, the volition of _his_ mind. All are able to see the difference between the power to remove the Secretary from office, and the power to control him, in all or any of his duties, while in office. The law charges the officer, whoever he may be, with the performance of certain duties. The President, with the consent of the Senate, appoints an individual to be such officer; and this individual he may remove, if he so please; but, until removed, he is the officer, and remains charged with the duties of his station, duties which nobody else can perform, and for the neglect or violation of which he is liable to be impeached.

The distinction is visible and broad between the power of removal and the power to control an officer not removed. The President, it is true, may terminate his political life; but he cannot control his powers and functions, and act upon him as a mere machine, while he is allowed to live. The power of control and direction, nowhere given, certainly, by any express provision of the Constitution or laws, is derived, by those who maintain it, from the right of removal; that is to say, it is a constructive power; it has no express warrant in the Constitution. A very important power, then, is raised by construction in the first place; and being thus raised, it becomes a fountain out of which other important powers, raised also by construction, are to be supplied. There is no little danger that such a mode of reasoning may be carried too far. It cannot be maintained that the power of direct control necessarily flows from the power of removal. Suppose it had been decided in 1789, when the question was debated, that the President does not possess the power of removal; will it be contended, that, in that case, his right of interference with the acts and duties of executive officers would be less than it now is? The reason of the thing would seem to be the other way. If the President may remove an incumbent when he becomes satisfied of his unfaithfulness and incapacity, there would appear to be less necessity to give him also a right of control, than there would be if he could not remove him.

We may try this question by supposing it to arise in a judicial proceeding. If the Secretary of the Treasury were impeached for removing the deposits, could he justify himself by saying that he did it by the President's direction? If he could, then no executive officer could ever be impeached who obeys the President; and the whole notion of making such officers impeachable at all would be farcical. If he could not so justify himself, (and all will allow he could not,) the reason can only be that the act of removal is his own act; the power, a power confided to him, for the just exercise of which the law looks to his discretion, his honesty, and his direct responsibility.

Now, Sir, the President wishes the world to understand that he himself decided on the question of the removal of the deposits; that he took the whole responsibility of the measure upon himself; that he wished it to be considered _his own act_; that he not only himself decided that the thing should be done, but regulated its details also, and named the day for carrying it into effect.

I have always entertained a very erroneous view of the partition of powers, and of the true nature of official responsibility under our Constitution, if this be not a plain case of the assumption of power.

The legislature had fixed a place, by law, for the keeping of the public money. They had, at the same time and by the same law, created and conferred a power of removal, to be exercised contingently. This power they had vested in the Secretary, by express words. The law did not say that the deposits should be made in the bank, unless the President should order otherwise; but it did say that they should be made there, unless the Secretary of the Treasury should order otherwise. I put it to the plain sense and common candor of all men, whether the discretion thus to be exercised over the subject was not the Secretary's own personal discretion; and whether, therefore, the interposition of the authority of another, acting directly and conclusively on the subject, deciding the whole question, even in its particulars and details, be not an assumption of power?

The Senate regarded this interposition as an encroachment by the executive on other branches of the government; as an interference with the legislative disposition of the public treasure. It was strongly and forcibly urged, yesterday, by the honorable member from South Carolina, that the true and only mode of preserving any balance of power, in mixed governments, is to keep an exact balance. This is very true, and to this end encroachment must be resisted at the first step. The question is, therefore, whether, upon the true principles of the Constitution, this exercise of power by the President can be justified. Whether the consequences be prejudicial or not, if there be an illegal exercise of power, it is to be resisted in the proper manner. Even if no harm or inconvenience result from transgressing the boundary, the intrusion is not to be suffered to pass unnoticed. Every encroachment, great or small, is important enough to awaken the attention of those who are intrusted with the preservation of a constitutional government. We are not to wait till great public mischiefs come, till the government is overthrown, or liberty itself put into extreme jeopardy. We should not be worthy sons of our fathers were we so to regard great questions affecting the general freedom. Those fathers accomplished the Revolution on a strict question of principle. The Parliament of Great Britain asserted a right to tax the Colonies in all cases whatsoever; and it was precisely on this question that they made the Revolution turn. The amount of taxation was trifling, but the claim itself was inconsistent with liberty; and that was, in their eyes, enough. It was against the recital of an act of Parliament, rather than against any suffering under its enactments, that they took up arms. They went to war against a preamble. They fought seven years against a declaration. They poured out their treasures and their blood like water, in a contest against an assertion which those less sagacious and not so well schooled in the principles of civil liberty would have regarded as barren phraseology, or mere parade of words. They saw in the claim of the British Parliament a seminal principle of mischief, the germ of unjust power; they detected it, dragged it forth from underneath its plausible disguises, struck at it; nor did it elude either their steady eye or their well-directed blow till they had extirpated and destroyed it, to the smallest fibre. On this question of principle, while actual suffering was yet afar off, they raised their flag against a power, to which, for purposes of foreign conquest and subjugation, Rome, in the height of her glory, is not to be compared; a power which has dotted over the surface of the whole globe with her possessions and military posts, whose morning drum-beat, following the sun, and keeping company with the hours, circles the earth with one continuous and unbroken strain of the martial airs of England.

The necessity of holding strictly to the principle upon which free governments are constructed, and to those precise lines which fix the partitions of power between different branches, is as plain, if not as cogent, as that of resisting, as our fathers did, the strides of the parent country against the rights of the Colonies; because, whether the power which exceeds its just limits be foreign or domestic, whether it be the encroachment of all branches on the rights of the people, or that of one branch on the rights of others, in either case the balanced and well-adjusted machinery of free government is disturbed, and, if the derangement go on, the whole system must fall.

But the case before us is not a case of merely theoretic infringement; nor is it one of trifling importance. Far otherwise. It respects one of the highest and most important of all the powers of government; that is to say, the custody and control of the public money. The act of removing the deposits, which I now consider as the President's act, and which his friends on this floor defend as his act, took the national purse from beneath the security and guardianship of the law, and disposed of its contents, in parcels, in such places of deposit as he chose to select. At this very moment, every dollar of the public treasure is subject, so far as respects its custody and safe-keeping, to his unlimited control. We know not where it is to-day; still less do we know where it may be to-morrow.

But, Mr. President, this is not all. There is another part of the case, which has not been so much discussed, but which appears to me to be still more indefensible in its character. It is something which may well teach us the tendency of power to move forward with accelerated pace, if it be allowed to take the first step. The Bank of the United States, in addition to the services rendered to the treasury, gave for its charter, and for the use of the public deposits, a *bonus* or outright sum of one million and a half of dollars. This sum was paid by the bank into the treasury soon after the commencement of its charter. In the act which passed both houses for renewing the charter, in 1832, it was provided that the bank, for the same consideration, should pay two hundred thousand dollars a year during the period for which it was proposed to renew it. A similar provision is in the bill which I asked leave to introduce some weeks ago. Now, Sir, this shows that the custody of the deposits is a benefit for which a bank may well afford to pay a large annual sum. The banks which now hold the deposits pay nothing to the public; they give no _bonus_, they pay no annuity. But this loss of so much money is not the worst part of the case, nor that which ought most to alarm us. Although they pay nothing to the public, they do pay, nevertheless, such sums, and for such uses, as may be agreed upon between themselves and the executive government. We are officially informed that an officer is appointed by the Secretary of the Treasury to inspect or superintend these selected banks; and this officer is compensated by a salary fixed by the executive, agreed to by the banks, and paid by them. I ask, Sir, if there can be a more irregular or a more illegal transaction than this? Whose money is it out of which this salary is paid? Is it not money justly due to the United States, and paid, because it is so due, for the advantage of holding the deposits? If a dollar is received on that account, is not its only true destination into the general treasury of the government? And who has authority, without law, to create an office, to fix a salary, and to pay that salary out of this money? Here is an inspector or supervisor of the deposit banks. But what law has provided for such an officer? What commission has he received? Who concurred in his appointment? What oath does he take? How is he to be punished or impeached if he colludes with any of these banks to embezzle the public money or defraud the government? The value of the use of this public money to the deposit banks is probably two hundred thousand dollars a year; or, if less than that, it is yet, certainly, a very great sum. May the President appoint whatever officers he pleases, with whatever duties he pleases, and pay them as much as he pleases, out of the moneys thus paid by the banks, for the sake of having the deposits?

Mr. President, the executive claim of power is exactly this, that the President may keep the money of the public in whatever banks he chooses, on whatever terms he chooses, and apply the sums which these banks are willing to pay for its use to whatever purposes he chooses. These sums are not to come into the general treasury. They are to be appropriated before they get there; they are never to be brought under the control of Congress; they are to be paid to officers and agents not known to the law, not nominated to the Senate, and responsible to nobody but the executive itself. I ask gentlemen if all this be lawful. Are they prepared to defend it? Will they stand up and justify it? In my opinion, Sir, it is a clear and most dangerous assumption of power. It is the creation of office without law; the appointment to office without consulting the Senate; the establishment of a salary without law; and the payment of that salary out of a fund which itself is derived from the use of the public treasures. This, Sir, is my other reason for concurring in the vote of the 28th of March; and on these grounds I leave the propriety of that vote, so far as I am concerned with it, to be judged of by the country.

But, Sir, the President denies the power of the Senate to pass any such resolution, on any ground whatever. Suppose the declaration contained in the resolution to be true; suppose the President had, in fact, assumed powers not granted to him; does the Senate possess the right to declare its opinion, affirming this fact, or does it not? I maintain that the Senate does possess such a power; the President denies it.

Mr. President, we need not look far, nor search deep, for the foundation of this right in the Senate. It is close at hand, and clearly visible. In the first place, it is the right of self-defence. In the second place, it is a right founded on the duty of representative bodies, in a free government, to defend the public liberty against encroachment. We must presume that the Senate honestly entertained the opinion expressed in the resolution of the 28th of March; and, entertaining that opinion, its right to express it is but the necessary consequence of its right to defend its own constitutional authority, as one branch of the government. This is its clear right, and this, too, is its imperative duty.

If one or both the other branches of the government happen to do that which appears to us inconsistent with the constitutional rights of the Senate, will any one say that the Senate is yet bound to be passive, and to be silent? to do nothing, and to say nothing? Or, if one branch appears to encroach on the rights of the other two, have these two no power of remonstrance, complaint, or resistance? Sir, the question may be put in a still more striking form. Has the Senate a right *to have an opinion* in a case of this kind? If it may have an opinion, how is that opinion to be ascertained but by resolution and vote? The objection must go the whole length; it must maintain that the Senate has not only no right to express opinions, but no right to form opinions, on the conduct of the executive government, though in matters intimately affecting the powers and duties of the Senate itself. It is not possible, Sir, that such a doctrine can be maintained for a single moment. All political bodies resist what they deem encroachments by resolutions expressive of their sentiments, and their purpose to resist such encroachments. When such a resolution is presented for its consideration, the question is, whether it be true; not whether the body has authority to pass it, admitting it to be true. The Senate, like other public bodies, is perfectly justifiable in defending, in this mode, either its legislative or executive authority. The usages of Parliament, the practice in our State legislatures and assemblies, both before and since the Revolution, and precedents in the Senate itself, fully maintain this right. The case of the Panama mission is in point. In that case, Mr. Branch, from North Carolina, introduced a resolution, which, after reciting that the President, in his annual message and in his communication to the Senate, had asserted that he possessed an authority to make certain appointments, _although the appointments had not been made_, went on to declare that "_a silent acquiescence on the part of this body may, at some future time, be drawn into dangerous precedent_"; and to resolve, therefore, that the President does not possess the right or power said to be claimed by him. This resolution was discussed, and finally laid on the table. But the question discussed was, whether the resolution was correct, in fact and principle; not whether the Senate had any right to pass such resolution. So far as I remember, no one pretended that, if the President had exceeded his authority, the Senate might not so declare by resolution. No one ventured to contend that, whether the rights of the Senate were invaded or not, the Senate must hold its peace.

The Protest labors strenuously to show that the Senate adopted the resolution of the 28th of March, under its *judicial* authority. The reason of this attempt is obvious enough. If the Senate, in its judicial character, has been trying the President, then he has not had a regular and formal trial; and, on that ground, it is hoped the public sympathy may be moved. But the Senate has acted not in its judicial, but in its legislative capacity. As a legislative body, it has defended its own just authority, and the authority of the other branch of the legislature. Whatever attacks our own rights and privileges, or whatever encroaches on the power of both houses, we may oppose and resist, by declaration, resolution, or other similar proceedings. If we look to the books of precedents, if we examine the journals of legislative bodies, we find everywhere instances of such proceedings.

It is to be observed, Sir, that the Protest imposes silence on the House of Representatives as well as on the Senate. It declares that no power is conferred on either branch of the legislature, to consider or decide upon official acts of the executive, for the purpose of censure, and without a view to legislation or impeachment. This, I think, Sir, is pretty high-toned pretension. According to this doctrine, neither house could assert its own rights, however the executive might assail them; neither house could point out the danger to the people, however fast executive encroachment might be extending itself, or whatever danger it might threaten to the public liberties. If the two houses of Congress may not express an opinion of executive conduct by resolution, there is the same reason why they should not express it in any other form, or by any other mode of proceeding. Indeed, the Protest limits both houses, expressly, to the case of impeachment. If the House of Representatives are not about to impeach the President, they have nothing to say of his measures or of his conduct; and unless the Senate are engaged in trying an impeachment, their mouths, too, are stopped. It is the practice of the President to send us an annual message, in which he rehearses the general proceedings of the executive for the past year. This message we refer to our committees for consideration. But, according to the doctrine of the Protest, they can express no opinion upon any executive proceeding upon which it gives information. Suppose the President had told us, in his last annual message, what he had previously told us in his cabinet paper, that the removal of the deposits was *his* act, done on *his* responsibility; and that the Secretary of the Treasury had exercised no discretion, formed no judgment, presumed to have no opinion whatever, on the subject. This part of the message would have been referred to the committee on finance; but what could they say? They think it shows a plain violation of the Constitution and the laws; but the President is not impeached; therefore they can express no censure. They think it a direct invasion of legislative power, but they must not say so. They may, indeed, commend, if they can. The grateful business of praise is lawful to them; but if, instead of commendation and applause, they find cause for disapprobation, censure, or alarm, the Protest enjoins upon them absolute silence.

Formerly, Sir, it was a practice for the President to meet both houses, at the opening of the session, and deliver a speech, as is still the usage of some of the State legislatures. To this speech there was an answer from each house$ and those answers expressed, freely, the sentiments of the house upon all the merits and faults of the administration. The discussion of the topics contained in the speech, and the debate on the answers, usually drew out the whole force of parties, and lasted sometimes a week. President Washington's conduct, in every year of his administration, was thus freely and publicly canvassed. He did not complain of it; he did not doubt that both houses had a perfect right to comment, with the utmost latitude, consistent with decorum, upon all his measures. Answers, or amendments to answers, were not unfrequently proposed, very hostile to his own course of public policy, if not sometimes bordering on disrespect. And when they did express respect and regard, there were votes ready to be recorded against the expression of those sentiments. To all this President Washington took no exception; for he well knew that these, and similar proceedings, belonged to the power of popular bodies. But if the President were now to meet us with a speech, and should inform us of measures, adopted by himself in the recess, which should appear to us the most plain, palpable, and dangerous violations of the Constitution, we must, nevertheless, either keep respectful silence, or fill our answer merely with courtly phrases of approbation.

Mr. President, I know not who wrote this Protest, but I confess I am astonished, truly astonished, as well at the want of knowledge which it displays of constitutional law, as at the high and dangerous pretensions which it puts forth. Neither branch of the legislature can express censure upon the President's conduct! Suppose, Sir, that we should see him enlisting troops and raising an army, can we say nothing, and do nothing? Suppose he were to declare war against a foreign power, and put the army and the fleet in action; are we still to be silent? Suppose we should see him borrowing money on the credit of the United States; are we yet to wait for impeachment? Indeed, Sir, in regard to this borrowing money on the credit of the United States, I wish to call the attention of the Senate, not only to what might happen, but to what has actually happened. We are informed that the Post-Office Department, a department over which the

President claims the same control as over the rest, *has actually borrowed near half a million of money on the credit of the United States.*

Mr. President, the first power granted to Congress by the Constitution is the power to lay taxes; the second, the power to borrow money on the credit of the United States. Now, Sir, where does the executive find its authority, in or through any department, to borrow money without authority of Congress? This proceeding appears to me wholly illegal, and reprehensible in a very high degree. It may be said that it is not true that this money is borrowed on the credit of the United States, but that it is borrowed on the credit of the Post-Office Department. But that would be mere evasion. The department is but a name. It is an office, and nothing more. The banks have not lent this money to any officer. If Congress should abolish the whole department to-morrow, would the banks not expect the United States to replace this borrowed money? The money, then, is borrowed on the credit of the United States, an act which Congress alone is competent to authorize. If the Post-Office Department may borrow money, so may the War Department and the Navy Department. If half a million may be borrowed, ten millions may be borrowed. What, then, if this transaction shall be justified, is to hinder the executive from borrowing money to maintain fleets and armies, or for any other purpose, at his pleasure, without any authority of law? Yet even this, according to the doctrine of the Protest, we have no right to complain of. We have no right to declare that an executive department has violated the Constitution and broken the law, by borrowing money on the credit of the United States. Nor could we make a similar declaration, if we were to see the executive, by means of this borrowed money, enlisting armies and equipping fleets. And yet, Sir, the President has found no difficulty, heretofore, in expressing his opinions, _in a paper not called for by the exercise of any official duty_, upon the conduct and proceedings of the two houses of Congress. At the commencement of this session, he sent us a message, commenting on the land bill which the two houses passed at the end of the last session. That bill he had not approved, nor had he returned it with objections. Congress was dissolved; and the bill, therefore, was completely dead, and could not be revived. No communication from him could have the least possible effect as an official act. Yet he saw fit to send a message on the subject, and in that message he very freely declares his opinion that the bill which had passed both houses _began with an entire subversion of every one of the compacts by which the United States became possessed of their Western domain_; that one of its provisions _was in direct and undisguised violation of the pledge given by Congress to the States_; that the Constitution provides that these compacts shall be untouched by the legislative power, which can only make needful rules and regulations; and that all beyond that is *an assumption of undelegated power.*

These are the terms in which the President speaks of an act of the two houses; not in an official paper, not in a communication which it was necessary for him to make to them; but in a message, adopted only as a mode through which to make public these opinions. After this, it would seem too late to enjoin on the houses of Congress a total forbearance from all comment on the measures of the executive.

Not only is it the right of both houses, or of either, to resist, by vote, declaration, or resolution, whatever it may deem an encroachment of executive power, but it is also undoubtedly the right of either house to oppose, in like manner, any encroachment by the other. The two houses have each its own appropriate powers and authorities, which it is bound to preserve. They have, too, different constituents. The members of the Senate are representatives of States; and it is in the Senate alone that the four-and-twenty States, as political bodies, have a direct influence in the legislative and executive powers of this government. He is a strange advocate of State rights, who maintains that this body, thus representing the States, and thus being the strictly federal branch of the legislature, may not assert and maintain all and singular its own powers and privileges, against either or both of the other branches.

If any thing be done or threatened derogatory to the rights of the States, as secured by the organization of the Senate, may we not lift up our voices against it? Suppose the House of Representatives should vote that the Senate ought not to propose amendments to revenue bills; would it be the duty of the Senate to take no notice of such proceeding? Or, if we were to see the President issuing commissions to office to persons who had never been nominated to the Senate, are we not to remonstrate?

Sir, there is no end of cases, no end of illustrations. The doctrines of the Protest, in this respect, cannot stand the slightest scrutiny; they are blown away by the first breath of discussion.

And yet, Sir, it is easy to perceive why this right of declaring its sentiments respecting the conduct of the executive is denied to either house, in its legislative capacity. It is merely that the Senate might be presented in the odious light of *trying* the President, judicially, without regular accusation or hearing. The

Protest declares that the President is _charged with a crime, and, without hearing or trial, found guilty and condemned_. This is evidently an attempt to appeal to popular feeling, and to represent the President as unjustly treated and unfairly tried. Sir, it is a false appeal. The President has not been tried at all; he has not been accused; he has not been charged with crime; he has not been condemned. Accusation, trial, and sentence are terms belonging to judicial proceedings. But the Senate has been engaged in no such proceeding. The resolution of the 28th of March was not an exercise of judicial power, either in form, in substance, or in intent. Everybody knows that the Senate can exercise no judicial power until articles of impeachment are brought before it. It is then to proceed, by accusation and answer, hearing, trial, and judgment. But there has been no impeachment, no answer, no hearing, no judgment. All that the Senate did was to pass a resolution, in legislative form, declaring its opinion of certain acts of the executive. This resolution imputed no crime; it charged no corrupt motive; it proposed no punishment. It was directed, not against the President personally, but against the act; and that act it declared to be, in its judgment, an assumption of authority not warranted by the Constitution.

It is in vain that the Protest attempts to shift the resolution to the judicial character of the Senate. The case is too plain for such an argument to be plausible. But, in order to lay some foundation for it, the Protest, as I have already said, contends that neither the Senate nor the House of Representatives can express its opinions on the conduct of the President, except in some form connected with impeachment; so that if the power of impeachment did not exist, these two houses, though they be representative bodies, though one of them be filled by the immediate representatives of the people, though they be constituted like other popular and representative bodies, could not utter a syllable, although they saw the executive either trampling on their own rights and privileges, or grasping at absolute authority and dominion over the liberties of the country! Sir, I hardly know how to speak of such claims of impunity for executive encroachment. I am amazed that any American citizen should draw up a paper containing such lofty pretensions; pretensions which would have been met with scorn in England, at any time since the Revolution of 1688. A man who should stand up, in either house of the British Parliament, to maintain that the house could not, by vote or resolution, maintain its own rights and privileges, would make even the Tory benches hang their heads for very shame.

There was, indeed, a time when such proceedings were not allowed. Some of the kings of the Stuart race would not tolerate them. A signal instance of royal displeasure with the proceedings of Parliament occurred in the latter part of the reign of James the First. The House of Commons had spoken, on some occasion, "of its own undoubted rights and privileges." The king thereupon sent them a letter, declaring that _he would not allow that they had any undoubted rights; but that what they enjoyed they might still hold by his own royal grace and permission_. Sir Edward Coke and Mr. Granville were not satisfied with this title to their privileges; and, under their lead, the house entered on its journals a resolution asserting its privileges, _as its own undoubted right_, and manifesting a determination to maintain them as such. This, says the historian, so enraged his Majesty, that he sent for the journal, had it brought into the Council, and there, in the presence of his lords and great officers of state, tore out the offensive resolution with his own royal hand. He then dissolved Parliament, and sent its most refractory members to the Tower. I have no fear, certainly, Sir, that this English example will be followed, on this occasion, to its full extent; nor would I insinuate that any thing outrageous has been thought of, or intended, except outrageous pretensions; but such pretensions I must impute to the author of this Protest, whoever that author may be. When this and the other house shall lose the freedom of speech and debate; when they shall surrender the rights of publicly and freely canvassing all important measures of the executive; when they shall not be allowed to maintain their own authority and their own privileges by vote, declaration, or resolution,--they will then be no longer free representatives of a free people, but slaves themselves, and fit instruments to make slaves of others.

The Protest, Mr. President, concedes what it doubtless regards as a liberal right of discussion to the people themselves. But its language, even in acknowledging this right of the *people* to discuss the conduct of their servants, is qualified and peculiar. The free people of the United States, it declares, have an undoubted right to discuss the official conduct of the President in such language and form as they may think proper, "subject only to the restraints of truth and justice." But, then, who is to be judge of this truth and justice? Are the people to judge for themselves, or are others to judge for them? The Protest is here speaking of *political* rights, and not moral rights; and if restraints are imposed on *political* rights, it must follow, of course, that others are to decide whenever the case arises whether these restraints have been violated. It is strange that the writer of the Protest did not perceive that, by using this language, he was pushing the President into a direct avowal of the doctrines of 1798. The text of the Protest and the text of the obnoxious act[1] of that year are nearly identical.

But, Sir, if the people have a right to discuss the official conduct of the executive, so have their representatives. We have been taught to regard a representative of the people as a sentinel on the watch-tower of liberty. Is he to be blind, though visible danger approaches? Is he to be deaf, though sounds of peril fill the air? Is he to be dumb, while a thousand duties impel him to raise the cry of alarm? Is he not, rather, to catch the lowest whisper which breathes intention or purpose of encroachment on the public liberties, and to give his voice breath and utterance at the first appearance of danger? Is not his eye to traverse the whole horizon with the keen and eager vision of an unhooded hawk, detecting, through all disguises, every enemy advancing, in any form, towards the citadel which he guards? Sir, this watchfulness for public liberty; this duty of foreseeing danger and proclaiming it; this promptitude and boldness in resisting attacks on the Constitution from any quarter; this defence of established landmarks; this fearless resistance of whatever would transcend or remove them,--all belong to the representative character, are interwoven with its very nature. If deprived of them, an active, intelligent, faithful agent of the people will be converted into an unresisting and passive instrument of power. A representative body, which gives up these rights and duties, gives itself up. It is a representative body no longer. It has broken the tie between itself and its constituents, and henceforth is fit only to be regarded as an inert, self-sacrificed mass, from which all appropriate principle of vitality has departed for ever.

I have thus endeavored to vindicate the right of the Senate to pass the resolution of the 28th of March, notwithstanding the denial of that right in the Protest.

But there are other sentiments and opinions expressed in the Protest, of the very highest importance, and which demand nothing less than our utmost attention.

The first object of a free people is the preservation of their liberty; and liberty is only to be preserved by maintaining constitutional restraints and just divisions of political power. Nothing is more deceptive or more dangerous than the pretence of a desire to simplify government. The simplest governments are despotisms; the next simplest, limited monarchies; but all republics, all governments of law, must impose numerous limitations and qualifications of authority, and give many positive and many qualified rights. In other words, they must be subject to rule and regulation. This is the very essence of free political institutions. The spirit of liberty is, indeed, a bold and fearless spirit; but it is also a sharp-sighted spirit, it is a cautious, sagacious, discriminating, far-seeing intelligence; it is jealous of encroachment, jealous of power, jealous of man. It demands checks; it seeks for guards; it insists on securities; it intrenches itself behind strong defences, and fortifies itself with all possible care against the assaults of ambition and passion. It does not trust the amiable weaknesses of human nature, and therefore it will not permit power to overstep its prescribed limits, though benevolence, good intent, and patriotic purpose come along with it. Neither does it satisfy itself with flashy and temporary resistance to illegal authority. Far otherwise. It seeks for duration and permanence. It looks before and after; and, building on the experience of ages which are past, it labors diligently for the benefit of ages to come. This is the nature of constitutional liberty; and this is *our* liberty, if we will rightly understand and preserve it. Every free government is necessarily complicated, because all such governments establish restraints, as well on the power of government itself as on that of individuals. If we will abolish the distinction of branches, and have but one branch; if we will abolish jury trials, and leave all to the judge; if we will then ordain that the legislator shall himself be that judge; and if we will place the executive power in the same hands, we may readily simplify government. We may easily bring it to the simplest of all possible forms, a pure despotism. But a separation of departments, so far as practicable, and the preservation of clear lines of division between them, is the fundamental idea in the creation of all our constitutions; and, doubtless, the continuance of regulated liberty depends on maintaining these boundaries.

In the progress, Sir, of the governments of the United States, we seem exposed to two classes of dangers or disturbances; one external, the other internal. It may happen that collisions arise between this government and the governments of the States. That case belongs to the first class. A memorable instance of this kind occurred last year. It was my conscientious opinion, on that occasion, that the authority claimed by an individual State[2] was subversive of the just powers of this government, and, indeed, incompatible with its existence. I gave a hearty co-operation, therefore, to measures which the crisis seemed to require. We have now before us what appears, to my judgment, to be an instance of the latter kind. A contest has arisen between different branches of the same government, interrupting their harmony, and threatening to disturb their balance. It is of the highest importance, therefore, to examine the question carefully, and to decide it justly.

The separation of the powers of government into three departments, though all our constitutions profess to be founded on it, has, nevertheless, never been perfectly established in any government of the world, and perhaps never can be. The general principle is of inestimable value, and the leading lines of distinction sufficiently plain; yet there are powers of so undecided a character, that they do not seem necessarily to range themselves under either head. And most of our constitutions, too, having laid down the general principle, immediately create exceptions. There do not exist, in the general science of government, or the received maxims of political law, such precise definitions as enable us always to say of a given power whether it be legislative, executive, or judicial. And this is one reason, doubtless, why the Constitution, in conferring power on all the departments, proceeds not by general definition, but by specific enumeration. And, again, it grants a power in general terms, but yet, in the same or some other article or section, imposes a limitation or qualification on the grant; and the grant and the limitation must, of course, be construed together. Thus the Constitution says that all legislative power, therein granted, shall be vested in Congress, which Congress shall consist of a Senate and a House of Representatives; and yet, in another article, it gives to the President a qualified negative over all acts of Congress. So the Constitution declares that the judicial power shall be vested in one Supreme Court, and such inferior courts as Congress may establish. It gives, nevertheless, in another provision, judicial power to the Senate; and, in like manner, though it declares that the executive power shall be vested in the President, using, in the immediate context, no words of limitation, yet it elsewhere subjects the treaty-making power, and the appointing power, to the concurrence of the Senate. The irresistible inference from these considerations is, that the mere nomination of a department, as one of the three great and commonly acknowledged departments of government, does not confer on that department any power at all. Notwithstanding the departments are called the legislative, the executive, and the judicial, we must yet look into the provisions of the Constitution itself, in order to learn, first, what powers the Constitution regards as legislative, executive, and judicial; and, in the next place, what portions or quantities of these powers are conferred on the respective departments; because no one will contend that *all* legislative power belongs to Congress, *all* executive power to the President, or *all* judicial power to the courts of the United States.

The first three articles of the Constitution, as all know, are taken up in prescribing the organization, and enumerating the powers, of the three departments. The first article treats of the legislature, and its first section is, "All legislative power, _herein granted_, shall be vested in a Congress of the United States, which shall consist of a Senate and House of Representatives." The second article treats of the executive power, and its first section declares that "the executive power shall be vested in a President of the United States of America." The third article treats of the judicial power, and its first section declares that "the judicial power of the United States shall be vested in one Supreme Court, and in such inferior courts as the Congress may, from time to time, ordain and establish."

It is too plain to be doubted, I think, Sir, that these descriptions of the persons or officers in whom the executive and the judicial powers are to be vested no more define the extent of the grant of those powers, than the words quoted from the first article describe the extent of the legislative grant to Congress. All these several titles, heads of articles, or introductory clauses, with the general declarations which they contain, serve to designate the departments, and to mark the general distribution of powers; but in all the departments, in the executive and judicial as well as in the legislative, it would be unsafe to contend for any specific power under such clauses.

If we look into the State constitutions, we shall find the line of distinction between the departments still less perfectly drawn, although the general principle of the distinction is laid down in most of them, and in some of them in very positive and emphatic terms. In some of these States, notwithstanding the principle of distribution is adopted and sanctioned, the legislature appoints the judges; and in others it appoints both the governor and the judges; and in others, again, it appoints not only the judges, but all other officers.

The inferences which, I think, follow from these views of the subject, are two: first, that the denomination of a department does not fix the limits of the powers conferred on it, nor even their exact nature; and, second (which, indeed, follows from the first), that in our American governments, the chief executive magistrate does not necessarily, and by force of his general character of supreme executive, possess the appointing power. He may have it, or he may not, according to the particular provisions applicable to each case in the respective constitutions.

The President appears to have taken a different view of this subject. He seems to regard the appointing power as originally and inherently in the executive, and as remaining absolute in his hands, except so far as the Constitution restrains it. This I do not agree to, and I shall have occasion hereafter to examine the question further. I have intended thus far only to insist on the high and indispensable duty of maintaining the division of power _as the Constitution has marked out that division_, and to oppose claims of authority not founded on express grants or necessary implication, but sustained merely by argument or inference from names or denominations given to departments.

Mr. President, the resolutions now before us declare, that the Protest asserts powers as belonging to the President inconsistent with the authority of the two houses of Congress, and inconsistent with the Constitution; and that the Protest itself is a breach of privilege. I believe all this to be true.

The doctrines of the Protest are inconsistent with the authority of the two houses, because, in my judgment, they deny the just extent of the law-making power. I take the Protest as it was sent to us, without inquiring how far the subsequent message has modified or explained it. It is singular, indeed, that a paper, so long in preparation, so elaborate in composition, and which is put forth for so high a purpose as the Protest avows, should not be able to stand an hour's discussion before it became evident that it was indispensably necessary to alter or explain its contents. Explained or unexplained, however, the paper contains sentiments which justify us, as I think, in adopting these resolutions.

In the first place, I think the Protest a clear breach of privilege. It is a reproof or rebuke of the Senate, in language hardly respectful, for the exercise of a power clearly belonging to it as a legislative body. It entirely misrepresents the proceedings of the Senate. I find this paragraph in it, among others of a similar tone and character: "A majority of the Senate, whose interference with the preliminary question has, for the best of all reasons, been studiously excluded, anticipate the action of the House of Representatives, assume not only the function which belongs exclusively to that body, but convert themselves into accusers, witnesses, counsel, and judges, and prejudge the whole case; thus presenting the appalling spectacle, in a free state, of judges going through a labored preparation for an impartial hearing and decision, by a previous *ex parte* investigation and sentence against the supposed offender."

Now, Sir, this paragraph, I am bound to say, is a total misrepresentation of the proceedings of the Senate. A majority of the Senate have not anticipated the House of Representatives; they have not assumed the functions of that body; they have not converted themselves into accusers, witnesses, counsel, or judges; they have made no *ex parte* investigation; they have given no sentence. This paragraph is an elaborate perversion of the whole design and the whole proceedings of the Senate. A Protest, sent to us by the President, against votes which the Senate has an unquestionable right to pass, and containing, too, such a misrepresentation of these votes as this paragraph manifests, is a breach of privilege.

But there is another breach of privilege. The President interferes between the members of the Senate and their constituents, and charges them with acting contrary to the will of those constituents. He says it is his right and duty to look to the journals of the Senate to ascertain who voted for the resolution of the 28th of March, and then to show that individual Senators have, by their votes on that resolution, disobeyed the instructions or violated the known will of the legislatures who appointed them. All this he claims as his right and his duty. And where does he find any such right or any such duty? What right has he to send a message to either house of Congress telling its members that they disobey the will of their constituents? Has any English sovereign since Cromwell's time dared to send such a message to Parliament? Sir, if he can tell us that some of us disobey our constituents, he can tell us that all do so; and if we consent to receive this language from him, there is but one remaining step, and that is, that since we thus disobey the will of our constituents, he should disperse us and send us home. In my opinion, the first step in this process is as distinct a breach of privilege as the last. If Cromwell's example shall be followed out, it will not be more clear then than it is now that the privileges of the Senate have been violated. There is yet something, Sir, which surpasses all this; and that is, that, after this direct interference, after pointing out those Senators whom he would represent as having disobeyed the known will of their constituents, _he disclaims all design of interfering at all_! Sir, who could be the writer of a message, which, in the first place, makes the President assert such monstrous pretensions, and, in the next line, affront the understanding of the Senate by disavowing all right to do that very thing which he is doing? If there be any thing, Sir, in this message, more likely than the rest of it to move one from his equanimity, it is this disclaimer of all design to interfere with the responsibility of members of the Senate to their constituents, after such interference had already been made, in the same paper, in the most objectionable and offensive form. If it were not for the purpose of telling these Senators that they disobeyed the will of the legislatures of the States they represent, *for what purpose was it* that the Protest has pointed out the four Senators, and paraded against them the sentiments of their legislatures? There can be no other purpose. The Protest says, indeed, that "these facts belong to the history of these proceedings"! To the history of what proceedings? To any proceeding to which the President was party? To any proceeding to which the Senate was party? Have they any thing to do with the resolution of the 28th of March? But it adds, that these facts *are important to the just development of the principles and interests involved in the proceedings.* All this might be said of any other facts. It is mere words. To what principles, to what interests, are these facts important? They can be important but in one point of view; and that is as proof, or evidence, that the Senators have disobeyed instructions, or acted against the known will of their constituents in disapproving the President's conduct. They have not the slightest bearing in any other way. They do not make the resolution of the Senate more or less true, nor its right to pass it more or less clear. Sir, these proceedings of the legislatures were introduced into this Protest for the very purpose, and no other, of showing that members of the Senate have acted contrary to the will of their constituents. Every man sees and knows this to have been the sole design; and any other pretence is a mockery to our understandings. And this purpose is, in my opinion, an unlawful purpose; it is an unjustifiable intervention between us and our constituents; and is, therefore, a manifest and flagrant breach of privilege.

In the next place, the assertions of the Protest are inconsistent with the just authority of Congress, because they claim for the President a power, independent of Congress, to possess the custody and control of the public treasures. Let this point be accurately examined; and, in order to avoid mistake, I will read the precise words of the Protest.

"The custody of the public property, under such regulations as may be prescribed by legislative authority, has always been considered an appropriate function of the executive department in this and all other governments. In accordance with this principle, every species of property belonging to the United States, (excepting that which is in the use of the several co-ordinate departments of the government, as means to aid them in performing their appropriate functions,) is in charge of officers appointed by the President, whether it be lands, or buildings, or merchandise, or provisions, or clothing, or arms and munitions of war. The superintendents and keepers of the whole are appointed by the President, and removable at his will.

"Public money is but a species of public property. It cannot be raised by taxation or customs, nor brought into the treasury in any other way except by law; but whenever or howsoever obtained, its custody always has been, and always must be, unless the Constitution be changed, intrusted to the executive department. No officer can be created by Congress, for the purpose of taking charge of it, whose appointment would not, by the Constitution, at once devolve on the President, and who would not be responsible to him for the faithful performance of his duties."

And, in another place, it declares that "Congress cannot, therefore, take out of the hands of the executive department the custody of the public property or money, without an assumption of executive power, and a subversion of the first principles of the Constitution." These, Sir, are propositions which cannot receive too much attention. They affirm, that the custody of the public money constitutionally and necessarily belongs to the executive; and that, until the Constitution is changed, Congress cannot take it out of his hands, nor make any provision for its custody, except by such superintendents and keepers as are appointed by the President and removable at his will. If these assertions be correct, we have, indeed, a singular constitution for a republican government; for we give the executive the control, the custody, and the possession of the public treasury, by original constitutional provision; and when Congress appropriates, it appropriates only what is already in the President's hands.

Sir, I hold these propositions to be sound in neither branch. I maintain that the custody of the public money does not necessarily belong to the executive, under this government; and I hold that Congress may so dispose of it, that it shall be under the superintendence of keepers not appointed by the President, nor removable at his will. I think it competent for Congress to declare, as Congress did declare in the bank charter, that the public deposits should be made in the bank. When in the bank, they were not kept by persons appointed by the President, or removable at his will. He could not change that custody; nor could it be changed at all, but according to provisions made in the law itself. There was, indeed, a provision in the law authorizing the *Secretary* to change the custody. But suppose there had been no such provision; suppose the contingent power had not been given to the Secretary; would it not have been a lawful enactment? Might not the law have provided that the public moneys should remain in the bank, until Congress itself should otherwise order, leaving no power of removal anywhere else? And if such provision had been made, what power, or custody, or control, would the President have possessed over them? Clearly, none at all. The act of May, 1800, directed custom-house bonds, in places where the bank which was then in existence was situated, or in which it had branches, to be deposited in the bank or its branches for collection, without the reservation to the Secretary, or anybody else, of any power of removal. Now, Sir, this was an unconstitutional law, if the Protest, in the part now under consideration, be correct; because it placed the public money in a custody beyond the control of the President, and in the hands of keepers not appointed by him, nor removable at his pleasure. One may readily discern, Sir, the process of reasoning by which the author of the Protest brought himself to the conclusion that Congress could not place the public moneys beyond the President's control. It is all founded on the power of appointment and the power of removal. These powers, it is supposed, must give the President complete control and authority over those who actually hold the money, and therefore must necessarily subject its custody, at all times, to his own individual will. This is the argument.

It is true, that the appointment of all public officers, with some exceptions, is, by the Constitution, given to the President, with the consent of the Senate; and as, in most cases, public property must be held by some officer, its keepers will generally be persons so appointed. But this is only the common, not a necessary consequence, of giving the appointing power to the President and Senate. Congress may still, if it shall so see fit, place the public treasure in the hand of no officer appointed by the President, or removable by him, but in hands quite beyond his control. Subject to one contingency only, it did this very thing by the charter of the present bank; and it did the same thing absolutely, and subject to no contingency, by the law of 1800. The Protest, in the first place, seizes on the fact that all officers must be appointed by the President, or on his nomination; it then assumes the next step, that all officers are, and _must be_, removable at his pleasure; and then, insisting that public money, like other public property, must be kept by _some public officer_, it thus arrives at the conclusion that it *must* always be in the hands of those who are appointed by the President, and who are removable at his pleasure. And it is very clear that the Protest means to maintain that the _tenure of office cannot be so regulated by law, as that public officers shall not be removable at the pleasure of the President_.

The President considers the right of removal as a fixed, vested, constitutional right, which Congress cannot limit, control, or qualify, until the Constitution shall be altered. This, Sir, is doctrine which I am not prepared to admit. I shall not now discuss the question, whether the law may not place the tenure of office beyond the reach of executive pleasure; but I wish merely to draw the attention of the Senate to the fact, that any such power in Congress is denied by the principles and by the words of the Protest. According to that paper, we live under a constitution by the provisions of which the public treasures are, necessarily and unavoidably, always under executive control; and as the executive may remove all officers, and appoint others, at least temporarily, without the concurrence of the Senate, he may hold those treasures, in the hands of persons appointed by himself alone, in defiance of any law which Congress has passed or can pass. It is to be seen, Sir, how far such claims of power will receive the approbation of the country. It is to be seen whether a construction will be readily adopted which thus places the public purse out of the guardianship of the immediate representatives of the people.

But, Sir, there is, in this paper, something even yet more strange than these extraordinary claims of power. There is a strong disposition, running through the whole Protest, to represent the executive department of this government as the peculiar protector of the public liberty, the chief security on which the people are to rely against the encroachment of other branches of the government. Nothing can be more manifest than this purpose. To this end, the Protest spreads out the President's official oath, reciting all its words in a formal quotation; and yet the oath of members of Congress is exactly equivalent. The President is to swear that he will "preserve, protect, and defend the Constitution"; and members of Congress are to swear that they will "support the Constitution." There are more words in one oath than the other, but the sense is precisely the same. Why, then, this reference to his official oath, and this ostentatious quotation of it? Would the writer of the Protest argue that the oath itself is any grant of power; or that, because the President is to "preserve, protect, and defend the Constitution," he is therefore to use what means he pleases for such preservation, protection, and defence, or any means except those which the Constitution and laws have specifically given him? Such an argument would be absurd; but if the oath be not cited for this preposterous purpose, with what design is it thus displayed on the face of the Protest, unless it be to support the general idea that the maintenance of the Constitution and the preservation of the public liberties are especially confided to the safe discretion, the sure moderation, the paternal guardianship, of executive power? The oath of the President contains three words, all of equal import; that is, that he will _preserve_, _protect_, and *defend* the Constitution. The oath of members of Congress is expressed in shorter phrase; it is, that they will *support* the Constitution. If there be any difference in the meaning of the two oaths, I cannot discern it; and yet the Protest solemnly and formally argues thus: "The duty of defending, so far as in him lies, the integrity of the Constitution, would, indeed, have resulted from the very nature of his office; but by thus expressing it in the official oath or affirmation, which, in this respect, differs from that of every other functionary, the founders of our republic have attested their sense of its importance, and have given to it a peculiar solemnity and force."

Sir, I deny the proposition, and I dispute the proof. I deny that the duty of defending the integrity of the Constitution is, in any peculiar sense, confided to the President; and I deny that the words of his oath furnish any argument to make good that proposition. Be pleased, Sir, to remember *against whom it is* that the President holds it *his* peculiar duty to defend the integrity of the Constitution. It is not against external force; it is not against a foreign foe; no such thing; _but it is against the representatives of the people and the representatives of the States_! It is against these that the founders of our republic have imposed on him the duty of defending the integrity of the Constitution; a duty, he says, of the importance of which they have attested their sense, and to which they have given peculiar solemnity and force, by expressing it in his official oath!

Let us pause, Sir, and consider this most strange proposition. The President is the chief executive magistrate. He is commander-in-chief of the army and navy; nominates all persons to office; claims a right to remove all at will, and to control all, while yet in office; dispenses all favors; and wields the whole patronage of the government. And the proposition is, that the duty of defending the integrity of the Constitution against the representatives of the States and against the representatives of the people, _results to him from the very nature of his office_; and that the founders of our republic have given to this duty, thus confided to him, peculiar solemnity and force!

Mr. President, the contest, for ages, has been to rescue Liberty from the grasp of executive power. Whoever has engaged in her sacred cause, from the days of the downfall of those great aristocracies which had stood between the king and the people to the time of our own independence, has struggled for the accomplishment of that single object. On the long list of the champions of human freedom, there is not one name dimmed by the reproach of advocating the extension of executive authority; on the contrary, the uniform and steady purpose of all such champions has been to limit and restrain it. To this end the spirit of liberty, growing more and more enlightened and more and more vigorous from age to age, has been battering, for centuries, against the solid butments of the feudal system. To this end, all that could be gained from the imprudence, snatched from the weakness, or wrung from the necessities of crowned heads, has been carefully gathered up, secured, and hoarded, as the rich treasures, the very jewels of liberty. To this end, popular and representative right has kept up its warfare against prerogative, with various success; sometimes writing the history of a whole age in blood, sometimes witnessing the martyrdom of Sidneys and Russells, often baffled and repulsed, but still gaining, on the whole, and holding what it gained with a grasp which nothing but the complete extinction of its own being could compel it to relinquish. At length, the great conquest over executive power, in the leading western states of Europe, has been accomplished. The feudal system, like other stupendous fabrics of past ages, is known only by the rubbish which it has left behind it. Crowned heads have been compelled to submit to the restraints of law, and the PEOPLE, with that intelligence and that spirit which make their voice resistless, have been able to say to prerogative, "Thus far shalt thou come, and no farther." I need hardly say, Sir, that into the full enjoyment of all which Europe has reached only through such slow and painful steps we sprang at once, by the Declaration of Independence, and by the establishment of free representative governments; governments borrowing more or less from the models of other free states, but strengthened, secured, improved in their symmetry, and deepened in their foundation, by those great men of our own country whose names will be as familiar to future times as if they were written on the arch of the sky.

Through all this history of the contest for liberty, executive power has been regarded as a lion which must be caged. So far from being the object of enlightened popular trust, so far from being considered the natural protector of popular right, it has been dreaded, uniformly, always dreaded, as the great source of its danger.

And now, Sir, who is he, so ignorant of the history of liberty, at home and abroad; who is he, yet dwelling in his contemplations among the principles and dogmas of the Middle Ages; who is he, from whose bosom all original infusion of American spirit has become so entirely evaporated and exhaled, that he shall put into the mouth of the President of the United States the doctrine that the defence of liberty *naturally results to* executive power, and is its peculiar duty? Who is he, that, generous and confiding towards power where it is most dangerous, and jealous only of those who can restrain it,--who is he, that, reversing the order of the state, and upheaving the base, would poise the pyramid of the political system upon its apex? Who is he, that, overlooking with contempt the guardianship of the representatives of the people, and with equal contempt the higher guardianship of the people themselves,--who is he that declares to us, through the President's lips, that the security for freedom rests in executive authority? Who is he that belies the blood and libels the fame of his own ancestors, by declaring that _they_, with solemnity of form, and force of manner, have invoked the executive power to come to the protection of liberty? Who is he that thus charges them with the insanity, or the recklessness, of putting the lamb beneath the lion's paw? No, Sir. No, Sir. Our security is in our watchfulness of executive power. It was the constitution of this department which was infinitely the most difficult part in the great work of creating our present government. To give to the executive department such power as should make it useful, and yet not such as should render it dangerous; to make it efficient, independent, and strong, and yet to prevent it from sweeping away every thing by its union of military and civil authority, by the influence of patronage, and office, and favor,--this, indeed, was difficult. They who had the work to do saw the difficulty, and we see it; and if we would maintain our system, we shall act wisely to that end, by preserving every restraint and every guard which the Constitution has provided. And when we, and those who come after us, have done all that we can do, and all that they can do, it will be well for us and for them, if some popular executive, by the power of patronage and party, and the power, too, of that very popularity, shall not hereafter prove an overmatch for all other branches of the government.

I do not wish, Sir, to impair the power of the President, as it stands written down in the Constitution, and as great and good men have hitherto exercised it. In this, as in other respects, I am for the Constitution as it is. But I will not acquiesce in the reversal of all just ideas of government; I will not degrade the character of popular representation; I will not blindly confide, where all experience admonishes me to be jealous; I will not trust executive power, vested in the hands of a single magistrate, to be the guardian of liberty. Having claimed for the executive the especial guardianship of the Constitution, the Protest proceeds to present a summary view of the powers which are supposed to be conferred on the executive by that instrument. And it is to this part of the message, Sir, that I would, more than to all others, call the particular attention of the Senate. I confess that it was only upon careful reperusal of the paper that I perceived the extent to which its assertions of power reach. I do not speak now of the President's claims of power as opposed to legislative authority, but of his opinions as to his own authority, duty, and responsibility, as connected with all other officers under the government. He is of opinion that the whole executive power is vested in him, and that he is responsible for its entire exercise; that among the duties imposed on him is that of "taking care that the laws be faithfully executed"; and that, "being thus made responsible for the entire action of the executive department, it is but reasonable that the power of appointing, overseeing, and controlling those who execute the laws, a power in its nature executive, should remain in his hands. It is, therefore, not only his right, but the Constitution makes it his duty, to 'nominate, and, by and with the advice and consent of the Senate, appoint,' all 'officers of the United States whose appointments are not in the Constitution otherwise provided for,' with a proviso that the appointment of inferior officers may be vested in the President alone, in the courts of justice, or in the heads of departments."

The first proposition, then, which the Protest asserts, in regard to the President's powers as executive magistrate, is, that, the general duty being imposed on him by the Constitution of taking care that the laws be faithfully executed, _he thereby becomes himself responsible for the conduct of every person employed in the government_; "for the entire action," as the paper expresses it, "of the executive department." This, Sir, is very dangerous logic. I reject the inference altogether. No such responsibility, nor any thing like it, follows from the general provision of the Constitution making it his duty to see the laws executed. If it did, we should have, in fact, but one officer in the whole government. The President would be everybody. And the Protest assumes to the President this whole responsibility for every other officer, for the very purpose of making the President everybody, of annihilating every thing like independence, responsibility, or _character_, in all other public agents. The whole responsibility is assumed, in order that it may be more plausibly argued that all officers of government are not agents of the law, but the President's agents, and therefore responsible to him alone. If he be responsible for the conduct of all officers, and they be responsible to him only, then it may be maintained that such officers are but his own agents, his substitutes, his deputies. The first thing to be done, therefore, is to assume the responsibility for all; and this you will perceive, Sir, is done, in the fullest manner, in the passages which I have read. Having thus assumed for the President the entire responsibility of the whole government, the Protest advances boldly to its conclusion, and claims, at once, absolute power over all individuals in office, as being merely the President's agents. This is the language: "The whole executive power being vested in the President, who is responsible for its exercise, it is a necessary consequence that he should have a right to employ agents of his own choice to aid him in the performance of his duties, and to discharge them when he is no longer willing to be responsible for their acts."

This, Sir, completes the work. This handsomely rounds off the whole executive system of executive authority. First, the President has the whole responsibility; and then, being thus responsible for all, he has, and ought to have, the whole power. We have heard of political _units_, and our American executive, as here represented, is indeed a *unit*. We have a charmingly simple government! Instead of many officers, in different departments, each having appropriate duties, and each responsible for his own duties, we are so fortunate as to have to deal with but one officer. The President carries on the government; all the rest are but sub-contractors. Sir, whatever *name* we give him, we have but ONE EXECUTIVE OFFICER. A Briareus sits in the centre of our system, and with his hundred hands touches every thing, moves every thing, controls every thing. I ask, Sir, Is this republicanism? Is this a government of laws? Is this legal responsibility?

According to the Protest, the very duties which every officer under the government performs are the duties of the President himself. It says that the President has a right to employ *agents* of his _own choice_, to aid HIM in the performance of HIS duties.

Mr. President, if these doctrines be true, it is idle for us any longer to talk about any such thing as a government of laws. We have no government of laws, not even the semblance or shadow of it; we have no legal responsibility. We have an executive, consisting of one person, wielding all official power, and which is, to every effectual purpose, completely *irresponsible*. The President declares that he is "responsible for the entire action of the executive department." Responsible? What does he mean by being "responsible"? Does he mean legal responsibility? Certainly not. No such thing. Legal responsibility signifies liability to punishment for misconduct or maladministration. But the Protest does not mean that the President is liable to be impeached and punished if a secretary of state should commit treason, if a collector of the customs should be guilty of bribery, or if a treasurer should embezzle the public money. It does not mean, and cannot mean, that he should be answerable for any such crime or such delinquency. What then, is its notion of that *responsibility* which it says the President is under for all officers, and which authorizes him to consider all officers as his own personal agents? Sir, it is merely responsibility to public opinion. It is a liability to be blamed; it is the chance of becoming unpopular, the danger of losing a re-election. Nothing else is meant in the world. It is the hazard of failing in any attempt or enterprise of ambition. This is all the responsibility to which the doctrines of the Protest hold the President subject.

It is precisely the *responsibility* under which Cromwell acted when he dispersed Parliament, telling its members, not in so many words, indeed, that they disobeyed the will of their constituents, but telling them that the people were sick of them, and that he drove them out "for the glory of God and the good of the nation." It is precisely the responsibility upon which Bonaparte broke up the popular assembly of France. I do not mean, Sir, certainly, by these illustrations, to insinuate designs of violent usurpation against the President; far from it; but I do mean to maintain, that such responsibility as that with which the Protest clothes him is no legal responsibility, no constitutional responsibility, no republican responsibility, but a mere liability to loss of office, loss of character, and loss of fame, if he shall choose to violate the laws and overturn the liberties of the country. It is such a responsibility as leaves every thing in his discretion and his pleasure.

Sir, it exceeds human belief that any man should put sentiments such as this paper contains into a public communication from the President to the Senate. They are sentiments which give us all one master. The Protest asserts an absolute right to remove all persons from office at pleasure; and for what reason? Because they are incompetent? Because they are incapable? Because they are remiss, negligent, or inattentive? No, Sir; these are not the reasons. But he may discharge them, one and all, simply because "he is no longer willing to be responsible for their acts"! It insists on an absolute right in the President to *direct and control* every act of every officer of the government, except the judges. It asserts this right of direct *control* over and over again. The President may go into the treasury, among the auditors and comptrollers, and *direct* them how to settle every man's account; what abatements to make from one, what additions to another. He may go into the custom-house, among collectors and appraisers, and may *control* estimates, reductions, and appraisements. It is true that these officers are sworn to discharge the duties of their respective offices honestly and fairly, according to their *own* best abilities; it is true, that many of them are liable to indictment for official misconduct, and others responsible, in suits of individuals, for damages and penalties, if such official misconduct be proved; but notwithstanding all this, the Protest avers that all these officers are but the _President's agents_; that they are but aiding *him* in the discharge of *his* duties; that *he* is responsible for their conduct, and that they are removable at his will and pleasure. And it is under this view of his own authority that the President calls the Secretaries *his* Secretaries, not once only, but repeatedly. After half a century's administration of this government, Sir;--after we have endeavored, by statute upon statute, and by provision following provision, to define and limit official authority; to assign particular duties to particular public servants; to define those duties; to create penalties for their violation; to adjust accurately the responsibility of each agent with his own powers and his own duties; to establish the prevalence of equal rule; to make the law, as far as possible, every thing, and individual will, as far as possible, nothing;--after all this, the astounding assertion rings in our ears, that, throughout the whole range of official agency, in its smallest ramifications as well as in its larger masses, there is but ONE RESPONSIBILITY, ONE DISCRETION, ONE WILL! True indeed is it, Sir, if these sentiments be maintained,--true indeed is it that a President of the United States may well repeat from Napoleon what he repeated from Louis the Fourteenth, "I am the state"!

The argument by which the writer of the Protest endeavors to establish the President's claim to this vast mass of accumulated authority, is founded on the provision of the Constitution that the executive power shall be vested in the President. No doubt the executive power is vested in the President; but what and how much executive power, and how limited? To this question I should answer, "Look to the Constitution, and see; examine the particulars of the grant, and learn what that executive power is which is given to the President, either by express words or by necessary implication." But so the writer of this Protest does not reason. He takes these words of the Constitution as being, of themselves, a general original grant of all executive power to the President, subject only to such express limitations as the Constitution prescribes. This is clearly the writer's view of the subject, unless, indeed, he goes behind the Constitution altogether, as some expressions would intimate, to search elsewhere for sources of executive power. Thus, the Protest says that it is not only the *right* of the President, but that the Constitution makes it his _duty_, to appoint persons to office; as if the *right* existed before the Constitution had created the *duty*. It speaks, too, of the power of removal, not as a power *granted* by the Constitution, but expressly as "an original executive power, *left* unchecked by the Constitution." How original? Coming from what source higher than the Constitution? I should be glad to know how the President gets possession of any power by a title earlier, or more _original_, than the grant of the Constitution; or what is meant by an *original* power, which the President possesses, and which the Constitution has *left* unchecked in his hands. The truth is, Sir, most assuredly, that the writer of the Protest, in these passages, was reasoning upon the British constitution, and not upon the Constitution of the United States. Indeed, he professes to found himself on authority drawn from the constitution of England. I will read, Sir, the whole passage. It is this:--

"In strict accordance with this principle, the power of removal, which, like that of appointment, is an original executive power, is left unchecked by the Constitution in relation to all executive officers, for whose conduct the President is responsible; while it is taken from him in relation to judicial officers, for whose acts he is not responsible. _In the government from which many of the fundamental principles of our system are derived, the head of the executive department originally had power to appoint and remove at will all officers, executive and judicial._ It was to take the judges out of this general power of removal, and thus make them independent of the executive, that the tenure of their offices was changed to good behavior. Nor is it conceivable why they are placed, in our Constitution, upon a tenure different from that of all other officers appointed by the executive, unless it be for the same purpose."

Mr. President, I do most solemnly protest (if I, too, may be permitted to make a protest) against this mode of reasoning. The analogy between the British constitution and ours, in this respect, is not close enough to guide us safely; it can only mislead us. It has entirely misled the writer of the Protest. The President is made to argue, upon this subject, as if he had some right *anterior* to the Constitution, which right is by that instrument checked, in some respects, and in other respects is left unchecked, but which, nevertheless, still derives its being from another source; just as the British king had, in the early ages of the monarchy, an uncontrolled right of appointing and removing all officers at pleasure, but which right, so far as it respects the judges, has since been checked and controlled by act of Parliament; the right being original and inherent, the *check* only imposed by law. Sir, I distrust altogether British precedents, authorities, and analogies, on such questions as this. We are not inquiring how far our Constitution has imposed checks on a pre-existing authority. We are inquiring what extent of power that Constitution has *granted*. The grant of power, the whole source of power, as well as the restrictions and limitations which are imposed on it, is made in and by the Constitution. It has no other origin. And it is this, Sir, which distinguishes our system so very widely and materially from the systems of Europe. *Our* governments are limited governments; limited in their origin, in their very creation; limited, because none but specific powers were ever granted, either to any department of government, or to the whole: *theirs* are limited, whenever limited at all, by reason of restraints imposed at different times on governments originally unlimited and despotic. Our American questions, therefore, must be discussed, reasoned on, decided, and settled, on the appropriate principles of our own constitutions, and not by inapplicable precedents and loose analogies drawn from foreign states.

Mr. President, in one of the French comedies, as you know, in which the dulness and prolixity of legal argument is intended to be severely satirized, while the advocate is tediously groping among ancient lore having nothing to do with his case, the judge grows impatient, and at last cries out to him to _come down to the flood_! I really wish, Sir, that the writer of this Protest, since he was discussing matters of the highest importance to us as Americans, and which arise out of our own peculiar Constitution, had kept himself, not only on this side the general deluge, but also on this side the Atlantic. I desire that the broad waves of that wide sea should continue to roll between us and the influence of those foreign principles and foreign precedents which he so eagerly adopts.

In asserting power for an American President, I prefer that he should attempt to maintain his assertions on American reasons. I know not, Sir, who the writer was (I wish I did); but whoever he was, it is manifest that he argues this part of his case, throughout, on the principles of the constitution of England. It is true, that, in England, the king is regarded as the original fountain of all honor and all office; and that anciently, indeed, he possessed all political power of every kind. It is true that this mass of authority, in the progress of that government, has been diminished, restrained, and controlled, by charters, by immunities, by grants, and by various modifications, which the friends of liberty have, at different periods, been able to obtain or to impose. All liberty, as we know, all popular privileges, as indeed the word itself imports, were formerly considered as favors and concessions from the monarch. But whenever and wherever civil freedom could get a foothold, and could maintain itself, these favors were turned into rights. Before and during the reigns of the princes of the Stuart family, they were acknowledged only as favors or privileges graciously allowed, although, even then, whenever opportunity offered, as in the instance to which I alluded just now, they were contended for as rights; and by the Revolution of 1688 they were acknowledged as the rights of Englishmen, by the prince who then ascended the throne, and as the condition on which he was allowed to sit upon it. But with us there never was a time when we acknowledged original, unrestrained, sovereign power over us. Our constitutions are not made to limit and restrain pre-existing authority. They are the instruments by which the people confer power on their own servants. If I may use a legal phrase, the people are grantors, not grantees. They give to the government, and to each branch of it, all the power it possesses, or can possess; and what is not given they retain. In England, before her revolution, and in the rest of Europe since, if we would know the extent of liberty or popular right, we must go to grants, to charters, to allowances and indulgences. But with us, we go to grants and to constitutions to learn the extent of the powers of government. No political power is more original than the Constitution; none is possessed which is not there granted; and the grant, and the limitations in the grant, are in the same instrument.

The powers, therefore, belonging to any branch of our government, are to be construed and settled, not by remote analogies drawn from other governments, but from the words of the grant itself, in their plain sense and necessary import, and according to an interpretation consistent with our own history and the spirit of our own institutions. I will never agree that a President of the United States holds the whole undivided power of office in his own hands, upon the theory that he is responsible for the entire action of the whole body of those engaged in carrying on the government and executing the laws. Such a responsibility is purely ideal, delusive, and vain. There is, there can be, no substantial responsibility, any further than every individual is answerable, not merely in his reputation, not merely in the opinion of mankind, but _to the law_, for the faithful discharge of his own appropriate duties. Again and again we hear it said that the President is responsible to the American people! that he is responsible to the bar of public opinion! For whatever he does, he assumes accountability to the American people! For whatever he omits, he expects to be brought to the high bar of public opinion! And this is thought enough for a limited, restrained, republican government! an undefined, undefinable, ideal responsibility to the public judgment!

Sir, if all this mean any thing, if it be not empty sound, it means no less than that the President may do any thing and every thing which he may expect to be tolerated in doing. He may go just so far as he thinks it safe to go; and Cromwell and Bonaparte went no farther. I ask again, Sir, is this legal responsibility? Is this the true nature of a government with written laws and limited powers? And allow me, Sir, to ask, too, if an executive magistrate, while professing to act under the Constitution, is restrained only by this responsibility to public opinion, what prevents him, on the same responsibility, from proposing a change in that Constitution? Why may he not say, "I am about to introduce new forms, new principles, and a new spirit; I am about to try a political experiment on a great scale; and when I get through with it, I shall be responsible to the American people, I shall be answerable to the bar of public opinion"?

Connected, Sir, with the idea of this airy and unreal responsibility to the public is another sentiment, which of late we hear frequently expressed; and that is, *that the President is the direct representative of the American people*. This is declared in the Protest in so many words. "The President," it says, "*is the direct representative of the American people*." Now, Sir, this is not the language of the Constitution. The Constitution nowhere calls him the representative of the American people; still less, their direct representative. It could not do so with the least propriety. He is not chosen directly by the people, but by a body of electors, some of whom are chosen by the people, and some of whom are appointed by the State legislatures. Where, then, is the authority for saying that the President is the _direct representative of the people_? The Constitution calls the members of the other house Representatives, and declares that they shall be chosen by the people; and there are no other direct or immediate representatives of the people in this government. The Constitution denominates the President simply the President of the United States; it points out the complex mode of electing him, defines his powers and duties, and imposes limits and restraints on his authority. With these powers and duties, and under these restraints, he becomes, when chosen, President of the United States. That is his character, and the denomination of his office. How is it, then, that, on this official character, thus cautiously created, limited, and defined, he is to engraft another and a very imposing character, namely, the character _of the direct representative of the American people_? I hold this, Sir, to be mere assumption, and dangerous assumption. If he is the representative of *all* the American people, he is the only representative which they all have. Nobody else presumes to represent all the people. And if he may be allowed to consider himself as the SOLE REPRESENTATIVE OF ALL THE AMERICAN PEOPLE, and is to act under no other responsibility than such as I have already described, then I say, Sir, that the government (I will not say the people) has already a master. I deny the sentiment, therefore, and I protest against the language; neither the sentiment nor the language is to be found in the Constitution of the country; and whoever is not satisfied to describe the powers of the President in the language of the Constitution may be justly suspected of being as little satisfied with the powers themselves. The President is President. His office and his name of office are known, and both are fixed and described by law. Being commander of the army and navy, holding the power of nominating to office and removing from office, and being by these powers the fountain of all patronage and all favor, what does he not become if he be allowed to superadd to all this the character of single representative of the American people? Sir, he becomes what America has not been accustomed to see, what this Constitution has never created, and what I cannot contemplate but with profound alarm. He who may call himself the single representative of a nation may speak in the name of the nation, may undertake to wield the power of the nation; and who shall gainsay him in whatsoever he chooses to pronounce to be the nation's will?

I will now, Sir, ask leave to recapitulate the general doctrines of this Protest, and to present them together. They are,--

That neither branch of the legislature can take up, or consider, for the purpose of censure, any official act of the President, without some view to legislation or impeachment;

That not only the passage, but the discussion, of the resolution of the Senate of the 28th of March, was unauthorized by the Constitution, and repugnant to its provisions;

That the custody of the public treasury always must be intrusted to the executive; that Congress cannot take it out of his hands, nor place it anywhere under such superintendents and keepers as are appointed by him, responsible to him, and removable at his will;

That the whole executive power is in the President, and that therefore the duty of defending the integrity of the Constitution _results to him from the very nature of his office_; and that the founders of our republic have attested their sense of the importance of this duty, and, by expressing it in his official oath, have given to it peculiar solemnity and force;

That, as he is to take care that the laws be faithfully executed, he is thereby made responsible for the entire action of the executive department, with the power of appointing, overseeing, and *controlling* those who execute the laws;

That the power of removal from office, like that of appointment, is an *original* executive power, and is *left* in his hands *unchecked* by the Constitution, except in the case of judges; that, being responsible for the exercise of the whole executive power, he has a right to employ agents of his own choice to assist *him* in the performance of *his* duties, and to discharge them when he is no longer willing to be responsible for their acts;

That the Secretaries are *his* Secretaries, and all persons appointed to offices created by law, except the judges, *his* agents, responsible to him, and removable at his pleasure;

And, finally, that he is the *direct representative of the American people.*

These, Sir, are some of the leading propositions contained in the Protest; and if they be true, then the government under which we live is an elective monarchy. It is not yet absolute; there are yet some checks and limitations in the Constitution and laws; but, in its essential and prevailing character, it is an elective monarchy.

Mr. President, I have spoken freely of this Protest, and of the doctrines which it advances; but I have spoken deliberately. On these high questions of constitutional law, respect for my own character, as well as a solemn and profound sense of duty, restrains me from giving utterance to a single sentiment which does not flow from entire conviction. I feel that I am not wrong. I feel that an inborn and inbred love of constitutional liberty, and some study of our political institutions, have not on this occasion misled me. But I have desired to say nothing that should give pain to the chief magistrate personally. I have not sought to fix arrows in his breast; but I believe him mistaken, altogether mistaken, in the sentiments which he has expressed; and I must concur with others in placing on the records of the Senate my disapprobation of those sentiments. On a vote which is to remain so long as any proceeding of the Senate shall last, and on a question which can never cease to be important while the Constitution of the country endures, I have desired to make public my reasons. They will now be known, and I submit them to the judgment of the present and of after times. Sir, the occasion is full of interest. It cannot pass off without leaving strong impressions on the character of public men. A collision has taken place which I could have most anxiously wished to avoid; but it was not to be shunned. We have not sought this controversy; it has met us, and been forced upon us. In my judgment, the law has been disregarded, and the Constitution transgressed; the fortress of liberty has been assaulted, and circumstances have placed the Senate in the breach; and, although we may perish in it, I know we shall not fly from it. But I am fearless of consequences. We shall hold on, Sir, and hold out, till the people themselves come to its defence. We shall raise the alarm, and maintain the post, till they whose right it is shall decide whether the Senate be a faction, wantonly resisting lawful power, or whether it be opposing, with firmness and patriotism, violations of liberty and inroads upon the Constitution.

[Footnote 1: Commonly called the Sedition Act, approved 14th July, 1798.]
[Footnote 2: South Carolina.]

THE APPOINTING AND REMOVING POWER.
DELIVERED IN THE SENATE OF THE UNITED STATES, ON THE 16TH OF FEBRUARY, 1835, ON THE PASSAGE OF THE BILL, ENTITLED "AN ACT TO REPEAL THE FIRST AND SECOND SECTIONS OF THE ACT TO LIMIT THE TERM OF SERVICE OF CERTAIN OFFICERS THEREIN NAMED."

Mr. President,--The professed object of this bill is the reduction of executive influence and patronage. I concur in the propriety of that object. Having no wish to diminish or to control, in the slightest degree, the constitutional and legal authority of the presidential office, I yet think that the indirect and rapidly increasing influence which it possesses, and which arises from the power of bestowing office and of taking it away again at pleasure, and from the manner in which that power seems now to be systematically exercised, is productive of serious evils.

The extent of the patronage springing from this power of appointment and removal is so great, that it brings a dangerous mass of private and personal interest into operation in all great public elections and public questions. This is a mischief which has reached, already, an alarming height. The principle of republican governments, we are taught, is public virtue; and whatever tends either to corrupt this principle, to debase it, or to weaken its force, tends, in the same degree, to the final overthrow of such governments. Our representative systems suppose, that, in exercising the high right of suffrage, the greatest of all political rights, and in forming opinions on great public measures, men will act conscientiously, under the influence of public principle and patriotic duty; and that, in supporting or opposing men or measures, there will be a general prevalence of honest, intelligent judgment and manly independence. These presumptions lie at the foundation of all hope of maintaining governments entirely popular. Whenever personal, individual, or selfish motives influence the conduct of individuals on public questions, they affect the safety of the whole system. When these motives run deep and wide, and come in serious conflict with higher, purer, and more patriotic purposes, they greatly endanger that system; and all will admit that, if they become general and overwhelming, so that all public principle is lost sight of, and every election becomes a mere scramble for office, the system inevitably must fall. Every wise man, in and out of government, will endeavor, therefore, to promote the ascendency of public virtue and public principle, and to restrain as far as practicable, in the actual operation of our institutions, the influence of selfish and private interests.

I concur with those who think, that, looking to the present, and looking also to the future, and regarding all the probabilities that await us in reference to the character and qualities of those who may fill the executive chair, it is important to the stability of government and the welfare of the people that there should be a check to the progress of official influence and patronage. The unlimited power to grant office, and to take it away, gives a command over the hopes and fears of a vast multitude of men. It is generally true, that he who controls another man's means of living controls his will. Where there are favors to be granted, there are usually enough to solicit for them; and when favors once granted may be withdrawn at pleasure, there is ordinarily little security for personal independence of character. The power of giving office thus affects the fears of all who are in, and the hopes of all who are out. Those who are *out* endeavor to distinguish themselves by active political friendship, by warm personal devotion, by clamorous support of men in whose hands is the power of reward; while those who are *in* ordinarily take care that others shall not surpass them in such qualities or such conduct as are most likely to secure favor. They resolve not to be outdone in any of the works of partisanship. The consequence of all this is obvious. A competition ensues, not of patriotic labors; not of rough and severe toils for the public good; not of manliness, independence, and public spirit; but of complaisance, of indiscriminate support of executive measures, of pliant subserviency and gross adulation. All throng and rush together to the altar of man-worship; and there they offer sacrifices, and pour out libations, till the thick fumes of their incense turn their own heads, and turn, also, the head of him who is the object of their idolatry.

The existence of parties in popular governments is not to be avoided; and if they are formed on constitutional questions, or in regard to great measures of public policy, and do not run to excessive length, it may be admitted that, on the whole, they do no great harm. But the patronage of office, the power of bestowing place and emoluments, creates parties, not upon any principle or any measure, but upon the single ground of personal interest. Under the direct influence of this motive, they form round a leader, and they go for "the spoils of victory." And if the party chieftain becomes the national chieftain, he is still but too apt to consider all who have opposed him as enemies to be punished, and all who have supported him as friends to be rewarded. Blind devotion to party, and to the head of a party, thus takes place of the sentiment of generous patriotism and a high and exalted sense of public duty.

Let it not be said, Sir, that the danger from executive patronage cannot be great, since the persons who hold office, or can hold office, constitute so small a portion of the whole people.

In the first place, it is to be remembered that patronage acts, not only on those who actually possess office, but on those also who expect it, or hope for it; and in the next place, office-holders, by their very situation, their public station, their connection with the business of individuals, their activity, their ability to help or to hurt according to their pleasure, their acquaintance with public affairs, and their zeal and devotion, exercise a degree of influence out of all proportion to their numbers.

Sir, we cannot disregard our own experience. We cannot shut our eyes to what is around us and upon us. No candid man can deny that a great, a very great change has taken place, within a few years, in the practice of the executive government, which has produced a corresponding change in our political condition. No one can deny that office, of every kind, is now sought with extraordinary avidity, and that the condition, well understood to be attached to every officer, high or low, is indiscriminate support of executive measures and implicit obedience to executive will. For these reasons, Sir, I am for arresting the further progress of this executive patronage, if we can arrest it; I am for staying the further contagion of this plague.

The bill proposes two measures. One is to alter the duration of certain offices, now limited absolutely to four years; so that the limitation shall be qualified or conditional. If the officer is in default, if his accounts are not settled, if he retains or misapplies the public money, information is to be given thereof, and thereupon his commission is to cease. But if his accounts are all regularly settled, if he collects and disburses the public money faithfully, then he is to remain in office, unless, for some other cause, the President sees fit to remove him. This is the provision of the bill. It applies only to certain enumerated officers, who may be called accounting officers; that is to say, officers who receive and disburse the public money. Formerly, all these officers held their places at the pleasure of the President. If he saw no just cause for removing them, they continued in their situations, no fixed period being assigned for the expiration of their commissions. But the act of 1820 limited the commissions of these officers to four years. At the end of four years, they were to go out, without any removal, however well they might have conducted themselves, or however useful to the public their further continuance in office might be. They might be nominated again, or might not; but their commissions expired.

Now, Sir, I freely admit that considerable benefit has arisen from this law. I agree that it has, in some instances, secured promptitude, diligence, and a sense of responsibility. These were the benefits which those who passed the law expected from it; and these benefits have, in some measure, been realized. But I think that this change in the tenure of office, together with some good, has brought along a far more than equivalent amount of evil. By the operation of this law, the President can deprive a man of office without taking the responsibility of removing him. The law itself vacates the office, and gives the means of rewarding a friend without the exercise of the power of removal at all. Here is increased power, with diminished responsibility. Here is a still greater dependence, for the means of living, on executive favor, and, of course, a new dominion acquired over opinion and over conduct. The power of removal is, or at least formerly was, a suspected and odious power. Public opinion would not always tolerate it; and still less frequently did it approve it. Something of character, something of the respect of the intelligent and patriotic part of the community, was lost by every instance of its unnecessary exercise. This was some restraint. But the law of 1820 took it all away. It vacated offices periodically, by its own operation, and thus added to the power of removal, which it left still existing in full force, a new and extraordinary facility for the extension of patronage, influence, and favoritism.

I would ask every member of the Senate if he does not perceive, daily, effects which may be fairly traced to this cause. Does he not see a union of purpose, a devotion to power, a co-operation in action, among all who hold office, quite unknown in the earlier periods of the government? Does he not behold, every hour, a stronger development of the principle of personal attachment, and a corresponding diminution of genuine and generous public feeling? Was indiscriminate support of party measures, was unwavering fealty, was regular suit and service, ever before esteemed such important and essential parts of official duty?

Sir, the theory of our institutions is plain; it is, that government is an agency created for the good of the people, and that every person in office is the agent and servant of the people. Offices are created, not for the benefit of those who are to fill them, but for the public convenience; and they ought to be no more in number, nor should higher salaries be attached to them, than the public service requires. This is the theory. But the difficulty in practice is, to prevent a direct reversal of all this; to prevent public offices from being considered as intended for the use and emolument of those who can obtain them. There is a headlong tendency to this, and it is necessary to restrain it by wise and effective legislation. There is still another, and perhaps a greatly more mischievous result, of extensive patronage in the hands of a single magistrate, to which I have already incidentally alluded; and that is, that men in office have begun to think themselves mere agents and servants of the appointing power, and not agents of the government or the country. It is, in an especial manner, important, if it be practicable, to apply some corrective to this kind of feeling and opinion. It is necessary to bring back public officers to the conviction, that they belong to the country, and not to any administration, nor to any one man. The army is the army of the country; the navy is the navy of the country; neither of them is either the mere instrument of the administration for the time being, nor of him who is at the head of it. The post-office, the land-office, the custom-house, are, in like manner, institutions of the country, established for the good of the people: and it may well alarm the lovers of free institutions, when all the offices in these several departments are spoken of, in high places, as being but "spoils of victory," to be enjoyed by those who are successful in a contest, in which they profess this grasping of the spoils to have been the object of their efforts.

This part of the bill, therefore, Sir, is a subject for fair comparison. We have gained something, doubtless, by limiting the commissions of these officers to four years. But have we gained as much as we have lost? And may not the good be preserved, and the evil still avoided? Is it not enough to say, that if, at the end of four years, moneys are retained, accounts unsettled, or other duties unperformed, the office shall be held to be vacated, without any positive act of removal?

For one, I think the balance of advantage is decidedly in favor of the present bill. I think it will make men more dependent on their own good conduct, and less dependent on the will of others. I believe it will cause them to regard their country more, their own duty more, and the favor of individuals less. I think it will contribute to official respectability, to freedom of opinion, to independence of character; and I think it will tend, in no small degree, to prevent the mixture of selfish and personal motives with the exercise of high political duties. It will promote true and genuine republicanism, by causing the opinion of the people respecting the measures of government, and the men in government, to be formed and expressed without fear or favor, and with a more entire regard to their true and real merits or demerits. It will be, so far as its effects reach, an auxiliary to patriotism and public virtue, in their warfare against selfishness and cupidity.

The second check on executive patronage contained in this bill is of still greater importance than the first. This provision is, that, whenever the President removes any of these officers from office, he shall state to the Senate the reasons for such removal. This part of the bill has been opposed, both on constitutional grounds and on grounds of expediency.

The bill, it is to be observed, expressly recognizes and admits the actual existence of the power of removal. I do not mean to deny, and the bill does not deny, that, at the present moment, the President may remove these officers at will, because the early decision adopted that construction, and the laws have since uniformly sanctioned it. The law of 1820, intended to be repealed by this bill, expressly affirms the power. I consider it, therefore, a settled point; settled by construction, settled by precedent, settled by the practice of the government, and settled by statute. At the same time, after considering the question again and again within the last six years, I am very willing to say, that, in my deliberate judgment, the original decision was wrong. I cannot but think that those who denied the power in 1789 had the best of the argument; and yet I will not say that I know myself so thoroughly as to affirm, that this opinion may not have been produced, in some measure, by that abuse of the power which has been passing before our eyes for several years. It is possible that this experience of the evil may have affected my view of the constitutional argument. It appears to me, however, after thorough and repeated and conscientious examination, that an erroneous interpretation was given to the Constitution, in this respect, by the decision of the first Congress; and I will ask leave to state, shortly, the reasons for that opinion, although there is nothing in this bill which proposes to disturb that decision.

The Constitution nowhere says one word of the power of removal from office, except in the case of conviction on impeachment. Wherever the power exists, therefore, except in cases of impeachment, it must exist as a constructive or incidental power. If it exists in the President alone, it must exist in him because it is attached to something else, or included in something else, or results from something else, which is granted to the President. There is certainly no specific grant; it is a power, therefore, the existence of which, if proved at all, is to be proved by inference and argument. In the only instance in which the Constitution speaks of removal from office, as I have already said, it speaks of it as the exercise of *judicial* power; that is to say, it speaks of it as one part of the judgment of the Senate, in cases of conviction on impeachment. No other mention is made, in the whole instrument, of any power of removal. Whence, then, is the power derived to the President?

It is usually said, by those who maintain its existence in the single hands of the President, that the power is derived from that clause of the Constitution which says, "The executive power shall be vested in a President." The power of removal, they argue, is, in its nature, an executive power; and, as the executive power is thus vested in the President, the power of removal is necessarily included.

It is true, that the Constitution declares that the executive power shall be vested in the President; but the first question which then arises is, _What is executive power? What is the degree, and what are the limitations?_ Executive power is not a thing so well known, and so accurately defined, as that the written constitution of a limited government can be supposed to have conferred it in the lump. What *is* executive power? What are its boundaries? What model or example had the framers of the Constitution in their minds, when they spoke of "executive power"? Did they mean executive power as known in England, or as known in France, or as known in Russia? Did they take it as defined by Montesquieu, by Burlamaqui, or by De Lolme? All these differ from one another as to the extent of the executive power of government. What, then, was intended by "the executive power"? Now, Sir, I think it perfectly plain and manifest, that, although the framers of the Constitution meant to confer executive power on the President, yet they meant to define and limit that power, and to confer no more than they did thus define and limit. When they say it shall be vested in a President, they mean that one magistrate, to be called a President, shall hold the executive authority; but they mean, further, that he shall hold this authority according to the grants and limitations of the Constitution itself.

They did not intend, certainly, a sweeping gift of prerogative. They did not intend to grant to the President whatever might be construed, or supposed, or imagined to be executive power; and the proof that they meant no such thing is, that, immediately after using these general words, they proceed specifically to enumerate his several distinct and particular authorities; to fix and define them; to give the Senate an essential control over the exercise of some of them, and to leave others uncontrolled. By the executive power conferred on the President, the Constitution means no more than that portion which itself creates, and which it qualifies, limits, and circumscribes.

A general survey of the frame of the Constitution will satisfy us of this. That instrument goes all along upon the idea of dividing the powers of government, so far as practicable, into three great departments. It describes the powers and duties of these departments in an article allotted to each. As first in importance and dignity, it begins with the legislative department. The first article of the Constitution, therefore, commences with the declaration, that "all legislative power herein granted shall be vested in a Congress of the United States, which shall consist of a Senate and House of Representatives," The article goes on to prescribe the manner in which Congress is to be constituted and organized, _and then proceeds to enumerate, specifically, the powers intended to be granted_; and adds the general clause, conferring such authority as may be necessary to carry granted powers into effect. Now, Sir, no man doubts that this is a limited legislature; that it possesses no powers but such as are granted by express words or necessary implication; and that it would be quite preposterous to insist that Congress possesses any particular legislative power, merely because it is, in its nature, a legislative body, if no grant can be found for it in the Constitution itself.

Then comes, Sir, the second article, creating an executive power; and it declares, that "the executive power shall be vested in a President of the United States." After providing for the mode of choosing him, it immediately proceeds to enumerate, specifically, the powers which he shall possess and exercise, and the duties which he shall perform. I consider the language of this article, therefore, precisely analogous to that in which the legislature is created; that is to say, I understand the Constitution as saying that "the executive power *herein granted* shall be vested in a President of the United States."

In like manner, the third article, or that which is intended to arrange the judicial system, begins by declaring that "the judicial power of the United States shall be vested in one Supreme Court, and in such inferior courts as the Congress may, from time to time, ordain and establish." But these general words do not show *what extent* of judicial power is vested in the courts of the United States. All that is left to be done, and is done, in the following sections, by express and well-guarded provisions.

I think, therefore, Sir, that very great caution is to be used, and the ground well considered, before we admit that the President derives any distinct and specific power from those general words which vest the executive authority in him. The Constitution itself does not rest satisfied with these general words. It immediately goes into particulars, and carefully enumerates the several authorities which the President shall possess. The very first of the enumerated powers is the command of the army and navy. This, most certainly, is an executive power. And why is it particularly set down and expressed, if any power was intended to be granted under the general words? This would pass, if any thing would pass, under those words. But enumeration, specification, particularization, was evidently the design of the framers of the Constitution, in this as in other parts of it. I do not, therefore, regard the declaration that the executive power shall be vested in a President as being any grant at all; any more than the declaration that the legislative power shall be vested in Congress constitutes, by itself, a grant of such power. In the one case, as in the other, I think the object was to describe and denominate the department, which should hold, respectively, the legislative and the executive authority; very much as we see, in some of the State constitutions, that the several articles are headed with the titles "legislative power," "executive power," "judicial power"; and this entitling of the articles with the name of the power has never been supposed, of itself, to confer any authority whatever. It amounts to no more than naming the departments.

If, then, the power of removal be admitted to be an executive power, still it must be sought for and found among the enumerated executive powers, or fairly implied from some one or more of them. It cannot be implied from the general words. The power of appointment was not left to be so implied; why, then, should the power of removal have been so left? They are both closely connected; one is indispensable to the other; why, then, was one carefully expressed, defined, and limited, and not one word said about the other? Sir, I think the whole matter is sufficiently plain. Nothing is said in the Constitution about the power of removal, because it is not a separate and distinct power. It is part of the power of appointment, naturally going with it or necessarily resulting from it. The Constitution or the laws may separate these powers, it is true, in a particular case, as is done in respect to the judges, who, though appointed by the President and Senate, cannot be removed at the pleasure of either or of both. So a statute, in prescribing the tenure of any other office, may place the officer beyond the reach of the appointing power. But where no other tenure is prescribed, and officers hold their places at will, that will is necessarily the will of the appointing power; because the exercise of the power of appointment at once displaces such officers. The power of placing one man in office necessarily implies the power of turning another out. If one man be Secretary of State, and another be appointed, the first goes out by the mere force of the appointment of the other, without any previous act of removal whatever. And this is the practice of the government, and has been, from the first. In all the removals which have been made, they have generally been effected simply by making other appointments. I cannot find a case to the contrary. There is no such thing as any distinct official act of removal. I have looked into the practice, and caused inquiries to be made in the departments, and I do not learn that any such proceeding is known as an entry or record of the removal of an officer from office; and the President could only act, in such cases, by causing some proper record or entry to be made, as proof of the fact of removal. I am aware that there have been some cases in which notice has been sent to persons in office that their services are, or will be, after a given day, dispensed with. These are usually cases in which the object is, not to inform the incumbent that he is _removed_, but to tell him that a successor either is, or by a day named will be, appointed. If there be any instances in which such notice is given without express reference to the appointment of a successor, they are few; and even in these, such reference must be implied; because in no case is there any distinct official act of removal, that I can find, unconnected with the act of appointment. At any rate, it is the usual practice, and has been from the first, to consider the appointment as producing the removal of the previous incumbent. When the President desires to remove a person from office, he sends a message to the Senate nominating some other person. The message usually runs in this form: "I nominate A.B. to be collector of the customs, &c., in the place of C.D., removed." If the Senate advise and consent to this nomination, C.D. is effectually out of office, and A.B. is in, in his place. The same effect would be produced, if the message should say nothing of any removal. Suppose A.B. to be Secretary of State, and the President to send us a message, saying merely, "I nominate C.D. to be Secretary of State." If we confirm this nomination, C.D. becomes Secretary of State, and A.B. is necessarily removed.

I have gone into these details and particulars, Sir, for the purpose of showing, that, not only in the nature of things, but also according to the practice of the government, the power of removal is incident to the power of appointment. It belongs to it, is attached to it, forms a part of it, or results from it.

If this be true, the inference is manifest. If the power of removal, when not otherwise regulated by Constitution or law, be part and parcel of the power of appointment, or a necessary incident to it, then whoever holds the power of appointment holds also the power of removal. But it is the President and the Senate, and not the President alone, who hold the power of appointment; and therefore, according to the true construction of the Constitution, it should be the President and Senate, and not the President alone, who hold the power of removal.

The decision of 1789 has been followed by a very strange and indefensible anomaly, showing that it does not rest on any just principle. The natural connection between the appointing power and the removing power has, as I have already stated, always led the President to bring about a removal by the process of a new appointment. This is quite efficient for his purpose, when the Senate confirms the new nomination. One man is then turned out, and another put in. But the Senate sometimes *rejects* the new nomination; and what then becomes of the old incumbent? Is he out of office, or is he still in? He has not been turned out by any exercise of the power of appointment, for no appointment has been made. That power has not been exercised. He has not been removed by any distinct and separate act of removal, for no such act has been performed, or attempted. Is he still in, then, or is he out? Where is he? In this dilemma, Sir, those who maintain the power of removal as existing in the President alone are driven to what seems to me very near absurdity. The incumbent has not been removed by the appointing power, since the appointing power has not been exercised. He has not been removed by any distinct and independent act of removal, since no such act has been performed.

They are forced to the necessity, therefore, of contending that the removal has been accomplished by the mere *nomination* of a successor; so that the removing power is made incident, not to the appointing power, but to one part of it; that is, to the *nominating* power. The nomination, not having been assented to by the Senate, it is clear, has failed, as the first step in the process of appointment. But though thus rendered null and void in its main object, as the first process in making an appointment, it is held to be good and valid, nevertheless, to bring about that which _results from an appointment_; that is, the removal of the person actually in office. In other words, the nomination produces the consequences of an appointment, or some of them, though it be itself no appointment, and effect no appointment. This, Sir, appears to me to be any thing but sound reasoning and just construction.

But this is not all. The President has sometimes sent us a nomination to an office already filled, and, before we have acted upon it, has seen fit to withdraw it. What is the effect of such a nomination? If a _nomination_, merely as such, turns out the present incumbent, then he is out, let what will become afterwards of the nomination. But I believe the President has acted upon the idea that a nomination made, and at any time afterwards withdrawn, does *not* remove the actual incumbent.

Sir, even this is not the end of the inconsistencies into which the prevailing doctrine has led. There have been cases in which nominations to offices already filled have come to the Senate, remained here for weeks, or months, the incumbents all the while continuing to discharge their official duties, and relinquishing their offices only when the nominations of their successors have been confirmed, and commissions issued to them; so that, if a nomination be confirmed, the *nomination itself* makes no removal; the removal then waits to be brought about by the *appointment*. But if the nomination be _rejected_, then the _nomination itself_, it is contended, has effected the removal. Who can defend opinions which lead to such results?

These reasons, Sir, incline me strongly to the opinion, that, upon a just construction of the Constitution, the power of removal is part of, or a necessary result from, the power of appointment, and, therefore, that it *ought to have been* exercised by the Senate concurrently with the President.

The argument may be strengthened by various illustrations. The Constitution declares that Congress may vest the appointment of inferior officers in the President alone, in the courts of law, or in the heads of departments; and Congress has passed various acts providing for appointments, according to this regulation of the Constitution. Thus the Supreme Court, and other courts of the United States, have authority to appoint their clerks; heads of departments also appoint their own clerks, according to statute provisions; and it has never been doubted that these courts, and these heads of departments, may remove their clerks at pleasure, although nothing is said in the laws respecting such power of removal. Now, it is evident that neither the courts nor the heads of departments acquire the right of removal under a general grant of executive power, for none such is made to them; nor upon the ground of any general injunction to see the laws executed, for no such general injunction is addressed to them. They nevertheless hold the power of removal, as all admit, and they must hold it, therefore, simply as incident to, or belonging to, the power of appointment. There is no other clause under which they can possibly claim it.

Again, let us suppose that the Constitution had given to the President the power of appointment, without consulting the Senate. Suppose it had said, "The President shall appoint ambassadors, other public ministers, judges of the Supreme Court, and all other officers of the United States." If the Constitution had stood thus, the President would unquestionably have possessed the power of removal, where the tenure of office was not fixed; and no man, I imagine, would in that case have looked for the removing power either in that clause which says the executive authority shall be vested in the President, or in that other clause which makes it his duty to see the laws faithfully executed. Everybody would have said, "The President possesses an uncontrolled power of appointment, and that necessarily carries with it an uncontrolled power of removal, unless some permanent tenure be given to the office by the Constitution, or by law."

And now, Sir, let me state, and examine, the main argument, on which the decision of 1789 appears to rest it.

The most plausible reasoning brought forward on that occasion may be fairly stated thus: "The executive power is vested in the President; this is the general rule of the Constitution. The association of the Senate with the President in exercising a particular function belonging to the executive power, is an exception to this general rule, and exceptions to general rules are to be taken strictly; therefore, though the Senate partakes of the appointing power, by express provision, yet, as nothing is said of its participation in the removing power, such participation is to be excluded."

The error of this argument, if I may venture to call it so, considering who used it,[1] lies in this. It supposes the power of removal to be held by the President under the general grant of executive power. Now, it is certain that the power of appointment is not held under that general grant, because it is particularly provided for, and is conferred, in express terms, on the President and Senate. If, therefore, the power of removal be a natural appendage to the power of appointment, then it is not conferred by the general words granting executive power to the President, but is conferred by the special clause which gives the appointing power to the President and Senate. So that the spirit of the very rule on which the argument of 1789, as I have stated it, relies, appears to me to produce a directly opposite result; for, if exceptions to a general rule are to be taken strictly, when expressed, it is still more clear, when they are not expressed at all, that they are not to be implied except on evident and clear grounds; and as the general power of appointment is confessedly given to the President and Senate, no exception is to be implied in favor of one part of that general power, namely, the removing part, unless for some obvious and irresistible reason. In other words, this argument which I am answering is not sound in its premises, and therefore not sound in its conclusion, if the grant of the power of appointment does naturally include also the power of removal, when this last power is not otherwise expressly provided for; because, if the power of removal belongs to the power of appointment, or necessarily follows it, then it has gone with it into the hands of the President and Senate; and the President does not hold it alone, as an implication or inference from the grant to him of general executive powers.

The true application of that rule of construction, thus relied on, would present the argument, I think, in this form: "The appointing power is vested in the President and Senate; this is the general rule of the Constitution. The removing power is part of the appointing power; it cannot be separated from the rest, but by supposing that an exception was intended; but all exceptions to general rules are to be taken strictly, even when expressed; and, for a much stronger reason, they are not to be implied, when not expressed, unless inevitable necessity of construction requires it."

On the whole, Sir, with the diffidence which becomes one who is reviewing the opinions of some of the ablest and wisest men of the age, I must still express my own conviction, that the decision of Congress in 1789, which separated the power of removal from the power of appointment, was founded on an erroneous construction of the Constitution, and that it has led to great inconsistencies, as well as to great abuses, in the subsequent, and especially in the more recent, history of the government.

Much has been said now, and much was said formerly, about the inconvenience of denying this power to the President alone. I agree that an argument drawn from this source may have weight, in a doubtful case; but it is not to be permitted that we shall presume the existence of a power merely because we think it would be convenient. Nor is there, I think, any such glaring, striking, or certain inconvenience as has been suggested. Sudden removals from office are seldom necessary; we see how seldom, by reference to the practice of the government under all administrations which preceded the present. And if we look back over the removals which have been made in the last six years, there is no man who can maintain that there is one case in a hundred in which the country would have suffered the least inconvenience if no removal had been made without the consent of the Senate. Party might have felt the inconvenience, but the country never. Many removals have been made (by new appointments) during the session of the Senate; and if there has occurred one single case, in the whole six years, in which the public convenience required the removal of an officer in the recess, such case has escaped my recollection. Besides, it is worthy of being remembered, when we are seeking for the true intent of the Constitution on this subject, that there is reason to suppose that its framers expected the Senate would be in session a much larger part of the year than the House of Representatives, so that its concurrence could generally be had, at once, on any question of appointment or removal.

But this argument, drawn from the supposed inconvenience of denying an absolute power of removal to the President, suggests still another view of the question. The argument asserts, that it must have been the intention of the framers of the Constitution to confer the power on the President, for the sake of convenience, and as an absolutely necessary power in his hands. Why, then, did they leave their intent doubtful? _Why did they not confer the power in express terms?_ Why were they thus totally silent on a point of so much importance?

Seeing that the removing power naturally belongs to the appointing power; seeing that, in other cases, in the same Constitution, its framers have left the one with the consequence of drawing the other after it,--if, in this instance, they meant to do what was uncommon and extraordinary, that, is to say, if they meant to separate and divorce the two powers, why did they not say so? Why did they not express their meaning in plain words? Why should they take up the appointing power, and carefully define it, limit it, and restrain it, and yet leave to vague inference and loose construction an equally important power, which all must admit to be closely connected with it, if not a part of it? If others can account for all this silence respecting the removing power, upon any other ground than that the framers of the Constitution regarded both powers as one, and supposed they had provided for them together, I confess I cannot. I have the clearest conviction, that they looked to no other mode of displacing an officer than by impeachment, or by the regular appointment of another person to the same place.

But, Sir, whether the decision of 1789 were right or wrong, the bill before us applies to the actually existing state of things. It recognizes the President's power of removal, in express terms, as it has been practically exercised, independently of the Senate. The present bill does not disturb the power; but I wish it not to be understood that the power is, even now, beyond the reach of legislation. I believe it to be within the just power of Congress to reverse the decision of 1789, and I mean to hold myself at liberty to act, hereafter, upon that question, as I shall think the safety of the government and of the Constitution may require. The present bill, however, proceeds upon the admission that the power does at present exist. Its words are:--

"Sec. 3. _And be it further enacted_, That, in all nominations made by the President to the Senate, to fill vacancies occasioned by the exercise of the President's power to remove the said officers mentioned in the second section of this act, the fact of the removal shall be stated to the Senate, at the same time that the nomination is made, with a statement of the reasons for which such officer may have been removed."

In my opinion, this provision is entirely constitutional, and highly expedient.

The regulation of the tenure of office is a common exercise of legislative authority, and the power of Congress in this particular is not at all restrained or limited by any thing contained in the Constitution, except in regard to judicial officers. All the rest is left to the ordinary discretion of the legislature.

Congress may give to offices which it creates (except those of judges) what duration it pleases. When the office is created, and is to be filled, the President is to nominate the candidate to fill it; but when he comes into the office, he comes into it upon the conditions and restrictions which the law may have attached to it.

If Congress were to declare by law that the Attorney-General, or the Secretary of State, should hold his office during good behavior, I am not aware of any ground on which such a law could be held unconstitutional. A provision of that kind in regard to such officers might be unwise, but I do not perceive that it would transcend the power of Congress.

If the Constitution had not prescribed the tenure of judicial office, Congress might have thought it expedient to give the judges just such a tenure as the Constitution has itself provided; that is to say, a right to hold during good behavior; and I am of opinion that such a law would have been perfectly constitutional. It is by law, in England, that the judges are made independent of the removing power of the crown. I do not think that the Constitution, by giving the power of appointment, or the power both of appointment and removal, to the President and Senate, intended to impose any restraint on the legislature, in regard to its authority of regulating the duties, powers, duration, or responsibility of office. I agree, that Congress ought not to do any thing which shall essentially impair that right of nomination and appointment of certain officers, such as ministers, judges, &c., which the Constitution has vested in the President and Senate. But while the power of nomination and appointment is left fairly where the Constitution has placed it, I think the whole field of regulation is open to legislative discretion. If a law were to pass, declaring that district attorneys, or collectors of customs, should hold their offices four years, unless removed on conviction for misbehavior, no one could doubt its constitutional validity; because the legislature is naturally competent to prescribe the tenure of office. And is a reasonable check on the power of removal any thing more than a qualification of the tenure of office? Let it be always remembered, that the President's removing power, as now exercised, is claimed and held under the general clause vesting in him the executive authority. It is implied, or inferred, from that clause alone.

Now, if it is properly derived from that source, since the Constitution does not say how it shall be limited, how defined, or how carried into effect, it seems especially proper for Congress, under the general provision of the Constitution which gives it authority to pass all laws necessary to carry into effect the powers conferred on any department, to regulate the subject of removal. And the regulation here required is of the gentlest kind. It only provides that the President shall make known to the Senate his reasons for removal of officers of this description, when he does see fit to remove them. It might, I think, very justly go farther. It might, and perhaps it ought, to prescribe the form of removal, and the proof of the fact. It might, I also think, declare that the President should only suspend officers, at pleasure, till the next meeting of the Senate, according to the amendment suggested by the honorable member from Kentucky; and, if the present practice cannot be otherwise checked, this provision, in my opinion, ought hereafter to be adopted. But I am content with the slightest degree of restraint which may be sufficient to arrest the totally unnecessary, unreasonable, and dangerous exercise of the power of removal. I desire only, for the present at least, that, when the President turns a man out of office, he should give his reasons for it to the Senate, when he nominates another person to fill the place. Let him give these reasons, and stand on them. If they are fair and honest, he need have no fear in stating them. It is not to invite any trial; it is not to give the removed officer an opportunity of defence; it is not to excite controversy and debate; it is simply that the Senate, and ultimately the public, may know the grounds of removal. I deem this degree of regulation, at least, necessary; unless we are willing to submit all these officers to an absolute and a perfectly irresponsible removing power; a power which, as recently exercised, tends to turn the whole body of public officers into partisans, dependants, favorites, sycophants, and man-worshippers.

Mr. President, without pursuing the discussion further, I will detain the Senate only while I recapitulate the opinions which I have expressed; because I am far less desirous of influencing the judgment of others, than of making clear the grounds of my own judgment.

I think, then, Sir, that the power of appointment naturally and necessarily includes the power of removal where no limitation is expressed, nor any tenure but that at will declared. The power of appointment being conferred on the President _and Senate_, I think the power of removal went along with it, and should have been regarded as a part of it, and exercised by the same hands. I think, consequently, that the decision of 1789, which *implied* a power of removal separate from the appointing power, was erroneous.

But I think the decision of 1789 has been established by practice, and recognized by subsequent laws, as the settled construction of the Constitution, and that it is our duty to act upon the case accordingly, for the present; without admitting that Congress may not, hereafter, if necessity shall require it, reverse the decision of 1789. I think the legislature possesses the power of regulating the condition, duration, qualification, and tenure of office, in all cases where the Constitution has made no express provision on the subject.

I am, therefore, of opinion, that it is competent for Congress to declare by law, as one qualification of the tenure of office, that the incumbent shall remain in place till the President shall remove him, for reasons to be stated to the Senate. And I am of opinion that this qualification, mild and gentle as it is, will have *some* effect in arresting the evils which beset the progress of the government, and seriously threaten its future prosperity.

These are the reasons for which I give my support to this bill.

NOTE.

This speech is singular among the speeches of Mr. Webster, as it exhibits him as a "Strict-Constructionist," and as a master of that peculiar kind of deductive reasoning which is commonly considered the special distinction of his great antagonist, Mr. Calhoun. In subtilty and refinement of argument it is fully the match of most of Mr. Calhoun's elaborate disquisitions. At the time of its delivery it excited the almost savage ire of John Quincy Adams, as will be seen by reference to the latter's "Diary." It was in connection with this speech that Mr. Adams speaks of "the rotten heart of Daniel Webster." How such a purely intellectual feat as this, one so entirely passionless and impersonal, should be referred to rottenness of heart, is one of the unexplained mysteries of the operations of Mr. Adams's understanding, when that understanding was misled by personal antipathy.

[Footnote 1: Mr. Madison. See the discussion in Gales and Seaton's Debates in Congress, Vol. I. p. 473 _et seq._]

ON THE LOSS OF THE FORTIFICATION BILL IN 1835.
A SPEECH DELIVERED IN THE SENATE OF THE UNITED STATES, ON THE 14TH OF JANUARY, 1836, ON MR. BENTON'S RESOLUTIONS FOR APPROPRIATING THE SURPLUS REVENUE TO NATIONAL DEFENCE.

It is not my purpose, Mr. President, to make any remark on the state of our affairs with France. The time for that discussion has not come, and I wait. We are in daily expectation of a communication from the President, which will give us light; and we are authorized to expect a recommendation by him of such measures as he thinks it may be necessary and proper for Congress to adopt. I do not anticipate him. In this most important and delicate business, it is the proper duty of the executive to go forward, and I, for one, do not intend either to be drawn or driven into the lead. When official information shall be before us, and when measures shall be recommended upon the proper responsibility, I shall endeavor to form the best judgment I can, and shall act according to its dictates.

I rise, now, for another purpose. This resolution has drawn on a debate upon the general conduct of the Senate during the last session of Congress, and especially in regard to the proposed grant of the three millions to the President on the last night of the session. My main object is to tell the story of this transaction, and to exhibit the conduct of the Senate fairly to the public view. I owe this duty to the Senate. I owe it to the committee with which I am connected; and although whatever is personal to an individual is generally of too little importance to be made the subject of much remark, I hope I may be permitted to say a few words in defence of my own reputation, in reference to a matter which has been greatly misrepresented.

This vote for the three millions was proposed by the House of Representatives as an amendment to the fortification bill; and the loss of that bill, three millions and all, is the charge which has been made upon the Senate, sounded over all the land, and now again renewed. I propose to give the true history of this bill, its origin, its progress, and its loss.

Before attempting that, however, let me remark, for it is worthy to be remarked and remembered, that the business brought before the Senate last session, important and various as it was, and both public and private, was all gone through with most uncommon despatch and promptitude. No session has witnessed a more complete clearing off and finishing of the subjects before us. The communications from the other house, whether bills or whatever else, were especially attended to in a proper season, and with that ready respect which is due from one house to the other. I recollect nothing of any importance which came to us from the House of Representatives, which was neglected, overlooked, or disregarded by the Senate.

On the other hand, it was the misfortune of the Senate, and, as I think, the misfortune of the country, that, owing to the state of business in the House of Representatives towards the close of the session, several measures which had been matured in the Senate, and passed into bills, did not receive attention, so as to be either agreed to or rejected, in the other branch of the legislature. They fell, of course, by the termination of the session.

Among these measures may be mentioned the following, viz.:--

THE POST-OFFICE REFORM BILL, which passed the Senate _unanimously_, and of the necessity for which the whole country is certainly now most abundantly satisfied;

THE CUSTOM-HOUSE REGULATIONS BILL, which also passed nearly unanimously, after a very laborious preparation by the Committee on Commerce, and a full discussion in the Senate;

THE JUDICIARY BILL, passed here by a majority of thirty-one to five, and which has again already passed the Senate at this session with only a single dissenting vote;

THE BILL INDEMNIFYING CLAIMANTS FOR FRENCH SPOLIATIONS BEFORE 1800;

THE BILL REGULATING THE DEPOSIT OF THE PUBLIC MONEY IN THE DEPOSIT BANKS;

THE BILL RESPECTING THE TENURE OF CERTAIN OFFICES, AND THE POWER OF REMOVAL FROM OFFICE; which has now again been passed to be engrossed, in the Senate, by a decided majority.

All these important measures, matured and passed in the Senate in the course of the session, and many others of less importance, were sent to the House of Representatives, and we never heard any thing more from them. They there found their graves.

It is worthy of being remarked, also, that the attendance of members of the Senate was remarkably full, particularly toward the end of the session. On the last day, every Senator was in his place till very near the hour of adjournment, as the journal will show. We had no breaking up for want of a quorum; no delay, no calls of the Senate; nothing which was made necessary by the negligence or inattention of the members of this body. On the vote of the three millions of dollars, which was taken at about eight o'clock in the evening, forty-eight votes were given, every member of the Senate being in his place and answering to his name. This is an instance of punctuality, diligence, and labor, continued to the very end of an arduous session, wholly without example or parallel.

The Senate, then, Sir, must stand, in the judgment of every man, fully acquitted of all remissness, all negligence, all inattention, amidst the fatigue and exhaustion of the closing hours of Congress. Nothing passed unheeded, nothing was overlooked, nothing forgotten, and nothing slighted.

And now, Sir, I would proceed immediately to give the history of the fortification bill, if it were not necessary, as introductory to that history, and as showing the circumstances under which the Senate was called on to transact the public business, first to refer to another bill which was before us, and to the proceedings which were had upon it.

It is well known, Sir, that the annual appropriation bills always originate in the House of Representatives. This is so much a matter of course, that no one ever looks to see such a bill first brought forward in the Senate. It is also well known, Sir, that it has been usual, heretofore, to make the annual appropriations for the Military Academy at West Point in the general bill which provides for the pay and support of the army. But last year the army bill did not contain any appropriation whatever for the support of West Point. I took notice of this singular omission when the bill was before the Senate, but presumed, and indeed understood, that the House would send us a separate bill for the Military Academy. The army bill, therefore, passed; but no bill for the Academy at West Point appeared. We waited for it from day to day, and from week to week, but waited in vain. At length, the time for sending bills from one house to the other, according to the joint rules of the two houses, expired, and no bill had made its appearance for the support of the Military Academy. These joint rules, as is well known, are sometimes suspended on the application of one house to the other, in favor of particular bills, whose progress has been unexpectedly delayed, but which the public interest requires to be passed. But the House of Representatives sent us no request to suspend the rules in favor of a bill for the support of the Military Academy, nor made any other proposition to save the institution from immediate dissolution. Notwithstanding all the talk about a war, and the necessity of a vote for the three millions, the Military Academy, an institution cherished so long, and at so much expense, was on the very point of being entirely broken up.

Now it so happened, Sir, that at this time there was another appropriation bill which had come from the House of Representatives, and was before the Committee on Finance here. This bill was entitled "An Act making appropriations for the civil and diplomatic expenses of the government for the year 1835."

In this state of things, several members of the House of Representatives applied to the committee, and besought us to save the Military Academy by annexing the necessary appropriations for its support to the bill for civil and diplomatic service. We spoke to them, in reply, of the unfitness, the irregularity, the incongruity, of this forced union of such dissimilar subjects; but they told us it was a case of absolute necessity, and that, without resorting to this mode, the appropriation could not get through. We acquiesced, Sir, in these suggestions. We went out of our way. We agreed to do an extraordinary and an irregular thing, in order to save the public business from miscarriage. By direction of the committee, I moved the Senate to add an appropriation for the Military Academy to the bill for defraying civil and diplomatic expenses. The bill was so amended; and in this form the appropriation was finally made.

But this was not all. This bill for the civil and diplomatic service, being thus amended by tacking the Military Academy to it, was sent back by us to the House of Representatives, where its length of tail was to be still much further increased. That house had before it several subjects for provision, and for appropriation, upon which it had not passed any bill before the time for passing bills to be sent to the Senate had elapsed. I was anxious that these things should, in some way, be provided for; and when the diplomatic bill came back, drawing the Military Academy after it, it was thought prudent to attach to it several of these other provisions. There were propositions to pave the streets in the city of Washington, to repair the Capitol, and various other things, which it was necessary to provide for; and they, therefore, were put into the same bill, by way of amendment to an amendment; that is to say, Mr. President, we had been prevailed on to amend their bill for defraying the salary of our ministers abroad, by adding an appropriation for the Military Academy, and they proposed to amend this our amendment by adding matter as germane to it as it was itself to the original bill. There was also the President's gardener. His salary was unprovided for; and there was no way of remedying this important omission, but by giving him place in the diplomatic service bill, among _chargés d'affaires_, envoys extraordinary, and ministers plenipotentiary. In and among these ranks, therefore, he was formally introduced by the amendment of the House, and there he now stands, as you will readily see by turning to the law.

Sir, I have not the pleasure to know this useful person; but should I see him, some morning, overlooking the workmen in the lawns, walks, copses, and parterres which adorn the grounds around the President's residence, considering the company into which we have introduced him, I should expect to see, at least, a small diplomatic button on his working jacket.

When these amendments came from the House, and were read at our table, though they caused a smile, they were yet adopted, and the law passed, almost with the rapidity of a comet, and with something like the same length of tail.

Now, Sir, not one of these irregularities or incongruities, no part of this jumbling together of distinct and different subjects, was in the slightest degree occasioned by any thing done, or omitted to be done, on the part of the Senate. Their proceedings were all regular; their decision was prompt, their despatch of the public business correct and reasonable. There was nothing of disorganization, nothing of procrastination, nothing evincive of a temper to embarrass or obstruct the public business. If the history which I have now truly given shows that one thing was amended by another, which had no sort of connection with it; that unusual expedients were resorted to; and that the laws, instead of arrangement and symmetry, exhibit anomaly, confusion, and the most grotesque associations, it is nevertheless true, that no part of all this was made necessary by us. We deviated from the accustomed modes of legislation only when we were supplicated to do so, in order to supply bald and glaring deficiencies in measures which were before us.

But now, Mr. President, let me come to the fortification bill, the lost bill, which not only now, but on a graver occasion, has been lamented like the lost Pleiad.

This bill, Sir, came from the House of Representatives to the Senate in the usual way, and was referred to the Committee on Finance. Its appropriations were not large. Indeed, they appeared to the committee to be quite too small. It struck a majority of the committee at once, that there were several fortifications on the coast, either not provided for at all, or not adequately provided for, by this bill. The whole amount of its appropriations was four hundred or four hundred and thirty thousand dollars. It contained no grant of three millions, and if the Senate had passed it the very day it came from the House, not only would there have been no appropriation of the three millions, but, Sir, none of these other sums which the Senate did insert in the bill. Others besides ourselves saw the deficiencies of this bill. We had communications with and from the departments, and we inserted in the bill every thing which any department recommended to us. We took care to be sure that nothing else was coming. And we then reported the bill to the Senate with our proposed amendments. Among these amendments, there was a sum of $75,000 for Castle Island in Boston harbor, $100,000 for defences in Maryland, and so forth. These amendments were agreed to by the Senate, and one or two others added, on the motion of members; and the bill, as thus amended, was returned to the House.

And now, Sir, it becomes important to ask, When was this bill, thus amended, returned to the House of Representatives? Was it unduly detained here, so that the House was obliged afterwards to act upon it suddenly? This question is material to be asked, and material to be answered, too, and the journal does satisfactorily answer it; for it appears by the journal that the bill was returned to the House of Representatives on Tuesday, the 24th of February, *one whole week before the close of the session.* And from Tuesday, the 24th of February, to Tuesday, the 3d day of March, we heard not one word from this bill. Tuesday, the 3d day of March, was, of course, the last day of the session. We assembled here at ten or eleven o'clock in the morning of that day, and sat until three in the afternoon, and still we were not informed whether the House had finally passed the bill. As it was an important matter, and belonged to that part of the public business which usually receives particular attention from the Committee on Finance, I bore the subject in my mind, and felt some solicitude about it, seeing that the session was drawing so near to a close. I took it for granted, however, as I had not heard any thing to the contrary, that the amendments of the Senate would not be objected to, and that, when a convenient time should arrive for taking up the bill in the House, it would be passed at once into a law, and we should hear no more about it. Not the slightest intimation was given, either that the executive wished for any larger appropriation, or that it was intended in the House to insert such larger appropriation. Not a syllable escaped from anybody, and came to our knowledge, that any further alteration whatever was intended in the bill.

At three o'clock in the afternoon of the 3d of March, the Senate took its recess, as is usual in that period of the session, until five o'clock. At five o'clock we again assembled, and proceeded with the business of the Senate until eight o'clock in the evening; and at eight o'clock in the evening, and not before, the clerk of the House appeared at our door, and announced that the House of Representatives had *disagreed* to one of the Senate's amendments, *agreed* to others; and to two of those amendments, namely, the fourth and fifth, it had agreed, *with an amendment of its own.*

Now, Sir, these fourth and fifth amendments of ours were, one, a vote of $75,000 for Castle Island in Boston harbor, and the other, a vote of $100,000 for certain defences in Maryland. And what, Sir, was the addition which the House of Representatives proposed to make, by way of "_amendment_" to a vote of $75,000 for repairing the works in Boston harbor? Here, Sir, it is:--

"_And be it further enacted_, That the sum of three millions of dollars be, and the same is hereby, appropriated, out of any money in the treasury not otherwise appropriated, to be expended, in whole or in part, under the direction of the President of the United States, for the military and naval service, including fortifications and ordnance, and the increase of the navy: _Provided_, such expenditures shall be rendered necessary for the defence of the country prior to the next meeting of Congress."

This proposition, Sir, was thus unexpectedly and suddenly put to us, at eight o'clock in the evening of the last day of the session. Unusual, unprecedented, extraordinary, as it obviously is, on the face of it, the manner of presenting it was still more extraordinary. The President had asked for no such grant of money; no department had recommended it; no estimate had suggested it; no reason whatever was given for it. No emergency had happened, and nothing new had occurred; every thing known to the administration, at that hour, respecting our foreign relations, had certainly been known to it for days and weeks.

With what propriety, then, could the Senate be called on to sanction a proceeding so entirely irregular and anomalous? Sir, I recollect the occurrences of the moment very well, and I remember the impression which this vote of the House seemed to make all round the Senate. We had just come out of executive session; the doors were but just opened; and I hardly remember that there was a single spectator in the hall or the galleries. I had been at the clerk's table, and had not reached my seat, when the message was read. All the Senators were in the chamber. I heard the message, certainly with great surprise and astonishment; and I immediately moved the Senate to *disagree* to this vote of the House. My relation to the subject, in consequence of my connection with the Committee on Finance, made it my duty to propose some course, and I had not a moment's doubt or hesitation what that course ought to be. I took upon myself, then, Sir, the responsibility of moving that the Senate should disagree to this vote, and I now acknowledge that responsibility. It might be presumptuous to say that I took a leading part, but I certainly took an early part, a decided part, and an earnest part, in rejecting this broad grant of three millions of dollars, without limitation of purpose or specification of object, called for by no recommendation, founded on no estimate, made necessary by no state of things which was known to us. Certainly, Sir, I took a part in its rejection; and I stand here, in my place in the Senate, to-day, ready to defend the part so taken by me; or, rather, Sir, I disclaim all defence, and all occasion of defence, and I assert it as meritorious to have been among those who arrested, at the earliest moment, this extraordinary departure from all settled usage, and, as I think, from plain constitutional injunction,--this indefinite voting of a vast sum of money to mere executive discretion, without limit assigned, without object specified, without reason given, and without the least control.

Sir, I am told, that, in opposing this grant, I spoke with warmth, and I suppose I may have done so. If I did, it was a warmth springing from as honest a conviction of duty as ever influenced a public man. It was spontaneous, unaffected, sincere. There had been among us, Sir, no consultation, no concert. There could have been none. Between the reading of the message and my motion to disagree, there was not time enough for any two members of the Senate to exchange five words on the subject. The proposition was sudden and perfectly unexpected. I resisted it, as irregular, as dangerous in itself, and dangerous in its precedent; as wholly unnecessary, and as violating the plain intention, if not the express words, of the Constitution. Before the Senate, then, I avowed, and before the country I now avow, my part in this opposition. Whatsoever is to fall on those who sanctioned it, of that let me have my full share.

The Senate, Sir, rejected this grant by a vote of TWENTY-NINE against nineteen. Those twenty-nine names are on the journal; and whensoever the EXPUNGING process may commence, or how far soever it may be carried, I pray it, in mercy, not to erase mine from that record. I beseech it, in its sparing goodness, to leave me that proof of attachment to duty and to principle. It may draw around it, over it, or through it, black lines, or red lines, or any lines; it may mark it in any way which either the most prostrate and fantastical spirit of _man-worship_, or the most ingenious and elaborate study of self-degradation, may devise, if only it will leave it so that those who inherit my blood, or who may hereafter care for my reputation, shall be able to behold it where it now stands.

The House, Sir, insisted on this amendment. The Senate adhered to its disagreement; the House asked a conference, to which request the Senate immediately acceded. The committee of conference met, and in a very short time came to an agreement. They agreed to recommend to their respective houses, as a substitute for the vote proposed by the House, the following:--

"As an additional appropriation for arming the fortifications of the United States, three hundred thousand dollars."

"As an additional appropriation for the repairs and equipment of ships of war of the United States, five hundred thousand dollars."

I immediately reported this agreement of the committee of conference to the Senate; but, inasmuch as the bill was in the House of Representatives, the Senate could not act further on the matter until the House should first have considered the report of the committee, decided thereon, and sent us the bill. I did not myself take any note of the particular hour of this part of the transaction. The honorable member from Virginia[1] says he looked at his watch at the time, and he knows that I had come from the conference, and was in my seat, at a quarter past eleven. I have no reason to think that he is under any mistake on this particular. He says it so happened that he had occasion to take notice of the hour, and well remembers it. It could not well have been later than this, as any one will be satisfied who will look at our journals, public and executive, and see what a mass of business was despatched after I came from the committee, and before the adjournment of the Senate. Having made the report, Sir, I had no doubt that both houses would concur in the result of the conference, and looked every moment for the officer of the House bringing the bill. He did not come, however, and I pretty soon learned that there was doubt whether the committee on the part of the House would report to the House the agreement of the conferees. At first, I did not at all credit this; but was confirmed by one communication after another, until I was obliged to think it true. Seeing that the bill was thus in danger of being lost, and intending at any rate that no blame should justly attach to the Senate, I immediately moved the following resolution:--

"_Resolved_, That a message be sent to the honorable the House of Representatives, respectfully to remind the House of the report of the committee of conference appointed on the disagreeing votes of the two houses on the amendment of the House to the amendment of the Senate to the bill respecting the fortifications of the United States."

You recollect this resolution, Sir, having, as I well remember, taken some part on the occasion.[2]

This resolution was promptly passed; the secretary carried it to the House, and delivered it. What was done in the House on the receipt of this message now appears from the printed journal. I have no wish to comment on the proceedings there recorded; all may read them, and each be able to form his own opinion. Suffice it to say, that the House of Representatives, having then possession of the bill, chose to retain that possession, and never acted on the report of the committee of conference. The bill, therefore, was lost. It was lost in the House of Representatives. It died there, and there its remains are to be found. No opportunity was given to the members of the House to decide whether they would agree to the report of the committee or not. From a quarter past eleven, when the report was agreed to, until two or three o'clock in the morning, the House remained in session. If at any time there was not a quorum of members present, the attendance of a quorum, we are to presume, might have been commanded, as there was undoubtedly a great majority of members still in the city.

But, Sir, there is one other transaction of the evening which I now feel bound to state, because I think it quite important on several accounts, that it should be known.

A nomination was pending before the Senate for a judge of the Supreme Court. In the course of the sitting, that nomination was called up, and, on motion, was indefinitely postponed. In other words, it was rejected; for an indefinite postponement is a rejection. The office, of course, remained vacant, and the nomination of another person to fill it became necessary. The President of the United States was then in the Capitol, as is usual on the evening of the last day of the session, in the chamber assigned to him, and with the heads of departments around him. When nominations are rejected under these circumstances, it has been usual for the President immediately to transmit a new nomination to the Senate; otherwise the office must remain vacant till the next session, as the vacancy in such case has not happened in the recess of Congress. The vote of the Senate, indefinitely postponing this nomination, was carried to the President's room by the secretary of the Senate. The President told the secretary that it was more than an hour past twelve o'clock, and that he could receive no further communications from the Senate, and immediately after, as I have understood, left the Capitol. The secretary brought back the paper containing the certified copy of the vote of the Senate, and indorsed thereon the substance of the President's answer, and also added, that, according to his own watch, it was quarter past one o'clock.

There are two views, Sir, in which this occurrence may well deserve to be noticed. One is as to the connection which it may perhaps have had with the loss of the fortification bill; the other is as to its general importance, as introducing a new rule, or a new practice, respecting the intercourse between the President and the two houses of Congress on the last day of the session.

On the first point, I shall only observe that the fact of the President's having declined to receive this communication from the Senate, and of his having left the Capitol, was immediately known in the House of Representatives. It was quite obvious, that, if he could not receive a communication from the Senate, neither could he receive a bill from the House of Representatives for his signature. It was equally obvious, that, if, under these circumstances, the House of Representatives should agree to the report of the committee of conference, so that the bill should pass, it must, nevertheless, fail to become a law for want of the President's signature; and that, in that case, the blame of losing the bill, on whomsoever else it might fall, could not be laid upon the Senate.

On the more general point, I must say, Sir, that this decision of the President, not to hold communication with the houses of Congress after twelve o'clock at night, on the 3d of March, is quite new. No such objection has ever been made before by any President. No one of them has ever declined communicating with either house at any time during the continuance of its session on that day. All Presidents heretofore have left with the houses themselves to fix their hour of adjournment, and to bring their session for the day to a close, whenever they saw fit.

It is notorious, in point of fact, that nothing is more common than for both houses to sit later than twelve o'clock, for the purpose of completing measures which are in the last stages of their progress. Amendments are proposed and agreed to, bills passed, enrolled bills signed by the presiding officers, and other important legislative acts performed, often at two or three o'clock in the morning. All this is very well known to gentlemen who have been for any considerable time members of Congress. And all Presidents have signed bills, and have also made nominations to the Senate, without objection as to time, whenever bills have been presented for signature, or whenever it became necessary to make nominations to the Senate, at any time during the session of the respective houses on that day.

And all this, Sir, I suppose to be perfectly right, correct, and legal. There is no clause of the Constitution, nor is there any law, which declares that the term of office of members of the House of Representatives shall expire at twelve o'clock at night on the 3d of March. They are to hold for two years, but the precise hour for the commencement of that term of two years is nowhere fixed by constitutional or legal provision. It has been established by usage and by inference, and very properly established, that, since the first Congress commenced its existence on the first Wednesday in March, 1789, which happened to be the fourth day of the month, therefore the 4th of March is the day of the commencement of each successive term; but no hour is fixed by law or practice. The true rule is, as I think, most undoubtedly, that the session held on the last day constitutes the last day for all legislative and legal purposes. While the session begun on that day continues, the day itself continues, according to the established practice both of legislative and judicial bodies. This could not well be otherwise. If the precise moment of actual time were to settle such a matter, it would be material to ask, Who shall settle the time? Shall it be done by public authority, or shall every man observe the tick of his own watch? If absolute time is to furnish a precise rule, the excess of a minute, it is obvious, would be as fatal as the excess of an hour. Sir, no bodies, judicial or legislative, have ever been so hypercritical, so astute to no purpose, so much more nice than wise, as to govern themselves by any such ideas. The session for the day, at whatever hour it commences, or at whatever hour it breaks up, is the legislative day. Every thing has reference to the commencement of that diurnal session. For instance, this is the 14th day of January; we assembled here to-day at twelve o'clock; our journal is dated January 14th, and if we should remain here until five o'clock to-morrow morning (and the Senate has sometimes sat so late), our proceedings would still bear date of the 14th of January; they would be so stated upon the journal, and the journal is a record, and is a conclusive record, so far as respects the proceedings of the body.

It is so in judicial proceedings. If a man were on trial for his life, at a late hour on the last day allowed by law for the holding of the court, and the jury should acquit him, but happened to remain so long in deliberation that they did not bring in their verdict till after twelve o'clock, is it all to be held for naught, and the man to be tried over again? Are all verdicts, judgments, and orders of courts null and void, if made after midnight on the day which the law prescribes as the last day? It would be easy to show by authority, if authority could be wanted for a thing the reason of which is so clear, that the day lasts while the daily session lasts. When the court or the legislative body adjourns for that day, the day is over, and not before. I am told, indeed, Sir, that it is true that, on this same 3d day of March last, not only were other things transacted, but that the bill for the repair of the Cumberland Road, an important and much litigated measure, actually received the signature of our presiding officer after twelve o'clock, was then sent to the President, and signed by him. I do not affirm this, because I took no notice of the time, or do not remember it if I did; but I have heard the matter so stated.

I see no reason, Sir, for the introduction of this new practice; no principle on which it can be justified, no necessity for it, no propriety in it. As yet, it has been applied only to the President's intercourse with the Senate. Certainly it is equally applicable to his intercourse with both houses in legislative matters; and if it is to prevail hereafter, it is of much importance that it should be known.

The President of the United States, Sir, has alluded to this loss of the fortification bill in his message at the opening of the session, and he has alluded, also, in the same message, to the rejection of the vote of the three millions. On the first point, that is, the loss of the whole bill, and the causes of that loss, this is his language: "Much loss and inconvenience have been experienced in consequence of the failure of the bill containing the ordinary appropriations for fortifications, which passed one branch of the national legislature at the last session, but was lost in the other."

If the President intended to say that the bill, having originated in the House of Representatives, passed the Senate, and was yet afterwards lost in the House of Representatives, he was entirely correct. But he has been wholly misinformed, if he intended to state that the bill, having passed the House, was lost in the Senate. As I have already stated, the bill was lost in the House of Representatives. It drew its last breath there. That House never let go its hold on it after the report of the committee of conference. But it held it, it retained it, and of course it died in its possession when the House adjourned. It is to be regretted that the President should have been misinformed in a matter of this kind, when the slightest reference to the journals of the two houses would have exhibited the correct history of the transaction.

I recur again, Mr. President, to the proposed grant of the three millions, for the purpose of stating somewhat more distinctly the true grounds of objection to that grant.

These grounds of objection were two; the first was, that no such appropriation had been recommended by the President, or any of the departments. And what made this ground the stronger was, that the proposed grant was defended, so far as it was defended at all, upon an alleged necessity, growing out of our foreign relations. The foreign relations of the country are intrusted by the Constitution to the lead and management of the executive government. The President not only is supposed to be, but usually is, much better informed on these interesting subjects than the houses of Congress. If there be danger of a rupture with a foreign state, he sees it soonest. All our ministers and agents abroad are but so many eyes, and ears, and organs to communicate to him whatsoever occurs in foreign places, and to keep him well advised of all which may concern the interests of the United States. There is an especial propriety, therefore, that, in this branch of the public service, Congress should always be able to avail itself of the distinct opinions and recommendations of the President. The two houses, and especially the House of Representatives, are the natural guardians of the people's money. They are to keep it sacred, and to use it discreetly. They are not at liberty to spend it where it is not needed, nor to offer it for any purpose till a reasonable occasion for the expenditure be shown. Now, in this case, I repeat again, the President had sent us no recommendation for any such appropriation; no department had recommended it; no estimate had contained it; in the whole history of the session, from the morning of the first day, down to eight o'clock in the evening of the last day, not one syllable had been said to us, not one hint suggested, showing that the President deemed any such measure either necessary or proper. I state this strongly, Sir, but I state it truly. I state the matter as it is; and I wish to draw the attention of the Senate and of the country strongly to this part of the case. I say again, therefore, that, when this vote for the three millions was proposed to the Senate, there was nothing before us showing that the President recommended any such appropriation. You very well know, Sir, that this objection was stated as soon as the message from the House was read. We all well remember that this was the very point put forth by the honorable member from Tennessee,[3] as being, if I may say so, the but-end of his argument in opposition to the vote. He said, very significantly, and very forcibly, "It is not asked for by those who best know what the public service requires; how, then, are we to presume that it is needed?" This question, Sir, was not answered then; it never has been answered since, it never can be answered satisfactorily.

But let me here again, Sir, recur to the message of the President. Speaking of the loss of the bill, he uses these words: "This failure was the more regretted, not only because it necessarily interrupted and delayed the progress of a system of national defence projected immediately after the last war, and since steadily pursued, but also because it contained a contingent appropriation, inserted in accordance with the views of the executive, in aid of this important object, and other branches of the national defence, some portions of which might have been most usefully applied during the past season."

Taking these words of the message, Sir, and connecting them with the fact that the President had made no recommendation to Congress of any such appropriation, it strikes me that they furnish matter for very grave reflection. The President says that this proposed appropriation was "in accordance with the views of the executive"; that it was "in aid of an important object"; and that "some portions of it might have been most usefully applied during the past season."

And now, Sir, I ask, if this be so, why was not this appropriation recommended to Congress by the President? I ask this question in the name of the Constitution of the United States; I stand on its own clear authority in asking it; and I invite all those who remember its injunctions, and who mean to respect them, to consider well how the question is to be answered.

Sir, the Constitution is not yet an entire dead letter. There is yet some form of observance of its requirements; and even while any degree of formal respect is paid to it, I must be permitted to continue the question, Why was not this appropriation recommended? It was in accordance with the President's views; it was for an important object; it might have been usefully expended. The President being of opinion, therefore, that the appropriation was necessary and proper, how is it that it was not recommended to Congress? For, Sir, we all know the plain and direct words in which the very first duty of the President is imposed by the Constitution. Here they are:--

"He shall, from time to time, give to the Congress information of the state of the Union, and recommend to their consideration such measures as he shall judge necessary and expedient."

After enumerating the *powers* of the President, this is the first, the very first *duty* which the Constitution gravely enjoins upon him. And now, Sir, in no language of taunt or reproach, in no language of party attack, in terms of no asperity or exaggeration, but called upon by the necessity of defending my own vote upon the subject, as a public man, as a member of Congress here in my place, and as a citizen who feels as warm an attachment to the Constitution of the country as any other can, I demand of any who may choose to give it an answer to this question: WHY WAS NOT THIS MEASURE, WHICH THE PRESIDENT DECLARES THAT HE THOUGHT NECESSARY AND EXPEDIENT, RECOMMENDED TO CONGRESS? And why am I, and why are other members of Congress, whose path of duty the Constitution says shall be enlightened by the President's opinions and communications, to be charged with want of patriotism and want of fidelity to the country, because we refused an appropriation which the

President, though it was in accordance with his views, and though he believed it important, would not, and did not, recommend to us? When these questions are answered to the satisfaction of intelligent and impartial men, then, and not till then, let reproach, let censure, let suspicion of any kind, rest on the twenty-nine names which stand opposed to this appropriation.

How, Sir, were we to know that this appropriation "was in accordance with the views of the executive"? He had not so told us, formally or informally. He had not only not recommended it to Congress, or either house of Congress, but nobody on this floor had undertaken to speak in his behalf. No man got up to say, "The President desires it; he thinks it necessary, expedient, and proper." But, Sir, if any gentleman had risen to say this, it would not have answered the requisition of the Constitution. Not at all. It is not by a hint, an intimation, the suggestion of a friend, that the executive duty in this respect is to be fulfilled. By no means. The President is to make a recommendation,--a public recommendation, an official recommendation, a responsible recommendation, not to one house, but to both houses; it is to be a recommendation to Congress. If, on receiving such recommendation, Congress fail to pay it proper respect, the fault is theirs. If, deeming the measure necessary and expedient, the President fails to recommend it, the fault is his, clearly, distinctly, and exclusively his. This, Sir, is the Constitution of the United States, or else I do not understand the Constitution of the United States.

Does not every man see how entirely unconstitutional it is that the President should communicate his opinions or wishes to Congress, on such grave and important subjects, otherwise than by a direct and responsible recommendation, a public and open recommendation, equally addressed and equally known to all whose duty calls upon them to act on the subject? What would be the state of things, if he might communicate his wishes or opinions privately to members of one house, and make no such communication to the other? Would not the two houses be necessarily put in immediate collision? Would they stand on equal footing? Would they have equal information? What could ensue from such a manner of conducting the public business, but quarrel, confusion, and conflict? A member rises in the House of Representatives, and moves a very large appropriation of money for military purposes. If he says he does it upon executive recommendation, where is his voucher? The President is not like the British king, whose ministers and secretaries are in the House of Commons, and who are authorized, in certain cases, to express the opinions and wishes of their sovereign. We have no king's servants; at least, we have none known to the Constitution. Congress can know the opinions of the President only as he officially communicates them. It would be a curious inquiry in either house, when a large appropriation is moved, if it were necessary to ask whether the mover represented the President, spoke his sentiments, or, in other words, whether what he proposed were "in accordance with the views of the executive." How could that be judged of? By the party he belongs to? Party is not quite strongly enough marked for that. By the airs he gives himself? Many might assume airs, if thereby they could give themselves such importance as to be esteemed authentic expositors of the executive will. Or is this will to be circulated in whispers; made known to the meetings of party men; intimated through the press; or communicated in any other form, which still leaves the executive completely irresponsible; so that, while executive purposes or wishes pervade the ranks of party friends, influence their conduct, and unite their efforts, the open, direct, and constitutional responsibility is wholly avoided? Sir, this is not the Constitution of the United States, nor can it be consistent with any constitution which professes to maintain separate departments in the government.

Here, then, Sir, is abundant ground, in my judgment, for the vote of the Senate, and here I might rest it. But there is also another ground. The Constitution declares that no money shall be drawn from the treasury but in consequence of appropriations made by law. What is meant by "_appropriations_"? Does not this language mean that particular sums shall be assigned by law to particular objects? How far this pointing out and fixing the particular objects shall be carried, is a question that cannot be settled by any precise rule. But "specific appropriation," that is to say, the designation of every object for which money is voted, as far as such designation is practicable, has been thought to be a most important republican principle. In times past, popular parties have claimed great merit from professing to carry this doctrine much farther, and to adhere to it much more strictly, than their adversaries. Mr. Jefferson, especially, was a great advocate for it, and held it to be indispensable to a safe and economical administration and disbursement of the public revenues.

But what have the friends and admirers of Mr. Jefferson to say to this _appropriation_? Where do they find, in this proposed grant of three millions, a constitutional designation of object, and a particular and specific application of money? Have they forgotten, all forgotten, and wholly abandoned even all pretence for specific appropriation? If not, how could they sanction such a vote as this? Let me recall its terms. They are, that "the sum of three millions of dollars be, and the same is hereby, appropriated, out of any money in the treasury not otherwise appropriated, to be expended, in whole or in part, under the direction of the President of the United States, for the military and naval service, including fortifications and ordnance, and the increase of the navy; provided such expenditures shall be rendered necessary for the defence of the country prior to the next meeting of Congress."

In the first place it is to be observed, that whether the money shall be used at all, or not, is made to depend on the discretion of the President. This is sufficiently liberal. It carries confidence far enough. But if there had been no other objections, if the objects of the appropriation had been sufficiently described, so that the President, if he expended the money at all, must expend it for purposes authorized by the legislature, and nothing had been left to his discretion but the question whether an emergency had arisen in which the authority ought to be exercised, I might not have felt bound to reject the vote. There are some precedents which might favor such a contingent provision, though the practice is dangerous, and ought not to be followed except in cases of clear necessity.

But the insurmountable objection to the proposed grant was, that it specified no objects. It was as general as language could make it. It embraced every expenditure that could be called either military or naval. It was to include "fortifications, ordnance, and the increase of the navy," but it was not confined to these. It embraced the whole general subject of military service. Under the authority of such a law, the President might repair ships, build ships, buy ships, enlist seamen, and do any thing and every thing else touching the naval service, without restraint or control.

He might repair such fortifications as he saw fit, and neglect the rest; arm such as he saw fit, and neglect the arming of others; or build new fortifications wherever he chose. But these unlimited powers over the fortifications and the navy constitute by no means the most dangerous part of the proposed authority; because, under that authority, his power to raise and employ land forces would be equally absolute and uncontrolled. He might levy troops, embody a new army, call out the militia in numbers to suit his own discretion, and employ them as he saw fit.

Now, Sir, does our legislation, under the Constitution, furnish any precedent for all this?

We make appropriations for the army, and we understand what we are doing, because it is "the army," that is to say, the army established by law. We make appropriations for the navy; they, too, are for "the navy," as provided for and established by law. We make appropriations for fortifications, but we say what fortifications, and we assign to each its intended amount of the whole sum. This is the usual course of Congress on such subjects; and why should it be departed from? Are we ready to say that the power of fixing the places for new fortifications, and the sum allotted to each; the power of ordering new ships to be built, and fixing the number of such new ships; the power of laying out money to raise men for the army; in short, every power, great or small, respecting the military and naval service, shall be vested in the President, without specification of object or purpose, to the entire exclusion of the exercise of all judgment on the part of Congress? For one, I am not prepared. The honorable member from Ohio, near me, has said, that if the enemy had been on our shores he would not have agreed to this vote. And I say, if the proposition were now before us, and the guns of the enemy were pointed against the walls of the Capitol, I would not agree to it.

The people of this country have an interest, a property, an inheritance, in this INSTRUMENT, against the value of which forty capitols do not weigh the twentieth part of one poor scruple. There can never be any necessity for such proceedings, but a feigned and false necessity; a mere idle and hollow pretence of necessity; least of all can it be said that any such necessity actually existed on the 3d of March. There was no enemy on our shores; there were no guns pointed against the Capitol; we were in no war, nor was there a reasonable probability that we should have war, unless we made it ourselves.

But whatever was the state of our foreign relations, is it not preposterous to say, that it was necessary for Congress to adopt this measure, and yet not necessary for the President to recommend it? Why should we thus run in advance of all our own duties, and leave the President completely shielded from his just responsibility? Why should there be nothing but trust and confidence on our side, and nothing but discretion and power on his?

Sir, if there be any philosophy in history, if human blood still runs in human veins, if man still conforms to the identity of his nature, the institutions which secure constitutional liberty can never stand long against this excessive personal confidence, against this devotion to men, in utter disregard both of principle and experience, which seem to me to be strongly characteristic of our times. This vote came to us, Sir, from the popular branch of the legislature; and that such a vote should come from such a branch of the legislature was amongst the circumstances which excited in me the greatest surprise and the deepest concern. Certainly, Sir, certainly I was not, on that account, the more inclined to concur. It was no argument with me, that others seemed to be rushing, with such heedless, headlong trust, such impetuosity of confidence, into the arms of executive power. I held back the more strongly, and would hold back the longer. I see, or I think I see,--it is either a true vision of the future, revealed by the history of the past, or, if it be an illusion, it is an illusion which appears to me in all the brightness and sunlight of broad noon,--that it is in this career of personal confidence, along this beaten track of _man-worship_, marked at every stage by the fragments of other free governments, that our own system is making progress to its close. A personal popularity, honorably earned at first by military achievements, and sustained now by party, by patronage, and by enthusiasm which looks for no ill, because it means no ill itself, seems to render men willing to gratify power, even before its demands are made, and to surfeit executive discretion, even in anticipation of its own appetite.

If, Sir, on the 3d of March last, it had been the purpose of both houses of Congress to create a military dictator, what formula had been better suited to their purpose than this vote of the House? It is true, we might have given more money, if we had had it to give. We might have emptied the treasury; but as to the *form* of the gift, we could not have bettered it. Rome had no better models. When we give our money _for any military purpose whatever_, what remains to be done? If we leave it with one man to decide, not only whether the military means of the country shall be used at all, but how they shall be used, and to what extent they shall be employed, what remains either for Congress or the people but to sit still and see how this dictatorial power will be exercised? On the 3d of March, Sir, I had not forgotten, it was impossible that I should have forgotten, the recommendation in the message at the opening of that session, that power should be vested in the President to issue letters of marque and reprisal against France, at his discretion, in the recess of Congress. Happily, this power was not granted; but suppose it had been, what would then have been the true condition of this government? Why, Sir, this condition is very shortly described. The whole war power would have been in the hands of the President; for no man can doubt a moment that reprisals would bring on immediate war; and the treasury, to the amount of this vote, in addition to all ordinary appropriations, would have been at his absolute disposal also. And all this in a time of peace. I beseech all true lovers of constitutional liberty to contemplate this state of things, and tell me whether such be a truly republican administration of this government. Whether particular consequences had ensued or not, is such an accumulation of power in the hands of the executive according to the spirit of our system? Is it either wise or safe? Has it any warrant in the practice of former times? Or are gentlemen ready to establish the practice, as an example for the benefit of those who are to come after us?

But, Sir, if the power to make reprisals, and this money from the treasury, had both been granted, is there not great reason to believe that we should have been now actually at war? I think there is great reason to believe this. It will be said, I know, that if we had armed the President with this power of war, and supplied him with this grant of money, France would have taken it for such a proof of spirit on our part, that she would have paid the indemnity without further delay. This is the old story, and the old plea. It is the excuse of every one who desires more power than the Constitution or the laws give him, that if he had more power he could do more good. Power is always claimed for the good of the people; and dictators are always made, when made at all, for the good of the people. For my part, Sir, I was content, and am content, to show France that we are prepared to maintain our just rights against her by the exertion of our power, when need be, according to the forms of our own Constitution; that, if we make war, we will make it constitutionally; and that we will trust all our interests, both in peace and war, to what the intelligence and the strength of the country may do for them, without breaking down or endangering the fabric of our free institutions.

Mr. President, it is the misfortune of the Senate to have differed with the executive on many great questions during the last four or five years. I have regretted this state of things deeply, both on personal and on public accounts; but it has been unavoidable. It is no pleasant employment, it is no holiday business, to maintain opposition against power and against majorities, and to contend for stern and sturdy principle, against personal popularity, against a rushing and overwhelming confidence, that, by wave upon wave and cataract after cataract, seems to be bearing away and destroying whatsoever would withstand it. How much longer we may be able to support this opposition in any degree, or whether we can possibly

hold out till the public intelligence and the public patriotism shall be awakened to a due sense of the public danger, it is not for me to foretell. I shall not despair to the last, if, in the mean time, we are true to our own principles. If there be a steadfast adherence to these principles, both here and elsewhere, if, one and all, they continue the rule of our conduct in the Senate, and the rallying-point of those who think with us and support us out of the Senate, I am content to hope on and to struggle on. While it remains a contest for the preservation of the Constitution, for the security of public liberty, for the ascendency of principles over men, I am willing to bear my part of it. If we can maintain the Constitution, if we can preserve this security for liberty, if we can thus give to true principle its just superiority over party, over persons, over names, our labors will be richly rewarded. If we fail in all this, they are already among the living who will write the history of this government, from its commencement to its close.
[Footnote 1: Mr. Leigh.][Footnote 2: Mr. King, of Alabama, was in the chair.]
[Footnote 3: Mr. White.]

RECEPTION AT NEW YORK.
A SPEECH DELIVERED AT NIBLO'S SALOON, IN NEW YORK, ON THE 15TH OF MARCH, 1837.

Mr. Chairman and Fellow-Citizens:--It would be idle in me to affect to be indifferent to the circumstances under which I have now the honor of addressing you.
I find myself in the commercial metropolis of the continent, in the midst of a vast assembly of intelligent men, drawn from all the classes, professions, and pursuits of life.
And you have been pleased, Gentlemen, to meet me, in this imposing manner, and to offer me a warm and cordial welcome to your city. I thank you. I feel the full force and importance of this manifestation of your regard. In the highly-flattering resolutions which invited me here, in the respectability of this vast multitude of my fellow-citizens, and in the approbation and hearty good-will which you have here manifested, I feel cause for profound and grateful acknowledgment.
To every individual of this meeting, therefore, I would now most respectfully make that acknowledgment; and with every one, as with hands joined in mutual greeting, I reciprocate friendly salutation, respect, and good wishes.
But, Gentlemen, although I am well assured of your personal regard, I cannot fail to know, that the times, the political and commercial condition of things which exists among us, and an intelligent spirit, awakened to new activity and a new degree of anxiety, have mainly contributed to fill these avenues and crowd these halls. At a moment of difficulty, and of much alarm, you come here as Whigs of New York, to meet one whom you believe to be bound to you by common principles and common sentiments, and pursuing, with you, a common object. Gentlemen, I am proud to admit this community of our principles, and this identity of our objects. You are for the Constitution of the country; so am I. You are for the Union of the States; so am I. You are for equal laws, for the equal rights of all men, for constitutional and just restraints on power, for the substance and not the shadowy image only of popular institutions, for a government which has liberty for its spirit and soul, as well as in its forms; and so am I. You feel that if, in warm party times, the executive power is in hands distinguished for boldness, for great success, for perseverance, and other qualities which strike men's minds strongly, there is danger of derangement of the powers of government, danger of a new division of those powers, in which the executive is likely to obtain the lion's part; and danger of a state of things in which the more popular branches of the government, instead of being guards and sentinels against any encroachments from the executive, seek, rather, support from its patronage, safety against the complaints of the people in its ample and all-protecting favor, and refuge in its power; and so I feel, and so I have felt for eight long and anxious years.
You believe that a very efficient and powerful cause in the production of the evils which now fall on the industrious and commercial classes of the community, is the derangement of the currency, the destruction of the exchanges, and the unnatural and unnecessary *misplacement* of the specie of the country, by unauthorized and illegal treasury orders. So do I believe. I predicted all this from the beginning, and from before the beginning. I predicted it all, last spring, when that was attempted to be done by law which was afterwards done by executive authority; and from the moment of the exercise of that executive authority to the present time, I have both foreseen and seen the regular progress of things under it, from inconvenience and embarrassment, to pressure, loss of confidence, disorder, and bankruptcies.
Gentlemen, I mean, on this occasion, to speak my sentiments freely on the great topics of the day. I have

nothing to conceal, and shall therefore conceal nothing. In regard to political sentiments, purposes, or objects, there is nothing in my heart which I am ashamed of; I shall throw it all open, therefore, to you, and to all men. [That is right, said some one in the crowd; let us have it, with no non-committal.] Yes, my friend, without non-committal or evasion, without barren generalities or empty phrase, without *if* or _but_, without a single touch, in all I say, bearing the oracular character of an Inaugural, I shall, on this occasion, speak my mind plainly, freely, and independently, to men who are just as free to concur or not to concur in my sentiments, as I am to utter them. I think you are entitled to hear my opinions freely and frankly spoken; but I freely acknowledge that you are still more clearly entitled to retain, and maintain, your own opinions, however they may differ or agree with mine.

It is true, Gentlemen, that I have contemplated the relinquishment of my seat in the Senate for the residue of the term, now two years, for which I was chosen. This resolution was not taken from disgust or discouragement, although some things have certainly happened which might excite both those feelings. But in popular governments, men must not suffer themselves to be permanently disgusted by occasional exhibitions of political harlequinism, or deeply discouraged, although their efforts to awaken the people to what they deem the dangerous tendency of public measures be not crowned with immediate success. It was altogether from other causes, and other considerations, that, after an uninterrupted service of fourteen or fifteen years, I naturally desired a respite. But those whose opinions I am bound to respect saw objections to a present withdrawal from Congress; and I have yielded my own strong desire to their convictions of what the public good requires.

Gentlemen, in speaking here on the subjects which now so much interest the community, I wish in the outset to disclaim all personal disrespect towards individuals. He[1] whose character and fortune have exercised such a decisive influence on our politics for eight years, has now retired from public station. I pursue him with no personal reflections, no reproaches. Between him and myself there has always existed a respectful personal intercourse. Moments have existed, indeed, critical and decisive upon the general success of his administration, in which he has been pleased to regard my aid as not altogether unimportant. I now speak of him respectfully, as a distinguished soldier, as one who, in that character, has done the state much service; as a man, too, of strong and decided character, of unsubdued resolution and perseverance in whatever he undertakes. In speaking of his civil administration, I speak without censoriousness, or harsh imputation of motives; I wish him health and happiness in his retirement; but I must still speak as I think of his public measures, and of their general bearing and tendency, not only on the present interests of the country, but also on the well-being and security of the government itself.

There are, however, some topics of a less urgent present application and importance, upon which I wish to say a few words, before I advert to those which are more immediately connected with the present distressed state of things.

My learned and highly-valued friend (Mr. Ogden) who has addressed me in your behalf, has been kindly pleased to speak of my political career as being marked by a freedom from local interests and prejudices, and a devotion to liberal and comprehensive views of public policy.

I will not say that this compliment is deserved. I will only say, that I have earnestly endeavored to deserve it. Gentlemen, the general government, to the extent of its power, is national. It is not consolidated, it does not embrace all powers of government. On the contrary, it is delegated, restrained, strictly limited.

But what powers it does possess, it possesses for the general, not for any partial or local good. It extends over a vast territory, embracing now six-and-twenty States, with interests various, but not irreconcilable, infinitely diversified, but capable of being all blended into political harmony.

He, however, who would produce this harmony must survey the whole field, as if all parts were as interesting to himself as they are to others, and with that generous, patriotic feeling, prompter and better than the mere dictates of cool reason, which leads him to embrace the whole with affectionate regard, as constituting, altogether, that object which he is so much bound to respect, to defend, and to love,--his country. We have around us, and more or less within the influence and protection of the general government, all the great interests of agriculture, navigation, commerce, manufactures, the fisheries, and the mechanic arts. The duties of the government, then, certainly extend over all this territory, and embrace all these vast interests. We have a maritime frontier, a sea-coast of many thousand miles; and while no one doubts that it is the duty of government to defend this coast by suitable military preparations, there are those who yet suppose that the powers of government stop at this point; and that as to works of peace and works of improvement, they are beyond our constitutional limits. I have ever thought otherwise. Congress has a right, no doubt, to declare war, and to provide armies and navies; and it has necessarily the right to build fortifications and batteries, to protect the coast from the effects of war. But Congress has authority also, and it is its duty, to regulate commerce, and it has the whole power of collecting duties on imports and tonnage. It must have ports and harbors, and dock-yards also, for its navies. Very early in the history of the government, it was decided by Congress, on the report of a highly respectable committee, that the transfer by the States to Congress of the power of collecting tonnage and other duties, and the grant of the authority to regulate commerce, charged Congress, necessarily, with the duty of maintaining such piers and wharves and lighthouses, and of making such improvements, as might have been expected to be done by the States, if they had retained the usual means, by retaining the power of collecting duties on imports. The States, it was admitted, had parted with this power; and the duty of protecting and facilitating commerce by these means had passed, along with this power, into other hands. I have never hesitated, therefore, when the state of the treasury would admit, to vote for reasonable appropriations, for breakwaters, lighthouses, piers, harbors, and similar public works, on any part of the whole Atlantic coast or the Gulf of Mexico, from Maine to Louisiana.

But how stands the inland frontier? How is it along the vast lakes and the mighty rivers of the North and West? Do our constitutional rights and duties terminate where the water ceases to be salt? or do they exist, in full vigor, on the shores of these inland seas? I never could doubt about this; and yet, Gentlemen, I remember even to have participated in a warm debate, in the Senate, some years ago, upon the constitutional right of Congress to make an appropriation for a pier in the harbor of Buffalo. What! make a harbor at Buffalo, where Nature never made any, and where therefore it was never intended any ever should be made! Take money from the people to run out piers from the sandy shores of Lake Erie, or deepen the channels of her shallow rivers! Where was the constitutional authority for this? Where would such strides of power stop? How long would the States have any power at all left, if their territory might be ruthlessly invaded for such unhallowed purposes, or how long would the people have any money in their pockets, if the government of the United States might tax them, at pleasure, for such extravagant projects as these? Piers, wharves, harbors, and breakwaters in the Lakes! These arguments, Gentlemen, however earnestly put forth heretofore, do not strike us with great power, at the present day, if we stand on the shores of Lake Erie, and see hundreds of vessels, with valuable cargoes and thousands of valuable lives, moving on its waters, with few shelters from the storm, except what is furnished by the havens created, or made useful, by the aid of government. These great lakes, stretching away many thousands of miles, not in a straight line, but with turns and deflections, as if designed to reach, by water communication, the greatest possible number of important points through a region of vast extent, cannot but arrest the attention of any one who looks upon the map. They lie connected, but variously placed; and interspersed, as if with studied variety of form and direction, over that part of the country. They were made for man, and admirably adapted for his use and convenience. Looking, Gentlemen, over our whole country, comprehending in our survey the Atlantic coast, with its thick population, its advanced agriculture, its extended commerce, its manufactures and mechanic arts, its varieties of communication, its wealth, and its general improvements; and looking, then, to the interior, to the immense tracts of fresh, fertile, and cheap lands, bounded by so many lakes, and watered by so many magnificent rivers, let me ask if such a MAP was ever before presented to the eye of any statesman, as the theatre for the exercise of his wisdom and patriotism? And let me ask, too, if any man is fit to act a part, on such a theatre, who does not comprehend the whole of it within the scope of his policy, and embrace it all as his country?

Again, Gentlemen, we are one in respect to the glorious Constitution under which we live. We are all united in the great brotherhood of American liberty. Descending from the same ancestors, bred in the same school, taught in infancy to imbibe the same general political sentiments, Americans all, by birth, education, and principle, what but a narrow mind, or woful ignorance, or besotted selfishness, or prejudice ten times blinded, can lead any of us to regard the citizens of any part of the country as strangers and aliens?

The solemn truth, moreover, is before us, that a common political fate attends us all.

Under the present Constitution, wisely and conscientiously administered, all are safe, happy, and renowned. The measure of our country's fame may fill all our breasts. It is fame enough for us all to partake in *her* glory, if we will carry her character onward to its true destiny. But if the system is broken, its fragments must fall alike on all. Not only the cause of American liberty, but the grand cause of liberty throughout the whole earth, depends, in a great measure, on upholding the Constitution and Union of these

States. If shattered and destroyed, no matter by what cause, the peculiar and cherished idea of United American Liberty will be no more for ever. There may be free states, it is possible, when there shall be separate states. There may be many loose, and feeble, and hostile confederacies, where there is now one great and united confederacy. But the noble idea of United American Liberty, of *our* liberty, such as our fathers established it, will be extinguished for ever. Fragments and shattered columns of the edifice may be found remaining; and melancholy and mournful ruins will they be. The august temple itself will be prostrate in the dust. Gentlemen, the citizens of this republic cannot sever their fortunes. A common fate awaits us. In the honor of upholding, or in the disgrace of undermining the Constitution, we shall all necessarily partake. Let us then stand by the Constitution as it is, and by our country as it is, one, united, and entire; let it be a truth engraven on our hearts, let it be borne on the flag under which we rally, in every exigency, that we have ONE COUNTRY, ONE CONSTITUTION, ONE DESTINY.

Gentlemen, of our interior administration, the public lands constitute a highly important part. This is a subject of great interest, and it ought to attract much more attention than it has hitherto received, especially from the people of the Atlantic States. The public lands are public property. They belong to the people of all the States. A vast portion of them is composed of territories which were ceded by individual States to the United States, after the close of the Revolutionary war, and before the adoption of the present Constitution. The history of these cessions, and the reasons for making them, are familiar to you. Some of the Old Thirteen possessed large tracts of unsettled lands within their chartered limits. The Revolution had established their title to these lands, and as the Revolution had been brought about by the common treasure and the common blood of all the Colonies, it was thought not unreasonable that these unsettled lands should be transferred to the United States, to pay the debt created by the war, and afterwards to remain as a fund for the use of all the States. This is the well-known origin of the title possessed by the United States to lands northwest of the River Ohio.

By treaties with France and Spain, Louisiana and Florida, containing many millions of acres of public land, have been since acquired. The cost of these acquisitions was paid, of course, by the general government, and was thus a charge upon the whole people. The public lands, therefore, all and singular, are national property; granted to the United States, purchased by the United States, paid for by all the people of the United States.

The idea, that, when a new State is created, the public lands lying within her territory become the property of such new State in consequence of her sovereignty, is too preposterous for serious refutation. Such notions have heretofore been advanced in Congress, but nobody has sustained them. They were rejected and abandoned, although one cannot say whether they may not be revived, in consequence of recent propositions which have been made in the Senate. The new States are admitted on express conditions, recognizing, to the fullest extent, the right of the United States to the public lands within their borders; and it is no more reasonable to contend that some indefinite idea of State sovereignty overrides all these stipulations, and makes the lands the property of the States, against the provisions and conditions of their own constitution, and the Constitution of the United States, than it would be, that a similar doctrine entitled the State of New York to the money collected at the custom-house in this city; since it is no more inconsistent with sovereignty that one government should hold lands, for the purpose of sale, within the territory of another, than it is that it should lay and collect taxes and duties within such territory. Whatever extravagant pretensions may have been set up heretofore, there was not, I suppose, an enlightened man in the whole West, who insisted on any such right in the States, when the proposition to cede the lands to the States was made, in the late session of Congress. The public lands being, therefore, the common property of all the people of all the States, I shall never consent to give them away to particular States, or to dispose of them otherwise than for the general good, and the general use of the whole country.

I felt bound, therefore, on the occasion just alluded to, to resist at the threshold a proposition to cede the public lands to the States in which they lie, on certain conditions. I very much regretted the introduction of such a measure, as its effect must be, I fear, only to agitate what was well settled, and to disturb that course of proceeding, in regard to the public lands, which forty years of experience have shown to be so wise, and so satisfactory in its operation, both to the people of the old States and to those of the new.

But, Gentlemen, although the public lands are not to be given away, nor ceded to particular States, a very liberal policy in regard to them ought certainly to prevail. Such a policy has prevailed, and I have steadily supported it, and shall continue to support it so long as I may remain in public life. The main object, in regard to these lands, is undoubtedly to settle them, so fast as the growth of our population, and its augmentation by emigration, may enable us to settle them.

The lands, therefore, should be sold, at a low price; and, for one, I have never doubted the right or expediency of granting portions of the lands themselves, or of making grants of money for objects of internal improvement connected with them.

I have always supported liberal appropriations for the purpose of opening communications to and through these lands, by common roads, canals, and railroads; and where lands of little value have been long in market, and, on account of their indifferent quality, are not likely to command a common price, I know no objection to a reduction of price, as to such lands, so that they may pass into private ownership. Nor do I feel any objections to removing those restraints which prevent the States from taxing the lands for five years after they are sold. But while, in these and all other respects, I am not only reconciled to a liberal policy, but espouse it and support it, and have constantly done so, I still hold the national domain to be the general property of the country, confined to the care of Congress, and which Congress is solemnly bound to protect and preserve for the common good.

The benefit derived from the public lands, after all, is, and must be, in the greatest degree, enjoyed by those who buy them and settle upon them. The original price paid to government constitutes but a small part of their actual value. Their immediate rise in value, in the hands of the settler, gives him competence. He exercises a power of selection over a vast region of fertile territory, all on sale at the same price, and that price an exceedingly low one. Selection is no sooner made, cultivation is no sooner begun, and the first furrow turned, than he already finds himself a man of property. These are the advantages of Western emigrants and Western settlers; and they are such, certainly, as no country on earth ever before afforded to her citizens. This opportunity of purchase and settlement, this certainty of enhanced value, these sure means of immediate competence and ultimate wealth,--all these are the rights and the blessings of the people of the West, and they have my hearty wishes for their full and perfect enjoyment.

I desire to see the public lands cultivated and occupied. I desire the growth and prosperity of the West, and the fullest development of its vast and extraordinary resources. I wish to bring it near to us, by every species of useful communication. I see, not without admiration and amazement, but yet without envy or jealousy, States of recent origin already containing more people than Massachusetts. These people I know to be part of ourselves; they have proceeded from the midst of us, and we may trust that they are not likely to separate themselves, in interest or in feeling, from their kindred, whom they have left on the farms and around the hearths of their common fathers.

A liberal policy, a sympathy with its interests, an enlightened and generous feeling of participation in its prosperity, are due to the West, and will be met, I doubt not, by a return of sentiments equally cordial and equally patriotic.

Gentlemen, the general question of revenue is very much connected with this subject of the public lands, and I will therefore, in a very few words, express my views on that point.

The revenue involves, not only the supply of the treasury with money, but the question of protection to manufactures. On these connected subjects, therefore, Gentlemen, as I have promised to keep nothing back, I will state my opinions plainly, but very shortly.

I am in favor of such a revenue as shall be equal to all the just and reasonable wants of the government; and I am decidedly opposed to all collection or accumulation of revenue beyond this point. An extravagant government expenditure, and unnecessary accumulation in the treasury, are both, of all things, to be most studiously avoided.

I am in favor of protecting American industry and labor, not only as employed in large manufactories, but also, and more especially, as employed in the various mechanic arts, carried on by persons of small capitals, and living by the earnings of their own personal industry. Every city in the Union, and none more than this, would feel severely the consequences of departing from the ancient and continued policy of the government respecting this last branch of protection. If duties were to be abolished on hats, boots, shoes, and other articles of leather, and on the articles fabricated of brass, tin, and iron, and on ready-made clothes, carriages, furniture, and many similar articles, thousands of persons would be immediately thrown out of employment in this city, and in other parts of the Union. Protection, in this respect, of our own labor against the cheaper, ill-paid, half-fed, and pauper labor of Europe, is, in my opinion, a duty which the country owes to its own citizens. I am, therefore, decidedly for protecting our own industry and our own labor.

In the next place, Gentlemen, I am of opinion, that, with no more than usual skill in the application of the well-tried principles of discriminating and specific duties, all the branches of national industry may be protected, without imposing such duties on imports as shall overcharge the treasury.

And as to the revenues arising from the sales of the public lands, I am of opinion that they ought to be set apart for the use of the States. The States need the money. The government of the United States does not need it. Many of the States have contracted large debts for objects of internal improvement, and others of them have important objects which they would wish to accomplish. The lands were originally granted for the use of the several States; and now that their proceeds are not necessary for the purposes of the general government, I am of opinion that they should go to the States, and to the people of the States, upon an equal principle. Set apart, then, the proceeds of the public lands for the use of the States; supply the treasury from duties on imports; apply to these duties a just and careful discrimination, in favor of articles produced at home by our own labor, and thus support, to a fair extent, our own manufactures. These, Gentlemen, appear to me to be the general outlines of that policy which the present condition of the country requires us to adopt.

Gentlemen, proposing to express opinions on the principal subjects of interest at the present moment, it is impossible to overlook the delicate question which has arisen from events which have happened in the late Mexican province of Texas. The independence of that province has now been recognized by the government of the United States. Congress gave the President the means, to be used when he saw fit, of opening a diplomatic intercourse with its government, and the late President immediately made use of those means.

I saw no objection, under the circumstances, to voting an appropriation to be used when the President should think the proper time had come; and he deemed, very promptly, it is true, that the time had already arrived. Certainly, Gentlemen, the history of Texas is not a little wonderful. A very few people, in a very short time, have established a government for themselves, against the authority of the parent state; and this government, it is generally supposed, there is little probability, at the present moment, of the parent state being able to overturn.

This government is, in form, a copy of our own. It is an American constitution, substantially after the great American model. We all, therefore, must wish it success; and there is no one who will more heartily rejoice than I shall, to see an independent community, intelligent, industrious, and friendly towards us, springing up, and rising into happiness, distinction, and power, upon our own principles of liberty and government. But it cannot be disguised, Gentlemen, that a desire, or an intention, is already manifested to annex Texas to the United States. On a subject of such mighty magnitude as this, and at a moment when the public attention is drawn to it, I should feel myself wanting in candor, if I did not express my opinion; since all must suppose that, on such a question, it is impossible that I should be without some opinion.

I say then, Gentlemen, in all frankness, that I see objections, I think insurmountable objections, to the annexation of Texas to the United States. When the Constitution was formed, it is not probable that either its framers or the people ever looked to the admission of any States into the Union, except such as then already existed, and such as should be formed out of territories then already belonging to the United States. Fifteen years after the adoption of the Constitution, however, the case of Louisiana arose. Louisiana was obtained by treaty with France, who had recently obtained it from Spain; but the object of this acquisition, certainly, was not mere extension of territory. Other great political interests were connected with it. Spain, while she possessed Louisiana, had held the mouths of the great rivers which rise in the Western States, and flow into the Gulf of Mexico. She had disputed our use of these rivers already, and with a powerful nation in possession of these outlets to the sea, it is obvious that the commerce of all the West was in danger of perpetual vexation. The command of these rivers to the sea was, therefore, the great object aimed at in the acquisition of Louisiana. But that acquisition necessarily brought territory along with it, and three States now exist, formed out of that ancient province.

A similar policy, and a similar necessity, though perhaps not entirely so urgent, led to the acquisition of Florida.

Now, no such necessity, no such policy, requires the annexation of Texas. The accession of Texas to our territory is not necessary to the full and complete enjoyment of all which we already possess. Her case, therefore, stands upon a footing entirely different from that of Louisiana and Florida. There being no necessity for extending the limits of the Union in that direction, we ought, I think, for numerous and powerful reasons, to be content with our present boundaries.

Gentlemen, we all see that, by whomsoever possessed, Texas is likely to be a slave-holding country; and I frankly avow my entire unwillingness to do anything that shall extend the slavery of the African race on this continent, or add other slave-holding States to the Union. When I say that I regard slavery in itself as a great moral, social, and political evil, I only use language which has been adopted by distinguished men, themselves citizens of slave-holding States. I shall do nothing, therefore, to favor or encourage its further extension. We have slavery already amongst us. The Constitution found it in the Union; it recognized it, and gave it solemn guaranties. To the full extent of these guaranties we are all bound, in honor, in justice, and by the Constitution. All the stipulations contained in the Constitution in favor of the slave-holding States which are already in the Union ought to be fulfilled, and, so far as depends on me, shall be fulfilled, in the fulness of their spirit and to the exactness of their letter. Slavery, as it exists in the States, is beyond the reach of Congress. It is a concern of the States themselves; they have never submitted it to Congress, and Congress has no rightful power over it. I shall concur, therefore, in no act, no measure, no menace, no indication of purpose, which shall interfere or threaten to interfere with the exclusive authority of the several States over the subject of slavery as it exists within their respective limits. All this appears to me to be matter of plain and imperative duty.

But when we come to speak of admitting new States, the subject assumes an entirely different aspect. Our rights and our duties are then both different.

The free States, and all the States, are then at liberty to accept or to reject. When it is proposed to bring new members into this political partnership, the old members have a right to say on what terms such new partners are to come in, and what they are to bring along with them. In my opinion, the people of the United States will not consent to bring into the Union a new, vastly extensive, and slave-holding country, large enough for half a dozen or a dozen States. In my opinion, they ought not to consent to it. Indeed, I am altogether at a loss to conceive what possible benefit any part of this country can expect to derive from such annexation. Any benefit to any part is at least doubtful and uncertain; the objections are obvious, plain, and strong. On the general question of slavery, a great portion of the community is already strongly excited. The subject has not only attracted attention as a question of politics, but it has struck a far deeper-toned chord. It has arrested the religious feeling of the country; it has taken strong hold on the consciences of men. He is a rash man indeed, and little conversant with human nature, and especially has he a very erroneous estimate of the character of the people of this country, who supposes that a feeling of this kind is to be trifled with or despised. It will assuredly cause itself to be respected. It may be reasoned with, it may be made willing, I believe it is entirely willing, to fulfil all existing engagements and all existing duties, to uphold and defend the Constitution as it is established, with whatever regrets about some provisions which it does actually contain. But to coerce it into silence, to endeavor to restrain its free expression, to seek to compress and confine it, warm as it is, and more heated as such endeavors would inevitably render it,-- should this be attempted, I know nothing, even in the Constitution or in the Union itself, which would not be endangered by the explosion which might follow.

I see, therefore, no political necessity for the annexation of Texas to the Union; no advantages to be derived from it; and objections to it of a strong, and, in my judgment, decisive character.

I believe it to be for the interest and happiness of the whole Union to remain as it is, without diminution and without addition.

Gentlemen, I pass to other subjects. The rapid advancement of the executive authority is a topic which has already been alluded to.

I believe there is serious cause of alarm from this source. I believe the power of the executive has increased, is increasing, and ought now to be brought back within its ancient constitutional limits. I have nothing to do with the motives which have led to those acts, which I believe to have transcended the boundaries of the Constitution. Good motives may always be assumed, as bad motives may always be imputed. Good intentions will always be pleaded for every assumption of power; but they cannot justify it, even if we were sure that they existed. It is hardly too strong to say, that the Constitution was made to guard the people against the dangers of good intention, real or pretended. When bad intentions are boldly avowed, the people will promptly take care of themselves. On the other hand, they will always be asked why they should resist or question that exercise of power which is so fair in its object, so plausible and patriotic in appearance, and which has the public good alone confessedly in view? Human beings, we may be assured, will generally exercise power when they can get it; and they will exercise it most undoubtedly, in popular governments, under pretences of public safety or high public interest. It may be very possible that good intentions do really sometimes exist when constitutional restraints are disregarded. There are men, in all ages, who mean to exercise power usefully; but who mean to exercise it. They mean to govern well; but they mean to govern. They promise to be kind masters; but they mean to be masters. They think there need be but little restraint upon themselves. Their notion of the public interest is apt to be quite closely connected with their own exercise of authority. They may not, indeed, always understand their own motives. The love of power may sink too deep in their own hearts even for their own scrutiny, and may pass with themselves for mere patriotism and benevolence.

A character has been drawn of a very eminent citizen of Massachusetts, of the last age, which, though I think it does not entirely belong to him, yet very well describes a certain class of public men. It was said of this distinguished son of Massachusetts, that in matters of politics and government he cherished the most kind and benevolent feelings towards the whole earth. He earnestly desired to see all nations well governed; and to bring about this happy result, he wished that the United States might govern the rest of the world; that Massachusetts might govern the United States; that Boston might govern Massachusetts; and as for himself, his own humble ambition would be satisfied by governing the little town of Boston.

I do not intend, Gentlemen, to commit so unreasonable a trespass on your patience as to discuss all those cases in which I think executive power has been unreasonably extended. I shall only allude to some of them, and, as being earliest in the order of time, and hardly second to any other in importance, I mention the practice of removal from all offices, high and low, for opinion's sake, and on the avowed ground of giving patronage to the President; that is to say, of giving him the power of influencing men's political opinions and political conduct, by hopes and by fears addressed directly to their pecuniary interests. The great battle on this point was fought, and was lost, in the Senate of the United States, in the last session of Congress under Mr. Adams's administration. After General Jackson was known to be elected, and before his term of office began, many important offices became vacant by the usual causes of death and resignation. Mr. Adams, of course, nominated persons to fill these vacant offices. But a majority of the Senate was composed of the friends of General Jackson; and, instead of acting on these nominations, and filling the vacant offices with ordinary promptitude, the nominations were postponed to a day beyond the 4th of March, for the purpose, openly avowed, of giving the patronage of the appointments to the President who was then coming into office. When the new President entered on his office, he withdrew these nominations, and sent in nominations of his own friends in their places. I was of opinion then, and am of opinion now, that that decision of the Senate went far to unfix the proper balance of the government. It conferred on the President the power of rewards for party purposes, or personal purposes, without limit or control. It sanctioned, manifestly and plainly, that exercise of power which Mr. Madison had said would deserve impeachment; and it completely defeated one great object, which we are told the framers of the Constitution contemplated, in the manner of forming the Senate; that is, that the Senate might be a body not changing with the election of a President, and therefore likely to be able to hold over him some check or restraint in regard to bringing his own friends and partisans into power with him, and thus rewarding their services to him at the public expense.

The debates in the Senate, on these questions, were long continued and earnest. They were of course in secret session, but the opinions of those members who opposed this course have all been proved true by the result. The contest was severe and ardent, as much so as any that I have ever partaken in; and I have seen some service in that sort of warfare.

Gentlemen, when I look back to that eventful moment, when I remember who those were who upheld this claim for executive power, with so much zeal and devotion, as well as with such great and splendid abilities, and when I look round now, and inquire what has become of these gentlemen, where they have found themselves at last, under the power which they thus helped to establish, what has become now of all their respect, trust, confidence, and attachment,--how many of them, indeed, have not escaped from being broken and crushed under the weight of the wheels of that engine which they themselves set in motion,--I feel that an edifying lesson may be read by those who, in the freshness and fulness of party zeal, are ready to confer the most dangerous power, in the hope that they and their friends may bask in its sunshine, while enemies only shall be withered by its frown.

I will not go into the mention of names. I will give no enumeration of persons; but I ask you to turn your minds back, and recollect who the distinguished men were who supported, in the Senate, General Jackson's administration for the first two years; and I will ask you what you suppose they think now of that power and that discretion which they so freely confided to executive hands. What do they think of the whole career of that administration, the commencement of which, and indeed the existence of which, owed so much to their own great exertions?

In addition to the establishment of this power of unlimited and causeless removal, another doctrine has been put forth, more vague, it is true, but altogether unconstitutional, and tending to like dangerous results. In some loose, indefinite, and unknown sense, the President has been called the *representative of the whole American people*. He has called himself so repeatedly, and been so denominated by his friends a thousand times. Acts, for which no specific authority has been found either in the Constitution or the laws, have been justified on the ground that the President is the representative of the whole American people. Certainly, this is not constitutional language. Certainly, the Constitution nowhere calls the President the universal representative of the people. The constitutional representatives of the people are in the House of Representatives, exercising powers of legislation. The President is an executive officer, appointed in a particular manner, and clothed with prescribed and limited powers. It may be thought to be of no great consequence, that the President should call himself, or that others should call him, the sole representative of all the people, although he has no such appellation or character in the Constitution. But, in these matters, words are things. If he is the people's representative, and as such may exercise power, without any other grant, what is the limit to that power? And what may not an unlimited representative of the people do? When the Constitution expressly creates representatives, as members of Congress, it regulates, defines, and limits their authority. But if the executive chief magistrate, merely because he is the executive chief magistrate, may assume to himself another character, and call himself the representative of the whole people, what is to limit or restrain this representative power in his hands?

I fear, Gentlemen, that if these pretensions should be continued and justified, we might have many instances of summary political logic, such as I once heard in the House of Representatives. A gentleman, not now living, wished very much to vote for the establishment of a Bank of the United States, but he had always stoutly denied the constitutional power of Congress to create such a bank. The country, however, was in a state of great financial distress, from which such an institution, it was hoped, might help to extricate it; and this consideration led the worthy member to review his opinions with care and deliberation. Happily, on such careful and deliberate review, he altered his former judgment. He came, satisfactorily, to the conclusion that Congress might incorporate a bank. The argument which brought his mind to this result was short, and so plain and obvious, that he wondered how he should so long have overlooked it. The power, he said, to create a bank, was either given to Congress, or it was not given. Very well. If it was given, Congress of course could exercise it; if it was not given, the people still retained it, and in that case, Congress, as the representatives of the people, might, upon an emergency, make free to use it.

Arguments and conclusions in substance like these, Gentlemen, will not be wanting, if men of great popularity, commanding characters, sustained by powerful parties, _and full of good intentions towards the public_, may be permitted to call themselves the universal representatives of the people.

But, Gentlemen, it is the _currency_, the currency of the country,--it is this great subject, so interesting, so vital, to all classes of the community, which has been destined to feel the most violent assaults of executive power. The consequences are around us and upon us. Not unforeseen, not unforetold, here they come, bringing distress for the present, and fear and alarm for the future. If it be denied that the present condition of things has arisen from the President's interference with the revenue, the first answer is, that, when he did interfere, just such consequences were predicted. It was then said, and repeated, and pressed upon the public attention, that that interference must necessarily produce derangement, embarrassment, loss of confidence, and commercial distress. I pray you, Gentlemen, to recur to the debates of 1832, 1833, and 1834, and then to decide whose opinions have proved to be correct. When the treasury experiment was first announced, who supported, and who opposed it? Who warned the country against it? Who were they who endeavored to stay the violence of party, to arrest the hand of executive authority, and to convince the people that this experiment was delusive; that its object was merely to increase executive power, and that its effect, sooner or later, must be injurious and ruinous? Gentlemen, it is fair to bring the opinions of political men to the test of experience. It is just to judge of them by their measures, and their opposition to measures; and for myself, and those political friends with whom I have acted, on this subject of the currency, I am ready to abide the test.

But before the subject of the currency, and its present most embarrassing state, is discussed, I invite your attention, Gentlemen, to the history of executive proceedings connected with it. I propose to state to you a series of facts; not to argue upon them, not to *mystify* them, nor to draw any unjust inference from them;

but merely to state the case, in the plainest manner, as I understand it. And I wish, Gentlemen, that, in order to be able to do this in the best and most convincing manner, I had the ability of my learned friend, (Mr. Ogden,) whom you have all so often heard, and who usually states his case in such a manner that, when stated, it is already very well argued.

Let us see, Gentlemen, what the train of occurrences has been in regard to our revenue and finances; and when these occurrences are stated, I leave to every man the right to decide for himself whether our present difficulties have or have not arisen from attempts to extend the executive authority. In giving this detail, I shall be compelled to speak of the late Bank of the United States; but I shall speak of it historically only. My opinion of its utility, and of the extraordinary ability and success with which its affairs were conducted for many years before the termination of its charter, is well known. I have often expressed it, and I have not altered it. But at present I speak of the bank only as it makes a necessary part in the history of events which I wish now to recapitulate.

Mr. Adams commenced his administration in March, 1825. He had been elected by the House of Representatives, and began his career as President under a powerful opposition. From the very first day, he was warmly, even violently, opposed in all his measures; and this opposition, as we all know, continued without abatement, either in force or asperity, through his whole term of four years. Gentlemen, I am not about to say whether this opposition was well or ill founded, just or unjust. I only state the fact as connected with other facts. The Bank of the United States, during these four years of Mr. Adams's administration, was in full operation. It was performing the fiscal duties enjoined on it by its charter; it had established numerous offices, was maintaining a large circulation, and transacting a vast business in exchange. Its character, conduct, and manner of administration were all well known to the whole country. Now there are two or three things worthy of especial notice. One is, that during the whole of this heated political controversy, from 1825 to 1829, the party which was endeavoring to produce a change of administration in the general government brought no charge of political interference against the Bank of the United States. If any thing, it was rather a favorite with that party generally. Certainly, the party, as a party, did not ascribe to it undue attachment to other parties, or to the then existing administration. Another important fact is, that, during the whole of the same period, those who had espoused the cause of General Jackson, and who sought to bring about a revolution under his name, did not propose the destruction of the bank, or its discontinuance, as one of the objects which were to be accomplished by the intended revolution. They did not tell the country that the bank was unconstitutional; they did not declare it unnecessary; they did not propose to get along without it, when they should come into power themselves. If individuals entertained any such purposes, they kept them much to themselves. The party, as a party, avowed none such. A third fact, worthy of all notice, is, that during this period there was no complaint about the state of the currency, either by the country generally or by the party then in opposition.

In March, 1829, General Jackson was inaugurated as President. He came into power on professions of reform. He announced reform of all abuses to be the great and leading object of his future administration; and in his inaugural address he pointed out the main subjects of this reform. But the bank was not one of them. It was not said by him that the bank was unconstitutional. It was not said that it was unnecessary or useless. It was not said that it had failed to do all that had been hoped or expected from it in regard to the currency.

In March, 1829, then, the bank stood well, very well, with the new administration. It was regarded, so far as appears, as entirely constitutional, free from political or party taint, and highly useful. It had as yet found no place in the catalogue of abuses to be reformed.

But, Gentlemen, nine months wrought a wonderful change. New lights broke forth before these months had rolled away; and the President, in his message to Congress in December, 1829, held a very unaccustomed language and manifested very unexpected purposes.

Although the bank had then five or six years of its charter unexpired, he yet called the attention of Congress very pointedly to the subject, and declared,--

1. That the constitutionality of the bank was well doubted by many;

2. That its utility or expediency was also well doubted;

3. That all must admit that it had failed to establish or maintain a sound and uniform currency; and

4. That the true bank for the use of the government of the United States would be a bank which should be founded on the revenues and credit of the government itself.

These propositions appeared to me, at the time, as very extraordinary, and the last one as very startling. A bank founded on the revenue and credit of the government, and managed and administered by the executive, was a conception which I had supposed no man holding the chief executive power in his own hands would venture to put forth.

But the question now is, what had wrought this great change of feeling and of purpose in regard to the bank. What events had occurred between March and December that should have caused the bank, so constitutional, so useful, so peaceful, and so safe an institution, in the first of these months, to start up into the character of a monster, and become so horrid and dangerous, in the last?

Gentlemen, let us see what the events were which had intervened. General Jackson was elected in December, 1828. His term was to begin in March, 1829. A session of Congress took place, therefore, between his election and the commencement of his administration.

Now, Gentlemen, the truth is, that during this session, and a little before the commencement of the new administration, a disposition was manifested by political men to interfere with the management of the bank. Members of Congress undertook to nominate or recommend individuals as directors in the branches or offices of the bank. They were kind enough, sometimes, to make out whole lists, or tickets, and to send them to Philadelphia, containing the names of those whose appointments would be satisfactory to General Jackson's friends. Portions of the correspondence on these subjects have been published in some of the voluminous reports and other documents connected with the bank, but perhaps have not been generally heeded or noticed. At first, the bank merely declined, as gently as possible, complying with these and similar requests. But like applications began to show themselves from many quarters, and a very marked case arose as early as June, 1829. Certain members of the Legislature of New Hampshire applied for a change in the presidency of the branch which was established in that State. A member of the Senate of the United States wrote both to the president of the bank and to the Secretary of the Treasury, strongly recommending a change, and in his letter to the Secretary hinting very distinctly at political considerations as the ground of the movement. Other officers in the service of the government took an interest in the matter, and urged a change; and the Secretary himself wrote to the bank, suggesting and recommending it. The time had come, then, for the bank to take its position. It did take it; and, in my judgment, if it had not acted as it did act, not only would those who had the care of it have been most highly censurable, but a claim would have been yielded to, entirely inconsistent with a government of laws, and subversive of the very foundations of republicanism.

A long correspondence between the Secretary of the Treasury and the president of the bank ensued. The directors determined that they would not surrender either their rights or their duties to the control or supervision of the executive government. They said they had never appointed directors of their branches on political grounds, and they would not remove them on such grounds. They had avoided politics. They had sought for men of business, capacity, fidelity, and experience in the management of pecuniary concerns. They owed duties, they said, to the government, which they meant to perform, faithfully and impartially, under all administrations; and they owed duties to the stockholders of the bank, which required them to disregard political considerations in their appointments. This correspondence ran along into the fall of the year, and finally terminated in a stern and unanimous declaration, made by the directors, and transmitted to the Secretary of the Treasury, that the bank would continue to be independently administered, and that the directors once for all refused to submit to the supervision of the executive authority, in any of its branches, in the appointment of local directors and agents. This resolution decided the character of the future. Hostility towards the bank, thenceforward, became the settled policy of the government; and the message of December, 1829, was the clear announcement of that policy. If the bank had appointed those directors, thus recommended by members of Congress; if it had submitted all its appointments to the supervision of the treasury; if it had removed the president of the New Hampshire branch; if it had, in all things, showed itself a complying, political, party machine, instead of an independent institution;--if it had done this, I leave all men to judge whether such an entire change of opinion, as to its constitutionality, its utility, and its good effects on the currency, would have happened between March and December.

From the moment in which the bank asserted its independence of treasury control, and its elevation above mere party purposes, down to the end of its charter, and down even to the present day, it has been the subject to which the selectest phrases of party denunciation have been plentifully applied.

But Congress manifested no disposition to establish a treasury bank. On the contrary, it was satisfied, and so was the country, most unquestionably, with the bank then existing. In the summer of 1832, Congress passed an act for continuing the charter of the bank, by strong majorities in both houses. In the House of Representatives, I think, two thirds of the members voted for the bill. The President gave it his negative; and as there were not two thirds of the Senate, though a large majority were for it, the bill failed to become a law.

But it was not enough that a continuance of the charter of the bank was thus refused. It had the deposit of the public money, and this it was entitled to, by law, for the few years which yet remained of its chartered term. But this it was determined it should not continue to enjoy. At the commencement of the session of 1832-33, a grave and sober doubt was expressed by the Secretary of the Treasury, in his official communication, whether the public moneys were safe in the custody of the bank! I confess, Gentlemen, when I look back to this suggestion, thus officially made, so serious in its import, so unjust, if not well founded, and so greatly injurious to the credit of the bank, and injurious, indeed, to the credit of the whole country, I cannot but wonder that any man of intelligence and character should have been willing to make it. I read in it, however, the first lines of another chapter. I saw an attempt was now to be made to remove the deposits of the public money from the bank, and such an attempt was made that very session. But Congress was not to be prevailed upon to accomplish the end by its own authority. It was well ascertained that neither house would consent to it. The House of Representatives, indeed, at the heel of the session, decided against the proposition by a very large majority.

The legislative authority having been thus invoked, and invoked in vain, it was resolved to stretch farther the long arm of executive power, and by that arm to reach and strike the victim. It so happened that I was in this city in May, 1833, and here learned, from a very authentic source, that the deposits would be removed by the President's order; and in June, as afterwards appeared, that order was given.

Now it is obvious, Gentlemen, that thus far the changes in our financial and fiscal system were effected, not by Congress, but by the executive; not by law, but by the will and the power of the President. Congress would have continued the charter of the bank; but the President negatived the bill. Congress was of opinion that the deposits ought not to be removed; but the President removed them. Nor was this all. The public moneys being withdrawn from the custody which the law had provided, by executive power alone, that same power selected the places for their future keeping. Particular banks, existing under State charters, were chosen. With these especial and particular arrangements were made, and the public moneys were deposited in their vaults. Henceforward these selected banks were to operate on the revenue and credit of the government; and thus the original scheme, promulgated in the annual message of December, 1829, was substantially carried into effect. Here were banks chosen by the treasury; all the arrangements with them made by the treasury; a set of duties to be performed by them to the treasury prescribed; and these banks were to hold the whole proceeds of the public revenue. In all this, Congress had neither part nor lot. No law had caused the removal of the deposits; no law had authorized the selection of deposit State banks; no law had prescribed the terms on which the revenues should be placed in such banks. From the beginning of the chapter to the end, it was all executive edict. And now, Gentlemen, I ask if it be not most remarkable, that, in a country professing to be under a government of laws, such great and important changes in one of its most essential and vital interests should be brought about without any change of law, without any enactment of the legislature whatever? Is such a power trusted to the executive of any government in which the executive is separated, by clear and well-defined lines, from the legislative department? The currency of the country stands on the same general ground as the commerce of the country. Both are intimately connected, and both are subjects of legal, not of executive, regulation.

It is worthy of notice, that the writers of the Federalist, in discussing the powers which the Constitution conferred on the President, made it matter of commendation, that it withdraws this subject altogether from his grasp. "He can prescribe no rules," say they, "concerning the commerce or *currency* of the country." And so we have been all taught to think, under all former administrations. But we have now seen that the President, and the President alone, does prescribe the rule concerning the currency. He makes it, and he alters it. He makes one rule for one branch of the revenue, and another rule for another. He makes one rule for the citizen of one State, and another for the citizen of another State. This, it is certain, is one part of the treasury order of July last.

But at last Congress interfered, and undertook to regulate the deposits of the public moneys. It passed the law of July, 1836, placing the subject under legal control, restraining the power of the executive, subjecting the banks to liabilities and duties, on the one hand, and securing them against executive favoritism, on the other. But this law contained another important provision; which was, that all the money in the treasury, beyond what was necessary for the current expenditures of the government, should be deposited with the States. This measure passed both houses by very unusual majorities, yet it hardly escaped a veto. It obtained only a cold assent, a slow, reluctant, and hesitating approval; and an early moment was seized to array against it a long list of objections. But the law passed. The money in the treasury beyond the sum of five millions was to go to the States. It has so gone, and the treasury for the present is relieved from the burden of a surplus. But now observe other coincidences. In the annual message of December, 1835, the President quoted the fact of the rapidly increasing sale of the public lands as proof of high national prosperity. He alluded to that subject, certainly with much satisfaction, and apparently in something of the tone of exultation. There was nothing said about monopoly, not a word about speculation, not a word about over-issues of paper, to pay for the lands. All was prosperous, all was full of evidence of a wise administration of government, all was joy and triumph.

But the idea of a deposit or distribution of the surplus money with the people suddenly damped this effervescing happiness. The color of the rose was gone, and every thing now looked gloomy and black. Now no more felicitation or congratulation, on account of the rapid sales of the public lands; no more of this most decisive proof of national prosperity and happiness. The executive Muse takes up a melancholy strain. She sings of monopolies, of speculation, of worthless paper, of loss both of land and money, of the multiplication of banks, and the danger of paper issues; and the end of the canto, the catastrophe, is, that lands shall no longer be sold but for gold and silver alone. The object of all this is clear enough. It was to diminish the income from the public lands. No desire for such a diminution had been manifested, so long as the money was supposed to be likely to remain in the treasury. But a growing conviction that some other disposition must be made of the surplus, awakened attention to the means of preventing that surplus. Toward the close of the last session, Gentlemen, a proposition was brought forward in Congress for such an alteration of the law as should admit payment for public lands to be made in nothing but gold and silver. The mover voted for his own proposition; but I do not recollect that any other member concurred in the vote. The proposition was rejected at once; but, as in other cases, that which Congress refused to do, the executive power did. Ten days after Congress adjourned, having had this matter before it, and having refused to act upon it by making any alteration in the existing laws, a treasury order was issued, commanding that very thing to be done which Congress had been requested and had refused to do. Just as in the case of the removal of the deposits, the executive power acted in this case also against the known, well understood, and recently expressed will of the representatives of the people. There never has been a moment when the legislative will would have sanctioned the object of that order; probably never a moment in which any twenty individual members of Congress would have concurred in it. The act was done without the assent of Congress, and against the well-known opinion of Congress. That act altered the law of the land, or purported to alter it, against the well-known will of the law-making power.

For one, I confess I see no authority whatever in the Constitution, or in any law, for this treasury order. Those who have undertaken to maintain it have placed it on grounds, not only different, but inconsistent and contradictory. The reason which one gives, another rejects; one confutes what another argues. With one it is the joint resolution of 1816 which gave the authority; with another, it is the law of 1820; with a third, it is the general superintending power of the President; and this last argument, since it resolves itself into mere power, without stopping to point out the sources of that power, is not only the shortest, but in truth the most just. He is the most sensible, as well as the most candid reasoner, in my opinion, who places this treasury order on the ground of the pleasure of the executive, and stops there. I regard the joint resolution of 1816 as mandatory; as prescribing a legal rule; as putting this subject, in which all have so deep an interest, beyond the caprice, or the arbitrary pleasure, or the discretion, of the Secretary of the Treasury. I believe there is not the slightest legal authority, either in that officer or in the President, to make a distinction, and to say that paper may be received for debts at the custom-house, but that gold and silver only shall be received at the land offices. And now for the sequel.

At the commencement of the last session, as you know, Gentlemen, a resolution was brought forward in the Senate for annulling and abrogating this order, by Mr. Ewing, of Ohio, a gentleman of much intelligence, of sound principles, of vigorous and energetic character, whose loss from the service of the country I regard as a public misfortune. The Whig members all supported this resolution, and all the members, I believe, with the exception of some five or six, were very anxious in some way to get rid of the treasury order. But Mr. Ewing's resolution was too direct. It was deemed a pointed and ungracious attack on executive policy. It must therefore be softened, modified, qualified, made to sound less harsh to the ears of men in power, and to assume a plausible, polished, inoffensive character. It was accordingly put into the plastic hands of friends of the executive to be moulded and fashioned, so that it might have the effect of ridding the country of the obnoxious order, and yet not appear to question executive infallibility. All this did not answer. The late President is not a man to be satisfied with soft words; and he saw in the measure, even as it passed the two houses, a substantial repeal of the order. He is a man of boldness and decision; and he respects boldness and decision in others. If you are his friend, he expects no flinching; and if you are his adversary, he respects you none the less for carrying your opposition to the full limits of honorable warfare. Gentlemen, I most sincerely regret the course of the President in regard to this bill, and certainly most highly disapprove it. But I do not suffer the mortification of having attempted to disguise and garnish it, in order to make it acceptable, and of still finding it thrown back in my face. All that was obtained by this ingenious, diplomatic, and over-courteous mode of enacting a law, was a response from the President and the Attorney-General, that the bill in question was obscure, ill penned, and not easy to be understood. The bill, therefore, was neither approved nor negatived. If it had been approved, the treasury order would have been annulled, though in a clumsy and objectionable manner. If it had been negatived, and returned to Congress, no doubt it would have been passed by two thirds of both houses, and in that way have become a law, and abrogated the order. But it was not approved, it was not returned; it was retained. It had passed the Senate in season; it had been sent to the House in season; but there it was suffered to lie so long without being called up, that it was completely in the power of the President when it finally passed that body; since he is not obliged to return bills which he does not approve, if not presented to him ten days before the end of the session. The bill was lost, therefore, and the treasury order remains in force. Here again the representatives of the people, in both houses of Congress, by majorities almost unprecedented, endeavored to abolish this obnoxious order. On hardly any subject, indeed, has opinion been so unanimous, either in or out of Congress. Yet the order remains.

And now, Gentlemen, I ask you, and I ask all men who have not voluntarily surrendered all power and all right of thinking for themselves, whether, from 1832 to the present moment, the executive authority has not effectually superseded the power of Congress, thwarted the will of the representatives of the people, and even of the people themselves, and taken the whole subject of the currency into its own grasp? In 1832, Congress desired to continue the bank of the United States, and a majority of the people desired it also; but the President opposed it, and his will prevailed. In 1833, Congress refused to remove the deposits; the President resolved upon it, however, and his will prevailed. Congress has never been willing to make a bank founded on the money and credit of the government, and administered, of course, by executive hands; but this was the President's object, and he attained it, in a great measure, by the treasury selection of deposit banks. In this particular, therefore, to a great extent, his will prevailed. In 1836, Congress refused to confine the receipts for public lands to gold and silver; but the President willed it, and his will prevailed. In 1837, both houses of Congress, by more than two thirds, passed a bill for restoring the former state of things by annulling the treasury order; but the President willed, notwithstanding, that the order should remain in force, and his will again prevailed. I repeat the question, therefore, and I would put it earnestly to every intelligent man, to every lover of our constitutional liberty, are we under the dominion of the law? or has the effectual government of the country, at least in all that regards the great interest of the currency, been in a single hand?

Gentlemen, I have done with the narrative of events and measures. I have done with the history of these successive steps, in the progress of executive power, towards a complete control over the revenue and the currency. The result is now all before us. These pretended reforms, these extraordinary exercises of power from an extraordinary zeal for the good of the people, what have they brought us to?

In 1829, the currency was declared to be _neither sound nor uniform_; a proposition, in my judgment, altogether at variance with the fact, because I do not believe there ever was a country of equal extent, in which paper formed any part of the circulation, that possessed a currency so sound, so uniform, so convenient, and so perfect in all respects, as the currency of this country, at the moment of the delivery of that message, in 1829.

But how is it now? Where has the improvement brought it? What has reform done? What has the great cry for hard money accomplished? Is the currency *uniform* now? Is money in New Orleans now as good, or nearly so, as money in New York? Are exchanges at par, or only at the same low rates as in 1829 and other years? Every one here knows that all the benefits of this experiment are but injury and oppression; all this reform, but aggravated distress.

And as to the *soundness* of the currency, how does that stand? Are the causes of alarm less now than in 1829? Is there less bank paper in circulation? Is there less fear of a general catastrophe? Is property more secure, or industry more certain of its reward? We all know, Gentlemen, that, during all this pretended warfare against all banks, banks have vastly increased. Millions upon millions of bank paper have been added to the circulation. Everywhere, and nowhere so much as where the present administration and its measures have been most zealously supported, banks have multiplied under State authority, since the decree was made that the Bank of the United States should be suffered to expire. Look at Mississippi, Missouri, Louisiana, Virginia, and other States. Do we not see that banking capital and bank paper are enormously increasing? The opposition to banks, therefore, so much professed, whether it be real or whether it be but pretended, has not restrained either their number or their issues of paper. Both have vastly increased.

And now a word or two, Gentlemen, upon this hard-money scheme, and the fancies and the delusions to which it has given birth. Gentlemen, this is a subject of delicacy, and one which it is difficult to treat with sufficient caution, in a popular and occasional address like this. I profess to be a _bullionist_, in the usual and accepted sense of that word. I am for a solid specie basis for our circulation, and for specie as a part of the circulation, so far as it may be practicable and convenient. I am for giving no value to paper, merely as paper. I abhor paper; that is to say, irredeemable paper, paper that may not be converted into gold or silver at the will of the holder. But while I hold to all this, I believe, also, that an exclusive gold and silver circulation is an utter impossibility in the present state of this country and of the world. We shall none of us ever see it; and it is credulity and folly, in my opinion, to act under any such hope or expectation. The States will make banks, and these will issue paper; and the longer the government of the United States neglects its duty in regard to measures for regulating the currency, the greater will be the amount of bank paper overspreading the country. Of this I entertain not a particle of doubt.

While I thus hold to the absolute and indispensable necessity of gold and silver, as the foundation of our circulation, I yet think nothing more absurd and preposterous, than unnatural and strained efforts to import specie. There is but so much specie in the world, and its amount cannot be greatly or suddenly increased. Indeed, there are reasons for supposing that its amount has recently diminished, by the quantity used in manufactures, and by the diminished products of the mines. The existing amount of specie, however, must support the paper circulations, and the systems of currency, not of the United States only, but of other nations also. One of its great uses is to pass from country to country, for the purpose of settling occasional balances in commercial transactions. It always finds its way, naturally and easily, to places where it is needed for these uses. But to take extraordinary pains to bring it where the course of trade does not bring it, where the state of debt and credit does not require it to be, and then to endeavor, by unnecessary and injurious regulations, treasury orders, accumulations at the mint, and other contrivances, there to retain it, is a course of policy bordering, as it appears to me, on political insanity. It is boasted that we have seventy-five or eighty millions of specie now in the country. But what more senseless, what more absurd, than this boast, if there is a balance against us abroad, of which payment is desired sooner than remittances of our own products are likely to make that payment? What more miserable than to boast of having that which is not ours, which belongs to others, and which the convenience of others, and our own convenience also, require that they should possess? If Boston were in debt to New York, would it be wise in Boston, instead of paying its debt, to contrive all possible means of obtaining specie from the New York banks, and hoarding it at home? And yet this, as I think, would be precisely as sensible as the course which the government of the United States at present pursues. We have, beyond all doubt, a great amount of specie in the country, but it does not answer its accustomed end, it does not perform its proper duty. It neither goes abroad to settle balances against us, and thereby quiet those who have demands upon us; nor is it so disposed of at home us to sustain the circulation to the extent which the circumstances of the times require. A great part of it is in the Western banks, in the land offices, on the roads through the wilderness, on the passages over the Lakes, from the land offices to the deposit banks, and from the deposit banks back to the land offices. Another portion is in the hands of buyers and sellers of specie; of men in the West, who sell land-office money to the new settlers for a high premium Another portion, again, is kept in private hands, to be used when circumstances shall tempt to the purchase of lands. And, Gentlemen, I am inclined to think, so loud has been the cry about hard money, and so sweeping the denunciation of all paper, that private holding, or hoarding, prevails to some extent in different parts of the country. These eighty millions of specie, therefore, really do us little good. We are weaker in our circulation, I have no doubt, our credit is feebler, money is scarcer with us, at this moment, than if twenty millions of this specie were shipped to Europe, and general confidence thereby restored.

Gentlemen, I will not say that some degree of pressure might not have come upon us, if the treasury order had not issued. I will not say that there has not been over-trading, and over-production, and a too great expansion of bank circulation. This may all be so, and the last-mentioned evil, it was easy to foresee, was likely to happen when the United States discontinued their own bank. But what I do say is, that, acting upon the state of things as it actually existed, and is now actually existing the treasury order has been, and now is productive of great distress. It acts upon a state of things which gives extraordinary force to its stroke, and extraordinary point to its sting. It arrests specie, when the free use and circulation of specie are most important; it cripples the banks, at a moment when the banks more than ever need all their means. It makes the merchant unable to remit, when remittance is necessary for his own credit, and for the general adjustment of commercial balances. I am not now discussing the general question, whether prices must not come down, and adjust themselves anew to the amount of bullion existing in Europe and America. I am dealing only with the measures of our own government on the subject of the currency, and I insist that these measures have been most unfortunate, and most ruinous in their effects on the ordinary means of our circulation at home, and on our ability of remittance abroad.

Their effects, too, on domestic exchanges, by deranging and misplacing the specie which is in the country, are most disastrous. Let him who has lent an ear to all these promises of a more uniform currency see how he can now sell his draft on New Orleans or Mobile. Let the Northern manufacturers and mechanics, those who have sold the products of their labor to the South, and heretofore realized the prices with little loss of exchange,--let them try present facilities. Let them see what reform of the currency has done for them. Let them inquire whether, in this respect, their condition is better or worse than it was five or six years ago.

Gentlemen, I hold this disturbance of the measure of value, and the means of payment and exchange, this derangement, and, if I may so say, this violation of the currency, to be one of the most unpardonable of political faults. He who tampers with the currency robs labor of its bread. He panders, indeed, to greedy capital, which is keen-sighted, and may shift for itself; but he beggars labor, which is honest, unsuspecting, and too busy with the present to calculate for the future. The prosperity of the working classes lives, moves, and has its being in established credit, and a steady medium of payment. All sudden changes destroy it. Honest industry never comes in for any part of the spoils in that scramble which takes place when the currency of a country is disordered. Did wild schemes and projects ever benefit the industrious? Did irredeemable bank paper ever enrich the laborious? Did violent fluctuations ever do good to him who depends on his daily labor for his daily bread? Certainly never. All these things may gratify greediness for sudden gain, or the rashness of daring speculation; but they can bring nothing but injury and distress to the homes of patient industry and honest labor. Who are they that profit by the present state of things? They are not the many, but the few. They are speculators, brokers, dealers in money, and lenders of money at exorbitant interest. Small capitalists are crushed, and, their means being dispersed, as usual, in various parts of the country, and this miserable policy having destroyed exchanges, they have no longer either money or credit. And all classes of labor partake, and must partake, in the same calamity. And what consolation for all this is it, that the public lands are paid for in specie? that, whatever embarrassment and distress pervade the country, the Western wilderness is thickly sprinkled over with eagles and dollars? that gold goes weekly from Milwaukie and Chicago to Detroit, and back again from Detroit to Milwaukie and Chicago, and performs similar feats of egress and regress, in many other instances, in the Western States? It is remarkable enough, that, with all this sacrifice of general convenience, with all this sky-rending clamor for government payments in specie, government, after all, never gets a dollar. So far as I know, the United States have not now a single specie dollar in the world. If they have, where is it? The gold and silver collected at the land offices is sent to the deposit banks; it is there placed to the credit of the government, and thereby becomes the property of the bank. The whole revenue of the government, therefore, after all, consists in mere bank credits; that very sort of security which the friends of the administration have so much denounced.

Remember, Gentlemen, in the midst of this deafening din against all banks, that, if it shall create such a panic as shall shut up the banks, it will shut up the treasury of the United States also.

Gentlemen, I would not willingly be a prophet of ill. I most devoutly wish to see a better state of things; and I believe the repeal of the treasury order would tend very much to bring about that better state of things. And I am of opinion, that, sooner or later, the order will be repealed. I think it must be repealed. I think the East, West, North, and South will demand its repeal. But, Gentlemen, I feel it my duty to say, that, if I should be disappointed in this expectation, I see no immediate relief to the distresses of the community. I greatly fear, even, that the worst is not yet.[2] I look for severer distresses; for extreme difficulties in exchange, for far greater inconveniences in remittance, and for a sudden fall in prices. Our condition is one which is not to be tampered with, and the repeal of the treasury order, being something which government can do, and which will do good, the public voice is right in demanding that repeal. It is true, if repealed now, the relief will come late. Nevertheless its repeal or abrogation is a thing to be insisted on, and pursued, till it shall be accomplished. This executive control over the currency, this power of discriminating, by treasury order, between one man's debt and another man's debt, is a thing not to be endured in a free country; and it should be the constant, persisting demand of all true Whigs, "Rescind the illegal treasury order, restore the rule of the law, place all branches of the revenue on the same grounds, make men's rights equal, and leave the government of the country where the Constitution leaves it, in the hands of the representatives of the people in Congress." This point should never be surrendered or compromised. Whatever is established, let it be equal, and let it be legal. Let men know, to-day, what money may be required of them to-morrow. Let the rule be open and public, on the pages of the statute-book, not a secret, in the executive breast.

Gentlemen, in the session which has now just closed, I have done my utmost to effect a direct and immediate repeal of the treasury order.

I have voted for a bill anticipating the payment of the French and Neapolitan indemnities by an advance from the treasury.

I have voted with great satisfaction for the restoration of duties on goods destroyed in the great conflagration in this city.

I have voted for a deposit with the States of the surplus which may be in the treasury at the end of the year. All these measures have failed; and it is for you, and for our fellow-citizens throughout the country, to decide whether the public interest would, or would not, have been promoted by their success.

But I find, Gentlemen, that I am committing an unpardonable trespass on your indulgent patience. I will pursue these remarks no further. And yet I cannot persuade myself to take leave of you without reminding you, with the utmost deference and respect, of the important part assigned to you in the political concerns of your country, and of the great influence of your opinions, your example, and your efforts upon the general prosperity and happiness.

Whigs of New York! Patriotic citizens of this great metropolis! Lovers of constitutional liberty, bound by interest and by affection to the institutions of your country, Americans in heart and in principle!--you are ready, I am sure, to fulfil all the duties imposed upon you by your situation, and demanded of you by your country. You have a central position; your city is the point from which intelligence emanates, and spreads in all directions over the whole land. Every hour carries reports of your sentiments and opinions to the verge of the Union. You cannot escape the responsibility which circumstances have thrown upon you. You must live and act, on a broad and conspicuous theatre, either for good or for evil to your country. You cannot shrink from your public duties; you cannot obscure yourselves, nor bury your talent. In the common welfare, in the common prosperity, in the common glory of Americans, you have a stake of value not to be calculated. You have an interest in the preservation of the Union, of the Constitution, and of the true principles of the government, which no man can estimate. You act for yourselves, and for the generations that are to come after you; and those who ages hence shall bear your names, and partake your blood, will feel, in their political and social condition, the consequences of the manner in which you discharge your political duties.

Having fulfilled, then, on your part and on mine, though feebly and imperfectly on mine, the offices of kindness and mutual regard required by this occasion, shall we not use it to a higher and nobler purpose? Shall we not, by this friendly meeting, refresh our patriotism, rekindle our love of constitutional liberty, and strengthen our resolutions of public duty? Shall we not, in all honesty and sincerity, with pure and disinterested love of country, as Americans, looking back to the renown of our ancestors, and looking forward to the interests of our posterity, here, to-night, pledge our mutual faith to hold on to the last to our professed principles, to the doctrines of true liberty, and to the Constitution of the country, let who will prove true, or who will prove recreant? Whigs of New York! I meet you in advance, and give you my pledge for my own performance of these duties, without qualification and without reserve. Whether in public life or in private life, in the Capitol or at home, I mean never to desert them. I mean never to forget that I have a country, to which I am bound by a thousand ties; and the stone which is to lie on the ground that shall cover me, shall not bear the name of a son ungrateful to his native land.

[Footnote 1: President Jackson.][Footnote 2: On the 10th of June following the delivery of this speech, all the banks in the city of New York, by common consent, suspended the payment of their notes in specie. On the next day, the same step was taken by the banks of Boston and the vicinity, and the example was followed by all the banks south of New York, as they received intelligence of the suspension of specie payments in that city. On the 15th of June, (just three months from the day this speech was delivered,) President Van Buren issued his proclamation calling an extra session of Congress for the first Monday of September.]

SLAVERY IN THE DISTRICT OF COLUMBIA.

REMARKS MADE IN THE SENATE OF THE UNITED STATES, ON THE 10TH OF JANUARY, 1838, UPON A RESOLUTION MOVED BY MR. CLAY AS A SUBSTITUTE FOR THE RESOLUTION OFFERED BY MR. CALHOUN ON THE SUBJECT OF SLAVERY IN THE DISTRICT OF COLUMBIA.

[On the 27th of December, 1837, a series of resolutions was moved in the Senate by Mr. Calhoun, on the subject of slavery. The fifth of the series was expressed in the following terms:--
"_Resolved_, That the intermeddling of any State, or States, or their citizens, to abolish slavery in this District, or any of the Territories, on the ground, or under the pretext, that it is immoral or sinful, or the passage of any act or measure of Congress with that view, would be a direct and dangerous attack on the institutions of all the slave-holding States."
These resolutions were taken up for discussion on several successive days. On the 10th of January, 1838, Mr. Clay moved the following resolution, as a substitute for the fifth of Mr. Calhoun's series:--
"_Resolved_, That the interference, by the citizens of any of the States, with the view to the abolition of slavery in this District, is endangering the rights and security of the people of the District; and that any act or measure of Congress, designed to abolish slavery in this District, would be a violation of the faith implied in the cessions by the States of Virginia and Maryland, a just cause of alarm to the people of the slave-holding States, and have a direct and inevitable tendency to disturb and endanger the Union."
On the subject of this amendment, Mr. Webster addressed the Senate as follows.]
Mr. President,--I cannot concur in this resolution. I do not know any matter of fact, or any ground of argument, on which this affirmation of plighted faith can be sustained. I see nothing by which Congress has tied up its hands, either directly or indirectly, so as to put its clear constitutional power beyond the exercise of its own discretion. I have carefully examined the acts of cession by the States, the act of Congress, the proceedings and history of the times, and I find nothing to lead me to doubt that it was the intention of all parties to leave this, like other subjects belonging to legislation for the ceded territory, entirely to the discretion and wisdom of Congress. The words of the Constitution are clear and plain. None could be clearer or plainer. Congress, by that instrument, has power to exercise exclusive jurisdiction over the ceded territory, in all cases whatsoever. The acts of cession contain no limitation, condition, or qualification whatever, except that, out of abundant caution, there is inserted a _proviso_ that nothing in the acts contained shall be construed to vest in the United States any right of property in the soil, so as to affect the rights of individuals therein, otherwise than as such individuals might themselves transfer their right of soil to the United States. The acts of cession declare, that the tract of country "is for ever ceded and relinquished to Congress and to the government of the United States, in full and absolute right and exclusive jurisdiction, as well of soil as of persons residing or to reside therein, pursuant to the tenor and effect of the eighth section of the first article of the Constitution of the United States."
Now, that section, to which reference is thus expressly made in these deeds of cession, declares, that Congress shall have power "to exercise exclusive legislation, in all cases whatsoever, over such district, not exceeding ten miles square, as may, by cession of particular States and the acceptance of Congress, become the seat of government of the United States."
Nothing, therefore, as it seems to me, can be clearer, than that the States making the cession expected Congress to exercise over the District precisely that power, and neither more nor less, which the Constitution had conferred upon it. I do not know how the provision, or the intention, either of the

Constitution in granting the power, or of the States in making the cession, could be expressed in a manner more absolutely free from all doubt or ambiguity.

I see, therefore, nothing in the act of cession, and nothing in the Constitution, and nothing in the history of this transaction, and nothing in any other transaction, implying any limitation upon the authority of Congress.

If the assertion contained in this resolution be true, a very strange result, as it seems to me, must follow. The resolution affirms that the faith of Congress is pledged, indefinitely. It makes no limitation of time or circumstance. If this be so, then it is an obligation that binds us for ever, as much as if it were one of the prohibitions of the Constitution itself. And at all times hereafter, even if, in the course of their history, availing themselves of events, or changing their views of policy, the States themselves should make provision for the emancipation of their slaves, the existing state of things could not be changed, nevertheless, in this District. It does really seem to me, that, if this resolution, in its terms, be true, though slavery in every other part of the world may be abolished, yet in the metropolis of this great republic it is established in perpetuity. This appears to me to be the result of the doctrine of plighted faith, as stated in the resolution.

In reply to Mr. Buchanan, Mr. Webster said:--#/

The words of the resolution speak for themselves. They require no comment. They express an unlimited plighted faith. The honorable member will so see if he will look at those words. The gentleman asks whether those who made the cession could have expected that Congress would ever exercise such a power. To this I answer, that I see no reason to doubt that the parties to the cession were as willing to leave this as to leave other powers to the discretion of Congress. I see not the slightest evidence of any especial fear, or any especial care or concern, on the part of the ceding States, in regard to this particular part of the jurisdiction ceded to Congress. And I think I can ask, on the other side, a very important question for the consideration of the gentleman himself, and for that of the Senate and the country; and that is, Would Congress have accepted the cession with any such restraint upon its constitutional power, either express or understood to be implied? I think not. Looking back to the state of things then existing, and especially to what Congress had so recently done, when it accepted the cession of the Northwestern Territory, I entertain no doubt whatever that Congress would have refused the cession altogether, if offered with any condition or understanding that its constitutional authority to exercise exclusive legislation over the District in all cases whatsoever should be abridged.

The Senate will observe that I am speaking solely to the point of plighted faith. Upon other parts of the resolution, and upon many other things connected with it, I have said nothing. I only resist the imposition of new obligations, or a new prohibition, not to be found, as I think, either in the Constitution or any act of Congress. I have said nothing on the expediency of abolition, immediate or gradual, or the reasons which ought to weigh with Congress should that question be proposed. I can, however, well conceive what would, as I think, be a natural and fair mode of reasoning on such an occasion.

When it is said, for instance, by way of argument, that Congress, although it have the power, ought not to take a lead in the business of abolition, considering that the interest which the United States have in the whole subject is vastly less than that which States have in it, I can understand the propriety and pertinency of the observation. It is, as far as it goes, a pertinent and appropriate argument, and I shall always be ready to give it the full weight belonging to it. When it is argued that, in a case so vital to the States, the States themselves should be allowed to maintain their own policy, and that the government of the United States ought not to do any thing which shall, directly or indirectly, shake or disturb that policy, this is a line of argument which I can understand, whatever weight I may be disposed to give to it; for I have always not only admitted, but insisted, that slavery within the States is a subject belonging absolutely and exclusively to the States themselves.

But the present is not an attempt to establish any such course of reasoning as this. The attempt is to set up a pledge of the public faith, to do the same office that a constitutional prohibition in terms would do; that is, to set up a direct bar, precluding all exercise of the discretion of Congress over the subject. It has been often said, in this debate, and I believe it is true, that a decided majority of the Senate do believe that Congress has a clear constitutional power over slavery in this District. But while this constitutional right is admitted, it is at the same moment attempted effectually to counteract, overthrow, and do away with it, by the affirmation of plighted faith, as asserted in the resolution before us.

Now, I have already said I know of nothing to support this affirmation. Neither in the acts of cession, nor in the act of Congress accepting it, nor in any other document, history, publication, or transaction, do I know of a single fact or suggestion supporting this proposition, or tending to support it. Nor has any gentleman, so far as I know, pointed out, or attempted to point out, any such fact, document, transaction, or other evidence. All is left to the general and repeated statement, that such a condition must have been intended by the States. Of all this I see no proof whatever. I see no evidence of any desire on the part of the States thus to limit the power of Congress, or thus to require a pledge against its exercise. And, indeed, if this were made out, the intention of Congress, as well as that of the States, must be inquired into. Nothing short of a clear and manifest intention of both parties, proved by proper evidence, can amount to plighted faith. The expectation or intent of one party, founded on something not provided for nor hinted at in the transaction itself, cannot plight the faith of the other party.

In short, I am altogether unable to see any ground for supposing that either party to the cession had any mental reservation, any unexpressed expectation, or relied on any implied, but unmentioned and unsuggested pledge, whatever. By the Constitution, if a district should be ceded to it for the seat of government, Congress was to have a right, in express terms, to exercise exclusive legislation, in all cases whatsoever. The cession was made and accepted in pursuance of this power. Both parties knew well what they were doing. Both parties knew that by the cession the States surrendered all jurisdiction, and Congress acquired all jurisdiction; and this is the whole transaction.

As to any provision in the acts of cession stipulating for the security of property, there is none, excepting only what I have already stated; the condition, namely, that no right of individuals to the soil should be construed to be transferred, but only the jurisdiction. But, no doubt, all rights of property ought to be duly respected by Congress, and all other legislatures.

And since the subject of compensation to the owners of emancipated slaves has been referred to, I take occasion to say, that if Congress should think that a wise, just, and politic legislation for this District required it to make compensation for slaves emancipated here, it has the same constitutional authority to make such compensation as to make grants for roads and bridges, almshouses, penitentiaries, and other similar objects, in the District. A general and absolute power of legislation carries with it all the necessary and just incidents belonging to such legislation.

Mr. Clay having made some remarks in reply, Mr. Webster rejoined:--#/

The honorable member from Kentucky asks the Senate to suppose the opposite case; to suppose that the seat of government had been fixed in a free State, Pennsylvania, for example; and that Congress had attempted to establish slavery in a district over which, as here, it had thus exclusive legislation. He asks whether, in that case, Congress could establish slavery in such a place. This mode of changing the question does not, I think, vary the argument; and I answer, at once, that, however improbable or improper such an act might be, yet, if the power were universal, absolute, and without restriction, it might unquestionably be so exercised. No limitation being expressed or intimated in the grant itself, or any other proceeding of the parties, none could be implied.

And in the other cases, of forts, arsenals, and dock-yards, if Congress has exclusive and absolute legislative power, it must, of course, have the power, if it could be supposed to be guilty of such folly, whether proposed to be exercised in a district within a free State, to establish slavery, or in a district in a slave State, to abolish or regulate it. If it be a district over which Congress has, as it has in this District, unlimited power of legislation, it seems to me that whatever would stay the exercise of this power, in either case, must be drawn from discretion, from reasons of justice and true policy, from those high considerations which ought to influence Congress in questions of such extreme delicacy and importance; and to all these considerations I am willing, and always shall be willing, I trust, to give full weight. But I cannot, in conscience, say that the power so clearly conferred on Congress by the Constitution, as a power to be exercised, like others, at its own discretion, is immediately taken away again by an implied faith that it shall not be exercised at all.

THE CREDIT SYSTEM AND THE LABOR OF THE UNITED STATES.
FROM THE SECOND SPEECH ON THE SUB-TREASURY, DELIVERED IN THE SENATE OF THE UNITED STATES, ON THE 12th OF MARCH, 1838.

Now, Mr. President, what I understand by the credit system is, that which thus connects labor and capital, by giving to labor the use of capital. In other words, intelligence, good character, and good morals bestow on those who have not capital a power, a trust, a confidence, which enables them to obtain it, and to employ it usefully for themselves and others. These active men of business build their hopes of success on their attentiveness, their economy, and their integrity. A wider theatre for useful activity is under their feet, and around them, than was ever open to the young and enterprising generations of men, on any other spot enlightened by the sun. Before them is the ocean. Every thing in that direction invites them to efforts of enterprise and industry in the pursuits of commerce and the fisheries. Around them, on all hands, are thriving and prosperous manufactures, an improving agriculture, and the daily presentation of new objects of internal improvement; while behind them is almost half a continent of the richest land, at the cheapest prices, under healthful climates, and washed by the most magnificent rivers that on any part of the globe pay their homage to the sea. In the midst of all these glowing and glorious prospects, they are neither restrained by ignorance, nor smitten down by the penury of personal circumstances. They are not compelled to contemplate, in hopelessness and despair, all the advantages thus bestowed on their condition by Providence. Capital they may have little or none, but CREDIT supplies its place; not as the refuge of the prodigal and the reckless; not as gratifying present wants with the certainty of future absolute ruin; but as the genius of honorable trust and confidence; as the blessing voluntarily offered to good character and to good conduct as the beneficent agent, which assists honesty and enterprise in obtaining comfort and independence.

Mr. President, take away this credit, and what remains? I do not ask what remains to the few, but to the many? Take away this system of credit, and then tell me what is left for labor and industry, but mere manual toil and daily drudgery? If we adopt a system that withdraws capital from active employment, do we not diminish the rate of wages? If we curtail the general business of society, does not every laboring man find his condition grow daily worse? In the politics of the day, Sir, we hear much said about divorcing the government from the banks; but when we abolish credit, we shall divorce labor from capital; and depend upon it, Sir, when we divorce labor from capital, capital is hoarded, and labor starves.

The declaration so often quoted, that "all who trade on borrowed capital ought to break," is the most aristocratic sentiment ever uttered in this country. It is a sentiment which, if carried out by political arrangement, would condemn the great majority of mankind to the perpetual condition of mere day-laborers. It tends to take away from them all that solace and hope which arise from possessing something which they can call their own. A man loves his own; it is fit and natural that he should do so; and he will love his country and its institutions, if he have some stake in that country, although it be but a very small part of the general mass of property. If it be but a cottage, an acre, a garden, its possession raises him, gives him self-respect, and strengthens his attachment to his native land. It is our happy condition, by the blessing of Providence, that almost every man of sound health, industrious habits, and good morals, can ordinarily attain, at least, to this degree of comfort and respectability; and it is a result devoutly to be wished, both for its individual and its general consequences.

But even to this degree of acquisition that credit of which I have already said so much is highly important, since its general effect is to raise the price of wages, and render industry productive. There is no condition so low, if it be attended with industry and economy, that it is not benefited by credit, as any one will find, if he will examine and follow out its operations.

Sir, if there be any aristocrats in Massachusetts, the people are all aristocrats; because I do not believe there is on earth, in a highly civilized society, a greater equality in the condition of men than exists there. If there be a man in the State who maintains what is called an equipage, has servants in livery, or drives four horses in his coach, I am not acquainted with him. On the other hand, there are few who are not able to carry their wives and daughters to church in some decent conveyance. It is no matter of regret or sorrow to us that few are very rich; but it is our pride and glory that few are very poor. It is our still higher pride, and our just boast, as I think, that all her citizens possess means of intelligence and education, and that, of all her productions, she reckons among the very chiefest those which spring from the culture of the mind and the heart.

Mr. President, one of the most striking characteristics of this age in the extraordinary progress which it has witnessed in popular knowledge. A new and powerful impulse has been acting in the social system of late, producing this effect in a most remarkable degree. In morals, in politics, in art, in literature, there is a vast accession to the number of readers and to the number of proficients. The present state of popular knowledge is not the result of a slow and uniform progress, proceeding through a lapse of years, with the same regular degree of motion. It is evidently the result of some new causes, brought into powerful action, and producing their consequences rapidly and strikingly. What, Sir, are these causes?

This is not an occasion, Sir, for discussing such a question at length; allow me to say, however, that the improved state of popular knowledge is but the necessary result of the improved condition of the great mass of the people. Knowledge is not one of our merely physical wants. Life may be sustained without it. But, in order to live, men must be fed and clothed and sheltered; and in a state of things in which one's whole labor can do no more than procure clothes, food, and shelter, he can have no time nor means for mental improvement. Knowledge, therefore, is not attained, and cannot be attained, till there is some degree of respite from daily manual toil and never-ending drudgery. Whenever a less degree of labor will produce the absolute necessaries of life, then there come leisure and means both to teach and to learn.

If this great and wonderful extension of popular knowledge be the result of an improved condition, it may, in the next place, well be asked, What are the causes which have thus suddenly produced that great improvement? How is it that the means of food, clothing, and shelter are now so much more cheaply and abundantly procured than formerly? Sir, the main cause I take to be the progress of scientific art, or a new extension of the application of science to art. This it is which has so much distinguished the last half-century in Europe and in America, and its effects are everywhere visible, and especially among us. Man has found new allies and auxiliaries in the powers of nature and in the inventions of mechanism.

The general doctrine of political economy is, that wealth consists in whatever is useful or convenient to man, and that labor is the producing cause of all this wealth. This is very true. But, then, what is labor? In the sense of political writers, and in common language, it means human industry; in a philosophical view, it may receive a much more comprehensive meaning. It is not, in that view, human toil only, the mere action of thews and muscles; but it is any active agency which, working upon the materials with which the world is supplied, brings forth products useful or convenient to man. The materials of wealth are in the earth, in the seas, and in their natural and unaided productions. Labor obtains these materials, works upon them, and fashions them to human use. Now it has been the object of scientific art, or of the application of science to art, to increase this active agency, to augment its power, by creating millions of laborers in the form of machines all but automatic, all to be diligently employed and kept at work by the force of natural powers. To this end these natural powers, principally those of steam and falling water, are subsidized and taken into human employment. Spinning-machines, power-looms, and all the mechanical devices, acting, among other operatives, in the factories and workshops, are but so many laborers. They are usually denominated labor-*saving* machines, but it would be more just to call them labor-*doing* machines. They are made to be active agents; to have motion, and to produce effect; and though without intelligence, they are guided by laws of science, which are exact and perfect, and they produce results, therefore, in general, more accurate than the human hand is capable of producing. When we look upon one of these, we behold a mute fellow-laborer, of immense power, of mathematical exactness, and of ever-during and unwearied effort. And while he is thus a most skilful and productive laborer, he is a non-consumer, at least beyond the wants of his mechanical being. He is not clamorous for food, raiment, or shelter, and makes no demands for the expenses of education. The eating and drinking, the reading and writing, and the clothes-wearing world, are benefited by the labors of these co-operatives, in the same way as if Providence had provided for their service millions of beings, like ourselves in external appearance, able to labor and to toil, and yet requiring little or nothing for their own consumption or subsistence; or rather, as if Providence had created a race of giants, each of whom, demanding no more for his support and consumption than a common laborer, should yet be able to perform the work of a hundred.

Now, Sir, turn back to the Massachusetts tables of production, and you will see that it is these automatic allies and co-operators, and these powers of nature, thus employed and placed under human direction, which have come, with such prodigious effect, to man's aid, in the great business of procuring the means of living, of comfort, and of wealth, and which have so swollen the products of her skilful industry. Look at these tables once more, Sir, and you will see the effects of labor, united with and acting upon capital. Look yet again, and you will see that credit, mutual trust, prompt and punctual dealings, and commercial confidence, are all mixed up as indispensable elements in the general system.

I will ask you to look yet once more, Sir, and you will perceive that general competence, great equality in human condition, a degree of popular knowledge and intelligence nowhere surpassed, if anywhere equalled, the prevalence of good moral sentiment, and extraordinary general prosperity, are the result of the whole. Sir, I have done with Massachusetts. I do not praise the old "Bay State" of the Revolution; I only present her as she is.

Mr. President, such is the state of things actually existing in the country, and of which I have now given you a sample. And yet there are persons who constantly clamor against this state of things. They call it aristocracy. They excite the poor to make war upon the rich, while in truth they know not who are either rich or poor. They complain of oppression, speculation, and the pernicious influence of accumulated wealth. They cry out loudly against all banks and corporations, and all the means by which small capitals become united, in order to produce important and beneficial results. They carry on a mad hostility against all established institutions. They would choke up the fountains of industry, and dry all its streams.

In a country of unbounded liberty, they clamor against oppression. In a country of perfect equality, they would move heaven and earth against privilege and monopoly. In a country where property is more equally divided than anywhere else, they rend the air with the shouting of agrarian doctrines. In a country where the wages of labor are high beyond all parallel, and where lands are cheap, and the means of living low, they would teach the laborer that he is but an oppressed slave. Sir, what can such men want? What do they mean? They can want nothing, Sir, but to enjoy the fruits of other men's labor. They can mean nothing but disturbance and disorder, the diffusion of corrupt principles, and the destruction of the moral sentiments and moral habits of society. A licentiousness of feeling and of action is sometimes produced by prosperity itself. Men cannot always resist the temptation to which they are exposed by the very abundance of the bounties of Providence, and the very happiness of their own condition; as the steed, full of the pasture, will sometimes throw himself against its enclosures, break away from its confinement, and, feeling now free from needless restraint, betake himself to the moors and barrens, where want, erelong, brings him to his senses, and starvation and death close his career.

REMARKS ON THE POLITICAL COURSE OF MR. CALHOUN, IN 1838.
FROM THE SAME SPEECH.

Having had occasion, Mr. President, to speak of nullification and the nullifiers, I beg leave to say that I have not done so for any purpose of reproach. Certainly, Sir, I see no possible connection, myself, between their principles or opinions, and the support of this measure.[1] They, however, must speak for themselves. They may have intrusted the bearing of their standard, for aught I know, to the hands of the honorable member from South Carolina; and I perceived last session what I perceive now, that in his opinion there is a connection between these projects of government and the doctrines of nullification. I can only say, Sir, that it will be marvellous to me, if that banner, though it be said to be tattered and torn, shall yet be lowered in obeisance, and laid at the footstool of executive power. To the sustaining of that power, the passage of this bill is of the utmost importance. The administration will regard its success as being to them, what Cromwell said the battle of Worcester was to him, "a crowning mercy." Whether gentlemen, who have distinguished themselves so much by their extreme jealousy of this government, shall now find it consistent with their principles to give their aid in effecting this consummation, remains to be seen.

The next exposition of the honorable gentleman's sentiments and opinions is in his letter of the 3d of November.

This letter, Sir, is a curiosity. As a paper describing political operations, and exhibiting political opinions, it is without a parallel. Its phrase is altogether military. It reads like a despatch, or a bulletin from head-quarters. It is full of attacks, assaults, and repulses. It recounts movements and counter-movements; speaks of occupying one position, falling back upon another, and advancing to a third; it has positions to cover enemies, and positions to hold allies in check. Meantime, the celerity of all these operations reminds one of the rapidity of the military actions of the king of Prussia, in the Seven Years' war. Yesterday, he was in the South, giving battle to the Austrian; to-day he is in Saxony, or Silesia. Instantly he is found to have traversed the Electorate, and is facing the Russian and the Swede on his northern frontier. If you look for his place on the map, before you find it he has quitted it. He is always marching, flying, falling back, wheeling, attacking, defending, surprising; fighting everywhere, and fighting all the time. In one particular, however, the campaigns described in this letter are conducted in a different manner from those of the great Frederick. I think we nowhere read, in the narrative of Frederick's achievements, of his taking a position to cover an enemy, or a position to hold an ally in check. These refinements in the science of tactics and of war are of more recent discovery.

Mr. President, public men must certainly be allowed to change their opinions, and their associations, whenever they see fit. No one doubts this. Men may have grown wiser; they may have attained to better and more correct views of great public subjects. It would be unfortunate, if there were any code which should oblige men, in public or private life, to adhere to opinions once entertained, in spite of experience and better knowledge, and against their own convictions of their erroneous character. Nevertheless, Sir, it must be acknowledged, that what appears to be a sudden, as well as a great change, naturally produces a shock. I confess that, for one, I was shocked when the honorable gentleman, at the last session, espoused this bill of the administration. And when I first read this letter of November, and, in the short space of a column and a half, ran through such a succession of political movements, all terminating in placing the honorable member in the ranks of our opponents, and entitling him to take his seat, as he has done, among them, if not at their head, I confess I felt still greater surprise. All this seemed a good deal too abrupt. Sudden movements of the affections, whether personal or political, are a little out of nature.

Several years ago, Sir, some of the wits of England wrote a mock play, intended to ridicule the unnatural and false feeling, the *sentimentality* of a certain German school of literature. In this play, two strangers are brought together at an inn. While they are warming themselves at the fire, and before their acquaintance is yet five minutes old, one springs up and exclaims to the other, "A sudden thought strikes me! Let us swear an eternal friendship!" This affectionate offer was instantly accepted, and the friendship duly sworn, unchangeable and eternal! Now, Sir, how long this eternal friendship lasted, or in what manner it ended, those who wish to know may learn by referring to the play.

But it seems to me, Sir, that the honorable member has carried his political sentimentality a good deal higher than the flight of the German school: for he appears to have fallen suddenly in love, not with strangers, but with opponents. Here we all had been, Sir, contending against the progress of executive power, and more particularly, and most strenuously, against the projects and experiments of the administration upon the currency. The honorable member stood among us, not only as an associate, but as a leader. We thought we were making some headway. The people appeared to be coming to our support and our assistance. The country had been roused, every successive election weakening the strength of the adversary, and increasing our own. We were in this career of success carried strongly forward by the current of public opinion, and only needed to hear the cheering voice of the honorable member,

"Once more unto the breach, dear friends, once more!"

and we should have prostrated for ever this anti-constitutional, anti-commercial, anti-republican, and anti-American policy of the administration. But instead of these encouraging and animating accents, behold! in the very crisis of our affairs, on the very eve of victory, the honorable member cries out to the enemy,--not to us, his allies, but to the enemy: "Hollo! A sudden thought strikes me! I abandon my allies! Now I think of it, they have always been my oppressors! I abandon them, and now let *you and me* swear an eternal friendship!" Such a proposition, from such a quarter, Sir, was not likely to be long withstood. The other party was a little coy, but, upon the whole, nothing loath. After proper hesitation, and a little decorous blushing, it owned the soft impeachment, admitted an equally sudden sympathetic impulse on its own side; and, since few words are wanted where hearts are already known, the honorable gentleman takes his place among his new friends amidst greetings and caresses, and is already enjoying the sweets of an eternal friendship.

In this letter, Mr. President, the writer says, in substance, that he saw, at the commencement of the last session, that affairs had reached the point when he and his friends, according to the course they should take, would reap the full harvest of their long and arduous struggle against the encroachments and abuses of the general government, or lose the fruits of all their labors. At that time, he says, State interposition (viz. Nullification) had overthrown the protective tariff and the American system, and put a stop to Congressional usurpation; that he had previously been united with the National Republicans; but that, in joining such allies, he was not insensible to the embarrassment of his position; that with them victory itself was dangerous, and that therefore he had been waiting for events; that now (that is to say, in September last) the joint attacks of the allies had brought down executive power; that the administration had become divested of power and influence, and that it was now clear that the combined attacks of the allied forces would utterly overthrow and demolish it. All this he saw. But he saw, too, as he says, that in that case the victory would inure, not to him or his cause, but to his allies and their cause. I do not mean to say that he spoke of personal victories, or alluded to personal objects, at all. He spoke of his cause.

He proceeds to say, then, that never was there before, and never, probably, will there be again, so fair an opportunity for himself and his friends to carry out _their own principles and policy_, and to reap the fruits of their long and arduous struggle. These principles and this policy, Sir, be it remembered, he represents, all along, as identified with the principles and policy of nullification. And he makes use of this glorious opportunity by refusing to join his late allies in any further attack on those in power, and rallying anew the old State-rights party to hold in check their old opponents, the National Republican party. This, he says, would enable him to prevent the complete ascendency of his allies, and to compel the Southern division of the administration party to occupy the ground of which he proposes to take possession, to wit, the ground of the old State-rights party. They will have, he says, no other alternative.

Mr. President, stripped of its military language, what is the amount of all this, but that, finding the administration weak, and likely to be overthrown, if the opposition continued with undiminished force, he went over to it, he joined it; intending to act, himself, upon nullification principles, and to compel the Southern members of the administration to meet him on those principles?--in other words, to make a nullification administration, and to take such part in it as should belong to him and his friends. He confesses, Sir, that in thus abandoning his allies, and taking a position to cover those in power, he perceived a shock would be created which would require some degree of resolution and firmness. In this he was right. A shock, Sir, has been created; yet there he is.

This administration, Sir, is represented as succeeding to the last, by an inheritance of principle. It professes to tread in the footsteps of its illustrious predecessor. It adopts, generally, the sentiments, principles, and opinions of General Jackson, _proclamation and all_; and yet, though he be the very prince of nullifiers, and but lately regarded as the chiefest of sinners, it receives the honorable gentleman with the utmost complacency. To all appearance, the delight is mutual; they find him an able leader, he finds them complying followers. But, Sir, in all this movement he understands himself. He means to go ahead, and to take them along. He is in the engine-car; he controls the locomotive. His hand regulates the steam, to increase or retard the speed at his discretion. And as to the occupants of the passenger-cars, Sir, they are as happy a set of gentlemen as one might desire to see of a summer's day. They feel that they are in progress; they hope they shall not be run off the track; and when they reach the end of their journey, they desire to be thankful!

The arduous struggle is now all over. Its richest fruits are all reaped; nullification embraces the sub-treasuries, and oppression and usurpation will be heard of no more.

On the broad surface of the country, Sir, there is a spot called "the Hermitage." In that residence is an occupant very well known, and not a little remarkable both in person and character. Suppose, Sir, the occupant of the Hermitage were now to open that door, enter the Senate, walk forward, and look over the chamber to the seats on the other side. Be not frightened, gentlemen; it is but fancy's sketch. Suppose he should thus come in among us, Sir, and see into whose hands has fallen the chief support of that administration, which was, in so great a degree, appointed by himself, and which he fondly relied on to maintain the principles of his own. If gentlemen were now to see his steady military step, his erect posture, his compressed lips, his firmly-knitted brow, and his eye full of fire, I cannot help thinking, Sir, they would all feel somewhat queer. There would be, I imagine, not a little awkward moving and shifting in their seats. They would expect soon to hear the roar of the lion, even if they did not feel his paw.

Sir, the spirit of union is particularly liable to temptation and seduction in moments of peace and prosperity. In war, this spirit is strengthened by a sense of common danger, and by a thousand recollections of ancient efforts and ancient glory in a common cause. But in the calms of a long peace, and in the absence of all apparent causes of alarm, things near gain an ascendency over things remote. Local interests and feelings overshadow national sentiments. Our attention, our regard, and our attachment are every moment solicited to what touches us closest, and we feel less and less the attraction of a distant orb. Such tendencies we are bound by true patriotism and by our love of union to resist. This is our duty; and the moment, in my judgment, has arrived when that duty should be performed. We hear, every day, sentiments and arguments which would become a meeting of envoys, employed by separate governments, more than they become the common legislature of a united country. Constant appeals are made to local interests, to geographical distinctions, and to the policy and the pride of particular States. It would sometimes appear as if it were a settled purpose to convince the people that our Union is nothing but a jumble of different and discordant interests, which must, erelong, be all resolved into their original state of separate existence; as if, therefore, it was of no great value while it should last, and was not likely to last long. The process of disintegration begins by urging as a fact the existence of different interests.

Sir, is not the end to which all this leads us obvious? Who does not see that, if convictions of this kind take possession of the public mind, our Union can hereafter be nothing, while it remains, but a connection without harmony; a bond without affection; a theatre for the angry contests of local feelings, local objects, and local jealousies? Even while it continues to exist in name, it may by these means become nothing but the mere form of a united government. My children, and the children of those who sit around me, may meet, perhaps, in this chamber, in the next generation; but if tendencies now but too obvious be not checked, they will meet as strangers and aliens. They will feel no sense of common interest or common country; they will cherish no common object of patriotic love. If the same Saxon language shall fall from their lips, it may be the chief proof that they belong to the same nation. Its vital principle exhausted and gone, its power of doing good terminated, the Union itself, become productive only of strife and contention, must ultimately fall, dishonored and unlamented.

The honorable member from Carolina himself habitually indulges in charges of usurpation and oppression against the government of his country. He daily denounces its important measures, in the language in which our Revolutionary fathers spoke of the oppressions of the mother country. Not merely against executive usurpation, either real or supposed, does he utter these sentiments, but against laws of Congress, laws passed by large majorities, laws sanctioned for a course of years by the people. These laws he proclaims, every hour, to be but a series of acts of oppression. He speaks of them as if it were an admitted fact, that such is their true character. This is the language he utters, these are the sentiments he expresses, to the rising generation around him. Are they sentiments and language which are likely to inspire our children with the love of union, to enlarge their patriotism, or to teach them, and to make them feel, that their destiny has made them common citizens of one great and glorious republic? A principal object in his late political movements, the gentleman himself tells us, was to _unite the entire South_; and against whom, or against what, does he wish to unite the entire South? Is not this the very essence of local feeling and local regard? Is it not the acknowledgment of a wish and object to create political strength by uniting political opinions geographically? While the gentleman thus wishes to unite the entire South, I pray to know, Sir, if he expects me to turn toward the polar star, and, acting on the same principle, to utter a cry of Rally! to the whole North? Heaven forbid! To the day of my death, neither he nor others shall hear such a cry from me.

Finally, the honorable member declares that he shall now march off, under the banner of State rights! March off from whom? March off from what? We have been contending for great principles. We have been struggling to maintain the liberty and to restore the prosperity of the country; we have made these struggles here, in the national councils, with the old flag, the true American flag, the Eagle, and the Stars and Stripes, waving over the chamber in which we sit. He now tells us, however, that he marches off under the State-rights banner!

Let him go. I remain. I am where I ever have been, and ever mean to be. Here, standing on the platform of the general Constitution, a platform broad enough and firm enough to uphold every interest of the whole country, I shall still be found. Intrusted with some part in the administration of that Constitution, I intend to act in its spirit, and in the spirit of those who framed it. Yes, Sir, I would act as if our fathers, who formed it for us and who bequeathed it to us, were looking on me; as if I could see their venerable forms bending down to behold us from the abodes above. I would act, too, as if the eye of posterity was gazing on me.

Standing thus, as in the full gaze of our ancestors and our posterity, having received this inheritance from the former, to be transmitted to the latter, and feeling that, if I am born for any good, in my day and generation, it is for the good of the whole country, no local policy or local feeling, no temporary impulse, shall induce me to yield my foothold on the Constitution of the Union. I move off under no banner not known to the whole American people, and to their Constitution and laws. No, Sir; these walls, these columns,

"shall fly From their firm base as soon as I."

I came into public life, Sir, in the service of the United States. On that broad altar, my earliest, and all my public vows, have been made. I propose to serve no other master. So far as depends on any agency of mine, they shall continue united States; united in interest and in affection; united in every thing in regard to which the Constitution has decreed their union; united in war, for the common defence, the common renown, and the common glory; and united, compacted, knit firmly together in peace, for the common prosperity and happiness of ourselves and our children.

[Footnote 1: The Sub-Treasury.]

REPLY TO MR. CALHOUN.
SPEECH DELIVERED IN THE SENATE OF THE UNITED STATES, ON THE 22D OF MARCH, 1838, IN ANSWER TO MR. CALHOUN.

[On Thursday, the 22d of March, Mr. Calhoun spoke at length in answer to Mr. Webster's speech of the 12th of March.

When he had concluded, Mr. Webster immediately rose, and addressed the Senate as follows.]

Mr. President,--I came rather late to the Senate this morning, and, happening to meet a friend on the Avenue, I was admonished to hasten my steps, as "the war was to be carried into Africa," and I was expected to be annihilated. I lost no time in following the advice, Sir, since it would be awkward for one to be annihilated without knowing any thing about it.

Well, Sir, the war has been carried into Africa. The honorable member has made an expedition into regions as remote from the subject of this debate as the orb of Jupiter from that of our earth. He has spoken of the tariff, of slavery, and of the late war. Of all this I do not complain. On the contrary, if it be his pleasure to allude to all or any of these topics, for any purpose whatever, I am ready at all times to hear him.

Sir, this carrying the war into Africa, which has become so common a phrase among us, is, indeed, imitating a great example; but it is an example which is not always followed with success. In the first place, every man, though he be a man of talent and genius, is not a Scipio; and in the next place, as I recollect this part of Roman and Carthaginian history,--the gentleman may be more accurate, but, as I recollect it, when Scipio resolved upon carrying the war into Africa, Hannibal was not at home. Now, Sir, I am very little like Hannibal, but I am at home; and when Scipio Africanus South-Caroliniensis brings the war into my territories, I shall not leave their defence to Asdrubal, nor Syphax, nor anybody else. I meet him on the shore, at his landing, and propose but one contest.

"Concurritur; horae Momento cita mors venit, aut victoria laeta."

Mr. President, I had made up my mind that, if the honorable gentleman should confine himself to a reply in the ordinary way, I would not say another syllable. But he has not done so. He has gone off into topics quite remote from all connection with revenue, commerce, finance, or sub-treasuries, and invites to a discussion which, however uninteresting to the public at the present moment, is too personal to be declined by me.

He says, Sir, that I undertook to compare my political character and conduct with his. Far from it. I attempted no such thing. I compared the gentleman's political opinions at different times with one another, and expressed decided opposition to those which he now holds. And I did, certainly, advert to the general tone and drift of the gentleman's sentiments and expressions for some years past, in their bearing on the Union, with such remarks as I thought they deserved; but I instituted no comparison between him and myself. He may institute one if he pleases, and when he pleases. Seeking nothing of this kind, I avoid nothing. Let it be remembered, that the gentleman began the debate, by attempting to exhibit a contrast between the present opinions and conduct of my friends and myself, and our recent opinions and conduct. Here is the first charge of inconsistency; let the public judge whether he has made it good. He says, Sir, that on several questions I have taken different sides, at different times; let him show it. If he shows any change of opinion, I shall be called on to give a reason, and to account for it. I leave it to the country to say whether, as yet, he has shown any such thing.

But, Sir, before attempting that, he has something else to say. He had prepared, it seems, to draw comparisons himself. He had intended to say something, if time had allowed, upon our respective opinions and conduct in regard to the war. If time had allowed! Sir, time does allow, time must allow. A general remark of that kind ought not to be, cannot be, left to produce its effect, when that effect is obviously intended to be unfavorable. Why did the gentleman allude to my votes or my opinions respecting the war at all, unless he had something to say? Does he wish to leave an undefined impression that something was done, or something said, by me, not now capable of defence or justification? something not reconcilable with true patriotism? He means that, or nothing. And now, Sir, let him bring the matter forth; let him take the responsibility of the accusation; let him state his facts. I am here to answer; I am here, this day, to answer. Now is the time, and now the hour. I think we read, Sir, that one of the good spirits would not bring against the Arch-enemy of mankind a railing accusation; and what is railing but general reproach, an imputation without fact, time, or circumstance? Sir, I call for particulars. The gentleman knows my whole conduct well; indeed, the journals show it all, from the moment I came into Congress till the peace. If I have done, then, Sir, any thing unpatriotic, any thing which, as far as love to country goes, will not bear comparison with his or any man's conduct, let it now be stated. Give me the fact, the time, the manner. He speaks of the war; that which we call the late war, though it is now twenty-five years since it terminated. He would leave an impression that I opposed it. How? I was not in Congress when war was declared, nor in public life anywhere. I was pursuing my profession, keeping company with judges and jurors, and plaintiffs and defendants. If I had been in Congress, and had enjoyed the benefit of hearing the honorable gentleman's speeches, for aught I can say, I might have concurred with him. But I was not in public life. I never had been, for a single hour; and was in no situation, therefore, to oppose or to support the declaration of war. I am speaking to the fact, Sir; and if the gentleman has any fact, let us know it. Well, Sir, I came into Congress during the war. I found it waged, and raging. And what did I do here to oppose it? Look to the journals. Let the honorable gentleman tax his memory. Bring up any thing, if there be any thing to bring up, not showing error of opinion, but showing want of loyalty or fidelity to the country. I did not agree to all that was proposed, nor did the honorable member. I did not approve of every measure, nor did he. The war had been preceded by the restrictive system and the embargo. As a private individual, I certainly did not think well of these measures. It appeared to me that the embargo annoyed ourselves as much as our enemies, while it destroyed the business and cramped the spirits of the people. In this opinion I may have been right or wrong, but the gentleman was himself of the same opinion. He told us the other day, as a proof of his independence of party on great questions, that he differed with his friends on the subject of the embargo. He was decidedly and unalterably opposed to it. It furnishes in his judgment, therefore, no imputation either on my patriotism, or on the soundness of my political opinions, that I was opposed to it also. I mean opposed in opinion; for I was not in Congress, and had nothing to do with the act creating the embargo. And as to opposition to measures for carrying on the war, after I came into Congress, I again say, let the gentleman specify; let him lay his finger on any thing calling for an answer, and he shall have an answer.

Mr. President, you were yourself in the House during a considerable part of this time. The honorable gentleman may make a witness of you. He may make a witness of anybody else. He may be his own witness. Give us but some fact, some charge, something capable in itself either of being proved or disproved. Prove any thing, state any thing, not consistent with honorable and patriotic conduct, and I am ready to answer it. Sir, I am glad this subject has been alluded to in a manner which justifies me in taking public notice of it; because I am well aware that, for ten years past, infinite pains has been taken to find something, in the range of these topics, which might create prejudice against me in the country. The journals have all been pored over, and the reports ransacked, and scraps of paragraphs and half-sentences have been collected, fraudulently put together, and then made to flare out as if there had been some discovery. But all this failed. The next resort was to supposed correspondence. My letters were sought for, to learn if, in the confidence of private friendship, I had ever said any thing which an enemy could make use of. With this view, the vicinity of my former residence has been searched, as with a lighted candle. New Hampshire has been explored, from the mouth of the Merrimack to the White Hills. In one instance a gentleman had left the State, gone five hundred miles off, and died. His papers were examined; a letter was found, and I have understood it was brought to Washington; a conclave was held to consider it, and the result was, that, if there was nothing else against Mr. Webster, the matter had better be let alone. Sir, I hope to make everybody of that opinion who brings against me a charge of want of patriotism. Errors of opinion can be found, doubtless, on many subjects; but as conduct flows from the feelings which animate the heart, I know that no act of my life has had its origin in the want of ardent love of country.

Sir, when I came to Congress, I found the honorable gentleman a leading member of the House of Representatives. Well, Sir, in what did we differ? One of the first measures of magnitude, after I came here, was Mr. Dallas's[1] proposition for a bank. It was a war measure. It was urged as being absolutely necessary to enable government to carry on the war. Government wanted revenue; such a bank, it was hoped, would furnish it; and on that account it was most warmly pressed and urged on Congress. You remember all this, Mr. President. You remember how much some persons supposed the success of the war and the salvation of the country depended on carrying that measure. Yet the honorable member from South Carolina opposed this bill. He now takes to himself a good deal of merit, none too much, but still a good deal of merit, for having defeated it. Well, Sir, I agreed with him. It was a mere paper bank; a machine for fabricating irredeemable paper. It was a new form for paper money; and instead of benefiting the country, I thought it would plunge it deeper and deeper in difficulty. I made a speech on the subject; it has often been quoted. There it is; let whoever pleases read and examine it. I am not proud of it for any ability it exhibits; on the other hand, I am not ashamed of it for the spirit which it manifests. But, Sir, I say again that the gentleman himself took the lead against this measure, this darling measure of the administration. I followed him; if I was seduced into error, or into unjustifiable opposition, there sits my seducer.

What, Sir, were other leading sentiments or leading measures of that day? On what other subjects did men differ? The gentleman has adverted to one, and that a most important one; I mean the navy. He says, and says truly, that at the commencement of the war the navy was unpopular. It was unpopular with his friends, who then controlled the politics of the country. But he says he differed with his friends; in this respect he resisted party influence and party connection, and was the friend and advocate of the navy. Sir, I commend him for it. He showed his wisdom. That gallant little navy soon fought itself into favor, and showed that no man who had placed reliance on it had been disappointed.

Well, Sir, in all this I was exactly of the opinion of the honorable gentleman.

Sir, I do not know when my opinion of the importance of a naval force to the United States had its origin. I can give no date to my present sentiments on this subject, because I never entertained different sentiments. I remember, Sir, that immediately after coming into my profession, at a period when the navy was most unpopular, when it was called by all sorts of hard names and designated by many coarse epithets, on one of those occasions on which young men address their neighbors, I ventured to put forth a boy's hand in defence of the navy. I insisted on its importance, its adaptation to our circumstances and to our national character, and its indispensable necessity, if we intended to maintain and extend our commerce. These opinions and sentiments I brought into Congress; and the first time in which I presumed to speak on the topics of the day, I attempted to urge on the House a greater attention to the naval service. There were divers modes of prosecuting the war. On these modes, or on the degree of attention and expense which should be bestowed on each, different men held different opinions. I confess I looked with most hope to the results of naval warfare, and therefore I invoked government to invigorate and strengthen that arm of the national defence. I invoked it to seek its enemy upon the seas, to go where every auspicious indication pointed, and where the whole heart and soul of the country would go with it.

Sir, we were at war with the greatest maritime power on earth. England had gained an ascendency on the seas over all the combined powers of Europe. She had been at war twenty years. She had tried her fortunes on the Continent, but generally with no success. At one time the whole Continent had been closed against her. A long line of armed exterior, an unbroken hostile array, frowned upon her from the Gulf of Archangel, round the promontory of Spain and Portugal, to the extreme point of Italy. There was not a port which an English ship could enter. Everywhere on the land the genius of her great enemy had triumphed. He had defeated armies, crushed coalitions, and overturned thrones; but, like the fabled giant, he was unconquerable only while he touched the land. On the ocean he was powerless. That field of fame was his adversary's, and her meteor flag was streaming in triumph over its whole extent.

To her maritime ascendency England owed every thing, and we were now at war with her. One of the most charming of her poets had said of her,--

"Her march is o'er the mountain waves, Her home is on the deep."

Now, Sir, since we were at war with her, I was for intercepting this march; I was for calling upon her, and paying our respects to her, at home; I was for giving her to know that we, too, had a right of way over the seas, and that our marine officers and our sailors were not entire strangers on the bosom of the deep. I was for doing something more with our navy than keeping it on our own shores, for the protection of our coasts and harbors; I was for giving play to its gallant and burning spirit; for allowing it to go forth upon the seas, and to encounter, on an open and an equal field, whatever the proudest or the bravest of the enemy could bring against it. I knew the character of its officers and the spirit of its seamen; and I knew that, in their hands, though the flag of the country might go down to the bottom, yet, while defended by them, that it could never be dishonored or disgraced.

Since she was our enemy, and a most powerful enemy, I was for touching her, if we could, in the very apple of her eye; for reaching the highest feather in her cap; for clutching at the very brightest jewel in her crown. There seemed to me to be a peculiar propriety in all this, as the war was undertaken for the redress of maritime injuries alone. It was a war declared for free trade and sailors' rights. The ocean, therefore, was the proper theatre for deciding this controversy with our enemy, and on that theatre it was my ardent wish that our own power should be concentrated to the utmost.

So much, Sir, for the war, and for my conduct and opinions as connected with it. And, as I do not mean to recur to this subject often, nor ever, unless indispensably necessary, I repeat the demand for any charge, any accusation, any allegation whatever, that throws me behind the honorable gentleman, or behind any other man, in honor, in fidelity, in devoted love to that country in which I was born, which has honored me, and which I serve. I, who seldom deal in defiance, now, here, in my place, boldly defy the honorable member to put his insinuation in the form of a charge, and to support that charge by any proof whatever. The gentleman has adverted to the subject of slavery. On this subject, he says, I have not proved myself a friend to the South. Why, Sir, the only proof is, that I did not vote for his resolutions.

Sir, this is a very grave matter; it is a subject very exciting and inflammable. I take, of course, all the responsibility belonging to my opinions; but I desire these opinions to be understood, and fairly stated. If I am to be regarded as an enemy to the South, because I could not support the gentleman's resolutions, be it so. I cannot purchase favor from any quarter, by the sacrifice of clear and conscientious convictions. The principal resolution declared that Congress had plighted its faith not to interfere either with slavery or the slave trade in the District of Columbia.

Now, Sir, this is quite a new idea. I never heard it advanced until this session. I have heard gentlemen contend that no such power was in the Constitution; but the notion, that, though the Constitution contained the power, yet Congress had plighted its faith not to exercise such a power, is an entire novelty, so far as I know. I must say, Sir, it appeared to me little else than an attempt to put a prohibition into the Constitution, because there was none there already. For this supposed plighting of the public faith, or the faith of Congress, I saw no ground, either in the history of the government, or in any one fact, or in any argument. I therefore could not vote for the proposition.

Sir, it is now several years since I took care to make my opinion known, that this government has, constitutionally, nothing to do with slavery, as it exists in the States. That opinion is entirely unchanged. I stand steadily by the resolution of the House of Representatives, adopted, after much consideration, at the commencement of the government, which was, that Congress has no authority to interfere in the emancipation of slaves, or in the treatment of them, within any of the States; it remaining with the several States alone to provide any regulations therein, which humanity and true policy may require. This, in my opinion, is the Constitution and the law. I feel bound by it. I have quoted the resolution often. It expresses the judgment of men of all parts of the country, deliberately and coolly formed; and it expresses my judgment, and I shall adhere to it. But this has nothing to do with the other constitutional question; that is to say, the mere constitutional question whether Congress has the power to regulate slavery and the slave trade in the District of Columbia.

On such a question, Sir, when I am asked what the Constitution is, or whether any power granted by it has been compromised away, or, indeed, could be compromised away, I must express my honest opinion, and always shall express it, if I say any thing, notwithstanding it may not meet concurrence either in the South, or the North, or the East, or the West. I cannot express by my vote what I do not believe. The gentleman has chosen to bring that subject into this debate, with which it has no concern; but he may make the most of it, if he thinks he can produce unfavorable impressions against me at the South from my negative to his fifth resolution. As to the rest of them, they were commonplaces, generally, or abstractions; in regard to which, one may well feel himself not called on to vote at all.

And now, Sir, in regard to the tariff. That is a long chapter, but I am quite ready to go over it with the honorable member.

He charges me with inconsistency. That may depend on deciding what inconsistency is, in respect to such subjects, and how it is to be proved. I will state the facts, for I have them in my mind somewhat more fully than the honorable member has himself presented them. Let us begin at the beginning. In 1816 I voted against the tariff law which then passed. In 1824 I again voted against the tariff law which was then proposed, and which passed. A majority of New England votes, in 1824, were against the tariff system.

The bill received but one vote from Massachusetts; but it passed. The policy was established. New England acquiesced in it; conformed her business and pursuits to it; embarked her capital, and employed her labor, in manufactures; and I certainly admit that, from that time, I have felt bound to support interests thus called into being, and into importance, by the settled policy of the government. I have stated this often here, and often elsewhere. The ground is defensible, and I maintain it.

As to the resolutions adopted in Boston in 1820, and which resolutions he has caused to be read, and which he says he presumes I prepared, I have no recollection of having drawn the resolutions, and do not believe I did. But I was at the meeting, and addressed the meeting, and what I said on that occasion was produced here, and read in the Senate, years ago.

The resolutions, Sir, were opposed to the commencing of a high tariff policy. I was opposed to it, and spoke against it; the city of Boston was opposed to it; the Commonwealth of Massachusetts was opposed to it. Remember, Sir, that this was in 1820. This opposition continued till 1824. The votes all show this. But in 1824 the question was decided; the government entered upon the policy; it invited men to embark their property and their means of living in it. Individuals thus encouraged have done this to a great extent; and therefore I say, so long as the manufactures shall need reasonable and just protection from government, I shall be disposed to give it to them. What is there, Sir, in all this, for the gentleman to complain of? Would he have us always oppose the policy adopted by the country on a great question? Would he have minorities never submit to the will of majorities?

I remember to have said, Sir, at the meeting in Faneuil Hall, that protection appeared to be regarded as incidental to revenue, and that the incident could not be carried fairly above the principal; in other words, that duties ought not to be laid for the mere object of protection. I believe that proposition to be substantially correct. I believe that, if the power of protection be inferred only from the revenue power, the protection could only be incidental.

But I have said in this place before, and I repeat it now, that Mr. Madison's publication after that period, and his declaration that the Convention did intend to grant the power of protection under the commercial clause, placed the subject in a new and a clear light. I will add, Sir, that a paper drawn up apparently with the sanction of Dr. Franklin, and read to a circle of friends at his house, on the eve of the assembling of the Convention, respecting the powers which the proposed new government ought to possess, shows plainly that, in regulating commerce, it was expected that Congress would adopt a course which should protect the manufactures of the North. He certainly went into the Convention himself under that conviction.

Well, Sir, and now what does the gentleman make out against me in relation to the tariff? What laurels does he gather in this part of Africa? I opposed the *policy* of the tariff, until it had become the settled and established policy of the country. I have never questioned the constitutional power of Congress to grant protection, except so far as the remark made in Faneuil Hall goes, which remark respects only the length to which protection might properly be carried, so far as the power is derived from the authority to lay duties on imports. But the policy being established, and a great part of the country having placed vast interests at stake in it, I have not disturbed it; on the contrary, I have insisted that it ought not to be disturbed. If there be inconsistency in all this, the gentleman is at liberty to blazon it forth; let him see what he can make of it. Here, Sir, I cease to speak of myself; and respectfully ask pardon of the Senate for having so long detained it upon any thing so unimportant as what relates merely to my own public conduct and opinions.

Sir, the honorable member is pleased to suppose that our spleen is excited, because he has interfered to snatch from us a victory over the administration. If he means by this any personal disappointment, I shall not think it worth while to make a remark upon it. If he means a disappointment at his quitting us while we were endeavoring to arrest the present policy of the administration, why then I admit, Sir, that I, for one, felt that disappointment deeply. It is the policy of the administration, its principles, and its measures, which I oppose. It is not persons, but things; not men, but measures. I do wish most fervently to put an end to this anti-commercial policy; and if the overthrow of the policy shall be followed by the political defeat of its authors, why, Sir, it is a result which I shall endeavor to meet with equanimity.

Sir, as to the honorable member's wresting the victory from us, or as to his ability to sustain the administration in this policy, there may be some doubt about that. I trust the citadel will yet be stormed, and carried, by the force of public opinion, and that no Hector will be able to defend its walls.

But now, Sir, I must advert to a declaration of the honorable member, which, I confess, did surprise me. The honorable member says, that, personally, he and myself have been on friendly terms, but that we always differed on great constitutional questions. Sir, this is astounding. And yet I was partly prepared for it; for I sat here the other day, and held my breath, while the honorable gentleman declared, and repeated, that he had always belonged to the State-rights party. And he means, by what he has declared to-day, that he has always given to the Constitution a construction more limited, better guarded, less favorable to the extension of the powers of this government, than that which I have given to it. He has always interpreted it according to the strict doctrines of the school of State rights! Sir, if the honorable member ever belonged, until very lately, to the State-rights party, the connection was very much like a secret marriage. And never was secret better kept. Not only were the espousals not acknowledged, but all suspicion was avoided. There was no known familiarity, or even kindness, between them. On the contrary, they acted like parties who were not at all fond of each other's company.

Sir, is there a man in my hearing, among all the gentlemen now surrounding us, many of whom, of both houses, have been here many years, and know the gentleman and myself perfectly,--is there one who ever heard, supposed, or dreamed that the honorable member belonged to the State-rights party before the year 1825? Can any such connection be proved upon him, can he prove it upon himself, before that time?

Sir, I will show you, before I resume my seat, that it was not until after the gentleman took his seat in the chair which you now occupy, that any public manifestation, or intimation, was ever given by him of his having embraced the peculiar doctrines of the State-rights party. The truth is, Sir, the honorable gentleman had acted a very important and useful part during the war. But the war terminated. Toward the end of the session of 1814-15, we received the news of peace. This closed the Thirteenth Congress. In the fall of 1815, the Fourteenth Congress assembled. It was full of ability, and the honorable gentleman stood high among its distinguished members. He remained in the House, Sir, through the whole of that Congress; and now, Sir, it is easy to show that, during those two years, the honorable gentleman took a decided lead in all those great measures which he has since so often denounced as unconstitutional and oppressive, the bank, the tariff, and internal improvements. The war being terminated, the gentleman's mind turned itself toward internal administration and improvement. He surveyed the whole country, contemplated its resources, saw what it was capable of becoming, and held a political faith not so narrow and contracted as to restrain him from useful and efficient action. He was, therefore, at once a full length ahead of all others in measures which were national, and which required a broad and liberal construction of the Constitution. This is historic truth. Of his agency in the bank, and other measures connected with the currency, I have already spoken, and I do not understand him to deny any thing I have said, in that particular. Indeed, I have said nothing capable of denial.

Now allow me a few words upon the tariff. The tariff of 1816 was distinctly a South Carolina measure. Look at the votes, and you will see it. It was a tariff for the benefit of South Carolina interests, and carried through Congress by South Carolina votes and South Carolina influence. Even the _minimum_, Sir, the so-much-reproached, the abominable _minimum_, that subject of angry indignation and wrathful rhetoric, is of Southern origin, and has a South Carolina parentage.

Sir, the contest on that occasion was chiefly between the cotton-growers at home, and the importers of cotton fabrics from India. These India fabrics were made from the cotton of that country. The people of this country were using cotton fabrics not made of American cotton, and, so far, they were diminishing the demand for such cotton. The importation of India cottons was then very large, and this bill was designed to put an end to it, and, with the help of the _minimum_, it did put an end to it. The cotton manufactures of the North were then in their infancy. They had some friends in Congress, but, if I recollect, the majority of Massachusetts members and of New England members were against this cotton tariff of 1816. I remember well, that the main debate was between the importers of India cottons, in the North, and the cotton-growers of the South. The gentleman cannot deny the truth of this, or any part of it. Boston opposed this tariff, and Salem opposed it, warmly and vigorously. But the honorable member supported it, and the law passed. And now be it always remembered, Sir, that that act passed on the professed ground of protection; that it had in it the *minimum* principle, and that the honorable member, and other leading gentlemen from his own State, supported it, voted for it, and carried it through Congress.

And now, Sir, we come to the doctrine of internal improvement, that other usurpation, that other oppression, which has come so near to justifying violent disruption of the government, and scattering the fragments of the Union to the four winds. Have the gentleman's State-rights opinions always kept him aloof from such unhallowed infringements of the Constitution? He says he always differed with me on constitutional questions. How was it in this most important particular? Has he here stood on the ramparts, brandishing his glittering sword against assailants, and holding out a banner of defiance? Sir, it is an indisputable truth, that he is himself the man, the *ipse* that first brought forward in Congress a scheme of general internal improvement, at the expense and under the authority of this government. He, Sir, is the very man, the _ipsissimus ipse_, who considerately, and on a settled system, began these unconstitutional measures, if they be unconstitutional. And now for the proof.

The act incorporating the Bank of the United States was passed in April, 1816. For the privileges of the charter, the proprietors of the bank were to pay to government a _bonus_, as it was called, of one million five hundred thousand dollars, in certain instalments. Government also took seven millions in the stock of the bank. Early in the next session of Congress, that is, in December, 1816, the honorable member moved, in the House of Representatives, that a committee be appointed to consider the propriety of setting apart this _bonus_, and also the dividends on the stock belonging to the United States, as a permanent fund for internal improvement. The committee was appointed, and the honorable member was made its chairman. He thus originated the plan, and took the lead in its execution. Shortly afterwards, he reported a bill carrying out the objects for which the committee had been appointed. This bill provided that the dividends on the seven millions of bank stock belonging to government, and also the whole of the _bonus_, should be permanently pledged as a fund for constructing roads and canals; and that this fund should be subject to such specific appropriations as Congress might subsequently make.

This was the bill; and this was the first project ever brought forward in Congress for a system of internal improvements. The bill goes the whole doctrine at a single jump. The Cumberland Road, it is true, was already in progress; and for that the gentleman had also voted. But there were, and are now, peculiarities about that particular expenditure which sometimes satisfy scrupulous consciences; but this bill of the gentleman's, without equivocation or saving clause, without if, or and, or but, occupied the whole ground at once, and announced internal improvement as one of the objects of this government, on a grand and systematic plan. The bill, Sir, seemed indeed too strong. It was thought by persons not esteemed extremely jealous of State rights to evince too little regard to the will of the States. Several gentlemen opposed the measure in that shape, on that account; and among them Colonel Pickering, then one of the Representatives from Massachusetts. Even Timothy Pickering could not quite sanction, or concur in, the honorable gentleman's doctrines to their full extent, although he favored the measure in its general character. He therefore prepared an amendment, as a substitute; and his substitute provided for two very important things not embraced in the original bill:--

First, that the proportion of the fund to be expended in each State, respectively, should be in proportion to the number of its inhabitants.

Second, that the money should be applied in constructing such roads, canals, and so forth, in the several States, as Congress might direct, *with the assent of the State*.

This, Sir, was Timothy Pickering's amendment to the gentleman's bill. And now, Sir, how did the honorable gentleman, who has always belonged to the State-rights party,--how did he treat this amendment, or this substitute? Which way do you think his State-rights doctrine led him? Why, Sir, I will tell you. He immediately rose, and moved to strike out the words "_with the assent of the State_"! Here is the journal under my hand, Sir; and here is the gentleman's motion. And certainly, Sir, it will be admitted that this motion was not of a nature to intimate that he was wedded to State rights. But the words were not struck out. The motion did not prevail. Mr. Pickering's substitute was adopted, and the bill passed the House in that form.

In committee of the whole on this bill, Sir, the honorable member made a very able speech both on the policy of internal improvements and the power of Congress over the subject. These points were fully argued by him. He spoke of the importance of the system, the vast good it would produce, and its favorable effect on the union of the States. "Let us, then," said he, "bind the republic together with a perfect system of roads and canals. Let us conquer space. It is thus the most distant parts of the republic will be brought within a few days' travel of the centre; it is thus that a citizen of the West will read the news of Boston still moist from the press."

But on the power of Congress to make internal improvements, ay, Sir, on the power of Congress, hear him! What were then his rules of construction and interpretation? How did he at that time read and understand the Constitution? Why, Sir, he said that "he was no advocate for refined arguments on the Constitution. The instrument was not intended as a thesis for the logician to exercise his ingenuity on. It ought to be construed with plain good-sense." This is all very just, I think, Sir; and he said much more in the same strain. He quoted many instances of laws passed, as he contended, on similar principles, and then added, that "he introduced these instances to prove the uniform sense of Congress and of the country (for they had not been objected to) as to our powers; and surely," said he, "they furnish better evidence of the true interpretation of the Constitution than the most refined and subtile arguments."

Here you see, Mr. President, how little original I am. You have heard me again and again contending in my place here for the stability of that which has been long settled; you have heard me, till I dare say you have been tired, insisting that the sense of Congress, so often expressed, and the sense of the country, so fully shown and so firmly established, ought to be regarded as having decided finally certain constitutional questions. You see now, Sir, what authority I have for this mode of argument. But while the scholar is learning, the teacher renounces. Will he apply his old doctrine now--I sincerely wish he would--to the question of the bank, to the question of the receiving of bank-notes by government, to the power of Congress over the paper currency? Will he admit that these questions ought to be regarded as decided by the settled sense of Congress and of the country? O, no! Far otherwise. From these rules of judgment, and from the influence of all considerations of this practical nature, the honorable member now takes these questions with him into the upper heights of metaphysics, into the regions of those refinements and subtile arguments which he rejected with so much decision in 1817, as appears by this speech. He quits his old ground of common-sense, experience, and the general understanding of the country, for a flight among theories and ethereal abstractions.

And now, Sir, let me ask, when did the honorable member relinquish these early opinions and principles of his? When did he make known his adhesion to the doctrines of the State-rights party? We have been speaking of transactions in 1816 and 1817. What the gentleman's opinions then were, we have seen. When did he announce himself a State-rights man? I have already said, Sir, that nobody knew of his claiming that character until after the commencement of 1825; and I have said so, because I have before me an address of his to his neighbors at Abbeville, in May of that year, in which he recounts, very properly, the principal incidents in his career as a member of Congress, and as head of a department; and in which he says that, as a member of Congress, he had given his zealous efforts in favor of a restoration of specie currency, of a due protection of those manufactures which had taken root during the war, and, finally, of a system for connecting the various parts of the country by a judicious system of internal improvement. He adds, that it afterwards became his duty, as a member of the administration, to aid in sustaining against the boldest assaults those very measures which, as a member of Congress, he had contributed to establish.

And now, Sir, since the honorable gentleman says he has differed with me on constitutional questions, will he be pleased to say what constitutional opinion I have ever avowed for which I have not his express authority? Is it on the bank power? the tariff power? the power of internal improvement? I have shown his votes, his speeches, and his conduct, on all these subjects, up to the time when General Jackson became a candidate for the Presidency. From that time, Sir, I know we have differed; but if there was any difference before that time, I call upon him to point it out, to declare what was the occasion, what the question, and what the difference. And if before that period, Sir, by any speech, any vote, any public proceeding, or by any mode of announcement whatever, he gave the world to know that he belonged to the State-rights party, I hope he will now be kind enough to produce it, or to refer to it, or to tell us where we may look for it.

Sir, I will pursue this topic no farther. I would not have pursued it so far, I would not have entered upon it at all, had it not been for the astonishment I felt, mingled, I confess, with something of warmer feeling, when the honorable gentleman declared that he had always differed with me on constitutional questions. Sir, the honorable member read a quotation or two from a speech of mine in 1816, on the currency or bank question. With what intent, or to what end? What inconsistency does he show? Speaking of the *legal* currency of the country, that is, the coin, I then said it was in a good state. Was not that true? I was speaking of the legal currency; of that which the law made a tender. And how is that inconsistent with any thing said by me now, or ever said by me? I declared then, he says, that the framers of this government were hard-money men. Certainly they were. But are not the friends of a convertible paper _hard-money men_, in every practical and sensible meaning of the term? Did I, in that speech, or any other, insist on excluding all convertible paper from the uses of society? Most assuredly I did not. I never quite so far lost my wits, I think. There is but a single sentence in that speech which I should qualify if I were to deliver it again, and that the honorable member has not noticed. It is a paragraph respecting the power of Congress over the circulation of State banks, which might perhaps need explanation or correction. Understanding it as applicable to the case then before Congress, all the rest is perfectly accordant with my present opinions. It is well known that I never doubted the power of Congress to create a bank; that I was always in favor of a bank, constituted on proper principles; that I voted for the bank bill of 1815; and that I opposed that of 1816 only on account of one or two of its provisions, which I and others hoped to be able to strike out. I am a hard-money man, and always have been, and always shall be. But I know the great use of such bank paper as is convertible into hard money on demand; which may be called specie paper, and which is equivalent to specie in value, and much more convenient and useful for common purposes. On the other hand, I abhor all irredeemable paper; all old-fashioned paper money; all deceptive promises; every thing, indeed, in the shape of paper issued for circulation, whether by government or individuals, which cannot be turned into gold and silver at the will of the holder.

But, Sir, I have insisted that government is bound to protect and regulate the means of commerce, to see that there is a sound currency for the use of the people. The honorable gentleman asks, What then is the limit? Must Congress also furnish all means of commerce? Must it furnish weights and scales and steelyards? Most undoubtedly, Sir, it must regulate weights and measures, and it does so. But the answer to the general question is very obvious. Government must furnish all that which none but government can furnish. Government must do that for individuals which individuals cannot do for themselves. That is the very end of government. Why else have we a government? Can individuals make a currency? Can individuals regulate money? The distinction is as broad and plain as the Pennsylvania Avenue. No man can mistake it, or well blunder out of it. The gentleman asks if government must furnish for the people ships, and boats, and wagons. Certainly not. The gentleman here only recites the President's message of September. These things, and all such things, the people can furnish for themselves; but they cannot make a currency; they cannot, individually, decide what shall be the money of the country. That, everybody knows, is one of the prerogatives, and one of the duties, of government; and a duty which I think we are most unwisely and improperly neglecting. We may as well leave the people to make war and to make peace, each man for himself, as to leave to individuals the regulation of commerce and currency.

Mr. President, there are other remarks of the gentleman of which I might take notice. But should I do so, I could only repeat what I have already said, either now or heretofore. I shall, therefore, not now allude to them. My principal purpose in what I have said has been to defend myself; that was my first object; and next, as the honorable member has attempted to take to himself the character of a strict constructionist, and a State-rights man, and on that basis to show a difference, not favorable to me, between his constitutional opinions and my own, heretofore, it has been my intention to show that the power to create a bank, the power to regulate the currency by other and direct means, the power to enact a protective tariff, and the power of internal improvement, in its broadest sense, are all powers which the honorable gentleman himself has supported, has acted on, and in the exercise of which, indeed, he has taken a distinguished lead in the counsels of Congress.

If this has been done, my purpose is answered. I do not wish to prolong the discussion, nor to spin it out into a colloquy. If the honorable member has any thing new to bring forward; if he has any charge to make, any proof, or any specification; if he has any thing to advance against my opinions or my conduct, my honor or patriotism, I am still at home. I am here. If not, then, so far as I am concerned, this discussion will here terminate.

I will say a few words, before I resume my seat, on the motion now pending. That motion is to strike out the specie-paying part of the bill. I have a suspicion, Sir, that the motion will prevail. If it should, it will leave a great vacuum; and how shall that vacuum be filled?

The part proposed to be struck out is that which requires all debts to government to be paid in specie. It makes a good provision for government, and for public men, through all classes. The Secretary of the Treasury, in his letter at the last session, was still more watchful of the interests of the holders of office. He assured us, that, bad as the times were, and notwithstanding the floods of bad paper which deluged the country, members of Congress should get gold and silver. In my opinion, Sir, this is beginning the use of good money in payments at the wrong end of the list. If there be bad money in the country, I think that Secretaries and other executive officers, and especially members of Congress, should be the last to receive any good money; because they have the power, if they will do their duty, and exercise it, of making the money of the country good for all. I think, Sir, it was a leading feature in Mr. Burke's famous bill for economical reform, that he provided, first of all, for those who are least able to secure themselves. Everybody else was to be well paid all they were entitled to, before the ministers of the crown, and other political characters, should have any thing. This seems to me very right. But we have a precedent, Sir, in our own country, more directly to the purpose; and as that which we now hope to strike out is the part of the bill furnished or proposed originally by the honorable member from South Carolina, it will naturally devolve on him to supply its place. I wish, therefore, to draw his particular attention to this precedent, which I am now about to produce.

Most members of the Senate will remember, that before the establishment of this government, and before or about the time that the territory which now constitutes the State of Tennessee was ceded to Congress, the inhabitants of the eastern part of that territory established a government for themselves, and called it the State of Franklin. They adopted a very good constitution, providing for the usual branches of legislative, executive, and judicial power. They laid and collected taxes, and performed other usual acts of legislation. They had, for the present, it is true, no maritime possessions, yet they followed the common forms in constituting high officers; and their governor was not only captain-general and commander-in-chief, but admiral also, so that the navy might have a commander when there should be a navy.

Well, Sir, the currency in this State of Franklin became very much deranged. Specie was scarce, and equally scarce were the notes of specie-paying banks. But the legislature did not propose any divorce of government and people; they did not seek to establish two currencies, one for men in office, and one for the rest of the community. They were content with neighbor's fare. It became necessary to pass what we should call now-a-days the civil-list appropriation bill. They passed such a bill; and when we shall have made a void in the bill now before us by striking out specie payments for government, I recommend to its friends to fill the gap, by inserting, if not the same provisions as were in the law of the State of Franklin, at least something in the same spirit.

The preamble of that law, Sir, begins by reciting, that the collection of taxes in specie had become very oppressive to the good people of the commonwealth, for the want of a circulating medium. A parallel case to ours, Sir, exactly. It recites further, that it is the duty of the legislature to hear, at all times, the prayer of their constituents, and apply as speedy a remedy as lies in their power. These sentiments are very just, and I sincerely wish there was a thorough disposition here to adopt the like.

Acting under the influence of these sound opinions, Sir, the legislature of Franklin passed a law for the support of the civil list, which, as it is short, I will beg permission to read. It is as follows:--

"_Be it enacted by the General Assembly of the State of Franklin, and it is hereby enacted by the authority of the same_, That, from the first day of January, A.D. 1789, the salaries of the civil officers of this commonwealth be as follows, to wit:

"His excellency, the governor, _per annum_, one thousand deer-skins; his honor, the chief justice, five hundred do. do.; the attorney-general, five hundred do. do.; secretary to his excellency the governor, five hundred raccoon do.; the treasurer of the State, four hundred and fifty otter do.; each county clerk, three hundred beaver do.; clerk of the house of commons, two hundred raccoon do.; members of assembly, _per diem_, three do. do.; justice's fee for signing a warrant, one muskrat do.; to the constable, for serving a warrant, one mink do.

"Enacted into a law this 18th day of October, 1788, under the great seal of the State.

"Witness his excellency, &c.

"_Governor, captain-general, commander-in-chief, and admiral in and over said State_."

This, Sir, is the law, the spirit of which I commend to gentlemen. I will not speak of the appropriateness of these several allowances for the civil list. But the example is good, and I am of opinion that, until Congress shall perform its duty, by seeing that the country enjoys a good currency, the same medium which the people are obliged to use, whether it be skins or rags, is good enough for its own members.

[Footnote 1: The Secretary of the Treasury.]

A UNIFORM SYSTEM OF BANKRUPTCY.

FROM A SPEECH DELIVERED IN THE SENATE OF THE UNITED STATES, ON THE 18TH OF MAY, 1840, ON THE PROPOSED AMENDMENT TO THE BILL ESTABLISHING A UNIFORM SYSTEM OF BANKRUPTCY.

Let me remind you, then, in the first place, Sir, that, commercial as the country is, and having experienced as it has done, and experiencing as it now does, great vicissitudes of trade and business, it is almost forty years since any law has been in force by which any honest man, failing in business, could be effectually discharged from debt by surrendering his property. The former bankrupt law was repealed on the 19th of

December, 1803. From that day to this, the condition of an insolvent, however honest and worthy, has been utterly hopeless, so far as he depended on any legal mode of relief. This state of things has arisen from the peculiar provisions of the Constitution of the United States, and from the omission by Congress to exercise this branch of its constitutional power. By the Constitution, the States are prohibited from passing laws impairing the obligation of contracts. Bankrupt laws impair the obligation of contracts, if they discharge the bankrupt from his debts without payment. The States, therefore, cannot pass such laws. The power, then, is taken from the States, and placed in our hands. It is true that it has been decided, that, in regard to contracts entered into after the passage of any State bankrupt law, between the citizens of the State having such law, and sued in the State courts, a State discharge may prevail. So far, effect has been given to State laws. I have great respect, habitually, for judicial decisions; but it has nevertheless, I must say, always appeared to me that the distinctions on which these decisions are founded are slender, and that they evade, without answering, the objections founded on the great political and commercial objects intended to be secured by this part of the Constitution. But these decisions, whether right or wrong, afford no effectual relief. The qualifications and limitations which I have stated render them useless, as to the purpose of a general discharge. So much of the concerns of every man of business is with citizens of other States than his own, and with foreigners, that the partial extent to which the validity of State discharges reaches is of little benefit.

The States, then, cannot pass effectual bankrupt laws; that is, effectual for the discharge of the debtor. There is no doubt that most, if not all, the States would now pass such laws, if they had the power; although their legislation would be various, interfering, and full of all the evils which the Constitution of the United States intended to provide against. But they have not the power; Congress, which has the power, does not exercise it. This is the peculiarity of our condition. The States would pass bankrupt laws, but they cannot; we can, but we will not. And between this want of power in the States and want of will in Congress, unfortunate insolvents are left to hopeless bondage. There are probably one or two hundred thousand debtors, honest, sober, and industrious, who drag out lives useless to themselves, useless to their families, and useless to their country, for no reason but that they cannot be legally discharged from debts in which misfortunes have involved them, and which there is no possibility of their ever paying. I repeat, again, that these cases have now been accumulating for a whole generation.

It is true they are not imprisoned; but there may be, and there are, restraint and bondage outside the walls of the jail, as well as in. Their power of earning is, in truth, taken away, their faculty of useful employment is paralyzed, and hope itself become extinguished. Creditors, generally, are not inhuman or unkind; but there will be found some who hold on, and the more a debtor struggles to free himself, the more they feel encouraged to hold on. The mode of reasoning is, that, the more honest the debtor may be, the more industrious, the more disposed to struggle and bear up against his misfortunes, the greater the chance is, that, in the end, especially if the humanity of others shall have led them to release him, their own debts may be finally recovered.

Now, in this state of our constitutional powers and duties, in this state of our laws, and with this actually existing condition of so many insolvents before us, it is not too serious to ask every member of the Senate to put it to his own conscience to say, whether we are not bound to exercise our constitutional duty. Can we abstain from exercising it? The States give to their own laws all the effect they can. This shows that they desire the power to be exercised. Several States have, in the most solemn manner, made known their earnest wishes to Congress. If we still refuse, what is to be done? Many of these insolvent persons are young men with young families. Like other men, they have capacities both for action and enjoyment. Are we to stifle all these for ever? Are we to suffer all these persons, many of them meritorious and respectable, to be pressed to the earth for ever, by a load of hopeless debt? The existing diversities and contradictions of State laws on the subject admirably illustrate the objects of this part of the Constitution, as stated by Mr. Madison; and they form that precise case for which the clause was inserted. The very evil intended to be provided against is before us, and around us, and pressing us on all sides. How can we, how dare we, make a perfect dead letter of this part of the Constitution, which we have sworn to support? The insolvent persons have not the power of locomotion. They cannot travel from State to State. They are prisoners. To my certain knowledge, there are many who cannot even come here to the seat of government, to present their petitions to Congress, so great is their fear that some creditor will dog their heels, and arrest them in some intervening State, or in this District, in the hope that friends will appear to save them, by payment of the debt, from imprisonment.

These are truths; not creditable to the country, but they are truths. I am sorry for their existence. Sir, there is one crime, quite too common, which the laws of man do not punish, but which cannot escape the justice of God; and that is, the arrest and confinement of a debtor by his creditor, with no motive on earth but the hope that some friend, or some relative, perhaps almost as poor as himself, his mother it may be, or his sisters, or his daughters, will give up all their own little pittance, and make beggars of themselves, to save him from the horrors of a loathsome jail. Human retribution cannot reach this guilt; human feeling may not penetrate the flinty heart that perpetrates it; but an hour is surely coming, with more than human retribution on its wings, when that flint shall be melted, either by the power of penitence and grace, or in the fires of remorse.

Sir, I verily believe that the power of perpetuating debts against debtors, for no substantial good to the creditor himself, and the power of imprisonment for debt, at least as it existed in this country ten years ago, have imposed more restraint on personal liberty than the law of debtor and creditor imposes in any other Christian and commercial country. If any public good were attained, any high political object answered, by such laws, there might be some reason for counselling submission and sufferance to individuals. But the result is bad, every way. It is bad to the public and to the country, which loses the efforts and the industry of so many useful and capable citizens. It is bad to creditors, because there is no security against preferences, no principle of equality, and no encouragement for honest, fair, and seasonable assignments of effects. As to the debtor, however good his intentions or earnest his endeavors, it subdues his spirit and degrades him in his own esteem; and if he attempts any thing for the purpose of obtaining food and clothing for his family, he is driven to unworthy shifts and disguises, to the use of other persons' names, to the adoption of the character of agent, and various other contrivances, to keep the little earnings of the day from the reach of his creditors. Fathers act in the name of their sons, sons act in the name of their fathers; all constantly exposed to the greatest temptation to misrepresent facts and to evade the law, if creditors should strike. All this is evil, unmixed evil. And what is it all for? Of what benefit to anybody? Who likes it? Who wishes it? What class of creditors desire it? What consideration of public good demands it?

Sir, we talk much, and talk warmly, of political liberty; and well we may, for it is among the chief of public blessings. But who can enjoy political liberty if he is deprived, permanently, of personal liberty, and the exercise of his own industry and his own faculties? To those unfortunate individuals, doomed to the everlasting bondage of debt, what is it that we have free institutions of government? What is it that we have public and popular assemblies? What is even this Constitution itself to them, in its actual operation, and as we now administer it? What is its aspect to them, but an aspect of stern, implacable severity? an aspect of refusal, denial, and frowning rebuke? nay, more than that, an aspect not only of austerity and rebuke, but, as they must think it, of plain injustice also, since it will not relieve them, nor suffer others to give them relief? What love can they feel towards the Constitution of their country, which has taken the power of striking off their bonds from their own paternal State governments, and yet, inexorable to all the cries of justice and of mercy, holds it unexercised in its own fast and unrelenting grasp? They find themselves bondsmen, because we will not execute the commands of the Constitution; bondsmen to debts they cannot pay, and which all know they cannot pay, and which take away the power of supporting themselves. Other slaves have masters, charged with the duty of support and protection; but their masters neither clothe, nor feed, nor shelter; they only bind.

But, Sir, the fault is not in the Constitution. The Constitution is beneficent as well as wise in all its provisions on this subject. The fault, I must be allowed to say, is in us, who have suffered ourselves quite too long to neglect the duty incumbent upon us. The time will come, Sir, when we shall look back and wonder at the long delay of this just and salutary measure. We shall then feel as we now feel when we reflect on that progress of opinion which has already done so much on another connected subject; I mean the abolition of imprisonment for debt. What should we say at this day, if it were proposed to re-establish arrest and imprisonment for debt, as it existed in most of the States even so late as twenty years ago? I mean for debt alone, for mere, pure debt, without charge or suspicion of fraud or falsehood.

Sir, it is about that length of time, I think, since you,[1] who now preside over our deliberations, began here your efforts for the abolition of imprisonment for debt; and a better work was never begun in the Capitol. Ever remembered and ever honored be that noble effort! You drew the attention of the public to the question, whether, in a civilized and Christian country, debt incurred without fraud, and remaining unpaid without fault, is a crime, and a crime fit to be punished by denying to the offender the enjoyment of the light of heaven, and shutting him up within four walls. Your own good sense, and that instinct of right feeling which often outruns sagacity, carried you at once to a result to which others were more slowly brought, but to which nearly all have at length been brought, by reason, reflection, and argument. Your movement led the way; it became an example, and has had a powerful effect on both sides of the Atlantic. Imprisonment for debt, or even arrest and holding to bail for mere debt, no longer exists in England; and former laws on the subject have been greatly modified and mitigated, as we all know, in our States. "Abolition of imprisonment for debt," your own words in the title of your own bill, has become the title of an act of Parliament.

Sir, I am glad of an occasion to pay you the tribute of my sincere respect for these your labors in the cause of humanity and enlightened policy. For these labors thousands of grateful hearts have thanked you; and other thousands of hearts, not yet full of joy for the accomplishment of their hopes, full, rather, at the present moment, of deep and distressing anxiety, have yet the pleasure to know that your advice, your counsel, and your influence will all be given in favor of what is intended for their relief in the bill before us.

Mr. President, let us atone for the omissions of the past by a prompt and efficient discharge of present duty. The demand for this measure is not partial or local. It comes to us, earnest and loud, from all classes and all quarters. The time is come when we must answer it to our own consciences, if we suffer longer delay or postponement. High hopes, high duties, and high responsibilities concentrate themselves on this measure and this moment. With a power to pass a bankrupt law, which no other legislature in the country possesses, with a power of giving relief to many, doing injustice to none, I again ask every man who hears me, if he can content himself without an honest attempt to exercise that power. We may think it would be better to leave the power with the States; but it was not left with the States; they have it not, and we cannot give it to them. It is in our hands, to be exercised by us, or to be for ever useless and lifeless. Under these circumstances, does not every man's heart tell him that he has a duty to discharge? If the final vote shall be given this day, and if that vote shall leave thousands of our fellow-citizens and their families, in hopeless and helpless distress, to everlasting subjection to irredeemable debt, can we go to our beds with satisfied consciences? Can we lay our heads upon our pillows, and, without self-reproach, supplicate the Almighty Mercy to forgive us our debts as we forgive our debtors? Sir, let us meet the unanimous wishes of the country, and proclaim relief to the unfortunate throughout the land. What should hinder? What should stay our hands from this good work? Creditors do not oppose it,--they apply for it; debtors solicit it, with an importunity, earnestness, and anxiety not to be described; the Constitution enjoins it; and all the considerations of justice, policy, and propriety, which are wrapped up in the phrase Public Duty, demand it, as I think, and demand it loudly and imperatively, at our hands. Sir, let us gratify the whole country, for once, with the joyous clang of chains, joyous because heard falling from the limbs of men. The wisest among those whom I address can desire nothing more beneficial than this measure, or more universally desired; and he who is youngest may not expect to live long enough to see a better opportunity of causing new pleasures and a happiness long untasted to spring up in the hearts of the poor and the humble. How many husbands and fathers are looking with hopes which they cannot suppress, and yet hardly dare to cherish, for the result of this debate! How many wives and mothers will pass sleepless and feverish nights, until they know whether they and their families shall be raised from poverty, despondency, and despair, and restored again to the circles of industrious, independent, and happy life!

Sir, let it be to the honor of Congress that, in these days of political strife and controversy, we have laid aside for once the sin that most easily besets us, and, with unanimity of counsel, and with singleness of heart and of purpose, have accomplished for our country one measure of unquestionable good.

[Footnote 1: Hon. Richard M. Johnson, Vice-President of the United States.]

"THE LOG CABIN CANDIDATE."
FROM A SPEECH DELIVERED AT THE GREAT MASS MEETING AT SARATOGA, NEW YORK, ON THE 12TH OF AUGUST, 1840.

But it is the cry and effort of the times to stimulate those who are called poor against those who are called rich; and yet, among those who urge this cry, and seek to profit by it, there is betrayed sometimes an occasional sneer at whatever savors of humble life. Witness the reproach against a candidate now before the people for their highest honors, that a log cabin, with plenty of hard cider, is good enough for him!

It appears to some persons, that a great deal too much use is made of the symbol of the log cabin. No man of sense supposes, certainly, that the having lived in a log cabin is any further proof of qualification for the Presidency, than as it creates a presumption that any one who, rising from humble condition, or under unfavorable circumstances, has been able to attract a considerable degree of public attention, is possessed of reputable qualities, moral and intellectual.

But it is to be remembered, that this matter of the log cabin originated, not with the friends of the Whig candidate, but with his enemies. Soon after his nomination at Harrisburg, a writer for one of the leading administration papers spoke of his "log cabin," and his use of "hard cider," by way of sneer and reproach. As might have been expected, (for pretenders are apt to be thrown off their guard,) this taunt at humble life proceeded from the party which claims a monopoly of the purest democracy. The whole party appeared to enjoy it, or, at least, they countenanced it by silent acquiescence; for I do not know that, to this day, any eminent individual or any leading newspaper attached to the administration has rebuked this scornful jeering at the supposed humble condition or circumstances in life, past or present, of a worthy man and a war-worn soldier. But it touched a tender point in the public feeling. It naturally roused indignation. What was intended as reproach was immediately seized on as merit. "Be it so! Be it so!" was the instant burst of the public voice. "Let him be the log cabin candidate. What you say in scorn, we will shout with all our lungs. From this day forward, we have our cry of rally; and we shall see whether he who has dwelt in one of the rude abodes of the West may not become the best house in the country!"

All this is natural, and springs from sources of just feeling. Other things, Gentlemen, have had a similar origin. We all know that the term "Whig" was bestowed in derision, two hundred years ago, on those who were thought too fond of liberty; and our national air of "Yankee Doodle" was composed by British officers, in ridicule of the American troops. Yet, erelong, the last of the British armies laid down its arms at Yorktown, while this same air was playing in the ears of officers and men. Gentlemen, it is only shallow-minded pretenders who either make distinguished origin matter of personal merit, or obscure origin matter of personal reproach. Taunt and scoffing at the humble condition of early life affect nobody, in this country, but those who are foolish enough to indulge in them, and they are generally sufficiently punished by public rebuke. A man who is not ashamed of himself need not be ashamed of his early condition. Gentlemen, it did not happen to me to be born in a log cabin; but my elder brothers and sisters were born in a log cabin, raised amid the snow-drifts of New Hampshire, at a period so early that, when the smoke first rose from its rude chimney, and curled over the frozen hills, there was no similar evidence of a white man's habitation between it and the settlements on the rivers of Canada. Its remains still exist. I make to it an annual visit. I carry my children to it, to teach them the hardships endured by the generations which have gone before them. I love to dwell on the tender recollections, the kindred ties, the early affections, and the touching narratives and incidents, which mingle with all I know of this primitive family abode. I weep to think that none of those who inhabited it are now among the living; and if ever I am ashamed of it, or if I ever fail in affectionate veneration for him who reared it, and defended it against savage violence and destruction, cherished all the domestic virtues beneath its roof, and, through the fire and blood of a seven years' revolutionary war, shrunk from no danger, no toil, no sacrifice, to serve his country, and to raise his children to a condition better than his own, may my name and the name of my posterity be blotted for ever from the memory of mankind!

ADDRESS TO THE LADIES OF RICHMOND.
REMARKS AT A PUBLIC RECEPTION BY THE LADIES OF RICHMOND, VIRGINIA, ON THE 5TH OF OCTOBER, 1840.

[The visit of Mr. Webster to Richmond was short, and his public engagements so numerous, as to put it out of his power to return the calls of his friends, or to pay his respects to their families. It was accordingly proposed that the ladies who might desire to do so should assemble in the "Log Cabin," and that he should there pay his respects to them collectively. The meeting was large, and the building quite full. On being introduced to them in a few appropriate remarks, by Mr. Lyons, Mr. Webster addressed them in the following speech.]

Ladies,--I am very sure I owe the pleasure I now enjoy to your kind disposition, which has given me the opportunity to present my thanks and my respects to you thus collectively, since the shortness of my stay in the city does not allow me the happiness of calling upon those, severally and individually, from members of whose families I have received kindness and notice. And, in the first place, I wish to express to you my deep and hearty thanks, as I have endeavored to do to your fathers, your husbands, and your brothers, for the unbounded hospitality I have received ever since I came among you. This is registered, I assure you, in a grateful heart, in characters of an enduring nature. The rough contests of the political world are not suited to the dignity and the delicacy of your sex; but you possess the intelligence to know how much of that happiness which you are entitled to hope for, both for yourselves and for your children, depends on the right administration of government, and a proper tone of public morals. That is a subject on which the moral perceptions of woman are both quicker and juster than those of the other sex. I do not speak of that administration of government whose object is merely the protection of industry, the preservation of civil liberty, and the securing to enterprise of its due reward. I speak of government in a somewhat higher point of view; I speak of it in regard to its influence on the morals and sentiments of the community. We live in an age distinguished for great benevolent exertion, in which the affluent are consecrating the means they possess to the endowment of colleges and academies, to the building of churches, to the support of religion and religious worship, to the encouragement of schools, lyceums, and athenaeums, and other means of general popular instruction. This is all well; it is admirable; it augurs well for the prospects of ensuing generations. But I have sometimes thought, that, amidst all this activity and zeal of the good and the benevolent, the influence of government on the morals and on the religious feelings of the community is apt to be overlooked or underrated. I speak, of course, of its indirect influence, of the power of its example, and the general tone which it inspires.

A popular government, in all these respects, is a most powerful institution; more powerful, as it has sometimes appeared to me, than the influence of most other human institutions put together, either for good or for evil, according to its character. Its example, its tone, whether of regard or disregard for moral obligation, is most important to human happiness; it is among those things which most affect the political morals of mankind, and their general morals also. I advert to this, because there has been put forth, in modern times, the false maxim, that there is one morality for politics, and another morality for other things; that, in their political conduct to their opponents, men may say and do that which they would never think of saying or doing in the personal relations of private life. There has been openly announced a sentiment, which I consider as the very essence of false morality, which declares that "all is fair in politics." If a man speaks falsely or calumniously of his neighbor, and is reproached for the offence, the ready excuse is this: "It was in relation to public and political matters; I cherished no personal ill-will whatever against that individual, but quite the contrary; I spoke of my adversary merely as a political man." In my opinion, the day is coming when falsehood will stand for falsehood, and calumny will be treated as a breach of the commandment, whether it be committed politically or in the concerns of private life.

It is by the promulgation of sound morals in the community, and more especially by the training and instruction of the young, that woman performs her part towards the preservation of a free government. It is generally admitted that public liberty, and the perpetuity of a free constitution, rest on the virtue and intelligence of the community which enjoys it. How is that virtue to be inspired, and how is that intelligence to be communicated? Bonaparte once asked Madame de Staël in what manner he could best promote the happiness of France. Her reply is full of political wisdom. She said, "Instruct the mothers of the French people." Mothers are, indeed, the affectionate and effective teachers of the human race. The mother begins her process of training with the infant in her arms. It is she who directs, so to speak, its first mental and spiritual pulsations. She conducts it along the impressible years of childhood and youth, and hopes to deliver it to the stern conflicts and tumultuous scenes of life, armed by those good principles which her child has received from maternal care and love.

If we draw within the circle of our contemplation the mothers of a civilized nation, what do we see? We behold so many artificers working, not on frail and perishable matter, but on the immortal mind, moulding and fashioning beings who are to exist for ever. We applaud the artist whose skill and genius present the mimic man upon the canvas; we admire and celebrate the sculptor who works out that same image in enduring marble; but how insignificant are these achievements, though the highest and the fairest in all the departments of art, in comparison with the great vocation of human mothers! They work, not upon the canvas that shall perish, or the marble that shall crumble into dust, but upon mind, upon spirit, which is to last for ever, and which is to bear, for good or evil, throughout its duration, the impress of a mother's plastic hand.

I have already expressed the opinion, which all allow to be correct, that our security for the duration of the free institutions which bless our country depends upon habits of virtue and the prevalence of knowledge and of education. The attainment of knowledge does not comprise all which is contained in the larger term of education. The feelings are to be disciplined; the passions are to be restrained; true and worthy motives are to be inspired; a profound religious feeling is to be instilled, and pure morality inculcated, under all circumstances. All this is comprised in education. Mothers who are faithful to this great duty will tell their children, that neither in political nor in any other concerns of life can man ever withdraw himself from the perpetual obligations of conscience and of duty; that in every act, whether public or private, he incurs a just responsibility; and that in no condition is he warranted in trifling with important rights and obligations. They will impress upon their children the truth, that the exercise of the elective franchise is a social duty, of as solemn a nature as man can be called to perform; that a man may not innocently trifle with his vote; that every free elector is a trustee, as well for others as himself; and that every man and every measure he supports has an important bearing on the interests of others, as well as on his own. It is in the inculcation of high and pure morals such as these, that, in a free republic, woman performs her sacred duty, and fulfils her destiny. The French, as you know, are remarkable for their fondness for sententious phrases, in which much meaning is condensed into a small space. I noticed lately, on the title-page of one of the books of popular instruction in France, this motto: "Pour instruction on the heads of the people! you owe them that baptism." And, certainly, if there be any duty which may be described by a reference to that great institute of religion,--a duty approaching it in importance, perhaps next to it in obligation,--it is this.
I know you hardly expect me to address you on the popular political topics of the day. You read enough, you hear quite enough, on those subjects. You expect me only to meet you, and to tender my profound thanks for this marked proof of your regard, and will kindly receive the assurances with which I tender to you, on parting, my affectionate respects and best wishes.

RECEPTION AT BOSTON.
A SPEECH MADE IN FANEUIL HALL, ON THE 30TH OF SEPTEMBER, 1842, AT A PUBLIC RECEPTION GIVEN TO MR. WEBSTER, ON HIS RETURN TO BOSTON, AFTER THE NEGOTIATION OF THE TREATY OF WASHINGTON.

[On the accession of General Harrison to the Presidency of the United States, on the 4th of March, 1841, Mr. Webster was called to the office of Secretary of State, in which, after the President's untimely death, he continued under Mr. Tyler for about two years. The relations of the country with Great Britain were at that time in a very critical position. The most important and difficult subject which engaged the attention of the government, while he filled the Department of State, was the negotiation of the treaty with Great Britain, which was signed at Washington on the 9th of August, 1842. The other members of General Harrison's Cabinet having resigned their places in the autumn of 1841, discontent was felt by some of their friends, that Mr. Webster should have consented to retain his. But as Mr. Tyler continued to place entire confidence in Mr. Webster's administration of the Department of State, the great importance of pursuing a steady line of policy in reference to foreign affairs, and especially the hope of averting a rupture with England by an honorable settlement of our difficulties with that country, induced Mr. Webster to remain at his post.
On occasion of a visit made by him to Boston, after the adjournment of Congress, in August, 1842, a number of his friends were desirous of manifesting their sense of the services which he had rendered to the country by pursuing this course. A public meeting of citizens was accordingly held in Faneuil Hall, on the 30th of September, 1842. At this meeting the following speech was made.]
I know not how it is, Mr. Mayor, but there is something in the echoes of these walls, or in this sea of upturned faces which I behold before me, or in the genius that always hovers over this place, fanning ardent and patriotic feeling by every motion of its wings,--I know not how it is, but there is something that excites me strangely, deeply, before I even begin to speak. It cannot be doubted that this salutation and greeting from my fellow-citizens of Boston is a tribute dear to my heart. Boston is indeed my home, my cherished home. It is now more than twenty-five years since I came to it with my family, to pursue, here in this enlightened metropolis, those objects of professional life for which my studies and education were designed to fit me. It is twenty years since I was invited by the citizens of Boston to take upon myself an

office of public trust in their service.[1] It gives me infinite pleasure to see here to-day, among those who hold the seats yielded to such as are more advanced in life, not a few of the gentlemen who were earnestly instrumental in inducing me to enter upon a course of life wholly unexpected, and to devote myself to the service of the public.

Whenever the duties of public life have withdrawn me from this home, I have felt it, nevertheless, to be the attractive spot to which all local affection tended. And now that the progress of time must shortly bring about the period, if it should not be hastened by the progress of events, when the duties of public life shall yield to the influences of advancing years, I cherish no hope more precious, than to pass here in these associations and among these friends what may remain to me of life; and to leave in the midst of you, fellow-citizens, partaking of your fortunes, whether for good or for evil, those who bear my name, and inherit my blood.

The Mayor has alluded, very kindly, to the exertions which I have made since I have held a position in the Cabinet, and especially to the results of the negotiation in which I have been recently engaged. I hope, fellow-citizens, that something has been done which may prove permanently useful to the public. I have endeavored to do something, and I hope my endeavors have not been in vain. I have had a hard summer's work, it is true, but I am not wholly unused to hard work. I have had some anxious days, I have spent some sleepless nights; but if the results of my efforts shall be approved by the community, I am richly compensated. My other days will be the happier, and my other nights will be given to a sweeter repose.

It was an object of the highest national importance, no doubt, to disperse the clouds which threatened a storm between England and America. For several years past there has been a class of questions open between the two countries, which have not always threatened war, but which have prevented the people from being assured of permanent peace.

His Honor the Mayor has paid a just tribute to that lamented personage, by whom, in 1841, I was called to the place I now occupy; and although, Gentlemen, I know it is in very bad taste to speak much of one's self, yet here, among my friends and neighbors, I wish to say a word or two on subjects in which I am concerned. With the late President Harrison I had contracted an acquaintance while we were both members of Congress, and I had an opportunity of renewing it afterwards in his own house, and elsewhere. I have made no exhibition or boast of the confidence which it was his pleasure to repose in me; but circumstances, hardly worthy of serious notice, have rendered it not improper for me to say on this occasion, that as soon as President Harrison was elected, without, of course, one word from me, he wrote to me inviting me to take a place in his Cabinet, leaving to me the choice of that place, and asking my advice as to the persons that should fill every other place in it. He expressed rather a wish that I should take the administration of the treasury, because, as he was pleased to say, I had devoted myself with success to the examination of the questions of currency and finance, and he felt that the wants of the country,--the necessities of the country, on the great subjects of currency and finance,--were moving causes that produced the revolution which had placed him in the presidential chair.

It so happened, Gentlemen, that my preference was for another place,--for that which I have now the honor to fill. I felt all its responsibilities; but I must say, that, with whatever attention I had considered the general questions of finance, I felt more competent and willing to undertake the duties of an office which did not involve the daily drudgery of the treasury.

I was not disappointed, Gentlemen, in the exigency which then existed in our foreign relations. I was not unaware of all the difficulties which hung over us; for although the whole of the danger was not at that moment developed, the cause of it was known, and it seemed as if an outbreak was inevitable. I allude now to that occurrence on the frontier of which the chairman has already spoken, which took place in the winter of 1841 the case of Alexander McLeod.

A year or two before, the Canadian government had seen fit to authorize a military incursion, for a particular purpose, within the territory of the United States. That purpose was to destroy a steamboat, charged with being employed for hostile purposes against its forces and the peaceable subjects of the crown. The act was avowed by the British government at home as a public act. Alexander McLeod, a person who individually could claim no regard or sympathy, happened to be one of the agents who, in a military character, performed the act of their sovereign. Coming into the United States some years after, he was arrested under a charge of homicide committed in this act, and was held to trial as for a private felony. According to my apprehensions, a proceeding of this kind was directly adverse to the well-settled doctrines of the public law. It could not but be received with lively indignation, not only by the British government, but among the people of England. It would be so received among us. If a citizen of the United States should as a military man receive an order of his government and obey it, (and he must either obey it or be hanged,) and should afterwards, in the territory of another power, which by that act he had offended, be tried for a violation of its law, as for a crime, and threatened with individual punishment, there is not a man in the United States who would not cry out for redress and for vengeance. Any elevated government, in a case like this, where one of its citizens, in the performance of his duty, incurs such menaces and danger, assumes the responsibility; any elevated government says, "The act was mine,--I am the man";--"Adsum qui feci, in me convertite ferrum."

Now, Gentlemen, information of the action of the British government on this subject was transmitted to us at Washington within a few days after the installation of General Harrison. I did not think that it was proper to make public then, nor is it important to say now, all that we knew on the subject; but I will tell you, in general terms, that if all that was known at Washington then had been divulged throughout the country, the value of the shipping interest of this city, and of every other interest connected with the commerce of the country, would have been depressed one half in six hours. I thought that the concussion might be averted, by holding up to view the principles of public law by which this question ought to be settled, and by demanding an apology for whatever had been done against those principles of public law by the British government or its officers. I thought we ought to put ourselves right in the first place, and then we could insist that they should do right in the next place. When in England, in the year 1839, I had occasion to address a large and respectable assemblage; and allusion having been made to the relations of things between the two countries, I stated then, what I thought and now think, that in any controversy which should terminate in war between the United States and England, the only eminent advantage that *either* would possess would be found in the rectitude of its cause. With the right on our side, we are a match for England; and with the right on her side, she is a match for us, or for anybody.

We live in an age, fellow-citizens, when there has been established among the nations a more elevated tribunal than ever before existed on earth; I mean the tribunal of the enlightened public opinion of the world. Governments cannot go to war now, either with or against the consent of their own subjects or people, without the reprobation of other states, unless for grounds and reasons justifying them in the general judgment of mankind. The judgment of civilization, of commerce, and of that heavenly light that beams over Christendom, restrains men, congresses, parliaments, princes, and people from gratifying the inordinate love of ambition through the bloody scenes of war. It has been wisely said, and it is true, that every settlement of national differences between Christian states by fair negotiation, without resort to arms, is a new illustration and a new proof of the benign influence of the Christian faith.

With regard to the terms of this treaty, and in relation to the other subjects connected with it, it is somewhat awkward for me to speak, because the documents connected with them have not been made public by authority. But I persuade myself, that, when the whole shall be calmly considered, it will be seen that there was throughout a fervent disposition to maintain the interest and honor of the country, united with a proper regard for the preservation of peace between us and the greatest commercial nation of the world.

Gentlemen, while I receive these commendations which you have bestowed, I have an agreeable duty to perform to others. In the first place, I have great pleasure in bearing testimony to the intelligent interest manifested by the President of the United States, under whose authority, of course, I constantly acted throughout the negotiation, and his sincere and anxious desire that it might result successfully. I take great pleasure in acknowledging here, as I will acknowledge everywhere, my obligations to him for the unbroken and steady confidence reposed in me through the whole progress of an affair not unimportant to the country, and infinitely important to my own reputation.

A negotiator disparaged, distrusted, treated with jealousy by his own government, would be indeed a very unequal match for a cool and sagacious representative of one of the proudest and most powerful monarchies of Europe, possessing in the fullest extent the confidence of his government, and authorized to bind it in concerns of the greatest importance. I shall never forget the frankness and generosity with which, after a full and free interchange of suggestions upon the subject, I was told by the President that on my shoulders rested the responsibility of the negotiation, and on my discretion and judgment should rest the lead of every measure. I desire also to speak here of the hearty co-operation rendered every day by the other gentlemen connected with the administration, from every one of whom I received important assistance. I speak with satisfaction, also, of the useful labors of all the Commissioners, although I need hardly say here, what has been already said officially, that the highest respect is due to the Commissioners from Maine and Massachusetts for their faithful adherence to the rights of their own States, mingled with a cordial co-operation in what was required by the general interests of the United States. And I hope I shall not be considered as trespassing on this occasion, if I speak of the happy selection made by England of a person to represent her government on this occasion,[2]--a thorough Englishman, understanding and appreciating the great objects and interests of his own government, of large and liberal views, and of such standing and weight of character at home, as to impress a feeling of approbation of his course upon both government and people. He was fully acquainted with the subject, and always, on all occasions, as far as his allegiance and duty permitted, felt and manifested good-will towards this country.

Aside from the question of the boundary, there were other important subjects to be considered, to which I know not whether this is a proper occasion to allude. When the results of the negotiation shall be fully before the public, it will be seen that these other questions have not been neglected, questions of great moment and importance to the country; and then I shall look with concern, but with faith and trust, for the judgment of that country upon them. It is but just to take notice of a very important act, intended to provide for such cases as McLeod's, for which the country is indebted to the Whig majorities in the two houses of Congress, acting upon the President's recommendation. Events showed the absolute necessity of removing into the national tribunals questions involving the peace and honor of the United States.

There yet remain, Gentlemen, several other subjects still unsettled with England. First, there is that concerning the trade between the United States and the possessions of England, on this continent and in the West Indies. It has been my duty to look into that subject, and to keep the run of it, as we say, from the arrangement of 1829 and 1830, until the present time. That arrangement was one unfavorable to the shipping interests of the United States, and especially so to the New England States. To adjust these relations is an important subject, either for diplomatic negotiation, or the consideration of Congress. One or both houses of Congress, indeed, have already called upon the proper department for a report upon the operations of that arrangement, and a committee of the House of Representatives has made a report, showing that some adjustment of these relations is of vital importance to the future prosperity of our navigating interests.

There is another question, somewhat more remote; that of the Northwest Boundary, where the possessions of the two countries touch each other upon the Pacific. There are evident public reasons why that question should be settled before the country becomes peopled.

There are also, Gentlemen, many open questions respecting our relations with other governments. Upon most of the other States of this continent, citizens of the United States have claims, with regard to which the delays already incurred have caused great injustice; and it becomes the government of the United States, by a calm and dignified course, and a deliberate and vigorous tone of administration of public affairs, to secure prompt justice to our citizens in these quarters.

I am here to-day as a guest. I was invited by a number of highly valued personal and political friends to partake with them of a public dinner, for the purpose of giving them an opportunity to pass the usual greeting of friends upon my return; of testifying their respect for my public services heretofore; and of exchanging congratulations upon the results of the late negotiation. It was at my instance that the proposed dinner took the form of this meeting, and, instead of meeting them at the festive board, I agreed to meet them, and those who chose to meet me with them, here. Still, the general character of the meeting seems not to be changed. I am here as a guest; here to receive greetings and salutations for particular services, and not under any intimation or expectation that I should address the gentlemen who invited me or others here, upon subjects not suggested by themselves. It would not become me to use the occasion for any more general purpose. Because, although I have a design, at some time not far distant, to make known my sentiments upon political matters generally, and upon the political state of the country and that of its several parties, yet I know very well that I should be trespassing beyond the bounds of politeness and propriety, should I enter upon this whole wide field now. I will not enter upon it, because the gentlemen who invited me entertain on many of these topics views different from my own, and they would very properly say, that they came here to meet Mr. Webster, to congratulate him upon the late negotiation, and to exchange sentiments upon matters about which they agreed with him; and that it was not in very correct taste for him to use the occasion to express opinions upon other subjects on which they differ. It is on that account that I shall forbear discussing political subjects at large, and shall endeavor to confine my remarks to what may be considered as affecting myself, directly or indirectly.

The Mayor was kind enough to say, that having, in his judgment, performed the duties of my own department to the satisfaction of my country, it might be left to me to take care of my own honor and reputation. I suppose that he meant to say, that in the present distracted state of the Whig party, and among the contrariety of opinions that prevail (if there be a contrariety of opinion) as to the course proper for *me* to pursue, the decision of that question might be left to myself. I am exactly of his opinion. I am quite of opinion that on a question touching my own honor and character, as I am to bear the consequences of the decision, I had a great deal better be trusted to make it. No man feels more highly the advantage of the advice of friends than I do; but on a question so delicate and important as that, I like to choose myself the friends who are to give me advice; and upon this subject, Gentlemen, I shall leave you as enlightened as I found you.

I give no pledges, I make no intimations, one way or the other; and I will be as free, when this day closes, to act as duty calls, as I was when the dawn of this day--(Here Mr. Webster was interrupted by tremendous applause. When silence was restored he continued:)

There is a delicacy in the case, because there is always delicacy and regret when one feels obliged to differ from his friends; but there is no embarrassment. There is no embarrassment, because, if I see the path of duty before me, I have that within me which will enable me to pursue it, and throw all embarrassment to the winds. A public man has no occasion to be embarrassed, if he is honest. Himself and his feelings should be to him as nobody and as nothing; the interest of his country must be to him as every thing; he must sink what is personal to himself, making exertions for his country; and it is his ability and readiness to do this which are to mark him as a great or as a little man in time to come.

There were many persons in September, 1841, who found great fault with my remaining in the President's Cabinet. You know, Gentlemen, that twenty years of honest, and not altogether undistinguished service in the Whig cause, did not save me from an outpouring of wrath, which seldom proceeds from Whig pens and Whig tongues against anybody. I am, Gentlemen, a little hard to coax, but as to being driven, that is out of the question. I chose to trust my own judgment, and thinking I was at a post where I was in the service of the country, and could do it good, I stayed there. And I leave it to you to-day to say, I leave it to my country to say, whether the country would have been better off if I had left also. I have no attachment to office. I have tasted of its sweets, but I have tasted of its bitterness. I am content with what I have achieved; I am more ready to rest satisfied with what is gained, than to run the risk of doubtful efforts for new acquisition.

I suppose I ought to pause here. (Cries of "Go on!") I ought, perhaps, to allude to nothing more, and I will not allude to any thing further than it may be supposed to concern myself, directly or by implication. Gentlemen, and Mr. Mayor, a most respectable convention of Whig delegates met in this place a few days since, and passed very important resolutions. There is no set of gentlemen in the Commonwealth, so far as I know them, who have more of my respect and regard. They are Whigs, but they are no better Whigs than I am. They have served the country in the Whig ranks; so have I, quite as long as most of them, though perhaps with less ability and success. Their resolutions on political subjects, as representing the Whigs of the State, are entitled to respect, so far as they were authorized to express opinion on those subjects, and no further. They were sent hither, as I supposed, to agree upon candidates for the offices of Governor and Lieutenant-Governor for the support of the Whigs of Massachusetts; and if they had any authority to speak in the name of the Whigs of Massachusetts to any other purport or intent, I have not been informed of it. I feel very little disturbed by any of those proceedings, of whatever nature; but some of them appear to me to have been inconsiderate and hasty, and their point and bearing can hardly be mistaken. I notice, among others, a declaration made, in behalf of all the Whigs of this Commonwealth, of "a full and final separation from the President of the United States." If those gentlemen saw fit to express their own sentiments to that extent, there was no objection. Whigs speak their sentiments everywhere; but whether they may assume a privilege to speak for others on a point on which those others have not given them authority, is another question. I am a Whig, I always have been a Whig, and I always will be one; and if there are any who would turn me out of the pale of that communion, let them see who will get out first. I am a Massachusetts Whig, a Faneuil Hall Whig, having breathed this air for five-and-twenty years, and meaning to breathe it as long as my life is spared. I am ready to submit to all decisions of Whig conventions on subjects on which they are authorized to make decisions; I know that great party good and great public good can only be so obtained. But it is quite another question whether a set of gentlemen, however respectable they may be as individuals, shall have the power to bind me on matters which I have not agreed to submit to their decision at all.

"A full and final separation" is declared between the Whig party of Massachusetts and the President. That is the text: it requires a commentary. What does it mean? The President of the United States has three years of his term of office yet unexpired. Does this declaration mean, then, that during those three years all the measures of his administration are to be opposed by the great body of the Whig party of Massachusetts, whether they are right or wrong? There are great public interests which require his attention. If the President of the United States should attempt, by negotiation, or by earnest and serious application to Congress, to make some change in the present arrangements, such as should be of service to those interests of navigation which are concerned in the colonial trade, are the Whigs of Massachusetts to give him neither aid nor succor? If the President of the United States shall direct the proper department to review the whole commercial policy of the United States, in respect of reciprocity in the indirect trade, to which so much of our tonnage is now sacrificed, if the amendment of this policy shall be undertaken by him, is there such a separation between him and the Whigs of Massachusetts as shall lead them and their representatives to oppose it. Do you know (there are gentlemen now here who do know) that a large proportion, I rather think more than one half, of the carrying trade between the empire of Brazil and the United States is enjoyed by tonnage from the North of Europe, in consequence of this ill-considered principle with regard to reciprocity. You might just as well admit them into the coasting trade. By this arrangement, we take the bread out of our children's mouths and give it to strangers. I appeal to you, Sir, (turning to Captain Benjamin Rich, who sat by him,) is not this true? (Mr. Rich at once replied, True!) Is every measure of this sort, for the relief of such abuses, to be rejected? Are we to suffer ourselves to remain inactive under every grievance of this kind until these three years shall expire, and through as many more as shall pass until Providence shall bless us with more power of doing good than we have now?

Again, there are now in this State persons employed under government, allowed to be pretty good Whigs, still holding their offices; collectors, district attorneys, postmasters, marshals. What is to become of them in this separation? Which side are they to fall? Are they to resign? or is this resolution to be held up to government as an invitation or a provocation to turn them out? Our distinguished fellow-citizen, who, with so much credit to himself and to his country, represents our government in England,[3]--is *he* expected to come home, on this separation, and yield his place to his predecessor,[4] or to somebody else? And in regard to the individual who addresses you,--what do his brother Whigs mean to do with him? Where do they mean to place me? Generally, when a divorce takes place, the parties divide their children. I am anxious to know where, in the case of this divorce, I shall fall. This declaration announces a full and final separation between the Whigs of Massachusetts and the President. If I choose to remain in the President's councils, do these gentlemen mean to say that I cease to be a Massachusetts Whig? I am quite ready to put that question to the people of Massachusetts.

I would not treat this matter too lightly, nor yet too seriously. I know very well that, when public bodies get together, resolutions can never be considered with any degree of deliberation. They are passed as they are presented. Who the honorable gentlemen were who drew this resolution I do not know. I suspect that they had not much meaning in it, and that they have not very clearly defined what little meaning they had. They were angry; they were resentful; they had drawn up a string of charges against the President,--a bill of indictment, as it were,--and, to close the whole, they introduced this declaration about "a full and final separation." I could not read this, of course, without perceiving that it had an intentional or unintentional bearing on my position; and therefore it was proper for me to allude to it here.

Gentlemen, there are some topics on which it has been my fortune to differ from my old friends. They may be right on these topics; very probably they are; but I am sure *I* am right in maintaining my opinions, such as they are, when I have formed them honestly and on deliberation. There seems to me to be a disposition to postpone all attempts to do good to the country to some future and uncertain day. Yet there is a Whig majority in each house of Congress, and I am of opinion that now is the time to accomplish what yet remains to be accomplished. Some gentlemen are for suffering the present Congress to expire; another Congress to be chosen, and to expire also; a third Congress to be chosen, and then, if there shall be a Whig majority in both branches, and a Whig President, they propose to take up highly important and pressing subjects. These are persons, Gentlemen, of more sanguine temperament than myself. "Confidence," says Lord Chatham, "is a plant of slow growth in an old bosom." He referred to confidence in men, but the remark is as true of confidence in predictions of future occurrences. Many Whigs see before us a prospect of more power, and a better chance to serve the country, than we now possess. Far along in the horizon, they discern mild skies and halcyon seas, while fogs and darkness and mists blind other sons of humanity from beholding all this bright vision. It was not so that we accomplished our last great victory, by simply brooding over a glorious Whig future. We succeeded in 1840, but not without an effort; and I know that nothing but union, cordial, sympathetic, fraternal union, can prevent the party that achieved that success from renewed prostration. It is not,--I would say it in the presence of the world,--it is not by premature and partial, by proscriptive and denunciatory proceedings, that this great Whig family can ever be kept together, or that Whig counsels can maintain their ascendency. This is perfectly plain and obvious. It was a party, from the first, made up of different opinions and principles, of gentlemen of every political complexion, uniting to make a change in the administration. They were men of strong State-rights principles, men of strong federal principles, men of extreme tariff, and men of extreme anti-tariff notions. What could be expected of such a party, unless animated by a spirit of conciliation and harmony, of union and sympathy? Its true policy was, from the first, and must be, unless it meditates its own destruction, to heal, and not to widen, the breaches that existed in its ranks. It consented to become united in order to save the country from a continuation of a ruinous course of measures. And the lesson taught by the whole history of the revolution of 1840 is the momentous value of conciliation, friendship, sympathy, and union. Gentlemen, if I understand the matter, there were four or five great objects in that revolution. And, in the first place, one great object was that of attempting to secure permanent peace between this country and England. For although, as I have said, we were not actually at war, we were subjected to perpetual agitations, which disturb the interests of the country almost as much as war. They break in upon men's pursuits, and render them incapable of calculating or judging of their chances of success in any proposed line or course of business. A settled peace was one of the objects of that revolution. I am glad if you think this is accomplished.

The next object of that revolution was an increase of revenue. It was notorious that, for the several last years, the expenditures for the administration of government had exceeded the receipts; in other words, government had been running in debt, and in the mean time the operation of the compromise act was still further and faster diminishing the revenue itself. A sound revenue was one of those objects; and that it has been accomplished, our thanks and praise are due to the Congress that has just adjourned.

A third object was protection, protection incidental to revenue, or consequent upon revenue. Now as to that, Gentlemen, much has been done, and I hope it will be found that enough has been done. And for this, too, all the Whigs who supported that measure in Congress are entitled to high praise: they receive mine, and I hope they do yours; it is right that they should. But let us be just. The French rhetoricians have a maxim, that there is nothing beautiful that is not true; I am afraid that some of our jubilant oratory would hardly stand the test of this canon of criticism. It is not true that a majority, composed of Whigs, could be found, in either house, in favor of the tariff bill. More than thirty Whigs, many of them gentlemen of lead and influence, voted against the law, from beginning to end, on all questions, direct and indirect; and it is not pleasant to consider what would have been the state of the country, the treasury, and the government itself, at this moment, if the law actually passed, for revenue and for protection, had depended on Whig votes alone. After all, it passed the House of Representatives by a single vote; and there is a good deal of _éclat_ about that single vote. But did not every gentleman who voted for it take the responsibility and deserve the honor of that single vote? Several gentlemen in the opposition thus befriended the bill; thus did our neighbor from the Middlesex District of this State,[5] voting for the tariff out and out, as steadily as did my honored friend, the member from this city.[6] We hear nothing of his "coming to the rescue," and yet he had that _one vote_, and held the tariff in his hand as absolutely as if he had had a presidential veto! And how was it in the Senate? It passed by one vote again there, and could not have passed at all without the assistance of the two Senators from Pennsylvania, of Mr. Williams of Maine, and of Mr. Wright of New York. Let us then admit the truth (and a lawyer may do that when it helps his case), that it was necessary that a large portion of the other party should come to the assistance of the Whigs to enable them to carry the tariff, and that, if this assistance had not been rendered, the tariff must have failed.

And this is a very important truth for New England. Her children, looking to their manufactures and industry for their livelihood, must rejoice to find the tariff, so necessary to these, no party question. Can they desire, can they wish, that such a great object as the protection of industry should become a party object, rising with party, and with the failure of the party that supported it going to the grave? This is a public, a national question. The tariff ought to be inwrought in the sentiments of all parties; and although I hope that the pre-eminence of Whig principles may be eternal, I wish to take bond and security, that we may make the protection of domestic industry more durable even than Whig supremacy.

Let us be true in another respect. This tariff has accomplished much, and is an honor to the men who passed it. But in regard to protection it has only restored the country to the state in which it was before the compromise act, and from which it fell under the operation of that act. It has repaired the consequences of that measure, and it has done *no more*. I may speak of the compromise act. My turn has come now. No measure ever passed Congress during my connection with that body that caused me so much grief and mortification. It was passed by a few friends joining the whole host of the enemy. I have heard much of the motives of that act. The personal motives of those that passed the act were, I doubt not, pure; and all public men are supposed to act from pure motives. But if by motives are meant the objects proposed by the act itself, and expressed in it, then I say, if those be the motives alluded to, they are worse than the act itself. The principle was bad, the measure was bad, the consequences were bad. Every circumstance, as well as every line of the act itself, shows that the design was to impose upon legislation a restraint that the Constitution had not imposed; to insert in the Constitution a new prohibitory clause, providing that, after the year 1842, no revenue should be collected except according to an absurd horizontal system, and none exceeding twenty per cent. It was then pressed through under the great emergency of the public necessities. But I may now recur to what I then said, namely, that its principle was false and dangerous, and that, when its time came, it would rack and convulse our system. I said we should not get rid of it without throes and spasms. Has not this been as predicted? We have felt the spasms and throes of this convulsion; but we have at last gone through them, and begin to breathe again. It is something that that act is at last got rid of; and the present tariff is deserving in this, that it is specific and discriminating, that it holds to common sense, and rejects and discards the principles of the compromise act, I hope for ever.

Another great and principal object of the revolution of 1840 was a restoration of the currency. Our troubles did not begin with want of money in the treasury, or under the sapping and mining operation of the compromise act. They are of earlier date. The trouble and distress of the country began with the *currency* in 1833, and broke out with new severity in 1837. Other causes of difficulty have since arisen, but the first great shock was a shock on the currency; and from the effect of this the country is not yet relieved. I hope the late act may yield competent revenue, and am sure it will do much for protection. But until you provide a better currency, so that you may have a universal one, of equal and general value throughout the land, I am hard to be persuaded that we shall see the day of our former prosperity. Currency, accredited currency, and easy and cheap internal exchanges,--until these things be obtained, depend upon it, the country will find no adequate relief.

And now, fellow-citizens, I will say a word or two on the history of the transactions on this subject. At the special session of Congress, the Secretary of the Treasury, Mr. Ewing, arranged a plan for a national bank. That plan was founded upon the idea of a large capital, furnished mainly by private subscriptions, and it included branches for local discounts. I need not advert, Gentlemen, to the circumstances under which this scheme was drawn up, and received, as it did, the approbation of the President and Cabinet, as the best thing that could be done. I need not remind you, that he whom we had all agreed should hold the second place in the government had been called to the head of it. I need not say that he held opinions wholly different from mine on the subjects which now came before us. But those opinions were fixed, and therefore it was thought the part of wisdom and prudence not to see how strong a case might be made against the President, but to get along as well as we might. With such views, Mr. Ewing presented his plan to Congress. As most persons will remember, the clause allowing the bank to establish branches provided that those branches might be placed in any State which should give its consent. I have no idea that there is any necessity for such a restriction. I believe Congress has the power to establish the branches without, as well as with, the consent of the States. But that clause, at most, was theoretical. I never could find anybody who could show any practical mischief resulting from it. Its opponents went upon the theory, which I do not exactly accord with, that an omission to exercise a power, in any case, amounts to a surrender of that power. At any rate, it was the best thing that could be done; and its rejection was the commencement of the disastrous dissensions between the President and Congress.

Gentlemen, it was exceedingly doubtful at the time when that plan was prepared whether the capital would be subscribed. But we did what we could about it. We asked the opinion of the leading merchants of the principal commercial cities. They were invited to Washington to confer with us. They expressed doubts whether the bank could be put into operation, but they expressed hopes also, and they pledged themselves to do the best they could to advance it. And as the commercial interests were in its favor, as the administration was new and fresh and popular, and the people were desirous to have something done, a great earnestness was felt that that bill should be tried.

It was sent to the Senate at the Senate's request, and by the Senate it was rejected. Another bill was reported in the Senate, without the provision requiring the consent of the States to branches, was discussed for six weeks or two months, and then could not pass even a Whig Senate. Here was the origin of distrust, disunion, and resentment.

I will not pursue the unhappy narrative of the latter part of the session of 1841. Men had begun to grow excited and angry and resentful. I expressed the opinion, at an early period, to all those to whom I was entitled to speak, that it would be a great deal better to forbear further action at present. That opinion, as expressed to the two Whig Senators from Massachusetts, is before the public. I wished Congress to give time for consultation to take place, for harmony to be restored; because I looked for no good, except from the united and harmonious action of all the branches of the Whig government. I suppose that counsel was not good, certainly it was not followed. I need not add the comment.

This brings us, as far as concerns the questions of currency, to the last session of Congress. Early in that session the Secretary of the Treasury sent in a plan of an exchequer. It met with little favor in either House, and therefore it is necessary for me, Gentlemen, lest the whole burden fall on others, to say that it had my hearty, sincere, and entire approbation. Gentlemen, I hope that I have not manifested through my public life a very overweening confidence in my own judgment, or a very unreasonable unwillingness to accept the views of others. But there are some subjects on which I feel entitled to pay some respect to my own opinion. The subject of currency, Gentlemen, has been the study of my life. Thirty years ago, a little before my entrance into the House of Representatives, the questions connected with a mixed currency, involving the proper relation of paper to specie, and the proper means of restricting an excessive issue of paper, came to be discussed by the most acute and well-disciplined understandings in England in Parliament. At that time, during the suspension of specie payments by the bank, when paper was fifteen per cent below par, Mr. Vansittart had presented his celebrated resolution, declaring that a bank-note was still worth the value expressed on its face; that the bank note had not depreciated, but that the price of bullion had risen. Lord Liverpool and Lord Castlereagh espoused this view, as we know, and it was opposed by the close reasoning of Huskisson, the powerful logic of Horner, and the practical sagacity and common sense of Alexander Baring, now Lord Ashburton. The study of those debates made me a bullionist. They convinced me that paper could not circulate safely in any country, any longer than it was immediately redeemable at the place of its issue. Coming into Congress the very next year, or the next but one after, and finding the finances of the country in a most deplorable condition, I then and ever after devoted myself, in preference to all other public topics, to the consideration of the questions relating to them. I believe I have read every thing of value that has been published since on those questions, on either side of the Atlantic. I have studied by close observation the laws of paper currency, as they have exhibited themselves in this and in other countries, from 1811 down to the present time. I have expressed my opinions at various times in Congress, and some of the predictions which I have made have not been altogether falsified by subsequent events. I must therefore be permitted, Gentlemen, without yielding to any flippant newspaper paragraph, or to the hasty ebullitions of debate in a public assembly, to say, that I believe the plan for an exchequer, as presented to Congress at its last session, is the *best* measure, the *only* measure for the adoption of Congress and the trial of the people. I am ready to stake my reputation upon it, and that is all that I have to stake. I am ready to stake my reputation, that, if this Whig Congress will take that measure and give it a fair trial, within three years it will be admitted by the whole American people to be the most beneficial measure of any sort ever adopted in this country, the Constitution only excepted.

I mean that they should take it as it was when it came from the Cabinet, not as it looked when the committees of Congress had laid their hands upon it. For when the committees of Congress had struck out the proviso respecting exchange, it was not worth a rush; it was not worth the parchment it would be engrossed upon. The great desire of this country is a general currency, a facility of exchange; a currency which shall be the same for you and for the people of Alabama and Louisiana, and a system of exchange which shall equalize credit between them and you, with the rapidity and facility with which steam conveys men and merchandise. That is what the country wants, what you want; and you have not got it. You have not got it, you cannot get it, but by some adequate provision of government. Exchange, ready exchange, that will enable a man to turn his Orleans means into money to-day, (as we have had in better times millions a year exchanged, at only three quarters of one per cent,) is what is wanted How are we to obtain this? A Bank of the United States founded on a private subscription is out of the question. That is an obsolete idea. The country and the condition of things have changed. Suppose that a bank were chartered with a capital of fifty millions, to be raised by private subscription. Would it not be out of all possibility to find the money? Who would subscribe? What would you get for shares? And as for the local discount, do you wish it? Do you, in State Street, wish that the nation should send millions of untaxed banking capital hither to increase your discounts? What, then, shall we do? People who are waiting for power to make a Bank of the United States may as well postpone all attempts to benefit the country to the incoming of the Jews.

What, then, shall we do? Let us turn to this plan of the exchequer, brought forward last year. It was assailed from all quarters. One gentleman did say, I believe, that by some possibility some good might come out of it, but in general it met with a different opposition from every different class. Some said it would be a perfectly lifeless machine,--that it was no system at all,--that it would do nothing, for good or evil; others thought that it had a great deal too much vitality, admitting that it would answer the purpose perfectly well for which it was designed, but fearing that it would increase the executive power: thus making it at once King Log and King Serpent. One party called it a ridiculous imbecility; the other, a dangerous giant, that might subvert the Constitution. These varied arguments, contradicting, if not refuting, one another, convinced me of one thing at least,--that the bill would not be adopted, nor even temperately and candidly considered. And it was not. In a manner quite unusual, it was discussed, assailed, denounced, before it was allowed to take the course of reference and examination.

The difficulties we meet in carrying out our system of constitutional government are indeed extraordinary. The Constitution was intended as an instrument of great political good; but we sometimes so dispute its meaning, that we cannot use it at all. One man will not have a bank, without the power of local discount, against the consent of the States; for that, he insists, would break the Constitution. Another will not have a bank with such a power, because he thinks that would break the Constitution. A third will not have an exchequer, with authority to deal in exchanges, because that would increase executive influence, and so might break the Constitution. And between them all, we are like the boatman who, in the midst of rocks and currents and whirlpools, will not pull one stroke for safety, lest he break his oar. Are we now looking for the time when we can charter a United States Bank with a large private subscription? When will that be? When confidence is restored. Are we, then, to do nothing to save the vessel from sinking, till the chances of the winds and waves have landed us on the shore? He is more sanguine than I am, who thinks that the time will soon come when the Whigs have more power to work effectually for the good of the country than they now have. The voice of patriotism calls upon them not to postpone, but to act at this moment, at the very next session; to make the best of their means, and to try. You say that the administration is responsible; why not, then, try the plan it has recommended. If it fails, let the President bear the responsibility. If you will not try this plan, why not propose something else?

Gentlemen, in speaking of events that have happened, I ought to say, and will, since I am making a full and free communication, that there is no one of my age, and I am no longer very young, who has written or spoken more against the abuse and indiscreet use of the veto power than I have. And there is no one whose opinions upon this subject are less changed. I presume it is universally known, that I have advised against the use of the veto power on every occasion when it has been used since I have been in the Cabinet. But I am, nevertheless, not willing to join those who seem more desirous to make out a case against the President, than of serving their country to the extent of their ability, vetoes notwithstanding. Indeed, at the close of the extra session, the received doctrine of many seemed to be, that they would undertake nothing until they could amend the Constitution so as to do away with this power. This was mere mockery. If we were now reforming the Constitution, we might wish for some, I do not say what, guards and restraints upon this power more than the Constitution at present contains; but no convention would recommend striking it out altogether. Have not the people of New York lately amended their constitution, so as to require, in certain legislative action, votes of two thirds? and is not this same restriction in daily use in the national House of Representatives itself, in the case of suspension of the rules? This constitutional power, therefore, is no greater a restraint than this body imposes on itself. But it is utterly hopeless to look for such an amendment; who expects to live to see its day? And to give up all practical efforts, and to go on with a general idea that the Constitution must be amended before anything can be done, was, I will not say trifling, but treating the great necessities of the people as of quite too little importance. This Congress accomplished, in this regard, nothing for the people. The exchequer plan which was submitted to it will accomplish some of the objects of the people, and especially the Whig people. I am confident of it; I know it. When a mechanic makes a tool, an axe, a saw, or a plane, and knows that the temper is good and the parts are well proportioned, he knows that it will answer its purpose. And I know that this plan will answer its purpose.

There are other objects which ought not to be neglected, among which is one of such importance that I will not now pass it by; I mean, the mortifying state of the public credit of this country at this time. I cannot help thinking, that if the statesmen of a former age were among us, if Washington were here, if John Adams, and Hamilton, and Madison were here, they would be deeply concerned and soberly thoughtful about the present state of the public credit of the country. In the position I fill, it becomes my duty to read, generally with pleasure, but sometimes with pain, communications from our public agents abroad. It is distressing to hear them speak of *their* distress at what they see and hear of the scorn and contumely with which the American character and American credit are treated abroad. Why, at this very time, we have a loan in the market, which, at the present rate of money and credit, ought to command in Europe one hundred and twenty-five per cent. Can we sell a dollar of it? And how is it with the credit of our own Commonwealth? Does it not find itself affected in its credit by the general state of the credit of the country? Is there nobody ready to make a movement in this matter? Is there not a man in our councils large enough, comprehensive enough in his views, to undertake at least to *present* this case before the American people, and thus do something to restore the public character for morals and honesty?

There are in the country some men who are indiscreet enough to talk of _repudiation_,--to advise their fellow-citizens to *repudiate* public debt. Does repudiation pay a debt? Does it discharge the debtor? Can it so modify a debt that it shall not be always binding, in law as well as in morals? No, Gentlemen; repudiation does nothing but add a sort of disrepute to acknowledged inability. It is our duty, so far as is in our power, to rouse the public feeling on the subject; to maintain and assert the universal principles of law and justice, and the importance of preserving public faith and credit. People say that the intelligent capitalists of Europe ought to distinguish between the United States government and the State governments. So they ought; but, Gentlemen, what does all this amount to? Does not the general government comprise the same people who make up the State governments? May not these Europeans ask us how long it may be before the national councils will repudiate public obligations?

The doctrine of repudiation has inflicted upon us a stain which we ought to feel worse than a wound; and the time has come when every man ought to address himself soberly and seriously to the correction of this great existing evil. I do not undertake to say what the Constitution allows Congress to do in the premises. I will only say, that if that great fund of the public domain properly and in equity belongs, as is maintained, to the States themselves, there are some means, by regular and constitutional laws, to enable and induce the States to save their own credit and the credit of the country.

Gentlemen, I have detained you much too long. I have wished to say, that, in my judgment, there remain certain important objects to engage our public and private attention, in the national affairs of the country. These are, the settlement of the remaining questions between ourselves and England; the great questions relating to the reciprocity principle; those relating to colonial trade; the most absorbing questions of the currency, and those relating to the great subject of the restoration of the national character and the public faith; these are all objects to which I am willing to devote myself, both in public and in private life. I do not expect that much of public service remains to be done by me; but I am ready, for the promotion of these objects, to act with sober men of any party, and of all parties. I am ready to act with men who are free from that great danger that surrounds all men of all parties,--the danger that patriotism itself, warmed and heated in party contests, will run into partisanship. I believe that, among the sober men of this country, there is a growing desire for more moderation of party feeling, more predominance of purely public considerations, more honest and general union of well-meaning men of all sides to uphold the institutions of the country and carry them forward.

In the pursuit of these objects, in public life or in a private station, I am willing to perform the part assigned to me, and to give them, with hearty good-will and zealous effort, all that may remain to me of strength and life.

[Footnote 1: The office of Representative in Congress.][Footnote 2: Lord Ashburton.]
[Footnote 3: Mr. Edward Everett.][Footnote 4: Mr. Andrew Stevenson.][Footnote 5: Mr. Parmenter.][Footnote 6: Mr. R.C. Winthrop.]

THE LANDING AT PLYMOUTH.
A SPEECH DELIVERED ON THE 22d OF DECEMBER, 1843, AT THE PUBLIC DINNER OF THE NEW ENGLAND SOCIETY OF NEW YORK, IN COMMEMORATION OF THE LANDING OF THE PILGRIMS.

[The great Pilgrim festival was celebrated on the 22d of December, 1843, by the New England Society of New York, with uncommon spirit and success. A commemorative oration was delivered in the morning by Hon. Rufus Choate, in a style of eloquence rarely equalled. The public dinner of the Society, at the Astor House, at which M.H. Grinnell, Esq. presided, was attended by a very large company, composed of the members of the Society and their invited guests. Several appropriate toasts having been given and responded to by the distinguished individuals present, George Griswold, Esq. rose to offer one in honor of Mr. Webster. After a few remarks complimentary to that gentleman, in reference to his services in refuting the doctrine of nullification and in averting the danger of war by the treaty of Washington, Mr. Griswold gave the following toast:--
"DANIEL WEBSTER,--the gift of New England to his country, his whole country, and nothing but his country."
This was received with great applause, and on rising to respond to it Mr. Webster was greeted with nine enthusiastic cheers, and the most hearty and prolonged approbation. When silence was restored, he spoke as follows.]
MR. PRESIDENT:--I have a grateful duty to perform in acknowledging the kindness of the sentiment thus expressed towards me. And yet I must say, Gentlemen, that I rise upon this occasion under a consciousness that I may probably disappoint highly raised, too highly raised expectations. In the scenes of this evening, and in the scene of this day, my part is an humble one. I can enter into no competition with the fresher geniuses of those more eloquent gentlemen, learned and reverend, who have addressed this Society. I may perform, however, the humbler, but sometimes useful, duty of contrast, by adding the dark ground of the picture, which shall serve to bring out the more brilliant colors.
I must receive, Gentlemen, the sentiment proposed by the worthy and distinguished citizen of New York before me, as intended to convey the idea that, as a citizen of New England, as a son, a child, a *creation* of New England, I may be yet supposed to entertain, in some degree, that enlarged view of my duty as a citizen of the United States and as a public man, which may, in some small measure, commend me to the regard of the whole country. While I am free to confess, Gentlemen, that there is no compliment of which I am more desirous to be thought worthy, I will add, that a compliment of that kind could have proceeded from no source more agreeable to my own feelings than from the gentleman who has proposed it,--an eminent merchant, the member of a body of eminent merchants, known throughout the world for their intelligence and enterprise. I the more especially feel this, Gentlemen, because, whether I view the present state of things or recur to the history of the past, I can in neither case be ignorant how much that profession, and its distinguished members, from an early day of our history, have contributed to make the country what it is, and the government what it is.
Gentlemen, the free nature of our institutions, and the popular form of those governments which have come down to us from the Rock of Plymouth, give scope to intelligence, to talent, enterprise, and public spirit, from all classes making up the great body of the community. And the country has received benefit in all its history and in all its exigencies, of the most eminent and striking character, from persons of the class to which my friend before me belongs. Who will ever forget that the first name signed to our ever-memorable and ever-glorious Declaration of Independence is the name of John Hancock, a merchant of Boston? Who will ever forget that, in the most disastrous days of the Revolution, when the treasury of the country was bankrupt, with unpaid navies and starving armies, it was a merchant,--Robert Morris of Philadelphia,--who, by a noble sacrifice of his own fortune, as well as by the exercise of his great financial abilities, sustained and supported the wise men of the country in council, and the brave men of the country in the field of battle? Nor are there wanting more recent instances. I have the pleasure to see near me, and near my friend who proposed this sentiment, the son of an eminent merchant of New England (Mr. Goodhue), an early member of the Senate of the United States, always consulted, always respected, in whatever belonged to the duty and the means of putting in operation the financial and commercial system of the country; and this mention of the father of my friend brings to my mind the memory of his great colleague, the early associate of Hamilton and of Ames, trusted and beloved by Washington, consulted on

all occasions connected with the administration of the finances, the establishment of the treasury department, the imposition of the first rates of duty, and with every thing that belonged to the commercial system of the United States,--George Cabot, of Massachusetts.

I will take this occasion to say, Gentlemen, that there is no truth better developed and established in the history of the United States, from the formation of the Constitution to the present time, than this,--that the mercantile classes, the great commercial masses of the country, whose affairs connect them strongly with every State in the Union and with all the nations of the earth, whose business and profession give a sort of nationality to their character,--that no class of men among us, from the beginning, have shown a stronger and firmer devotion to whatsoever has been designed, or to whatever has tended, to preserve the union of these States and the stability of the free government under which we live. The Constitution of the United States, in regard to the various municipal regulations and local interests, has left the States individual, disconnected, isolated. It has left them their own codes of criminal law; it has left them their own system of municipal regulations. But there was one great interest, one great concern, which, from the very nature of the case, was no longer to be left under the regulations of the then thirteen, afterwards twenty, and now twenty-six States, but was committed, necessarily committed, to the care, the protection, and the regulation of one government; and this was that great unit, as it has been called, the commerce of the United States. There is no commerce of New York, no commerce of Massachusetts, none of Georgia, none of Alabama or Louisiana. All and singular, in the aggregate and in all its parts, is the commerce of the United States, regulated at home by a uniform system of laws under the authority of the general government, and protected abroad under the flag of our government, the glorious _E Pluribus Unum_, and guarded, if need be, by the power of the general government all over the world. There is, therefore, Gentlemen, nothing more cementing, nothing that makes us more cohesive, nothing that more repels all tendencies to separation and dismemberment, than this great, this common, I may say this overwhelming interest of one commerce, one general system of trade and navigation, one everywhere and with every nation of the globe. There is no flag of any particular American State seen in the Pacific seas, or in the Baltic, or in the Indian Ocean. Who knows, or who hears, there of your proud State, or of my proud State? Who knows, or who hears, of any thing, at the extremest north or south, or at the antipodes,--in the remotest regions of the Eastern or Western Sea,--who ever hears, or knows, of any thing but an American ship, or of any American enterprise of a commercial character that does not bear the impression of the American Union with it?

It would be a presumption of which I cannot be guilty, Gentlemen, for me to imagine for a moment, that, among the gifts which New England has made to our common country, I am any thing more than one of the most inconsiderable. I readily bring to mind the great men, not only with whom I have met, but those of the generation before me, who now sleep with their fathers, distinguished in the Revolution, distinguished in the formation of the Constitution and in the early administration of the government, always and everywhere distinguished; and I shrink in just and conscious humiliation before their established character and established renown; and all that I venture to say, and all that I venture to hope may be thought true, in the sentiment proposed, is, that, so far as mind and purpose, so far as intention and will, are concerned, I may be found among those who are capable of embracing the whole country of which they are members in a proper, comprehensive, and patriotic regard. We all know that the objects which are nearest are the objects which are dearest; family affections, neighborhood affections, social relations, these in truth are nearest and dearest to us all; but whosoever shall be able rightly to adjust the graduation of his affections, and to love his friends and his neighbors, and his country, as he ought to love them, merits the commendation pronounced by the philosophic poet upon him

"Qui didicit patriae quid debeat, et quid amicis."

Gentlemen, it has been my fortune, in the little part which I have acted in public life, for good or for evil to the community, to be connected entirely with that government which, within the limits of constitutional power, exercises jurisdiction over all the States and all the people. My friend at the end of the table on my left has spoken pleasantly to us to-night of the reputed miracles of tutelar saints. In a sober sense, in a sense of deep conviction, I say that the emergence of this country from British domination, and its union under its present form of government beneath the general Constitution of the country, if not a miracle, is, I do not say the most, but one of the most fortunate, the most admirable, the most auspicious occurrences, which have ever fallen to the lot of man. Circumstances have wrought out for us a state of things which, in other times and other regions, philosophy has dreamed of, and theory has proposed, and speculation has suggested, but which man has never been able to accomplish. I mean the government of a great nation over a vastly extended portion of the surface of the earth, _by means of local institutions for local purposes, and general institutions for general purposes_. I know of nothing in the history of the world, notwithstanding the great league of Grecian states, notwithstanding the success of the Roman system, (and certainly there is no exception to the remark in modern history,)--I know of nothing so suitable on the whole for the great interests of a great people spread over a large portion of the globe, as the provision of local legislation for local and municipal purposes, with, not a confederacy, nor a loose binding together of separate parts, but a limited, positive general government for positive general purposes, over the whole. We may derive eminent proofs of this truth from the past and the present. What see we to-day in the agitations on the other side of the Atlantic? I speak of them, of course, without expressing any opinion on questions of politics in a foreign country; but I speak of them as an occurrence which shows the great expediency, the utility, I may say the necessity, of local legislation. If, in a country on the other side of the water (Ireland), there be some who desire a severance of one part of the empire from another, under a proposition of repeal, there are others who propose a continuance of the existing relation under a federative system: and what is this? No more, and no less, than an approximation to that system under which we live, which for local, municipal purposes shall have a local legislature, and for general purposes a general legislature.

This becomes the more important when we consider that the United States stretch over so many degrees of latitude,--that they embrace such a variety of climate,--that various conditions and relations of society naturally call for different laws and regulations. Let me ask whether the legislature of New York could wisely pass laws for the government of Louisiana, or whether the legislature of Louisiana could wisely pass laws for Pennsylvania or New York? Everybody will say, "No." And yet the interests of New York and Pennsylvania and Louisiana, in whatever concerns their relations between themselves and their general relations with all the states of the world, are found to be perfectly well provided for, and adjusted with perfect congruity, by committing these general interests to one common government, the result of popular general elections among them all.

I confess, Gentlemen, that having been, as I have said, in my humble career in public life, employed in that portion of the public service which is connected with the general government, I have contemplated, as the great object of every proceeding, not only the particular benefit of the moment, or the exigency of the occasion, but the preservation of this system; for I do consider it so much the result of circumstances, and that so much of it is due to fortunate concurrence, as well as to the sagacity of the great men acting upon those occasions,--that it is an experiment of such remarkable and renowned success,--that he is a fool or a madman who would wish to try that experiment a second time. I see to-day, and we all see, that the descendants of the Puritans who landed upon the Rock of Plymouth; the followers of Raleigh, who settled Virginia and North Carolina; he who lives where the truncheon of empire, so to speak, was borne by Smith; the inhabitants of Georgia; he who settled under the auspices of France at the mouth of the Mississippi; the Swede on the Delaware, the Quaker of Pennsylvania,--all find, at this day, their common interest, their common protection, their common _glory_, under the united government, which leaves them all, nevertheless, in the administration of their own municipal and local affairs, to be Frenchmen, or Swedes, or Quakers, or whatever they choose. And when one considers that this system of government, I will not say has produced, because God and nature and circumstances have had an agency in it,--but when it is considered that this system has not prevented, but has rather encouraged, the growth of the people of this country from three millions, on the glorious 4th of July, 1776, to seventeen millions now, who is there that will say, upon this hemisphere,--nay, who is there that will stand up in any hemisphere, who is there in any part of the world, that will say that the great experiment of a united republic has *failed* in America?

And yet I know, Gentlemen, I feel, that this united system is held together by strong tendencies to union, at the same time that it is kept from too much leaning toward consolidation by a strong tendency in the several States to support each its own power and consideration. In the physical world it is said, that
"All nature's difference keeps all nature's peace,"
and there is in the political world this same harmonious difference, this regular play of the positive and negative powers, (if I may so say,) which, at least for one glorious half-century, has kept us as we have been kept, and made us what we are.

But, Gentlemen, I must not allow myself to pursue this topic. It is a sentiment so commonly repeated by me upon all public occasions, and upon all private occasions, and everywhere, that I forbear to dwell upon it now. It is the union of these States, it is the system of government under which we live, beneath the Constitution of the United States, happily framed, wisely adopted, successfully administered for fifty years,--it is mainly this, I say, that gives us power at home and credit abroad. And, for one, I never stop to consider the power or wealth or greatness of a State. I tell you, Mr. Chairman, I care nothing for your Empire State as such. Delaware and Rhode Island are as high in my regard as New York. In population, in power, in the government over us, you have a greater share. You would have the same share if you were divided into forty States. It is not, therefore, as a State sovereignty, it is only because New York is a vast portion of the whole American people, that I regard this State, as I always shall regard her, as respectable and honorable. But among State sovereignties there is no preference; there is nothing high and nothing low; every State is independent and every State is equal. If we depart from this great principle, then are we no longer one people; but we are thrown back again upon the Confederation, and upon that state of things in which the inequality of the States produced all the evils which befell us in times past, and a thousand ill-adjusted and jarring interests.

Mr. President, I wish, then, without pursuing these thoughts, without especially attempting to produce any fervid impression by dwelling upon them, to take this occasion to answer my friend who has proposed the sentiment, and to respond to it by saying, that whoever would serve his country in this our day, with whatever degree of talent, great or small, it may have pleased the Almighty Power to give him, he cannot serve it, he will not serve it, unless he be able, at least, to extend his political designs, purposes, and objects, till they shall comprehend the whole country of which he is a servant.

Sir, I must say a word in connection with that event which we have assembled to commemorate. It has seemed fit to the dwellers in New York, New-Englanders by birth or descent, to form this society. They have formed it for the relief of the poor and distressed, and for the purpose of commemorating annually the great event of the settlement of the country from which they spring. It would be great presumption in me to go back to the scene of that settlement, or to attempt to exhibit it in any colors, after the exhibition made to-day; yet it is an event that in all time since, and in all time to come, and more in times to come than in times past, must stand out in great and striking characteristics to the admiration of the world. The sun's return to his winter solstice, in 1620, is the epoch from which he dates his first acquaintance with the small people, now one of the happiest, and destined to be one of the greatest, that his rays fall upon; and his annual visitation, from that day to this, to our frozen region, has enabled him to see that progress, _progress_, was the characteristic of that small people. He has seen them from a handful, that one of his beams coming through a key-hole might illuminate, spread over a hemisphere which he cannot enlighten under the slightest eclipse. Nor, though this globe should revolve round him for tens of hundreds of thousands of years, will he see such another incipient colonization upon any part of this attendant upon his mighty orb. What else he may see in those other planets which revolve around him we cannot tell, at least until we have tried the fifty-foot telescope which Lord Rosse is preparing for that purpose.

There is not, Gentlemen, and we may as well admit it, in any history of the past, another epoch from which so many great events have taken a turn; events which, while important to us, are equally important to the country from whence we came. The settlement of Plymouth--concurring, I always wish to be understood, with that of Virginia--was the settlement of New England by colonies of Old England. Now, Gentlemen, take these two ideas and run out the thoughts suggested by both. What has been, and what is to be, Old England? What has been, what is, and what may be, in the providence of God, _New_ England, with her neighbors and associates? I would not dwell, Gentlemen, with any particular emphasis upon the sentiment, which I nevertheless entertain, with respect to the great diversity in the races of men. I do not know how far in that respect I might not encroach on those mysteries of Providence which, while I adore, I may not comprehend; but it does seem to me to be very remarkable, that we may go back to the time when New England, or those who founded it, were _subtracted_ from Old England; and both Old England and New England went on, nevertheless, in their mighty career of progress and power.

Let me begin with New England for a moment. What has resulted, embracing, as I say, the nearly contemporaneous settlement of Virginia,--what has resulted from the planting upon this continent of two or three slender colonies from the mother country? Gentlemen, the great epitaph commemorative of the character and the worth, the discoveries and glory, of Columbus, was, that he had _given a new world to the crowns of Castile and Aragon_. Gentlemen, this is a great mistake. It does not come up at all to the great merits of Columbus. He gave the territory of the southern hemisphere to the crowns of Castile and Aragon; but as a place for the plantation of colonies, as a place for the habitation of men, as a place to which laws and religion, and manners and science, were to be transferred, as a place in which the creatures of God should multiply and fill the earth, under friendly skies and with religious hearts, he gave it to the whole world, he gave it to universal man! From this seminal principle, and from a handful, a hundred saints, blessed of God and ever honored of men, landed on the shores of Plymouth and elsewhere along the coast, united, as I have said already more than once, in the process of time, with the settlement at Jamestown, has sprung this great people of which we are a portion.

I do not reckon myself among quite the oldest of the land, and yet it so happens that very recently I recurred to an exulting speech or oration of my own, in which I spoke of my country as consisting of nine millions of people. I could hardly persuade myself that within the short time which had elapsed since that epoch our population had doubled; and that at the present moment there does exist most unquestionably as great a probability of its continued progress, in the same ratio, as has ever existed in any previous time. I do not know whose imagination is fertile enough, I do not know whose conjectures, I may almost say, are *wild* enough to tell what may be the progress of wealth and population in the United States in half a century to come. All we know is, here is a people of from seventeen to twenty millions, intelligent, educated, freeholders, freemen, republicans, possessed of all the means of modern improvement, modern science, arts, literature, with the world before them! There is nothing to check them till they touch the shores of the Pacific, and then, they are so much accustomed to water, that _that's_ a facility, and no obstruction!

So much, Gentlemen, for this branch of the English race; but what has happened, meanwhile, to England herself since the period of the departure of the Puritans from the coast of Lincolnshire, from the English Boston? Gentlemen, in speaking of the progress of English power, of English dominion and authority, from that period to the present, I shall be understood, of course, as neither entering into any defence or any accusation of the policy which has conducted her to her present state. As to the justice of her wars, the necessity of her conquests, the propriety of those acts by which she has taken possession of so great a portion of the globe, it is not the business of the present occasion to inquire. _Neque teneo, neque refello._ But I speak of them, or intend to speak of them, as facts of the most extraordinary character, unequalled in the history of any nation on the globe, and the consequences of which may and must reach through a thousand generations. The Puritans left England in the reign of James the First. England herself had then become somewhat settled and established in the Protestant faith, and in the quiet enjoyment of property, by the previous energetic, long, and prosperous reign of Elizabeth. Her successor was James the Sixth of Scotland, now become James the First of England; and here was a union of the crowns, but not of the kingdoms,--a very important distinction. Ireland was held by a military power, and one cannot but see that at that day, whatever may be true or untrue in more recent periods of her history, Ireland was held by England by the two great potencies, the power of the sword and the power of confiscation. In other respects, England was nothing like the England which we now behold. Her foreign possessions were quite inconsiderable. She had some hold on the West India Islands; she had Acadia, or Nova Scotia, which King James granted, by wholesale, for the endowment of the knights whom he created by hundreds. And what has been her progress? Did she then possess Gibraltar, the key to the Mediterranean? Did she possess a port in the Mediterranean? Was Malta hers? Were the Ionian Islands hers? Was the southern extremity of Africa, was the Cape of Good Hope, hers? Were the whole of her vast possessions in India hers? Was her great Australian empire hers? While that branch of her population which followed the western star, and under its guidance committed itself to the duty of settling, fertilizing, and peopling an unknown wilderness in the West, were pursuing their destinies, other causes, providential doubtless, were leading English power eastward and southward, in consequence and by means of her naval prowess, and the extent of her commerce, until in our day we have seen that within the Mediterranean, on the western coast and at the southern extremity of Africa, in Arabia, in hither India and farther India, she has a population *ten times* as great as that of the British Isles two centuries ago. And recently, as we have witnessed,--I will not say with how much truth and justice, policy or impolicy, I do not speak at all to the morality of the action, I only speak to the _fact_,--she has found admission into China, and has carried the Christian religion and the Protestant faith to the doors of three hundred millions of people.

It has been said that whosoever would see the Eastern world before it turns into a Western world must make his visit soon, because steamboats and omnibuses, commerce, and all the arts of Europe, are extending themselves from Egypt to Suez, from Suez to the Indian seas, and from the Indian seas all over the explored regions of the still farther East.

Now, Gentlemen. I do not know what practical views or what practical results may take place from this great expansion of the power of the two branches of Old England. It is not for me to say. I only can see, that on this continent *all* is to be _Anglo-American_ from Plymouth Rock to the Pacific seas, from the north pole to California. That is certain; and in the Eastern world, I only see that you can hardly place a finger on a map of the world and be an *inch* from an English settlement.

Gentlemen, if there be any thing in the supremacy of races, the experiment now in progress will develop it. If there be any truth in the idea, that those who issued from the great Caucasian fountain, and spread over Europe, are to react on India and on Asia, and to act on the whole Western world, it may not be for us, nor our children, nor our grandchildren, to see it, but it will be for our descendants of some generation to see the extent of that progress and dominion of the favored races.

For myself, I believe there is no limit fit to be assigned to it by the human mind, because I find at work everywhere, on both sides of the Atlantic, under various forms and degrees of restriction on the one hand, and under various degrees of motive and stimulus on the other hand, in these branches of a common race, the great principle _of the freedom of human thought, and the respectability of individual character_. I find everywhere an elevation of the character of man as man, an elevation of the individual as a component part of society. I find everywhere a rebuke of the idea, that the many are made for the few, or that government is any thing but an *agency* for mankind. And I care not beneath what zone, frozen, temperate, or torrid; I care not of what complexion, white or brown; I care not under what circumstances of climate or cultivation,--if I can find a race of men on an inhabitable spot of earth whose general sentiment it is, and whose general feeling it is, that government is made for man,--man, as a religious, moral, and social being,--and not man for government, there I know that I shall find prosperity and happiness.

Gentlemen, I forbear from these remarks. I recur with pleasure to the sentiment which I expressed at the commencement of my observations. I repeat the gratification which I feel at having been referred to on this occasion by a distinguished member of the mercantile profession; and without detaining you further, I beg to offer as a sentiment,--

"_The mercantile interest of the United States_, always and everywhere friendly to a united and free government."

Mr. Webster sat down amid loud and repeated applause; and immediately after, at the request of the President, rose and said:--#/

Gentlemen, I have the permission of the President to call your attention to the circumstance that a distinguished foreigner is at the table to-night, Mr. Aldham; a gentleman, I am happy to say, of my own hard-working profession, and a member of the English Parliament from the great city of Leeds. A traveller in the United States, in the most unostentatious manner, he has done us the honor, at the request of the Society, to be present to-night. I rise, Gentlemen, to propose his health. He is of that Old England of which I have been speaking; of that Old England with whom we had some fifty years ago rather a serious family quarrel,--terminated in a manner, I believe, not particularly disadvantageous to either of us. He will find in this, his first visit to our country, many things to remind him of his own home, and the pursuits in which he is engaged in that home. If he will go into our courts of law, he will find those who practise there referring to the same books of authority, acknowledging the same principles, discussing the same subjects which he left under discussion in Westminster Hall. If he go into our public assemblies, he will find the same rules of procedure--possibly not always quite as regularly observed--as he left behind him in that house of Parliament of which he is a member. At any rate, he will find us a branch of that great family to which he himself belongs, and I doubt not that, in his sojourn among us, in the acquaintances he may form, the notions he may naturally imbibe, he will go home to his own country somewhat better satisfied with what he has seen and learned on this side of the Atlantic, and somewhat more convinced of the great importance to both countries of preserving the peace that at present subsists between them. I propose to you, Gentlemen, the health of Mr. Aldham.

Mr. Aldham rose and said:--"Mr. President and Gentlemen of the New England Society, I little expected to be called on to take a part in the proceedings of this evening; but I am very happy in being afforded an opportunity of expressing my grateful acknowledgments for the very cordial hospitality which you have extended to me, and the very agreeable intellectual treat with which I have been favored this evening. It was with no little astonishment that I listened to the terms in which I was introduced to you by a gentleman whom I so much honor (Mr. Webster). The kind and friendly terms in which he referred to me were, indeed, quite unmerited by their humble object, and nothing, indeed, could have been more inappropriate. It is impossible for any stranger to witness such a scene as this without the greatest interest. It is the celebration of an event which already stands recorded as one of the most interesting and momentous occurrences which ever took place in the annals of our race. And an Englishman especially cannot but experience the deepest emotion as he regards such a scene. Every thing which he sees, every emblem employed in this celebration, many of the topics introduced, remind him most impressively of that community of ancestry which exists between his own countrymen and that great race which peoples this continent, and which, in enterprise, ingenuity, and commercial activity,--in all the elements indeed of a great and prosperous nation,--is certainly not exceeded, perhaps not equalled, by any other nation on the face of the globe. Gentlemen, I again thank you for the honor you have done me, and conclude by expressing the hope that the event may continue to be celebrated in the manner which its importance and interest merit."

Mr. Aldham sat down amid great applause.

THE CHRISTIAN MINISTRY AND THE RELIGIOUS INSTRUCTION OF THE YOUNG.
A SPEECH DELIVERED IN THE SUPREME COURT AT WASHINGTON, ON THE 20TH OF FEBRUARY, 1844, IN THE GIRARD WILL CASE.

[The heirs at law of the late Stephen Girard, of Philadelphia, instituted a suit in October, 1836, in the Circuit Court of the Eastern District of Pennsylvania, sitting as a court of equity, to try the question of the validity of his will. In April, 1841, the cause came on for hearing in the Circuit Court, and was decided in favor of the will. The case was carried by appeal to the Supreme Court of the United States, at Washington, where it was argued by General Jones and Mr. Webster for the complainants and appellants, and by Messrs. Binney and Sergeant for the validity of the will.

The following speech was made by Mr. Webster in the course of the trial at Washington. A deep impression was produced upon the public mind by those portions of it which enforced the intimate connection of the Christian ministry with the business of instruction, and the necessity of founding education on a religious basis.

This impression resulted in the following correspondence:--

"_Washington, February 13, 1844._

"SIR,--Enclosed is a copy of certain proceedings of a meeting held in reference to your argument in the Supreme Court of the case arising out of the late Mr. Girard's will. In communicating to you the request contained in the second resolution, we take leave to express our earnest hope that you may find it convenient to comply with that request.

"We are, Sir, with high consideration, yours, very respectfully,

"P.R. FENDALL, } HORACE STRINGFELLOW,} JOSHUA N. DANFORTH, } R.R. GURLEY, } WILLIAM RUGGLES, } _Committee._ JOEL S. BACON, } THOMAS SEWALL, } WILLIAM B. EDWARDS, }

"HON. DANIEL WEBSTER."

"At a meeting of a number of citizens, belonging to different religious denominations, of Washington and its vicinity, convened to consider the expediency of procuring the publication of so much of Mr. Webster's argument before the Supreme Court of the United States, in the case of François F. Vidal et al., Appellants, v. The Mayor, Aldermen, and Citizens of Philadelphia, and Stephen Girard's Executors, as relates to that part of Mr. Girard's will which excludes ministers of religion from any station or duty in the college directed by the testator to be founded, and denies to them the right of visiting said college; the object of the meeting having been stated by Professor Sewall in a few appropriate remarks, the Hon. Henry L. Ellsworth was elected chairman, and the Rev. Isaac S. Tinsley secretary.

"Whereupon it was, on motion, unanimously resolved,

"1st. That, in the opinion of this meeting, the powerful and eloquent argument of Mr. Webster, on the before-mentioned clause of Mr. Girard's will, demonstrates the vital importance of Christianity to the success of our free institutions, and its necessity as the basis of all useful moral education; and that the general diffusion of that argument among the people of the United States is a matter of deep public interest.

"2d. That a committee of eight persons, of the several Christian denominations represented in this meeting, be appointed to wait on Mr. Webster, and, in the name and on behalf of this meeting, to request him to prepare for the press the portion referred to of his argument in the Girard case; and, should he consent to do so, to cause it to be speedily published and extensively disseminated.

"The following gentlemen were appointed the committee under the second resolution: Philip R. Fendall, Esq., Rev. Horace Stringfellow, Rev. Joshua N. Danforth, Rev. R. Randolph Gurley, Professor William Ruggles, Rev. President J.S. Bacon, Doctor Thomas Sewall, Rev. William B. Edwards.

"The meeting then adjourned.

"H.L. ELLSWORTH, *Chairman* "ISAAC S. TINSLEY, *Secretary*."

"_Washington, February 13, 1844._

"GENTLEMEN,--I have the honor to acknowledge the receipt of your communication. Gentlemen connected with the public press have, I believe, reported my speech in the case arising under Mr. Girard's will. I will look over the report of that part of it to which you refer, so far as to see that it is free from material errors, but I have not leisure so to revise it as to give it the form of a careful or regular composition.

"I am, Gentlemen, with very true regard, your obedient servant,

"DANIEL WEBSTER.

"To Messrs. P.R. FENDALL, HORACE STRINGFELLOW, JOSHUA N. DANFORTH, R.R. GURLEY, WILLIAM RUGGLES, JOEL S. BACON, THOMAS SEWALL, WILLIAM B. EDWARDS."]

The following mottoes were prefixed to this speech, in the original pamphlet edition.

"_Socrates._ If, then, you wish public measures to be right and noble, *virtue* must be given by you to the citizens.

"_Alcibiades._ How could any one deny that?

"_Socrates._ _Virtue_, therefore, is that which is to be first possessed, both by you and by every other person who would have direction and care, not only for himself and things dear to himself, but for the state and things dear to the state.

"_Alcibiades._ You speak truly.

"_Socrates._ To act justly and wisely (both you and the state), YOU MUST ACT ACCORDING TO THE WILL OF GOD.

"_Alcibiades._ It is so."--_Plato._

"Sic igitur hoc a principio persuasum civibus, dominos esse omnium rerum ac moderatores, deos."--_Cicero de Legibus._

"We shall never be such fools as to call in an enemy to the substance of any system, to supply its defects, or to perfect its construction."

"If our religious tenets should ever want a further elucidation, we shall not call on atheism to explain them. We shall not light up our temple from that unhallowed fire."

"We know, and it is our pride to know, that man is, by his constitution, a religious animal."--_Burke._

MAY IT PLEASE YOUR HONORS:--

It is not necessary for me to narrate, in detail, the numerous provisions of Mr. Girard's will. This has already been repeatedly done by other counsel, and I shall content myself with stating and considering those parts only which are immediately involved in the decision of this cause.

The will is drawn with apparent care and method, and is regularly divided into clauses. The first nineteen clauses contain various devises and legacies to relatives, to other private individuals and to public bodies. By the twentieth clause the whole residue of his estate, real and personal, is devised and bequeathed to the "mayor, aldermen, and citizens of Philadelphia," in trust for the several uses to be after mentioned and declared.

The twenty-first clause contains the devise or bequest to the college, in these words:--

"And so far as regards the residue of my personal estate in trust, as to two millions of dollars, part thereof, to apply and expend so much of that sum as may be necessary in erecting, as soon as practicably may be, in the centre of my square of ground, between High and Chestnut Streets, and Eleventh and Twelfth Streets, in the city of Philadelphia, (which square of ground I hereby devote for the purpose hereinafter stated, and for no other, for ever,) a permanent college, with suitable out-buildings sufficiently spacious for the residence and accommodation of at least three hundred scholars, and the requisite teachers and other persons necessary in such an institution as I direct to be established, and in supplying the said college and out-buildings with decent and suitable furniture, as well as books, and all things needful to carry into effect my general design."

The testator then proceeds to direct that the college shall be constructed of the most durable materials, avoiding needless ornament, and attending chiefly to the strength, convenience, and neatness of the whole; and gives directions, very much in detail, respecting the form of the building, and the size and fashion of the rooms. The whole square, he directs, shall be enclosed with a solid wall, at least fourteen inches thick and ten feet high, capped with marble, and guarded with irons on the top, so as to prevent persons from getting over; and there are to be two places of entrance into the square, with two gates at each, one opening inward and the other outward, those opening inward to be of iron, and those opening outward to be of wood-work, lined with sheet-iron.

The testator then proceeds to give his directions respecting the institution, laying down his plan and objects in several articles. The third article is in these words:--

"3. As many poor white male orphans, between the ages of six and ten years, as the said income shall be adequate to maintain, shall be introduced into the college as soon as possible; and from time to time, as there may be vacancies, or as increased ability from income may warrant, others shall be introduced."

The fifth direction is as follows:--

"5. No orphan should be admitted until the guardians, or directors of the poor, or a proper guardian or other competent authority, shall have given, by indenture, relinquishment, or otherwise, adequate power to the mayor, aldermen, and citizens of Philadelphia, or to directors or others by them appointed, to enforce, in relation to each orphan, every proper restraint, and to prevent relations or others from interfering with or withdrawing such orphan from the institution."

By the sixth article, or direction, preference is to be given, first, to orphans born in Philadelphia; second, to those born in other parts of Pennsylvania; third, to those born in the city of New York; and, lastly, to those born in the city of New Orleans.

By the seventh article, it is declared, that the orphans shall be lodged, fed, and clothed in the college; that they shall be instructed in the various branches of a sound education, comprehending reading, writing, grammar, arithmetic, geography, navigation, surveying, practical mathematics, astronomy, natural, chemical, and experimental philosophy, and the French and Spanish languages, and such other learning and science as the capacities of the scholars may merit or want. The Greek and Latin languages are not forbidden, but are not recommended.

By the ninth article it is declared, that the boys shall remain in the college till they arrive at between fourteen and eighteen years of age, when they shall be bound out by the city government to suitable occupations, such as agriculture, navigation, and the mechanical trades.

The testator proceeds to say, that he necessarily leaves many details to the city government; and then adds, "There are, however, some restrictions which I consider it my duty to prescribe, and to be, amongst others, conditions on which my bequest for said college is made, and to be enjoyed."

The second of these restrictions is in the following words:--

"Secondly. I enjoin and require _that no ecclesiastic, missionary, or minister, of any sect whatever, shall ever hold or exercise any station or duty whatever in the said college; nor shall any such person ever be admitted for any purpose, or as a visitor, within the premises appropriated to the purposes of the said college_.

"In making this restriction, I do not mean to cast any reflection upon any sect or person whatsoever; but, as there is such a diversity of opinion amongst them, I desire to keep the tender minds of the orphans who are to derive advantage from this bequest free from the excitement which clashing doctrines and sectarian controversy are so apt to produce; my desire is, that all the instructors and teachers in the college shall take pains to instil into the minds of the scholars _the purest principles of morality_, so that on their entrance into active life they may, *from inclination* and habit, evince _benevolence towards their fellow-creatures, and a love of truth, sobriety, and industry_, adopting at the same time such religious tenets as their *matured reason* may enable them to prefer."

The testator having, after the date of his will, bought a house in Penn Township, with forty-five acres of land, he made a codicil, by which he directed the college to be built on this estate, instead of the square mentioned in the will, and the whole establishment to be made thereon, just as if he had in his will devoted the estate to that purpose. The city government has accordingly been advised that the whole forty-five acres must be enclosed with the same high wall as was provided in the will for the square in the city.

I have now stated, I believe, all the provisions of the will which are material to the discussion of that part of the case which respects the character of the institution.

The first question is, whether this devise can be sustained, otherwise than as a charity, and by that special aid and assistance by which courts of equity support gifts to charitable uses.

If the devise be a good limitation at law, if it require no exercise of the favor which is bestowed on privileged testaments, then there is already an end to the question. But I take it that this point is conceded. The devise is void, according to the general rules of law, on account of the uncertainty in the description of those who are intended to receive its benefits.

"Poor white male orphan children" is so loose a description, that no one can bring himself within the terms of the bequest, so as to say that it was made in his favor. No individual can acquire any right or interest; nobody, therefore, can come forward as a party, in a court of law, to claim participation in the gift. The bequest must stand, if it stand at all, on the peculiar rules which equitable jurisprudence applies to charities. This is clear.

I proceed, therefore, to submit, and most conscientiously to argue, a question, certainly one of the highest which this court has ever been called upon to consider, and one of the highest, and most important, in my opinion, ever likely to come before it. That question is, _whether, in the eye of equitable jurisprudence, this devise be a charity at all_. I deny that it is so. I maintain, that neither by judicial decisions nor by correct reasoning on general principles can this devise or bequest be regarded as a charity. This part of the argument is not affected by the particular judicial system of Pennsylvania, or the question of the power of her courts to uphold and administer charitable gifts. The question which I now propose respects the inherent, essential, and manifest character of the devise itself. In this respect, I wish to express myself clearly, and to be correctly and distinctly understood. What I have said I shall stand by, and endeavor to maintain; namely, that in the view of a court of equity this devise *is no charity at all*. It is no charity, because the plan of education proposed by Mr. Girard is derogatory to the Christian religion; tends to weaken men's reverence for that religion, and their conviction of its authority and importance; and therefore, in its general character, tends to mischievous, and not to useful ends.

The proposed school is to be founded on plain and clear principles, and for plain and clear objects, of infidelity. This cannot well be doubted; and a gift, or devise, for such objects, is not a charity, and as such entitled to the well-known favor with which charities are received and upheld by the courts of Christian countries.

In the next place, the object of this bequest is against the public policy of the State of Pennsylvania, in which State Christianity is declared to be the law of the land. For that reason, therefore, as well as the other, the devise ought not to be allowed to take effect.

These are the two propositions which it is my purpose to maintain, on this part of the case.

This scheme of instruction begins by attempting to attach reproach and odium to the whole clergy of the country. It places a brand, a stigma, on every individual member of the profession, without an exception. No minister of the Gospel, of any denomination, is to be allowed to come within the grounds belonging to this school, on any occasion, or for any purpose whatever. They are all rigorously excluded, as if their mere presence might cause pestilence. We have heard it said that Mr. Girard, by this will, distributed his charity without distinction of sect or party. However that may be, Sir, he certainly has dealt out opprobrium to the whole profession of the clergy, without regard to sect or party.

By this will, no minister of the Gospel of any sect or denomination whatever can be authorized or allowed to hold any office within the college; and not only that, but no minister or clergyman of any sect can, for any purpose whatever, enter within the walls that are to surround this college. If a clergyman has a sick nephew, or a sick grandson, he cannot, upon any pretext, be allowed to visit him within the walls of the college. The provision of the will is express and decisive. Still less may a clergyman enter to offer consolation to the sick, or to unite in prayer with the dying.

Now, I will not arraign Mr. Girard or his motives for this. I will not inquire into Mr. Girard's opinions upon religion. But I feel bound to say, the occasion demands that I should say, that this is the most opprobrious, the most insulting and unmerited stigma, that ever was cast, or attempted to be cast, upon the preachers of Christianity, from north to south, from east to west, through the length and breadth of the land, in the history of the country. When have they deserved it? Where have they deserved it? How have they deserved it? They are not to be allowed even the ordinary rights of hospitality; not even to be permitted to put their foot over the threshold of this college!

Sir, I take it upon myself to say, that in no country in the world, upon either continent, can there be found a body of ministers of the Gospel who perform so much service to man, in such a full spirit of self-denial, under so little encouragement from government of any kind, and under circumstances almost always much straitened and often distressed, as the ministers of the Gospel in the United States, of all denominations. They form no part of any established order of religion; they constitute no hierarchy; they enjoy no peculiar privileges. In some of the States they are even shut out from all participation in the political rights and privileges enjoyed by their fellow-citizens. They enjoy no tithes, no public provision of any kind. Except here and there, in large cities, where a wealthy individual occasionally makes a donation for the support of public worship, what have they to depend upon? They have to depend entirely on the voluntary contributions of those who hear them.

And this body of clergymen has shown, to the honor of their own country and to the astonishment of the hierarchies of the Old World, that it is practicable in free governments to raise and sustain by voluntary contributions alone a body of clergymen, which, for devotedness to their sacred calling, for purity of life and character, for learning, intelligence, piety, and that wisdom which cometh from above, is inferior to none, and superior to most others.

I hope that our learned men have done something for the honor of our literature abroad. I hope that the courts of justice and members of the bar of this country have done something to elevate the character of the profession of the law. I hope that the discussions above (in Congress) have done something to meliorate the condition of the human race, to secure and extend the great charter of human rights, and to strengthen and advance the great principles of human liberty. But I contend that no literary efforts, no adjudications, no constitutional discussions, nothing that has been done or said in favor of the great interests of universal man, has done this country more credit, at home and abroad, than the establishment of our body of clergymen, their support by voluntary contributions, and the general excellence of their character for piety and learning.

The great truth has thus been proclaimed and proved, a truth which I believe will in time to come shake all the hierarchies of Europe, that the voluntary support of such a ministry, under free institutions, is a practicable idea.

And yet every one of these, the Christian ministers of the United States, is by this devise denied the privileges which are at the same time open to the vilest of our race; every one is shut out from this, I had almost said _sanctum_, but I will not profane that word by such a use of it.

Did a man ever live that had a respect for the Christian religion, and yet had no regard for *any one* of its ministers? Did that system of instruction ever exist, which denounced the whole body of Christian teachers, and yet called itself a system of Christianity?

The learned counsel on the other side see the weak points of this case. They are not blind. They have, with the aid of their great learning, industry, and research, gone back to the time of Constantine, they have searched the history of the Roman emperors, the Dark Ages, and the intervening period, down to the settlement of these colonies; they have explored every nook and corner of religious and Christian history, to find out the various meanings and uses of Christian charity; and yet, with all their skill and all their research, they have not been able to discover any thing which has ever been regarded as a Christian charity, that sets such an opprobrium upon the forehead of all its ministers. If, with all their endeavors, they can find any one thing which has been so regarded, _they may have their college_, and make the most of it. But the thing does not exist; it _never had a being_; history does not record it, common sense revolts at it. It certainly is not necessary for me to make an ecclesiastical argument in favor of this proposition. The thing is so plain, that it must instantly commend itself to your honors.

It has been said that Mr. Girard was charitable. I am not now going to controvert this. I hope he was. I hope he has found his reward. It has also been asked, "Cannot Mr. Girard be allowed to have his own will, to devise his property according to his own desire?" Certainly he can, in any legal devise, and the law will sustain him therein. But it is not for him to overturn the law of the land. The law cannot be altered to please Mr. Girard. He found that out, I believe, in two or three instances in his lifetime. Nor can the law be altered on account of the magnitude and munificence of the bounty. What is the value of that bounty, however great or munificent, which touches the very foundations of human society, which touches the very foundations of Christian charity, which touches the very foundations of public law, and the Constitution, and the whole welfare of the state?

And now, let me ask, What is, in contemplation of law, "a charity"? The word has various significations. In the larger and broader sense, it means the kindly exercise of the social affections, all the good feelings which man entertains towards man. Charity is love. This is that charity of which St. Paul speaks, that charity which covereth the sins of men, "that suffereth all things, hopeth all things." In a more popular sense, charity is alms-giving or active benevolence.

But the question for your honors to decide here is, What is a charity, or a charitable use, in contemplation of law? To answer this inquiry, we are generally referred to the objects enumerated in the 43d of Elizabeth. The objects enumerated in that statute, and others analogous to them, are charities in the sense of equitable jurisprudence.

There is no doubt that a school of learning is a charity. It is one of those mentioned in the statutes. Such a school of learning as was contemplated by the statutes of Elizabeth is a charity; and all such have borne that name and character to this day. I mean to confine myself to that description of charity, the statute charity, and to apply it to this case alone.

The devise before us proposes to establish, as its main object, a school of learning, a college. There are provisions, of course, for lodging, clothing, and feeding the pupils, but all this is subsidiary. The great object is the instruction of the young; although it proposes to give the children better food and clothes and lodging, and proposes that the system of education shall be somewhat better than that which is usually provided for the poor and destitute in our public institutions generally.

The main object, then, is to establish a school of learning for children, beginning with them at a very tender age, and retaining them (namely, from six years to eighteen) till they are on the verge of manhood, when they will have expended more than one third part of the average duration of human life. For if the college takes them at six, and keeps them till they are eighteen, a period of twelve years will be passed within its walls; more than a third part of the average of human life. These children, then, are to be taken almost before they learn their alphabet, and be discharged about the time that men enter on the active business of life. At six, many do not know their alphabet. John Wesley did not know a letter till after he was six years old, and his mother then took him on her lap, and taught him his alphabet at a single lesson. There are many parents who think that any attempt to instil the rudiments of education into the mind of a child at an earlier age, is little better than labor thrown away.

The great object, then, which Mr. Girard seemed to have in view, was to take these orphans at this very tender age, and to keep them within his walls until they were entering manhood. And this object I pray your honors steadily to bear in mind.

I never, in the whole course of my life, listened to any thing with more sincere delight, than to the remarks of my learned friend who opened this cause, on the nature and character of true charity. I agree with every word he said on that subject. I almost envy him his power of expressing so happily what his mind conceives so clearly and correctly. He is right when he speaks of it as an emanation from the Christian religion. He is right when he says that it has its origin in the word of God. He is right when he says that it was unknown throughout all the world till the first dawn of Christianity. He is right, pre-eminently right, in all this, as he was pre-eminently happy in his power of clothing his thoughts and feelings in appropriate forms of speech. And I maintain, that, in any institution for the instruction of youth, where the authority of God is disowned, and the duties of Christianity derided and despised, and its ministers shut out from all participation in its proceedings, there can no more be charity, true charity, found to exist, than evil can spring out of the Bible, error out of truth, or hatred and animosity come forth from the bosom of perfect love. No, Sir! No, Sir! If charity denies its birth and parentage, if it turns infidel to the great doctrines of the Christian religion, if it turns unbeliever, it is no longer charity! There is no longer charity, either in a Christian sense or in the sense of jurisprudence; for it separates itself from the fountain of its own creation. There is nothing in the history of the Christian religion; there is nothing in the history of English law, either before or after the Conquest; there can be found no such thing as a school of instruction in a Christian land, from which the Christian religion has been, of intent and purpose, rigorously and opprobriously excluded, and yet such school regarded as a charitable trust or foundation. This is the first instance on record. I do not say that there may not be charity schools in which religious instruction is not provided. I need not go that length, although I take that to be the rule of the English law. But what I do say, and repeat, is, that a school for the instruction of the young, which sedulously and reproachfully excludes Christian knowledge, is no charity, either on principle or authority, and is not, therefore, entitled to the character of a charity in a court of equity. I have considered this proposition, and am ready to stand by it.

I will not say that there may not be a charity for instruction, in which there is no positive provision for the Christian religion. But I do say, and do insist, that there is no such thing in the history of religion, no such thing in the history of human law, as a charity, a school of instruction for children, from which the

Christian religion and Christian teachers are excluded, as unsafe and unworthy intruders. Such a scheme is deprived of that which enters into the very essence of human benevolence, when that benevolence contemplates instruction, that is to say, religious knowledge, connected with human knowledge. It is this which causes it to be regarded as a charity; and by reason of this it is entitled to the special favor of the courts of law. This is the vital question which must be decided by this court. It is vital to the understanding of what the law is, it is vital to the validity of this devise.

If this be true, if there can be no charity in that plan of education which opposes Christianity, then that goes far to decide this case. I take it that this court, in looking at this subject, will see the important bearing of this point upon it. The learned counsel said that the State of Pennsylvania was not an infidel State. It is true that she is not an infidel State. She has a Christian origin, a Christian code of laws, a system of legislation founded on nothing else, in many of its important bearings upon human society, than the belief of the people of Pennsylvania, their firm and sincere belief, in the divine authority and great importance of the truths of the Christian religion. And she should the more carefully seek to preserve them pure.

Now, let us look at the condition and prospects of these tender children, who are to be submitted to this experiment of instruction without Christianity. In the first place, they are orphans, have no parents to guide or instruct them in the way in which they should go, no father, no religious mother, to lead them to the pure fount of Christianity; *they are orphans*. If they were only poor, there might be somebody bound by ties of human affection to look after their spiritual welfare; to see that they imbibed no erroneous opinions on the subject of religion; that they run into no excessive improprieties of belief as well as conduct. The child would have its father or mother to teach it to lisp the name of its Creator in prayer, or hymn His praise. But in this experimental school of instruction, if the orphans have any friends or connections able to look after their welfare, it shuts them out. It is made the duty of the governors of the institution, on taking the child, so to make out the indentures of apprenticeship as to keep him from any after interference in his welfare on the part of guardians or relatives; to keep them from withdrawing him from the school, or interfering with his instruction whilst he is in the school, in any manner whatever.

The school or college is to be surrounded by high walls; there are to be two gates in these walls, and no more; they are to be of iron within, and iron bound or covered without; thus answering more to the description of a castle than a school-house. The children are to be thus guarded for twelve years in this, I do not mean to say a prison, nor do I mean to say that this is exactly close confinement; but it is much closer confinement than ordinarily is met with, under the rules of any institution at present, and has a resemblance to the monastic institutions of past ages, rather than to any school for instruction at this period, at least in this country.

All this is to be within one great enclosure; all that is done for the bodily or mental welfare of the child is to be done within this great wall. It has been said that the children could attend public worship elsewhere. Where is the proof of this? There is no such provision in the devise; there is nothing said about it in any part of Mr. Girard's will; and I shall show presently that any such thing would be just as adverse to Mr. Girard's whole scheme, as it would be that the doctrines of Christianity should be preached within the walls of the college.

These children, then, are taken before they know the alphabet. They are kept till the period of early manhood, and then sent out into the world to enter upon its business and affairs. By this time the character will have been stamped. For if there is any truth in the Bible, if there is any truth in those oracles which soar above all human authority, or if any thing be established as a general fact, by the experience of mankind, in this first third of human life the character is formed. And what sort of a character is likely to be made by this process, this experimental system of instruction?

I have read the two provisions of Mr. Girard's will in relation to this feature of his school. The first excludes the Christian religion and all its ministers from its walls. The second explains the whole principles upon which he purposes to conduct his school. It was to try an experiment in education, never before known to the Christian world. It had been recommended often enough among those who did not belong to the Christian world. But it was never known to exist, never adopted by anybody even professing a connection with Christianity. And I cannot do better, in order to show the tendency and object of this institution, than to read from a paper by Bishop White, which has been referred to by the other side.

In order to a right understanding of what was Mr. Girard's real intention and original design, we have only to read carefully the words of the clause I have referred to. He enjoins that no ministers of religion, of any sects, shall be allowed to enter his college, on any pretence whatever. Now, it is obvious, that by sects he means Christian sects. Any of the followers of Voltaire or D'Alembert may have admission into this school whenever they please, because they are not usually spoken of as "sects." The doors are to be opened to the opposers and revilers of Christianity, in every form and shape, and shut to its supporters. While the voice of the upholders of Christianity is never to be heard within the walls, the voices of those who impugn Christianity may be raised high and loud, till they shake the marble roof of the building. It is no less derogatory thus to exclude the one, and admit the other, than it would be to make a positive provision and all the necessary arrangements for lectures and lessons and teachers, for all the details of the doctrines of infidelity. It is equally derogatory, it is the same in principle, thus to shut the door to one party, and open the door to the other.

We must reason as to the probable results of such a system according to natural consequences. They say, on the other side, that infidel teachers will not be admitted in this school. How do they know that? What is the inevitable tendency of such an education as is here prescribed? What is likely to occur? The court cannot suppose that the trustees will act in opposition to the directions of the will. If they accept the trust, they must fulfil it, and carry out the details of Mr. Girard's plan.

Now, what is likely to be the effect of this system on the minds of these children, thus left solely to its pernicious influence, with no one to care for their spiritual welfare in this world or the next? They are to be left entirely to the tender mercies of those who will try upon them this experiment of moral philosophy or philosophical morality. Morality without sentiment; benevolence towards man, without a sense of responsibility towards God; the duties of this life performed, without any reference to the life which is to come; this is Mr. Girard's theory of useful education.

Half of these poor children may die before the term of their education expires. Still, those who survive must be brought up imbued fully with the inevitable tendencies of the system.

It has been said that there may be lay preachers among them. Lay preachers! This is ridiculous enough in a country of Christianity and religion. [Here some one handed Mr. Webster a note.] A friend informs me that four of the principal religious sects in this country, the Episcopalians, Presbyterians, Methodists, and Baptists, allow no lay preachers; and these four constitute a large majority of the religious and Christian portion of the people of the United States. And, besides, lay preaching would be just as adverse to Mr. Girard's original object and whole plan as professional preaching, *provided it should be Christianity which should be preached*.

It is plain, as plain as language can be made, that he did not intend to allow the minds of these children to be troubled about religion of any kind, whilst they were within the college. And why? He himself assigns the reason. Because of the difficulty and trouble, he says, that might arise from the multitude of sects, and creeds, and teachers, and the various clashing doctrines and tenets advanced by the different preachers of Christianity. Therefore his desire as to these orphans is, that their minds should be kept free from all bias of any kind in favor of any description of Christian creed, till they arrived at manhood, and should have left the walls of his school.

Now, are not laymen equally sectarian in their views with clergymen? And would it not be just as easy to prevent sectarian doctrines from being preached by a clergyman, as from being taught by a layman? It is idle, therefore, to speak of lay preaching.

MR. SERGEANT here rose, and said that they on their side had not uttered one word about lay preaching. It was lay teaching they spoke of.

Well, I would just as soon take it that way as the other, *teaching* as preaching. Is not the teaching of laymen as sectarian as the preaching of clergymen? What is the difference between unlettered laymen and lettered clergymen in this respect? Every one knows that laymen are as violent controversialists as clergymen, and the less informed the more violent. So this, while it is a little more ridiculous, is equally obnoxious. According to my experience, a layman is just as likely to launch out into sectarian views, and to advance clashing doctrines and violent, bigoted prejudices, as a professional preacher, and even more so. Every objection to professional religious instruction applies with still greater force to lay teaching. As in other cases, so in this, the greatest degree of candor is usually found accompanying the greatest degree of knowledge. Nothing is more apt to be positive and dogmatical than ignorance.

But there is no provision in any part of Mr. Girard's will for the introduction of any lay teaching on religious matters whatever. The children are to get their religion when they leave his school, and they are to have nothing to do with religion before they do leave it. They are then to choose their religious opinions, and not before.

MR. BINNEY. "Choose their tenets" is the expression.

Tenets are opinions, I believe. The mass of one's religious tenets makes up one's religion.

Now, it is evident that Mr. Girard meant to found a school of morals, without any reference to, or connection with, religion. But, after all, there is nothing original in this plan of his. It has its origin in a deistical source, but not from the highest school of infidelity. Not from Bolingbroke, or Shaftesbury, or Gibbon; not even from Voltaire or D'Alembert. It is from two persons who were probably known to Mr. Girard in the early part of his life; it is from Mr. Thomas Paine and Mr. Volney. Mr. Thomas Paine, in his "Age of Reason," says: "Let us devise means to establish schools of instruction, that we may banish the ignorance that the ancient _régime_ of kings and priests has spread among the people. Let us propagate morality, unfettered by superstition."

MR. BINNEY. What do you get that from?

The same place that Mr. Girard got this provision of his will from, Paine's "Age of Reason." The same phraseology in effect is here. Paine disguised his real meaning, it is true. He said: "Let us devise means to establish schools to propagate morality, unfettered by *superstition*." Mr. Girard, who had no disguise about him, uses plain language to express the same meaning. In Mr. Girard's view, *religion* is just that thing which Mr. Paine calls *superstition*. "Let us establish schools of morality," said he, "unfettered by religious tenets. Let us give these children a system of pure morals before they adopt any religion." The ancient _régime_ of which Paine spoke as obnoxious was that of kings and priests. That was the popular way he had of making any thing obnoxious that he wished to destroy. Now, if he had *merely* wished to get rid of the dogmas which he says were established by kings and priests, if he had no desire to abolish the Christian religion itself, he could have thus expressed himself: "Let us rid ourselves of the errors of kings and priests, and plant morality on the plain text of the Christian religion, with the simplest forms of religious worship."

I do not intend to leave this part of the cause, however, without a still more distinct statement of the objections to this scheme of instruction. This is due, I think, to the subject and to the occasion; and I trust I shall not be considered presumptuous, or as trenching upon the duties which properly belong to another profession. But I deem it due to the cause of Christianity to take up the notions of this scheme of Mr. Girard, and show how mistaken is the idea of calling it a charity. In the first place, then, I say, this scheme is derogatory to Christianity, because it rejects Christianity from the education of youth, by rejecting its teachers, by rejecting the ordinary agencies of instilling the Christian religion into the minds of the young. I do not say that, in order to make this a charity, there should be a positive provision for the teaching of Christianity, although, as I have already observed, I take that to be the rule in an English court of equity. But I need not, in this case, claim the whole benefit of that rule. I say it is derogatory, because there is a positive rejection of Christianity; because it rejects the ordinary means and agencies of Christianity. He who rejects the ordinary means of accomplishing an end, means to defeat that end itself, or else he has no meaning. And this is true, although the means originally be means of human appointment, and not attaching to or resting on any higher authority.

For example, if the New Testament had contained a set of principles of morality and religion, without reference to the means by which those principles were to be established, and if in the course of time a system of means had sprung up, become identified with the history of the world, become general, sanctioned by continued use and custom, then he who should reject those means would design to reject, and would reject, that morality and religion themselves.

This would be true in a case where the end rested on divine authority, and human agency devised and used the means. But if the means themselves be of divine authority also, then the rejection of them is a direct rejection of that authority.

Now, I suppose there is nothing in the New Testament more clearly established by the Author of Christianity, than the appointment of a Christian ministry. The world was to be evangelized, was to be brought out of darkness into light, by the influences of the Christian religion, spread and propagated by the instrumentality of man. A Christian ministry was therefore appointed by the Author of the Christian religion himself, and it stands on the same authority as any other part of his religion. When the lost sheep of the house of Israel were to be brought to the knowledge of Christianity, the disciples were commanded to go forth into all the cities, and to preach "that the kingdom of heaven is at hand." It was added, that whosoever would not receive them, nor hear their words, it should be more tolerable for Sodom and Gomorrha than for them. And after his resurrection, in the appointment of the great mission to the whole human race, the Author of Christianity commanded his disciples that they should "go into all the world, and preach the Gospel to every creature." This was one of his last commands; and one of his last promises was the assurance, "Lo, I am with you alway, even to the end of the world!" I say, therefore, there is nothing set forth more authentically in the New Testament than the appointment of a Christian ministry; and he who does not believe this does not and cannot believe the rest.

It is true that Christian ministers, in this age of the world, are selected in different ways and different modes by different sects and denominations. But there are, still, ministers of all sects and denominations. Why should we shut our eyes to the whole history of Christianity? Is it not the preaching of ministers of the Gospel that has evangelized the more civilized part of the world? Why do we at this day enjoy the lights and benefits of Christianity ourselves? Do we not owe it to the instrumentality of the Christian ministry? The ministers of Christianity, departing from Asia Minor, traversing Asia, Africa, and Europe, to Iceland, Greenland, and the poles of the earth, suffering all things, enduring all things, hoping all things, raising men everywhere from the ignorance of idol worship to the knowledge of the true God, and everywhere bringing life and immortality to light through the Gospel, have only been acting in obedience to the Divine instruction; they were commanded to go forth, and they have gone forth, and they still go forth. They have sought, and they still seek, to be able to preach the Gospel to every creature under the whole heaven. And where was Christianity ever received, where were its truths ever poured into the human heart, where did its waters, springing up into everlasting life, ever burst forth, except in the track of a Christian ministry? Did we ever hear of an instance, does history record an instance, of any part of the globe Christianized by lay preachers, or "lay teachers"? And, descending from kingdoms and empires to cities and countries, to parishes and villages, do we not all know, that wherever Christianity has been carried, and wherever it has been taught, by human agency, that agency was the agency of ministers of the Gospel? It is all idle, and a mockery, to pretend that any man has respect for the Christian religion who yet derides, reproaches, and stigmatizes all its ministers and teachers. It is all idle, it is a mockery, and an insult to common sense, to maintain that a school for the instruction of youth, from which Christian instruction by Christian teachers is sedulously and rigorously shut out, is not deistical and infidel both in its purpose and in its tendency. I insist, therefore, that this plan of education is, in this respect, derogatory to Christianity, in opposition to it, and calculated either to subvert or to supersede it.

In the next place, this scheme of education is derogatory to Christianity, because it proceeds upon the presumption that the Christian religion is not the only true foundation, or any necessary foundation, of morals. The ground taken is, that religion is not necessary to morality, that benevolence may be insured by habit, and that all the virtues may nourish, and be safely left to the chance of flourishing, without touching the waters of the living spring of religious responsibility. With him who thinks thus, what can be the value of the Christian revelation? So the Christian world has not thought; for by that Christian world, throughout its broadest extent, it has been, and is, held as a fundamental truth, that religion is the only solid basis of morals, and that moral instruction not resting on this basis is only a building upon sand. And at what age of the Christian era have those who professed to teach the Christian religion, or to believe in its authority and importance, not insisted on the absolute necessity of inculcating its principles and its precepts upon the minds of the young? In what age, by what sect, where, when, by whom, has religious truth been excluded from the education of youth? Nowhere; never. Everywhere, and at all times, it has been, and is, regarded as essential. It is of the essence, the vitality, of useful instruction. From all this Mr. Girard dissents. His plan denies the necessity and the propriety of religious instruction as a part of the education of youth. He dissents, not only from all the sentiments of Christian mankind, from all common conviction, and from the results of all experience, but he dissents also from still higher authority, the word of God itself. My learned friend has referred, with propriety, to one of the commands of the Decalogue; but there is another, a first commandment, and that is a precept of religion, and it is in subordination to this that the moral precepts of the Decalogue are proclaimed. This first great commandment teaches man that there is one, and only one, great First Cause, one, and only one, proper object of human worship. This is the great, the ever fresh, the overflowing fountain of all revealed truth. Without it, human life is a desert, of no known termination on any side, but shut in on all sides by a dark and impenetrable horizon. Without the light of this truth, man knows nothing of his origin, and nothing of his end. And when the Decalogue was delivered to the Jews, with this great announcement and command at its head, what said the inspired lawgiver? that it should be kept from children? that it should be reserved as a communication fit only for mature age? Far, far otherwise. "And these words, which I command thee this day, shall be in thy heart. And thou shalt teach them diligently unto thy children, and shall talk of them when thou sittest in thy house, and when thou walkest by the way, when thou liest down, and when thou risest up."

There is an authority still more imposing and awful. When little children were brought into the presence of the Son of God, his disciples proposed to send them away; but he said, "Suffer little children to come unto me." Unto _me_; he did not send them first for lessons in morals to the schools of the Pharisees, or to the unbelieving Sadducees, nor to read the precepts and lessons *phylacteried* on the garments of the Jewish priesthood; he said nothing of different creeds or clashing doctrines; but he opened at once to the youthful mind the everlasting fountain of living waters, the only source of eternal truths: "Suffer little children to come *unto me*." And that injunction is of perpetual obligation. It addresses itself to-day with the same earnestness and the same authority which attended its first utterance to the Christian world. It is of force everywhere, and at all times. It extends to the ends of the earth, it will reach to the end of time, always and everywhere sounding in the ears of men, with an emphasis which no repetition can weaken, and with an authority which nothing can supersede: "Suffer little children to come unto me."

And not only my heart and my judgment, my belief and my conscience, instruct me that this great precept should be obeyed, but the idea is so sacred, the solemn thoughts connected with it so crowd upon me, it is so utterly at variance with this system of philosophical *morality* which we have heard advocated, that I stand and speak here in fear of being influenced by my feelings to exceed the proper line of my professional duty. Go thy way at this time, is the language of philosophical morality, and I will send for thee at a more convenient season. This is the language of Mr. Girard in his will. In this there is neither religion nor reason.

The earliest and the most urgent intellectual want of human nature is the knowledge of its origin, its duty, and its destiny. "Whence am I, what am I, and what is before me?" This is the cry of the human soul, so soon as it raises its contemplation above visible, material things.

When an intellectual being finds himself on this earth, as soon as the faculties of reason operate, one of the first inquiries of his mind is, "Shall I be here always?" "Shall I live here for ever?" And reasoning from what he sees daily occurring to others, he learns to a certainty that his state of being must one day be changed. I do not mean to deny, that it may be true that he is created with this consciousness; but whether it be consciousness, or the result of his reasoning faculties, man soon learns that he must die. And of all sentient beings, he alone, so far as we can judge, attains to this knowledge. His Maker has made him capable of learning this. Before he knows his origin and destiny, he knows that he is to die. Then comes that most urgent and solemn demand for light that ever proceeded, or can proceed, from the profound and anxious broodings of the human soul. It is stated, with wonderful force and beauty, in that incomparable composition, the book of Job: "For there is hope of a tree, if it be cut down, that it will sprout again, and that the tender branch thereof will not cease; that, through the scent of water, it will bud, and bring forth boughs like a plant. _But if a man die, shall he live again?_" And that question nothing but God, and the religion of God, can solve. Religion does solve it, and teaches every man that he is to live again, and that the duties of this life have reference to the life which is to come. And hence, since the introduction of Christianity, it has been the duty, as it has been the effort, of the great and the good, to sanctify human knowledge, to bring it to the fount, and to baptize learning into Christianity; to gather up all its productions, its earliest and its latest, its blossoms and its fruits, and lay them all upon the altar of religion and virtue.

Another important point involved in this question is, What becomes of the Christian Sabbath, in a school thus established? I do not mean to say that this stands exactly on the same authority as the Christian religion, but I mean to say that the observance of the Sabbath is a part of Christianity in all its forms. All Christians admit the observance of the Sabbath. All admit that there is a Lord's day, although there may be a difference in the belief as to which is the right day to be observed. Now, I say that in this institution, under Mr. Girard's scheme, the ordinary observance of the Sabbath could not take place, because the ordinary means of observing it are excluded. I know that I shall be told here, also, that lay teachers would come in again; and I say again, in reply, that, where the ordinary means of attaining an end are excluded, the intention is to exclude the end itself. There can be no Sabbath in this college, there can be no religious observance of the Lord's day; for there are no means for attaining that end. It will be said, that the children would be permitted to go out. There is nothing seen of this permission in Mr. Girard's will. And I say again, that it would be just as much opposed to Mr. Girard's whole scheme to allow these children to go out and attend places of public worship on the Sabbath day, as it would be to have ministers of religion to preach to them within the walls; because, if they go out to hear preaching, they will hear just as much about religious controversies, and clashing doctrines, and more, than if appointed preachers officiated in the college. His object, as he states, was to keep their minds free from all religious doctrines and sects, and he would just as much defeat his ends by sending them out as by having religious instruction within. Where, then, are these little children to go? Where can they go to learn the truth, to reverence the Sabbath? They are far from their friends, they have no one to accompany them to any place of worship, no one to show them the right from the wrong course; their minds must be kept clear from all bias on the subject, and they are just as far from the ordinary observance of the Sabbath as if there were no Sabbath day at all. And where there is no observance of the Christian Sabbath there will of course be no public worship of God. In connection with this subject I will observe, that there has been recently held a large convention of clergymen and laymen in Columbus, Ohio, to lead the minds of the Christian public to the importance of a more particular observance of the Christian Sabbath; and I will read, as part of my argument, an extract from their address, which bears with peculiar force upon this case.

"It is alike obvious that the Sabbath exerts its salutary power by making the population acquainted with the being, perfections, and laws of God; with our relations to him as his creatures, and our obligations to him as rational, accountable subjects, and with our character as sinners, for whom his mercy has provided a Saviour; under whose government we live to be restrained from sin and reconciled to God, and fitted by his word and spirit for the inheritance above."

"It is by the reiterated instruction and impression which the Sabbath imparts to the population of a nation, by the moral principle which it forms, by the conscience which it maintains, by the habits of method, cleanliness, and industry it creates, by the rest and renovated vigor it bestows on exhausted human nature, by the lengthened life and higher health it affords, by the holiness it inspires, and cheering hopes of heaven, and the protection and favor of God, which its observance insures, that the Sabbath is rendered the moral conservator of nations."

"The omnipresent influence the Sabbath exerts, however, by no secret charm or compendious action, upon masses of unthinking minds; but by arresting the stream of worldly thoughts, interests, and affections, stopping the din of business, unlading the mind of its cares and responsibilities, and the body of its burdens, while God speaks to men, and they attend, and hear, and fear, and learn to do his will.

"You might as well put out the sun, and think to enlighten the world with tapers, destroy the attraction of gravity, and think to wield the universe by human powers, as to extinguish the moral illumination of the Sabbath, and break this glorious main-spring of the moral government of God."

And I would ask, Would any Christian man consider it desirable for his orphan children, after his death, to find refuge within this asylum, under all the circumstances and influences which will necessarily surround its inmates? Are there, or will there be, any Christian parents who would desire that their children should be placed in this school, to be for twelve years exposed to the pernicious influences which must be brought to bear on their minds? I very much doubt if there is any Christian father who hears me this day, and I am quite sure that there is no Christian mother, who, if called upon to lie down on the bed of death, although sure to leave her children as poor as children can be left, who would not rather trust them, nevertheless, to the Christian charity of the world, however uncertain it has been said to be, than place them where their physical wants and comforts would be abundantly attended to, but away from the solaces and consolations, the hopes and the grace, of the Christian religion. She would rather trust them to the mercy and kindness of that spirit, which, when it has nothing else left, gives a cup of cold water in the name of a disciple; to that spirit which has its origin in the fountain of all good, and of which we have on record an example the most beautiful, the most touching, the most intensely affecting, that the world's history contains, I mean the offering of the poor widow, who threw her two mites into the treasury. "And he looked up, and saw the rich men casting their gifts into the treasury; and he saw also a certain poor widow casting in thither two mites. And he said, Of a truth I say unto you, that this poor widow hath cast in more than they all; for all these have, of their abundance, cast in unto the offerings of God: but she of her penury hath cast in all the living that she had." What more tender, more solemnly affecting, more profoundly pathetic, than this charity, this offering to God, of a farthing! We know nothing of her name, her family, or her tribe. We only know that she was a poor woman, and a widow, of whom there is nothing left upon record but this sublimely simple story, that, when the rich came to cast their proud offerings into the treasury, this poor woman came also, and cast in her two mites, which made a farthing! And that example, thus made the subject of divine commendation, has been read, and told, and gone abroad everywhere, and sunk deep into a hundred millions of hearts, since the commencement of the Christian era, and has done more good than could be accomplished by a thousand marble palaces, because it was charity mingled with true benevolence, given in the fear, the love, the service, and honor of God; because it was charity, that had its origin in religious feeling; because it was a gift to the honor of God!

Cases have come before the courts, of bequests, in last wills, made or given to God, without any more specific direction; and these bequests have been regarded as creating charitable uses. But can that be truly called a charity which flies in the face of all the laws of God and all the usages of Christian man? I arraign no man for mixing up a love of distinction and notoriety with his charities. I blame not Mr. Girard because he desired to raise a splendid marble palace in the neighborhood of a beautiful city, that should endure for ages, and transmit his name and fame to posterity. But his school of learning is not to be valued, because it has not the chastening influences of true religion; because it has no fragrance of the spirit of Christianity. It is not a charity, for it has not that which gives to a charity for education its chief value. It will, therefore, soothe the heart of no Christian parent, dying in poverty and distress, that those who owe to him their being may be led, and fed, and clothed by Mr. Girard's bounty, at the expense of being excluded from all the means of religious instruction afforded to other children, and shut up through the most interesting period of their lives in a seminary without religion, and with moral sentiments as cold as its own marble walls.

I now come to the consideration of the second part of this clause in the will, that is to say, the reasons assigned by Mr. Girard for making these restrictions with regard to the ministers of religion; and I say that these are much more derogatory to Christianity than the main provision itself, excluding them. He says that there are such a multitude of sects and such diversity of opinion, that he will exclude all religion and all its ministers, in order to keep the minds of the children free from clashing controversies. Now, does not this tend to subvert all belief in the utility of teaching the Christian religion to youth at all? Certainly, it is a broad and bold denial of such utility. To say that the evil resulting to youth from the differences of sects and creeds overbalances all the benefits which the best education can give them, what is this but to say that the branches of the tree of religious knowledge are so twisted, and twined, and commingled, and all run so much into and over each other, that there is therefore no remedy but to lay the axe at the root of the tree itself? It means that, and nothing less! Now, if there be any thing more derogatory to the Christian religion than this, I should like to know what it is. In all this we see the attack upon religion itself, made on its ministers, its institutions, and its diversities. And that is the objection urged by all the lower and more vulgar schools of infidelity throughout the world. In all these schools, called schools of Rationalism in Germany, Socialism in England, and by various other names in various countries which they infest, this is the universal cant. The first step of all these philosophical moralists and regenerators of the human race is to attack the agency through which religion and Christianity are administered to man. But in this there is nothing new or original. We find the same mode of attack and remark in Paine's "Age of Reason." At page 336 he says: "The Bramin, the follower of Zoroaster, the Jew, the Mahometan, the Church of Rome, the Greek Church, the Protestant Church, split into several hundred contradictory sectaries, preaching, in some instances, damnation against each other, all cry out, 'Our holy religion!'"

We find the same view in Volney's "Ruins of Empires." Mr. Volney arrays in a sort of semicircle the different and conflicting religions of the world. "And first," says he, "surrounded by a group in various fantastic dresses, that confused mixture of violet, red, white, black, and speckled garments, with heads shaved, with tonsures, or with short hairs, with red hats, square bonnets, pointed mitres, or long beards, is the standard of the Roman Pontiff. On his right you see the Greek Pontiff, and on the left are the standards of two recent chiefs (Luther and Calvin), who, shaking off a yoke that had become tyrannical, had raised altar against altar in their reform, and wrested half of Europe from the Pope. Behind these are the subaltern sects, subdivided from the principal divisions. The Nestorians, Eutychians, Jacobites, Iconoclasts, Anabaptists, Presbyterians, Wickliffites, Osiandrians, Manicheans, Pietists, Adamites, the Contemplatives, the Quakers, the Weepers, and a hundred others, all of distinct parties, persecuting when strong, tolerant when weak, hating each other in the name of the God of peace, forming such an exclusive heaven in a religion of universal charity, damning each other to pains without end in a future state, and realizing in this world the imaginary hell of the other."

Can it be doubted for an instant that sentiments like these are derogatory to the Christian religion? And yet on grounds and reasons _exactly these_, not *like* these, but EXACTLY these, Mr. Girard founds his excuse for excluding Christianity and its ministers from his school. He is a tame copyist, and has only raised marble walls to perpetuate and disseminate the principles of Paine and of Volney. It has been said that Mr. Girard was in a difficulty; that he was the judge and disposer of his own property. We have nothing to do with his difficulties. It has been said that he must have done as he did do, because there could be no agreement otherwise. Agreement? among whom? about what? He was at liberty to do what he pleased with his own. He had to consult no one as to what he should do in the matter. And if he had wished to establish such a charity as might obtain the especial favor of the courts of law, he had only to frame it on principles not hostile to the religion of the country.

But the learned gentleman went even further than this, and to an extent that I regretted; he said that there was as much dispute about the Bible as about any thing else in the world. No, thank God, that is not the case!

MR. BINNEY. The disputes about the meaning of words and passages; you will admit that?

Well, there is a dispute about the translation of certain words; but if this be true, there is just as much dispute about it out of Mr. Girard's institution as there would be in it. And if this plan is to be advocated and sustained, why does not every man keep his children from attending all places of public worship until they are over eighteen years of age? He says that a prudent parent keeps his child from the influence of sectarian doctrines, by which I suppose him to mean those tenets that are opposed to his own. Well, I do not know but what that plan is as likely to make bigots as it is to make any thing else. I grant that the mind of youth should be kept pliant, and free from all undue and erroneous influences; that it should have as much play as is consistent with prudence; but put it where it can obtain the elementary principles of religious truth; at any rate, those broad and general precepts and principles which are admitted by all Christians. But here in this scheme of Mr. Girard, all sects and all creeds are denounced. And would not a prudent father rather send his child where he could get instruction under any form of the Christian religion, than where he could get none at all? There are many instances of institutions, professing one leading creed, educating youths of different sects. The Baptist college in Rhode Island receives and educates youths of all religious sects and all beliefs. The colleges all over New England differ in certain minor points of belief, and yet that is held to be no ground for excluding youth with other forms of belief, and other religious views and sentiments.

But this objection to the multitude and differences of sects is but the old story, the old infidel argument. It is notorious that there are certain great religious truths which are admitted and believed by all Christians. All believe in the existence of a God. All believe in the immortality of the soul. All believe in the responsibility, in another world, for our conduct in this. All believe in the divine authority of the New Testament. Dr. Paley says that a single word from the New Testament shuts up the mouth of human questioning, and excludes all human reasoning. And cannot all these great truths be taught to children without their minds being perplexed with clashing doctrines and sectarian controversies? Most certainly they can.

And, to compare secular with religious matters, what would become of the organization of society, what would become of man as a social being, in connection with the social system, if we applied this mode of reasoning to him in his social relations? We have a constitutional government, about the powers, and limitations, and uses of which there is a vast amount of differences of belief. Your honors have a body of laws, now before you, in relation to which differences of opinion, almost innumerable, are daily spread before the courts; in all these we see clashing doctrines and opinions advanced daily, to as great an extent as in the religious world.

Apply the reasoning advanced by Mr. Girard to human institutions, and you will tear them all up by the root; as you would inevitably tear all divine institutions up by the root, if such reasoning is to prevail. At the meeting of the first Congress there was a doubt in the minds of many of the propriety of opening the session with prayer; and the reason assigned was, as here, the great diversity of opinion and religious belief. At length Mr. Samuel Adams, with his gray hairs hanging about his shoulders, and with an impressive venerableness now seldom to be met with, (I suppose owing to the difference of habits,) rose in that assembly, and, with the air of a perfect Puritan, said that it did not become men, professing to be Christian men, who had come together for solemn deliberation in the hour of their extremity, to say that there was so wide a difference in their religious belief, that they could not, as one man, bow the knee in prayer to the Almighty, whose advice and assistance they hoped to obtain. Independent as he was, and an enemy to all prelacy as he was known to be, he moved that the Rev. Mr. Duché, of the Episcopal Church, should address the Throne of Grace in prayer. And John Adams, in a letter to his wife, says that he never saw a more moving spectacle. Mr. Duché read the Episcopal service of the Church of England, and then, as if moved by the occasion, he broke out into extemporaneous prayer. And those men, who were then about to resort to force to obtain their rights, were moved to tears; and floods of tears, Mr. Adams says, ran down the cheeks of the pacific Quakers who formed part of that most interesting assembly. Depend upon it, where there is a spirit of Christianity, there is a spirit which rises above forms, above ceremonies, independent of sect or creed, and the controversies of clashing doctrines.

The consolations of religion can never be administered to any of these sick and dying children in this college. It is said, indeed, that a poor, dying child can be carried out beyond the walls of the school. He can be carried out to a hostelry, or hovel, and there receive those rites of the Christian religion which cannot be performed within those walls, even in his dying hour! Is not all this shocking? What a stricture is it upon this whole scheme! What an utter condemnation! A dying youth cannot receive religious solace within this seminary of learning!

But, it is asked, what could Mr. Girard have done? He could have done, as has been done in Lombardy by the Emperor of Austria, as my learned friend has informed us, where, on a large scale, the principle is established of teaching the elementary principles of the Christian religion, of enforcing human duties by divine obligations, and carefully abstaining in all cases from interfering with sects or the inculcation of sectarian doctrines. How have they done in the schools of New England? There, as far as I am acquainted with them, the great elements of Christian truth are taught in every school. The Scriptures are read, their authority taught and enforced, their evidences explained, and prayers usually offered.

The truth is, that those who really value Christianity, and believe in its importance, not only to the spiritual welfare of man, but to the safety and prosperity of human society, rejoice that in its revelations and its teachings there is so much which mounts above controversy, and stands on universal acknowledgment. While many things about it are disputed or are dark, they still plainly see its foundation, and its main pillars; and they behold in it a sacred structure, rising up to the heavens. They wish its general principles, and all its great truths, to be spread over the whole earth. But those who do not value Christianity, nor believe in its importance to society or individuals, cavil about sects and schisms, and ring monotonous changes upon the shallow and so often refuted objections founded on alleged variety of discordant creeds and clashing doctrines. I shall close this part of my argument by reading extracts from an English writer, one of the most profound thinkers of the age, a friend of reformation in the government and laws, John Foster, the friend and associate of Robert Hall. Looking forward to the abolition of the present dynasties of the Old World, and desirous to see how the order and welfare of society is to be preserved in the absence of present conservative principles, he says:--

"Undoubtedly the zealous friends of popular education account knowledge valuable absolutely, as being the apprehension of things as they are; a prevention of delusions; and so far a fitness for right volitions. But they consider religion (besides being itself the primary and infinitely the most important part of knowledge) as a principle indispensable for securing the full benefit of all the rest. It is desired, and endeavored, that the understandings of these opening minds may be taken possession of by just and solemn ideas of their relation to the Eternal Almighty Being; that they may be taught to apprehend it as an awful reality, that they are perpetually under his inspection; and, as a certainty, that they must at length appear before him in judgment, and find in another life the consequences of what they are in spirit and conduct here. It is to be impressed on them, that his will is the supreme law, that his declarations are the most momentous truth known on earth, and his favor and condemnation the greatest good and evil. Under an ascendency of this divine wisdom it is, that their discipline in any other knowledge is designed to be conducted; so that nothing in the mode of their instruction may have a tendency contrary to it, and every thing be taught in a manner recognizing the relation with it, as far as shall consist with a natural, unforced way of keeping the relation in view. Thus it is sought to be secured, that, as the pupil's mind grows stronger, and multiplies its resources, and he therefore has necessarily more power and means for what is wrong, there may be luminously presented to him, as if celestial eyes visibly beamed upon him, the most solemn ideas that can enforce what is right."

"Such is the discipline meditated for preparing the subordinate classes to pursue their individual welfare, and act their part as members of the community...."

"All this is to be taught, in many instances directly, in others by reference for confirmation, from the Holy Scriptures, from which authority will also be impressed, all the while, the principles of religion. And religion, while its grand concern is with the state of the soul towards God and eternal interests, yet takes every principle and rule of morals under its peremptory sanction; making the primary obligation and responsibility be towards God, of every thing that is a duty with respect to men. So that, with the subjects of this education, the sense of *propriety* shall be _conscience_; the consideration of how they ought to be regulated in their conduct as a part of the community shall be the recollection that their Master in heaven dictates the laws of that conduct, and will judicially hold them amenable for every part of it."

"And is not a discipline thus addressed to the purpose of fixing religious principles in ascendency, as far as that difficult object is within the power of discipline, and of infusing a salutary tincture of them into whatever else is taught, the right way to bring up citizens faithful to all that deserves fidelity in the social compact?...

"Lay hold on the myriads of juvenile spirits before they have time to grow up through ignorance, into a reckless hostility to social order; train them to sense and good morals; inculcate the principles of religion, simply and solemnly, as religion, as a thing directly of divine dictation, and not as if its authority were chiefly in virtue of human institutions; let the higher orders, generally, make it evident to the multitude that they are desirous to raise them in value, and promote their happiness; and then, *whatever* the demands of the people as a body, thus improving in understanding and sense of justice, shall come to be, and *whatever* modification their preponderance may ultimately enforce on the great social arrangements, it will be infallibly certain that there never *can* be a love of disorder, an insolent anarchy, a prevailing spirit of revenge and devastation. Such a conduct of the ascendent ranks would, in this nation at least, secure that, as long as the world lasts, there never would be any formidable commotion, or violent sudden changes. All those modifications of the national economy to which an improving people would aspire, and would deserve to obtain, would be gradually accomplished, in a manner by which no party would be wronged, and all would be the happier."[1]

I not only read this for the excellence of its sentiments and their application to the subject, but because they are the results of the profound meditations of a man who is dealing with popular ignorance. Desirous of, and expecting, a great change in the social system of the Old World, he is anxious to discover that conservative principle by which society can be kept together when crowns and mitres shall have no more influence. And he says that the only conservative principle must be, and is, RELIGION! the authority of God! his revealed will! and the influence of the teaching of the ministers of Christianity!

Mr. Webster here stated that he would, on Monday, bring forward certain references and legal points bearing on this view of the case.

The court then adjourned.

SECOND DAY.

The seven judges all took their seats at eleven o'clock, and the court was opened.

Mr. Binney observed to the court, that he had omitted to notice, in his argument, that, in regard to the statutes of Uniformity and Toleration in England, whilst the Jewish Talmuds for the propagation of Judaism alone were not sustained by those statutes, yet the Jewish Talmuds for the maintenance of the poor were sustained thereby. And the decisions show that, where a gift had for its object the maintenance and education of poor Jewish children, the statutes sustained the devise. In proof of this he quoted 1 Ambler, by Blunt, p. 228, case of De Costa, &c. Also, the case of Jacobs v. Gomperte, in the notes. Also, in the notes, 2 Swanston, p. 487, same case of De Costa, &c. Also, 7 Vesey, p. 423, case of Mo Catto v. Lucardo. Also, Sheppard, p. 107, and Boyle, p. 43.

Another case was that of a bequest given to an object abroad, and in the decision the Master of the Rolls considered that religious instruction was not a necessary part of education. See, also, the case of The Attorney-General v. The Dean and Canons of Christ Church, Jacobs, p. 485.

Mr. Binney then quoted from Noah Webster the definition of the word "tenets," to show that Mr. Webster did not give the right definition when he said that "tenets" meant "religion."

Mr. Webster then rose and said:--#/

The arguments of my learned friend, may it please your honors, in relation to the Jewish laws as tolerated by the statutes, go to maintain my very proposition; that is, that no school for the instruction of youth in any system which is in any way derogatory to the Christian religion, or for the teaching of doctrines that are in any way contrary to the Christian religion, is, or ever was, regarded as a charity by the courts. It is true that the statutes of Toleration regarded a devise for the maintenance of poor Jewish children, to give them food and raiment and lodging, as a charity. But a devise for the teaching of the Jewish religion to poor children, that should come into the Court of Chancery, would not be regarded as a charity, or entitled to any peculiar privileges from the court.

When I stated to your honors, in the course of my argument on Saturday, that all denominations of Christians had some mode or provision for the appointment of teachers of Christianity amongst them, I meant to have said something about the Quakers. Although we know that the teachers among them come into their office in a somewhat peculiar manner, yet there are preachers and teachers of Christianity provided in that peculiar body, notwithstanding its objection to the mode of appointing teachers and preachers by other Christian sects. The place or character of a Quaker preacher is an office and appointment as well known as that of a preacher among any other denomination of Christians.

I have heretofore argued to show that the Christian religion, its general principles, must ever be regarded among us as the foundation of civil society; and I have thus far confined my remarks to the tendency and effect of the scheme of Mr. Girard (if carried out) upon the Christian religion. But I will go farther, and say that this school, this scheme or system, in its tendencies and effects, is opposed to all religions, of every kind. I will not now enter into a controversy with my learned friend about the word "tenets," whether it signify opinions or dogmas, or whatever you please. Religious tenets, I take it, and I suppose it will be generally conceded, mean religious opinions; and if a youth has arrived at the age of eighteen, and has no religious tenets, it is very plain that he has no religion. I do not care whether you call them dogmas, tenets, or opinions. If the youth does not entertain dogmas, tenets, or opinions, or opinions, tenets, or dogmas, on religious subjects, then he has no religion at all. And this strikes at a broader principle than when you merely look at this school in its effect upon Christianity alone. We will suppose the case of a youth of eighteen, who has just left this school, and has gone through an education of philosophical morality, precisely in accordance with the views and expressed wishes of the donor. He comes then into the world to choose his religious tenets. The very next day, perhaps, after leaving school, he comes into a court of law to give testimony as a witness. Sir, I protest that by such a system he would be disfranchised. He is asked, "What is your religion?" His reply is, "O, I have not yet chosen any; I am going to look round, and see which suits me best." He is asked, "Are you a Christian?" He replies, "That involves religious tenets, and as yet I have not been allowed to entertain any." Again, "Do you believe in a future state of rewards and punishments?" And he answers, "That involves sectarian controversies, which have carefully been kept from me." "Do you believe in the existence of a God?" He answers, that there are clashing doctrines involved in these things, which he has been taught to have nothing to do with; that the belief in the existence of a God, being one of the first questions in religion, he is shortly about to think of that proposition. Why, Sir, it is vain to talk about the destructive tendency of such a system; to argue upon it is to insult the understanding of every man; _it is mere, sheer, low, ribald, vulgar deism and infidelity_![2] It opposes all that is in heaven, and all on earth that is worth being on earth. It destroys the connecting link between the creature and the Creator; it opposes that great system of universal benevolence and goodness that binds man to his Maker. _No religion till he is eighteen!_ What would be the condition of all our families, of all our children, if religious fathers and religious mothers were to teach their sons and daughters no religious tenets till they were eighteen? What would become of their morals, their character, their purity of heart and life, their hope for time and eternity? What would become of all those thousand ties of sweetness, benevolence, love, and Christian feeling, that now render our young men and young maidens like comely plants growing up by a streamlet's side,--the graces and the grace of opening manhood, of blossoming womanhood? What would become of all that now renders the social circle lovely and beloved? What would become of society itself? How could it exist? And is that to be considered a charity which strikes at the root of all this; which subverts all the excellence and the charms of social life; which tends to destroy the very foundation and frame-work of society, both in its practices and in its opinions; which subverts the whole decency, the whole morality, as well as the whole Christianity and government, of society? No, Sir! no, Sir!

And here let me turn to the consideration of the question, What is an oath? I do not mean in the variety of definitions that may be given to it as it existed and was practised in the time of the Romans, but an oath as it exists at present in our courts of law; as it is founded on a degree of consciousness that there is a Power above us that will reward our virtues and punish our vices. We all know that the doctrine of the English law is, that in the case of every person who enters court as a witness, be he Christian or Hindoo, there must be a firm conviction on his mind that falsehood or perjury will be punished, either in this world or the next, or he cannot be admitted as a witness. If he has not this belief, he is disfranchised. In proof of this, I refer your honors to the great case of Ormichund against Barker, in Lord Chief Justice Willes's report. There this doctrine is clearly laid down. But in no case is a man allowed to be a witness that has no belief in future rewards and punishments for virtues or vices, nor ought he to be. We hold life, liberty, and property in this country upon a system of oaths; oaths founded on a religious belief of some sort. And that system which would strike away the great substratum, destroy the safe possession of life, liberty, and property, destroy all the institutions of civil society, cannot and will not be considered as entitled to the protection of a court of equity. It has been said, on the other side, that there was no teaching *against* religion or Christianity in this system. I deny it. The whole testament is one bold proclamation against Christianity and religion of every creed. The children are to be brought up in the principles declared in that testament. They are to learn to be suspicious of Christianity and religion; to keep clear of it, that their youthful heart may not become susceptible of the influences of Christianity or religion in the slightest degree. They are to be told and taught that religion is not a matter for the heart or conscience, but for the decision of the cool judgment of mature years; that at that period when the whole Christian world deem it most desirable to instil the chastening influences of Christianity into the tender and comparatively pure mind and heart of the child, ere the cares and corruptions of the world have reached and seared it,--at that period the child in this college is to be carefully excluded therefrom, and to be told that its influence is pernicious and dangerous in the extreme. Why, the whole system is a constant preaching against Christianity and against religion, and I insist that there is no charity, and can be no charity, in that system of instruction from which Christianity is excluded. I perfectly agree with what my learned friend says in regard to the monasteries of the Old World, as seats of learning to which we are all indebted at the present day. Much of our learning, almost all of our early histories, and a vast amount of literary treasure, were preserved therein and emanated therefrom. But we all know, that although these were emphatically receptacles for literature of the highest order, yet they were always connected with Christianity, and were always regarded and conducted as religious establishments.

Going back as far as the statutes of Henry the Fourth, as early as 1402,[3] in the act respecting charities, we find that one hundred years before the Reformation, in Catholic times, in the establishment of every charitable institution, there was to be proper provision for religious instruction. Again, after the time of the Reformation, when those monastic institutions were abolished, in the 1st Edw. VI. ch. 14, we find certain *chantries* abolished, and their funds appropriated to the instruction of youth in the grammar schools founded in that reign, which Lord Eldon says extended all over the kingdom. In all these we find provision for religious instruction, the dispensation of the same being by a teacher or preacher. In 2 Swanston, p. 529, the case of the Bedford Charity, Lord Eldon gives a long opinion, in the course of which he says, that in these schools care is taken to educate youth in the Christian religion, and in all of them the New Testament is taught, both in Latin and Greek. Here, then, we find that the great and leading provision, both before and after the Reformation, was to connect the knowledge of Christianity with human letters. And it will be always found that a school for instruction of youth, to possess the privileges of a charity, must be provided with religious instruction.

For the decision, that the essentials of Christianity are part of the common law of the land, I refer your honors to 1 Vernon, p. 293, where Lord Hale, who cannot be suspected of any bigotry on this subject, says, that to decry religion, and call it a cheat, tends to destroy all religion; and he also declares Christianity to be part of the common law of the land. Mr. N. Dane, in his Abridgment, ch. 219, recognizes the same principle. In 2 Strange, p. 834, case of The King v. Wilson, the judges would not suffer it to be debated that writing against religion generally is an offence at common law. They laid stress upon the word "generally," because there might arise differences of opinion between religious writers on points of doctrine, and so forth. So in Taylor's case, 3 Merivale, p. 405, by the High Court of Chancery, these doctrines were recognized and maintained. The same doctrine is laid down in 2 Burn's Ecclesiastical Law, p. 95, Evans v. The Chamberlain of London; and in 2 Russell, p. 501, The Attorney-General v. The Earl of Mansfield.

There is a case of recent date, which, if the English law is to prevail, would seem conclusive as to the character of this devise. It is the case of The Attorney-General v. Cullum, 1 Younge and Collyer's Reports, p. 411. The case was heard and decided in 1842, by Sir Knight Bruce, Vice-Chancellor. The reporter's abstract, or summary, of the decision is this: "COURTS OF EQUITY, IN THIS COUNTRY, WILL NOT SANCTION ANY SYSTEM OF EDUCATION IN WHICH RELIGION IS NOT INCLUDED."

The charity in question in that case was established in the reign of Edward the Fourth, for the benefit of the community and poor inhabitants of the town of Bury St. Edmunds. The objects of the charity were various:

for relief of prisoners, educating and instructing poor people, for food and raiment for the aged and impotent, and others of the same kind. There were uses, also, now deemed superstitious, such as praying for the souls of the dead. In this, and in other respects, the charity required revision, to suit it to the habits and requirements of modern times; and a scheme was accordingly set forth for such revision by the master, under the direction of the court. By this scheme there were to be schools, and these schools were to be closed on Sundays, although the Scriptures were to be read daily on other days. This was objected to, and it was insisted, on the other hand, that the masters and mistresses of the schools should be members of the Church of England; that they should, on every Lord's day, give instruction in the doctrines of the Church to those children whose parents might so desire; but that all the scholars should be required to attend public worship every Lord's day in the parish church, _or other place of worship, according to their respective creeds_.

The Vice-Chancellor said, that the term "education" was properly understood, by all the parties, to comprehend religious instruction; that the objection to the scheme proposed by the master was not that it did not provide for religious instruction according to the doctrines of the Church of England, but that it did not provide for religious instruction at all. In the course of the hearing, the Vice-Chancellor said, that any scheme of education, without religion, would be worse than a mockery. The parties afterwards agreed, that the masters and mistresses should be members of the Church of England; that every school day the master should give religious instruction, during one hour, to all the scholars, _such religious instruction to be confined to the reading and explanation of the Scriptures_; that on every Lord's day he should give instruction in the liturgy, catechism, and articles of the Church of England, and that the scholars should attend church every Lord's day, *unless they were children of persons not in communion with the Church of England*. In giving the sanction of the court to this arrangement, the Vice-Chancellor said, that he wished to have it distinctly understood that the ground on which he had proceeded was not a preference of one form of religion to another, but the necessity, if the matter was left to him judicially, to adopt the course of requiring the teachers to be members of the Church of England.

This case clearly shows, that, at the present day, a school, founded by a charity, for the instruction of children, cannot be sanctioned by the courts as a charity, unless the scheme of education includes religious instruction. It shows, too, that this general requisition of the law is independent of a church establishment, and that it is not religion in any particular form, but religion, religious and Christian instruction in some form, which is held to be indispensable. It cannot be doubted how a charity for the instruction of children would fare in an English court, the scheme of which should carefully and sedulously exclude all religious or Christian instruction, and profess to establish morals on principles no higher than those of enlightened Paganism.

Enough, then, your honors, has been said on this point; and I am willing that inquiry should be prosecuted to any extent of research to controvert this position, that a school of education for the young, which rejects the Christian religion, cannot be sustained as a charity, so as to entitle it to come before the courts of equity for the privileges which they have power to confer on charitable bequests.

Mr. Webster then replied to the remarks of Mr. Binney, in relation to the Liverpool Blue Coat School, and read from the report of Mr. Bache on education in Europe, Mr. Bache having been sent abroad by the city of Philadelphia to investigate this whole matter of education.

If Mr. Girard had established such a school as that, it would have been free from all those objections that have been raised against it. This Liverpool Blue Coat School, though too much of a religious party character, is strictly a church establishment. It is a school established on a peculiar foundation, that of the Madras system of Dr. Bell. It is a monitorial school; those who are advanced in learning are to teach the others in religion, as well as secular knowledge. It is strictly a religious school, and the only objection is, that in its instruction it is too much confined to a particular sect.

Mr. Binney observed that there was no provision made for clergymen.

That is true, because the scheme of the school is monitorial, in which the more advanced scholars instruct the others. But religious instruction is amply and particularly provided for.

Mr. Webster then referred to Shelford, p. 105, and onward, under the head "Jews," in the fourth paragraph, where, he stated, the whole matter, and all the cases, as regarded the condition and position of the Jews respecting various charities, were given in full.

He then referred to the Smithsonian legacy, which had been mentioned, and which he said was no charity at all, nor any thing like a charity. It was a gift to Congress, to be disposed of as Congress saw fit, for scientific purposes.

He then replied, in a few words, to the arguments of Mr. Binney in relation to the University of Virginia; and said that, although there was no provision for religious instruction in that University, yet he supposed it would not be contended for a moment that the University of Virginia was a charity, or that it came before the courts claiming of the law of that State protection as such. It stood on its charter.

I repeat again, before closing this part of my argument, the proposition, important as I believe it to be, for your honors' consideration, that the proposed school, in its true character, objects, and tendencies, is derogatory to Christianity and religion. If it be so, then I maintain that it cannot be considered a charity, and as such entitled to the just protection and support of a court of equity. I consider this the great question for the consideration of this court. I may be excused for pressing it on the attention of your honors. It is one which, in its decision, is to influence the happiness, the temporal and the eternal welfare, of one hundred millions of human beings, alive and to be born, in this land. Its decision will give a hue to the apparent character of our institutions; it will be a comment on their spirit to the whole Christian world. I again press the question to your honors: _Is a clear, plain, positive system for the instruction of children, founded on clear and plain objects of infidelity, a charity in the eye of the law, and as such entitled to the privileges awarded to charities in a court of equity?_ And with this, I leave this part of the case.

THIRD DAY.

I shall now, may it please your honors, proceed to inquire whether there is, in the State of Pennsylvania, any settled public policy to which this school, as planned by Mr. Girard in his will, is in opposition; for it follows, that, if there be any settled public policy in the laws of Pennsylvania on this subject, then any school, or scheme, or system, which tends to subvert this public policy, cannot be entitled to the protection of a court of equity. It will not be denied that there is a general public policy in that, as in all States, drawn from its history and its laws. And it will not be denied that any scheme or school of education which directly opposes this is not to be favored by the courts. Pennsylvania is a free and independent State. She has a popular government, a system of trial by jury, of free suffrage, of vote by ballot, of alienability of property. All these form part of the general public policy of Pennsylvania. Any man who shall go into that State can speak and write as much as he pleases against a popular form of government, freedom of suffrage, trial by jury, and against any or all of the institutions just named; he may decry civil liberty, and assert the divine right of kings, and still he does nothing criminal; but if, to give success to such efforts, special power from a court of justice is required, it will not be granted to him. There is not one of these features of the general public policy of Pennsylvania against which a school might not be established and preachers and teachers employed to teach. That might in a certain sense be considered a school of education, but it would not be a charity. And if Mr. Girard, in his lifetime, had founded schools and employed teachers to preach and teach in favor of infidelity, or against popular government, free suffrage, trial by jury, or the alienability of property, there was nothing to stop him or prevent him from so doing. But where any one or all of these come to be provided for a school or system as a charity, and come before the courts for favor, then in neither one, nor all, nor any, can they be favored, because they are opposed to the general public policy and public law of the State.

These great principles have always been recognized; and they are no more part and parcel of the public law of Pennsylvania than is the Christian religion. We have in the charter of Pennsylvania, as prepared by its great founder, William Penn,--we have in his "great law," as it was called, the declaration, that the preservation of Christianity is one of the great and leading ends of government. This is declared in the charter of the State. Then the laws of Pennsylvania, the statutes against blasphemy, the violation of the Lord's day, and others to the same effect, proceed on this great, broad principle, that the preservation of Christianity is one of the main ends of government. This is the general public policy of Pennsylvania. On this head we have the case of Updegraph v. The Commonwealth,[4] in which a decision in accordance with this whole doctrine was given by the Supreme Court of Pennsylvania. The solemn opinion pronounced by that tribunal begins by a general declaration that Christianity is, and has always been, part of the common law of Pennsylvania.

I have said, your honors, that our system of oaths in all our courts, by which we hold liberty and property, and all our rights, is founded on or rests on Christianity and a religious belief. In like manner the affirmation of Quakers rests on religious scruples drawn from the same source, the same feeling of religious responsibility.

The courts of Pennsylvania have themselves decided that a charitable bequest, which counteracts the public policy of the State, cannot be sustained. This was so ruled in the often cited case of the Methodist Church v. Remington. There, the devise was to the Methodist Church generally, extending through the States and into Canada, and the trust was declared void on this account alone; namely, that it was inconsistent with the public policy of the State, inconsistent with the general spirit of the laws of Pennsylvania. But is there any comparison to be made between that ground on which a devise to a church is declared void, namely, as inconsistent with the public policy of the State, and the case of a devise which undermines and opposes the whole Christian religion, and derides all its ministers; the one tending to destroy all religion, and the other being merely against the spirit of the legislation and laws of the State, and the general public policy of government, in a very subordinate matter? Can it be shown that this devise of a piece of ground to the Methodist Church can be properly set aside, and declared void on general grounds, and not be shown that such a devise as that of Mr. Girard, which tends to overturn as well as oppose the public policy and laws of Pennsylvania, can also be set aside?

Sir, there are many other American cases which I could cite to the court in support of this point of the case. I will now only refer to 8 Johnson, page 291.

It is the same in Pennsylvania as elsewhere, the general principles and public policy are sometimes established by constitutional provisions, sometimes by legislative enactments, sometimes by judicial decisions, and sometimes by general consent. But however they may be established, there is nothing that we look for with more certainty than this general principle, that Christianity is part of the law of the land. This was the case among the Puritans of New England, the Episcopalians of the Southern States, the Pennsylvania Quakers, the Baptists, the mass of the followers of Whitefield and Wesley, and the Presbyterians; all brought and all adopted this great truth, and all have sustained it. And where there is any religious sentiment amongst men at all, this sentiment incorporates itself with the law. _Every thing declares it._ The massive cathedral of the Catholic; the Episcopalian church, with its lofty spire pointing heavenward; the plain temple of the Quaker; the log church of the hardy pioneer of the wilderness; the mementos and memorials around and about us; the consecrated graveyards, their tombstones and epitaphs, their silent vaults, their mouldering contents; all attest it. _The dead prove it as well as the living._ The generations that are gone before speak to it, and pronounce it from the tomb. We feel it. All, all, proclaim that Christianity, general, tolerant Christianity, Christianity independent of sects and parties, that Christianity to which the sword and the fagot are unknown, general, tolerant Christianity, is the law of the land.

Mr. Webster, having gone over the other points in the case, which were of a more technical character, in conclusion, said:--#/

I now take leave of this cause. I look for no good whatever from the establishment of this school, this college, this scheme, this experiment of an education in "practical morality," unblessed by the influences of religion. It sometimes happens to man to attain by accident that which he could not achieve by long-continued exercise of industry and ability. And it is said even of the man of genius, that by chance he will sometimes "snatch a grace beyond the reach of art." And I believe that men sometimes do mischief, not only beyond their intent, but beyond the ordinary scope of their talents and ability. In my opinion, if Mr. Girard had given years to the study of a mode by which he could dispose of his vast fortune so that no good could arise to the general cause of charity, no good to the general cause of learning, no good to human society, and which should be most productive of protracted struggles, troubles, and difficulties in the popular counsels of a great city, he could not so effectually have attained that result as he has by this devise now before the court. It is not the result of good fortunes, but of bad fortunes, which have overriden and cast down whatever of good might have been accomplished by a different disposition. I believe that this plan, this scheme, was unblessed in all its purposes, and in all its original plans. Unwise in all its frame and theory, while it lives it will lead an annoyed and troubled life, and leave an unblessed memory when it dies. If I could persuade myself that this court would come to such a decision as, in my opinion, the public good and the law require, and if I could believe that any humble efforts of my own had contributed in the least to lead to such a result, I should deem it the crowning mercy of my professional life.

[Footnote 1: Foster's Essay on the Evils of Popular Ignorance, Section IV.]

[Footnote 2: The effect of this remark was almost electric, and some one in the court-room broke out in applause.][Footnote 3: 2 Pickering, p. 433.][Footnote 4: 11 Sergeant & Rawle, p. 394.]

MR. JUSTICE STORY.[1]

[At a meeting of the Suffolk Bar, held in the Circuit Court Room, Boston, on the morning of the 12th of September, the day of the funeral of Mr. Justice Story, Chief Justice Shaw having taken the chair and announced the object of the meeting, Mr. Webster rose and spoke substantially as follows.]

Your solemn announcement, Mr. Chief Justice, has confirmed the sad intelligence which had already reached us, through the public channels of information, and deeply afflicted us all.

JOSEPH STORY, one of the Associate Justices of the Supreme Court of the United States, and for many years the presiding judge of this Circuit, died on Wednesday evening last, at his house in Cambridge, wanting only a few days for the completion of the sixty-sixth year of his age.

This most mournful and lamentable event has called together the whole Bar of Suffolk, and all connected with the courts of law or the profession. It has brought you, Mr. Chief Justice, and your associates of the Bench of the Supreme Court of Massachusetts, into the midst of us; and you have done us the honor, out of respect to the occasion, to consent to preside over us, while we deliberate on what is due, as well to our own afflicted and smitten feelings, as to the exalted character and eminent distinction of the deceased judge. The occasion has drawn from his retirement, also, that venerable man, whom we all so much respect and honor, (Judge Davis,) who was, for thirty years, the associate of the deceased upon the same Bench. It has called hither another judicial personage, now in retirement, (Judge Putnam,) but long an ornament of that Bench of which you are now the head, and whose marked good fortune it is to have been the professional teacher of Mr. Justice Story, and the director of his early studies. He also is present to whom this blow comes near; I mean, the learned judge (Judge Sprague) from whose side it has struck away a friend and a highly venerated official associate. The members of the Law School at Cambridge, to which the deceased was so much attached, and who returned that attachment with all the ingenuousness and enthusiasm of educated and ardent youthful minds, are here also, to manifest their sense of their own severe deprivation, as well as their admiration of the bright and shining professional example which they have so loved to contemplate,--an example, let me say to them, and let me say to all, as a solace in the midst of their sorrows, which death hath not touched and which time cannot obscure.

Mr. Chief Justice, one sentiment pervades us all. It is that of the most profound and penetrating grief, mixed, nevertheless, with an assured conviction, that the great man whom we deplore is yet with us and in the midst of us. He hath not wholly died. He lives in the affections of friends and kindred, and in the high regard of the community. He lives in our remembrance of his social virtues, his warm and steady friendships, and the vivacity and richness of his conversation. He lives, and will live still more permanently, by his words of written wisdom, by the results of his vast researches and attainments, by his imperishable legal judgments, and by those juridical disquisitions which have stamped his name, all over the civilized world, with the character of a commanding authority. "Vivit, enim, vivetque semper; atque etiam latius in memoria hominum et sermone versabitur, postquam ab oculis recessit."

Mr. Chief Justice, there are consolations which arise to mitigate our loss, and shed the influence of resignation over unfeigned and heart-felt sorrow. We are all penetrated with gratitude to God that the deceased lived so long; that he did so much for himself, his friends, the country, and the world; that his lamp went out, at last, without unsteadiness or flickering. He continued to exercise every power of his mind without dimness or obscuration, and every affection of his heart with no abatement of energy or warmth, till death drew an impenetrable veil between us and him. Indeed, he seems to us now, as in truth he is, not extinguished or ceasing to be, but only withdrawn; as the clear sun goes down at its setting, not darkened, but only no longer seen.

This calamity, Mr. Chief Justice, is not confined to the bar or the courts of this Commonwealth. It will be felt by every bar throughout the land, by every court, and indeed by every intelligent and well-informed man in or out of the profession. It will be felt still more widely, for his reputation had a still wider range. In the High Court of Parliament, in every tribunal in Westminster Hall, in the judicatories of Paris and Berlin, of Stockholm and St. Petersburg, in the learned universities of Germany, Italy, and Spain, by every eminent jurist in the civilized world, it will be acknowledged that a great luminary has fallen from the firmament of public jurisprudence.

Sir, there is no purer pride of country than that in which we may indulge when we see America paying back the great debt of civilization, learning, and science to Europe. In this high return of light for light and mind for mind, in this august reckoning and accounting between the intellects of nations, Joseph Story was destined by Providence to act, and did act, an important part. Acknowledging, as we all acknowledge, our obligations to the original sources of English law, as well as of civil liberty, we have seen in our generation copious and salutary streams turning and running backward, replenishing their original fountains, and giving a fresher and a brighter green to the fields of English jurisprudence. By a sort of reversed hereditary transmission, the mother, without envy or humiliation, acknowledges that she has received a valuable and cherished inheritance from the daughter. The profession in England admits with frankness and candor, and with no feeling but that of respect and admiration, that he whose voice we have so recently heard within these walls, but shall now hear no more, was, of all men who have yet appeared, most fitted by the comprehensiveness of his mind, and the vast extent and accuracy of his attainments, to compare the codes of nations, to trace their differences to difference of origin, climate, or religious or political institutions, and to exhibit, nevertheless, their concurrence in those great principles upon which the system of human civilization rests.

Justice, Sir, is the great interest of man on earth. It is the ligament which holds civilized beings and civilized nations together. Wherever her temple stands, and so long as it is duly honored, there is a foundation for social security, general happiness, and the improvement and progress of our race. And whoever labors on this edifice with usefulness and distinction, whoever clears its foundations, strengthens its pillars, adorns its entablatures, or contributes to raise its august dome still higher in the skies, connects himself, in name, and fame, and character, with that which is and must be as durable as the frame of human society.

All know, Mr. Chief Justice, the pure love of country which animated the deceased, and the zeal, as well as the talent, with which he explained and defended her institutions. His work on the Constitution of the United States is one of his most eminently successful labors. But all his writings, and all his judgments, all his opinions, and the whole influence of his character, public and private, leaned strongly and always to the support of sound principles, to the restraint of illegal power, and to the discouragement and rebuke of licentious and disorganizing sentiments. "Ad rempublicam firmandam, et ad stabiliendas vires, et sanandum populum, omnis ejus pergebat institutio."

But this is not the occasion, Sir, nor is it for me to consider and discuss at length the character and merits of Mr. Justice Story, as a writer or a judge. The performance of that duty, with which this Bar will no doubt charge itself, must be deferred to another opportunity, and will be committed to abler hands. But in the homage paid to his memory, one part may come with peculiar propriety and emphasis from ourselves. We have known him in private life. We have seen him descend from the bench, and mingle in our friendly circles. We have known his manner of life, from his youth up. We can bear witness to the strict uprightness and purity of his character, his simplicity and unostentatious habits, the ease and affability of his intercourse, his remarkable vivacity amidst severe labors, the cheerful and animating tones of his conversation, and his fast fidelity to friends. Some of us, also, can testify to his large and liberal charities, not ostentatious or casual, but systematic and silent,--dispensed almost without showing the hand, and falling and distilling comfort and happiness, like the dews of heaven. But we can testify, also, that in all his pursuits and employments, in all his recreations, in all his commerce with the world, and in his intercourse with the circle of his friends, the predominance of his judicial character was manifest. He never forgot the ermine which he wore. The judge, the judge, the useful and distinguished judge, was the great picture which he kept constantly before his eyes, and to a resemblance of which all his efforts, all his thoughts, all his life, were devoted. We may go the world over, without finding a man who shall present a more striking realization of the beautiful conception of D'Aguesseau: "C'est en vain que l'on cherche à distinguer en lui la personne privée et la personne publique; un même esprit les anime, un même objet les réunit; l'homme, le père de famille, le citoyen, tout est en lui consacré à la gloire du magistrat."

Mr. Chief Justice, one may live as a conqueror, a king, or a magistrate; but he must die as a man. The bed of death brings every human being to his pure individuality; to the intense contemplation of that deepest and most solemn of all relations, the relation between the creature and his Creator. Here it is that fame and renown cannot assist us; that all external things must fail to aid us; that even friends, affection, and human love and devotedness, cannot succor us. This relation, the true foundation of all duty, a relation perceived and felt by conscience and confirmed by revelation, our illustrious friend, now deceased, always acknowledged. He reverenced the Scriptures of truth, honored the pure morality which they teach, and clung to the hopes of future life which they impart. He beheld enough in nature, in himself, and in all that can be known of things seen, to feel assured that there is a Supreme Power, without whose providence not a sparrow falleth to the ground. To this gracious being he trusted himself for time and for eternity; and the last words of his lips ever heard by mortal ears were a fervent supplication to his Maker to take him to himself.

[Footnote 1: The following letter of dedication to the mother of Judge Story accompanied these remarks in the original edition:--

"_Boston, September 15, 1845._

"VENERABLE MADAM,--I pray you to allow me to present to you the brief remarks which I made before the Suffolk Bar, on the 12th instant, at a meeting occasioned by the sudden and afflicting death of your distinguished son. I trust, dear Madam, that as you enjoyed through his whole life constant proofs of his profound respect and ardent filial affection, so you may yet live long to enjoy the remembrance of his virtues and his exalted reputation.

"I am, with very great regard, "Your obedient servant, "DANIEL WEBSTER.

"TO MADAM STORY."]

THE RHODE ISLAND GOVERNMENT.

AN ARGUMENT MADE IN THE SUPREME COURT OF THE UNITED STATES, ON THE 27TH OF JANUARY, 1848, IN THE DORR REBELLION CASES.

[The facts necessary to the understanding of these cases are sufficiently set forth in the commencement of Mr. Webster's argument. The event out of which the cases arose is known in popular language as the *Dorr Rebellion*. The first case (that of Martin Luther against Luther M. Borden and others) came up by writ of error from the Circuit Court of Rhode Island, in which the jury, under the rulings of the court (Mr. Justice Story), found a verdict for the defendants; the second case (that of Rachel Luther against the same defendants) came up by a certificate of a division of opinion. The allegations, evidence, and arguments were the same in both cases.

The first case was argued by Mr. Hallet and Mr. Clifford (Attorney-General) for the plaintiffs in error, and by Mr. Whipple and Mr. Webster for the defendants in error. Mr. Justice Catron, Mr. Justice Daniel, and Mr. Justice McKinley were absent from the court, in consequence of ill health. Chief Justice Taney delivered the opinion of the court, affirming the judgment of the court below in the first case, and dismissing the second for want of jurisdiction. Mr. Justice Woodbury dissented, and delivered a very elaborate opinion in support of his view of the subject.]

There is something novel and extraordinary in the case now before the court. All will admit that it is not such a one as is usually presented for judicial consideration.

It is well known, that in the years 1841 and 1842 political agitation existed in Rhode Island. Some of the citizens of that State undertook to form a new constitution of government, beginning their proceedings towards that end by meetings of the people, held without authority of law, and conducting those proceedings through such forms as led them, in 1842, to say that they had established a new constitution and form of government, and placed Mr. Thomas W. Dorr at its head. The previously existing, and then existing, government of Rhode Island treated these proceedings as nugatory, so far as they went to establish a new constitution; and criminal, so far as they proposed to confer authority upon any persons to interfere with the acts of the existing government, or to exercise powers of legislation, or administration of the laws. All will remember that the state of things approached, if not actual conflict between men in arms, at least the "perilous edge of battle." Arms were resorted to, force was used, and greater force threatened. In June, 1842, this agitation subsided. The new government, as it called itself, disappeared from the scene of action. The former government, the Charter government, as it was sometimes styled, resumed undisputed control, went on in its ordinary course, and the peace of the State was restored.

But the past had been too serious to be forgotten. The legislature of the State had, at an early stage of the troubles, found it necessary to pass special laws for the punishment of the persons concerned in these proceedings. It defined the crime of treason, as well as smaller offences, and authorized the declaration of martial law. Governor King, under this authority, proclaimed the existence of treason and rebellion in the State, and declared the State under martial law. This having been done, and the ephemeral government of Mr. Dorr having disappeared, the grand juries of the State found indictments against several persons for having disturbed the peace of the State, and one against Dorr himself for treason. This indictment came on in the Supreme Court of Rhode Island in 1844, before a tribunal admitted on all hands to be the legal judicature of the State. He was tried by a jury of Rhode Island, above all objection, and after all challenge. By that jury, under the instructions of the court, he was convicted of treason, and sentenced to imprisonment for life.

Now an action is brought in the courts of the United States, and before your honors, by appeal, in which it is attempted to prove that the characters of this drama have been oddly and wrongly cast; that there has been a great mistake in the courts of Rhode Island. It is alleged, that Mr. Dorr, instead of being a traitor or an insurrectionist, was the real governor of the State at the time; that the force used by him was exercised in defence of the constitution and laws, and not against them; that he who opposed the constituted authorities was not Mr. Dorr, but Governor King; and that it was *he* who should have been indicted, and tried, and sentenced. This is rather an important mistake, to be sure, if it be a mistake. "Change places," cries poor Lear, "_change places_, and _handy-dandy_, which is the justice and which the thief?" So our learned opponents say, "Change places, and, _handy-dandy_, which is the governor and which the rebel?" The aspect of the case is, as I have said, novel. It may perhaps give vivacity and variety to judicial investigations. It may relieve the drudgery of perusing briefs, demurrers, and pleas in bar, bills in equity and answers, and introduce topics which give sprightliness, freshness, and something of an uncommon public interest to proceedings in courts of law.

However difficult it may be, and I suppose it to be *wholly* impossible, that this court should take judicial cognizance of the questions which the plaintiff has presented to the court below, yet I do not think it a matter of regret that the cause has come hither. It is said, and truly said, that the case involves the consideration and discussion of what are the true principles of government in our American system of public liberty. This is very right. The case does involve these questions, and harm can never come from their discussion, especially when such discussion is addressed to reason and not to passion; when it is had before magistrates and lawyers, and not before excited masses out of doors. I agree entirely that the case does raise considerations, somewhat extensive, of the true character of our American system of popular liberty; and although I am constrained to differ from the learned counsel who opened the cause for the plaintiff in error, on the principles and character of that American liberty, and upon the true characteristics of that American system on which changes of the government and constitution, if they become necessary, are to be made, yet I agree with him that this case does present them for consideration.

Now, there are certain principles of public liberty, which, though they do not exist in all forms of government, exist, nevertheless, to some extent, in different forms of government. The protection of life and property, the _habeas corpus_, trial by jury, the right of open trial, these are principles of public liberty existing in their best form in the republican institutions of this country, but, to the extent mentioned, existing also in the constitution of England. Our American liberty, allow me to say, therefore, has an ancestry, a pedigree, a history. Our ancestors brought to this continent all that was valuable, in their judgment, in the political institutions of England, and left behind them all that was without value, or that was objectionable. During the colonial period they were closely connected of course with the colonial system; but they were Englishmen, as well as colonists, and took an interest in whatever concerned the mother country, especially in all great questions of public liberty in that country. They accordingly took a deep concern in the Revolution of 1688. The American colonists had suffered from the tyranny of James the Second. Their charters had been wrested from them by mockeries of law, and by the corruption of judges in the city of London; and in no part of England was there more gratification, or a more resolute feeling, when James abdicated and William came over, than in the American colonies. All know that Massachusetts immediately overthrew what had been done under the reign of James, and took possession of the colonial fort in the harbor of Boston in the name of the new king.

When the United States separated from England, by the Declaration of 1776, they departed from the political maxims and examples of the mother country, and entered upon a course more exclusively American. From that day down, our institutions and our history relate to ourselves. Through the period of the Declaration of Independence, of the Confederation, of the Convention, and the adoption of the Constitution, all our public acts are records out of which a knowledge of our system of American liberty is to be drawn.

From the Declaration of Independence, the governments of what had been colonies before were adapted to their new condition. They no longer owed allegiance to crowned heads. No tie bound them to England. The whole system became entirely popular, and all legislative and constitutional provisions had regard to this new, peculiar, American character, which they had assumed. Where the form of government was already well enough, they let it alone. Where reform was necessary, they reformed it. What was valuable, they retained; what was essential, they added, and no more. Through the whole proceeding, from 1776 to the latest period, the whole course of American public acts, the whole progress of this American system, was marked by a peculiar conservatism. The object was to do what was necessary, and no more; and to do that with the utmost temperance and prudence.

Now, without going into historical details at length, let me state what I understand the American principles to be, on which this system rests.

First and chief, no man makes a question, that the people are the source of all political power. Government is instituted for their good, and its members are their agents and servants. He who would argue against this must argue without an adversary. And who thinks there is any peculiar merit in asserting a doctrine like this, in the midst of twenty millions of people, when nineteen millions nine hundred and ninety-nine thousand nine hundred and ninety-nine of them hold it, as well as himself? There is no other doctrine of government here; and no man imputes to another, and no man should claim for himself, any peculiar merit for asserting what everybody knows to be true, and nobody denies. Why, where else can we look but to the people for political power, in a popular government? We have no hereditary executive, no hereditary branch of the legislature, no inherited masses of property, no system of entails, no long trusts, no long family settlements, no primogeniture. Every estate in the country, from the richest to the poorest, is divided among sons and daughters alike. Alienation is made as easy as possible; everywhere the transmissibility of property is perfectly free. The whole system is arranged so as to produce, as far as unequal industry and enterprise render it possible, a universal equality among men; an equality of rights absolutely, and an equality of condition, so far as the different characters of individuals will allow such equality to be produced. He who considers that there may be, is, or ever has been, since the Declaration of Independence, any person who looks to any other source of power in this country than the people, so as to give peculiar merit to those who clamor loudest in its assertion, must be out of his mind, even more than Don Quixote. His imagination was only perverted. He saw things not as they were, though what he saw were things. He saw windmills, and took them to be giants, knights on horseback. This was bad enough; but whoever says, or speaks as if he thought, that anybody looks to any other source of political power in this country than the people, must have a stronger and wilder imagination, for he sees nothing but the creations of his own fancy. He stares at phantoms.

Well, then, let all admit, what none deny, that the only source of political power in this country is the people. Let us admit that they are _sovereign_, for they are so; that is to say, the aggregate community, the collected will of the people, is sovereign. I confess that I think Chief Justice Jay spoke rather paradoxically than philosophically, when he said that this country exhibited the extraordinary spectacle of many sovereigns and no subjects. The people, he said, are all sovereigns; and the peculiarity of the case is that they have no subjects, except a few colored persons. This must be rather fanciful. The aggregate community is sovereign, but that is not *the* sovereignty which acts in the daily exercise of sovereign power. The people cannot act daily as the people. They must establish a government, and invest it with so much of the sovereign power as the case requires; and this sovereign power being delegated and placed in the hands of the government, that government becomes what is popularly called THE STATE. I like the old-fashioned way of stating things as they are; and this is the true idea of a state. It is an organized government, representing the collected will of the people, as far as they see fit to invest that government with power. And in that respect it is true, that, though *this* government possesses sovereign power, it does not possess *all* sovereign power; and so the State governments, though sovereign in some respects, are not so in all. Nor could it be shown that the powers of both, as delegated, embrace the whole range of what might be called sovereign power. We usually speak of the States as sovereign States. I do not object to this. But the Constitution never so styles them, nor does the Constitution speak of the government here as the *general* or the *federal* government. It calls this government the United States; and it calls the State governments State governments. Still the fact is undeniably so; legislation is a sovereign power, and is exercised by the United States government to a certain extent, and also by the States, according to the forms which they themselves have established, and subject to the provisions of the Constitution of the United States.

Well, then, having agreed that all power is originally from the people, and that they can confer as much of it as they please, the next principle is, that, as the exercise of legislative power and the other powers of government immediately by the people themselves is impracticable, they must be exercised by REPRESENTATIVES of the people; and what distinguishes American governments as much as any thing else from any governments of ancient or of modern times, is the marvellous felicity of their representative system. It has with us, allow me to say, a somewhat different origin from the representation of the commons in England, though that has been worked up to some resemblance of our own. The representative system in England had its origin, not in any supposed rights of the people themselves, but in the necessities and commands of the crown. At first, knights and burgesses were summoned, often against their will, to a Parliament called by the king. Many remonstrances were presented against sending up these representatives; the charge of paying them was, not unfrequently, felt to be burdensome by the people. But the king wished their counsel and advice, and perhaps the presence of a popular body, to enable him to make greater headway against the feudal barons in the aristocratic and hereditary branch of the legislature. In process of time these knights and burgesses assumed more and more a popular character, and became, by degrees, the guardians of popular rights. The people through them obtained protection against the encroachments of the crown and the aristocracy, till in our day they are understood to be the representatives of the people, charged with the protection of their rights. With us it was always just so. Representation has always been of this character. The power is with the people; but they cannot exercise it in masses or _per capita_; they can only exercise it by their representatives. The whole system with us has been popular from the beginning.

Now, the basis of this representation is suffrage. The right to choose representatives is every man's part in the exercise of sovereign power; to have a voice in it, if he has the proper qualifications, is the portion of political power belonging to every elector. That is the beginning. That is the mode in which power emanates from its source, and gets into the hands of conventions, legislatures, courts of law, and the chair of the executive. It begins in suffrage. Suffrage is the delegation of the power of an individual to some agent.

This being so, then follow two other great principles of the American system.

1. The first is, that the right of suffrage shall be guarded, protected, and secured against force and against fraud; and,

2. The second is, that its exercise shall be prescribed by previous law; its qualifications shall be prescribed by previous law; the time and place of its exercise shall be prescribed by previous law; the manner of its exercise, under whose supervision (always sworn officers of the law), is to be prescribed. And then, again, the results are to be certified to the central power by some certain rule, by some known public officers, in some clear and definite form, to the end that two things may be done: first, that every man entitled to vote may vote; second, that his vote may be sent forward and counted, and so he may exercise his part of sovereignty, in common with his fellow-citizens.

In the exercise of political power through representatives we know nothing, we never have known any thing, but such an exercise as should take place through the prescribed forms of law. When we depart from that, we shall wander as widely from the American track as the pole is from the track of the sun.

I have said that it is one principle of the American system, that the people limit their governments, National and State. They do so; but it is another principle, equally true and certain, and, according to my judgment of things, equally important, that the people often *limit themselves*. They set bounds to their own power. They have chosen to secure the institutions which they establish against the sudden impulses of mere majorities. All our institutions teem with instances of this. It was their great conservative principle, in constituting forms of government, that they should secure what they had established against hasty changes by simple majorities. By the fifth article of the Constitution of the United States, Congress, two thirds of both houses concurring, may propose amendments of the Constitution; or, on the application of the legislatures of two thirds of the States, may call a convention; and amendments proposed in either of these forms must be ratified by the legislatures or conventions of three fourths of the States. The fifth article of the Constitution, if it was made a topic for those who framed the "people's constitution" of Rhode Island, could only have been a matter of reproach. It gives no countenance to any of their proceedings, or to any thing like them. On the contrary, it is one remarkable instance of the enactment and application of that great American principle, that the constitution of government should be cautiously and prudently interfered with, and that changes should not ordinarily be begun and carried through by bare majorities.

But the people limit themselves also in other ways. They limit themselves in the first exercise of their political rights. They limit themselves, by all their constitutions, in two important respects; that is to say, in regard to the qualifications of _electors_, and in regard to the qualifications of the *elected*. In every State, and in all the States, the people have precluded themselves from voting for everybody they might wish to vote for; they have limited their own right of choosing. They have said, We will elect no man who has not such and such qualifications. We will not vote ourselves, unless we have such and such qualifications. They have also limited themselves to certain prescribed forms for the conduct of elections. They must vote at a particular place, at a particular time, and under particular conditions, or not at all. It is in these modes that we are to ascertain the will of the American people; and our Constitution and laws know no other mode. We are not to take the will of the people from public meetings, nor from tumultuous assemblies, by which the timid are terrified, the prudent are alarmed, and by which society is disturbed. These are not American modes of signifying the will of the people, and they never were. If any thing in the country, not ascertained by a regular vote, by regular returns, and by regular representation, has been established, it is an exception, and not the rule; it is an anomaly which, I believe, can scarcely be found.

It is true that at the Revolution, when all government was immediately dissolved, the people got together, and what did they do? Did they exercise sovereign power? They began an inceptive organization, the object of which was to bring together representatives of the people, who should form a government. This was the mode of proceeding in those States where their legislatures were dissolved. It was much like that had in England upon the abdication of James the Second. He ran away, he abdicated. He threw the great seal into the Thames. I am not aware that, on the 4th of May, 1842, any great seal was thrown into Providence River! But James abdicated, and King William took the government; and how did he proceed? Why, he at once requested all who had been members of the old Parliament, of any regular Parliament in the time of Charles the Second, to assemble. The Peers, being a standing body, could of course assemble; and all they did was to recommend the calling of a convention, to be chosen by the same electors, and composed of the same numbers, as composed a Parliament. The convention assembled, and, as all know, was turned into a Parliament. This was a case of necessity, a revolution. Don't we call it so? And why? Not merely because a new sovereign then ascended the throne of the Stuarts, but because there was a change in the organization of the government. The legal and established succession was broken. The convention did not assemble under any preceding law. There was a _hiatus_, a syncope, in the action of the body politic. This was revolution, and the Parliaments that assembled afterwards referred their legal origin to that revolution.

Is it not obvious enough, that men cannot get together and count themselves, and say they are so many hundreds and so many thousands, and judge of their own qualifications, and call themselves the people, and set up a government? Why, another set of men, forty miles off, on the same day, with the same propriety, with as good qualifications, and in as large numbers, may meet and set up another government; one may meet at Newport and another at Chepachet, and both may call themselves the people. What is this but anarchy? What liberty is there here, but a tumultuary, tempestuous, violent, stormy liberty, a sort of South American liberty, without power except in its spasms, a liberty supported by arms to-day, crushed by arms to-morrow? Is that *our* liberty?

The regular action of popular power, on the other hand, places upon public liberty the most beautiful face that ever adorned that angel form. All is regular and harmonious in its features, and gentle in its operation. The stream of public authority, under American liberty, running in this channel, has the strength of the Missouri, while its waters are as transparent as those of a crystal lake. It is powerful for good. It produces no tumult, no violence, and no wrong;--

"Though deep, yet clear; though gentle, yet not dull; Strong, without rage; without o'erflowing, full."

Another American principle growing out of this, and just as important and well settled as is the truth that the people are the source of power, is, that, when in the course of events it becomes necessary to ascertain the will of the people on a new exigency, or a new state of things or of opinion, the legislative power provides for that ascertainment by an ordinary act of legislation. Has not that been our whole history? It would take me from now till the sun shall go down to advert to all the instances of it, and I shall only refer to the most prominent, and especially to the establishment of the Constitution under which you sit. The old Congress, upon the suggestion of the delegates who assembled at Annapolis in May, 1786, recommended to the States that they should send delegates to a convention to be holden at Philadelphia to form a Constitution. No article of the old Confederation gave them power to do this; but they did it, and the States did appoint delegates, who assembled at Philadelphia, and formed the Constitution. It was communicated to the old Congress, and that body recommended to the States to make provision for calling the people together to act upon its adoption. Was not that exactly the case of passing a law to ascertain the will of the people in a new exigency? And this method was adopted without opposition, nobody suggesting that there could be any other mode of ascertaining the will of the people.

My learned friend went through the constitutions of several of the States. It is enough to say, that, of the old thirteen States, the constitutions, with but one exception, contained no provision for their own amendment. In New Hampshire there was a provision for taking the sense of the people once in seven years. Yet there is hardly one that has not altered its constitution, and it has been done by conventions called by the legislature, as an ordinary exercise of legislative power. Now what State ever altered its constitution in any other mode? What alteration has ever been brought in, put in, forced in, or got in anyhow, by resolutions of mass meetings, and then by applying force? In what State has an assembly, calling itself the people, convened without law, without authority, without qualifications, without certain officers, with no oaths, securities, or sanctions of any kind, met and made a constitution, and called it the constitution of the STATE? There must be some authentic mode of ascertaining the will of the people, else all is anarchy. It resolves itself into the law of the strongest, or, what is the same thing, of the most numerous for the moment, and all constitutions and all legislative rights are prostrated and disregarded.

But my learned adversary says, that, if we maintain that the people (for he speaks in the name and on behalf of the people, to which I do not object) cannot commence changes in their government but by some previous act of legislation, and if the legislature will not grant such an act, we do in fact follow the example of the Holy Alliance, "the doctors of Laybach," where the assembled sovereigns said that all changes of government must proceed from sovereigns; and it is said that we mark out the same rule for the people of Rhode Island.

Now will any man, will my adversary here, on a moment's reflection, undertake to show the least resemblance on earth between what I have called the American doctrine, and the doctrine of the sovereigns at Laybach? What do I contend for? I say that the will of the people must prevail, when it is ascertained; but there must be some legal and authentic mode of ascertaining that will; and then the people may make what government they please. Was that the doctrine of Laybach? Was not the doctrine there held this,--that the *sovereigns* should say what changes shall be made? Changes must proceed from them; new constitutions and new laws emanate from them; and all the people had to do was to submit. That is what they maintained. All changes began with the sovereigns, and ended with the sovereigns. Pray, at about the time that the Congress of Laybach was in session, did the allied powers put it to the people of Italy to say what sort of change they would have? And at a more recent date, did they ask the citizens of Cracow what change they would have in their constitution? Or did they take away their constitution, laws, and liberties, by their own sovereign act? All that is necessary here is, that the will of the people should be ascertained, by some regular rule of proceeding, prescribed by previous law. But when ascertained, that will is as sovereign as the will of a despotic prince, of the Czar of Muscovy, or the Emperor of Austria himself, though not quite so easily made known. A ukase or an edict signifies at once the will of a despotic prince; but that will of the people, which is here as sovereign as the will of such a prince, is not so quickly ascertained or known; and thence arises the necessity for suffrage, which is the mode whereby each man's power is made to tell upon the constitution of the government, and in the enactment of laws.

One of the most recent laws for taking the will of the people in any State is the law of 1845, of the State of New York. It begins by recommending to the people to assemble in their several election districts, and proceed to vote for delegates to a convention. If you will take the pains to read that act, it will be seen that New York regarded it as an ordinary exercise of legislative power. It applies all the penalties for fraudulent voting, as in other elections. It punishes false oaths, as in other cases. Certificates of the proper officers were to be held conclusive, and the will of the people was, in this respect, collected essentially in the same manner, supervised by the same officers, under the same guards against force and fraud, collusion and misrepresentation, as are usual in voting for State or United States officers.

We see, therefore, from the commencement of the government under which we live, down to this late act of the State of New York, one uniform current of law, of precedent, and of practice, all going to establish the point that changes in government are to be brought about by the will of the people, assembled under such legislative provisions as may be necessary to ascertain that will, truly and authentically.

In the next place, may it please your honors, it becomes very important to consider what bearing the Constitution and laws of the United States have upon this Rhode Island question. Of course the Constitution of the United States recognizes the existence of States. One branch of the legislature of the

United States is composed of Senators, appointed by the States, in their State capacities. The Constitution of the United States[1] says that "the United States shall guarantee to each State a republican form of government, and shall protect the several States against invasion; and on application of the legislature, or of the executive when the legislature cannot be convened, against domestic violence." Now, I cannot but think this a very stringent article, drawing after it the most important consequences, and all of them *good* consequences. The Constitution, in the section cited, speaks of States as having existing legislatures and existing executives; and it speaks of cases in which violence is practised or threatened against the State, in other words, "domestic violence"; and it says the State shall be protected. It says, then, does it not? that the existing government of a State shall be protected. My adversary says, if so, and if the legislature would not call a convention, and if, when the people rise to make a constitution, the United States step in and prohibit them, why, the rights and privileges of the people are checked, controlled. Undoubtedly. The Constitution does not proceed on the *ground* of revolution; it does not proceed on any *right* of revolution; but it does go on the idea, that, within and under the Constitution, no new form of government can be established in any State, without the authority of the existing government.

Admitting the legitimacy of the argument of my learned adversary, it would not authorize the inference he draws from it, because his own case falls within the same range. He has proved, he thinks, that there was an existing government, a paper government, at least; a rightful government, as he alleges. Suppose it to be rightful, in his sense of right. Suppose three fourths of the people of Rhode Island to have been engaged in it, and ready to sustain it. What then? How is it to be done without the consent of the previous government? How is the fact, that three fourths of the people are in favor of the new government, to be legally ascertained? And if the existing government deny that fact, and if that government hold on, and will not surrender till displaced by force, and if it is threatened by force, then the case of the Constitution arises, and the United States must aid the government that is in, because an attempt to displace a government by force is "domestic violence." It is the exigency provided for by the Constitution. If the existing government maintain its post, though three fourths of the State have adopted the new constitution, is it not evident enough that the exigency arises in which the constitutional power here must go to the aid of the existing government? Look at the law of 28th February, 1795.[2] Its words are, "And in case of an insurrection in any State, _against the government thereof_, it shall be lawful for the President of the United States, on application of the legislature of such State, or of the executive (when the legislature cannot be convened), to call forth such number of the militia of any other State or States, as may be applied for, as he may judge sufficient to suppress such insurrection." Insurrection against the *existing* government is, then, the thing to be suppressed.

But the law and the Constitution, the whole system of American institutions, do not contemplate a case in which a resort will be necessary to proceedings _aliunde_, or outside of the law and the Constitution, for the purpose of amending the frame of government. They go on the idea that the States are all republican, that they are all representative in their forms, and that these popular governments in each State, the annually created creatures of the people, will give all proper facilities and necessary aids to bring about changes which the people may judge necessary in their constitutions. They take that ground and act on no other supposition. They assume that the popular will in all particulars will be accomplished. And history has proved that the presumption is well founded.

This, may it please your honors, is the view I take of what I have called the American system. These are the methods of bringing about changes in government.

Now, it is proper to look into this record, and see what the questions are that are presented by it, and consider,--

1. Whether the case is one for judicial investigation at all; that is, whether this court can try the matters which the plaintiff has offered to prove in the court below; and,

2. In the second place, whether many things which he did offer to prove, if they could have been and had been proved, were not acts of criminality, and therefore no justification; and,

3. Whether all that was offered to be proved would show that, in point of fact, there had been established and put in operation any new constitution, displacing the old charter government of Rhode Island.

The declaration is in trespass. The writ was issued on the 8th of October, 1842, in which Martin Luther complains that Luther M. Borden and others broke into his house in Warren, Rhode Island, on the 29th of June, 1842, and disturbed his family and committed other illegal acts.

The defendant answers, that large numbers of men were in arms, in Rhode Island, for the purpose of overthrowing the government of the State, and making war upon it; and that, for the preservation of the government and people, martial law had been proclaimed by the Governor, under an act of the legislature, on the 25th of June, 1842. The plea goes on to aver, that the plaintiff was aiding and abetting this attempt to overthrow the government, and that the defendant was under the military authority of John T. Child, and was ordered by him to arrest the plaintiff; for which purpose he applied at the door of his house, and being refused entrance he forced the door.

The action is thus for an alleged trespass, and the plea is justification under the law of Rhode Island. The plea and replications are as usual in such cases in point of form. The plea was filed at the November term of 1842, and the case was tried at the November term of 1843, in the Circuit Court in Rhode Island. In order to make out a defence, the defendant offered the charter of Rhode Island, the participation of the State in the Declaration of Independence, its uniting with the Confederation in 1778, its admission into the Union in 1790, its continuance in the Union and its recognition as a State down to May, 1843, when the constitution now in force was adopted. Here let it be particularly remarked, that Congress admitted Rhode Island into the Constitution under this identical old charter government, thereby giving sanction to it as a republican form of government. The defendant then refers to all the laws and proceedings of the Assembly, till the adoption of the present constitution of Rhode Island. To repel the case of the defendant, the plaintiff read the proceedings of the old legislature, and documents to show that the idea of changing the government had been entertained as long ago as 1790. He read also certain resolutions of the Assembly in 1841, memorials praying changes in the constitution, and other documents to the same effect. He next offered to prove that suffrage associations were formed throughout the State in 1840 and 1841, and that steps were taken by them for holding public meetings; and to show the proceedings had at those meetings. In the next place, he offered to prove that a mass convention was held at Newport, attended by over four thousand persons, and another at Providence, at which over six thousand attended, at which resolutions were passed in favor of the change. Then he offered to prove the election of delegates; the meeting of the convention in October, 1841, and the draughting of the Dorr constitution; the reassembling in 1841, the completion of the draught, its submission to the people, their voting upon it, its adoption, and the proclamation on the 13th of January, 1842, that the constitution so adopted was the law of the land.

That is the substance of what was averred as to the formation of the Dorr constitution. The plaintiff next offered to prove that the constitution was adopted by a large majority of the qualified voters of the State; that officers were elected under it in April, 1842; that this new government assembled on the 3d of May; and he offered a copy of its proceedings. He sets forth that the court refused to admit testimony upon these subjects, and to these points; and ruled that the old government and laws of the State were in full force and power, and then existing, when the alleged trespass was made, and that they justified the acts of the defendants, according to their plea.

I will give a few references to other proceedings of this new government. The new constitution was proclaimed on the 13th of January, 1842, by some of the officers of the convention. On the 13th of April, officers were appointed under it, and Mr. Dorr was chosen governor. On Tuesday, the 3d of May, the new legislature met, was organized, and then, it is insisted, the new constitution became the law of the land. The legislature sat through that whole day, morning and evening; adjourned; met the next day, and sat through all that day, morning and evening, and did a great deal of paper business. It went through the forms of choosing a Supreme Court, and transacting other business of a similar kind, and on the evening of the 4th of May it adjourned, to meet again on the first Monday of July, in Providence,

"And word spake never more."

It never reassembled. This government, then, whatever it was, came into existence on the *third* day of May, and went out of existence on the *fourth* day of May.

I will now give some references concerning the new constitution authorized by the government, the old government, and which is now the constitution of Rhode Island. It was framed in November, 1842. It was voted upon by the people on the 21st, 22d, and 23d days of November, was then by them accepted, and became by its own provisions the constitution of Rhode Island on the first Tuesday of May, 1843.

Now, what, in the mean time, had become of Mr. Dorr's government? According to the principle of its friends, they are forced to admit that it was superseded by the new, that is to say, the present government, because the people accepted the new government. But there was no new government till May, 1843. According to them, then, there was an *interregnum* of a whole year. If Mr. Dorr had had a government, what became of it? If it ever came in, what put it out of existence? Why did it not meet on the day to which it had adjourned? It was not displaced by the new constitution, because that had not been agreed upon in convention till November. It was not adopted by the people till the last of November, and it did not go into operation till May. What then had become of Mr. Dorr's government?

I think it is important to note that the new constitution, established according to the prescribed forms, came thus into operation in May, 1843, and was admitted by all to be the constitution of the State. What then happened in the State of Rhode Island? I do not mean to go through all the trials that were had after this ideal government of Mr. Dorr ceased to exist; but I will ask attention to the report of the trial of Dorr for treason, which took place in 1844, before all the judges of the Supreme Court of the State. He was indicted in August, 1842, and the trial came on in March, 1844. The indictment was found while the charter government was in force, and the trial was had under the new constitution. He was found guilty of treason. And I turn to the report of the trial now, to call attention to the language of the court in its charge, as delivered by Chief Justice Durfee. I present the following extract from that charge:--

"It may be, Gentlemen, that he really believed himself to be the governor of the State, and that he acted throughout under this delusion. However this may go to extenuate the offence, it does not take from it its legal guilt. It is no defence to an indictment for the violation of any law for the defendant to come into court and say, 'I thought that I was but exercising a constitutional right, and I claim an acquittal on the ground of mistake,' Were it so, there would be an end to all law and all government. Courts and juries would have nothing to do but to sit in judgment upon indictments, in order to acquit or excuse. The accused has only to prove that he has been systematic in committing crime, and that he thought that he had a right to commit it; and, according to this doctrine, you must acquit. The main ground upon which the prisoner sought for a justification was, that a constitution had been adopted by a majority of the male adult population of this State, voting in their primary or natural capacity or condition, and that he was subsequently elected, and did the acts charged, as governor under it. He offered the votes themselves to prove its adoption, which were also to be followed by proof of his election. This evidence we have ruled out. Courts and juries, Gentlemen, do not count votes to determine whether a constitution has been adopted or a governor elected, or not. Courts take notice, without proof offered from the bar, what the constitution is or was, and who is or was the governor of their own State. It belongs to the legislature to exercise this high duty. It is the legislature which, in the exercise of its delegated sovereignty, counts the votes and declares whether a constitution be adopted or a governor elected, or not; and we cannot revise and reverse their acts in this particular, without usurping their power. Were the votes on the adoption of our present constitution now offered here to prove that it was or was not adopted; or those given for the governor under it, to prove that he was or was not elected; we could not receive the evidence ourselves, we could not permit it to pass to the jury. And why not? Because, if we did so, we should cease to be a mere judicial, and become a political tribunal, with the whole sovereignty in our hands. Neither the people nor the legislature would be sovereign. We should be sovereign, or you would be sovereign; and we should deal out to parties litigant, here at our bar, sovereignty to this or that, according to rules or laws of our own making, and heretofore unknown in courts.

"In what condition would this country be, if appeals could be thus taken to courts and juries? *This* jury might decide one way, and *that* another, and the sovereignty might be found here to-day, and there to-morrow. Sovereignty is above courts or juries, and the creature cannot sit in judgment upon its creator. Were this instrument offered as the constitution of a foreign state, we might, perhaps, under some circumstances, require proof of its existence; but, even in that case, the fact would not be ascertained by counting the votes given at its adoption, but by the certificate of the secretary of state, under the broad seal of the state. This instrument is not offered as a foreign constitution, and this court is bound to know what the constitution of the government is under which it acts, without any proof even of that high character. We know nothing of the existence of the so-called 'people's constitution' as law, and there is no proof before you of its adoption, and of the election of the prisoner as governor under it; and you can return a verdict only on the evidence that has passed to you."

Having thus, may it please your honors, attempted to state the questions as they arise, and having referred to what has taken place in Rhode Island, I shall present what further I have to say in three propositions:--

1st. I say, first, that the matters offered to be proved by the plaintiff in the court below are not of judicial cognizance; and proof of them, therefore, was properly rejected by the court.

2d. If all these matters could be, and had been, legally proved, they would have constituted no defence, because they show nothing but an *illegal* attempt to overthrow the government of Rhode Island.

3d. No proof was offered by the plaintiff to show that, in fact, another government had gone into operation, by which the Charter government had become displaced.

And first, these matters are not of judicial cognizance. Does this need arguing? Are the various matters of fact alleged, the meetings, the appointment of committees, the qualifications of voters,--is there any one of all these matters of which a court of law can take cognizance in a case in which it is to decide on sovereignty? Are fundamental changes in the frame of a government to be thus proved? The thing to be proved is a change of the sovereign power. Two legislatures existed at the same time, both claiming power to pass laws. Both could not have a legal existence. What, then, is the attempt of our adversaries? To put down one sovereign government, and to put another up, by facts and proceedings in regard to elections out of doors, unauthorized by any law whatever. Regular proceedings for a change of government may in some cases, perhaps, be taken notice of by a court; but this court must look elsewhere than out of doors, and to public meetings, irregular and unauthorized, for the decision of such a question as this. It naturally looks to that authority under which it sits here, to the provisions of the Constitution which have created this tribunal, and to the laws by which its proceedings are regulated. It must look to the acts of the government of the United States, in its various branches.

This Rhode Island disturbance, as everybody knows, was brought to the knowledge of the President of the United States[3] by the public authorities of Rhode Island; and how did he treat it? The United States have guaranteed to each State a republican form of government. And a law of Congress has directed the President, in a constitutional case requiring the adoption of such a proceeding, to call out the militia to put down domestic violence, and suppress insurrection. Well, then, application was made to the President of the United States, to the executive power of the United States. For, according to our system, it devolves upon the executive to determine, in the first instance, what are and what are not governments. The President recognizes governments, foreign governments, as they appear from time to time in the occurrences of this changeful world. And the Constitution and the laws, if an insurrection exists against the government of any State, rendering it necessary to appear with an armed force, make it his duty to call out the militia and suppress it.

Two things may here be properly considered. The first is, that the Constitution declares that the United States shall protect every State against domestic violence; and the law of 1795, making provision for carrying this constitutional duty into effect in all proper cases, declares, that, "in case of an insurrection in any State against the government thereof, it shall be lawful for the President of the United States to call out the militia of other States to suppress such insurrection." These constitutional and legal provisions make it the indispensable duty of the President to decide, in cases of commotion, what is the rightful government of the State. He cannot avoid such decision. And in this case he decided, of course, that the existing government, the charter government, was the rightful government. He could not possibly have decided otherwise.

In the next place, if events had made it necessary to call out the militia, and the officers and soldiers of such militia, in protecting the existing government, had done precisely what the defendants in this case did, could an action have been maintained against them? No one would assert so absurd a proposition.

In reply to the requisition of the Governor, the President stated that he did not think it was yet time for the application of force; but he wrote a letter to the Secretary of War, in which he directed him to confer with the Governor of Rhode Island; and, whenever it should appear to them to be necessary, to call out from Massachusetts and Connecticut a militia force sufficient to *terminate at once* this insurrection, by the authority of the government of the United States. We are at no loss, therefore, to know how the executive government of the United States treated this insurrection. It was regarded as fit *to be suppressed.* That is manifest from the President's letters to the Secretary of War and to Governor King.

Now, the eye of this court must be directed to the proceedings of the general government, which had its attention called to the subject, and which did institute proceedings respecting it. And the court will learn from the proceedings of the executive branch of the government, and of the two chambers above us, how the disturbances in Rhode Island were regarded; whether they were looked upon as the establishment of any government, or as a mere pure, unauthorized, unqualified *insurrection* against the authority of the existing government of the State.

I say, therefore, that, upon that ground, these facts are not facts which this court can inquire into, or which the court below could try; because they are facts going to prove (if they prove any thing) the establishment of a new sovereignty; and that is a question to be settled elsewhere and otherwise. From the very nature of the case, it is not a question to be decided by judicial inquiry. Take, for example, one of the points which it involves. My adversary offered to prove that the constitution was adopted by a majority of the people of Rhode Island; by a large majority, as he alleges. What does this offer call on your honors to do? Why, to ascertain, by proof, what is the number of citizens of Rhode Island, and how many attended the meetings at which the delegates to the convention were elected; and then you have to add them all up, and prove by testimony the qualifications of every one of them to be an elector. It is enough to state such a proposition to show its absurdity. As none such ever was sustained in a court of law, so none can be or ought to be sustained. Observe that minutes of proceedings can be no proof, for they were made by no authentic persons; registers were kept by no warranted officers; chairmen and moderators were chosen without authority. In short, there are no official records; there is no testimony in the case but parol. Chief Justice Durfee has stated this so plainly, that I need not dwell upon it.

But, again, I say you cannot look into the facts attempted to be proved, because of the certainty of the continuance of the old government till the new and legal constitution went into effect on the 3d of May, 1843. To prove that there was another constitution of two days' duration would be ridiculous. And I say that the decision of Rhode Island herself, by her legislature, by her executive, by the adjudication of her highest court of law, on the trial of Dorr, has shut up the whole case. Do you propose,--I will not put it in that form,--but would it be proper for this court to reverse that adjudication? That declares that the judges of Rhode Island know nothing of the "People's Constitution." Is it possible, then, for this court, or for the court below, to know any thing of it?

It appears to me that, if there were nothing else in the case, the proceedings of Rhode Island herself must close everybody's mouth, in the court and out of it. Rhode Island is competent to decide the question herself, and everybody else ought to be bound by her decision. And she has decided it.

And it is but a branch of this to say, according to my second proposition,--

2. That if every thing offered had been proved, if in the nature of the case these facts and proceedings could have been received as proof, the court could not have listened to them, because every one of them is regarded by the State in which they took place as a *criminal* act. Who can derive any authority from acts declared to be criminal? The very proceedings which are now set up here show that this pretended constitution was founded upon acts which the legislature of the State had provided punishment for, and which the courts of the State have punished. All, therefore, which the plaintiff has attempted to prove, are acts which he was not allowed to prove, because they were criminal in themselves, and have been so treated and punished, so far as the State government, in its discretion, has thought proper to punish them.

3. Thirdly, and lastly, I say that there is no evidence offered, nor has any distinct allegation been made, that there was an actual government established and put in operation to displace the Charter government, even for a single day. That is evident enough. You find the whole embraced in those two days, the 3d and 4th of May. The French revolution was thought to be somewhat rapid. That took *three* days. But this work was accomplished in two. It is all there, and what is it? Its birth, its whole life, and its death were accomplished in forty-eight hours. What does it appear that the members of this government did? Why, they voted that A should be treasurer, and C, secretary, and Mr. Dorr, governor; and chose officers of the Supreme Court. But did ever any man under that authority attempt to exercise a particle of official power? Did any man ever bring a suit? Did ever an officer make an arrest? Did any act proceed from any member of this government, or from any agent of it, to touch a citizen of Rhode Island in his person, his safety, or his property, so as to make the party answerable upon an indictment or in a civil suit? Never. It never performed one single act of government. It never did a thing in the world! All was patriotism, and all was paper; and with patriotism and with paper it went out on the 4th of May, admitting itself to be, as all must regard it, a contemptible _sham_!

I have now done with the principles involved in this case, and the questions presented on this record.

In regard to the other case, I have but few words to say. And, first, I think it is to be regretted that the court below sent up such a list of points on which it was divided. I shall not go through them, and shall leave it to the court to say whether, after they shall have disposed of the first cause, there is any thing left. I shall only draw attention to the subject of martial law; and in respect to that, instead of going back to martial law as it existed in England at the time the charter of Rhode Island was granted, I shall merely observe that martial law confers power of arrest, of summary trial, and prompt execution; and that when it has been proclaimed, the land becomes a camp, and the law of the camp is the law of the land. Mr. Justice Story defines martial law to be the law of war, a resort to military authority in cases where the civil law is not sufficient; and it confers summary power, not to be used arbitrarily or for the gratification of personal feelings of hatred or revenge, but for the preservation of order and of the public peace. The officer clothed with it is to judge of the degree of force that the necessity of the case may demand; and there is no limit to this, except such as is to be found in the nature and character of the exigency.

I now take leave of this whole case. That it is an interesting incident in the history of our institutions, I freely admit. That it has come hither is a subject of no regret to me. I might have said, that I see nothing to complain of in the proceedings of what is called the Charter government of Rhode Island, except that it might perhaps have discreetly taken measures at an earlier period for revising the constitution. If in that delay it erred, it was the error into which prudent and cautious men would fall. As to the enormity of freehold suffrage, how long is it since Virginia, the parent of States, gave up her freehold suffrage? How long is it since nobody voted for governor in New York without a freehold qualification? There are now States in which no man can vote for members of the upper branch of the legislature who does not own fifty acres of land. Every State requires more or less of a property qualification in its officers and electors; and it is for discreet legislation, or constitutional provisions, to determine what its amount shall be. Even the Dorr constitution had a property qualification. According to its provisions, for officers of the State, to be sure, anybody could vote; but its authors remembered that taxation and representation go together, and therefore they declared that no man, in any town, should vote to lay a tax for town purposes who had not the means to pay his portion. It said to him, You cannot vote in the town of Providence to levy a tax for repairing the streets of Providence; but you may vote for governor, and for thirteen representatives from the town of Providence, and send them to the legislature, and there they may tax the people of Rhode Island at their sovereign will and pleasure.

I believe that no harm can come of the Rhode Island agitation in 1841, but rather good. It will purify the political atmosphere from some of its noxious mists, and I hope it will clear men's minds from unfounded notions and dangerous delusions. I hope it will bring them to look at the regularity, the order, with which we carry on what, if the word were not so much abused, I would call our *glorious* representative system of popular government. Its principles will stand the test of this crisis, as they have stood the test and torture of others. They are exposed always, and they always will be exposed, to dangers. There are dangers from the extremes of too much and of too little popular liberty; from monarchy, or military despotism, on one side, and from licentiousness and anarchy on the other. This always will be the case. The classical navigator had been told that he must pass a narrow and dangerous strait:

"Dextrum Scylla latus, laevum implacata Charybdis, Obsidet."

Forewarned he was alive to his danger, and knew, by signs not doubtful, where he was, when he approached its scene:

"Et gemitum ingentem pelagi, pulsataque saxa, Audimus longe, fractasque ad litora voces; Exsultantque vada, atque aestu miscentur arenae. ... Nimirum haec ilia Charybdis!"

The long-seeing sagacity of our fathers enables us to know equally well where we are, when we hear the voices of tumultuary assemblies, and see the turbulence created by numbers meeting and acting without the restraints of law; and has most wisely provided constitutional means of escape and security. When the established authority of government is openly contemned; when no deference is paid to the regular and authentic declarations of the public will; when assembled masses put themselves above the law, and, calling themselves the people, attempt by force to seize on the government; when the social and political order of the state is thus threatened with overthrow, and the spray of the waves of violent popular commotion lashes the stars,--our political pilots may well cry out:

"Nimirum haec illa Charybdis!"

The prudence of the country, the sober wisdom of the people, has thus far enabled us to carry this Constitution, and all our constitutions, through the perils which have surrounded them, without running upon the rocks on one side, or being swallowed up in the eddying whirlpools of the other. And I fervently hope that this signal happiness and good fortune will continue, and that our children after us will exercise a similar prudence, and wisdom, and justice; and that, under the Divine blessing, our system of free government may continue to go on, with equal prosperity, to the end of time.

[Footnote 1: Art. IV. § 4.][Footnote 2: Statutes at Large, Vol. I. p. 424.][Footnote 3: Mr. Tyler.]

OBJECTS OF THE MEXICAN WAR.

A SPEECH DELIVERED IN THE SENATE OF THE UNITED STATES, ON THE 23D OF MARCH, 1848, ON THE BILL FROM THE HOUSE OF REPRESENTATIVES FOR RAISING A LOAN OF SIXTEEN MILLIONS OF DOLLARS.

[On the 2d of February, 1848, the treaty called a "treaty of peace, friendship, limits, and settlement, between the United States of America and the Mexican Republic," was signed at Guadalupe Hidalgo. This treaty, with the advice and consent of the Senate, was ratified by the President of the United States on the 16th of March. In the mean time, a bill, introduced into the House of Representatives on the 18th of February, to authorize a loan of sixteen millions of dollars for the purpose of carrying on the war, passed through that house, and was considered in the Senate. Other war measures were considered and adopted by the two houses, after the signature and ratification of the treaty. On the 23d of March, the Sixteen Million Loan Bill being under consideration, Mr. Webster spoke as follows.]

MR. PRESIDENT,--On Friday a bill passed the Senate for raising ten regiments of new troops for the further prosecution of the war against Mexico; and we have been informed that that measure is shortly to be followed, in this branch of the legislature, by a bill to raise twenty regiments of volunteers for the same service. I was desirous of expressing my opinions against the object of these bills, against the supposed necessity which leads to their enactment, and against the general policy which they are apparently designed to promote. Circumstances personal to myself, but beyond my control, compelled me to forego, on that day, the execution of that design. The bill now before the Senate is a measure for raising money to meet the exigencies of the government, and to provide the means, as well as for other things, for the pay and support of these thirty regiments.

Sir, the scenes through which we have passed, and are passing, here, are various. For a fortnight the world supposes we have been occupied with the ratification of a treaty of peace, and that within these walls, "the world shut out," notes of peace, and hopes of peace, nay, strong assurances of peace, and indications of peace, have been uttered to console and to cheer us. Sir, it has been over and over stated, and is public, that we have ratified a treaty, of course a treaty of peace, and, as the country has been led to suppose, not of an uncertain, empty, and delusive peace, but of real and substantial, a gratifying and an enduring peace, a peace which would stanch the wounds of war, prevent the further flow of human blood, cut off these enormous expenses, and return our friends, and our brothers, and our children, if they be yet living, from the land of slaughter, and the land of still more dismal destruction by climate, to our firesides and our arms. Hardly have these halcyon notes ceased upon our ears, when, in resumed public session, we are summoned to fresh warlike operations; to create a new army of thirty thousand men for the further prosecution of the war; to carry the war, in the language of the President, still more dreadfully into the vital parts of the enemy, and to press home, by fire and sword, the claims we make, and the grounds which we insist upon, against our fallen, prostrate, I had almost said, our ignoble enemy. If we may judge from the opening speech of the honorable Senator from Michigan, and from other speeches that have been made upon this floor, there has been no time, from the commencement of the war, when it has been more urgently pressed upon us, not only to maintain, but to increase, our military means; not only to continue the war, but to press it still more vigorously than at present.

Pray, what does all this mean? Is it, I ask, confessed, then,--is it confessed that we are no nearer a peace than we were when we snatched up this bit of paper called, or miscalled, a treaty, and ratified it? Have we yet to fight it out to the utmost, as if nothing pacific had intervened?

I wish, Sir, to treat the proceedings of this and of every department of the government with the utmost respect. The Constitution of this government, and the exercise of its just powers in the administration of the laws under it, have been the cherished object of all my unimportant life. But, if the subject were not one too deeply interesting, I should say our proceedings here may well enough cause a smile. In the ordinary transaction of the foreign relations of this and of all other governments, the course has been to negotiate first, and to ratify afterwards. This seems to be the natural order of conducting intercourse between foreign states. We have chosen to reverse this order. We ratify first, and negotiate afterwards. We set up a treaty, such as we find it and choose to make it, and then send two ministers plenipotentiary to negotiate thereupon in the capital of the enemy. One would think, Sir, the ordinary course of proceeding much the juster; that to negotiate, to hold intercourse, and come to some arrangement, by authorized agents, and then to submit that arrangement to the sovereign authority to which these agents are responsible, would be always the most desirable method of proceeding. It strikes me that the course we have adopted is strange, is even *grotesque*. So far as I know, it is unprecedented in the history of diplomatic intercourse. Learned gentlemen on the floor of the Senate, interested to defend and protect this course, may, in their extensive reading, have found examples of it. I know of none.

Sir, we are in possession, by military power, of New Mexico and California, countries belonging hitherto to the United States of Mexico. We are informed by the President that it is his purpose to retain them, to consider them as territory fit to be attached to these United States of America; and our military operations and designs now before the Senate are to enforce this claim of the executive of the United States. We are to compel Mexico to agree that the part of her dominions called New Mexico, and that called California, shall be ceded to us. We are in possession, as is said, and she shall yield her title to us. This is the precise object of this new army of thirty thousand men. Sir, it is the identical object, in my judgment, for which the war was originally commenced, for which it has hitherto been prosecuted, and in furtherance of which this treaty is to be used but as one means to bring about this general result; that general result depending, after all, on our own superior power, and on the necessity of submitting to any terms which we may prescribe to fallen, fallen, fallen Mexico!

Sir, the members composing the other house, the more popular branch of the legislature, have all been elected since, I had almost said the fatal, I will say the remarkable, events of the 11th and 13th days of May, 1846. The other house has passed a resolution affirming that "the war with Mexico was begun unconstitutionally and unnecessarily by the executive government of the United States." I concur in that sentiment; I hold that to be the most recent and authentic expression of the will and opinion of the majority of the people of the United States.

There is, Sir, another proposition, not so authentically announced hitherto, but, in my judgment, equally true and equally capable of demonstration; and that is, that this war was begun, has been continued, and is now prosecuted, for the great and leading purpose of the acquisition of new territory, out of which to bring new States, with their Mexican population, into this our Union of the United States.

If unavowed at first, this purpose did not remain unavowed long. However often it may be said that we did not go to war for conquest,

"credat Judaeus Apella, Non ego,"

yet the moment we get possession of territory we must retain it and make it our own. Now I think that this original object has not been changed, has not been varied. Sir, I think it exists in the eyes of those who originally contemplated it, and who began the war for it, as plain, as attractive to them, and from which they no more avert their eyes now than they did then or have done at any time since. We have compelled a treaty of cession; we know in our consciences that it is compelled. We use it as an instrument and an agency, in conjunction with other instruments and other agencies of a more formidable and destructive character, to enforce the cession of Mexican territory, to acquire territory for new States to be added to this Union. We know, every intelligent man knows, that there is no stronger desire in the breast of a Mexican citizen than to retain the territory which belongs to the republic. We know that the Mexican people will part with it, if part they must, with regret, with pangs of sorrow. That we know; we know it is all forced; and therefore, because we know it must be forced, because we know that (whether the government, which we consider our creature, do or do not agree to it) the Mexican people will never accede to the terms of this treaty but through the impulse of absolute necessity, and the impression made upon them by absolute and irresistible force, therefore we purpose to overwhelm them with another army. We purpose to raise another army of ten thousand regulars and twenty thousand volunteers, and to pour them in and upon the Mexican people.

Now, Sir, I should be happy to agree, notwithstanding all this tocsin, and all this cry of all the Semproniuses in the land, that *their* "voices are still for war,"--I should be happy to agree, and substantially I do agree, to the opinion of the Senator from South Carolina. I think I have myself uttered the sentiment, within a fortnight, to the same effect, that, after all, _the war with Mexico is substantially over_, that there can be no more fighting. In the present state of things, my opinion is that the people of this country will not sustain the war. They will not go for its heavy expenses; they will not find any gratification in putting the bayonet to the throats of the Mexican people. For my part, I hope the ten regiment bill will never become a law. Three weeks ago I should have entertained that hope with the utmost confidence; events instruct me to abate my confidence. I still *hope* it will not pass.

And here, I dare say, I shall be called by some a "Mexican Whig." The man who can stand up here and say that he hopes that what the administration projects, and the further prosecution of the war with Mexico requires, may not be carried into effect, must be an enemy to his country, or what gentlemen have considered the same thing, an enemy to the President of the United States, and to his administration and his party. He is a Mexican. Sir, I think very badly of the Mexican character, high and low, out and out; but names do not terrify me. Besides, if I have suffered in this respect, if I have rendered myself subject to the reproaches of these stipendiary presses, these hired abusers of the motives of public men, I have the honor, on this occasion, to be in very respectable company. In the reproachful sense of that term, I don't know a greater Mexican in this body than the honorable Senator from Michigan, the chairman of the Committee on Military Affairs.

MR. CASS. Will the gentleman be good enough to explain what sort of a Mexican I am?

On the resumption of the bill in the Senate the other day, the gentleman told us that its principal object was to frighten Mexico; it would touch his humanity too much to hurt her! He would frighten her--

MR. CASS. Does the gentleman affirm that I said that?

Yes; twice.

MR. CASS. No, Sir, I beg your pardon, I did not say it. I did not say it would touch my humanity to hurt her.

Be it so.

MR. CASS. Will the honorable Senator allow me to repeat my statement of the object of the bill? I said it was twofold: first, that it would enable us to prosecute the war, if necessary; and, second, that it would show Mexico we were prepared to do so; and thus, by its moral effect, would induce her to ratify the treaty. The gentleman said, that the principal object of the bill was to frighten Mexico, and that this would be more humane than to harm her.

MR. CASS. That's true.

Well, Sir, the remarkable characteristic of that speech, that which makes it so much a Mexican speech, is, that the gentleman spoke it in the hearing of Mexico, as well as in the hearing of this Senate. We are accused here, because what we say is heard by Mexico, and Mexico derives encouragement from what is said here. And yet the honorable member comes forth and tells Mexico that the principal object of the bill is to frighten her! The words have passed along the wires; they are on the Gulf, and are floating away to Vera Cruz; and when they get there, they will signify to Mexico, "After all, ye good Mexicans, my principal object is to frighten you; and to the end that you may not be frightened too much, I have given you this indication of my purpose."

But, Sir, in any view of this case, in any view of the proper policy of this government, to be pursued according to any man's apprehension and judgment, where is the necessity for this augmentation, by regiments, of the military force of the country? I hold in my hand here a note, which I suppose to be substantially correct, of the present military force of the United States. I cannot answer for its entire accuracy, but I believe it to be substantially according to fact. We have twenty-five regiments of regular troops, of various arms; if full, they would amount to 28,960 rank and file, and including officers to 30,296 men. These, with the exception of six or seven hundred men, are now all out of the United States and in field service in Mexico, or _en route_ to Mexico. These regiments are not full; casualties and the climate have sadly reduced their numbers. If the recruiting service were now to yield ten thousand men, it would not more than fill up these regiments, so that every brigadier and colonel and captain should have his appropriate and his full command. Here is a call, then, on the country now for the enlistment of ten thousand men, to fill up the regiments in the foreign service of the United States.

I understand, Sir, that there is a report from General Scott; from General Scott, a man who has performed the most brilliant campaign on recent military record, a man who has warred against the enemy, warred against the climate, warred against a thousand unpropitious circumstances, and has carried the flag of his country to the capital of the enemy, honorably, proudly, _humanely_, to his own permanent honor, and the great military credit of his country,--General Scott; and where is he? At Puebla! at Puebla, undergoing an inquiry before his inferiors in rank, and other persons without military rank while the high powers he has exercised, and exercised with so much distinction, are transferred to another, I do not say to one unworthy of them, but to one inferior in rank, station, and experience to himself.

But General Scott reports, as I understand, that, in February, there were twenty thousand regular troops under his command and _en route_, and we have thirty regiments of volunteers for the war. If full, this would make thirty-four thousand men, or, including officers, thirty-five thousand. So that, if the regiments were full, there is at this moment a number of troops, regular and volunteer, of not less than fifty-five or sixty thousand men, including recruits on the way. And with these twenty thousand men in the field, of regular troops, there were also ten thousand volunteers; making, of regulars and volunteers under General Scott, thirty thousand men. The Senator from Michigan knows these things better than I do, but I believe this is very nearly the fact. Now all these troops are regularly officered; there is no deficiency, in the line or in the staff, of officers. They are all full. Where there is any deficiency it consists of men.

Now, Sir, there may be a plausible reason for saying that there is difficulty in recruiting at home for the supply of deficiency in the volunteer regiments. It may be said that volunteers choose to enlist under officers of their own knowledge and selection; they do not incline to enlist as individual volunteers, to join regiments abroad, under officers of whom they know nothing. There may be something in that; but pray what conclusion does it lead to, if not to this, that all these regiments must moulder away, by casualties or disease, until the privates are less in number than the officers themselves.

But however that may be with respect to volunteers, in regard to recruiting for the regular service, in filling up the regiments by pay and bounties according to existing laws, or new laws, if new ones are necessary, there is no reason on earth why we should now create five hundred new officers, for the purpose of getting ten thousand more men. The officers are already there; in that respect there is no deficiency. All that is wanted is men, and there is place for the men; and I suppose no gentleman, here or elsewhere, thinks that recruiting will go on faster than would be necessary to obtain men to fill up the deficiencies in the regiments abroad.

But now, Sir, what do we want of a greater force than we have in Mexico? I am not saying, What do we want of a force greater than we can supply? but, What is the object of bringing these new regiments into the field? What do we propose? There is no army to fight. I suppose there are not five hundred men under arms in any part of Mexico; probably not half that number, except in one place. Mexico is prostrate. It is not the government that resists us. Why, it is notorious that the government of Mexico is on our side, that it is an instrument by which we hope to establish such a peace, and accomplish such a treaty, as we like. As far as I understand the matter, the government of Mexico owes its life and breath and being to the support of our arms, and to the hope, I do not say how inspired, that somehow or other, and at no distant period, she will have the pecuniary means of carrying it on, from our three millions, or our twelve millions, or from some of our other millions.

What do we propose to do, then, with these thirty regiments which it is designed to throw into Mexico? Are we going to cut the throats of her people? Are we to thrust the sword deeper and deeper into the "vital parts" of Mexico? What is it proposed to do? Sir, I can see no object in it; and yet, while we are pressed and urged to adopt this proposition to raise ten and twenty regiments, we are told, and the public is told, and the public believes, that we are on the verge of a safe and an honorable peace. Every one looks every morning for tidings of a confirmed peace, or of confirmed hopes of peace. We gather it from the administration, and from every organ of the administration from Dan to Beersheba. And yet warlike preparations, the incurring of expenses, the imposition of new charges upon the treasury, are pressed here, as if peace were not in all our thoughts, at least not in any of our expectations.

Now, Sir, I propose to hold a plain talk to-day; and I say that, according to my best judgment, the object of the bill is patronage, office, the gratification of friends. This very measure for raising ten regiments creates four or five hundred officers; colonels, subalterns, and not them only, for for all these I feel some respect, but there are also paymasters, contractors, persons engaged in the transportation service, commissaries, even down to sutlers, _et id genus omne_, people who handle the public money without facing the foe, one and all of whom are true descendants, or if not, true representatives, of Ancient Pistol, who said,

"I shall sutler be Unto the camp, and profits will accrue."

Sir, I hope, with no disrespect for the applicants, and the aspirants, and the patriots (and among them are some sincere patriots) who would fight for their country, and those others who are not ready to fight, but who are willing to be paid,--with due respect for all of them according to their several degrees and their merits, I hope they will all be disappointed. I hope that, as the pleasant season advances, the whole may find it for their interest to place themselves, of mild mornings, in the cars, and take their destination to their respective places of honorable private occupation and of civil employment. They have my good wishes that they may find the way to their homes from the Avenue and the Capitol, and from the purlieus of the President's house, in good health themselves, and that they may find their families all very happy to receive them.

But, Sir, to speak more seriously, this war was waged for the object of creating new States, on the southern frontier of the United States, out of Mexican territory, and with such population as could be found resident thereupon. I have opposed this object. I am against all accessions of territory to form new States. And this is no matter of sentimentality, which I am to parade before mass meetings or before my constituents at home. It is not a matter with me of declamation, or of regret, or of expressed repugnance. It is a matter of firm, unchangeable purpose. I yield nothing to the force of circumstances that have occurred, or that I can consider as likely to occur. And therefore I say, Sir, that, if I were asked to-day whether, for the sake of peace, I would take a treaty for adding two new States to the Union on our southern border, I would say, _No!_ distinctly, No! And I wish every man in the United States to understand that to be my judgment and my purpose.

I said upon our *southern* border, because the present proposition takes that locality. I would say the same of the western, the northeastern, or of any other border. I resist to-day, and for ever, and to the end, any proposition to add any foreign territory, south or west, north or east, to the States of this Union, as they are constituted and held together under the Constitution. I do not want the colonists of England on the north; and as little do I want the population of Mexico on the south. I resist and reject all, and all with equal resolution. Therefore I say, that, if the question were put to me to-day, whether I would take peace under the present state of the country, distressed as it is, during the existence of a war odious as this is, under circumstances so afflictive as now exist to humanity, and so disturbing to the business of those whom I represent,--I say still, if it were put to me whether I would have peace, with new States, I would say, No! no! And that because, Sir, in my judgment, there is no necessity of being driven into that dilemma. Other gentlemen think differently. I hold no man's conscience; but I mean to make a clean breast of it myself; and I protest that I see no reason, I believe there is none, why we cannot obtain as safe a peace, as honorable and as prompt a peace, without territory as with it. The two things are separable. There is no necessary connection between them. Mexico does not wish us to take her territory, while she receives our money. Far from it. She yields her assent, if she yields it at all, reluctantly, and we all know it. It is the result of force, and there is no man here who does not know that. And let me say, Sir, that, if this Trist paper shall finally be rejected in Mexico, it is most likely to be because those who under our protection hold the power there cannot persuade the Mexican Congress or people to agree to this cession of territory. The thing most likely to break up what we now expect to take place is the repugnance of the Mexican people to part with their territory. They would prefer to keep their territory, and that we should keep our money; as I prefer we should keep our money, and they their territory. We shall see. I pretend to no powers of prediction. I do not know what may happen. The times are full of strange events. But I think it certain that, if the treaty which has gone to Mexico shall fail to be ratified, it will be because of the aversion of the Mexican Congress, or the Mexican people, to cede the territory, or any part of it, belonging to their republic.

I have said that I would rather have no peace for the present, than have a peace which brings territory for new States; and the reason is, that we shall get peace as soon without territory as with it, more safe, more durable, and vastly more honorable to us, the great republic of the world.

But we hear gentlemen say, We must have some territory, the people demand it. I deny it; at least, I see no proof of it whatever. I do not doubt that there are individuals of an enterprising character, disposed to emigrate, who know nothing about New Mexico but that it is far off, and nothing about California but that it is still farther off, who are tired of the dull pursuits of agriculture and of civil life; that there are hundreds and thousands of such persons to whom whatsoever is new and distant is attractive. They feel the spirit of borderers; and the spirit of a borderer, I take it, is to be tolerably contented with his condition where he is, until somebody goes to regions beyond him; and then he is all eagerness to take up his traps and go still farther than he who has thus got in advance of him. With such men the desire to emigrate is an irresistible passion. At least so thought that sagacious observer of human nature, M. de Talleyrand, when he travelled in this country in 1794.

But I say I do not find anywhere any considerable and respectable body of persons who want more territory, and such territory. Twenty-four of us last year in this house voted against the prosecution of the war for territory, because we did not want it, both Southern and Northern men. I believe the Southern gentlemen who concurred in that vote found themselves, even when they had gone against what might be supposed to be local feelings and partialities, sustained on the general policy of not seeking territory, and by the acquisition of territory bringing into our politics certain embarrassing and embroiling questions and considerations. I do not learn that they suffered from the advocacy of such a sentiment. I believe they were supported in it; and I believe that through the greater part of the South, and even of the Southwest, there is no prevalent opinion in favor of acquiring territory, and such territory, and of the augmentation of our population by such an accession. And such, I need not say, is, if not the undivided, the preponderating sentiment of all the North.

But it is said we must take territory for the sake of peace. We must take territory. It is the will of the President. If we do not now take what he offers, we may fare worse. Mr. Polk will take no less, that he is fixed upon, He is immovable. He--has--put--down--his--foot! Well, Sir, he put it down upon "fifty-four forty," but it didn't stay. I speak of the President, as of all Presidents, without disrespect. I know of no reason why his opinion and his will, his purpose, declared to be final, should control us, any more than our purpose, from equally conscientious motives, and under as high responsibilities, should control him. We think he is firm, and will not be moved. I should be sorry, Sir, very sorry indeed, that we should entertain more respect for the firmness of the individual at the head of the government than we entertain for our own firmness. He stands out against us. Do we fear to stand out against him? For one, I do not. It appears to me to be a slavish doctrine. For one, I am willing to meet the issue, and go to the people all over this broad land. Shall we take peace without new States, or refuse peace without new States? I will stand upon that, and trust the people. And I do that because I think it right, and because I have no distrust of the people. I am not unwilling to put it to their sovereign decision and arbitration. I hold this to be a question vital, permanent, elementary, in the future prosperity of the country and the maintenance of the Constitution; and I am willing to trust that question to the people. I prefer that it should go to them, because, if what I take to be a great constitutional principle, or what is essential to its maintenance, is to be broken down, let it be the act of the people themselves; it shall never be my act. I, therefore, do not distrust the people. I am willing to take their sentiment, from the Gulf to the British Provinces, and from the ocean to the Missouri: Will you continue the war for territory, to be purchased, after all, at an enormous price, a price a thousand times the value of all its purchases, or take peace, contenting yourselves with the honor we have reaped by the military achievements of the army? Will you take peace without territory, and preserve the integrity of the Constitution of the country? I am entirely willing to stand upon that question. I will therefore take the issue: _Peace, with no new States, keeping our own money ourselves, or war till new States shall be acquired, and vast sums paid._ That is the true issue. I am willing to leave that before the people and to the people, because it is a question for themselves. If they support me and think with me, very well. If otherwise, if they will have territory and add new States to the Union, let them do so; and let them be the artificers of their own fortune, for good or for evil.

But, Sir, we tremble before executive power. The truth cannot be concealed. We tremble before executive power! Mr. Polk will take no less than this. If we do not take this, the king's anger may kindle, and he will give us what is worse.

But now, Sir, who and what is Mr. Polk? I speak of him with no manner of disrespect. I mean, thereby, only to ask who and what is the President of the United States for the current moment. He is in the last year of his administration. Formally, officially, it can only be drawn out till the fourth of March, while really and substantially we know that two short months will, or may, produce events that will render the duration of that official term of very little importance. We are on the eve of a Presidential election. That machinery which is employed to collect public opinion or party opinion will be put in operation two months hence. We shall see its result. It may be that the present incumbent of the Presidential office will be again presented to his party friends and admirers for their suffrages for the next Presidential term. I do not say how probable or improbable this is. Perhaps it is not entirely probable. Suppose this not to be the result, what then? Why, then Mr. Polk becomes as absolutely insignificant as any respectable man among the public men of the United States. Honored in private life, valued for his private character, respectable, never eminent, in public life, he will, from the moment a new star arises, have just as little influence as you or I; and, so far as I am concerned, that certainly is little enough.

Sir, political partisans, and aspirants, and office-seekers, are not sunflowers. They do not "turn to their god when he sets The same look which they turned when he rose."

No, Sir, if the respectable gentleman now at the head of the government be nominated, there will be those who will commend his consistency, who will be bound to maintain it, for the interest of his party friends will require it. It will be done. If otherwise, who is there in the whole length and breadth of the land that will care for the consistency of the present incumbent of the office? There will then be new objects. "Manifest destiny" will have pointed out some other man. Sir, the eulogies are now written, the commendations are already elaborated. I do not say every thing fulsome, but every thing panegyrical, has already been written out, with *blanks* for names, to be filled when the convention shall adjourn. When "manifest destiny" shall be unrolled, all these strong panegyrics, wherever they may light, made beforehand, laid up in pigeon-holes, studied, framed, emblazoned, and embossed, will all come out; and then there will be found to be somebody in the United States whose merits have been strangely overlooked, marked out by Providence, a kind of miracle, while all will wonder that nobody ever thought of him before, as a fit, and the only fit, man to be at the head of this great republic!

I shrink not, therefore, from any thing that I feel to be my duty, from any apprehension of the importance and imposing dignity, and the power of will, ascribed to the present incumbent of office. But I wish we possessed that power of will. I wish we had that firmness. Yes, Sir, I wish we had adherence. I wish we could gather something from the spirit of our brave forces, who have met the enemy under circumstances most adverse and have stood the shock. I wish we could imitate Zachary Taylor in his bivouac on the field of Buena Vista. He said he "would remain for the night; he would feel the enemy in the morning, and try his position." I wish, before we surrender, we could make up *our* minds to "*feel* the enemy, and try his position," and I think we should find him, as Taylor did, under the early sun, on his way to San Luis Potosi. That is my judgment.

But, Sir, I come to the all-absorbing question, more particularly, of the creation of New States.

Some years before I entered public life, Louisiana had been obtained under the treaty with France. Shortly after, Florida was obtained under the treaty with Spain. These two countries were situated on our frontier, and commanded the outlets of the great rivers which flow into the Gulf. As I have had occasion to say, in the first of these instances, the President of the United States[1] supposed that an amendment of the Constitution was required. He acted upon that supposition. Mr. Madison was Secretary of State, and, upon the suggestion of the President, proposed that the proper amendment to the Constitution should be submitted, to bring Louisiana into the Union. Mr. Madison drew it, and submitted it to Mr. Adams, as I have understood. Mr. Madison did not go upon any general idea that new States might be admitted; he did not proceed to a general amendment of the Constitution in that respect. The amendment which he proposed and submitted to Mr. Adams was a simple declaration, by a new article, that "the Province of Louisiana is hereby declared to be part and parcel of the United States." But public opinion, seeing the great importance of the acquisition, took a turn favorable to the affirmation of the power. The act was acquiesced in, and Louisiana became a part of the Union, without any amendment of the Constitution.

On the example of Louisiana, Florida was admitted.

Now, Sir, I consider those transactions as passed, settled, legalized. There they stand as matters of political history. They are facts against which it would be idle at this day to contend.

My first agency in matters of this kind was upon the proposition for admitting Texas into this Union. That I thought it my duty to oppose, upon the general ground of opposing all formation of new States out of foreign territory, and, I may add, and I ought to add in justice, of States in which slaves were to be represented in the Congress of the United States. I was opposed to this on the ground of its inequality. It happened to me, Sir, to be called upon to address a political meeting in New York, in 1837, soon after the recognition of Texan Independence. I state now, Sir, what I have often stated before, that no man, from the first, has been a more sincere well-wisher to the government and the people of Texas than myself. I looked upon the achievement of their independence in the battle of San Jacinto as an extraordinary, almost a marvellous, incident in the affairs of mankind. I was among the first disposed to acknowledge her independence. But from the first, down to this moment, I have opposed, as far as I was able, the annexation of new States to this Union. I stated my reasons on the occasion now referred to, in language which I have now before me, and which I beg to present to the Senate.

Mr. Webster here read the passage from his speech at Niblo's Saloon, New York, which will be found in a previous part of this work, pages 429, 430, beginning, "But it cannot be disguised, Gentlemen, that a desire, or an intention, is already manifested to annex Texas to the United States."

Well, Sir, for a few years I held a position in the executive administration of the government. I left the Department of State in 1843, in the month of May. Within a month after, another (an intelligent gentleman, for whom I cherished a high respect, and who came to a sad and untimely end) had taken my place, I had occasion to know, not officially, but from circumstances, that the annexation of Texas was taken up by Mr. Tyler's administration as an administration measure. It was pushed, pressed, insisted on; and I believe the honorable gentleman to whom I have referred[2] had something like a passion for the accomplishment of this purpose. And I am afraid that the President of the United States[3] at that time suffered his ardent feelings not a little to control his more prudent judgment. At any rate, I saw, in 1843, that annexation had become a purpose of the administration. I was not in Congress nor in public life. But, seeing this state of things, I thought it my duty to admonish the country, so far as I could, of the existence of that purpose. There are gentlemen at the North, many of them, there are gentlemen now in the Capitol, who know that, in the summer of 1843, being fully persuaded that this purpose was embraced with zeal and determination by the executive department of the government of the United States, I thought it my duty, and asked them to concur with me in the attempt, to make that purpose known to the country. I conferred with gentlemen of distinction and influence. I proposed means for exciting public attention to the question of annexation, before it should have become a party question; for I had learned that, when any topic becomes a party question, it is in vain to argue upon it.

But the optimists and the quietists, and those who said, All things are well, and let all things alone, discouraged, discountenanced, and repressed any such effort. The North, they said, could take care of itself; the country could take care of itself, and would not sustain Mr. Tyler in his project of annexation. When the time should come, they said, the power of the North would be felt, and would be found sufficient to resist and prevent the consummation of the measure. And I could now refer to paragraphs and articles in the most respectable and leading journals of the North, in which it was attempted to produce the impression that there was no danger; there could be no addition of new States, and men need not alarm themselves about that.

I was not in Congress, Sir, when the preliminary resolutions, providing for the annexation of Texas, passed. I only know that, up to a very short period before the passage of those resolutions, the impression in that part of the country of which I have spoken was, that no such measure could be adopted. But I have found, in the course of thirty years' experience, that whatever measures the executive government may embrace and push are quite likely to succeed in the end. There is always a giving way somewhere. The executive government acts with uniformity, with steadiness, with entire unity of purpose. And sooner or later, often enough, and, according to my construction of our history, quite too often, it effects its purposes. In this way it becomes the predominating power of the government.

Well, Sir, just before the commencement of the present administration, the resolutions for the annexation of Texas were passed in Congress. Texas complied with the provisions of those resolutions, and was here, or the case was here, on the 22d day of December, 1845, for her final admission into the Union, as one of the States. I took occasion then to say, that I hoped I had shown all proper regard for Texas; that I had been certainly opposed to annexation; that, if I should go over the whole matter again, I should have nothing new to add; that I had acted, all along, under the unanimous declaration of all parties, and of the legislature of Massachusetts; that I thought there must be some limit to the extent of our territories, and that I wished this country should exhibit to the world the example of a powerful republic, without greediness and hunger of empire. And I added, that while I held, with as much faithfulness as any citizen of the country, to all the original arrangements and compromises of the Constitution under which we live, I never could, and I never should, bring myself to be in favor of the admission of any States into the Union as slave-holding States; and I might have added, any States at all, to be formed out of territories not now belonging to us.

Now, as I have said, in all this I acted under the resolutions of the State of Massachusetts, certainly concurrent with my own judgment, so often repeated, and reaffirmed by the unanimous consent of all men of all parties, that I could not well go through the series, pointing out, not only the impolicy, but the unconstitutionality, of such annexation. If a State proposes to come into the Union, and to come in as a slave State, then there is an augmentation of the inequality in the representation of the people; an inequality already existing, with which I do not quarrel, and which I never will attempt to alter, but shall preserve as long as I have a vote to give, or any voice in this government, because it is a part of the original compact. Let it stand. But then there is another consideration of vastly more general importance even than that; more general, because it affects all the States, free and slave-holding; and it is, that, if States formed out of territories thus thinly populated come into the Union, they necessarily and inevitably break up the relation existing between the two branches of the government, and destroy its balance. They break up the intended relation between the Senate and the House of Representatives. If you bring in new States, any State that comes in must have two Senators. She may come in with fifty or sixty thousand people, or more. You may have, from a particular State, more Senators than you have Representatives. Can any thing occur to disfigure and derange the form of government under which we live more signally than that? Here would be a Senate bearing no proportion to the people, out of all relation to them, by the addition of new States; from some of them only one Representative, perhaps, and two Senators, whereas the larger States may have ten, fifteen, or even thirty Representatives, and but two Senators. The Senate, augmented by these new Senators coming from States where there are few people, becomes an odious oligarchy. It holds power without any adequate constituency. Sir, it is but "borough-mongering" upon a large scale. Now, I do not depend upon theory; I ask the Senate and the country to look at facts, to see where we were when we made our departure three years ago, and where we now are; and I leave it to the imagination to conjecture where we shall be.

We admitted Texas,--one State for the present; but, Sir, if you refer to the resolutions providing for the annexation of Texas, you find a provision that it shall be in the power of Congress hereafter to make four new States out of Texan territory. Present and prospectively, five new States, with ten Senators, may come into the Union out of Texas. Three years ago we did this; we now propose to make two States.

Undoubtedly, if we take, as the President recommends, New Mexico and California, there must then be four new Senators. We shall then have provided, in these territories out of the United States along our southern borders, for the creation of States enough to send fourteen Senators into this chamber. Now, what will be the relation between these Senators and the people they represent, or the States from which they come? I do not understand that there is any very accurate census of Texas. It is generally supposed to contain one hundred and fifty thousand persons. I doubt whether it contains above one hundred thousand. MR. MANGUM. It contains one hundred and forty-nine thousand.

My honorable friend on my left says, a hundred and forty-nine thousand. I put it down, then, one hundred and fifty thousand. Well, Sir, Texas is not destined, probably, to be a country of dense population. We will suppose it to have at the present time a population of near one hundred and fifty thousand. New Mexico may have sixty or seventy thousand inhabitants; say seventy thousand. In California, there are not supposed to be above twenty-five thousand men; but undoubtedly, if this territory should become ours, persons from Oregon, and from our Western States, will find their way to San Francisco, where there is some good land, and we may suppose they will shortly amount to sixty or seventy thousand. We will put them down at seventy thousand. Then the whole territory in this estimate, which is as high as any man puts it, will contain two hundred and ninety thousand persons, and they will send us, whenever we ask for them, fourteen Senators; a population less than that of the State of Vermont, and not the eighth part of that of New York. Fourteen Senators, and not as many people as Vermont, and no more people than New Hampshire! and not so many people as the good State of New Jersey!

But then, Sir, Texas claims to the line of the Rio Grande, and if it be her true line, why then of course she absorbs a considerable part, nay, the greater part, of the population of what is now called New Mexico. I do not argue the question of the true southern or western line of Texas; I only say, that it is apparent to everybody who will look at the map, and learn any thing of the matter, that New Mexico cannot be divided by this river, the Rio Grande, which is a shallow, fordable, insignificant stream, creeping along through a narrow valley, at the base of enormous mountains. New Mexico must remain together; it must be a State, with its seventy thousand people, and so it will be; and so will California.

But then, Sir, suppose Texas to remain a unit, and but one State for the present; still we shall have three States, Texas, New Mexico, and California. We shall have six Senators, then, for less than three hundred thousand people. We shall have as many Senators for three hundred thousand people in that region as we have for New York, Pennsylvania, and Ohio, with four or five millions of people; and that is what we call an equal representation! Is not this enormous? Have gentlemen considered this? Have they looked at it? Are they willing to look it in the face, and then say they embrace it? I trust, Sir, the people will look at it and consider it. And now let me add, that this disproportion can never be diminished; it must remain for ever. How are you going to diminish it? Why, here is Texas, with a hundred and forty-nine thousand people, with one State. Suppose that population should flow into Texas, where will it go? Not to any dense point, but to be spread over all that region, in places remote from the Gulf, in places remote from what is now the capital of Texas; and therefore, as soon as there are in other portions of Texas people enough within our common construction of the Constitution and our practice in respect to the admission of States, my honorable friend from Texas[4] will have a new State, and I have no doubt he has chalked it out already.

As to New Mexico, its population is not likely to increase. It is a settled country; the people living along in the bottom of the valley on the sides of a little stream, a garter of land only on one side and the other, filled by coarse landholders and miserable *peons*. It can sustain, not only under this cultivation, but under any cultivation that our American race would ever submit to, no more people than are there now. There will, then, be two Senators for sixty thousand inhabitants in New Mexico to the end of our lives and to the end of the lives of our children.

And how is it with California? We propose to take California, from the forty-second degree of north latitude down to the thirty-second. We propose to take ten degrees along the coast of the Pacific. Scattered along the coast for that great distance are settlements and villages and ports; and in the rear all is wilderness and barrenness, and Indian country. But if, just about San Francisco, and perhaps Monterey, emigrants enough should settle to make up one State, then the people five hundred miles off would have another State. And so this disproportion of the Senate to the people will go on, and must go on, and we cannot prevent it.

I say, Sir, that, according to my conscientious conviction, we are now fixing on the Constitution of the United States, and its frame of government, a monstrosity, a disfiguration, an enormity! Sir, I hardly dare trust myself. I don't know but I may be under some delusion. It may be the weakness of my eyes that forms this monstrous apparition. But, if I may trust myself, if I can persuade myself that I am in my right mind, then it does appear to me that we in this Senate have been and are acting, and are likely to be acting hereafter, and immediately, a part which will form the most remarkable epoch in the history of our country. I hold it to be enormous, flagrant, an outrage upon all the principles of popular republican government, and on the elementary provisions of the Constitution under which we live, and which we have sworn to support.

But then, Sir, what relieves the case from this enormity? What is our reliance? Why, it is that we stipulate that these new States shall only be brought in at a suitable time. And pray, what is to constitute the suitableness of time? Who is to judge of it? I tell you, Sir, that suitable time will come when the preponderance of party power here makes it necessary to bring in new States. Be assured it will be a suitable time when votes are wanted in this Senate. We have had some little experience of that. Texas came in at a "suitable time," a *very* suitable time! Texas was finally admitted in December, 1845. My friend near me here, for whom I have a great regard, and whose acquaintance I have cultivated with pleasure,[5] took his seat in March, 1846, with his colleague. In July, 1846, these two Texan votes turned the balance in the Senate, and overthrew the tariff of 1842, in my judgment the best system of revenue ever established in this country. Gentlemen on the opposite side think otherwise. They think it fortunate. They think that was a suitable time, and they mean to take care that other times shall be equally suitable. I understand it perfectly well. That is the difference of opinion between me and these honorable gentlemen. To their policy, their objects, and their purposes the time was _suitable_, and the aid was efficient and decisive.

Sir, in 1850 perhaps a similar question may be agitated here. It is not likely to be before that time, but agitated it will be then, unless a change in the administration of the government shall take place. According to my apprehension, looking at general results as flowing from our established system of commerce and revenue, in two years from this time we shall probably be engaged in a new revision of our system: in the work of establishing, if we can, a tariff of specific duties; of protecting, if we can, our domestic industry and the manufactures of the country; in the work of preventing, if we can, the overwhelming flood of foreign importations. Suppose that to be part of the future: that would be exactly the "suitable time," if necessary, for two Senators from New Mexico to make their appearance here!

But, again, we hear another halcyon, soothing tone, which quiets none of my alarms, assuages none of my apprehensions, commends me to my nightly rest with no more resignation. And that is, the plea that we may trust the popular branch of the legislature, we may look to the House of Representatives, to the Northern and Middle States and even the sound men of the South, and trust them to take care that States be not admitted sooner than they should be, or for party purposes. I am compelled, by experience, to distrust all such reliances. If we cannot rely on ourselves, when we have the clear constitutional authority competent to carry us through, and the motives intensely powerful, I beg to know how we can rely on others. Have we more reliance on the patriotism, the firmness, of others, than on our own?

Besides, experience shows us that things of this sort may be *sprung* upon Congress and the people. It was so in the case of Texas. It was so in the Twenty-eighth Congress. The members of that Congress were not chosen to decide the question of annexation or no annexation. They came in on other grounds, political and party, and were supported for reasons not connected with that question. What then? The administration sprung upon them the question of annexation. It obtained a *snap* judgment upon it, and carried the measure of annexation. That is indubitable, as I could show by many instances, of which I shall state only one. Four gentlemen from the State of Connecticut were elected before the question arose, belonging to the dominant party. They had not been here long before they were committed to annexation; and when it was known in Connecticut that annexation was in contemplation, remonstrances, private, public, and legislative, were uttered, in tones that any one could hear who could hear thunder. Did they move them? Not at all. Every one of them voted for annexation! The election came on, and they were turned out, to a man. But what did those care who had had the benefit of their votes? Such agencies, if it be not more proper to call them such instrumentalities, retain respect no longer than they continue to be useful.

Sir, we take New Mexico and California; who is weak enough to suppose that there is an end? Don't we hear it avowed every day, that it would be proper also to take Sonora, Tamaulipas, and other provinces of Northern Mexico? Who thinks that the hunger for dominion will stop here of itself? It is said, to be sure, that our present acquisitions will prove so lean and unsatisfactory, that we shall seek no further. In my judgment, we may as well say of a rapacious animal, that, if he has made one unproductive hunt, he will not try for a better foray.

But further. There are some things one can argue against with temper, and submit to, if overruled, without mortification. There are other things that seem to affect one's consciousness of being a sensible man, and to imply a disposition to impose upon his common sense. And of this class of topics, or pretences, I have never heard of any thing, and I cannot conceive of any thing, more ridiculous in itself, more absurd, and more affrontive to all sober judgment, than the cry that we are getting indemnity by the acquisition of New Mexico and California. I hold they are not worth a dollar; and we pay for them vast sums of money! We have expended, as everybody knows, large treasures in the prosecution of the war; and now what is to constitute this indemnity? What do gentlemen mean by it? Let us see a little how this stands. We get a country; we get, in the first instance, a cession, or an acknowledgment of boundary, (I care not which way you state it,) of the country between the Nueces and the Rio Grande. What this country is appears from a publication made by a gentleman in the other house.[6] He speaks of the country in the following manner:--

"The country from the Nueces to the valley of the Rio Grande is poor, sterile, sandy, and barren, with not a single tree of any size or value on our whole route. The only tree which we saw was the musquit-tree, and very few of these. The musquit is a small tree, resembling an old and decayed peach-tree. The whole country may be truly called a perfect waste, uninhabited and uninhabitable. There is not a drop of running water between the two rivers, except in the two small streams of San Salvador and Santa Gertrudis, and these only contain water in the rainy season. Neither of them had running water when we passed them. The *chaparral* commences within forty or fifty miles of the Rio Grande. This is poor, rocky, and sandy; covered with prickly-pear, thistles, and almost every sticking thing, constituting a thick and perfectly impenetrable undergrowth. For any useful or agricultural purpose, the country is not worth a *sous*.

"So far as we were able to form any opinion of this desert upon the other routes which had been travelled, its character, everywhere between the two rivers, is pretty much the same. We learned that the route pursued by General Taylor, south of ours, was through a country similar to that through which we passed; as also was that travelled by General Wool from San Antonio to Presidio on the Rio Grande. From what we both saw and heard, the whole command came to the conclusion which I have already expressed, that it was worth *nothing*. I have no hesitation in saying, that I would not hazard the life of one valuable and useful man for every foot of land between San Patricio and the valley of the Rio Grande. The country is not now, and can never be, of the *slightest value*."

Major Gaines has been there lately. He is a competent observer. He is contradicted by nobody. And so far as that country is concerned, I take it for granted that it is not worth a dollar.

Now of New Mexico, what of that! Forty-nine fiftieths, at least, of the whole of New Mexico, are a barren waste, a desert plain of mountain, with no wood, no timber. Little fagots for lighting a fire are carried thirty or forty miles on mules. There is no fall of rain there, as in temperate climates. It is Asiatic in scenery altogether: enormously high mountains, running up some of them ten thousand feet, with narrow valleys at their bases, through which streams sometimes trickle along. A strip, a garter, winds along, through which runs the Rio Grande, from far away up in the Rocky Mountains to latitude 33°, a distance of three or four hundred miles. There these sixty thousand persons reside. In the mountains on the right and left are streams which, obeying the natural tendency as tributaries, should flow into the Rio Grande, and which, in certain seasons, when rains are abundant, do, some of them, actually reach the Rio Grande; while the greater part always, and all for the greater part of the year, never reach an outlet to the sea, but are absorbed in the sands and desert plains of the country. There is no cultivation there. There is cultivation where there is artificial watering or irrigation, and nowhere else. Men can live only in the narrow valley, and in the gorges of the mountains which rise round it, and not along the course of the streams which lose themselves in the sands.

Now there is no public domain in New Mexico, not a foot of land, to the soil of which we shall obtain title. Not an acre becomes ours when the country becomes ours. More than that, the country is as full of people, such as they are, as it is likely to be. There is not the least thing in it to invite settlement from the fertile valley of the Mississippi. And I undertake to say, there would not be two hundred families of persons who would emigrate from the United States to New Mexico, for agricultural purposes, in fifty years. They could not live there. Suppose they were to cultivate the lands; they could only make them productive in a slight degree by irrigation or artificial watering. The people there produce little, and live on little. That is not the characteristic, I take it, of the people of the Eastern or of the Middle States, or of the Valley of the Mississippi. They produce a good deal, and they consume a good deal.

Again, Sir, New Mexico is not like Texas. I have hoped, and I still hope, that Texas will be filled up from among ourselves, not with Spaniards, not with _peons_; that its inhabitants will not be Mexican landlords, with troops of slaves, predial or otherwise.

Mr. Rusk here rose, and said that he disliked to interrupt the Senator, and therefore he had said nothing while he was describing the country between the Nueces and the Rio Grande; but he wished now to say, that, when that country comes to be known, it will be found to be as valuable as any part of Texas. The valley of the Rio Grande is valuable from its source to its mouth. But he did not look upon *that* as indemnity; he claimed that as the *right* of Texas. So far as the Mexican population is concerned, there is a good deal of it in Texas; and it comprises many respectable persons, wealthy, intelligent, and distinguished. A good many are now moving in from New Mexico, and settling in Texas.

I take what I say from Major Gaines. But I am glad to hear that any part of New Mexico is fit for the foot of civilized man. And I am glad, moreover, that there are some persons in New Mexico who are not so blindly attached to their miserable condition as not to make an effort to come out of their country, and get into a better.

Sir, I would, if I had time, call the attention of the Senate to an instructive speech made in the other house by Mr. Smith of Connecticut. He seems to have examined all the authorities, to have conversed with all the travellers, to have corresponded with all our agents. His speech contains communications from all of them; and I commend it to every man in the United States who wishes to know what we are about to acquire by the annexation of New Mexico.

New Mexico is secluded, isolated, a place by itself, in the midst and at the foot of vast mountains, five hundred miles from the settled part of Texas, and as far from anywhere else! It does not belong anywhere! It has no *belongings* about it! At this moment it is absolutely more retired and shut out from communication with the civilized world than Hawaii or any of the other islands of the Pacific sea. In seclusion and remoteness, New Mexico may press hard on the character and condition of Typee. And its people are infinitely less elevated, in morals and condition, than the people of the Sandwich Islands. We had much better have Senators from Oahu. They are far less intelligent than the better class of our Indian neighbors. Commend me to the Cherokees, to the Choctaws; if you please, speak of the Pawnees, of the Snakes, the Flatfeet, of any thing but the *Digging* Indians, and I will be satisfied not to take the people of New Mexico. Have they any notion of our institutions, or of *any* free institutions? Have they any notion of popular government? Not the slightest! Not the slightest on earth! When the question is asked, What will be their constitution? it is farcical to talk of such people making a constitution for themselves. They do not know the meaning of the term, they do not know its import. They know nothing at all about it; and I can tell you, Sir, that when they are made a Territory, and are to be made a State, such a constitution as the executive power of this government may think fit to send them will be sent, and will be adopted. The constitution of our *fellow citizens* of New Mexico will be framed in the city of Washington.

Now what says in regard to all Mexico Colonel Hardin, that most lamented and distinguished officer, honorably known as a member of the other house, and who has fallen gallantly fighting in the service of his country? Here is his description:--

"The whole country is miserably watered. Large districts have no water at all. The streams are small, and at great distances apart. One day we marched on the road from Monclova to Parras thirty-five miles without water, a pretty severe day's marching for infantry.

"Grass is very scarce, and indeed there is none at all in many regions for miles square. Its place is supplied with prickly-pear and thorny bushes. There is not one acre in two hundred, more probably not one in five hundred, of all the land we have seen in Mexico, which can ever be cultivated; the greater portion of it is the most desolate region I could ever have imagined. The pure granite hills of New England are a paradise to it, for they are without the thorny briers and venomous reptiles which infest the barbed barrenness of Mexico. The good land and cultivated spots in Mexico are but dots on the map. Were it not that it takes so very little to support a Mexican, and that the land which is cultivated yields its produce with little labor, it would be surprising how its sparse population is sustained. All the towns we have visited, with perhaps the exception of Parras, are depopulating, as is also the whole country.

"The people are on a par with their land. One in two hundred or five hundred is rich, and lives like a nabob; the rest are _peons_, or servants sold for debt, who work for their masters, and are as subservient as the slaves of the South, and look like Indians, and, indeed, are not more capable of self-government. One man, Jacobus Sanchez, owns three fourths of all the land our column has passed over in Mexico. We are told we have seen the best part of Northern Mexico; if so, the whole of it is not worth much.

"I came to Mexico in favor of getting or taking enough of it to pay the expenses of the war. I now doubt whether all Northern Mexico is worth the expenses of our column of three thousand men. The expenses of the war must be enormous; we have paid enormous prices for every thing, much beyond the usual prices of the country."

There it is. That's all North Mexico; and New Mexico is not the better part of it.

Sir, there is a recent traveller, not unfriendly to the United States, if we may judge from his work, for he speaks well of us everywhere; an Englishman, named Ruxton. He gives an account of the morals and the manners of the population of New Mexico. And, Mr. President and Senators, I shall take leave to introduce you to these soon to be your respected _fellow-citizens_ of New Mexico:--

"It is remarkable that, although existing from the earliest times of the colonization of New Mexico, a period of two centuries, in a state of continual hostility with the numerous savage tribes of Indians who surround their territory, and in constant insecurity of life and property from their attacks, being also far removed from the enervating influences of large cities, and, in their isolated situation, entirely dependent upon their own resources, the inhabitants are totally destitute of those qualities which, for the above reasons, we might naturally have expected to distinguish them, and are as deficient in energy of character and physical courage as they are in all the moral and intellectual qualities. In their social state but one degree removed from the veriest savages, they might take a lesson even from these in morality and the conventional decencies of life. Imposing no restraint on their passions, a shameless and universal concubinage exists, and a total disregard of morality, to which it would be impossible to find a parallel in any country calling itself civilized. A want of honorable principle, and consummate duplicity and treachery, characterize all their dealings. Liars by nature, they are treacherous and faithless to their friends, cowardly and cringing to their enemies; cruel, as all cowards are, they unite savage ferocity with their want of animal courage; as an example of which, their recent massacre of Governor Bent, and other Americans, may be given, one of a hundred instances."

These, Sir, are soon to be our beloved countrymen!

Mr. President, for a good many years I have struggled in opposition to every thing which I thought tended to strengthen the arm of executive power. I think it is growing more and more formidable every day. And I think that by yielding to it in this, as in other instances, we give it a strength which it will be difficult hereafter to resist. I think that it is nothing less than the fear of executive power which induces us to acquiesce in the acquisition of territory; fear, _fear_, and nothing else.

In the little part which I have acted in public life, it has been my purpose to maintain the people of the United States, what the Constitution designed to make them, _one people_, one in interest, one in character, and one in political feeling. If we depart from that, we break it all up. What sympathy can there be between the people of Mexico and California and the inhabitants of the Valley of the Mississippi and the Eastern States in the choice of a President? Do they know the same man? Do they concur in any general constitutional principles? Not at all.

Arbitrary governments may have territories and distant possessions, because arbitrary governments may rule them by different laws and different systems. Russia may rule in the Ukraine and the provinces of the Caucasus and Kamtschatka by different codes, ordinances, or ukases. We can do no such thing. They must be of us, *part* of us, or else strangers.

I think I see that in progress which will disfigure and deform the Constitution. While these territories remain territories, they will be a trouble and an annoyance; they will draw after them vast expenses; they will probably require as many troops as we have maintained during the last twenty years to defend them against the Indian tribes. We must maintain an army at that immense distance. When they shall become States, they will be still more likely to give us trouble.

I think I see a course adopted which is likely to turn the Constitution of the land into a deformed monster, into a curse rather than a blessing; in fact, a frame of an unequal government, not founded on popular representation, not founded on equality, but on the grossest inequality; and I think that this process will go on, or that there is *danger* that it will go on, until this Union shall fall to pieces. I resist it, to-day and always! Whoever falters or whoever flies, I continue the contest!

I know, Sir, that all the portents are discouraging. Would to God I could auspicate good influences! Would to God that those who think with me, and myself, could hope for stronger support! Would that we could stand where we desire to stand! I see the signs are sinister. But with few, or alone, my position is fixed. If there were time, I would gladly awaken the country. I believe the country might be awakened, although it may be too late. For myself, supported or unsupported, by the blessing of God, I shall do my duty. I see well enough all the adverse indications. But I am sustained by a deep and a conscientious sense of duty; and while supported by that feeling, and while such great interests are at stake, I defy auguries, and ask no omen but my country's cause!

[Footnote 1: Mr. Jefferson.][Footnote 2: Mr. Upshur.][Footnote 3: Mr. Tyler.][Footnote 4: Mr. Rusk.][Footnote 5: Mr. Rusk.] [Footnote 6: Major Gaines.]

EXCLUSION OF SLAVERY FROM THE TERRITORIES.
REMARKS MADE IN THE SENATE OF THE UNITED STATES, ON THE 12TH OF AUGUST, 1848.

[In the course of the first session of the Thirtieth Congress, a bill passed the House of Representatives to organize a government for the Territory of Oregon. This bill received several amendments on its passage through the Senate, and among them one moved by Mr. Douglass of Illinois, on the 10th of August, by which the eighth section of the law of the 6th of March, 1820, for the admission of Missouri, was revived and adopted, as a part of the bill, and declared to be "in full force, and binding, for the future organization of the territories of the United States, in the same sense and with the same understanding with which it was originally adopted."

This, with some of the other amendments of the Senate, was disagreed to by the House. On the return of the bill to the Senate, a discussion arose, and continued for several days, on the question of agreement or disagreement with the amendments of the House to the Senate's amendments.

The principal subject of this discussion was whether the Senate would recede from the above-mentioned amendment moved by Mr. Douglass, which was finally decided in the affirmative. In these discussions, a considerable portion of which was of a conversational character, Mr. Webster took a leading part; but of most of what was said by him, as by other Senators, no report has been preserved. The session of the Senate at which the last and most animated discussion of this subject took place, nominally on Saturday of the 12th of August, was prolonged till ten o'clock, A.M., of Sunday, the 13th. In the course of the debate on this day Mr. Webster spoke as follows.]

I am very little inclined to prolong this debate, and I hope I am utterly disinclined to bring into it any new warmth or excitement. I wish to say a few words, however, first, upon the question as it is presented to us, as a parliamentary question; and secondly, upon the general political questions involved in the debate.

As a question of parliamentary proceeding, I understand the case to be this. The House of Representatives sent us a bill for the establishment of a territorial government in Oregon; and no motion has been made in the Senate to strike out any part of that bill. The bill purporting to respect Oregon, simply and alone, has not been the subject of any objection in this branch of the legislature. The Senate has proposed no important amendment to this bill, affecting Oregon itself; and the honorable member from Missouri[1] was right, entirely right, when he said that the amendment now under consideration had no relation to Oregon. That is perfectly true; and therefore the amendment which the Senate has adopted, and the House has disagreed to, has no connection with the immediate subject before it. The truth is, that it is an amendment by which the Senate wished to have now a public, legal declaration, not respecting Oregon, but respecting the newly acquired territories of California and New Mexico. It wishes now to make a line of slavery, which shall include those new territories. The amendment says that the line of the "Missouri Compromise" shall be the line to the Pacific, and then goes on to say, in the language of the bill as it now stands, that the Ordinance of 1787 shall be applicable to Oregon; and therefore I say that the amendment proposed is foreign to the immediate object of the bill. It does nothing to modify, restrain, or affect, in any way, the government which we propose to establish over Oregon, or the condition or character of that government, or of the people under it. In a parliamentary view, this is the state of the case.

Now, Sir, this amendment has been attached to this bill by a strong majority of the Senate. That majority had the right, as it had the power, to pass it. The House disagreed to that amendment. If the majority of the Senate, who attached it to the bill, are of opinion that a conference with the House will lead to some adjustment of the question, by which this amendment, or something equivalent to it, may be adopted by the House, it is very proper for them to urge a conference. It is very fair, quite parliamentary, and there is not a word to be said against it. But my position is that of one who voted against the amendment, who thinks that it ought not to be attached to this bill; and therefore I naturally vote for the motion to get rid of it, that is, "to recede."

So much for the parliamentary question. Now there are two or three political questions arising in this case, which I wish to state dispassionately; not to argue, but to state. The honorable member from Georgia,[2] for whom I have great respect, and with whom it is my delight to cultivate personal friendship, has stated, with great propriety, the importance of this question. He has said, that it is a question interesting to the South and to the North, and one which may very well also attract the attention of mankind. He has not stated any part of this too strongly. It is such a question. Without doubt, it is a question which may well attract the attention of mankind. On the subjects involved in this debate, the whole world is not now asleep. It is wide awake; and I agree with the honorable member, that, if what is now proposed to be done by us who resist this amendment is, as he supposes, unjust and injurious to any portion of this community, or against its constitutional rights, that injustice should be presented to the civilized world, and we, who concur in the proceeding, ought to submit ourselves to its rebuke. I am glad that the honorable gentleman proposes to refer this question to the great tribunal of Modern Civilization, as well as the great tribunal of the American People. It is proper. It is a question of magnitude enough, of interest enough, to all the civilized nations of the earth, to call from those who support the one side or the other a statement of the grounds upon which they act.

Now I propose to state as briefly as I can the grounds upon which I proceed, historical and constitutional; and will endeavor to use as few words as possible, so that I may relieve the Senate from hearing me at the earliest possible moment. In the first place, to view the matter historically. This Constitution, founded in 1787, and the government under it, organized in 1789, do recognize the existence of slavery in certain States then belonging to the Union, and a particular description of slavery. I hope that what I am about to say may be received without any supposition that I intend the slightest disrespect. But this particular description of slavery does not, I believe, now exist in Europe, nor in any other civilized portion of the habitable globe. It is not a predial slavery. It is not analogous to the case of the *predial* slaves, or slaves *glebae adscripti* of Russia, or Hungary, or other states. It is a peculiar system of personal slavery, by which the person who is called a slave is transferable as a chattel, from hand to hand. I speak of this as a fact; and that is the fact. And I will say further, perhaps other gentlemen may remember the instances, that although slavery, as a system of servitude attached to the earth, exists in various countries of Europe, I am not at the present moment aware of any place on the globe in which this property of man in a human being as a slave, transferable as a chattel, exists, except America. Now, that it existed, in the form in which it still exists, in certain States, at the formation of this Constitution, and that the framers of that instrument, and those who adopted it, agreed that, as far as it existed, it should not be disturbed or interfered with by the new general government, there is no doubt.

The Constitution of the United States recognizes it as an existing fact, an existing relation between the inhabitants of the Southern States. I do not call it an "institution," because that term is not applicable to it; for that seems to imply a voluntary establishment. When I first came here, it was a matter of frequent reproach to England, the mother country, that slavery had been entailed upon the colonies by her, against their consent, and that which is now considered a cherished "institution" was then regarded as, I will not say an _evil_, but an entailment on the Colonies by the policy of the mother country against their wishes. At any rate, it stands upon the Constitution. The Constitution was adopted in 1788, and went into operation in 1789. When it was adopted, the state of the country was this: slavery existed in the Southern States; there was a very large extent of unoccupied territory, the whole Northwestern Territory, which, it was understood, was destined to be formed into States; and it was then determined that no slavery should exist in this territory. I gather now, as a matter of inference from the history of the time and the history of the debates, that the prevailing motives with the North for agreeing to this recognition of the existence of slavery in the Southern States, and giving a representation to those States founded in part upon their slaves, rested on the supposition that no acquisition of territory would be made to form new States on the southern frontier of this country, either by cession or conquest. No one looked to any acquisition of new territory on the southern or southwestern frontier. The exclusion of slavery from the Northwestern Territory and the prospective abolition of the foreign slave trade were generally, the former unanimously, agreed to; and on the basis of these considerations, the South insisted that where slavery existed it should not be interfered with, and that it should have a certain ratio of representation in Congress. And now, Sir, I am one, who, believing such to be the understanding on which the Constitution was framed, mean to abide by it.

There is another principle, equally clear, by which I mean to abide; and that is, that in the Convention, and in the first Congress, when appealed to on the subject by petitions, and all along in the history of this government, it was and has been a conceded point, that slavery in the States in which it exists is a matter of State regulation exclusively, and that Congress has not the least power over it, or right to interfere with it. Therefore I say, that all agitations and attempts to disturb the relations between master and slave, by persons not living in the slave States, are unconstitutional in their spirit, and are, in my opinion, productive of nothing but evil and mischief. I countenance none of them. The manner in which the governments of those States where slavery exists are to regulate it, is for their own consideration, under their responsibility to their constituents, to the general laws of propriety, humanity, and justice, and to God. Associations formed elsewhere, springing from a feeling of humanity, or any other cause, have nothing whatever to do with it, nor right to interfere with it. They have never received any encouragement from me, and they never will. In my opinion, they have done nothing but delay and defeat their own professed objects.

I have now stated, as I understand it, the condition of things upon the adoption of the Constitution of the United States. What has happened since? Sir, it has happened that, above and beyond all contemplation or expectation of the original framers of the Constitution, or the people who adopted it, foreign territory has been acquired by cession, first from France, and then from Spain, on our southern frontier. And what has been the result? Five slave-holding States have been created and added to the Union, bringing ten Senators into this body, (I include Texas, which I consider in the light of a foreign acquisition also,) and up to this hour in which I address you, not one free State has been admitted to the Union from all this acquired territory!

MR. BERRIEN (in his seat). Yes, Iowa.

Iowa is not yet in the Union. Her Senators are not here. When she comes in, there will be one to five, one free State to five slave States, formed out of new territories. Now, it seems strange to me that there should be any complaint of injustice exercised by the North toward the South. Northern votes have been necessary, they have been ready, and they have been given, to aid in the admission of these five new slave-holding States. These are facts; and as the gentleman from Georgia has very properly put it as a case in which we are to present ourselves before the world for its judgment, let us now see how we stand. I do not represent the North. I state my own case; and I present the matter in that light in which I am willing, as an individual member of Congress, to be judged by civilized humanity. I say then, that, according to true history, the slave-holding interest in this country has not been a disfavored interest; it has not been disfavored by the North. The North has concurred to bring in these five slave-holding States out of newly acquired territory, which acquisitions were not at all in the contemplation of the Convention which formed the Constitution, or of the people when they agreed that there should be a representation of three fifths of the slaves in the then existing States.

Mr. President, what is the result of this? We stand here now, at least I do, for one, to say, that, considering there have been already five new slave-holding States formed out of newly acquired territory, and only one non-slave-holding State, at most, I do not feel that I am called on to go further; I do not feel the obligation to yield more. But our friends of the South say, You deprive us of all our rights. We have fought for this territory, and you deny us participation in it. Let us consider this question as it really is; and since the honorable gentleman from Georgia proposes to leave the case to the enlightened and impartial judgment of mankind, and as I agree with him that it is a case proper to be considered by the enlightened part of mankind, let us see how the matter in truth stands. Gentlemen who advocate the case which my honorable friend from Georgia, with so much ability, sustains, declare that we invade their rights, that we deprive them of a participation in the enjoyment of territories acquired by the common services and common exertions of all. Is this true? How deprive? Of what do we deprive them? Why, they say that we deprive them of the privilege of carrying their slaves, as slaves, into the new territories. Well, Sir, what is the amount of that? They say that in this way we deprive them of the opportunity of going into this acquired territory with their property. Their "property"? What do they mean by "property"? We certainly do not deprive them of the privilege of going into these newly acquired territories with all that, in the general estimate of human society, in the general, and common, and universal understanding of mankind, is esteemed property. Not at all. The truth is just this. They have, in their own States, peculiar laws, which create property in persons. They have a system of local legislation on which slavery rests; while everybody agrees that it is against natural law, or at least against the common understanding which prevails among men as to what is natural law.

I am not going into metaphysics, for therein I should encounter the honorable member from South Carolina,[3] and we should find "no end, in wandering mazes lost," until after the time for the adjournment of Congress. The Southern States have peculiar laws, and by those laws there is property in slaves. This is purely local. The real meaning, then, of Southern gentlemen, in making this complaint, is, that they cannot go into the territories of the United States carrying with them their own peculiar local law, a law which creates property in persons. This, according to their own statement, is all the ground of complaint they have. Now here, I think, gentlemen are unjust towards us. How unjust they are, others will judge; generations that will come after us will judge. It will not be contended that this sort of personal slavery exists by general law. It exists only by local law. I do not mean to deny the validity of that local law where it is established; but I say it is, after all, local law. It is nothing more. And wherever that local law does not extend, property in persons does not exist. Well, Sir, what is now the demand on the part of our Southern friends? They say, "We will carry our local laws with us wherever we go. We insist that Congress does us injustice unless it establishes in the territory in which we wish to go our own local law." This demand I for one resist, and shall resist. It goes upon the idea that there is an inequality, unless persons under this local law, and holding property by authority of that law, can go into new territory and there establish that local law, to the exclusion of the general law. Mr. President, it was a maxim of the civil law, that, between slavery and freedom, freedom should always be presumed, and slavery must always be proved. If any question arose as to the *status* of an individual in Rome, he was presumed to be free until he was proved to be a slave, because slavery is an exception to the general rule. Such, I suppose, is the general law of mankind. An individual is to be presumed to be free, until a law can be produced which creates ownership in his person. I do not dispute the force and validity of the local law, as I have already said; but I say, it is a matter to be proved; and therefore, if individuals go into any part of the earth, it is to be proved that they are not freemen, or else the presumption is that they are.

Now our friends seem to think that an inequality arises from restraining them from going into the territories, unless there be a law provided which shall protect their ownership in persons. The assertion is, that we create an inequality. Is there nothing to be said on the other side in relation to inequality? Sir, from the date of this Constitution, and in the counsels that formed and established this Constitution, and I suppose in all men's judgment since, it is received as a settled truth, that slave labor and free labor do not exist well together. I have before me a declaration of Mr. Mason, in the Convention that formed the Constitution, to that effect. Mr. Mason, as is well known, was a distinguished member from Virginia. He says that the objection to slave labor is, that it puts free white labor in disrepute; that it causes labor to be regarded as derogatory to the character of the free white man, and that the free white man despises to work, to use his expression, where slaves are employed. This is a matter of great interest to the free States, if it be true, as to a great extent it certainly is, that wherever slave labor prevails free white labor is excluded or discouraged. I agree that slave labor does not necessarily exclude free labor totally. There is free white labor in Virginia, Tennessee, and other States, where most of the labor is done by slaves. But it necessarily loses something of its respectability, by the side of, and when associated with, slave labor. Wherever labor is mainly performed by slaves, it is regarded as degrading to freemen. The freemen of the North, therefore, have a deep interest in keeping labor free, exclusively free, in the new territories.

But, Sir, let us look further into this alleged inequality. There is no pretence that Southern people may not go into territory which shall be subject to the Ordinance of 1787. The only restraint is, that they shall not carry slaves thither, and continue that relation. They say this shuts them altogether out. Why, Sir, there can be nothing more inaccurate in point of fact than this statement. I understand that one half the people who settled Illinois are people, or descendants of people, who came from the Southern States. And I suppose that one third of the people of Ohio are those, or descendants of those, who emigrated from the South; and I venture to say, that, in respect to those two States, they are at this day settled by people of Southern origin in as great a proportion as they are by people of Northern origin, according to the general numbers and proportion of people, South and North. There are as many people from the South, in proportion to the whole people of the South, in those States, as there are from the North, in proportion to the whole people of the North. There is, then, no exclusion of Southern people; there is only the exclusion of a peculiar local law. Neither in principle nor in fact is there any inequality.

The question now is, whether it is not competent to Congress, in the exercise of a fair and just discretion, considering that there have been five slave-holding States added to this Union out of foreign acquisitions, and as yet only one free State, to prevent their further increase. That is the question. I see no injustice in it. As to the power of Congress, I have nothing to add to what I said the other day. Congress has full power over the subject. It may establish any such government, and any such laws, in the territories, as in its discretion it may see fit. It is subject, of course, to the rules of justice and propriety; but it is under no constitutional restraints.

I have said that I shall consent to no extension of the area of slavery upon this continent, nor to any increase of slave representation in the other house of Congress. I have now stated my reasons for my conduct and my vote. We of the North have already gone, in this respect, far beyond all that any Southern man could have expected, or did expect, at the time of the adoption of the Constitution. I repeat the statement of the fact of the creation of five new slave-holding States out of newly acquired territory. We have done that which, if those who framed the Constitution had foreseen, they never would have agreed to slave representation. We have yielded thus far; and we have now in the House of Representatives twenty persons voting upon this very question, and upon all other questions, who are there only in virtue of the representation of slaves.

Let me conclude, therefore, by remarking, that, while I am willing to present this as showing my own judgment and position, in regard to this case, and I beg it to be understood that I am speaking for no other than myself, and while I am willing to offer it to the whole world as my own justification, I rest on these propositions: First, That when this Constitution was adopted, nobody looked for any new acquisition of territory to be formed into slave-holding States. Secondly, That the principles of the Constitution prohibited, and were intended to prohibit, and should be construed to prohibit, all interference of the general government with slavery as it existed and as it still exists in the States. And then, looking to the operation of these new acquisitions, which have in this great degree had the effect of strengthening that interest in the South by the addition of these five States, I feel that there is nothing unjust, nothing of which any honest man can complain, if he is intelligent, and I feel that there is nothing with which the civilized world, if they take notice of so humble a person as myself, will reproach me, when I say, as I said the other day, that I have made up my mind, for one, that under no circumstances will I consent to the further extension of the area of slavery in the United States, or to the further increase of slave representation in the House of Representatives.

[Footnote 1: Mr. Benton.][Footnote 2: Mr. Berrien.][Footnote 3: Mr. Calhoun.]

SPEECH AT MARSHFIELD.
DELIVERED AT A MEETING OF THE CITIZENS OF MARSHFIELD, MASS., ON THE 1ST OF
SEPTEMBER, 1848.

[The following correspondence explains the occasion of the meeting at Marshfield, at which the following
speech was delivered.
"Marshfield, Mass., Aug. 2, 1848.
"HON. DANIEL WEBSTER:--
"Dear Sir,--The undersigned, Whigs and fellow-citizens of yours, are desirous of seeing and conferring
with you on the subject of our national policy, and of hearing your opinions freely expressed thereon. We
look anxiously on the present aspect of public affairs, and on the position in which the Whig party, and
especially Northern Whigs, are now placed. We should be grieved indeed to see General Cass--so decided
an opponent of all those measures which we think essential to the honor and interests of the country and
the prosperity of all classes--elected to the chief magistracy. On the other hand, it is not to be concealed,
that there is much discontent with the nomination made by the late Philadelphia Convention, of a Southern
man, a military man, fresh from bloody fields, and known only by his sword, as a Whig candidate for the
Presidency.
"So far as is in our humble ability, we desire to preserve the Union and the Whig party, and to perpetuate
Whig principles; but we wish to see also that these principles may be preserved, and this Union
perpetuated, in a manner consistent with the rights of the Free States, and the prevention of the farther
extension of the slave power; and we dread the effects of the precedent, which we think eminently
dangerous, and as not exhibiting us in a favorable light to the nations of the earth, of elevating a mere
military man to the Presidency.
"We think a crisis is upon us; and we would gladly know how we may best discharge our duties as true
Americans, honest men, and good Whigs. To you, who have been so long in public life, and are able from
your great experience and unrivalled ability to give us information and advice, and upon whom, as
neighbors and friends, we think we have some claims, we naturally look, and we should be exceedingly
gratified if, in any way, public or private, you would express your opinion upon interesting public
questions now pending, with that boldness and distinctness with which you are accustomed to declare your
sentiments. If you can concur with our wishes, please signify to us in what manner it would be most
agreeable to you that they should be carried into effect.
"With very great regard, your obedient servants,
"DANIEL PHILLIPS, GEORGE LEONARD, GEO. H. WETHERBEE, and many others."
To this invitation Mr. Webster returned the following reply:--
"_Marshfield, Aug. 3, 1848._
"GENTLEMEN,--I have received your letter. The critical state of things at Washington obliges me to think
it my duty to repair thither immediately and take my seat in the Senate, notwithstanding the state of my
health and the heat of the weather render it disagreeable for me to leave home.
"I cannot, therefore, comply with your wishes at present; but on my return, if such should continue to be
your desire, I will meet you and the other Whigs of Marshfield, in an unceremonious manner, that we may
confer upon the topics to which your letter relates.
"I am, Gentlemen, with esteem and friendship,
"Your obliged fellow-citizen,
"DANIEL WEBSTER.
"To Messrs. DANIEL PHILLIPS, GEORGE LEONARD, GEO. H. WETHERBEE, and others."
Soon after Mr. Webster's return from Washington, it was arranged that the meeting should take place at the
"Winslow House," the ancient seat of the Winslow family, now forming a part of Mr. Webster's farm at
Marshfield, on Friday, the first day of September.]
Although it is not my purpose, during the present recess of Congress, frequently to address public
assemblies on political subjects, I have felt it my duty to comply with your request, as neighbors and
townsmen, and to meet you to-day; and I am not unwilling to avail myself of this occasion to signify to the
people of the United States my opinions upon the present state of our public affairs. I shall perform that
duty, certainly with great frankness, I hope with candor. It is not my intention to-day to endeavor to carry
any point, to act as any man's advocate, to put up or put down anybody. I wish, and I propose, to address

you in the language and in the spirit of conference and consultation. In the present extraordinary crisis of our public concerns, I desire to hold no man's conscience but my own. My own opinions I shall communicate, freely and fearlessly, with equal disregard to consequences, whether they respect myself or respect others.

We are on the eve of a highly important Presidential election. In two or three months the people of this country will be called upon to elect an executive chief magistrate of the United States; and all see, and all feel, that great interests of the country are to be affected, for good or evil, by the results of that election. Of the interesting subjects over which the person who shall be elected must necessarily exercise more or less control, there are especially three, vitally connected, in my judgment, with the honor and happiness of the country. In the first place, the honor and happiness of the country imperatively require that there shall be a chief magistrate elected who shall not plunge us into further wars of ambition and conquest. In the second place, in my judgment, the interests of the country and the feeling of a vast majority of the people require that a President of these United States should be elected, who will neither use official influence to promote, nor feel any desire in his heart to promote, the further extension of slavery in this community, or its further influence in the public councils. In the third place, if I have any just estimate, if an experience not now a short one in public affairs has enabled me to know any thing of what the public interest demands, the state of the country requires an essential reform in the system of revenue and finance such as shall restore the prosperity, by prompting the industry and fostering the labor of the country, in its various branches. There are other things important, but I will not allude to them. These three I hold to be essential.

There are three candidates presented to the choice of the American people. General Taylor is the Whig candidate, standing upon the nomination of the Whig Convention; General Cass is the candidate of the opposing and now dominant party in the country; and a third candidate is presented in the person of Mr. Van Buren, by a convention of citizens assembled at Buffalo, whose object, or whose main object, as it appears to me, is contained in one of those considerations which I have mentioned, and that is, the prevention of the further increase of slavery;--an object in which you and I, Gentlemen, so far as that goes, entirely concur with them, I am sure.

Most of us who are here to-day are Whigs, National Whigs, Massachusetts Whigs, Old Colony Whigs, and Marshfield Whigs, and if the Whig nomination made at Philadelphia were entirely satisfactory to the people of Massachusetts and to us, our path of duty would be plain. But the nomination of a candidate for the Presidency made by the Whig Convention at Philadelphia is not satisfactory to the Whigs of Massachusetts. That is certain, and it would be idle to attempt to conceal the fact. It is more just and more patriotic, it is more manly and practical, to take facts as they are, and things as they are, and to deduce our own conviction of duty from what exists before us. However respectable and distinguished in the line of his own profession, or however estimable as a private citizen, General Taylor is a military man, and a military man merely. He has had no training in civil affairs. He has performed no functions of a civil nature under the Constitution of his country. He has been known and is known, only by his brilliant achievements at the head of an army. Now the Whigs of Massachusetts, and I among them, are of opinion that it was not wise, nor discreet, to go to the army for the selection of a candidate for the Presidency of the United States. It is the first instance in their history in which any man of mere military character has been proposed for that high office. General Washington was a great military character; but by far a greater civil character. He had been employed in the councils of his country, from the earliest dawn of the Revolution. He had been in the Continental Congress, and he had established a great character for civil wisdom and judgment. After the war, as you know, he was elected a member of that convention which formed the Constitution of the United States; and it is one of the most honorable tributes ever paid to him, that by that assembly of good and wise men he was selected to preside over their deliberations. And he put his name first and foremost to the Constitution under which we live. President Harrison was bred a soldier, and at different periods of his life rendered important military services. But President Harrison, nevertheless, was for a much greater period of his life employed in civil than in military service. For twenty years he was either governor of a Territory, member of one or the other house of Congress, or minister abroad; and discharged all these duties to the satisfaction of his country. This case, therefore, stands by itself; without a precedent or justification from any thing in our previous history. It is for this reason, as I imagine, that the Whigs of Massachusetts feel dissatisfied with this nomination. There may be other reasons, there are others; they are, perhaps, of less importance, and more easily to be answered. But this is a well-founded objection; and in my opinion it ought to have prevailed, and to have prevented this nomination. I know enough of history to see the dangerous tendency of such resorts to military popularity.

But, if I may borrow a mercantile expression, I may now venture to say, that there is another side to this account. The impartiality with which I propose to discharge my duty to-day requires that it should be stated. And, in the first place, it is to be considered, that General Taylor has been nominated by a Whig convention, held in conformity with the usages of the Whig party, and, so far as I know, fairly nominated. It is to be considered, also, that he is the only Whig before the people, as a candidate for the Presidency; and no citizen of the country, with any effect, can vote for any other Whig, let his preferences be what they might or may.

In the next place, it is proper to consider the personal character of General Taylor, and his political opinions, relations, and connections, so far as they are known. In advancing to a few observations on this part of the case, I wish everybody to understand that I have no personal acquaintance whatever with General Taylor. I never saw him but once, and that but for a few moments in the Senate. The sources of information are open to you, as well as to me, from which I derive what I know of his character and opinions. But I have endeavored to obtain access to those sources. I have endeavored to inform and instruct myself by communication with those who have known him in his profession as a soldier, in his associations as a man, in his conversations and opinions on political subjects; and I will tell you frankly what I think of him, according to the best lights which I have been able to obtain.

I need not say, that he is a skilful, brave, and gallant soldier. That is admitted by all. With me, all that goes but very little way to make out the proper qualifications for President of the United States. But what is more important, I believe that he is an entirely honest and upright man. I believe that he is modest, clear-headed, of independent and manly character, possessing a mind trained by proper discipline and self-control. I believe that he is estimable and amiable in all the relations of private life. I believe that he possesses a reputation for equity and fair judgment, which gives him an influence over those under his command beyond what is conferred by the authority of station. I believe that he is a man possessing the confidence and attachment of all who have been near him and know him. And I believe, that, if elected President, he will do his best to relieve the country from present evils, and guard it against future dangers. So much for what I think of the personal character of General Taylor.

I will say, too, that, so far as I have observed, his conduct since he has been a candidate for the office of President has been irreproachable. I hear no intrigue imputed to him, no contumelious treatment of rivals. I do not find him making promises or holding out hopes to any men or any party. I do not find him putting forth any pretensions of his own, and therefore I think of him very much as he seems to think of himself, that he is an honest man, of an independent mind and of upright intentions. And as for the subject of his qualifications for the Presidency, he has himself nothing to say about it.

And now, friends and fellow-townsmen, with respect to his political opinions and relations, I can say at once, that I believe him to be a Whig; I believe him to hold to the main doctrines of the Whig party. To think otherwise would be to impute to him a degree of tergiversation and fraudulent deception of which I suppose him to be entirely incapable.

Gentlemen, it is worth our while to consider in what manner General Taylor has become a candidate for the Presidency of the United States. It would be a great mistake to suppose that he was made such merely by the nomination of the Philadelphia Convention. He had been nominated for the Presidency in a great many States, by various conventions and meetings of the people, a year before the convention at Philadelphia assembled. The whole history of the world shows, whether in the most civilized or the most barbarous ages, that the affections and admiration of mankind are at all times easily carried away towards successful military achievements. The story of all republics and of all free governments shows this. We know in the case now before us, that so soon as brilliant success had attended General Taylor's operations on the Rio Grande, at Palo Alto, and Monterey, spontaneous nominations of him sprang up.

And here let me say, that, generally, these were Whig nominations. Not universally, but generally, these nominations, made at various times before the meeting of the Philadelphia Convention, were Whig nominations. General Taylor was esteemed, from the moment that his military achievements brought him into public notice, as a Whig general. You all remember, that when we were discussing his merits in Congress, upon the question of giving thanks to the army under his command, and to himself, among other objections, the friends and supporters of Mr. Polk's administration denounced him as being, and because he was, a Whig general. My friends near me, whom I am happy to see here, belonging to the House of Representatives, will remember that a leading man of the party of the administration declared in his place in Congress, that the policy of the administration, connected with the Mexican war, would never prosper, till the President recalled those Whig generals, Scott and Taylor. The policy was a Democratic policy. The argument was, that the men to carry out this policy should be Democratic men; the officers to fight the battles should be Democratic officers; and on that ground, the ordinary vote of thanks was refused to General Taylor, on the part of the friends of the administration.

Let me remark, in the next place, that there was no particular purpose connected with the advancement of slavery entertained, generally, by those who nominated him. As I have said, they were Whig nominations, more in the Middle and Northern than in the Southern States, and by persons who never entertained the slightest desire, by his nomination, or by any other means, to extend the area of slavery of the human race, or the influence of the slave-holding States in the councils of the nation. The Quaker city of Philadelphia nominated General Taylor, the Whigs all over the Union nominated him, with no such view. A great convention was assembled in New York, of highly influential and respectable gentlemen, very many of them well known to me, and they nominated General Taylor with no such view. General Taylor's nomination was hailed, not very extensively, but by some enthusiastic and not very far-seeing people in the Commonwealth of Massachusetts. There were, even among us, in our own State, Whigs quite early enough, certainly, in manifesting their confidence in this nomination; a little too early, it may be, in uttering notes of exultation for the anticipated triumph. It would have been better if they had waited.

Now the truth is, Gentlemen,--and no man can avoid seeing it, unless, as sometimes happens, the object is too near our eyes to be distinctly discerned,--the truth is, that in these nominations, and also in the nomination at Philadelphia, in these conventions, and also in the convention at Philadelphia, General Taylor was nominated exactly for this reason;--that, believing him to be a Whig, they thought he could be chosen more easily than any other Whig. This is the whole of it. That sagacious, wise, far-seeing doctrine of availability lies at the bottom of the whole matter. So far, then, from imputing any motive to these conventions over the country, or to the convention in Philadelphia, as operating on a majority of the members, to promote slavery by the nomination of General Taylor, I do not believe a word of it,--not one word. I see that one part of what is called the Platform of the Buffalo Convention says that the candidates before the public were nominated under the dictation of the slave power. I do not believe a word of it.

In the first place, a very great majority of the convention at Philadelphia was composed of members from the Free States. By a very great majority they might have nominated anybody they chose. But the Free States did not choose to nominate a Free State man, or a Northern man. Even our neighbors, the States of New England, with the exception of New Hampshire and a part of Maine, neither proposed nor concurred in the nomination of any Northern man. Vermont would hear of nothing but the nomination of a Southern and slave-holding candidate. Connecticut was of the same mind, and so was Rhode Island. The North made no demand, nor presented any request for a Northern candidate, nor attempted any union among themselves for the purpose of promoting the nomination of such a candidate. They were content to take their choice among the candidates of the South. It is preposterous, therefore, to pretend that a candidate from the Slave States has been forced upon the North by Southern dictation.

In the next place, it is true that there were persons from New England who were extremely zealous and active in procuring the nomination of General Taylor, but they were men who would cut off their right hands before they would do any thing to promote slavery in the United States. I do not admire their policy; indeed I have very little respect for it, understand that; but I acquit them of bad motives. I know the leading men in that convention. I think I understand the motives that governed them. Their reasoning was this: "General Taylor is a Whig: not eminent in civil life, not known in civil life, but still a man of sound Whig principles. Circumstances have given him a reputation and _éclat_ in the country. If he shall be the Whig candidate, he will be chosen; and with him there will come into the two houses of Congress an augmentation of Whig strength. The Whig majority in the House of Representatives will be increased. The Democratic majority in the Senate will be diminished." That was the view, and such was the motive, however wise or however unwise, that governed a very large majority of those who composed the convention at Philadelphia. In my opinion, this was a wholly unwise policy; it was short-sighted and temporizing on questions of great principles. But I acquit those who adopted it of any such motives as have been ascribed to them, and especially of what has been ascribed to them in a part of this Buffalo Platform. Such, Gentlemen, are the circumstances connected with the nomination of General Taylor. I only repeat, that those who had the greatest agency originally in bringing him before the people were Whig conventions and Whig meetings in the several States, Free States, and that a great majority of that convention which nominated him in Philadelphia was from the Free States, and might have rejected him if they had chosen, and selected anybody else on whom they could have united.

This is the case, Gentlemen, as far as I can discern it, and exercising upon it as impartial a judgment as I can form,--this is the case presented to the Whigs, so far as respects the personal fitness and personal character of General Taylor, and the circumstances which have caused his nomination. If we were weighing the propriety of nominating such a person to the Presidency, it would be one thing; if we are considering the expediency, or I may say the necessity (which to some minds may seem to be the case), of well-meaning and patriotic Whigs supporting him after he is nominated, that is quite another thing.

This leads us to the consideration of what the Whigs of Massachusetts are to do, or such of them as do not see fit to support General Taylor. Of course they must vote for General Cass, or they must vote for Mr. Van Buren, or they must omit to vote at all. I agree that there are cases in which, if we do not know in what direction to move, we ought to stand still till we do. I admit that there are cases in which, if one does not know what to do, he had better not do he knows not what. But on a question so important to ourselves and the country, on a question of a popular election under constitutional forms, in which it is impossible that every man's private judgment can prevail, or every man's private choice succeed, it becomes a question of conscientious duty and patriotism, what it is best to do upon the whole.

Under the practical administration of the Constitution of the United States, there cannot be a great range of personal choice in regard to the candidate for the Presidency. In order that their votes may be effective, men must give them for some one of those who are prominently before the public. This is the necessary result of our forms of government and of the provisions of the Constitution. The people are therefore brought sometimes to the necessity of choosing between candidates neither of whom would be their original, personal choice.

Now, what is the contingency? What is the alternative presented to the Whigs of Massachusetts? In my judgment, fellow-citizens, it is simply this; the question is between General Taylor and General Cass. And that is the only question. I am no more skilled to foresee political occurrences than others. I judge only for myself. But, in my opinion, there is not the least probability of any other result than the choice of General Taylor or General Cass. I know that the enthusiasm of a new-formed party, that the popularity of a new-formed name, without communicating any new-formed idea, may lead men to think that the sky is to fall, and that larks are suddenly to be taken. I entertain no such expectations. I speak without disrespect of the Free Soil party. I have read their platform, and though I think there are some unsound places in it, I can stand on it pretty well. But I see nothing in it both new and valuable. "What is valuable is not new, and what is new is not valuable." If the term Free Soil party, or Free Soil men, designate those who are fixed, and unalterably fixed, in favor of the restriction of slavery, are so to-day and were so yesterday, and have been so for some time, then I hold myself to be as good a Free Soil man as any of the Buffalo Convention. I pray to know who is to put beneath my feet a freer soil than that upon which I have stood ever since I have been in public life? I pray to know who is to make my lips freer than they always have been, or to inspire into my breast a more resolute and fixed determination to resist the advances and encroachments of the slave power, than has inhabited it since I for the first time opened my mouth in the councils of the country? The gentlemen at Buffalo have placed at the head of their party Mr. Van Buren, a gentleman for whom I have all the respect that I ought to entertain for one with whom I have been associated, in some degree, in public life for many years, and who has held the highest offices in the country. But really, speaking for myself, if I were to express confidence in Mr. Van Buren and his politics on any question, and most especially this very question of slavery, I think the scene would border upon the ludicrous, if not upon the contemptible. I never proposed any thing in my life of a general and public nature, that Mr. Van Buren did not oppose. Nor has it happened to me to support any important measure proposed by him. If he and I now were to find ourselves together under the Free Soil flag, I am sure that, with his accustomed good nature, he would laugh. If nobody were present, we should both laugh at the strange occurrences and stranger jumbles of political life that should have brought us to sit down cosily and snugly, side by side, on the same platform. That the leader of the Free Spoil party should so suddenly have become the leader of the Free Soil party would be a joke to shake his sides and mine.

Gentlemen, my first acquaintance in public life with Mr. Van Buren was when he was pressing with great power the election of Mr. Crawford to the Presidency, against Mr. Adams. Mr. Crawford was not elected, and Mr. Adams was. Mr. Van Buren was in the Senate nearly the whole of that administration; and during the remainder of it he was Governor of the State of New York. It is notorious that he was the soul and centre, throughout the whole of Mr. Adams's term, of the opposition made to him. He did more to prevent Mr. Adams's re-election in 1828, and to obtain General Jackson's election, than any other man,--yes, than any *ten* other men in the country.

General Jackson was chosen, and Mr. Van Buren was appointed his Secretary of State. It so happened that in July, 1829, Mr. McLane went to England to arrange the controverted, difficult, and disputed point on the subject of the colonial trade. Mr. Adams had held a high tone on that subject. He had demanded, on the ground of reciprocity and right, the introduction of our products into all parts of the British territory, freely, in our own vessels, since Great Britain was allowed to bring her produce into the United States upon the same terms. Mr. Adams placed this demand upon the ground of reciprocity and justice. Great Britain would not yield. Mr. Van Buren, in his instructions to Mr. McLane, told him to yield that question of right, and to solicit the free admission of American produce into the British colonies, on the ground of privilege and favor; intimating that there had been a change of parties, and that this favor ought not to be refused to General Jackson's administration because it had been demanded on the ground of right by Mr. Adams's. This is the sum and substance of the instruction.

Well, Gentlemen, it was one of the most painful duties of my life, on account of this, to refuse my assent to Mr. Van Buren's nomination. It was novel in our history, when an administration changes, for the new administration to seek to obtain privileges from a foreign power on the assertion that they have abandoned the ground of their predecessors. I suppose that such a course is held to be altogether undignified by all public men. When I went into the Department of State under General Harrison, I found in the conduct of my predecessor many things that I could have wished had been otherwise. Did I retract a jot or tittle of what Mr. Forsyth had said? I took the case as he had left it, and conducted it upon the principles which he left. I should have considered that I disgraced myself if I had said, "Pray, my Lord Ashburton, we are more rational persons than our predecessors, we are more considerate than they, and intend to adopt an entirely opposite policy. Consider, my dear Lord, how much more friendly, reasonable, and amiable we are than our predecessors."

But now, on this very subject of the extension of the slave power, I would by no means do the least injustice to Mr. Van Buren. If he has come up to some of the opinions expressed in the platform of the Buffalo Convention, I am very glad of it. I do not mean to say that there may not be very good reasons for those of his own party who cannot conscientiously vote for General Cass to vote for him, because I think him much the least dangerous of the two. But, in truth, looking at Mr. Van Buren's conduct as President of the United States, I am amazed to find that he should be placed at the head of a party professing to be, beyond all other parties, friends of liberty and enemies of African slavery in the Southern States. Why, the very first thing that Mr. Van Buren did after he was President was to declare, that, if Congress interfered with slavery in the District of Columbia, he would apply the veto to their bills. Mr. Van Buren, in his inaugural address, quotes the following expression from his letter accepting his nomination: "I must go into the Presidential chair the inflexible and uncompromising opponent of every attempt on the part of Congress to abolish slavery in the District of Columbia against the wishes of the slave-holding States; and also with a determination equally decided to resist the slightest interference with it in the States where it exists." He then proceeds: "I submitted also to my fellow-citizens, with fulness and frankness, the reasons which led me to this determination. The result authorizes me to believe that they have been approved and are confided in by a majority of the people of the United States, including those whom they most immediately affect. It now only remains to add, that no bill conflicting with these views can even receive my constitutional sanction."

In the next place, we know that Mr. Van Buren's casting vote was given for a law of very doubtful propriety,--a law to allow postmasters to open the mails and see if there was any incendiary matter in them, and, if so, to destroy it. I do not say that there was no constitutional power to pass such a law. Perhaps the people of the South thought it was necessary to protect themselves from incitements to insurrection. So far as any thing endangers the lives and property of the South, so far I agree that there may be such legislation in Congress as shall prevent such results.

But, Gentlemen, no man has exercised a more controlling influence on the conduct of his friends in this country than Mr. Van Buren. I take it that the most important event in our time tending to the extension of slavery and its everlasting establishment on this continent, was the annexation of Texas, in 1844. Where was Mr. Van Buren then? Let me ask, Three or four years ago, where was he THEN? Every friend of Mr. Van Buren, so far as I know, supported the measure. The two Senators from New York supported it, and the members of the House of Representatives from New York supported it, and nobody resisted it but Whigs. And I say in the face of the world, I say in the face of those connected with, or likely to be benefited by, the Buffalo Convention,--I say to all of them, that there has been no party of men in this country which has firmly and sternly resisted the progress of the slave power but the Whigs.

Why, look to this very question of the annexation of Texas. We talk of the dictation of the slave power! At least they do, I do not. I do not allow that anybody dictates to me. They talk of the triumph of the South over the North! There is not a word of truth or reason in the whole of it. I am bound to say on my conscience, that, of all the evils inflicted upon us by these acquisitions of slave territory, the North has borne its full part in the infliction. Northern votes, in full proportion, have been given in both houses for the acquisition of new territory, in which slavery existed. We talk of the North. There has for a long time been no North. I think the North Star is at last discovered; I think there will be a North; but up to the recent session of Congress there has been no North, no geographical section of the country, in which there has been found a strong, conscientious, and *united* opposition to slavery. No such North has existed.

Pope says, you know,

"Ask where's the North? At York, 'tis on the Tweed; In Scotland, at the Orcades; and there, At Greenland, Zembla, or the Lord knows where."

Now, if there has heretofore been such a *North* as I have described, a North strong in opinion and united in action against slavery,--if such a *North* has existed anywhere, it has existed "the Lord knows where," I do not. Why, on this very question of the admission of Texas, it may be said with truth, that the North let in Texas. The Whigs, North and South, resisted Texas. Ten Senators from slave-holding States, of the Whig party, resisted Texas. Two, only, as I remember, voted for it. But the Southern Whig votes against Texas were overpowered by the Democratic votes from the Free States, and from New England among the rest. Yes, if there had not been votes from New England in favor of Texas, Texas would have been out of the Union to this day. Yes, if men from New England had been true, Texas would have been nothing but Texas still. There were four votes in the Senate from New England in favor of the admission of Texas, Mr. Van Buren's friends, Democratic members: one from Maine; two from New Hampshire; one from Connecticut. Two of these gentlemen were confidential friends of Mr. Van Buren, and had both been members of his cabinet. They voted for Texas; and they let in Texas, against Southern Whigs and Northern Whigs. That is the truth of it, my friends. Mr. Van Buren, by the wave of his hand, could have kept out Texas. A word, a letter, though it had been even shorter than General Cass's letter to the Chicago Convention, would have been enough, and would have done the work. But he was silent.

When Northern members of Congress voted, in 1820, for the Missouri Compromise, against the known will of their constituents, they were called "Dough Faces." I am afraid, fellow-citizens, that the generation of "dough faces" will be as perpetual as the generation of men.

In 1844, as we all know, Mr. Van Buren was a candidate for the Presidency, on the part of the Democratic party, but lost the nomination at Baltimore. We now learn, from a letter from General Jackson to Mr. Butler, that Mr. Van Buren's claims were superseded, because, after all, the South thought that the accomplishment of the annexation of Texas might be more safely intrusted to Southern hands. We all know that the Northern portion of the Democratic party were friendly to Mr. Van Buren. Our neighbors from New Hampshire, and Maine, and elsewhere, were Van Buren men. But the moment it was ascertained that Mr. Polk was the favorite of the South, and the favorite of the South upon the ground I have mentioned, as a man more certain to bring about the annexation of Texas than Mr. Van Buren, these friends of Mr. Van Buren in the North all "caved in,"--not a man of them stood. Mr. Van Buren himself wrote a letter very complimentary to Mr. Polk and Mr. Dallas, and found no fault with the nomination.

Now, Gentlemen, if they were "dough faces" who voted for the Missouri Compromise, what epithet should describe these men, here in our New England, who were so ready, not only to change or abandon him whom they most cordially wished to support, but did so in order to make more sure the annexation of Texas. They nominated Mr. Polk at the request of gentlemen from the South, and voted for him, through thick and thin, till the work was accomplished, and Mr. Polk elected. For my part, I think that "dough faces" is an epithet not sufficiently reproachful. Such persons are dough faces, with dough heads, and dough hearts, and dough souls; they are *all* dough; the coarsest potter may mould them to vessels of honor or dishonor,--most readily to vessels of _dis_honor.

But what do we now see? Repentance has gone far. There are among these very people, these very gentlemen, persons who espouse, with great zeal, the interests of the Free Soil party. I hope their repentance is as sincere as it appears to be. I hope it is honest conviction, and not merely a new chance for power, under a new name and a new party. But, with all their pretensions, and with all their patriotism, I see dough still sticking on the cheeks of some of them. And therefore I have no confidence in them, not a particle. I do not mean to say, that the great mass of the people, especially those who went to the Buffalo Convention from this State, have not the highest and purest motives. I think they act unwisely, but I acquit them of dishonest intentions. But with respect to others, and those who have been part and parcel in the measures which have brought new slave territory into this Union, I distrust them all. If they repent, let them, before we trust them, do works worthy of repentance.

I have said, Gentlemen, that in my opinion, if it were desirable to place Mr. Van Buren at the head of government, there is no chance for him. Others are as good judges as I am. But I am not able to say that I see any State in the Union in which there is a reasonable probability that he will get the vote. There may be. Others are more versed in such statistics than I am. But I see none, and therefore I think that we are reduced to a choice between General Cass and General Taylor. You may remember, that in the discussions of 1844, when Mr. Birney was drawing off votes from the Whig candidate, I said that every vote for Mr. Birney was half a vote for Mr. Polk. Is it not true that the vote of the Liberty party taken from Mr. Clay's vote in the State of New York made Mr. Polk President? That is as clear as any historical fact. And in my judgment, it will be so now. I consider every Whig vote given to Mr. Van Buren, as directly aiding the election of Mr. Cass. Mark, I say, *Whig* vote. There may be States in which Mr. Van Buren may draw from the other side largely. But I speak of Whig votes, in this State and in any State. And I am of opinion, that any such vote given to Mr. Van Buren inures to the benefit of General Cass.

Now as to General Cass, Gentlemen. We need not go to the Baltimore platform to instruct ourselves as to what his politics are, or how he will conduct the government. General Cass will go into the government, if at all, chosen by the same party that elected Mr. Polk; and he will "follow in the footsteps of his illustrious predecessor." I hold him, I confess, in the present state of the country, to be the most dangerous man on whom the powers of the executive chief magistracy could well be conferred. He would consider himself, not as conservative, not as protective to present institutions, but as belonging to the party of Progress. He believes in the doctrine of American destiny; and that that destiny is, to go through wars and invasions, and maintain vast armies, to establish a great, powerful, domineering government over all this continent. We know that, if Mr. Cass could have prevented it, the treaty with England in 1842 would not have been made. We know that, if Mr. Cass could have prevented it, the settlement of the Oregon question would not have been accomplished in 1846. We know that General Cass could have prevented the Mexican war; and we know that he was first and foremost in pressing that war. We know that he is a man of talent, of ability, of some celebrity as a statesman, in every way superior to his predecessor, if he should be the successor of Mr. Polk. But I think him a man of rash politics, pushed on by a rash party, and committed to a course of policy, as I believe, not in consistency with the happiness and security of the country. Therefore it is for you, and for me, and for all of us, Whigs, to consider whether, in this state of the case, we can or cannot, we will or will not, give our votes for the Whig nomination. I leave that to every man's conscience. I have endeavored to state the case as it presents itself to me.

Gentlemen, before General Taylor's nomination, I stated always, when the subject was mentioned by my friends, that I did not and could not recommend the nomination of a military man to the people of the United States for the office of President. It was against my conviction of what was due to the best interests of the country, and to the character of the republic. I stated always, at the same time, that if General Taylor should be nominated by the Whig Convention, fairly, I should not oppose his election. I stand now upon the same declaration. General Taylor has been nominated fairly, as far as I know, and I cannot, therefore, and shall not, oppose his election. At the same time, there is no man who is more firmly of opinion that such a nomination was not fit to be made. But the declaration that I would not oppose General Taylor, if nominated by the Whig party, was of course subject, in the nature of things, to some exceptions. If I believed him to be a man who would plunge the country into further wars for any purpose of ambition or conquest, I would oppose him, let him be nominated by whom he might. If I believed that he was a man who would exert his official influence for the further extension of the slave power, I would oppose him, let him be nominated by whom he might. But I do not believe either. I believe that he has been, from the first, opposed to the policy of the Mexican war, as improper, impolitic, and inexpedient. I believe, from the best information I can obtain,--and you will take this as my own opinion, Gentlemen,--I believe, from the best information I can obtain, that he has no disposition to go to war, or to form new States in order to increase the limits of slavery.

Gentlemen, so much for what may be considered as belonging to the Presidency as a national question. But the case by no means stops here. We are citizens of Massachusetts. We are Whigs of Massachusetts. We have supported the present government of the State for years, with success; and I have thought that most Whigs were satisfied with the administration of the State government in the hands of those who have had it. But now it is proposed, I presume, on the basis of the Buffalo Platform, to carry this into the State elections, as well as into the national elections. There is to be a nomination of a candidate for Governor, against Mr. Briggs, or whoever may be nominated by the Whigs; and there is to be a nomination of a candidate for Lieutenant-Governor, against Mr. Reed, or whoever may be nominated by the Whigs; and there are to be nominations against the present members of Congress. Now, what is the utility or the necessity of this? We have ten members in the Congress of the United States. I know not ten men of any party who are more zealous, and firm, and inflexible in their opposition against slavery in any form. And what will be the result of opposing their re-election? Suppose that a considerable number of Whigs secede from the Whig party, and support a candidate of this new party, what will be the result? Do we not know what has been the case in this State? Do we not know that this district has been unrepresented from month to month, and from year to year, because there has been an opposition to as good an antislavery man as breathes the air of this district? On this occasion, and even in his own presence, I may allude to our Representative, Mr. Hale. Do we want a man to give a better vote in Congress than Mr. Hale gives? Why, I undertake to say that there is not one of the Liberty party, nor will there be one of this new party, who will have the least objection to Mr. Hale, except that he was not nominated by themselves. Ten to one, if the Whigs had not nominated him, they would have nominated him themselves; doubtless they would, if he had come into their organization, and called himself a third party man.

Now, Gentlemen, I remember it to have occurred, that, on very important questions in Congress, the vote was lost for want of two or three members which Massachusetts might have sent, but which, in consequence of the division of parties, she did not send. And now I foresee that, if in this district any considerable number of Whigs think it their duty to join in the support of Mr. Van Buren, and in the support of gentlemen whom that party may nominate for Congress, the same thing will take place, and we shall be without a representative, in all probability, in the first session of the next Congress, when the battle is to be fought on this very slavery question. The same is likely to happen in other districts. I am sure that honest, intelligent, and patriotic Whigs will lay this consideration to their consciences, and judge of it as they think they ought to do.

Gentlemen, I will detain you but a moment longer. You know that I gave my vote in Congress against the treaty of peace with Mexico, because it contained these cessions of territory, and brought under the authority of the United States, with a pledge of future admission into the Union, the great, vast, and almost unknown countries of New Mexico and California.

In the session before the last, one of the Southern Whig Senators, Mr. Berrien of Georgia, had moved a resolution, to the effect that the war ought not to be continued for the purposes of conquest and acquisition. The resolution declared that the war with Mexico ought not to be prosecuted by this government with any view to the dismemberment of that republic, or to the acquisition, by conquest, of any portion of her territory. That proposition he introduced into the Senate, in the form of a resolution; and I believe that every Whig Senator but one voted for it. But the Senators belonging to the Locofoco or Democratic party voted against it. The Senators from New York voted against it. General Cass, from the free State of Michigan, Mr. Fairfield, from Maine, Mr. Niles, from Connecticut, and others, voted against it, and the vote was lost. That is, these gentlemen,--some of them very prominent friends of Mr. Van Buren, and ready to take the field for him,--these very gentlemen voted not to exclude territory that might be obtained by conquest. They were willing to bring in the territory, and then have a squabble and controversy whether it should be slave or free territory. I was of opinion that the true and safe policy was, to shut out the whole question by getting no territory, and thereby keep off all controversy. The territory will do us no good, if free; it will be an encumbrance, if free. To a great extent, it will produce a preponderance in favor of the South in the Senate, even if it be free. Let us keep it out, therefore. But no. We will make the acquisition, bring in the territory, and manage it afterwards. That was the policy.

Gentlemen, in an important crisis in English history, in the reign of Charles the Second, when the country was threatened by the accession to the throne of a prince, then called the Duke of York, who was a bigot to the Roman Catholic religion, a proposition was made to exclude him from the crown. Some said that was a very rash measure, brought forward by very rash men; that they had better admit him, and then put limitations upon him, chain him down, restrict him. When the debate was going on, a member is reported to have risen and expressed his sentiments by rather a grotesque comparison, but one of considerable force:--

"I hear a lion, in the lobby roar! Say, Mr. Speaker, shall we shut the door, And keep him out; or shall we let him in, And see if we can get him out again?"

I was for shutting the door and keeping the lion out. Other more confident spirits, who are of the character of Van Amburgh, were for letting him in, and disturbing all the interests of the country. When this Mexican treaty came before the Senate, it had certain clauses ceding New Mexico and California to the United States. A Southern gentleman, Mr. Badger, of North Carolina, moved to strike out those clauses. Now you understand, that if a motion to strike out a clause of a treaty be supported by one third, it will be struck out; that is, two thirds of the Senate must vote for each clause, in order to have it retained. The vote on this question of striking out stood 38 to 14, not quite one third being against the cession, and so the clause was retained. And why were there not one third? Just because there were four New England Senators voting for these new territories. That is the reason.

I hope I am as ardent an advocate for peace as any man living; but I would not be carried away by the desire for peace to commit an act which I believed highly injurious, likely to have consequences of a permanent character, and indeed to endanger the existence of the government. Besides, I believed that we could have struck out the cessions of territory, and had peace just as soon. And I would be willing to go before the people and leave it to them to say, whether they would carry on the war any longer for acquisition of territory. If they would, then they were the artificers of their own fortunes. I was not afraid of the people on that subject. But if this course had continued the war somewhat longer, I would have preferred that result, rather than that those territories lying on our southern border should come in hereafter as new States. I should speak, perhaps, with more confidence, if some Whigs of the North had not voted for the treaty. My own opinion was then clear and decisive. For myself I thought the case a perfectly plain one, and no man has yet stated a reason to convince me to the contrary.

I voted to strike out the articles of cession. They would have been struck out if four of the New England Senators had not voted against the motion. I then voted against the ratification of the treaty, and that treaty would have failed if three New England Senators had not voted for it, and Whig Senators too. I should do the same thing again, and with much more resolution. I would have run a still greater risk, I would have endured a still greater shock, I would have risked anything, rather than have been a participator in any measure which should have a tendency to annex Southern territory to the States of the Union. I hope it will be remembered, in all future time, that on this question of the accession of these new territories of almost boundless extent, I voted against them, and against the treaty which contained them, notwithstanding all inducements to the contrary, and all the cries, which I thought hasty and injudicious, of "Peace! Peace on any terms!" I will add, that those who voted against the treaty were gentlemen from so many parts of the country, that its rejection would have been an act rather of national than of local resistance. There were votes against it from both parties, and from all parties, the South and the West, the North and the East. What we wanted was a few more New England votes.

Gentlemen, after I had the honor of receiving the invitation to meet my fellow-citizens, I found it necessary, in the discharge of my duty, though with great inconvenience to my health, to be present at the closing scenes of the session. You know what there transpired. You know the important decision that was made in both houses of Congress, in regard to Oregon. The immediate question respected Oregon, or rather the bill respected Oregon, but the question more particularly concerned these new territories. The effect of the bill as passed in the Senate was to establish these new territories as slave-holding States. The House disagreed. The Senate receded from their ground, and the bill passed, establishing Oregon as a free Territory, and making no provision for the newly acquired territories on the South. My vote, and the reasons I gave for it, are known to the good people of Massachusetts, and I have not heard that they have expressed any particular disapprobation of them.

But this question is to be resumed at the first session of the next Congress. There is no probability that it will be settled at the next session of this Congress. But at least at the first session of the next Congress this question will be resumed. It will enter at this very period into all the elections of the South.

And now I venture to say, Gentlemen, two things; the first well known to you, that General Cass is in favor of what is called the Compromise Line, and is of opinion that the Wilmot Proviso, or the Ordinance of

1787, which excludes slavery from territories, ought not to be applied to territories lying south of 36° 30'. He announced this before he was nominated, and if he had not announced it, he would have been 36° 30' farther off from being nominated. In the next place, he will do all he can to establish that compromise line; and lastly, which is a matter of opinion, in my conscientious belief he will establish it.

Give him the power and the patronage of the government, let him exercise it over certain portions of the country whose representatives voted on this occasion to put off that question for future consideration; let him have the power of this government with his attachments, with his inducements, and we shall see the result. I verily believe, that unless there is a renewed strength, an augmented strength, of Whig votes in Congress, he will accomplish his purpose. He will surely have the Senate, and with the patronage of the government, with every interest which he can bring to bear, co-operating with every interest which the South can bring to bear, he will establish the compromise line. We cry safety before we are out of the woods, if we feel that the danger respecting the territories is over.

Gentlemen, I came here to confer with you as friends and countrymen, to speak my own mind and hear yours; but if we all should speak, and occupy as much time as I have, we should make a late meeting. I shall detain you no longer. I have been long in public life, longer, far longer than I shall remain there. I have had some participation for more than thirty years in the councils of the nation. I profess to feel a strong attachment to the liberty of the United States, to the Constitution and free institutions of this country, to the honor, and I may say the glory, of my native land. I feel every injury inflicted upon it, almost as a personal injury. I blush for every fault which I think I see committed in its public councils, as if they were faults or mistakes of my own. I know that, at this moment, there is no object upon earth so much attracting the gaze of the intelligent and civilized nations of the earth as this great republic. All men look at us, all men examine our course, all good men are anxious for a favorable result to this great experiment of republican liberty. We are on a hill and cannot be hid. We cannot withdraw ourselves either from the commendation or the reproaches of the civilized world. They see us as that star of empire which half a century ago was represented as making its way westward. I wish they may see it as a mild, placid, though brilliant orb, moving athwart the whole heavens to the enlightening and cheering of mankind; and not as a meteor of fire and blood terrifying the nations.

JEREMIAH MASON.

[The death of the Hon. Jeremiah Mason, one of the most eminent members of the legal profession in the United States, took place at Boston, on the 14th of October, 1848. At a meeting of the Bar of the County of Suffolk, Mass., held on the 17th instant, appropriate resolutions in honor of the deceased, accompanied with a few eloquent observations, were introduced by Mr. Choate, and unanimously adopted. It was voted by the meeting, that Mr. Webster should be requested to present these resolutions to the Supreme Judicial Court at its next term in Boston.

In compliance with this request, at the opening of the next term of the court, on the 14th of November, 1848, prayer having been offered, Mr. Webster rose and spoke as follows.]

May it please your Honors,--JEREMIAH MASON, one of the counsellors of this court, departed this life on the 14th of October, at his residence in this city. The death of one of its members, so highly respected, so much admired and venerated, could not fail to produce a striking impression upon the members of this bar; and a meeting was immediately called, at which a member of this court, just on the eve of leaving the practice of his profession for a seat on the bench,[1] presided; and resolutions expressive of the sense entertained by the bar of the high character of the deceased, and of sincere condolence with those whom his loss touched more nearly, were moved by one of his distinguished brethren, and adopted with entire unanimity. My brethren have appointed me to the honorable duty of presenting these resolutions to this court; and it is in discharge of that duty that I rise to address you, and pray that the resolutions which I hold in my hand may be read by the clerk.

The clerk of the court then read the resolutions, as follows:--

"_Resolved_, That the members of this bar have heard with profound emotion of the decease of the Honorable Jeremiah Mason, one of the most eminent and distinguished of the great men who have ever adorned this profession; and, as well in discharge of a public duty, as in obedience to the dictates of our private feelings, we think it proper to mark this occasion by some attempt to record our estimate of his pre-eminent abilities and high character.

"_Resolved_, That the public character and services of Mr. Mason demand prominent commemoration; that, throughout his long life, whether as a private person or in public place, he maintained a wide and various intercourse with public men, and cherished a constant and deep interest in public affairs, and by his vast practical wisdom and sagacity, the fruit of extraordinary intellectual endowments, matured thought, and profound observation, and by the soundness of his opinions and the comprehensiveness and elevated tone of his politics, he exerted at all times a great and most salutary influence upon the sentiments and policy of the community and the country; and that, as a Senator in the Congress of the United States during a period of many years, and in a crisis of affairs which demanded the wisdom of the wisest and the civil virtues of the best, he was distinguished among the most eminent men of his country for ability in debate, for attention to all the duties of his great trust, for moderation, for prudence, for fidelity to the obligations of that party connection to which he was attached, for fidelity still more conspicuous and still more admirable to the higher obligations of a thoughtful and enlarged patriotism.

"_Resolved_, That it was the privilege of Mr. Mason to come to the bar when the jurisprudence of New England was yet in its infancy; that he brought to its cultivation great general ability, and a practical sagacity, logical power, and patient research,--constituting altogether a legal genius, rarely if ever surpassed; that it was greatly through his influence that the growing wants of a prosperous State were met and satisfied by a system of common law at once flexible and certain, deduced by the highest human wisdom from the actual wants of the community, logically correct, and practically useful; that in the fact that the State of New Hampshire now possesses such a system of law, whose gladsome light has shone on other States, are seen both the product and the monument of his labors, less conspicuous, but not less real, than if embodied in codes and institutes bearing his name; yet that, bred as he was to the common law, his great powers, opened and liberalized by its study and practice, enabled him to grasp readily, and wield with entire ease, those systems of equity, applicable to the transactions of the land or the sea, which, in recent times, have so much meliorated and improved the administration of justice in our country.

"_Resolved_, That as respects his practice as a counsellor and advocate at this bar, we would record our sense of his integrity, prudence, fidelity, depth of learning, knowledge of men and affairs, and great powers of persuading kindred minds; and we know well, that, when _he_ died, there was extinguished one of the few great lights of the old common law.

"_Resolved_, That Mr. Webster be requested to present these resolutions to the Supreme Judicial Court, at its next term, in Boston; and the District Attorney of the United States be requested to present them to the Circuit Court of the United States now in session.

"_Resolved_, That the Secretary communicate to the family of Mr. Mason a copy of these resolutions, together with the respectful sympathy of the bar."

The proprieties of this occasion (continued Mr. Webster) compel me, with whatever reluctance, to refrain from the indulgence of the personal feelings which arise in my heart, upon the death of one with whom I have cultivated a sincere, affectionate, and unbroken friendship, from the day when I commenced my own professional career, to the closing hour of his life. I will not say, of the advantages which I have derived from his intercourse and conversation, all that Mr. Fox said of Edmund Burke; but I am bound to say, that of my own professional discipline and attainments, whatever they may be, I owe much to that close attention to the discharge of my duties which I was compelled to pay, for nine successive years, from day to day, by Mr. Mason's efforts and arguments at the same bar. _Fas est ab hoste doceri_; and I must have been unintelligent, indeed, not to have learned something from the constant displays of that power which I had so much occasion to see and to feel.

It is the more appropriate duty of the present moment to give some short notice of his life, character, and the qualities of his mind and heart, so that he may be presented as an example to those who are entering upon or pursuing the same career. Four or five years ago, Mr. Mason drew up a biography of himself, from the earliest period of his recollection to the time of his removal to Portsmouth, in 1797; which is interesting, not only for the information it gives of the mode in which the habits of his life were formed, but also for the manner of its composition.

He was born on the 27th day of April, 1768, at Lebanon in Connecticut. His remotest ancestor in this country was Captain John Mason (an officer who had served with distinction in the Netherlands, under Sir Thomas Fairfax), who came from England in 1630, and settled at Dorchester in the Colony of Massachusetts. His great-grandfather lived at Haddam. His grandfather, born in 1705, lived at Norwich, and died in the year 1779. Mr. Mason remembered him, and recollected his character, as that of a respectable and deeply religious man. His ancestor on the maternal side was James Fitch, a learned divine, who came from England and settled in Saybrook, but removed to Lebanon, where he died. A Latin epitaph, in the ancient burying-ground of that town, records his merits. One of his descendants held a large tract of land in the parish of Goshen, in the town of Lebanon, by grant from the Indians; one half of which, near a century afterwards, was bequeathed to his daughter, Elizabeth Fitch, the mother of Mr. Mason. To this property Mr. Mason's father removed soon after his marriage, and there he died, in 1813. The title of this land was obtained from Uncas, an Indian sachem in that neighborhood, by the great-grandfather of Mr. Mason's mother, and has never been alienated from the family. It is now owned by Mr. Mason's nephew, Jeremiah Mason, the son of his eldest brother James. The family has been distinguished for longevity; the average ages of Mr. Mason's six immediate ancestors having exceeded eighty-three years each. Mr. Mason was the sixth of nine children, all of whom are now dead.

Mr. Mason's father was a man of intelligence and activity, of considerable opulence, and highly esteemed by the community. At the commencement of the Revolutionary war, being a zealous Whig, he raised and commanded a company of minute-men, as they were called, and marched to the siege of Boston. Here he rendered important service, being stationed at Dorchester Heights, and engaged in fortifying that position. In the autumn of that year, he was promoted to a colonelcy, and joined the army with his regiment, in the neighborhood of New York. At the end of the campaign, he returned home out of health, but retained the command of his regiment, which he rallied and brought out with celerity and spirit when General Arnold assaulted and burned New London. He became attached to military life, and regretted that he had not at an early day entered the Continental service. Colonel Mason was a good man, affectionate to his family, kind and obliging to his neighbors, and faithful in the observance of all moral and religious duties.

Mr. Mason's mother was distinguished for a good understanding, much discretion, the purity of her heart and affections, and the exemplary kindness and benevolence of her life. It was her great anxiety to give all her children the best education, within the means of the family, which the state of the country would allow; and she was particularly desirous that Jeremiah should be sent to college. "In my recollection of my mother," says Mr. Mason, "she was the personification of love, kindness, and benevolence."

Destined for an education and for professional life, Mr. Mason was sent to Yale College, at sixteen years of age; his preparatory studies having been pursued under "Master Tisdale," who had then been forty years at the head of a school in Lebanon, which had become distinguished, and among the scholars of which were the Wheelocks, afterwards Presidents of Dartmouth College. He was graduated in 1784, and performed a part in the Commencement exercises, which greatly raised the expectation of his friends, and gratified and animated his love for distinction. "In the course of a long and active life," says he, "I recollect no occasion when I have experienced such elevation of feeling." This was the effect of that spirit of emulation which incited the whole course of his life of usefulness. There is now prevalent among us a morbid and sickly notion, that emulation, even as honorable rivalry, is a debasing passion, and not to be encouraged. It supposes that the mind should be left without such excitement, in a dreamy and undisturbed state, flowing or not flowing, according to its own impulse, without such aids as are furnished by the rivalry of one with another. For one, I do not believe in this. I hold to the doctrine of the old school, as to this part of education. Quinctilian says: "Sunt quidam, nisi institeris, remissi; quidam imperio indignantur: quosdam continet metus, quosdam debilitat: alios continuatio extundit, in aliis plus impetus facit. Mihi ille detur puer, quem laus excitet, quem gloria juvet, qui victus fleat; hic erit alendus ambitu, hunc mordebit objurgatio, hunc honor excitabit; in hoc desidiam nunquam verebor." I think this is sound sense and just feeling.

Mr. Mason was destined for the law, and commenced the study of that profession with Mr. Baldwin, a gentleman who has lived to perform important public and private duties, has served his country in Congress, and on the bench of the Supreme Court of Connecticut, and still lives to hear the account of the peaceful death of his distinguished pupil. After a year, he went to Vermont, in whose recently established tribunals he expected to find a new sphere for the gratification of ambition, and the employment of talents. He studied in the office of Stephen Rowe Bradley, afterwards a Senator in Congress; and was admitted to the bar, in Vermont and New Hampshire, in the year 1791.

He began his career in Westmoreland, a few miles below Walpole, at the age of twenty-three; but in 1794, three years afterwards, removed to Walpole, as being a larger village, where there was more society and more business. There was at that time on the Connecticut River a rather unusual number of gentlemen, distinguished for polite accomplishments and correct tastes in literature, and among them some well known to the public as respectable writers and authors. Among these were Mr. Benjamin West, Mr. Dennie, Mr. Royall Tyler, Mr. Jacobs, Mr. Samuel Hunt, Mr. J.W. Blake, Mr. Colman (who established, and for a long time edited, the "New York Evening Post"), and Mr. Olcott. In the association with these gentlemen, and those like them, Mr. Mason found an agreeable position, and cultivated tastes and habits of the highest character.

About this period, he made a journey to Virginia, on some business connected with land titles, where he had much intercourse with Major-General Henry Lee; and, on his return, he saw President Washington, at Philadelphia, and was greatly struck by the urbanity and dignity of his manner. He heard Fisher Ames make his celebrated speech upon the British treaty. All that the world has said with regard to the extraordinary effect produced by that speech, and its wonderful excellence, is fully confirmed by the opinion of Mr. Mason. He speaks of it as one of the highest exhibitions of popular oratory that he had ever witnessed; popular, not in any low sense, but popular as being addressed to a popular body, and high in all the qualities of sound reasoning and enlightened eloquence.

Mr. Mason was inclined to exercise his abilities in a larger sphere. He had at this time made the acquaintance of Aaron Burr and Alexander Hamilton. The former advised Mr. Mason to remove himself to New York. His own preference was for Boston; but he thought, that, filled as it then was by distinguished professional ability, it was too crowded to allow him a place. That was a mistake. On the contrary, the bar of this city, with the utmost liberality and generosity of feeling and sentiment, have always been ready to receive, with open arms, every honorable acquisition to the dignity and usefulness of the profession, from other States. Mr. Mason, however, removed to Portsmouth in the autumn of 1797; and, as was to be expected, his practice soon became extensive. He was appointed Attorney-General in 1802. About that time, the late learned and lamented Chief Justice Smith retired from his professional duties, to take his place as a judge; and Mr. Mason became the acknowledged head of his profession. He resigned the office of Attorney-General, three or four years afterwards, to the great regret of the court, the bar, and the country. As a prosecuting officer, he was courteous, inflexible, and just; careful that the guilty should not escape, and that the honest should be protected. He was impartial, almost judicial, in the administration of his great office. He had no morbid eagerness for conviction; and never permitted, as sometimes occurs, an unworthy wrangling between the official power prosecuting, and the zeal of the other party defending. His official course produced exactly the ends it was designed to do. The honest felt safe; but there was a trembling and fear in the evil disposed, that the transgressed law would be vindicated.

Very much confined to his profession, he never sought office or political elevation. Yet he held decided opinions upon all political questions, and cultivated acquaintance with all the leading subjects of the day; and no man was more keenly alive than he to whatever occurred, at home or abroad, involving the great interests of the civilized world.

His political principles, opinions, judgments, were framed upon those of the men of the times of Washington. From these, to the last, he never swerved. The copy was well executed. His conversation on subjects of state was as instructive and interesting as upon professional topics. He had the same reach of thought, and exhibited the same comprehensive mind, and sagacity quick and far seeing, with regard to political things and men, as he did in professional affairs. His influence was, therefore, hardly the less from the fact that he was not actively engaged in political life. There was an additional weight given to his judgment, arising from his being a disinterested beholder only. The looker-on can sometimes form a more independent and impartial opinion of the course and results of the contest, than those who are actually engaged in it.

But at length, in June, 1813, he was persuaded to accept the post of a Senator of the United States, and took his seat that month. He was in Congress during the sessions of 1813 and 1814. Those were very exciting times; party spirit ran very high, and each party put forward its most prominent and gifted men. Both houses were filled by the greatest intellects of the country. Mr. Mason found himself by the side of Rufus King, Giles, Goldsborough, Gore, Barbour, Daggett, Hunter, and other distinguished public men. Among men of whatever party, and however much some of them differed from him in opinion or political principle, there was not one of them all but felt pleasure if he spoke, and respected his uncommon ability and probity, and his fair and upright demeanor in his place and station. He took at once his appropriate position. Of his associates and admirers in the other house, there are some eminent persons now living who were occasional listeners to his speeches and much struck with his ability; together with Pickering, Benson, Pitkin, Stockton, Lowndes, Gaston, and Hopkinson, now all deceased, who used to flock to hear him, and always derived deep gratification and instruction from his talents, character, and power.

He resigned his seat in the Senate in 1817. His published speeches are not numerous. The reports of that day were far less complete than now, and comparatively few debates were preserved and revised. It was a remarkable truth, that he always thought far too lightly of himself and all his productions. I know that he was with difficulty persuaded to prepare his speeches in Congress for publication; and in this memorial of himself which I have before me he says, with every appearance and feeling of sincerity, that he "has never acted any important part in life, but has felt a deep interest in the conduct of others."

His two main speeches were, first, one of great vigor, in the Senate, in February, 1814, on the Embargo, just before that policy was abandoned. The other was later, in December, 1815, shortly before the peace, on Mr. Giles's Conscription Bill, in which he discussed the subject of the enlistment of minors; and the clause authorizing such enlistment was struck out upon his motion.

He was afterwards for several years a member of the New Hampshire Legislature, and assisted in revising the code of that State. He paid much attention to the subject of the judicature, and performed his services fully to the satisfaction of the State; and the result of his labors was warmly commended. In 1824 he was again a candidate for the Senate of the United States. The election was to be made by the concurrent vote of the two branches of the Legislature. In the popular branch he was chosen by a strong vote. The Senate, however, non-concurred; by which means the election was lost,--a loss to the country, not to him,--by force of circumstances and agencies not now or ever fit to be recalled or remembered.

He continued to reside for many years in Portsmouth. His residence in that ancient town was a happy one. He was happy in his family and in the society of the town, surrounded by agreeable neighbors, respected by the bar and the court, and standing at the head of his profession. He had a great love of conversation. He took pleasure in hearing others talk, and gave an additional charm by the freshness, agreeableness, and originality of his own observations. His warm hospitality left him never alone, and his usefulness was felt as much within the walls of the homes, as of the tribunals, of Portsmouth. There are yet many in that town who love him and his; many who witnessed, as children, and recollect, the enthusiasm with which he was greeted by their fathers and mothers; and all in New Hampshire old enough to remember him will feel what we feel here on this occasion.

Led at last partly by the desire of exerting his abilities in a larger sphere of usefulness, and partly by the fact of the residence here of beloved domestic connections, he came to this city, and entered upon the performance of his professional duties in 1832. Of the manner in which he discharged those duties, this court is the most competent judge. You, Mr. Chief Justice, and the venerable associate who usually occupies a place at your right,[2] have been witnesses of the whole. You know the fidelity with which he observed his duty to the court, as well as his duty to his clients. In learning, assiduity, respect for the bench, uprightness, and integrity, he stood as an example to the bar. You know the general probity and talent with which he performed, for so many years, the duty of a counsellor of this court.

I should hardly trust myself to make any analysis of Mr. Mason's mind. I may be a partial judge. But I may speak of what I myself admire and venerate. The characteristics of Mr. Mason's mind, as I think, were real greatness, strength, and sagacity. He was great through strong sense and sound judgment, great by comprehensive views of things, great by high and elevated purposes. Perhaps sometimes he was too cautious and refined, and his distinctions became too minute; but his discrimination arose from a force of intellect, and quick-seeing, far-reaching sagacity, everywhere discerning his object and pursuing it steadily. Whether it was popular or professional, he grasped a point and held it with a strong hand. He was sarcastic sometimes, but not frequently; not frothy or petulant, but cool and vitriolic. Unfortunate for him on whom his sarcasm fell!

His conversation was as remarkable as his efforts at the bar. It was original, fresh, and suggestive; never dull or indifferent. He never talked when he had nothing to say. He was particularly agreeable, edifying, and instructive to all about him; and this was the charm of the social intercourse in which he was connected.

As a professional man, Mr. Mason's great ability lay in the department of the common law. In this part of jurisprudence he was profoundly learned. He had drunk copiously from its deepest springs; and he had studied with diligence and success the departures from the English common law which had taken place in this country, either necessarily, from difference of condition, or positively, by force of our own statutes. In his addresses, both to courts and juries, he affected to despise all eloquence, and certainly disdained all ornament; but his efforts, whether addressed to one tribunal or the other, were marked by a degree of clearness, directness, and force not easy to be equalled. There were no courts of equity, as a separate and distinct jurisdiction, in New Hampshire, during his residence in that State. Yet the equity treatises and equity reports were all in his library, not "wisely ranged for show," but for constant and daily consultation; because he saw that the common law itself was growing every day more and more liberal, that equity principles were constantly forcing themselves into its administration and within its rules; that the subjects of litigation in the courts were constantly becoming, more and more, such as escaped from the technicalities and the trammels of the common law, and offered themselves for discussion and decision on the broader principles of general jurisprudence. Mr. Mason, like other accomplished lawyers, and more than most, admired the searching scrutiny and the high morality of a court of equity; and felt the instruction and edification resulting from the perusal of the judgments of Lord Hardwicke, Lord Eldon, and Sir William Grant, as well as of those of great names in our own country, not now among the living.

Among his early associates in New Hampshire, there were many distinguished men. Of those now dead were Mr. West, Mr. Gordon, Edward St. Loe Livermore, Peleg Sprague, William K. Atkinson, George Sullivan, Thomas W. Thompson, and Amos Kent; the last of these having been always a particular personal friend. All of these gentlemen in their day held high and respectable stations, and were eminent as lawyers of probity and character.

Another contemporary and friend of Mr. Mason was Mr. Timothy Bigelow, a lawyer of reputation, a man of probity and honor, attractive by his conversation, and highly agreeable in his social intercourse. Mr. Bigelow, we all know, was of this State, in which he filled high offices with great credit; but, as a counsellor and advocate, he was constant in his attendance on the New Hampshire courts. Having known Mr. Bigelow from my early youth, I have pleasure in recalling the mutual regard and friendship which I know to have subsisted between him and the subject of these remarks. I ought not to omit Mr. Wilson and Mr. Betton, in mentioning Mr. Mason's contemporaries at the bar. They were near his own age, and both well known as lawyers and public men.

Mr. Mason, while yet in New Hampshire, found himself engaged in causes in which that illustrious man, Samuel Dexter, also appeared. The late Mr. Justice Story was still more frequently at the bar of that State; and, at a period somewhat earlier, your great and distinguished predecessor, Chief Justice Parsons, occasionally presented himself before the courts at Portsmouth or Exeter, and he is known to have entertained a very high regard, personal and professional, as well for Mr. Mason as for the late Chief Justice Smith.

Among those still living, with whom Mr. Mason was on terms of intimacy, and with whom he associated at the bar, were Messrs. Plumer, Arthur Livermore, Samuel Bell, and Charles H. Atherton. If these respected men could be here to-day, every one of them would unite with us in our tribute of love and veneration to his memory.

But, Sir, political eminence and professional fame fade away and die with all things earthly. Nothing of character is really permanent but virtue and personal worth. These remain. Whatever of excellence is wrought into the soul itself belongs to both worlds. Real goodness does not attach itself merely to this life; it points to another world. Political or professional reputation cannot last for ever; but a conscience void of offence before God and man is an inheritance for eternity. _Religion_, therefore, is a necessary and indispensable element in any great human character. There is no living without it. Religion is the tie that connects man with his Creator, and holds him to his throne. If that tie be all sundered, all broken, he floats away, a worthless atom in the universe; its proper attractions all gone, its destiny thwarted, and its whole future nothing but darkness, desolation, and death. A man with no sense of religious duty is he whom the Scriptures describe, in such terse but terrific language, as living "without God in the world." Such a man is out of his proper being, out of the circle of all his duties, out of the circle of all his happiness, and away, far, far away, from the purposes of his creation.

A mind like Mr. Mason's, active, thoughtful, penetrating, sedate, could not but meditate deeply on the condition of man below, and feel its responsibilities. He could not look on this mighty system,
"This universal frame, thus wondrous fair,"
without feeling that it was created and upheld by an Intelligence, to which all other intelligences must be responsible. I am bound to say, that in the course of my life I never met with an individual, in any profession or condition of life, who always spoke, and always thought, with such awful reverence of the power and presence of God. No irreverence, no lightness, even no too familiar allusion to God and his attributes, ever escaped his lips. The very notion of a Supreme Being was, with him, made up of awe and

solemnity. It filled the whole of his great mind with the strongest emotions. A man like him, with all his proper sentiments and sensibilities alive in him, must, in this state of existence, have something to believe and something to hope for; or else, as life is advancing to its close and parting, all is heart-sinking and oppression. Depend upon it, whatever may be the mind of an old man, old age is only really happy, when, on feeling the enjoyments of this world pass away, it begins to lay a stronger hold on those of another. Mr. Mason's religious sentiments and feelings were the crowning glories of his character. One, with the strongest motives to love and venerate him, and the best means of knowledge, says:--

"So far as my memory extends, he always showed a deep conviction of the divine authority of the Holy Scriptures, of the institutions of Christianity, and of the importance of personal religion. Soon after his residence in Boston, he entered the communion of the Church, and has continued since regularly to receive the Lord's Supper. From that time, he also habitually maintained domestic worship, morning and evening. The death of two of his sons produced a deep impression upon his mind, and directed it in an increased degree to religious subjects.

"Though he was always reserved in the expression of religious feeling, still it has been very apparent, for several years, that his thoughts dwelt much upon his practical religious duties, and especially upon preparation for another world. Within three or four years, he frequently led the conversation to such subjects; and during the year past, immediate preparation for his departure has been obviously the constant subject of his attention. His expressions in regard to it were deeply humble; and, indeed, the very humble manner in which he always spoke of himself was most marked.

"I have observed, of late years, an increasing tenderness in his feelings and manner, and a desire to impress his family with the conviction that he would not remain long with them. His allusions of this kind have been repeated, even when apparently in his usual health; and they indicated the current of his thoughts.

"He retained his consciousness till within a few hours of his death, and made distinct replies to every question put to him. He was fully aware that his end was near; and in answer to the question, 'Can you now rest with firm faith upon the merits of your Divine Redeemer?' he said, 'I trust I do, upon what else can I rest?'

"At another time, in reply to a similar question, he said, '_Of course_, I have no other ground of hope.' We did not often speak to him during those last three days, but had no doubt that he was entirely conscious of his state, knew that his family were all near, and that his mind was free from anxiety. He could not speak with ease, and we were unwilling to cause him the pain of exertion. His whole life, marked by uniform greatness, wisdom, and integrity, his deep humility, his profound reverence for the Divine Majesty, his habitual preparation for death, his humble trust in his Saviour, left nothing to be desired for the consolation of his family under this great loss. He was gradually prepared for his departure. His last years were passed in calm retirement; and he died as he wished to die, with his faculties unimpaired, without great pain, with his family around his bed, the precious promises of the Gospel before his mind, without lingering disease, and yet not suddenly called away."

Such, Mr. Chief Justice, was the life, and such the death, of JEREMIAH MASON. For one, I could pour out my heart like water, at the recollection of his virtues and his friendship, and in the feeling of his loss. I would embalm his memory in my best affections. His personal regard, so long continued to me, I esteem one of the greatest blessings of my life; and I hope that it may be known hereafter, that, without intermission or coolness through many years, and until he descended to his grave, Mr. Mason and myself were friends.

Mr. Mason died in old age; not by a violent stroke from the hand of death, not by a sudden rupture of the ties of nature, but by a gradual wearing out of his constitution. He enjoyed through life, indeed, remarkable health. He took competent exercise, loved the open air, and, avoiding all extreme theories or practice, controlled his conduct and habits of life by the rules of prudence and moderation. His death was therefore not unlike that described by the angel, admonishing Adam:--

"I yield it just, said Adam, and submit. But is there yet no other way, besides These painful passages, how we may come To death, and mix with our connatural dust?

"There is, said Michael, if thou well observe The rule of 'Not too much,' by temperance taught, In what thou eat'st and drink'st; seeking from thence Due nourishment, not gluttonous delight; Till many years over thy head return, So mayst thou live; till, like ripe fruit, thou drop Into thy mother's lap; or be with ease Gathered, not harshly plucked; for death mature. This is old age."

[Footnote 1: Mr. Justice Richard Fletcher.][Footnote 2: Mr. Justice Wilde.]

KOSSUTH.
FROM A SPEECH DELIVERED IN BOSTON, ON THE 7TH OF NOVEMBER, 1849, AT A FESTIVAL OF THE NATIVES OF NEW HAMPSHIRE ESTABLISHED IN MASSACHUSETTS.

We have all had our sympathies much enlisted in the Hungarian effort for liberty. We have all wept at its failure. We thought we saw a more rational hope of establishing free government in Hungary than in any other part of Europe, where the question has been in agitation within the last twelve months. But despotic power from abroad intervened to suppress that hope.

And, Gentlemen, what will come of it I do not know. For my part, at this moment, I feel more indignant at recent events connected with Hungary than at all those which passed in her struggle for liberty. I see that the Emperor of Russia demands of Turkey that the noble Kossuth and his companions shall be given up, to be dealt with at his pleasure. And I see that this demand is made in derision of the established law of nations. Gentlemen, there is something on earth greater than arbitrary or despotic power. The lightning has its power, and the whirlwind has its power, and the earthquake has its power; but there is something among men more capable of shaking despotic thrones than lightning, whirlwind, or earthquake, and that is, the excited and aroused indignation of the whole civilized world. Gentlemen, the Emperor of Russia holds himself to be bound by the law of nations, from the fact that he negotiates with civilized nations, and that he forms alliances and treaties with them. He professes, in fact, to live in a civilized age, and to govern an enlightened nation. I say, that if, under these circumstances, he shall perpetrate so great a violation of national law as to seize these Hungarians and to execute them, he will stand as a criminal and malefactor in the view of the public law of the world. The whole world will be the tribunal to try him, and he must appear before it, and hold up his hand, and plead, and abide its judgment.

The Emperor of Russia is the supreme lawgiver in his own country, and, for aught I know, the executor of that law also. But, thanks be to God, he is not the supreme lawgiver or executor of national law, and every offence against that is an offence against the rights of the civilized world. If he breaks that law in the case of Turkey, or any other case, the whole world has a right to call him out, and to demand his punishment. Our rights as a nation, like those of other nations, are held under the sanction of national law; a law which becomes more important from day to day; a law which none, who profess to agree to it, are at liberty to violate. Nor let him imagine, nor let any one imagine, that mere force can subdue the general sentiment of mankind. It is much more likely to diffuse that sentiment, and to destroy the power which he most desires to establish and secure.

Gentlemen, the bones of poor John Wickliffe were dug out of his grave, seventy years after his death, and burnt for his heresy; and his ashes were thrown upon a river in Warwickshire. Some prophet of that day said:

"The Avon to the Severn runs, The Severn to the sea, And Wickliffe's dust shall spread abroad, Wide as the waters be."

Gentlemen, if the blood of Kossuth is taken by an absolute, unqualified, unjustifiable violation of national law, what will it appease, what will it pacify? It will mingle with the earth, it will mix with the waters of the ocean, the whole civilized world will snuff it in the air, and it will return with awful retribution on the heads of those violators of national law and universal justice. I can not say when, or in what form; but depend upon it, that, if such an act take place, then thrones, and principalities, and powers, must look out for the consequences.

And now, Gentlemen, let us do our part; let us understand the position in which we stand, as the great republic of the world, at the most interesting era of its history. Let us consider the mission and the destiny which Providence seems to have designed for us, and let us so take care of our own conduct, that, with irreproachable hearts, and with hands void of offence, we may stand up whenever and wherever called upon, and, with a voice not to be disregarded, say, This shall not be done, at least not without our protest.

THE CONSTITUTION AND THE UNION.
A SPEECH DELIVERED IN THE SENATE OF THE UNITED STATES, ON THE 7TH OF MARCH, 1850.

[On the 25th of January, 1850, Mr. Clay submitted a series of resolutions to the Senate, on the subject of slavery, in connection with the various questions which had arisen in consequence of the acquisition of Mexican territory. These resolutions furnished the occasion of a protracted debate. On Wednesday, the 6th of March, Mr. Walker of Wisconsin engaged in the discussion, but, owing to the length of time taken up by repeated interruptions, he was unable to finish his argument. In the mean time it had been generally understood that Mr. Webster would, at an early day, take an opportunity of addressing the Senate on the present aspect of the slavery question, on the dangers to the Union of the existing agitation, and on the terms of honorable adjustment. In the expectation of hearing a speech from him on these all-important topics, an immense audience assembled in the Senate-Chamber at an early hour of Thursday, the 7th of March. The floor, the galleries, and the antechambers of the Senate were crowded, and it was with difficulty that the members themselves were able to force their way to their seats.

At twelve o'clock the special order of the day was announced, and the Vice-President stated that Mr. Walker of Wisconsin was entitled to the floor. That gentleman, however, rose and said:--

"Mr. President, this vast audience has not come together to hear me, and there is but one man, in my opinion, who can assemble such an audience. They expect to hear him, and I feel it to be my duty, therefore, as it is my pleasure, to give the floor to the Senator from Massachusetts. I understand it is immaterial to him upon which of these questions he speaks, and therefore I will not move to postpone the special order."

Mr. Webster then rose, and, after making his acknowledgments to the Senators from Wisconsin (Mr. Walker) and New York (Mr. Seward) for their courtesy in yielding the floor to him, delivered the following speech, which, in consideration of its character and of the manner in which it was received throughout the country, has been entitled a speech for "the Constitution and the Union." In the pamphlet edition it was dedicated in the following terms to the people of Massachusetts:--

WITH THE HIGHEST RESPECT, AND THE DEEPEST SENSE OF OBLIGATION, I DEDICATE THIS SPEECH TO THE PEOPLE OF MASSACHUSETTS.

"HIS EGO GRATIORA DICTU ALIA ESSE SCIO; SED ME VERA PRO GRATIS LOQUI, ETSI MEUM INGENIUM NON MONERET, NECESSITAS COGIT. VELLEM, EQUIDEM, VOBIS PLACERE; SED MULTO MALO VOS SALVOS ESSE, QUALICUMQUE ERGA ME ANIMO FUTURI ESTIS."

DANIEL WEBSTER.]

Mr. President,--I wish to speak to-day, not as a Massachusetts man, nor as a Northern man, but as an American, and a member of the Senate of the United States. It is fortunate that there is a Senate of the United States; a body not yet moved from its propriety, not lost to a just sense of its own dignity and its own high responsibilities, and a body to which the country looks, with confidence, for wise, moderate, patriotic, and healing counsels. It is not to be denied that we live in the midst of strong agitations, and are surrounded by very considerable dangers to our institutions and government. The imprisoned winds are let loose. The East, the North, and the stormy South combine to throw the whole sea into commotion, to toss its billows to the skies, and disclose its profoundest depths. I do not affect to regard myself, Mr. President, as holding, or as fit to hold, the helm in this combat with the political elements; but I have a duty to perform, and I mean to perform it with fidelity, not without a sense of existing dangers, but not without hope. I have a part to act, not for my own security or safety, for I am looking out for no fragment upon which to float away from the wreck, if wreck there must be, but for the good of the whole, and the preservation of all; and there is that which will keep me to my duty during this struggle, whether the sun and the stars shall appear, or shall not appear, for many days. I speak to-day for the preservation of the Union. "Hear me for my cause." I speak to-day, out of a solicitous and anxious heart, for the restoration to the country of that quiet and that harmony which make the blessings of this Union so rich, and so dear to us all. These are the topics that I propose to myself to discuss; these are the motives, and the sole motives, that influence me in the wish to communicate my opinions to the Senate and the country; and if I can do any thing, however little, for the promotion of these ends, I shall have accomplished all that I expect.

Mr. President, it may not be amiss to recur very briefly to the events which, equally sudden and extraordinary, have brought the country into its present political condition. In May, 1846, the United States declared war against Mexico. Our armies, then on the frontiers, entered the provinces of that republic, met and defeated all her troops, penetrated her mountain passes, and occupied her capital. The marine force of the United States took possession of her forts and her towns, on the Atlantic and on the Pacific. In less than two years a treaty was negotiated, by which Mexico ceded to the United States a vast territory, extending seven or eight hundred miles along the shores of the Pacific, and reaching back over the mountains, and across the desert, until it joins the frontier of the State of Texas. It so happened, in the distracted and feeble condition of the Mexican government, that, before the declaration of war by the United States against Mexico had become known in California, the people of California, under the lead of American officers, overthrew the existing Mexican provincial government, and raised an independent flag. When the news arrived at San Francisco that war had been declared by the United States against Mexico, this independent flag was pulled down, and the stars and stripes of this Union hoisted in its stead. So, Sir, before the war was over, the forces of the United States, military and naval, had possession of San Francisco and Upper California, and a great rush of emigrants from various parts of the world took place into California in 1846 and 1847. But now behold another wonder.

In January of 1848, a party of Mormons made a discovery of an extraordinarily rich mine of gold, or rather of a great quantity of gold, hardly proper to be called a mine, for it was spread near the surface, on the lower part of the south, or American, branch of the Sacramento. They attempted to conceal their discovery for some time; but soon another discovery of gold, perhaps of greater importance, was made, on another part of the American branch of the Sacramento, and near Sutter's Fort, as it is called. The fame of these discoveries spread far and wide. They inflamed more and more the spirit of emigration towards California, which had already been excited; and adventurers crowded into the country by hundreds, and flocked towards the Bay of San Francisco. This, as I have said, took place in the winter and spring of 1848. The digging commenced in the spring of that year, and from that time to this the work of searching for gold has been prosecuted with a success not heretofore known in the history of this globe. You recollect, Sir, how incredulous at first the American public was at the accounts which reached us of these discoveries but we all know, now, that these accounts received, and continue to receive, daily confirmation, and down to the present moment I suppose the assurance is as strong, after the experience of these several months, of the existence of deposits of gold apparently inexhaustible in the regions near San Francisco, in California, as it was at any period of the earlier dates of the accounts.

It so happened, Sir, that although, after the return of peace, it became a very important subject for legislative consideration and legislative decision to provide a proper territorial government for California, yet differences of opinion between the two houses of Congress prevented the establishment of any such territorial government at the last session. Under this state of things, the inhabitants of California, already amounting to a considerable number, thought it to be their duty, in the summer of last year, to establish a local government. Under the proclamation of General Riley, the people chose delegates to a convention, and that convention met at Monterey. It formed a constitution for the State of California, which, being referred to the people, was adopted by them in their primary assemblages. Desirous of immediate connection with the United States, its Senators were appointed and Representatives chosen, who have come hither, bringing with them the authentic constitution of the State of California; and they now present themselves, asking, in behalf of their constituents, that it may be admitted into this Union as one of the United States. This constitution, Sir, contains an express prohibition of slavery, or involuntary servitude, in the State of California. It is said, and I suppose truly, that, of the members who composed that convention, some sixteen were natives of, and had been residents in, the slave-holding States, about twenty-two were from the non-slaveholding States, and the remaining ten members were either native Californians or old settlers in that country. This prohibition of slavery, it is said, was inserted with entire unanimity.

It is this circumstance, Sir, the prohibition of slavery, which has contributed to raise, I do not say it has wholly raised, the dispute as to the propriety of the admission of California into the Union under this constitution. It is not to be denied, Mr. President, nobody thinks of denying, that, whatever reasons were assigned at the commencement of the late war with Mexico, it was prosecuted for the purpose of the acquisition of territory, and under the alleged argument that the cession of territory was the only form in which proper compensation could be obtained by the United States, from Mexico, for the various claims and demands which the people of this country had against that government. At any rate, it will be found that President Polk's message, at the commencement of the session of December, 1847, avowed that the war was to be prosecuted until some acquisition of territory should be made. As the acquisition was to be south of the line of the United States, in warm climates and countries, it was naturally, I suppose, expected by the South, that whatever acquisitions were made in that region would be added to the slave-holding portion of the United States. Very little of accurate information was possessed of the real physical character, either of California or New Mexico, and events have not turned out as was expected. Both California and New Mexico are likely to come in as free States; and therefore some degree of disappointment and surprise has resulted. In other words, it is obvious that the question which has so long harassed the country, and at some times very seriously alarmed the minds of wise and good men, has come upon us for a fresh discussion,--the question of slavery in these United States.

Now, Sir, I propose, perhaps at the expense of some detail and consequent detention of the Senate, to review historically this question, which, partly in consequence of its own importance, and partly, perhaps mostly, in consequence of the manner in which it has been discussed in different portions of the country, has been a source of so much alienation and unkind feeling between them.

We all know, Sir, that slavery has existed in the world from time immemorial. There was slavery, in the earliest periods of history, among the Oriental nations. There was slavery among the Jews; the theocratic government of that people issued no injunction against it. There was slavery among the Greeks; and the ingenious philosophy of the Greeks found, or sought to find, a justification for it exactly upon the grounds which have been assumed for such a justification in this country; that is, a natural and original difference among the races of mankind, and the inferiority of the black or colored race to the white. The Greeks justified their system of slavery upon that idea, precisely. They held the African and some of the Asiatic tribes to be inferior to the white race; but they did not show, I think, by any close process of logic, that, if this were true, the more intelligent and the stronger had therefore a right to subjugate the weaker.

The more manly philosophy and jurisprudence of the Romans placed the justification of slavery on entirely different grounds. The Roman jurists, from the first and down to the fall of the empire, admitted that slavery was against the natural law, by which, as they maintained, all men, of whatsoever clime, color, or capacity, were equal; but they justified slavery, first, upon the ground and authority of the law of nations, arguing, and arguing truly, that at that day the conventional law of nations admitted that captives in war, whose lives, according to the notions of the times, were at the absolute disposal of the captors, might, in exchange for exemption from death, be made slaves for life, and that such servitude might descend to their posterity. The jurists of Rome also maintained, that, by the civil law, there might be servitude or slavery, personal and hereditary; first, by the voluntary act of an individual, who might sell himself into slavery; secondly, by his being reduced into a state of slavery by his creditors, in satisfaction of his debts; and, thirdly, by being placed in a state of servitude or slavery for crime. At the introduction of Christianity, the Roman world was full of slaves, and I suppose there is to be found no injunction against that relation between man and man in the teachings of the Gospel of Jesus Christ or of any of his Apostles. The object of the instruction imparted to mankind by the Founder of Christianity was to touch the heart, purify the soul, and improve the lives of individual men. That object went directly to the first fountain of all the political and social relations of the human race, as well as of all true religious feeling, the individual heart and mind of man.

Now, Sir, upon the general nature and influence of slavery there exists a wide difference of opinion between the northern portion of this country and the southern. It is said on the one side, that, although not the subject of any injunction or direct prohibition in the New Testament, slavery is a wrong; that it is founded merely in the right of the strongest; and that it is an oppression, like unjust wars, like all those conflicts by which a powerful nation subjects a weaker to its will; and that, in its nature, whatever may be said of it in the modifications which have taken place, it is not according to the meek spirit of the Gospel. It is not "kindly affectioned"; it does not "seek another's, and not its own"; it does not "let the oppressed go free." These are sentiments that are cherished, and of late with greatly augmented force, among the people of the Northern States. They have taken hold of the religious sentiment of that part of the country, as they have, more or less, taken hold of the religious feelings of a considerable portion of mankind. The South, upon the other side, having been accustomed to this relation between the two races all their lives, from their birth, having been taught, in general, to treat the subjects of this bondage with care and kindness, and I believe, in general, feeling great kindness for them, have not taken the view of the subject which I have mentioned. There are thousands of religious men, with consciences as tender as any of their brethren at the North, who do not see the unlawfulness of slavery; and there are more thousands, perhaps, that, whatsoever they may think of it in its origin, and as a matter depending upon natural right, yet take things as they are, and, finding slavery to be an established relation of the society in which they live, can see no way in which, let their opinions on the abstract question be what they may, it is in the power of the present generation to relieve themselves from this relation. And candor obliges me to say, that I believe they are just as conscientious, many of them, and the religious people, all of them, as they are at the North who hold different opinions.

The honorable Senator from South Carolina[1] the other day alluded to the separation of that great religious community, the Methodist Episcopal Church. That separation was brought about by differences of opinion upon this particular subject of slavery. I felt great concern, as that dispute went on, about the result. I was in hopes that the difference of opinion might be adjusted, because I looked upon that religious denomination as one of the great props of religion and morals throughout the whole country, from Maine to Georgia, and westward to our utmost western boundary. The result was against my wishes and against my hopes. I have read all their proceedings and all their arguments; but I have never yet been able to come to the conclusion that there was any real ground for that separation; in other words, that any good could be produced by that separation. I must say I think there was some want of candor and charity. Sir, when a question of this kind seizes on the religious sentiments of mankind, and comes to be discussed in religious assemblies of the clergy and laity, there is always to be expected, or always to be feared, a great degree of excitement. It is in the nature of man, manifested by his whole history, that religious disputes are apt to become warm in proportion to the strength of the convictions which men entertain of the magnitude of the questions at issue. In all such disputes, there will sometimes be found men with whom every thing is absolute; absolutely wrong, or absolutely right. They see the right clearly; they think others ought so to see it, and they are disposed to establish a broad line, of distinction between what is right and what is wrong. They are not seldom willing to establish that line upon their own convictions of truth and justice; and are ready to mark and guard it by placing along it a series of dogmas, as lines of boundary on the earth's surface are marked by posts and stones. There are men who, with clear perceptions, as they think, of their own duty, do not see how too eager a pursuit of one duty may involve them in the violation of others, or how too warm an embracement of one truth may lead to a disregard of other truths equally important. As I heard it stated strongly, not many days ago, these persons are disposed to mount upon some particular duty, as upon a war-horse, and to drive furiously on and upon and over all other duties that may stand in the way. There are men who, in reference to disputes of that sort, are of opinion that human duties may be ascertained with the exactness of mathematics. They deal with morals as with mathematics; and they think what is right may be distinguished from what is wrong with the precision of an algebraic equation. They have, therefore, none too much charity towards others who differ from them. They are apt, too, to think that nothing is good but what is perfect, and that there are no compromises or modifications to be made in consideration of difference of opinion or in deference to other men's judgment. If their perspicacious vision enables them to detect a spot on the face of the sun, they think that a good reason why the sun should be struck down from heaven. They prefer the chance of running into utter darkness to living in heavenly light, if that heavenly light be not absolutely without any imperfection. There are impatient men; too impatient always to give heed to the admonition of St. Paul, that we are not to "do evil that good may come"; too impatient to wait for the slow progress of moral causes in the improvement of mankind. They do not remember that the doctrines and the miracles of Jesus Christ have, in eighteen hundred years, converted only a small portion of the human race; and among the nations that are converted to Christianity, they forget how many vices and crimes, public and private, still prevail, and that many of them, public crimes especially, which are so clearly offences against the Christian religion, pass without exciting particular indignation. Thus wars are waged, and unjust wars. I do not deny that there may be just wars. There certainly are; but it was the remark of an eminent person, not many years ago, on the other side of the Atlantic, that it is one of the greatest reproaches to human nature that wars are sometimes just. The defence of nations sometimes causes a just war against the injustice of other nations. In this state of sentiment upon the general nature of slavery lies the cause of a great part of those unhappy divisions, exasperations, and reproaches which find vent and support in different parts of the Union.

But we must view things as they are. Slavery does exist in the United States. It did exist in the States before the adoption of this Constitution, and at that time. Let us, therefore, consider for a moment what was the state of sentiment, North and South, in regard to slavery, at the time this Constitution was adopted. A remarkable change has taken place since; but what did the wise and great men of all parts of the country think of slavery then? In what estimation did they hold it at the time when this Constitution was adopted? It will be found, Sir, if we will carry ourselves by historical research back to that day, and ascertain men's opinions by authentic records still existing among us, that there was then no diversity of opinion between the North and the South upon the subject of slavery. It will be found that both parts of the country held it equally an evil,--a moral and political evil. It will not be found that, either at the North or at the South, there was much, though there was some, invective against slavery as inhuman and cruel. The great ground of objection to it was political; that it weakened the social fabric; that, taking the place of free labor, society became less strong and labor less productive; and therefore we find from all the eminent men of the time the clearest expression of their opinion that slavery is an evil. They ascribed its existence here, not without truth, and not without some acerbity of temper and force of language, to the injurious policy of the mother country, who, to favor the navigator, had entailed these evils upon the Colonies. I need hardly refer, Sir, particularly to the publications of the day. They are matters of history on the record. The eminent men, the most eminent men, and nearly all the conspicuous politicians of the South, held the same sentiments,--that slavery was an evil, a blight, a scourge, and a curse. There are no terms of reprobation of slavery so vehement in the North at that day as in the South. The North was not so much excited against it as the South; and the reason is, I suppose, that there was much less of it at the North, and the people did not see, or think they saw, the evils so prominently as they were seen, or thought to be seen, at the South. Then, Sir, when this Constitution was framed, this was the light in which the Federal Convention viewed it. That body reflected the judgment and sentiments of the great men of the South. A member of the other house, whom I have not the honor to know, has, in a recent speech, collected extracts from these public documents. They prove the truth of what I am saying, and the question then was, how to deal with it, and how to deal with it as an evil. They came to this general result. They thought that slavery could not be continued in the country if the importation of slaves were made to cease, and therefore they provided that, after a certain period, the importation might be prevented by the act of the new government. The period of twenty years was proposed by some gentleman from the North, I think, and many members of the Convention from the South opposed it as being too long. Mr. Madison especially was somewhat warm against it. He said it would bring too much of this mischief into the country to allow the importation of slaves for such a period. Because we must take along with us, in the whole of this discussion, when we are considering the sentiments and opinions in which the constitutional provision originated, that the conviction of all men was, that, if the importation of slaves ceased, the white race would multiply faster than the black race, and that slavery would therefore gradually wear out and expire. It may not be improper here to allude to that, I had almost said, celebrated opinion of Mr. Madison. You observe, Sir, that the term _slave_, or _slavery_, is not used in the Constitution. The Constitution does not require that "fugitive slaves" shall be delivered up. It requires that persons held to service in one State, and escaping into another, shall be delivered up. Mr. Madison opposed the introduction of the term _slave_, or _slavery_, into the Constitution; for he said that he did not wish to see it recognized by the Constitution of the United States of America that there could be property in men.

Now, Sir, all this took place in the Convention in 1787; but connected with this, concurrent and contemporaneous, is another important transaction, not sufficiently attended to. The Convention for framing this Constitution assembled in Philadelphia in May, and sat until September, 1787. During all that time the Congress of the United States was in session at New York. It was a matter of design, as we know, that the Convention should not assemble in the same city where Congress was holding its sessions. Almost all the public men of the country, therefore, of distinction and eminence, were in one or the other of these two assemblies; and I think it happened, in some instances, that the same gentlemen were members of both bodies. If I mistake not, such was the case with Mr. Rufus King, then a member of Congress from Massachusetts. Now, at the very time when the Convention in Philadelphia was framing this Constitution, the Congress in New York was framing the Ordinance of 1787, for the organization and government of the territory northwest of the Ohio. They passed that Ordinance on the 13th of July, 1787, at New York, the very month, perhaps the very day, on which these questions about the importation of slaves and the character of slavery were debated in the Convention at Philadelphia. So far as we can now learn, there was a perfect concurrence of opinion between these two bodies; and it resulted in this Ordinance of 1787, excluding slavery from all the territory over which the Congress of the United States had jurisdiction, and that was all the territory northwest of the Ohio. Three years before, Virginia and other States had made a cession of that great territory to the United States; and a most munificent act it was. I never reflect upon it without a disposition to do honor and justice, and justice would be the highest honor, to Virginia, for the cession of her northwestern territory. I will say, Sir, it is one of her fairest claims to the respect and gratitude of the country, and that, perhaps, it is only second to that other claim which belongs to her,--that from her counsels, and from the intelligence and patriotism of her leading statesmen, proceeded the first idea put into practice of the formation of a general constitution of the United States. The Ordinance of 1787 applied to the whole territory over which the Congress of the United States had jurisdiction. It was adopted two years before the Constitution of the United States went into operation; because the Ordinance took effect immediately on its passage, while the Constitution of the United States, having been framed, was to be sent to the States to be adopted by their conventions; and then a government was to be organized under it. This Ordinance, then, was in operation and force when the Constitution was adopted, and the government put in motion, in April, 1789.

Mr. President, three things are quite clear as historical truths. One is, that there was an expectation that, on the ceasing of the importation of slaves from Africa, slavery would begin to run out here. That was hoped and expected. Another is, that, as far as there was any power in Congress to prevent the spread of slavery in the United States, that power was executed in the most absolute manner, and to the fullest extent. An honorable member,[2] whose health does not allow him to be here to-day--

A SENATOR. He is here.

I am very happy to hear that he is; may he long be here, and in the enjoyment of health to serve his country! The honorable member said, the other day, that he considered this Ordinance as the first in the series of measures calculated to enfeeble the South, and deprive them of their just participation in the benefits and privileges of this government. He says, very properly, that it was enacted under the old Confederation, and before this Constitution went into effect; but my present purpose is only to say, Mr. President, that it was established with the entire and unanimous concurrence of the whole South. Why, there it stands! The vote of every State in the Union was unanimous in favor of the Ordinance, with the exception of a single individual vote, and that individual vote was given by a Northern man. This Ordinance prohibiting slavery for ever northwest of the Ohio has the hand and seal of every Southern member in Congress. It was therefore no aggression of the North on the South. The other and third clear historical truth is, that the Convention meant to leave slavery in the States as they found it, entirely under the authority and control of the States themselves.

This was the state of things, Sir, and this the state of opinion, under which those very important matters were arranged, and those three important things done; that is, the establishment of the Constitution of the United States with a recognition of slavery as it existed in the States; the establishment of the ordinance for the government of the Northwestern Territory, prohibiting, to the full extent of all territory owned by the United States, the introduction of slavery into that territory, while leaving to the States all power over slavery in their own limits; and creating a power, in the new government, to put an end to the importation of slaves, after a limited period. There was entire coincidence and concurrence of sentiment between the North and the South, upon all these questions, at the period of the adoption of the Constitution. But opinions, Sir, have changed, greatly changed; changed North and changed South. Slavery is not regarded in the South now as it was then. I see an honorable member of this body paying me the honor of listening to my remarks;[3] he brings to my mind, Sir, freshly and vividly, what I have learned of his great ancestor, so much distinguished in his day and generation, so worthy to be succeeded by so worthy a grandson, and of the sentiments he expressed in the Convention in Philadelphia.[4]

Here we may pause. There was, if not an entire unanimity, a general concurrence of sentiment running through the whole community, and especially entertained by the eminent men of all parts of the country. But soon a change began, at the North and the South, and a difference of opinion showed itself; the North growing much more warm and strong against slavery, and the South growing much more warm and strong in its support. Sir, there is no generation of mankind whose opinions are not subject to be influenced by what appear to them to be their present emergent and exigent interests. I impute to the South no particularly selfish view in the change which has come over her. I impute to her certainly no dishonest view. All that has happened has been natural. It has followed those causes which always influence the human mind and operate upon it. What, then, have been the causes which have created so new a feeling in favor of slavery in the South, which have changed the whole nomenclature of the South on that subject, so that, from being thought and described in the terms I have mentioned and will not repeat, it has now become an institution, a cherished institution, in that quarter; no evil, no scourge, but a great religious, social, and moral blessing, as I think I have heard it latterly spoken of? I suppose this, Sir, is owing to the rapid growth and sudden extension of the COTTON plantations of the South. So far as any motive consistent with honor, justice, and general judgment could act, it was the COTTON interest that gave a new desire to promote slavery, to spread it, and to use its labor. I again say that this change was produced by causes which must always produce like effects. The whole interest of the South became connected, more or less, with the extension of slavery. If we look back to the history of the commerce of this country in the early years of this government, what were our exports? Cotton was hardly, or but to a very limited extent, known. In 1791 the first parcel of cotton of the growth of the United States was exported, and amounted only to 19,200 pounds.[5] It has gone on increasing rapidly, until the whole crop may now, perhaps, in a season of great product and high prices, amount to a hundred millions of dollars. In the years I have mentioned, there was more of wax, more of indigo, more of rice, more of almost every article of export from the South, than of cotton. When Mr. Jay negotiated the treaty of 1794 with England, it is evident from the twelfth article of the treaty, which was suspended by the Senate, that he did not know that cotton was exported at all from the United States.

Well, Sir, we know what followed. The age of cotton became the golden age of our Southern brethren. It gratified their desire for improvement and accumulation, at the same time that it excited it. The desire grew by what it fed upon, and there soon came to be an eagerness for other territory, a new area or new areas for the cultivation of the cotton crop; and measures leading to this result were brought about rapidly, one after another, under the lead of Southern men at the head of the government, they having a majority in both branches of Congress to accomplish their ends. The honorable member from South Carolina[6] observed that there has been a majority all along in favor of the North. If that be true, Sir, the North has acted either very liberally and kindly, or very weakly; for they never exercised that majority efficiently five times in the history of the government, when a division or trial of strength arose. Never. Whether they were outgeneralled, or whether it was owing to other causes, I shall not stop to consider; but no man acquainted with the history of the Union can deny that the general lead in the politics of the country, for three fourths of the period that has elapsed since the adoption of the Constitution, has been a Southern lead.

In 1802, in pursuit of the idea of opening a new cotton region, the United States obtained a cession from Georgia of the whole of her western territory, now embracing the rich and growing States of Alabama and Mississippi. In 1803 Louisiana was purchased from France, out of which the States of Louisiana, Arkansas, and Missouri have been framed, as slave-holding States. In 1819 the cession of Florida was made, bringing in another region adapted to cultivation by slaves. Sir, the honorable member from South Carolina thought he saw in certain operations of the government, such as the manner of collecting the revenue, and the tendency of measures calculated to promote emigration into the country, what accounts for the more rapid growth of the North than the South. He ascribes that more rapid growth, not to the operation of time, but to the system of government and administration established under this Constitution. That is matter of opinion. To a certain extent it may be true; but it does seem to me that, if any operation of the government can be shown in any degree to have promoted the population, and growth, and wealth of the North, it is much more sure that there are sundry important and distinct operations of the government, about which no man can doubt, tending to promote, and which absolutely have promoted, the increase of the slave interest and the slave territory of the South. It was not time that brought in Louisiana; it was the act of men. It was not time that brought in Florida; it was the act of men. And lastly, Sir, to complete those acts of legislation which have contributed so much to enlarge the area of the institution of slavery, Texas, great and vast and illimitable Texas, was added to the Union as a slave State in 1845; and that, Sir, pretty much closed the whole chapter, and settled the whole account.

That closed the whole chapter and settled the whole account, because the annexation of Texas, upon the conditions and under the guaranties upon which she was admitted, did not leave within the control of this government an acre of land, capable of being cultivated by slave labor, between this Capitol and the Rio Grande or the Nueces, or whatever is the proper boundary of Texas; not an acre. From that moment, the whole country, from this place to the western boundary of Texas, was fixed, pledged, fastened, decided, to be slave territory for ever, by the solemn guaranties of law. And I now say, Sir, as the proposition upon which I stand this day, and upon the truth and firmness of which I intend to act until it is overthrown, that there is not at this moment within the United States, or any territory of the United States, a single foot of land, the character of which, in regard to its being free territory or slave territory, is not fixed by some law, and some irrepealable law, beyond the power of the action of the government. Is it not so with respect to

Texas? It is most manifestly so. The honorable member from South Carolina, at the time of the admission of Texas, held an important post in the executive department of the government; he was Secretary of State. Another eminent person of great activity and adroitness in affairs, I mean the late Secretary of the Treasury,[7] was a conspicuous member of this body, and took the lead in the business of annexation, in co-operation with the Secretary of State; and I must say that they did their business faithfully and thoroughly; there was no botch left in it. They rounded it off, and made as close joiner-work as ever was exhibited. Resolutions of annexation were brought into Congress, fitly joined together, compact, efficient, conclusive upon the great object which they had in view, and those resolutions passed.

Allow me to read a part of these resolutions. It is the third clause of the second section of the resolution of the 1st of March, 1845, for the admission of Texas, which applies to this part of the case. That clause is as follows:--

"New States, of convenient size, not exceeding four in number, in addition to said State of Texas, and having sufficient population, may hereafter, by the consent of said State, he formed out of the territory thereof, which shall be entitled to admission under the provisions of the Federal Constitution. And such States as may be formed out of that portion of said territory lying south of thirty-six degrees thirty minutes north latitude, commonly known as the Missouri Compromise line, shall be admitted into the Union with or without slavery, as the people of each State asking admission may desire; and in such State or States as shall be formed out of said territory north of said Missouri Compromise line, slavery or involuntary servitude (except for crime) shall be prohibited."

Now what is here stipulated, enacted, and secured? It is, that all Texas south of 36° 30', which is nearly the whole of it, shall be admitted into the Union as a slave State. It was a slave State, and therefore came in as a slave State; and the guaranty is, that new States shall be made out of it, to the number of four, in addition to the State then in existence and admitted at that time by these resolutions, and that such States as are formed out of that portion of Texas lying south of 36° 30' may come in as slave States. I know no form of legislation which can strengthen this. I know no mode of recognition that can add a tittle of weight to it. I listened respectfully to the resolutions of my honorable friend from Tennessee.[8] He proposed to recognize that stipulation with Texas. But any additional recognition would weaken the force of it; because it stands here on the ground of a contract, a thing done for a consideration. It is a law founded on a contract with Texas, and designed to carry that contract into effect. A recognition now, founded not on any consideration, or any contract, would not be so strong as it now stands on the face of the resolution. I know no way, I candidly confess, in which this government, acting in good faith, as I trust it always will, can relieve itself from that stipulation and pledge, by any honest course of legislation whatever. And therefore I say again, that, so far as Texas is concerned, in the whole of that State south of 36° 30', which, I suppose, embraces all the territory capable of slave cultivation, there is no land, not an acre, the character of which is not established by law; a law which cannot be repealed without the violation of a contract, and plain disregard of the public faith.

I hope, Sir, it is now apparent that my proposition, so far as it respects Texas, has been maintained, and that the provision in this article is clear and absolute; and it has been well suggested by my friend from Rhode Island,[9] that that part of Texas which lies north of 36° 30' of north latitude, and which may be formed into free States, is dependent, in like manner, upon the consent of Texas, herself a slave State.

Now, Sir, how came this? How came it to pass that within these walls, where it is said by the honorable member from South Carolina that the free States have always had a majority, this resolution of annexation, such as I have described it, obtained a majority in both houses of Congress? Sir, it obtained that majority by the great number of Northern votes added to the entire Southern vote, or at least nearly the whole of the Southern vote. The aggregate was made up of Northern and Southern votes. In the House of Representatives there were about eighty Southern votes and about fifty Northern votes for the admission of Texas. In the Senate the vote for the admission of Texas was twenty-seven, and twenty-five against it; and of those twenty-seven votes, constituting the majority, no less than thirteen came from the free States, and four of them were from New England. The whole of these thirteen Senators, constituting within a fraction, you see, one half of all the votes in this body for the admission of this immeasurable extent of slave territory, were sent here by free States.

Sir, there is not so remarkable a chapter in our history of political events, political parties, and political men as is afforded by this admission of a new slave-holding territory, so vast that a bird cannot fly over it in a week. New England, as I have said, with some of her own votes, supported this measure. Three fourths of the votes of liberty-loving Connecticut were given for it in the other house, and one half here. There was one vote for it from Maine, but, I am happy to say, not the vote of the honorable member who addressed the Senate the day before yesterday,[10] and who was then a Representative from Maine in the House of Representatives; but there was one vote from Maine, ay, and there was one vote for it from Massachusetts, given by a gentleman then representing, and now living in, the district in which the prevalence of Free Soil sentiment for a couple of years or so has defeated the choice of any member to represent it in Congress. Sir, that body of Northern and Eastern men who gave those votes at that time are now seen taking upon themselves, in the nomenclature of politics, the appellation of the Northern Democracy. They undertook to wield the destinies of this empire, if I may give that name to a republic, and their policy was, and they persisted in it, to bring into this country and under this government all the territory they could. They did it, in the case of Texas, under pledges, absolute pledges, to the slave interest, and they afterwards lent their aid in bringing in these new conquests, to take their chance for slavery or freedom. My honorable friend from Georgia,[11] in March, 1847, moved the Senate to declare that the war ought not to be prosecuted for the conquest of Territory, or for the dismemberment of Mexico. The whole of the Northern Democracy voted against it. He did not get a vote from them. It suited the patriotic and elevated sentiments of the Northern Democracy to bring in a world from among the mountains and valleys of California and New Mexico, or any other part of Mexico, and then quarrel about it; to bring it in, and then endeavor to put upon it the saving grace of the Wilmot Proviso. There were two eminent and highly respectable gentlemen from the North and East, then leading gentlemen in the Senate, (I refer, and I do so with entire respect, for I entertain for both of those gentlemen, in general, high regard, to Mr. Dix of New York and Mr. Niles of Connecticut,) who both voted for the admission of Texas. They would not have that vote any other way than as it stood; and they would have it as it did stand. I speak of the vote upon the annexation of Texas. Those two gentlemen would have the resolution of annexation just as it is, without amendment; and they voted for it just as it is, and their eyes were all open to its true character. The honorable member from South Carolina who addressed us the other day was then Secretary of State. His correspondence with Mr. Murphy, the Chargé d'Affaires of the United States in Texas, had been published. That correspondence was all before those gentlemen, and the Secretary had the boldness and candor to avow in that correspondence, that the great object sought by the annexation of Texas was to strengthen the slave interest of the South. Why, Sir, he said so in so many words--

MR. CALHOUN. Will the honorable Senator permit me to interrupt him for a moment?

Certainly.

MR. CALHOUN. I am very reluctant to interrupt the honorable gentleman; but, upon a point of so much importance, I deem it right to put myself *rectus in curia*. I did not put it upon the ground assumed by the Senator. I put it upon this ground: that Great Britain had announced to this country, in so many words, that her object was to abolish slavery in Texas, and, through Texas, to accomplish the abolition of slavery in the United States and the world. The ground I put it on was, that it would make an exposed frontier, and, if Great Britain succeeded in her object, it would be impossible that that frontier could be secured against the aggressions of the Abolitionists; and that this government was bound, under the guaranties of the Constitution, to protect us against such a state of things.

That comes, I suppose, Sir, to exactly the same thing. It was, that Texas must be obtained for the security of the slave interest of the South.

MR. CALHOUN. Another view is very distinctly given.

That was the object set forth in the correspondence of a worthy gentleman not now living,[12] who preceded the honorable member from South Carolina in the Department of State. There repose on the files of the Department, as I have occasion to know, strong letters from Mr. Upshur to the United States Minister in England, and I believe there are some to the same Minister from the honorable Senator himself, asserting to this effect the sentiments of this government; namely, that Great Britain was expected not to interfere to take Texas out of the hands of its then existing government and make it a free country. But my argument, my suggestion, is this: that those gentlemen who composed the Northern Democracy when Texas was brought into the Union saw clearly that it was brought in as a slave country, and brought in for the purpose of being maintained as slave territory, to the Greek Kalends. I rather think the honorable gentleman who was then Secretary of State might, in some of his correspondence with Mr. Murphy, have suggested that it was not expedient to say too much about this object, lest it should create some alarm. At any rate, Mr. Murphy wrote to him that England was anxious to get rid of the constitution of Texas, because it was a constitution establishing slavery; and that what the United States had to do was to aid the people of Texas in upholding their constitution; but that nothing should be said which should offend the fanatical men of the North. But, Sir, the honorable member did avow this object himself, openly, boldly, and manfully; he did not disguise his conduct or his motives.

MR. CALHOUN. Never, never.

What he means he is very apt to say.

MR. CALHOUN. Always, always.

And I honor him for it.

This admission of Texas was in 1845. Then in 1847, *flagrante bello* between the United States and Mexico, the proposition I have mentioned was brought forward by my friend from Georgia, and the Northern Democracy voted steadily against it. Their remedy was to apply to the acquisitions, after they should come in, the Wilmot Proviso. What follows? These two gentlemen,[13] worthy and honorable and influential men, (and if they had not been they could not have carried the measure,) these two gentlemen, members of this body, brought in Texas, and by their votes they also prevented the passage of the resolution of the honorable member from Georgia, and then they went home and took the lead in the Free Soil party. And there they stand, Sir! They leave us here, bound in honor and conscience by the resolutions of annexation; they leave us here, to take the odium of fulfilling the obligations in favor of slavery which they voted us into, or else the greater odium of violating those obligations, while they are at home making capital and rousing speeches for free soil and no slavery. And therefore I say, Sir, that there is not a chapter in our history, respecting public measures and public men, more full of what would create surprise, more full of what does create in my mind, extreme mortification, than that of the conduct of the Northern Democracy on this subject.

Mr. President, sometimes, when a man is found in a new relation to things around him and to other men, he says the world has changed, and that he has not changed. I believe, Sir, that our self-respect leads us often to make this declaration in regard to ourselves when it is not exactly true. An individual is more apt to change, perhaps, than all the world around him. But under the present circumstances, and under the responsibility which I know I incur by what I am now stating here, I feel at liberty to recur to the various expressions and statements, made at various times, of my own opinions and resolutions respecting the admission of Texas, and all that has followed. Sir, as early as 1836, or in the early part of 1837, there was conversation and correspondence between myself and some private friends on this project of annexing Texas to the United States; and an honorable gentleman with whom I have had a long acquaintance, a friend of mine, now perhaps in this chamber, I mean General Hamilton, of South Carolina, was privy to that correspondence. I had voted for the recognition of Texan independence, because I believed it to be an existing fact, surprising and astonishing as it was, and I wished well to the new republic; but I manifested from the first utter opposition to bringing her, with her slave territory, into the Union. I happened, in 1837, to make a public address to political friends in New York, and I then stated my sentiments upon the subject. It was the first time that I had occasion to advert to it; and I will ask a friend near me to have the kindness to read an extract from the speech made by me on that occasion. It was delivered in Niblo's Saloon, in 1837.

Mr. Greene then read the following extract from the speech of Mr. Webster to which he referred:--

"Gentlemen, we all see that, by whomsoever possessed, Texas is likely to be a slave-holding country; and I frankly avow my entire unwillingness to do any thing that shall extend the slavery of the African race on this continent, or add other slave-holding States to the Union. When I say that I regard slavery in itself as a great moral, social, and political evil, I only use language which has been adopted by distinguished men, themselves citizens of slave-holding States. I shall do nothing, therefore, to favor or encourage its further extension. We have slavery already amongst us. The Constitution found it in the Union; it recognized it, and gave it solemn guaranties. To the full extent of these guaranties we are all bound, in honor, in justice, and by the Constitution. All the stipulations contained in the Constitution in favor of the slave-holding States which are already in the Union ought to be fulfilled, and, so far as depends on me, shall be fulfilled, in the fulness of their spirit, and to the exactness of their letter. Slavery, as it exists in the States, is beyond the reach of Congress. It is a concern of the States themselves; they have never submitted it to Congress, and Congress has no rightful power over it. I shall concur, therefore, in no act, no measure, no menace, no indication of purpose, which shall interfere or threaten to interfere with the exclusive authority of the several States over the subject of slavery as it exists within their respective limits. All this appears to me to be matter of plain and imperative duty.

"But when we come to speak of admitting new States, the subject assumes an entirely different aspect. Our rights and our duties are then both different....

"I see, therefore, no political necessity for the annexation of Texas to the Union; no advantages to be derived from it; and objections to it of a strong, and, in my judgment, decisive character."

I have nothing, Sir, to add to, or to take from, those sentiments. That speech, the Senate will perceive, was made in 1837. The purpose of immediately annexing Texas at that time was abandoned or postponed; and it was not revived with any vigor for some years. In the mean time it happened that I had become a member of the executive administration, and was for a short period in the Department of State. The annexation of Texas was a subject of conversation, not confidential, with the President and heads of departments, as well as with other public men. No serious attempt was then made, however, to bring it about. I left the Department of State in May, 1843, and shortly after I learned, though by means which were no way connected with official information, that a design had been taken up of bringing Texas, with her slave territory and population, into this Union. I was in Washington at the time, and persons are now here who will remember that we had an arranged meeting for conversation upon it. I went home to Massachusetts and proclaimed the existence of that purpose, but I could get no audience and but little attention. Some did not believe it, and some were too much engaged in their own pursuits to give it any heed. They had gone to their farms or to their merchandise, and it was impossible to arouse any feeling in New England, or in Massachusetts, that should combine the two great political parties against this annexation; and, indeed, there was no hope of bringing the Northern Democracy into that view, for their leaning was all the other way. But, Sir, even with Whigs, and leading Whigs, I am ashamed to say, there was a great indifference towards the admission of Texas, with slave territory, into this Union.

The project went on. I was then out of Congress. The annexation resolutions passed on the 1st of March, 1845; the legislature of Texas complied with the conditions and accepted the guaranties; for the language of the resolution is, that Texas is to come in "upon the conditions and under the guaranties herein prescribed." I was returned to the Senate in March, 1845, and was here in December following, when the acceptance by Texas of the conditions proposed by Congress was communicated to us by the President, and an act for the consummation of the union was laid before the two houses. The connection was then not completed. A final law, doing the deed of annexation ultimately, had not been passed; and when it was put upon its final passage here, I expressed my opposition to it, and recorded my vote in the negative; and there that vote stands, with the observations that I made upon that occasion.[14] Nor is this the only occasion on which I have expressed myself to the same effect. It has happened that, between 1837 and this time, on various occasions, I have expressed my entire opposition to the admission of slave States, or the acquisition of new slave territories, to be added to the United States. I know, Sir, no change in my own sentiments, or my own purposes, in that respect. I will now ask my friend from Rhode Island to read another extract from a speech of mine made at a Whig Convention in Springfield, Massachusetts, in the month of September, 1847.

Mr. Greene here read the following extract:--

"We hear much just now of a *panacea* for the dangers and evils of slavery and slave annexation, which they call the 'Wilmot Proviso.' That certainly is a just sentiment, but it is not a sentiment to found any new party upon. It is not a sentiment on which Massachusetts Whigs differ. There is not a man in this hall who holds to it more firmly than I do, nor one who adheres to it more than another.

"I feel some little interest in this matter, Sir. Did not I commit myself in 1837 to the whole doctrine, fully, entirely? And I must be permitted to say that I cannot quite consent that more recent discoverers should claim the merit and take out a patent.

"I deny the priority of their invention. Allow me to say, Sir, it is not their thunder....

"We are to use the first and the last and every occasion which offers to oppose the extension of slave power.

"But I speak of it here, as in Congress, as a political question, a question for statesmen to act upon. We must so regard it. I certainly do not mean to say that it is less important in a moral point of view, that it is not more important in many other points of view; but as a legislator, or in any official capacity, I must look at it, consider it, and decide it as a matter of political action."

On other occasions, in debates here, I have expressed my determination to vote for no acquisition, cession, or annexation, north or south, east or west. My opinion has been, that we have territory enough, and that we should follow the Spartan maxim, "Improve, adorn what you have," seek no further. I think that it was in some observations that I made on the three-million loan bill that I avowed this sentiment. In short, Sir, it has been avowed quite as often, in as many places, and before as many assemblies, as any humble opinions of mine ought to be avowed.

But now that, under certain conditions, Texas is in the Union, with all her territory, as a slave State, with a solemn pledge, also, that, if she shall be divided into many States, those States may come in as slave States south of 36° 30', how are we to deal with this subject? I know no way of honest legislation, when the proper time comes for the enactment, but to carry into effect all that we have stipulated to do. I do not entirely agree with my honorable friend from Tennessee,[15] that, as soon as the time comes when she is entitled to another representative, we should create a new State. On former occasions, in creating new States out of territories, we have generally gone upon the idea that, when the population of the territory amounts to about sixty thousand, we would consent to its admission as a State. But it is quite a different thing when a State is divided, and two or more States made out of it. It does not follow in such a case that the same rule of apportionment should be applied. That, however, is a matter for the consideration of Congress, when the proper time arrives. I may not then be here; I may have no vote to give on the occasion; but I wish it to be distinctly understood, that, according to my view of the matter, this government is solemnly pledged, by law and contract, to create new States out of Texas, with her consent, when her population shall justify and call for such a proceeding, and, so far as such States are formed out of Texan territory lying south of 36° 30', to let them come in as slave States. That is the meaning of the contract which our friends, the Northern Democracy, have left us to fulfil; and I, for one, mean to fulfil it, because I will not violate the faith of the government. What I mean to say is, that the time for the admission of new States formed out of Texas, the number of such States, their boundaries, the requisite amount of population, and all other things connected with the admission, are in the free discretion of Congress, except this; to wit, that, when new States formed out of Texas are to be admitted, they have a right, by legal stipulation and contract, to come in as slave States.

Now, as to California and New Mexico, I hold slavery to be excluded from those territories by a law even superior to that which admits and sanctions it in Texas. I mean the law of nature, of physical geography, the law of the formation of the earth. That law settles for ever, with a strength beyond all terms of human enactment, that slavery cannot exist in California or New Mexico. Understand me, Sir; I mean slavery as we regard it; the slavery of the colored race as it exists in the Southern States. I shall not discuss the point, but leave it to the learned gentlemen who have undertaken to discuss it; but I suppose there is no slavery of that description in California now. I understand that _peonism_, a sort of penal servitude, exists there, or rather a sort of voluntary sale of a man and his offspring for debt; an arrangement of a peculiar nature known to the law of Mexico. But what I mean to say is, that it is as impossible that African slavery, as we see it among us, should find its way, or be introduced, into California and New Mexico, as any other natural impossibility. California and New Mexico are Asiatic in their formation and scenery. They are composed of vast ridges of mountains, of great height, with broken ridges and deep valleys. The sides of these mountains are entirely barren; their tops capped by perennial snow. There may be in California, now made free by its constitution, and no doubt there are, some tracts of valuable land. But it is not so in New Mexico. Pray, what is the evidence which every gentleman must have obtained on this subject, from information sought by himself or communicated by others? I have inquired and read all I could find, in order to acquire information on this important subject. What is there in New Mexico that could, by any possibility, induce anybody to go there with slaves? There are some narrow strips of tillable land on the borders of the rivers; but the rivers themselves dry up before midsummer is gone. All that the people can do in that region is to raise some little articles, some little wheat for their _tortillas_, and that by irrigation. And who expects to see a hundred black men cultivating tobacco, corn, cotton, rice, or any thing else, on lands in New Mexico, made fertile only by irrigation?

I look upon it, therefore, as a fixed fact, to use the current expression of the day, that both California and New Mexico are destined to be free, so far as they are settled at all, which I believe, in regard to New Mexico, will be but partially for a great length of time; free by the arrangement of things ordained by the Power above us. I have therefore to say, in this respect also, that this country is fixed for freedom, to as many persons as shall ever live in it, by a less repealable law than that which attaches to the right of holding slaves in Texas; and I will say further, that, if a resolution or a bill were now before us, to provide a territorial government for New Mexico, I would not vote to put any prohibition into it whatever. Such a prohibition would be idle, as it respects any effect it would have upon the territory; and I would not take pains uselessly to reaffirm an ordinance of nature, nor to re-enact the will of God. I would put in no Wilmot Proviso for the mere purpose of a taunt or a reproach. I would put into it no evidence of the votes of superior power, exercised for no purpose but to wound the pride, whether a just and a rational pride, or an irrational pride, of the citizens of the Southern States. I have no such object, no such purpose. They would think it a taunt, an indignity; they would think it to be an act taking away from them what they regard as a proper equality of privilege. Whether they expect to realize any benefit from it or not, they would think it at least a plain theoretic wrong; that something more or less derogatory to their character and their rights had taken place. I propose to inflict no such wound upon anybody, unless something essentially important to the country, and efficient to the preservation of liberty and freedom, is to be effected. I repeat, therefore, Sir, and, as I do not propose to address the Senate often on this subject, I repeat it because I wish it to be distinctly understood, that, for the reasons stated, if a proposition were now here to establish a government for New Mexico, and it was moved to insert a provision for a prohibition of slavery, I would not vote for it.

Sir, if we were now making a government for New Mexico, and anybody should propose a Wilmot Proviso, I should treat it exactly as Mr. Polk treated that provision for excluding slavery from Oregon. Mr. Polk was known to be in opinion decidedly averse to the Wilmot Proviso; but he felt the necessity of establishing a government for the Territory of Oregon. The proviso was in the bill, but he knew it would be entirely nugatory; and, since it must be entirely nugatory, since it took away no right, no describable, no tangible, no appreciable right of the South, he said he would sign the bill for the sake of enacting a law to form a government in that Territory, and let that entirely useless, and, in that connection, entirely senseless, proviso remain. Sir, we hear occasionally of the annexation of Canada; and if there be any man, any of the Northern Democracy, or any one of the Free Soil party, who supposes it necessary to insert a Wilmot Proviso in a territorial government for New Mexico, that man would of course be of opinion that it is necessary to protect the everlasting snows of Canada from the foot of slavery by the same overspreading wing of an act of Congress. Sir, wherever there is a substantive good to be done, wherever there is a foot of land to be prevented from becoming slave territory, I am ready to assert the principle of the exclusion of slavery. I am pledged to it from the year 1837; I have been pledged to it again and again; and I will perform those pledges; but I will not do a thing unnecessarily that wounds the feelings of others, or that does discredit to my own understanding.

Now, Mr. President, I have established, so far as I proposed to do so, the proposition with which I set out, and upon which I intend to stand or fall; and that is, that the whole territory within the former United States, or in the newly acquired Mexican provinces, has a fixed and settled character, now fixed and settled by law which cannot be repealed,--in the case of Texas without a violation of public faith, and by no human power in regard to California or New Mexico; that, therefore, under one or other of these laws, every foot of land in the States or in the Territories has already received a fixed and decided character.

Mr. President, in the excited times in which we live, there is found to exist a state of crimination and recrimination between the North and South. There are lists of grievances produced by each, and those grievances, real or supposed, alienate the minds of one portion of the country from the other, exasperate the feelings, and subdue the sense of fraternal affection, patriotic love, and mutual regard. I shall bestow a little attention, Sir, upon these various grievances existing on the one side and on the other. I begin with complaints of the South. I will not answer, further than I have, the general statements of the honorable Senator from South Carolina, that the North has prospered at the expense of the South in consequence of the manner of administering this government, in the collecting of its revenues, and so forth. These are disputed topics, and I have no inclination to enter into them. But I will allude to other complaints of the South, and especially to one which has in my opinion just foundation; and that is, that there has been found at the North, among individuals and among legislators, a disinclination to perform fully their constitutional duties in regard to the return of persons bound to service who have escaped into the free States. In that respect, the South, in my judgment, is right, and the North is wrong. Every member of every Northern legislature is bound by oath, like every other officer in the country, to support the Constitution of the United States; and the article of the Constitution[16] which says to these States that they shall deliver up fugitives from service is as binding in honor and conscience as any other article. No man fulfils his duty in any legislature who sets himself to find excuses, evasions, escapes from this constitutional obligation. I have always thought that the Constitution addressed itself to the legislatures of the States or to the States themselves. It says that those persons escaping to other States "shall be delivered up," and I confess I have always been of the opinion that it was an injunction upon the States themselves. When it is said that a person escaping into another State, and coming therefore within the jurisdiction of that State, shall be delivered up, it seems to me the import of the clause is, that the State itself, in obedience to the Constitution, shall cause him to be delivered up. That is my judgment. I have always entertained that opinion, and I entertain it now. But when the subject, some years ago, was before the Supreme Court of the United States, the majority of the judges held that the power to cause fugitives from service to be delivered up was a power to be exercised under the authority of this government. I do not know, on the whole, that it may not have been a fortunate decision. My habit is to respect the result of judicial deliberations and the solemnity of judicial decisions. As it now stands, the business of seeing that these fugitives are delivered up resides in the power of Congress and the national judicature, and my friend at the head of the Judiciary Committee[17] has a bill on the subject now before the Senate, which, with some amendments to it, I propose to support, with all its provisions, to the fullest extent. And I desire to call the attention of all sober-minded men at the North, of all conscientious men, of all men who are not carried away by some fanatical idea or some false impression, to their constitutional obligations. I put it to all the sober and sound minds at the North as a question of morals and a question of conscience. What right have they, in their legislative capacity or any other capacity, to endeavor to get round this Constitution, or to embarrass the free exercise of the rights secured by the Constitution to the persons whose slaves escape from them? None at all; none at all. Neither in the forum of conscience, nor before the face of the Constitution, are they, in my opinion, justified in such an attempt. Of course it is a matter for their consideration. They probably, in the excitement of the times, have not stopped to consider of this. They have followed what seemed to be the current of thought and of motives, as the occasion arose, and they have neglected to investigate fully the real question, and to consider their constitutional obligations; which, I am sure, if they did consider, they would fulfil with alacrity. I repeat, therefore, Sir, that here is a well-founded ground of complaint against the North, which ought to be removed, which it is now in the power of the different departments of this government to remove; which calls for the enactment of proper laws authorizing the judicature of this government, in the several States, to do all that is necessary for the recapture of fugitive slaves and for their restoration to those who claim them. Wherever I go, and whenever I speak on the subject, and when I speak here I desire to speak to the whole North, I say that the South has been injured in this respect, and has a right to complain; and the North has been too careless of what I think the Constitution peremptorily and emphatically enjoins upon her as a duty.

Complaint has been made against certain resolutions that emanate from legislatures at the North, and are sent here to us, not only on the subject of slavery in this District, but sometimes recommending Congress to consider the means of abolishing slavery in the States. I should be sorry to be called upon to present any resolutions here which could not be referable to any committee or any power in Congress; and therefore I should be unwilling to receive from the legislature of Massachusetts any instructions to present resolutions expressive of any opinion whatever on the subject of slavery, as it exists at the present moment in the States, for two reasons: first, because I do not consider that the legislature of Massachusetts has any thing to do with it; and next, because I do not consider that I, as her representative here, have any thing to do with it. It has become, in my opinion, quite too common; and if the legislatures of the States do not like that opinion, they have a great deal more power to put it down than I have to uphold it; it has become, in my opinion, quite too common a practice for the State legislatures to present resolutions here on all subjects and to instruct us on all subjects. There is no public man that requires instruction more than I do, or who requires information more than I do, or desires it more heartily; but I do not like to have it in too imperative a shape. I took notice, with pleasure, of some remarks made upon this subject, the other day, in the Senate of Massachusetts, by a young man of talent and character, of whom the best hopes may be entertained. I mean Mr. Hillard. He told the Senate of Massachusetts that he would vote for no instructions whatever to be forwarded to members of Congress, nor for any resolutions to be offered expressive of the sense of Massachusetts as to what her members of Congress ought to do. He said that he saw no propriety in one set of public servants giving instructions and reading lectures to another set of public servants. To his own master each of them must stand or fall, and that master is his constituents. I wish these sentiments could become more common. I have never entered into the question, and never shall, as to the binding force of instructions. I will, however, simply say this: if there be any matter pending in this body, while I am a member of it, in which Massachusetts has an interest of her own not adverse to the general interests of the country, I shall pursue her instructions with gladness of heart and with all the efficiency which I can bring to the occasion. But if the question be one which affects her interest, and at the same time equally affects the interests of all the other States, I shall no more regard her particular wishes or instructions than I should regard the wishes of a man who might appoint me an arbitrator or referee to decide some question of important private right between him and his neighbor, and then *instruct* me to decide in his favor. If ever there was a government upon earth it is this government, if ever there was a body upon earth it is this body, which should consider itself as composed by agreement of all, each member appointed by some, but organized by the general consent of all, sitting here, under the solemn obligations of oath and conscience, to do that which they think to be best for the good of the whole.

Then, Sir, there are the Abolition societies, of which I am unwilling to speak, but in regard to which I have very clear notions and opinions. I do not think them useful. I think their operations for the last twenty years have produced nothing good or valuable. At the same time, I believe thousands of their members to be honest and good men, perfectly well-meaning men. They have excited feelings; they think they must do something for the cause of liberty; and, in their sphere of action, they do not see what else they can do than to contribute to an Abolition press, or an Abolition society, or to pay an Abolition lecturer. I do not mean to impute gross motives even to the leaders of these societies; but I am not blind to the consequences of their proceedings. I cannot but see what mischiefs their interference with the South has produced. And is it not plain to every man? Let any gentleman who entertains doubts on this point recur to the debates in the Virginia House of Delegates in 1832, and he will see with what freedom a proposition made by Mr. Jefferson Randolph for the gradual abolition of slavery was discussed in that body. Every one spoke of slavery as he thought; very ignominious and disparaging names and epithets were applied to it. The debates in the House of Delegates on that occasion, I believe, were all published. They were read by every colored man who could read; and to those who could not read, those debates were read by others. At that time Virginia was not unwilling or afraid to discuss this question, and to let that part of her population know as much of the discussion as they could learn. That was in 1832. As has been said by the honorable member from South Carolina, these Abolition societies commenced their course of action in 1835. It is said, I do not know how true it may be, that they sent incendiary publications into the slave States; at any rate, they attempted to arouse, and did arouse, a very strong feeling; in other words, they created great agitation in the North against Southern slavery. Well, what was the result? The bonds of the slaves were bound more firmly than before, their rivets were more strongly fastened. Public opinion, which in Virginia had begun to be exhibited against slavery, and was opening out for the discussion of the question, drew back and shut itself up in its castle. I wish to know whether anybody in Virginia can now talk openly as Mr. Randolph, Governor McDowell, and others talked in 1832, and sent their remarks to the press? We all know the fact, and we all know the cause; and every thing that these agitating people have done has been, not to enlarge, but to restrain, not to set free, but to bind faster, the slave population of the South.[18]

Again, Sir, the violence of the Northern press is complained of. The press violent! Why, Sir, the press is violent everywhere. There are outrageous reproaches in the North against the South, and there are reproaches as vehement in the South against the North. Sir, the extremists of both parts of this country are violent; they mistake loud and violent talk for eloquence and for reason. They think that he who talks loudest reasons best. And this we must expect, when the press is free, as it is here, and I trust always will be; for, with all its licentiousness and all its evil, the entire and absolute freedom of the press is essential to the preservation of government on the basis of a free constitution. Wherever it exists there will be foolish and violent paragraphs in the newspapers, as there are, I am sorry to say, foolish and violent speeches in both houses of Congress. In truth, Sir, I must say that, in my opinion, the vernacular tongue of the country has become greatly vitiated, depraved, and corrupted by the style of our Congressional debates. And if it were possible for those debates to vitiate the principles of the people as much as they have depraved their tastes, I should cry out, "God save the Republic!"

Well, in all this I see no solid grievance, no grievance presented by the South, within the redress of the government, but the single one to which I have referred; and that is, the want of a proper regard to the injunction of the Constitution for the delivery of fugitive slaves.

There are also complaints of the North against the South. I need not go over them particularly. The first and gravest is, that the North adopted the Constitution, recognizing the existence of slavery in the States, and recognizing the right, to a certain extent, of the representation of slaves in Congress, under a state of sentiment and expectation which does not now exist; and that, by events, by circumstances, by the eagerness of the South to acquire territory and extend her slave population, the North finds itself, in regard to the relative influence of the South and the North, of the free States and the slave States, where it never did expect to find itself when they agreed to the compact of the Constitution. They complain, therefore, that, instead of slavery being regarded as an evil, as it was then, an evil which all hoped would be extinguished gradually, it is now regarded by the South as an institution to be cherished, and preserved, and extended; an institution which the South has already extended to the utmost of her power by the acquisition of new territory.

Well, then, passing from that, everybody in the North reads; and everybody reads whatsoever the newspapers contain; and the newspapers, some of them, especially those presses to which I have alluded, are careful to spread about among the people every reproachful sentiment uttered by any Southern man bearing at all against the North; every thing that is calculated to exasperate and to alienate; and there are many such things, as everybody will admit, from the South, or some portion of it, which are disseminated among the reading people; and they do exasperate, and alienate, and produce a most mischievous effect upon the public mind at the North. Sir, I would not notice things of this sort appearing in obscure quarters; but one thing has occurred in this debate which struck me very forcibly. An honorable member from Louisiana addressed us the other day on this subject. I suppose there is not a more amiable and worthy gentleman in this chamber, nor a gentleman who would be more slow to give offence to anybody, and he did not mean in his remarks to give offence. But what did he say? Why, Sir, he took pains to run a contrast between the slaves of the South and the laboring people of the North, giving the preference, in all points of condition, and comfort, and happiness, to the slaves of the South. The honorable member, doubtless, did not suppose that he gave any offence, or did any injustice. He was merely expressing his opinion. But does he know how remarks of that sort will be received by the laboring people of the North? Why, who are the laboring people of the North? They are the whole North. They are the people who till their own farms with their own hands; freeholders, educated men, independent men. Let me say, Sir, that five sixths of the whole property of the North is in the hands of the laborers of the North; they cultivate their farms, they educate their children, they provide the means of independence. If they are not freeholders, they earn wages; these wages accumulate, are turned into capital, into new freeholds, and small capitalists are created. Such is the case, and such the course of things, among the industrious and frugal. And what can these people think when so respectable and worthy a gentleman as the member from Louisiana undertakes to prove that the absolute ignorance and the abject slavery of the South are more in conformity with the high purposes and destiny of immortal, rational human beings, than the educated, the independent free labor of the North?

There is a more tangible and irritating cause of grievance at the North. Free blacks are constantly employed in the vessels of the North, generally as cooks or stewards. When the vessel arrives at a Southern port, these free colored men are taken on shore, by the police or municipal authority, imprisoned, and kept in prison till the vessel is again ready to sail. This is not only irritating, but exceedingly unjustifiable and oppressive. Mr. Hoar's mission, some time ago, to South Carolina, was a well-intended effort to remove this cause of complaint. The North thinks such imprisonments illegal and unconstitutional; and as the cases occur constantly and frequently, they regard it as a great grievance.

Now, Sir, so far as any of these grievances have their foundation in matters of law, they can be redressed, and ought to be redressed; and so far as they have their foundation in matters of opinion, in sentiment, in mutual crimination and recrimination, all that we can do is to endeavor to allay the agitation, and cultivate a better feeling and more fraternal sentiments between the South and the North.

Mr. President, I should much prefer to have heard from every member on this floor declarations of opinion that this Union could never be dissolved, than the declaration of opinion by anybody, that, in any case, under the pressure of any circumstances, such a dissolution was possible. I hear with distress and anguish the word "secession," especially when it falls from the lips of those who are patriotic, and known to the country, and known all over the world, for their political services. Secession! Peaceable secession! Sir, your eyes and mine are never destined to see that miracle. The dismemberment of this vast country without convulsion! The breaking up of the fountains of the great deep without ruffling the surface! Who is so foolish, I beg everybody's pardon, as to expect to see any such thing? Sir, he who sees these States, now revolving in harmony around a common centre, and expects to see them quit their places and fly off without convulsion, may look the next hour to see the heavenly bodies rush from their spheres, and jostle against each other in the realms of space, without causing the wreck of the universe. There can be no such thing as a peaceable secession. Peaceable secession is an utter impossibility. Is the great Constitution under which we live, covering this whole country,--is it to be thawed and melted away by secession, as the snows on the mountain melt under the influence of a vernal sun, disappear almost unobserved, and run off? No, Sir! No, Sir! I will not state what might produce the disruption of the Union; but, Sir, I see as plainly as I see the sun in heaven what that disruption itself must produce; I see that it must produce war, and such a war as I will not describe, *in its twofold character.*

Peaceable secession! Peaceable secession! The concurrent agreement of all the members of this great republic to separate! A voluntary separation, with alimony on one side and on the other. Why, what would be the result? Where is the line to be drawn? What States are to secede? What is to remain American? What am I to be? An American no longer? Am I to become a sectional man, a local man, a separatist, with no country in common with the gentlemen who sit around me here, or who fill the other house of Congress? Heaven forbid! Where is the flag of the republic to remain? Where is the eagle still to tower? or is he to cower, and shrink, and fall to the ground? Why, Sir, our ancestors, our fathers and our grandfathers, those of them that are yet living amongst us with prolonged lives, would rebuke and reproach us; and our children and our grandchildren would cry out shame upon us, if we of this generation should dishonor these ensigns of the power of the government and the harmony of that Union which is every day felt among us with so much joy and gratitude. What is to become of the army? What is to become of the navy? What is to become of the public lands? How is each of the thirty States to defend itself? I know, although the idea has not been stated distinctly, there is to be, or it is supposed possible that there will be, a Southern Confederacy. I do not mean, when I allude to this statement, that any one seriously contemplates such a state of things. I do not mean to say that it is true, but I have heard it suggested elsewhere, that the idea has been entertained, that, after the dissolution of this Union, a Southern Confederacy might be formed. I am sorry, Sir, that it has ever been thought of, talked of, or dreamed of, in the wildest flights of human imagination. But the idea, so far as it exists, must be of a separation, assigning the slave States to one side and the free States to the other. Sir, I may express myself too strongly, perhaps, but there are impossibilities in the natural as well as in the physical world, and I hold the idea of a separation of these States, those that are free to form one government, and those that are slave-holding to form another, as such an impossibility. We could not separate the States by any such line, if we were to draw it. We could not sit down here to-day and draw a line of separation that would satisfy any five men in the country. There are natural causes that would keep and tie us together, and there are social and domestic relations which we could not break if we would, and which we should not if we could.

Sir, nobody can look over the face of this country at the present moment, nobody can see where its population is the most dense and growing, without being ready to admit, and compelled to admit, that erelong the strength of America will be in the Valley of the Mississippi. Well, now, Sir, I beg to inquire what the wildest enthusiast has to say on the possibility of cutting that river in two, and leaving free States at its source and on its branches, and slave States down near its mouth, each forming a separate government? Pray, Sir, let me say to the people of this country, that these things are worthy of their pondering and of their consideration. Here, Sir, are five millions of freemen in the free States north of the river Ohio. Can anybody suppose that this population can be severed, by a line that divides them from the territory of a foreign and an alien government, down somewhere, the Lord knows where, upon the lower banks of the Mississippi? What would become of Missouri? Will she join the *arrondissement* of the slave States? Shall the man from the Yellowstone and the Platte be connected, in the new republic, with the man who lives on the southern extremity of the Cape of Florida? Sir, I am ashamed to pursue this line of remark. I dislike it, I have an utter disgust for it. I would rather hear of natural blasts and mildews, war, pestilence, and famine, than to hear gentlemen talk of secession. To break up this great government! to dismember this glorious country! to astonish Europe with an act of folly such as Europe for two centuries has never beheld in any government or any people! No, Sir! no, Sir! There will be no secession! Gentlemen are not serious when they talk of secession.

Sir, I hear there is to be a convention held at Nashville. I am bound to believe that, if worthy gentlemen meet at Nashville in convention, their object will be to adopt conciliatory counsels; to advise the South to forbearance and moderation, and to advise the North to forbearance and moderation; and to inculcate principles of brotherly love and affection, and attachment to the Constitution of the country as it now is. I believe, if the convention meet at all, it will be for this purpose; for certainly, if they meet for any purpose hostile to the Union, they have been singularly inappropriate in their selection of a place. I remember, Sir, that, when the treaty of Amiens was concluded between France and England, a sturdy Englishman and a distinguished orator, who regarded the conditions of the peace as ignominious to England, said in the House of Commons, that, if King William could know the terms of that treaty, he would turn in his coffin! Let me commend this saying of Mr. Windham, in all its emphasis and in all its force, to any persons who shall meet at Nashville for the purpose of concerting measures for the overthrow of this Union over the bones of Andrew Jackson!

Sir, I wish now to make two remarks, and hasten to a conclusion. I wish to say, in regard to Texas, that if it should be hereafter, at any time, the pleasure of the government of Texas to cede to the United States a portion, larger or smaller, of her territory which lies adjacent to New Mexico, and north of 36° 30' of north latitude, to be formed into free States, for a fair equivalent in money or in the payment of her debt, I think it an object well worthy the consideration of Congress, and I shall be happy to concur in it myself, if I should have a connection with the government at that time.

I have one other remark to make. In my observations upon slavery as it has existed in this country, and as it now exists, I have expressed no opinion of the mode of its extinguishment or melioration. I will say, however, though I have nothing to propose, because I do not deem myself so competent as other gentlemen to take any lead on this subject, that if any gentleman from the South shall propose a scheme, to be carried on by this government upon a large scale, for the transportation of free colored people to any colony or any place in the world, I should be quite disposed to incur almost any degree of expense to accomplish that object. Nay, Sir, following an example set more than twenty years ago by a great man,[19] then a Senator from New York, I would return to Virginia, and through her to the whole South, the money received from the lands and territories ceded by her to this government, for any such purpose as to remove, in whole or in part, or in any way to diminish or deal beneficially with, the free colored population of the Southern States. I have said that I honor Virginia for her cession of this territory. There have been received into the treasury of the United States eighty millions of dollars, the proceeds of the sales of the public lands ceded by her. If the residue should be sold at the same rate, the whole aggregate will exceed two hundred millions of dollars. If Virginia and the South see fit to adopt any proposition to relieve themselves from the free people of color among them, or such as may be made free, they have my full consent that the government shall pay them any sum of money out of the proceeds of that cession which may be adequate to the purpose.

And now, Mr. President, I draw these observations to a close. I have spoken freely, and I meant to do so. I have sought to make no display. I have sought to enliven the occasion by no animated discussion, nor have I attempted any train of elaborate argument. I have wished only to speak my sentiments, fully and at length, being desirous, once and for all, to let the Senate know, and to let the country know, the opinions and sentiments which I entertain on all these subjects. These opinions are not likely to be suddenly changed. If there be any future service that I can render to the country, consistently with these sentiments and opinions, I shall cheerfully render it. If there be not, I shall still be glad to have had an opportunity to disburden myself from the bottom of my heart, and to make known every political sentiment that therein exists.

And now, Mr. President, instead of speaking of the possibility or utility of secession, instead of dwelling in those caverns of darkness, instead of groping with those ideas so full of all that is horrid and horrible, let us come out into the light of day; let us enjoy the fresh air of Liberty and Union; let us cherish those hopes which belong to us; let us devote ourselves to those great objects that are fit for our consideration and our action; let us raise our conceptions to the magnitude and the importance of the duties that devolve upon us; let our comprehension be as broad as the country for which we act, our aspirations as high as its certain destiny; let us not be pygmies in a case that calls for men. Never did there devolve on any generation of men higher trusts than now devolve upon us, for the preservation of this Constitution and the harmony and peace of all who are destined to live under it. Let us make our generation one of the strongest and brightest links in that golden chain which is destined, I fondly believe, to grapple the people of all the States to this Constitution for ages to come. We have a great, popular, constitutional government, guarded by law and by judicature, and defended by the affections of the whole people. No monarchical throne presses these States together, no iron chain of military power encircles them; they live and stand under a government popular in its form, representative in its character, founded upon principles of equality, and so constructed, we hope, as to last for ever. In all its history it has been beneficent; it has trodden down no man's liberty; it has crushed no State. Its daily respiration is liberty and patriotism; its yet youthful veins are full of enterprise, courage, and honorable love of glory and renown. Large before, the country has now, by recent events, become vastly larger. This republic now extends, with a vast breadth, across the whole continent. The two great seas of the world wash the one and the other shore. We realize, on a mighty scale, the beautiful

description of the ornamental border of the buckler of Achilles:--
"Now, the broad shield complete, the artist crowned With his last hand, and poured the ocean round; In living silver seemed the waves to roll, And beat the buckler's verge, and bound the whole."

NOTE.
Letter from Mr. Webster to the Editors of the National Intelligencer, enclosing Extracts from a Letter of the late Dr. Channing.
Washington, February 15, 1851.
MESSRS. GALES AND SEATON
Having occasion recently to look over some files of letters written several years ago, I happened to fall on one from the late Rev. Dr. W.E. Channing. It contains passages which I think, coming from such a source, and written at such a time, would be interesting to the country. I have therefore extracted them, and send them to you for publication in your columns.
Yours respectfully, DANIEL WEBSTER.

Boston, May 14, 1828.
MY DEAR SIR.
I wish to call your attention to a subject of general interest.
A little while ago, Mr. Lundy of Baltimore, the editor of a paper called "The Genius of Universal Emancipation," visited this part of the country, to stir us up to the work of abolishing slavery at the South, and the intention is to organize societies for this purpose. I know few objects into which I should enter with more zeal, but I am aware how cautiously exertions are to be made for it in this part of the country. I know that our Southern brethren interpret every word from this region on the subject of slavery as an expression of hostility. I would ask if they cannot be brought to understand us better, and if we can do any good till we remove their misapprehensions. It seems to me that, before moving in this matter, we ought to say to them distinctly, "We consider slavery as your calamity, not your crime, and we will share with you the burden of putting an end to it. We will consent that the public lands shall be appropriated to this object; or that the general government shall be clothed with power to apply a portion of revenue to it."
I throw out these suggestions merely to illustrate my views. We must first let the Southern States see that we are their *friends* in this affair; that we sympathize with them, and, from principles of patriotism and philanthropy, are willing to share the toil and expense of abolishing slavery, or I fear our interference will avail nothing. I am the more sensitive on this subject from my increased solicitude for the preservation of the Union. I know no public interest so important as this. I ask from the general government hardly any other boon than that it will hold us together, and preserve pacific relations and intercourse among the States. I deprecate every thing which sows discord and exasperates sectional animosities. If it will simply keep us at peace, and will maintain in full power the national courts, for the purpose of settling quietly among citizens of different States questions which might otherwise be settled by arms, I shall be satisfied. My fear in regard to our efforts against slavery is, that we shall make the case worse by rousing sectional pride and passion for its support, and that we shall only break the country into two great parties, which may shake the foundations of government.
I have written to you because your situation gives you advantages which perhaps no other man enjoys for ascertaining the method, if any can be devised, by which we may operate beneficially and safely in regard to slavery. Appeals will probably be made soon to the people here, and I wish that wise men would save us from the rashness of enthusiasts, and from the perils to which our very virtues expose us.
With great respect, your friend,
WM. E. CHANNING
HON. DANIEL WEBSTER.
[Footnote 1: Mr. Calhoun.][Footnote 2: Mr. Calhoun.][Footnote 3: Mr. Mason of Virginia.]
[Footnote 4: See Madison Papers, Vol. III. pp. 1390, 1428, _et seq._]
[Footnote 5: Seybert's Statistics, p. 92. A small parcel of cotton found its way to Liverpool from the United States in 1784, and was refused admission, on the ground that it could not be the growth of the United States.][Footnote 6: Mr. Calhoun.][Footnote 7: Mr. Walker.]
[Footnote 8: Mr. Bell.][Footnote 9: Mr. Greene.][Footnote 10: Mr. Hamlin.][Footnote 11: Mr. Berrien.][Footnote 12: Mr. Upshur.][Footnote 13: Messrs. Niles of Connecticut and Dix of New

York.][Footnote 14: See the remarks on the Admission of Texas, in Webster's Works, Vol. V. p. 55.][Footnote 15: Mr. Bell.][Footnote 16: Art. IV. Sect. 2, § 2.][Footnote 17: Mr. Mason.] [Footnote 18: See Note at the end of the Speech.][Footnote 19: Mr. Rufus King.]

RECEPTION AT BUFFALO.
A SPEECH DELIVERED BEFORE A LARGE ASSEMBLY OF THE CITIZENS OF BUFFALO AND THE COUNTY OF ERIE, AT A PUBLIC RECEPTION ON THE 22D OF MAY, 1851.

Fellow-Citizens of the City of Buffalo,--I am very glad to see you; I meet you with pleasure. It is not the first time that I have been in Buffalo, and I have always come to it with gratification. It is at a great distance from my own home. I am thankful that circumstances have enabled me to be here again, and I regret that untoward events deprived me of the pleasure of being with you when your distinguished fellow-citizen, the President of the United States, visited you, and received from you, as he deserved, not only a respectful, but a cordial and enthusiastic welcome. The President of the United States has been a resident among you for more than half his life. He has represented you in the State and national councils. You know him and all his relations, both public and private, and it would be bad taste in me to say any thing of him, except that I wish to say, with emphasis, that, since my connection with him in the administration of the government of the United States, I have fully concurred with him in all his great and leading measures. This might be inferred from the fact that I have been one of his ordinary advisers. But I do not wish to let it rest on that presumption; I wish to declare that the principles of the President, as set forth in his annual message, his letters, and all documents and opinions which have proceeded from him, or been issued by his authority, in regard to the great question of the times,--all these principles are my principles; and if he is wrong in them, I am, and always shall be.

Gentlemen, it has been suggested to me that it would be agreeable to the citizens of Buffalo, and their neighbors in the county of Erie, that I should state to you my opinions, whatever may be their value, on the present condition of the country, its prospects, its hopes, and its dangers; and, fellow-citizens, I intend to do that, this day, and this hour, as far as my strength will permit.

Gentlemen, believe me, I know where I am. I know to whom I am speaking. I know for whom I am speaking. I know that I am here in this singularly prosperous and powerful section of the United States, Western New York, and I know the character of the men who inhabit Western New York. I know they are sons of liberty, one and all; that they sucked in liberty with their mothers' milk; inherited it with their blood; that it is the subject of their daily contemplation and watchful thought. They are men of unusual equality of condition, for a million and a half of people. There are thousands of men around us, and here before us, who till their own soil with their own hands; and others who earn their own livelihood by their own labor in the workshops and other places of industry; and they are independent, in principle and in condition, having neither slaves nor masters, and not intending to have either. These are the men who constitute, to a great extent, the people of Western New York. But the school-house, I know, is among them. Education is among them. They read, and write, and think. Here, too, are women, educated, refined, and intelligent; and here are men who know the history of their country, and the laws of their country, and the institutions of their country; and men, lovers of liberty always, and yet lovers of liberty under the Constitution of the country, and who mean to maintain that Constitution with all their strength. I hope these observations will satisfy you that I know where I am, under what responsibility I speak, and before whom I appear; and I have no desire that any word I shall say this day shall be withholden from you, or your children, or your neighbors, or the whole world; for I speak before you and before my country, and, if it be not too solemn to say so, before the great Author of all things.

Gentlemen, there is but one question in this country now; or, if there be others, they are but secondary, or so subordinate that they are all absorbed in that great and leading question; and that is neither more nor less than this: Can we preserve the union of the States, not by coercion, not by military power, not by angry controversies,--but can we of this generation, you and I, your friends and my friends,--can we so preserve the union of these States, by such administration of the powers of the Constitution as shall give content and satisfaction to all who live under it, and draw us together, not by military power, but by the silken cords of mutual, fraternal, patriotic affection? That is the question, and no other. Gentlemen, I believe in party distinctions. I am a party man. There are questions belonging to party in which I take an interest, and there are opinions entertained by other parties which I repudiate; but what of all that? If a house be divided against itself, it will fall, and crush everybody in it. We must see that we maintain the government which is over us. We must see that we uphold the Constitution, and we must do so without regard to party.

Now how did this question arise? The question is for ever misstated. I dare say, if you know much of me, or of my course of public conduct, for the last fourteen months, you have heard of my attending Union meetings, and of my fervent admonitions at Union meetings. Well, what was the object of those meetings? What was their purpose? The object and purpose have been designedly or thoughtlessly misrepresented. I had an invitation, some time since, to attend a Union meeting in the county of Westchester; I could not go, but wrote a letter. Well, some wise man of the East said he did not think it was very necessary to hold Union meetings in Westchester. He did not think there were many disunionists about Tarrytown! And so in many parts of the country, there is a total misapprehension of the purpose and object of these Union meetings. Every one knows, that there is not a county, or a city, or a hamlet in the State of New York, that is ready to go out of the Union, but only some small bodies of fanatics. There is no man so insane in the State, not fit for a lunatic asylum, as to wish it. But that is not the point. We all know that every man and every neighborhood, and all corporations, in the State of New York, except those I have mentioned, are attached to the Union, and have no idea of withdrawing from it. But that is not, I repeat, the point. The question, fellow-citizens, (and I put it to you now as the real question,) the question is, Whether you and the rest of the people of the great State of New York, and of all the States, will so adhere to the Constitution, will so enact and maintain laws to preserve that instrument, that you will not only remain in the Union yourselves, but permit your brethren to remain in it, and help to perpetuate it? That is the question. Will you concur in measures necessary to maintain the Union, or will you oppose such measures? That is the whole point of the case.

There are thirty or forty members of Congress from New York; you have your proportion in the United States Senate. We have many members of Congress from New England. Will they maintain the laws that are passed for the administration of the Constitution, and respect the rights of the South, so that the Union may be held together; and not only so that we may not go out of it ourselves, which we are not inclined to do, but so that, by maintaining the rights of others, they may also remain in the Union? Now, Gentlemen, permit me to say, that I speak of no concessions. If the South wish any concession from me, they will not get it; not a hair's breadth of it. If they come to my house for it, they will not find it, and the door will be shut; I concede nothing. But I say that I will maintain for them, as I will maintain for you, to the utmost of my power, and in the face of all danger, their rights under the Constitution, and your rights under the Constitution. And I shall never be found to falter in one or the other. It is obvious to every one, and we all know it, that the origin of the great disturbance which agitates the country is the existence of slavery in some of the States; but we must meet the subject; we must consider it; we must deal with it earnestly, honestly, and justly. From the mouth of the St. John's to the confines of Florida, there existed, in 1775, thirteen colonies of English origin, planted at different times, and coming from different parts of England, bringing with them various habits, and establishing, each for itself, institutions entirely different from the institutions which they left, and in many cases from each other. But they were all of English origin. The English language was theirs, Shakepeare and Milton were theirs, the common law of England was theirs, and the Christian religion was theirs; and these things held them together by the force of a common character. The aggressions of the parent state compelled them to assert their independence. They declared independence, and that immortal act, pronounced on the 4th of July, 1776, made them independent.

That was an act of union by the United States in Congress assembled. But this act of itself did nothing to establish over them a general government. They had a Congress. They had Articles of Confederation to prosecute the war. But thus far they were still, essentially, separate and independent each of the other. They had entered into a simple confederacy, and nothing more. No State was bound by what it did not itself agree to, or what was done according to the provisions of the confederation. That was the state of things, Gentlemen, at that time. The war went on; victory crowned the American arms; our independence was acknowledged. The States were then united together under a confederacy of very limited powers. It could levy no taxes. It could not enforce its own decrees. It was a confederacy, instead of a united government. Experience showed that this was insufficient and inefficient. Accordingly, beginning as far back almost as the close of the war, measures were taken for the formation of a united government, a government in the strict sense of the term, a government that could pass laws binding on the individual citizens of all the States, and which could enforce those laws by its executive powers, having them interpreted by a judicial power belonging to the government itself, and yet a government strictly limited in its nature. Well, Gentlemen, this led to the formation of the Constitution of the United States, and that instrument was framed on the idea of a limited government. It proposed to leave, and did leave, the different domestic institutions of the several States to themselves. It did not propose consolidation. It did not propose that the laws of Virginia should be the laws of New York, or that the laws of New York should be the laws of Massachusetts. It proposed only that, for certain purposes and to a certain extent, there should be a united government, and that that government should have the power of executing its own laws. All the rest was left to the several States.

We now come, Gentlemen, to the very point of the case. At that time slavery existed in the Southern States, entailed upon them in the time of the supremacy of British laws over us. There it was. It was obnoxious to the Middle and Eastern States, and honestly and seriously disliked, as the records of the country will show, by the Southern States themselves. Now, how was it to be dealt with? Were the Northern and Middle States to exclude from the government those States of the South which had produced a Washington, a Laurens, and other distinguished patriots, who had so truly served, and so greatly honored, the whole country? Were they to be excluded from the new government because they tolerated the institution of slavery? Your fathers and my fathers did not think so. They did not see that it would be of the least advantage to the slaves of the Southern States, to cut off the South from all connection with the North. Their views of humanity led to no such result; and of course, when the Constitution was framed and established, and adopted by you, here in New York, and by New England, it contained an express provision of security to the persons who lived in the Southern States, in regard to fugitives who owed them service; that is to say, it was stipulated that the fugitive from service or labor should be restored to his master or owner if he escaped into a free State. Well, that had been the history of the country from its first settlement. It was a matter of common practice to return fugitives before the Constitution was formed. Fugitive slaves from Virginia to Massachusetts were restored by the people of Massachusetts. At that day there was a great system of apprenticeship at the North, and many apprentices at the North, taking advantage of circumstances, and of vessels sailing to the South, thereby escaped; and they were restored on proper claim and proof. That led to a clear, express, and well-defined provision in the Constitution of the country on the subject. Now I am aware that all these things are well known; that they have been stated a thousand times; but in these days of perpetual discontent and misrepresentation, to state things a thousand times is not enough; for there are persons whose consciences, it would seem, lead them to consider it their duty to deny, misrepresent, falsify, and cover up truths.

Now these are words of the Constitution, fellow-citizens, which I have taken the pains to transcribe therefrom, so that he who runs may read:--

"NO PERSON HELD TO SERVICE OR LABOR IN ONE STATE, UNDER THE LAWS THEREOF, ESCAPING INTO ANOTHER, SHALL, IN CONSEQUENCE OF ANY LAW OR REGULATION THEREIN, BE DISCHARGED FROM SUCH SERVICE OR LABOR, BUT SHALL BE DELIVERED UP ON CLAIM OF THE PARTY TO WHOM SUCH SERVICE OR LABOR MAY BE DUE."

Is there any mistake about that? Is there any forty-shilling attorney here to make a question of it? No. I will not disgrace my profession by supposing such a thing. There is not, in or out of an attorney's office in the county of Erie, or elsewhere, one who could raise a doubt, or a particle of a doubt, about the meaning of this provision of the Constitution. He may act as witnesses do, sometimes, on the stand. He may wriggle, and twist, and say he cannot tell, or cannot remember. I have seen many such efforts in my time, on the part of witnesses, to falsify and deny the truth. But there is no man who can read these words of the Constitution of the United States, and say they are not clear and imperative. "No person," the Constitution says, "held to service or labor in one State, under the laws thereof, escaping into another, shall, in consequence of any law or regulation therein, be discharged from such service or labor, but shall be delivered up on claim of the party to whom such service or labor may be due." Why, you may be told by forty conventions in Massachusetts, in Ohio, in New York, or elsewhere, that, if a colored man comes here, he comes as a freeman; that is a *non sequitur*. It is not so. If he comes as a fugitive from labor, the Constitution says he is not a freeman, and that he shall be delivered up to those who are entitled to his service.

Gentlemen, that is the Constitution of the United States. Do we, or do we not, mean to conform to it, and to execute that part of the Constitution as well as the rest of it? I believe there are before me here members of Congress. I suppose there may be here members of the State legislature, or executive officers under the

State government. I suppose there may be judicial magistrates of New York, executive officers, assessors, supervisors, justices of the peace, and constables before me. Allow me to say, Gentlemen, that there is not, that there cannot be, any one of these officers in this assemblage, or elsewhere, who has not, according to the form of the usual obligation, bound himself by a solemn oath to support the Constitution. They have taken their oaths on the Holy Evangelists of Almighty God, or by uplifted hand, as the case may be, or by a solemn affirmation, as is the practice in some cases; but among all of them there is not a man who holds, nor is there any man who can hold, any office in the gift of the United States, or of this State, or of any other State, who does not bind himself, by the solemn obligation of an oath, to support the Constitution of the United States. Well, is he to tamper with that? Is he to palter? Gentlemen, our political duties are as much matters of conscience as any other duties; our sacred domestic ties, our most endearing social relations, are no more the subjects for conscientious consideration and conscientious discharge, than the duties we enter upon under the Constitution of the United States. The bonds of political brotherhood, which hold us together from Maine to Georgia, rest upon the same principles of obligation as those of domestic and social life.

Now, Gentlemen, that is the plain story of the Constitution of the United States, on the question of slavery. I contend, and have always contended, that, after the adoption of the Constitution, any measure of the government calculated to bring more slave territory into the United States was beyond the power of the Constitution, and against its provisions. That is my opinion, and it always has been my opinion. It was inconsistent with the Constitution of the United States, or thought to be so, in Mr. Jefferson's time, to attach Louisiana to the United States. A treaty with France was made for that purpose. Mr. Jefferson's opinion at that moment was, that an alteration of the Constitution was necessary to enable it to be done. In consequence of considerations to which I need not now refer, that opinion was abandoned, and Louisiana was admitted by law, without any provision in, or alteration of, the Constitution. At that time I was too young to hold any office, or take any share in the political affairs of the country. Louisiana was admitted as a slave State, and became entitled to her representation in Congress on the principle of a mixed basis. Florida was afterwards admitted. Then, too, I was out of Congress. I had formerly been a member, but had ceased to be so. I had nothing to do with the Florida treaty, or the admission of Florida. My opinion remains unchanged, that it was not within the original scope or design of the Constitution to admit new States out of foreign territory; and, for one, whatever may be said at the Syracuse Convention, or at any other assemblage of insane persons, I never would consent, and never have consented, that there should be one foot of slave territory beyond what the old thirteen States had at the time of the formation of the Union. Never, never! The man cannot show his face to me, and say he can prove that I ever departed from that doctrine. He would sneak away, and slink away, or hire a mercenary press to cry out, What an apostate from liberty Daniel Webster has become! But he knows himself to be a hypocrite and a falsifier.

But, Gentlemen, I was in public life when the proposition to annex Texas to the United States was brought forward. You know that the revolution in Texas, which separated that country from Mexico, occurred in the year 1835 or 1836. I saw then, and I do not know that it required any particular foresight, that it would be the very next thing to bring Texas, which was designed to be a slave-holding State, into this Union. I did not wait. I sought an occasion to proclaim my utter aversion to any such measure, and I determined to resist it with all my strength to the last. On this subject, Gentlemen, you will bear with me, if I now repeat, in the presence of this assembly, what I have before spoken elsewhere. I was in this city in the year 1837, and, some time before I left New York on that excursion from which I returned to this place, my friends in New York were kind enough to offer me a public dinner as a testimony of their regard. I went out of my way, in a speech delivered in Niblo's Saloon, on that occasion, for the purpose of showing that I anticipated the attempt to annex Texas as a slave territory, and said it should be opposed by me to the last extremity. Well, there was the press all around me,--the Whig press and the Democratic press. Some spoke in terms commendatory enough of my speech, but all agreed that I took pains to step out of my way to denounce in advance the annexation of Texas as slave territory to the United States. I said on that occasion:--

"Gentlemen, we all see that, by whomsoever possessed, Texas is likely to be a slave-holding country; and I frankly avow my entire unwillingness to do any thing that shall extend the slavery of the African race on this continent, or add other slave-holding States to the Union. When I say that I regard slavery in itself as a great moral, social, and political evil, I only use language which has been adopted by distinguished men, themselves citizens of slave-holding States. I shall do nothing, therefore, to favor or encourage its further extension. We have slavery already amongst us. The Constitution found it in the Union; it recognized it, and gave it solemn guaranties. To the full extent of these guaranties we are all bound, in honor, in justice, and by the Constitution. All the stipulations contained in the Constitution in favor of the slave-holding States which are already in the Union ought to be fulfilled, and, so far as depends on me, shall be fulfilled, in the fulness of their spirit and to the exactness of their letter. Slavery, as it exists in the States, is beyond the reach of Congress. It is a concern of the States themselves; they have never submitted it to Congress, and Congress has no rightful power over it. I shall concur, therefore, in no act, no measure, no menace, no indication of purpose, which shall interfere or threaten to interfere with the exclusive authority of the several States over the subject of slavery as it exists within their respective limits. All this appears to me to be matter of plain and imperative duty. But when we come to speak of admitting new States, the subject assumes an entirely different aspect. Our rights and our duties are then both different. The free States, and all the States, are then at liberty to accept or to reject. When it is proposed to bring new members into this political partnership, the old members have a right to say on what terms such new partners are to come in, and what they are to bring along with them. In my opinion, the people of the United States will not consent to bring into the Union a new, vastly extensive, and slave-holding country, large enough for half a dozen or a dozen States. In my opinion they ought not to consent to it."

Gentlemen, I was mistaken; Congress did consent to the bringing in of Texas. They did consent, and I was a false prophet. Your own State consented, and the majority of the representatives of New York consented. I went into Congress before the final consummation of the deed, and there I fought, holding up both my hands, and urging, with a voice stronger than it now is, my remonstrances against the whole of it. But you would have it so, and you did have it so. Nay, Gentlemen, I will tell the truth, whether it shames the Devil or not. Persons who have aspired high as lovers of liberty, as eminent lovers of the Wilmot Proviso, as eminent Free Soil men, and who have mounted over our heads, and trodden us down as if we were mere slaves, insisting that they are the only true lovers of liberty, they are the men, the very men, that brought Texas into this Union. This is the truth, the whole truth, and nothing but the truth, and I declare it before you, this day. Look to the journals. Without the consent of New York, Texas would not have come into the Union, either under the original resolutions or afterwards. But New York voted for the measure. The two Senators from New York voted for it, and decided the question; and you may thank them for the glory, the renown, and the happiness of having five or six slave States added to the Union. Do not blame me for it. Let them answer who did the deed, and who are now proclaiming themselves the champions of liberty, crying up their Free Soil creed, and using it for selfish and deceptive purposes. They were the persons who aided in bringing in Texas. It was all fairly told to you, both beforehand and afterwards. You heard Moses and the prophets, but if one had risen from the dead, such was your devotion to that policy, at that time, you would not have listened to him for a moment. I do not, of course, speak of the persons now here before me, but of the general political tone in New York, and especially of those who are now Free Soil apostles. Well, all that I do not complain of; but I will not now, or hereafter, before the country, or the world, consent to be numbered among those who introduced new slave power into the Union. I did all in my power to prevent it.

Then, again, Gentlemen, the Mexican war broke out. Vast territory was acquired, and the peace was made; and, much as I disliked the war, I disliked the peace more, because it brought in these territories. I wished for peace indeed, but I desired to strike out the grant of territory on the one side, and the payment of the $12,000,000 on the other. That territory was unknown to me; I could not tell what its character might be. The plan came from the South. I knew that certain Southern gentlemen wished the acquisition of California, New Mexico, and Utah, as a means of extending slave power and slave population. Foreseeing a sectional controversy, and, as I conceived, seeing how much it would distract the Union, I voted against the treaty with Mexico. I voted against the acquisition. I wanted none of her territory, neither California, New Mexico, nor Utah. They were rather ultra-American, as I thought. They were far from us, and I saw that they might lead to a political conflict, and I voted against them all, against the treaty and against the peace, rather than have the territories. Seeing that it would be an occasion of dispute, that by the controversy the whole Union would be agitated, Messrs. Berrien, Badger, and other respectable and distinguished men of the South, voted against the acquisition, and the treaty which secured it; and if the men of the North had voted the same way, we should have been spared all the difficulties that have grown out of it. We should have had peace without the territories.

Now there is no sort of doubt, Gentlemen, that there were some persons in the South who supposed that

California, if it came into the Union at all, would come in as a slave State. You know the extraordinary events which immediately occurred, and the impulse given to emigration by the discovery of gold. You know that crowds of Northern people immediately rushed to California, and that an African slave could no more live there among them, than he could live on the top of Mount Hecla. Of necessity it became a free State, and that, no doubt, was a source of much disappointment to the South. And then there were New Mexico and Utah; what was to be done with them? Why, Gentlemen, from the best investigation I had given to the subject, and the reflection I had devoted to it, I was of the opinion that the mountains of New Mexico and Utah could no more sustain American slavery than the snows of Canada. I saw it was impossible. I thought so then; it is quite evident now. Therefore, when it was proposed in Congress to apply the Wilmot Proviso to New Mexico and Utah, it appeared to me just as absurd as to apply it here in Western New York. I saw that the snow-capped hills, the eternal mountains, and the climate of those countries would never support slavery. No man could carry a slave there with any expectation of profit. It could not be done; and as the South regarded the Proviso as merely a source of irritation, and as designed by some to irritate, I thought it unwise to apply it to New Mexico or Utah. I voted accordingly, and who doubts now the correctness of that vote? The law admitting those territories passed without any proviso. Is there a slave, or will there ever be one, in either of those territories? Why, there is not a man in the United States so stupid as not to see, at this moment, that such a thing was wholly unnecessary, and that it was only calculated to irritate and to offend. I am not one who is disposed to create irritation, or give offence among brethren, or to break up fraternal friendship, without cause. The question was accordingly left legally open, whether slavery should or should not go to New Mexico or Utah. There is no slavery there, it is utterly impracticable that it should be introduced into such a region, and utterly ridiculous to suppose that it could exist there. No one, who does not mean to deceive, will now pretend it can exist there.

Well, Gentlemen, we have a race of agitators all over the country; some connected with the press, some, I am sorry to say, belonging to the learned professions. They agitate; their livelihood consists in agitating; their freehold, their copyhold, their capital, their all in all, depend on the excitement of the public mind. The events now briefly alluded to were going on at the commencement of the year 1850. There were two great questions before the public. There was the question of the Texan boundary, and of a government for Utah and New Mexico, which I consider as one question; and there was the question of making a provision for the restoration of fugitive slaves. On these subjects, I have something to say. Texas, as you know, established her independence of Mexico by her revolution and the battle of San Jacinto, which made her a sovereign power. I have already stated to you what I then anticipated from the movement, namely, that she would ask to come into the Union as a slave State. We admitted her in 1845, and we admitted her as a slave State. We admitted her also with an undefined boundary; remember that. She claimed by conquest the whole of that territory commonly called New Mexico, east of the Rio Grande. She claimed also those limits which her constitution had declared and marked out as the proper limits of Texas. This was her claim, and when she was admitted into the United States, the United States did not define her territory. They admitted her as she was. We took her as she defined her own limits, and with the power of making four additional slave States. I say "we," but I do not mean that I was one; I mean the United States admitted her.

What, then, was the state of things in 1850? There was Texas claiming all, or a great part, of that which the United States had acquired from Mexico as New Mexico. She claimed that it belonged to her by conquest and by her admission into the United States, and she was ready to maintain her claim by force of arms. Nor was this all. A man must be ignorant of the history of the country who does not know, that, at the commencement of 1850, there was great agitation throughout the whole South. Who does not know that six or seven of the largest States of the South had already taken measures looking toward secession; were preparing for disunion in some way? They concurred apparently, at least some of them, with Texas, while Texas was prepared or preparing to enforce her rights by force of arms. Troops were enlisted by her, and many thousand persons in the South disaffected towards the Union, or desirous of breaking it up, were ready to make common cause with Texas; to join her ranks, and see what they could make in a war to establish the right of Texas to New Mexico. The public mind was disturbed. A considerable part of the South was disaffected towards the Union, and in a condition to adopt any course that should be violent and destructive.

What then was to be done, as far as Texas was concerned? Allow me to say, Gentlemen, there are two sorts of foresight. There is a military foresight, which sees what will be the result of an appeal to arms; and there is also a statesmanlike foresight, which looks not to the result of battles and carnage, but to the results of political disturbances, the violence of faction carried into military operations, and the horrors attendant on civil war. I never had a doubt, that, if the administration of General Taylor had gone to war, and had sent troops into New Mexico, the Texan forces would have been subdued in a week. The power on one side was far superior to all the power on the other. But what then? What if Texan troops, assisted by thousands of volunteers from the disaffected States, had gone to New Mexico, and had been defeated and turned back? Would that have settled the boundary question? Now, Gentlemen, I wish I had ten thousand voices. I wish I could draw around me the whole people of the United States, and I wish I could make them all hear what I now declare on my conscience as my solemn belief, before the Power who sits on high, and who will judge you and me hereafter, that, if this Texan controversy had not been settled by Congress in the manner it was, by the so-called adjustment measures, civil war would have ensued; blood, American blood, would have been shed; and who can tell what would have been the consequences? Gentlemen, in an honorable war, if a foreign foe invade us, if our rights are threatened, if it be necessary to defend them by arms, I am not afraid of blood. And if I am too old myself, I hope there are those connected with me by ties of relationship who are young, and willing to defend their country to the last drop of their blood. But I cannot express the horror I feel at the shedding of blood in a controversy between one of these States and the government of the United States, because I see in it a total and entire disruption of all those ties that make us a great and happy people. Gentlemen, this was the great question, the leading question, at the commencement of the year 1850.

Then there was the other matter, and that was the Fugitive Slave Law. Let me say a word about that. Under the provisions of the Constitution, during Washington's administration, in the year 1793, there was passed, by general consent, a law for the restoration of fugitive slaves. Hardly any one opposed it at that period; it was thought to be necessary, in order to carry the Constitution into effect; the great men of New England and New York all concurred in it. It passed, and answered all the purposes expected from it, till about the year 1841 or 1842, when the States interfered to make enactments in opposition to it. The act of Congress said that State magistrates might execute the duties of the law. Some of the States passed enactments imposing a penalty on any State officers who exercised authority under the law, or assisted in its execution; others denied the use of their jails to carry the law into effect; and, in general, at the commencement of the year 1850, it had become absolutely indispensable that Congress should pass some law for the execution of this provision of the Constitution, or else give up that provision entirely. That was the question. I was in Congress when it was brought forward. I was for a proper law. I had, indeed, proposed a different law; I was of opinion that a summary trial by a jury might be had, which would satisfy the people of the North, and produce no harm to those who claimed the service of fugitives; but I left the Senate, and went to another station, before any law was passed. The law of 1850 passed. Now I undertake, as a lawyer, and on my professional character, to say to you, and to all, that the law of 1850 is decidedly more favorable to the fugitive than General Washington's law of 1793; and I will tell you why. In the first place, the present law places the power in much higher hands; in the hands of independent judges of the Supreme and Circuit Courts, and District Courts, and of commissioners who are appointed to office for their legal learning. Every fugitive is brought before a tribunal of high character, of eminent ability, of respectable station. In the second place, when a claimant comes from Virginia to New York, to say that one A or one B has run away, or is a fugitive from service or labor, he brings with him a record of the court of the county from which he comes, and that record must be sworn to before a magistrate, and certified by the county clerk, and bear an official seal. The affidavit must state that A or B had departed under such and such circumstances, and had gone to another State; and that record under seal is, by the Constitution of the United States, entitled to full credit in every State. Well, the claimant or his agent comes here, and he presents to you the seal of the court in Virginia, affixed to a record of his declaration, that A or B had escaped from service. He must then prove that the fugitive is here. He brings a witness; he is asked if this is the man, and he proves it; or, in nine cases out of ten, the fact would be admitted by the fugitive himself. Such is the present law; and, much opposed and maligned as it is, it is more favorable to the fugitive slave than the law enacted during Washington's administration, in 1793, which was sanctioned by the North as well as by the South. The present violent opposition has sprung up in modern times. From whom does this clamor come? Why, look at the proceedings of the antislavery conventions; look at their resolutions. Do you find among those persons who oppose this Fugitive Slave Law any admission whatever, that any law ought to be passed to carry into effect the solemn stipulations of the Constitution? Tell me any such case;

tell me if any resolution was adopted by the convention at Syracuse favorable to the carrying out of the Constitution. Not one! The fact is, Gentlemen, they oppose the constitutional provision; they oppose the whole! Not a man of them admits that there ought to be any law on the subject. They deny, altogether, that the provisions of the Constitution ought to be carried into effect. Look at the proceedings of the antislavery conventions in Ohio, Massachusetts, and at Syracuse, in the State of New York. What do they say? "That, so help them God, no colored man shall be sent from the State of New York back to his master in Virginia!" Do not they say that? And, to the fulfilment of that they "pledge their lives, their fortunes, and their sacred honor." Their sacred honor! They pledge their sacred honor to violate the Constitution; they pledge their sacred honor to commit treason against the laws of their country!

I have already stated, Gentlemen, what your observation of these things must have taught you. I will only recur to the subject for a moment, for the purpose of persuading you, as public men and private men, as good men and patriotic men, that you ought, to the extent of your ability and influence, to see to it that such laws are established and maintained as shall keep you, and the South, and the West, and all the country, together, on the terms of the Constitution. I say, that what is demanded of us is to fulfil our constitutional duties, and to do for the South what the South has a right to demand.

Gentlemen, I have been some time before the public. My character is known, my life is before the country. I profess to love liberty as much as any man living; but I profess to love American liberty, that liberty which is secured to the country by the government under which we live; and I have no great opinion of that other and higher liberty which disregards the restraints of law and of the Constitution. I hold the Constitution of the United States to be the bulwark, the only bulwark, of our liberties and of our national character, I do not mean that you should become slaves under the Constitution. That is not American liberty. That is not the liberty of the Union for which our fathers fought, that liberty which has given us a right to be known and respected all over the world. I mean only to say, that I am for constitutional liberty. It is enough for me to be as free as the Constitution of the country makes me.

Now, Gentlemen, let me say, that, as much as I respect the character of the people of Western New York, as much as I wish to retain their good opinion, if I should ever hereafter be placed in any situation in public life, let me tell you now that you must not expect from me the slightest variation, even of a hair's breadth, from the Constitution of the United States. I am a Northern man. I was born at the North, educated at the North, have lived all my days at the North. I know five hundred Northern men to one Southern man. My sympathies, all my sympathies, my love of liberty for all mankind, of every color, are the same as yours. My affections and hopes in that respect are exactly like yours. I wish to see all men free, all men happy. I have few personal associations out of the Northern States. My people are your people. And yet I am told sometimes that I am not a friend of liberty, because I am not a Free Soil man. What am I? What was I ever? What shall I be hereafter, if I could sacrifice, for any consideration, that love of American liberty which has glowed in my breast since my infancy, and which, I hope, will never leave me till I expire?

Gentlemen, I regret that slavery exists in the Southern States; but it is clear and certain that Congress has no power over it. It may be, however, that, in the dispensations of Providence, some remedy for this evil may occur, or may be hoped for hereafter. But, in the mean time, I hold to the Constitution of the United States, and you need never expect from me, under any circumstances, that I shall falter from it; that I shall be otherwise than frank and decisive. I would not part with my character as a man of firmness and decision, and honor and principle, for all that the world possesses. You will find me true to the North, because all my sympathies are with the North. My affections, my children, my hopes, my everything, are with the North. But when I stand up before my country, as one appointed to administer the Constitution of the country, by the blessing of God I will be just.

Gentlemen, I expect to be libelled and abused. Yes, libelled and abused. But it does not disturb me. I have not lost a night's rest for a great many years from any such cause. I have some talent for sleeping. And why should I not expect to be libelled? Is not the Constitution of the United States libelled and abused? Do not some people call it a covenant with hell? Is not Washington libelled and abused? Is he not called a bloodhound on the track of the African negro? Are not our fathers libelled and abused by their own children? And ungrateful children they are. How, then, shall I escape? I do not expect to escape; but, knowing these things, I impute no bad motive to any men of character and fair standing. The great settlement measures of the last Congress are laws. Many respectable men, representatives from your own State and from other States, did not concur in them. I do not impute any bad motive to them. I am ready to believe they are Americans all. They may not have thought these laws necessary; or they may have thought that they would be enacted without their concurrence. Let all that pass away. If they are now men who will stand by what is done, and stand up for their country, and say that, as these laws were passed by a majority of the whole country, we must stand by them and live by them, I will respect them all as friends.

Now, Gentlemen, allow me to ask of you, What do you think would have been the condition of the country, at this time, if these laws had not been passed by the last Congress? if the question of the Texas boundary had not been settled? if New Mexico and Utah had been left as desert-places, and no government had been provided for them? And if the other great object to which State laws had opposed so many obstacles, the restoration of fugitives, had not been provided for, I ask, what would have been the state of this country now? You men of Erie County, you men of New York, I conjure you to go home to-night and meditate on this subject. What would have been the state of this country, now, at this moment, if these laws had not been passed? I have given my opinion that we should have had a civil war. I refer it to you, therefore, for your consideration; meditate on it; do not be carried away by any abstract notions or metaphysical ideas; think practically on the great question, What would have been the condition of the United States at this moment, if we had not settled these agitating questions? I repeat, in my opinion, there would have been a civil war.

Gentlemen, will you allow me, for a moment, to advert to myself? I have been a long time in public life; of course, not many years remain to me. At the commencement of 1850, I looked anxiously at the condition of the country, and I thought the inevitable consequence of leaving the existing controversies unadjusted would be civil war. I saw danger in leaving Utah and New Mexico without any government, a prey to the power of Texas. I saw the condition of things arising from the interference of some of the States in defeating the operation of the Constitution in respect to the restoration of fugitive slaves. I saw these things, and I made up my mind to encounter whatever might betide me in the attempt to avert the impending catastrophe. And allow me to add something which is not entirely unworthy of notice. A member of the House of Representatives told me that he had prepared a list of one hundred and forty speeches which had been made in Congress on the slavery question. "That is a very large number, my friend," I said; "but how is that?" "Why," said he, "a Northern man gets up and speaks with considerable power and fluency until the Speaker's hammer knocks him down. Then gets up a Southern man, and he speaks with more warmth. He is nearer the sun, and he comes out with the greater fervor against the North. He speaks his hour, and is in turn knocked down. And so it has gone on, until I have got one hundred and forty speeches on my list." "Well," said I, "where are they, and what are they?" "If the speaker," said he, "was a Northern man, he held forth against slavery; and if he was from the South, he abused the North; and all these speeches were sent by the members to their own localities, where they served only to aggravate the local irritation already existing. No man reads both sides. The other side of the argument is not heard; and the speeches sent from Washington in such prodigious numbers, instead of tending to conciliation, do but increase, in both sections of the Union, an excitement already of the most dangerous character."

Gentlemen, in this state of things, I saw that something must be done. It was impossible to look with indifference on a danger of so formidable a character. I am a Massachusetts man, and I bore in mind what Massachusetts has ever been to the Constitution and the Union. I felt the importance of the duty which devolved upon one to whom she had so long confided the trust of representing her in either house of Congress. As I honored her, and respected her, I felt that I was serving her in my endeavors to promote the welfare of the whole country.

And now suppose, Gentlemen, that, on the occasion in question, I had taken a different course. If I may allude so particularly to an individual so insignificant as myself, suppose that, on the 7th of March, 1850, instead of making a speech that would, so far as my power went, reconcile the country, I had joined in the general clamor of the Antislavery party. Suppose I had said, "I will have nothing to do with any accommodation; we will admit no compromise; we will let Texas invade New Mexico; we will leave New Mexico and Utah to take care of themselves; we will plant ourselves on the Wilmot Proviso, let the consequences be what they may." Now, Gentlemen, I do not mean to say that great consequences would have followed from such a course on my part; but suppose I had taken such a course. How could I be blamed for it? Was I not a Northern man? Did I not know Massachusetts feelings and prejudices? But what of that? I am an American. I was made a whole man, and I did not mean to make myself half a one. I felt that I had a duty to perform to my country, to my own reputation; for I flattered myself that a service of forty years had given me some character, on which I had a right to repose for my justification in the performance of a duty attended with some degree of local unpopularity. I thought it my duty to pursue this course, and I did not care what was to be the consequence. I felt it was my duty, in a very alarming crisis, to come out; to go for my country, and my whole country; and to exert any power I had to keep that country together. I cared for nothing, I was afraid of nothing, but I meant to do my duty. Duty performed makes a man happy; duty neglected makes a man unhappy. I therefore, in the face of all discouragements and all dangers, was ready to go forth and do what I thought my country, your country, demanded of me. And, Gentlemen, allow me to say here to-day, that if the fate of John Rogers had stared me in the face, if I had seen the stake, if I had heard the fagots already crackling, by the blessing of Almighty God I would have gone on and discharged the duty which I thought my country called upon me to perform. I would have become a martyr to save that country.

And now, Gentlemen, farewell. Live and be happy. Live like patriots, live like Americans. Live in the enjoyment of the inestimable blessings which your fathers prepared for you; and if any thing that I may do hereafter should be inconsistent, in the slightest degree, with the opinions and principles which I have this day submitted to you, then discard me for ever from your recollection.

THE ADDITION TO THE CAPITOL.
AN ADDRESS DELIVERED AT THE LAYING OF THE CORNER-STONE OF THE ADDITION TO THE CAPITOL, ON THE 4th OF JULY, 1851.[1]

Fellow-Citizens,--I greet you well; I give you joy, on the return of this anniversary; and I felicitate you, also, on the more particular purpose of which this ever-memorable day has been chosen to witness the fulfilment. Hail! all hail! I see before and around me a mass of faces, glowing with cheerfulness and patriotic pride. I see thousands of eyes turned towards other eyes, all sparkling with gratification and delight. This is the New World! This is America! This is Washington! and this the Capitol of the United States! And where else, among the nations, can the seat of government be surrounded, on any day of any year, by those who have more reason to rejoice in the blessings which they possess? Nowhere, fellow-citizens! assuredly, nowhere! Let us, then, meet this rising sun with joy and thanksgiving!

This is that day of the year which announced to mankind the great fact of American Independence. This fresh and brilliant morning blesses our vision with another beholding of the birthday of our nation; and we see that nation, of recent origin, now among the most considerable and powerful, and spreading over the continent from sea to sea.

Among the first colonists from Europe to this part of America, there were some, doubtless, who contemplated the distant consequences of their undertaking, and who saw a great futurity. But, in general, their hopes were limited to the enjoyment of a safe asylum from tyranny, religious and civil, and to respectable subsistence, by industry and toil. A thick veil hid our times from their view. But the progress of America, however slow, could not but at length awaken genius, and attract the attention of mankind.

In the early part of the second century of our history, Bishop Berkeley, who, it will be remembered, had resided for some time in Newport, in Rhode Island, wrote his well-known "Verses on the Prospect of Planting ARTS and LEARNING in AMERICA." The last stanza of this little poem seems to have been produced by a high poetical inspiration:--

"Westward the course of empire takes its way; The four first acts already past, A fifth shall close the drama with the day: Time's noblest offspring is the last."

This extraordinary prophecy may be considered only as the result of long foresight and uncommon sagacity; of a foresight and sagacity stimulated, nevertheless, by excited feeling and high enthusiasm. So clear a vision of what America would become was not founded on square miles, or on existing numbers, or on any common laws of statistics. It was an intuitive glance into futurity; it was a grand conception, strong, ardent, glowing, embracing all time since the creation of the world, and all regions of which that world is composed, and judging of the future by just analogy with the past. And the inimitable imagery and beauty with which the thought is expressed, joined to the conception itself, render it one of the most striking passages in our language.

On the day of the Declaration of Independence our illustrious fathers performed the first scene in the last great act of this drama; one in real importance infinitely exceeding that for which the great English poet invokes

"A muse of fire, ... A kingdom for a stage, princes to act, And monarchs to behold the swelling scene!"

The Muse inspiring our fathers was the Genius of Liberty, all on fire with a sense of oppression, and a resolution to throw it off; the whole world was the stage, and higher characters than princes trod it; and, instead of monarchs, countries and nations and the age beheld the swelling scene. How well the characters were cast, and how well each acted his part, and what emotions the whole performance excited, let history, now and hereafter, tell.

At a subsequent period, but before the Declaration of Independence, the Bishop of St. Asaph published a discourse, in which the following remarkable passages are found:--

"It is difficult for man to look into the destiny of future ages; the designs of Providence are vast and complicated, and our own powers are too narrow to admit of much satisfaction to our curiosity. But when we see many great and powerful causes constantly at work, we cannot doubt of their producing proportionable effects.

"The colonies in North America have not only taken root and acquired strength, *but seem hastening with an accelerated progress to such a powerful state as may introduce a new and important change in human affairs.*

"Descended from ancestors of the most improved and enlightened part of the Old World, they receive, as it were by inheritance, all the improvements and discoveries of their mother country. And it happens fortunately for them to commence their flourishing state at a time when the human understanding has attained to the free use of its powers, and has learned to act with vigor and certainty. They may avail themselves, not only of the experience and industry, but even of the errors and mistakes, of former days. Let it be considered for how many ages a great part of the world appears not to have thought at all; how many more they have been busied in forming systems and conjectures, while reason has been lost in a labyrinth of words, and they never seem to have suspected on what frivolous matters their minds were employed.

"And let it be well understood what rapid improvements, what important discoveries, have been made, in a few years, by a few countries, with our own at their head, which have at last discovered the right method of using their faculties.

"May we not reasonably expect that a number of provinces possessed of these advantages and quickened by mutual emulation, with only the common progress of the human mind, should very considerably enlarge the boundaries of science?

"The vast continent itself, over which they are gradually spreading, may be considered as a treasure yet untouched of natural productions that shall hereafter afford ample matter for commerce and contemplation. And if we reflect what a stock of knowledge may be accumulated by the constant progress of industry and observation, fed with fresh supplies from the stores of nature, assisted sometimes by those happy strokes of chance which mock all the powers of invention, and sometimes by those superior characters which arise occasionally to instruct and enlighten the world, it is difficult even to imagine to what height of improvement their discoveries may extend.

"_And perhaps they may make as considerable advances in the arts of civil government and the conduct of life._ We have reason to be proud, and even jealous, of our excellent constitution; but those equitable principles on which it was formed, an equal representation (the best discovery of political wisdom), and a just and commodious distribution of power, which with us were the price of civil wars, and the rewards of the virtues and sufferings of our ancestors, descend to them as a natural inheritance, without toil or pain.

"_But must they rest here, as in the utmost effort of human genius? Can chance and time, the wisdom and the experience of public men, suggest no new remedy aqainst the evils_ which vices and ambition are perpetually apt to cause? May they not hope, without presumption, to preserve a greater zeal for piety and public devotion than we have alone? For sure it can hardly happen to them, as it has to us, that, when religion is best understood and rendered most pure and reasonable, then should be the precise time when many cease to believe and practise it, and all in general become most indifferent to it.

"May they not possibly be more successful than their mother country has been in preserving that reverence and authority which are due to the laws? to those who make, and to those who execute them? _May not a method be invented of procuring some tolerable share of the comforts of life to those inferior useful ranks of men to whose industry we are indebted for the whole? Time and discipline may discover some means to correct the extreme inequalities of condition between the rich and the poor, so dangerous to the innocence and happiness of both._ They may fortunately be led by habit and choice to despise that luxury which is considered with us the true enjoyment of wealth. They may have little relish for that ceaseless hurry of amusements which is pursued in this country without pleasure, exercise, or employment. And perhaps, after trying some of our follies and caprices, and rejecting the rest, they may be led by reason and experiment to that old simplicity which was first pointed out by nature, and has produced those models which we still admire in arts, eloquence, and manners. _The diversity of new scenes and situations, which so many growing states must necessarily pass through, may introduce changes in the fluctuating opinions and manners of men which we can form no conception of_; and not only the gracious disposition of Providence, but the visible preparation of causes, seems to indicate strong tendencies towards a general improvement."

Fellow-citizens, this "gracious disposition of Providence," and this "visible preparation of causes," at length brought on the hour for decisive action. On the 4th of July, 1776, the Representatives of the United States of America, in Congress assembled, declared that these United Colonies are, and of right ought to be, FREE AND INDEPENDENT STATES.

This Declaration, made by most patriotic and resolute men, trusting in the justice of their cause and the protection of Heaven, and yet made not without deep solicitude and anxiety, has now stood for seventy-five years, and still stands. It was sealed in blood. It has met dangers, and overcome them; it has had enemies, and conquered them; it has had detractors, and abashed them all; it has had doubting friends, but it has cleared all doubts away; and now, to-day, raising its august form higher than the clouds, twenty millions of people contemplate it with hallowed love, and the world beholds it, and the consequences which have followed from it, with profound admiration.

This anniversary animates and gladdens and unites all American hearts. On other days of the year we may be party men, indulging in controversies, more or less important to the public good; we may have likes and dislikes, and we may maintain our political differences, often with warm, and sometimes with angry feelings. But to-day we are Americans all; and all nothing but Americans. As the great luminary over our heads, dissipating mists and fogs, now cheers the whole hemisphere, so do the associations connected with this day disperse all cloudy and sullen weather in the minds and hearts of true Americans. Every man's heart swells within him; every man's port and bearing become somewhat more proud and lofty, as he remembers that seventy-five years have rolled away, and that the great inheritance of liberty is still his; his, undiminished and unimpaired; his in all its original glory; his to enjoy, his to protect, and his to transmit to future generations.

Fellow-citizens, this inheritance which we enjoy to-day is not only an inheritance of liberty, but of our own peculiar American liberty. Liberty has existed in other times, in other countries, and in other forms. There has been a Grecian liberty, bold and powerful, full of spirit, eloquence, and fire; a liberty which produced multitudes of great men, and has transmitted one immortal name, the name of Demosthenes, to posterity. But still it was a liberty of disconnected states, sometimes united, indeed, by temporary leagues and confederacies, but often involved in wars between themselves. The sword of Sparta turned its sharpest edge against Athens, enslaved her, and devastated Greece; and, in her turn, Sparta was compelled to bend before the power of Thebes. And let it ever be remembered, especially let the truth sink deep into all American minds, that it was the WANT OF UNION among her several states which finally gave the mastery of all Greece to Philip of Macedon.

And there has also been a Roman liberty, a proud, ambitious, domineering spirit, professing free and popular principles in Rome itself, but, even in the best days of the republic, ready to carry slavery and chains into her provinces, and through every country over which her eagles could be borne. What was the liberty of Spain, or Gaul, or Germany, or Britain, in the days of Rome? Did true constitutional liberty then exist? As the Roman empire declined, her provinces, not instructed in the principles of free popular government, one after another declined also, and when Rome herself fell, in the end, all fell together.

I have said, Gentlemen, that our inheritance is an inheritance of American liberty. That liberty is characteristic, peculiar, and altogether our own. Nothing like it existed in former times, nor was known in the most enlightened states of antiquity; while with us its principles have become interwoven into the minds of individual men, connected with our daily opinions, and our daily habits, until it is, if I may so say, an element of social as well as of political life; and the consequence is, that to whatever region an American citizen carries himself, he takes with him, fully developed in his own understanding and experience, our American principles and opinions, and becomes ready at once, in co-operation with others, to apply them to the formation of new governments. Of this a most wonderful instance may be seen in the history of the State of California.

On a former occasion I ventured to remark, that "it is very difficult to establish a free conservative government for the equal advancement of all the interests of society. What has Germany done, learned Germany, more full of ancient lore than all the world beside? What has Italy done? What have they done who dwell on the spot where Cicero lived? They have not the power of self-government which a common town-meeting, with us, possesses.... Yes, I say that those persons who have gone from our town-meetings to dig gold in California are more fit to make a republican government than any body of men in Germany or Italy; because they have learned this one great lesson, that there is no security without law, and that, under the circumstances in which they are placed, where there is no military authority to cut their throats, there is no sovereign will but the will of the majority; that, therefore, if they remain, they must submit to that will." And this I believe to be strictly true.

Now, fellow-citizens, if your patience will hold out, I will venture, before proceeding to the more appropriate and particular duties of the day, to state, in a few words, what I take these American political principles in substance to be. They consist, as I think, in the first place, in the establishment of popular governments, on the basis of representation; for it is plain that a pure democracy, like that which existed in some of the states of Greece, in which every individual had a direct vote in the enactment of all laws, cannot possibly exist in a country of wide extent. This representation is to be made as equal as circumstances will allow. Now, this principle of popular representation, prevailing either in all the branches of government, or in some of them, has existed in these States almost from the days of the settlements at Jamestown and Plymouth; borrowed, no doubt, from the example of the popular branch of the British legislature. The representation of the people in the British House of Commons was, however, originally very unequal, and is yet not equal. Indeed, it may be doubted whether the appearance of knights and burgesses, assembling on the summons of the crown, was not intended at first as an assistance and support to the royal prerogative, in matters of revenue and taxation, rather than as a mode of ascertaining popular opinion. Nevertheless, representation had a popular origin, and savored more and more of the character of that origin, as it acquired, by slow degrees, greater and greater strength, in the actual government of the country. The constitution of the House of Commons was certainly a form of representation, however unequal; numbers were counted, and majorities prevailed; and when our ancestors, acting upon this example, introduced more equality of representation, the idea assumed a more rational and distinct shape. At any rate, this manner of exercising popular power was familiar to our fathers when they settled on this continent. They adopted it, and generation has risen up after generation, all acknowledging it, and all learning its practice and its forms.

The next fundamental principle in our system is, that the will of the majority, fairly expressed through the means of representation, shall have the force of law; and it is quite evident that, in a country without thrones or aristocracies or privileged castes or classes, there can be no other foundation for law to stand upon.

And, as the necessary result of this, the third element is, that the law is the supreme rule for the government of all. The great sentiment of Alcaeus, so beautifully presented to us by Sir William Jones, is absolutely indispensable to the construction and maintenance of our political systems:--

"What constitutes a state? Not high-raised battlement or labored mound, Thick wall or moated gate; Not cities proud, with spires and turrets crowned; Not bays and broad-armed ports, Where, laughing at the storm, rich navies ride; Not starred and spangled courts, Where low-browed baseness wafts perfume to pride. No: MEN, high-minded MEN, With powers as far above dull brutes endued, In forest, brake, or den, As beasts excel cold rocks and brambles rude: Men who their duties know, But know their rights, and, knowing, dare maintain; Prevent the long-aimed blow, And crush the tyrant while they rend the chain: These constitute a state; And SOVEREIGN LAW, that state's collected will, O'er thrones and globes elate Sits empress, crowning good, repressing ill."

And, finally, another most important part of the great fabric of American liberty is, that there shall be written constitutions, founded on the immediate authority of the people themselves, and regulating and restraining all the powers conferred upon government, whether legislative, executive, or judicial.

This, fellow-citizens, I suppose to be a just summary of our American principles, and I have on this occasion sought to express them in the plainest and in the fewest words. The summary may not be entirely exact, but I hope it may be sufficiently so to make manifest to the rising generation among ourselves, and to those elsewhere who may choose to inquire into the nature of our political institutions, the general theory upon which they are founded.

And I now proceed to add, that the strong and deep-settled conviction of all intelligent persons amongst us is, that, in order to support a useful and wise government upon these popular principles, the general education of the people, and the wide diffusion of pure morality and true religion, are indispensable. Individual virtue is a part of public virtue. It is difficult to conceive how there can remain morality in the government when it shall cease to exist among the people; or how the aggregate of the political institutions, all the organs of which consist only of men, should be wise, and beneficent, and competent to inspire confidence, if the opposite qualities belong to the individuals who constitute those organs, and make up that aggregate.

And now, fellow-citizens, I take leave of this part of the duty which I proposed to perform; and, once more felicitating you and myself that our eyes have seen the light of this blessed morning, and that our ears have heard the shouts with which joyous thousands welcome its return, and joining with you in the hope that every revolving year may renew these rejoicings to the end of time, I proceed to address you, shortly, upon the particular occasion of our assembling here to-day.

Fellow-citizens, by the act of Congress of the 30th of September, 1850, provision was made for the extension of the Capitol, according to such plan as might be approved by the President of the United States, and for the necessary sums to be expended, under his direction, by such architect as he might appoint. This measure was imperatively demanded, for the use of the legislative and judiciary departments, the public libraries, the occasional accommodation of the chief executive magistrate, and for other objects. No act of Congress incurring a large expenditure has received more general approbation from the people. The President has proceeded to execute this law. He has approved a plan; he has appointed an architect; and all things are now ready for the commencement of the work.

The anniversary of national independence appeared to afford an auspicious occasion for laying the foundation-stone of the additional building. That ceremony has now been performed by the President himself, in the presence and view of this multitude. He has thought that the day and the occasion made a united and imperative call for some short address to the people here assembled; and it is at his request that I have appeared before you to perform that part of the duty which was deemed incumbent on us.

Beneath the stone is deposited, among other things, a list of which will be published, the following brief account of the proceedings of this day, in my handwriting:--

"On the morning of the first day of the seventy-sixth year of the Independence of the United States of America, in the city of Washington, being the 4th day of July, 1851, this stone, designed as the corner-stone of the extension of the Capitol, according to a plan approved by the President, in pursuance of an act of Congress, was laid by

"MILLARD FILLMORE,

"PRESIDENT OF THE UNITED STATES,

"assisted by the Grand Master of the Masonic Lodges, in the presence of many members of Congress, of officers of the Executive and Judiciary Departments, National, State, and District, of officers of the army and navy, the corporate authorities of this and neighboring cities, many associations, civil and military and masonic, members of the Smithsonian Institution and National Institute, professors of colleges and teachers of schools of the District, with their students and pupils, and a vast concourse of people from places near and remote, including a few surviving gentlemen who witnessed the laying of the corner-stone of the Capitol by President Washington, on the 18th day of September, A.D. 1793.

"If, therefore, it shall be hereafter the will of God that this structure shall fall from its base, that its foundation be upturned, and this deposit brought to the eyes of men, be it then known, that on this day the Union of the United States of America stands firm, that their Constitution still exists unimpaired, and with all its original usefulness and glory; growing every day stronger and stronger in the affections of the great body of the American people, and attracting more and more the admiration of the world. And all here assembled, whether belonging to public life or to private life, with hearts devoutly thankful to Almighty God for the preservation of the liberty and happiness of the country, unite in sincere and fervent prayers that this deposit, and the walls and arches, the domes and towers, the columns and entablatures, now to be erected over it, may endure for ever!

"GOD SAVE THE UNITED STATES OF AMERICA!

"DANIEL WEBSTER,

"*Secretary of State of the United States.*"

Fellow-citizens, fifty-eight years ago Washington stood on this spot to execute a duty like that which has now been performed. He then laid the corner-stone of the original Capitol. He was at the head of the government, at that time weak in resources, burdened with debt, just struggling into political existence and respectability, and agitated by the heaving waves which were overturning European thrones. But even then, in many important respects, the government was strong. It was strong in Washington's own great character; it was strong in the wisdom and patriotism of other eminent public men, his political associates and fellow-laborers; and it was strong in the affections of the people. Since that time astonishing changes have been wrought in the condition and prospects of the American people; and a degree of progress witnessed with which the world can furnish no parallel. As we review the course of that progress, wonder and amazement arrest our attention at every step. The present occasion, although allowing of no lengthened remarks, may yet, perhaps, admit of a short comparative statement of important subjects of national interest as they existed at that day, and as they now exist. I have adopted for this purpose the tabular form of statement, as being the most brief and significant.

COMPARATIVE TABLE.

Year 1793. Year 1851.

Number of States 15 31 Representatives and Senators in Congress 135 295 Population of the United States 3,929,328 23,267,498 Population of Boston 18,038 136,871 Population of Baltimore 13,503 169,054 Population of Philadelphia 42,520 409,045 Population of New York (city) 33,121 515,507 Population of Washington . . . 40,075 Population of Richmond 4,000 27,582 Population of Charleston 16,359 42,983 Amount of receipts into the Treasury $5,720,624 $52,312,980 Amount of expenditures $7,529,575 $48,005,879 Amount of imports $31,000,000 $215,725,995 Amount of exports $26,109,000 $217,517,130 Amount of tonnage (tons) 520,764 3,772,440 Area of the United States in square miles 805,461 3,314,365 Rank and file of the army 5,120 10,000 Militia (enrolled) . . . 2,006,456 Navy of the United States (vessels) (None.) 76 Navy armament (ordnance) . . . 2,012 Treaties and conventions with foreign powers 9 90 Light-houses and light-boats 12 372 Expenditures for ditto $12,061 $529,265 Area of the Capitol 1/2 acre. 4-1/8 acres. Number of miles of railroad in operation . . . 10,287 Cost of ditto . . . $306,607,954 Number of miles in course of construction . . . 10,092 Lines of electric telegraph, in miles . . . 15,000 Number of post-offices 209 21,551 Number of miles of post-route 5,642 196,290 Amount of revenue from post-offices $104,747 $6,727,867 Amount of expenditures of Post-Office Department $72,040 $6,024,567 Number of miles of mail transportation . . . 52,465,724 Number of colleges 19 121 Public libraries 35 694 Volumes in ditto 75,000 2,201,632 School libraries . . . 10,000 Volumes in ditto . . . 2,000,000 Emigrants from Europe to the United States 10,000 299,610 Coinage at the Mint $9,664 $52,019,465

In respect to the growth of Western trade and commerce, I extract a few sentences from a very valuable address before the Historical Society of Ohio, by William D. Gallagher, Esq., 1850:--

"A few facts will exhibit as well as a volume the wonderful growth of Western trade and commerce. Previous to the year 1800, some eight or ten keel-boats, of twenty or twenty-five tons each, performed all the carrying trade between Cincinnati and Pittsburg. In 1802 the first government vessel appeared on Lake Erie. In 1811 the first steamboat (the Orleans) was launched at Pittsburg. In 1826 the waters of Michigan were first ploughed by the keel of a steamboat, a pleasure trip to Green Bay being planned and executed in the summer of this year. In 1832 a steamboat first appeared at Chicago. At the present time the entire number of steamboats running on the Mississippi and Ohio and their tributaries is more probably over than under six hundred, the aggregate tonnage of which is not short of one hundred and forty thousand; a larger number of steamboats than England can claim, and a greater steam commercial marine than that employed by Great Britain and her dependencies."

And now, fellow-citizens, having stated to you this infallible proof of the growth and prosperity of the nation, I ask you, and I would ask every man, whether the government which has been over us has proved itself an infliction or a curse to the country, or any part of it?

Ye men of the South, of all the original Southern States, what say you to all this? Are you, or any of you, ashamed of this great work of your fathers? Your fathers were not they who storied the prophets and killed them. They were among the prophets; they were of the prophets; they were themselves the prophets.

Ye men of Virginia, what do you say to all this? Ye men of the Potomac, dwelling along the shores of that river on which WASHINGTON lived and died, and where his remains now rest, ye, so many of whom may see the domes of the Capitol from your own homes, what say ye?

Ye men of James River and the Bay, places consecrated by the early settlement of your Commonwealth, what do you say? Do you desire, from the soil of your State, or as you travel to the North, to see these halls vacated, their beauty and ornaments destroyed, and their national usefulness gone for ever?

Ye men beyond the Blue Ridge, many thousands of whom are nearer to this Capitol than to the seat of government of your own State, what do you think of breaking this great association into fragments of States and of people? I know that some of you, and I believe that you all, would be almost as much shocked at the announcement of such a catastrophe, as if you were to be informed that the Blue Ridge itself would soon totter from its base. And ye men of Western Virginia, who occupy the great slope from the top of the Alleghanies to Ohio and Kentucky, what benefit do you propose to yourselves by disunion? If you "secede," what do you "secede" from, and what do you "accede" to? Do you look for the current of the Ohio to change, and to bring you and your commerce to the tidewaters of Eastern rivers? What man in his senses can suppose that you would remain part and parcel of Virginia a month after Virginia should have ceased to be part and parcel of the United States?

The secession of Virginia! The secession of Virginia, whether alone or in company, is most improbable, the greatest of all improbabilities. Virginia, to her everlasting honor, acted a great part in framing and establishing the present Constitution. She has had her reward and her distinction. Seven of her noble sons have each filled the Presidency, and enjoyed the highest honors of the country. Dolorous complaints come up to us from the South, that Virginia will not head the march of secession, and lead the other Southern States out of the Union. This, if it should happen, would be something of a marvel, certainly, considering how much pains Virginia took to lead these same States into the Union, and considering, too, that she has partaken as largely of its benefits and its government as any other State.

And ye men of the other Southern States, members of the Old Thirteen; yes, members of the Old Thirteen; that always touches my regard and my sympathies; North Carolina, Georgia, South Carolina! What page in your history, or in the history of any one of you, is brighter than those which have been recorded since the Union was formed? Or through what period has your prosperity been greater, or your peace and happiness better secured? What names even has South Carolina, now so much dissatisfied, what names has she of which her intelligent sons are more proud than those which have been connected with the government of the United States? In Revolutionary times, and in the earliest days of this Constitution, there was no State more honored, or more deserving of honor. Where is she now? And what a fall is there, my countrymen! But I leave her to her own reflections, commending to her, with all my heart, the due consideration of her own example in times now gone by.

Fellow-citizens, there are some diseases of the mind as well as of the body, diseases of communities as well as diseases of individuals, that must be left to their own cure; at least it is wise to leave them so until the last critical moment shall arrive.

I hope it is not irreverent, and certainly it is not intended as reproach, when I say, that I know no stronger expression in our language than that which describes the restoration of the wayward son,--"he came to himself." He had broken away from all the ties of love, family, and friendship. He had forsaken every thing which he had once regarded in his father's house. He had forsworn his natural sympathies, affections, and habits, and taken his journey into a far country. He had gone away from himself and out of himself. But misfortunes overtook him, and famine threatened him with starvation and death. No entreaties from home followed him to beckon him back; no admonition from others warned him of his fate. But the hour of reflection had come, and nature and conscience wrought within him, until at length "*he came to himself.*" And now, ye men of the new States of the South! You are not of the original thirteen. The battle had been fought and won, the Revolution achieved, and the Constitution established, before your States had any existence as States. You came to a prepared banquet, and had seats assigned you at table just as honorable as those which were filled by older guests. You have been and are singularly prosperous; and if any one should deny this, you would at once contradict his assertion. You have bought vast quantities of choice and excellent land at the lowest price; and if the public domain has not been lavished upon you, you yourself will admit that it has been appropriated to your own uses by a very liberal hand. And yet in some of these States, not in all, persons are found in favor of a dissolution of the Union, or of secession from it. Such opinions are expressed even where the general prosperity of the community has been the most rapidly advanced. In the flourishing and interesting State of Mississippi, for example, there is a large party which insists that her grievances are intolerable, that the whole body politic is in a state of suffering; and all along, and through her whole extent on the Mississippi, a loud cry rings that her only remedy is "Secession," "Secession." Now, Gentlemen, what infliction does the State of Mississippi suffer under? What oppression prostrates her strength or destroys her happiness? Before we can judge of the proper remedy, we must know something of the disease; and, for my part, I confess that the real evil existing in the case appears to me to be a certain inquietude or uneasiness growing out of a high degree of prosperity and consciousness of wealth and power, which sometimes lead men to be ready for changes, and to push on unreasonably to still higher elevation. If this be the truth of the matter, her political doctors are about right. If the complaint spring from over-wrought prosperity, for that disease I have no doubt that secession would prove a sovereign remedy.

But I return to the leading topic on which I was engaged. In the department of invention there have been wonderful applications of science to arts within the last sixty years. The spacious hall of the Patent Office is at once the repository and proof of American inventive art and genius. Their results are seen in the numerous improvements by which human labor is abridged.

Without going into details, it may be sufficient to say, that many of the applications of steam to locomotion and manufactures, of electricity and magnetism to the production of mechanical motion, the electrical telegraph, the registration of astronomical phenomena, the art of multiplying engravings, the introduction and improvement among us of all the important inventions of the Old World, are striking indications of the progress of this country in the useful arts. The net-work of railroads and telegraphic lines by which this vast country is reticulated have not only developed its resources, but united emphatically, in metallic bands, all parts of the Union. The hydraulic works of New York, Philadelphia, and Boston surpass in extent and importance those of ancient Rome.

But we have not confined our attention to the immediate application of science to the useful arts. We have entered the field of original research, and have enlarged the bounds of scientific knowledge.

Sixty years ago, besides the brilliant discoveries of Franklin in electricity, scarcely any thing had been done among us in the way of original discovery. Our men of science were content with repeating the experiments and diffusing a knowledge of the discoveries of the learned of the Old World, without attempting to add a single new fact or principle to the existing stock. Within the last twenty-five or thirty years a remarkable improvement has taken place in this respect. Our natural history has been explored in all its branches; our geology has been investigated with results of the highest interest to practical and theoretical science. Discoveries have been made in pure chemistry and electricity, which have received the approbation of the world. The advance which has been made in meteorology in this country, within the last twenty years, is equal to that made during the same period in all the world besides.

In 1793 there was not in the United States an instrument with which a good observation of the heavenly bodies could be made. There are now instruments at Washington, Cambridge, and Cincinnati equal to those at the best European observatories, and the original discoveries in astronomy within the last five years, in this country, are among the most brilliant of the age. I can hardly refrain from saying, in this connection, that the "Celestial Mechanics" of La Place has been translated and commented upon by Bowditch.

Our knowledge of the geography and topography of the American continent has been rapidly extended by the labor and science of the officers of the United States army, and discoveries of much interest in distant seas have resulted from the enterprise of the navy.

In 1807, a survey of the coast of the United States was commenced, which at that time it was supposed no American was competent to direct. The work has, however, grown within the last few years, under a native superintendent, in importance and extent, beyond any enterprise of the kind ever before attempted.

These facts conclusively prove that a great advance has been made among us, not only in the application of science to the wants of ordinary life, but in science itself, in its highest branches, in its adaptation to satisfy the cravings of the immortal mind.

In respect to literature, with the exception of some books of elementary education, and some theological treatises, of which scarcely any but those of Jonathan Edwards have any permanent value, and some works on local history and politics, like Hutchinson's Massachusetts, Jefferson's Notes on Virginia, the Federalist, Belknap's New Hampshire, and Morse's Geography, and a few others, America had not produced a single work of any repute in literature. We were almost wholly dependent on imported books. Even our Bibles and Testaments were, for the most part, printed abroad. The book trade is now one of the greatest branches of business, and many works of standard value, and of high reputation in Europe as well as at home, have been produced by American authors in every department of literary composition.

While the country has been expanding in dimensions, in numbers, and in wealth, the government has applied a wise forecast in the adoption of measures necessary, when the world shall no longer be at peace, to maintain the national honor, whether by appropriate displays of vigor abroad, or by well-adapted means of defence at home. A navy, which has so often illustrated our history by heroic achievements, though in peaceful times restrained in its operations to narrow limits, possesses, in its admirable elements, the means of great and sudden expansion, and is justly looked upon by the nation as the right arm of its power. An army, still smaller, but not less perfect in its detail, has on many a field exhibited the military aptitudes and prowess of the race, and demonstrated the wisdom which has presided over its organization and government.

While the gradual and slow enlargement of these respective military arms has been regulated by a jealous watchfulness over the public treasure, there has, nevertheless, been freely given all that was needed to perfect their quality; and each affords the nucleus of any enlargement that the public exigencies may demand, from the millions of brave hearts and strong arms upon the land and water.

The navy is the active and aggressive element of national defence; and, let loose from our own sea-coast, must display its power in the seas and channels of the enemy. To do this, it need not be large; and it can never be large enough to defend by its presence at home all our ports and harbors. But, in the absence of the navy, what can the regular army or the volunteer militia do against the enemy's line-of-battle ships and steamers, falling without notice upon our coast? What will guard our cities from tribute, our merchant-vessels and our navy-yards from conflagration? Here, again, we see a wise forecast in the system of defensive measures which, especially since the close of the war with Great Britain, has been steadily followed by our government.

While the perils from which our great establishments had just escaped were yet fresh in remembrance, a system of fortifications was begun, which now, though not quite complete, fences in our important points with impassable strength. More than four thousand cannon may at any moment, within strong and permanent works, arranged with all the advantages and appliances that the art affords, be turned to the protection of the sea-coast, and be served by the men whose hearths they shelter. Happy for us that it is so, since these are means of security that time alone can supply, and since the improvements of maritime warfare, by making distant expeditions easy and speedy, have made them more probable, and at the same time more difficult to anticipate and provide against. The cost of fortifying all the important points of our coast, as well upon the whole Atlantic as the Gulf of Mexico, will not exceed the amount expended on the fortifications of Paris.

In this connection one most important facility in the defence of the country is not to be overlooked; it is the extreme rapidity with which the soldiers of the army, and any number of the militia corps, may be brought to any point where a hostile attack shall at any time be made or threatened.

And this extension of territory embraced within the United States, increase of its population, commerce, and manufactures, development of its resources by canals and railroads, and rapidity of intercommunication by means of steam and electricity, have all been accomplished without overthrow of, or danger to, the public liberties, by any assumption of military power; and, indeed, without any permanent increase of the army, except for the purpose of frontier defence, and of affording a slight guard to the public property; or of the navy, any further than to assure the navigator that, in whatsoever sea he shall sail his ship, he is protected by the stars and stripes of his country. This, too, has been done without the shedding of a drop of blood for treason or rebellion; while systems of popular representation have regularly been supported in the State governments and in the general government; while laws, national and State, of such a character have been passed, and have been so wisely administered, that I may stand up here to-day, and declare, as I now do declare, in the face of all the intelligent of the age, that, for the period which has elapsed from the day that Washington laid the foundation of this Capitol to the present time, there has been no country upon earth in which life, liberty, and property have been more amply and steadily secured, or more freely enjoyed, than in these United States of America. Who is there that will deny this? Who is there prepared with a greater or a better example? Who is there that can stand upon the foundation of facts, acknowledged or proved, and assert that these our republican institutions have not answered the true ends of government beyond all precedent in human history?

There is yet another view. There are still higher considerations. Man is an intellectual being, destined to immortality. There is a spirit in him, and the breath of the Almighty hath given him understanding. Then only is he tending toward his own destiny, while he seeks for knowledge and virtue, for the will of his Maker, and for just conceptions of his own duty. Of all important questions, therefore, let this, the most important of all, be first asked and first answered: In what country of the habitable globe, of great extent and large population, are the means of knowledge the most generally diffused and enjoyed among the people? This question admits of one, and only one, answer. It is here; it is here in these United States; it is among the descendants of those who settled at Jamestown; of those who were pilgrims on the shore of Plymouth; and of those other races of men, who, in subsequent times, have become joined in this great American family. Let one fact, incapable of doubt or dispute, satisfy every mind on this point. The population of the United States is twenty-three millions. Now, take the map of the continent of Europe and spread it out before you. Take your scale and your dividers, and lay off in one area, in any shape you please, a triangle, square, circle, parallelogram, or trapezoid, and of an extent that shall contain one hundred and fifty millions of people, and there will be found within the United States more persons who do habitually read and write than can be embraced within the lines of your demarcation.

But there is something even more than this. Man is not only an intellectual, but he is also a religious being, and his religious feelings and habits require cultivation. Let the religious element in man's nature be neglected, let him be influenced by no higher motives than low self-interest, and subjected to no stronger restraint than the limits of civil authority, and he becomes the creature of selfish passion or blind fanaticism.

The spectacle of a nation powerful and enlightened, but without Christian faith, has been presented, almost within our own day, as a warning beacon for the nations.

On the other hand, the cultivation of the religious sentiment represses licentiousness, incites to general benevolence and the practical acknowledgment of the brotherhood of man, inspires respect for law and order, and gives strength to the whole social fabric, at the same time that it conducts the human soul upward to the Author of its being.

Now, I think it may be stated with truth, that in no country, in proportion to its population, are there so many benevolent establishments connected with religious instruction, Bible, Missionary, and Tract Societies, supported by public and private contributions, as in our own. There are also institutions for the education of the blind, of idiots, of the deaf and dumb; for the reception of orphan and destitute children, and the insane; for moral reform, designed for children and females respectively; and institutions for the reformation of criminals; not to speak of those numerous establishments, in almost every county and town in the United States, for the reception of the aged, infirm, and destitute poor, many of whom have fled to our shores to escape the poverty and wretchedness of their condition at home.

In the United States there is no church establishment or ecclesiastical authority founded by government. Public worship is maintained either by voluntary associations and contributions, or by trusts and donations of a charitable origin.

Now, I think it safe to say, that a greater portion of the people of the United States attend public worship, decently clad, well behaved, and well seated, than of any other country of the civilized world. Edifices of religion are seen everywhere. Their aggregate cost would amount to an immense sum of money. They are, in general, kept in good repair, and consecrated to the purposes of public worship. In these edifices the people regularly assemble on the Sabbath day, which, by all classes, is sacredly set apart for rest from secular employment and for religious meditation and worship, to listen to the reading of the Holy Scriptures, and discourses from pious ministers of the several denominations.

This attention to the wants of the intellect and of the soul, as manifested by the voluntary support of schools and colleges, of churches and benevolent institutions, is one of the most remarkable characteristics of the American people, not less strikingly exhibited in the new than in the older settlements of the country. On the spot where the first trees of the forest were felled, near the log cabins of the pioneers, are to be seen rising together the church and the school-house. So has it been from the beginning, and God grant that it may thus continue!

"On other shores, above their mouldering towns, In sullen pomp, the tall cathedral frowns; Simple and frail, our lowly temples throw Their slender shadows on the paths below; Scarce steal the winds, that sweep the woodland tracks, The larch's perfume from the settler's axe, Ere, like a vision of the morning air, His slight-framed steeple marks the house of prayer. Yet Faith's pure hymn, beneath its shelter rude, Breathes out as sweetly to the tangled wood, As where the rays through blazing oriels pour On marble shaft and tessellated floor."

Who does not admit that this unparalleled growth in prosperity and renown is the result, under Providence, of the union of these States under a general Constitution, which guarantees to each State a republican form of government, and to every man the enjoyment of life, liberty, and the pursuit of happiness, free from civil tyranny or ecclesiastical domination?

And, to bring home this idea to the present occasion, who does not feel that, when President Washington laid his hand on the foundation of the first Capitol, he performed a great work of perpetuation of the Union and the Constitution? Who does not feel that this seat of the general government, healthful in its situation, central in its position, near the mountains whence gush springs of wonderful virtue, teeming with Nature's richest products, and yet not far from the bays and the great estuaries of the sea, easily accessible and generally agreeable in climate and association, does give strength to the union of these States? that this city, bearing an immortal name, with its broad streets and avenues, its public squares and magnificent edifices of the general government, erected for the purpose of carrying on within them the important business of the several departments, for the reception of wonderful and curious inventions, for the preservation of the records of American learning and genius, of extensive collections of the products of nature and art, brought hither for study and comparison from all parts of the world,--adorned with numerous churches, and sprinkled over, I am happy to say, with many public schools, where all the children of the city, without distinction, have the means of obtaining a good education, and with academies and colleges, professional schools and public libraries,--should continue to receive, as it has heretofore received, the fostering care of Congress, and should be regarded as the permanent seat of the national government? Here, too, a citizen of the great republic of letters,[2] a republic which knows not the metes and bounds of political geography, has prophetically indicated his conviction that America is to exercise a wide and powerful influence in the intellectual world, by founding in this city, as a commanding position in the field of science and literature, and placing under the guardianship of the government, an institution "for the increase and diffusion of knowledge among men."

With each succeeding year new interest is added to the spot; it becomes connected with all the historical associations of our country, with her statesmen and her orators, and, alas! its cemetery is annually enriched by the ashes of her chosen sons.

Before us is the broad and beautiful river, separating two of the original thirteen States, which a late President, a man of determined purpose and inflexible will, but patriotic heart, desired to span with arches of ever-enduring granite, symbolical of the firmly cemented union of the North and the South. That President was General Jackson.

On its banks repose the ashes of the Father of his Country, and at our side, by a singular felicity of position, overlooking the city which he designed, and which bears his name, rises to his memory the marble column, sublime in its simple grandeur, and fitly intended to reach a loftier height than any similar structure on the surface of the whole earth.

Let the votive offerings of his grateful countrymen be freely contributed to carry this monument higher and still higher. May I say, as on another occasion, "Let it rise; let it rise till it meet the sun in his coming; let the earliest light of the morning gild it, and parting day linger and play on its summit!"

Fellow-citizens, what contemplations are awakened in our minds as we assemble here to re-enact a scene like that performed by Washington! Methinks I see his venerable form now before me, as presented in the glorious statue by Houdon, now in the Capitol of Virginia. He is dignified and grave; but concern and anxiety seem to soften the lineaments of his countenance. The government over which he presides is yet in the crisis of experiment. Not free from troubles at home, he sees the world in commotion and in arms all around him. He sees that imposing foreign powers are half disposed to try the strength of the recently established American government. We perceive that mighty thoughts, mingled with fears as well as with hopes, are struggling within him. He heads a short procession over these then naked fields; he crosses yonder stream on a fallen tree; he ascends to the top of this eminence, whose original oaks of the forest stand as thick around him as if the spot had been devoted to Druidical worship, and here he performs the appointed duty of the day.

And now, fellow-citizens, if this vision were a reality; if Washington actually were now amongst us, and if he could draw around him the shades of the great public men of his own day, patriots and warriors, orators and statesmen, and were to address us in their presence, would he not say to us: "Ye men of this generation, I rejoice and thank God for being able to see that our labors and toils and sacrifices were not in vain. You are prosperous, you are happy, you are grateful; the fire of liberty burns brightly and steadily in your hearts, while DUTY and the LAW restrain it from bursting forth in wild and destructive conflagration. Cherish liberty, as you love it; cherish its securities, as you wish to preserve it. Maintain the Constitution which we labored so painfully to establish, and which has been to you such a source of inestimable blessings. Preserve the union of the States, cemented as it was by our prayers, our tears, and our blood. Be true to God, to your country, and to your duty. So shall the whole Eastern world follow the morning sun to contemplate you as a nation; so shall all generations honor you, as they honor us; and so shall that Almighty Power which so graciously protected us, and which now protects you, shower its everlasting blessings upon you and your posterity."

Great Father of your Country! we heed your words; we feel their force as if you now uttered them with lips of flesh and blood. Your example teaches us, your affectionate addresses teach us, your public life teaches us, your sense of the value of the blessings of the Union. Those blessings our fathers have tasted, and we have tasted, and still taste. Nor do we intend that those who come after us shall be denied the same high fruition. Our honor as well as our happiness is concerned. We cannot, we dare not, we will not, betray our sacred trust. We will not filch from posterity the treasure placed in our hands to be transmitted to other generations. The bow that gilds the clouds in the heavens, the pillars that uphold the firmament, may disappear and fall away in the hour appointed by the will of God; but until that day comes, or so long as our lives may last, no ruthless hand shall undermine that bright arch of Union and Liberty which spans the continent from Washington to California.

Fellow-citizens, we must sometimes be tolerant to folly, and patient at the sight of the extreme waywardness of men; but I confess that, when I reflect on the renown of our past history, on our present prosperity and greatness, and on what the future hath yet to unfold, and when I see that there are men who can find in all this nothing good, nothing valuable, nothing truly glorious, I feel that all their reason has fled away from them, and left the entire control over their judgment and their actions to insanity and fanaticism; and more than all, fellow-citizens, if the purposes of fanatics and disunionists should be accomplished, the patriotic and intelligent of our generation would seek to hide themselves from the scorn of the world, and go about to find dishonorable graves.

Fellow-citizens, take _courage_; be of *good cheer*. We shall come to no such ignoble end. We shall live, and not die. During the period allotted to our several lives, we shall continue to rejoice in the return of this anniversary. The ill-omened sounds of fanaticism will be hushed; the ghastly spectres of *Secession* and *Disunion* will disappear; and the enemies of united constitutional liberty, if their hatred cannot be appeased, may prepare to have their eyeballs seared as they behold the steady flight of the American eagle, on his burnished wings, for years and years to come.

President Fillmore, it is your singularly good fortune to perform an act such as that which the earliest of your predecessors performed fifty-eight years ago. You stand where he stood; you lay your hand on the corner-stone of a building designed greatly to extend that whose corner-stone he laid. Changed, changed is every thing around. The same sun, indeed, shone upon his head which now shines upon yours. The same broad river rolled at his feet, and bathes his last resting-place, that now rolls at yours. But the site of this city was then mainly an open field. Streets and avenues have since been laid out and completed, squares and public grounds enclosed and ornamented, until the city which bears his name, although comparatively inconsiderable in numbers and wealth, has become quite fit to be the seat of government of a great and united people.

Sir, may the consequences of the duty which you perform so auspiciously to-day, equal those which flowed from his act. Nor this only; may the principles of your administration, and the wisdom of your political conduct, be such, as that the world of the present day, and all history hereafter, may be at no loss to perceive what example you have made your study.

Fellow-citizens, I now bring this address to a close, by expressing to you, in the words of the great Roman orator, the deepest wish of my heart, and which I know dwells deeply in the hearts of all who hear me:

"Duo modo haec opto; unum, UT MORIENS POPULUM ROMANUM LIBERUM RELINQUAM; hoc mihi majus a diis immortalibus dari nihil potest: alterum, ut ita cuique eveniat, ut de republicâ quisque mereatur."

And now, fellow-citizens, with hearts void of hatred, envy, and malice towards our own countrymen, or any of them, or towards the subjects or citizens of other governments, or towards any member of the great family of man; but exulting, nevertheless, in our own peace, security, and happiness, in the grateful remembrance of the past, and the glorious hopes of the future, let us return to our homes, and with all humility and devotion offer our thanks to the Father of all our mercies, political, social, and religious.

[Footnote 1: The following motto stands upon the title-page of the original pamphlet edition:--
"Stet Capitolium Fulgens; late nomen in ultimas Extendat oras."]

[Footnote 2: Hugh Smithson, whose munificent bequest has been applied to the foundation of "The Smithsonian Institution."]

APPENDIX.

IMPRESSMENT.
Mr. Webster to Lord Ashburton.
Department of State, Washington, August 8, 1842.
My Lord,--We have had several conversations on the subject of impressment, but I do not understand that your Lordship has instructions from your government to negotiate upon it, nor does the government of the United States see any utility in opening such negotiation, unless the British government is prepared to renounce the practice in all future wars.

No cause has produced to so great an extent, and for so long a period, disturbing and irritating influences on the political relations of the United States and England, as the impressment of seamen by British cruisers from American merchant-vessels.

From the commencement of the French Revolution to the breaking out of the war between the two countries in 1812, hardly a year elapsed without loud complaint and earnest remonstrance. A deep feeling of opposition to the right claimed, and to the practice exercised under it, and not unfrequently exercised without the least regard to what justice and humanity would have dictated, even if the right itself had been admitted, took possession of the public mind of America, and this feeling, it is well known, co-operated most powerfully with other causes to produce the state of hostilities which ensued.

At different periods, both before and since the war, negotiations have taken place between the two governments, with the hope of finding some means of quieting these complaints. At some times, the effectual abolition of the practice has been requested and treated of; at other times, its temporary suspension; and at other times, again, the limitation of its exercise, and some security against its enormous abuses.

A common destiny has attended these efforts; they have all failed. The question stands at this moment where it stood fifty years ago. The nearest approach to a settlement was a convention proposed in 1803, and which had come to the point of signature, when it was broken off in consequence of the British government insisting that the *narrow seas* should be expressly excepted out of the sphere over which the contemplated stipulation against impressment should extend. The American Minister, Mr. King, regarded this exception as quite inadmissible, and chose rather to abandon the negotiation than to acquiesce in the doctrine which it proposed to establish.

England asserts the right of impressing British subjects, in time of war, out of neutral merchant-vessels, and of deciding by her visiting officers who, among the crews of such merchant-vessels, are British subjects. She asserts this as a legal exercise of the prerogative of the crown; which prerogative is alleged to be founded on the English law of the perpetual and indissoluble allegiance of the subject, and his obligation under all circumstances, and for his whole life, to render military service to the crown whenever required.

This statement, made in the words of eminent British jurists, shows at once that the English claim is far broader than the basis or platform on which it is raised. The law relied on is English law; the obligations insisted on are obligations existing between the crown of England and its subjects. This law and these obligations, it is admitted, may be such as England may choose they shall be. But then they must be confined to the parties. Impressment of seamen out of and beyond English territory, and from on board the ships of other nations, is an interference with the rights of other nations; is further, therefore, than English prerogative can legally extend; and is nothing but an attempt to enforce the peculiar law of England beyond the dominions and jurisdiction of the crown. The claim asserts an extra-territorial authority for the law of British prerogative, and assumes to exercise this extra-territorial authority, to the manifest injury and annoyance of the citizens and subjects of other states, on board their own vessels, on the high seas. Every merchant-vessel on the seas is rightfully considered as part of the territory of the country to which it belongs. The entry, therefore, into such vessel, being neutral, by a belligerent, is an act of force, and is, _prima facie_, a wrong, a trespass, which can be justified only when done for some purpose allowed to form a sufficient justification by the law of nations. But a British cruiser enters an American merchant-vessel in order to take therefrom supposed British subjects; offering no justification, therefore, under the law of nations, but claiming the right under the law of England respecting the king's prerogative. This cannot be defended. English soil, English territory, English jurisdiction, is the appropriate sphere for the operation of English law. The ocean is the sphere of the law of nations; and any merchant-vessel on the seas is by that law under the protection of the laws of her own nation, and may claim immunity, unless in cases in which that law allows her to be entered or visited.

If this notion of perpetual allegiance, and the consequent power of the prerogative, was the law of the world; if it formed part of the conventional code of nations, and was usually practised, like the right of visiting neutral ships, for the purpose of discovering and seizing enemy's property, then impressment might be defended as a common right, and there would be no remedy for the evil till the national code should be altered. But this is by no means the case. There is no such principle incorporated into the code of nations. The doctrine stands only as English law, not as a national law; and English law cannot be of force beyond English dominion. Whatever duties or relations that law creates between the sovereign and his subjects can be enforced and maintained only within the realm, or proper possessions or territory of the sovereign.

There may be quite as just a prerogative right to the property of subjects as to their personal services, in an exigency of the state; but no government thinks of controlling by its own laws property of its subjects situated abroad; much less does any government think of entering the territory of another power for the purpose of seizing such property and applying it to its own uses. As laws, the prerogatives of the crown of England have no obligation on persons or property domiciled or situated abroad.

"When, therefore," says an authority not unknown or unregarded on either side of the Atlantic, "we speak of the right of a state to bind its own native subjects everywhere, we speak only of its own claim and exercise of sovereignty over them when they return within its own territorial jurisdiction, and not of its right to compel or require obedience to such laws, on the part of other nations, within their own territorial sovereignty. On the contrary, every nation has an exclusive right to regulate persons and things within its own territory, according to its sovereign will and public polity."

The good sense of these principles, their remarkable pertinency to the subject now under consideration, and the extraordinary consequences resulting from the British doctrine, are signally manifested by that which we see taking place every day. England acknowledges herself overburdened with population of the poorer classes. Every instance of the emigration of persons of those classes is regarded by her as a benefit. England, therefore, encourages emigration; means are notoriously supplied to emigrants, to assist their conveyance, from public funds; and the New World, and most especially these United States, receive the many thousands of her subjects thus ejected from the bosom of their native land by the necessities of their condition. They come away from poverty and distress in over-crowded cities, to seek employment, comfort, and new homes in a country of free institutions, possessed by a kindred race, speaking their own language, and having laws and usages in many respects like those to which they have been accustomed; and a country which, upon the whole, is found to possess more attractions for persons of their character and condition than any other on the face of the globe. It is stated that, in the quarter of the year ending with June last, more than twenty-six thousand emigrants left the single port of Liverpool for the United States, being four or five times as many as left the same port within the same period for the British colonies and all other parts of the world. Of these crowds of emigrants, many arrive in our cities in circumstances of great destitution, and the charities of the country, both public and private, are severely taxed to relieve their immediate wants. In time they mingle with the new community in which they find themselves, and seek means of living. Some find employment in the cities, others go to the frontiers, to cultivate lands reclaimed from the forest; and a greater or less number of the residue, becoming in time naturalized citizens, enter into the merchant service under the flag of their adopted country.

Now, my Lord, if war should break out between England and a European power, can any thing be more unjust, any thing more irreconcilable to the general sentiments of mankind, than that England should seek out these persons, thus encouraged by her and compelled by their own condition to leave their native homes, tear them away from their new employments, their new political relations, and their domestic connections, and force them to undergo the dangers and hardships of military service for a country which has thus ceased to be their own country? Certainly, certainly, my Lord, there can be but one answer to this question. Is it not far more reasonable that England should either prevent such emigration of her subjects, or that, if she encourage and promote it, she should leave them, not to the embroilment of a double and contradictory allegiance, but to their own voluntary choice, to form such relations, political or social, as they see fit, in the country where they are to find their bread, and to the laws and institutions of which they are to look for defence and protection?

A question of such serious importance ought now to be put at rest. If the United States give shelter and protection to those whom the policy of England annually casts upon their shores,--if, by the benign influences of their government and institutions, and by the happy condition of the country, those emigrants become raised from poverty to comfort, finding it easy even to become landholders, and being allowed to partake in the enjoyment of all civil rights,--if all this may be done, (and all this is done, under the countenance and encouragement of England herself,) is it not high time that, yielding that which had its origin in feudal ideas as inconsistent with the present state of society, and especially with the intercourse and relations subsisting between the Old World and the New, England should at length formally disclaim all right to the services of such persons, and renounce all control over their conduct?

But impressment is subject to objections of a much wider range. If it could be justified in its application to those who are declared to be its only objects, it still remains true that, in its exercise, it touches the political rights of other governments, and endangers the security of their own native subjects and citizens. The sovereignty of the state is concerned in maintaining its exclusive jurisdiction and possession over its merchant-ships on the seas, except so far as the law of nations justifies intrusion upon that possession for special purposes; and all experience has shown, that no member of a crew, wherever born, is safe against impressment when a ship is visited.

The evils and injuries resulting from the actual practice can hardly be overstated, and have ever proved themselves to be such as should lead to its relinquishment, even if it were founded in any defensible principle. The difficulty of discriminating between English subjects and American citizens has always been found to be great, even when an honest purpose of discrimination has existed. But the lieutenant of a man-of-war, having necessity for men, is apt to be a summary judge, and his decisions will be quite as significant of his own wants and his own power as of the truth and justice of the case. An extract from a letter of Mr. King, of the 13th of April, 1797, to the American Secretary of State, shows something of the enormous extent of these wrongful seizures.

"Instead of a few, and these in many instances equivocal cases, I have," says he, "since the month of July past, made application for the discharge from British men-of-war of two hundred and seventy-one seamen, who, stating themselves to be Americans, have claimed my interference. Of this number, eighty-six have been ordered by the Admiralty to be discharged, thirty-seven more have been detained as British subjects or as American volunteers, or for want of proof that they are Americans, and to my applications for the discharge of the remaining one hundred and forty-eight I have received no answer; the ships on board of which these seamen were detained having, in many instances, sailed before an examination was made in consequence of my application.

"It is certain that some of those who have applied to me are not American citizens, but the exceptions are, in my opinion, few, and the evidence, exclusive of certificates, has been such as, in most cases, to satisfy me that the applicants were real Americans, who have been forced into the British service, and who, with singular constancy, have generally persevered in refusing pay or bounty, though in some instances they have been in service more than two years."

But the injuries of impressment are by no means confined to its immediate subjects, or the individuals on whom it is practised. Vessels suffer from the weakening of their crews, and voyages are often delayed, and not unfrequently broken up, by subtraction from the number of necessary hands by impressment. And what is of still greater and more general moment, the fear of impressment has been found to create great difficulty in obtaining sailors for the American merchant service in times of European war. Seafaring men, otherwise inclined to enter into that service, are, as experience has shown, deterred by the fear of finding themselves erelong in compulsory military service in British ships of war. Many instances have occurred, fully established by proof, in which raw seamen, natives of the United States, fresh from the fields of agriculture, entering for the first time on shipboard, have been impressed before they made the land, placed on the decks of British men-of-war, and compelled to serve for years before they could obtain their release, or revisit their country and their homes. Such instances become known, and their effect in discouraging young men from engaging in the merchant service of their country can neither be doubted nor wondered at. More than all, my Lord, the practice of impressment, whenever it has existed, has produced, not conciliation and good feeling, but resentment, exasperation, and animosity between the two great commercial countries of the world.

In the calm and quiet which have succeeded the late war, a condition so favorable for dispassionate consideration, England herself has evidently seen the harshness of impressment, even when exercised on seamen in her own merchant service, and she has adopted measures calculated, if not to renounce the power or to abolish the practice, yet at least to supersede its necessity by other means of manning the royal navy more compatible with justice and the rights of individuals, and far more conformable to the spirit and sentiments of the age.

Under these circumstances, the government of the United States has used the occasion of your Lordship's pacific mission to review this whole subject, and to bring it to your notice and that of your government. It has reflected on the past, pondered the condition of the present, and endeavored to anticipate, so far as might be in its power, the probable future; and I am now to communicate to your Lordship the result of these deliberations.

The American government, then, is prepared to say that the practice of impressing seamen from American vessels cannot hereafter be allowed to take place. That practice is founded on principles which it does not recognize, and is invariably attended by consequences so unjust, so injurious, and of such formidable magnitude, as cannot be submitted to.

In the early disputes between the two governments on this so long contested topic, the distinguished person to whose hands were first intrusted the seals of this department[1] declared, that "the simplest rule will be, that the vessel being American shall be evidence that the seamen on board are such."

Fifty years' experience, the utter failure of many negotiations, and a careful reconsideration, now had, of the whole subject, at a moment when the passions are laid, and no present interest or emergency exists to bias the judgment, have fully convinced this government that this is not only the simplest and best, but the only rule, which can be adopted and observed, consistently with the rights and honor of the United States and the security of their citizens. That rule announces, therefore, what will hereafter be the principle maintained by their government. In every regularly documented American merchant-vessel the crew who navigate it will find their protection in the flag which is over them.

This announcement is not made, my Lord, to revive useless recollections of the past, nor to stir the embers from fires which have been, in a great degree, smothered by many years of peace. Far otherwise. Its purpose is to extinguish those fires effectually, before new incidents arise to fan them into flame. The communication is in the spirit of peace, and for the sake of peace, and springs from a deep and conscientious conviction that high interests of both nations require this so long contested and controverted subject now to be finally put to rest. I persuade myself that you will do justice to this frank and sincere avowal of motives, and that you will communicate your sentiments in this respect to your government.

This letter closes, my Lord, on my part, our official correspondence; and I gladly use the occasion to offer you the assurance of my high and sincere regard.

DANIEL WEBSTER.

LORD ASHBURTON, &c., &c., &c.

Lord Ashburton to Mr. Webster_

Washington, August 9, 1842.

Sir,--The note you did me the honor of addressing me the 8th instant, on the subject of impressment, shall be transmitted without delay to my government, and will, you may be assured, receive from them the deliberate attention which its importance deserves.

The object of my mission was mainly the settlement of existing subjects of difference; and no differences have or could have arisen of late years with respect to impressment, because the practice has, since the peace, wholly ceased, and cannot, consistently with existing laws and regulations for manning her Majesty's navy, be, under the present circumstances, renewed.

Desirous, however, of looking far forward into futurity to anticipate even possible causes of disagreement, and sensible of the anxiety of the American people on this grave subject of past irritation, I should be sorry in any way to discourage the attempt at some settlement of it; and, although without authority to enter upon it here during the limited continuance of my mission, I entertain a confident hope that this task may be accomplished, when undertaken with the spirit of candor and conciliation which has marked all our late negotiations.

It not being our intention to endeavor now to come to any agreement on this subject, I may be permitted to abstain from noticing at length your very ingenious arguments relating to it, and from discussing the graver matters of constitutional and international law growing out of them. These sufficiently show that the question is one requiring calm consideration; though I must, at the same time, admit that they prove a strong necessity of some settlement for the preservation of that good understanding which, I trust, we may flatter ourselves that our joint labors have now succeeded in establishing.

I am well aware that the laws of our two countries maintain opposite principles respecting allegiance to the sovereign. America, receiving every year by thousands the emigrants of Europe, maintains the doctrine suitable to her condition, of the right of transferring allegiance at will. The laws of Great Britain have maintained from all time the opposite doctrine. The duties of allegiance are held to be indefeasible; and it is believed that this doctrine, under various modifications, prevails in most, if not in all, the civilized states of Europe.

Emigration, the modern mode by which the population of the world peaceably finds its level, is for the benefit of all, and eminently for the benefit of humanity. The fertile deserts of America are gradually advancing to the highest state of cultivation and production, while the emigrant acquires comfort which his own confined home could not afford him.

If there were any thing in our laws or our practice on either side tending to impede this march of providential humanity, we could not be too eager to provide a remedy; but as this does not appear to be the case, we may safely leave this part of the subject without indulging in abstract speculations having no material practical application to matters in discussion between us.

But it must be admitted that a serious practical question does arise, or, rather, has existed, from practices formerly attending the mode of manning the British navy in times of war. The principle is, that all subjects of the crown are, in case of necessity, bound to serve their country, and the seafaring man is naturally taken for the naval service. This is not, as is sometimes supposed, any arbitrary principle of monarchical government, but one founded on the natural duty of every man to defend the life of his country; and all the analogy of your laws would lead to the conclusion, that the same principle would hold good in the United States if their geographical position did not make its application unnecessary.

The very anomalous condition of the two countries with relation to each other here creates a serious difficulty. Our people are not distinguishable; and, owing to the peculiar habits of sailors, our vessels are very generally manned from a common stock. It is difficult, under these circumstances, to execute laws which at times have been thought to be essential for the existence of the country, without risk of injury to others. The extent and importance of those injuries, however, are so formidable, that it is admitted that some remedy should, if possible, be applied; at all events, it must be fairly and honestly attempted. It is true, that during the continuance of peace no practical grievance can arise; but it is also true, that it is for that reason the proper season for the calm and deliberate consideration of an important subject. I have much reason to hope that a satisfactory arrangement respecting it may be made, so as to set at rest all apprehension and anxiety; and I will only further repeat the assurance of the sincere disposition of my government favorably to consider all matters having for their object the promoting and maintaining undisturbed kind and friendly feelings with the United States.

I beg, Sir, on this occasion of closing the correspondence with you connected with my mission, to express the satisfaction I feel at its successful termination, and to assure you of my high consideration and personal esteem and regard.

ASHBURTON.

HON. DANIEL WEBSTER, &c., &c., &c.

[Footnote 1: Mr. Jefferson.]

THE RIGHT OF SEARCH.

Mr. Webster to Mr. Everett.

Department of State, Washington, March 28, 1843.

Sir,--I transmit to you with this despatch a message from the President of the United States to Congress, communicated on the 27th of February, and accompanied by a report made from this department to the President, of the substance of a despatch from Lord Aberdeen to Mr. Fox, which was by him read to me on the 24th ultimo.

Lord Aberdeen's despatch, as you will perceive, was occasioned by a passage in the President's message to Congress at the opening of its late session. The particular passage is not stated by his Lordship; but no mistake will be committed, it is presumed, in considering it to be that which was quoted by Sir Robert Peel and other gentlemen in the debate in the House of Commons, on the answer to the Queen's speech, on the 3d of February.

The President regrets that it should have become necessary to hold a diplomatic correspondence upon the subject of a communication from the head of the executive government to the legislature, drawing after it, as in this case, the further necessity of referring to observations made by persons in high and responsible stations, in debates of public bodies. Such a necessity, however, seems to be unavoidably incurred in consequence of Lord Aberdeen's despatch; for, although the President's recent message may be regarded as a clear exposition of his opinions on the subject, yet a just respect for her Majesty's government, and a disposition to meet all questions with promptness, as well as with frankness and candor, require that a formal answer should be made to that despatch.

The words in the message at the opening of the session which are complained of, it is supposed, are the following: "Although Lord Aberdeen, in his correspondence with the American envoys at London, expressly disclaimed all right to detain an American ship on the high seas, even if found with a cargo of slaves on board, and restricted the British pretension to a mere claim to visit and inquire, yet it could not well be discerned by the Executive of the United States how such visit and inquiry could be made without detention on the voyage, and consequent interruption to the trade. It was regarded as the right of search, presented only in a new form and expressed in different words; and I therefore felt it to be my duty distinctly to declare, in my annual message to Congress, that no such concession could be made, and that the United States had both the will and the ability to enforce their own laws, and to protect their flag from being used for purposes wholly forbidden by those laws, and obnoxious to the moral censure of the world."

This statement would tend, as Lord Aberdeen thinks, to convey the supposition, not only that the question of the right of search had been disavowed by the British plenipotentiary at Washington, but that Great Britain had made concessions on that point.

Lord Aberdeen is entirely correct in saying that the claim of a right of search was not discussed during the late negotiation, and that neither was any concession required by this government, nor made by that of her Britannic Majesty.

The eighth and ninth articles of the treaty of Washington constitute a mutual stipulation for concerted efforts to abolish the African slave-trade. The stipulation, it may be admitted, has no other effects on the pretensions of either party than this: Great Britain had claimed as a *right* that which this government could not admit to be a _right_, and, in the exercise of a just and proper spirit of amity, a mode was resorted to which might render unnecessary both the assertion and the denial of such claim.

There probably are those who think that what Lord Aberdeen calls a right of visit, and which he attempts to distinguish from the right of search, ought to have been expressly acknowledged by the government of the United States. At the same time, there are those on the other side who think that the formal surrender of such right of visit should have been demanded by the United States as a precedent condition to the negotiation for treaty stipulations on the subject of the African slave-trade. But the treaty neither asserts the claim in terms, nor denies the claim in terms; it neither formally insists upon it, nor formally renounces it. Still, the whole proceeding shows that the object of the stipulation was to avoid such differences and disputes as had already arisen, and the serious practical evils and inconveniences which, it cannot be denied, are always liable to result from the practice which Great Britain had asserted to be lawful. These evils and inconveniences had been acknowledged by both governments. They had been such as to cause much irritation, and to threaten to disturb the amicable sentiments which prevailed between them. Both governments were sincerely desirous of abolishing the slave-trade; both governments were equally desirous of avoiding occasion of complaint by their respective citizens and subjects; and both governments regarded the eighth and ninth articles as effectual for their avowed purpose, and likely, at the same time, to preserve all friendly relations, and to take away causes of future individual complaints. The treaty of Washington was intended to fulfil the obligations entered into by the treaty of Ghent. It stands by itself; is clear and intelligible. It speaks its own language, and manifests its own purpose. It needs no interpretation, and requires no comment. As a fact, as an important occurrence in national intercourse, it may have important bearings on existing questions respecting the public law; and individuals, or perhaps governments, may not agree as to what these bearings really are. Great Britain has discussions, if not controversies, with other great European states upon the subject of visit or search. These states will naturally make their own commentary on the treaty of Washington, and draw their own inferences from the fact that such a treaty has been entered into. Its stipulations, in the mean time, are plain, explicit, and satisfactory to both parties, and will be fulfilled on the part of the United States, and, it is not doubted, on the part of Great Britain also, with the utmost good faith.

Holding this to be the true character of the treaty, I might, perhaps, excuse myself from entering into the consideration of the grounds of that claim of a right to visit merchant-ships for certain purposes, in time of peace, which Lord Aberdeen asserts for the British government, and declares that it can never surrender. But I deem it right, nevertheless, and no more than justly respectful toward the British government, not to leave the point without remark.

In his recent message to Congress, the President, referring to the language of Lord Aberdeen in his note to Mr. Everett of the 20th of December, 1841, and in his late despatch to Mr. Fox, says: "These declarations may well lead us to doubt whether the apparent difference between the two governments is not rather one of definition than of principle."

Lord Aberdeen, in his note to you of the 20th of December, says: "The undersigned again renounces, as he has already done in the most explicit terms, any right on the part of the British government to search American vessels in time of peace. The right of search, except when specially conceded by treaty, is a pure belligerent right, and can have no existence on the high seas during peace. The undersigned apprehends, however, that the right of search is not confined to the verification of the nationality of the vessel, but also extends to the object of the voyage and the nature of the cargo. The sole purpose of the British cruisers is to ascertain whether the vessels they meet with are really American or not. The right asserted has, in truth, no resemblance to the right of search, either in principle or practice. It is simply a right to satisfy the party who has a legitimate interest in knowing the truth, that the vessel actually is what her colors announce. This right we concede as freely as we exercise. The British cruisers are not instructed to detain American vessels under any circumstances whatever; on the contrary, they are ordered to abstain from all interference with them, be they slavers or otherwise. But where reasonable suspicion exists that the American flag has been abused for the purpose of covering the vessel of another nation, it would appear scarcely credible, had it not been made manifest by the repeated protestations of their representative, that the government of the United States, which has stigmatized and abolished the trade itself, should object to the adoption of such means as are indispensably necessary for ascertaining the truth."

And in his recent despatch to Mr. Fox his Lordship further says: "That the President might be assured that Great Britain would always respect the just claims of the United States. That the British government made no pretension to interfere in any manner whatever, either by detention, visit, or search, with vessels of the United States, known or believed to be such, but that it still maintained, and would exercise when necessary, its own right to ascertain the genuineness of any flag which a suspected vessel might bear; that if, in the exercise of this right, either from involuntary error, or in spite of every precaution, loss or injury should be sustained, a prompt reparation would be afforded; but that it should entertain, for a single instant, the notion of abandoning the right itself, would be quite impossible."

This, then, is the British claim, as asserted by her Majesty's government.

In his remarks in the speech already referred to, in the House of Commons, the first minister of the crown said: "There is nothing more distinct than the right of visit is from the right of search. Search is a belligerent right, and not to be exercised in time of peace, except when it has been conceded by treaty. The right of search extends not only to the vessel, but to the cargo also. The right of visit is quite distinct from this, though the two are often unfounded. The right of search, with respect to American vessels, we entirely and utterly disclaim; nay, more, if we knew that an American vessel were furnished with all the materials requisite for the slave-trade, if we knew that the decks were prepared to receive hundreds of human beings within a space in which life is almost impossible, still we should be bound to let that American vessel pass on. But the right we claim is to know whether a vessel pretending to be American, and hoisting the American flag, be *bona fide* American."

The President's message is regarded as holding opinions in opposition to these.

The British government, then, supposes that the right of visit and the right of search are essentially distinct in their nature, and that this difference is well known and generally acknowledged; that the difference between them consists in their different objects and purposes: one, the visit, having for its object nothing but to ascertain the nationality of the vessel; the other, the search, by an inquisition, not only into the nationality of the vessel, but the nature and object of her voyage, and the true ownership of her cargo.

The government of the United States, on the other hand, maintains that there is no such well-known and acknowledged, nor, indeed, any broad and generic difference between what has been usually called visit, and what has been usually called search; that the right of visit, to be effectual, must come, in the end, to include search; and thus to exercise, in peace, an authority which the law of nations only allows in times of war. If such well-known distinction exists, where are the proofs of it? What writers of authority on public law, what adjudications in courts of admiralty, what public treaties, recognize it? No such recognition has presented itself to the government of the United States; but, on the contrary, it understands that public writers, courts of law, and solemn treaties have, for two centuries, used the words "visit" and "search" in the same sense. What Great Britain and the United States mean by the "right of search," in its broadest sense, is called by Continental writers and jurists by no other name than the "right of visit." Visit, therefore, as it has been understood, implies not only a right to inquire into the national character, but to detain the vessel, to stop the progress of the voyage, to examine papers, to decide on their regularity and authenticity, and to make inquisition on board for enemy's property, and into the business which the vessel is engaged in. In other words, it describes the entire right of belligerent visitation and search. Such a right is justly disclaimed by the British government in time of peace. They, nevertheless, insist on a right which they denominate a right of visit, and by that word describe the claim which they assert. It is proper, and due to the importance and delicacy of the questions involved, to take care that, in discussing them, both governments understand the terms which may be used in the same sense. If, indeed, it should be manifest that the difference between the parties is only verbal, it might be hoped that no harm would be done; but the government of the United States thinks itself not justly chargeable with excessive jealousy, or with too great scrupulosity in the use of words, in insisting on its opinion that there is no such distinction as the British government maintains between visit and search; and that there is no right to visit in time of peace, except in the execution of revenue laws or other municipal regulations, in which cases the right is usually exercised near the coast, or within the marine league, or where the vessel is justly suspected of violating the law of nations by piratical aggression; but, wherever exercised, it is a right of search.

Nor can the United States government agree that the term "right" is justly applied to such exercise of power as the British government thinks it indispensable to maintain in certain cases. The right asserted is a right to ascertain whether a merchant-vessel is justly entitled to the protection of the flag which she may happen to have hoisted, such vessel being in circumstances which render her liable to the suspicion, first, that she is not entitled to the protection of the flag; and secondly, that, if not entitled to it, she is, either by the law of England, as an English vessel, or under the provisions of treaties with certain European powers, subject to the supervision and search of British cruisers. And yet Lord Aberdeen says, "that if, in the exercise of this right, either from involuntary error, or in spite of every precaution, loss or injury should be sustained, a prompt reparation would be afforded."

It is not easy to perceive how these consequences can be admitted justly to flow from the fair exercise of a clear right. If injury be produced by the exercise of a right, it would seem strange that it should be repaired, as if it had been the effect of a wrongful act. The general rule of law certainly is, that, in the proper and prudent exercise of his own right, no one is answerable for undesigned injuries. It may be said that the right is a qualified right; that it is a right to do certain acts of force at the risk of turning out to be wrong-doers, and of being made answerable for all damages. But such an argument would prove every trespass to be matter of right, subject only to just responsibility. If force were allowed to such reasoning in other cases, it would follow that an individual's right in his own property was hardly more than a well-founded claim for compensation if he should be deprived of it. But compensation is that which is rendered for injury, and is not commutation, or forced equivalent, for acknowledged rights. It implies, at least in its general interpretation the commission of some wrongful act.

But, without pressing further these inquiries into the accuracy and propriety of definitions and the use of words, I proceed to draw your attention to the thing itself, and to consider what these acts are which the British government insists its cruisers have a right to perform, and to what consequences they naturally and necessarily tend. An eminent member of the House of Commons[1] thus states the British claim, and his statement is acquiesced in and adopted by the first minister of the crown:--

"The claim of this country is for the right of our cruisers to ascertain whether a merchant-vessel is justly entitled to the protection of the flag which she may happen to have hoisted, such vessel being in circumstances which rendered her liable to the suspicion, first, that she was not entitled to the protection of the flag; and, secondly, if not entitled to it, she was, either under the law of nations or the provisions of treaties, subject to the supervision and control of our cruisers."

Now the question is, *By what means* is this ascertainment to be effected?

As we understand the general and settled rules of public law, in respect to ships of war sailing under the authority of their government, "to arrest pirates and other public offenders," there is no reason why they may not approach any vessels descried at sea for the purpose of ascertaining their real characters. Such a right of approach seems indispensable for the fair and discreet exercise of their authority; and the use of it cannot he justly deemed indicative of any design to insult or injure those they approach, or to impede them in their lawful commerce. On the other hand, it is as clear that no ship is, under such circumstances, bound to lie by or wait the approach of any other ship. She is at full liberty to pursue her voyage in her own way, and to use all necessary precautions to avoid any suspected sinister enterprise or hostile attack. Her right to the free use of the ocean is as perfect as that of any other ship. An entire equality is presumed to exist. She has a right to consult her own safety, but at the same time she must take care not to violate the rights of others. She may use any precautions dictated by the prudence or fears of her officers, either as to delay, or the progress or course of her voyage; but she is not at liberty to inflict injuries upon other innocent parties simply because of conjectural dangers.

But if the vessel thus approached attempts to avoid the vessel approaching, or does not comply with her commander's order to send him her papers for his inspection, nor consent to be visited or detained, what is next to be done? Is force to be used? And if force be used, may that force be lawfully repelled? These questions lead at once to the elemental principle, the essence of the British claim. Suppose the merchant-vessel be in truth an American vessel engaged in lawful commerce, and that she does not choose to be detained. Suppose she resists the visit. What is the consequence? In all cases in which the belligerent right of visit exists, resistance to the exercise of that right is regarded as just cause of condemnation, both of vessel and cargo. Is that penalty, or what other penalty, to be incurred by resistance to visit in time of peace? Or suppose that force be met by force, gun returned for gun, and the commander of the cruiser, or some of his seamen be killed; what description of offence will have been committed? It would be said, in behalf of the commander of the cruiser, that he mistook the vessel for a vessel of England, Brazil, or Portugal; but does this mistake of his take away from the American vessel the right of self-defence? The writers of authority declare it to be a principle of natural law, that the privilege of self-defence exists against an assailant who mistakes the object of his attack for another whom he had a right to assail.

Lord Aberdeen cannot fail to see, therefore, what serious consequences might ensue, if it were to be admitted that this claim to visit, in time of peace, however limited or defined, should be permitted to exist as a strict matter of right; for if it exist as a right, it must be followed by corresponding duties and obligations, and the failure to fulfil those duties would naturally draw penal consequences after it, till erelong it would become, in truth, little less, or little other, than the belligerent right of search.

If visit or visitation be not accompanied by search, it will be in most cases merely idle. A sight of papers may be demanded, and papers may be produced. But it is known that slave-traders carry false papers, and different sets of papers. A search for other papers, then, must be made where suspicion justifies it, or else the whole proceeding would be nugatory. In suspicious cases, the language and general appearance of the crew are among the means of ascertaining the national character of the vessel. The cargo on board, also, often indicates the country from which she comes. Her log-books, showing the previous course and events of her voyage, her internal fitting up and equipment, are all evidences for her, or against her, on her allegation of character. These matters, it is obvious, can only be ascertained by rigorous search.

It may be asked, If a vessel may not be called on to show her papers, why does she carry papers? No doubt she may be called on to show her papers; but the question is, Where, when, and by whom? Not in time of peace, on the high seas, where her rights are equal to the rights of any other vessel, and where none has a right to molest her. The use of her papers is, in time of war, to prove her neutrality when visited by belligerent cruisers; and in both peace and war, to show her national character, and the lawfulness of her voyage, in those ports of other countries to which she may proceed for purposes of trade.

It appears to the government of the United States, that the view of this whole subject which is the most naturally taken is also the most legal, and most in analogy with other cases. British cruisers have a right to detain British merchantmen for certain purposes; and they have a right, acquired by treaty, to detain merchant-vessels of several other nations for the same purposes. But they have no right at all to detain an American merchant-vessel. This Lord Aberdeen admits in the fullest manner. Any detention of an American vessel by a British cruiser is therefore a wrong, a trespass; although it may be done under the belief that she was a British vessel, or that she belonged to a nation which had conceded the right of such detention to the British cruisers, and the trespass therefore an involuntary trespass. If a ship of war, in thick weather, or in the darkness of the night, fire upon and sink a neutral vessel, under the belief that she is an enemy's vessel, this is a trespass, a mere wrong; and cannot be said to be an act done under any right, accompanied by responsibility for damages. So if a civil officer on land have process against one individual, and through mistake arrest another, this arrest is wholly tortious; no one would think of saying that it was done under any lawful exercise of authority, subject only to responsibility, or that it was any thing but a mere trespass, though an unintentional trespass. The municipal law does not undertake to lay down beforehand any rule for the government of such cases; and as little, in the opinion of the government of the United States, does the public law of the world lay down beforehand any rule for the government of cases of involuntary trespasses, detentions, and injuries at sea; except that in both classes of cases law and reason make a distinction between injuries committed through mistake and injuries committed by design, the former being entitled to fair and just compensation, the latter demanding exemplary damages, and sometimes personal punishment. The government of the United States has frequently made known its opinion, which it now repeats, that the practice of detaining American vessels, though subject to just compensation if such detention afterward turn out to have been without good cause, however guarded by instructions, or however cautiously exercised, necessarily leads to serious inconvenience and injury. The amount of loss cannot be always well ascertained. Compensation, if it be adequate in the amount, may still necessarily be long delayed; and the pendency of such claims always proves troublesome to the governments of both countries. These detentions, too, frequently irritate individuals, cause warm blood, and produce nothing but ill effects on the amicable relations existing between the countries. We wish, therefore, to put an end to them, and to avoid all occasions for their recurrence.

On the whole, the government of the United States, while it has not conceded a mutual right of visit or search, as has been done by the parties to the quintuple treaty of December, 1841, does not admit that, by the law and practice of nations, there is any such thing as a right of visit, distinguished by well-known rules and definitions from the right of search.

It does not admit that visit of American merchant-vessels by British cruisers is founded on any right, notwithstanding the cruiser may suppose such vessel to be British, Brazilian, or Portuguese. We cannot but see that the detention and examination of American vessels by British cruisers has already led to consequences, and fear that, if continued, it would still lead to further consequences, highly injurious to the lawful commerce of the United States.

At the same time, the government of the United States fully admits that its flag can give no immunity to pirates, nor to any other than to regularly documented American vessels. It was upon this view of the whole case, and with a firm conviction of the truth of these sentiments, that it cheerfully assumed the duties contained in the treaty of Washington; in the hope that thereby causes of difficulty and difference might be altogether removed, and that the two powers might be enabled to act concurrently, cordially, and effectually for the suppression of a traffic which both regard as a reproach upon the civilization of the age, and at war with every principle of humanity and every Christian sentiment.

The government of the United States has no interest, nor is it under the influence of any opinions, which should lead it to desire any derogation of the just authority and rights of maritime power. But in the convictions which it entertains, and in the measures which it has adopted, it has been governed solely by a sincere desire to support those principles and those practices which it believes to be conformable to public law, and favorable to the peace and harmony of nations.

Both houses of Congress, with a remarkable degree of unanimity, have made express provisions for carrying into effect the eighth article of the treaty. An American squadron will immediately proceed to the coast of Africa. Instructions for its commander are in the course of preparation, and copies will be furnished to the British government; and the President confidently believes, that the cordial concurrence of the two governments in the mode agreed on will be more effectual than any efforts yet made for the suppression of the slave-trade.

You will read this despatch to Lord Aberdeen, and, if he desire it, give him a copy.

I am, Sir, &c., &c.

DANIEL WEBSTER.

EDWARD EVERETT, ESQ., &c., &c., &c.

[Footnote 1: Mr. Wood, now Sir Charles Wood, Chancellor of the Exchequer.]

LETTERS TO GENERAL CASS ON THE TREATY OF WASHINGTON.

Mr. Webster to General Cass.

Department of State, Washington, August 29, 1842.

Sir,--You will see by the enclosed the result of the negotiations lately had in this city between this department and Lord Ashburton. The treaty has been ratified by the President and Senate.

In communicating to you this treaty, I am directed by the President to draw your particular attention to those articles which relate to the suppression of the African slave-trade.

After full and anxious consideration of this very delicate subject, the government of the United States has come to the conclusion which you will see expressed in the President's message to the Senate accompanying the treaty.

Without intending or desiring to influence the policy of other governments on this important subject, this government has reflected on what was due to its own character and position, as the leading maritime power on the American continent, left free to make choice of such means for the fulfilment of its duties as it should deem best suited to its dignity. The result of its reflections has been, that it does not concur in measures which, for whatever benevolent purpose they may be adopted, or with whatever care and moderation they may be exercised, have yet a tendency to place the police of the seas in the hands of a single power. It chooses rather to follow its own laws with its own sanction, and to carry them into execution by its own authority. Disposed to act in the spirit of the most cordial concurrence with other nations for the suppression of the African slave-trade, that great reproach of our times, it deems it to be right, nevertheless, that this action, though concurrent, should be independent, and it believes that from this independence it will derive a greater degree of efficiency.

You will perceive, however, that, in the opinion of this government, cruising against slave-dealers on the coast of Africa is not all which is necessary to be done in order to put an end to the traffic. There are markets for slaves, or the unhappy natives of Africa would not be seized, chained, and carried over the ocean into slavery. These markets ought to be shut. And, in the treaty now communicated to you, the high contracting parties have stipulated "that they will unite, in all becoming representations and remonstrances, with any and all powers within whose dominions such markets are allowed to exist; and that they will urge upon all such powers the propriety and duty of closing such markets effectually, at once and for ever."

You are furnished, then, with the American policy in regard to this interesting subject. First, independent but cordially concurrent efforts of maritime states to suppress, as far as possible, the trade on the coast, by means of competent and well-appointed squadrons, to watch the shores and scour the neighboring seas. Secondly, concurrent, becoming remonstrance with all governments who tolerate within their territories markets for the purchase of African negroes. There is much reason to believe that, if other states, professing equal hostility to this nefarious traffic, would give their own powerful concurrence and co-operation to these remonstrances, the general effect would be satisfactory, and that the cupidity and crimes of individuals would at length cease to find both their temptation and their reward in the bosom of Christian states, and in the permission of Christian governments.

It will still remain for each government to revise, execute, and make more effectual its own municipal laws against its subjects or citizens who shall be concerned in, or in any way give aid or countenance to others concerned in this traffic.

You are at liberty to make the contents of this despatch known to the French government.

I have, &c.

DANIEL WEBSTER.

LEWIS CASS, ESQ., &c., &c., &c.

Mr. F. Webster to General Cass.

Department of State, Washington, October 11, 1842.

Sir,--I have to acknowledge the receipt of your despatch of the 17th of September last, requesting permission to return home.

I have submitted the despatch to the President, and am by him directed to say, that although he much regrets that your own wishes should, at this time, terminate your mission to the court of France, where for a long period you have rendered your country distinguished service, in all instances to its honor and to the satisfaction of the government, and where you occupy so favorable a position, from the more than ordinary good intelligence which is understood to subsist between you, personally, and the members of the French government, and from the esteem entertained for you by its illustrious head; yet he cannot refuse your request to return once more to your home and your country, so that you can pay that attention to your personal and private affairs which your long absence and constant employment in the service of your government may now render most necessary.

I have, Sir, to tender you, on behalf of the President, his most cordial good wishes, and am, &c.
FLETCHER WEBSTER, *Acting Secretary of State*.
LEWIS CASS, ESQ., &c., &c., &c.

Mr. Webster to General Cass.
Department of State, Washington, November 14, 1842.
Sir,--I have the honor to acknowledge the receipt of your despatch of the 3d of October, brought by the "Great Western," which arrived at New York on the 6th instant.

It is probable you will have embarked for the United States before my communication can now reach you; but as it is thought proper that your letter should be answered, and as circumstances may possibly have occurred to delay your departure, this will be transmitted to Paris in the ordinary way.

Your letter has caused the President considerable concern. Entertaining a lively sense of the respectable and useful manner in which you have discharged, for several years, the duties of an important foreign mission, it occasions him real regret and pain, that your last official communication should be of such a character as that he cannot give to it his entire and cordial approbation.

It appears to be intended as a sort of protest, a remonstrance, in the form of an official despatch, against a transaction of the government to which you were not a party, in which you had no agency whatever, and for the results of which you were no way answerable. This would seem an unusual and extraordinary proceeding. In common with every other citizen of the republic, you have an unquestionable right to form opinions upon public transactions, and the conduct of public men; but it will hardly be thought to be among either the duties or the privileges of a minister abroad to make formal remonstrances and protests against proceedings of the various branches of the government at home, upon subjects in relation to which he himself has not been charged with any duty or partaken any responsibility.

The negotiation and conclusion of the treaty of Washington were in the hands of the President and Senate. They had acted upon this important subject according to their convictions of duty and of the public interest, and had ratified the treaty. It was a thing done; and although your opinion might be at variance with that of the President and Senate, it is not perceived that you had any cause of complaint, remonstrance, or protest, more than any other citizen who might entertain the same opinion.

In your letter of the 17th of September, requesting your recall, you observe: "The mail by the steam-packet which left Boston the 1st instant has just arrived, and has brought intelligence of the ratification of the treaties recently concluded with Great Britain. All apprehensions, therefore, of any immediate difficulties with that country are at an end, and I do not see that any public interest demands my further residence in Europe. I can no longer be useful here, and the state of my private affairs requires my presence at home. Under these circumstances, I beg you to submit to the President my wish for permission to retire from this mission, and to return to the United States without delay."

As you appeared at that time not to be acquainted with the provisions of the treaty, it was inferred that your desire to return home proceeded from the conviction _that, inasmuch as all apprehensions of immediate differences with Great Britain were at an end_, you would no longer be useful at Paris. Placing this interpretation on your letter, and believing, as you yourself allege, that your long absence abroad rendered it desirable for you to give some attention to your private affairs in this country, the President lost no time in yielding to your request, and, in doing so, signified to you the sentiments of approbation which he entertained for your conduct abroad. You may, then, well imagine the great astonishment which the declaration contained in your despatch of the 3d of October, that you could no longer remain in France honorably to yourself or advantageously to the country, and that the proceedings of this government had placed you in a false position, from which you could escape only by returning home, created in his mind. The President perceives not the slightest foundation for these opinions. He cannot see how your usefulness as minister to France should be terminated by the settlement of difficulties and disputes between the United States and Great Britain. You have been charged with no duties connected with the settlement of these questions, or in any way relating to them, beyond the communication to the French government of the President's approbation of your letter of the 13th of February, written without previous instructions from this department. This government is not informed of any other act or proceeding of yours connected with any part of the subject, nor does it know that your official conduct and character have become in any other way connected with the question of the right of search; and that letter having been approved, and the French government having been so informed, the President is altogether at a loss to understand how you can regard yourself as placed in a false position. If the character or conduct of any one was to be affected, it could only be the character and conduct of the President himself. The government has done nothing, most assuredly, to place you in a false position. Representing your country at a foreign court, you saw a transaction about to take place between the government to which you were accredited and another power, which you thought might have a prejudicial effect on the interest of your own country. Thinking, as it is to be presumed, that the case was too pressing to wait for instructions, you presented a protest against that transaction, and our government approved your proceeding. This is your only official connection with the whole subject. If after this the President had sanctioned the negotiation of a treaty, and the Senate had ratified it, containing provisions in the highest degree objectionable, however the government might be discredited, your exemption from all blame and censure would have been complete. Having delivered your letter of the 13th of February to the French government, and having received the President's approbation of that proceeding, it is most manifest that you could be in no degree responsible for what should be done afterward, and done by others. The President, therefore, cannot conceive what particular or personal interest of yours was affected by the subsequent negotiation here, or how the treaty, the result of that negotiation, should put an end to your usefulness as a public minister at the court of France, or in any way affect your official character or conduct.

It is impossible not to see that such a proceeding as you have seen fit to adopt might produce much inconvenience, and even serious prejudice, to the public interests. Your opinion is against the treaty, a treaty concluded and formally ratified; and, to support that opinion, while yet in the service of the government, you put a construction on its provisions such as your own government does not put upon them, such as you must be aware the enlightened public of Europe does not put upon them, and such as England herself has not put upon them as yet, so far as we know.

It may become necessary hereafter to publish your letter, in connection with other correspondence of the mission; and although it is not to be presumed that you looked to such publication, because such a presumption would impute to you a claim to put forth your private opinions upon the conduct of the President and Senate, in a transaction finished and concluded, through the imposing form of a public despatch, yet, if published, it cannot be foreseen how far England might hereafter rely on your authority for a construction favorable to her own pretensions, and inconsistent with the interest and honor of the United States. It is certain that you would most sedulously desire to avoid any such attitude. You would be slow to express opinions, in a solemn and official form, favorable to another government, and on the authority of which opinions that other government might hereafter found new claims or set up new pretensions. It is for this reason, as well as others, that the President feels so much regret at your desire of placing your construction of the provisions of the treaty, and your objections to those provisions, according to your construction, upon the records of the government.

Before examining the several objections suggested by you, it may be proper to take notice of what you say upon the course of the negotiation. In regard to this, having observed that the national dignity of the United States had not been compromised down to the time of the President's message to the last session of Congress, you proceed to say: "But England then urged the United States to enter into a conventional arrangement, by which we might be pledged to concur with her in measures for the suppression of the slave-trade. Till then we had executed our own laws in our own way. But, yielding to this application, and departing from our former principle of avoiding European combinations upon subjects not American, we stipulated in a solemn treaty, that we would carry into effect our own laws, and fixed the minimum force we would employ for that purpose."

The President cannot conceive how you should have been led to adventure upon such a statement as this. It is but a tissue of mistakes. England did not urge the United States to enter into this conventional arrangement. The United States yielded to no application from England. The proposition for abolishing the slave-trade, as it stands in the treaty, was an American proposition; it originated with the executive government of the United States, which cheerfully assumes all its responsibility. It stands upon it as its own mode of fulfilling its duties, and accomplishing its objects. Nor have the United States departed, in this treaty, in the slightest degree, from their former principles of avoiding European combinations upon subjects not American, because the abolition of the African slave-trade is an American subject as emphatically as it is a European subject; and indeed more so, inasmuch as the government of the United States took the first great steps in declaring that trade unlawful, and in attempting its extinction. The abolition of this traffic is an object of the highest interest to the American people and the American government; and you seem strangely to have overlooked altogether the important fact, that nearly thirty years ago, by the treaty of Ghent, the United States bound themselves by solemn compact with England, to continue "their efforts to promote its entire abolition," both parties pledging themselves by that treaty to use their best endeavors to accomplish so desirable an object.

Again, you speak of an important concession made to the renewed application of England. But the treaty, let it be repeated, makes no concession to England whatever. It complies with no demand, grants no application, conforms to no request. All these statements, thus by you made, and which are so exceedingly erroneous, seem calculated to hold up the idea, that in this treaty your government has been acting a subordinate, or even a complying part.

The President is not a little startled that you should make such totally groundless assumptions of fact, and then leave a discreditable inference to be drawn from them. He directs me not only to repel this inference as it ought to be repelled, but also to bring to your serious consideration and reflection the propriety of such an assumed narration of facts as your despatch, in this respect, puts forth.

Having informed the department that a copy of the letter of the 24th of August, addressed by me to you, had been delivered to M. Guizot, you proceed to say: "In executing this duty, I felt too well what was due to my government and country to intimate my regret to a foreign power that some declaration had not preceded the treaty, or some stipulation accompanied it, by which the extraordinary pretension of Great Britain to search our ships at all times and in all places, first put forth to the world by Lord Palmerston on the 27th of August, 1841, and on the 13th of October following again peremptorily claimed as a right by Lord Aberdeen, would have been abrogated, as equally incompatible with the laws of nations and with the independence of the United States. I confined myself, therefore, to a simple communication of your letter."

It may be true that the British pretension leads necessarily to consequences as broad and general as your statement. But it is no more than fair to state that pretension in the words of the British government itself, and then it becomes matter of consideration and argument how broad and extensive it really is. The last statement of this pretension, or claim, by the British government, is contained in Lord Aberdeen's note to Mr. Stevenson of the 13th of October, 1841. It is in these words:--

"The undersigned readily admits, that to visit and search American vessels in time of peace, when that right of search is not granted by treaty, would be an infraction of public law, and a violation of national dignity and independence. But no such right is asserted. We sincerely desire to respect the vessels of the United States, but we may reasonably expect to know what it really is that we respect. Doubtless the flag is *prima facie* evidence of the nationality of the vessel; and, if this evidence were in its nature conclusive and irrefragable, it ought to preclude all further inquiry. But it is sufficiently notorious that the flags of all nations are liable to be assumed by those who have no right or title to bear them. Mr. Stevenson himself fully admits the extent to which the American flag has been employed for the purpose of covering this infamous traffic. The undersigned joins with Mr. Stevenson in deeply lamenting the evil; and he agrees with him in thinking that the United States ought not to be considered responsible for this abuse of their flag. But if all inquiry be resisted, even when carried no further than to ascertain the nationality of the vessel, and impunity be claimed for the most lawless and desperate of mankind, in the commission of this fraud, the undersigned greatly fears that it may be regarded as something like an assumption of that responsibility which has been deprecated by Mr. Stevenson....

"The undersigned renounces all pretension on the part of the British government to visit and search American vessels in time of peace. Nor is it as American that such vessels are ever visited; but, it has been the invariable practice of the British navy, and, as the undersigned believes, of all navies in the world, to ascertain by visit the real nationality of merchant-vessels met with on the high seas, if there be good reason to apprehend their illegal character....

"The undersigned admits, that, if the British cruiser should possess a knowledge of the American character of any vessel, his visitation of such vessel would be entirely unjustifiable. He further admits, that so much respect and honor are due to the American flag, that no vessel bearing it ought to be visited by a British cruiser, except under the most grave suspicions and well-founded doubts of the genuineness of its character.

"The undersigned, although with pain, must add, that if such visit should lead to the proof of the American origin of the vessel, and that she was avowedly engaged in the slave-trade, exhibiting to view the manacles, fetters, and other usual implements of torture, or had even a number of these unfortunate beings on board, no British officer could interfere further. He might give information to the cruisers of the United

States, but it could not be in his own power to arrest or impede the prosecution of the voyage and the success of the undertaking.

"It is obvious, therefore, that the utmost caution is necessary in the exercise of this right claimed by Great Britain. While we have recourse to the necessary, and, indeed, the only means for detecting imposture, the practice will be carefully guarded and limited to cases of strong suspicion. The undersigned begs to assure Mr. Stevenson that the most precise and positive instructions have been issued to her Majesty's officers on this subject."

Such are the words of the British claim or pretension; and it stood in this form at the delivery of the President's message to Congress in December last; a message in which you are pleased to say that the British pretension was promptly met and firmly resisted.

I may now proceed to a more particular examination of the objections which you make to the treaty.

You observe that you think a just self-respect required of the government of the United States to demand of Lord Ashburton a distinct renunciation of the British claim to search our vessels previous to entering into any negotiation. The government has thought otherwise; and this appears to be your main objection to the treaty, if, indeed, it be not the only one which is clearly and distinctly stated. The government of the United States supposed that, in this respect, it stood in a position in which it had no occasion to demand any thing, or ask for any thing, of England. The British pretension, whatever it was, or however extensive, was well known to the President at the date of his message to Congress at the opening of the last session. And I must be allowed to remind you how the President treated this subject in that communication.

"However desirous the United States may be," said he, "for the suppression of the slave-trade, they cannot consent to interpolations into the maritime code at the mere will and pleasure of other governments. We deny the right of any such interpolation to any one, or all the nations of the earth, without our consent. We claim to have a voice in all amendments or alterations of that code; and when we are given to understand, as in this instance, by a foreign government, that its treaties with other nations cannot be executed without the establishment and enforcement of new principles of maritime police, to be applied without our consent, we must employ a language neither of equivocal import nor susceptible of misconstruction. American citizens prosecuting a lawful commerce in the African seas, under the flag of their country, are not responsible for the abuse or unlawful use of that flag by others; nor can they rightfully, on account of any such alleged abuses, be interrupted, molested, or detained while on the ocean; and if thus molested and detained while pursuing honest voyages in the usual way, and violating no law themselves, they are unquestionably entitled to indemnity."

This declaration of the President stands: not a syllable of it has been, or will be, retracted. The principles which it announces rest on their inherent justice and propriety, on their conformity to public law, and, so far as we are concerned, on the determination and ability of the country to maintain them. To these principles the government is pledged, and that pledge it will be at all times ready to redeem.

But what is your own language on this point? You say, "This claim (the British claim), thus asserted and supported, was promptly met and firmly repelled by the President in his message at the commencement of the last session of Congress; and in your letter to me approving the course I had adopted in relation to the question of the ratification by France of the quintuple treaty, you consider the principles of that message as the established policy of the government." And you add, "So far, our national dignity was uncompromitted." If this be so, what is there which has since occurred to compromit this dignity? You shall yourself be judge of this; because you say, in a subsequent part of your letter, that "the mutual rights of the parties are in this respect wholly untouched." If, then, the British pretension had been promptly met and firmly repelled by the President's message; if, so far, our national dignity had not been compromitted; and if, as you further say, our rights remain wholly untouched by any subsequent act or proceeding, what ground is there on which to found complaint against the treaty?

But your sentiments on this point do not concur with the opinions of your government. That government is of opinion that the sentiments of the message, which you so highly approve, are reaffirmed and corroborated by the treaty, and the correspondence accompanying it. The very object sought to be obtained, in proposing the mode adopted for abolishing the slave-trade, was to take away all pretence whatever for interrupting lawful commerce by the visitation of American vessels. Allow me to refer you, on this point, to the following passage in the message of the President to the Senate, accompanying the treaty:--

"In my message at the commencement of the present session of Congress, I endeavored to state the principles which this government supports respecting the right of search and the immunity of flags. Desirous of maintaining those principles fully, at the same time that existing obligations should be fulfilled, I have thought it most consistent with the dignity and honor of the country that it should execute its own laws and perform its own obligations by its own means and its own power. The examination or visitation of the merchant-vessels of one nation by the cruisers of another, for any purposes except those known and acknowledged by the law of nations, under whatever restraints or regulations it may take place, may lead to dangerous results. It is far better by other means to supersede any supposed necessity, or any motive, for such examination or visit. Interference with a merchant-vessel by an armed cruiser is always a delicate proceeding, apt to touch the point of national honor, as well as to affect the interests of individuals. It has been thought, therefore, expedient, not only in accordance with the stipulations of the treaty of Ghent, but at the same time as removing all pretext on the part of others for violating the immunities of the American flag upon the seas, as they exist and are defined by the law of nations, to enter into the articles now submitted to the Senate.

"The treaty which I now submit to you proposes no alteration, mitigation, or modification of the rules of the law of nations. It provides simply, that each of the two governments shall maintain on the coast of Africa a sufficient squadron to enforce, separately and respectively, the laws, rights, and obligations of the two countries for the suppression of the slave-trade."

In the actual posture of things, the President thought that the government of the United States, standing on its own rights and its own solemn declarations, would only weaken its position by making such a demand as appears to you to have been expedient. We maintain the public law of the world as we receive it and understand it to be established. We defend our own rights and our own honor, meeting all aggression at the boundary. Here we may well stop.

You are pleased to observe, that "under the circumstances of the assertion of the British claim, in the correspondence of the British secretaries, and of its denial by the President of the United States, the eyes of Europe were upon these two great naval powers; one of which had advanced a pretension, and avowed her determination to enforce it, which might at any moment bring them into collision."

It is certainly true that the attention of Europe has been very much awakened, of late years, to the general subject, and quite alive, also, to whatever might take place in regard to it between the United States and Great Britain. And it is highly satisfactory to find, that, so far as we can learn, the opinion is universal that the government of the United States has fully sustained its rights and its dignity by the treaty which has been concluded. Europe, we believe, is happy to see that a collision, which might have disturbed the peace of the whole civilized world, has been avoided in a manner which reconciles the performance of a high national duty, and the fulfilment of positive stipulations, with the perfect immunity of flags and the equality of nations upon the ocean. I must be permitted to add, that, from every agent of the government abroad who has been heard from on the subject, with the single exception of your own letter, (an exception most deeply regretted,) as well as from every part of Europe where maritime rights have advocates and defenders, we have received nothing but congratulation. And at this moment, if the general sources of information may be trusted, our example has recommended itself already to the regard of states the most jealous of British ascendency at sea; and the treaty against which you remonstrate may soon come to be esteemed by them as a fit model for imitation.

Toward the close of your despatch, you are pleased to say: "By the recent treaty we are to keep a squadron upon the coast of Africa. We have kept one there for years; during the whole term, indeed, of these efforts to put a stop to this most iniquitous commerce. The effect of the treaty is, therefore, to render it obligatory upon us by a convention, to do what we have long done voluntarily; to place our municipal laws, in some measure, beyond the reach of Congress." Should the effect of the treaty be to place our municipal laws, in some measure, beyond the reach of Congress, it is sufficient to say that all treaties containing obligations necessarily do this. All treaties of commerce do it; and, indeed, there is hardly a treaty existing, to which the United States are party, which does not, to some extent, or in some way, restrain the legislative power. Treaties could not be made without producing this effect.

But your remark would seem to imply that, in your judgment, there is something derogatory to the character and dignity of the country in thus stipulating with a foreign power for a concurrent effort to execute the laws of each. It would be a sufficient refutation of this objection to say, that, if in this arrangement there be any thing derogatory to the character and dignity of one party, it must be equally derogatory, since the stipulation is perfectly mutual, to the character and dignity of both. But it is derogatory to the character and dignity of neither. The objection seems to proceed still upon the implied ground that the abolition of the slave-trade is more a duty of Great Britain, or a more leading object with her, than it is or should be with us; as if, in this great effort of civilized nations to do away the most cruel traffic that ever scourged or disgraced the world, we had not as high and honorable, as just and merciful, a part to act, as any other nation upon the face of the earth. Let it be for ever remembered, that in this great work of humanity and justice the United States took the lead themselves. This government declared the slave-trade unlawful; and in this declaration it has been followed by the great powers of Europe. This government declared the slave-trade to be piracy; and in this, too, its example has been followed by other states. This government, this young government, springing up in this new world within half a century, founded on the broadest principles of civil liberty, and sustained by the moral sense and intelligence of the people, has gone in advance of all other nations in summoning the civilized world to a common effort to put down and destroy a nefarious traffic reproachful to human nature. It has not deemed, and it does not deem, that it suffers any derogation from its character or its dignity, if, in seeking to fulfil this sacred duty, it act, as far as necessary, on fair and equal terms of concert with other powers having in view the same praiseworthy object. Such were its sentiments when it entered into the solemn stipulations of the treaty of Ghent; such were its sentiments when it requested England to concur with us in declaring the slave-trade to be piracy; and such are the sentiments which it has manifested on all other proper occasions.

In conclusion, I have to repeat the expression of the President's deep regret at the general tone and character of your letter, and to assure you of the great happiness it would have afforded him if, concurring with the judgment of the President and Senate, concurring with what appears to be the general sense of the country, concurring in all the manifestations of enlightened public opinion in Europe, you had seen nothing in the treaty of the 9th of August to which you could not give your cordial approbation.

I have, &c.

DANIEL WEBSTER.

LEWIS CASS, ESQ., &c., &c., &c.

Mr. Webster to General Cass.

Department of State, Washington, December 20, 1842.

Sir,--Your letter of the 11th instant has been submitted to the President. He directs me to say, in reply, that he continues to regard your correspondence, of which this letter is part, as being quite irregular from the beginning. You had asked leave to retire from your mission; the leave was granted by the President, with kind and friendly remarks upon the manner in which you had discharged its duties. Having asked for this honorable recall, which was promptly given, you afterward addressed to this department your letter of the 3d of October, which, however it may appear to you, the President cannot but consider as a remonstrance, a protest, against the treaty of the 9th of August; in other words, an attack upon his administration for the negotiation and conclusion of that treaty. He certainly was not prepared for this. It came upon him with no small surprise, and he still feels that you must have been, at the moment, under the influence of temporary impressions, which he cannot but hope have ere now worn away.

A few remarks upon some of the points of your last letter must now close the correspondence.

In the first place, you object to my having called your letter of October 3d a "protest or remonstrance" against a transaction of the government, and observe that you must have been unhappy in the mode of expressing yourself, if you were liable to this charge.

What other construction your letter will bear, I cannot perceive. The transaction was *finished*. No letter or remarks of yourself, or any one else, could undo it, if desirable. Your opinions were unsolicited. If given as a citizen, then it was altogether unusual to address them to this department in an official despatch; if as a public functionary, the whole subject-matter was quite aside from the duties of your particular station. In your letter you did not propose any thing _to be done_, but objected to what had been done. You did not suggest any method of remedying what you were pleased to consider a defect, but stated what you thought to be reasons for fearing its consequences. You declared that there had been, in your opinion, an omission to assert American rights; to which omission you gave the department to understand that you would never have consented.

In all this there is nothing but protest and remonstrance; and, though your letter be not formally entitled such, I cannot see that it can be construed, in effect, as any thing else; and I must continue to think, therefore, that the terms used are entirely applicable and proper.

In the next place, you say: "You give me to understand that the communications which have passed between us on this subject are to be published, and submitted to the great tribunal of public opinion."
It would have been better if you had quoted my remark with entire correctness. What I said was, not that the communications which have passed between us *are to be* published, or *must* be published, but that "it may become necessary hereafter to publish your letter, in connection with other correspondence of the mission; and, although it is not to be presumed that you looked to such publication, because such a presumption would impute to you a claim to put forth your private opinions upon the conduct of the President and Senate, in a transaction finished and concluded, through the imposing form of a public despatch, yet, if published, it cannot be foreseen how far England might hereafter rely on your authority for a construction favorable to her own pretensions, and inconsistent with the interest and honor of the United States."

In another part of your letter you observe: "The publication of my letter, which is to produce this result, is to be the act of the government, and not my act. But if the President should think that the slightest injury to the public interest would ensue from the disclosure of my views, the letter may be buried in the archives of the department, and thus forgotten and rendered harmless."

To this I have to remark, in the first place, that instances have occurred in other times, not unknown to you, in which highly important letters from ministers of the United States, in Europe, to their own government, have found their way into the newspapers of Europe, when that government itself held it to be inconsistent with the interest of the United States to make such letters public.

But it is hardly worth while to pursue a topic like this.

You are pleased to ask: "Is it the duty of a diplomatic agent to receive all the communications of his government, and to carry into effect their instructions _sub silentio_, whatever may be his own sentiments in relation to them; or is he not bound, as a faithful representative, to communicate freely, but respectfully, his own views, that these may be considered, and receive their due weight, in that particular case, or in other circumstances involving similar considerations? It seems to me that the bare enunciation of the principle is all that is necessary for my justification. I am speaking now of the propriety of my action, not of the manner in which it was performed. I may have executed the task well or ill. I may have introduced topics unadvisedly, and urged them indiscreetly. All this I leave without remark. I am only endeavoring here to free myself from the serious charge which you bring against me. If I have misapprehended the duties of an American diplomatic agent upon this subject, I am well satisfied to have withdrawn, by a timely resignation, from a position in which my own self-respect would not permit me to remain. And I may express the conviction, that there is no government, certainly none this side of Constantinople, which would not encourage rather than rebuke the free expression of the views of their representatives in foreign countries."

I answer, certainly not. In the letter to which you were replying it was fully stated, that, "in common with every other citizen of the republic, you have an unquestionable right to form opinions upon public transactions and the conduct of public men. But it will hardly be thought to be among either the duties or the privileges of a minister abroad to make formal remonstrances and protests against proceedings of the various branches of the government at home, upon subjects in relation to which he himself has not been charged with any duty, or partaken any responsibility."

You have not been requested to bestow your approbation upon the treaty, however gratifying it would have been to the President to see that, in that respect, you united with other distinguished public agents abroad. Like all citizens of the republic, you are quite at liberty to exercise your own judgment upon that as upon other transactions. But neither your observations nor this concession cover the case. They do not show, that, as a public minister abroad, it is a part of your official functions, in a public despatch, to remonstrate against the conduct of the government at home in relation to a transaction in which you bore no part, and for which you were in no way answerable. The President and Senate must be permitted to judge for themselves in a matter solely within their control. Nor do I know that, in complaining of your protest against their proceedings in a case of this kind, any thing has been done to warrant, on your part, an invidious and unjust reference to Constantinople. If you could show, by the general practice of diplomatic functionaries in the civilized part of the world, and more especially, if you could show by any precedent drawn from the conduct of the many distinguished men who have represented the government of the United States abroad, that your letter of the 3d of October was, in its general object, tone, and character, within the usual limits of diplomatic correspondence, you may be quite assured that the President would not have recourse to the code of Turkey in order to find precedents the other way.

You complain that, in the letter from this department of the 14th of November, a statement contained in yours of the 3d of October is called a tissue of mistakes, and you attempt to show the impropriety of this appellation. Let the point be distinctly stated, and what you say in reply be then considered.

In your letter of October 3d you remark, that "England then urged the United States to enter into a conventional arrangement, by which we might be pledged to concur with her in measures for the suppression of the slave-trade. Until then, we had executed our own laws in our own way; but, yielding to this application, and departing from our former principle of avoiding European combinations upon subjects not American, we stipulated in a solemn treaty that we would carry into effect our own laws, and fixed the minimum force we would employ for that purpose."

The letter of this department of the 14th of November, having quoted this passage, proceeds to observe, that "the President cannot conceive how you should have been led to adventure upon such a statement as this. It is but a tissue of mistakes. England did not urge the United States to enter into this conventional arrangement. The United States yielded to no application from England. The proposition for abolishing the slave-trade, as it stands in the treaty, was an American proposition; it originated with the executive government of the United States, which cheerfully assumes all its responsibility. It stands upon it as its own mode of fulfilling its duties and accomplishing its objects. Nor have the United States departed in the slightest degree from their former principles of avoiding European combinations upon subjects not American; because the abolition of the African slave-trade is an American subject as emphatically as it is a European subject, and, indeed, more so, inasmuch as the government of the United States took the first great step in declaring that trade unlawful, and in attempting its extinction. The abolition of this traffic is an object of the highest interest to the American people and the American government; and you seem strangely to have overlooked altogether the important fact, that nearly thirty years ago, by the treaty of Ghent, the United States bound themselves, by solemn compact with England, to continue their efforts to promote its entire abolition; both parties pledging themselves by that treaty to use their best endeavors to accomplish so desirable an object."

Now, in answer to this, you observe in your last letter: "That the particular mode in which the governments should act in concert, as finally arranged in the treaty, was suggested by yourself, I never doubted. And if this is the construction I am to give to your denial of my correctness, there is no difficulty upon the subject. The question between us is untouched. All I said was, that England continued to prosecute the matter; that she presented it for negotiation, and that we thereupon consented to its introduction. And if Lord Ashburton did not come out with instructions from his government to endeavor to effect some arrangement upon this subject, the world has strangely misunderstood one of the great objects of his mission, and I have misunderstood that paragraph in your first note, where you say that Lord Ashburton comes with full powers to negotiate and settle all matters in discussion between England and the United States. But the very fact of his coming here, and of his acceding to any stipulations respecting the slave-trade, is conclusive proof that his government were desirous to obtain the co-operation of the United States. I had supposed that our government would scarcely take the initiative in this matter, and urge it upon that of Great Britain, either in Washington or in London. If it did so, I can only express my regret, and confess that I have been led inadvertently into an error."

It would appear from all this, that that which, in your first letter, appeared as a direct statement of facts, of which you would naturally be presumed to have had knowledge, sinks at last into inferences and conjectures. But, in attempting to escape from some of the mistakes of this tissue, you have fallen into others. "All I said was," you observe, "that England continued to prosecute the matter; that she presented it for negotiation, and that we thereupon consented to its introduction." Now the English minister no more presented this subject for negotiation than the government of the United States presented it. Nor can it be said that the United States consented to its introduction in any other sense than it may be said that the British minister consented to it. Will you be good enough to review the series of your own assertions on this subject, and see whether they can possibly be regarded merely as a statement of your own inferences? Your only authentic fact is a general one, that the British minister came clothed with full power to negotiate and settle all matters in discussion. This, you say, is conclusive proof that his government was desirous to obtain the co-operation of the United States respecting the slave-trade; and then you infer that England continued to prosecute this matter, and presented it for negotiation, and that the United States consented to its introduction; and give to this inference the shape of a direct statement of a fact.

You might have made the same remarks, and with the same propriety, in relation to the subject of the "Creole," that of impressment, the extradition of fugitive criminals, or any thing else embraced in the treaty or in the correspondence, and then have converted these inferences of your own into so many facts. And it is upon conjectures like these, it is upon such inferences of your own, that you make the direct and formal statement in your letter of the 3d of October, that "England then urged the United States to enter into a conventional arrangement, by which we might be pledged to concur with her in measures for the suppression of the slave-trade. Until then, we had executed our own laws in our own way; but, yielding to this application, and departing from our former principle of avoiding European combinations upon subjects not American, we stipulated in a solemn treaty that we would carry into effect our own laws, and fixed the minimum force we would employ for that purpose."

The President was well warranted, therefore, in requesting your serious reconsideration and review of that statement.

Suppose your letter to go before the public unanswered and uncontradicted; suppose it to mingle itself with the general political history of the country, as an official letter among the archives of the Department of State, would not the general mass of readers understand you as reciting facts, rather than as drawing your own conclusions? as stating history, rather than as presenting an argument? It is of an incorrect narrative that the President complains. It is that, in your hotel at Paris, you should undertake to write a history of a very delicate part of a negotiation carried on at Washington, with which you had nothing to do, and of the history of which you had no authentic information; and which history, as you narrate it, reflects not a little on the independence, wisdom, and public spirit of the administration.

As of the history of this part of the negotiation you were not well informed, the President cannot but think it would have been more just in you to have refrained from any attempt to give an account of it.

You observe, further: "I never mentioned in my despatch to you, nor in any manner whatever, that our government had conceded to that of England the right to search our ships. That idea, however, pervades your letter, and is very apparent in that part of it which brings to my observation the possible effect of my views upon the English government. But in this you do me, though I am sure unintentionally, great injustice. I repeatedly state that the recent treaty leaves the rights of the parties as it found them. My difficulty is not that we have made a positive concession, but that we have acted unadvisedly in not making the abandonment of this pretension a previous condition to any conventional arrangement upon the general subject."

On this part of your letter I must be allowed to make two remarks.

The first is, inasmuch as the treaty gives no color or pretext whatever to any right of searching our ships, a declaration against such a right would have been no more suitable to this treaty than a declaration against the right of sacking our towns in time of peace, or any other outrage.

The rights of merchant-vessels of the United States on the high seas, as understood by this government, have been clearly and fully asserted. As asserted, they will be maintained; nor would a declaration such as you propose have increased either its resolution or its ability in this respect. The government of the United States relies on its own power, and on the effective support of the people, to assert successfully all the rights of all its citizens, on the sea as well as on the land; and it asks respect for these rights not as a boon or favor from any nation. The President's message, most certainly, is a clear declaration of what the country understands to be its rights, and his determination to maintain them; not a mere promise to negotiate for these rights, or to endeavor to bring other powers into an acknowledgment of them, either express or implied. Whereas, if I understand the meaning of this part of your letter, you would have advised that something should have been offered to England which she might have regarded as a benefit, but coupled with such a declaration or condition as that, if she received the boon, it would have been a recognition by her of a claim which we make as matter of right. The President's view of the proper duty of the government has certainly been quite different. Being convinced that the doctrine asserted by this government is the true doctrine of the law of nations, and feeling the competency of the government to uphold and enforce it for itself, he has not sought, but, on the contrary, has sedulously avoided, to change this ground, and to place the just rights of the country upon the assent, express or implied, of any power whatever.

The government thought no skilfully extorted promises necessary in any such cases. It asks no such pledges of any nation. If its character for ability and readiness to protect and defend its own rights and dignity is not sufficient to preserve them from violation, no interpolation of promise to respect them, ingeniously woven into treaties, would be likely to afford such protection. And as our rights and liberties depend for existence upon our power to maintain them, general and vague protests are not likely to be more effectual than the Chinese method of defending their towns, by painting grotesque and hideous figures on the walls to fright away assailing foes.

My other remark on this portion of your letter is this:--

Suppose a declaration to the effect that this treaty should not be considered as sacrificing any American rights had been appended, and the treaty, thus fortified, had been sent to Great Britain, as you propose; and suppose that that government, with equal ingenuity, had appended an equivalent written declaration that it should not be considered as sacrificing any British right, how much more defined would have been the rights of either party, or how much clearer the meaning and interpretation of the treaty, by these reservations on both sides? Or, in other words, what is the value of a protest on one side, balanced by an exactly equivalent protest on the other?

No nation is presumed to sacrifice its rights, or give up what justly belongs to it, unless it expressly stipulates that, for some good reason or adequate consideration, it does make such relinquishment; and an unnecessary asseveration that it does not intend to sacrifice just rights would seem only calculated to invite aggression. Such proclamations would seem better devised for concealing weakness and apprehension, than for manifesting conscious strength and self-reliance, or for inspiring respect in others.

Toward the end of your letter you are pleased to observe: "The rejection of a treaty, duly negotiated, is a serious question, to be avoided whenever it can be without too great a sacrifice. Though the national faith is not actually committed, still it is more or less engaged. And there were peculiar circumstances, growing out of long-standing difficulties, which rendered an amicable arrangement of the various matters in dispute with England a subject of great national interest. But the negotiation of a treaty is a far different subject. Topics are omitted or introduced at the discretion of the negotiators, and they are responsible, to use the language of an eminent and able Senator, for 'what it contains and what it omits.' This treaty, in my opinion, omits a most important and necessary stipulation; and therefore, as it seems to me, its negotiation, in this particular, was unfortunate for the country."

The President directs me to say, in reply to this, that in the treaty of Washington no topics were omitted, and no topics introduced, at the mere discretion of the negotiator; that the negotiation proceeded from step to step, and from day to day, under his own immediate supervision and direction; that he himself takes the responsibility for what the treaty contains and what it omits, and cheerfully leaves the merits of the whole to the judgment of the country.

I now conclude this letter, and close this correspondence, by repeating once more the expression of the President's regret that you should have commenced it by your letter of the 3d of October.

It is painful to him to have with you any cause of difference. He has a just appreciation of your character and your public services at home and abroad. He cannot but persuade himself that you must be aware yourself, by this time, that your letter of October was written under erroneous impressions, and that there is no foundation for the opinions respecting the treaty which it expresses; and that it would have been far better on all accounts if no such letter had been written.

I have, &c.

DANIEL WEBSTER.

LEWIS CASS, ESQ., *Late Minister of the United States at Paris.*

THE HÜLSEMANN LETTER.

[As the authorship of this remarkable paper has sometimes been imputed to another person, it may be proper to give the facts respecting its preparation, although they involve nothing more important than a question of literary interest.

Mr. Webster, as has been stated, arrived at Marshfield on the 9th of October, 1850, where he remained for the space of two weeks. He brought with him the papers relating to this controversy with Austria. Before he left Washington, he gave to Mr. Hunter, a gentleman then and still filling an important post in the Department of State, verbal instructions concerning some of the points which would require to be touched in an answer to Mr. Hülsemann's letter of September 30th, and requested Mr. Hunter to prepare a draft of such an answer. This was done, and Mr. Hunter's draft of an answer was forwarded to Mr. Webster at Marshfield. On the 20th of October, 1850, Mr. Webster, being far from well, addressed a note to Mr. Everett,[1] requesting him also to prepare a draft of a reply to Mr. Hülsemann, at the same time sending to

Mr. Everett a copy of Mr. Hülsemann's letter and of President Taylor's message to the Senate relating to Mr. Mann's mission to Hungary.[2] On the 21st Mr. Webster went to his farm in Franklin, New Hampshire, where he remained until the 4th of November. While there he received from Mr. Everett a draft of an answer to Mr. Hülsemann, which was written by Mr. Everett between the 21st and the 24th of October.

Soon after Mr. Webster's death, it was rumored that the real author of "the Hülsemann letter" was Mr. Hunter,--a rumor for which Mr. Hunter himself was in no way responsible. At a later period, in the summer of 1853, the statement obtained currency in the newspapers that Mr. Everett wrote this celebrated despatch, and many comments were made upon the supposed fact that Mr. Everett had claimed its authorship. The facts are, that, while at Franklin, Mr. Webster, with Mr. Hunter's and Mr. Everett's drafts both before him, went over the whole subject, making considerable changes in Mr. Everett's draft, striking out entire paragraphs with his pen, altering some phrases, and writing new paragraphs of his own, but adopting Mr. Everett's draft as the basis of the official paper; a purpose which he expressed to Mr. Everett on his return to Boston toward Washington. Subsequently, when he had arrived in Washington, Mr. Webster caused a third draft to be made, in the State Department, from Mr. Everett's paper and his own additions and alterations. On this third draft he made still other changes and additions, and, when the whole was completed to his own satisfaction, the official letter was drawn out by a clerk, was submitted to the President, and, being signed by Mr. Webster, was sent to Mr. Hülsemann.[3]

There are, no doubt, passages and expressions in this letter which are in a tone not usual with Mr. Webster in his diplomatic papers. How he himself regarded the criticisms that might be made upon it may be seen from the following note:--

[TO MR. TICKNOR.]

"Washington, January 16, 1851.

"My dear Sir,--If you say that my Hülsemann letter is boastful and rough, I shall own the soft impeachment. My excuse is twofold: 1. I thought it well enough to speak out, and tell the people of Europe who and what we are, and awaken them to a just sense of the unparalleled growth of this country. 2. I wished to write a paper which should touch the national pride, and make a man feel *sheepish* and look *silly* who should speak of disunion. It is curious enough but it is certain, that Mr. Mann's private instructions were seen, somehow, by Schwarzenberg.

"Yours always truly,

"DANIEL WEBSTER."[4]

Department of State, Washington, December 21, 1850.

The undersigned, Secretary of State of the United States, had the honor to receive, some time ago, the note of Mr. Hülsemann, Chargé d'Affaires of his Majesty, the Emperor of Austria, of the 30th of September. Causes, not arising from any want of personal regard for Mr. Hülsemann, or of proper respect for his government, have delayed an answer until the present moment. Having submitted Mr. Hülsemann's letter to the President, the undersigned is now directed by him to return the following reply.

The objects of Mr. Hülsemann's note are, first, to protest, by order of his government, against the steps taken by the late President of the United States to ascertain the progress and probable result of the revolutionary movements in Hungary; and, secondly, to complain of some expressions in the instructions of the late Secretary of State to Mr. A. Dudley Mann, a confidential agent of the United States, as communicated by President Taylor to the Senate on the 28th of March last.

The principal ground of protest is founded on the idea, or in the allegation, that the government of the United States, by the mission of Mr. Mann and his instructions, has interfered in the domestic affairs of Austria in a manner unjust or disrespectful toward that power. The President's message was a communication made by him to the Senate, transmitting a correspondence between the executive government and a confidential agent of its own. This would seem to be itself a domestic transaction, a mere instance of intercourse between the President and the Senate, in the manner which is usual and indispensable in communications between the different branches of the government. It was not addressed either to Austria or Hungary; nor was it a public manifesto, to which any foreign state was called on to reply. It was an account of its transactions communicated by the executive government to the Senate, at the request of that body; made public, indeed, but made public only because such is the common and usual course of proceeding. It may be regarded as somewhat strange, therefore, that the Austrian Cabinet did not perceive that, by the instructions given to Mr. Hülsemann, it was itself interfering with the domestic concerns of a foreign state, the very thing which is the ground of its complaint against the United States. This department has, on former occasions, informed the ministers of foreign powers, that a communication from the President to either house of Congress is regarded as a domestic communication, of which, ordinarily, no foreign state has cognizance; and in more recent instances, the great inconvenience of making such communications the subject of diplomatic correspondence and discussion has been fully shown. If it had been the pleasure of his Majesty, the Emperor of Austria, during the struggles in Hungary, to have admonished the provisional government or the people of that country against involving themselves in disaster, by following the evil and dangerous example of the United States of America in making efforts for the establishment of independent governments, such an admonition from that sovereign to his Hungarian subjects would not have originated here a diplomatic correspondence. The President might, perhaps, on this ground, have declined to direct any particular reply to Mr. Hülsemann's note; but out of proper respect for the Austrian government, it has been thought better to answer that note at length; and the more especially, as the occasion is not unfavorable for the expression of the general sentiments of the government of the United States upon the topics which that note discusses.

A leading subject in Mr. Hülsemann's note is that of the correspondence between Mr. Hülsemann and the predecessor of the undersigned, in which Mr. Clayton, by direction of the President, informed Mr Hülsemann "that Mr. Mann's mission had no other object in view than to obtain reliable information as to the true state of affairs in Hungary, by personal observation." Mr. Hülsemann remarks, that "this explanation can hardly be admitted, for it says very little as to the cause of the anxiety which was felt to ascertain the chances of the revolutionists." As this, however, is the only purpose which can, with any appearance of truth, be attributed to the agency; as nothing whatever is alleged by Mr. Hülsemann to have been either done or said by the agent inconsistent with such an object, the undersigned conceives that Mr. Clayton's explanation ought to be deemed, not only admissible, but quite satisfactory.

Mr. Hülsemann states, in the course of his note, that his instructions to address his present communication to Mr. Clayton reached Washington about the time of the lamented death of the late President, and that he delayed from a sense of propriety the execution of his task until the new administration should be fully organized; "a delay which he now rejoices at, as it has given him the opportunity of ascertaining from the new President himself, on the occasion of the reception of the diplomatic corps, that the fundamental policy of the United States, so frequently proclaimed, would guide the relations of the American government with other powers." Mr. Hülsemann also observes, that it is in his power to assure the undersigned "that the Imperial government is disposed to cultivate relations of friendship and good understanding with the United States."

The President receives this assurance of the disposition of the Imperial government with great satisfaction; and, in consideration of the friendly relations of the two governments thus mutually recognized, and of the peculiar nature of the incidents by which their good understanding is supposed by Mr. Hülsemann to have been for a moment disturbed or endangered, the President regrets that Mr. Hülsemann did not feel himself at liberty wholly to forbear from the execution of instructions, which were of course transmitted from Vienna without any foresight of the state of things under which they would reach Washington. If Mr. Hülsemann saw, in the address of the President to the diplomatic corps, satisfactory pledges of the sentiments and the policy of this government in regard to neutral rights and neutral duties, it might, perhaps, have been better not to bring on a discussion of past transactions. But the undersigned readily admits that this was a question fit only for the consideration and decision of Mr. Hülsemann himself; and although the President does not see that any good purpose can be answered by reopening the inquiry into the propriety of the steps taken by President Taylor to ascertain the probable issue of the late civil war in Hungary, justice to his memory requires the undersigned briefly to restate the history of those steps, and to show their consistency with the neutral policy which has invariably guided the government of the United States in its foreign relations, as well as with the established and well-settled principles of national intercourse, and the doctrines of public law.

The undersigned will first observe, that the President is persuaded his Majesty, the Emperor of Austria, does not think that the government of the United States ought to view with unconcern the extraordinary events which have occurred, not only in his dominions, but in many other parts of Europe, since February, 1848. The government and people of the United States, like other intelligent governments and communities, take a lively interest in the movements and the events of this remarkable age, in whatever part of the world they may be exhibited. But the interest taken by the United States in those events has not proceeded from any disposition to depart from that neutrality toward foreign powers, which is among the deepest principles and the most cherished traditions of the political history of the Union. It has been the necessary effect of the unexampled character of the events themselves, which could not fail to arrest the attention of the contemporary world, as they will doubtless fill a memorable page in history.

But the undersigned goes further, and freely admits that, in proportion as these extraordinary events appeared to have their origin in those great ideas of responsible and popular government, on which the American constitutions themselves are wholly founded, they could not but command the warm sympathy of the people of this country. Well-known circumstances in their history, indeed their whole history, have made them the representatives of purely popular principles of government. In this light they now stand before the world. They could not, if they would, conceal their character, their condition, or their destiny. They could not, if they so desired, shut out from the view of mankind the causes which have placed them, in so short a national career, in the station which they now hold among the civilized states of the world. They could not, if they desired it, suppress either the thoughts or the hopes which arise in men's minds, in other countries, from contemplating their successful example of free government. That very intelligent and distinguished personage, the Emperor Joseph the Second, was among the first to discern this necessary consequence of the American Revolution on the sentiments and opinions of the people of Europe. In a letter to his minister in the Netherlands in 1787, he observes, that "it is remarkable that France, by the assistance which she afforded to the Americans, gave birth to reflections on freedom." This fact, which the sagacity of that monarch perceived at so early a day, is now known and admitted by intelligent powers all over the world. True, indeed, it is, that the prevalence on the other continent of sentiments favorable to republican liberty is the result of the reaction of America upon Europe; and the source and centre of this reaction has doubtless been, and now is, in these United States.

The position thus belonging to the United States is a fact as inseparable from their history, their constitutional organization, and their character, as the opposite position of the powers composing the European alliance is from the history and constitutional organization of the government of those powers. The sovereigns who form that alliance have not unfrequently felt it their right to interfere with the political movements of foreign states; and have, in their manifestoes and declarations, denounced the popular ideas of the age in terms so comprehensive as of necessity to include the United States, and their forms of government. It is well known that one of the leading principles announced by the allied sovereigns, after the restoration of the Bourbons, is, that all popular or constitutional rights are holden no otherwise than as grants and indulgences from crowned heads. "Useful and necessary changes in legislation and administration," says the Laybach Circular of May, 1821, "ought only to emanate from the free will and intelligent conviction of those whom God has rendered responsible for power; all that deviates from this line necessarily leads to disorder, commotions, and evils far more insufferable than those which they pretend to remedy." And his late Austrian Majesty, Francis the First, is reported to have declared, in an address to the Hungarian Diet, in 1820, that "the whole world had become foolish, and, leaving their ancient laws, were in search of imaginary constitutions." These declarations amount to nothing less than a denial of the lawfulness of the origin of the government of the United States, since it is certain that that government was established in consequence of a change which did not proceed from thrones, or the permission of crowned heads. But the government of the United States heard these denunciations of its fundamental principles without remonstrance, or the disturbance of its equanimity. This was thirty years ago.

The power of this republic, at the present moment, is spread over a region one of the richest and most fertile on the globe, and of an extent in comparison with which the possessions of the house of Hapsburg are but as a patch on the earth's surface. Its population, already twenty-five millions, will exceed that of the Austrian empire within the period during which it may be hoped that Mr. Hülsemann may yet remain in the honorable discharge of his duties to his government. Its navigation and commerce are hardly exceeded by the oldest and most commercial nations; its maritime means and its maritime power may be seen by Austria herself, in all seas where she has ports, as well as they may be seen, also, in all other quarters of the globe. Life, liberty, property, and all personal rights, are amply secured to all citizens, and protected by just and stable laws; and credit, public and private, is as well established as in any government of Continental Europe; and the country, in all its interests and concerns, partakes most largely in all the improvements and progress which distinguish the age. Certainly, the United States may be pardoned, even by those who profess adherence to the principles of absolute government, if they entertain an ardent affection for those popular forms of political organization which have so rapidly advanced their own prosperity and happiness, and enabled them, in so short a period, to bring their country, and the hemisphere to which it belongs, to the notice and respectful regard, not to say the admiration, of the civilized world. Nevertheless, the United States have abstained, at all times, from acts of interference with the political changes of Europe. They cannot, however, fail to cherish always a lively interest in the fortunes of nations struggling for institutions like their own. But this sympathy, so far from being necessarily a hostile feeling toward any of the parties to these great national struggles, is quite consistent with amicable relations with them all. The Hungarian people are three or four times as numerous as the inhabitants of these United States were when the American Revolution broke out. They possess, in a distinct language, and in other respects, important elements of a separate nationality, which the Anglo-Saxon race in this country did not possess; and if the United States wish success to countries contending for popular constitutions and national independence, it is only because they regard such constitutions and such national independence, not as imaginary, but as real blessings. They claim no right, however, to take part in the struggles of foreign powers in order to promote these ends. It is only in defence of his own government, and its principles and character, that the undersigned has now expressed himself on this subject. But when the people of the United States behold the people of foreign countries, without any such interference, spontaneously moving toward the adoption of institutions like their own, it surely cannot be expected of them to remain wholly indifferent spectators.

In regard to the recent very important occurrences in the Austrian empire, the undersigned freely admits the difficulty which exists in this country, and is alluded to by Mr. Hülsemann, of obtaining accurate information. But this difficulty is by no means to be ascribed to what Mr. Hülsemann calls, with little justice, as it seems to the undersigned, "the mendacious rumors propagated by the American press." For information on this subject, and others of the same kind, the American press is, of necessity, almost wholly dependent upon that of Europe; and if "mendacious rumors" respecting Austrian and Hungarian affairs have been anywhere propagated, that propagation of falsehoods has been most prolific on the European continent, and in countries immediately bordering on the Austrian empire. But, wherever these errors may have originated, they certainly justified the late President in seeking true information through authentic channels.

His attention was first particularly drawn to the state of things in Hungary by the correspondence of Mr. Stiles, Chargé d'Affaires of the United States at Vienna. In the autumn of 1848, an application was made to this gentleman, on behalf of Mr. Kossuth, formerly Minister of Finance for the Kingdom of Hungary by Imperial appointment, but, at the time the application was made, chief of the revolutionary government. The object of this application was to obtain the good offices of Mr. Stiles with the Imperial government, with a view to the suspension of hostilities. This application became the subject of a conference between Prince Schwarzenberg, the Imperial Minister for Foreign Affairs, and Mr. Stiles. The Prince commended the considerateness and propriety with which Mr. Stiles had acted; and, so far from disapproving his interference, advised him, in case he received a further communication from the revolutionary government in Hungary, to have an interview with Prince Windischgrätz, who was charged by the Emperor with the proceedings determined on in relation to that kingdom. A week after these occurrences, Mr. Stiles received, through a secret channel, a communication signed by L. Kossuth, President of the Committee of Defence, and countersigned by Francis Pulszky, Secretary of State. On the receipt of this communication, Mr. Stiles had an interview with Prince Windischgrätz, "who received him with the utmost kindness, and thanked him for his efforts toward reconciling the existing difficulties." Such were the incidents which first drew the attention of the government of the United States particularly to the affairs of Hungary, and the conduct of Mr. Stiles, though acting without instructions in a matter of much delicacy, having been viewed with satisfaction by the Imperial government, was approved by that of the United States.

In the course of the year 1848, and in the early part of 1849, a considerable number of Hungarians came to the United States. Among them were individuals representing themselves to be in the confidence of the revolutionary government, and by these persons the President was strongly urged to recognize the existence of that government. In these applications, and in the manner in which they were viewed by the President, there was nothing unusual; still less was there any thing unauthorized by the law of nations. It is the right of every independent state to enter into friendly relations with every other independent state. Of course, questions of prudence naturally arise in reference to new states, brought by successful revolutions into the family of nations; but it is not to be required of neutral powers that they should await the recognition of the new government by the parent state. No principle of public law has been more frequently acted upon, within the last thirty years, by the great powers of the world, than this. Within that period, eight or ten new states have established independent governments, within the limits of the colonial dominions of Spain, on this continent; and in Europe the same thing has been done by Belgium and Greece. The existence of all these governments was recognized by some of the leading powers of Europe, as well as by the United States, before it was acknowledged by the states from which they had separated themselves. If, therefore, the United States had gone so far as formally to acknowledge the independence of Hungary, although, as the result has proved, it would have been a precipitate step, and one from which no benefit would have resulted to either party; it would not, nevertheless, have been an act against the law of nations, provided they took no part in her contest with Austria. But the United States did no such thing. Not only did they not yield to Hungary any actual countenance or succor, not only did they not show their ships of war in the Adriatic with any menacing or hostile aspect, but they studiously abstained from every thing which had not been done in other cases in times past, and contented themselves with instituting an inquiry into the truth and reality of alleged political occurrences. Mr. Hülsemann incorrectly states, unintentionally certainly, the nature of the mission of this agent, when he says that "a United States agent had been despatched to Vienna with orders to watch for a favorable moment to recognize the Hungarian republic, and to conclude a treaty of commerce with the same." This, indeed, would have been a lawful object, but Mr. Mann's errand was, in the first instance, purely one of inquiry. He had no power to act, unless he had first come to the conviction that a firm and stable Hungarian government existed. "The principal object the President has in view," according to his instructions, "is to obtain minute and reliable information in regard to Hungary, in connection with the affairs of adjoining countries, the probable issue of the present revolutionary movements, and the chances we may have of forming commercial arrangements with that power favorable to the United States." Again, in the same paper, it is said: "The object of the President is to obtain information in regard to Hungary, and her resources and prospects, with a view to an early recognition of her independence and the formation of commercial relations with her." It was only in the event that the new government should appear, in the opinion of the agent, to be firm and stable, that the President proposed to recommend its recognition.

Mr. Hülsemann, in qualifying these steps of President Taylor with the epithet of "hostile," seems to take for granted that the inquiry could, in the expectation of the President, have but one result, and that favorable to Hungary. If this were so, it would not change the case. But the American government sought for nothing but truth; it desired to learn the facts through a reliable channel. It so happened, in the chances and vicissitudes of human affairs, that the result was adverse to the Hungarian revolution. The American agent, as was stated in his instructions to be not unlikely, found the condition of Hungarian affairs less prosperous than it had been, or had been believed to be. He did not enter Hungary, nor hold any direct communication with her revolutionary leaders. He reported against the recognition of her independence, because he found she had been unable to set up a firm and stable government. He carefully forbore, as his instructions required, to give publicity to his mission, and the undersigned supposes that the Austrian government first learned its existence from the communications of the President to the Senate.

Mr. Hülsemann will observe from this statement, that Mr. Mann's mission was wholly unobjectionable, and strictly within the rule of the law of nations and the duty of the United States as a neutral power. He will accordingly feel how little foundation there is for his remark, that "those who did not hesitate to assume the responsibility of sending Mr. Dudley Mann on such an errand should, independent of considerations of propriety, have borne in mind that they were exposing their emissary to be treated as a spy." A spy is a person sent by one belligerent to gain secret information of the forces and defences of the other, to be used for hostile purposes. According to practice, he may use deception, under the penalty of being lawfully hanged if detected. To give this odious name and character to a confidential agent of a neutral power, bearing the commission of his country, and sent for a purpose fully warranted by the law of nations, is not only to abuse language, but also to confound all just ideas, and to announce the wildest and most extravagant notions, such as certainly were not to have been expected in a grave diplomatic paper; and the President directs the undersigned to say to Mr. Hülsemann, that the American government would regard such an imputation upon it by the Cabinet of Austria as that it employs spies, and that in a quarrel none of its own, as distinctly offensive, if it did not presume, as it is willing to presume, that the word used in the original German was not of equivalent meaning with "spy" in the English language, or that in some other way the employment of such an opprobrious term may be explained. Had the Imperial government of

Austria subjected Mr. Mann for the treatment of a spy, it would have placed itself without the pale of civilized nations; and the Cabinet of Vienna may be assured, that if it had carried, or attempted to carry, any such lawless purpose into effect, in the case of an authorized agent of this government, the spirit of the people of this country would have demanded immediate hostilities to be waged by the utmost exertion of the power of the republic, military and naval.

Mr. Hülsemann proceeds to remark, that "this extremely painful incident, therefore, might have been passed over, without any written evidence being left on our part in the archives of the United States, had not General Taylor thought proper to revive the whole subject by communicating to the Senate, in his message of the 18th [28th] of last March, the instructions with which Mr. Mann had been furnished on the occasion of his mission to Vienna. The publicity which has been given to that document has placed the Imperial government under the necessity of entering a formal protest, through its official representative, against the proceedings of the American government, lest that government should construe our silence into approbation, or toleration even, of the principles which appear to have guided its action and the means it has adopted." The undersigned reasserts to Mr. Hülsemann, and to the Cabinet of Vienna, and in the presence of the world, that the steps taken by President Taylor, now protested against by the Austrian government, were warranted by the law of nations and agreeable to the usages of civilized states. With respect to the communication of Mr. Mann's instructions to the Senate, and the language in which they are couched, it has already been said, and Mr. Hülsemann must feel the justice of the remark, that these are domestic affairs, in reference to which the government of the United States cannot admit the slightest responsibility to the government of his Imperial Majesty. No state, deserving the appellation of independent, can permit the language in which it may instruct its own officers in the discharge of their duties to itself to be called in question under any pretext by a foreign power.

But even if this were not so, Mr. Hülsemann is in an error in stating that the Austrian government is called an "iron rule" in Mr. Mann's instructions. That phrase is not found in the paper; and in respect to the honorary epithet bestowed in Mr. Mann's instructions on the late chief of the revolutionary government of Hungary, Mr. Hülsemann will bear in mind that the government of the United States cannot justly be expected, in a confidential communication to its own agent, to withhold from an individual an epithet of distinction of which a great part of the world thinks him worthy, merely on the ground that his own government regards him as a rebel. At an early stage of the American Revolution, while Washington was considered by the English government as a rebel chief, he was regarded on the Continent of Europe as an illustrious hero. But the undersigned will take the liberty of bringing the Cabinet of Vienna into the presence of its own predecessors, and of citing for its consideration the conduct of the Imperial government itself. In the year 1777 the war of the American Revolution was raging all over these United States. England was prosecuting that war with a most resolute determination, and by the exertion of all her military means to the fullest extent. Germany was at that time at peace with England; and yet an agent of that Congress, which was looked upon by England in no other light than that of a body in open rebellion, was not only received with great respect by the ambassador of the Empress Queen at Paris, and by the minister of the Grand Duke of Tuscany (who afterwards mounted the Imperial throne), but resided in Vienna for a considerable time; not, indeed, officially acknowledged, but treated with courtesy and respect; and the Emperor suffered himself to be persuaded by that agent to exert himself to prevent the German powers from furnishing troops to England to enable her to suppress the rebellion in America. Neither Mr. Hülsemann nor the Cabinet of Vienna, it is presumed, will undertake to say that any thing said or done by this government in regard to the recent war between Austria and Hungary is not borne out, and much more than borne out, by this example of the Imperial Court. It is believed that the Emperor Joseph the Second habitually spoke in terms of respect and admiration of the character of Washington, as he is known to have done of that of Franklin; and he deemed it no infraction of neutrality to inform himself of the progress of the revolutionary struggle in America, or to express his deep sense of the merits and the talents of those illustrious men who were then leading their country to independence and renown. The undersigned may add, that in 1781 the courts of Russia and Austria proposed a diplomatic congress of the belligerent powers, to which the commissioners of the United States should be admitted.

Mr. Hülsemann thinks that in Mr. Mann's instructions improper expressions are introduced in regard to Russia; but the undersigned has no reason to suppose that Russia herself is of that opinion. The only observation made in those instructions about Russia is, that she "has chosen to assume an attitude of interference, and her immense preparations for invading and reducing the Hungarians to the rule of

Austria, from which they desire to be released, gave so serious a character to the contest as to awaken the most painful solicitude in the minds of Americans." The undersigned cannot but consider the Austrian Cabinet as unnecessarily susceptible in looking upon language like this as a "hostile demonstration." If we remember that it was addressed by the government to its own agent, and has received publicity only through a communication from one department of the American government to another, the language quoted must be deemed moderate and inoffensive. The comity of nations would hardly forbid its being addressed to the two imperial powers themselves. It is scarcely necessary for the undersigned to say, that the relations of the United States with Russia have always been of the most friendly kind, and have never been deemed by either party to require any compromise of their peculiar views upon subjects of domestic or foreign polity, or the true origin of governments. At any rate, the fact that Austria, in her contest with Hungary, had an intimate and faithful ally in Russia, cannot alter the real nature of the question between Austria and Hungary, nor in any way affect the neutral rights and duties of the government of the United States, or the justifiable sympathies of the American people. It is, indeed, easy to conceive, that favor toward struggling Hungary would be not diminished, but increased, when it was seen that the arm of Austria was strengthened and upheld by a power whose assistance threatened to be, and which in the end proved to be, overwhelmingly destructive of all her hopes.

Toward the conclusion of his note Mr. Hülsemarnn remarks, that "if the government of the United States were to think it proper to take an indirect part in the political movements of Europe, American policy would be exposed to acts of retaliation, and to certain inconveniences which would not fail to affect the commerce and industry of the two hemispheres." As to this possible fortune, this hypothetical retaliation, the government and people of the United States are quite willing to take their chances and abide their destiny. Taking neither a direct nor an indirect part in the domestic or intestine movements of Europe, they have no fear of events of the nature alluded to by Mr. Hülsemann. It would be idle now to discuss with Mr. Hülsemann those acts of retaliation which he imagines may possibly take place at some indefinite time hereafter. Those questions will be discussed when they arise; and Mr. Hülsemann and the Cabinet at Vienna may rest assured, that, in the mean time, while performing with strict and exact fidelity all their neutral duties, nothing will deter either the government or the people of the United States from exercising, at their own discretion, the rights belonging to them as an independent nation, and of forming and expressing their own opinions, freely and at all times, upon the great political events which may transpire among the civilized nations of the earth. Their own institutions stand upon the broadest principles of civil liberty; and believing those principles and the fundamental laws in which they are embodied to be eminently favorable to the prosperity of states, to be, in fact, the only principles of government which meet the demands of the present enlightened age, the President has perceived, with great satisfaction, that, in the constitution recently introduced into the Austrian empire, many of these great principles are recognized and applied, and he cherishes a sincere wish that they may produce the same happy effects throughout his Austrian Majesty's extensive dominions that they have done in the United States.

The undersigned has the honor to repeat to Mr. Hülsemann the assurance of his high consideration.
DANIEL WEBSTER.
THE CHEVALIER J.G. HÜLSEMANN, _Chargé d'Affaires of Austria, Washington_.
[Footnote 1: Mr. Everett had then resigned the Presidency of Harvard College.]
[Footnote 2: Whether Mr. Hunter's draft was also sent to Mr. Everett, I do not know. The internal evidence would seem to indicate that it was; but the fact is not material.]
[Footnote 3: I have seen, I believe, all the documents in relation to this matter; viz. Mr. Hunter's draft, Mr. Everett's (in his handwriting, with Mr. Webster's erasures), the third draft, made at the department under Mr. Webster's directions, and the original added paragraphs, written by Mr. Webster with his own hand. To those who are curious about the question of _authorship_, it is needful only to say that Mr. Webster adopted Mr. Everett's draft as the basis of the official letter, but that the official letter is a much more vigorous, expanded, and complete production than Mr. Everett's draft. It is described in a note written by Mr. Everett to one of the literary executors, in 1853, as follows: "It can be stated truly that what Mr. Webster did himself to the letter was very considerable; and that he added one half in bulk to the original draft; and that his additions were of the most significant character. It was very carefully elaborated in the department by him, till he was authorized to speak of it as he did at the Kossuth dinner...."
This refers to what Mr. Webster said in his speech at the Kossuth banquet, in Washington, January 7, 1852:--

"May I be so egotistical as to say that I have nothing new to say on the subject of Hungary? Gentlemen, in the autumn of the year before last, out of health, and retired to my paternal home among the mountains of New Hampshire, I was, by reason of my physical condition, confined to my house; but I was among the mountains, whose native air I was bound to inspire. Nothing saluted my senses, nothing saluted my mind, or my sentiments, but freedom, full and entire; and there, gentlemen, near the graves of my ancestors, I wrote a letter, which most of you have seen, addressed to the Austrian _chargé d'affaires_. I can say nothing of the ability displayed in that letter, but, as to its principles, while the sun and moon endure, I stand by them."]

[Footnote 4: From Hon. George T. Curtis's Life of Daniel Webster, Vol. II. pp. 535-537.]

Made in the USA
Middletown, DE
19 November 2018